PART I

From Covenant to
Community

JUDAISM, CHRISTIANITY, AND ISLAM

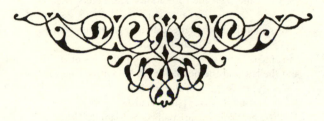

The Classical Texts
and Their Interpretation

F. E. PETERS

Princeton University Press
Princeton, New Jersey

Published by Princeton University Press, 41 William Street,
Princeton, New Jersey 08540
In the United Kingdom: Princeton University Press, Oxford

Library of Congress Cataloging-in-Publication Data

Peters, F. E. (Francis E.)
Judaism, Christianity, and Islam : the classical texts
and their interpretation / F.E. Peters.
p.   cm.
Also published simultaneously in 3 separate volumes.
Includes index.
Contents: pt. 1. From covenant to community — pt. 2. The word
and the law and the people of God — pt. 3. The works
of the spirit.
ISBN 0-691-07356-2 (acid-free paper)
1. Judaism. 2. Christianity. 3. Islam. I. Title.
BL80.2.P455   1990b
291—dc20   90-36669

This book has been composed in Linotron Perpetua type

Princeton University Press books are printed on acid-free
paper, and meet the guidelines for permanence and durability
of the Committee on Production Guidelines for Book
Longevity of the Council on Library Resources

Printed in the United States of America by Princeton
University Press, Princeton, New Jersey

1   3   5   7   9   10   8   6   4   2

For
Barakat Ahmad

in whose true spirit this work was conceived,
and to whose joyfully recollected memory
it is now gratefully dedicated

Contents

vii

PART II

The Word and the Law and the People of God

CONTENTS

PART III

The Works of the Spirit

Introduction 793

Preface

"Hear, O Israel," the Lord said to His Chosen People near the beginning of their extraordinary relationship. And that is the matter of this book: what His people heard from the Lord and how they understood it. Not merely the original Israelites, but His other peoples, the Christians and Muslims: they too chosen, as they say; they too, as they claim, authentic "sons of Abraham."

What they heard when God spoke to them is not difficult to discover. Jews, Christians, and Muslims alike felt strongly and thought carefully enough about it to preserve the words of God inside the covers of a Book, or rather, three books—the Bible, the New Testament, and the Quran—which they eye somewhat uneasily in each other's hands. So it is in the first instance God's words that have been reproduced here, not in their entirety—the integral texts are readily enough available—but in extracts and, more importantly, in a manner that will make it somewhat simpler to comprehend the other element of what is undertaken in this work: How did the Jews, Christians, and Muslims understand what they had heard?

The words of God to Abraham and later to Moses on Sinai, they all heard. The Bible is Scripture for all three religious communities, and indeed it is the basis of each's claim to be God's own people. But each group understood those words differently, whether as a basis of belief or as a directive to action. And even in each group's own, more particular and privileged communication with or from God—the Jews' Mishna, for example, or the letters of Paul, or the traditions from the Prophet Muhammad—there is little enough agreement within the community itself on what exactly God meant or what precisely was the good to be done or the evil to be avoided.

What I have attempted is to lay out the kinds of issues these three intimately related groups chiefly thought about, the questions that most interested them, and particularly such matters as might encourage comparison among the three; I have then selected standard or well-known or important texts to illustrate those matters. Jews, Christians, and Muslims all thought about the Law of God, for example, and how God ought to be worshiped, about authority and the authorities, about angels and heaven and hell; each group attempted on occasion to state what it believed and to make its members somehow conform to it; and most consequential of all perhaps, the three religious communities shared an invincible conviction that God's revelation to them was not confined to that revered and well-guarded Book we call Scripture.

This is obviously not a history of Judaism, Christianity, and Islam, and even less of the three communities of believers. The historically minded will doubtless be puzzled, and perhaps dismayed, at the sometimes odd juxtaposition of authorities or events. I have no remedy for either the puzzlement or the dismay except to refer them to histories of the faiths or the communities, of which there is certainly no lack. Here the objective is to keep the three communities of believers in one line of sight and to focus on each through a single topic that interested them all. Thus, after the first four chapters, which follow a rough time line, the presentation moves to a topical arrangement that violates the chronological order at almost every turn but has the advantage, I hope, of hearing each group out on subjects of parallel or mutual or polemical concern.

It is, in any event, the same way the sources themselves deal with the matter. Though Scripture is often cast in the form of history, not many of those who came after viewed the sacred books through the eyes of the historian. There is the Jew Josephus, yes, and the Christian Eusebius, and Muhammad's biographer Ibn Ishaq. But for the rest, the authors represented in these pages are chiefly lawyers, theologians, priests, and visionaries—Jewish, Christian, and Muslim believers who were disinterested in the past as past, since for them the past was, like the Torah in the Talmud and like the Bible in both the Gospels and the Quran, eternally present. In reading the third-century rabbis, for example, one cannot really tell that there was no longer a Temple in Jerusalem and that no priests had made sacrifice there for more than a century, much less when that catastrophic destruction took place or what merely human acts contributed to it.

Nor were those same authorities much interested in the present as present. We catch contemporary reflections, of course, but their primary concern was not to bring us up to date on the present state of the People of God, on how well or poorly the Law of God was being observed. Our authors tell us, for example, that there were rules governing the conduct of Christians and Jews living under Islam; but they do not tell us, as other kinds of sources do, which regulations were actually in force and for whom, or which were simply on the books. Since the "books" in question are likely to have been holy books or equally holy traditions, to be on them or in them was what really mattered and not how many "commoners of the land" were actually fornicating, killing their neighbors, or violating the Sabbath. We have ways of discovering, or guessing about, the latter, but not from our lawyers and divines, who had more important things to concern them.

In reproducing rather than retelling Scripture, I have allowed God speak for Himself, and I have extended the courtesy to the Jews, Christians, and Muslims as well. And those children of a voluble God have spoken, sometimes clearly and eloquently; at times obscurely, perhaps because they did not understand or perhaps because they chose not to say; sometimes gently and sometimes rudely, especially when they are speaking of each other. I have kept my own explanations to a minimum on the simple principle that all these "Peoples of the Book" are capable of and should be permitted to speak for themselves. I have supplied some factual data, provided contexts where such seemed required, and attempted some explanatory transitions across what is a somewhat discontinuous terrain. Much is missing, to be sure: saints are often more interesting than their writings and religious art more striking than tracts on iconoclasm. God's own preference for history over theology is well known.

I have made here almost no judgments about authenticity: these are the received texts, scriptural and otherwise, of each community. And I have tried, despite strong professional and personal inclinations to the contrary, not to seduce the reader into the enormous historical and textual problems that almost every one of these texts—and often every line and every single word of them—has raised over the centuries among believers and nonbelievers alike. Thus there are no traces here of the revelations of Julius Wellhausen or Ignaz Goldziher, no echoes of the prophetic voices of Rudolf Bultmann or Joseph Schacht, of Jacob Neusner or Patricia Crone, no sign of "P" or "E" or "J" or the even more celebrated "Q". And finally, I have attempted to reduce technical vocabulary, particularly of the transliterated variety, to an absolute minimum: lovers of *halakha* and *hadith* will have to be served elsewhere.

This work was originally composed as a companion for my *Children of Abraham: Judaism, Christianity, Islam*. It is in a sense the flesh to the latter's bone, and, in the ineluctable manner of flesh, has put on quite a bit of weight in the process. Nor is the order exactly the same as in that earlier work. Here the matter is divided into three parts: From Covenant to

Community; The Word and the Law and the People of God; The Works of the Spirit. But even though the arrangement is different, the same general topics are covered. More important, the time parameters of the earlier work are this one's as well: we begin here literally at the beginning, but break off while each religious complex is still in its "classical" or, perhaps less provocatively, its "scholastic" period. To put it another way, this collection ends before the great movements of modernism and reform touched—at different moments and in differing degrees—Judaism, Christianity, and Islam and rendered them different. Not everyone will be happy with such a peremptory leave-taking, particularly those who prefer the reformed to the traditional versions of these communities. No matter. Given the limitations of the guide, it cannot be otherwise.

The only abbreviations requiring explanation are: B.C.E. = Before the Common Era, and C.E. = the Common Era. The M prefix before a title means Mishna; BT = Babylonian Talmud and JT = Jerusalem or Palestinian Talmud.

The texts used for this work have all been published in one place or another, often in many places since, as I have said, my objective throughout is to place before the reader the "classical texts" of the three religious communities. They are not only published; most of them are very well known to the members of the community whose heritage they are. Thus they have also been translated out of their original Hebrew and Aramaic, Greek and Latin, Arabic and Persian into a variety of other languages, including English. The question is not where to find the texts but which to choose and whose version to prefer.

Of the translations used in compiling this dossier, some are mine and some, as noted in the Acknowledgments, are from other hands. Where I have used others' versions, I have generally modified them only to the extent of standardizing names—the English word "God" has replaced the translators' untranslated "Allah" throughout, for example—and of reducing all dates to those of the Common Era.

Stockport, New York

Acknowledgments

Translations of the Hebrew Bible are derived from *A New Translation of the Holy Scriptures according to the Massoretic Text*, second edition, Philadelphia: Jewish Publication Society of America, 1982.

Translations of the biblical apocrypha are derived from *The Apocryphal Old Testament*, edited by H.D.F. Sparks, Oxford: Clarendon Press, 1984.

Translations of the deutero-canonical books and the New Testament are derived from *The New English Bible with the Apocrypha*, corrected impression of the second edition, New York: Oxford University Press, 1972. Translations of the New Testament apocrypha are derived from Edgar Hennecke and Wilhelm Schneemelcher (eds.), *New Testament Apocrypha*, 2 vols., translated by R. McLean Wilson et al., Philadelphia: Westminster Press, 1963–1965.

Translations of the Quran are derived from Ahmed Ali, *Al-Qur'an*, Princeton: Princeton University Press, 1988.

A Brief Chronology

B.C.E. is an abbreviation of "Before the Common Era" and C.E. of the "Common Era." The Common Era is that of the Gregorian calendar, where time is measured before or after what was thought to be the birth year of Jesus: in Latin, *Anno Domini*, the "Year of the Lord," abbreviated A.D. In fact, Jesus' date of birth is now placed in or about 4 B.C.E.

Muslims also use a "before" and "after" system. In their case the watershed date is that of the *Hijrah* or Emigration of Muhammad from Mecca to Medina in 622 C.E., called in the West A.H., or *Anno Hegirae*.

Jewish time reckoning is only "after," that is, from the Creation of the World, normally understood to be about 4000 years B.C.E.

B.C.E.

ca. 1700	God's Covenant with Abraham
ca. 1200	The exodus from Egypt; the giving of the Torah to Moses on Mount Sinai
ca. 1000	David, king of the Israelites, captures Jerusalem and makes it his capital
ca. 970	Solomon builds the First Temple in Jerusalem
621	Josiah centralizes all Jewish worship in the Temple in Jerusalem
587	Babylonians under Nebuchadnezzar carry Israelites into exile in Babylon; the destruction of Solomon's Temple
538	Exiles return to Judea; Ezra; Nehemiah; rebuilding of Jerusalem Temple
332	Alexander the Great in the Near East; Greek dynasties rule Palestine
ca. 280	Translation of Bible in Greek: the "Septuagint"
200	The Seleucid dynasty of Syria replaces the Ptolemies as rulers of Palestine
175–164	Antiochus IV Epiphanes; profanation of the Temple
164	Maccabean revolt; Jewish independence
164–37	The Hasmonean dynasty rules Palestine

37–4	Herod the Great, king of Judea
ca. 25–45 C.E.	Philo in Alexandria
20	Herod begins restoration of the Temple
ca. 4	Birth of Jesus in Bethlehem

C.E.

6	Romans take over direct rule of Judea
26–36	Pontius Pilate, Roman prefect of Judea
ca. 30	Execution of Jesus in Jerusalem
the 50s	Letters of Paul
ca. 60–70	Composition of Mark, earliest of the Gospels
ca. 62	Death of James in Jerusalem and Peter and Paul in Rome
66	Jewish insurrection in Palestine; flight of Yohanan ben Zakkai to Jabneh (Jamnia) and of Jewish Christians to the Transjordan
70	Romans under Titus destroy Herod's Temple
ca. 80–100	Remaining three canonical Gospels written
ca. 100	Death of the Jewish historian Josephus
135	Second Jewish revolt in Palestine; Jerusalem leveled and Jews forbidden to live there
ca. 200	Widespread persecutions of Christians in the Roman Empire; redaction of the Mishna by Judah "the Prince"
ca. 250	Antony, the first hermit, withdraws to the desert of Egypt
303	Last violent persecution of Christians by Diocletian
313	Constantine, the first Christian emperor, suspends persecution of Christians
318	Pachomius founds the first monastery, or community of ascetics, in Egypt
325	First ecumenical council of the Christian Church at Nicea
330	Constantine and his mother Helena begin the conversion of Jerusalem into a Christian holy city
340	First Christian monasteries founded in the West
381	Decree establishing Christianity as the official religion of the Roman Empire
399	Death of the Christian mystic Evagrius of Pontus
410	Visigoths sack Rome
425	Office of Nasi, or Patriarch, abolished in the Roman Empire
430	Death of Augustine, Latin theologian of Hippo in North Africa
451	Ecumenical council of Chalcedon
ca. 500	Completion of the *gemaras* at Tiberias and (ca. 600) in Iraq: thus the final versions of the "Jerusalem" and "Babylonian" Talmuds
ca. 535	Benedict founds his monastery at Monte Cassino
ca. 570	Birth of Muhammad at Mecca

1134–1204	Moses Maimonides, Jewish theologian and lawyer
1187	Muslims under Saladin retake Jerusalem
1198	Death of the Muslim philosopher Ibn Rushd (Averroes)
1225–1274	Thomas Aquinas; the height of medieval Christian theology in the West
ca. 1300	Compilation of the *Zohar*, the primary work of Kabbala
1323	Pope Boniface VIII publishes the bull *Unam Sanctam*
1377	Ibn Khaldun's *Prolegomenon to History*
1453	Constantinople falls to the Turks
1492	Christian reconquest of Spain completed; Jewish migrations to Islamic lands in North Africa and the Near East
1488–1575	Joseph Caro, author of *Shulhan Aruch*
1517	Luther posts his controversial theses; beginning of the Protestant Reformation

Judaism,
Christianity,
and Islam

Introduction

The Bible begins at the creation of the world, and there is surely a lesson in that. But the Jews—to use our word rather than theirs at this point—begin their own proper history not where the Bible begins, nor where the modern historian might seek them out—when the "Hebrews" emerge as a distinct racial, ethnic, cultural, or linguistic group—but at quite another moment that stands recorded and underlined in the biblical book called Genesis. The account falls in the twelfth chapter of that work, when God speaks to, and in the end concludes a covenant with, a man thereafter called Abraham. In Genesis the covenant is still only a promise, with no immediate boon save an heir, though Abraham is called upon to perform the simple but painful condition laid down by the Lord: the circumcision of himself and all the males, slave and free, of his household. But the promise of future reward is quite specific: Abraham and his descendants would have an ongoing, expanding, and even glorious tribal identity and, more, a land of their own, surely a heady vision for what must have been a marginal clan of nomads wandering the byways of the Middle East: a Chosen People and a Promised Land, a twin identity that forever thereafter both explained the past and underwrote the future for the Jews.

If we listen to the Christians and the Muslims, their history too began in that same moment of promise to Abraham. They too are the offspring of that selfsame promise, siblings, perhaps, of the Jews, but only as Isaac was to Ishmael or Jacob to Esau: the replacement issue of the first-born son. Christians and Muslims are constrained by the immutable givens of history, their history, to yield to the Jews the title of the first-born of Abraham; they themselves are instead, they would insist, his *rightful* heirs.

The Bible is the record of that famous covenant, *the* Covenant as it concerns these three communities, the story of God's offer and its acceptance and of the glories and the pains of that pioneer people called, in clan fashion, the Children of Israel, as they struggled under its charge from tribe to people to nation. And it is more: the Bible is the charter document of the three faiths, viewed directly and studied carefully by Jews and

Christians alike for its lessons on the past and its presentiments of the future, and regarded by Muslims through its reissue in the Quran. The claims of the three stand or fall on its understanding. It is also the past of all of them, something that must be made to yield sense no less than satisfaction.

Then it ends. Beyond the return from Exile and beyond Daniel there is no Bible, no sacred text to carry the Covenant forward. There is history, surely, some of it holy if not sacred, like the books of Maccabees; much of it religious, like the abundant, though noncanonical, "apocrypha" produced by the rapidly and radically changing times from the arrival of Alexander to the birth of Jesus. Both Jews and Christians pick their way through the historical debris of those days: the Jews curiously, looking beyond to the Mishna and Talmud, the five-centuries-distant documents of a renewed Covenant; the Christians anxiously, for there if anywhere, in those centuries from the Exile to the Romans, lies the embryonic tissue that shaped and sustained the birth of the Christian movement in the first century C.E. If the Christians are the newborn of the Covenant, they are also children of the age of the Apocrypha and carry its sectarian and apocalyptic sensibilities full upon them. The Muslims, finally, have looked away. Their perception of the career of the Chosen Peoples takes leave of mere history after the Exile. Muslim sacred history knows and cares nothing of the age of the Apocrypha, the doings, religious or otherwise, of the Greeks and the Romans. It looks briefly at Jesus and then passes on, oblivious of Church and Synagogue, to the sixth-century call of the Last Messenger of the Covenant.

We shall not look away here. We shall follow God's Chosen People across the difficult passage that leads from Daniel to Jesus, from "Israelite," with its antique ring, to "Jew," with its modern one. It is a troubled time, when Israel takes on new and powerful political foes: the Hellenistic monarchies and finally the Romans (the last, one is tempted to say, secular sovereigns that Jews will know until modern times, though the truth is that Rome was not so much secular as pagan, a condition that by hindsight seemed almost benign). It was also the era when the Children of Abraham met not so much a religious foe, which the old paganism was, as a genuine rival, Hellenism, which showed forth even at that time and that place all the dangerously attractive traits that were later described as "rationalism," or "modernism," or "humanism." It was in fact all those things, and it presented itself to the Jews to challenge and beguile them, as it later would to both Christianity and Islam in turn.

4

The "lives" of Jesus and Muhammad are then set out as their follow-ers read and understand them. Although there are formal, biographical similarities, the accounts are fundamentally discontinuous. Both derive from literary works, but the first, the Gospels, are part of the Christians' Scripture, and rightly so, since they present what were judged to be sacral events. Muhammad's life emerges from a traditional biography—Muslim Scripture, the Quran, is quite otherwise—where the miraculous elements are intrusive. The Christian cannot but study the "Good News of Jesus Christ," since the sacred work of Jesus is revealed therein; the Muslim reads the "Life of the Prophet of God" simply as an act of piety: revela-tion lies elsewhere.

At that point, the death of Muhammad in 632 C.E., the primary data are complete, the covenantal evidence is in. And the argument begins. Or rather, continues, since the debate over the Covenant and its heirs had begun deep within Jewish history, before there were Muslims or even Christians. The Israelites had early fashioned a dream of a "kingdom of priests," a dream that found only fitful fulfillment as long as there was a "kingdom of kings." But the Israelite monarchy disappeared forever in the debris of Herod's successors, and that longed-for priesthood of all believers found a second life in the program of the Pharisees. The Phari-saic ideal prevailed under the rabbis, revitalized perhaps by its very sur-vival. At the outset the Christians had appeared to share that same dream, for polemical and competitive reasons if for no other. Once separated from the main body of the Jews, however, the course of the Christian community took a quite different turn. It became what the Israelites had once been: a community of priests. Christianity was born, just barely, in the age of Temple Judaism and remained faithful to that model, which may have been, not entirely by coincidence, far more congenial than the purified and separatist Torah Judaism of the rabbis to the Gentiles enter-ing the Church in increasing numbers in the second and third centuries of the new era.

By 200 C.E. Jews and Christians stood as communities apart, the first deeply transformed from the remote days of the monarchy by the experi-ence of the Exile, its encounter with Hellenism, its apocalyptic moment in the face of Roman imperial might, and, in the end, its argument with its own Christians, sectarians at first, then schismatics, and finally apos-tates from what was understood as normative Judaism in the second century C.E. Jews had embarked upon their long Second Exile, a life of near invisibility in the city and countryside, pacifist and parochial, meditative and self-contemplative, aliens in lands of their masters, eventually their Christian and Muslim masters. The Christians, on the other hand, stood poised on the brink of explosive growth in numbers, in public and private power, and in architectural, liturgical, and theological grandeur— a growth unchecked in the East until the rise of Islam.

The separation of Jews and Christians was a painful process and left a continuing legacy of hostility between the two groups. But it had another, rather odd effect. If the Jews were not an entirely admired minority in the Roman Empire—two major Jewish insurrections made their political loyalty more than a little suspect in Roman eyes—they were a protected one, the beneficiaries of various exemptions, many of them going back to Greek days, from the empire's laws and customs. It took some time, but once the Christians were finally identified as a separate religious community from the Jews, they escaped some of the odium and all of the protections that had been the Jewish lot. The Christians, as it turned out, were as stiff-necked as the Jews on the matter of monotheism, and they had to pay the price: there were Roman religious persecutions of the Christians of varying scope and duration throughout the third century C.E. The Christians weathered them and in the end converted their persecutors, something the Jews had been unable or had forsworn to do. The consequence was enormous and longstanding: after the conversion of Constantine, many Christians lived out more than a millennium as subjects of a Christian Roman Empire, full-fledged citizens and rather comfortably at home in both the City of God and the City of Man.

The Christians' dual estate, the catholic Christian church and the catholic Christian empire, grew increasingly alike in the fourth, fifth, and sixth centuries. Roman law held its ground against the growing body of Church law; but the administrative style of the empire, with its centralized governance and its hierarchization of authority, was echoed in the Church. Bishops and provincial governors, patriarchs and prefects—the jurisdiction was almost identical. There lacked only a counterpart of the emperor himself, or perhaps two, since there was often a twin *imperium* in Rome and Constantinople. Predictably, that lack too was filled, and the long and destructive controversy, and the subsequent schism, over the issue of an "imperial bishop," an absolute primate in Rome—or perhaps in Constantinople—shook the Christian Church for centuries to come.

In its growth to community maturity, Islam faced the same problem of identity and authority. What was easy for the Prophet and his generation was not so for their successors. The political and social organism that constituted Islam as surely as the body of believers grew with spectacular speed and dimension. The growth to political maturity, which had taken many centuries for Israel amid peoples who were enemies but not rivals and which had occurred in Christianity only after a breathing space of nearly three centuries, was a lightening-like process in Islam: empire descended like a crown upon Muslim heads within decades of the Prophet's death, an empire that thrust the new community into the company of a powerful, confident, and nearly fully grown Christendom. Even within the lifetime of Muhammad, the Islamic community had had Christian and Jewish subjects; shortly those same subjects outnumbered their masters in a newly expanded "Abode of Islam" that reached from Spain around the southern Mediterranean basin eastward to the Indus.

But who should rule such a creation? A prophet or a king? A political Caliph or a charismatic Imam? The issue flamed early and persisted late. There was scarcely time to think, so rapid was the progress of Islam's political fortunes; but there were some who from the outset stood against the secularizing flood of event for a spiritual Islam governed not by the strongest but by the spiritual best, the very men, it was maintained, who had been signaled by the Prophet himself: his cousin and son-in-law Ali and after him his heirs. This was the position of the "Party of Ali," the Shi'at Ali or Shi'ites, and they maintained it staunchly in the face of centuries of actual rule by the titled, the rich, and the powerful, namely the consensually agreed-upon Caliphs of Sunni Islam.

1. The Covenant and the History of the Chosen People

1. "In the Beginning"

The Bible is the foundation of men's belief in the One True God, the one and the same deity that is called Yahweh by the Jews, Our Father who is in heaven by the Christians, and Allah by the Muslims. And whether memorized, ignored, transcended, or superseded, it was and remained the charter and testament of all the children of Abraham.

Abraham does not appear at the outset, however; the Bible begins absolutely, "in the beginning," truly the very beginning, before the world was. Abraham still lay many generations in the future.

When God began to create the heaven and the earth—the earth being unformed and void, with darkness over the surface of the deep and a wind from God sweeping over the water—God said, "Let there be light"; and there was light. God saw that the light was good, and God separated the light from the darkness. God called the light Day, and the darkness He called Night. And there was evening and there was morning, a first day. (Genesis 1:1–5)

So the Bible starts bereshit, "in the beginning," not of history but of the world, whence the book called Genesis proceeds, day by day, through God's creation of the earth, the heavens and their bodies, all living creatures beneath the waters and in the air above.

God said, "Let the earth bring forth every kind of living creature: cattle, creeping things, and wild beasts of every kind." And it was so. God made wild beasts of every kind and cattle of every kind, and all kinds of creeping things of the earth. And God saw that this was good. And God said, "Let us make man in our image, after our likeness. They shall rule the fish of the sea, the birds of the sky, the cattle, the whole earth, and all the creeping things that creep on earth." And God created man in His image, in the image of God He created him; male and female He created them. God blessed them and God said to them, "Be fertile and increase, fill the earth and master it; and rule the fish of the sea, the birds of the sky, and all the living things that creep on earth. . . ."

God said, "See, I give you every seed-bearing plant that is upon all the earth, and every tree that has seed-bearing fruit; they shall be yours for food. And to all the animals on land, to all the birds of the sky, and to everything that creeps on earth, in which there is the breath of life, [I give] all the green plants for food." And it was so. And God saw all that He had made, and found it very good. And there was evening and there was morning, the sixth day. . . .

Such is the story of heaven and earth when they were created. (Genesis 1:24–2:4)

It was by no means the whole story. This account of the making of the world and its denizens offered by Genesis, though it is quite detailed in its own way, was endlessly explained in the sequel; details were added; its silences filled; its unposed questions answered out of men's ever deepening understanding of how God worked and how the world worked.

Part of that understanding came from other sources that had little to do with the Bible, other peoples' stories about how the world began—the Babylonians' and Egyptians', for example—and, more consequentially in the long run, other peoples' demonstrations about how the world must have come into being. The Greeks, with whom all the children of Abraham would eventually come into contact, had a number of such demonstrations, scientific in both their intent and their effect, and Jews, Christians, and Muslims have devoted, and still devote, a substantial degree of their attention and energies to refuting or reconciling them.

2. The Quran on Creation

The Christians accepted Genesis as Scripture—that is, God's true word—and so their account of Creation is identical with that of the Jews, though it was read, of course, in a Greek or later a Latin translation, and often commented upon in a very different way. For the Muslims, on the other hand, the scripture called the Quran superseded the Book of Genesis; and though its source is the same as that in Genesis, God Himself, there are obvious differences in detail in its view of Creation.

It was God who raised the skies without support, as you can see, and assumed His throne, and enthralled the sun and the moon (so that) each runs to a predetermined course. He disposes all affairs, distinctly explaining every sign that you may be certain of the meeting with your Lord.

And it was He who stretched the earth and placed upon it stabilisers and rivers; and made two of a pair of every fruit; (and) He covers up the day with the night. In these are signs for those who reflect.

On the earth are tracts adjoining one another, and vineyards, fields of corn and date-palm trees, some forked and some with single trunks, yet all irrigated with the selfsame water, though We make some more excellent than others in fruit. There are surely signs in them for those who understand. (Quran 13:2–4)

Much of the "biblical" material in the Quran, or perhaps better, the Torah material in the Quran—the Quran is in its entirety "Bible" to the Muslim—is not presented in a continuous narrative line in the manner of Genesis but often simply alluded to, frequently to support or illustrate another point. Hence the subject of Creation comes up in different places, as here again in Quran 32, where the moral conse-quences to Creation are homiletically drawn at the beginning and the end.

It is God who created the heavens and the earth and all that lies between them, in six spans, then assumed all authority. You have no protector other than Him, nor any intercessor. Will you not be warned even then? He regulates all affairs from high to low, then they rise to perfection step by step in a (heavenly) day whose measure is a thousand years in your reckoning. Such is He, the knower of the unknown and the known, the mighty and the merciful, who made all things He created excellent; and first fashioned man from clay, then made his offspring from the extract of base fluid, then proportioned and breathed into him His spirit, and gave you the senses of hearing, sight and feeling, and yet how little are the thanks you offer. (Quran 32:4–9)

It is already apparent that, among other differences between Genesis and the Quran, there is the matter of chronology, as the Muslims themselves were well aware.

The people of the Torah [that is, the Jews] say that God began the work of Creation on Sunday and finished on Saturday, when He took His seat upon the Throne, and so they take that as their holy day. The Chris-tians say the beginning (of Creation) fell on a Monday and the ending on Sunday, when He took His seat on the Throne, so they take that as their holy day. Ibn Abbas [a companion of Muhammad and an active transmit-ter of traditions from the Prophet] said that the beginning was on a Saturday and the ending on a Friday, so that the taking of His seat was also on a Friday, and for that reason we keep it as a holy day. It was said by the Prophet, may God bless him and give him peace, "Friday is the mistress among the days. It is more excellent in God's sight than either the Breaking of the Fast (at the end of Ramadan) or the Feast of Sacrifice (in connection with the Pilgrimage liturgy). On it occurred five special things, to wit: Adam was created, on it his spirit was breathed into him, he was wedded, he died, and on it will come the Final Hour. No human ever asks his Lord for anything on Friday but that God gives him what he asks." Another version of this Prophetic tradition reads: ". . . ask, so long as it is not something forbidden." (Al-Kisa'i, *Stories of the Prophets*) [JEFFERY 1962: 171–172]

3. Adam and Eve

We return to the second chapter of the Book of Genesis, to the account of the creation of Adam and Eve.

When the Lord God made earth and heaven—when no shrub of the field was yet on earth and no grasses of the field had yet sprouted, because the Lord God had not sent rain upon the earth and there was no man to till the soil, but a flow would well up from the ground and water the whole surface of the earth—the Lord God formed man [in Hebrew *adam*] from the dust of the earth. He blew into his nostrils the breath of life, and man became a living being.

The Lord God planted a garden in Eden, in the east, and placed there the man whom He had formed. And from the ground the Lord God caused to grow every tree that was pleasing to the sight and good for food, with the tree of life in the middle of the garden, and the tree of knowledge of good and bad. . . .

The Lord God took the man and placed him in the garden of Eden, to till it and tend it. And the Lord God commanded the man, saying, "Of every tree of the garden you are free to eat; but as for the tree of knowledge of good and bad, you must not eat of it; for as soon as you eat of it, you shall die."

The Lord God said, "It is not good for man to be alone. I will make a fitting helper for him." And the Lord God formed out of the earth all the wild beasts and all the birds of the sky. He brought them to the man to see what he would call them, and whatever the man called each living creature, that would be its name. And the man gave names to all cattle and to the birds of the sky and to all the wild beasts; but for Adam no fitting helper was found. So the Lord God cast a deep sleep upon the man;

and while he slept, He took one of his ribs and closed up the flesh at that spot. And the Lord God fashioned the rib that He had taken from the man into a woman; and He brought her to the man. Then the man said: "This one at last is bone of my bones, and flesh of my flesh. This one shall be called Woman [in Hebrew *ishshah*], for from man [*ish*] was she taken." Hence a man leaves his father and mother and clings to his wife, so that they become one flesh. Now they were both naked, the man and his wife, yet they felt no shame. (Genesis 2:5–25)

4. The Christians Regard Eve

From the very outset of their tradition, beginning with Paul, the Christians showed considerable interest in the text of Genesis. Adam in particular, the prototype of Christ, and, to a somewhat lesser extent, his mate Eve served a number of purposes for Christians. Paul, for example, in his first Letter to the Corinthians, works the changes on the meaning of the word "head," all woven around Genesis 2:5–25, to illustrate the role of women in the Church and in the world.

I wish you to understand that, while every man has Christ for his Head, woman's head is man, as Christ's Head is God. A man who keeps his head covered when he prays or prophesies brings shame on his head; a woman, on the contrary, brings shame on her head if she prays or prophesies bareheaded. . . . A man has no need to cover his head, because man is the image of God and the mirror of His glory, whereas woman reflects the glory of man. For man did not originally spring from woman, but woman was made out of man; and man was not created for woman's sake, but woman for the sake of man; and therefore it is woman's duty to have a sign of authority on her head, out of regard for the angels. And yet, in Christ's fellowship woman is as essential to man as man to woman. If woman was made out of man, it is through woman that man now comes to be; and God is the source of all. (Paul, *To the Corinthians* 1.11: 3–12)

The Christian bishop Augustine (d. 430 C.E.) also contemplated this scene of Creation, but from a far wider theological perspective.

From the words (of Paul) "Till we come to a perfect man, to the measure of the fullness of Christ" (Eph. 4:13), and from his words "Conformed to the image of the Son of God" (Rom. 8:29), some conclude that women shall not rise as women (at the final resurrection), but that all shall be men, because God made man only of earth and woman of the man. For my part, they seem to be wiser who make no doubt that both sexes shall rise. For there shall be no lust, which is now the cause of confusion. For before they sinned, the man and woman were naked and were not ashamed. From those bodies, then, vice shall be withdrawn, while nature shall be preserved. And the sex of woman is not a vice, but nature. It shall then indeed be superior to carnal intercourse and child-bearing; nevertheless, the female members shall remain adapted not to the old uses but to a new beauty which, so far from provoking lust, now extinct, shall excite praise to the wisdom and clemency of God, who both made what was not and delivered from corruption what He made.

For at the beginning of the human race the woman was made of a rib taken from the side of the man while he slept; for it seemed fit that even then Christ and his Church should be foreshadowed in this event. For that sleep of the man was the death of Christ, whose side, as he hung lifeless upon the cross, was pierced with a spear, and there flowed from it blood and water, and these we know to be the sacraments from which the Church is "built up." For the Scripture used this very word, not saying "He formed" or "He framed," but "built her up into a woman" (Gen. 2:22); whence also the Apostle (Paul) speaks of the "building up" of the body of Christ (Eph. 4:12), which is the Church.

The woman therefore, is the creature of God even as the man, and by her creation from man is unity commended; and the manner of her creation prefigured, as has been said, Christ and the Church. He, then, who created both sexes, will restore both. (Augustine, *City of God* 22.17) [AUGUSTINE 1948: 2.636–637]

5. The Original Sin and Its Transmission

The chief interest of this chapter of Genesis, at least for Jews and Christians—the Muslims, as we shall soon see, were far more interested in the fall of the angels—was its description of the "original sin" and what followed from it.

Now the serpent was the shrewdest of all the wild beasts that the Lord God had made. He said to the woman, "Did God really say: You shall not eat of any tree of the garden?" The woman replied to the serpent, "We may eat of the fruit of the other trees of the garden. It is only about the fruit of the tree in the middle of the garden that God said: You shall not eat of it or touch it, lest you die." And the serpent said to the woman, "You are not going to die, but God knows that as soon as you eat of it your eyes will be opened and you will be like divine beings who know good and bad." When the woman saw that the tree was good for eating and a delight to the eyes, and that the tree was desirable as a source of wisdom, she took of the its fruit and ate. She also gave some to her husband, and he ate. Then the eyes of both of them were opened and they perceived that they were naked; and they sewed together fig leaves and made themselves loincloths. (Genesis 3:1–7)

We stand here before a base text of the Jewish understanding of sin, for it was from this act of Adam that sin entered the world and forever altered human nature.

Once he [that is, Adam] had transgressed, death raged beyond his time, mourning acquired its name, sorrow was prepared, suffering was created, toil received its full measure. Pride began to take up its residence. Sheol demanded to revitalize itself with blood and seized children. The desire of parents was created; the greatness of humanity was diminished and goodness grew faint. (2 Baruch 56:6)

If Adam was the first to sin and brought death upon all those who did not yet exist in his time, nevertheless, each of those born of him has prepared for himself the punishment to come or prepared glory for himself. . . . We are all our own Adams. (2 Baruch 44:15–19)

Both texts, which confirm the reality of "original sin" and at the same time vindicate human freedom, are from the "Apocalypse of Baruch," a Jewish work of the era just after 70 C.E. and so almost contemporary with the similar but profoundly different meditation of the former Pharisee Paul on Adam's sin.

It was through one man that sin entered the world, and through sin death, and thus death pervaded the whole human race inasmuch as all men have sinned. (Paul, *To the Romans* 5:12)

This is the terse summary of Paul, who is hurrying on to other things, to Jesus, the second Adam, who freed mankind of this universal grip of sin (see Chapter 3 below). For a more elaborate Christian explanation of the consequences of Adam's sin we must turn back to Augustine.

The first men would not have suffered death if they had not sinned. . . . But having become sinners, they were so punished with death that whatever sprang from their stock should also be punished with the same death. For nothing could be born of them other than what they themselves had been. The condemnation changed their nature for the worse in proportion to the greatness of their sin, so that what was previously a punishment in the man who had first sinned, became part of the nature in others who were born. . . . In the first man, then, the whole human nature was to be transmitted by the woman to posterity when that conjugal union received the divine sentence of its own condemnation, and what man became, not when he was created but when he sinned and was punished, this he propagated, so far as the origin of sin and death are concerned.

For God, the author of all natures, not of vices, created man upright; but man, being by his own will corrupted and justly condemned, begot corrupted and condemned children. For we were all in that one man when we were all that one man, who fell into sin by the woman who had been made from him before the sin. For not yet was the particular form created and distributed to us, in which we as individuals were to live; but already the seminal nature was there from which we were to be propagated; and when this was vitiated by sin and bound by the chain of death and justly condemned, man could not be born of man in any other state. And thus from the bad use of free will there originated a whole series of evils, which with its train of miseries conducts the human race from its depraved origin, as from a corrupt root, on to the destruction of the second death, which has no end, those alone excepted who are freed by the grace of God. (Augustine, *City of God* 13.13–14)

[AUGUSTINE 1948: 2:255–256]

The bodily or genetic transmission of the original sin, which was variously defined by medieval authorities as "a langor of nature" or "an inordinate disposition arising from the destruction of the harmony which was essential to original justice," was obviously a troublesome matter, as Thomas Aquinas's (d. 1277 C.E.) address to the question indicates.

In endeavoring to explain how the sin of our first parent could be transmitted by way of origin to his descendants, various writers have gone about it in various ways. For some, considering that the subject of sin is in the rational soul, maintained that the rational soul is transmitted with the semen, so that an infected soul would seem to produce other infected souls. Others, rejecting this as erroneous, endeavored to show how the guilt of the parents' souls can be transmitted to the children, even though the soul itself is not transmitted, from the fact that defects of the body are transmitted from parent to child. . . . Now since the body is proportioned to the soul, and since the soul's defects are experienced in the body, and vice versa, in like manner, they say, a culpable defect of the soul is passed on to the child through the transmission of semen, although the semen itself is not the subject of guilt.

But all these explanations are insufficient. For granted that some bodily defects are transmitted by way of origin from parent to child, and granted that even some defects of the soul are transmitted, in consequence, because of a defect in a bodily disposition, as in the case of idiots begetting idiots, nevertheless, the fact of having an inherited defect seems to exclude the notion of guilt, which is essentially something voluntary. Therefore, even granted that the rational soul were transmitted (genetically), from the very fact that the stain on the child's soul is not in its will, it would cease to be a guilty stain implicating its subject in punishment; for as Aristotle says (*Ethics* 3, 5), "no one blames a man born blind; one rather takes pity on him."

The path around the difficulty of explaining the genetic inheritance of a spiritual disposition passes through one of the theologians' most familiar and friendly territories, the argument from analogy. Thomas continues:

Therefore we must explain this matter otherwise, by saying that all men born of Adam may be considered one man inasmuch as they have one common nature, which they receive from their first parents. Even as in political matters all who are members of one community are reputed as one body, and the whole community as one man. . . . Accordingly, the multitude of men born of Adam are so many members of one body. Now the action of one member of the body, of the hand, for instance, is voluntary, not by the will of the hand but by the will of the soul, the first mover of the body's members. Therefore, a murder which the hand commits would not be imputed as a sin to the hand considered by itself apart from the body, but it is imputed to it as something belonging to man and moved by man's first moving principle. In this way, then, the disorder which is in this man born of Adam is voluntary, not by his will, but by the will of his first parent, who, by the movement of generation, moves all who originate from him, even as the soul's will moves all the body's members to their actions.

Hence the sin which is thus transmitted by the first parent to his descendants is called *original*, just as the sin that flows from the soul into the bodily members is called *actual*. And just as the actual sin that is committed by a member of the body is not the sin of that member, except insomuch as that member is a part of the man, . . . so original sin is not the sin of this person, except insomuch as this person receives his nature from his first parent. (Thomas Aquinas, *Summa Theologica* I/2, ques. 81, art. 1) [AQUINAS 1945: 2:665–666]

But the contemporary biology did at least exonerate Eve.

It would seem that if Eve and not Adam had sinned, their children would still have contracted original sin. For we contract original sin from our parents, insofar as we were once in them. . . . Now a man pre-exists in his mother as well as in his father. Therefore a man would have contracted original sin from his mother's sin as well as from his father's.

Not so, says Thomas in answer to his own objection.

Original sin is transmitted by the first parent insofar as he is the mover in the begetting of his children. And so it has been said that if anyone were begotten only materially of human flesh, he would not contract original sin, Now it is evident that, in the opinion of the experts, the active principle of generation is from the father; so that if Eve and not Adam had sinned, their children would not have contracted original sin. . . . The child pre-exists in its father as in its active principle, and in its mother as in its material and passive principle. (Thomas Aquinas, *Summa Theologica* I/2 ques. 81, art. 5) [AQUINAS 1945: 2:671–672]

6. Paradise Lost

They [that is, Adam and his wife] heard the sound of the Lord God moving about in the garden at the breezy time of day; and the man and his wife hid from the Lord God among the trees of the garden. The Lord God called out to the man and said to him, "Where are you?" He replied, "I heard the sound of You in the garden, and I was afraid because I was naked, so I hid." Then He asked, "Who told you that you were naked? Did you eat of the tree from which I had forbidden you to eat?" The man said, "The woman You put at my side—she gave me of the tree, and I ate." And the Lord God said to the woman, "What is this you have done!" The woman replied, "The serpent duped me, and I ate." Then the Lord God said to the serpent,

> "Because you did this,
> More cursed shall you be
> Than all cattle
> And all the wild beasts:
> On your belly shall you crawl
> And dirt shall you eat
> All the days of your life.
> I will put enmity
> Between you and the woman,
> And between your offspring and hers;
> They shall strike at your head,
> And you shall strike at their heel."

And to the woman He said,

> "I will make most severe
> Your pangs in childbearing;
> In pain shall you bear children.
> Yet your urge shall be for your husband,
> And he shall rule over you."

To Adam He said, "Because you did as your wife said and ate of the tree about which I commanded you, 'You shall not eat of it,'

> Cursed be the ground because of you;
> By toil shall you eat of it
> All the days of your life
> Thorns and thistles shall it sprout for you.
> but your food shall be the grasses of the field;
> By the sweat of your brow
> Shall you get bread to eat,
> Until you return to the ground—
> For from it you were taken.
> For dust you are,
> And to dust you shall return."

The man named his wife Eve, because she was the mother of all the living. And the Lord God made garments of skins for Adam and his wife, and clothed them.

And the Lord God said, "Now that the man has become like one of us, knowing good and bad, what if he should stretch out his hand and take also from the tree of life and eat, and live forever!" So the Lord God banished him from the garden of Eden, to till the soil from which he was taken. He drove the man out, and stationed east of the garden of Eden the cherubim and the fiery ever-turning sword, to guard the way to the tree of life. (Genesis 3:8–24)

And their descendants will inherit the same moral consequences, Augustine assures us.

Justly is shame very specially connected with this lust; justly too these (sexual) members themselves, being moved and restrained not (any longer) at our will, but by a certain independent autocracy, so to speak, are called *pudenda* or "shameful." For as it is written, "They were naked and were not ashamed" (Gen. 2:25)—not that their nakedness was unknown to them, but because nakedness was not yet shameful, because not yet did lust move those members without the will's consent; nor yet did the flesh by its disobedience testify against the disobedience of man. For they were not created blind, as the unenlightened vulgar fancy; for Adam saw the animals and gave them names, and of Eve we read, "The woman saw that the tree was good for food and it was pleasant to the eyes" (Gen. 3:6). Their eyes, therefore, were open, but were not open to this, that is to say, were not observant so as to recognize what was conferred on them by the garment of grace, for they had no consciousness of their members warring against their will.

But when they were stripped of this grace, that their disobedience might be punished by fit retribution, there began in the movement of their bodily members a shameless novelty which made their nakedness indecent: it at once made them observant and made them ashamed. And therefore, after they violated God's command by open transgression, it is written: "And the eyes of both of them were opened and they discovered that they were naked; so they stitched fig leaves together and made themselves loincloths."

"The eyes of both of them were opened," not to see, for they already saw, but to discern between the good they had lost and the evil into which they had fallen. And therefore also the tree itself which they were forbidden to touch was called the tree of the knowledge of good and evil from this circumstance, that if they ate of it, it would impart to them this knowledge. For the discomfort of sickness reveals the pleasure of health. "They knew," there, "that they were naked," naked of that grace that prevented them from being ashamed of bodily nakedness, while the law of sin offered no resistance to their mind. And thus they obtained a knowledge of which they would have lived in blissful ignorance had they, in trustful obedience to God, declined to commit that offense which involved them in the hurtful effects of unfaithfulness and disobedience. And therefore, being ashamed of the disobedience of their own flesh, which bore witness to their disobedience even as it punished it, "they stitched fig leaves together and made themselves loincloths," that is, cinctures for their privy parts. . . . Shame modestly covered that which lust disobediently moved in opposition to the will, which was thus punished for its own disobedience. Consequently all nations, being propagated from one stock, have so strong an instinct to cover the shameful parts that some barbarians do not uncover them even in the bath but wash with their drawers on. (Augustine, *City of God* 14.17)
[AUGUSTINE 1948: 2.262–263]

What was there, Augustine asks, that was so terrible about this particular offense that it should have such long-reaching consequences?

If one finds a difficulty in understanding why other sins do not alter human nature as it was altered by the transgression of those first human beings, so that on account of it this nature is subject to the great corruption we feel and see, and to death, and is distracted and tossed with so many furious and contending emotions, and is certainly far different from what it was before sin, even though it was (even) then lodged in an animal body—if, I say, anyone is moved by this, he ought not to think that this sin was a small and light one because it was committed about food, and neither bad nor noxious except because it was forbidden; for in that spot of singular felicity God could not have created or planted any evil thing. But by the precept He gave, God commended obedience, which is, in a way, the mother and guardian of all the virtues in the reasonable creature, which was so created that submission is advantageous to it, while the fulfillment of its own will in preference to the Creator's is destruction. And as this commandment enjoined abstinence from one kind of food in the midst of great abundance of other kinds was so easy to keep—so light a burden to the memory—and, above all, found no resistance to its observance in lust, which only afterwards sprung up as the penal consequence of sin, the iniquity of violating it was all the greater in proportion to the ease with which it might have been kept.

Our first parents fell into open disobedience because already they were secretly corrupted; for the evil act had never been done had not an evil will preceded it. And what is the origin of that evil will but pride? . . . And what is pride but the craving for undue exaltation? And this is undue exaltation, when the soul abandons Him to whom it ought to cleave as its end and becomes an end to itself. This happens when it becomes its own satisfaction. And it does so when it falls away from that unchangeable good which ought to satisfy it more than itself. This falling away is spontaneous; for if the will had remained steadfast in the love of that higher and changeless good by which it was illumined to intelligence and kindled into love, it would not have turned away to find satisfaction in itself, and so become frigid and benighted; the woman would not have believed that the serpent spoke the truth, nor would the man have preferred the request of his wife to the command of God, nor would he have supposed that it was a venial transgression to cling to the partner of his life even in a partnership of sin. (Augustine, *City of God* 14.12–13)

[AUGUSTINE 1948: 2:257–258]

7. Adam and the Fall of the Angels
in the Quran

Christians found the chief moral implications of Genesis in the story of Adam's fall and banishment. Muslims too read the Creation story in a moral manner, chiefly because the Quran presented it from precisely that perspective. Here, however, the emphasis is not on the fall of Adam but on the sin of the angels.

He made for you all that lies within the earth, then turning to the firmament He proportioned several skies: He has a knowledge of everything.

And when the work of Creation was completed, there followed this dialogue in heaven.

Remember when the Lord said to the angels, "I have to place a trustee [Arabic *khalifa*, Caliph] on the earth," they said, "Will You place one there who would create disorder and shed blood, while we intone Your litanies and sanctify Your name?" And God said, "I know what you do not know." Then He gave Adam the knowledge of the nature and reality of all things and everything, and set them before the angels and said, "Tell me the names of these if you are truthful." And they said, "Glory to You, (O Lord), knowledge we have none save what You have given us, for You are all-knowing and all-wise."

Then He said to Adam, "Convey to them their names." And when he had told them, God said, "Did I not I tell you that I know the unknown of the heavens and the earth, and I know what you disclose and know what you hide."

Remember, when We asked the angels to bow in homage to Adam, they all bowed but Iblis, who disdained and turned insolent, and so became a disbeliever.

And We said to Adam, "Both you and your spouse will live in the Garden, eat freely to your fill wherever you like, but approach not this tree or you will become transgressors."

But Satan tempted them and had them banished from the (happy) state they were in. And We said, "Go, one the enemy of the other, and live on the the earth the time ordained, and fend for yourselves."

Then his Lord sent commands to Adam and turned toward him: Indeed He is compassionate and kind. (Quran 2:29–37)

8. The Summons of Abraham

The Book of Genesis leaves Adam and pursues its narrative through the story of Cain and Abel. It then traces the line of Adam through Seth, then Enoch (of whom we shall hear again), down to Noah and the generation of the Flood. The history of Noah's sons Shem, Ham, and Japheth is told; and finally, after the story of the Tower of Babel, the biblical account reaches the immediate ancestors of Abraham.

Now this is the line of Terah: Terah begot Abram, Nahor, and Haran; and Haran begot Lot. Haran died in the lifetime of his father Terah, in his native land, Ur of the Chaldeans. Abram and Nahor took to themselves wives, the name of Abram's wife being Sarai and that of Nahor's wife Milcah, the daughter of Haran, the father of Milcah and Iscah. Now Sarai was barren, she had no child.

Terah took his son Abram, his grandson Lot the son of Haran, and his daughter-in-law Sarai, the wife of his son Abram, and they set out together from Ur of the Chaldeans for the land Canaan; but when they had come as far as Haran, they settled there. The days of Terah came to 205 years; and Terah died in Haran.

The Lord said to Abram, "Go forth from your native land and from your father's house to the land that I will show you.

> I will make of you a great nation,
> And I will bless you;
> I will make your name great,
> And you shall be a blessing.
> I will bless those who bless you
> And curse him that curses you;
> And all the families of the earth
> Shall bless themselves by you."

Abram went forth as the Lord had commanded him, and Lot went with him. Abram was seventy-five years old when he left Haran. Abram took his wife Sarai and his brother's son Lot, and all the wealth that they had amassed, and the persons that they acquired in Haran; and they set out for the land of Canaan.

So Abram ends his long migration from his Iraqi homeland at "Ur of the Chaldeans" to Canaan, the future Land of the Promise.

Abram passed through the land as far as the site of Shechem, at the terebinth of Moreh. The Canaanites were then in the land. When they arrived in the land of Canaan, the Lord appeared to Abram and said, "I will give this land to your offspring." And he built an altar there to the Lord who had appeared to him. From there he moved on to the hill country east of Bethel and pitched his tent, with Bethel on the west and Ai on the east; and he built there an altar to the Lord and invoked the Lord by name. Then Abram journeyed by stages toward the Negeb. (Genesis 11:27–12:9)

9. Melchizedek, High Priest of Salem

After a spell in Egypt, Abraham and his family returned to the land of the Canaanites and made his home at the terebinths of Mamre, in a place called Hebron, where he was immediately caught up in the wars of the local princes and rulers. It was during his return home from one of those campaigns near Damascus that the following incident took place.

When he [that is, Abram] returned from defeating Cherdorlaomer and the kings with him, the king of Sodom came out to meet him in the Valley of Shaveh, which is the Valley of the King. And Melchizedek, king of Salem, brought out bread and wine; he was a priest of God Most High. He blessed him, saying,

> "Blessed be Abram of God Most High,
> Creator of heaven and earth.
> And blessed be God Most High,
> Who has delivered your foes into your hand."

And [Abram] gave him a tenth of everything. (Genesis 14:17–20)

10. A Christian Appreciation of Melchizedek

With those few words the mysterious Melchizedek, "priest of God Most High," disappears from the historical narrative of Genesis as abruptly as he had entered it, though assuredly not from the thoughts of the Jews, who quickly identified him with Shem, the son of Noah, and understood that he was king of Jerusalem. But even more consequentially, Melchizedek reappears in a Messianic context in Psalm 110:4.

The Lord has sworn and will not change His purpose: You [that is, the Messiah, since it is he who is being addressed] are a priest forever, in the succession of Melchizedek.

There the Christians found Melchizedek and used him for their own purposes. This is how the author of the New Testament's Letter to the Hebrews *understood him.*

This Melchizedek, king of Salem, priest of God Most High, met Abraham returning from the rout of the kings and blessed him; and Abraham gave him a tithe of everything as his portion. His name, in the first place, means "king of righteousness"; next he is king of Salem, that is, "king of peace." He has no father, no mother, no lineage; his years have no beginning, his life no end. He is like the Son of God: he remains a priest for all time.

Consider how great he must be for Abraham the patriarch to give him a tithe of the finest of the spoil. The descendants of Levi who take the priestly office are commanded by the Law to receive tithes from the people, that is, from their kinsmen, although they too are descendants of Abraham. But Melchizedek, though he does not trace his descent from them, has received tithes from Abraham himself, and given his blessing to the man who received the promises; and beyond all dispute the lesser is always blessed by the greater. (Hebrews 7:1–7)

11. The Covenant and the Promised Land

Melchizedek was assuredly neither the center nor the point of these chapters of Genesis. *The narrative is heading toward quite another climax, and it has to do with Abram, as he was still being called.*

Some time later, the word of the Lord came to Abram in a vision, saying,

> "Fear not, Abram,
> I am a shield to you;
> Your reward shall be very great."

But Abram said, "O Lord God, what can You give me, seeing that I shall die childless, and the one in charge of my household is Dammesek Eliezer!" Abram said further, "Since You have granted me no offspring, my steward shall be my heir." The word of the Lord came to him in reply, "That one shall not be your heir; none but your very own issue shall be your heir." He took him outside and said, "Look toward heaven and count the stars, if you are able to count them." And He added, "So shall your offspring be." And because he put his trust in the Lord, He reckoned it to his merit. (Genesis 15:1–6)

On that day the Lord made a covenant with Abram, saying, "To your offspring I give this land, from the river of Egypt to the great river, the river Euphrates: the Kenites, the Kenizzites, the Kadmonites, the Hittites, the Perizzites, the Rephaim, the Amorites, the Canaanites, the Girgashites, and the Jebusites." (Genesis 15:17–21)

12. The Birth of Ishmael

The rest of the Bible, and the New Testament and Quran as well, has to do with the fulfillment of this promise made to the descendants of Abraham. Jews, Christians, and Muslims would all one day claim to be the true progeny and heir to Abraham. But that same question of birthright arose in the patriarch's own lifetime.

Sarai, Abram's wife, had borne him no children. She had an Egyptian maid servant whose name was Hagar. And Sarai said to Abram, "Look, the Lord has kept me from bearing. Consort with my maid; perhaps I shall have a son through her." And Abram heeded Sarai's request. So Sarai, Abram's wife, took her maid, Hagar the Egyptian— after Abram had dwelt in the land of Canaan ten years—and gave her to her husband Abram as concubine. He cohabited with Hagar and she conceived; and when she saw that she had conceived, her mistress was lowered in her esteem. And Sarai said to Abram, "The wrong done me is your fault! I myself put my maid in your bosom; now that she sees that she is pregnant, I am lowered in her esteem. The Lord decide between you and me!" Abram said to Sarai, "Your maid is in your hands. Deal with her as you think right." Then Sarai treated her harshly, and she ran away from her.

An angel of the Lord found her by a spring of water in the wilderness, the spring on the road to Shur, and said, "Hagar, slave of Sarai, where have you come from, and where are you going?" And she said, "I am running away from my mistress Sarai."

And the angel of the Lord said to her, "Go back to your mistress, and submit to her harsh treatment." And the angel of the Lord said to her.

"I will greatly increase your offspring
And they shall be too many to count."

The angel of the Lord said to her further,

"Behold, you are with child
And shall bear a son;
You shall call him Ishmael,
For the Lord has paid heed to your suffering.

He shall be a wild ass of a man;
His hand against everyone,
And everyone's hand against him;
He shall dwell alongside of all his kinsmen."

Hagar bore a son to Abram, and Abram gave the son that Hagar bore him the name Ishmael. Abram was eighty-six years old when Hagar bore Ishmael to Abram. (Genesis 16:1–16)

13. The Covenant

This was all prelude. The Promise came to Abraham thirteen years later, and it concerned not Ishmael but another, yet unborn child of the elderly Abraham.

When Abram was ninety-nine years old, the Lord appeared to Abram and said to him, "I am El Shaddai. Walk in My ways and be blameless. I will establish My covenant between Me and you, and I will make you exceedingly numerous."

Abram threw himself on his face; and God spoke to him further, "As for Me, this is My covenant with you: You shall be the father of a multitude of nations. And you shall no longer be called Abram, but your name shall be Abraham, for I make you the father of a multitude of nations. I will make you exceedingly fertile, and make nations of you; and kings shall come forth from you. I will maintain My covenant between Me and you, and your offspring to come, as an everlasting covenant throughout the ages, to be God to you and your offspring to come. I give the land you sojourn in to you and your offspring to come, all the land of Canaan, as an everlasting possession. I will be their God." (Genesis 17:1–8)

God further said to Abraham, "As for you, you and your offspring to come throughout the ages shall keep My covenant. Such shall be the covenant between Me and you and your offspring to follow which you shall keep: every male among you shall be circumcised. You shall circumcise the flesh of your foreskin, and that shall be the sign of the covenant between Me and you. And throughout the generations, every male among you shall be circumcised at the age of eight days. As for the homeborn slave and the one bought from an outsider who is not of your offspring, they must be circumcised, homeborn and purchased alike. Thus shall My covenant be marked in your flesh as an everlasting pact. And if any male who is uncircumcised fails to circumcise the flesh of his foreskin, that person shall be cut off from his kin; he has broken My covenant." (Genesis 17:9–14)

Thus the Covenant was sealed by circumcision. There remained, however, the question of the heir.

And God said to Abraham, "As for your wife Sarai, you shall not call her Sarai, but her name shall be Sarah. I will bless her; indeed, I will give you a son by her. I will bless her so that we shall give rise to nations; rulers of peoples shall issue from her." Abraham threw himself on his face and laughed, as he said to himself, "Can a child be born to a man a hundred years old, or can Sarah bear a child at ninety?" And Abraham said to God, "Oh that Ishmael might live by Your favor!" God said, "Nevertheless, Sarah your wife shall bear you a son, and you shall name him Isaac; and I will maintain My covenant with him as an everlasting covenant for his offspring to come. As for Ishmael, I have heeded you. I hereby bless him. I will make him fertile and exceedingly numerous. He shall be the father of twelve chieftains, and I will make of him a great nation. But My covenant I will maintain with Isaac, whom Sarah shall bear to you at this season next year." And when He was done speaking with him, God was gone from Abraham.

Then Abraham took his son Ishmael, and all his homeborn slaves and all those he had bought, every male in Abraham's household, and he circumcised the flesh of their foreskins on that very day, as God had spoken to him. Abraham was ninety-nine years old when he circumcised the flesh of his foreskin, and his son Ishmael was thirteen years old when he was circumcised in the flesh of his foreskin. (Genesis 17:15–25)

14. Ishmael and the Ishmaelites

The Lord took note of Sarah as He had promised, and the Lord did for Sarah as He had spoken. Sarah conceived and bore a son to Abraham in his old age, at the set time of which God had spoken. Abraham gave his newborn son, whom Sarah had borne him, the name of Isaac. And when his son Isaac was eight days old, Abraham circumcised him, as God had commanded him. Now Abraham was a hundred years old when his son Isaac was born to him. Sarah said, "God has brought me laughter; everyone who hears will laugh at me." And she added,

"Who would have said to Abraham
that Sarah would suckle children!
Yet I have borne a son in his old age."

The child grew up and was weaned, and Abraham held a great feast on the day that Isaac was weaned.

Sarah saw the son whom Hagar the Egyptian had borne to Abraham playing. She said to Abraham, "Cast out that slave woman and her son, for the son of that slave shall not share in the inheritance with my son Isaac." The matter distressed Abraham greatly, for it concerned a son of his. But God said to Abraham, "Do not be distressed over the boy or your slave; whatever Sarah tells you, do as she says, for it is through Isaac that offspring shall be continued for you. As for the son of the slave woman, I will make a nation of him, too, for he is your seed."

Ishmael, then, is to be neither glorified nor entirely rejected.

Early the next morning Abraham took some bread and a skin of water, and gave them to Hagar. He placed them on her shoulder, together with the child, and sent her away. And she wandered about in the wilderness of Beer-sheba. When the water was gone from the skin, she left the child under one of the bushes, and went and sat down at a distance, a bowshot away; for she thought, "Let me not look on as the child dies." And sitting thus afar, she burst into tears.

God heard the cry of the boy, and an angel of God called to Hagar from heaven and said to her, "What troubles you, Hagar? Fear not, for God has heeded the cry of the boy where he is. Come, lift up the boy and hold him by the hand, for I will make a great nation of him." Then God opened her eyes and she saw a well of water. She went and filled the skin with water, and let the boy drink. God was with the boy and he grew up; he dwelt in the wilderness and became a bowman. He lived in the wilderness of Paran [that is, in Sinai]; and his mother got a wife for him from the land of Egypt. (Genesis 21:1–21)

Genesis returns to the subject of Ishmael one final time in Chapter 25.

This is the line of Ishmael, Abraham's son, whom Hagar the Egyptian, Sarah's slave, bore to Abraham. These are the names of the sons of Ishmael, by their names, in the order of their birth: Nebaioth, the first-born of Ishmael, Kedar, Abdeel, Mibsam, Mishma, Dumah, Massa, Hadad, Tema, Jetur, Naphish, and Kedmah. These are the sons of Ishmael and these are their names by their villages and by their encampments: twelve chieftains of as many tribes. These were the years of the life of Ishmael: one hundred and thirty-seven years; then he breathed his last and died, and was gathered to his kin. They dwelt from Havilah, by Shur, which is close to Egypt, all the way to Asshur; they camped alongside all their kinsman. (Genesis 25:12–18)

15. The Arabs as Ishmaelites

This is the end of the story in the canonical Scripture. But when the anonymous Pharisee sat down sometime between 135 and 105 B.C.E. to retell the story of Abraham, Isaac, and Jacob under the name of "The Book of Jubilees," he knew somewhat more than what Genesis revealed about the descendants of Ishmael. First, Abraham summoned Ishmael and his twelve sons, Isaac and his two, and the sons of another of his women, Keturah, and bade them to continue to observe circumcision, to avoid all fornication, uncleanness, and intermarriage with the Canaanite population of the land. The passage then concludes.

And he [that is, Abraham] gave gifts to Ishmael and his sons, and to the sons of Keturah, and he sent them away from his son Isaac, and he gave his son Isaac everything. And Ishmael and his sons, and the sons of Keturah and their sons, went together and settled between Paran to the borders of Babylon, in all the land that is toward the East, facing the desert. And these mingled with each other, and they were called Arabs and Ishmaelites. (Jubilees 20:11–13)

Four or five centuries later, the Babylonian rabbis were imagining a series of lawsuits that would have taken place before Alexander the Great when that conqueror entered Palestine in the 330s B.C.E. Three peoples laid claim against the Jews to the land of Israel: the Phoenicians, who claimed descent from the original Canaanites; the Egyptians, who claimed they had been robbed by the children of Israel at the time of the Exodus; and finally "the Ishmaelites and the Ketureans," who had an obvious, if partial, claim on the land as the other heirs of Abraham. A rabbi named Gebiha ben Pesiha requests permission to go and plead the Jews' case before Alexander, so that if it is lost people might say, "You have defeated one of our ignorant men," while, if he prevails, it will be said that "the Law of Moses our Teacher has defeated them."

So they gave him permission and he went and pleaded against them. "Whence do you adduce your proof?" he asked them [that is, the Ishmaelites and Ketureans]. "From the Torah," they replied. "Then I too," he said, "will bring proof only from the Torah, for it is written, 'And Abraham gave all that he had to Isaac. But to the sons of the concubines which Abraham had, Abraham gave gifts' (Gen. 25: 1–4); if a father made a bequest to the children in his lifetime and sent them away from each other, has one any claim on the other?"

What gifts? Rabbi Jeremiah ben Abba said: This teaches that he imparted to them the (secrets of the) unholy arts [that is, of sorcery and demonology]. (BT.Sanhedrin 91a)

It may be doubted that any such case actually occurred. What is certain, however, is that the genealogy of the Arabs as descendants of Ishmael was well established, and widely disseminated, long before the coming of Islam. Josephus says that the Arabs were circumcised at the age of thirteen "because Ishmael, the founder of their race, born to Abraham's concubine, was circumcised at that age" (Antiquities 1.12.2), and that the sons of Ishmael "occupied the whole country extending from the Euphrates to the Red Sea and called it Nabatene, and it is these who conferred their name on the Arab nation and its tribes in honor of both their own prowess and the fame of Abraham" (Antiquities 1.12.4). And finally, this is how the story of the Ishmaelites is presented in the Church History *of Sozomen about 440 C.E. The author had just been discussing "Saracens," a common name for Arabs before and after Islam.*

This tribe (of Saracens) takes its origins from Ishmael the son of Abraham and had that appellation as well: the ancients called them Ishmaelites from their ancestry. And to avoid the charge of bastardy and the low birth of the mother of Ishmael, they called themselves "Sara-cens" as if descended from Abraham's wife Sarah. Possessing this kind of descent, all of them are circumcised like the Hebrews and abstain from the flesh of swine and observe among themselves many of the latter's customs. Nor should one think that they have always lived in the same manner, whether by reason of the passage of time or by their intercourse with the surrounding peoples. For it was long after them that Moses legislated, and then only for those who went out of Egypt. Those who lived near the Ishmaelites, being demon worshipers, likely destroyed the Ishmaelites' ancestral way of life, the only norm by which the ancient Hebrews lived before the Mosaic legislation, relying on unwritten customs. Those same demons the Ishmaelites too doubtless reverenced, and they especially honored them and called upon them in the manner of the cult practices of their neighbors and so demonstrated the reason why they neglected their ancestral laws. The passage of a long time caused them to forget some and allow others to grow antiquated. Afterwards some of them became acquainted with the Jews and learned whence they had come. They reverted back to their ancestry and took up the Hebrew customs and laws. From that time many among them still live in the Jewish fashion. (Sozomen, *Church History* 6.38.1–13)

That same descent was re-established in the Quran, which puts not only Ishmael but also his father Abraham at Mecca in the patriarchal era. And if the identification of Ishmael as the father of the Arabs was useful for Muhammad, it served equally well for Jewish exegetes living under Islam, as is graphically illustrated by the meditations of this anonymous tenth-century rabbi on Genesis, which are rather more direct than is usual in this genre.

It says: "And he [that is, Ishmael] shall be a man like the wild ass." (Gen. 16:12), that is to say, like an animal that dwells in the desert, so your son Ishmael will find shelter in the desert. And with this, she [Hagar] realized that Ishmael her son would have no portion in the land of Canaan, short of a foothold. With this statement he [God?] disabused her of her view and so obliged her to return and submit to Sarah because the promises (made to Abraham) would not be fulfilled in her son.

And when Abraham and Sarah heard this statement from her, they rejoiced, understanding that he would still be blessed by other seed, from her or from another woman, because Sarah was an old woman, and that the promise would be fulfilled. Sarah too was astonished to hear Hagar, imagining that Abraham would have a child from her or from another woman.

Then the announcement was made that Abraham would have another son, and he was Isaac and it was he of whom the promises had been spoken.

And it says: "His hand shall be against every man" (ibid.), meaning that at the end of his lifetime Ishmael will enter a settled area and will dwell in settlements, and will reign over settlements and rule nations. Of this it is written in Daniel (11:24), "In time of peace he will overrun the richest districts of the province and succeed in doing what his fathers and forefathers failed to do, distributing spoil, booty, and property to his followers, etc." At first he will come forth with only a few people and he will manipulate with plots and cunning, as it says, "he will enter into fraudulent alliances, and although the people behind him are but few, he will rise to power" (Dan. 11:23). And he will stretch his arm upon the nations, as it says: "His hand shall be against every man." This is what Zechariah has said (6:4), "(The chariot) with the roan horse went forth (to the east), and they were eager to go and range over the whole earth." So he said, "Go and range over the earth," and they did so.

The roan horses are the Ishmaelites from whom some Arab tribes emerged with the "Defective." They took the kingship from the Midianites, from (the Shah) Yazdgard [635–651 C.E.], of whom it is written (Dan. 11:21), "A contemptible creature will succeed," and he is called (ibid. 7:8) "the Little Horn," of which it is said, "and three of the first horns were uprooted to make way for it" (ibid.).

And there was no nation in the world that had happen to it what happened to Ishmael. No one spoke like it, as it was written (ibid.), "And a mouth speaking great things." Of its leaders it is said (Dan. 8:23), "a king shall appear, harsh and grim, a master of stratagem." At first the Ishmaelite nation lived in the desert and did not have the "yoke of kingship," as it is written, "a wild ass used to the wilderness snuffing the wind in her lust." And when this nation grew up it entered the settled areas and imposed its yoke on kingdoms and on deserts. And they did not leave these places and they are in their hands up to this day, a period of 372 years [from the Hijra, that is, 982 C.E.]. . . . And just as the saying "His hand shall be against every man" was fulfilled, so shall the saying "and every man's hand shall be against him" will (also) be fulfilled, as it is written in Habakkuk (2:8), "Because you have plundered many mighty nations, all the rest of the world will plunder you." (MS Adler 7320)

[SOKOLOW 1981: 313–316]

16. The Binding of Isaac

We return to the narrative in Genesis:

Sometime afterward, God put Abraham to the test. He said to him, "Abraham," and he answered, "Here I am." And He said, "Take your son, your favored one, Isaac, whom you love, and go to the land of Moriah, and offer him there as a burnt offering on one of the heights which I will point out to you." So early next morning, Abraham saddled his ass and took with him two of his servants and his son Isaac. He split wood for the burnt offering, and he set out for the place of which God had told him. On the third day Abraham looked up and saw the place from afar. Then Abraham said to his servants, "You stay here with the ass. The boy and I will go up there; we will worship and we will return to you."

Abraham took the wood for the burnt offering and put it on his son Isaac. He himself took the firestone and the knife; and the two walked off together. Then Isaac said to his father Abraham, "Father!" And he answered, "Yes, my son." And he said, "Here are the firestone and the wood; but where is the sheep for the burnt offering?" And Abraham said, "God will see to the sheep for His burnt offering, my son." And the two of them walked on together.

They arrived at the place of which God had told him. Abraham built an altar there; he laid out the wood; he bound his son Isaac; he laid him on the altar, on top of the wood. And Abraham picked up the knife to slay his son. Then an angel of the Lord called to him from heaven. "Abraham! Abraham!" And he answered, "Here I am." And he said, "Do not raise your hand against the boy, or do anything to him. For now I know that you fear God, since you have not withheld your son, your favored one, from Me." When Abraham looked up, his eye fell upon a ram, caught in the thicket by its horns. So Abraham went and took the ram and offered it up as a burnt offering in place of his son. And Abraham named that site Adonai Jireh, hence the present saying, "On the mount of the Lord there is vision."

To this point the account appears to describe a somewhat arbitrary test to which the Lord had put Abraham's conviction. In the immediate sequel it becomes clear that the test of the "binding of Isaac" was the act whereby Abraham and his descendants "merited" the Promise that God had made to them, which is now renewed:

The angel of the Lord called to Abraham a second time from heaven and said, "By Myself I swear, the Lord declares: because you have done this and have not withheld your son, your favored one, I will bestow My blessing upon you and make your descendants as numerous as the stars of heaven and the sands on the seashore; and your descendants shall seize the gates of their foes. All the nations of the earth shall bless themselves by your descendants, because you have obeyed My command. . . ."

Then the angel of the Lord called from heaven a second time to Abraham: "This is the word of the Lord: By My Own Self I swear: inasmuch as you have done this and have not withheld your son, your only son, I will bless you abundantly and greatly multiply your descendants until they are as numerous as the stars in the sky and the grains of sand on the seashore. Your descendants shall possess the cities of their enemies. All nations on earth shall pray to be blessed as your descendants are blessed, and this because you have obeyed Me." (Genesis 22:1–18)

17. The Christian as the Offspring of Abraham

Abraham is, of course, the crucial figure in the entire history of the Covenant, as we shall see again and again. The Jews, founding themselves on the simple sense of Genesis, regarded themselves as natural heirs of both Abraham and the Covenant. For the Christian and Muslim contestants, however, the point had to be argued, and strenuously. This is the classic Christian argument, perhaps taken from the preaching of John the Baptist, who had admonished his fellow Jews: "Do not presume to say to yourselves, 'We have Abraham as a father.' I tell you, God can make children of Abraham out of these stones here" (Matt. 3:9). Here Paul explains.

What, then, are we to say about Abraham, our ancestor in the natural line? If Abraham was justified by anything he had done, then he had ground for pride. But he had no such ground before God; for what does Scripture say? "Abraham put his faith in God, and that faith was counted to him as righteousness." Now if a man does a piece of work, his wages are not "counted" to him as a favor; they are paid as a debt. But if without any work to his credit he simply puts his faith in him who acquits the guilty, then his faith is indeed "counted as righteousness" (Gen. 15:6).

Paul connects the Promise directly with Abraham's monotheistic faith and not, as the passage in Genesis 22:16–18 suggests, on his perfect obedience in the matter of the "binding of Isaac."

Consider, we say "Abraham's faith was counted as righteousness"; in what circumstances was it so counted? Was he circumcised at the time or not? He was not yet circumcised but uncircumcised; and he later received the symbolic rite of circumcision as a hallmark of the righteousness which faith had given him when he was still uncircumcised. Consequently, he is the father of all who have faith when uncircumcised, so that righteousness is "counted" to them; and at the same time he is the father of such of the circumcised as do not rely on their circumcision alone but also walk in the footsteps of the faith which our father Abraham had while he was yet uncircumcised.

For it was not through law that Abraham, or his posterity, was given the promise that the world would be their inheritance, but through the righteousness that came from faith. For if those who hold by the law, and they alone, are heirs, then faith is empty and the promise goes for nothing, because law can bring only retribution. But where there is no law, there can be no breach of law. The promise was made on the ground of faith, in order that it might be a matter of sheer grace, and that it might be valid for all Abraham's posterity, not only for those who hold by the law, but for those also who have the faith of Abraham. For he is the father of us all, as Scripture says, "I have appointed you to be the father of many nations." This promise, then, was valid before God, the God in whom he put his faith, the God who makes the dead live and summons things that are not yet in existence as if they already were. . . . Without any weakening of his faith he contemplated his own body, as good as dead (for he was about a hundred years old) and the deadness of Sarah's womb, and never doubted God's promise in unbelief, but, strong in faith, gave honor to God, in the firm conviction of his power to do what he had promised. And that is why Abraham's faith was "counted to him as righteousness."

Those words were written not for Abraham's sake alone, but for our sake too: it is to be "counted" in the same way to us who have faith in the God who raised Jesus our Lord from the dead; for he was given up to death for our misdeeds, and raised to life to justify us. (Paul, *To the Romans* 4:1–25)

That the circumcision of Abraham was simply a sign—a "symbolic rite," as Paul called it—and did not constitute his justification was argued from a different point of view by the Christian Justin in his debate with the rabbi Trypho or Tarphon sometime about 150 C.E.

If circumcision had been necessary as you [that is, Trypho and the Jews] suppose, God would not have created Adam uncircumcised, nor would He have looked with favor upon the sacrifice of Abel which he offered in uncircumcision, nor would Enoch have been pleasing to God in uncircumcision. . . . Lot, uncircumcised, was delivered out of Sodom. . . . Noah is the father of the human race; but with his children, while he was uncircumcised, he entered into the ark. Melchizedek, the priest of the Most High, was uncircumcised, to whom Abraham, the first to receive circumcision after the flesh, gave tithes, and Melchizedek blessed him. It was according to his succession [that is, Melchizedek] that God declared through David that he would make him a priest forever. . . .

We are constrained to concede that Abraham accepted circumcision as a sign and not as righteousness by both Scripture and the events themselves. It was rightly said of his people that whoever was not circumcised by the eighth day would be cut off from his tribe. But the fact that the female gender cannot receive circumcision is an argument that it was given as a sign and not as the work of justice, for God so made women that as far as regards justice and virtue, they likewise are capable of full observance. (Justin, *Dialogue with Trypho* 19, 23)

18. The New Covenant and the Old: The Christian View

The Christians were hardly in a position to deny, even if they had been so inclined, that a Covenant had been sealed between God and Abraham and his descendants and that those latter were, in some sense, the Jews. What they could and did do was take their point of departure from a well-known text of Jeremiah (Jer. 31:31–34, cited in Chapter 2 below) and argue that there would be a second or New Covenant to supersede the first.

Had that first Covenant been faultless, there would have been no need to look for a second in its place. But God, finding fault with them, says, "The days are coming, says the Lord, when I will conclude a new Covenant with the House of Israel and the House of Judah. It will not be like the Covenant I made with their forefathers when I took them by the hand to lead them out of Egypt; because they did not abide by the terms of that Covenant, and I abandoned them, says the Lord. For the Covenant I will make with the house of Israel after these those days, says the Lord, is this: I will set my laws in their understanding and write them on their hearts; and I will be their God and they will be my people . . . " (Jer. 31:31–34). By speaking of a new Covenant, He has pronounced the first one old; and anything that is growing old and aging will shortly disappear. (Hebrews 8:7–13)

19. The Rabbinic Response: There Will Be No New Covenant

The Jews were not much inclined to argue this or any other point with the Christians, though perhaps the Christian claim to a New Testament lies somewhere behind this kind of text.

It is written, "For this commandment is not in heaven" (Deut. 30:11–12). Moses said to the Israelites, "Lest you should say, Another Moses is to arise and to bring us another Law from heaven; therefore I make it known to you now that it is not in heaven." Rabbi Hanina said: The Law and all the implements by which it has been carried out have been given, namely, modesty, beneficence, uprightness and reward. (*Deuteronomy Rabbah* 8.6)

20. The Quran's Account of the Covenant

The Muslim for his part was not constrained to argue the case of his spiritual descent from Genesis; he had his own account of the Covenant in the Quran. It begins with Abraham in a state of idolatry, of "associating," as the Quran puts it, other gods with the One True God.

Remember when Abraham said to Azar, his father: "Why do you take idols for gods? I certainly find you and your people in error." Thus We showed to Abraham the visible and invisible world of the heavens and the earth, that he could be among those who believe. When the night came with her covering of darkness, he saw a star, and (Azar, his father) said, "This is my Lord." But when the star set, (Abraham) said, "I love not those that wane." When (Azar) saw the moon rise all aglow, he said, "This is my Lord." But even as the moon set, (Abraham) said; "If my Lord had not shown me the way, I would surely have gone astray." When (Azar) saw the sun rise all resplendent, he said, "My Lord is surely this, and the greatest of them all." But the sun also set, and (Abraham) said, "O my people, I am through with those you associate with God. I have truly turned my face toward Him who created the heavens and the earth: I have chosen one way and I am not a idolater."

His people argued and he said, "Do you argue with me about God? He has guided me already, and I fear not what you associate with Him, unless my Lord wills, for held within the knowledge of my Lord is everything. Will you not reflect? And why should I fear those you associate with Him when you fear not associating others with God for which He has sent down no sanction? Tell me whose way is the way of peace, if you have the knowledge. They alone have peace who believe, and do not intermix belief with denial, and are guided on the right path.

This is the argument We gave to Abraham against his people. We exalt whosoever We please in rank by degrees. Your Lord is wise and all-knowing. And We gave him Isaac and Jacob and guided them, as We had guided Noah before them, and of his descendants, David and Solomon and Job and Joseph and Moses and Aaron. Thus do We reward those who are upright and do good. Zachariah and John We guided, and guided Jesus and Elias who were all among the upright. And we gave guidance to Ishmael, Elisha and Jonah and Lot; and We favored them over all the other people of the world, as We did some of their fathers and progeny and brethren, and chose them, and showed them the right path.

This is God's guidance: He guides among His creatures whom He will. If they had associated others with Him, surely vain would have been all they did. Those are the people to whom We gave the Book and the Law and the Prophethood. But if they reject these things We shall entrust them to a people who will not deny. (Quran 6:74–89)

21. Abraham as the First Muslim

Abraham ... prayed: "Accept this from us, O Lord, for You hear and know everything; and make us submitters (muslimin) to your will and make our progeny a people submissive to You (*ummah muslimah*). Teach us the way of worship and forgive our trespasses, for You are compassionate and merciful; and send, O Lord, an apostle from among them to impart Your message to them, to teach them the Book and the wisdom, and correct them in every way; for indeed You are mighty and wise."

And who will turn away from the religion of Abraham but one dull of soul? We made him the chosen one here in the world, and one of the best in the world to come, (for) when his Lord said to him, "Submit" (*aslim*)," he replied: "I submit (*aslamtu*) to the Lord of all the worlds." And Abraham left this legacy to his sons, and to Jacob, and said, "O my sons, God has chosen this as the faith for you. Do not die but as those who have submitted to God (*muslimuna*)."

Were you present at the hour of Jacob's death? "What will you worship after me?" he asked his sons, and they answered, "We shall worship your God and the God of your fathers, of Abraham and Ishmael and Isaac, the one and only God, and to Him we are submitters (*muslimuna*)."

Those were the people, and they have passed away. Theirs is the reward for what they did, and yours will be for what you do. You will not be questioned about their deeds.

And they say, "Become Jews or become Christians, and find the right way." Say: "No, we follow the religion of Abraham, the upright, who was not an idolater." (Quran 2:127–135)

According to the Life of the Apostle of God, *this is how Muhammad himself urged the matter in respect to both the Jewish and the Christian claims to be the sons of Abraham, and so of the Covenant.*

The Jewish rabbis and the Christians of Najran, when they were before the Apostle (in Medina), broke into disputing. The Jews said that Abraham was nothing but a Jew. The Christians said that he was nothing but a Christian. So God revealed concerning them (Quran 3:55–58): "O People of the Scripture, why will you argue about Abraham, when the Torah and the Gospel were not revealed until after him. Have you then no sense? . . ."

Abraham was not a Jew nor not yet a Christian, but he was an upright man who surrendered to God, and he was not of the idolaters. Lo! those of mankind who have the best claim to Abraham are those who followed him, and this Prophet and those who believe (with him); and God is the Protecting Friend of the believers. (*Life* 383–384)

[IBN ISHAQ 1955:260]

22. Jacob's Dream

To return once again to the account in Genesis of Isaac's two sons, Esau and Jacob, it was through the latter that the Covenant would be fulfilled. But Isaac's wife, Rebecca, feared that the young man would marry one of the local Hittite women, and so Jacob was sent away eastward, back along the route traced by his grandfather Abraham.

So Isaac sent for Jacob and blessed him. He instructed him, saying, "You shall not take a wife from among the Canaanite women. Up, go to Paddan-aram, to the house of Bethuel, your mother's father, and take a wife from among the daughters of Laban, your mother's brother. May El Shaddai bless you, make you fertile and numerous, so that you become an assembly of peoples. May He grant the blessing of Abraham to you and your offspring that you may possess the land where you are sojourning, which God gave to Abraham. . . ."

Jacob left Beer-sheba, and set out for Haran. He came upon a certain place and stopped there for the night, for the sun had set. Taking one of the stones of that place, he put it under his head and lay down in that place. He had a dream; a stairway was set on the ground and its top reached to the sky, and angels of God were going up and down on it. And the Lord was standing beside him and He said, "I am the Lord, the God of your father Abraham and the God of Isaac: the ground on which you are lying I will give to you and to your offspring. Your descendants shall be as the dust of the earth; you shall spread out to the west and to the east, to the north and to the south. All the families of the earth shall bless themselves by you and your descendants. Remember, I am with you: I will protect you wherever you go and will bring you back to this land. I will not leave you until I have done what I have promised you."

Jacob awoke from his sleep and said, "Surely the Lord is present in this place, and I did not know it!" Shaken, he said, "How awesome is this place! This is none other than the abode of God, and that is the gateway to heaven." Early in the morning, Jacob took the stone that he had put under his head and set it up as a pillar and poured oil on the top of it. He named the site Bethel; but previously the name of the city had been Luz.

Jacob made a vow, saying, "If God remains with me, if He protects me on this journey that I am making, and gives me bread to eat and clothing to wear, and if I return safe to my father's house—the Lord shall be my God. And this stone, which I have set up as a pillar, shall be God's

abode; and of all that You give me, I will set aside a tithe for You."
(Genesis 28:1–23)

This was by no means the only stone marking the presence of God in the Middle East. We shall observe another at Mecca: the black stone embedded in the Arabs' Beth-El, the House of God called the Ka ͨ ba.

23. Jacob Becomes Israel

Jacob finds not one wife but two among Laban's daughters in Paddan-aram, and eventually he and Rachel and Leah and their children return to the lands of Abraham and Isaac in Canaan. On the way, Jacob has another encounter with the divine.

That same night he arose, and taking his two wives, his two maid servants, and his eleven children, he crossed the ford of the Jabbok. After taking them across the stream, he sent across all his possessions. Jacob was left alone. And a man wrestled with him until the break of dawn. When he saw that he had not prevailed against him, he wrenched Jacob's hip at its socket, so that the socket of his hip was strained as he wrestled with him.

Then he said, "Let me go, for dawn is breaking." But he answered, "I will not let you go, unless you bless me." Said the other, "What is your name?" He replied, "Jacob." Said he, "Your name shall no longer be Jacob, but Israel, for you have striven with beings divine and human, and have prevailed." Jacob asked, "Pray tell me your name." But he said, "You must not ask my name!" And he took leave of him there. So Jacob named the place Peniel, meaning, "I have seen a divine being face to face, yet my life has been preserved." The sun rose upon him as he passed Penuel, limping on his hip.

The anonymous narrator or later editor then adds his own legal gloss to the text of Genesis.

That is why the children of Israel to this day do not eat the thigh muscle that is on the socket of the hip, since Jacob's hip socket was wrenched at the thigh muscle. (Genesis 32:22–32)

24. The Descendants of Jacob

Now the sons of Jacob were twelve in number. The sons of Leah: Reuben—Jacob's firstborn—Simeon, Levi, Judah, Issachar, and Zebulun. The sons of Rachel: Joseph and Benjamin. The sons of Bilhah, Rachel's maid: Dan and Naphtali. And the sons of Zilpah, Leah's maid: Gad and Asher. These are the sons of Jacob who were born to him in Paddan-aram.

And Jacob came to his father Isaac at Mamre, at Kiriath-arba, now Hebron, where Abraham and Isaac had sojourned. Isaac was a hundred and eighty years old when he breathed his last and died. He was gathered to his kin in ripe old age, and he was buried by his sons his sons Esau and Jacob. (Genesis 35:23–29)

In the years that follow, Jacob and his offspring, the "Children of Israel," migrate into Egypt, where they serve the Pharaoh and where Joseph rises to high position at the royal court.

Thus Israel settled in the country of Egypt, in the region of Goshen; they acquired holdings in it, and were fertile and increased greatly.

Jacob lived seventeen years in the land of Egypt, so that the span of Jacob's life came to one hundred and forty-seven years. And when the time approached for Israel to die, he summoned his son Joseph to him, "Do me this favor, place your hand under my thigh as a pledge of your steadfast loyalty: please do not bury me in Egypt. When I lie down with my fathers, take me up from Egypt and bury me in their burial place." He replied, "I will do as you have spoken." And he said, "Swear to me." And he swore to him. Then Israel bowed at the head of the bed. (Genesis 47:27–31)

So it was done. Jacob was embalmed in the Egyptian manner and then taken for burial.

"In the cave which is in the field of Ephron the Hittite, the cave which is in the field of Machpelah, facing Mamre, in the land of Canaan, the field that Abraham bought from Ephron the Hittite for a burial site— there Abraham and his wife Sarah were buried; there Isaac and his wife Rebekah were buried; and there I buried Leah." (Genesis 49:29–31)

The blissful period of the vizirate of Joseph in Egypt did not last, however.

Joseph died, and all his brothers, and all that generation. But the Israelites were fertile and prolific; they multiplied and increased very greatly, so that the land was filled with them.

A new king arose over Egypt, who did not know Joseph. And he said to his people, "Look, the Israelite people are much too numerous for us. Let us deal shrewdly with them, so that they may not increase; otherwise in the event of war they may join our enemies in fighting against us and rise from the ground." So they set taskmasters over them to oppress them with forced labor; and they built garrison cities for Pharaoh: Pithom and

Raamses. But the more they were oppressed, the more they increased and spread out, so that the [Egyptians] came to dread the Israelites.

The Egyptians ruthlessly imposed upon the Israelites the various labors that they made them perform. Ruthlessly they made life bitter for them with harsh labor at mortar and bricks and with all sorts of tasks in the field. (Exodus 1:6–14)

25. Moses in Egypt

A long time after that, the king of Egypt died. The Israelites were groaning under the bondage and cried out; and their cry for help from the bondage rose up to God. God heard their moaning, and God remembered His covenant with Abraham and Isaac and Jacob. God looked upon the Israelites, and God took notice of them. (Exodus 2:23–25)

God's chosen instrument for the liberation of Israel from Egypt was Moses, a descendant of Levi who had been adopted and raised at the Pharaoh's court.

Now Moses, tending the flock of his father-in-law Jethro, the priest of Midian, drove the flock into the wilderness, and came to Horeb, the mountain of God. An angel of the Lord appeared to him in a blazing fire out of a bush. He gazed, and there was a bush all aflame, yet the bush was not consumed. When the Lord saw that he had turned aside to look, God called to him out of the bush: "Moses! Moses!" He answered, "Here I am." And He said, "Do not come closer. Remove your sandals from your feet, for the place on which you stand is holy ground. I am," He said, "the God of your father, the God of Abraham, the God of Isaac, and the God of Jacob." And Moses hid his face, for he was afraid to look at God.

And the Lord continued, "I have marked well the plight of My people in Egypt and have heeded their outcry because of their taskmasters; yes, I am mindful of their sufferings. I have come down to rescue them from the Egyptians and to bring them out of that land to a good and spacious land, a land flowing with milk and honey, the home of the Canaanites, the Hittites, the Amorites, the Perizzites, the Hivites, and the Jebusites. Now the cry of the Israelites has reached Me; moreover, I have seen how the Egyptians oppress them. Come, therefore, I will send you to the Pharaoh, and you shall free My people, the Israelites, from Egypt."

Moses said to God, "When I come to the Israelites and say to them 'The God of your fathers has sent me to you,' and they ask me, 'What is His name?' what shall I say to them?" And God said to Moses, "Ehyeh-Asher-Ehyeh" [possibly, "I Am That I Am"]. He continued, "Thus shall you say to the Israelites, 'Ehyeh sent me to you.' " And God said further to Moses, "Thus shall you speak to the Israelites: The Lord, the God of your fathers, the God of Abraham, the God of Isaac, and the God of Jacob, has sent me to you:

This shall be My name forever,
This My appellation for all eternity.

Go and assemble the elders of Israel and say to them: the Lord, the God of your fathers, the God of Abraham, Isaac, and Jacob, has appeared to me and said, 'I have taken note of you and of what is being done to you in Egypt, and I have declared: I will take you out of the misery of Egypt.' " (Exodus 3:1–35)

Moses has little success with his fellow Israelites, and even less with the Pharaoh.

Afterward Moses and Aaron went and said to Pharaoh, "Thus says the Lord, the God of Israel: Let My people go that they may celebrate a festival for Me in the wilderness." But Pharaoh said, "Who is the Lord that I should heed Him and let Israel go?" (Exodus 5:1–2)

The Lord said to Moses and Aaron, "When Pharaoh speaks to you and says, 'Produce your marvel,' you shall say to Aaron, 'Take your rod and cast it down before Pharaoh.' It shall turn into a serpent." So Moses and Aaron came before Pharaoh and did just as the Lord had commanded: Aaron cast down his rod in the presence of Pharaoh and his courtiers, and it turned into a serpent. Then Pharaoh, for his part, summoned the wise men and the sorcerers; and the Egyptian magicians, in turn, did the same with their spells: each cast down his rod, and they turned into serpents. But Aaron's rod swallowed their rods. Yet Pharaoh's heart stiffened and he did not heed them, as the Lord had said. (Exodus 7:8–13)

The Pharaoh must be persuaded, and so the Lord sends a series of plagues and portents upon the Land of Egypt (Exod. 7:14–10:29). The Pharaoh is frightened but unmoved. Then comes the final, crushing punishment.

Moses said, "Thus says the Lord: Toward midnight I will go forth among the Egyptians, and every first-born in the land of Egypt shall die, from the first-born of Pharaoh who sits on his throne to the first-born of the slave girl who is behind the millstones; and all the first-born of the cattle. And there shall be a loud cry in all the land of Egypt, such as had never been or will ever be again; but not a dog shall snarl at any of the Israelites, at man or beast—in order that you may know that the Lord makes a distinction between Egypt and Israel." (Exodus 11:4–7)

The Israelites, forewarned, ate a hasty late-night meal, the prototype of the later Passover (Exod. 12:1–27), and fled the land of Egypt. Four hundred and thirty years of slavery were over.

26. Moses and the Pharaoh in the Quran

The story of Moses' confrontation with the Pharaoh in Egypt is one of the most often repeated biblical tales in the Quran. It was a marvelous story, surely, filled with wonders, but it also emphasized a point on which Muhammad felt strongly: the punishment reserved for those who disbelieve and mistreat God's prophets. This is one of the later Quranic versions of the story.

(After these apostles) . . . We sent Moses with Our miracles to Pharaoh and his nobles, who acted unjustly in their regard. See then the end of the authors of evil. And Moses said, "O Pharaoh, I have been sent by the Lord of all the worlds; I am duty bound to speak nothing of God but the truth. I have brought from your Lord a clear sign; so let the people of Israel depart with me." He said, "If you brought a sign, then display it, if what you say is true."

At this Moses threw down his staff and lo, it became a live serpent. And he drew forth his hand, and behold, it looked white to those who beheld it. The nobles of the Pharaoh said: "He surely is a clever magician. He wishes to drive you away from your land." "So what do you advise?" They said: "Put him and his brother off awhile, and send out heralds to the cities to bring all the wise magicians to you."

The magicians came to Pharaoh. They said, "Is there a reward for us if we succeed?" "Yes," he said, "you will be among the honored." So they said. "O Moses, you may cast your spell first, or we shall cast ours." "You cast it first," answered Moses. When they cast their spell, they bewitched the eyes of the people and petrified them by conjuring up a great charm.

We said to Moses, "Throw down your staff," and it swallowed up their conjurations in no time. Thus the truth was upheld and the falsehood that they practiced was exposed. Thus there and then they were vanquished and overthrown, humiliated. The sorcerers fell to the ground in homage and said; "We have come to believe in the Lord of the worlds, the Lord of Moses and Aaron. . . ."

Then the leaders of Pharaoh's people said to him: "Will you allow Moses and his people to create disorder in the land and discard you and your gods?" He said, "We shall now slay their sons and spare their women, and subdue them." Moses said to his people: "Invoke the help of

45

God and be firm. The earth belongs to God, He can make whom He wills among His creatures inherit it. The future is theirs who take heed for themselves." "We were oppressed," they said, "before you came to us and since you have come to us." He answered: "It may be well that God will soon destroy your enemy and make you inherit the land, and then see how you behave."

Already We afflicted the people of Pharaoh with famine and the dearth of everything that they might take heed. Yet, when good came their way, they said, "It is our due," but when misfortune befell them, they put the omen down to Moses and those who were with him. But surely the omen was with God, yet most of them did not understand. They said: "Whatsoever the sign you have brought us, we shall not believe in you."

So We let loose on them floods and locusts, and vermin and frogs and blood—how many different signs. But they still remained arrogant, for they were a people full of sin.

Yet when punishment overtook them, they said, "O Moses, invoke your God for us as you have been enjoined. If the torment is removed, we shall certainly believe in you and let the People of Israel go with you." But no sooner was the punishment withdrawn for a time to enable them to make good their promise than they broke it. So we took vengeance on them and drowned them in the sea for rejecting Our signs and not heeding them. (Quran 7:103–136)

27. Paul Interprets the Exodus

After escaping across the parted waters of the Red Sea, which engulfed the pursuing Egyptians, the Israelites wandered for forty years in the wilderness of Sinai, now saved from starvation by the Lord, now chastised for their lapses into idolatry and infidelity to the Covenant. This is how the Christian Paul read the major events— and the lessons—of the Exodus.

You should understand, my brothers, that our ancestors were all under the pillar of cloud, and all of them passed through the Red Sea; and so they all received baptism into the fellowship of Moses in cloud and sea. They all ate the same supernatural food [that is, the manna in the desert], and all drank the same supernatural drink; I mean, they all drank from the supernatural rock that accompanied their travels [cf. Exod. 17:6]—and that rock was Christ. And yet most of them were not accepted by God, for the desert was strewn with their corpses.

These events happened as symbols to warn us not to set our desires on evil things, as they did. Do not be idolaters, like some of them; as Scripture has it, "the people sat down to feast and rose up to revel." Let us not commit fornication, as some of them did—and twenty-three thousand died on one day [Num. 25:9]. Let us not put the power of the Lord to the test, as some of them did—and were destroyed by serpents [cf. Num. 21:6]. Do not grumble against God, as some of them did—and were destroyed by the Destroyer [cf. Num. 16:49]. All these things that happened to them were symbolic and were recorded for our benefit as a warning. For upon us the fulfillment of the ages has come. (Paul, *To the Corinthians* 1.10:1–11)

28. Biblical Miracles

The miraculous feeding of the Israelites with manna and the supply of water from a rock struck by Moses' staff, Paul read typologically as Christ—perhaps by implication as a foreshadowing of the Eucharist (cf. John 6:30). His Alexandrian contemporary Philo, another Hellenized Jew of the Diaspora, used the same events as an occasion to give his views on miracles.

Though this supply of food never failed and continued to be enjoyed in abundance, a serious scarcity of water again occurred. Sore-pressed by this, their mood turned to desperation, whereupon Moses, taking the sacred staff with which he accomplished the signs in Egypt, under inspiration smote the steep rock with it. It may be the rock contained originally a spring and now had its artery clean severed, or perhaps then for the first time a body of water collected in it through hidden channels was forced out by the impact. Whichever is the case, it opened under the violence of the stream and spouted out its contents.

Philo was aware, then, that apparent miracles were subject to rationalization. That was not the interpretation he chose however.

If anyone disbelieves these things, he neither knows God nor has ever sought to know Him; for if he did, he would at once have perceived, yes, perceived with a firm apprehension, that these extraordinary and seemingly incredible events are but child's play to God. He has but to turn his eyes to things which are really great and worthy of his earnest contemplation: the creation of heaven and the rhythmic movements of the planets and the fixed stars; the light that shines upon us from the sun by day and from the moon by night . . . the yearly seasons with their well-marked diversities and other beauties innumerable. He who should wish to describe the several parts, or rather any one of the cardinal parts of the universe, would find life too short, even if his years were prolonged beyond those of all other men. But these things, though truly marvelous, are held in little account because they are familiar. Not so with the unfamiliar; though they be but small matters, we give way before what seems so strange and, drawn by their novelty, regard them with amazement. (Philo, *Life of Moses* 1.210–213)

29. The Death of Moses

For all the services he rendered to the Lord and for all the privileges granted to him, including the reception of the tablets of the Law on Sinai and an extraordinary vision of God, Moses was not destined to enter the Land of the Promise to which he had led his and God's people.

Moses went up from the steppes of Moab to Mount Nebo, to the summit of Pisgah, opposite Jericho, and the Lord showed him the whole land: Gilead as far as Dan; all Naphtali; the land of Ephraim and Manasseh; the whole land of Judah as far as the Western Sea; the Negeb; and the Plain—the Valley of Jericho, the city of palm trees—as far as Zoar. And the Lord said to him, "This is the land of which I swore to Abraham, Isaac, and Jacob, 'I will give it to your offspring.' I have let you see it with your own eyes, but you shall not cross there."

And then his death, or his presumed death.

So Moses the servant of the Lord died there, in the land of Moab, at the command of the Lord. He buried him in the valley in the land of Moab, near Beth-peor; and no one knows his burial place to this day. Moses was a hundred and twenty years old when he died; his eyes were undimmed and his vigor unabated. And the Israelites bewailed Moses in the steppes of Moab for thirty days.

The period of wailing and mourning for Moses came to an end. Now Joshua son of Nun was filled with the spirit of wisdom because Moses had laid his hands upon him; and the Israelites heeded him, doing as the Lord had commanded Moses.

Never again did there arise in Israel a prophet like Moses whom the Lord singled out, face to face, for the various signs and portents that the Lord sent to him to display in the land of Egypt, against Pharaoh and all his courtiers and his whole country, and for all the great might and awesome power that Moses displayed before all Israel. (Deuteronomy 34:1–12)

30. The Promised Land:
The Covenant Recalled and Renewed

We resume the narrative at a point late in the life of Moses' successor, Joshua, the son of Nun, when the Israelites were already in possession of substantial parts of the land that had been promised to them.

Much later, after the Lord had given Israel rest from all the enemies around them, and when Joshua was old and well advanced in years, Joshua summoned all Israel, their elders and commanders, their magistrates and officials, and said to them: "I have grown old and am advanced in years. You have seen all that the Lord your God has done to all those nations on your account, for it was the Lord your God who fought for you. See, I have allotted to you, by your tribes, (the territory of) these nations that still remain, and that of all the nations that I have destroyed, from the Jordan to the Mediterranean Sea in the west. The Lord your God Himself will thrust them out on your account and drive them out to make way for you, and you shall occupy their land as the Lord your God promised you."

That was the Lord's part of the Covenant. The Israelites are then instructed on their responsibilities.

But be most resolute to observe faithfully all that is written in the book of the Teaching of Moses, without ever deviating from it to the right or to the left, and without intermingling with these nations which are left among you. Do not utter the names of their gods or swear by them; do not serve them or bow down to them. But hold fast to the Lord your God as you have done to this day.

The Lord has driven out great, powerful nations on your account, and not a man has withstood you to this day. A single man of you would put a thousand to flight, for the Lord your God Himself has been fighting for you, as He promised you. For your own sakes, therefore, be most mindful to love the Lord your God. For should you turn away and attach yourselves to the remnant of those nations—to those that are left among you—and intermarry with them, you joining them and they joining you, know for certain that the Lord your God will not continue to drive these nations out before you. (Joshua 23:1–13)

In the wake of this pointed reminder from the Lord, Joshua assembled at Shechem all the tribes of Israel and their leaders for a formal ceremony of renewal. After recalling all the events that had befallen them from the days of Abraham to the present, Joshua continues.

Now, therefore, revere the Lord and serve Him with undivided loyalty; put away the gods that your forefathers served beyond the Euphrates and in Egypt, and serve the Lord. Or, if you are loath to serve the Lord, choose this day which ones you are going to serve—the gods that your forefathers served beyond the Euphrates, or those of the Amorites in whose land you are settled; but I and my household will serve the Lord."

In reply, the people declared, "Far be it from us to forsake the Lord and serve other gods! For it was the Lord our God who brought us and our fathers up from the land of Egypt, the house of bondage, and who wrought those wondrous signs before our very eyes, and guarded us all along the way that we traveled and among all the peoples through whose midst we passed. And then the Lord drove out before us all the peoples— the Amorites—that inhabited the country. We too will serve the Lord, for He is our God."

Joshua, however, said to the people, "You will not be able to serve the Lord, for He is a holy God. He is a jealous God; He will not forgive your transgressions and your sins. If you forsake the Lord and serve alien gods, He will turn and deal harshly with you and make an end of you, after having been gracious to you." But the people replied to Joshua, "No we will serve the Lord!' Thereupon Joshua said to the people, "You are witnesses against yourselves that you have by your own act chosen to serve the Lord." "Yes, we are!" they responded. "Then put away the alien gods that you have among you and direct your hearts to the Lord, the God of Israel." And the people declared to Joshua, "We will serve none but the Lord our God and we will obey none but Him."

On that day at Shechem, Joshua made a covenant for the people and he made a fixed rule for them. Joshua recorded all this in a book of divine instruction. He took a great stone and set it up at the foot of the oak in the sacred precinct of the Lord; and Joshua said to all the people, "See, this very stone shall be a witness against us, for it heard all the words that the Lord spoke to us; it shall be a witness against you, lest you break faith with your God." Joshua then dismissed the people to their allotted portions. (Joshua 24:14–28)

31. Saul: A King for Israel

The Israelites conquered the Land of the Promise as a tribal confederation and for many generations continued to live under that form of loose confederacy, with occasional leaders called "Judges" arising as opportunity presented or crisis de-

manded. In this settled land of settled peoples other models of government presented themselves, and eventually the people demanded a king. According to the biblical account, the request was granted only reluctantly by the Lord, whose choice fell upon Saul, "a young man in his prime; there was no better man among the Israelites than he. He was a head taller than any of his fellows" (1 Sam. 9:2). The Lord communicated His will to Samuel.

Now the day before Saul came, the Lord had revealed the following to Samuel: "At this time tomorrow, I will send a man to you from the territory of Benjamin, and you shall anoint him ruler of My people Israel. He will deliver My people from the hands of the Philistines; for I have taken note of My people, their outcry has come to Me." (1 Samuel 9: 15–17)

Samuel took a flask of oil and poured some on Saul's head and kissed him, and said, "The Lord herewith anoints you ruler over His own people." (1 Samuel 10:1)

And Samuel said to the people, "Do you see the one whom the Lord had chosen? There is none like him among all the people." And all the people acclaimed him, shouting, "Long live the king!"

Samuel expounded to the people the rules of the monarchy and recorded them in a document which he deposited before the Lord. Samuel then sent the people back to their homes. (1 Samuel 10:24–25)

32. "Obedience Is Better Than Sacrifice"

Saul ruled as king over Israel for twenty-two years, but he did not enjoy divine favor to the end. The Lord had commanded him to destroy the neighboring Amelekites utterly, "men and women, children and babes in arms, herds and flocks, camels and asses" (1 Sam. 15:3). The people were not spared, as commanded, but Saul kept the flocks and herds. God's reaction followed swiftly.

The word of the Lord then came to Samuel: "I regret that I made Saul king, for he has turned away from Me and has not carried out My commands." Samuel was distressed and he entreated the Lord all night long. Early in the morning Samuel went to meet Saul. Samuel was told, "Saul went to Carmel, where he erected a monument for himself; then he left and went on down to Gilgal."

When Samuel came to Saul, Saul said to him, "Blessed are you of the Lord! I have fulfilled the Lord's command." "Then what," demanded Samuel, "is this bleating of sheep in my ears, and the lowing of oxen that I hear?" Saul answered, "They were brought from the Amelekites, for the troops spared the choicest of the sheep and oxen for sacrificing to the Lord your God. And we proscribed the rest." Samuel said to Saul, "Stop! Let me tell you what the Lord said to me last night!" "Speak!" he replied. And Samuel said, "You may look small to yourself, but you are the head of the tribes of Israel. The Lord anointed you king over Israel, and the Lord sent you on a mission, saying, 'Go and proscribe the sinful Amelekites; make war on them until you have exterminated them.' Why did you disobey the Lord and swoop down on the spoil in defiance of the Lord's will?" Saul said to Samuel, "But I did obey the Lord! I performed the mission on which the Lord sent me: I captured King Agag of Amalek, and I proscribed Amalek, and the troops took from the spoil some sheep and oxen—the best of what had been proscribed—to sacrifice to the Lord your God at Gilgal." But Samuel said:

> "Does the Lord delight in burnt offerings and sacrifices
> As much as in obedience to the Lord's command?
> Surely, obedience is better than sacrifice,
> Compliance than the fat of rams.
> For rebellion is like the sin of divination,
> Defiance, like the iniquity of teraphim.
> Because you rejected the Lord's command,
> He has rejected you as king."

. . . But Samuel said to him, "The Lord has this day torn the kingship over Israel away from you and has given it to another who is worthier than you." (1 Samuel 15:10–28)

33. David, King of Israel

The better man was David, a young shepherd of the family of Jesse in Bethlehem. He was anointed by Samuel at God's own command in a private ceremony (1 Sam. 16:12–13) and thereafter began a spectacular rise as a warrior for Israel against the Philistines. Saul soon took notice and attempted to kill the man he had already identified as his rival. David fled, and even after Saul and his three sons were slain by the Philistines at Mount Gilboa, David still had to contend with Abner, Saul's chief commander, and other supporters of the house of Saul. There was a civil war, and only when Abner and his forces were defeated was David, then ruling at Hebron, acknowledged as king by all the Israelites.

All the tribes of Israel come to David at Hebron and said, "We are your own flesh and blood. Long before now, when Saul was king over us, it was you who led Israel in war; and the Lord said to you: You shall shepherd My people Israel; you shall be ruler of Israel." All the elders of Israel came to the king at Hebron, and King David made a pact with them in Hebron before the Lord. And they anointed David king over Israel.

David was thirty years old when he became king, and he reigned forty years. In Hebron he reigned over all Israel and Judah thirty-three years. (2 Samuel 5:1–5)

34. The Ark Installed in Jerusalem

After his consecration as king over all the Israelites, David captured the Jebusite city of Jerusalem not far from Hebron, an event noted almost casually in the second book of Samuel.

. . . David captured the stronghold and renamed it the City of David; David also fortified the surrounding area, from the Millo inward. David kept growing stronger, for the Lord, the God of Hosts, was with him. (2 Samuel 5:7–10)

In the biblical narrative far more attention is given to another, more pregnant event in the history of David and Jerusalem: the transfer of the Ark of the Covenant to the king's new capital. The first attempt to move it there was stymied by an accident, and the arrival of the Ark was delayed for three months. The Ark meanwhile rested in the house of Obed-edom, a man of Gath in Philistia.

It was reported to King David: "The Lord has blessed Obed-edom's house and all that belongs to him because of the Ark of God." Thereupon David went and brought up the Ark of God from the house of Obed-edom to the City of David, amid rejoicing. When the bearers of the Ark of the Lord had moved forward six paces, he sacrificed an ox and a fatling. David whirled with all his might before the Lord; David was girt with a linen ephod. Thus David and all the House of Israel brought up the Ark of the Lord with shouts and with blasts of the horn.

As the Ark of the Lord entered the City of David, Michal daughter of Saul looked out of the window and saw King David leaping and whirling before the Lord; and she despised him for it.

They brought in the Ark of the Lord and set it up in its place inside the tent which David had pitched for it, and David sacrificed burnt offerings and offerings of well-being before the Lord. When David finished sacrificing the burnt offerings of well-being, he blessed the people in the name of the Lord of Hosts. And he distributed among all the people—the entire multitude of Israel, man and woman alike—a loaf of bread, a cake made in a pan, and a raisin cake. (2 Samuel 6:12–19)

35. The Establishment of the House of David

When the king was settled in his palace and the Lord had granted him safety from all the enemies around him, the king said to the prophet Nathan: "Here I am dwelling in a house of cedar, while the Ark of the Lord abides in a tent!" Nathan said to the king, "Go and do whatever you have in mind, for the Lord is with you."

But that same night the word of the Lord came to Nathan: "Go and say to my servant David: Thus said the Lord: Are you the one to build a house for Me to dwell in? From the day that I brought the People of Israel out of Egypt to this day I have not dwelt in a house, but have moved about in Tent and Tabernacle. As I moved about wherever the Israelites went, did I ever reproach any of the tribal leaders whom I appointed to care for My people of Israel: Why have you not built Me a house of cedar?"

. . . "When your days are done and you lie with your fathers, I will raise up your offspring after you, one of your own issue, and I will establish his kingship. He shall build a house for My name, and I will establish his royal throne forever." (2 Samuel 7:1–13)

36. The Threshing Floor on Mount Moriah

David, now filled with assurance, determines to take a census of his people, this despite God's warning that he should not do so.

But afterward David reproached himself for having numbered the people. And David said to the Lord, "I have sinned grievously in what I have done. Please, O Lord, remit the guilt of your servant, for I have acted foolishly."

The Lord sends a pestilence upon Israel as a punishment for David's folly. Seventy thousand people die.

But when the angel extended his hand against Jerusalem to destroy it, the Lord renounced further punishment and said to the angel who was destroying the people, "Enough! Stay your hand!" The angel of the Lord was then by the threshing floor of Araunah the Jebusite.

When David saw the angel who was striking down the people, he said to the Lord, "I alone am guilty, I alone have done wrong; but these poor sheep, what have they done? Let your hand fall upon me and my father's house!"

Gad [the seer of David] came to David the same day and said to him, "Go and set up an altar to the Lord on the threshing floor of Araunah the Jebusite." David went up, following Gad's instructions, as the Lord had commanded. Araunah looked out and saw the king and his courtiers approaching him. So Araunah went out and bowed low to the king, with his face to the ground. And Araunah asked, "Why has my lord the king come to his servant?" David replied, "To buy the threshing floor from you, that I may build an altar to the Lord and that the plague against my people may be checked." And Araunah said to David, "Let my lord the king take it and offer up whatever he sees fit. Here are oxen for a burnt offering, and the threshing boards and the gear of the oxen for wood. All this, O king, Araunah gives to Your Majesty. And may the Lord your God," Araunah added, "respond to you with favor!" But the king replied to Araunah, "No, I will buy them from you at a price. I cannot sacrifice to the Lord my God burnt offerings that have cost me nothing." So David bought the threshing floor and the oxen for fifty shekels of silver. And David built there an altar to the Lord and sacrificed burnt offerings and offerings of well-being. The Lord responded to the plea for the land, and the plague against Israel was checked. (2 Samuel 24:10–25)

There is nothing in this account to suggest that we have to do here with anything more than a simple threshing ground that was rendered holy by a secondary act of divine providence that had occurred there—secondary in the sense that God had not manifested Himself but rather that the sword of His avenging angel was stayed in that place. David built an altar there, and as we shall see, that otherwise unnoteworthy Jebusite threshing floor at the highest point of Mount Moriah became the site and center of the principal and then the unique Jewish sanctuary in the land of Israel.

37. Solomon and the Temple

Apparently David had more royal and elaborate plans for that place atop Mount Moriah in Jerusalem than the erection of a mere altar. The narrative in 2 Samuel suggests a Davidic temple and then turns aside to other matters. The parallel account in the books called Chronicles, where Araunah is called Ornan, is both specific and detailed.

At that time, when David saw that the Lord had answered him at the threshing floor of Ornan the Jebusite, then he sacrificed there—for the tabernacle of the Lord, which Moses had made in the wilderness, and the altar of burnt offerings, were at that time in the shrine at Gibeon, and

David was unable to go to it to worship the Lord because he was terrified by the sword of the angel of the Lord. David said, "Here will be the House of the Lord and here the altar of burnt offerings for Israel."

David gave orders to assemble the aliens living in the land of Israel, and assigned them to be hewers, to quarry and dress stones for building the house of God. Much iron for nails for the doors of the gates and for clasps did David lay aside, and so much copper it could not be weighed, and cedar logs without number—for the Sidonian and the Tyrians brought many cedar logs to David.

For David thought, "My son Solomon is an untried youth, and the House to be built for the Lord is to be made exceedingly great to win fame and glory throughout all the lands; let me then lay aside material for him." So David laid aside much material before he died. (1 Chronicles 21:28–22:5)

David gave his son Solomon the plan of the porch and its houses, its storerooms and its upper chambers and inner chambers; and of the place of the Ark-cover; and the plan of all that he had by the spirit: of the courts of the House of the Lord and all its surrounding chambers. . . . "All this that the Lord made me understand by His hand on me, I give to you in writing—the plan of all the works." (1 Chronicles 28:11–19)

By this account, then, it was David himself who, under the guidance of the Lord, drew up the plans for the Temple that was to rise on the summit of the eastern hill of Jerusalem. But like Moses detained from entering the Land of Promise, it was reserved for another to build the House of the Lord, David's son Solomon.

38. The Wisdom of Solomon

Solomon was noted for far more than the construction of the Temple in the later traditions of the Jews, Christians, and Muslims. He personified wisdom and mastery of the practical arts, some of them indeed beyond ordinary human competence. This is how the king appeared in the eyes of the medieval Jewish scholar Nachmanides (d. ca. 1270 C.E.).

King Solomon, peace be upon him, whom the Lord had given wisdom and knowledge, derived it all from the Torah, and from it he studied until he knew the secret of all things created, even of the forces and characteristics of plants, so that he wrote even a Book of Medicine, as it is written, "And he spoke of trees, from the cedar that is in Lebanon to the hyssop that springs out of the wall" (1 Kings 5:13).

The Jewish tradition did in fact credit a number of works to Solomon, including the canonical Book of Proverbs and a noncanonical "Wisdom of Solomon," which Nachmanides refers to next.

Now I have seen the Aramaic translation of the book called "The Great Wisdom of Solomon," and in it is written: ". . . It is the Lord alone who gives knowledge that contains no falsehood, (enabling one) to know how the world arose, the composition of the constellations, the beginning, the end and the middle of times, the angles at the ends of the constellations, and how the seasons are produced by the movement of the heavens and the fixed positions of the stars, the benign nature of cattle and the fierceness of wild beasts, the power of the wind and the thoughts of man, the relationship of trees and the powers of roots; everything hidden and everything revealed I know."

All this Solomon knew from the Torah, and he found everything in it—in its simple meanings, in the subtleties of its expressions and its letters and strokes. . . .

Scripture likewise relates concerning him, "And Solomon's wisdom excelled the wisdom of all the children of the East and all the wisdom of Egypt" (1 Kings 5:10). That is to say, he was better versed than they in divination and enchanting, for this was their wisdom, as it is said, "For they are replenished from the East, and with soothsayers like the Philistines" (Isa. 2:6). What was the wisdom of the children of the East? They knew and were crafty in the divination of birds. "And all the wisdom of Egypt" means that Solomon was better versed in sorcery, which is the wisdom of Egypt and the nature of growing things. As is known from the Book of Egyptian Agriculture, the Egyptians were very well versed in the matter of planting and grafting different species. Thus the Sages have said: "Solomon even planted peppers in the Land of Israel. How was he able to plant them? Solomon was a wise man, and he knew the essence of the foundation of the world. Why was this? It is written, 'Out of Sion, the perfected of beauty, the Lord has shone forth' (Ps. 50:2). Out of Sion the whole world was perfected. How is this known? Why (else) was it called 'the Stone of Foundation'? Because the world was founded from it. Now Solomon knew which of its arteries extended to Ethiopia, and upon it he planted peppers, and immediately it produced fruits, for so he says, 'And I planted trees in them of all kinds of fruits' (Eccles. 2:5)." (Nachmanides, *Commentary on Genesis*) [NACHMANIDES 1971:12–13]

Solomon is mentioned more than once in the Quran, including a long passage (Quran 27:15–44) describing an encounter between the Israelite king and the queen of Saba or Sheba in the Yemen. Invariably in the Muslim sources, as in the Jewish ones, Solomon is depicted as possessing extraordinary power, though with a somewhat different implication regarding its source, since for the Muslims his power included control over the jinn, those preternaturally gifted spirits who stand just below the angels in God's creation and are often associated with the magical arts, as was Solomon himself. It was the jinn, for example, who assisted Solomon in building the Temple in Jerusalem, as these verses of the Quran appear to reflect.

We (subjugated) the wind to Solomon. Its morning journey took one month, and its evening one month. We made a spring of molten brass to flow for him; and many *jinns* labored for him by the will of his Lord. Any one of them who turned from Our command was made to taste the torment of blazing fire. They made for him whatever he wished, synagogues and statues, dishes large as water troughs, and cauldrons firmly fixed (on ovens); and We said: "O house of David, act and give thanks. But few among My creatures are thankful." (Quran 34:12–13)

With this provocative Quranic portrait before them, the later Muslim commentators supplied many additional details, like these on the seal and ring of Solomon.

Ibn Ishaq says that when Solomon died the satans wrote different kinds of magic in a book, which they then sealed with a seal similar Solomon's. On the cover they wrote, "This is what Asaf ibn Barkhiya the prophet wrote for King Solomon." The book was then buried under Solomon's throne, and when the Jews later discovered it, they claimed that Solomon was a magician. Another tradition handed down on the authority of Ibn Ishaq asserts that God deprived Solomon of his kingship and immediately groups of both men and *jinn* apostatized. When, however, God returned the kingship to him, they returned once again to the true faith. Then Solomon collected all the books of magic and buried them under his throne. Satan later brought them out, and it was thought that these books had been sent down by God to Solomon. Thus they followed these books, claiming that they were Scripture. (Tabari, *Commentary* on Quran 2:102)

Solomon was the focus of many legendary stories in Islam, which, as one Quranic expert said, "God alone knows best whether they are true." True or not, they were popular. In this one, for example, Solomon kills the king of Sidon and then takes his daughter, named Jarada, to wife. Jarada professed her belief in the One True God, "and Solomon loved her." His new wife declined, however, into inconsolable grief for her dead father.

So Solomon ordered the satans to fashion an image of her father and dress it in his clothes. Jarada and her servants went and worshiped this image every morning and evening, as was customary in her father's king-dom. When (his vizier) Asaf reported this to Solomon, the king ordered the idol destroyed and he punished the woman. Then he went out to a deserted place to be alone. Ashes were scattered before him and he sat himself down on them, humiliating himself in penance before God.

On another occasion Solomon had a slave girl named Amina who became a mother by him. Once, when he went out to purify himself or to sleep with one of his wives, he entrusted Amina with the signet ring in which his power lay. She had it for a whole day and then the satan who lives in the sea came to her. This *jinn*, whose name was Sakhr, and who had proved useful to Solomon in the building of the Temple, came to her in the form of Solomon himself and said to her, "Amina, give me my signet ring!" Then he put the ring on his finger and sat down on Solo-mon's throne. This ring placed under his command the birds, the *jinn* and men. Also he changed the outward appearance of (the genuine) Solomon so that when the latter came to Amina to get back his ring, she mistook him for a stranger and drove him off.

Solomon . . . wandered among the houses as a beggar. Whenever he said, "I am Solomon," people responded by throwing dirt at him and reviling him. Then he went to the fishermen, who employed him to assist them in the hauling in of fish; for this he was paid two fish a day. Solomon remained in this condition for forty days, that is, for as long as idolatry continued to be practiced in his house.

Asaf and the notables of Israel did not acknowledge the sovereignty of the *jinn* [who had usurped Solomon's throne], but when Asaf ques-tioned the wives of Solomon about (the impostor), they answered: "He excuses none of us from sex when she is menstruating, nor does he purify himself afterwards."

The impostor is thus unmasked by his violation of the code of ritual purity. He throws the signet ring of Solomon into the sea, where it is swallowed by a fish. The fish comes into the hands of Solomon, the fishmongers' apprentice, who discovers the ring and so regains his powers. The commentator concludes:

Religious scholars reject such interpretations and claim that they belong to the lying stories of the Jews. The *jinns* are incapable of such acts: it is a thoroughly detestable notion that God should give the *jinn* such power over His servants so that they could change the laws (for the community), or that He should give them such power over the wives of the Prophets so that they would commit adultery with them. It is true that there might have been a different law for statues, since God did say in the Quran, "The *jinn* made for Solomon whatever he wished—palaces, statues . . ." (Quran 34:13), but it is impossible to believe that God would permit his prophet to bow down before an idol. Should something take place (in Solomon's kingdom of which he is) unaware, then certainly he was not held responsible. (Zamakhshari, *Commentary* on Quran 38:34)

39. The House Divided: Judah and Israel

Immediately upon the death of Solomon, his splendid kingdom began to disintegrate. Solomon's foolish son Rehoboam managed to cling to the Judean patrimony, but the northern territories, called "Israel," fell into the hands of one who had already run afoul of Solomon: Jeroboam son of Nebat.

Rehoboam went to Shechem, for all Israel had come to Shechem to acclaim him as king. Jeroboam son of Nebat learned of it while he was still in Egypt; for Jeroboam had fled from King Solomon, and had settled in Egypt. They sent for him; and Jeroboam and all the assembly of Israel came and spoke to Rehoboam as follows: "Your father made our yoke heavy. Now lighten the harsh labor and the heavy yoke which your father laid on us, and we will serve you." (1 Kings 12:1–4)

When they returned, Rehoboam had his answer ready.

"My father made your yoke heavy, but I will add to your yoke; my father flogged you with whips, but I will flog you with scorpions. . . ."

When all Israel saw that the king had not listened to them, the people answered the king:

> "We have no portion in David,
> No share in Jesse's son!
> To your tents, O Israel!
> Now look to your own House, O David."

So the Israelites returned to their homes. But Rehoboam continued to reign over the Israelites who lived in the towns of Judah.

King Rehoboam sent Adoram, who was in charge of the forced labor, but all Israel pelted him to death with stones. Thereupon King Rehoboam hurriedly mounted his chariot and fled to Jerusalem. Thus Israel revolted against the House of David, as is still the case.

When all Israel heard that Jeroboam had returned, they sent messengers and summoned him to the assembly and made him king over all Israel. Only the tribe of Judah remained loyal to the House of David. (1 Kings 12:14–20)

Thus a political schism occurred in the body of Israel. It was compounded by an overt abrogation of the Covenant, what the author of Kings calls "a sin in Israel."

Jeroboam fortified Shechem in the hill country of Ephraim and resided there; he moved out from there and fortified Penuel. Jeroboam said to himself, "Now the kingdom may well return to the House of David. If these people still go up to offer sacrifices at the House of the Lord in Jerusalem, the hearts of these people will turn back to their master, King Rehoboam of Judah; they will kill me and go back to King Rehoboam of Judah." So the king took counsel and made two golden calves. He said to the people, "You have been going up to Jerusalem long enough. This is your god, O Israel, who brought you up from the land of Egypt!" He set up one in Bethel and placed the other in Dan. That proved to be a cause of guilt. . . .

He stationed at Bethel the priests of the shrines that he had appointed to sacrifice to the calves which he had made. And Jeroboam established a festival on the fifteenth day of the eighth month; in imitation of the festival in Judah, he established one at Bethel, and he ascended the altar (there). On the fifteenth day of the eighth month—the month in which he had contrived of his own mind to establish a festival for the Israelites—Jeroboam ascended the altar which he had made in Bethel.

As he ascended the altar to present an offering, a man of God arrived at Bethel from Judah at the command of the Lord. While Jeroboam was standing on the altar to present the offering, the man of God, at the command of the Lord, cried out against the altar: "O altar, altar! Thus said the Lord: A son shall be born to the House of David, Josiah by name; and he shall slaughter upon you the priests of the shrines who bring offerings upon you. And human bones shall be burned upon you."

And the priestly authors of the books of the Kings do not hesitate to attach the moral:

Even after this incident, Jeroboam did not turn back from his evil way, but kept on appointing priests for the shrines from the ranks of the people. He ordained as priests of the shrines anyone who so desired. Thereby the House of Jeroboam incurred guilt—to their utter annihilation from the face of the earth. (1 Kings 12:25–13:34)

Nor was it in northern Israel alone that a breach of the Covenant occurred.

Meanwhile, Rehoboam son of Solomon had become king in Judah. Rehoboam was forty-one years old when he became king, and he reigned seventeen years in Jerusalem—the city the Lord had chosen out of all the tribes of Israel to establish His name there. His mother's name was Naamah the Ammonitess. Judah did what was displeasing to the Lord, and angered Him more than their fathers had done by the sins that they committed. They too built for themselves shrines, pillars, and sacred posts on every high hill and under every leafy tree; there were also male prostitutes in the land. (Judah) imitated all the abhorrent practices of the nations which the Lord had dispossessed before the Israelites.

In the fifth year of King Rehoboam, King Shishak of Egypt marched against Jerusalem and carried off the treasure of the House of the Lord and the treasures of the royal palace. He carried off everything; he even carried off all the golden shields that Solomon had made. (1 Kings 14: 21–26)

40. Years of Infidelity, Disaster, Waiting

The theodicy of the Israelite chroniclers is a straightforward one: if Israel sins through infidelity to the Covenant, Israel will be punished. Since the days of Jeroboam, the northern kingdom of Israel was a breeding ground for such infidelity. When God's punishment finally came, it came in the form of the Assyrians.

In the twelfth year of King Ahaz of Judah, Hoshea son of Elah became king over Israel in Samaria—for nine years. He did what was displeasing to the Lord, though not as much as the kings of Israel who preceded him. King Shalmaneser marched against him, and Hoshea became his vassal and paid him tribute. But the king of Assyria caught Hoshea in an act of treachery: he had sent envoys to King So of Egypt, and he had not paid the tribute of the king of Assyria, as in previous years. And the king of Assyria arrested him and put him in prison. Then the king of Assyria marched against the whole land; he came to Samaria and besieged it for three years. In the ninth year of Hoshea, the king of Assyria captured Samaria [721 B.C.E.]. He deported the Israelites to Assyria and settled them in Halah, at the (River) Habor, at the River Gozen, and in the towns of Media.

Viewed in the sight of the Lord, the southern kingdom of Judah was little better in its observance of the terms of the Covenant. Yet the Lord postponed His judgment on Judah, perhaps because a just king had at last come to the throne in Jerusalem.

In the third year of King Hoshea son of Elah of Israel, Hezekiah son of King Ahaz of Judah became king (in Judah). He was twenty-five years old when he became king, and he reigned in Jerusalem twenty-nine years.

. . . He did what was pleasing to the Lord, just as his father David had done. He abolished the shrines and smashed the pillars and cut down the sacred post. He also broke into pieces the bronze serpent which Moses had made [cf. Num. 21:4–9], for until that time the Israelites had been offering sacrifices to it; it was called Nehushtan. He trusted only in the Lord the God of Israel; there was none like him among all the kings of Judah after him, nor among those before him. (2 Kings 18:1–5)

Such was the reputation of Hezekiah that a millennium afterwards rabbis in Babylonia were discussing the question of whether in fact he had been the Messiah (see Chapter 2 below). According to 2 Kings, "the Lord was with him and he prospered in all that he undertook." What he undertook was to throw off the sovereignty of the king of Assyria, an act of defiance that brought the Assyrians not once but twice to the threshold of Jerusalem. On the first occasion Hezekiah submitted and averted calamity by the payment of large penalties. But the next time, in 701 B.C.E, the Lord had to intervene directly—it is one of the last times in the long history of the Israelites that such intervention occurs—against the Assyrians camped outside the walls of Jerusalem.

That night an angel of the Lord went out and struck down one hundred and eighty-five thousand in the Assyrian camp, and the following morning they were all dead corpses.

So King Sennacherib of Assyria broke camp and retreated, and stayed in Nineveh. (2 Kings 19:35–36)

The saintly Hezekiah was succeeded by his sin-laden son Manasseh, who possesses the blackest reputation in the entire annals of the kings of Israel.

Manasseh was twelve years old when he became king, and he reigned fifty-five years in Jerusalem. . . . He did what was displeasing to the Lord, following the abhorrent practices of the nations which the Lord had dispossessed before the Israelites. He rebuilt shrines which his father Hezekiah had destroyed; he erected altars for Baal and made a sacred post, as King Ahab of Israel had done. He bowed down to all the host of heaven and worshiped them, and he built altars for them in the House of the Lord, of which the Lord had said, "I will establish My name in Jerusalem." He built altars for all the hosts of heaven in the two courts of the House of the Lord. . . . The sculptured image of Asherah which he made, he placed in the House concerning which the Lord had said to David and to his son Solomon, "In this House and in Jerusalem, which I chose out of all the tribes of Israel, I will establish My name forever." (2 Kings 21:1–7)

41. The Reforms of Josiah

Now, if ever, the Lord's judgment should have come. But the theologically satisfying denouement of the destruction of Jerusalem that should have occurred during the fifty-five years of Manasseh's defilement of the city and the land was postponed once again, perhaps because of the presence of a just king, in this case Josiah (640–609 B.C.E.), the grandson of Manasseh, who "did right in the eyes of the Lord; he followed closely in the footsteps of his forefather David, swerving neither right nor left" (2 Kings 22:1–2). Well established in the eighteenth year of his rule, in 622 B.C.E. the king put his hand to the task and in the sequel brought about one of the momentous turning points in the history of Jewish cult practice.

Then the high priest Hilikiah said to the scribe Shaphan, "I have found a scroll of the Teaching in the House of the Lord." And Hilikiah gave the scroll to Shaphan, who read it. . . . The scribe Shaphan also told the king, "The high priest Hilikiah has given me a scroll"; and Shaphan read it to the king.

When the king heard the contents of the scroll of the Teaching, he rent his clothes. And the king gave orders to the priest Hilikiah, and to Ahikam son of Shaphan, Achbor son of Michaiah, the scribe Shaphan, and Saiah the king's minister: "Go, inquire of the Lord on my behalf, and on behalf of the people, and on behalf of all Judah, concerning the words of this scroll that has been found. For great indeed must be the wrath of the Lord that has been kindled against us, because our fathers did not obey the words of this scroll to do all that had been prescribed for us." (2 Kings 22:8–13)

The "book of the law" may have been the core of the one included in the Bible under the name of Deuteronomy, or "The Second Book of Law." The discovery was read as a divine signal for reform, a conclusion confirmed when king and minister consulted Huldah the prophetess "at her home in the Mishneh quarter of Jerusalem" (2 Kings 22:14). They were admonished that unless the terms of the Covenant are restored, God's wrath will descend upon the nation.

At the king's summons, all the elders of Judah and Jerusalem assembled before him. The king went up to the House of the Lord, together with all the men of Judah and all the inhabitants of Jerusalem, and the priests and prophets—all the people, young and old. And he read to them the entire text of the covenant scroll which had been found in the House of the Lord. The king stood by the pillar and solemnized the covenant before the Lord: that they would follow the Lord and observe His commandments, His injunctions, and His laws with all their heart and soul;

that they should fulfill all the terms of this covenant as inscribed upon the scroll. And all the people entered into the covenant.

Then the king ordered the high priest Hilikiah, the priests of the second rank, and the guards of the threshold to bring out of the Temple of the Lord all the objects made for Baal and Asherah and all the host of heaven. He burned them outside Jerusalem in the fields of Kidron, and he removed the ashes to Bethel. He suppressed the idolatrous priests whom the kings of Judah had appointed to make offerings at the shrines in the towns of Judah and in the environs of Jerusalem, and those who made offerings to Baal, to the sun and moon and constellations—all the host of heaven. He brought out the (image of Asherah) from the House of the Lord to the Kidron Valley outside Jerusalem, and burned it in the Kidron Valley; he beat it to dust and scattered its dust over the burial ground of the common people. He tore down the cubicles of the male prostitutes in the House of the Lord, at the place where the women wore coverings for Asherah. (2 Kings 23:1–7)

And then, as a final step in a process of cultic centralization that had begun with David's choice of Jerusalem as his capital and his placing of the Ark on Mount Moriah, Josiah decreed that the Temple of Jerusalem should be the sole place where the Israelites might offer sacrifice to their God.

He brought all the priests from the towns of Judah [to Jerusalem] and defiled the shrines where the priests had been making offerings— from Geba to Beer-sheba. He also demolished the shrines of the gates, which were at the entrance of the gate of Joshua, the city prefect, which were on a person's left (as he entered) the city gate. The priests of the shrines, however, did not ascend the altar of the Lord in Jerusalem, but they ate unleavened bread along with their kinsmen.

The king commanded all the people, "Offer the Passover sacrifice to the Lord your God as prescribed in this scroll of the Covenant." Now the Passover sacrifice had not been offered in that manner in the days of the chieftains who ruled Israel, or during the days of the kings of Israel and the kings of Judah. Only in the eighteenth year of King Josiah (622 B.C.E.) was such a Passover sacrifice offered in that manner to the Lord in Jerusalem. (2 Kings 23:8–9, 21–23)

42. "The End, The End, It Comes, It Comes"

The cult of the Lord was saved for the moment, but there could be no political salvation for Israel. Shishak and the Egyptians had already shown the Israelite monarchies for the fragile things they were. As we have seen, Samaria and the heart of the northern kingdom finally fell to the Assyrians in 721 B.C.E. Later, in 701 B.C.E., when Hezekiah was king in Judah, Jerusalem narrowly escaped destruction when the Assyrians held it under siege. The great powers in turn swirled through Palestine: Assyria, Egypt, and finally Babylonia.

The Israelite kings did what they could, now strengthening the defenses of the city, now attempting to buy off the attackers. They may have had some hope of weathering the storm, but there were others who saw the approaching disaster in different terms and knew with the certainty of inspiration that there was no way of averting the Lord's judgment on Israel.

Then the hand of the Lord came upon me there, and He said to me, "Arise, go out to the valley, and there I will speak with you." I arose and went out to the valley, and there stood the Presence of the Lord, like the Presence that I had seen at the Chebar Canal; and I flung myself down on my face. And a spirit entered into me and set me upon my feet. And He spoke to me, and said to me, "Go, shut yourself up in your house. As for you, O mortal, cords have been placed upon you, and you have been bound with them, and you shall not go out among them. And I will make your tongue cleave to your palate, and you shall be dumb; you shall not be a reprover to them, for they are a rebellious breed. But when I speak with you, I will open your mouth and you shall say to them, 'Thus says the Lord God!' He who listens will listen, and he who does not will not—for they are a rebellious breed." (Ezekiel 3:22–27)

The man taken "captive" by God on the bank of the Chebar Canal in Babylonia was Ezekiel, and the year may have been about 593 B.C.E. The Babylonians had already attacked Jerusalem once; the future, the Lord warned His prophet, would be even worse.

Thus said the Lord God: I set this Jerusalem in the midst of nations, with countries round her. But she rebelled against My rules and My laws, acting more wickedly than the nations and the countries round her; she rejected My rules and disobeyed My laws . . . thus said the Lord God: I, in turn, am going to deal with you, and I will execute judgments in your midst in the sight of the nations. On account of all your abominations, I will do among you what I have never done, and the like of which I will never do again.

Assuredly, parents shall eat their children in your midst, and children shall eat their parents. I will execute judgments against you, and I will scatter all your survivors in every direction.

Assuredly, as I live—said the Lord God—because you defiled My Sanctuary with all your detestable things and all your abominations, I in turn will shear (you) away and show no pity. I in turn will show no compassion. (Ezekiel 5:5–11)

The word of the Lord came to me: You, O mortal, [say:] Thus said the Lord God to the land of Israel: Doom! Doom is coming upon the four corners of the land. Now doom is upon you! I will let loose My anger against you and judge you according to your ways; I will requite you for all your abominations. I will show you no pity and no compassion; but I will requite you for your ways and for the abominations in your midst. And you shall know that I am the Lord.

Thus said the Lord God: A singular disaster; a disaster is coming. Doom is coming! The hour of doom is coming! It stirs against you; the end, the end, it comes, it comes. (Ezekiel 7:1–6)

2. From Israelite to Jew: The Post-Exilic Reconstruction

1. Ruin and Exile

He [that is, Nebuchadnezzar, king of Babylon] exiled all of Jerusalem: all the commanders and all the warriors—ten thousand exiles—as well as all the craftsmen and smiths; only the poorest people in the land were left. He deported Jehoiachin to Babylon; and the king's wives and officers and the notables of the land were brought as exiles from Jerusalem to Babylon. . . .

And the king of Babylon appointed Mattaniah, Jehoiachin's uncle, king in his place, changing his name to Zedekiah. (2 Kings 24:14–17)

This was in 597 B.C.E., and the Judean vassal Zedekiah was intended to serve his Babylonian master on the latter's own terms. Such must not have been the case, however, since ten years later we once again find Nebuchadnezzar standing before the walls of Jerusalem. There was resistance on the part of the decimated Israelites. But the city fell, as inevitably it had to, and on this occasion the punishment was not looting or the exaction of tribute but the wholesale destruction of the city and another draft of exiles for Babylon.

And in the ninth year of his reign, on the tenth day of the tenth month, Nebuchadnezzar moved against Jerusalem with his whole army. He besieged it; and they built towers against it all around. The city continued in a state of siege until the eleventh year of King Zedekiah. By the ninth day [of the fourth month; 587 B.C.E.] the famine had become acute in the city; there was no food left for the common people. Then the wall of the city was breached. All the soldiers (left the city) by night through the gate between the double walls which is near the king's garden. . . .

Zedekiah was captured near Jericho, brought back to Jerusalem, and blinded.

In the fifth month, on the seventh day of the month, in the nine-teenth year of Nebuchadnezzar king of Babylon, Nebuzaradan, captain of the king's bodyguard, came to Jerusalem and set fire to the House of the Lord and the royal palace; all the houses in the city, including the mansion of Gedaliah, were burnt down. The Chaldean forces of the captain of the guard pulled down the walls all around Jerusalem. Nebuzaradan, captain of the guard, deported the rest of the people left in the city, those who had deserted to the king of Babylon and any remaining artisans. He left only the weakest class of people to be vinedressers and laborers. (2 Kings 25:1–12)

2. The Quran Reflects on the Destruction of the Temple

The Quran knew that the Temple in Jerusalem was twice destroyed; and although the text is somewhat opaque in its allusion, most of the commentators took the two events to refer to the Babylonian and probably to the earlier Assyrian assault on the city rather than to the Roman assault in 70 C.E.

We [that is, as always, God] announced to the Children of Israel in the Book: "You will surely create disorder twice in the land, and become exceedingly arrogant." So when the time of the first prediction came, We sent against you Our creatures full of martial might, who ransacked your cities; and the prediction was fulfilled. Then We gave you a chance against them, and strengthened you with wealth and children and increased your numbers, and said: "If you do good, you do so for your own good; if you do ill, you will do it for your own loss." So, when the time of the second prediction comes, (We shall rouse another people) to shame you, and enter the Temple as they had the first time, and to destroy what they conquered utterly. (Quran 17:4–7)

3. Life and the Glory of God Returns to Israel

If Ezekiel had foreseen the blackest days of the end, he also saw, in another vision-ary transport, a new beginning and, in an extraordinary image, literally a new life.

When I have cleansed you of all your iniquities, I will people your settlements, and the ruined places shall be rebuilt; and the desolate land, after lying waste in the sight of every passerby, shall again be tilled. And men shall say, "That land, once ruined, desolate, and ravaged, is now populated and fortified." . . .

Thus said the Lord God: Moreover, in this I will respond to the House of Israel and act for their sake: I will multiply their people like sheep. As Jerusalem is filled with sacrificial sheep during her festivals, so shall the ruined cities be filled with flocks of people. And they shall know that I am the Lord.

The hand of the Lord came upon me. He took me out by the spirit of the Lord and set me down in the valley. It was full of bones. He led me all around them; they were very many of them spread over the valley, and they were very dry. He said to me, "O mortal, can these bones live again?" I replied, "O Lord God, only You know." And He said to me, "Prophesy over these bones and say to them, O dry bones, hear the word of the Lord!" Thus said the Lord God to these bones: I will cause breath to enter you and you shall live again. I will lay sinews upon you and cover you with flesh, and form skin over you. And I will put breath into you, and you shall live again. And you shall know that I am the Lord.

I prophesied as I had been commanded. And while I was prophesying, suddenly there was a sound of rattling, and the bones came together, bone to matching bone. I looked, and there were sinews on them, and flesh had grown, and skin had formed over them; but there was no breath in them. Then He said to me, "Prophesy to the breath, prophesy, O mortal! Say to the breath; Thus said the Lord God: Come, O breath, from the four winds, and breathe into these slain, that they may live again." I prophesied as He commanded me. The breath entered them, and they came to life and stood up on their feet, a vast multitude. (Ezekiel 36:33–37:11)

Nor was that the end of the wonder. The Lord Himself, Ezekiel was shown, would return to the seat of His former glory in Jerusalem, to a new, purified Jerusalem and to a new Temple, whose very plan is given by the Lord to His prophet.

Then he led me to a gate, the gate that faced east. And there, coming from the east with a roar like the roar of mighty waters, was the Presence of the God of Israel, and the earth was lit up by His Presence. The vision was like the vision I had seen when I came to destroy the city, the very same vision that I had seen by the Chebar Canal. Forthwith, I fell on my face.

The Presence of the Lord entered the Temple by the gate that faced eastward. A spirit carried me into the inner court, and lo, the Presence of the Lord filled the Temple; and I heard speech addressed to me from the Temple, though (the) man was standing beside me. It said to me:

O mortal, this is the place of My throne and the place for the soles of My feet, where I will dwell in the midst of the people Israel forever. The House of Israel and their kings must not again defile My holy name by their apostasy and by the corpses of their kings at their death. . . .

(Now) you, O mortal, describe the Temple to the House of Israel, and let them measure its design. But let them be ashamed of their iniquities: When they are ashamed of all they have done, make known to them the plan of the Temple and its layout, its exits and entrances—its entire plan, and all the laws and instructions pertaining to its entire plan. Write it down before their eyes, that they may faithfully follow its entire plan and all its laws. Such are the instructions for the Temple on top of the mountain: the entire area of its enclosure shall be most holy. Thus far the instructions for the Temple. (Ezekiel 43:1–12)

4. Israel: A New Covenant

Ezekiel was a true visionary, and in his apocalyptic sight the restoration of both Israel and Jerusalem appears to be God's work alone. But the destruction of the Holy City and its Temple and the carrying off of large numbers of Israelites into exile in Babylon were events of such obvious magnitude for a people who had always regarded themselves under God's special dispensation that they provoked changes that ran deeper into the life of the community than Ezekiel's transcendent vision could have stooped to encompass. Adjustments had to be made in cult and institution. New reflections and new tones, some despairing and some expectant, were heard among the religious leaders of the people. These leaders were themselves new figures: not, as often before, warriors, kings, and priests, but, like Ezekiel, prophets of the Almighty Himself. And what they were saying was at once disturbing and hopeful.

Thus said the Lord:

> "Restrain your voice from weeping,
> Your eyes from shedding tears;
> For there is a reward for your labor . . .
> They shall return from the enemy's land.
> And there is hope for your future . . .
> Your children shall return to their country."
> (Jeremiah 31:16–17)

Christians, as we have already seen, took those words to refer not to a renewal after the Exile but to a far more profound redrawing of the Covenant in their own day.

See, a time is coming—declares the Lord—when I will make a new covenant with the House of Israel and the House of Judah. It will not be like the covenant I made with their fathers, when I took them by the hand to lead them out of the land of Egypt, a covenant which they broke, so that I rejected them—declares the Lord. But such is the covenant I will make with the House of Israel after these days—declares the Lord: I will put My Teaching into their innermost being and inscribe it upon their hearts. Then I will be their God, and they shall be My people. No longer will they need to teach one another and say to one another, "Heed the Lord"; for all of them, from the least of them to the greatest shall heed Me—declares the Lord. (Jeremiah 31:31-34)

5. The Redeemer of Israel

Jeremiah's interest was in a new Covenant. Another prophet, Isaiah, had a vision that was at once more startling and more personal: there is to be a mediator, a redeemer for Israel sent by God Himself, and it this very person who speaks in the following passage.

> Listen, O coastlands, to me,
> And give heed, O nations afar:
> The Lord appointed me before I was born,
> He named me while I was in my mother's womb.
> He made my mouth shaped like a sharpened blade,
> He hid me in the shadow of His hand,
> And He made me like a polished arrow;
> He concealed me in His quiver.
> And He said to me, "You are My servant,
> Israel in whom I glory."
> I thought, "I have labored in vain,
> I have spent my strength for empty breath."
> But my case rested with the Lord,
> My recompense was in the hands of my God.
> And now the Lord has resolved—
> He who formed me in the womb to be His servant—
> To bring back Jacob to Himself,
> That Israel may be restored to Him.
> And I have been honored in the sight of the Lord,
> My God has been my strength.
> For He has said:

"It is too little that you should be My servant
In that I raise up the tribes of Jacob
And restore the survivors of Israel:
I will also make you a light of nations,
That My salvation may reach the ends of the earth."
([Second] Isaiah 49:1–6)

6. The Suffering Servant

Here too there was much for the Christians to ponder.

> Indeed, My servant shall prosper,
> Be exalted and raised to great heights.
> Just as the many were appalled at him—
> So marred was his appearance, unlike that of man,
> His form, beyond human semblance—
> Just so he shall startle many nations.
> Kings shall be silenced because of him,
> For they shall see what has not been told them,
> Shall behold what they never have heard.
>
> Who can believe what we have heard?
> Upon whom has the arm of the Lord been revealed?
> For he has grown, by His favor, like a tree-crown,
> Like a tree-trunk out of arid ground.
> He had no form or beauty, that we should look at him:
> No charm, that we should find him pleasing.

He was despised, shunned by men,
A man of suffering, familiar with disease.
As one who hid his face from us,
He was despised, we held him of no account.
Yet it was our sickness that he was bearing,
Our suffering that he endured.
We accounted him plagued,
Smitten and afflicted by God;
But he was wounded because of our sins,
Crushed because of our iniquities.
He bore the chastisement that made us whole,
And by his bruises we were healed.
We all went astray like sheep,
Each going his own way;

And the Lord visited upon him
The guilt of all of us.

He was maltreated, yet he was submissive,
He did not open his mouth;
Like a sheep being led to slaughter,
Like an ewe, dumb before those who shear her,
He did not open his mouth.
By oppressive judgment he was taken away,
Who could describe his abode?
For he was cut off from the land of the living
Through the sin of My people, who deserved the punishment.
And his grave was set among the wicked,
And with the rich, in his death—
Though he had done no injustice
And had spoken no falsehood.
But the Lord chose to crush him by disease,
That, if he made himself an offering for guilt,
He might see offspring and have long life,
And that through him the Lord's purpose might prosper.
Out of his anguish he shall see it;
He shall enjoy it to the full through his devotion.
My righteous servant makes the many righteous,
It is their punishment that he bears;
Assuredly, I will give him the many as his portion,
He shall receive the multitude as his spoil.
For he exposed himself to death
And was numbered among the sinners,
Whereas he bore the guilt of the many
And made intercession for sinners.
([Second] Isaiah 52:13–53:12)

7. The Return

Eventually, in the turning world of Near Eastern politics, the invincible Babylonians met their own doom. They were replaced by a new Iranian power, the Achaemenians, and with the change of dynasty in Iraq and Iran there was a change of circumstances for the Israelites as well.

In the first year of King Cyrus of Persia [538 B.C.E.], when the word of the Lord spoken by Jeremiah was fulfilled, the Lord roused the spirit of King Cyrus of Persia to issue a proclamation throughout his realm by word of mouth and in writing as follows:

Thus said King Cyrus of Persia: The Lord God of Heaven has given me all the kingdoms of the earth and has charged me with building Him a house in Jerusalem, which is in Judah. Anyone of you of all His people—may his God be with him, and let him go up to Jerusalem that is in Judah and build the House of the Lord God of Israel, the God that is in Jerusalem; and all who stay behind, wherever he may be living, let the people of his place assist him with silver, gold, goods, and livestock, beside the freewill offering to the House of God that is in Jerusalem. (Ezra 1:1–4)

8. The Cult of the Lord Restored

Among the first of the projects undertaken by the returnees was the restoration of the sacrificial worship of the God of Israel in the only place where that was now possible, on the Temple mount in Jerusalem.

When the seventh month arrived—the Israelites being settled in their towns—the entire people assembled as one man in Jerusalem. Then Jeshua son of Jozadak and his brother priests, and Zerubbabel son of Shealtiel and his brothers set to and built the altar of the God of Israel to offer burnt offerings upon it as is written in the Teaching of Moses, the man of God. They set up the altar on its site because they were in fear of the peoples of the land, and they offered burnt offerings upon it to the Lord, burnt offerings every morning and evening. Then they celebrated the festival of Tabernacles as is written, with its daily burnt offerings in the proper quantities, on each day as is prescribed for it, followed by the regular burnt offering and the offerings for the new moons and for all the sacred fixed times of the Lord and whatever freewill offerings were made to the Lord. From the first day of the seventh month they began to make burnt offerings to the Lord, though the foundation of the Temple of the Lord had not been laid. . . .

In the second year after their arrival at the House of God, at Jerusalem, in the second month, Zerubbabel son of Shealtiel and Jeshua son of Jozadak, and the rest of their brother priests and Levites, and all who had come from the captivity to Jerusalem . . . appointed Levites . . . to supervise the work. . . .

When the builders had laid the foundation of the Temple of the Lord, priests in their vestments with trumpets, and Levites sons of Asaph with cymbals were stationed to give praise to the Lord, as King David of Israel had ordained. . . . All the people raised a great shout extolling the Lord because the foundation of the House of the Lord had been laid. Many of the priests and Levites and the chiefs of the clans, the old men who had seen the first house, wept loudly at the sight of the founding of this house. Many others shouted joyously at the top of their voices. The people could not distinguish the shouts of joy from the people's weeping, for the people raised a great shout, the sound of which could be heard from afar. (Ezra 3:1–13)

9. The Second Temple

The cult of the Lord had been restored, but there was still no temple in Jerusalem, and the task of rebuilding it figures nowhere in the plans of Nehemiah, the chief political architect of the new Jerusalem, whose post was, however, a purely civil one. The temple initiative came from quite another source, the prophets Haggai and Zechariah, and with explicit permission of the Shah Darius.

Now you, Tattenai, governor of the province of Beyond the River (Euphrates), Shethar-bozenai, and your colleagues, the officials of the province of Beyond the River, stay away from that place. Allow the work of this House of God to go on; let the governor of the Jews and the elders of the Jews rebuild this House of God on its site.

Moreover, this Jewish temple in Jerusalem would be built with a subsidy from the imperial exchequer of Iran.

And I hereby issue an order concerning what you must do to help these elders of the Jews rebuild this House of God: the expenses are to be paid to these men with dispatch out of the resources of the king, derived from the taxes of the province of Beyond the River, so that the work not be stopped. They are to be given daily, without fail, whatever they need of young bulls, rams, or lambs as burnt offerings for the God of Heaven, and wheat, salt, wine, and oil, at the order of the priests in Jerusalem, so that they may offer pleasing sacrifices to the God of heaven and pray for the life of the king and his sons. . . .

Then Tattenai, (Achaemenian) governor of the province of Beyond the River, Shethar-bozenai, and their colleagues carried out with dispatch what King Darius had written. So the elders of the Jews progressed in the building, urged on by the prophesying of Haggai the prophet and Zechariah son of Iddo, and they brought the building (of the Temple) to completion under the aegis of the God of Israel and by the order of Cyrus and

Darius and King Artaxerxes of Persia. The house was finished on the third of the month of Adar in the sixth year of the reign of King Darius. (Ezra 6:6–15)

Thus we are given to believe that Zerubbabel's Temple stood where Solomon's had before it. We have no reason to think otherwise. But even though we are assured through Haggai that people old enough to remember Solomon's building found the new Temple not unlike the old (Haggai 2:3), it is difficult to think of this as anything but a validation of authenticity. Solomon's resources and ambitions in the tenth century B.C.E. were substantially greater than those of Zerubbabel in the fifth, and the Second Temple, like the rebuilt Jerusalem, must have reflected the straitened circumstances of the people who lived there, as those priests and Levites and elders whom we saw weeping in disappointment at the sight of the new Temple's foundations poignantly attest.

But a fresh start had been made in Jerusalem, and the hopes earlier expressed by Isaiah seemed to Zechariah, the prophet of this age who was present at the momentous beginnings, now at last close to fulfillment.

Thus said the Lord of Hosts: Take courage, you who now hear these words which the prophets spoke when the foundations were laid for the rebuilding of the Temple, the House of the Lord of Hosts.

Thus said the Lord: I have returned to Zion, and I will dwell in Jerusalem. Jerusalem will be called the City of Faithfulness, and the mount of the Lord of Hosts the Holy Mount.

Thus said the Lord of Hosts: There shall yet be old men and women in the squares of Jerusalem, each with staff in hand because of their great age. And the squares of the city shall be crowded with boys and girls playing in the squares. . . . I will rescue My people from the lands of the east and from the lands of the west, and I will bring them home to dwell in Jerusalem. They shall be My people, and I will be their God—in truth and sincerity. (Zechariah 8:3–8)

10. The Mosaic Law Renewed

Finally, the Mosaic constitution of the restored Jewish theocracy had once again to be promulgated, and it is here perhaps that Ezra, the prototype of the class of Jewish Torah scholars later called rabbis, enters the story of Jerusalem.

After these events, during the reign of King Artaxerxes of Persia, Ezra son of Seriah . . . came up from Babylon, a scribe expert in the Teaching of Moses which the Lord God of Israel had given, whose request the king had granted in its entirety, thanks to the benevolence of the Lord toward him. . . . For Ezra had dedicated himself to study the Teaching of the Lord so as to observe it, and to teach laws and rules to Israel. (Ezra 7:1–10)

When the seventh month arrived—the Israelites being (settled) in their towns—the entire people assembled as one man in the square behind the Water Gate, and they asked Ezra the scribe to bring the scroll of the Teaching of Moses with which the Lord had charged Israel. On the first day of the seventh month, Ezra the priest brought the Teaching before the congregation, men and women and all who could listen with understanding. He read from it, facing the square before the Water Gate, from the first light until midday, to the men and the women and those who could understand; the ears of all the people were given to the scroll of the Teaching.

Ezra the scribe stood upon a wooden tower made for the purpose. . . . Ezra opened the scroll in the sight of all the people, for he was above all the people; as he opened it, all the people answered, "Amen, Amen," with hands upraised. Then they bowed their heads and prostrated themselves before the Lord with their faces to the ground. Jeshua, Bani, Sherebiah, Jamin, Akkub, Shabbethai, Hodiah, Maaseiah, Kelita, Azariah, Jozabad, Hanan, Pelaiah, and the Levites explained the Teaching to the people, while the people stood in their places. They read from the scroll of the Teaching of God, translating it and giving the sense (in Aramaic); so they understood the reading. (Nehemiah 8:1–8)

On the twenty-fourth day of this month, the Israelites assembled, fasting, in sackcloth, and with earth upon them. Those of the stock of Israel separated themselves from all foreigners, and stood and confessed their sins and the iniquities of their fathers. Standing in their places, they read from the scroll of the teaching of the Lord their God for one-fourth of the day, and for another fourth they confessed and prostrated themselves before the Lord their God. . . .

". . . We make this pledge and put it in writing; And on the sealed copy (are subscribed) our officials, our Levites, and our priests. . . .

"And the rest of the people, the priests, the Levites, the gatekeepers, the singers, the temple servants, and all who separated themselves from the peoples of the lands to (follow) the Teaching of God, their wives, sons and daughters, all who know enough to understand, join with their noble brothers, and take an oath with sanctions to follow the Teaching of God, given through Moses the servant of God, and to observe carefully all the

commandments of the Lord our Lord, His rules and laws." (Nehemiah
9:1–3; 10:1–30)

11. An Edict of Toleration

*The Israelites had been restored to Palestine but not to sovereignty over that land.
They were subjects of the Persian shah and then, in the wake of Alexander the
Great's progress across Asia, a province to be fought over by his Greek successors in
Egypt and Syria, the Ptolemies and Seleucids. The latter finally triumphed, and by
200 B.C.E. the Seleucid Antiochus III (223–187 B.C.E.) was firmly in control of
Palestine, together with most of western Asia.*

When Antiochus [III] the Great reigned over Asia it was the lot of
the Jews to undergo great hardships through the devastation of their land,
as did also the inhabitants of Coele-Syria. For while he was at war with
Ptolemy Philopator and with his son Ptolemy, surnamed Epiphanes, and
whether he was victorious or defeated, they experienced the same fate.
. . . But not long afterward Antiochus defeated (the Egyptian general)
Scopas in a battle near the sources of the Jordan [200 B.C.E.] and destroyed
a greater part of his army. And later, when Antiochus took possession of
the cities in Coele-Syria which Scopas had held, and Samaria, the Jews of
their own will went over to him and admitted him to their city and made
abundant provision for his entire army and his elephants; and they readily
joined his forces in besieging the (Egyptian) garrison which had been left
by Scopas in the citadel of Jerusalem. Accordingly, Antiochus, considering it just to requite the zeal and exertions of the Jews on his behalf, wrote
to his governors and Friends (of the King), bearing witness to the Jews
concerning the good treatment he had received at their hands and announcing the rewards which he had decided to give them on that account. (Josephus, *Antiquities* 12.3.3)

*Josephus then reproduces Antiochus' letter, which carries us directly into the com-
plex and often tortured relations between the Jerusalem Jews and their Greco-
Macedonian sovereigns in Antioch.*

King Antiochus to Ptolemy, greetings. Since the Jews, beginning
from the time that we entered their territory, have testified to their zeal
in our regard, and since, from our arrival in their city they have received
us in a magnificent manner and came out to meet us with their senate
[*gerousia*, literally Council of Elders], have contributed generously to the
upkeep of our soldiers and our elephants, and have assisted us in captur-

ing the Egyptian garrison in the citadel (*akra*), we have judged it proper that we too should respond to those good offices by restoring their city destroyed by the misfortunes of war and repopulating it by bringing back all those people dispersed from it.

And like past sovereigns of the land of Israel, the Seleucids too would subsidize the daily Temple offerings.

First we have decided by reasons of piety to furnish for the sacrifices a contribution of sacrificial offerings and wine and oil and incense to the value of 20,000 drachmas of silver, and of flour of grain in sacred artabas according to the measure of the country, 1,460 mediamni of wheat and 375 mediamni of salt. I wish all these contributions be furnished them as I have commanded and that the work on the Temple be achieved, the stoas and whatever else needs be built. Let wood be provided from both Judea itself and from among the other peoples and from the Lebanon, without being taxed. Likewise for the other things required to make the restoration of the Temple outstanding.

All of that people will be governed according to their ancestral laws, and their Council of Elders and priests and scribes of the Temple and the sacred chanters will be exempt from the capitation tax, the crown tax and that on salt. And so that the city might more quickly be repopulated, I grant to those who now live in it and those who will return until the month of Hyperberetaios to be exempt from tax for a period of three years. Further we exempt them in the future from one-third of the taxes in order to compensate them for their losses. As for those who have been taken from the city and reduced to slavery, to them and their offspring we grant their freedom and bid their goods be restored to them. (Josephus, *Antiquities* 12.3.3)

Finally, the authority of Seleucid sovereignty was placed behind the proper observation of the Mosaic Law.

Now these [Josephus continues] were the contents of the letter. And out of reverence for the Temple he also published throughout the kingdom a grave and holy public notice with these terms. "It is prohibited for any foreigner to go into the sanctuary forbidden to the Jews themselves, except for those who have been purified and are so permitted according to the ancestral law. It is prohibited to bring into the city either horse meat or the flesh of a mule or a wild or domesticated ass, of the panther, the fox or the hare, or in general of any of the animals forbidden to the Jews. It is prohibited bringing in their skins. Nor can they be raised in the city. It is prohibited using any but traditionally butchered animals, from among which it is also prescribed that the sacrifices for God be chosen. Whoever shall transgress any one of these (prohibitions) shall pay to the priests a fine of 3,000 silver drachmas." (Josephus, *Antiquities* 12.3.4)

12. The Hellenization of Jerusalem

Onto this apparently agreeable scene came in "that wicked man" Antiochus IV, surnamed, in the ordinary grandiose style of the times, "Epiphanes," the "God-Made-Manifest." The mise-en-scène is provided by the first Book of Maccabees:

Alexander (the Great) had reigned twelve years when he died [323 B.C.E.]. His generals took over the government, each in his own province. On his death they were all crowned as kings, and their descendants succeeded them for many years. They brought untold miseries upon the world.

A scion of this stock was that wicked man Antiochus Epiphanes, son of King Antiochus (III). He had been a hostage in Rome before he succeeded to the throne in the year 137 of the Greek era [175 B.C.E.]. At that time there appeared in Israel a group of renegade Jews who incited the people. "Let us enter into a covenant with the Gentiles round about," they said, "because disaster after disaster has overtaken us since we segregated ourselves from them." The people thought this a good argument, and some of them in their enthusiasm went to the king and received authority to introduce non-Jewish laws and customs. They built a sports stadium in Gentile style in Jerusalem. They removed the marks of their circumcision and they repudiated the holy Covenant. They intermarried with Gentiles and abandoned themselves to evil ways. (1 Maccabees 1: 7–16)

The author of the first Book of Maccabees had the advantage of considerable hind-sight on the matter of Antiochus IV. But, as the text readily admits, the Greek king had neither planted the enthusiasm for things Greek among the Jews of Jerusalem nor even encouraged them to pursue that enthusiasm by introducing some of the hallmarks of urban Hellenism into the city. The initiative came from within, from the "Hellenizers" among the Jews in what was by then a large, populous, and prosperous city, as contemporary sources attest.

Jews were spreading all over the eastern Mediterranean, and their prosperity was shared by Jerusalem, or at least by the upper class constituted by the higher priesthoods and most intimately connected with the Holy City's chief and almost unique business, the Temple. And with prosperity came attraction to the life and the mores of the people who had brought it, the Hellenes. Not their gods, certainly, which every Jew despised, but that easily identified style that manifested itself in the art and the architecture that was beginning to fill the Near Eastern landscape and in that manner of life that was on prominent and attractive display in Alexandria, where many Jews now lived. Hellenism had no need of Antiochus Epiphanes to make its case: the Jews themselves reached out for it, and the Seleucid sovereign was happy to oblige.

13. Antioch-at-Jerusalem

The assimilation of the Jewish upper classes, particularly the priests, to the new Hellenism was complicated by a powerful rivalry for the chief post of that land, the High Priesthood. When High Priest Onias died, he was succeeded by his brother Jesus or Jeshua, who had Hellenized his name to Jason. How the matter was arranged is explained by Maccabees.

But when Seleucus was dead [in 175 B.C.E.] and had been succeeded by Antiochus, known as Epiphanes, Jason, Onias' brother, obtained the High Priesthood by corrupt means. He petitioned the king and promised him 360 talents in silver coin immediately and 80 talents from future revenues. In addition he undertook to pay another 150 talents for the authority to institute a sports stadium, to arrange for the education of young men there, and to enroll in Jerusalem a group to be known as "Antiochenes." The king agreed, and as soon as he had seized the High Priesthood, Jason made the Jews conform to the Greek way of life.

He set aside the royal privileges established for the Jews through the agency of John, the father of that Eupolemus who negotiated a treaty of friendship and alliance with the Romans. He abolished the lawful way of life and introduced practices which were against the law. He lost no time in establishing a sports stadium at the foot of the citadel itself, and he made the most outstanding of the young men assume the Greek athlete's hat. So Hellenism reached a high point with the introduction of foreign customs through the boundless wickedness of the impious Jason, no true High Priest. As a result, the priests no longer had any enthusiasm for their duties at the altar, but despised the Temple and neglected the sacrifices; and in defiance of the Law they eagerly contributed to the expenses of the wrestling school whenever the opening gong called them. They placed no honor on their hereditary dignities, but cared above everything for Hellenic honors. (2 Maccabees 4:7–16)

Josephus has his own, somewhat more political version of the same events, which now includes Jason's younger brother.

About this same time the High Priest Onias also died, and Antiochus gave the high priesthood to his brother, for the son whom Onias had left was still an infant. . . . Jesus, however—this was the brother of Onias—was deprived of the high priesthood when the king became angry with him and gave it to his youngest brother, named Onias. . . . Now Jesus changed his name to Jason while Onias was called Menelaus. And when the former High Priest Jesus rose up against Menelaus, who was appointed after him, the populace was divided between the two, the [pro–Seleucid] Tobiads being on the side of Menelaus, while the majority of the people supported Jason; and being hard pressed by him, Menelaus and the Tobiads withdrew, and going to Antiochus informed him that they wished to abandon their country's laws and the way of life prescribed by these and to follow the king's laws and adopt the Greek way of life. (Josephus, *Antiquities* 12.5.1, 2)

14. The Abomination of Desolation

About this time [that is, 170–169 B.C.E.] Antiochus undertook his second invasion of Egypt. . . . Upon a false report of Antiochus' death, Jason collected no less than a thousand men and made a surprise attack upon Jerusalem. The defenders on the wall were driven back and the city was finally taken; Menelaus took refuge in the citadel, and Jason continued to massacre his fellow citizens without pity. . . . He did not, however, gain control of the government; he gained only dishonor as the result of his plot, and returned again as a fugitive to Ammonite territory. . . .

When news of this reached the king (Antiochus), it became clear to him that Judea was in a state of rebellion. So he set out from Egypt in a savage mood, took Jerusalem by storm, and ordered his troops to cut down without mercy everyone they met and to slaughter those who took refuge in the houses. Young and old were massacred, girls and infants butchered. By the end of three days their losses had amounted to eighty thousand, and as many sold into slavery.

Not satisfied with this, the king had the audacity to enter the holiest Temple on earth, guided by Menelaus, who had turned traitor both to his religion and his country. He laid impious hands on the sacred vessels; his desecrating hands swept together the votive offerings which other kings had set up to enhance the splendor and fame of the shrine. (2 Maccabees 5:1–16)

1 Maccabees adds a few details on the spoliation of the Temple.

In his arrogance he entered the Temple and carried off the golden altar, the lampstand with all its equipment, the table for the Bread of the Presence, the sacred cups and bowls, the golden censers, the curtain and the crowns. He stripped off all the gold plating from the Temple front. He seized the silver, gold, and precious vessels, and whatever secret treasures he found, he took them all with him when he left for his own country. (1 Maccabees 1:21–24)

Sometime about 174 B.C.E. Antiochus had elevated Jerusalem to the high status of polis. In his anger at what seemed like a transparent act of treason committed while he was at war with Egypt, and after another disastrous foray into Egypt in 168, in the following year he degraded the city to the lowest and most humiliating rank of all, that of a military colony, in effect an occupied city under martial law. He then banned the very practice of Judaism.

Two years later the king sent to the towns of Judea a high revenue official, who arrived at Jerusalem with a powerful force. His language was friendly, but full of guile. For, once he had gained the city's confidence, he suddenly attacked it. He dealt it a heavy blow and killed many Israelites, plundering the city and setting it ablaze. He pulled down houses and walls on every side; women and children were made prisoners, and the cattle seized.

The City of David was turned into a citadel, enclosed by a high, stout wall with strong towers, and garrisoned by impious foreigners and renegades. Having made themselves secure, they accumulated arms and provisions, and deposited there the massed plunder of Jerusalem. There they lay in ambush, a lurking threat to the Temple and a perpetual menace to Israel. (1 Maccabees 1:29–36)

Moreover, he forbade them to offer the daily sacrifices which they used to offer to God in accordance with their law, and after plundering the entire city, he killed some of the people and some he took captive together with their women and children, so that the number of those taken alive came to ten thousand. And he burnt the finest parts of the city and pulling down the walls, built the Citadel in the Lower City; for it was high enough to overlook the Temple and it was for this reason that he fortified it with high walls and towers and stationed a Macedonian garrison there. Nonetheless, there remained in the Akra those of the people who were impious and of bad character and at their hands the citizens were destined to suffer terrible things. (Josephus, *Antiquities* 12.5.4)

The king then issued a decree throughout his empire: his subjects were all to become one people and abandon their own laws and religion.

The nations everywhere complied with the royal command, and many in Israel accepted the foreign worship, sacrificing to idols and profaning the sabbath. Moreover, the king sent agents with written orders to Jerusalem and the towns of Judea. Ways and customs foreign to the country were to be introduced. Burnt offerings, sacrifices and libations in the Temple were forbidden. . . .

Such was the decree which the king issued to all his subjects. He appointed superintendents over all of the people and instructed the towns of Judea to offer sacrifice, town by town. People thronged to their side in large numbers, every one of them a traitor to the law. (1 Maccabees 1:41–64)

This was a full-scale pogrom, indeed, an attempt to exterminate the Jewish religion, quite unlike anything Jerusalem had experienced before. And though there are trails of political clues across the acts of Antiochus, there can be no certainty that they lead to either the full or the true story of the events of 167 B.C.E. This is how they were read by one Jew, the prophetic author of the Book of Daniel.

At the appointed time, he [Antiochus] will again invade the south [that is, Egypt], but the second time will not be like the first. Ships from Kittim [Rome] will come against him. He will be checked, and will turn back, raging against the holy covenant. Having done his pleasure, he will then attend to those who forsake the holy covenant. Forces will be levied by him; they will desecrate the Temple, the fortress; they will abolish the regular offering and set up the appalling abomination. (Daniel 11:29–31)

And so in fact it happened.

. . . King Antiochus sent an elderly Athenian to force the Jews to abandon their ancestral customs and no longer regulate their lives according to the laws of God. He was also commissioned to pollute the Temple at Jerusalem and dedicate it to Olympian Zeus, and to dedicate the sanctuary on Mount Gerizim to Zeus, God of Hospitality, following the practice of the local inhabitants.

This evil hit them hard and was a severe trial. The Gentiles filled the Temple with licentious revelry; they took their pleasure with prostitutes and had intercourse with women in the sacred precincts. They brought forbidden things inside, and heaped the altar with impure offerings prohibited by the law. It was forbidden either to observe the Sabbath or keep the traditional festivals, or to admit being a Jew at all. On the monthly celebration of the king's birthday, the Jews were driven by brute force to eat the entrails of the sacrificial victims; and on the feast of Dionysus they were forced to wear ivy wreaths and join the procession in his honor. (2 Maccabees 6:1–7)

On the 15th day of the month of Kislev in the year 145 [7 December 167 B.C.E.] the "Abomination of Desolation" was set up on the altar. Pagan altars were built throughout the towns of Judea; incense was offered at the doors of houses and in the streets. All scrolls of the Law which were found were torn up and burnt. Anyone discovered in possession of a Book of the Covenant, or conforming to the Law, was put to death by the king's sentence. . . .

On the twenty-fifth day of the month they offered sacrifice on the pagan altar which was on top of the altar of the Lord. (1 Maccabees 1: 54–60)

15. The Maccabean Restoration

The origins and early unfolding of the Maccabean rebellion against Seleucid oppression do not directly concern us here. Jerusalem continued to be held by a Syrian garrison and their Jewish sympathizers in the Akra. There was an early and brief Maccabean occupation of the Holy City, but permanent reappropriation awaited more convincing military triumphs over the Syrian forces, as occurred at Bethsura in 164 B.C.E. Only then could Jerusalem be entered and the Temple restored.

But Judas and his brothers said: "Now that our enemies have been crushed, let us go up to Jerusalem to cleanse the Temple and rededicate it." So the whole army was assembled and went up to Mount Sion. There they found the Temple laid waste, the altar profaned, the gates burnt down, the courts overgrown like a thicket or wooded hillside, and the priests' rooms in ruin. . . .

Then Judas detailed troops to engage the garrison of the citadel while he cleansed the Temple. He selected priests without blemish, devoted to the Law, and they purified the Temple, removing to an unclean place the stones which defiled it. They discussed what to do with the altar of burnt offering, which was profaned, and rightly decided to demolish it, for fear it might become a standing reproach to them because it had been defiled by the Gentiles. They therefore pulled down the altar and stored away the stones in a fitting place on the Temple hill, until a prophet should arise who could be consulted about them. They took unhewn stones, as the law commands, and built a new altar on the model of the previous one. They rebuilt the Temple and restored its interior, and consecrated the Temple courts. . . .

Then early on the twenty-fifth day of the ninth month, the month Kislev, in the year 148 [164 B.C.E.] sacrifice was offered as the Law commands on the newly made altar of burnt offerings. On the anniversary of the day when the Gentiles had profaned it, on that very day, it was rededicated, with hymns of thanksgiving, to the music of harps and lutes and cymbals. All the people prostrated themselves, worshiping and praising Heaven that their cause had prospered.

They celebrated the rededication of the altar for eight days; there was great rejoicing and they brought burnt offerings and sacrificed peace offerings and thank offerings. They decorated the front of the Temple with golden wreaths and ornamental shields. They renewed the gates and the priests' rooms, and fitted them with doors. There was great merry-making among the people, and the disgrace brought on them by the Gentiles was removed.

Then Judas, his brothers, and the whole congregation of Israel decreed that the rededication of the altar should be observed with joy and gladness at the same season of each year, for eight days, beginning on the twenty-fifth of Kislev. (1 Maccabees 4:36–59)

16. A Muslim Tells the Story of Hanukka

One of the motives behind the writing of Maccabees may have been to popularize among Diaspora communities this feast of the "Purification of the Temple" and so to glorify the still new dynasty responsible for it. And despite its lack of biblical authority—the books of Maccabees were never included in the canon of the Bible—the festival of Hanukka, as it was called, did enjoy some measure of popularity, at least in Jerusalem, where it was celebrated in Jesus' day as the "Festival of Lights" (John 10:22).

Another measure of the success of Hanukka is the number of stories and legends that grew up around the event, like the "Acts of the Maccabean Martyrs" included in 2 Maccabees 6:9–7:42. This, for example, is how the Muslim scholar Biruni heard the story in the early eleventh century, when he included it in his Traces of the Past *in the section on "Festivals and Fasts of the Jews."*

The 25th of Kislev. Beginning of the feast *Hanukka,* that is, purification. It lasts eight days, during which they [that is, the Jews] light lamps at the door of the hall: on the first night one lamp for each inhabitant of the house, on the second night two lamps, on the third night three, etc., and finally eight lamps on the eighth night, by which they mean to express their thanks toward God from day to day for the purification and sanctification of Jerusalem.

The origin is this: Antiochus, the king of the Greeks, had subdued and maltreated them during a long period. It was his custom to violate the women, before they were led to their spouses, in a subterranean vault. From this vault two cords led outside, where two bells were fixed at their ends. When, then, he wanted a woman, he rang the right bell, and the woman entered; when he had done with her he rang the left bell and dismissed her. Further there was an Israelite who had eight sons, and a daughter whom another Israelite had demanded in marriage. Now when the young man asked to marry her, the father of the bride said: "Give me time, for I stand between two things. If we give my daughter to you, she will be dishonored by the cursed tyrant, and she will no longer be a lawful bride for you. And if she does not submit to Antiochus, he will make me perish." For this state of things he blamed and reviled his sons, who became greatly excited and angry. But the youngest of them jumped up, dressed himself like a woman, hid a dagger in his clothes, and went to the gate of the king, behaving like the whores. Now, the tyrant rang the right bell, and he was ushered into his presence; there being along with him, he killed him and cut off his head; then he rang the left bell and was let out, and stuck up the head somewhere. Therefore the Israelites celebrate a feast on that and the following (seven) days, corresponding to the number of the brothers of this youth. But God knows best. (Biruni, *Traces of the Past*) [BIRUNI 1879: 271–272]

17. The New Covenant at Qumran

Although the Covenant concluded by the Lord with Abraham—and through him, his descendants—was the charter document of the Children of Israel as the Chosen People, it was neither the first nor the last such contract made or renewed between God and the Israelites. In the pre-Exilic period Joshua son of Nun had presided over just such a renewal (see Chapter 1 above), and in more recent times we have seen how Ezra had presided over a formal covenantal renewal in Jerusalem and how Jeremiah had predicted other, more sweeping revisions of the agreement between the Lord and His people.

Christianity regarded itself as one such latter-day revision in the form of a "New Covenant"; but as we now know from the discovery of the Dead Sea Scrolls and their related documents, it was not the first. Whatever the exact identification of those Jewish sectaries who lived in community at Qumran near the Dead Sea, and whatever their precise relationship with the group Josephus and others call the "Essenes" or their fellow covenanters who produced the "Damascus Rule" at about the same time, it is certain that there were within the body of Palestinian Jews some priestly pietists who disagreed with the current interpretation of the Law on a number of points, including the ritual prescriptions governing Temple sacrifice. Their disagreement was sufficiently strong and deeply principled that it led them to separate themselves from the rest of the Jews and constitute themselves a true priestly Israel, the only participants in the New Covenant.

The Damascus Rule undertakes to describe, in its extremely allusive way, the events leading to this new dispensation. The "time of desolation," it appears likely, was the Hasmonean era, and the critical event in the schism may well have been the promotion of Jonathan in 152 B.C.E. to the position of High Priest by the Seleucid Alexander Balas.

And at the time of the desolation of the land there arose removers of the bond who led Israel astray. And the land was ravaged because they preached rebellion against the commandments of God given by the hand of Moses and of His holy anointed ones, and because they prophesied lies to turn Israel away from God. But God remembered the Covenant with the forefathers, and He raised from Aaron [that is, from among the hereditary priesthoods] men of discernment and from Israel [that is, from the lay community] men of wisdom, and He caused them to hear. And they dug the Well: "the well which the nobles of the people delved with the stave" (Num. 21:18).

This sectarian view of history rests, as often in both this document and the Qumran library, on a privileged reading of Scripture, in this instance of a text of Numbers, which the Damascus Rule directly proceeds to gloss.

The "Well" is the Law, and those who dug it were the converts of Israel who went out of the land of Judah to sojourn in the land of Damascus. God called them all "princes" because they sought Him, and their renown was disputed by no man. The "stave" is the Interpreter of the Law, of whom Isaiah said, "He made a tool for His work" (Isa. 54:16); and the "nobles of the people" are those who came to dig the "Well" with the staves with which "the stave" ordained that they should walk in all the age of wickedness—and without them they shall find nothing—until he comes who shall teach righteousness at the end of days.

None of those brought into the Covenant shall enter the Temple to light His altar in vain. They shall bar the door, inasmuch as God has said, "Who among you will bar its door?" And, "You shall not light My altar in vain" (Mal. 1:10). They shall take care to act according to the exact interpretation of the Law during the age of wickedness. They shall separate from the sons of the Pit, and shall keep away from the unclean riches of wickedness acquired by vow or anathema or from the Temple treasure; they shall not rob the poor of His people, to make widows their prey or of the fatherless their victim (Isa. 10:2). They shall distinguish between clean and unclean, and shall proclaim the difference between holy and profane. They shall keep the Sabbath day according to its exact interpretation, and the feasts and the Day of Fasting according to the findings of the members of the New Covenant of the land of Damascus. (*The Damascus Rule* 5–6) [VERMES 1968: 102–103])

One plausible interpretation of the "land of Damascus" is that it refers to the Qumran community. That community had, at any rate, a similar view of the New Covenant, whose ideals and renewal are described in the opening passages of the "Community Rule."

The Master shall teach the saints to live [according to] the Book of the Community Rule, that they may seek God with a whole heart and soul, and do what is right and good before Him as He commanded by the hand of Moses and all His servants the Prophets; that they may love all that He has chosen and hate all that He has rejected; that they may abstain from all evil and hold fast to all good; that they may practice truth, righteousness and justice upon earth and no longer stubbornly follow a sinful heart and lustful eyes, committing all manner of evil. . . .

All those who freely devote themselves to His truth shall bring all their knowledge, powers and possessions into the Community of God, that they may purify their knowledge in the truth of God's precepts and order their powers according to His ways of perfection and all their possessions according to His righteous counsel. They shall not depart from any command of God concerning their times; they shall be neither early nor late for their appointed times; they shall stray neither to the right nor the left of any of His true precepts. All who embrace the Community Rule shall enter into the Covenant before God to obey all His commandments so that they may not abandon him during the dominion of Satan because of fear or error or affliction.

On entering the Covenant, the Priests and the Levites shall bless the God of salvation and all His faithfulness, and all those entering the Covenant shall say after them "Amen, Amen!"

Then the Priests shall recite the favors God manifested in His mighty deeds and declare all His merciful grace to Israel, and all the Levites shall recite the iniquities of the children of Israel, all their guilty rebellions and sins during the dominion of Satan. And after them, all those entering the Covenant shall confess and say, "We have strayed! We have disobeyed!" (*Community Rule* 1) [VERMES 1968: 71–72]

What the Community Rule calls the "dominion of Satan" is the present age, from which the members of the community attempted to hold themselves apart. This evil will one day come to an end, and the truth will be restored.

But in the mysteries of His understanding, and in His glorious wisdom, God has ordained an end for falsehood, and at the time of the visitation He will destroy it forever. Then truth, which has wallowed in the ways of wickedness during the dominion of falsehood until the appointed time of judgment, shall arise in the world forever. God will then purify every deed of Man with His truth. He will refine for Himself the human frame by rooting out all spirit of falsehood from the bounds of the flesh. He will cleanse him of all wicked deeds with the spirit of holiness; like purifying waters He will shed upon him the spirit of truth to cleanse him of all abomination and falsehood. And he shall be plunged into the spirit of purification that he may instruct the upright in the knowledge of the Most High and teach the wisdom of the sons of heaven to the perfect way. For God has chosen them for an everlasting Covenant and all the glory of Adam shall be theirs. There shall be no more lies and all the works of falsehood will be put to shame. (*Community Rule* 4)

[VERMES 1968: 77–78]

18. Herod the Great
(37–4 B.C.E.)

The inglorious end of the glorious Maccabean beginning came a scant century later in the person of the two sons of Alexander Janneus (103–76 B.C.E.), the then reigning sovereign of the Hasmonean house, as the later royal Maccabees were known. Their names were Aristobulus and Hyrcanus, and their qualifications for ruling Judea were perhaps doubtful. The question was in any event moot, since the Romans by then held all the East in fief, and it was they who would choose and control the ruler of Israel. In the summer of 47 B.C.E. Julius Caesar came in person to Palestine and held audience with his Judean clients.

After listening to both (sons), Caesar declared Hyrcanus the better candidate for the High Priesthood and allowed Antipater [Hyrcanus' vizier] to choose his own office. Antipater left it to the bestower of the honor to decide its magnitude, and was appointed Commissioner of all Judea, with authority to rebuild the walls of the metropolis [that is,

Jerusalem]. These honors Caesar ordered to be engraved in the Capitol, to commemorate his own justice and Antipater's splendid services.

As soon as Antipater had escorted Caesar out of Palestine, he returned to Judea. There he began rebuilding the wall of the metropolis which Pompey had torn down [in 63 B.C.E.], and proceeded to suppress disturbances in various parts of the country, using in every case both threats and advice. . . . While he [Antipater] talked in this way he was organizing the country along his own lines, knowing that Hyrcanus was too lethargic and spineless to be a real king. Phasael, his eldest son, he appointed governor of Jerusalem and its district; the next one, Herod, he sent with equal authority into Galilee, though he was quite young. (Josephus, *War* 1.10.3–4)

Thus arrived Herod, aged twenty-six, on the stage of Jewish history, the middle son of an Idumean adventurer named Antipater who had risen by his own skill, cunning, and ambition to be effective ruler of the Jewish Temple state in Judea. In 43 B.C.E. Antipater was murdered by an Arab rival from the Transjordan. It took Herod five years to navigate a civil war in Rome and a Parthian invasion of Palestine and secure his father's place. In 39 B.C.E. he was nominated king of Judea by action of the Roman Senate, and two years later he besieged and captured Jerusalem and so took possession of his kingdom, which he ruled with loyalty to Rome and cruelty to his subjects until his death in 4 B.C.E.

The extraordinary Herod dominates much of Josephus' narrative in both the Antiquities *and the* Jewish War, *not without a certain admiration on the part of the historian.*

In the fifteenth year of his reign [or the eighteenth, according to the *Antiquities*; see below] Herod restored the existing Sanctuary (in Jerusalem) and around it enclosed an area double the former size, keeping no account of the cost and achieving a magnificence beyond compare. This could be seen particularly in the great colonnades that ran around the entire Temple and the fortress that towered over it to the north. The former were completely new structures, the latter an extremely costly reconstruction, as luxurious as a palace, and named Antonia in honor of Antony. Herod's own palace, built in the Upper city, consisted of two very large and very lovely buildings which made even the Sanctuary seem insignificant; these he named after his friends, one Caesareum, one Agrippeum. (Josephus, *War* 1.21.1)

If ever a man was full of family affection, that man was Herod. In memory of his father he founded a city, choosing a site in the loveliest plain in his kingdom with an abundance of rivers and trees and naming it Antipatris; and the fortress overlooking Jericho he refortified, making it outstandingly strong and beautiful, and dedicated it to his mother under the name of Cypros. To his brother Phasael he erected the tower in Jerusalem that took his name. . . . He also founded another city in the valley running north from Jericho and called it Phasaelis. . . .

After this spate of building he extended his generosity to a great many cities outside his boundaries. For Tripolis, Damascus and Ptolemais he provided gymnasia, for Byblos, a wall, for Beirut and Tyre, halls, colonnades, temples and marketplaces, for Sidon and Damascus, theaters, for the coastal Laodicea, an aqueduct, for Ascalon, baths, magnificent fountains, and cloistered quadrangles remarkable for both scale and craftsmanship; in other places he dedicated woods and parks. . . . And the wide street in Syrian Antioch, did he not pave—two and a quarter miles of it—with polished marble and to keep the rain off furnish it with a colonnade from end to end?

It may be argued that all these benefits were enjoyed only by the particular community favored; but his endowment of Elis was a gift not only to Greece in general but to every corner of the civilized world reached by the fame of the Olympic Games. Seeing that the games were declining for lack of funds and that the sole relic of ancient Greece was slipping away, he not only acted as president of the quadrennial meeting held when he happened to be on his way to Rome, but he also endowed them for all time with an income large enough to ensure that his presidency should never be forgotten. (Josephus, *War* 1.21.9–12)

19. Herod Rebuilds the Temple

It is not those other ecumenical works of that prodigious builder Herod that concern us here, but rather his chief legacy to his own Jewish subjects: the Temple in Jerusalem.

It was at this time [of Augustus' visit to Syria in 20 B.C.E.], in the eighteenth year of his reign, . . . that Herod undertook an extraordinary work, the reconstructing of the Temple of God at his own expense, enlarging its precincts and raising it to a more imposing height. For he believed that the accomplishment of this task would be the most notable of all the things achieved by him, as indeed it was, and would be great enough to assure his eternal remembrance. (Josephus, *Antiquities* 15.11.1)

And while the unlikelihood of his realizing his hope did not disturb (the people), they were dismayed by the thought that he might tear down the whole edifice and not have sufficient means to bring his project (of rebuilding it) to completion. . . . Since they felt this way, the king spoke encouragingly to them, saying that he would not pull down the Temple (of Zerubbabel) before having ready all the materials needed for its completion. And these assurances he did not belie. For he prepared a thousand wagons to carry the stones, selected 10,000 of the most skilled workmen, purchased priestly robes for a thousand priests and trained some as masons and others as carpenters, and began the construction only after all these preparations had been diligently made by him.

Moreover, according to the Mishna, the king arranged that the Temple liturgy was not disturbed at any time during the work.

Rabbi Eliezer said: I have heard a tradition that while they were building the Temple they made curtains for the Temple and curtains for the courtyards, but they built (the walls of) the Temple outside (the curtains), (the walls of the courtyards) they built within (the curtains). (M.Eduyoth 8:6)

Josephus' account of the construction of the Temple continues.

After removing the old foundations, he [Herod] laid down others, and upon these he erected the Temple, which was a hundred cubits in length . . . and twenty more in height, but in the course of time this dropped as the foundations subsided. And this part we decided to raise again in the time of Nero. The Temple was built of hard, white stones, each of which was about twenty-five cubits in length, eight in height and twelve in width. And the whole of it, as also in the Royal Portico, either side was the lowest, while the middle portion was the highest, so that it was visible at a distance of many stades to those who inhabited the country, especially those who lived opposite or happened to approach it. . . . And he surrounded the Temple with very large porticoes, all of which he made in proportion (to the Temple), and he surpassed his predecessors in spending money, so that it was thought that no one else had adorned the Temple so splendidly.

(The Temple sanctuary and its porticoes) were supported by a great wall and the wall itself was the greatest ever heard of by man. The hill was a rocky ascent that sloped gently up toward the eastern part of the city to the topmost peak. The hill our first king Solomon [or "our king Solomon first"] with God-given wisdom surrounded with great works above at the top. And below, beginning at the foot, where a deep ravine runs round it, he (Herod) surrounded it with enormous stones bound together with lead. He cut off more and more of the area within as (the wall) became greater in depth, so that the size and height of the structure, which was square, were immense, and the great size of the stones was seen along the front [that is, outside] surface, while the iron clamps in the inside assured that the joints would remain permanently united.

When the work reached the top of the hill, he leveled off the summit and filled in the hollow spaces near the walls, and made the upper surfaces smooth and even throughout. Such was the whole enclosure, having a circumference of four stades, each side taking up the length of a stade. Within this wall and on the very summit there ran another wall of stone, which had on the eastern ridge a double portico of the same length as the wall, and it faced the doors of the Temple, for this lay within it. This portico many of the earlier kings adorned. Round about the entire Temple were fixed the spoils taken from the barbarians, and all these King Herod dedicated, adding those which he took from the (Nabatean) Arabs. (Josephus, *Antiquities* 15.11.24)

Again, in the War:

Though the Temple . . . was seated on a strong hill, the level area on its summit originally barely sufficed for shrine and altar, the ground around it being precipitous and steep. But king Solomon, the actual founder of the Temple, having walled up the eastern side, a single portico was reared on this made ground; on its other sides the sanctuary remained exposed. In the course of the ages, however, through the constant additions of people to the embankment, the hilltop by this process of leveling up was widened. They further broke down the north wall and thus took in an area as large as the whole Temple area subsequently occupied. Then, after having enclosed the hill from its base on (the other) three sides, and accomplished a task greater than they could ever have hoped to achieve—a task upon which long ages were spent by them as well as all their sacred treasures, though replenished by the tributes offered to God from every quarter of the world—they built around the original block the upper courts and the lower Temple enclosure. The latter, where its foundations were lowest, they built up from a depth of three hundred cubits; at some spots this figure was exceeded. The whole depth of the foundations was not, however, apparent, for they filled up a considerable part of the ravines, wishing to level the narrow alleys of the town. Blocks of stone were used in building measuring forty cubits; for lavish funds and popular enthusiasm led to incredible enterprise, and a task seemingly interminable was through perseverance and in time actually achieved. (Josephus, *War* 5.5.1)

Josephus proceeds to describe the gates into the Temple complex, and the Mishna too names and locates them.

In the western part of the court (of the Temple) there were four gates. The first led to the palace over the intervening ravine, two others led to the suburbs, and the last led to the other part of the (Upper) city, from which it was separated by many steps going down into the ravine and from here up again to the hill. For the city lay opposite the Temple, being in the form of a theater and being bordered by a deep ravine along its whole southern side. The fourth front of this (court), facing south, also had gates in the middle, and had over it the Royal Portico, which had three aisles extending in length from the eastern to the western ravine. And it was a structure more noteworthy than any under the sun. For while the depth of the ravine was great, and no one who bent over to look into it from above could bear to look down to the bottom, the height of the portico standing over it was so very great that anyone looking down from its rooftop, combining the two elevations, he would become dizzy and his vision would be unable to reach the end of so measureless a depth. (Josephus, *Antiquities* 15.11.5)

There are five gates to the Temple Mount: the two Huldah Gates on the south that served for coming in and for going out; the Kiponus gate on the west that served for coming in and going out; the Tadi Gate on the north which was not used at all; the eastern on which was portrayed [or sculpted] the Palace of Shushan. Through this the High Priest who burned the (Red) Cow and the heifer and all (the priests) who aided him went forth to the Mount of Olives. (M.Middoth 1:3)

20. The Annexation of Judea to the Roman Empire

Whatever his own subjects thought of him, Herod was a useful and obliging client to his Roman masters, not least for his capacity and willingness to maintain order, if not peace, in his own turbulent kingdom. He cost the Romans little and gave a substantial return. How substantial appeared immediately after his death in 4 B.C.E. In his own plans for his succession, Herod's choice for Judea fell upon his son Archelaus. As the ineffective Archelaus was preparing to go to Rome to secure his appointment as king—"because Caesar was to have control of all the settlements he [Herod] had made"—disturbances broke out in Jerusalem, and at his departure the Roman governor of Syria had to intervene with a legion to quell them. Archelaus' appointment did not pass uncontested. A delegation of Jews went to Rome and rehearsed Herod's crimes against the people.

... That, in short the Jews had borne more calamities from Herod, in a few years, than had their forefathers during all that interval of time that had passed since they had come out of Babylon, and returned home, in the reign of Xerxes. ... Whereupon, they prayed that the Romans would have compassion upon the remains of Judea and not expose what was left of them to such as would barbarously tear them to pieces, and that they would join their country to (the province of) Syria and administer the government by their own commanders. (Josephus, *War* 2.6.2)

The Romans were willing to oblige on this occasion, and in 6 C.E. Judea was joined to the province of Syria and thereafter administered by a Roman prefect.

21. The View from the Diaspora

Elsewhere around the Mediterranean, where the Jews lived in colonies in the lands of others, they had passed, like those lands themselves, directly from Greek to Roman sovereignty. The largest of those Jewish communities that constituted what was called "the Diaspora" was in Egypt. We do not know a great deal about it; people appear to have prospered, particularly in Alexandria, though in a milieu that on occasion displayed profoundly anti-Jewish sentiments. One of the more violent outbursts took place in Alexandria in 38 C.E., when there were attacks upon the Jewish quarters: synagogues were broken into, statues of Emperor Caligula erected there, and the Jews officially denounced as "aliens and foreigners." Here Philo, the chief spokesman of the Alexandrian Jews and the head of a Jewish delegation to the emperor in 39 C.E., undertakes to set straight the record on the Jews for the benefit of his sovereign in Rome.

It was perfectly clear that the rumor of the overthrow of the synagogues beginning at Alexandria would spread at once to the rest of Egypt and speed from Egypt to the East and the nations of the East ... and to the West and the nations of the West. For so populous are the Jews that no one country can contain them, and therefore they settle in very many of the most prosperous countries in Europe and Asia, both in the islands and on the mainland, and while they hold the Holy City where stands the sacred Temple of the Most High God to be their mother city, yet those which are theirs by inheritance from their fathers, grandfathers and ancestors even farther back, are in each case accounted by them to be their fatherland in which they were born and reared, while to some of them they have come at the time of their foundation as immigrants to the satisfaction of the founders. It was feared, then, that people everywhere might take their cue from Alexandria and outrage their Jewish fellow citizens by rioting against their synagogues and ancestral customs.

There follows a somewhat curious argument: if their synagogues are closed or destroyed, the Jews will have no place to thank their Roman benefactors appropriately!

Now the Jews, though naturally well-disposed for peace, could not be expected to remain quiet whatever happened, not only because with all men the determination to fight for their institutions outweighs even the danger to life, but also because they are the only people under the sun who, by losing their meetinghouses, were losing also what what they would have valued as worth dying many thousands of deaths, namely their means of showing reverence to their benefactors, since they no longer had the sacred buildings where they could set forth their thankfulness. And they might have said to their enemies, "You have failed to see that you are not adding to, but taking from, the honor given to our masters; and you do not understand that everywhere in the habitable world the religious veneration of the Jews for the Augustan house has its basis, as all may see, in the meetinghouses; and if we have these destroyed, no place, no method is left to us for paying this homage. If we neglect to pay it when our institutions permit, we should deserve the utmost penalty for not tendering our requital with all due fullness. But if we fall short because it is forbidden by our own laws, which Augustus also was well pleased to confirm, I do not see what offense, either small or great, can be laid to our charge. The only thing for which we might be blamed would be that we transgressed, though involuntarily, by not defending ourselves against defections from our customs. . . .

"What we have described is an act of aggression by bitterly hostile and crafty plotters in which the authors of the outrages would not appear to be acting unjustly and the sufferers could not oppose them in safety. For surely, my good sirs, there is no honor given by overthrowing the laws, disturbing ancestral customs, outraging fellow citizens, and teaching the inhabitants of other cities to disregard the claims of fellow feeling." (Philo, *Against Flaccus* 7.45–52)

22. Divine Wisdom

With the return from exile in the last decades of the sixth century B.C.E., the historical narrative of the canonical books of the Bible comes to an end. Thereafter the continuous voice of prophetic history is stilled. What follow are accounts of partisan religious pleaders who did not find their way into the canon—like the various books of Maccabees—or made no pretense to that status—like the un-

ashamedly secular Josephus, who preferred to follow in the steps of Thucydides rather than those of the authors of Kings.

The past was still open to contemplation, however, even revalorization, and one notable feature of that new understanding of God's working in history is reflected in the appearance of the personified figure of Divine Wisdom, who was present at creation and whose providential hand was guiding the destiny of the Children of Israel. We see it first in the canonical book called "The Proverbs of Solomon," whose author or editor passes over Law, Temple, and Priesthood to focus on a new theme:

> The Lord created me at the beginning of His course
> As the first of His works of old.
> In the distant past I was fashioned,
> At the beginning, at the origin of earth.
> There was still no deep when I was brought forth,
> No springs rich in water;
> Before [the foundation of] the mountains were sunk,
> Before the hills I was born.
> He had not yet made earth and fields,
> Or the world's first clumps of clay.
> I was there when He set the heavens into place;
> When He fixed the horizon upon the deep;
> When He made the heavens above firm,
> And the fountains of the deep gushed forth;
> When He assigned the sea its limits,
> So that its waters never transgress His command;
> When He fixed the foundations of the earth,
> I was with Him as a confidant,
> A source of delight every day,
> Rejoicing before Him at all times,
> Rejoicing in the inhabited world,
> Finding delight with mankind.
> (Proverbs 8:22–31)

Jesus ben Sira, sometime about 180 B.C.E., writes with the just cited text before him.

> Hear the praise of Wisdom from her own mouth,
> as she speaks with pride among her own people,
> before the assembly of the Most High
> and in the presence of the heavenly host:

"I am the Word which was spoken by the Most High;
it was I who covered the earth like a mist.
My dwelling place was in high heaven;
my throne was in a pillar of cloud.
Alone I made a circuit of the sky
and traversed the depths of the abyss.
The waves of the sea, the whole earth,
every people and nation are under my sway.
Among them all I looked for a home:
in whose territory was I to settle?
Then the Creator of the universe laid a command upon me:
my Creator decreed where I should dwell.
He said, "Make your home in Jacob;
find your heritage in Israel."
Before time began He created me,
and I shall remain forever.
In the sacred tent I ministered in His presence,
and so I came to be established in Sion.
Thus He settled me in the city He loved
and gave me authority in Jerusalem.
I took root among the people whom the Lord had honored
by choosing them to be his special possession.
There I grew like a cedar of Lebanon,
like a cypress on the slopes of Hermon,
like a date-palm at Engedi,
like roses at Jericho.
I drew like a fair olive tree in vale,
or like a plane tree planted beside the water. . . .

"Come to me, you who desire me,
eat your full of my fruit.
The memory of me is sweeter than syrup,
the possession of me is sweeter than the honey
dripping from the comb.
Whoever feeds on me will be hungry for more,
and whoever drinks from me will thirst for more.
To obey me is to be safe from disgrace;
those who work in wisdom will not go astray."
(Wisdom of Jesus ben Sira [Ecclesiasticus] 24:1–22)

23. The Vision of Daniel

The visionary style was not new in Israel—we have already seen an example in the Exilic prophet Ezekiel—but what was more typical, and urgent, was the transcendental quality of what these latter-day seers saw. They were experiencing a New Age, terrible and glorious in turn, a trial and a fulfillment of Israel on some level of experience far different from that of history.

One such work that was included in the Jewish canon was the prophecy attributed to a certain Daniel. The time purports to be that of the Exile, but the circumstances of the book are transparently those of the second century B.C.E., when the Greeks were in the land of Israel. The trials of Daniel at the court of Nebuchadnezzar take up the first six books of the work, at which point there is a somewhat abrupt shift into another mode:

In the first year of King Belshazzar of Babylon, Daniel saw a dream and a vision of his mind in bed; afterward he wrote down the dream. Beginning the account, Daniel related the following:

"In my vision at night, I saw the four winds of heaven stirring up the great sea. Four mighty beasts different from each other emerged from the sea. The first was like a lion but had eagles' wings. As I looked on, its wings were plucked off, and it was lifted off the ground and set on its feet like a man and given the mind of a man. Then I saw a second, different beast, which was like a bear but raised on one side, and with three fangs in its mouth among its teeth; it was told, "Arise, eat much meat!" After that, as I looked on, there was another one, like a leopard, and it had on its back four wings like those of a bird; the beast had four heads, and dominion was given to it. After that, as I looked on in the night vision, there was a fourth beast—fearsome, dreadful, and very powerful, with great iron teeth—that devoured and crushed, and stamped the remains with its feet. It was different from all the other beasts which had gone before it; and it had ten horns. While I was gazing upon these horns, a new little horn sprouted up among them; three of the older horns were uprooted to make room for it. There were eyes in this horn like those of a man, and a mouth that spoke arrogantly. As I looked on,

> Thrones were set in place,
> And the Ancient of Days took his seat.
> His garment was like lamb's wool.
> And the hair of his head was like lamb's wool.
> His throne was tongues of flame;
> Its wheels were blazing fire.

A river of fire streamed forth before Him;
Thousands upon thousands served Him;
Myriads upon myriads attended Him;
The court sat and the books were opened.

"I looked on. Then, because of the arrogant words that the horn spoke, the beast was killed as I looked on; its body was destroyed and it was consigned to the flames. The dominion of the other beasts was taken away, but an extension of life was given to them for a time and season. As I looked on, in the night vision,

One like a human being
Came with the clouds of heaven;
He reached the Ancient of Days
And was presented to Him.
Dominion, glory, and kingship were given to him;
All peoples and nations of every language must serve him.

His dominion is an everlasting dominion that
shall not pass away.
And his kingship, one that shall not be destroyed.

"As for me, Daniel, my spirit was disturbed within me and the vision of my mind alarmed me. I approached one of the attendants and asked him the true meaning of all this. He gave me this interpretation of the matter: 'These great beasts, four in number, (mean) four kingdoms will arise out of the earth; then holy ones of the Most High will receive the kingdom, and will possess the kingdom forever—forever and ever.' Then I wanted to ascertain the true meaning of the fourth beast, which was different from them all, very fearsome, with teeth of iron, claws of bronze that devoured and crushed, and stamped the remains; and of the ten horns on its head; and of the new one that sprouted, to make room for which three fell—the horn that had eyes, and a mouth that spoke arrogantly, and which was more conspicuous than its fellows. (I looked on as that horn made war with the holy ones and overcame them, until the Ancient of Days came and judgment was rendered in favor of the holy ones of the Most High, for the time had come, and the holy ones took possession of the kingdom.) This is what he said: 'The fourth beast (means)—there will be a fourth kingdom upon the earth which will be different from all the other kingdoms; it will devour the whole earth, tread it down, and crush it. And the ten horns (mean)—from that kingdom, ten kings will arise, and after them another will arise. He will be different from the former ones, and will bring low three kings. He will speak words against the Most High, and will harass the holy ones of the Most High. He will think of changing times and laws, and they will be delivered into his power for a time, times, and half a time. Then the court will sit and his dominion will be taken away, to be destroyed and abolished for all time. The kingship and dominion and grandeur belonging to all the kingdoms under heaven will be given to the people of the holy ones of the Most High. Their kingdom shall be an everlasting kingdom, and all dominions shall serve and obey them.' Here the account ends. I, Daniel, was very alarmed by my thoughts, and my face darkened; and I could not put the matter out of my mind." (Daniel 7:1–28)

Here, then, is a vision not of the End Time but of a historical resolution, though mediated in heaven. The vision is allegorical and supplies its own interpretation—"These great beasts, four in number, [mean] four kingdoms"—at least to the extent of telling us that the context is political. Which kingdoms are meant, we are left to guess. Most commentators have supposed that the reference is to the Babylonian, Median, Persian, and Greek kingdoms and that within the latter the "little horn" is Antiochus Epiphanes.

This is plausible, and it would seem equally plausible that by the "Ancient in Years" is meant God Himself. Daniel does not ask and the anonymous interpreter offers no explanation of the "One like a human being / Came with the clouds of heaven," to whom "Dominion, glory and kingship" were given. Here too, however, it seems likely from the text that the "saints" of the people of Israel are thus personified.

24. Jewish Voices in the First Christian Century

One way of bringing a new understanding to the now classical texts of the biblical canon was to retell them in the disguise of one of the earlier prophets, as was done in the book called Jubilees, in those attributed to Enoch, Baruch, and Ezra, and in those circulated under the name of Solomon. All of these anonymous authors concealed under older names were addressing the present, of course. In some cases they attempted to peer into the future, since one of the predominant modes of post-Exilic literature—when it was not dispensing a mild terrestrial wisdom, often in the current Hellenic style, or a more transcendental appeal to a personified Divine Wisdom—was "unveiling" the future in the form of visions of the End Time.

The historical Baruch was a contemporary of Jeremiah, best known for having written down that latter prophet's utterances. But in the first century of the Christian era the name became a popular magnet for apocalypses, and a number of them circulated under his name. One of them, preserved only in Syriac and generally called 2 Baruch, is of special interest in that it represents a Jewish voice, or rather a number of Jewish voices, contemporary to Paul, the destruction of Jerusalem, and the growth of the Christian movement.

Whatever happens then will happen to the whole earth; so that all who are alive will experience it. For at that time I will protect only those who are found in those days in this land. And it shall be that when all is accomplished that was to come to pass in the twelve periods before the end, the Messiah shall then begin to be revealed. And Behemoth shall appear from his place and Leviathan shall ascend from the sea—those two great monsters I created on the fifth day of creation and have kept until then; and then they shall serve as food for all that survive. . . . And those who have been hungry will rejoice; and also, they shall see marvels every day. . . .

And it shall come to pass after this, when the time of the presence of the Messiah on earth has run its course, that he will return in glory to the heavens. Then all who have died and have set their hopes on him will rise again. And it shall come to pass at that time that the treasuries will be opened in which is preserved the number of the souls of the righteous, and they will come out, and the multitude of souls will appear together in one single assembly; and those who are first will rejoice and those who are last will not be cast down. For each of them will know that the predetermined end of the times has come. But the souls of the wicked, when they see all this, will be the more discomforted. For they will know that their torment is upon them and that their perdition has arrived. (2 Baruch 29–30)

Another such work was the so-called Psalms of Solomon, written about the time Pompey and the Romans took and sacked Jerusalem in 63 B.C.E.

Behold, O Lord, and raise up for them their king, the son of David.
For the time You did foresee, O God, that he may reign over Israel
                    Your servant.
And gird him with strength, that he may shatter unrighteous rulers
And purify Jerusalem of the nations which trample her down in
                    destruction.
In wisdom, in righteousness, may he expel sinners from the inheritance.
May he smash the sinners' arrogance like a potter's vessel.
With a rod of iron may he break in pieces all their substance:
 May he destroy the lawless nations by the word of his mouth.
So that, at his rebuke, nations before him;

And may he reprove sinners by the word of their own hearts.
And he shall gather together a holy people, whom he shall lead
                  in righteousness,
And he shall judge the tribes of the people which has been sanctified
                  by the Lord his God.
And he shall not permit unrighteousness to lodge any more in
                  their midst,
Nor shall there dwell with them any man with knowledge of wickedness,
For he shall know them, that they are all sons of their God. . . .

And he shall be a righteous king, taught by God, over them,
And there shall be no unrighteousness in his days in their midst,
For all shall be holy and their king the anointed Lord. . . .

He will bless the people of the Lord with wisdom and joy,
And he himself is pure from sin, so that he may rule a great people,
That he may rebuke rulers, and remove sinners by the might of his word.
And during his days he shall not be weakened, relying upon his God;
For God created him strong in the holy spirit,
And wise in prudent counsel, together with strength and righteousness.
And the blessing of the Lord is with him providing strength,
And he shall not be weakened.
His hope is upon the Lord;
Who then can prevail against him?
(Psalms of Solomon 17:23–39)

25. The Son of Man

The first Book of Enoch is a composite that includes a number of visions, with one of them, the second, expressed in the form of parables. These are difficult to date, but for all their later popularity with Christians, they appear to have been composed well before the time of Jesus and perhaps as long as a century or more before his day. This is how the second vision begins.

    The second vision which he saw, the vision of wisdom, which Enoch the son of Jared, the son of Mahalel, the son of Cainan, the son of Enosh, the son of Seth, the son of Adam, saw. And this is the beginning of the words of wisdom which I raised my voice to speak and say to those who dwell on the dry ground: Hear me, you men of old, and see, you who come after, the words of the Holy One which I will speak before the Lord of Spirits. It would have been better to have said these things before, but from those who come after we will not withhold the beginning of wisdom. Until now there has not been given by the Lord of Spirits such wisdom as I have now received in accordance with my insight, in accordance with the wish of the Lord of Spirits by whom the lot of eternal life has been given me. And three Parables were imparted to me, and I raised my voice and said to those who dwell on the dry ground. (1 Enoch 37:1–5)

All three parables are filled with Messianic associations, where the titles of "The Anointed One," "The Righteous One," "The Elected One" are all applied to him. In addition, the second and third bear a number of references to the more unusual "Son of Man," the same designation that appears to be used in a Messianic context in the Gospel of Mark.

And at that hour that Son of Man was named in the presence of the Lord of Spirits, and his name was named before the Head of Days. Even before the sun and the constellations were created, before the stars of the heaven were made, his name was named before the Lord of Spirits. He will be a staff to the righteous and the holy, that they may lean on him and not fall, and he shall be the light of the nations, and he will be the hope of those who grieve in their hearts. All who dwell upon the dry ground will fall down and worship before him, and they will bless, and praise, and celebrate with psalms the name of the Lord of Spirits. And because of this he was chosen and hidden before him, before the world was created, and forever. But the wisdom of the Lord of Spirits has revealed him to the holy and righteous, for he has kept safe the lot of the righteous, for they have hated and rejected this world of iniquity, and all its works and ways they have hated in the name of the Lord of Spirits; for in his name they are saved, and he is the one who will require their lives. (1 Enoch 48:2–7)

And they had great joy, and they blessed and glorified and exalted because the name of that Son of Man has been revealed to them. And he sat on the throne of his glory, and the whole judgment was given to the Son of Man, and he will cause the sinners to pass away and be destroyed from the face of the earth. And those who have led astray the world will be bound in chains, and will be shut up in the assembly place of their destruction, and all their works will pass away from the face of the earth. And from then on there will be nothing corruptible, for that Son of Man has appeared, and has sat on the throne of his glory, and everything evil will pass away and go from before him; and the word of that Son of Man will be strong before the Lord of Spirits. This is the third Parable of Enoch. (1 Enoch 69:26–29)

And from the end of the third parable:

And that angel came to me and greeted me with his voice and said to me: "You are the Son of Man who was born to righteousness, and righteousness remains over you, and the righteousness of the Head of Days will not leave you." And he said to me, "He proclaims peace to you in the name of the world which is to come; for from there peace has come out from the creation of the world; and so you will have it for ever and for ever and ever. And all will walk according to your way, inasmuch as righteousness will never leave you; with you will be their dwelling, and with you their lot, and they will never be separated from you for ever and ever and ever. And so there will be length of days with that Son of Man, and the righteous will have peace and an upright way in the name of the Lord of Spirits for ever and ever." (1 Enoch 71:14–17)

26. The Rabbis Discuss the Messiah

Many of these freewheeling apocalyptic writings run down in time to about 200 C.E., when the Mishna was being put together as the authoritative codex of the Jewish Oral Law. Tracts like Baruch and Enoch are visionary, poetical, and often ecstatic, while the rabbis represented in the Mishna, and those who sat down in the yeshivas or academies to study it, were primarily concerned with the prescriptions of the Law. Their interests, if not their methods, occasionally converged, however. One such point of convergence is the question of the Messiah. Rabbi Judah's Mishna does not pay a great deal of formal attention to the issue, but one passage in that text dealing with "the world to come" prompted Messianic speculation by the next generation of rabbis in a Mishnaic text that we will see again in Chapter 5 below in a different context.

All Israelites have a share in the world to come, for it is written, "Your people also shall be all righteous, they shall inherit the land forever; the branch of My planting, the work of My hands that I might be glorified" (Isa. 60:21). And these are they who have no share in the world that is to come: he that says that there is no resurrection of the dead prescribed in the Law, and he that says that the Law is not from heaven, and an Epicurean [that is, a skeptic or doubter]. Rabbi Akiba says: Also he that reads non-canonical books, or that utters a charm over a wound. . . . Abba Saul says: Also he that pronounces the Name (of God) with its proper letters. (M.Sanhedrin 10:1)

The discussion of this in the Babylonian Talmud winds about until it at length reaches the Messianic question.

Rabbi Nahman said to Rabbi Isaac, "Have you heard when the Bar Nafle [possibly the "Son of the Clouds" of Dan. 7:13] will come?" "Who is Bar Nafle?" he asked. "Messiah," he answered. "Do you call Messiah Bar Nafle?" "Even so," he rejoined, "as it is written, 'In that day I will raise up a tabernacle of David that is fallen [in Hebrew *ha-nofeleth*, of the same root as "Nafle"]' (Amos 9:11)." He replied, "Thus has Rabbi Yohanan said: 'In the generation when the Son of David [that is, the Messiah] will come, scholars will be few in number, and as for the rest, their eyes will fail through sorrow and grief. Multitudes of troubles and evil decrees will be promulgated anew, each new evil coming with haste before the other has ended.' " (BT.Sanhedrin 96b–97a)

Thus we are launched on a long discussion not so much of the character, personality, or even the work of the Messiah as of the characteristics of the Messianic era and when that time might be expected to come. The discourse goes on.

Our Rabbis taught: In the seven-year cycle at the end of which the Son of David will come—in the first year this verse will be fulfilled: "And I will cause it to rain on one city and cause it not to rain on another city" (Amos 4:7); in the second the arrows of hunger will be sent forth; in the third, a great famine, in the course of which men, women and children, pious men and saints, will die and the Torah will be forgotten by its students; in the fourth, partial plenty; in the fifth, great plenty, when men will eat, drink and rejoice; in the sixth, heavenly sounds; in the seventh, wars, and at the conclusion of the seven-year cycle the Son of David will come." Rabbi Joseph demurred: But so many such seven-year cycles have passed, yet he has not come! Abaye retorted: Were there then heavenly sounds in the sixth and wars in the seventh? Moreover, have they been in this order?

It has been taught, Rabbi Judah said: In the generation when the Son of David comes, the House of Assembly will be for harlots, Galilee in ruins, Gablan lie desolate, the border inhabitants wander about from city to city, receiving no hospitality, the wisdom of the scribes in disfavor, God-fearing men despised, people dog-faced, and truth entirely lacking, as it is written, "Yes, truth fails and he that departs from evil makes himself a prey" (Isa. 59:15).

There may have been some attempt at a historical identification of these rather generalized circumstances, but they are not included in the text. At some points, however, there may have been more specific events behind the words, as in this remark, which may reflect the spread of Christianity, "heresy," through the Roman Empire, the "kingdom" of the text, or even the whole world.

It has been taught, Rabbi Nehemiah said: In the generation of Messiah's coming impudence will increase, esteem be perverted, the wine yield its fruits and yet wine be dear, and the Kingdom will be converted to heresy, with none to rebuke them. This supports Rabbi Isaac, who said: The Son of David will not come until the whole world is converted to the belief of the heretics. Raba said: What verse proves this? "It [that is, the leprosy] is all turned white; he is clean" (Lev. 13:13).

Here the reference to the Hasmoneans, the Herodians, and the revolt of Bar Kokhba in 132–135 C.E. is unmistakable.

It has been taught: Rabbi Nathan said: This verse pierces and descends to the very abyss: "For the vision is yet for an appointed time, but at the end it shall speak and not lie; though he tarry, yet wait for him, because it will surely come; it will not tarry" (Hab. 2:3). Not as our Masters, who interpreted the verse "until a time and times and the dividing of time" (Dan. 7:25); nor as Rabbi Simlai, who expounded the verse "You feed them with the bread of tears, and give them tears to drink a third time" (Ps. 80:6); nor as Rabbi Akiba, who expounded the verse "Yet once, it is a little while and I will shake the heavens and the earth" (Hag. 2:6); but the first dynasty [that is, the Hasmoneans] shall last seventy years, the second [the Herodian] fifty-two, and the reign of Bar Koziba [or Bar Kokhba] two and a half years.

But there was, after all, no great certainty, and even a certain display of wit.

Rab said: The world was created only on David's account. Samuel said: On Moses' account. Rabbi Yohanan said: For the sake of the Messiah. What is the Messiah's name? The School of Rabbi Shilah said: His name is Shiloh, for it is written, "Until Shiloh comes" (Gen. 49:10). The School of Rabbi Yannai said: His name is Yinnon, for it is written, "His name shall endure forever; before the sun, his name was Yinnon" (Ps. 72:17). The School of Rabbi Haninah maintained: His name is Haninah, as it is written, "Where I will not give you Haninah" (Jer. 16:13). Others say: His name is Menahem the son of Hezekiah, for it is written, "Because Menahem [or "The Comforter"], who would relieve my soul, is far away" (Lam. 1:16).

This last suggestion—that the Messiah was, not will be, Menahem the son of Hezekiah—carries us into an entirely new position: there will be no future Messiah because he has already come.

Rabbi Hillel said: There shall be no Messiah for Israel because they have already enjoyed him in the days of Hezekiah. Rabbi Joseph said: May

God forgive him (for saying so). Now when did Hezekiah flourish? During the first Temple. Yet Zechariah, prophesying in the days of the second [that is, after the Exile], proclaimed: "Rejoice greatly, O daughter of Sion, O daughter of Jerusalem; behold, the king comes to you! He is just and, having salvation, lowly; and riding upon an ass, and upon a colt, the foal of an ass" (Zech. 9:9). (BT. Sanhedrin 97a–99a)

It is tempting to think that here too the spread of Christianity, with its own Messianic claims, had influenced the rethinking of the Messianic question by Rabbi Hillel. This opinion that the Messiah had already come did not in any event find a great deal of support in either rabbinical or later circles, but it does bring us full circle to the beginnings of Messianic speculation in Israel. The time of troubles from which release would come may well have been the Assyrian invasion at the end of the seventh century B.C.E., as we have seen, and Hezekiah may indeed have been Isaiah's candidate for the instrument of that release. A millennium later the troubles were still political, though they now bore a Roman face, and a savior-king was just as urgently required.

27. The Rabbis Preach the Suffering Redeemer

The Pesikta Rabbati *is an assembly of rabbinic meditations on the Torah lessons read in the synagogue throughout the year on the Sabbath. Although this collection was not finally put together until Islamic times, the material in it is mostly Talmudic. The homiletic approach, it is obvious, is not very different from that taken by the discussions of the Messiah in the Talmud itself. We begin with the Sabbath lesson.*

> Arise, shine, for your Lord is come,
> And the glory of the Lord is risen upon you.
> For behold, darkness will cover the earth,
> And gross darkness the peoples; but upon you
> The Lord will arise, and His glory shall be
> Seen upon you. (Isa. 60:1–2)

These words are to be considered in the light of what David king of Israel was inspired by the Holy Spirit to say: "For with You is the fountain of life; in Your light do we see light" (Ps. 36:10). . . . What is meant by "in Your light we see light"? What light is it that the congregation of Israel looks for as from a watchtower? It is the light of the Messiah, of which it is said, "And God saw the light and it was good" (Gen. 1:4). This verse proves that the Holy One, blessed be He, contemplated the Messiah and his works before the world was created, and then under His throne of glory put away the Messiah until the time of the generation in which he will appear.

Satan asked the Holy One, blessed be He: Master of the universe, for whom is the light which is put away under Your throne of glory? God replied: For him who will turn you back and put you to utter shame. Satan said: Master of the universe, show him to me. God replied: Come and see him. And when he saw him, Satan was shaken, and he fell upon his face and said: Surely this is the Messiah who will cause me and the counterparts in heaven of the princes of the earth's nations to be swallowed up in Gehenna. . . . In that hour all princely counterparts of the nations in agitation will say to Him: Master of the universe, who is this through whose power we are to be swallowed up? What is his name? What kind of being is he?

The Holy One, blessed be He, will reply: He is the Messiah, and his name is Ephraim, My true Messiah, who will pull himself up straight and will pull up straight his generation, and who will give light to the eyes of Israel and deliver his people; and no nation or people will be able to withstand him. . . .

(At the time of the Messiah's creation) the Holy One, blessed be He, will tell him in detail what will befall him: There are souls that have been put away with you under My throne, and it is their sins which will bend you down under a yoke of iron and make you like a calf whose eyes grow dim with suffering and will choke your spirit as with a yoke; because of the sins of those souls your tongue will cleave to the roof of your mouth. Are you willing to endure such things?

The Messiah will ask the Holy One, blessed be He: Will my suffering last many years? The Holy One, blessed be He, will reply: Upon your life and the life of My head, it is a period of seven years which I have decreed for you. But if your soul is sad at the prospect of your suffering, I shall at this moment banish those sinful souls. The Messiah will say: Master of the universe, with joy in my soul and gladness in my heart I take this suffering upon myself, provided that not one soul in Israel perish; that not only those who are alive to be saved in my days, but also those who are dead, who died from the days of Adam up to the time of the redemption; and that not only those to be saved in my days, but also those who died as abortions; and that not only those to be saved in my days, but all those whom You have thought to create but were not created. Such are the things I desire, and for these I am ready to take upon myself (whatever You decree).

The following passage from the same section seems to be from a later stratum of comment and to refer to contemporary events, possibly sometime just before the Muslim conquest of the Near East in the seventh century C.E.

Rabbi Isaac taught: In the year in which the king Messiah reveals himself, all the kings of the nations of the earth will be at strife with one another. The king of Persia will make war against the king of Arabia, and this king of Arabia will go to Edom and take counsel of the Edomites [who are usually the Romans or Byzantines in this context]. Thereupon the king of Persia will again lay the whole world waste. . . . And Israel, agitated and frightened, will say: Where shall we go, where shall we come? God will reply: My children, be not afraid, the time of your redemption is come. And this latter redemption will not be like your previous redemption, for following your previous redemption you suffered anguish and enslavement by the kingdoms; as for this redemption— following this one you will have no anguish or enslavement by the kingdoms.

Our Masters taught: When the Messiah appears, he will come stand on the roof of the Temple and will make a proclamation to Israel, saying: Meek ones, the day of your redemption is come. And if you do not believe me, behold my light which rises upon you, as it is said, "Arise, shine, for your light is come, and the glory of the Lord is risen upon you." And it has risen only upon you and not the nations of the earth, as it is said, "For behold, darkness shall cover the earth, and gross darkness the peoples; but upon you the Lord shall rise, and His glory shall be seen upon you." (*Pesikta Rabbati* 36:1–2) [PESIKTA RABBATI 1968: 2:676–683]

28. A Seventh-Century Messianic Apocalypse

There may indeed have been heightened Messianic expectations at the beginning of the Muslim era, just as there were at the time of the Roman occupation of Palestine. Among the debris of documents preserved in the storeroom of the medieval synagogue of Cairo is a poem that provides an apocalyptic vision of what it was like when the Arabs—here, as often, the "Ishmaelites"—suddenly descended on the Holy City in the seventh century. It is couched in the familiar opaque language of apocalypses, but the references are sufficiently clear—to the Byzantines or Romans as "Edomites," for example—to enable us to date it very close to 638 C.E.:

On that day when the Messiah, son of David, will come
To a downtrodden people
These signs will be seen in the world and will be brought forth:

Earth and heaven will wither,
And the sun and the moon will be blemished,
And the dwellers in the Land (of Israel) will be struck silent.

The king of the West and the king of the East
Will be ground one against the other,
And the armies of the king of the West will hold firm in the Land.
And a king will go forth from the land of Yoqtan [Arabia]
And his armies will seize the Land,
The dwellers of the world will be judged
And the heavens will rain dust on the earth,
And winds will spread in the Land.
Gog and Magog will incite one another
And kindle fear in the heart of the Gentiles.
And Israel will be freed of all their sins
And will no more be kept far from the house of prayer.

Blessings and consolations will be showered on them,
And they will be engraved on the Book of Life.
The Kings from the land of Edom will be no more,
And the people of Antioch will rebel and make peace
And Maʿuziya [Tiberias] and Samaria will be consoled,
And Acre and Galilee will be shown mercy.
Edomites and Ishmaelites will fight in the valley of Acre
Till the horses sink in blood and panic.
Gaza and her daughters will be stoned
And Ascalon and Ashod will be terror-stricken.

Israel will go forth from the City and turn eastwards,
And taste no bread for five and four days.
And their Messiah will be revealed and they will be consoled.
And they will share pleasant secrets with their King
And they will raise praises to their King;
And all the wicked will not rise up in the Judgment.

(LEWIS 1976: 198)

29. Later Messianic Thinking

The rabbis of the Babylonian schools of the fourth and fifth centuries C.E. were somewhat vague on the functions of the Messiah to come. The destructive events of 70–135 C.E., when the city of Jerusalem was twice retaken and sacked by a Roman army, made the arrival of a political savior for Israel seem increasingly implausible

*at best; and after the followers of Jesus the Messiah left the body of the Jewish
community and began to enjoy enormous success among the Gentiles, Messianic
expectations among the Jews had necessarily to reshape themselves. Some of that
rethinking may have quietly occurred among the generations of scholars who completed the Talmuds, but that was by no means the end of it. This, for example, is
how the question of the Messiah of Israel appeared first to Saadya (d. 942 C.E.), the
gaon, or head, of the yeshiva in Iraq, and then to Maimonides, writing toward the
end of the twelfth century C.E., also within Islam. The Christian claims are not very
far from their thoughts and in both instances are addressed directly. First, Saadya:*

There are so-called Jews who assert that the prophetic promises and
messages of comfort were all fulfilled at the time of the Second Temple
and have been entirely abrogated in that nothing remains of their promise. These people base their opinion on a fundamentally wrong conception. They say that the emphatic assurances of salvation which we find in
the Scripture [that is, in the Prophets] . . . were all given on condition that
the obedience of the people would be complete. They said that this was
similar to the promise which our teacher Moses gave to Israel . . . and that
on account of their sins their kingdom came to an end and vanished; in
the same way, some of the Messianic promises, they say were fulfilled at
the time of the Second Temple [that is, in the era after the Exile] and then
vanished, whereas others did not come to pass at all on account of the sins
of the people.

*In the first part of his refutation of this position Saadya attacks the notion that the
promises of salvation to Israel, whether before the Exile or after, were in any way
"stipulated" or "conditioned." He then turns to the notion that the Messianic Age
has in fact occurred.*

(1) In the Messianic Age it is expected that all creatures will believe
in God and proclaim His unity, as it is said, "And the Lord shall be king
over all the earth; and in that day shall the Lord be one and His Name
One" (Zech. 14:9), but do we not see them still clinging to their errors
and their denial of God? (2) In the Messianic Age the faithful are supposed
to be free and not forced to pay tribute in money and food to other
nations, as it says, "The Lord has sworn by His right hand. . . . Surely I
will no more give your grain to be food for your enemies; and strangers
shall not drink your wine for which you have labored" (Isa. 62:8). But do
we not see that every nation is compelled to pay tribute and obedience
to the nation to which it is subject? (3) In the Messianic Age we expect
the abolition of wars between men and complete disarmament, as it says,
"And they shall beat their swords into plowshares, and their spears into

pruning hooks; nation shall not lift up sword against nation, neither shall they learn war any more" (Isa. 2:4). But do we not see the nations fighting and contending with each other more violently than ever before? Should one try to explain that the Scripture only means to say that there will be no more wars under the banner of religion, is it not the fact that religious wars and quarrels are today more intensive than ever? (4) In the Messianic Age animals are expected to live peacefully one beside the other, the wolf feeding the lamb, the lion eating straw, and the young child playing with a snake and a basilisk . . . (Isa. 11:6–9), whereas we see that the evil nature of wild animals is still the same and they have not changed in any way. Again, should someone explain that Scripture only means to say that the wicked people will live peacefully alongside the virtuous, the facts are precisely to the contrary. For nowadays the tyranny and violence of the strong against the weak are more ruthless than ever before.

All these facts prove conclusively that the prophetic messages of comfort have not yet been fulfilled. Our refutation of the opinion held by the people we have referred to applies also to the Christians. (Saadya, *Book of Doctrines and Beliefs* 8.3) [SAADYA 1945: 175–179]

Maimonides, two and a half centuries later, on the same subject:

King Messiah will arise and restore the kingdom of David to its former state and original sovereignty. He will rebuild the sanctuary (of the Temple) and gather the dispersed of Israel. All the ancient laws will be reinstituted in his days; sacrifices will again be offered; the Sabbatical and Jubilee years will again be observed in accordance with the commandments set forth in the Law.

He who does not believe in the restoration or does not look forward to the coming of the Messiah denies not only the teachings of the prophets but also those of the Law and Moses our Teacher, for Scripture reaffirms the rehabilitation of Israel, as it is said: "Then the Lord your God will turn your captivity, and have compassion on you and will return and gather you . . . and the Lord your God will bring you into the land which your fathers possessed" (Deut. 30:3–5). These words stated in Scripture include all that the prophets said (on the subject). They recur in the section treating of Balaam (Num. 22–24). The prophecy in that section bears upon the two Messiahs: the first, namely David, who saved Israel from the hand of their enemies; and the later Messiah, a descendent of David, who will achieve the final salvation of Israel. . . .

Do not think that King Messiah will have to perform signs and wonders, bring anything new into being, revive the dead, or do similar things. It is not so. Rabbi Akiba was a great sage, a teacher of Mishna, yet he was also the armor bearer of Bar Kozba [or Bar Koziba or Kokhba, the leader of the Jewish insurrection of 135 C.E.]. He affirmed that the latter was King Messiah; he and all the wise men of his generation shared this belief until Bar Kozba was slain in (his) iniquity, when it became known he was not the Messiah. Yet the rabbis had not asked him for a sign or a token. The general principle is: This Law of ours with its statutes and ordinances is not subject to change. It is for ever and all eternity; it is not to be added to or taken away from. . . .

If there arises a king from the house of David who meditates on the Torah, occupies himself with the commandments, as did his ancestor David, observes the precepts prescribed in the Written and Oral Law, prevails upon Israel to walk in the way of Torah and repair its breaches, and fights the battles of the Lord, it may be assumed that he is the Messiah. If he does these things and (further) succeeds, rebuilds the sanctuary on its site and gathers the dispersed of Israel, he is beyond all doubt the Messiah.

The text then continues, though this passage is removed in some of the versions of the Mishneh Torah.

But if he does not meet with success, or is slain, it is obvious that he is not the Messiah promised in the Torah. He is to be regarded like all the other wholehearted and worthy kings of the house of David who died and whom the Holy One, blessed be He, raised up to test the multitude, as it is written, "And some of them that are wise shall stumble, to refine among them, and to purify, and to make white, even to the end of the end; for it is yet for the time appointed" (Dan. 11:35).

Even of Jesus of Nazareth, who imagined that he was the Messiah and was put to death by the court, Daniel had prophesied, as it is written, "And the children of the violent among your people shall lift themselves up to establish the vision, but they shall stumble" (Dan. 11:14). For has there ever been a greater stumbling than this? All the prophets affirmed that the Messiah would redeem Israel, save them, gather their dispersed, and confirm the commandments. But he caused Israel to be destroyed by their sword, their remnant to be dispersed and humiliated. He was instrumental in changing the Torah and causing the world to err and service another besides God.

But it is beyond the human mind to fathom the designs of the Creator, for our ways are not His ways, neither are our thoughts His thoughts. All these matters relating to Jesus of Nazareth and the Ish-

maelite [that is, Muhammad] who came after him, only served to clear the way for King Messiah, to prepare the whole world to worship God with one accord, as it is written, "For then will I turn to the peoples a pure language, that they may call upon the name of the Lord to serve Him with one consent" (Zeph. 3:9). Thus the Messianic hope, the Torah, and the commandments have become familiar topics, topics of conversation (among the inhabitants) of the far isles and many peoples, uncircumcised of heart and flesh. These are discussing these matters and the commandments of the Torah. Some say, "These commandments were true, but have lost their validity and are no longer binding"; others declare that they had an esoteric meaning and were not intended to be taken literally, that the Messiah has already come and revealed their their occult significance. But when the true King Messiah will appear and succeed, be exalted and lifted up, they will forthwith recant and realize that they have inherited naught but lies from their fathers, that their prophets and forebears have led them astray. (Maimonides, *Mishneh Torah* 14.11)
[MAIMONIDES 1965]

Let no one think that in the days of the Messiah any of the laws of nature will be set aside, or any innovation introduced into creation. The world will follow its normal course. The words of Isaiah, "And the wolf will dwell with the lamb, and the leopard lie down with the kid" (11:6), are to be understood figuratively, meaning that Israel will live securely among the wicked of the heathens, who are likened to wolves and leopards. . . . They will accept the true religion, and will neither plunder nor destroy, and together with Israel earn a comfortable living in a legitimate way, as it is written, "And the lion shall eat straw with the ox" (Isa. 11:7). All similar expressions used in connection with the Messianic age are metaphorical. In the days of King Messiah the full meaning of these metaphors and their allusions will become clear to all. . . .

Some of our sages say that the coming of Elijah will precede the advent of the Messiah. But no one is in a position to know the details of this and similar things until they come to pass. They are not explicitly stated by the prophets. Nor have the rabbis any traditions with regard to these matters. They are guided solely by what the scriptural texts seem to apply. Hence there is divergence of opinion on the subject. Be that as it may, neither the exact sequence of those events nor the details thereof constitute religious dogmas. No one should occupy himself with the legendary themes or spend much time on homiletic statements bearing on this and like subjects. . . .

The Sages and the prophets did not long for the days of the Messiah that Israel might exercise dominion over the world, or rule over the heathens, or be exalted by the nations, or that it might eat and drink and rejoice. Their aspiration was that Israel might be free to devote itself to the Law and its wisdom, with no one to oppress or disturb it, and thus be worthy of life in the world to come. (Maimonides, *Mishneh Torah* 14.12) [MAIMONIDES 1965]

30. A Muslim Savant Makes His Own Calculations on the Era of the Messiah

The first and most famous of the beginnings of antiquity is the fact of the creation of mankind. But among those who have a book of divine revelation, such as the Jews, Christians and Magians, and their various sects, there exists such a difference of opinion as to the nature of this fact, and as to the question of how to date from it, the like of which is not allowable for eras. Everything, the knowledge of which is connected with the beginning of creation and the history of bygone generations, is mixed up with falsifications and myths, because it belongs to a far remote age, because a long interval separates us from it, and because the student is incapable of keeping it in memory and of fixing it. God says, "Have they not got the stories about those who were before them? None but God knows them" (Quran 9:71). Therefore it is becoming not to admit any account of a similar subject, if it is not attested by a book whose correctness can be relied upon, or from a tradition for which the conditions of authenticity, according to the prevalent opinion, furnish grounds for belief.

On this note of exasperation the Muslim scientist Biruni (d. 1048 C.E.), whom we have already heard on the subject of Hanukka, opens his study of the chronology of ancient nations. The beginning of the world was indeed buried in the remote past; but as Biruni was well aware, it was ideology as much as chronology that was at work in determining the date of creation.

The Jews and the Christians differ widely on this subject (of the era of creation); for, according to the doctrine of the Jews, the time between Adam and Alexander is 3,448 years, while according to the Christian doctrine, it is 5,180 years. The Christians reproach the Jews with having diminished the number of years with the view of making the appearance of Jesus fall in the middle of the seven millennia, which are according to their view, the time of the duration of the world, so as not to coincide with the time at which, as the prophets after Moses had prophesied, the birth of Jesus from a pure virgin at the end of time would take place. . . .

The Jews expect the coming of the Messiah, who was promised to them at the end of 1,335 years after Alexander, expecting it like something which they know for certain. . . . This expectation was based on the assumption that the beginning of this era [that is, the era of Alexander the Great] coincided with the time when the sacrifices were abolished, when no more divine revelation was received, and no more prophets were sent. Then they referred to the Hebrew word of God in the fifth book of the Torah (Deut. 31:18), "I, God, shall be concealing my being until that day." And they counted the (numerical value of) letters of the words for "be concealing," which gives the sum of 1,335. This they declared to be the time during which no inspiration from heaven was received and the sacrifices were abolished, which is what is meant by God's "concealing" Himself. . . .

In order to support what they maintain, they quote two passages in the book of Daniel: "Since the time when the sacrifice was abolished until impurity comes to destruction it is 1,290 (days)" (Dan. 12:11), and the next following passage (Dan. 12:12), "Therefore happy the man who hopes to reach to 1,335 (days)." Some people explain the difference of 45 years in these two passages so as to refer the former (1,290) to the beginning of the rebuilding of Jerusalem, and the latter (1,335) to the time when the rebuilding would be finished. According to other, the first number is the date of the birth of the Messiah, while the latter is the date of his public appearance.

Further, the Jews say, when Jacob bestowed his blessing on Judah (Gen. 49:10), he informed him that the rule would always remain with his sons till the coming of him to whom the rule belongs. So in these words he told him that the rule would remain with his descendants until the appearance of the expected Messiah. And now the Jews add that this is really the case; that the rule has not been taken from them. For the *Resh Galuta*, that is, the "Chief of the Exiles" who had been banished from their homes in Jerusalem, is the master of every Jew in the world, the ruler whom they obey in all countries, whose order is carried out under most circumstances.

As to what the Jews think of the continuance of rule in the family of Judah, and which they transfer to the leadership of the exiles, we must remark that if was correct to extend the word "rule" to similar leadership by way of analogy, the Magians, the Sabians and others would partake of this, and neither the other Israelites nor other nations would be exempt therefrom. Because no class of men, not even the lowest, are without a sort of rule and leadership with relation to others who are inferior to them.

As to that which they derive from the book of Daniel . . . the first passage, "since the time when the sacrifices were abolished . . . is 1,290," admits of being referred, first, to the first destruction of Jerusalem; and, secondly, to the second destruction, which happened, however, 385 years *after* the accession of Alexander. Therefore the Jews have not the slightest reason to commence (the calculations on the coming of the Messiah) with that date which they have announced [that is, the era of Alexander the Great]. (Biruni, *Traces of the Past*) [BIRUNI 1879: 16–21]

3. The Good News of Jesus Christ

1. What Is the Good News?

From Paul, servant of Christ Jesus, Apostle by God's call, set apart for the service of the Good News. This Good News God announced before in Sacred Scriptures through His prophets. It is about His Son: on the human level he was born of David's stock, but on the level of the spirit, the Holy Spirit, he was declared Son of God by a mighty act in that he rose from the dead: it is about Jesus Christ our Lord. (Paul, *To the Romans* 1:1–4)

For Paul, the "Good News" was precisely that: the announcement of an event. But for the early Christians that same "Good News"—in Greek, euangelion; in English, the Gospel—was something more. It was the text, or rather, the four texts or books that proclaimed the event on early and good authority: the books of Matthew and John, disciples of Jesus; of Mark, a follower of Peter; and of Luke, the companion of Paul. They are our chief sources on the life and teachings of Jesus of Nazareth.

2. The Genealogy of Jesus

The bloodlines of Jesus of Nazareth are given in two of those four Gospels that record the main outlines of his life and teachings. In Luke 3:23–38 his genealogy is carried back to Adam. In Matthew, who was concerned with establishing Jesus' Messianic credentials, Jesus' ancestors are traced back to David, from whose line the Messiah will come, and then eventually to Abraham, the father of all believers.

A table of the descent of Jesus Christ, son of David, son of Abraham.

Abraham was the father of Isaac, Isaac of Jacob, Jacob of Judah and his brothers, Judah of Perez and Zarah—their mother was Tamar—Perez of Hezron, Hezron of Ram, Ram of Amminadab, Amminadab of

Nahshon, Nahshon of Salma, Salma of Boaz—his mother was Rahab—Boaz of Obed—his mother was Ruth—Obed of Jesse, and Jesse was the father of King David.

David was the father of Solomon—his mother had been the wife of Uriah—Solomon of Rehoboam, Rehoboam of Abijah, Abijah of Asa, Asa of Jehoshaphat, Jehoshaphat of Joram, Joram of Azariah, Azariah of Jotham, Jotham of Ahaz, Ahaz of Hezekiah, Hezekiah of Menasseh, Menasseh of Amon, Amon of Josiah, and Josiah was the father of Jeconiah and his brothers at the time of the deportation to Babylon.

After the deportation Jeconiah was the father of Shealtiel, Shealtiel of Zerubbabel, Zerubbabel of Abiud, Abiud of Eliakim, Eliakim of Azor, Azor of Zadok, Zadok of Achim, Achim of Eliud, Eliud of Eliezer, Eliezer of Matthan, Matthan of Jacob, Jacob of Joseph, the husband of Mary, who gave birth to Jesus called Messiah.

There were fourteen generations in all from Abraham to David, fourteen from David until the deportation to Babylon, and fourteen from the deportation to the Messiah. (Matthew 1:1–17)

3. Two Miraculous Conceptions: John and Jesus

In all three of the Synoptic Gospels—Matthew, Mark, and Luke—the figure of John, called "the Baptizer," precedes the adult Jesus onto the scene in Palestine. Luke, in fact, gives a circumstantial account of the birth of John before he describes Jesus' own nativity.

In the days of Herod, king of Judea [37–4 B.C.E.], there was a priest named Zechariah, of the division of the priesthood called after Abijah. His wife was also of priestly descent; her name was Elizabeth. Both of them were upright and devout, blamelessly observing all the commandments and ordinances of the Lord.

Once, when it was the turn of his division and he was there to take part in the divine service, it fell to his lot, by priestly custom, to enter the sanctuary of the Lord and offer incense; and the whole congregation was at prayer outside. It was the hour of the incense offering. There appeared to him an angel of the Lord, standing at the right of the altar of incense. At this sight Zechariah was startled, and fear overcame him. But the angel said to him, "Do not be afraid, Zechariah; your prayer has been heard; your wife Elizabeth will bear a son, and you shall name him John. Your heart will thrill with joy, and many will be glad that he was born, for he will be great in the eyes of the Lord. He will never touch wine or strong drink. From his very birth he will be filled with the Holy Spirit; and he will bring back many Israelites to the Lord their God. He will go before him as a forerunner, possessed by the spirit and power of Elijah, to reconcile father and child, to convert the rebellious to the ways of the righteous, to prepare a people that will be fit for the Lord."

Zechariah said to the angel, "How can I be sure of this? I am an old man and my wife is well on in years."

The angel replied, "I am Gabriel; I stand in attendance upon God, and I have been sent to speak to you and bring you this good news. But now listen: you will lose your powers of speech and remain silent until the days when these things happen to you, because you have not believed me, though at their proper time my words will be proved true. . . ."

When his period of duty was completed Zechariah returned home. After this his wife Elizabeth conceived, and for five months she lived in seclusion, thinking, "This is the Lord's doing; now at last He has deigned to take away my reproach from among men."

In the sixth month the angel Gabriel was sent from God to a town in Galilee called Nazareth, with a message for a girl betrothed to a man named Joseph, a descendant of David; the girl's name was Mary. The angel went in and said to her, "Greetings, most favored one! The Lord is with you." But she was deeply troubled by what he said and wondered what this greeting might mean. Then the angel said to her, "Do not be afraid, Mary, for God has been gracious to you; you shall conceive and bear a son, and you shall give him the name Jesus. He will be great; he will bear the title 'Son of the Most High'; the Lord God will give him the throne of his ancestor David, and he will be king over Israel forever; his reign shall never end." "How can this be?" Mary said; "I am still a virgin." The angel answered, "The Holy Spirit will come upon you, and the power of the Most High will overshadow you; and for that reason the holy child to be born from you will be called 'Son of God.' Moreover, your kinswoman Elizabeth has herself conceived a son in her old age; and she who was reputed barren is now in her sixth month, for God's promises can never fail." "Here am I," said Mary; "I am the Lord's servant; as you have spoken, so be it." And the angel left. (Luke 1:5–38)

4. The Quranic Versions

The Quranic account of Jesus begins with the birth of Mary, here identified as the daughter of Imran. In Numbers 26:58–59 Imran is the name of the father of Moses, Aaron, and their sister Mary, and so there may be some confusion here between the mother of Jesus and the sister of Moses.

Remember when the wife of Imran said: "O Lord, I offer You what I carry in my womb in dedication to your service, accept it for You hear all and know every thing."

And when she had given birth to the child, she said, "O Lord, I have delivered but a girl"—but God knew better what she had delivered; the boy could not be as that girl was—"I have named her Mary, (she said) and I give her into Your keeping. Preserve her and her children from Satan the ostracized."

Her Lord accepted her graciously and she grew up with excellence, and was given into the care of Zechariah. Whenever Zechariah came to see her in the chamber, he found her provided with food, and he asked: "Where did this come from, O Mary?" And she said, "From God who gives food in abundance to whomsoever He will."

Then Zechariah prayed to his Lord: "O Lord, bestow on me offspring, virtuous and good, for You answer all prayers." Then the angels said to him as he stood in the chamber in prayer: "God sends you good tidings of John, who will confirm a thing from God and be noble, continent, and a prophet, and one of those who are upright and do good."

He said: "O Lord, how can I have a son when I am old and my wife is barren?" "Thus," came the answer, "God does as He wills." And Zechariah said: "Give me a token, O Lord, My Lord." "The token will be," was the reply, "that you will speak to no man for three days except by signs; and remember your Lord much, and pray at evening and sunrise."

The angels said: "O Mary, indeed God has favored you and made you immaculate, and has chosen you from all the women of the world. So adore your Lord, O Mary, and pay homage and bow with those who bow in prayer."

This is news of the Unknown that We send you, for you were not there when they cast lots with quills to determine who would take care of Mary, nor when they disputed it. When the angels said: "O Mary, God gives you news of a thing from Him, for rejoicing, (news of one) whose name will be Messiah, Jesus son of Mary, illustrious in this world and the next, and one among the honored, who will speak to the people when in the cradle and in the prime of life, and will be among the upright and the doers of good."

She said: "How can I have a son, O Lord, when no man has touched me?" He said: "That is how God creates what He wills. When He decrees a thing, He says 'Be!' and it is. And He will teach him the Law and the judgment, and the Torah and the Gospel." (Quran 3:35–48)

And again:

Commemorate Mary in the Book. When she withdrew from her family people to a place in the east, and took cover from them. We sent a spirit of Ours to her who appeared before her in the concrete form of a man.

"I seek refuge in the Merciful from you, if you fear Him," she said. He replied: "I am only a messenger from your Lord (sent) to bestow a good son on you." "How can I have a son," she said, "when no man has touched me, nor am I sinful?" He said: "Thus will it be. Your Lord said: 'It will be easy for Me,' that 'We shall make him a sign for men and a blessing from Us.' This is a thing already decreed."

When she conceived him she went away to a distant place. (Quran 19:16–22)

5. The Question of the Virgin Birth

This is the story of the birth of the Messiah. Mary his mother was betrothed to Joseph. Before their wedding she found that she was with child by the Holy Spirit. Being a man of principle, and at the same time wanting to save her from exposure, Joseph desired to have the marriage contract set aside quietly. He had resolved on this when an angel of the Lord appeared to him in a dream. "Joseph, son of David," said the angel, "do not be afraid to take Mary home with you as your wife. It was by the Holy Spirit that she conceived this child. She will bear a son; and you shall give him the name Jesus for he shall save the people from their sins." All this happened to fulfill what the Lord declared through the prophet, "The virgin will conceive and bear a son and he shall be called Emmanuel" (Isa. 7:14), a name which means "God is with us." Rising from sleep Joseph did as the angel had directed him; he took Mary home to be his wife but had no intercourse with her until her son was born. (Matthew 1:18–25)

If Muslims were quite prepared to accept this account of the miraculous conception of Jesus as presented in the Gospel of Matthew, Jews were not. The rabbis, whenever they do mention Jesus, maintain that he was the illegitimate son of a quite human father; and, as will be seen, even some heretical Jewish-Christian groups likewise denied the Virgin Birth. The only place where we can get close to an actual Jewish and Christian discussion of the issue is in the Dialogue with Trypho, *written by the Gentile Christian Justin in the middle of the second century* C.E. *The arguments, drawn from philology and comparative religion, are placed by Justin in Rabbi Trypho's mouth, of course, but they are plausibly genuine.*

Trypho responded, "The passage [from Isa. 7:14 cited in Matthew's text above] does not say, 'Behold a virgin shall conceive in the womb and bring forth a son,' but rather 'Behold, a young woman shall conceive . . .' The whole prophecy is to be applied to Hezekiah, and it can be demonstrated that the events happened to Hezekiah according to the prophecy [see Chapter 2 above]. And in the myths of those who are called the Greeks it is related that Perseus was born of Danae while she was a virgin after he who is called Zeus among them had flowed into her in the form of a stream of gold. You should be ashamed of peddling the same tales as the Greeks; you should say rather that this Jesus was a human being born as a human being from human beings, and if you are attempting to demonstrate from the Scriptures that he is the Christ [that is, the Messiah], you should say that he earned the appointment as Christ by his perfect behavior in obedience to the Law, but in no event should you dare to tell fairy tales, in which case you are convicted of the same futility as the Greeks."

I replied to this . . . "Be assured, Trypho, that the very stories which the one who is called the devil deceitfully caused to be told among the Greeks, just as he operated through the sages of Egypt and the false prophets in the time of Elijah, have confirmed my understanding and faith in the Scriptures. For when they say that Dionysus was born as the son of Zeus as the result of his intercourse with Semele, and when they tell us that this same Dionysus was the inventor of wine, and that he was torn to pieces and rose again and went up to heaven, and when they introduce an ass into his mysteries, do I not recognize that he has imitated the prophecy spoken beforehand by the Patriarch Jacob and recorded by Moses (Gen. 49:11–12)?"

"When those who pass down the mysteries of Mithras [Justin continues] maintain that he was born from a rock and call the place a cave where they initiate into their traditions those who believe in him, do I not perceive that in this case they are imitating the saying of Daniel that 'A stone cut without hands from a great mountain' (Dan. 2:34), and a similar passage in Isaiah (33:16), the whole of whose utterances they attempted to imitate? For they have arranged that words encouraging right conduct should be spoken in their rites?" (Justin, *Dialogue with Trypho*)

6. The Birth of Jesus in Bethlehem

In those days a decree was issued by the Emperor Augustus for a registration to be made throughout the Roman world. This was the first registration of its kind; it took place when Quirinius was governor of Syria. For this purpose everyone made his way to his own town; and so Joseph went up to Judea from the town of Nazareth in Galilee, to register at the city of David, called Bethlehem, because he was of the house of David by descent; and with him went Mary, who was betrothed to him. She was expecting a child, and while they were there the time came for her baby to be born, and she gave birth to a son, her firstborn. She wrapped him in his swaddling clothes and laid him in a manger, because there was no room for them to lodge in the house. (Luke 2:1–7)

Eight days later the time came to circumcise him, and he was given the name Jesus, the name given by the angel before he was conceived. Then after their purification had been completed in accordance with the Law of Moses, they brought him up to Jerusalem to present him to the Lord, as prescribed in the Law of the Lord: "Every firstborn male shall be deemed to belong to the Lord" (Lev. 12:1–8), and also to make the offering as stated in the Law, "a pair of turtle doves or two young pigeons."

There was at that time in Jerusalem a man called Simeon. This man was upright and devout, one who watched and waited for the restoration of Israel, and the Holy Spirit was upon him. It had been disclosed to him by the Holy Spirit that he would not see death until he had seen the Lord's Messiah. Guided by the spirit he came into the Temple, and when the parents brought in the child Jesus to do for him what was customary under the Law, he took him in his arms, praised God and said:

"This day, Master, You give your servant his discharge in peace; now your promise is fulfilled. For I have seen with my own eyes the deliverance which You have made ready in full view of all the nations: A light that will be a revelation to the heathen and glory to your people Israel."

The child's father and mother were full of wonder at what was being said about him. Simeon blessed them and said to Mary, his mother, "This child is destined to be a sign which men reject; and you too will be pierced to the heart. Many in Israel will stand or fall because of him, and thus the secret thoughts of men will be laid bare."

. . . When they had done everything prescribed by the Law of the Lord, they returned to Galilee to their own town of Nazareth. The child grew big and strong and full of wisdom and God's favor was upon him. (Luke 2:21–40)

The last sentence is all we know of Jesus from the time of his circumcision until the point, some three decades later, when he makes his first public appearance in the life of Israel. It occurs at a ford of the river Jordan, and the protagonist of the scene is a Jewish revivalist named John.

7. John and the Baptism of Jesus

About that time John the Baptist appeared as a preacher in the Judean wilderness; his theme was: "Repent, for the kingdom of Heaven is upon you." It was of him that the prophet Isaiah spoke (Isa. 40:3) when he said, "A voice crying aloud in the wilderness, 'Prepare a way for the Lord; clear a straight path for him.' "

John's clothing was a rough coat of camel's hair, with a leather belt around his waist, and his food was locusts and honey. They flocked to him from Jerusalem, from all Judea, and the whole Jordan valley, and were baptized by him in the River Jordan, confessing their sins."

When he saw many of the Pharisees and Sadducees coming for baptism he said to them: "You vipers' brood! Who warned you to escape from the coming tribulation? Then prove your repentance by the fruit it bears, and do not presume to say to yourselves 'We have Abraham as our father.' I tell you that God can make children of Abraham out of these stones here. Already the axe is laid to the roots of the trees; and every tree that fails to produce good fruit is cut down and thrown into the fire. I baptize you with water, for repentance; but the one who comes after me is mightier than I. I am not fit to take off his shoes. He will baptize you with the Holy Spirit and with fire. His shovel is ready in his hand and he will winnow his threshing floor; the wheat he will gather into his granary; but he will burn the chaff on a fire that can never go out."

Then Jesus arrived at the Jordan from Galilee and came to John to be baptized by him. John tried to dissuade him. "Do you come to me?" he said. "I need rather to be baptized by you." Jesus replied: "Let it be so for the present; we do well to conform in this way with all that God requires." John then allowed him to come. After baptism Jesus came up out of the water at once, and at that moment heaven opened; he saw the Spirit of God descending like a dove to alight upon him; and a voice from heaven was heard saying, "This is my Son, my Beloved, on whom my favor rests." (Matthew 3:1–17)

We can follow the career of John to its end, since both the Gospels and Josephus supply details. Of John, Josephus says the following.

He was a good man and exhorted the Jews to lead righteous lives, practice justice toward one another and piety toward God, and so to join in baptism. In his view this was a necessary preliminary if baptism was to be acceptable to God. They must not use it to gain pardon for the sins they have committed, but as a consecration of the body, implying that the soul was thoroughly purified beforehand by right behavior. When many others joined the crowds about him, for they were greatly moved on hearing his words, Herod (Antipas; 4 B.C.E.–39 C.E.) feared that John's great influence over the people would lead to a rebellion—for they seemed already willing to do anything he might advise. Herod decided therefore that it would be much better to strike first and to be rid of him before his work led to an uprising than to wait for an upheaval, become involved in a difficult situation and see his mistake. Accordingly John was sent as a prisoner to (the fortress) Machaerus . . . because of Herod's suspicious temper, and was there put to death. (Josephus, *Antiquities* 18.5.2)

8. The Ministry Begins

When he heard that John had been arrested (by Herod Antipas), Jesus withdrew to Galilee; and leaving Nazareth he went and settled in Capernaum on the Sea of Galilee, in the district of Zebulun and Naphtali. This was to fulfill the passage in the prophet Isaiah (9: 1–2) which tells of "the land of Zebulun, the land of Naphtali, the Way of the Sea, the land beyond Jordan, heathen Galilee," and says, "The people that lived in darkness saw a great light; light dawned on the dwellers of the land of death's dark shadow."

From that day Jesus began to proclaim his message: "Repent, for the kingdom of Heaven is upon you."

Jesus was walking by the Sea of Galilee when he saw two brothers, Peter and his brother Andrew, casting a net into the lake, for they were fishermen. Jesus said to them, "Come with me, and I will make you fishers of men." And at once they left their nets and followed him.

He went on, and saw another pair of brothers, James son of Zebedee and his brother John; they were in the boat with their father Zebedee, overhauling their nets. He called them and at once they left their boat and followed him.

He went round the whole of Galilee teaching in the synagogues, preaching the gospel of the Kingdom, and curing whatever illness or infirmity there was among the people. His fame reached the whole of Syria, and sufferers from every kind of illness, racked with pain, possessed by devils, epileptic or paralyzed, were all brought to him and he cured them. Great crowds followed him, from Galilee and the Ten Towns, from Jerusalem and Judea and the Transjordan. (Matthew 4:12–35)

9. The Family of Jesus

Not much is said of the family of Jesus in the Gospels, but on a few occasions early in his public ministry we are given brief, sometimes surprising glances at his household.

On the third day there was a wedding at Cana in Galilee. The mother of Jesus was there, and Jesus and his disciples were guests also. The wine gave out, so Jesus' mother said to him, "They have no wine left." He said, "Your concern, mother, is not mine. My hour has not yet come." His mother said to the servants, "Do whatever he tells you." There were six stone water jars standing near, of the kind used for Jewish rites of purification; each held from twenty to thirty gallons. Jesus said to the servants, "Fill the jars with water," and they filled them to the brim. "Now draw some off," he said, "and take it to the steward of the feast"; and they did so. The steward tasted the water, now turned into wine, not knowing the source, though the servants who had drawn the water knew. He hailed the bridegroom and said, "Everyone serves the best wine first, and waits until the guests have drunk freely before serving the poorer sort; but you have kept the best wine till now."

This deed at Cana in Galilee is the first of the signs by which Jesus revealed his glory and led his disciples to believe in him. (John 2:1–11)

He entered a house; and once more such a crowd collected round that they had no chance to eat. When his family heard of this, they set out to take charge of him; for people were saying that he was out of his mind. (Mark 3:20–21)

"I tell you this [Jesus said], no sin, no slander is beyond forgiveness for men; but whoever slanders the Holy Spirit can never be forgiven; he is guilty of eternal sin." He said this because they had declared that he was possessed by an unclean spirit. Then his mother and his brothers arrived, and remaining outside sent in a message asking him to come out to them. "Your mother and your brothers are outside asking for you." He replied,

"Who is my mother, who are my brothers?" And looking around at those who were sitting in the circle about him, he said, "Here are my mother and my brothers. Whoever does the will of God is my brother, my sister, my mother." (Mark 3:28–35)

He left that place and went to his home town (of Nazareth) accompanied by his disciples. When the Sabbath came he began to teach in the synagogue, and the large congregation that heard him were amazed and said, "Where does he get it from?" and "What wisdom is this that has been given him?" and "How does he work such miracles? Is not this the carpenter, the son of Mary, the brother of James and Joseph and Judas and Simon? And are not his sisters here with us?" So they fell foul of him. Jesus said to them, "A prophet will always be held in honor except in his home town, and among his kinsmen and his own family." He would work no miracles there, except that he put his hands on a few sick people and healed them; and he was taken aback by their want of faith. (Mark 6:1–6)

The plain sense of this latter passage is that Jesus had brothers and sisters, all presumably younger, if we accept the Gospel account of his birth. Church tradition did not understand it so, however. At some point—it is difficult to say precisely when—it began to be affirmed not only that Mary was a virgin before and even in the birth of Jesus, as the Gospels state, but also that she remained so for the rest of her life. Leo, bishop of Rome (440–461 C.E.), put it this way in one of his sermons.

Christ was born by a new birth, conceived of a virgin, born of a virgin, without benefit of the concupiscence of paternal flesh and without injury to maternal integrity. By origin different but in nature similar, it was brought about not by normal human usage but by the divine power that a virgin conceived him, and a virgin bore him and a virgin she remained. (Leo, *Sermon* 22.2)

There are earlier attestations to this belief about the mother of Jesus, and at least one of them was elicited by an opposing point of view. A certain Helvidius maintained that Jesus indeed had brothers and sisters according to the flesh, James, the first head of the church in Jerusalem, being notable among them. The assertion brought this reply from the Latin theologian and biblical scholar Jerome in 383 C.E.

We believe that God was born of a virgin because that is what we read; that Mary married after that birth we do not believe because that we do not read. Nor do we assert this in order to condemn marriage; indeed virginity itself is one of the fruits of marriage. . . . You say that Mary did not remain a virgin (after the birth of Jesus); I prefer to say that Joseph himself was a virgin through Mary, so that from a virginal union a virgin son was born. (Jerome, *Against Helvidius* 19)

10. Jesus the Healer

A substantial part of the Gospels is given over to an account of the years that Jesus spent in Galilee preaching his message of the Kingdom in public and private and performing miraculous acts, most of them healing, that began to attract attention to him in ever-widening circles.

That day, in the evening, he [Jesus] said to them [his disciples], "Let us cross over to the other side of the lake (of Galilee)." So they left the crowd and they took him with them in the boat where he had been sitting, and there were other boats accompanying him. A heavy squall came on and the waves broke over the boat until it was all but swamped. Now he was asleep in the stern on a cushion; they roused him and said, "Master, we are sinking! Do you not care?" He awoke, rebuked the wind and said to the sea, "Hush! Be still!" The wind dropped and there was a dead calm. He said to them, "Why are you such cowards? Have you no faith even now?" They were awestruck and said to one another, "Who can this be? Even the wind and the sea obey him."

So they came to the other side of the lake, into the country of the Gerasenes. As he stepped ashore, a man possessed by an unclean spirit came up to him from among the tombs where he had been dwelling. He could no longer be controlled. Even chains were useless; he had often been fettered and chained up, but he had snapped his chains and broken the fetters. No one was strong enough to master him. And so, unceasingly, night and day, he would cry aloud among the tombs and on the hillsides and cut himself with stones. When he saw Jesus in the distance, he ran and flung himself down before him, shouting loudly, "'What do you want with me, Jesus, Son of the Most High God? In God's name do not torment me," for Jesus was already saying to him, "Out, unclean spirit, come out of this man." Jesus asked him, "What is your name?" "My name is Legion," he said, "there are so many of us." And he begged hard that Jesus would not send them out of the country.

Now there happened to be a large herd of pigs feeding on the hillside, and the spirits begged him, "Send us among the pigs and let us go into them." He gave them leave, and the unclean spirits came out and went into the pigs. And the herd of about two thousand rushed over the edge into the lake and were drowned. The men in charge of them took to their heels and carried the news to the town and the countryside, and the people came out to see what had happened. They came to Jesus and saw the madman who had been possessed by the legion of devils sitting there clothed and in his right mind; and they were afraid. The spectators told them how the madman had been cured and what had happened to the pigs. Then they begged Jesus to leave the district. . . .

As soon as Jesus had returned by boat to the other shore, a great crowd once more gathered round him. While he was still by the lakeside, the president of one of the synagogues came up, Jairus by name, and when he saw him, he threw himself down at his feet and pleaded with him. "My little daughter," he said, "is at death's door. I beg you to come and to lay your hands on her and to cure her and save her life." So Jesus went with him, accompanied by a great crowd that pressed upon him.

Among them was a woman who had suffered from hemorrhages for twelve years; and in spite of long treatment by many doctors on which she had spent all she had, there had been no improvement. On the contrary, she had grown worse. She had heard what people were saying about Jesus, so she came up behind in the crowd and touched his cloak. For she said to herself, if I touch even his clothes I shall be healed. And then and there the source of her hemorrhages dried up and she knew in herself that she was cured of her trouble. At the same time, Jesus, aware that power had gone out of him, turned round in the crowd and asked, "Who touched my clothes?" His disciples said to him, "You see the crowd pressing upon you and yet you ask 'Who touched me?' " Meanwhile he was looking around to see who had done it. And the woman, trembling with fear when she grasped what had happened to her, came and fell at his feet and told him the whole truth. He said to her, "My daughter, your faith has cured you. Go in peace, free forever from this trouble."

While he was still speaking, a message came from the president's house, "Your daughter is dead. Why trouble the Rabbi further?" But Jesus, overhearing the message as it was delivered, said to the president of the synagogue, "Do not be afraid; only have faith." After this he allowed no one to accompany him, except Peter and James and James' brother John. They came to the president's house, where they found a great commotion, with loud crying and wailing. So he went in and said to them, "Why the crying and commotion? The child is not dead; she is asleep." And they only laughed at him. But after turning all the others out, he took the child's father and mother and his own companions and went in where the child was lying. Then, taking hold of her hand, he said to her "*talitha, qum*," which means "Get up, my child." Immediately the girl got up and walked about—she was about twelve years old. At that they were beside themselves in amazement. He gave strict orders to let no one hear about it, and told them to give her something to eat. (Mark 4:33–5:43)

11. The Public Preacher

When he [Jesus] saw the crowds he went up the hill. There he took his seat, and when his disciples had gathered round him, he began to address them, and this is the teaching he gave:

How blest are those who know their need of God; the kingdom of Heaven is theirs.

How blest are the sorrowful; they shall find consolation.

How blest are those of gentle spirit; they shall have the earth for their possession.

How blest are those who hunger and thirst to see right prevail; they shall be satisfied.

How blest are those who show mercy; mercy shall be shown to them.

How blest are those whose hearts are pure; they shall see God.

How blest are the peacemakers; God shall call them His sons.

How blessed are those who have suffered persecution for the cause of right; the kingdom of Heaven is theirs.

How blest are you when you suffer insults and persecution and every kind of calumny for my sake. Accept it with gladness and exultation, for you have a reward in heaven; in the same way they persecuted the prophets before you.

You are the salt to the world. And if the salt becomes tasteless, how is its saltness to be restored? It is now good for nothing except to be thrown away and trodden underfoot.

You are light for all the world. A town that stands on a hill cannot be hidden. When a lamp is lit, it is not put under a bushel but on the lampstand, where it gives light to everyone in the house. And you, like the lamp, must shed light among your fellows, so that, when they see the good you do, they may give praise to your Father in heaven. (Matthew 5:1–16)

"Not everyone who calls me 'Lord, Lord,' will enter the kingdom of Heaven, but only those who do the will of my heavenly Father. When that day comes, many will say to me, 'Lord, Lord, did we not prophesy in your name, cast out devils in your name, and in your name perform many miracles?' Then I will tell them to their face, 'I never knew you; out of my sight, you and your wicked ways!' " . . .

When Jesus had finished this discourse the people were astounded at his teaching; unlike their own teachers, he taught with a note of authority. (Matthew 7:21–29)

12. The Parables of the Kingdom

On another occasion he began to teach by the lakeside. The crowd that gathered round him was so large that he had to get into a boat on the lake, and there he sat, with the whole crowd on the beach right down to the water's edge. And he taught them many things in parables. . . .

When he was alone the Twelve and others who were around him questioned him about the parables. He replied, "To you the secret of the kingdom of God has been given; but to those who are outside, everything comes by way of parables, so that, as Scripture says (Isa. 6:9–10), they may look and look and see nothing, they may hear and hear but understand nothing; otherwise they would turn to God and be forgiven."

He said, "The kingdom of God is like this. A man scatters seed on the land; he goes to bed at night and wakes up in the morning, and the seed sprouts and grows, he knows not how. The ground produces a crop by itself, first the blade, then the ear, then the full-grown grain in the ear. But as soon as the crop is ripe he plies the sickle because harvest time has come."

He also said, "How shall we picture the kingdom of God, or by what parable shall we describe it? It is like the mustard seed, which is smaller than any seed in the ground at its sowing, but once sown, it springs up and grows taller than any other plant, and forms branches so large that the birds can settle in its shade."

With many such parables he would give them his message, so far as they were able to receive it. He never spoke to them except in parables; but privately to his disciples he explained everything. (Mark 4:1–14)

13. Jesus' Instructions to His Disciples

Then he called his twelve disciples to him and gave them authority to cast out unclean spirits and to cure every kind of ailment and disease.

These are the names of the twelve Apostles: first Simon, also called Peter, and his brother Andrew; James, son of Zebedee, and his brother John; Philip and Bartholomew, Thomas and Matthew the tax gatherer; James son of Alpheus; Thaddeus, Simon, a member of the Zealot party [or, a man zealous for the Law], and Judas Iscariot, the man who betrayed him.

These twelve Jesus sent out with the following instructions: "Do not take the road to Gentile lands, and do not enter any Samaritan town; but go rather to the lost sheep of the house of Israel. And as you go, proclaim the message: 'The kingdom of Heaven is upon you.' Heal the sick, raise the dead, cleanse lepers, cast out devils. You received without cost; give without charge. . . .

"Whoever will acknowledge you, I will acknowledge him before my Father in heaven, and whoever disowns me before men, I will disown him before my Father in heaven.

"You must not think that I have come to bring peace to the earth. I have not come to bring peace but a sword. I have come to set a man against his father, a daughter against her mother, a son's wife against his mother-in-law; and a man will find his enemies under his own roof. No man is worthy of me who cares more for a father or a mother than for me; no man is worthy of me who cares for son or daughter; no man is worthy of me who does not take up his cross and follow in my footsteps. By gaining his life, a man will lose it; by losing his life for my sake, he will gain it. . . ."

When Jesus had finished giving his twelve disciples their instructions, he left that place and went to teach and preach in neighboring towns. (Matthew 10:1–11:1)

14. The Demand for Signs

Both Jesus and Muhammad were asked for signs to validate their message. Neither was very eager to comply.

At this some of the doctors of the Law and the Pharisees said, "Master, we would like you to show us a sign." He answered: "It is a wicked, godless generation that asks for a sign. And the only sign that will be given it is the sign of the prophet Jonah. Jonah was in the sea monster's belly for three days and three nights, and in the same way the Son of Man will be three days and three nights in the bowels of the earth. At the Judgment, when this generation is on trial, the men of Nineveh will appear against it and ensure its condemnation, for they repented at the teaching of Jonah." (Matthew 12:38–40)

And Muhammad:

They say: "How is it no signs were sent down to him from his Lord?" Say: "The signs are with God. I am only a warner, plain and simple." (Quran 29:50)

The issue raised in this verse was subsequently taken up by the Quranic commentators.

"The signs are with God": This means that God sends down from among them only what He wishes, and if He had wanted to send down the sign which they demanded, then he would have done so.

"I am only a warner": This means that I, Muhammad, am commissioned to warn and to make this warning clear through the sign [that is, the Quran] which has been given to me. It is not for me to choose among God's signs, so that it would be in my power to say, "Send down to me one of this kind and not one of that kind!" Besides, I know that each sign has a lasting purpose, and each sign is as good as that of anyone else in this regard. (Zamakhshari, *The Unveiler, ad loc.*)

15. The Bread of Life

Jesus did in fact point to a sign, one that provoked a strong response not only from his opponents but even from his followers.

They said "What sign can you give us to see, so that we may believe you? What is the work you do? Our ancestors had manna to eat in the desert; as Scripture says, 'He gave them bread from heaven to eat.' " Jesus answered, "I tell you this; the truth is not that Moses gave you the bread from heaven, but that my Father gives you the real bread from heaven. The bread that God gives comes down from heaven and brings life to the world." They said to him, "Sir, give us this bread now and always." Jesus said to them, "I am the bread of life. Whoever comes to me shall never be hungry, and whoever believes in me shall never be thirsty. But you, as I said, do not believe, though you have seen. All that the Father gives me will come to me, and the man who comes to me I will never turn away. I have come down from heaven, to do not my own will but the will of Him who sent me. It is his will that I should not lose even one of all that He has given me, but raise them all up on the Last Day. For it is my Father's will that everyone who looks upon the Son and puts his faith in him shall possess eternal life; and I will raise him up on the Last Day."

At this the Jews began to murmur disapprovingly because he said "I am the bread which came down from heaven." They said, "Surely this is

Jesus son of Joseph; we know his father and his mother. How can he now say 'I have come down from heaven'?" Jesus answered, "Stop murmuring among yourselves. No man can come to me unless he is drawn by the Father who sent me; and I will raise him up on the Last Day. It is written in the prophets: 'And they shall all be taught by God.' Anyone who has listened to the Father and learns from him comes to me. I do not mean that anyone has seen the Father. He who has come from God has seen the Father and he alone. In truth, in very truth, I tell you, the believer possesses eternal life. Your forefathers ate the manna in the desert and they are dead. I am speaking of the bread that comes down from heaven; if anyone eats this bread he shall live forever. Moreover, the bread which I will give you is my own flesh; I give it for the life of the world."

This led to a fierce dispute among the Jews. "How can this man give us his flesh to eat?" they said. Jesus replied, "In truth, in very truth I tell you, unless you eat the flesh of the Son of Man and drink his blood, you can have no life in you. Whoever eats my flesh and drinks my blood possesses eternal life, and I will raise him up on the Last Day. My flesh is real food; my blood is real drink. Whoever eats my flesh and drinks my blood dwells continually in me and I dwell in him. As the living Father sent me, and I live because of the Father, so he who eats me shall live because of me. This is the bread which came down from heaven; and it is not like the bread which our fathers ate: they are dead, but whoever eats this bread will live forever."

This was spoken in synagogue when Jesus was teaching in Capernaum. Many of his disciples on hearing it exclaimed, "This is more than we can stomach! Why listen to such talk?" Jesus was aware that his disciples were murmuring about it and asked them, "Does this shock you? What if you see the Son of Man ascending to the place where he was before? The spirit alone gives life; the flesh is of no avail. The words which I have spoken to you are both spirit and life. And yet there are some of you who have no faith." For Jesus knew all along who were without faith and who was to betray him. So he said, "This is why I told you that no one can come to me unless it has been granted to him by the Father."

From that time many of his disciples withdrew and no longer went about with him. So Jesus asked the Twelve, "Do you also want to leave me?" Simon Peter answered him, "Lord, to whom shall we go? Your words are words of eternal life. We have faith and we know you are the Holy One of God." (John 6:30–69)

16. The Heavenly Table in the Quran

In the Gospel, as we have seen, the doubters of Jesus' role and mission ask for a heavenly sign and cite Moses' reception of manna in the desert as just such a sign. In the Quran too a sign is demanded of Jesus.

Said Jesus son of Mary: "O God our Lord, send down a table well laid out with food from the skies so that this day may be a day of feast for the earlier among us and the later, and a token from You. Give us our (daily) bread, for you are the best of all givers of food."

And God said: "I shall send it down to you; but if any of you disbelieve after this, I shall inflict such punishment on him as I never shall inflict on any other creature." (Quran 5:114–115)

The Muslim commentators on the Quran were uncertain of the exact meaning of this passage, as indeed are we. What, for example, is the meaning of "may be a day of feast"? Tabari (d. 923 C.E.), one of the earliest and most abundant of the Islamic exegetes, explains the disagreement and offers his solutions.

The commentators are in disagreement concerning the interpretation of God's words "which may be a day of feast." Some think that the meaning is: Send down upon us a table and we will henceforth take the day on which it comes down as a feast day which we and our descendants will hold in esteem. . . . Others think the meaning is: Send down upon us a table from which we will all eat together. . . . Still others say that when God here speaks of a feast day, it is meant not in the sense of a festival but in the sense of a benefit which God is vouchsafing us, and an argument and a proof as well. Among these interpretations, that which comes nearest to being correct is the one which includes the following meaning: Send down upon us a table which will be a feast day for us, in that we will pray and worship our Lord on the day that it comes down, just as the people used to do on their feast days. Thus the meaning which we affirm corresponds to the normal usage that people associate with the word "feast day" in their speech and not with the interpretation that reads it "a benefit from God," since the meaning of God's speech is always to be be interpreted as lying closer to the ordinary manner of speaking of the one who makes the request than to some significance inaccessible or unknown to the speaker. . . .

The commentators likewise disagree on whether or not the table was (actually) sent down (from heaven) and concerning what was on it. Some say that it was sent down with fish and other food and that the people ate from it. Then, after its descent, the table was taken up again because of (certain) innovations they (that is, the Christians) introduced in their relationship to God. . . . Others say that it came down with fruit from Paradise. . . . Still others say that on it lay every kind of food except meat. . . . Still others hold that that God did not send down a table to the Children of Israel. Those who maintain this view have another disagreement among themselves. Many say that this may be nothing more than a figure that God has offered to His creatures to inhibit their demanding (divine) signs from the prophets of God. . . .

In our view, however, the correct interpretation is as follows: God (actually) sent down the table to those who asked Jesus to request it from his Lord. We hold this because of the information we have received on this point from the Messenger of God, his companions, and after them the exegetes. . . . Furthermore, God breaks no promise, and there will not be any contradiction in what He announces. Thus God announced in His Book that He will fulfill the request of His prophet Jesus when He says: "In truth I do send it down on you." . . . As to what was on the table, it is correct to say that there was (some kind of) food on it. It could have been fish and bread, or it could have been fruit from Paradise. There is no advantage in knowing exactly what it was, nor is there any harm in not knowing, as long as the conclusions drawn from the verse correspond with the external wording of the revelation. (Tabari, *Commentary*, *ad loc.*)

One fairly consistent Muslim interpretation of the miracle of the Table was to associate it with the multiplication of the loaves and fishes, here told in Matthew's version.

When he heard what had happened Jesus withdrew privately by boat to a lonely place; but the people heard of it and came after him in crowds by land from the towns. When he came ashore, he saw a great crowd; his heart went out for them, and he cured those of them who were sick. When it grew late the disciples came up to him and said: "This is a lonely place and the day has gone; send the people off to the villages to buy themselves food." He answered: "There is no need for them to go; give them something to eat yourselves." "All we have here," they said, "is five loaves and two fishes." "Let me have them," he replied. So he told the people to sit down on the grass; then, taking the five loaves and the two fishes, he looked up to heaven, said the blessing, broke the loaves and gave them to the disciples; and the disciples gave them to the people. They all ate to their hearts' content; and the scraps left over, which they picked up, were enough to fill twelve great baskets. Some five thousand men shared in this meal, to say nothing of women and children. (Matthew 14:13–21)

Some early Muslim authorities offered their own versions of the miracle of the Table.

Muqatil and al-Kalbi say that God answered Jesus, on whom be peace, saying: "Behold, I am sending it down to you as you requested, but whosoever eats of that food and does not believe, I will make him an example and a curse and a warning to those who will come after." They said, "We agree," so Jesus summoned Simon, the brass worker, who was the most worthy of the Apostles, and asked, "Have you any food?" He answered, "I have two small fishes and six loaves." Jesus said, "Give them to me." Then Jesus broke them into little bits and said, "Sit down in the meadow in rows of ten persons a row." Then Jesus stood up and prayed to God Most High, and God answered him, sending down blessing on them, so that they became excellent bread and excellent fish. Then Jesus arose and went and began to distribute to each row what his fingers could carry. Then he said, "Eat in the name of God," and straightway the food became so plentiful that it was up to their knees. So they ate what God willed, and there was still some left over, even though the people numbered five thousand and more. Then all the people said, "We bear witness that you are the servant of God and His Messenger." (Tha ͑alibi, *Stories of the Prophets*)

17. Two Alien Encounters

One of the issues that would exercise the early community of Jesus' followers, as we shall see, was the question of carrying his message and extending his redemptive role into the world of the non-Jew. On at least two occasions in his life Jesus had extended contact with such non-Jews in a didactic context, one a Gentile woman in the region of Tyre and Sidon and the other a Samaritan woman at a well near Shechem.

Jesus then withdrew to the region of Tyre and Sidon. And a Canaanite woman from those parts came up to him crying out, "Sir! Have pity on me, Son of David; my daughter is tormented by a devil." But he said not a word in reply. His disciples came and urged him, "Send her away; see how she comes shouting after us." Jesus replied, "I was sent to the lost sheep of the house of Israel, and to them alone." But the woman came and fell at his feet and cried, "Help me, sir." To this Jesus replied, "It is not right to take the children's bread and throw it to the dogs." "True, sir," she answered; "and yet the dogs eat the scraps that fall from the master's table." Hearing this Jesus replied, "Woman, what faith you have! Be it as you wish." And from that moment her daughter was restored to health. (Matthew 15:21–28)

Since the fall of the Kingdom of Israel to the Assyrians in 721 C.E. and the resettlement of pagans in the region of Samaria, the natives of that region were not accepted by the Judeans as true Jews. As a result, they built their own temple atop Mount Gerizim near Shechem. Most Jews avoided the region and its hostile inhabitants by passing between Judea and Galilee via the Transjordan, but on this occasion Jesus and his disciples took the more direct route northward.

A report now reached the Pharisees: "Jesus is winning and baptizing more disciples than John"; although in fact it was only the disciples who were baptizing and not Jesus himself. When Jesus learned this, he left Judea and set out once more for Galilee. He had to pass through Samaria, and on his way came to a Samaritan town called Sychar [that is, Shechem], near the plot of ground which Jacob gave to his son Joseph and the spring called "Jacob's Well." It was about noon and Jesus, tired after his journey, sat down by the well.

The disciples had gone away to the town to buy food. Meanwhile a Samaritan woman came to draw water. Jesus said to her, "Give me a drink." The Samaritan woman said, "What! You, a Jew, ask a drink of me, a Samaritan woman?" Jews and Samaritans, it should be noted, do not use vessels in common. Jesus answered her, "If only you knew what God gives and who it is that is asking you for a drink, you would have asked him and he would have given you living water." "Sir," the woman said, "you have no bucket and this well is deep. How can you give me 'living water'? Are you a greater man than Jacob our ancestor, who gave us the well and drank from it himself, he and his sons, and his cattle too?" Jesus said, "Everyone who drinks this water will be thirsty again, but whoever drinks the water that I shall give him will never suffer thirst any more. The water that I shall give him will be an inner spring always welling up for eternal life." "Sir," said the woman, "give me that water, and then I shall not be thirsty, nor have to come all this way to draw."

Jesus replied, "Go home, call your husband and come back." She answered, "I have no husband." "You are right," said Jesus, "in saying that you have no husband, for, although you have had five husbands, the man with whom you are now living is not your husband; you told me the truth there." "Sir," she replied, "I can see that you are a prophet. Our fathers worshiped on this mountain, but you Jews say that the temple where God should be worshiped is in Jerusalem." "Believe me," said Jesus, "the time is coming when you will worship the Father neither on this mountain nor in Jerusalem. You Samaritans worship without knowing what you worship, while we worship what we know. It is from the Jews that salvation comes. But the time approaches, indeed it is already here, when those who are real worshipers will worship the Father in spirit and in truth. Such are the worshipers whom the Father wants. God is spirit, and those who worship Him must worship in spirit and truth." The woman answered, "I know that Messiah—that is, Christ—is coming. When he comes he will tell us everything." Jesus said, "I am he, I who am speaking to you now." (John 4:1–26)

18. Peter's Confession of Jesus' Messiahship

Jesus' self-confession of his Messiahship in Samaria had its sequel in another, equally dramatic event.

When he came to the territory of Caesarea Philippi, Jesus asked his disciples, "Who do men say that the Son of Man is?" They answer, "Some say John the Baptist, others Elijah, others Jeremiah, or one of the prophets." "And you," he asked, "who do you say I am?" Simon Peter answered: "You are the Messiah, the Son of the Living God." Then Jesus said, "Simon, son of Jonah, you are favored indeed! You did not learn that from mortal man; it was revealed to you by my heavenly Father. And I say this to you: You are Peter, the Rock; and on this rock I will build my church and the powers of death will never conquer it. I will give you the keys of the kingdom of Heaven; what you forbid on earth will be forbidden in heaven; and what you allow on earth will be allowed in heaven." He then gave his disciples strict orders not to tell anyone that he was the Messiah. (Matthew 16:13–21)

19. The Last Days of Jesus

They were on the road, going up to Jerusalem, Jesus leading the way; and the disciples were filled with awe, while those who followed behind were afraid. He took the Twelve aside and began to tell them what was to happen to him. "We are now going to Jerusalem," he said, "and the Son of Man will be given up to the chief priests and the doctors of the Law. They will condemn him to death and hand him over to the foreign power. He will be mocked and spat upon, flogged and killed; and three days afterwards he will rise again." (Mark 10:32–34)

So begins Jesus' final visit to Jerusalem. Although he had been to the Holy City on occasion—how often or for how long is difficult to say on the Gospel evidence—he had labored during most of his brief career in his native region of Galilee. But as the end that he had anticipated approached sometime about 30 C.E., it would be played out not in the towns around the Sea of Galilee but in the heart and center of Judaism, in Jerusalem, and the Roman prefect Pilate would be one of its chief actors. And with Jesus' final journey to Jerusalem to celebrate the Passover, so moves the focus of the four Gospels that chronicle his ministry and his teaching to that same city.

They were now nearing Jerusalem; and when they reached Bethphage at the Mount of Olives, Jesus sent two disciples with these instructions: "Go to the village opposite, where you will at once find a donkey tethered with her foal beside her; untie them and bring them to me. If anyone speaks to you, say 'Our Master needs them' and he will let you take them at once." This was to fulfill the prophecy which says: "Tell the daughter of Sion, 'Here is your king, who comes to you in gentleness, riding on an ass, riding on the foal of a beast of burden.' "

It is Passover, and Jerusalem is filled with people from the other towns of Judea, from Galilee, and from the entire Diaspora.

The disciples went and did as Jesus had directed, and brought the donkey and her foal; they laid their cloaks on them and Jesus mounted. Crowds of people carpeted the road with their cloaks, and some cut branches from the trees to spread in his path. Then the crowd that went ahead and the others that came behind raised the shout: "Hosanna to the Son of David! Blessings on him who comes in the name of the Lord! Hosanna in the heavens!"

When he entered Jerusalem the whole city went wild with excitement. "Who is this?" people asked, and the crowd replied, "This is the prophet Jesus, from Nazareth in Galilee."

Jesus then went into the Temple and drove out all who were buying and selling in the Temple precincts; he upset the tables of the moneychangers and the seats of the dealers in pigeons; and said to them: "Scripture says, 'My House shall be called a house of prayer,' but you are making it a robbers' cave." (Matthew 21:1–17)

John continues the story.

His disciples recalled the words of Scripture, "Zeal for thy house will destroy me." The Jews challenged Jesus: "What sign," they asked, "can you show us as authority for your action?" "Destroy this Temple," Jesus replied, "and in three days I will raise it again." They said, "It has taken forty-six years to build this Temple. Are you going to raise it again in three days?" But the Temple he was speaking of was his body. After his resurrection his disciples recalled what he had said, and they believed the Scripture and the words that Jesus had spoken. (John 2:17–22)

As he was leaving the Temple, one of his disciples exclaimed, "Look, Master, what huge stones! What fine buildings!" Jesus said to him, "You see these great buildings? Not one stone will be left upon another; all will be thrown down." (Mark 13:1–2)

"O Jerusalem, Jerusalem, Jerusalem, the city that murders the prophets and stones the messengers sent to her! How often have I longed to gather your children, as a hen gathers her brood under her wings; but you would not let me. Look, look! There is your Temple, forsaken by God. And I tell you, you shall never see me until the time when you say 'Blessings on him who comes in the name of the Lord.'" (Matthew 23:37–39)

20. The Plot against Jesus

According to John, the events leading to the arrest and execution of Jesus were set in train somewhat before the last Passover. Jesus was in Bethany, where he had raised Lazarus, the brother of Martha and Mary, from the dead (John 11:1–44).

Now many of the Jews who had come to visit Mary and had seen what Jesus did, put their faith in him. But some of them went off to the Pharisees and reported what he had done. Thereupon the chief priests and the Pharisees convened a meeting of the Council. "What action are we taking?" they said. "This man is performing many signs. If we leave him alone like this the whole populace will believe in him. Then the Romans will come and sweep away our Temple and our nation." But one of them, Caiaphas, who was High Priest that year, said, "You know nothing whatever; you do not use your judgment; it is more to your interest that one man should die for the people than that the whole nation should be destroyed." He did not say this of his own accord, but as the High Priest in office that year, he was prophesying that Jesus would die for the nation—would die not for the nation alone but to gather together the scattered children of God. So from that day on they plotted his death. (John 11: 45–53)

The Jewish Passover was now at hand, and many people went up from the country to Jerusalem to purify themselves before the festival. They looked out for Jesus, and as they stood in the Temple they asked one another, "What do you think? Perhaps he is not coming to the festival." Now the chief priests and the Pharisees had given orders that anyone who knew where he was should give information, so that they might arrest him. [And Mark adds: "It must not be during the Passover," they said, "or we should have rioting among the people."] (John 11:55–57)

21. "I Am in the Father and the Father Is in Me"

On the evening of Thursday, the day for the preparation for Passover (or somewhat earlier, according to John), Jesus gathered with his disciples in an upper room in Jerusalem to celebrate the Passover Seder with them. The meal marked, among other things, the institution of the Eucharist. The Synoptics' account is quite brief, but John includes in his narrative of Jesus' last supper a long and moving discourse to his disciples. It follows immediately upon the departure of Judas, the Apostle who was to betray him.

When he had gone out Jesus said, "Now the Son is glorified, and in him God is glorified. If God is glorified in him, God will also glorify him in Himself; and He will glorify him now. My children, for a little longer I am with you; then you will look for me, and as I told the Jews, so I tell you now, where I am going you cannot come. I give you a new commandment: love one another; as I have loved you, so you are to love one another. If there is this love among you, then all will know you are my disciples. . . .

"Set your troubled hearts at rest. Trust in God always; trust also in me. There are many dwelling places in my Father's house; if it were not so, I should have told you; for I am going there on purpose to prepare a place for you. And if I go and prepare a place for you, I shall come again and receive you to myself, so that where I am you may be also; and my way there is known to you." Thomas said, "Lord, we do not know where you are going, so how can we know the way?" Jesus replied, "I am the way; I am the truth and I am the life; no one comes to the Father except by me.

"If you knew me you would know my Father too. From now on you do know Him; you have seen Him." Philip said to him, "Lord, show us the Father and we ask no more." Jesus answered, "Have I been all this time with you, Philip, and you still do not know me? Anyone who has seen me has seen the Father. Then how can you say 'Show us the Father'? Do you not believe that I am in the Father and the Father is in me? I am not myself the source of the words I speak to you: it is the Father who dwells in me doing His own work. Believe me when I say that I am in the Father and the Father is in me; or else accept the evidence of the deeds themselves. In truth, in very truth I tell you, he who has faith in me will do what I am doing; and he will do greater things still because I am going to the Father. Indeed anything you ask in my name I will do, so that the Father may be gloried in the Son. If you ask anything in my name, I will do it.

"If you love me you will obey my commands; and I will ask the Father and He will give you another to be your Advocate, who will be with you forever, the Spirit of truth. The world cannot receive him, because the world neither sees nor knows him; but you know him because he dwells with you and is in you. I will not leave you bereft; I am coming back to you. In a little while the world will see me no longer, but you will see me; because I live, you too will live; then you will know that I am in my Father, and you in me and I in you. The man who has received my commands and obeys them, he it is who loves me; and he who loves me will be loved by my Father; and I will love him and disclose myself to him. . . .

"Peace is my parting gift to you, my own peace, such as the world cannot give. Set your troubled hearts at rest, and banish your fears. You hear me say 'I am going away, and coming back to you.' If you loved me you would be glad to hear that I was going to the Father, for the Father is greater than I. I have told you now, beforehand, so that when it happens you may have faith." (John 13:31–14:29)

22. "This Is My Commandment . . . "

"I am the real vine, and my Father is the gardener. Every barren branch of mine He cuts away; and every fruiting branch he cleans, to make it more fruitful still. You have already been cleansed by the word I have spoken to you. Dwell in me, as I in you. No branch can bear fruit by itself, but only if it remains united with the vine; no more can you bear fruit unless you remain united with me.

"I am the vine, and you are the branches. He who dwells in me, as I dwell in him, bears much fruit; for apart from me you can do nothing. He who does not dwell in me is thrown away like a withered branch. The withered branches are heaped together, thrown on the fire, and burnt.

"If you dwell in me, and my words dwell in you, ask what you will and you shall have it. This is my Father's glory, that you may bear fruit in plenty and so be my disciples. As the Father has loved me, so I have loved you. Dwell in my love. If you heed my commands, you will dwell in my love, as I have heeded my Father's commands and dwell in His love.

"I have spoken thus to you, so that my joy may be in you, and your joy complete. This is my commandment: love one another as I have loved you. There is no greater love than this, that a man should lay down his life for his friends. You are my friends, if you do what I command you. I call you servants no longer; a servant does not know what his master is about. I have called you friends because I have disclosed to you everything that I heard from my Father. You did not choose me; I chose you; I appointed you to go on and bear fruit, fruit that shall last, so that the Father may give you all that you ask in my name. This is my commandment to you: love one another." (John 15:1–17)

23. "The Victory Is Mine;
I Have Conquered the World"

"Till now I have been using figures of speech; a time is coming when I shall no longer use figures but tell you of the Father in plain words. When that day comes you will make your request in my name, and I do not say that I shall pray to the Father for you, for the Father loves you Himself, because you have loved me and believed that I came from God. I came from the Father and came into the world. Now I am leaving the world again and going to the Father." His disciples said, "Why this is plain speaking; this is no figure of speech. We are certain now that you know everything, and do not need to be questioned; because of this we believe that you have come from God."

Jesus answered, "Do you now believe? Look, the hour is coming, has indeed already come, when you are all to be scattered, each to his home, leaving me alone. Yet I am not alone, because the Father is with me. I have told you all this that you may find peace. In the world you will have trouble. But courage! The victory is mine; I have conquered the world." (John 16:25–33)

24. The Arrest of Jesus

When the meal was finished, Jesus and his disciples left. It was by then late Thursday evening.

After singing the Passover Hymn, they went out to the Mount of Olives. . . . When they reached a place called Gethsemane, he [Jesus] said to his disciples, "Sit here while I pray." And he took Peter and James and John with him. Horror and dismay came over him and he said to them, "My heart is ready to break with grief; stop here and stay awake." Then he went forward a little and threw himself upon the ground, and prayed that, if it were possible, this hour might pass him by. "Abba, Father," he said, "all things are possible to you; take this cup away from me. Yet, not what I will, but You will."

He came back and found them asleep; and he said to Peter, "Asleep, Simon? Were you not able to stay awake for one hour? Stay awake, all of you, and pray that you may be spared the test. The spirit is willing but the flesh is weak." Once more he went away and prayed. On his return he found them asleep again, for their eyes were heavy; and they did not know how to answer him. A third time he came and said to them, "Still sleeping? Still taking your ease? Enough! The hour has come. The Son of Man is betrayed to sinful men. Up, let us go forward! My betrayer is upon us."

Suddenly, while he was still speaking, Judas, one of the Twelve, appeared, and with him a crowd armed with swords and cudgels, sent by the chief priests, lawyers and elders. Now the traitor had agreed with them upon a signal. "The one I kiss is your man; seize him and get him safely away." When he reached the spot, he stepped forward at once and said to Jesus, "Rabbi," and kissed him. Then they seized him and held him fast. One of the party drew his sword and struck at the High Priest's servant, cutting off his ear. Then Jesus spoke. "Do you take me for a bandit, that you have come out with swords and cudgels to arrest me? Day after day I was within your reach as I taught in the Temple, and you did not lay hands on me. But let the Scriptures be fulfilled." Then the disciples all deserted him and ran away.

Among those following was a young man with nothing on but a linen cloth. They tried to seize him; but he slipped out of the linen cloth and ran away naked. (Mark 14:26–52)

25. The Sanhedrin Trial

Jesus was led off under arrest to the house of Caiaphas the High Priest where the lawyers and elders were assembled. . . . The chief priests and the elders tried to find some allegation against Jesus on which a death sentence could be based; but they failed to find one, though many came forward with false evidence. Finally two men alleged that he had said "I can pull down the Temple of God and rebuild it in three days." At this the High Priest rose and said to him, "Have you no answer to the charge that these witnesses bring against you?" But Jesus kept silence. The High Priest then said, "By the living God I charge you to tell us: Are you the Messiah, the Son of God?" Jesus replied, "The words are yours. But I tell you this: from now on, you will see the Son of Man seated at the right hand of God and coming on the clouds of heaven." At these words the High Priest tore his robes and exclaimed, "Blasphemy! Need we call further witnesses? You have heard the blasphemy. What is your opinion?" "He is guilty," they answered; "he should die." Then they spat in his face and struck him with their fists; and others said, "Now, Messiah, if you are a prophet, tell us who hit you." (Matthew 26:30–50)

The meeting at the house of the High Priest may have been a preliminary hearing, at least according to Luke, who puts the formal Sanhedrin trial early on the next day, Friday.

When day broke, the elders of the nation, chief priests and doctors of the Law assembled, and he was brought before their Council. "Tell us," they said, "are you the Messiah?" "If I tell you," he replied, "you will not believe me; and if I ask questions, you will not answer. But from now on the Son of Man will be seated at the right hand of Almighty God." "You are the Son of God, then?" they all said, and he replied, "It is you who say I am." They said, "Need we call further witnesses? We have heard it ourselves from his own lips." (Luke 22:66–71)

The Mishnaic tractate called "Sanhedrin" devotes considerable detail to the procedures to be followed in cases held before that body, though we cannot be certain which, if any of them, were operative in Jesus' own day nearly two centuries earlier.

In non-capital cases they hold the trial during the daytime and the verdict may be reached during the night; in capital cases they hold the trial during the daytime and the verdict also must be reached during the daytime. In non-capital cases the verdict, whether of acquittal or of conviction, may be reached the same day; in capital cases a verdict of acquittal may be reached the same day, but a verdict of conviction not until the following day. Therefore trials may not be held on the eve of the Sabbath or on the eve of a festival day. (M.Sanhedrin 4:1)

And on the charge of blasphemy:

The Lord spoke to Moses and said, Take the man who blasphemed out of the camp. Everyone who heard him shall put a hand on his head, and then all the community shall stone him to death. You shall say to the Israelites: When any man whatever blasphemes his God, he shall accept responsibility for his sin. Whoever utters the name of the Lord shall be put to death: all the community shall stone him; alien or native, if he utters the Name, he shall be put to death. (Leviticus 24:13–16)

The blasphemer is not culpable unless he pronounces the Name itself. Rabbi Joshua ben Karha says: On every day (of the trial) they examined the witnesses with a substituted name, (such as) "May Yosi smite Yosi." When sentence was to be given they did not declare him guilty of death (on the grounds of evidence given) with the substituted name but they sent out all the people and asked the chief among the witnesses and said to him, "Say expressly what you heard," and he says it; and the judges stand up on their feet and rend their garments, and they may not mend them again. And the second witness says, "I also heard the like," and the third says, "I also heard the like." (M.Sanhedrin 7:5)

26. Jesus before Pilate

John's chronology of the events of the arrest and execution of Jesus is somewhat different from that presented by the Synoptics. Here, for example, it is clear that the events were taking place before the Passover Supper; according to the Synoptics, Jesus had taken that meal with his disciples before his arrest.

From Caiaphas Jesus was led into the Governor's headquarters. It was now early morning, and the Jews themselves stayed outside the head-quarters to avoid defilement, so that they could eat the Passover meal. So Pilate went out to them and asked, "What charge do you bring against this man?" "If he were not a criminal," they replied, "we should not have brought him before you." Pilate said, "Take him away and try him by your own law." The Jews answered, "We are not allowed to put any man to death." Thus they ensured the fulfillment of the words by which Jesus indicated the manner of his death. (John 18:28–32)

If the response given in John does not address itself to the specific charges, Luke's narrative does, beginning immediately after the Friday morning trial before the Sanhedrin.

With that the whole assembly [that is, of the Sanhedrin] rose, and they brought him before Pilate. They opened the case against him by saying, "We found this man subverting our nation, opposing the payment of taxes to Caesar and claiming to be Messiah, a king." Pilate asked him, "Are you the king of the Jews?" He replied, "The words are yours." Pilate then turned to the chief priests and the crowd. "I find no case for this man to answer." But they insisted: "His teaching is causing disaffection among the people all through Judea. It started from Galilee and has spread as far as this city."

When Pilate heard this, he asked if the man was a Galilean, and on learning that he belonged to Herod's [Antipas'] jurisdiction, he remitted the case to him. When Herod saw Jesus he was greatly pleased; having heard about him, he had long been wanting to see him and had been hoping to see some miracle performed by him. He questioned him at some length without getting any reply; but the chief priests and lawyers appeared and pressed the case against him vigorously. Then Herod and his troops treated him with contempt and ridicule and sent him back to Pilate dressed in a gorgeous robe. That same day Herod and Pilate became friends; till then there had been a standing feud between them. (Luke 23:1–12)

Pilate, perhaps in an effort to confront the crowd with an unacceptable alternative, offers the release of either Jesus or a notorious criminal called Bar Abbas, "who had committed murder in the recent uprising" (Mark 15:7), possibly the one mentioned in Luke 13:1–2.

At the festival season it was the Governor's custom to release one prisoner chosen by the people. There was then in custody a man of some notoriety, called Jesus Bar Abbas. When they were assembled, Pilate said to them, "Which would you like me to release to you—Jesus Bar Abbas, or Jesus called the Messiah?" For he knew that it was out of malice that they had brought Jesus before him.

While Pilate was sitting in court a message came to him from his wife: "Have nothing to do with this innocent man; I was much troubled on his account in my dreams last night."

Meanwhile the chief priests and elders had persuaded the crowd to ask for the release of Bar Abbas and to have Jesus put to death. So when the Governor asked, "Which of the two do you wish me to release to you?" they said, "Bar Abbas." "Then what am I to do with Jesus who is called Messiah?" asked Pilate; and with one voice they answered, "Crucify him!" "Why, what harm has he done?" Pilate asked; but they shouted all the louder, "Crucify him!"

Pilate could see that nothing was being gained and a riot was start-ing; so he took water and washed his hands in the full view of the people, saying, "My hands are clean of this man's blood; see to that yourselves." And with one voice the people cried, "His blood be upon us and upon our children." He then released Bar Abbas to them; but he had Jesus flogged and handed over to be crucified. Pilate's soldiers then took Jesus into the governor's headquarters, where they collected the whole company round him. They stripped him and dressed him in a scarlet mantle; and plaiting a crown of thorns they placed it on his head, with a cane in his right hand. Falling on their knees before him they jeered at him: "Hail, King of the Jews!" They spat on him, and used the cane to beat him about the head. When they had finished their mockery, they took off the mantle and dressed him in his own clothes. (Matthew 27:24–31)

Once more Pilate came out and said to the Jews, "Here he is; I am bringing him out to let you know that I find no case against him"; and Jesus came out, wearing the crown of thorns and the purple cloak. "Be-hold the man!" said Pilate. The chief priests and their henchmen saw him and shouted, "Crucify him! Crucify him!" "Take him and crucify him yourselves," said Pilate; "for my part, I find no no case against him." The Jews answered, "We have a law, and by that law he ought to die because he has claimed to be the Son of God."

When Pilate heard that, he was more afraid than ever, and going back into his headquarters, he asked Jesus, "Where have you come from?" But Jesus gave him no answer. "Do you refuse to speak to me?" said Pilate. "Surely you know that I have authority to release you, and I have authority to crucify you?" "You would have no authority at all over me," Jesus replied, "if it had not been granted to you from above; and therefore the deeper guilt lies with the man who handed me over to you." From that moment Pilate tried to release him; but the Jews kept shouting, "If you let this man go, you are no friend to Caesar; any man who claims to be king is defying Caesar." When Pilate heard what they were saying, he brought Jesus out and took his seat on the tribunal at the place known as "The Pavement"—"Gabbatha" in the language of the Jews. It was the eve of Passover, about noon. Pilate said to the Jews, "Here is your king." They shouted, "Away with him! Crucify him!" "Crucify your king?" said Pilate. "We have no king but Caesar," the Jews replied. Then at last, to satisfy them, he handed Jesus over to be crucified. (John 19:4–16)

27. The Crucifixion

Jesus was now taken in charge and carrying his own cross, went out to the Place of the Skull, as it is called—or, in the Jews' language "Golgotha"—where they crucified him, and with him two others ["bandits," Mark calls them], one on the right, one on the left, and Jesus between them. And Pilate wrote an inscription to be fastened on the cross; it read, "Jesus of Nazareth, King of the Jews." This inscription was read by many Jews, because the place where Jesus was crucified was not far from the city, and the inscription was in Hebrew, Latin and Greek. . . . The soldiers, having crucified Jesus, took possession of his clothes, and divided them into four parts, one for each soldier, leaving out the tunic. (John 19:17–23)

The passersby hurled abuse at him: they wagged their heads and cried, "You would pull the Temple down, would you, and build it in three days? Come down from the cross and save yourself, if you are indeed the Son of God." So too the chief priests with the lawyers and elders mocked at him. "He saved others," they said, "but he cannot save himself. King of Israel indeed! Let him come down now from the cross, and then we will believe him. Did he trust in God? Let God rescue him, if he wants him—for he said he was God's Son." Even the bandits who were crucified with him taunted him in the same way.

From midday a darkness fell over the whole land, which lasted until three in the afternoon; and about three Jesus cried aloud *"Eli, Eli, lema sabachthani?"* which means "My God, my God, why hast thou forsaken me?" Some of the bystanders, on hearing this, said, "He is calling Elijah." One of the soldiers then ran at once and fetched a sponge, which he soaked in sour wine, and held it to his lips at the end of a cane. But the others said, "Let us see if Elijah will come to save him." Jesus again gave a loud cry and breathed his last. At that moment the curtain of the Temple was torn in two from top to bottom. There was an earthquake, the rocks split and the graves opened, and many of God's saints were raised from sleep; and coming out of their graves after his resurrection they entered the Holy City where many saw them. (Matthew 27:39–53)

Because it was the eve of Passover, the Jews were anxious that the bodies should not remain on the cross for the coming Sabbath, since that Sabbath was a day of great solemnity. So they requested Pilate to have the legs broken and the bodies taken down. The soldiers accordingly came to the first of his fellow victims and to the second, and they broke their legs.

But when they came to Jesus they found that he was already dead, so they did not break his legs. But one of the soldiers stabbed his side with a lance, and at once there was a flow of blood and water. (John 19:31–34)

28. Josephus on Jesus

The Jewish Antiquities *of the Jewish historian Flavius Josephus, who wrote after the destruction of Jerusalem in 70 C.E., cover most of the events that took place in Palestine during the lifetime of Jesus. In the Greek manuscripts of that work there occurs in Book 17 a passage concerning Jesus.*

About this time there lived Jesus, a wise man, if indeed one ought to call him a man. For he was one who wrought surprising feats and was a teacher of such people as accept the truth gladly. He won over many Jews and many of the Greeks. He was the Messiah. When Pilate, upon hearing him accused by men of the highest standing among us, had condemned him to be crucified, those who had in the first place come to love him did not cease. On the third day he appeared to them restored to life. For the prophets of God had prophesied these and many other marvelous things about him. And the tribe of the Christians, so called after him, has still up to now not disappeared. (Josephus, *Antiquities* 17.3.3)

This celebrated passage, with its open acknowledgment of Jesus' Messiahship and its not very subtle Christian coloring throughout, has long provoked suspicion that either a complete forgery or a series of interpolations had taken place. The latter is not an unlikely possibility, particularly in the light of such latter-day versions as the following, found in a tenth-century Arab Christian historian, Agapius of Manbij, who is patently quoting from the Antiquities *and may have had before him the authentic text of Josephus. It was one, at any rate, closer to what we might imagine Josephus and not a Christian author to have written.*

Similarly Josephus the Hebrew. For he says in the treatises that he has written on the governance of the Jews:

"At this time there was a wise man who was called Jesus. And his conduct was good, and (he) was known to be virtuous. And many people from among the Jews and the other nations became his disciples. Pilate condemned him to be crucified and to die. And those who had become his disciples did not desert his discipleship. They reported that he had appeared to them three days after his crucifixion and that he was alive; accordingly, he was perhaps the Messiah concerning whom the prophets have recounted wonders." (Agapius, *Kitab al-ʿUnwan*, 239–240)

[PINES 1971: 16]

29. The Rabbis on the Life and Death of Jesus

The life and death of Jesus of Nazareth did not pass completely unnoticed in the rabbinic writings, though the references are generally oblique and were for the most part excised from later editions of the Talmuds and related texts. The following remarks on Ben Stada or Ben Pandera, elsewhere identified as "Jeshua ben Pandera," are not atypical of the kinds of passages that have been identified, not without argument, as references to Jesus.

"He who cuts upon his flesh." It is a tradition that Rabbi Eliezer said to the Wise, "Did not Ben Stada bring spells from Egypt in a cut which was upon his flesh?" They said to him, "He was a fool and they do not bring a proof from a fool." Ben Stada is Ben Pandera. Rab Hisda said, "The husband was Stada, the paramour was Pandera." The husband was Pappos ben Yehudah, the mother was Stada. The mother was Miriam, the dresser of women's hair, as they say in Pumbeditha, "Such a one has been false to her husband." (BT.Sanhedrin 67a)

These allusions, particularly as they refer to the death of Jesus, most often occur in the context of the Mishnaic treatise "Sanhedrin," which is concerned with that tribunal's jurisdiction and procedures in capital cases.

In regard to all who are worthy of death according to the Torah, they do not use concealment against them, except in the case of the deceiver. How do they deal with him? They put two disciples of the wise in the inner chamber and he sits in the outer chamber, and they light the lamp so that they shall see him and hear his voice. And thus they did to Ben Stada in Lydda; two disciples of the wise were chosen for him, and they brought him to the Beth Din and stoned him. [Or, as in B.Sanhedrin 67b, "they hung him on the eve of Passover."] (Tosefta Sanhedrin 10:11)

And it was taught: On the eve of the Passover Jeshua [the Nazarene] was hanged. For forty days before the execution took place a herald went forth and cried, "He is going forth to be stoned because he has practiced sorcery and enticed Israel to apostasy. Anyone who can say anything in his favor, let him come and plead on his behalf." And since nothing was brought forward in his favor, he was hanged on the eve of Passover. Ulla retorted, "Do you suppose that he was one for whom a defense could be made? Was he not an enticer, concerning whom Scripture says, 'Neither shall you spare, neither shall thou conceal him' (Deut. 13:9). With Jeshua however it was different, for he was connected with the government [or royalty—that is, influential]." (BT.Sanhedrin 43a)

The following comment, attributed to the second-century Rabbi Meir, may also, despite the lack of names, refer to Jesus' crucifixion.

Rabbi Meir used to say, What is the meaning of "For a curse of God is he that is hung" (Deut. 21:23)? [It is like the case of] two brothers, twins, who resembled each other. One ruled over the whole world, the other took to robbery. After a time the one who took to robbery was caught, and they crucified him on a cross. And everyone who passed to and fro said, "It seems that the king is crucified." Therefore it is said "A curse of God is he that is hung." (Tosefta Sanhedrin 9:7)

30. The Quranic Account of the Crucifixion

For Muslims, who regard Jesus as one of the greatest of the prophets, the alleged crucifixion did not occur—not, at any rate, with Jesus as the victim.

And (the Jews were punished) because they said: "We killed the Christ, Jesus son of Mary, who was an apostle of God"; but they neither killed him nor crucified him, though it so appeared to them. Those who disagree in the matter are only lost in doubt. They have no knowledge of it other than conjecture, for surely they did not kill him. (Quran 4:157–158)

The classical Muslim exegetical tradition on the Quran's account of the alleged crucifixion of Jesus is represented by al-Baydawi (d. 1286 C.E.), and it illustrates the somewhat uncertain attempts to explain what actually occurred in Jerusalem during that Passover in 30 C.E.

There is a story that a group of Jews insulted Jesus and his mother, whereupon he appealed to God against them. When God transformed those (who had insulted them) into monkeys and swine, the Jews took counsel to kill Jesus. Then God told Jesus that He would raise him up to heaven, and so Jesus said to his disciples: "Who among you will agree to take a form similar to mine and die (in my place) and be crucified and then go (straight) to paradise?" A man among them offered himself, so God changed him into a form resembling Jesus', and he was killed and crucified.

Others say that a man pretended (to be a believer) in Jesus' presence but then went off and denounced him, whereupon God changed the man into form similar to that of Jesus, and then he was seized and crucified. (Baydawi, *Commentary*, ad loc.)

The thesis was not a Muslim innovation. It had been put forward by the Christian Gnostic Valentinus sometime about 140 C.E.

So Jesus did not suffer (on the cross), but a certain Simon of Cyrene was constrained to bear his cross for him, and it was Simon who was crucified in ignorance and error, since he had been transformed by Jesus to look like himself, so that people thought he was Jesus, while Jesus took on the appearance of Simon and stood by and mocked them. (Ireneus, *Against the Heresies* 1:24.4)

31. The Burial

We return to the Gospel accounts of the events immediately following Jesus' execution.

After that Pilate was approached by Joseph of Arimathea, a disciple of Jesus, but a secret disciple for fear of the Jews, who asked to be allowed to remove the body of Jesus. Pilate gave the permission so Joseph came and took the body away. He was joined by Nicodemus, the man who had first visited Jesus by night, who brought with him a mixture of myrrh and aloes, more than half a hundredweight. They took the body of Jesus and wrapped it, with the spices, in strips of linen cloth according to Jewish burial customs. Now at the place where he had been crucified there was a garden, and in the garden a new tomb, not yet used for burial. There, because the tomb was near at hand and it was the eve of the Jewish Sabbath, they laid Jesus. (John 19:38–42)

So Joseph bought a linen sheet, took him down from the cross and wrapped him in the sheet. Then he laid him in a tomb cut out of the rock, and rolled a stone against the entrance. And Mary of Magdala and Mary the mother of Joseph were watching and saw where he was laid. (Mark 15:46–47)

32. The Resurrection

The account of the Resurrection, or rather, the testimony that the Resurrection had occurred, is quite brief in all four of the Gospels.

When the Sabbath was over, Mary of Magdala, Mary the mother of James, and Salome brought aromatic oils intending to go and anoint him; and very early on the Sunday morning, just after sunrise, they came to the tomb. They were wondering among themselves who would roll away the stone for them from the entrance of the tomb, when they looked up and saw that the stone, huge as it was, had been rolled back already. They went into the tomb, where they saw a youth sitting on the right-hand side, wearing a white robe; and they were dumbfounded. But he said to them, "Fear nothing; you are looking for Jesus of Nazareth, who was crucified. He has been raised again; he is not here; look, there is the place where they laid him. But go and give this message to his disciples and Peter: 'He is going before you into Galilee; there you will see him, as he told you.'" Then they went and ran away from the tomb, beside themselves with terror. They said nothing to anybody, for they were afraid.

When he had risen from the dead early on Sunday morning he appeared first to Mary of Magdala, from whom he had formerly cast out seven devils. She went and carried the news to his mourning and sorrowful followers, but when they were told that he was alive and that she had seen him, they did not believe it. (Mark 16:1–11)

Matthew is somewhat more circumstantial.

Next day, the morning after that same Friday, the chief priests and the Pharisees came in a body to Pilate: "Your excellency," they said, "we recall how that imposter said while he was still alive, 'I am to be raised again after three days.' So will you give orders for the grave to be made secure until the third day? Otherwise his disciples may come, steal the body, and then tell the people that he has been raised from the dead; and the final deception will be worse than the first." "You may have your guard," said Pilate; "go and make it secure as best you can." So they went and made the grave secure; they sealed the stone and left the guard in charge.

The Sabbath was over, and it was about daybreak on Sunday, when Mary of Magdala and the other Mary came to look at the grave. Suddenly there was a violent earthquake; an angel of the Lord descended from heaven; he came to the stone and rolled it away, and sat himself down on it. His face shone like lightning; his garments were white as snow. At the sight of him the guards shook with fear and lay like the dead.

The angel then addressed the women: "You," he said, "have nothing to fear. I know you are looking for Jesus, who was crucified. He is not here; he has been raised again, as he said he would be. Come and see the place where he was laid, and then go quickly and tell his disciples: 'He has been raised from the dead and is going before you into Galilee; there you will see him.' That is what I had to tell you."

They hurried away from the tomb in awe and great joy, and ran to tell his disciples. Suddenly Jesus was there in their path. He gave them his greeting, and they came up and clasped his feet, falling prostrate before him. Then Jesus said to them, "Do not be afraid. Go and take word to my brothers that they are to leave for Galilee. They will see me there."

The women had started on their way when some of the guard went into the city and reported to the chief priests everything that had happened. After meeting with the elders and conferring together, the chief priests offered the soldiers a substantial bribe and told them to say, "His disciples came by night and stole his body, while we were asleep." They added, "If this should reach the Governor's ears, we will put matters right with him and see that you do not suffer." So they took the money and did as they were told. This story became widely known, and is current in Jewish circles to this day. (Matthew 27:62–28:15)

33. The Ascension

Luke begins his Acts of the Apostles by referring his patron, a certain Theophilus, back to his earlier work, the Gospel!

In the first part of my work, Theophilus, I wrote all that Jesus did and taught from the beginning until the day when, after giving instructions through the Holy Spirit to the apostles whom he had chosen, he was taken up to heaven. He showed himself to these men after his death and gave ample proof that he was alive: over a period of forty days he appeared to them and taught them about the kingdom of God. While he was in their company he told them not to leave Jerusalem. "You must wait," he said, "for the promise made by my Father, about which you have heard me speak: John, as you know, baptized with water, but you will be baptized with the Holy Spirit, and within the next few days.

". . . You will bear witness for me in Jerusalem, and all of Judea and Samaria, and away to the ends of the earth." When he had said this, as they watched, he was lifted up, and a cloud removed him from their sight. . . . Then they returned to Jerusalem from the hill called Olivet, which is near Jerusalem, no farther than a Sabbath day's journey. Entering the city they went to the room upstairs where they were lodging: Peter and John and James and Andrew, Philip and Thomas, Bartholomew and Matthew, James son of Alpheus and Simon the Zealot and Judas son of James. All these were constantly at prayer together, and with them a group of women, including Mary the mother of Jesus, and his brothers. (Acts 1:1–14)

34. Peter on Jesus as the Messiah

Almost immediately after the Ascension, the Apostles took to the streets of Jerusalem and began to announce that the recently executed Jesus of Nazareth was risen from the dead and was indeed the Messiah. The Acts of the Apostles has preserved an early version of that message as preached by Peter to his fellow Jews in Jerusalem.

The God of Abraham, Isaac and Jacob, the God of our fathers, has given the highest honor to his servant Jesus, whom you committed to trial and repudiated in Pilate's court—repudiated the one who was holy and righteous when Pilate had decided to release him. You begged as a favor the release of a murderer, and killed him who had led the way to life. But God raised him from the dead; of that we are witnesses. . . .

And now, my friends, I know quite well that you acted in ignorance, and so did your rulers; but this is how God fulfilled what he had foretold in the utterances of the prophets: that his Messiah should suffer. Repent then and turn to God, so that your sins may be wiped out. Then the Lord may grant you a time of recovery and send you the Messiah that he has already appointed, that is, Jesus. He must be received into heaven until the time of universal restoration comes, of which God spoke by his holy prophets. Moses said, "The Lord God will raise a prophet for you from among yourselves as he raised me; you shall listen to everything he says to you, and anyone who refuses to listen to that prophet must be extirpated from Israel" (Deut. 18:15–19). And so said all the prophets, from Samuel onwards; with one voice they all predicted this present time.

You are the heirs of the prophets: you are within the Covenant which God made with your fathers, when he said to Abraham, "And in your offspring all the families on earth shall find blessing." When God raised up his Servant, he sent him to you first, to bring you blessings by turning every one of you from your wicked ways. (Acts 3:13–26)

35. Jesus Explained to the Pagans

Peter spoke to believing Jews familiar with the general tenor of their own Scriptures and willing at least to entertain the notion that Jesus was the fulfillment of the promises made in those Scriptures. Among a pagan audience the matter was quite different, as Paul discovered when he reached Athens. The time is in the fifties of the first century C.E.

Now while Paul was waiting for them [that is, his traveling companions] at Athens, he was exasperated to see how the city was filled with idols. So he argued in the synagogue with the Jews and Gentile worshipers, and also in the city square every day with the casual passersby. And some of the Epicurean and Stoic philosophers joined issue with him. Some said, "What can this charlatan be trying to say?"; others, "He would appear to be a propagandist for foreign deities"—this because he was preaching about Jesus and Resurrection. So they took him and brought him before the Court of the Areopagus and said, "May we know what this new doctrine is that you propound? You are introducing ideas that sound strange to us, and we should like to know what they mean." Now the Athenians in general and the foreigners there had no time for anything but talking or hearing about the latest novelty.

Then Paul stood up before the Court of the Areopagus and said: "Men of Athens, I see that in everything that concerns religion you are uncommonly scrupulous. For as I was going round looking at the objects of your worship, I noticed among other things an altar bearing the inscription 'To an Unknown God.' What you worship and do not know, that is what I now proclaim. The God who created the world and everything in it, and who is Lord of heaven and earth, does not live in shrines made by men. It is not because He lacks anything that He accepts service at men's hands, for He is Himself the universal giver of life and breath and all else. He created every race of men of one stock, to inhabit the whole earth's surface. He fixed the epochs of their history and the limits of their territory. They were to seek God and, it might be, touch and find Him; though indeed He is not far from each one of us, for in Him we live and move, in Him we exist; as some of your own poets have said, 'We are also His offspring.' As God's offspring, then, we ought not to suppose that the deity is like an image in gold or silver or stone, shaped by human craftsmanship and design. As for the times of ignorance, God has overlooked them; but now He commands mankind, all men everywhere, to repent, because He has fixed the day on which He will have the world judged, by a man of His own choosing; of this He has given assurance to all by raising him from the dead."

When they heard about the raising of the dead, some scoffed; and others said, "We will hear you on this subject some other time." And so Paul left the assembly. (Acts 17:16–33)

Paul's was a public speech, delivered under the limitations of time and place by a man not notoriously patient of such limitations. The same case was made to the pagans from a somewhat different angle by the converted philosopher Justin in the more expansive context of a literary Apologia *addressed to the Roman emperor. The date is now about a century after Paul stood before the Athenians.*

There were among the Jews certain men who were prophets of God, through whom the prophetic spirit published beforehand things that were to come to pass before they happened. And their prophecies, as they were spoken and when they were uttered, the kings who were among the Jews at those times carefully preserved in their possession, after they had been arranged by the prophets themselves in their own Hebrew language. . . . They are also in the possession of all Jews throughout the world. . . . In these books of the prophets we found the coming of Jesus our Christ foretold, born of a virgin, growing up to manhood, and healing every disease and every sickness, and raising the dead, and being hated and unrecognized and crucified, and dying, and rising again and ascending into heaven, and both being in fact and called the Son of God, and that certain persons should be sent by him to every race of men to publish these things, and that rather among the Gentiles (than among the Jews) men would believe in him. And he was predicted before he appeared, first 5,000 years before, and again 3,000, then 2,000, then 1,000, and yet again 800; for according to the succession of generations prophets after prophets arose.

Though we have many other prophecies, we say nothing of them, judging these sufficient for the persuasion of those who have ears capable of hearing and understanding; and considering also that that these persons are able to see that we do not make assertions for which we are incapable of bringing forth proof, like those fables that are told of the reputed sons of Zeus. For why should we believe of a crucified man that he is the firstborn of the Unbegotten God and himself will pass judgment on the whole human race unless we found testimonies concerning him published before he came and was born as a man and unless we saw that things had happened exactly so? (Justin, *Apology* 1.31.53)

36. Jesus, Messiah of Israel?

That some Jews, perhaps many, accepted the Messianic claims made by Jesus and then by his followers on his behalf is manifest from the spread of his community first in Palestine and then through the Diaspora synagogues where those claims were preached and argued. That many more Jews did not accept them is equally clear from the rift that developed between the Jewish community at large and the "Chris-

tians," as they came to be called, who had sprung from its midst. And although a Jewish polemicist might derisively dismiss the Christians' developing theology of Jesus as the Son of God, the case that Jesus of Nazareth was in fact the Messiah promised to and long awaited by the Children of Israel was made out of the Jewish Scriptures themselves and so had to be treated more carefully. The Jewish response to the Messianic claims on behalf of Jesus of Nazareth can be gauged from these much later remarks by the medieval Jewish scholar Maimonides.

But if he (who claims to be the Messiah) does not meet with success, or is slain, it is obvious that he is not the Messiah promised in the Torah. He is to be regarded like all the other wholehearted and worthy kings of the house of David who died and whom the Holy One, blessed be He, raised up to test the multitude, as it is written, "And some of them that are wise shall stumble, to refine among them, and to purify, and to make white, even to the end of the end; for it is yet for the time appointed" (Dan. 11:35).

Even of Jesus of Nazareth, who imagined that he was the Messiah and who was put to death by the court, Daniel had prophesied, as it is written, "And the children of the violent among your people shall lift themselves up to establish the vision, but they shall stumble" (Dan. 11:14). For has there ever been a greater stumbling than this? All the prophets affirmed that the Messiah would redeem Israel, save them, gather their dispersed, and confirm the commandments. But he caused Israel to be destroyed by the sword, their remnant to be dispersed and humiliated. He was instrumental in changing the Torah and causing the world to err and serve another besides God. (Maimonides, *Mishneh Torah* 14.11) [MAIMONIDES 1965]

Maimonides could also be more direct, and more polemical, as in his Letter to the Yemen.

There arose a new sect which combined the two previously mentioned methods (of foiling the will of God), namely, conquest and polemic, into one, because it believed that this procedure would be the more effective in removing every trace of the Jewish nation and its religion. And so it determined to make its own claim to prophecy and to found a new faith, contrary to our divine religion, and to contend that it too was God-given. It hoped by this to sow doubts and confusion, since one (religion) is opposed to the other, and yet both supposedly emanate from a divine source, which would lead to the destruction of both religions. Such is the remarkable plan contrived by a man who is both envious and dangerous. He will attempt to kill his enemy and to save his own life, but when he finds it impossible to attain both objectives, he will contrive a plan that will kill them both.

The first to have adopted this sort of plan was Jesus the Nazarene, may his bones be ground to dust! He was a Jew by reason of the fact that his mother was a Jewess, even though his father was a Gentile. For in accordance with the principle of our law, a child born of a Jewess and a Gentile, or a Jewess and a slave, is legitimate. And so it is only figuratively that Jesus is called illegitimate. He constrained people to believe he was a prophet sent by God to clarify problems in the Torah, and that he was the Messiah who had been predicted by every seer. He interpreted the Torah and its precepts in such a fashion as to lead to their total annulment, to the abolition of all its commandments and to violation of its prohibitions. The sages, of blessed memory, since they become aware of his plans before his reputation spread among our people, meted out to him an appropriate punishment.

Daniel had already referred to him [that is, Jesus] when he predicted the downfall of a wicked and heretic man among the Jews who would seek to destroy the Law, claim prophecy for himself, pretend to work miracles and claim that he is the Messiah, as it is written, "Also the children of the impudent among your people shall make bold to claim prophecy, but they shall fall" (Dan. 11:14). (Maimonides, *Letter to the Yemen*)

37. A Muslim Has Some Arithmetic Problems

We have seen in Chapter 2 above that the Muslim scientist Biruni (d. 1048 C.E.) had difficulties with the Jews' calculations on the date of their expected Messiah. He has no fewer with the Christians' arithmetic.

These are the doubts and difficulties which beset the assertions of the Jews. Those, however, which attach to the schemes of the Christians are even more numerous and conspicuous. For even if the Jews granted to them that the coming of the Messiah would take place seventy "weeks of years" (Dan. 9:24) after the vision of Daniel, we must remark that the appearance of Jesus the son of Mary did not take place at that time. The reason is this: The Jews agree to fix the interval between the exodus of the Israelites from Egypt and the era of Alexander at 1,000 complete years. From passages in the books of the Prophets they have inferred that the interval between the exodus from Egypt and the building of Jerusalem is 480 years; and the interval between the building and the destruction by

Nebuchadnezzar 410 years, and that it remained in a ruined state for 70 years. Now this gives the sum of 960 years (after the exodus) as the date for the vision of Daniel, and as a remainder of the above-mentioned millennium, 40 years. Further, Jews and Christians unanimously suppose that the birth of Jesus son of Mary took place in the year 304 of the era of Alexander. Therefore, if we use their own chronology, the birth of Jesus the son of Mary took place 344 years after the vision of Daniel and the rebuilding of Jerusalem, that is, about 49 "weeks of years." From his birth till the time when he began preaching are four and a half more. Hence it is evident that the birth of Jesus precedes the date which they have assumed (as the time of the birth of the Messiah). (Al-Biruni, *Traces of the Past*) [BIRUNI 1879: 21]

38. A Jewish Reflection on the Christians' Role in History

In the same passage of the Mishneh Torah *where he addressed Jesus' Messianic claims, Maimonides turned briefly to the larger question of God's purpose in permitting the spread of such claims.*

But it is beyond the human mind to fathom the designs of the Creator, for our ways are not His ways, neither are our thoughts His thoughts. All these matters relating to Jesus of Nazareth and the Ishmaelite (that is, Muhammad) who came after him, only served to clear the way for King Messiah, to prepare the whole world to worship God with one accord, as it is written, "For then will I turn to the peoples a pure language, that they may call upon the name of the Lord to serve Him with one consent" (Zeph. 3:9). Thus the Messianic hope, the Torah, and the commandments have become familiar topics, topics of conversation (among the inhabitants) of the far isles and many peoples, uncircumcised of heart and flesh. They are discussing these matters and the commandments of the Torah. Some say, "These commandments were true, but have lost their validity and are no longer binding"; others declare that they had an esoteric meaning and were not intended to be taken literally; that the Messiah has already come and revealed their their occult significance. But when the true King Messiah will appear and succeed, be exalted and lifted up, they will forthwith recant and realize that they have inherited naught but lies from their fathers, that their prophets and forebears have led them astray. (Maimonides, *Mishneh Torah* 14.11)

39. John on Jesus as the Word of God

The case for and against Jesus as the Messiah of Israel was one argued by and for Jews. But the claims by and about Jesus did not end there, as the opening verses of the Gospel of John reveal.

When all things began, the Word already was. The Word dwelt with God, and what God was, the Word was. The Word, then, was with God at the beginning, and through him all things came to be; no single thing was created without him. All that came to be was alive with his life, and that life was the light on men. The light shines on in the dark, and the darkness has never mastered it.

There appeared a man named John, sent from God; he came as a witness, to testify to the light, that all might become believers through him. He was not himself the light; he came to bear witness to the light. The real light which enlightens every man was even then coming into the world.

He was in the world; but the world, though it owed its being to him, did not recognize him. He entered his own realm, and his own did not receive him. But to all who did receive him, to those who have yielded him their allegiance, he gave the right to become children of God, not born of any human stock, or by the fleshly desire of an earthly father, but the offspring of God Himself. So the Word became flesh; he came to dwell among us, and we saw his glory, such glory as befits the Father's only Son, full of grace and truth. (John 1:1–14)

40. A Muslim Interpretation of John

Although there were other differences among the three religions, this assertion of the divinity of Jesus in the opening lines of John's Gospel appeared to Jews and Muslims to repudiate the monotheism that stood at the very heart of the faith of Abraham. The Jew would reject the claim simply: there was no need to deal with the Gospel as such. The Muslim's task, on the other hand, was exegetical: to defend the Gospel, which was authentic revelation, but refute the Christians' understanding of it as a proclamation of Jesus' divinity. The task was taken up by the Muslim theologian al-Ghazali (d. 1111 C.E.), onetime professor of Islamic law in Baghdad.

We now turn to a final point and shall examine one of the critical points upon which Christians rely to prove the Divinity of Jesus, upon whom be peace, the opening verses of John's Gospel: "In the beginning was the Word" and so on and so forth, to the end of the passage: "And the Word was made flesh and dwelt among us, and we beheld his glory."

Ghazali's approach to this text is to demonstrate that the expression "the Word," which the Christians apply to Jesus throughout the passage, applies rather to God understood with the attributes of knowledge or speech. This Ghazali can do with relative ease in the opening verses of John. What must then be navigated, however, is the closing formula of the passage: "And the Word was made flesh." Here Ghazali resorts to allegorical interpretation.

The "Word" in their system stands for the essence regarded as an attribute of knowledge or speech. . . . It therefore indicates the essence qualified by knowledge or speech. This usage is by no means peculiar to God; a dubious expression, however confused it may be, may quite properly and accurately be used to denote each particular thing to which it is applied. So "the Word" can be employed to connote the essence as defined by knowledge or speech, without any implication of the essence having the attribute of corporeality or being dissociated from that attribute. Consequently, at the beginning of the passage the expression "the Word" is applied to the knower as dissociated from corporeality in fact, that is, to God; while at the end of this passage the same term is also applied to the knower or the speaker as possessing the attribute of corporeality in fact, that is to say, to God's Messenger. Therefore the phrase "and the Word became flesh" means that the God-Knower had previously been called "the Word" in a manner dissociated from corporeality, but now that same term was being applied to a knower possessing the attribute of corporeality, to wit, the Messenger. . . .

. . . It is established that it is the Truth, glorious be His Name, who lightens with His Light "every man who comes" and unveils for him every secret; that much is clearly stated in this text: "to bear witness of the Light. That was the true Light that lights every man." The phrase "He was in the world" may well qualify "the Light," and also the Truth, glorious is His name; for Almighty God's guidance, His making clear every secret and His unveiling every ambiguity—that has never ceased to dwell in the world. The words "and the world was made by him" qualify the Truth, blessed be His Name; that has been explicitly stated at the beginning of the chapter: "All things were made by Him."

I should like to know what grounds there are for taking this to refer to Jesus, upon whom be peace, in the face of the clear statement occurring at the beginning of the chapter, describing God: "and without Him was not anything made that was made." The words "he came to his own" mean "to the Truth's own appeared His Light, to wit, His guidance and direction; since it is by His Light that every man is guided to follow the right path. . . ."

"To them He gave the power to become sons of God": it would have been more natural to say "to become His sons," only the writer avoided that, preferring the explicit mention of the revered Name God, because of the noble relationship, in order to make a deeper impression on the souls of his readers. After that he said: "even to them that believe in His name, who were born, not of blood, nor of the will of the flesh, nor of the will of man, but of God," meaning that this sonship by virtue of which they obtained that noble relationship was not of the order of those sonships which are apt to result from the wills of men and their attention to women, with the resultant formation of flesh and blood, but rather the meaning is that the extreme nearness and compassion of God towards them. Finally, the writer connects up again with the beginning of the chapter, making it clear that it is a property of the Word, from which the idea of the Knower is derived, to be applied, whether that Knower is dissociated from corporeality, such as the Essence of the Creator, or not dissociated, as with the essence of the Messenger. (Ghazali, *The Elegant Refutation*) [ARBERRY 1964: 300–306]

41. Paul on Jesus as the Image and the Son of God

Thus Ghazali was at some pains to separate the Father, who created all, from the "son," Jesus, who is His messenger. Christians felt no such constraint, of course, and Paul and the author of Hebrews were eager to explain all the nuances of the relationship between the Father and His only begotten Son.

He rescued us from the domain of the darkness and brought us away into the kingdom of his dear Son, in whom our release is secured and our sins forgiven. He is the image of the invisible God; his is the primacy over all created things. In him everything in heaven and on earth was created, not only things visible but also the invisible order of thrones, sovereignties, authorities and powers; the whole universe has been created through him and for him. And he exists before everything and all things are held together in him. He is, moreover, the head of the body, the Church. He is its origin, the first to return from the dead, to be in all things alone supreme. For in him the complete being of God, by God's own choice, came to dwell. Through him God chose to reconcile the whole universe to himself, making peace through the shedding of his blood upon the cross—to reconcile all things, whether on earth or in heaven, through him alone. (Paul, *To the Colossians* 1:13–20)

When in former times God spoke to our forefathers, He spoke in fragmentary and varied fashion through the prophets. But in these latter days He has spoken to us in the Son whom He made heir to the whole universe and through whom He created all orders of existence: the Son who is the effulgence of God's splendor and the stamp of God's very being, and sustains the universe by his word of power. When he had brought about the purgation of sins, he took his seat at the right hand of Majesty on high, raised as far above the angels as the title he has inherited is above theirs. For God never said to any angel, "Thou art My Son; this day have I begotten thee," or again, "I will be Father to him and he will be My son" (Ps. 110:1). (Hebrews 1:1–6)

The divine nature was his from the first; but he did not prize his equality with God, but made himself nothing, assuming the nature of a slave. Bearing the human likeness, revealed in human shape, he humbled himself, and in obedience accepted even death—death on a cross. Therefore God raised him to the heights and bestowed on him the name above all names, that at the name of Jesus every knee should bow—in heaven, on earth, and in the depths—and every tongue should confess "Jesus Christ is Lord," to the glory of God the Father. (Paul, *To the Philippians* 2:6–11)

42. The Second Adam

Christians saw the New Covenant foreshadowed on almost every page of the Old. According to Paul, one of the earliest of those biblical prototypes of Jesus was Adam. He uses the comparison to make two different points, one spiritual and one moral.

If there is such a thing as an animal body, there is also a spiritual body. It is in this sense that Scripture says, "The first man, Adam, became an animate man," whereas the last Adam has become a life-giving spirit. Observe, the spiritual does not come first; the animal body comes first, and then the spiritual. The first man was made "of the dust of the earth"; the second man is from heaven. The man made of dust is the pattern of all men of dust, and the heavenly man is the pattern of all the heavenly. As we have worn the likeness of the man born of dust, so we shall wear the likeness of the heavenly man. (Paul, *To the Corinthians* 1.15:44–49)

Again, in his letter to the Romans, contrasting the Old Law and the New, the rule of sin and the rule of grace, Paul enlarges on the theology of redemption.

It was through one man that sin entered the world, and through sin death, and thus death pervaded the whole human race, inasmuch as all men have sinned. For sin was already in the world before there was law, though in the absence of law no reckoning is kept of sin. But death held sway from Adam to Moses, even over those who had not sinned as Adam did, by disobeying a direct command—and Adam foreshadows the Man who was to come.

But God's grace is out of all proportion to Adam's wrongdoing. For if the wrongdoing of that one man brought death upon so many, its effect is vastly exceeded by the grace of God and the gift that came to so many by the grace of the one man, Jesus Christ. And again, the gift of God is not to be compared in its effect with that one man's sin. For the judicial action, following upon the one offense, issued in a verdict of condemnation, but the act of grace, following upon so many misdeeds, issued in a verdict of acquittal. For if by the wrongdoing of that one man death established its reign, through a single sinner, so much more shall those who receive in far greater measure God's grace and His gift of righteousness, live and reign through the one man, Jesus Christ. (Paul, *To the Romans* 5:12–17)

43. Jesus Christ, God and Man and Mediator between Them

John's meditation on Jesus as the pre-existent Word of God and Paul's on Jesus as the second Adam are brought together in this work of Ireneus, bishop of Lyons about 175 C.E.

Since it has been clearly demonstrated that the Word, which existed in the beginning with God, and by whom all things were made, who was also present with the human race, was in these latter days, according to the time appointed by the Father, united to His own workmanship, having been made a man subject to suffering, every objection is set aside on the part of those who say "If Christ were born at that time, He did not exist before that time." For I have shown that the Son of God did not then begin to be, since he existed with his Father always; but when he was incarnate, and was made man, he began afresh the long line of human beings, and furnished us in a brief and comprehensive fashion with salvation; so that what we had lost in Adam, namely to be according to the image and likeness of God, that we might recover in Jesus Christ.

Jesus caused human nature to cleave to and become one with God, as we have said. For if man had not overcome the adversary of man, the enemy would not have been legitimately overcome. And again, if God had not given salvation, we could not have had it securely. And if man had not been united to God, he could never have become a partaker in incorruptibility. For it was incumbent upon the mediator between God and man, by his relationship to both, to bring about a friendship and concord, and to present man to God and to reveal God to man. For in what way could we be partakers of the adoption of sons if we had not received from him, through the Son, that fellowship that refers to himself, if the Word, having been made flesh, had not entered into communion with us? Wherefore he passed through every stage of life, restoring to all communication with God. (Ireneus, *Against the Heresies* 3.18.1.7)

44. Muhammad on Jesus

While still in Mecca, before his emigration to Medina in 622 C.E., Muhammad was often engaged by his opponents in polemical disputations. One such, reported in his Life, *had to do with Jesus.*

Ask him (a certain Abdullah suggested), "Is everything which is worshiped besides God in Gehenna along with those who worship it? We (Quraysh) worship angels; the Jews worship Uzayr [that is, Ezra]; and the Christians worship Jesus Son of Mary." Al-Walid and others with him in the assembly marveled at Abdullah's words and thought that he had argued convincingly. When the Apostle (Muhammad) was told of this he said, "Everyone who wishes to be worshiped to the exclusion of God will indeed be with those who worship him. But they worship only satans and those whom they [the satans] have ordered to be worshiped. So God revealed (the verses) 'Those who have received kindness from Us in the past will be removed far from it (the pains of damnation) and will not hear its sound and they abide eternally in their heart's desire' (Quran 21: 101). This refers to Jesus Son of Mary and Uzayr and those rabbis and monks who have lived in obedience to God, whom the erring people worship as lords beside God. . . ."

Then He [that is, God] mentions Jesus Son of Mary (in the Quran) and says, "He was nothing but a slave to whom We showed favor and made him an example to the Children of Israel. If We had wished We could have made (even) for you angels to act as vice-regents in the earth. Verily, there is knowledge of the Final Hour, so doubt not about it but follow Me. This is an upright path" (Quran 43:59–61), that is, the signs which I gave him (Jesus) in raising the dead and healing the sick, therein is sufficient proof of (his) knowledge of the Final Hour. God is saying, "Doubt not about it but follow Me. This is an upright path." (*Life* 236–237) [IBN ISHAQ 1955: 163–164]

Apart from the Quran, Jesus appears in a variety of contexts in the teachings of Muhammad. Here, for example, is a tradition reported of the Prophet, one that provides a kind of doctrinal summary of the beliefs of the Muslim, with considerable emphasis on Jesus.

It is narrated on the authority of Ubadah ibn Samit that the Messenger of God, may peace be upon him, observed: He who has said: "There is no god but the God, that He is One and there is no associate with Him, that Muhammad is His servant and His Messenger, that the Anointed One (that is, Christ) is His servant and the son of His slave girl, and he (Christ) is His Word, which He communicated to Mary, and is His Spirit, that Paradise is a fact and Hell is a fact," him God will cause to enter Paradise through which of its eight doors he would like. (Muslim, *Sahih* 1.11.43)

45. Pentecost and the Descent of the Holy Spirit

We return to the account of the Acts of the Apostles immediately following the Ascension of Jesus.

While the day of Pentecost [that is, the Jewish feast of Weeks, fifty days after the Passover when Jesus was executed] was running its course they were all together in one place when suddenly there came from the sky a noise like that of a strong driving wind, which filled the whole house where they were sitting. And there appeared to them tongues like flames of fire, dispersed among them and resting on each one. And they were all filled with the Holy Spirit and began to talk in other tongues, as the Spirit gave them power of utterance.

Now there were living in Jerusalem devout Jews drawn from every nation under heaven; and at this sound the crowd gathered, all bewildered because each one heard his own language spoken. They were amazed and in their astonishment exclaimed, "Why these are all Galileans, are they not, these men who are speaking? Parthians, Medes, Elamites; inhabitants of Mesopotamia, of Judea and Cappadocia, of Pontus and Asia, of Phrygia and Pamphylia, of Egypt and the districts of Libya round Cyrene; visitors from Rome, both Jews and proselytes, Cretans and Arabs, we hear them telling in our own tongues the great things God has done." (Acts 2:1–11)

46. A Muslim Account of Pentecost

Wahb [an early convert to Islam] and others among the People of the Book say that when God raised Jesus, on whom be peace, to Himself, he remained in heaven seven days. Then God said to him: "Behold, your enemies the Jews have precluded you from (keeping) your promise to your companions, so descend to them and give them your testament. Go down also to Mary Magdalen for there is no one who has wept for you or grieved for you as she has. Go down, therefore, to her and announce yourself to her, that she may be the first one to find you. Then bid her gather the Apostles to you so that you may send them out into the world as preachers summoning to God Most High. . . .

When God bade Jesus descend to her seven days after his ascension, he went down to her and the mountain blazed with light as he came down. Then she gathered to him the Apostles, whom he sent out into the world as summoners to God. After this God took him up (again), clothed him with feathers, dressed him in light, and removed from him his desire for food and drink. So he flew about with the angels around the Throne, being of human and angelic kind, earthly and heavenly. Then the Apostles dispersed to where he had bidden each one of them to go. The night in which he descended is the night which the Christians celebrate. They say that he sent Peter to Rome, Andrew and Matthew to the land where the inhabitants eat men, Thomas and Levi to the Orient, Philip and Judas to Qayrawan and Africa, John to Ephesus, the place of the Companions of the Cave (Quran 18), the two James to Jerusalem, which is Aelia, the land of the Holy House, Bartholomew to Arabia, that is, to the Hejaz, Simon to the land of the Berbers. Each one of the Apostles who was thus sent out was made able to speak the language of those to whom Jesus sent him. (Tha'alibi, *Stories of the Prophets*) [JEFFERY 1962: 594–595]

47. The Apostles Examined by the Sanhedrin

The account in the Acts of the Apostles of events in Jerusalem after the Ascension of Jesus continues.

They [the disciples of Jesus] used to meet by common consent in Solomon's Portico (of the Temple), no one from outside their number venturing to join with them. But people in general spoke highly of them, and more than that, numbers of men and women were added to their ranks as believers in the Lord. In the end the sick were actually carried out into the streets and laid there on beds and stretchers, so that even the shadow of Peter might fall on one or another as he passed by. And the people from the towns round about Jerusalem flocked in, bringing those who were ill or harassed by unclean spirits, and all of them were cured.

Then the High Priest and his colleagues, the Sadducean party as it then was, were goaded into action by jealousy. They proceeded to arrest the Apostles, and put them in official custody.

The Apostles are released by a miracle, but the Temple gendarmerie take them into custody once again.

So they brought them and stood them before the Council [or Sanhedrin, that is, "the full senate of the Israelite nation"] and the High Priest began his examination. "We expressly ordered you," he said, "to desist from your teaching in that name, and what has happened? You have filled Jerusalem with your teaching, and you are trying to make us responsible for that man's death." Peter replied for himself and the Apostles. "We must obey God rather than men. The God of our fathers raised up Jesus whom you have done to death by hanging him on a gibbet. He it is whom God has exalted by his own hand as leader and savior, to grant Israel repentance and forgiveness of sins. And we are witnesses to all this, and so is the Holy Spirit given by God to those who are obedient to him."

This touched them to the raw, and they wanted to put them to death. But a member of the Council rose to his feet, a Pharisee named Gamaliel, a teacher of the Law held in high regard by all the people [and one of Paul's mentors; see below]. He moved that the men be put outside for a while. Then he said, "Men of Israel, be cautious in deciding what to do with these men. . . . Leave them alone. For if this idea of theirs or its execution is of human origin, it will collapse; but if it is from God, you will never be able to put them down, and you risk finding yourselves at war with God."

They took his advice. They sent for the Apostles and had them flogged; then they ordered them to give up speaking in the name of Jesus, and discharged them. So the Apostles went out of the Council rejoicing that they had been found worthy to suffer indignity for the sake of the Name. And every day they went steadily on with their teaching in the

Temple and in private houses, telling the good news of Jesus the Messiah. (Acts 5:12–42)

48. The "Hellenists"

During this period, when disciples were growing in number, there was disagreement between those who spoke Greek and those who spoke the language of the Jews. The former party complained that their widows were being overlooked in the daily distribution. . . . (So) they elected Stephen, a man full of faith and the Holy Spirit, Philip, Prochorus, Nicanor, Timon, Parmenas, and Nicolas of Antioch, a former convert to Judaism. These they presented to the apostles, who prayed and laid hands on them. The word of God now spread more and more widely; the number of disciples in Jerusalem went on increasing rapidly, and very many of the priests adhered to the Faith. Stephen, who was full of grace and power, began to work great miracles and signs among the people. But some members of the synagogue called the Synagogue of the Freedmen, comprising Cyrenians and Alexandrians and people from Cilicia and Asia, came forward and argued with Stephen, but could not hold their own against the inspired wisdom with which he spoke. (Acts 6:1–10)

49. Stephen and Paul

Precisely one of those "Hellenists," Greek-acculturated Jews from the Diaspora, provoked the next crisis for the followers of Jesus in Jerusalem. The performance of signs and wonders might inspire admiration, astonishment, and even belief, but Stephen's long and critical catechesis of the Jewish elders in Jerusalem aroused somewhat different feelings.

This (speech of Stephen's) touched them to the raw and they ground their teeth with fury. But Stephen, filled with the Holy Spirit, and gazing intently up to heaven, saw the glory of God, and Jesus standing at God's right hand. "Look," he said, "there is a rift in the sky. I can see the Son of Man standing at God's right hand!" At this they gave a great shout and stopped their ears. Then they made one rush at him, and flinging him out of the city, set about stoning him. The witnesses laid their coats at the feet of a young man named Saul. So they stoned Stephen, and as they did so, he called out, "Lord Jesus, receive my spirit." Then he fell on his knees and cried aloud, "Lord, do not hold this sin against them," and with that he died. And Saul was among those who approved of his murder. (Acts 7:54–8:1)

50. The Conversion of Paul

Christianity thus had its first martyr. More important, there appears dramatically and for the first time the figure of Paul, here still called Saul. His well-known conversion through a vision of Jesus on the road to Damascus followed, as described in Acts 9 and again, with added autobiographical detail, in Acts 22.

"I am a true-born Jew [Paul explained to a hostile crowd collected in the Temple at Jerusalem], a native of Tarsus in Cilicia. I was brought up in this city, and as a pupil of Gamaliel I was thoroughly trained in every point of our ancestral law. I have always been ardent in God's service, as you are all today, and so I began to persecute this movement to the death, arresting its followers, men and women alike, and putting them in chains. For this I have as witnesses the High Priest and the whole Council of Elders. I was given letters from them to our fellow Jews at Damascus, and had started out to bring the Christians there to Jerusalem as prisoners for punishment; and this is what happened.

"I was on the road and nearing Damascus, when suddenly about midday a great light flashed from the sky all around me and I heard a voice saying to me, 'Saul, Saul, why do you persecute me?' I answered, 'Tell me, Lord, who you are.' 'I am Jesus of Nazareth,' he said, 'whom you are persecuting.' My companions saw the light but did not hear the voice that spoke to me. 'What shall I do, Lord?' I said, and the Lord replied, 'Get up and continue your journey to Damascus; there you will be told of all the tasks that are laid upon you.' As I had been blinded by the brilliance of that light, my companions led me by the hand, and so I came to Damascus." (Acts 22:1–11)

As the days mounted up, the Jews (of Damascus) hatched a plot against his life; but their plans became known to Saul. They kept watch on the city gates day and night so that they might murder him. But his converts took him one night and let him down by the wall, lowering him in a basket. When he reached Jerusalem he tried to join the body of the disciples there; but they were all afraid of him, because they did not believe that he was really a convert. Barnabas, however, took him by the hand and introduced him to the apostles. . . . Saul now stayed with them, moving about freely in Jerusalem. He spoke out openly and boldly in the name of the Lord, talking and debating with the Greek-speaking Jews. But they planned to murder him, and when the brethren learned of this they escorted him to Caesarea and saw him off to Tarsus. (Acts 9:23–30)

That is the version of Paul's coming to Jerusalem in Acts. Paul's own account in his letters is considerably different.

You have heard what my manner of life was when I was still a practicing Jew: how savagely I persecuted the Church of God and tried to destroy it; and how in the practice of our national religion I was outstripping many of my Jewish contemporaries in my boundless devotions to the traditions of my ancestors. But then in his good pleasure God, who had set me apart from birth and called me through his grace, chose to reveal his Son to me and through me, in order that I might proclaim him among the Gentiles. When that happened, without consulting any human being, without going up to Jerusalem to see those who were Apostles before me, I went off at once to Arabia, and afterwards returned to Damascus. Three years later did I go up Jerusalem to get to know Cephas [Peter]. I stayed with him for a fortnight, without seeing any of the other Apostles, except James, the Lord's brother. What I write is plain truth; before God I am not lying. (Paul, *To the Galatians* 1:13–20)

51. The Gospel According to Peter

One of the earliest explanations of Jesus and his message occurs early in the Acts of the Apostles, where Peter is invited to Caesarea.

At Caesarea there was a man named Cornelius, a centurion of the Italian Cohort, as it was called. He was a religious man, and he and his whole family joined in the worship of God. He gave generously to help the Jewish people, and was regular in his prayers to God. (Acts 10:1–2)

Peter, summoned by a vision, accompanies Cornelius' servants to Caesarea.

Cornelius was expecting them and had called together his relatives and close friends. When Peter arrived, Cornelius came to meet him and bowed to the ground in deep reverence. But Peter raised him up to his feet and said, "Stand up; I am a man like anyone else." Still talking with him he went in and found a large gathering. He said to them, "I need not tell you that a Jew is forbidden by his religion to visit or associate with a man of another race; yet God has shown clearly that I must not call any man profane or unclean. That is why I came here without demur when you sent for me." (Acts 10:17–29)

Peter then unfolds the "Good News of Jesus."

I now see how true it is that God has no favorites, but that in every nation the man who is God-fearing and does what is right is acceptable to Him. He sent his word to the Israelites and gave the good news of peace through Jesus Christ, who is Lord of all. I need not tell you what happened lately all over the land of the Jews starting from Galilee after the baptism proclaimed by John. You know about Jesus of Nazareth, how God anointed him with the Holy Spirit and with power. He went about doing good and healing all who were oppressed by the devil, for God was with him. And we can bear witness to what he did in the Jewish country- side and in Jerusalem. He was put to death by hanging on a gibbet; but God raised him to life on the third day, and allowed him to appear, not to the whole people, but to witnesses whom God had chosen in ad- vance—to us who ate and drank with him after he rose from the dead. He commanded us to proclaim him to the people and affirm that he is the one who has been designated by God as the judge of the living and the dead. It is to him that all the prophets testify, declaring that everyone who trusts him receives forgiveness of sins through his name. (Acts 10:34–43)

52. The Gentile Issue

The issue raised by Peter's consorting with Gentiles, even with the God-fearing and sympathetic Cornelius, did not simply disappear. Peter was called to account on his return to Jerusalem: "You have been visiting men who are uncircumcised, and sitting at table with them!" (Acts 11:3). Only after he told the brethren about his vision were their misgivings temporarily allayed.

"Hardly had I begun speaking," Peter explained, "when the Holy Spirit came upon them, just as upon us at the beginning. Then I recalled what the Lord had said: 'John baptized with water, but you will be bap- tized with the Holy Spirit.' God gave them no less of a gift than He gave us when we put our trust in the Lord Jesus Christ. Then how could I possibly stand in God's way?"

When they heard this their doubts were silenced. They gave praise to God and said, "This means that God has given life-giving repentance to the Gentiles also." (Acts 11:16–18)

Now certain persons who had come down (to Antioch) from Judea began to teach the brotherhood that those who were not circumcised in accordance with the Mosaic practice could not be saved. That brought them into fierce dissension and controversy with Paul and Barnabas. And so it was arranged that these two and some others from Antioch should go up to Jerusalem and see the apostles and elders about this question. . . .

When they reached Jerusalem they were welcomed by the church and the apostles and elders, and reported all that God had done through them. Then some of the Pharisaic party who had become believers came forward and said, "They must be circumcised and told to keep the Law of Moses."

The question was discussed at length. Peter expressed a preference for the lenient view; then James, "the brother of the Lord," speaks.

My judgment therefore is that we should impose no irksome restrictions on those of the Gentiles who are turning to God but instruct them by letter to abstain from things polluted by contact with idols, from fornication, from anything that has been strangled and from blood. Moses, after all, has never lacked for spokesmen in every town for generations past; he is read in the synagogues Sabbath by Sabbath. (Acts 15:1–21)

53. Jews and Gentiles

Paul gives his own, more personal reflections on these same events in his letter to the Galatians.

These men of repute (in the Jerusalem church) did not prolong the consultation, but on the contrary acknowledged that I had been entrusted with the Gospel for Gentiles as surely as Peter had been entrusted with the Gospel for Jews. For God whose action made Peter an Apostle to the Jews, also made me an Apostle to the Gentiles. Recognizing, then, the favor thus bestowed on me, those reputed pillars of our society, James, Cephas [that is, Peter] and John, accepted Barnabas and myself as partners, and shook hands upon it, agreeing that we should go to the Gentiles while they went to the Jews. All they asked was that we should keep their poor in mind, which was the very thing I made it my business to do.

But when Cephas came to Antioch, I opposed him to his face, because he was clearly in the wrong. For until certain persons came from James (in Jerusalem) he was taking his meals with Gentile Christians; but when they came he drew back and began to hold himself apart, because he was afraid of the advocates of circumcision. The other Jewish Christians showed the same lack of principle; even Barnabas was carried away and played false like the rest. But when I saw that their conduct did not square with the truth of the Gospel, I said to Cephas, before the whole congregation, "If you, a Jew born and bred, live like a Gentile and not like a Jew, how can you insist that Gentiles must live like Jews?"

We ourselves are Jews by birth, not Gentiles and sinners. But we know that that no man is justified by doing what the Law demands, but only through faith in Christ Jesus; so we too have put our faith in Jesus Christ, in order that we might be justified through this faith and not through deeds dictated by law; for by such deeds, Scripture says, no mortal man shall be justified.

If now, in seeking to be justified in Christ, we ourselves no less than the Gentiles turn out to be sinners against the Law, does that mean that Christ is an abettor of sin? No, never! No, if I start building up a system which I have pulled down, then it is that I show myself up as a transgressor of the Law. For through the Law I died to law—to live for God. I have been crucified with Christ: the life I live is not my life, but the life which Christ lives in me; and my present bodily life is lived by faith in the Son of God, who loved me and gave himself up for me. I will not nullify the grace of God; if righteousness comes by Law, then Christ died for nothing. (Paul, *To the Galatians* 2:6–21)

54. Paul's Mission and God's Hidden Purpose

As we shall see, this issue of Jews and Gentiles will have a long history in the Christian Church. Aquinas was still pondering these particular events in Acts and Galatians in the thirteenth century. Paul too had reason to give them thought later in his apostolic career.

I, Paul, who in the cause of you Gentiles am now the prisoner of Jesus Christ—for surely you have heard how God has assigned the gift of his grace to me for your benefit. It was by a revelation that His secret was made known to me. I have already written a brief account of this, and by reading it you may perceive that I understand the secret of Christ. In former generations this was not disclosed to the human race; but now it has been revealed by inspiration to his dedicated apostles and prophets, that through the Gospel the Gentiles are the joint heirs with the Jews, part of the same body, sharers together in the promise made in Christ Jesus. Such is the gospel of which I was made a minister, by God's gift, bestowed unmerited on me in the working of his power.

To me, who am less than the least of all God's people, He has granted by His grace the privilege of proclaiming to the Gentiles the good news of the unfathomable riches of Christ, and of bringing to light how this hidden purpose was to be put into effect. It was hidden for long ages in God the creator of the universe, in order that now, through the Church, the wisdom of God in all its varied forms might be made known to the rulers and authorities in the realms of heaven. This is in accord with his age-long purpose, which He achieved in Christ Jesus our Lord. (Paul, *To the Ephesians* 3:1–11)

55. The Arrest of Paul

After the community meeting in Jerusalem, Paul departs for a long round of mission-ary visits through the eastern Mediterranean. Finally, he and Luke, who is now using "we" in the account in Acts, reach Jerusalem.

So we reached Jerusalem where the brotherhood welcomed us gladly. Next day Paul paid a visit to James; we were with him, and all the elders attended. He greeted them, and then described in detail all that God had done among the Gentiles through his ministry. When they heard this they [James and the elders] gave praise to God. Then they said to Paul, "You see, brother, how many thousands of converts we have amongst the Jews, all of them staunch upholders of the Law. Now they have been given certain information about you: it is said that you teach all the Jews in the Gentile world to turn their backs on Moses, telling them to give up circumcising their children and following our way of life. What is the position, then? They are sure to hear that you have arrived. You must therefore do as we tell you. We have four men here who are under a vow; take them with you and go through the ritual purification with them, paying their expenses, after which they may shave their heads. Then everyone will know there is nothing in the stories that were told about you, but that you are a practicing Jew and keep the Law yourself." . . . So Paul took the four men and next day, having gone through the ritual purification with them, he went into the Temple to give notice of the date when the period of purification would end and the offering be made for each of them. (Acts 21:15–26)

But just before the seven days were up, the Jews from the province of Asia saw him in the Temple. They stirred up the whole crowd, and seized him, shouting, "Men of Israel, help, help! This is the fellow who spreads his doctrine all over the world, attacking our people, our Law, and this sanctuary. On top of all this he has brought Gentiles into the Temple and profaned this holy place." For they had previously seen Tro-phimus the Ephesian with him in the city and assumed that Paul had brought him into the Temple.

The whole city was in turmoil, and people came running from all directions. They seized Paul and dragged him out of the Temple; and at once the doors [of the Court of the Israelites] were shut. While they were clamoring for his death, a report reached the officer commanding the cohort (in the Fortress Antonia) that all Jerusalem was in an uproar. He immediately took a force of soldiers with their centurions and came down on the rioters at the double. As soon as they saw the commandant and his troops they stopped beating Paul. The commandant stepped forward, arrested him and ordered him to be shackled with two chains. He then asked who the man was and what he had been doing. Some in the crowd shouted one thing, some another. As he could not get at the truth because of the hubbub, he ordered him to be taken into the barracks. When Paul reached the steps [up to the Antonia], he had to be carried by the soldiers because of the violence of the crowd. For the whole crowd was at their heels yelling "Kill him!"

Just before Paul was taken into the barracks he said to the commandant, "May I have a word with you?" The commandant said, "So you speak Greek, do you? Then you are not the Egyptian who started a revolt some time ago and led a force of four thousand terrorists into the wilds?" Paul replied, "I am a Jew, a Tarsian from Cilicia, a citizen of no mean city. I ask your permission to speak to the people." When permission had been given, Paul stood on the steps and with a gesture called for the attention of the people. As soon as quiet was restored, he addressed them in the Jewish language: "Brothers and fathers, give me a hearing while I make my defense before you." When they heard him speaking to them in their own language, they listened more quietly. "I am a true-born Jew," he said, "a native of Tarsus in Cilicia. I was brought up in this city, and as a pupil of Gamaliel I was thoroughly trained in every point of our ancestral law." (Acts 21:7–22:4)

Paul proceeds to describe his conversion and his return from Damascus to Jerusalem, when he had another vision of Jesus, who said, "Go, I am sending you far away to the Gentiles."

Up to this point they had given him a hearing but now they began shouting, "Down with him! A scoundrel like that is better dead!" And as they were yelling and waving their cloaks and flinging dust in the air, the commandant ordered him to be brought into the barracks and gave instructions to examine him by flogging and find out what reason there was for such an outcry against him. But when they tied him up for the lash, Paul said to the centurion who was standing there, "Can you legally flog a man who is a Roman citizen and moreover who has not been found guilty?" When the centurion heard this, he went and reported it to the commandant. "What do you mean to do?" he said. "This man is a Roman citizen." The commandant came to Paul. "Tell me, are you a Roman citizen?" he asked. "Yes," said he. The commandant rejoined, "It cost me a large sum to acquire citizenship." Paul said, "But it was mine by birth." Then those who were about to examine him withdrew hastily, and the commandant himself was alarmed when he realized that Paul was a Roman citizen and that he had put him in irons. (Acts 22:22–29)

The commandant of the Antonia garrison planned to have a hearing before the Sanhedrin in Jerusalem, but threats to Paul's life caused him to send the prisoner under heavy escort to Caesarea to the governor Felix. The date was sometime shortly before 60 C.E., and it marked the end of Paul's association with Jerusalem.

56. The Great War Begins

In 64 C.E., Gessius Florus, the last Roman prefect for Judea and the unwitting provocateur of the destruction of the Holy City, takes up his post. From the beginning, Florus had little understanding of or sympathy with his subjects in Judea, who were in fact never very far from sedition. The trouble began when a number of Jews were arrested in Caesarea.

The citizens of Jerusalem, though they took this affair badly, yet they restrained their passion. But Florus acted as if he had been hired to fan the war into flame, and sent some men to take seventeen talents out of the sacred treasure (of the Temple), on the pretense that Caesar required them. At this the people became immediately disturbed and ran in a body to the Temple with great shouting and called upon Caesar by name and begged him to free them from the tyranny of Florus. Some of the more seditious cried out against Florus himself and blamed him severely. They carried about a basket and solicited small change for him, as if he were a poor man without possessions. Far from being ashamed of his greed for money, he became further enraged and was provoked to get even more. Instead of going to Caesarea, as he ought to have done, and damping the flames of war there . . . he marched quickly with a force of cavalry and infantry against Jerusalem, that he might gain his objective by force of Roman arms and drain the city dry.

Once in the city Florus summoned the elders and leaders of the Jews and demanded the guilty be handed over to him. Apologies were made, and they protested, "it was no wonder that in so great a crowd there should be some rasher than they ought to have been and, by reason of their age, foolish as well."

Florus was all the more provoked at this, and called out aloud from his soldiers to loot the Upper Market, and to slay whomever they met there. The soldiers, who found this order of their commander agreeable to their own sense of greed, plundered not only the (public) place where they were sent but broke into houses and killed the inhabitants. The citizens fled down the alleys and the soldiers killed those they caught and looted in every way conceivable. They also arrested many of the peaceable citizens and brought them before Florus, whom he first had whipped and then crucified. (Josephus, *War* 2.14.6–9)

This was in April or May 66 C.E., the beginning of a long-postponed and now increasingly inevitable confrontation between the Romans and the Jews of Jerusalem. The critical moment was at hand.

Eleazer, the son of Ananias the High Priest, a very bold young man, who was also at that time the superintendent of the Temple, persuaded those who were officiating in the divine services to accept no gift or sacrifice on behalf of any foreigner. And this was the true beginning of our war with the Romans, for they rejected the sacrifice of Caesar on this account. When many of the high priests and leaders begged them not to omit this sacrifice, which was customary for them to offer for their rulers, they would not be persuaded. (Josephus, *War* 2.17.2)

When the (Jewish) leaders in Jerusalem perceived that the sedition was too difficult for them to put down, and that the danger that would arise from the Romans would descend in the first place upon their shoulders, they tried to clear themselves and sent representatives, some to Florus . . . and others to Agrippa . . . and they requested that both of them should come with an army to the city and cut off the revolt while it was still possible. Now this terrible message was good news to Florus, and since it was his intent that there should be a war, he gave no answer to the delegates. But Agrippa was equally solicitous for the rebels and for those against whom the war would be fought; he wanted to save the Jews for the Romans and the Temple for the Jews. He was also aware that a war would not be to his own advantage and so he sent 2,000 horsemen to the assistance of the people. . . .

At this the (Jewish) leaders and the high priests, as well as those others who wanted peace, took courage and seized the Upper City, since the rebels had already occupied the Lower City and the Temple.

The next day Agrippa's cavalry are driven out of the Upper City by the rebels.

. . . [They] set fire to the house of Ananias the High Priest and to the palace of Agrippa and Berenice. After which they spread the fire to the place where the archives were kept and quickly burned the due bills belonging to creditors and so dissolved the obligation of paying debts. This was done to gain the allegiance of the many who profited thereby and to persuade the poorer citizens to join the insurrection with impunity against the wealthy.

The next day they . . . made an assault upon the Antonia and besieged the garrison within it for two days, and then took the garrison and slew them and set the citadel on fire, after which they marched against the palace [that, is Herod's former palace, the Roman pretorium] where the king's soldiers had fled. (Josephus, *War* 2.17.4–7)

57. Fugitives from the City

Finally, all the forces of resistance, Roman and Agrippan, are driven from Jerusalem, and the city rests entirely in the possession of the rebels. Others had departed as well, among them the small community of Christians in Jerusalem.

The members of the Jerusalem church, by means of an oracle given by revelation to acceptable persons there, were ordered to leave the country before the war (of 66–70 C.E.) began and settle in a town in the Peraea (in the Transjordan) called Pella. To Pella those who believed in Christ migrated from Jerusalem; and as if holy men had abandoned the royal metropolis of the Jews and the entire Jewish land, the judgment of God at last overtook them for the abominable crimes against Christ and His Apostles, completely blotting out that wicked generation from among men. (Eusebius, *Church History* 3.5)

Somewhat later in the war:

Now when Vespasian came to destroy Jerusalem, he said to the inhabitants, "Fools, why do you seek to destroy this city and why do you seek to burn the Temple? For what do I ask you but that you send me one bow or one arrow and I shall go away from you?" They then said to him, "Even as we went forth against the first two who were here before you and slew them, so shall we go forth against you and slay you."

And when Rabban Yohanan ben Zakkai heard this, he sent for the men of Jerusalem and said to them, "My children, why do you destroy this city, and why do you seek to destroy the Temple? For what is it that he asks of you?" . . .

Vespasian had men stationed inside the walls of Jerusalem. Every word which they overheard they would write down, attach it to an arrow and shoot it over the wall, saying that Rabban Yohanan ben Zakkai was one of the emperor's friends.

Now after Rabban Yohanan ben Zakkai had spoken to them one day, two days, and three days, and they would still not listen to him, he sent for his disciples, Rabbi Eliezer and Rabbi Joshua.

"My sons," he said, "arise and take me out of here. Make a coffin for me that I may lie in it."

Rabbi Eliezer took the head of the coffin and Rabbi Joshua took hold of the foot, and they began carrying him as the sun set until they reached the gates of Jerusalem. "Who is this?" the gatekeepers demanded. "It is a dead man," they replied. "Do you not know that the dead may not be held overnight in Jerusalem?" "If it is a dead man," the gatekeepers said to them, "take him out." So they took him out. (*The Fathers According to Rabbi Nathan* 4) [ABOTH RABBI NATHAN 1955: 35–36]

Thus Rabbi Yohanan ben Zakkai, who eventually went on to Jabneh to found the academy from which much of rabbinic Judaism was later to flow, escaped, like the Christian elders, from a Jerusalem destined for ruin and so preserved intact institutions that would return there at a later date and shape the spiritual reconstruction of the city and, indeed, the entire Jewish tradition.

4. Muhammad, the Prophet of God

1. Muhammad's Descent from Adam

Like the Synoptic Gospels' presentation of Jesus, the standard Muslim life of Muhammad, the Life of the Apostle of God, *which was composed out of earlier materials by Ibn Ishaq (d. 768 C.E.) and then re-edited by Ibn Hisham (d. 843 C.E.), begins with a genealogy, here, as in Luke 3:23–38, stretching back to the father of all mankind.*

This is the book of the life of the Messenger of God:

Muhammad was the son of Abdullah, son of Abd al-Muttalib, whose name was Shayba, son of Hashim, whose name was Amr, son of Abd al-Manaf, whose name was al-Mughira, son of Qusayy, whose name was Zayd, son of Kilab, son of Murra, son of Ka'b, son of Lu'ayy, son of Ghalib, son of Fikr, son of Malik, son of al-Nadr, son of Kinana, son of Khuzayma, son of Mudrika, whose name was Amir, son of Ilyas, son of Mudar, son of Nizar, son of Ma'add, son of Adnan, son of Udd or Udad, son of Muqawwam, son of Nahur, son of Tayrah, son of Ya'rub, son of Yashjub, son of Nabit, son of Ishmael, son of Abraham, the Friend of the Compassionate One, son of Tarih, who is Azar, son of Nahur, son of Sarugh, son of Ra'u, son of Falikh, son of Aybar, son of Shalikh, son of Arfakhshad, son of Shem, son of Noah, son of Lamk, son of Matthuselah, son of Enoch, who is the prophet Idris, according to what is alleged, though God knows best, he was the first of the sons of Adam to whom prophecy and writing with a pen were given, son of Yard, son of Mahlil, son of Cain, son of Yanish, son of Seth, son of Adam. (Ibn Ishaq, *Life* 3) [IBN ISHAQ 1955: 3]

CHAPTER 4

2. The Birth of the Prophet

After this prelude on the remote past, the standard life of the Prophet sets the historical scene by laying out various traditions about early Mecca: how Abraham and Ishmael came to build the House of the Lord there and how Ishmael's descendants were forced to leave the place and lapsed back into paganism. After some additional material on south Arabia, the narrative turns directly to the birth of the Prophet.

It is alleged in popular stories, and only God knows the truth, that Amina, daughter of Wahb, mother of God's Apostle, used to say when she was pregnant with God's Apostle, that a voice said to her, "You are pregnant with the lord of this people, and when he is born say 'I put him in the care of the One away from the evil of every envyer'; then call him Muhammad." As she was pregnant with him she saw a light come forth from her by which she could see the castles of Busra in Syria. Shortly afterwards Abdullah, the Apostle's father, died while his mother was still pregnant. (*Life* 102) [IBN ISHAQ 1955: 69]

The Messenger was born on Monday, the 12th of First Rabi꜄ in the Year of the Elephant [570 C.E.]. . . . Salih b. Ibrahim . . . said that his tribesmen said that Hassan ibn Thabit said: "I was a well-grown boy of seven or eight, understanding all that I heard, when I heard a Jew calling out at the top of his voice from the top of a fort in Yathrib [Medina] 'O company of Jews!' until they all came together and called out 'Confound you! What is the matter?' He answered, 'Tonight has a star risen under which Ahmad is to be born.' "

After his birth his mother (Amina) sent to tell his grandfather Abd al-Muttalib that she had given birth to a boy and asked him to come and look at him. When he came she told him what she had seen when she conceived him and what was said to her and what she was ordered to call him. It is alleged that Abd al-Muttalib took him before (the idol) Hubal in the middle of the Ka꜄ba, where he stood and prayed to God, thanking him for this gift. Then he brought him out and delivered him to his mother, and he tried to find foster mothers [or wet nurses] for him. (*Life* 103) [IBN ISHAQ 1955: 70]

Finally the boy Muhammad undergoes a purification at the hands of more than human agents, then is weighed and found worthy of his future role.

Thawr ibn Yazid . . . told me that some of the Apostle's companions asked him to tell them about himself. He said: "I am what Abraham my

189

father prayed for and the good news of my brother Jesus. When my mother was carrying me she saw a light proceeding from her which showed her the castles of Syria. I was suckled among the Banu Saʿd ibn Bakr, and while I was with a (foster) brother of mine behind our tents shepherding the lambs, two men in white raiment came to me with a gold basin full of snow. Then they seized me and opened my belly, extracted my heart and split it; then they extracted a black drop from it and threw it away; then they washed my heart and my belly with the snow until they had thoroughly cleaned them. Then one said to the other, weigh him against ten of his people; they did and I outweighed them. Then they weighed me against a hundred and then a thousand and I outweighed them. He said 'Leave him alone, for by God, if you weigh him against all his people he would outweigh them.' " (*Life* 106) [IBN ISHAQ 1955: 72]

3. The Christian Monk Bahira Identifies Muhammad

When Muhammad was six, his mother, Amina, died, whereupon he was sent to live with his grandfather. Two years later Abd al-Muttalib died as well, and Muhammad was then put into the care of his paternal uncle, Abu Talib. Thus we are introduced in a somewhat offhand manner to the commercial climate of Mecca in which Muhammad would continue to share for most of his adult life. The point of the story is other, however. In the passage cited above the Prophet's birth was acknowledged by a Jew, who saw his sign in the stars; here a Christian monk recognizes Muhammad in the flesh as the one of whom Scripture had spoken.

Abu Talib had planned to go on a merchant caravan to Syria, and when all preparations had been made for the journey, the Messenger of God, so they allege, attached himself closely to him so that he took pity on him and said that he would take him with him. . . . When the caravan reached Busra in Syria there was a monk there in his cell by the name of Bahira, who was well versed in the knowledge of the Christians. . . . They had often passed by him in the past and he never spoke to them or took any notice of them until this year, and when they stopped near his cell he made a great feast for them . . . and sent word to them, "I have prepared food for you, O men of Quraysh, and I should like you all to come, great and small, bond and free." One of them said to him, "By God, Bahira, something extraordinary has happened today; you used not to treat us so, and we have often passed by you. What has befallen you today?" He answered, "You are right in what you say, but you are my guests and I wish to honor you and give you food so that you may eat."

So they gathered together with him, leaving the Messenger of God behind with the baggage under the tree, on account of his extreme youth. When Bahira looked at the people he did not see the mark which he knew and found in his books, so he said, "Do not let one of you remain behind and not come to my feast." . . . One of the men of Quraysh said, "By al-Lat and al-Uzza, we are to blame for leaving behind the son of Abdullah ibn Abd al-Muttalib." Then he got up and embraced him and made him sit with the people. When Bahira saw him he stared at him closely, looking at his body and finding traces of his description (in the Christian books). When people had finished eating and had gone away, Bahira got up and said to him, "Boy, I now ask you by al-Lat and al-Uzza to answer my question." Now Bahira said this only because he had heard his people swearing by these goddesses. They allege that the Messenger of God said to him, "Do not ask me by al-Lat and al-Uzza, for by God nothing is more hateful to me than those two." Bahira answered, "Then, by God, tell me what I ask"; he replied, "Ask me what you like," so he began to question him about what happened in his waking and in his sleep, and his habits and affairs generally, and what the Messenger of God told him coincided with what Bahira knew of his description. Then he looked at his back and saw the seal of prophethood between his shoulders in the very place described in his book.

When he had finished he went to his uncle Abu Talib . . . and said, "Take your nephew back to his country and guard him carefully against the Jews, for, by God! if they see him and know about him what I know, they will do him evil; a great future lies before this nephew of yours, so take him home quickly." (*Life* 115–116) [IBN ISHAQ 1955: 79–81]

4. The Scriptural Prediction of the Coming of the Prophet of Islam

The boy Muhammad's identification and acknowledgment by the Christian monk Bahira was a popular story in Islam, and the motif of the future holy man identified in the child can be paralleled from the infancy and boyhood accounts of Moses and Jesus, among others. Although such stories may be no more than the stuff of legend, there is a similar but theologically quite different question that is proposed for meditation by the Quran itself, namely, God's own foreshadowing of the coming of His prophet Muhammad in Scripture. It is God who speaks here.

Those who follow the messenger, the unlettered Prophet, described in the Torah and the Gospel, who bids things noble and forbids things vile, makes lawful what is clean, and prohibits what is foul, who relieves them of their burdens and the yoke that lies upon them, those who believe and honor and help him, and follow the light sent with him, are those who will attain their goal. (Quran 7:157)

In this first passage God in the Quran makes explicit though unspecified reference to the Bible and the Gospels as announcing the coming of a future prophet, "whose name shall be Ahmad." In another passage the same sentiments are expressed from the mouth of Jesus.

And when Jesus son of Mary said: "O Children of Israel, I am sent to you by God to confirm the Torah (sent) before me, and to give you good tidings of an apostle who will come after me, whose name is Ahmad (the praised one)." Yet, when he has come to them with clear proofs, they say: "This is only magic." (Quran 61:6)

On the second of these passages, the classical Quranic commentaries have this to say.

According to Ka'b al-Ahbar [a rabbi who was an early convert to Islam and the attributed source of much of the material on Judaism in the early Islamic tradition], it is related that the disciples of Jesus asked: "O Spirit of God, will there be another religious community after us?" and that Jesus then said: "Yes, the community of Ahmad. It will comprise people who are wise, knowing, devout and pious, as if they were all prophets in religious knowledge. They will be content with modest sustenance from God, and He will be pleased with a modest conduct on their part." (Zamakhshari, *The Unveiler, ad loc.*)

". . . whose name is Ahmad . . . ": that is, Muhammad. The meaning is: My [that is, Jesus'] religion exists by reason of holding on firmly to the books of God and His prophets. And so Jesus mentions (only) the very first of the well-known books, concerning which the earlier prophets rendered judgment, and only that prophet who (as the last) constitutes the seal of those who are sent by God. (Baydawi, *Commentary, ad loc.*)

The Muslim scientist and chronologer Biruni (d. 1048 C.E.) argues the case somewhat more rigorously in his Traces of the Past. *His point of departure is the chief biblical proof-text for the Muslims' contention that Muhammad had been foretold in earlier Scripture, namely this passage in Isaiah.*

God ordered him to set a watchman on the watchtower, that he might declare what he should see. Then he said: I see a man riding on an ass and a man riding on a camel. And one of them came forward crying and speaking: Babylon is fallen, and its graven images are broken. (Isaiah 21:6–9)

Biruni begins:

This is a prophecy regarding the Messiah, the "man riding on an ass," and regarding Muhammad, the "man riding on a camel," because in consequence of the latter's appearance, Babylon has fallen, its idols have been broken, its castles have been shattered, and its empire has perished. There are many passages in this book of Isaiah predicting Muhammad, being rather hints (than explicit texts), but easily admitting of a clear interpretation. And despite all this, the Jews' obstinacy in clinging to their error induces them to devise and maintain things which are not acknowledged by men in general, to wit, that the "man riding on a camel" is Moses and not Muhammad. But what connection have Moses and his people with Babylon? And did that happen to Moses and to his people after him which happened to Muhammad and his companions in Babylon? By no means! If the Jews had escaped one by one from the Babylonians, they would have considered it a sufficient prize to return (to their country), even though in a desperate condition.

This testimony (of Isaiah) is confirmed in the fifth book of Moses, which is called Deuteronomy: "I will raise them up a prophet like yourself from among their brethren, and will put My word in his mouth. And he shall speak to them all that I command him. And whoever will not heed the word of him who speaks in My name, I shall take revenge on him" (Deut. 21:6–9). Now I should like to know whether there are other brethren of the sons of Isaac except the sons of Ishmael? If they say that the brethren of the sons of Israel are the children of Esau, we ask only: Has there been raised among *them* a man like Moses—in the times after Moses—of the same description and resembling him?

Does not also the following passage from the same book, of which this is a translation, bear testimony to Muhammad: "The Lord came from Mount Sinai, and rose up to us from Seir, and He shone from Mount Paran, accompanied by ten thousand saints at His right hand" (Deut. 33:2)? The terms of this passage are hints for the establishing of the proof that the (anthropomorphic) descriptions inherent in them cannot be referred to the essence of the Creator, nor to His qualities, He being high above such things. His coming from Mount Sinai means His secret conversation with Moses there; His riding up from Seir means the appearance of the Messiah; and His shining forth from Paran, where Ishmael grew up and married, means the coming of Muhammad from there as the last of the founders of religions, accompanied by legions of saints, who were sent down from heaven to help, being marked with certain badges. He who refuses to accept this interpretation, for which all evidence has borne testimony, is required to prove what kinds of mistakes there are in it. "But he whose companion is Satan, woe to him for such a companion" (Quran 4:42). (al-Biruni, *Traces of the Past*)

[BIRUNI 1879: 22–23]

5. Maimonides Replies

The issue of the scriptural predictions of the coming of Muhammad as a prophet, and the related one of the Jews and Christians tampering with those texts, was to be a rich source of polemic among Muslims, Christians, and Jews. The Christians had built their case for the Messiahship of Jesus on biblical prophecy, and in the passage just cited the Quran invokes just such a foretelling on the part of another postbiblical prophet, Jesus son of Mary. But that evidence merely opened the discussion. If the Bible had foretold the coming of Jesus, had it not also foreshadowed the Prophet of Islam? Where? On the basis of Quran 7:156–157 Muslims had of necessity to argue that it had, and it was their search for confirmatory texts that lay behind this response of the Spanish scriptural scholar and philosopher Maimonides (d. 1204 C.E.), written to his fellow Jews in the Yemen and reassuring them that the Muslim claim was absurd.

In your letter you mention that the emissary [apparently a Jewish apostate to Islam] has incited a number of people to believe that several verses in Scripture allude to the Madman [Muhammad], such as "multiply exceedingly" (Gen. 17:20); "he shone forth from Mount Paran" (Deut. 33:2); "a prophet from the midst of you" (Deut. 18:15); and the promise to Ishmael, "I will make him a great nation" (Gen. 17:20). These arguments have been rehashed so often that they have become nauseating. It is not enough to declare that they are altogether feeble; more, to cite these verses as proofs is ridiculous and absurd in the extreme. For these are not matters that can confuse the minds of anyone. Neither the untutored multitude, nor even the very apostates who delude others with them, believe in them or entertain any illusions about them. Their purpose in citing these verses is to win favor in the eyes of the Gentiles by demonstrating that they believe the statement in the Quran that Muhammad was mentioned in the Torah. But the Muslims themselves put no faith in their arguments: they neither accept nor cite them, because they are manifestly so fallacious.

Inasmuch as the Muslims could not find a single proof in the entire Bible, nor any reference, nor even a possible allusion to their prophet which they could utilize, they were compelled to accuse us, saying, "You have altered the text of the Torah and expunged from it every trace of the name of Muhammad." They could find nothing stronger than this ignominious argument, the falseness of which is easily demonstrated to one and all by the following facts. First, the Scripture was translated into Syriac, Greek, Persian and Latin hundreds of years before the appearance of Muhammad. Second, there is a uniform tradition regarding the text of the Bible both in the East and in the West, with the result that no differences in the text exist at all, not even in the vocalization, for they are all correct. Nor do any differences affecting the meaning exist. The motive for their accusation lies, therefore, in the absence of any allusion to Muhammad in the Torah. (Maimonides, *Letter to the Yemen*)

6. Marriage with Khadija

We return to Ibn Ishaq's Life of the Apostle of God.

The Messenger of God grew up, God protecting and keeping him from the vileness of heathenism because He wished to honor him with Apostleship, until he grew up to be the finest of his people in manliness, the best in character, most noble in lineage, the best neighbor, the most kind, truthful, reliable, the furthest removed from filthiness and corrupt morals, through loftiness and nobility, so that he was known among his people as "the trustworthy" because of the good qualities which God had implanted in him. (*Life* 117) [IBN ISHAQ 1955: 81]

Next we are introduced to Khadija, Muhammad's longtime and, for as long as she lived, his only wife. The motifs of Muhammad the successful and the acknowledged future holy man continue to be entwined in the narrative.

Khadija was a merchant woman of dignity and wealth. She used to hire men to carry merchandise outside the country on a profit-sharing basis, for the Quraysh were a people given to commerce. Now when she heard about the Prophet's truthfulness, trustworthiness and honorable character, she sent for him and proposed that he should take her goods to Syria and trade with them, while she would pay him more than she paid others. He was to take a lad called Maysara. The Messenger of God accepted the proposal and the two set forth until they came to Syria.

The Messenger stopped in the shade of a tree near a monk's cell, when the monk came up to Maysara and asked him who the man was resting under the tree. He told him he was of the Quraysh, the people who held the sanctuary (in Mecca), and the monk exclaimed: "None but a prophet ever sat beneath this tree."

Then the Prophet sold the goods he had brought and bought what he wanted to buy and began the return journey to Mecca. The story goes that at the height of noon, when the heat was intense as he rode his beast, Maysara saw two angels shading the Messenger from the sun's rays. When he brought Khadija her property she sold it and it amounted to double or thereabouts. Maysara for his part told her about the two angels who had shaded him and of the monk's words.

Now Khadija was a determined, noble and intelligent woman possessing the properties with which God willed to honor her. So when Maysara told her those things she sent to the Messenger of God and—so the story goes—said "O son of my uncle, I like you because of our relationship and your high reputation among your people, your trustworthiness and good character and truthfulness." Then she proposed marriage. Now Khadija at that time was the best-born woman in the Quraysh, of the greatest dignity, and also the richest. All the people were eager to get possession of her wealth if were possible. . . .

The Messenger of God told his uncles of Khadija's proposal, and his his uncle Hamza ibn Abd al-Muttalib went with him to Khuwaylid ibn Asad and asked for her hand and he married her. She was the mother of all the Apostle's children except Ibrahim, namely, al-Qasim [whence he was known as Abu al-Qasim], al-Tahir, al-Tayyib, Zaynab, Ruqayya, Umm Kulthum and Fatima. Al-Qasim, al-Tayyib and al-Tahir died in the time of paganism. All his daughters lived into Islam and embraced it, and migrated with him to Medina. (*Life* 119–121) [IBN ISHAQ 1955: 82–83]

7. The Kaʿba Rebuilt

The center of the pre-Islamic religious cult in Mecca (later incorporated into Islamic ritual as well) was the Kaʿba or "cube," a square building in the midst of the sacred precinct or haram. *It had a black meteoric rock embedded in one of its corners.*

The Quraysh decided to rebuild the Kaʿba when the Messenger was thirty-five years of age. They were planning to roof it and feared to demolish it, for it was made of loose stones about a man's height, and they wanted to raise it and roof it because men had stolen part of the treasure of the Kaʿba which used to be in a well in the middle of it. . . .

Now a ship belonging to a Greek merchant had been cast ashore at Jedda and became a total wreck. They took its timbers and got ready to roof the Kaʿba (with them). It happened that in Mecca there was a Copt who was a carpenter, so everything they needed was at hand. . . . The people were afraid to demolish the temple, however, and withdrew in awe from it. Al-Walid ibn al-Mughira said, "I will begin the demolition." So he took a pick ax, went up to it, saying the while, "O God, do not be afraid, O God, we intend only what is best." Then he demolished the part at the two corners. That night the people watched, saying, "We will look out; if he is struck down, we won't destroy any more of it and will restore it as it was; but if nothing happens to him, then God is pleased with what we are doing and we will demolish it." In the morning al-Walid returned to the work of demolition and the people worked with him until they got down to the foundation of Abraham (Quran 2:127). They came upon green stones like camel's humps joined to one another. . . . I was told that the Quraysh found in the corner a writing in Syriac. They could not understand it until a Jew read it for them. It was as follows: "I am God, the Lord of the Bakka. I created it on the day that I created heaven and earth and formed the sun and the moon, and I surrounded it with seven pious angels. It will stand while its two mountains stand, a blessing to its people with milk and water," and I was told that they found in the *maqam* [a stone, and a shrine, sacred to Abraham in Islamic tradition] a writing, "Mecca is God's holy house, its sustenance comes to it from three directions; let its people not be the first to profane it. . . ."

The tribes of Quraysh gathered stones for the building, each tribe collecting them and building by itself until the building was finished up to the (location of the) black stone, where controversy arose, since each tribe wanted to lift it into its place, until they went their several ways formed alliances and got ready for battle.

They agree to accept the arbitration of the next man to enter into the sanctuary. It was Muhammad.

When they saw him they said, "This is the trustworthy one. We are satisfied. This is Muhammad." When they came to him and they informed him of the matter he said, "Give me a cloak," and when it was brought to him he took the black stone and placed it inside it and said that each tribe should take hold of an end of the cloak and lift it together. They did this so that when they got it into position he placed it with his own hand, and then building went on above it. (*Life* 122–125) [IBN ISHAQ 1955: 84–86]

8. The Religion of Abraham

It seems likely that the stories of Abraham's association with Mecca were circulating before the Quran began making reference to them. How or when that connection came to be, we cannot even guess, since there is no evidence that Jews or Christians lived in Muhammad's native city. But there were some type of monotheists there, or so the Arab tradition informs us, though the word used to describe them, hanif, remains somewhat mysterious.

One day when the Quraysh had assembled on a feast day to venerate and circumambulate the idol to which they offered sacrifices, this being a feast which they held annually, four men drew apart and agreed to keep their counsel in the bonds of friendship. There were Waraqa ibn Nawfal, Ubaydallah ibn Jahsh, Uthman ibn al-Hawarith and Zayd ibn Amr. They were of the opinion that their people had corrupted the religion of their father Abraham, and that the stone they went around was of no account; it could neither hear, nor see, nor hurt, nor help. "Find for yourselves a religion," they said, "for by God you have none." So they went their several ways in the lands, seeking the Hanifiyya, the religion of Abraham.

Waraqa attached himself to Christianity and studied its Scriptures until he had completely mastered them. Ubaydallah went on searching until Islam came; then he migrated with the Muslims to Abyssinia, taking with him his wife who was a Muslim, Umm Habiba. When he arrived there he adopted Christianity, parted from Islam, and died a Christian in Abyssinia. . . . Uthman ibn al-Hawarith went to the Byzantine emperor and became a Christian. He was given a high office there. Zayd ibn Amr stayed as he was: he accepted neither Judaism or Christianity. He abandoned the religion of his people and abstained from idols, animals that had died, and things offered to idols. He forbade the killing of infant daughters, saying that he worshiped the God of Abraham, and he publicly rebuked his people for their practices. (*Life* 143–144) [IBN ISHAQ 1955: 98–99]

9. Muhammad's Call and First Revelation

Like the hanifs, Muhammad too may have been a man struggling toward belief—until God once again intervened in history. Our source is the Prophet's biographer, Ibn Ishaq.

When Muhammad the Messenger of God reached the age of forty [ca. 610 C.E.], God sent him in compassion to mankind as "a bearer of good news and a warner to all men" (Quran 34:28). Now God had made a covenant with every prophet whom He had sent before him that he should believe in Him, testify to His truth, and help Him against His adversaries, and He required of them that they should transmit that to everyone who believed in them and they carried out their obligations in that respect. . . .

Al-Zuhri related from Urwa ibn Zubayr that Aisha told him that when God desired to honor Muhammad and have mercy on His servants by means of him, the first sign of prophethood vouchsafed to the Messenger was true visions, resembling the brightness of daybreak, which were shown to him in his sleep. And God, she said, made him love solitude so that he liked nothing better than to be alone.

Abd al-Malik ibn Abdullah, who had a retentive memory, related to me from a certain scholar that the Apostle, at the time when God willed to bestow His grace upon him and endow him with prophethood, would go forth for his affair and journey far afield until he reached the glens of Mecca and the valleys where no house was in sight; and not a stone or a tree that he passed but would say, "Peace unto you, O Messenger of God." And the Messenger would turn to his right and his left and look behind him and he would see naught but trees and stones. Thus he stayed seeing and hearing so long as it pleased God that he should stay. Then Gabriel came to him with the gift of God's grace while he was on (Mount) Hira in the month of Ramadan.

. . . Ubayd ibn Umayr related . . . that the Messenger would pray in seclusion on Hira every year for a month to practice *tahannuth* as was the custom of the Quraysh in heathen days. *Tahannuth* is religious devotion. . . .

Wahb ibn Kaysan told me that Ubayd told him: Every year during that month the Messenger would pray in seclusion and give food to the poor that came to him. And when he completed the month and returned from his seclusion, even before entering his house he would go to the Kaʿba and walk around it seven times or as often as it pleased God. Then he would go back to his house.

(Thus it went) until in the year when God sent him, in the month of Ramadan when God willed concerning him what He willed of His grace, the Messenger set forth for (Mount) Hira as was his custom, and his family was with him. When it was the night on which God honored him with his mission and showed mercy on His servants thereby, Gabriel brought him the command of God. "He came to me," said the Messenger of God, "while I was asleep, with a coverlet of brocade on which was some writing, and said, 'Recite!' I said, 'What shall I recite?' He pressed me with it so tightly that I thought it was death; then he let me go and said 'Recite!' I said, 'What shall I recite?' He pressed me with it a third time so that I thought it was death and said 'Recite!' I said, 'What then shall I recite?'—and this I said only to deliver myself from him, lest he should do the same to me again. He said:

> 'Recite: In the name of your Lord who created,
> Who created man from an embryo.
> Recite: Your Lord is the most beneficent,
> Who taught by the pen,
> Taught man what he did not know.' "
> (Quran 96:1–5)

According to Ibn Ishaq's account, then, the verses included in the Quran as Sura or Chapter 96 constituted the earliest of the revelations given to Muhammad. But the matter of the earliest revelation is not so certain. The narrative continues.

So I recited it and he departed from me. And I awoke from my sleep, and it was as though these words were written on my heart. When I was midway on the mountain, I heard a voice from heaven saying, "O Muhammad, thou art the Messenger of God and I am Gabriel." I raised my head toward heaven to see who was speaking, and behold, there was Gabriel with feet astride the horizon saying, "O Muhammad, thou art the Messenger of God and I am Gabriel." . . . And I continued standing there, neither advancing nor turning back until Khadija sent her messengers in search of me, and they gained the high ground above Mecca and returned to her all the while I was standing in the same place. Then he parted from me and I from him, returning to my family. (*Life*, 150–153)

[IBN ISHAQ 1955: 104–106]

This last incident is echoed in the Quran, though in a slightly different form.

> So he acquired poise and balance,
> And reached the highest pinnacle.
> Then he drew near and drew closer
> Until a space of two bow arcs or less remained,
> When He revealed to His votary what He revealed.
> (Quran 53:6–10)

The events of this critical moment in the life of the Prophet are described in various forms in the traditions circulating in the early Islamic community.

Muhammad ibn Umar informed us . . . on the authority of Aisha: The beginning of the revelations to the Apostle of God, may God bless him, was in the form of true dreams. . . . They came to him like daybreak. She said: he remained in this condition for as long as God willed. He liked solitude; nothing was dearer to him. He would retire to the cave of Hira taking provisions for several nights, after which he returned to his family. Then he would come to Khadija to take provisions again until the truth dawned on him while he was in the cave of Hira.

Muhammad ibn Umar informed us ... on the authority of Ibn Abbas: When, at that time, the Apostle of God, may God bless him, was at Ajyad, he saw an angel, with one foot on the other, in the horizon, and calling: "O Muhammad. I am Gabriel, O Muhammad. I am Gabriel." The Apostle of God, may God bless him, was terrified. Whenever he raised his head toward the heaven he saw him; so he returned hastily to Khadija and conveyed this information to her. He said: "O Khadija! By God, I never hated anything so much as idols and soothsayers; and I am afraid that I shall myself become a soothsayer. . . ."

She informs him he has nothing to fear.

Yahya ibn Abbad said ... I think on the authority of Ibn Abbas: "In truth the Prophet, may God bless him, said; 'O Khadija, I hear sounds and see light and I fear I am mad.' "

Once again Khadija assures him he has nothing to fear on this score. There is still another version, once again from Muhammad ibn Umar, that derives finally from the authority of Ibn Abbas.

In truth, after the first revelation to the Apostle of God, may God bless him, that came at Hira, the coming of revelations remained suspended for a few days. Since he did not see Gabriel he was much grieved; he went to Thabir and at another time to Hira with the intention of throwing himself down. When the Apostle of God, may God bless him. was intending to do this from one of these mountains, he heard a sound coming from heaven. The Apostle of God, may God bless him, paused for a moment because of the thunderous sound, then he raised his head and behold, it was Gabriel seated in a chair between the earth and the sky. He was saying: "O Muhammad, you are truly the Apostle of God and I am Gabriel." The Apostle of God, may God bless him, returned and God had cooled his eye and strengthened his heart; thereafter revelations followed one after the other. (Ibn Sa'd, *Tabaqat* I/1 129–130)

We return to Ibn Ishaq's version of events. Waraqa ibn Nawfal, it will be recalled, was earlier identified as one of the hanifs. He now re-enters the account at a crucial point.

And I came to Khadija and sat by her thigh and drew close to her. She said, "O Abu al-Qasim, where have you been? By God, I sent my messengers in search of you, and they reached the high ground above

Mecca and returned to me (without seeing you)." Then I told her what I had seen, and she said, "Rejoice, O son of my uncle, and be of good heart. Verily, by Him in whose hand is Khadija's soul, I have hopes that you will be the prophet of this people." Then she rose and gathered her garments about her and set forth to her cousin Waraqa ibn Nawfal, who had become a Christian and read the Scriptures and learned from those that follow the Torah and the Gospel. And when she related to him what the Messenger of God told her he had seen and heard, Waraqa cried, "Holy! Holy! Holy! Verily, by Him in whose hand is Waraqa's soul, if you have spoken to me the truth, O Khadija, there has come to him the greatest *Namus* [Gk. *nomos*, law, likely the Torah, though not understood as such by the tradition] who came to Moses previously, and behold, he is the prophet of this people. Bid him be of good heart." So Khadija returned to the Prophet of God and told him what Waraqa had said. (*Life* 153–154) [IBN ISHAQ 1955: 106–107]

10. Sadness, Doubt, Consolation

Muhammad, for his part, was not so certain of what had befallen him. The traditional Life *leaves little doubt that it was Khadija who supported him through this difficult period of doubt and hesitation.*

Khadija believed in him and accepted as true what he had brought from God, and helped him in his work. She was the first to believe in God and His Messenger and in the truth of his message. By her, God lightened the burden of His Prophet. He had never met with contradiction and charges of falsehood (before), which saddened him, but God comforted him by her when he went home. She strengthened him, lightened his burden, proclaimed his truth, and belittled men's opposition. May God Almighty have mercy on her!

. . . Then the revelations stopped for a time so that the Messenger of God was distressed and grieved. Then Gabriel brought him the Sura of the Morning (Sura 93), in which his Lord, who had so honored him, swore that He had not forsaken him and did not hate him. God said, "By the morning and the night, when it is still, thy Lord has not forsaken or hated thee," meaning that He has not left you, forsaken you or hated you after having loved you. "And verily, the latter end is better for you than the beginning," that is, what I have for you when you return to Me is better than the honor which I have given you in the world. "And the Lord will give you and satisfy you," that is, of victory in this world and reward in the next. "Did he not find you an orphan and give you refuge, going astray and guided you, found you poor and made you rich?" God thus told him how He had begun to honor him in his earthly life, and His kindness to him as an orphan and wandering astray, and His delivering him from all that by His compassion.

"Do not oppress the orphan and do not repel the beggar," that is, do not be a tyrant or proud or harsh or mean toward the weakest of God's creatures. "Speak of the kindness of thy Lord," that is, tell about the kindness of God in giving you prophecy, mention it and call men to it.

So the Messenger began to mention secretly God's kindness to him and to his servants in the matter of prophecy to everyone among his people whom he could trust. (*Life* 155–156) [IBN ISHAQ 1955: 111–112]

11. The Conversion of Ali

This was not yet public preaching, but Muhammad's own firm conviction and the urgency of his message began to have its effect, although at first in a limited circle. Ali, the son of Abu Talib and cousin of the Prophet, and later one of the great heroes of Islam, embraced the new faith. But the reaction of his father illustrates the enormous social difficulty of a Meccan rejecting the "tradition of his fathers" for the new "tradition of the Prophet."

Ali was the first male to believe in the Apostle, to pray with him and to believe in his divine message, when he was a boy of ten. God favored him in that he was brought up in the care of the Messenger before Islam began. . . .

A traditionist mentioned that when the time of prayer came the Messenger used to go out to the glens of Mecca accompanied by Ali, who went unbeknown to his father, and his uncles and the rest of the people. There they used to pray the ritual prayers and return at nightfall. This went on as long as God intended that it should, until one day Abu Talib came upon them while they were praying and said to the Apostle, "O nephew, what is this religion which I see you practicing?" He replied, "O uncle, this is the religion of God, His angels, His Apostles, and the religion of our father Abraham." Or, as he said, "God sent me as a Messenger to mankind, and you, my uncle, most deserve that I should teach you the truth and call you to guidance, and you are the most worthy to respond and help me," or words to that effect. His uncle replied, "I cannot give up the religion of my fathers which they followed, but by God, you shall never meet anything to distress you so long as I live." They (also) mention that he said to Ali, "My boy, what is this religion of yours?" He answered, "I believe in God and the Messenger of God, and I declare that what he has brought is true, and I pray to God with him and follow him." (*Life* 158–160) [IBN ISHAQ 1955: 114]

12. The Earliest Public Preaching of Islam

People began to accept Islam, both men and women, in large numbers until the fame of it was spread throughout Mecca, and it began to be talked about. Then God commanded His Messenger to declare the truth of what he had received and to make known his commands to men and to call them to Him. Three years had elapsed from the time that the Messenger concealed his state until God commanded him to publish His religion, according to information which has reached me. Then God said, "Proclaim what you have been ordered and turn aside the polytheists" (Quran 15: 94). And again, "Warn your family, your nearest relations, and lower your wing to the followers who follow you" (Quran 26:214–215). And "Say, I am the one who warns plainly" (Quran 15:9). (*Life* 166) [IBN ISHAQ 1955: 117]

The 114 suras or chapters of the Quran were eventually arranged pretty much in reverse order of their length, and so it is difficult to be exact about the precise sequence or chronology of the revelations to Muhammad. There is, however, general agreement among both Muslim and non-Muslim scholars on some of the earliest of them, and they offer an insight into the tenor and tone of the Prophet's preaching to his contemporaries in Mecca.

> You, enfolded in your mantle!
> Arise and warn!
> Glorify your Lord,
> Purify your inner self,
> And banish all trepidation.
> Do not bestow favors in expectation of return,
> And persevere in the way of your Lord.
> For when the trumpet blows
> It will be a day of distress,
> Dolorous for the unbelievers.
> Leave him to Me alone whom I created,
> And gave him abundant wealth
> And sons always present by his side,

And made things easy for them.
Yet he wants that I should give him more.
Never! He is refractory of our signs.
I shall inflict on him hardship,
For he had thought and calculated.
May he be accursed, how he planned!
May he be accursed, how he plotted!
Then he looked around,
And frowned and puckered his brow,
Then turned his back and waxed proud,
And said: "This is nothing but the magic of old,
Nothing more than the speech of a man!"
I will cast him into the fire of Hell.
What do you think Hell-fire is?
It leaves nothing, nor does it spare;
It glows and burns the skin. . . .
(Quran 74:1–29)

I call to witness the early hours of the morning,
And the night when dark and still,
Your Lord has neither left you, nor despises you.
What is to come is better for you than what has gone before;
For your Lord will certainly give you, and you will be content.
Did He not find you an orphan, and take care of you?
Did He not find you perplexed and show you the way?
Did He not find you poor and enrich you?
So do not oppress the orphan,
And do not drive the beggar away,
And keep recounting the favors of your Lord.
(Quran 93)

Say: O you unbelievers,
I do not worship what you worship,
Nor do you worship Who I worship;
Nor will I worship what you worship,
Nor will you worship Who I worship.
To you your way; to me my way.
(Quran 109)

Say: He is God, the one the most unique,
God the immanently indispensable.

He has begotten no one, and is begotten of none.
There is no one comparable to Him.
(Quran 112)

Have you seen him who denies the Day of Judgment?
It is he who pushes the orphan away,
And does not induce others to feed the needy.
Woe to those who pray,
But who are oblivious in their moral duties,
Who dissimulate,
And withhold the necessities (from others).
(Quran 107)

I call to witness the heavens and the night star—
How will you comprehend what the night star is?
It is the star that shines with a piercing brightness—
That over each soul there is a guardian.
Let man consider what he was made of:
He was created of spurting water
Issuing from between the backbone and the ribs.
God has certainly the power to bring him back (from the dead).
The day all secrets are examined
He will have no strength or helper.
So I call to witness the rain-producing sky,
And the earth which opens up,
That this Quran is a distinctive word
And no trifle.
They are hatching up a plot, (Muhammad,)
But I too am devising a plan.
So bear with unbelievers with patience and give them a respite
                              for a while.
(Quran 86)

Recite, in the name of your Lord who created,
Created man from an embryo;
Recite! For your Lord is most beneficent,
Who taught by the pen,
Taught man what he did not know.
And yet, but yet man is rebellious,
For he thinks he is sufficient in himself.
Surely your returning is to your Lord.

Have you seen him who restrains
A votary when he turns to his devotions?
Have you thought that if he denies and turns away,
Does he not know that God sees?
And yet indeed if he does not desist We shall drag him by the
    forelock,
By the lying, the sinful forelock!
So let him summon his associates,
And we shall call the guards of Hell!
Beware! Do not obey him, but bow in adoration and draw near
    (to your Lord).

(Quran 96)

The Message of these early suras of the Quran is clear and direct: God, who created the world and mankind, will require an accounting from His creation on the Last Day. The insolent, the worldly, the greedy will be cast into Hell; the generous and obedient will be rewarded with Paradise. The appropriate human response, then, is submission—in Arabic islam—*to the will of God and the directions of His Prophet.*

13. The Opposition of the Quraysh

Since the Quraysh have been united,
United to fit out caravans winter and summer.
Let them worship the Lord of this House,
Who provided them against destitution, and gave them security
    from fear.

(Quran 106)

The earliest Meccan Muslims—literally, "those who have submitted," the same term used of Abraham and his descendants—did not include many of the powerful first families of Mecca, those same Quraysh who sent forth their summer and winter caravans to trade in Syria and the Yemen. The Meccan merchant aristocracy continued to be what it had always been in living memory: the worshipers of idols, a great many of which were collected in the haram, *or sacred enclosure that surrounded the Ka'ba in the midst of Mecca.*

When the Messenger openly displayed Islam as God ordered him, his people did not withdraw or turn against him, so far as I have heard, until he spoke disparagingly of their gods. When he did that they took great offense and resolved unanimously to treat him as an enemy, except those whom God had protected by Islam from such evil, but they were a despised minority. Abu Talib his uncle treated the Messenger kindly and protected him, the latter continuing to obey God's commands, nothing turning him back. When the Quraysh saw that he would not yield to them and insulted their gods and that his uncle treated him kindly and stood up in his defense and would not give him up to them, some of their leading men went to Abu Talib. . . . They said, "O Abu Talib, your nephew has cursed our gods, insulted our religion, mocked our way of life and accused our forefathers of error. Either you must stop him or you must let us get at him, for you yourself are in the same position as we are in opposition to him and we will rid you of him." He gave them a conciliatory reply and a soft answer and they went away.

The Messenger continued on his way, making public God's religion and calling men to it. In consequence his relations with the Quraysh deteriorated and men withdrew from him in enmity. They were always talking about him and inciting one another against him. Then they went to Abu Talib a second time and said, "You have a high and lofty position among us, and we have asked you to put a stop to your nephew's activities but you have not done so. By God, we cannot endure that our fathers should be reviled, our customs mocked and our gods insulted. Until you rid us of him we will fight the pair of you until one side perishes," or words to that effect. Thus saying, they went off. Abu Talib was deeply distressed at the breach with his people and their enmity, but he could not desert the Messenger and give him up to them.

Mecca was still very much a tribal society, and the message of Muhammad inevitably raised the specter of schisms running across the complex lines of patronage and clientage in the city.

Then the Quraysh incited people against the companions of the Messenger who had become Muslims. Every tribe fell upon the Muslims among them, beating them and seducing them from their religion. God protected His Messenger from them through his uncle, who, when he saw what the Quraysh were doing, called upon the Banu Hashim and the Banu al-Muttalib to stand with him in protecting the Apostle. This they agreed to do, with the exception of Abu Lahab, the accursed enemy of God. (*Life* 166–170) [IBN ISHAQ 1955: 118–120]

14. The Prophet Characterized

When the annual fair was due, a number of the Quraysh came to al-Walid ibn al-Mughira, who was a man of some standing, and he addressed them in these words: "The time of the fair has come round again, and representatives of the Arabs will come to you and they will have heard about this fellow of yours. So agree on one opinion (concerning him) without dispute so that none may contradict the other." They replied, "You give us your opinion about him." He said, "No, you speak and I will listen." They said, "He is a seer." Al-Walid said, "By God, he is not, for he has not the unintelligent murmuring and rhymed speech of the seer." "Then he is possessed," they said. "No, he is not that," al-Walid replied. "We have seen possessed people and here is no choking, spasmodic movements and whispering." "Then he is a poet," they said. "No, he is no poet," al-Walid said, "for we know poetry in all its forms and meters." "Then he is a sorcerer." "No, we have seen sorcerers and their sorcery, and here is no blowing and no knots." "Then what are we to say, O Abu Abd al-Shams?" they asked. He replied, "By God, his speech is sweet, his root is a palm tree whose branches are fruitful and everything you have said would be recognized as false. The nearest thing to such in your saying is that he is a sorcerer, who has brought a message by which he separates a man from his father or from his brother, or from his wife, or from his family." (*Life* 171) [IBN ISHAQ 1955: 121]

15. Attempted Negotiations

Islam began to spread in Mecca among men and women of the tribes of the Quraysh, though the Quraysh were imprisoning and seducing as many of the Muslims as they could. A traditionist told me from Saʿid ibn Jubayr and from Ikrima, freedman of Abdullah ibn Abbas, that the leading men of every clan of the Quraysh . . . decided to send for Muhammad and to negotiate and argue with him so that they could not be held to blame on his account in the future. When they sent for him the Messenger of God came quickly because he thought that what he had (earlier) said to them had made an impression, for he was most zealous for their welfare and their wicked ways pained him. When he came and sat down with them, they explained that they had sent for him in order that they could talk together. No Arab had ever treated his tribe as he had treated them, and they repeated the charges which have been mentioned on several occasions. If it was money he wanted, they would make him richest of them all; if it was honor, he should be their prince; if it was sovereignty, they would make him king; if it was a spirit that had got possession of him, then they would exhaust their means in finding medicine to cure him.

These broad promises were likely neither sincere nor altogether practical, but they attest to the magnitude of the threat that Muhammad was thought to pose to the social and commercial equilibrium of Mecca, a city that had combined trade and pilgrimage to its shrine into a profitable enterprise.

The Messenger replied that he had no such intention. He sought not money nor honor nor sovereignty, but God had sent him as an Apostle, and revealed a book to him, and commanded him to become an announcer and a warner. He had brought the message of his Lord and given them good advice. If they took it, then they would have a portion of this world and the next; if they rejected it, he could only patiently await the outcome until God decided between them, or words to that effect.

"Well, Muhammad," they said, "if you won't accept any of our propositions, you know that no people are more short of land and water and live a harder life than we, so ask your Lord, who sent you, to remove us from these mountains which shut us in, and to straighten out our country for us, and to open up in it rivers like those of Syria and Iraq, and to resurrect for us our forefathers—and let there be among those who are resurrected Qusayy ibn Kilab, for he was a true shaykh—so that we may ask them whether what you say is true or false." . . . He replied that he had not been sent to them with such an object. He had conveyed to them God's message and they could either accept it with advantage or reject it and await God's judgment. They said that if he could not do that for them, let him do something for himself. Ask God to send an angel with him to confirm what he said and to contradict them; to make him gardens and castles and treasures of gold and silver to satisfy his obvious wants, since he stood in the street as they did and he sought a livelihood as they did. . . . He replied that he would not do it, and would not ask for such things, for he was not sent to do so, and he repeated what he had said before. . . . They said, "Did not your Lord know that we would sit with you and ask you these questions, so that He might come to you and instruct you how to answer, and tell you what He was going to do with us, if we did not accept your message? Information has reached us that you are taught by this fellow in al-Yamama called al-Rahman ["The Compassionate"], and by God we will never believe in the Rahman. Our conscience is clear, by God, we will not leave you and our treatment of you until either we destroy you or you destroy us." (*Life* 187–189)

[IBN ISHAQ 1955: 133–134]

16. Persecution and Emigration to Abyssinia

Then the Quraysh showed the enmity to all those who followed the Apostle; every clan which included Muslims attacked them, imprisoning and beating them, allowing them no food or drink, and exposing them to the burning heat of Mecca so as to seduce them from their religion. Some gave way under pressure of persecution and others resisted them, being protected by God. . . . It was that evil man Abu Jahl who stirred up the Meccans against them. When he heard that a man had become a Muslim, if he was a man of social importance and had relations to defend him, he (merely) reprimanded him and poured scorn on him, saying, "You have forsaken the religion of your father who is better than you. We will declare you a blockhead and brand you a fool and destroy your reputation." If he was a merchant he said, "We will boycott your goods and reduce you to beggary." If he was a person of no social importance, he beat him and incited the people against him. (*Life* 205–207)

[IBN ISHAQ 1955: 143–145]

When the Messenger saw the affliction of his companions and, though he (himself) escaped it because of his standing with God and his uncle Abu Talib, he could not protect them, he said to them: "If you were to go to Abyssinia it would be better for you, for the king (there) will not tolerate injustice and it is a friendly country, until such time as God shall relieve you from your distress." Thereupon his companions went to Abyssinia, being afraid of apostasy and fleeing to God with their religion. This was the first *hijra* [emigration] in Islam.

The choice of Abyssinia across the Red Sea as a place of refuge for the beleaguered Muslims is somewhat surprising, but only because we are so scantily instructed by our sources on the larger commercial connections of Mecca. Abyssinia had long since embraced Christianity, a religion to which Muhammad may have felt an affinity. But Abyssinia was also a rising commercial exporter in the shifting international trade of the sixth and seventh centuries, and the tiny band of Muslim expatriates may well have been sent there to explore commercial possibilities. Whatever the case, the Quraysh sent their own deputation to convince the Christian king of Abyssinia, called the Negus, to send the Muslims back. The Negus holds a public hearing on the matter and requests an explanation of Islam.

When they [the Muslims] came into the royal presence, they found the king had summoned his bishops with their sacred books exposed around him. He asked them what was the religion for which they had forsaken their people, without entering into his religion or any other. Abu

Ja'far ibn Abi Talib answered, "O King, we were an uncivilized people, worshiping idols, eating corpses, committing abominations, breaking natural ties, treating guests badly, and our strong devoured our weak. Thus we were until God sent us a Messenger whose lineage, truth, trustworthiness and clemency we know. He summoned us to acknowledge God's unity and to worship Him and renounce the stones and images which our fathers formerly worshiped. He commanded us to speak the truth, be faithful to our engagements, mindful of the ties of kinship and kindly hospitality, and to refrain from crimes and bloodshed. He forbade us to commit abominations and to speak lies, and to devour the property of orphans, and to vilify chaste women. He commanded us to worship God alone and not to associate anything with Him, and he gave us orders about prayer, almsgiving and fasting. We confessed his truth and believed in him, and we followed him in what he had brought from God, and we worshiped God alone without associating aught with Him. We treated as forbidden what he forbade and as lawful what he declared lawful. . . ."

The Negus asked if they had with them anything which had come from God. When Ja'far said he had, the Negus commanded him to read it to him, so he read him a passage from the sura called "Mary" (19). The Negus wept until his beard was wet and the bishops wept until their scrolls were wet, when they heard what was read to them. Then the Negus said, "Of a truth, this and what Jesus brought have come from the same niche. You two (Quraysh) may go, for by God, I will never give them [the Muslims] up and they shall not be betrayed. (*Life* 208–220)
[IBN ISHAQ 1955: 146–148]

17. A Famous Conversion

Abdullah ibn Abi Najih, the Meccan, from his companions Ata and Mujahid, or other narrators, said that the conversion of Umar [Umar ibn al-Khattab, the second Caliph, 634–644 C.E.], according to what he himself used to say, happened thus:

"I was far from Islam. I was a winebibber in the heathen period, used to love it and rejoice in it. We used to have a meeting place in al-Hazwara where the Quraysh used to gather. . . . I went out one night, making for my boon companions in that gathering, but when I got there, there was no one present, so I thought it would be a good thing if I went to so-and-so, the wineseller, who was selling wine in Mecca at that time, in the hope that I might get something to drink from him. I could not find him either, so I thought it would be a good thing if I went around the

Ka'ba seven or seventy times. So I came to the sanctuary intending to go round the Ka'ba, and there was the Messenger standing praying. As he prayed he faced Syria [that is, Jerusalem], putting the Ka'ba between himself and Syria. His position was between the black stone and the southern corner. When I saw him I thought it would be a good thing if I could listen to Muhammad so as to hear what he said. If I came near to listen to him I would frighten him, so I came from the direction of the Hijr [a low stone porch near the Ka'ba] . . . until I stood facing him in the path of his direction of prayer, there being nothing between us but the covering of the Ka'ba.

"When I heard the Quran my heart was softened and I wept, and Islam entered into me; but I remained in my place until the Messenger had finished his prayer. Then he went away. . . . I followed him until he got between the house of Abbas and Ibn Azhar, where I overtook him. When he heard my voice he recognized me and supposed that I had followed him only to ill treat him, so he repelled me, saying 'What has brought you here at this hour?' I replied that I had come to believe in God and His Messenger and what he had brought from God. He gave thanks to God and said, 'God has guided you.' Then he rubbed my breast and prayed that I might be steadfast. Afterwards I left him. He went into his house." (*Life* 227–230) [IBN ISHAQ 1955: 157–158]

18. The Boycott

When the Quraysh perceived that the Apostle's companions had settled in a land in peace and safety and that the Negus had protected those who had sought refuge with him, and that Umar had become a Muslim and that he and Hamza were on the side of the Messenger and his companions, and that Islam had begun to spread among the tribes, they came together and decided among themselves to write a document in which they would put a boycott on the Banu Hashim and the Banu Muttalib that no one should marry their women or give women for them to marry; and that no one should either buy from them or sell to them, and when they agreed on that they wrote it in a deed. Then they solemnly agreed on the points and hung the deed up in the middle of the Ka'ba to remind them of their obligations.

The point does not appear to have been so much to starve Muhammad and his followers into submission as to exclude them from the commercial life of that very commercial city.

... Meanwhile the Messenger was exhorting his people night and day, secretly and publicly, openly proclaiming God's command without fear of anyone. His uncle and the rest of the Banu Hashim gathered round him and protected him from the attacks of the Quraysh, who when they saw they could not get at him, mocked and laughed and disputed with him. The Quran began to come down concerning the wickedness of the Quraysh and those who showed enmity to him, some by name and some only referred to in general. (*Life* 230–233) [IBN ISHAQ 1955: 159–161]

19. Muhammad's Night Journey

Deceived by false reports of the conversion of the Quraysh, many of the emigrants return from Abyssinia. Although the Quraysh showed no signs of relenting on religious grounds, their boycott against the Banu Hashim and the Banu Muttalib did in effect collapse. It is at this point that the Life *inserts the account of the famous "Night Journey" of the Prophet referred to in Sura 17:1 of the Quran.*

Glory be to Him who took His votary by night from the Sacred Mosque to the distant Mosque, whose precincts We have blessed, that We may show him some of Our signs. Verily, He is the all-hearing and all-seeing.

The Life *fills out the details.*

The following account reached me from Abdullah b. Mas'ud and Abu Sa'id al-Khudri and Aisha the Prophet's wife and Mu'awiya b. Abi Sufyan and al-Hasan al-Basri and Ibn Shihab al-Zuhri and Qatada and other traditionists as well as Umm Hani, daughter of Abu Talib. It is pieced together in the story that follows, each one contributing something of what he was told about what had happened when the Prophet was taken on the Night Journey. The matter of the place of the journey and what is said about it is a searching test and a matter of God's power and authority wherein is a lesson for the intelligent, and guidance and mercy and strengthening to those who believe. It was certainly an act of God by which He took him by night in whatever way He pleased to show him signs which He willed him to see so that he witnessed His mighty sovereignty and power by which He does what He wills to do.

Though there may have been, as this text hints, some hesitations about the destination of this journey by night, there soon developed a consensus that the "distant shrine" of Quran 17:1 was in fact the site of the former Temple in Jerusalem.

According to what I have heard, Abdullah ibn Mas'ud used to say: Buraq [the steed that carried Muhammad; see below], whose every stride carried it as far as its eye could reach and on which earlier prophets had ridden, was brought to the Messenger and he was mounted on it. His companion (Gabriel) went with him to see the wonders between heaven and earth, until he came to Jerusalem's Temple. There he found Abraham the Friend of God, Moses and Jesus assembled with a company of prophets and prayed with them. Then he was brought three vessels containing milk, wine and water respectively. The Messenger said: "I heard a voice saying when these were offered to me, If he takes the water he will be drowned and his people also; if he takes the wine he will go astray and his people also; and if he tastes the milk, he will be rightly guided and his people also. So I took the vessel containing the milk and drank it. Gabriel said to me, 'You have been rightly guided, and so will your people be, Muhammad.' "

In the manner of Arab historians, Ibn Ishaq provides another version of the same event, this one from Hasan al-Basri [d. 728 C.E.], a purported eyewitness to some of the circumstances, though he must have been a very small child at the time.

I was told that al-Hasan al-Basri said that the Messenger of God said: "While I was sleeping in the Hijr [a kind of semicircular stone porch close by the Ka'ba], Gabriel came and stirred me with his foot. I sat up but saw nothing and lay down again. He came a second time and stirred me with his foot. I sat up but saw nothing and lay down again. He came to me the third time and stirred me with his foot. I sat up and he took hold of my arm and I stood beside him and he brought me out to the door of the shrine and there was a white animal, half mule and half donkey with wings on its side with which it propelled its feet, putting down each forefoot at the limit of its sight, and he mounted me on it. Then he went out with me, keeping close by my side."

In his story al-Hasan continued: "The Messenger and Gabriel went their way until they arrived at the shrine at Jerusalem. There he found Abraham, Moses and Jesus among a company of the prophets. The Messenger acted as their leader in prayer. . . . Then the Messenger returned to Mecca and in the morning he told the Quraysh what had happened. Most of them said: 'By God, this is a plain absurdity! A caravan takes a month to go to Syria and a month to return and can Muhammad do the return journey in one night?' At this many Muslims gave up their faith; some went to Abu Bakr and said: 'What do you think of your friend now, Abu Bakr? He alleges he went to Jerusalem last night and prayed there and came back to Mecca.' Abu Bakr replied that they were lying about the Apostle. But they replied that he was at that very moment in the shrine telling the people about it. Abu Bakr said: 'If he says so, then it must be true. And what is so surprising in that? He tells me that communications from God from heaven to earth come to him in an hour of a day or night and I believe him, and that is more extraordinary than that at which you boggle!'

"Abu Bakr then went to the Messenger and asked him if these reports were true, and when he said they were, he asked him to describe Jerusalem to him." Al-Hasan said that [as a small child] he was lifted up so that he could see the Messenger speaking as he told Abu Bakr what Jerusalem was like. Whenever Muhammad described a part of it, Abu Bakr said: "That's true. I testify that you are the Messenger of God!" until he had completed the description, and then the Messenger said: "And you, Abu Bakr, are the Witness to Truth."

But the entire incident of the Night Journey was, as Ibn Ishaq had warned at the outset, a grave trial of faith for some of the early Muslims.

Al-Hasan continued: "God sent down the verse (Quran 13:62) concerning those who had left Islam on this account: 'We made you a vision which we showed you only for a test to men and the accursed tree in the Quran. We put them in fear, but it only adds to their heinous error.' " Such is al-Hasan's story. (*Life* 263–265) [IBN ISHAQ 1955: 181–182]

This celebrated Night Journey, a frequent subject of Islamic art and legend, is the cornerstone of Muslim attachment to Jerusalem.

20. The Death of Khadija and Abu Talib (619 C.E.)

Khadija and Abu Talib died in the same year, and with Khadija's death troubles followed fast on each other's heels, for she had been a faithful support for him in Islam, and he used to tell her all his troubles. With the death of Abu Talib he lost a strength and stay in his personal life and a defense and protection against his tribe. Abu Talib died some three years before he migrated to Medina (in 622 C.E.), and it was then that the Quraysh began to treat him in an offensive way which they would not have dared to follow in his uncle's lifetime. (*Life* 276–277)
[IBN ISHAQ 1955: 191]

Muhammad had married Khadija in 595 C.E., when he was twenty-five and she forty. She bore him a number of sons, all of whom died in infancy, and four daughters—Zaynab, Ruqayya, Umm Kulthum, and Fatima. In the years that followed Khadija's death, and when he was in his fifties, Muhammad married Sawda, Abu Bakr's daughter Aisha, Umar's daughter Hafsa, Hind, Zaynab daugh-

ter of Jahsh, Umm Salama, Juwayriyya, Ramla or Umm Habiba, Safiyya, and Maymuna. None of them bore him children, however, though he had a son, Ibrahim, by his Coptic concubine, Mary. Ibrahim too died in infancy.

21. The Pledge at Aqaba

Help was suddenly proferred from an unexpected source: by visitors from the oasis of Yathrib, some 275 miles to the north of Mecca. Yathrib, later named "The medina [city] *of the Prophet," or simply Medina, was an agricultural settlement of mixed Arab and Jewish population. Here, too, as had happened earlier, the Jews were quick to recognize and possibly appropriate (or reject) the Prophet of Islam.*

When God wished to display His religion openly and to glorify His Prophet and to fulfill His promise to him, the time came when he met a number of "Helpers" [that is, future converts to Islam at Medina] at one of the (Meccan) fairs. . . . They said that when the Messenger met them he learned by inquiry that they were of the (tribe of the) Khazraj and were allies of the Jews (there). He invited them to sit with him and he expounded to them Islam and recited the Quran to them. Now God had prepared the way for Islam in that they [the Khazraj] lived side by side with the Jews (of Medina), who were people of the Scriptures and knowledge, while they themselves were polytheists and idolaters. They had often raided them in their district and whenever bad feelings arose the Jews used to say to them, "A Prophet will be sent soon. His day is at hand. We shall follow him and kill you by his aid just as Ad and Iram perished." So when they [the Khazraj] heard the Apostle's message they said to one another, "This is the very Prophet of whom the Jews warned us. Don't let them get to him before us!" Thereupon they accepted his teaching and became Muslims, saying, "We have left our people, for no tribe is so divided by hatred and rancor as they. Perhaps God will unite them through you. So let us go to them and invite them to this religion of yours; and if God unites them in it, then no man will be mightier than you." Thus saying they returned to Medina as believers.

In the following year twelve "Helpers" attended the fair and met at al-Aqaba (a place near Mecca)—this was the first Aqaba—where they gave the Messenger the "pledge of women" (cf. Quran 60:12). . . . "I was present at Aqaba [one of the participants reported]. There were twelve of us and we pledged ourselves to the Prophet after the manner of women and that was before (the obligation of) war was enjoined, the undertaking being that we should associate nothing with God; we should not steal; we should not commit fornication; nor kill our offspring; we should not slander our neighbors; we should not disobey him (Muhammad) in what was right. If we fulfilled this, paradise would be ours; if we committed any of these sins, it was for God to punish or forgive us as He pleased. . . ."

(The next year) the Muslim "Helpers" came to the fair with the pilgrims of their people who were polytheists. They met the Messenger at Aqaba during the days following upon the day of the (Hajj) sacrifice, when God intended to honor them and to help His Messenger and strengthen Islam and to humiliate heathenism and its devotees. . . . Ma'bad ibn Ka'b told me that his brother Abdullah had told him that his father Ka'b ibn Malik said: ". . . We slept that night among our people in the caravan until, when a third of the night had passed, we went stealing softly like sandgrouse to our appointment with the Messenger as far as the gully by al-Aqaba. There were seventy-three men with two of our women. . . . We gathered together in the gully, waiting until the Messenger came with his uncle al-Abbas, who was at that time a polytheist, though he wanted to be present at his nephew's business and make certain that he received a firm guarantee.

"When we sat down al-Abbas was the first to speak and said: 'O people of Khazraj—the Arabs used that term to cover the tribes of both the Khazraj and the Aws. You know Muhammad's situation among us. We have protected him from his own people who think as we do about him. He lives in honor and safety among his people, but he will turn to you and join you. If you think you can be faithful to what you promised him and protect him from his opponents, then assume the burden you have undertaken. But if you think you will betray and abandon him after he has gone out with you, then leave him now, for he is safe where he is.' We replied, 'We have heard what you say. You speak, O Apostle, and choose for yourself and for your Lord what you wish.'

"The Messenger spoke and recited the Quran and invited me to God and recommended Islam, and then said: 'I invite your allegiance on the basis that you protect me as you would your women and children.' Al-Bara took his hand and said: 'By Him who sent you with the truth, we will protect you as we protect our women. We give our alliance and we are men of war possessing arms which have been passed on from father to son.' While al-Bara was speaking, Abu al-Haytham ibn al-Tayyihan interrupted him and said: 'O Apostle, we have ties with other men—he meant the Jews—and if we sever them, perhaps when we have done that and God will have given us victory, will you return to your people and leave us?' The Messenger smiled and said, 'No, blood is blood and blood not to be paid for is blood not to be paid for. I am of you and you are of me. I will war against those who war against you and be at peace with those at peace with you.' " (*Life* 288–297) [IBN ISHAQ 1955: 198–204]

22. A Turn to Armed Resistance

The Messenger had not been given permission to fight or allowed to shed blood before the second (pledge of) Aqaba. He had simply been ordered to call men to God and to endure insult and forgive the innocent. The Quraysh had persecuted his followers, seducing some from their religion and exiling others from their country. They had to choose whether to give up their religion, be mistreated at home, or to flee the country, some to Abyssinia, others to Medina.

When the Quraysh became insolent toward God and rejected His gracious purpose, accused His Prophet of lying, and ill treated and exiled those who served Him and proclaimed His unity, believed in His Prophet and held fast to His religion, He gave permission for His Messenger to fight and protect himself against those who wronged them and treated them badly.

The first verse which was sent down on this subject from what I have heard from Urwa ibn al-Zubayr and other learned persons was:

"Permission is granted those (to take up arms) who fight because they were oppressed. God is certainly able to give help to those who were driven away from their homes for no other reason than that they said 'Our Lord is God.' And if God had not restrained some men through some others, monasteries, churches, synagogues and mosques, where the name of God is honored most, would have been razed. God will surely help those who help Him. —Verily, God is all-powerful and all-mighty— Those who would be firm in devotion, pay the tithe, and enjoin what is good and forbid what is wrong, if we give them authority in the land. But the result of things rests with God." (Quran 22:39–41)

The meaning is: "I have allowed them to fight only because they were unjustly treated, while their sole offense against men is that they worship God. When they are in the ascendent they will establish prayer, pay the poor tax, enjoin kindness and forbid iniquity, that is, the Prophet and his companions, all of them." Then God sent down to him (the verse): "Fight so there is no more persecution," that is, until no believer is seduced from his religion, "and the religion is God's," that is, until God alone is worshiped. (Quran 2:193).

This permission to fight, to turn from passive to active resistance to the Quraysh, was no trifling matter, as its divine sanction shows. The Quraysh's commercial enterprises were protected by their own religiously sanctioned prohibitions against violence and bloodshed during the months of pilgrimage and the annual fairs that were connected with it.

When God had given permission to fight, and this clan of the "Helpers" had pledged their support to him in Islam and to help him and his followers, and the Muslims had taken refuge with them, the Messenger commanded his companions to emigrate to Medina and to link up with their brethren the "Helpers." "God will make for you brethren and houses in which you may be safe." So they went out in companies, and the Messenger stayed in Mecca waiting for the Lord's permission to leave Mecca and migrate to Medina. (*Life* 313–314) [IBN ISHAQ 1955: 212–213]

23. The Emigration to Medina
(622 C.E.)

The arrangements were now complete, and the emigration of Muslims to Mecca began, though gradually and with great caution.

After his companions had left, the Messenger stayed at Mecca waiting for permission to emigrate. Except for Abu Bakr and Ali, none of his supporters were left but those who were under restraint and those who had been forced to apostatize. The former kept asking the Messenger for permission to emigrate and he would answer, "Don't be in a hurry; it may be that God will give you a companion." Abu Bakr hoped that it would be Muhammad himself.

When the Quraysh saw that the Messenger (now) had a party and companions not of their tribe and outside their territory, and that his companions had migrated to join them, and knew that they had settled in a new home and had gained protectors, they feared that the Messenger might join them, since they knew that he had decided to fight them. So they assembled in their council chamber, the house of Qusayy ibn Kilab, where all their important business was conducted, to take counsel what they should do in regard to the Apostle, for they were now in fear of him.

As with the Pharisaic opposition to Jesus, we are at a loss to explain why the Quraysh should have so feared Muhammad and his few followers. In both instances there may have been more than meets the eye or than the sources could or would tell us. With Jesus, the hidden background may well have been political; here, equally likely, it was commercial. The Quraysh not only feared for their souls; Muhammad was perceived as a potentially dangerous rival to the prosperity of the Mecca Trading Company.

(After a discussion of various possibilities) Abu Jahl said that he had a plan that had not been suggested hitherto, namely that each clan should provide a young, powerful, well-born aristocratic warrior; that each of them should be equipped with a sharp sword; and that each of them should strike a blow at him and kill him. Thus they would be relieved of him, and the responsibility for his blood would lie on all the clans. The Banu Abd al-Manaf could not fight them all and would accept the blood money to which they would all contribute. . . . Having come to a decision, the people dispersed.

Then Gabriel came to the Messenger and said, "Do not sleep tonight on the bed on which you usually sleep." Before much of the night had passed they [the deputized assassins] assembled at his door waiting for him to go to sleep so they might fall upon him. When the Messenger saw what they were doing, he told Ali to lie on his bed and wrap himself in his green Hadrami mantle; for no harm would befall him. He himself used to sleep in that mantle. . . .

According to what I have been told, none knew when the Messenger left except Ali and Abu Bakr and the latter's family. I have heard that the Messenger told Ali about his departure and ordered him to stay behind in Mecca in order to return goods which men had deposited with the Apostle, for anyone in Mecca who had property which he was anxious about left it with him because of his notorious honesty and trustworthiness.

When the Messenger decided to go he came to Abu Bakr and the two of them left by a window in the back of the latter's house and made for a cave on Thawr, a mountain below Mecca. Having entered, Abu Bakr ordered his son Abdullah to listen to what people were saying and to come to them by night with the day's news. . . . The two of them stayed in the cave for three days. When the Quraysh missed the Messenger they offered a hundred she-camels to anyone who would bring them back. During the day Abdullah was listening to the plans and conversations and would come at night with the news.

After three days in hiding, Muhammad and Abu Bakr ride in secrecy to Medina.

Muhammad ibn Ja'far ibn al-Zubayr from Urwa ibn al-Zubayr from Abd al-Rahman ibn Uwaymir ibn Sa' told me, saying, Men of my tribe who were the Apostle's companions told me: "When we heard that the Messenger had left Mecca and we were eagerly expecting his arrival, we used to go out after morning prayers to the lava tract beyond our land to await him. This we did until there was no more shade left, then we went indoors in the hot season. On the day the Messenger arrived we had sat as we always had until there being no more shade we went inside, and it was then that the Prophet arrived. The first to see him was a Jew. He had seen what we were in the habit of doing and that we were expecting the arrival of the Apostle, and he called out at the top of his voice, 'O Banu Qayla, your luck has come!' So we went out to greet the Apostle, who was in the shadow of a palm tree with Abu Bakr, who was of like age. Now most of us had never seen the Messenger and as the people crowded around him they did not know him from Abu Bakr until the shade left him and Abu Bakr got up with his mantle and shielded him from the sun, and then we knew."

Ali stayed in Mecca for three days and nights until he restored the deposits which the Prophet held. This done, he joined the Messenger and (also) lodged at Kulthum's house. . . . The Messenger ordered that a mosque be built and he stayed with Abu Ayyub until the mosque and his houses were completed. The Messenger joined in the activity to encourage the Muslims to work and both the (Meccan) "Emigrants" and the (Medinese) "Helpers" labored hard. . . . The Messenger stayed in Medina from the month of First Rabiʿ to Safar of the following year until his mosque and his quarters were built. This tribe of the "Helpers" all accepted Islam, and every house of the "Helpers" accepted Islam except Khatma, Waqif, Waʾil and Umayya who were Aws Allah, a clan of the Aws who clung to their paganism. (*Life* 323–340) [IBN ISHAQ 1955: 221–230]

24. The Constitution of Medina

Included in Ibn Ishaq's Life of the Prophet *is a document that purports to record the political arrangements contracted between Muhammad and his partisans and the citizens of Medina. There is little reason to doubt its authenticity, since it constitutes Medina the kind of "protected" enclave found elsewhere in Arabia, though here not around a shrine, as at Mecca, for example, but on the authority of a recognized holy man. The contracting parties agreed to recognize Muhammad as their leader and to accept his judgments. In so doing, they were acknowledging, as was the Prophet himself, that they were one community, or* umma, *not yet uniquely composed of Muslims but committed to defend its joint interests, or what was now defined to be the common good.*

The Messenger wrote a document concerning the "Emigrants" and the "Helpers" in which he made a friendly agreement with the Jews and established them in their religion and their property, and stated the reciprocal obligations as follows: In the Name of God, the Compassionate, the Merciful. This is a document from Muhammad the Prophet (concerning the relations) between the believers and Muslims of the Quraysh and Yathrib [Medina], and those who followed them and joined them and labored with them. They are one community to the exclusion of all men. The Quraysh emigrants according to their present custom shall pay all the blood money within their number and shall redeem their prisoners with the kindness and justice common among believers. . . .

A believer shall not take as an ally the freedman of another Muslim against him. The God-fearing believers shall be against the rebellious or him who spreads injustice or sin or enmity or corruption between believers. A believer shall not slay a believer for the sake of an unbeliever, nor shall he aid an unbeliever against a believer. God's protection is one, the least of them may give protection to a stranger on their behalf. Believers are friends one to the other to the exclusion of outsiders. To the Jew who follows us belongs help and equality. He shall not be wronged nor his enemies aided. The peace of believers is indivisible and no separate peace shall be made when believers are fighting in the way of God. Conditions must be fair and equitable to all. . . .

The Jews must bear their expenses and the Muslims their expenses. Each must help the other against anyone who attacks the people of this document. They must seek mutual advice and consultation, and loyalty is a protection against treachery. A man is not liable for his ally's misdeeds. The wronged must be helped. The Jews must pay with the believers so long as war lasts. Yathrib [Medina] shall be sanctuary for the people of this document. . . . If any dispute or controversy should arise it must be referred to God and to Muhammad the Messenger of God. (*Life* 341–343) [IBN ISHAQ 1955: 231–233]

25. Jewish Opposition

Almost as soon as the Prophet and his followers had settled down in Medina, or Yathrib, as it was still called at that time, his relations with the Jews of the place began to deteriorate. Soon after his first great victory over his Meccan rivals at Badr Wells, the conflict with the Jews turned to open warfare, as we shall see. But commercial, religious, and psychological differences may have surfaced even before. Muhammad, after all, claimed to be a prophet in the tradition of Moses and the Torah. In the Jewish community of Medina he encountered, perhaps contrary to his own expectations, a rebuff from the contemporary partisans of that same tradition.

About this time the Jewish rabbis showed hostility to the Messenger in envy, hatred and malice, because God had chosen His Messenger from the Arabs. They were joined by men from (the Arab tribes of) al-Aws and al-Khazraj who had obstinately clung to their heathen religion. They were hypocrites, clinging to the polytheism of their fathers, denying the resurrection; yet when Islam appeared and their people flocked to it they were compelled to accept it to save their lives. But in secret they were hypocrites whose inclination was toward the Jews because these latter considered the Messenger a liar and strove against Islam.

It was the Jewish rabbis who used to annoy the Prophet with questions and introduce confusion, so as to confound the truth with falsity. The (verses of the) Quran used to come down in reference to questions of theirs, though some of the questions about what was allowed and forbidden came from the Muslims themselves.... The first hundred verses of the Sura of the Cow (2:1–100) came down in reference to these Jewish rabbis and the hypocrites of the Aws and Khazraj, according to what I have been told, and God knows best. (*Life* 351)

[IBN ISHAQ 1955: 239–240]

26. A Turning Away from the Jews

There follows in the Life *(363–400 [IBN ISHAQ 1955: 247–270]) an extended situational exegesis of Sura 2 of the Quran, which is Islam's most considerable meditation on the Jewish past and the newly revealed Islamic present in God's plan for mankind. Included in this same sura is a radical new development in the liturgical life of Muhammad and his followers.*

The foolish will now ask and say: "What has made the faithful turn them away from the direction of prayer toward which they used to pray?" Say: "To God belongs the East and the West, and He guides who so wills to the path that is straight."

Thus We have made you a community of the middle path that you act as witness over man, the Prophet is witness over you. We decreed the prayer-direction to which you faced before that We may know who follow the Apostle and who turn away in haste. It [that is, the change in the direction of prayer] was a hard test, except for those who were guided by God. But God will not suffer your faith to go to waste, for God is to men full of mercy and grace.

We have seen you turning your face to the heavens. We shall turn you toward a prayer-direction that will please you. So turn toward the

Holy Mosque, and turn toward it wherever you be. And those who are recipients of the Book surely know that this is the truth from their Lord, and God is not negligent of all that you do.

Even though you bring all the proof to the People of the Book, they will not face to the direction you turn to, nor you theirs, nor will they follow each other's direction. And if you follow their whims after all the knowledge that has reached you, then surely you will be among the transgressors. (Quran 2:142–145)

There was little agreement among the Muslim Quranic commentators on how to construe these verses on the change of the Muslims' direction of prayer. The standard Commentary of Tabari (d. 923 C.E.), for example, gives the reader a number of choices, no one of them greatly different from the others.

On the authority of Iqrima and Hasan al-Basri: The first command to be abrogated in the Quran was that concerning the direction of prayer. This was because the Prophet (first) preferred the Rock of the Holy House of Jerusalem, which was the prayer-direction of the Jews. The Prophet faced it for seventeen months (after his arrival in Medina) in the hope that the Jews would believe in him and follow him. Then God said: "Say: 'To God belongs the East and the West. . . .' "

Al-Rabi° ibn Anas relates on the authority of Abu al-Aliya: The Prophet of God was given his choice of turning his face (in prayer) toward whichever direction he wished. He chose the Holy House in Jerusalem so that the People of the Book might be conciliated. This was his prayer-direction for sixteen months (after his arrival in Medina); all the while, however, he kept turning his face toward the heavens until God turned him toward the House [that is, the Ka°ba].

It is related, on the other hand, on the authority of Ibn Abbas: When the Apostle of God migrated to Medina, most of whose inhabitants were Jews, God ordered him to (pray) with his face toward Jerusalem, and the Jews were glad. The Prophet faced that way for someting more than ten months, but he loved the prayer-direction of Abraham [that is, the Ka°ba]. So he used to pray to God and gaze into the heavens until God sent down (the verse), "We have seen you turning your face toward heaven" (2:144). The Jews became suspicious and said, "What has turned them away from the direction of prayer toward which they used to pray?" And so God sent down (the verse), "Say: To God belongs the East and the West." (Tabari, *Commentary, ad loc.*)

All these reports attempt to reconcile the Quranic verses with what was understood to be the position of Muhammad vis-à-vis the Jews of Medina. It was not the only way of approaching the problem, of course. Nisaburi (d. 1327 C.E.) illustrates the more "spiritual" reading of history favored by Sufi authors.

It is because the servant must turn his face toward and serve Him. It is also in order that unity and harmony among the people and faith may be established. It is as though the Exalted One says, "O man of faith! You are my servant, the Kaʿba is My House and the prayers are My service. Your heart is My Throne and Paradise is My noble abode. Turn your face toward My house and your heart to Me, so that I may grant you My noble abode." The Jews faced the west, which is the direction of the setting lights.... The Christians faced the east, which is the direction of the rising of lights ... but the people of faith faced the manifestation of lights, which is Mecca. From Mecca is Muhammad, and from him were lights created, and for his sake the circling spheres were set on their course. The west is the prayer-direction of Moses and the east is the prayer-direction of Jesus; between them is the prayer-direction of Abraham and Muhammad, for the best of things is that which is in the middle position. (Nisaburi, *Marvels of the Qurʾan* 3.8) [AYOUB 1984: 169]

27. The Battle at the Badr Wells

Once established in Medina, the Prophet turned his attention to the Quraysh of Mecca. Following some preliminary skirmishes, the first major confrontation took place at the wells of Badr near Medina in 624 C.E. When Muhammad received news of the passage there of a Quraysh caravan, "he summoned the Muslims and said, 'This is the Quraysh caravan containing their property. Go out and attack it; perhaps God will give it as prey.' The people answered his summons, some eagerly, others reluctantly because they had not thought that the Messenger would go to war" (Life 428 [IBN ISHAQ 1955: 289]). The Quraysh heard of the intended attack and mobilized their own forces, thus setting up a major confrontation between the Muslims and their opponents at Mecca. During the preliminaries, when Muhammad was positioning his forces, the following interesting incident is reported.

Al-Hubab ibn al-Mundhir ibn al-Jamuh said to the Apostle: "Is this the place which God has ordered you to occupy, so that we can neither advance nor withdraw from it, or is it a matter of opinion and military tactics?" When Muhammad replied that it was the latter al-Hubab pointed out to him that this was not the place to stop but that they should go on to the water hole nearest the enemy and halt there, stop up the wells beyond it and construct a cistern for themselves so that they would have plenty of water.... The Messenger agreed that it was an excellent plan and it was immediately carried out. (*Life* 439) [IBN ISHAQ 1955: 296–297]

The fighting begins, and at first it goes badly for the outnumbered Muslims. The Prophet rallies his troops with this promise.

Then the Messenger went forth to the people and incited them, saying, "By God in whose hand is the soul of Muhammad, no man will be slain this day fighting against them (the Quraysh) with steadfast courage, advancing and not retreating, but God will cause him to enter Paradise." (*Life* 445) [IBN ISHAQ 1955: 300]

The Muslims were victorious, with a great effect on their own and the Quraysh's morale for the rest of the struggle between them. The jubilation that followed was tempered only by a quarrel about the distribution of the rich spoils.

They ask you (O Muhammad), about the spoils of war. Say: The spoils of war belong to God and the Apostle, so keep your duty to God and adjust the matter of your difference and obey God and his Apostle, if you are true believers. (Quran 8:1)

Thus the event is referred to in the opening verse of Sura 8, called "The Spoils." Most of the sura is in fact devoted to the events surrounding the battle of Badr and is interpreted at length in the Life *(476–485 [IBN ISHAQ 1955: 321–327]).*

28. The Affair of the Banu Qaynuqa‵

After the success at Badr, the issue of the Jews of Medina surfaced once again, or at least as it concerned one tribe of them, the Banu Qaynuqa‵.

Meanwhile there was the affair of the Banu Qaynuqa‵. The Messenger assembled them in their market and addressed them as follows: "O Jews, beware lest God bring upon you the vengeance He brought upon the Quraysh and become Muslims. You know I am the Prophet who has been sent—you will find that in your Scriptures and God's covenant with you." They replied, "O Muhammad, you seem to think that we are your people. Do not deceive yourself because you encountered a people with no knowledge of war and got the better of them; for by God, if we fight you, you will find that we are real men!"

A freedman of the family of Zayd ibn Thabit from Sa‵id ibn Jubayr from Iqrima from Ibn Abbas told me that the latter said that the following verses came down about them: "Say to those who disbelieve: You will be vanquished and gathered to Hell, an evil resting place. You have already had a sign in the two forces which met," that is, the Apostle's companions at Badr and the Quraysh. "One force fought in the way of God; the other, disbelievers, thought they saw double their own force with their very eyes. God strengthens with His help whomever He wills. Verily in that is an example for the discerning" (Quran 3:12–13).

Asim ibn Umar ibn Qatada said that the Banu Qaynuqaʿ were the first of the Jews to break their agreement with the Messenger and to go to war (with him), between Badr and (the battle of) Uhud, and the Messenger besieged them until they surrendered unconditionally. Abdullah ibn Ubayy went to him when God put them in his power and said, "O Muhammad, deal kindly with my clients"—the Banu Qaynuqaʿ were allies of Khazraj—but the Messenger put him off. He repeated the words and the Messenger turned away from him, whereupon Abdullah thrust his hand into the collar of the Apostle's robe; the Messenger was so angry that his face became almost black. He said, "Confound you, let me go." Abdullah answered, "No, by God, I will not let you go until you deal kindly with my clients. Four hundred men without mail and three hundred mailed protected me from all my enemies; would you cut them down in one morning? By God, I am a man who fears that circumstances may change." The Messenger said, "You can have them."

. . . (Thus) when the Banu Qaynuqaʿ fought against the Messenger Abdullah ibn Ubayy espoused their cause and defended them, but Ubada ibn al-Samit, who had the same alliance with them as had Abdullah, went to the Messenger and renounced all responsibility for them in favor of God and His Apostle, saying, "O Messenger of God, I take God and His Messenger as my friends, and I renounce my agreement and friendship with these unbelievers." It was concerning him and Abdullah ibn Ubayy that this passage from the Sura of the Table came down: "O you who believe, take not Jews and Christians as friends. They are friends one of another. Who of you takes them as friends is one of them. God will not guide the unjust people. You can see those in whose heart there is sickness," that is, Abdullah ibn Ubayy when he said "I fear a change of circumstances." Acting hastily in regard to them, they say we fear a change of circumstances may overtake us. Perhaps God will bring victory or an act from Him so that they will be sorry for their secret thoughts, and those who believe will say, Are these those who swore by God their most binding oath that they were surely with you? As for God's words, "Verily God and His Messenger are your friends, and those who believe, who perform prayer, give alms and bow down in homage," they refer to Ubada taking God and His Messenger and the believers as his friends and renouncing his agreement and friendship with the Banu Qaynuqaʿ: "Those who take God and His Messenger and the believers as friends, they are God's party, they are victorious" (Quran 3:51–56). (*Life 545–547*) [IBN ISHAQ 1955: 363–364]

29. The Battle of Uhud

The triumph of Badr was followed in the next year by a full-scale attack of three thousand foot soldiers and two hundred cavalry mustered by the Quraysh for an assault on Medina. The severe setback that resulted for the Muslims is commemorated as the Battle of Uhud.

The Muslims were put to flight and the enemy slew many of them. It was a day of trial and testing in which God honored several with martyrdom, until the enemy got at the Messenger, who was struck with a stone so that he fell on his side and one of his teeth was smashed, his face gashed and his lip injured. The man who wounded him was Utba ibn Abi Waqqas. (*Life 571*) [IBN ISHAQ 1955: 380]

According to what Salih ibn Kaysan told me, Hind, the daughter of Utba, and the women with her stopped to mutilate the Apostle's dead companions. They cut off their ears and noses and Hind made them into anklets and collars. . . . She cut out Hamza's liver and chewed it, but she was not able to swallow it and threw it away. Then she mounted a high rock and shrieked at the top of her voice:

> "We have paid you back for Badr
> And a war that follows a war is always violent.
> I could not bear the loss of Utba
> Nor my brother and his uncle and my firstborn.
> I have slaked my vengeance and fulfilled my vow. . . ."

When (the Quraysh leader) Abu Sufyan wanted to leave, he went to the top of the mountain and shouted loudly, saying, "You have done a fine work. Victory in war goes by turns: today is in exchange for the day of Badr. Show your superiority, Hubal," that is, vindicate your religion. The Messenger told Umar to go up and answer him and say, "God is most high and most glorious. We are not equal: our dead are in paradise, yours are in hell." At this answer Abu Sufyan said to Umar, "Come up here to me." The Messenger told him to go and see what Abu Sufyan was up to. When he came Abu Sufyan said, "I adjure you by God, Umar, have we killed Muhammad?" "By God, you have not, he is listening to what you are saying right now," Umar replied. Abu Sufyan said, "I regard you as more truthful and reliable than Ibn Qami'a," referring to the latter's claim that he had killed Muhammad. (*Life 581–583*) [IBN ISHAQ 1955: 385–386]

30. The Deportation of the Banu al-Nadir

Just as in the sequel of Badr, when Muhammad turned to the Jewish tribe of the Qaynuqa, so the direct or indirect consequence of Uhud was the expulsion of a second Jewish tribe from the Medina association, the Banu al-Nadir. In this case the provocation was the report of a threat by members of the Banu al-Nadir against the Prophet's life. The response was prompt and direct: an assault on their redoubts in the Medina oasis.*

The Jews took refuge in their forts and the Messenger ordered the palm trees should be cut down and burnt. And they [the Banu al-Nadir] called out to him, "O Muhammad, you have prohibited wanton destruction and blamed those guilty of it. Why then are you cutting down and burning our palm trees?" Now there were a number of the (Arab tribe of the) Banu Awf ibn al-Khazraj . . . who had sent to the Banu al-Nadir saying, "Stand firm and protect yourselves, for we will not betray you. If you are attacked we will fight with you and if you are turned out we will go with you." Accordingly they waited for the help they had promised, but they [the Banu Awf] did nothing and God cast terror into their hearts. The Banu al-Nadir then asked the Messenger to deport them and to spare their lives on condition that they could retain all their property which they could carry on camels, armor excepted, and he agreed. So they loaded their camels with what they could carry. Men were destroying their houses down to the lintel of the door, which they put on the back of their camels and went off with it. Some went to Khaybar and others went to Syria. . . .

Abdullah ibn Abi Bakr told me that he was told that the Banu al-Nadir carried off their women and children and property with tambourines and pipes and singing girls playing behind them. . . . They went with such pomp and splendor as had never been seen in any tribe in their days. They left their property to the Messenger and it became his personal possession to dispose of as he wished. He divided it among the first emigrants (from Mecca to Medina), to the exclusion of the "Helpers." . . .

Concerning the Banu al-Nadir, the Sura of the Exile (59) came down in which is recorded how God wreaked his vengeance on them and gave His Messenger power over them and how He dealt with them. (*Life* 652–654) [IBN ISHAQ 1955: 437–438]

31. The Battle of the Trench (627 C.E.)

A number of Jews who had formed a party against the Apostle . . .
went to the Quraysh at Mecca and invited them to join them in an attack
upon the Messenger so they could get rid of him together. The Quraysh
said, "You, O Jews, are the first people of Scripture and know the nature
of our dispute with Muhammad. Is our religion the best or is his?" They
replied that certainly the Quraysh's religion was better than Muhammad's and had a better claim to be in the right. And it was in this
connection that God sent down (the verses of the Quran): "Have you not
considered those to whom a part of Scripture was given and yet believe
in idols and false deities and say to those who disbelieve, these are more
rightly guided than those who believe? . . . We gave the family of Abraham the Scripture and the wisdom and We gave them a great kingdom
and some of them believed in it and some of them turned from it, and hell
is sufficient for (their) burning" (Quran 4:51–54).

These words (of the Jews) rejoiced the Quraysh and they responded
gladly to their invitation to fight the Apostle, and they assembled and
made their preparations. Then that company of Jews went off to Ghatafan of Qays Aylan and invited them to fight the Messenger and told them
that they would act in concert with them and that the Quraysh had
followed their lead in the matter; so they too joined in with them. . . .

When the Messenger heard of their intention he drew a trench
around Medina and worked at it himself, encouraging the Muslims with
hope of reward in heaven. The Muslims worked very hard with him, but
the disaffected held back and began to hide their real object by working
slackly and stealing away to their families without the Apostle's permission or knowledge.

When the Messenger had finished the trench, the Quraysh came and
encamped where the torrent beds of Ruma meet between al-Juruf and
Zughaba with ten thousand of their black mercenaries and their followers
from the Banu Kinana and the people of Tihama. Ghatafan too came with
their followers from Najd and halted at Dhanab Naqma toward the direction of Uhud. The Messenger and the Muslims came out with three
thousand men having Salᶜ at their backs. He pitched his camp there with
the trench between him and his foes, and he gave orders for the women
and children to be taken up to the forts (of the oasis). . . .

The situation became serious and fear was everywhere. The enemy
came at them from above and below until the believers imagined vain

things and disaffection was rife among the disaffected, to the point that Mu'attib ibn Qushayr said, "Muhammad used to promise that we would eat the treasures of Khusraw and Caesar and today not one of us can feel safe going to the privy!" It reached such a point that Aws ibn al-Qayzi, one of the Banu Haritha ibn al-Harith, said to the people, "Our houses are exposed to the enemy"—this he said before a large gathering of his people—"so let us go out and return to our home, for it is outside Medina." The Messenger and the polytheists remained (facing each other) twenty days and more, nearly a month, without fighting except for some shooting with arrows and the siege. (*Life* 669–676) [IBN ISHAQ 1955: 450–454]

Muhammad and his followers were dispirited, but the morale in the camp of the Quraysh was at an even lower pitch. Soon the alliance began to disintegrate. In the end the siege was broken off, and the attackers returned to their homes.

32. The Banu Qurayza

One of the reasons for the failure of the siege at the trench was the unwillingness of the remaining Jewish tribe of the oasis, the Banu Qurayza, to take an active part in the Quraysh assault. On the Muslim side, however, restraint was not construed as sympathy.

According to what al-Zuhri told me, at the time of the noon prayers Gabriel came to the Messenger wearing an embroidered turban and riding on a mule with a saddle covered with a piece of brocade. He asked the Messenger if he had abandoned fighting, and when he said he had, Gabriel said that the angels had not yet laid aside their arms and that he had just come from pursuing the enemy. "God commands you, Muhammad, to go to the Banu Qurayza. I am about to go to them and shake their stronghold. . . ."

The Messenger besieged them for twenty-five nights until they were sore pressed and God cast terror into their hearts. . . . And when they felt sure that the Messenger would not leave them until he had made an end to them, (their leader) Ka'b ibn Asad said to them: "O Jews, you can see what has happened to you. I offer you three alternatives. Take which you please. We will follow this man and accept him as true, for by God it is plain to you that he is a prophet who has been sent and that it is he that you find mentioned in your Scripture; and then your lives, your property, your women and children will be saved." They said, "We will never abandon the laws of the Torah and never change it for another." He said, "Then if you will not accept this suggestion, let us kill our wives and children and send men with their swords drawn against Muhammad and his companions, leaving no encumbrances behind us, and let God decide between us and Muhammad. If we perish, we perish, and we shall not leave children behind us to cause anxiety. If we conquer, we can acquire other wives and children." They said, "Should we kill those poor creatures? What would be the good of life when they were dead?" He said, "Then if you will not accept this suggestion, tonight is the eve of the Sabbath and it may well be that Muhammad and his companions will feel secure from us, so come down and perhaps we can take Muhammad and his companions by surprise." They said, "Are we to profane our Sabbath and do on the Sabbath what those before us of whom you well know did and were turned into apes?" He answered, "Not a single man among you from the day of your birth has ever passed a night resolved to do what he knows ought to be done."

Then the Banu Qurayza sent to the Messenger saying, "Send us Abu Lubaba (of the Banu Aws) . . . for they were allies of the Aws, that we may consult him." So the Messenger sent him to them, and when they saw him they got up to meet him. The women and children went up to him weeping in his face, and he felt pity for them. They said, "O Abu Lubaba, do you think we should submit to Muhammad's judgment?" He said "Yes," but pointed his hand to his throat, signifying slaughter. Abu Lubaba (later) said, "My feet had not moved from the spot before I knew that I had been false to God and His Apostle." Then he left them and did not go to the Messenger but bound himself to one of the pillars in the mosque saying, "I will not leave this place until God forgives me for what I have done," and he promised that he would never go to the Banu Qurayza and would never be seen in a town in which he had betrayed God and His Apostle.

When the Aws, the former patrons of the Banu Qurayza, somewhat hesitantly asked for leniency—they recalled what had happened in the case of the other Jewish clients at Medina—Muhammad asked them if they would be content if one of their own number passed judgment on the Banu Qurayza. They said they would. A certain Sa'd ibn Mu'adh was chosen.

Sa'd said: "I give judgment that the men should be killed, the property divided, and the women and children taken as captives. . . ."

Then the Banu Qurayza surrendered themselves and the Messenger confined them in the quarter of Bint al-Harith, a woman of the Banu al-Najjar. Then the Messenger went out to the market of Medina—which is still the market today—and dug trenches in it. Then he sent for them and struck off their heads in those trenches as they were brought out to him in batches. Among them was the enemy of God Huyayy ibn Aktab and Ka'b ibn Asas their chief. There were 600 or 700 in all, though some put the figure as high as 800 or 900. As they were being taken out in batches to the Apostle, they asked Ka'b what he thought would be done to them. He replied, "Will you never understand? Don't you see that the summoner never stops and those who are taken away never return? By God, it is death!" This went on until the Messenger made an end to them. (*Life* 684–690) [IBN ISHAQ 1955: 641–464]

33. The Affair at Hudaybiyya

The Messenger stayed in Medina during the months of Ramadan and Shawwal (in 628 C.E.) and then went out on the 'umra (or lesser pilgrimage) in Dhu al-Qa'da with no intention of making war. He called together the Arabs and the neighboring bedouin to march with him, fearing that the Quraysh (in Mecca) would oppose him with arms or prevent his visiting the shrine, as they actually did. Many of the Arabs held back from him, and he went out with the Emigrants and the Helpers and such of the Arabs as stuck to him. He took the sacrificial victims with him and donned the pilgrim garb so that all would know that he did not intend war and that his purpose was to visit the shrine and venerate it. . . .

In his tradition al-Zuhri said: When the Messenger had rested (at Hudaybiyya near Mecca), Budayl ibn Warqa al-Khuza'i came to him with some men of the Khuza'a and asked him what he had come for. He told them he had not come for war but to go on pilgrimage and visit the sacred precincts. . . . Then they returned to the Quraysh and told them what they had heard; but the Quraysh suspected them and spoke roughly to them, "He may not come out wanting war, but by God, he will never come in here against our will nor will the Arabs ever see that we allowed it." The Khaza'a were in fact the Apostle's confidants, both the Muslims and the non-Muslims among them, and they kept him informed of everything that went on in Mecca. . . .

. . . Then they (the Quraysh of Mecca) sent Urwa ibn Mas'ud al-Thaqafi to the Apostle. . . . He came to the Messenger and sat before him and said: "Muhammad, you have collected a mixed people together and then brought them against your own people to destroy them? By God, I think I see you deserted by these people here tomorrow." Now Abu

Bakr was sitting behind the Messenger and he said, "Go suck al-Lat's tits! Should we desert him?" . . . Then Urwa began to take hold of the Apostle's beard as he talked to him. Al-Mughira ibn Shuʿba was standing by the Apostle's head clad in mail and he began to hit Urwa's hand as he held the Apostle's beard saying, "Take your hand away from the Apostle's face before you lose it!" Urwa said, "Confound you, how rough and rude you are!" The Messenger smiled and when Urwa asked who the man was he told him that it was his brother's son Urwa ibn Shuʿba, and Urwa said, "You wretch, it was only yesterday that I was wiping your behind!"

The Messenger told him what he told the others, namely that he had not come out for war. Urwa then got up from the Apostle's presence, having noted how his companions treated him. Whenever he performed his ablutions, they ran to get the water he used; if he spat, they ran to it; if a hair of his head fell out, they ran to pick it up. So he returned to the Quraysh and said, "I have seen Khusraw in his kingdom and Caesar in his kingdom and the Negus in his kingdom, but never have I seen a king among a people like Muhammad is among his companions."

Muhammad decided to try a more direct approach: to send one of his own followers into Mecca to convince the Quraysh of his peaceful intentions. The one chosen was Uthman, the future third Caliph of Islam (644–656 C.E.) and a man well connected in Mecca.

As Uthman entered or was about to enter Mecca, Aban ibn Saʿid met him and carried him in front of him (on his mount) and gave him protection until he could convey the Apostle's message to them. Having heard what Uthman had to say, the Quraysh said: "If you wish to circumambulate the shrine, then go ahead." He for his part said he would not until Muhammad did so, and so the Quraysh kept him prisoner with them. The Messenger and the Muslims were informed, however, that Uthman had been killed.

Abdullah ibn Abi Bakr told me that when the Messenger heard that Uthman had been killed, he said that he would not leave until they fought the enemy, and he summoned the men to pledge themselves to this. The pledge of al-Ridwan took place under a tree. Men used to say that Muhammad took their pledge unto death, but Jabir ibn Abdullah said that it was not a pledge unto death but an undertaking not to run away. . . . Then the Messenger heard that the news about Uthman was false. (*Life* 741–746) [IBN ISHAQ 1955: 499–504]

34. The Armistice

... Then the Quraysh sent Suhayl ibn Amr to the Messenger with
instructions to make peace with him on condition that he returned (to
Medina) this year so that none of the Arabs could say that he had made
a forcible entry. ... After a long discussion peace was made and nothing
remained but to write the document. Umar leaped up and went to Abu
Bakr saying, "Is he not God's Messenger and are we not Muslims, and are
not they polytheists?" to which Abu Bakr agreed, and he went on, "Then
why should we agree to what is demeaning to our religion?" Abu Bakr
replied, "Follow what he says, for I bear witness that he is God's Apostle." Umar said, "And so do I." Then he went to the Messenger and put
the same questions, to which the Messenger answered, "I am God's slave
and His Apostle. I will not go against His commandment and He will not
make me a loser." Umar used to say (afterwards), "I have not ceased
giving alms and fasting and praying and freeing slaves because of what I
did that day and for fear of what I had said, when I hoped that (my plan)
would be better."

Then the Messenger summoned Ali and told him to write, "In the
name of God, the Compassionate, the Merciful." Suhayl said, "I do not
recognize this; write rather, In thy name, O God." The Messenger told
Ali to write the latter and he did so. Then he said, "Write: This is what
Muhammad, Messenger of God, has agreed with Suhayl ibn Amr." Suhayl
said, "If I confessed that you were God's Messenger I would not have
fought you. Write your own name and the name of your father." The
Messenger said, "Write: This is what Muhammad ibn Abdullah has
agreed with Suhayl ibn Amr: they have agreed to lay aside war for ten
years during which men can be safe and refrain from hostilities on condition that if anyone comes to Muhammad without the permission of his
guardian he will return him to them; and if anyone of those with Muhammad returns to the Quraysh they will not return him to him. We will not
show enmity one to another and there shall be no secret reservation or
bad faith. He who wishes to enter into a bond or agreement with Muhammad may do so and whoever wishes to enter into a bond or agreement with the Quraysh may do so."

The Messenger then went on his way back (to Medina), and when
he was halfway the Sura of the Victory came down: "We have given you
a signal victory that God may forgive you your past sin and the sin which

is to come and may complete His favor upon you and guide you on an upright path" (Quran 48:1–2). . . .

No previous victory in Islam was greater than this. There was nothing but battle when men met; but when there was an armistice and war was abolished and men met in safety and held discussion, none talked about Islam intelligently without entering it. In those two years double or more than double as many entered Islam as ever before. (*Life* 746– 751) [IBN ISHAQ 1955: 504–507]

35. Khaybar and Fadak

There followed almost immediately a raid upon the Jewish oasis of Khaybar in the north. The resistance was determined but unavailing, and the terms of the capitulation were not lost on the occupants of Fadak, another nearby oasis.

The Messenger besieged the people of Khaybar in their two forts al-Watih and al-Salalim until when they could hold out no longer they asked him to let them go and spare their lives, and he did so. Now the Messenger had already taken possession of all their property . . . except what belonged to these two forts. When the people of Fadak heard of what had happened they sent to the Messenger asking him to let them go (as well) and to spare their lives and they would leave him their property, and he did so. . . . When the people of Khaybar surrendered on these conditions they asked the Messenger to employ them on the property, with a half share of (future) produce, saying, "We know more about it than you and are better farmers." The Messenger agreed to this arrangement on the condition that "if we wish to expel you, we will expel you." He made a similar arrangement with the men of Fadak, except that Khaybar became war spoils for all the Muslims, while Fadak was the personal property of the Messenger because they had not attacked it with horses and camels. (*Life* 763–764) [IBN ISHAQ 1955: 515–516]

36. The Pilgrimage Fulfilled

When the Messenger returned from Khaybar to Medina he stayed there from the first Rabiʿ until Shawwal, sending out raiding parties and expeditions. Then in Dhu al-Qaʿda—the month in which the polytheists had prevented him from making the pilgrimage (in the preceding year)— he went out to make the "fulfilled pilgrimage" in place of the lesser pilgrimage from which they had excluded him. Those Muslims who had been excluded with him went out in A.H. 7 [February 629 C.E.] and when the Meccans heard it, they got out of his way. . . .

. . . The Messenger married Maymuna daughter of al-Harith on that journey when he was on pilgrimage. (His uncle) al-Abbas gave her to him in marriage [and probably became a Muslim at the same time]. The Messenger remained three days in Mecca. Huwaytib ibn Abd al-Uzza with a few Quraysh came to him on the third day because the Quraysh had entrusted him with the duty of sending the Messenger out of Mecca. They said, "Your time is up, so get out from among us." The Messenger answered, "How would it harm you if you were to let me stay and I gave a wedding feast among you and prepared food and you came too?" They replied, "We don't need your food, so get out." So the Messenger went out and left Abu Rafiʿ his client in charge of Maymuna until he brought her to him in Sarif. (*Life* 788–790) [IBN ISHAQ 1955: 530–531]

37. "The Truth Has Come and Falsehood Has Passed Away"

The breaking of the armistice concluded between Muhammad and the Quraysh of Mecca at Hudaybiyya in 628 C.E. came about not through the principals themselves but by an altercation between two of their bedouin allies. The violation might have been settled in other ways perhaps—the Quraysh appeared willing to negotiate— but in 630 Muhammad judged the occasion fit and the time appropriate for settling accounts with the polytheists of Mecca once and for all.

The Messenger ordered preparations to be made for a foray and Abu Bakr came in to see his daughter (and Muhammad's wife) Aisha as she was moving some of the Apostle's gear. He asked her if the Messenger had ordered her to get things ready and she said he had and that her father had better get ready too. She told him that she did not know where the troops were going, however. Later the Messenger informed the men that he was going to Mecca and ordered them to make preparations. He said, "O God, take their eyes and ears from the Quraysh that we may take them by surprise in their land," and the men got themselves ready. (*Life* 808) [IBN ISHAQ 1955: 544]

The surprise prayed for by Muhammad was granted him, along with other good fortune: Abu Sufyan, the Quraysh leader, was captured by chance before the Muslims reached Mecca and persuaded, despite continuing doubts, to save himself and embrace Islam. The Meccans' will to resist was at a low ebb.

The Messenger had instructed his commanders when they entered Mecca only to fight those who resisted them, except for a small number [perhaps only four] who were to be killed even if they were found beneath the curtains of the Ka'ba itself. . . . The Messenger after arriving in Mecca, once the populace had settled down, went to the shrine and went round it seven times on his camel, touching the black stone with a stick which he had in his hand. This done, he summoned Uthman ibn Talha and took the keys of the Ka'ba from him, and when the door was opened for him, he went in. There he found a dove made of wood. He broke it in his hands and threw it away. . . . (According to another account) the Messenger entered Mecca on the day of the conquest and it contained 360 idols which Iblis [or Satan] had strengthened with lead. The Messenger was standing by them with a stick in his hand, saying, "The truth has come and falsehood has passed away" (Quran 17:81). Then he pointed at them with his stick and they collapsed on their backs one after another.

When the Messenger had prayed the noon prayer on the day of the conquest (of Mecca), he ordered that all the idols which were around the Ka'ba should be collected and burned with fire and broken up. . . . The Quraysh had put pictures in the Ka'ba, including two of Jesus son of Mary and of Mary, on both of whom be peace. Ibn Shihab said: Asma the daughter of Shaqr said that a woman of the Banu Ghassan had joined in the pilgrimage of the Arabs and when she saw a picture of Mary in the Ka'ba she said: "My father and my mother be your ransom! (Mary), you are surely an Arab woman!" The Messenger ordered that the pictures be erased, except those of Jesus and Mary.

A traditionist told me that the Messenger stood at the door of the Ka'ba and said: "There is no god but God alone; He has no associates. He has made good His promise and helped His servant. He alone has put to flight the confederates. Every claim of privilege or blood or property are abolished by me except the custody of the shrine and the watering of the pilgrims. . . . O Quraysh, God has taken from you the haughtiness of paganism and its veneration of ancestors. Man springs from Adam and Adam from dust." Then he recited them this verse: "O men, we created you male and female and made you into peoples and tribes that you may know one another; in truth, the most noble of you in God's sight is the most pious . . . " to the end of the passage (Quran 49:13). Then he added, "O Quraysh, what do you think I am about to do to you?" They replied, "Good, for you are a noble brother, son of a noble brother." He said, "Go your way; you are freed." (*Life* 818–821) [IBN ISHAQ 1955: 550–553]

38. Consolidation of Gains

Troops were despatched to the neighborhood of Mecca to smash the others idols revered in the holy places around that holy city. Then suddenly there came the last real challenge to Muhammad's political supremacy: a bedouin confederation mustered its last forces and marched against the Prophet. The encounter occurred at a place called Hunayn. Although at first there was panic in the Muslim ranks, their numerical superiority finally prevailed, and the bedouin were routed.

God has given you victory on many fields, and on the day of Hunayn, when you exulted in your numbers, though they availed you nothing, and the earth, vast as it was, was straitened for you. Then you turned back in flight. Then God sent down His peace of reassurance on His Messenger and upon the believers, and sent down hosts you could not see, and punished those who did not believe. Such is the reward of disbelievers. (Quran 9:25–26)

Even before the occupation of Mecca, Muhammad had been casting his net of raids and expeditions in an ever wider arc. After the battle of Hunayn, toward the end of that same eventful year of 630 C.E. (his last surviving son, the infant Ibrahim, born of the Egyptian Christian concubine named Mary, also died in that year), he prepared his troops for an expedition northward and deep across the frontiers of the Byzantine Empire to the town of Tabuk. Although it may have revealed to Muhammad the weakness of his international rivals, the raid was not an entirely successful enterprise in its organization or in its fulfillment, as many passages in Sura 9 of the Quran testify.

39. A Miracle of Muhammad

One event reported on the course of Muhammad's long journey into Byzantine territory is worth noting. Although it occurs in the canonical collection of traditions concerning the Prophet, it is not entirely typical. Contrary to most of the accounts of his life and deeds, this report attributes to Muhammad superhuman powers, albeit they are displayed at the quite explicit urging of Umar.

It is narrated either on the authority of Abu Hurayra or that of Abu Sa'id Khudri. The narrator A'mash has narrated this tradition with a little bit of doubt (about the original source). He [that is, the narrator] said: During the time of the Tabuk expedition (provisions) ran short and the men (of the army) suffered starvation. They said: Messenger of God, would you permit us to slay our camels? We would eat them and use their fat. The Messenger of God, may peace be upon him, said: Do as you please. He [the narrator] said: Then Umar came and said: Messenger of God, if you do that, the riding animals would become short. But (rather) summon them along with the provisions left to them. Then invoke God's blessings on them. It is hoped God will bless them. The Messenger of God replied in the affirmative.

He [the narrator] said: He called for a leather mat to be used as a tablecloth and spread it out. Then the people came, along with the remaining portions of their provisions. He [the narrator] said: One was coming with a handful of sorghum, another with a handful of dates, still another with a portion of bread, till small quantities of these were collected on the tablecloth. He [the narrator] said: Then the Messenger of God invoked blessings (on them) and said: Fill your utensils with these provisions. He [the narrator] said: They filled the vessels to the brim with them, and no one among the army was left even with a single empty vessel. He [the narrator] said: They ate their fill and there was still a surplus. Upon this the Messenger of God, may peace be upon him, remarked: I bear testimony that there is no god but the God and I am the Messenger of God. The man who meets his Lord without entertaining any doubt about these two (truths) would never be kept away from Paradise. (Muslim, *Sahih* 1:11.42)

40. The Submission of the Idolaters

Upon Muhammad's return from this far-reaching raid to the north, the bedouin continued to make their peace, political and religious, with him, though with some caution:

In deciding their attitude to Islam the Arabs were only waiting to see what happened to this clan of the Quraysh and the Apostle. For the Quraysh were the leaders and guides of men, the people of the sacred shrine (of Mecca), and the pure stock of Ishmael son of Abraham; and the leading Arabs did not contest this. It was the Quraysh who had declared war on the Messenger and opposed him; and when Mecca was occupied and the Quraysh became subject to him and he subdued them to Islam, and the Arabs knew they could not fight the Messenger or display enmity toward him, they entered into God's religion "in batches" as God said, coming to him from all directions. (*Life* 933) [IBN ISHAQ 1955: 628]

Submission to the Prophet of Islam and his God was not always simple or easy, since the social, political, and psychological price of disavowing the customs of their own past was a large one. The Thaqif, for example, were willing to "make their submis-

sion and accept Islam on the Apostle's conditions provided they could get a document guaranteeing their land and their people and their animals." They got their document, but that was by no means the end of the matter.

Among the things they asked the Messenger was that they should be allowed to retain their idol al-Lat undestroyed for three years. The Messenger refused and they continued to ask him for a year or two (grace), and he refused. Finally they asked for a month (dispensation) after their return home, but he refused to agree to any set time. All that they wanted, as they were trying to show, was to be safe from their fanatics and women and children by leaving al-Lat, and they did not want to frighten their people by destroying her until they had (all) accepted Islam. The Messenger refused this, but he sent Abu Sufyan and al-Mughira to destroy her (for them). They also asked him that he would excuse them from prayer and that they would not have to break the idol with their own hands. The Messenger said: "We excuse you from breaking your idols with your own hands, but as for prayer, there is no good in a religion which has no prayers." They said that they would perform them, though they were demeaning. (*Life* 916) [IBN ISHAQ 1955: 613–614]

41. A Primer on Islam

As each new tribe embraced Islam, their duties and responsibilities as Muslims had to be spelled out for them. One case in particular gives us an opportunity to observe what was understood as "Islam" in those days.

Now the Messenger had sent to them [the Banu al-Harith, Christians of the city of Najran in the Yemen] . . . Amr ibn Hazm to instruct them in religion and to teach them the customary practice (*sunna*) and the institutions of Islam and to collect their alms. And he wrote Amr a letter in which he gave him his orders and injunctions as follows:

"In the Name of God, the Compassionate, the Merciful. This is a clear announcement from God and His Apostle. O you who believe, be faithful to your agreements. The instructions of Muhammad the Prophet, the Messenger of God, to Amr ibn Hazm when he sent him to the Yemen. He orders him to observe piety toward God in all his doings for God is with those who are pious and who do well; and he commanded him to behave with truth as God commanded him; and that he should give people the good news and command them to follow it and to teach men the Quran and instruct them in it and to forbid men to do wrong so that none but the pure should touch the Quran, and he should instruct men in their privileges and obligations and be lenient with them when they behave aright and severe on injustice, since God hates injustice and has forbidden it. 'The curse of God is on the evildoers' (Quran 5:1).

"Give men the good news of paradise and the way to earn it, and warn them of hell and the way to earn it, and make friends with men so that they may be instructed in religion. Teach men the rites of the pilgrimage (*hajj*), its customs and its obligation and what God has ordered about it: the greater pilgrimage is the *hajj* and the lesser pilgrimage is the ʿumra. Prohibit men from praying in one small garment, unless it be a garment whose ends are doubled over their shoulders, and forbid men from squatting in one garment which exposes their person to the air, and forbid them to twist the head of the hair on the back of the neck (in a pigtail).

"If there is a quarrel between men, forbid them to appeal to tribes and families, and let their appeal be to God. And those who do not appeal to God but to tribes and families, let them be smitten with the sword until their appeal is to God. Command men to perform the ablutions, their faces, their hands to the elbows and their feet to the ankles, and let them wipe their heads as God ordered. And command prayer at the proper time with bowing, prostration and humble reverence: prayer at daybreak; at noon when the sun declines; in the afternoon when the sun is descending; at evening when the night approaches, not delaying it until the stars appear in the sky; later at the beginning of the night. Order them to hasten to the mosques when they are summoned, and to wash when they go to them.

"Order them to subtract from the booty God's fifth and whatever alms are enjoined on the Muslims from land: a tenth of what the fountains water and the sky waters and a twentieth of what the bucket waters; and for every ten camels (they own), two sheep; and for every twenty camels, four sheep; for every forty cows, one cow; for every thirty cows, a bull or a cow calf; for every forty sheep at grass, one sheep. This is what God enjoined on the believers in the matters of alms (*zakat*). He who adds thereto, it is a merit to him.

"A Jew or a Christian who becomes a sincere Muslim of his own accord and obeys the religion of Islam is a believer with the same rights and the same obligations. If one of them holds fast to his own religion, he is not to be turned from it. Every adult (non-Muslim), male or female, bond or free, must pay a gold dinar or its equivalent in clothes. He who does this has the guarantee of God and His Apostle; he who withholds it is the enemy of God and His Messenger and all believers." (*Life* 961–962) [IBN ISHAQ 1955: 646–648]

42. The Farewell Pilgrimage

At the beginning of the year 632 C.E., the year of his death, Muhammad went on his final pilgrimage. The details were lovingly cherished, since they served as the foundation of all future performances of this ritual, which is a solemn obligation upon all Muslims. Ibn Ishaq passes over these in his Life; *he reproduces instead what turned out to be the Prophet's final discourse.*

In the beginning of Dhu al-Qaʿda the Messenger prepared to make the pilgrimage and ordered his men to get ready. Abd al-Rahman ibn al-Qasim from his father, from Aisha, the Prophet's wife, told me that the Messenger went on pilgrimage on the 25th of Dhu al-Qaʿda (20 February 632 C.E.).

(In its course) the Messenger showed the men the rites and taught them the customs of the Pilgrimage. He made a speech in which he made things clear. He praised and glorified God, then he said: "O men, listen to my words. I do not know whether I shall ever meet you in this place again after this year. Your blood and your property are sacrosanct until you meet your Lord, as this day and this month are holy. You will surely meet your Lord and He will ask you of your works. I have told you so. He who has a pledge, let him return it to him who entrusted it to him; all usury is abolished, but you have your capital. Wrong not and you shall not be wronged. . . . All blood shed in the period of paganism is to be left unavenged. . . . Satan despairs of ever being worshiped in your land, but if he can be obeyed in anything short of worship, he will be pleased in matters you may be disposed to think of little account, so beware of him in your religion. . . .

"You have rights over your wives and they have rights over you. You have the right that they should not defile your bed and that they should not behave with open unseemliness. If they do, God allows you to put them in separate rooms and to beat them, though not with severity. If they refrain from these things, they have the right to their food and clothing with kindness. Lay injunctions on women kindly, for they are your prisoners, having no control of their persons. You have taken them only in trust from God, and you have the enjoyment of their persons by the words of God. So understand my words, O men, for I have told you. I have left you something with which, if you hold fast to it, you will never fall into error, a plain indication, the Book of God and the practices of His Prophet, so give good heed to what I say.

"Know that every Muslim is a Muslim's brother, and that (all) the Muslims are brethren. It is only lawful to take from a brother what he gives you willingly, so wrong not each other. O God, have I not told you?" (*Life* 968—969) [IBN ISHAQ 1955: 650–651]

43. Muhammad's Illness and Death
(June 632 C.E.)

Abdullah ibn Umar from Ubayd al-Jubayr, from Abdullah ibn Amr ibn al-As, from Abu Muwayhiba, a freedman of the Apostle, said: In the middle of the night the Messenger sent for me and told me that he was ordered to pray for the dead in this cemetery and that I was to go with him. I went, and when he stood among them he said: "Peace upon you, O people of the graves! Happy are you that you are so much better off than men here. Dissensions have come like waves of darkness one after the other, the last being worse than the first." Then he turned to me and said, "I have been given the choice between keys of the treasuries of this world and a long life here followed by Paradise, or meeting my Lord and Paradise (at once)." I urged him to choose the former, but he said he had chosen the latter. Then he prayed for the dead and went away. Then it was that the illness through which God took him began . . .

Al-Zuhri said that Abdullah ibn Ka'b ibn Malik told him that the messenger said on the day that he asked God's forgiveness for the men of the battle of Uhud, "O Emigrants, behave kindly to the Helpers, for other men increase but they in the nature of things cannot grow more numerous. They were my constant comfort and support. So treat their good men well and forgive those of them who were remiss." Then he came down and entered his house and his pain increased until he was exhausted. Then some of his wives gathered to him, Umm Salama and Maymuna, and some of the wives of the Muslims, among them Asma daughter of Umays, and his uncle Abbas was with him, and they agreed to force him to take some of the medicine. Abbas said, "Let me force him," but it was they who did it. When he recovered he asked . . . why they had done that. His uncle said, "We were afraid that you would get pleurisy." He replied, "That is a disease God would not afflict me with." . . .

Al-Zuhri said, Hamza ibn Abdullah ibn Umar told me that Aisha said: "When the Prophet became seriously ill, he ordered the people to tell Abu Bakr to superintend the prayers. Aisha told him that Abu Bakr was a delicate man with a weak voice who wept much when he read the Quran. He [Muhammad] repeated his order nonetheless and I repeated my objections. He said, 'You are like Joseph's companions; tell him to preside at prayers.' My only reason for saying what I did was that I wanted (my father) Abu Bakr to be spared this task, because I knew the people would never like a man who occupied the Apostle's place and would blame him for every misfortune that occurred, and I wanted Abu Bakr spared that."

Al-Zuhri said that Anas ibn Malik told him that on the Monday on which God took His Messenger he went out to the people as they were praying the morning prayer. The curtain was lifted and the door opened and out came the Messenger and stood at the door of Aisha's room. The Muslims were almost seduced from their prayers at seeing him, and he motioned to them that they should continue their prayers. The Messenger smiled with joy when he marked their demeanor at prayer, and I never saw him with a nobler expression than he had on that day. Then he went back and the people went away thinking that the Messenger had recovered from his illness. . . .

Ya'qub ibn Utba from al-Zuhri from Urwa from (Muhammad's wife) Aisha said: The Messenger came back to me from the mosque that day and lay on my lap. A man of Abu Bakr's family came in to me with a toothpick in his hand. The Messenger looked at it in such a way that I knew he wanted it, and when I asked him if he wanted me to give it to him, he said yes. So I took it and chewed it to soften it for him and gave it to him. He rubbed his teeth with it more energetically than I had ever seen him rub them before. Then he laid it down. I found him heavy on my breast, and as I looked into his face, lo, his eyes were fixed and he was saying, "No, the most Exalted Companion is of Paradise." I said, "You were given the choice and you have chosen, by Him who sent you with the truth!" And so the Messenger was taken. . . .

Al-Zuhri said, and Sa'id ibn al-Musayyib from Abu Hurayra told me: When the Messenger was dead Umar got up (in the mosque) and said: "Some of the disaffected will allege that the Messenger is dead, but by God, he is not dead: he has gone to his Lord as Moses son of Imran went and was hidden [on Sinai] from his people for forty days. By God, the Messenger will return as Moses returned and will cut off the hands and feet of men who allege that the Messenger is dead." When Abu Bakr heard what had happened he came to the door of the mosque as Umar was speaking to the people. He paid no attention but went into Aisha's room to the Apostle, who was lying covered by a mantle of Yemeni cloth. He went and uncovered his face and kissed him saying, "You are dearer than my father and mother. You have tasted the death that God had decreed; a second death will never overtake you."

Then he replaced the mantle over the Apostle's face and went out. Umar was still speaking and Abu Bakr said, "Gently, Umar, be quiet." But Umar refused and went on talking, and when Abu Bakr saw that he would not be silent, he went forward himself to the people who, when they heard his words, came to him and left Umar. Giving thanks and praise to God, he said: "O men, if anyone worships Muhammad, Muhammad is dead; if anyone worships God, God is alive, immortal." Then he recited this verse: "Muhammad is nothing but an Apostle. Apostles have passed away before him. Can it be that if he were to die or be killed you would turn back on your heels? He who turns back does no harm to God and God will reward the grateful" (Quran 3:144). By God, it was as if the people did not know that this verse had not come down until Abu Bakr recited it that day. The people took it from him and it was constantly on their tongues. Umar said, "By God, when I heard Abu Bakr recite those words I was dumbfounded so that my legs would not bear me and I fell to the ground realizing that the Messenger was indeed dead." (*Life* 1000–1013) [IBN ISHAQ 1955: 678–683].

44. The Beginning of the Muslim Era

In his Traces of the Past *the Muslim chronographer Biruni (d. 1048 C.E.) reports the traditions concerning the beginning of the reckoning of a special era for Muslims.*

The era of the Hijra [or Emigration] of the Prophet Muhammad from Mecca to Medina is based upon lunar years, in which the commencements of months are determined by the (actual) appearance of the new moon and not by calculation. It is used by the whole Muslim world. The circumstances under which this point was adopted as an epoch and not the time when the Prophet was either born, or was entrusted with his divine mission, or died, were the following. Maymun ibn Mihran relates that Umar ibn al-Khattab [Caliph, 634–644 C.E.], when people one day handed him a check payable in the month of Sha'ban, said: "Which Sha'ban is meant? The one in which we are or the next Sha'ban?"

Thereupon he assembled the Companions of the Prophet and asked their advice regarding the matter of chronology, which troubled his mind. . . . Then Umar spoke to the Companions of the Prophet: "Establish a mode of dating for the intercourse of people." Now some said, "Date according to the era of the Greeks, for they date according to the era of Alexander." Others objected that this mode was too lengthy, and said, "Date according to the era of the Persians." But then it was objected that as soon as a new king arises among the Persians he abolishes the era of his predecessor. So they could not come to an agreement.

Aisha relates that Abu Musa al-Ash'ari wrote to Umar ibn al-Khattab: "You send us letters without a date." Umar had already organized the (government) registers, had established the taxes and regulations, and was in want of an era, not liking the old ones. On this occasion he assembled the Companions and took their advice. Now the most authentic date, which involves no obscurities or possible mishaps, seemed to be the date of the Hijra of the Prophet, and of his arrival at Medina on Monday, the eighth day of the month First Rabi', while the beginning of the year was a Thursday. Now he adopted this epoch and fixed thereby the dates in all his affairs. This happened in 17 of the Era of the Hijra [that is, 638 C.E.].

The reason why Umar selected this event as an epoch, and not the time of the birth of the Prophet, or the time when he was entrusted with his divine mission, is this, that regarding those two dates there was such a divergency of opinion as did not allow it to be made the basis of something which must be agreed upon universally. . . . Considering further that after the Hijra the affairs of Islam were thoroughly established, while heathenism decreased, that the Prophet was saved from the calamities prepared for him by the infidels of Mecca, and that after the Hijra his conquests followed each other in rapid succession, we come to the conclusion that the Hijra was to the Prophet what to kings is their accession and their taking possession of the whole sovereign power. (al-Biruni, *Traces of the Past* [BIRUNI 1879: 34–35]

45. Muhammad and Islam: An Early Christian Summary

The rapid Muslim conquest of the Near East made the Christians there quickly aware of the military and political aspects of the new Islamic society under which they would henceforward live. It took somewhat longer for them to come to an understanding, however imperfect, of the religious message that stood behind the conquest. The earliest to have attempted to put Islam into some kind of religious perspective was the Christian monk and theologian John of Damascus. He was well equipped to do so, since his family had already served in the Muslim administration of his native city, and John himself appears to have known Arabic and to have studied not only the Quran but also the Prophetic traditions. The result was a full-scale polemical assault on the new religion, which is taken up in Chapters 100–101 of John's On Heresies, *written in 743* C.E., *a little more than a century after the death of Muhammad.*

There is also the still-prevailing deceptive superstition of the Ishmaelites, the forerunner of the Antichrist. It takes its origin from Ishmael, who was born to Abraham from Hagar, and that is why they also call them Hagarenes and Ishmaelites. They also call them Saracens, allegedly for having been sent away by Sarah empty; for Hagar said to the angel, "Sarah has sent me away empty." These then were the idolators, and they venerated the morning star and Aphrodite, whom notably they called *Khabar* in their own language, which means "great"; therefore until the time of (the Emperor) Heraclius they were undoubtedly idolators.

From that time a false prophet appeared among them, surnamed Mamed, who, having been casually exposed to the Old and the New Testament, and supposedly encountered an Arian monk, formed a heresy of his own. And after, by pretense, he managed to make the people think of him as a God-fearing fellow, he spread rumors that a Scripture was brought down to him from heaven. Thus, having drafted some pronouncements in his book, worthy (only) of laughter, he handed it down to them in order that they might comply with it.

He says that there exists one God, Maker of all, who was neither begotten nor has He begotten. He says that Christ is the Word of God and His Spirit, created and a servant, and that he was born without a seed from Mary, the sister of Moses and Aaron. For, he says, the Word of God and the Spirit entered Mary and she gave birth to Jesus who was a prophet and a servant of God. And that the Jews, having themselves violated the Law, wanted to crucify him and after they arrested him they crucified his shadow; but Christ himself, they say, was not crucified nor did he die; for God took him up to Himself into heaven because He loved him. And this is what he says, that when Jesus went up to the heavens, God questioned him, saying: "O Jesus, did you say that 'I am the Son of God and God'?" And Jesus, they say, answered: "Be merciful to me, Lord; You know that I did not say so, nor will I boast that I am your servant;

but men who have gone astray wrote that I made the statement, and they said lies against me and they have been in error." And God, they say, answered him: "I knew that you would not say this thing."

If this was one of the earliest Christian experiences of the Muslim religion, it must also have been the Muslims' first encounter with a sophisticated Christian refutation of their claims.

And although he (Muhammad) includes in this writing many more absurdities worthy of laughter, he insists that this was brought down to him from God. And we ask: "And which is the one who gives witness, that God has given to him the Scriptures? And which of the prophets foretold that such a prophet would arise? And because they are surprised and at a loss, (we tell them) that Moses received the Law by the side of Mount Sinai in the sight of all the people when God appeared in a cloud and fire and darkness and storm, and that all the prophets, starting from Moses and onward, foretold of the advent of Christ and that Christ is God and that the Son of God will come by taking up flesh and that he will be crucified and that he will die and that he will be asked to judge the living and the dead alike." And when, then, we ask, "How is it that your prophet did not come this way, by having others bearing witness to him . . . so that you too have an assurance?" they reply that God does whatever He pleases. "This," we say, "is what we also know; but how did the Scripture come down to your prophet, this is what we are asking?" And they answer that while he was asleep the Scripture came down upon him. . . .

Moreover, they call us "Associators" because, they say, we introduce beside God an associate to Him by saying that Christ is the Son of God and God. To whom we answer that this is what the prophets and Scripture have handed down to us; and you, as you claim, accept the prophets. If therefore we say that Christ is the Son of God, they also were wrong who taught and handed it down to us so. And some of them mention that we have added such things, by having allegorized the prophets. Others hold that the Jews, out of hatred, deceived us with writings which supposedly originated from the prophets, so that we might get lost. . . .

They also defame us as being idolators because we venerate the Cross, which they despise; and we respond to them: "How is it that you rub yourselves against a stone by your *Chabatha* [that is, the Ka'ba], and you express your adoration for the stone by kissing it?" And some of them answer that it was because Abraham had intercourse with Hagar on it; others, because he tied his camel around it when he was about to sacrifice

Isaac. And we respond to them: "Since the Scripture says that there was a wooded mountain and timber, from which Abraham cut even for the holocaust of Isaac, and that he also left the asses behind with the servants, whence, then, is your idle tale? For in that place (of the Haram) there is neither wood from a forest nor do asses pass through." And they are embarrassed. They maintain nonetheless that the stone is of Abraham. Then we respond: "Suppose that it is of Abraham, as you foolishly maintain; are you not ashamed to kiss it for the sole reason that Abraham had intercourse with a woman upon it, or because he tied his camel to it, and yet you blame us for venerating the Cross of Christ, through which the power of the demons and the deceit of the devil has been destroyed?" This, then, which they call "stone" is the head of Aphrodite, whom they used to venerate (and) whom they called Chaber, on which those who understand it exactly can see traces of engraving even to this day.

John then turns his attention to the Quran, on which he is obviously informed in some detail. Equally obviously, his choice of details—Sura 4 contains 177 verses— is dictated by polemical considerations. Moreover, the themes he chose were to have an extremely long life in the Christian argument against Islam.

This Muhammad, as has been mentioned, composed many idle tales, on each one of which he prefixed a title, like for example the discourse (called) "The Woman" (Sura 4) in which he clearly legislates that one may have four wives and, if he can, one thousand concubines, as many as he can maintain beside his four wives; and that one can divorce whomsoever he pleases, if he so wishes, and have another (wife in her place). He made this law because of the following case (Quran 33:37). Muhammad had a comrade named Zayd. This man had a beautiful wife with whom Muhammad fell in love. While they were once sitting together Muhammad said to him, "O you, God has commanded me to take your wife." And he (Zayd) replied, "You are a Messenger; do as God has told you; take my wife."

After mocking the story of a camel that turns up in a number of suras (7:77; 26:141–159; 101:14), John touches upon "The Table Spread" of Sura 5:114.

Muhammad also talks about the Discourse of the Table. He says that Christ requested from God a table, and it was given to him. Because, he says, He told him, "I have given to you and your (companions) an incorruptible table."

Also the Discourse of the Cow (Sura 2), and several other tales worthy of laughter, which, because of their number, I think I should skip.

He made a law that they and the women should be circumcised, and he commanded (them) neither to observe the Sabbath, nor to be baptized and, on the one hand, to eat what was forbidden in the Law and, on the other, to abstain from others (which the Law permits); he also forbade the drinking of wine altogether. (John of Damascus, *On Heresies* 100–101) [SAHAS 1972: 133–141]

46. Maimonides on Muhammad

We have already seen in Chapter 2 the common interpretation of the "little horn" of Daniel's apocalyptic vision as referring to Antiochus Epiphanes. That connection, however, is nowhere stated explicitly in the text—an attractive ambiguity that permitted the vision to be later construed in other, no less political ways. After the seventh century of the Christian era one commonplace interpretation of the prophecy was that it referred to the rise of Islam, as we have noted in one exegetical text. It was also understood in that fashion by Maimonides (d. 1204 C.E.), the Jewish scholar who spent all of his life under Islamic sovereignty.

This event [that is, the rise of Islam] was predicted in the divinely inspired prophecy of Daniel, according to which a person would one day appear with a religion similar to the true one, and with a book of Scriptures and oral communications, and he will arrogantly pretend that God has granted a revelation to him, and indeed that he has spoken with Him, as well as other extravagant claims. In this manner, when he was describing the rise of the Arab kingdom after the fall of the Roman Empire (in the seventh century C.E.), he referred to the appearance of the Madman (Muhammad) and his victories over the Roman, Persian and Byzantine Empires in his vision of the horn which grew and became long and strong. This is clear from a verse which can be understood by the masses as well as by the select few. Since this interpretation is borne out by the facts of history, no other meaning can be attributed to the following verse: "I considered the horns, and behold, there came among them another horn, a little one, before which three of the first horns were plucked up by the roots; and behold, in this horn were eyes like the eyes of man, and a mouth speaking great things" (Dan. 7:8).

Now consider how remarkably apt is the imagery (of this verse). Daniel says he saw a small horn that was growing. When it became longer, even remarkably longer, it cast down before it the (other) three horns and behold, in the side of the horn there were two eyes like the eyes of a man, and a mouth speaking bold words. This obviously refers to someone who will found a new religion similar to the divine Law, and make claims to a revelation of a Scripture, and to prophecy. He will, furthermore, attempt to alter and abolish the Law, as it is said, "And he will seek to change the seasons and the law" (Dan. 7:25). (Maimonides, *Letter to the Yemen*)

47. A Muslim's Appreciation of Muhammad

Both the Christian John of Damascus and the Jew Maimonides are hostile witnesses on the Prophet of Islam. The Prophet appeared quite differently in the eyes of his followers, of course, and the accents of reverence and respect of the earliest of them still echo through the pages of Ibn Ishaq's Life of the Apostle of God. *Nor did the reverence or the respect diminish over the centuries. This, for example, is how Muhammad and his work appeared in the eyes of al-Damiri, an Egyptian writer who died in 1405 C.E.*

Historians record that the first who ever undertook to be a true leader of the (Arab) people was the Prophet, upon whom be God's blessing and peace. God sent him after a long break (in the succession of Messengers) to be a mercy to mankind, and he delivered His message. He strove with true diligence in the cause of God, gave proper advice to the people, and served his Lord till death came to him. He was the most favored of all creatures, the noblest of the Messengers, the Prophet of Mercy, the leader of convinced believers, who on the Day will bear the Standard of Praise, be the general intercessor, occupy the glorious station, have the pool which many will frequent, and gather under his banner Adam and all who came after him.

He is the best of Prophets and his community is the best of communities. His Companions are, after the Prophets, the choicest of mankind, and his is the noblest of sects. He performed astonishing miracles, possessed great natural abilities, had a sound and powerful intelligence, a most distinguished genealogy, and perfect beauty. His generosity was boundless, his bravery unchallengeable, his forbearance excessive, his knowledge profitable, his actions ever honorable, his fear of God complete, his piety sublime. He was the most eloquent of men, perfect in every respect, and the furthest of all mankind from things base and vicious. Of him the poet has said:

> "None like Muhammad has the Merciful ever created,
> Nor such, to my thinking, will He ever again create."

Aisha, with whom may God be pleased, said: "The Prophet, upon whom be God's blessing and peace, when he was at home used to be at the service of his household, that is, he used to act as servant to them. He used to delouse his own clothes and patch them, mend his own sandals and serve himself. He used to see to the feeding of his own domestic camel, sweep the house with a broom, hobble the camel, eat with the servant and help her knead her dough, and used to carry his own purchases home from the market." Moreover, he, upon whom be God's blessing and peace, used to be continually in grief, ever occupied by anxious thought, never having any rest. . . .

It is said that his death, upon him be God's blessing and peace, took place after God had perfected our religion for us and brought to completion His favor to us, at midday on the 12th of the month of First Rabi in the year 11 A.H. [632 C.E.], when he, upon whom be God's blessing and peace, was sixty-three years of age. Ali ibn Abi Talib took charge of washing him for burial, and he was interred in the apartment of Aisha, the Mother of the Believers, with whom may God be pleased. (Damiri, *The Book of Animals* 1.40–41) [JEFFERY 1962: 331–332]

5. "A Kingdom of Priests and a Holy Nation"

From Adam to Abraham, the Bible sketches what appears to be a history of all mankind, as viewed from the perspective of that time and that place. But when the account reaches the generation of Abraham, God pronounces a choice, or, perhaps, since the notion of exclusion is not stressed in the narrative at that point, God displays His particular favor toward Abraham and his descendants. That favor was to be shown in two ways, both highly appropriate to the small seminomadic clan constituted by Abraham and his family: they would increase in number, and they would someday come into possession of a land of their own. For his part, Abraham was bound to the circumcision of the males among his kin. What else might be required of the children of Abraham by way of reciprocation for the favor of God is not spelled out in Genesis, but over the following half-millennium or so, when the biblical account focuses almost exclusively upon Abraham's clan, those details are supplied: the Promise is succeeded by a Covenant, and the terms it imposed upon the growing number of those who called themselves "Children of Israel" were laid down in their fullest form by the Lord once Moses had led the Israelites from their bondage in Egypt.

1. Holiness and the Covenant

To put it most generally, the Children of Israel were set apart by virtue of their holiness: they will be, in God's own striking phrase, a "nation of priests."

On the third new moon after the Israelites had gone forth from the land of Egypt, on that very day, they entered the wilderness of Sinai. Having journeyed from Rephidim, they entered the wilderness of Sinai and encamped in the wilderness. Israel encamped there in front of the mountain, and Moses went up to God. The Lord called to him from the mountain, saying, "Thus shall you say to the house of Jacob and declare

255

to the children of Israel. 'You have seen what I did to the Egyptians, how I bore you on eagles' wings and brought you to Me. Now, then, if you will obey Me faithfully and keep My Covenant, you shall be My treasured possession among all the peoples. Indeed, all the earth is Mine, but you shall be to Me a kingdom of priests and a holy nation.' These are the words that you shall speak to the children of Israel." (Exodus 19:1–6)

The Lord spoke to Moses, saying: Speak to the Israelite people and say to them:

"I am the Lord your God. You shall not copy the practices of the land of Egypt where you dwelt, or of the land of Canaan to which I am taking you; nor shall you follow their laws. My rules alone shall you observe, and faithfully follow My laws: I am the Lord your God.

"You shall keep My laws and My rules, by the pursuit of which man shall live: I am the Lord." (Leviticus 18:1–5)

Do not defile yourselves in any of those ways [described in Lev. 18:6–23], for it is by such that the nations which I am casting out before you defiled themselves. Thus the land became defiled; and I called it to account for its iniquity, and the land spewed out its inhabitants. But you, unlike them, must keep My laws and My rules, and you must not do any of those abhorrent things, neither the citizen nor the stranger who resides among you; for all these abhorrent things were done by the people who were in the land before you and the land became defiled. So let not the land spew you out for defiling it, as it spewed out the nations that came before you. All who do any of these abhorrent things—such persons shall be cut off from their people. You shall keep my charge not to engage in any of the abhorrent practices that were carried out before you, and you shall not defile yourselves through them: I am the Lord your God. (Leviticus 18:24–30)

2. God's Final Punishment of Disobedience

That these are not simply counsels or recommendations is likewise made unmistakably clear.

And if, despite this, you disobey Me and remain hostile to Me, I will act against you in wrathful hostility; I for my part will discipline you seven times for your sins. You shall eat the flesh of your sons and the flesh of your daughters. I will destroy your cult places and cut down your incense stands, and I will heap your carcasses upon your lifeless fetishes. I will spurn you. I will lay your cities in ruin and make your sanctuaries deso-

late, and I will not savor your pleasing odors. I will make the land deso-
late, so that your enemies who settle in it shall be appalled by it. And you
I will scatter among the nations and I will unsheath the sword against you.
Your land shall become a desolation and your cities a ruin. . . . As for
those of you who survive, I will cast a faintness into their hearts in the
land of their enemies. The sound of a driven leaf shall put them to flight.
Fleeing as though from the sword, they shall fall though none pursues.
With no one pursuing, they shall stumble over one another as before the
sword. You shall not be able to stand your ground before your enemies,
but you shall perish among the nations; and the land of your enemies shall
consume you.

. . . Then at last shall their obdurate heart humble itself, and they
shall atone for their iniquity. Then will I remember My Covenant with
Jacob; I will remember also My Covenant with Isaac, and also My Covenant with Abraham; and I will remember the land. . . . Even then, when
they are in the land of their enemies, I will not reject them or spurn them
so as to destroy them, annulling My Covenant with them: for I am the
Lord their God. I will remember in their favor the Covenant with the
ancients, whom I freed from the land of Egypt in the sight of their nations
to be their God: I, the Lord.

These are the laws, rules and directions that the Lord established,
through Moses on Mount Sinai, between Himself and the Israelite people.
(Leviticus 26:27–46)

3. The Chosen People

*God had settled His Covenant, with all its demands, promised rewards, and threat-
ened punishments, on the children of Abraham—Isaac in the first generation, and
then Jacob and his offspring. And despite intimations by the prophets and insistence
by the Christians of an extension to the Gentiles, there it remained, at least in Jewish
eyes. Counterclaims to the notion of a "chosen people" come up in an interesting
context in a dialogue written by Judah Halevi in 1130–1140 C.E., when Christians
were on the offensive in Spain, the author's homeland, and in possession of the holy
places in Jerusalem. The questioner is an imaginary king of Khazars who is investigating the claims of various religions, and the respondent is a rabbi who speaks for
Judah Halevi himself.*

The Khazar King: . . . The perfection of his [Moses'] work was
marred by the fact that his book was written in Hebrew, which made it
unintelligible to the peoples of Sind, India and Khazar. They would,
therefore, be unable to practice all his laws until some centuries had

elapsed, or they had been prepared for it by changes of conquest or alliance, but not through the revelation of the prophet himself, or another who would stand up for him and testify to his law.

The Rabbi: Moses invited only *his* people and those of his own tongue to accept the law, while God promised that at all times there should be prophets to expound His law. This He did as long as they found favor in His sight and His presence was with them.

The Khazar King: Would it not have been better or more commensurate with divine wisdom if all mankind had been guided on the true path?

The Rabbi: Or would it not have been best for all animals to have been reasonable beings? You have apparently forgotten what we said previously concerning Adam's progeny, and how the spirit of divine prophecy rested on one person (in each generation), who was chosen from his brethren and was the essence of his father. It was he on whom this divine light was concentrated. He was the kernel, while the others were as husks which had no share in it. (All) the sons of Jacob were, however, distinguished from other people by godly qualities, which made them, so to speak, an angelic caste. . . . We do not deny that the good actions of any man, to whichever people he may belong, will be rewarded by God. But the priority belongs to people who are near God during their life, and we estimate the rank they occupy after death accordingly.

After this preliminary exploration of the concept of a chosen people and its limitations, the discussion turns in the direction of the social consequences of such a notion. Do we not have a right to expect that God's people of choice would be so signaled by their position in the world, the Khazar king asks.

The Rabbi: I see you reproaching us with our degradation and poverty, while the best of other religions boast of both (high station in this world and the next). Do they not glorify him [that is, Jesus] who said: "He who strikes you on the right cheek, turn to him the left also; and he who takes your coat, let him have your shirt as well" (Matt. 5:39–40)? He and his friends and followers, after hundreds of years of contumely, flogging and slaying, attained their well-known success, and in the very things they glorify. This is also the history of the founder of Islam [that is, Muhammad] and his friends, who eventually prevailed and became powerful. The nations boast of these, but not of those kings whose power and might are great, whose walls are strong and whose chariots are terrible. Yet our relation to God is a closer one than if we had reached greatness already on earth.

The Khazar King: This might be so, if your humility were voluntary; but it is involuntary, and if you had power you would slay.

The Rabbi: You have touched our weak spot, O King of the Khazars. If the majority of us, as you say, would learn humility toward God and His Law from our low station, Providence would not have forced us to bear it for such a long period. Only the smallest portion (of us) thinks this; the majority may expect reward, because they bear their degradation, partly from necessity, partly from their own free will. . . . If we bear our exile and degradation for God's sake, as is meet, we shall be the pride of the generation which will come with the Messiah, and accelerate the day of deliverance we hope for.

Now we do not allow anyone who embraces our religion theoretically by means of word alone to take equal rank with ourselves, but demand actual self-sacrifice, purity, knowledge, circumcision and numerous religious ceremonies. The convert must adopt our way of life entirely. . . . Those, however, who become Jews do not take equal rank with born Israelites, who are specially privileged to attain to prophecy, while the former can only achieve something by learning from them, and become pious and learned, but never prophets. (Judah Halevi, *The Khazar King*) [HALEVI 1905: 72–79]

4. A Muslim Wonders about the "Children of God"

When the Muslim essayist al-Jahiz (d. 868 C.E.), in his Refutation of the Christians, *came to the question of Jesus as Son of God, he was quickly drawn into the larger question of the divine paternity and the use made of it by the Jews in their Covenant history.*

In general, we cannot grant that God has a son, either by carnal begetting or by adoption. To concede that would be to manifest enormous ignorance, indeed, to commit blasphemy. Thus, if God is Jacob's father, then He must be Joseph's grandfather, and once we admit that He can be a father and a grandfather, even without conceding actual (physical) paternity, and introduce some complication or otherwise lessen His divine majesty and magnitude, we are then forced to concede that He is a paternal and maternal uncle; for if it is proper (as in the case of Jacob) to call God father by reason of His mercy, His affection for a person of His own choosing and His willingness to raise him, then it must be equally appropriate for someone who wishes to honor Him and acknowledge His superiority and mastery over the whole of creation to call him brother and find a companion and friend for Him. Now this is lawful only for someone who does not acknowledge God's greatness and man's insignificance compared to Him. . . .

There is another side to this question, which will show you how well based my argument is. Had God known that in the Books which He revealed to the Israelites the following words occurred: "Your father was my firstborn, and you are the children of my firstborn," he would not have been angry when they said: "We are God's children." For how could God's son's son be anything else than God's grandson? That would have been a mark of complete respect and perfect love, all the more because He Himself said in the Torah, "The Israelites are the children of My firstborn son." Thus it is clear that when the (pagan) Arabs asserted that the angels were God's daughters (Quran 16:59), God regarded this belief as a grave sin and manifested His anger against those who had said it, even though He was well aware that they did not impute them to Him as the offspring of His flesh. How then can we suppose that God declared beforehand to His creatures that Jacob was His son, like Solomon, or Ezra or Jesus? God is too great to have paternity among His attributes, and man is too contemptible to claim to have been begotten of God. (Jahiz, *Refutation of the Christians* 143–144)

5. The Restoration of Israel's Holiness after the Exile

The restoration of Israel in Judea after 538 B.C.E. required more than simply bringing back numbers of the former population. The Israelites had also to be reconstituted as a community, a complex act that involved in the first instance the revival of the worship of the God of Israel in the sanctified place atop Mount Moriah, the rebuilding of the Temple, and the restoration of the priesthoods and Levitical orders—in short, a renewal of the Covenant (see Chapter 2 above). But if renewal and restoration were one part of the program, purification, and thus inevitably separation, was another. A fastidious observance of the Sabbath commandment was one instrument to achieve this end, as we shall see, but the problem of mixed marriages, whether of the returnees or of those Israelites who had remained behind in Judea, was perhaps more complex and its solution in the end more painful. The narrative is Ezra's.

. . . The officers approached me, saying, "The people of Israel and the priests and Levites have not separated themselves from the peoples of the land whose abhorrent practices are like those of the Canaanites, the Hittites, the Perizzites, the Jebusites, the Ammonites, the Moabites, the Egyptians and the Amorites. They have taken their daughters as wives for

themselves and for their sons, so that the holy seed has become inter-
mingled with the peoples of the land; and it is the officers and prefects
who have taken the lead in this trespass."

When I heard this, I rent my garment and robe, I tore hair out of my
head and beard, and I sat desolate. Around me gathered all who were
concerned with the words of the God of Israel because of the returning
exiles' trespass, while I sat desolate until the evening offering. At the time
of the evening offering I ended my self-affliction; still in my torn garments
and robe, I got down on my knees and spread out my hands to the Lord
my God. . . . "Bondsmen we are, though even in our bondage God has
not forsaken us, but has disposed the king of Persia favorably toward us,
to furnish us with sustenance and to raise again the House of our God,
repairing its ruins and giving us a hold in Judah and Jerusalem.

"Now, what can we say in the face of this, O our God, for we have
forsaken your commandments, which You gave us through Your servants
the prophets when You said, 'The land which you are about to possess is
a land unclean through uncleanness of the peoples of the land, through
their abhorrent practices with which they, in their impurity, have filled
it from one end to the other. Now, then, do not give your daughters in
marriage to their sons or let their daughters marry your sons; do nothing
for their well-being or their advantage, then you will be strong and enjoy
the bounty of the land and bequeath it to your children forever.' " (Ezra
9:1–12)

While Ezra was praying and making confession, weeping and pros-
trating himself before the House of God, a very great crowd of Israelites
gathered about him, men, women and children; the people were weeping
bitterly. Then Shecaniah son of Jehiel of the family of Elam spoke up and
said to Ezra, "We have trespassed against God by bringing into our homes
foreign women from the peoples of the land; but there is still hope for
Israel despite this. Now, then, let us make a covenant with our God to
expel all these women and those who have been born to them, in accordance with the bidding of the Lord and of all who are concerned over the
commandment of our God, and let the Torah be obeyed. Take action, for
the responsibility is yours and we are with you. Act with resolve!"

. . . Then a proclamation was issued in Judah and Jerusalem that all
who had returned from the exile should assemble in Jerusalem, and that
anyone who did not come in three days would, by a decision of the
officers and elders, have his property confiscated and himself excluded
from the congregation of the returning exiles.

All the men of Judah and Benjamin assembled in Jerusalem in three days; it was the ninth month, the twentieth of the month. All the people sat in the square of the House of God, trembling on account of the event and because of the rains. Then Ezra the priest got up and said to them, "You have trespassed by bringing home foreign women, thus aggravating the guilt of Israel. So now, make confession to the Lord, God of your fathers, and do His will, and separate yourselves from the peoples of the land and from the foreign women."

The entire congregation responded in a loud voice, "We must surely do just as you say. However, many people are involved, and it is the rainy season; it is not possible to remain in the open, nor is this the work of a day or two, because we have transgressed extensively in this matter. Let our officers remain on behalf of the entire congregation, and all our townspeople who have brought home foreign women shall appear before them at scheduled times, together with the elders and judges of each town, in order to avert the burning anger of our God from us on this account. . . . "

The returning exiles did so. Ezra and the men who were the chiefs of the ancestral clans—all listed by name—sequestered themselves on the first day of the tenth month to study the matter. By the first day of the first month they were done with all the men who had brought home foreign women. (Ezra 9:1–10:17)

In the Book of Nehemiah, as well, the problem of the intermingling of the Israelites with foreigners in their land is raised and addressed, at first as part of the people's formal renewal of their Covenant with God.

(We) . . . take an oath with sanctions to follow the Torah of God . . . namely: we will not give our daughters in marriage to the peoples of the land, or take their daughters for our sons. The peoples of the land who bring their wares and all sorts of foodstuffs for sale on the sabbath day— we will not buy from them on the sabbath or a holy day. We will forgo (the produce of) the seventh year, and every outstanding debt. (Nehemiah 10:30–31).

Later it is Nehemiah himself who speaks.

At that time I saw men in Judah treading winepresses on the sabbath, and others bringing heaps of grain and loading them on asses, also wine, grapes, figs, and all sorts of goods, and bringing them into Jerusalem on the sabbath. I admonished them there and then for selling provisions. Tyrians who lived there brought fish and all sorts of wares and sold them on the sabbath to the Judahites in Jerusalem. I censured the nobles of

Judah, saying to them, "What evil thing is this that you are doing, profaning the sabbath day! This is what your ancestors did, and for it God brought all this misfortune on this city; and now you give cause for further wrath against Israel by profaning the sabbath!"

When shadows filled the gateways of Jerusalem at the approach of the sabbath, I gave orders that the doors be closed, and ordered them not to be opened until after the sabbath. I stationed some of my servants at the gates, so that no goods should enter on the sabbath. . . . I gave orders to the Levites to purify themselves and come and guard the gates, to preserve the sanctity of the sabbath. . . .

Also at that time, I saw that Jews had married Ashodite, Ammonite and Moabite women; a good number of their children spoke the language of Ashod and the language of those various peoples, and did not know how to speak Judean. I censured them, cursed them, flogged them, tore out their hair, and adjured them by God, saying, "You shall not give your daughters in marriage to their sons, or take any of their daughters for your sons or yourselves. It was just in such things that King Solomon of Israel sinned! Among the many nations there was not a king like him, and so well loved was he by his God that God made him king of all Israel, yet foreign wives caused even him to sin. How, then, can we acquiesce in your doing this great wrong, breaking faith with our God by marrying foreign women?"

One of the sons of Joiada son of the high priest Eliashib was a son-in-law of Sanballat the Horonite; I drove him away from me. Remember to their discredit, O God, how they polluted the priesthood, the covenant of the priests and Levites. I purged them of every foreign element, and arranged for the priests and Levites to work each at his tasks by shifts, and for the wood offering (to be brought) at fixed times, and for the firstfruits. (Nehemiah 13:15–31)

6. Conversion

As related by Ezra and Nehemiah, the return of the Israelites from exile in Babylonia was accompanied by an effort to restore Judaism to its older ethnic basis by dissolving the marriages that had inevitably occurred between the Jews living abroad and the native non-Jewish peoples who were their hosts. But not all the Jews had returned from Babylon; nor did other Jews cease to choose or to be constrained to a life outside the geographical boundaries of Eretz Israel. From the perspective of the "ethnic purists," the growth of Diaspora Judaism led to the inevitable dilution of the tribal heritage of the Covenant. But it also gave rise to an increasing interest in Judaism on the part of the Gentiles, most notably perhaps from the Hellenes and the Hellenized, with their own new sophistication and openness to the previously scorned manners and customs of the "barbarians." The phenomenon was remarked upon by the historian Josephus, writing toward the end of the first Christian century.

There is not one city, Greek or barbarian, to which our custom of abstaining from work on the seventh day has not spread, and where the fasts and the lighting of lamps and many of our prohibitions in the matter of food are not observed. Moreover, they attempt to imitate our unanimity, our liberal charities, our devoted labor in the crafts, our endurance under persecution on behalf of our laws. (Josephus, *Against Apion* 2.38)

The Jews were not oblivious to what was happening or, as it appears, indifferent to it. Matthew has Jesus say in the course of a long diatribe against the Pharisees, "Alas for you, lawyers and Pharisees, hypocrites! You travel over sea and land to make one convert; and when you have won him, you make him twice as fit for hell as yourselves" (Matt. 24:15). Post-Exilic Judaism unmistakably encouraged conversion, for a time at least, and set out the provisions whereby the Gentile might become, by affiliation, a member of the Chosen People.

Rabbi says: Just as Israel did not enter the Covenant except through three things, through circumcision, through immersion and through the acceptance of sacrifice, so it was the same with the proselytes. (Sifre on Numbers 108)

The "acceptance of sacrifice" makes it certain that we are dealing here with a pre–70 C.E. perspective on the conditions of conversion, just as the following Talmudic text, which sets forth the actual procedure of formal conversion and yet makes no mention of sacrifice, must reflect the conditions prevailing after the destruction of the Temple.

Our rabbis taught: A proselyte who comes to convert at this time, we say to him: Why did you decide to convert? Do you know that Israel at this time is afflicted, oppressed, downtrodden, and rejected, and that tribulations are visited upon them? If he says, "I am aware, but I am unworthy," we accept him immediately, and we make known to him a few of the lighter commandments and a few of the weightier commandments, and we make known to him the penalty for transgression of gleaning (the poor man's share of the harvest), the forgotten (sheaves), the corner, and the poor man's tithe. And we make known to him the punishment for violating the commandments. . . . And just as we make known to him the punishment for violating the commandments, so also we make known to him their reward. . . . We are not too lengthy with him nor are we too detailed. If he accepts this, we circumcise him immediately. . . . Once he has recovered (from circumcision), we immerse him immediately. And two scholars stand over him and make known to him some of the lighter and some of the weightier commandments. If he is immersed validly, he is like an Israelite in all matters. (In the case of a woman) women position her in the water up to her neck, and two scholars stand outside and make known to her some of the lighter commandments and some of the weightier commandments. (BT.Yebamoth 47a–b)

7. The Pharisaic Program: Separate as Holy

Despite the Lord's avowed intention of creating all Israel as "a nation of priests," the Torah legislation given to the Israelites seems to envision a body of priests maintaining a special and high degree of purity within Israelite society. If the cited passages in Exodus and Leviticus were the ideal, then many centuries passed before it was constituted, if not a reality, then at least a possibility. The responsibility for this profound transformation at the heart of Judaism appears to have been the work of that somewhat mysterious group of men called Pharisees, the same who were so severely taken to task by Jesus. There would be no mystery to the Pharisees if we were simply to read Josephus' clear and coherent description.

The Jews, from the most ancient times, had three philosophies pertaining to their traditions, that of the Essenes, that of the Sadducees, and thirdly, that of a group called the Pharisees. . . . The Pharisees simplify their standard of living, making no concession to luxury. They follow the guidance of that which their doctrine has selected and transmitted as good, attaching the chief importance to the observance of those commandments which it has seen fit to dictate to them. They show respect and deference to their elders, nor do they rashly presume to contradict their proposals.

Though they postulate that everything is brought about by fate, still they do not deprive the human will of the pursuit of what is in man's power, since it was God's good pleasure that there should be a fusion and that the will of man with his virtue and vice should be admitted to the council chamber of fate. They believe that souls have the power to survive death and that there are rewards and punishments under the earth for those who have led lives of virtue and vice: eternal imprisonment is the lot of evil souls, while the good souls receive an easy passage to a new life. Because of these views they are, as a matter of fact, extremely influential among the townsfolk; and all prayers and sacred rites of divine worship are performed according to their exposition. This is the great tribute that the inhabitants of the cities, by practicing the highest ideals both in their way of living and in their discourse, have paid to the excellence of the Pharisees. (Josephus, *Antiquities* 18.11–13)

According to Josephus, then, the Pharisees were a party of Jews who enjoyed a great deal of popular support in the centuries immediately preceding and following the beginning of the Christian era. They were characterized not only by their theological positions, such as a belief in the afterlife, but also by their respect for and devotion to the Law, both the written Torah and the oral "traditions from the Fathers." The Gospels, as we shall see, are more polemical and disapproving of them than Josephus, who was himself, after all, one of their number. Yet the Gospels' portrait of the Pharisees is not so very different: the Pharisees are punctilious observers of the Law who seek to impose their standards of observance on the whole people.

Neither Josephus nor the Gospels explain the meaning of "Pharisaioi," a transparently foreign term transcribed in Greek. When we turn to the rabbinic sources, we do not find the same transcription; but there occurs throughout a term that easily suggests itself as the original of "Pharisees," namely, perushim, *literally "the Separate" or "the Separated." We might be willing to accept this identification of "Pharisees" and the Perushim except for two chief reasons. First, in those rabbinic sources the Perushim do not appear as a cohesive party or association, as they clearly are in the Greek-language texts. Second, the rabbis do not speak very highly of them or of their opinions, which they might reasonably be expected to do of men who were their unmistakable predecessors in the exaltation and refinement of the Law. The matter is not simple, however, as we have already seen. In many texts the rabbinic program hovers over the notion of "separateness," with close verbal associations with* perushim, *as in these rabbinic comments on the Torah's expression "a holy people."*

"Holy": that is, holy and sanctified, *separated* from the world and their abominations. (Mekilta on Exodus 19:9)

"For I am the Lord your God, you shall sanctify yourselves and be holy, for I am holy": that is, even as I am holy, so you shall be holy; even as I am *separate*, so also shall you be *separated* (*perushim*). (Sifra on Leviticus 11:44)

"You shall sanctify yourselves and be holy": this means the sanctification which consists in *separation* from the heathen. It is nothing other than the sanctification which consists in observing all the commandments, as it says, "You shall be holy." (Sifra on Leviticus 20:7)

"As I am holy, so you shall be (holy)": that is, as I am *separate*, so you shall be *separated* (*perushim*). If you are *separated* from the nations, you belong to me . . . but if you are not, then you belong to Nebuchadnezzar, king of Babylon, and his companions. (Sifra on Leviticus 20:26)

Separateness from the surrounding heathen is a commonplace prescription repeated again and again in Scripture, as we have seen. What the Pharisees brought to the advice was an attitude toward the heathen within Israel, that is, those people, Jews by birth, whose lack of strict observance rendered them unclean and so unholy, like the "publicans and sinners" with whom Jesus dined. These are the am ha-Aretz, the "commoners of the land" who appear and reappear as the target of the Perushim and of the rabbis themselves throughout the rabbinic writings.

Our rabbis taught: Who is an *am ha-Aretz?* Whoever does not recite the *Shema* morning and evening with its accompanying benedictions. So according to Rabbi Meir. The Sages say, "Whoever does not put on phylacteries." Ben Azzai says, "Whoever has not fringe upon his garment." Rabbi Jonathan ben Joseph says, "Whoever has sons and does not rear them to study Torah." Others say, "Even if he learnt Torah and Mishna and did not attend upon rabbinic scholars, he is an *am ha-Aretz.* If he learned Scripture but not Mishna, he is a boor; if he learnt neither Scripture nor Mishna, concerning him Scripture declares, 'I will sow Israel and Judah with the seed of man and the seed of cattle' (Jer. 31:27)." (BT. Sotah 22a)

8. Jesus on the Pharisees

Although Jesus may have agreed with the end, and indeed even with many of the means, he did not much approve of either the attitudes or the example of the Pharisees of his day. For some of his many criticisms of the Pharisees recorded in the Gospels, we can look particularly to Matthew.

Jesus addressed the people and his disciples in these words: "The doctors of the Law and the Pharisees sit in the chair of Moses: therefore do what they tell you; pay attention to their words. But do not follow their practice; for they say one thing and do another. They make up heavy packs and pile them on men's shoulders, but do not lift a finger to lift the load themselves. Whatever they do is done for show. They go about with broad phylacteries and with large fringe upon their robes; they like to have places of honor at feasts and the chief seats in the synagogues, to be greeted respectfully in the streets, and to be addressed as 'rabbi.' " (Matthew 23:1–7)

Alas for you, lawyers and Pharisees, hypocrites! You pay tithes (even) of mint and dill and cumin; but you have overlooked the weightier demands of the Law, justice, mercy and good faith. It is those you should have practiced, without neglecting the others. Blind guides! You strain off a gnat (from your drink), yet gulp down a camel!

Alas for you, lawyers and Pharisees, hypocrites! You clean the outside of the cup and dish, which you have filled inside by robbery and self-indulgence. Clean the inside of the cup first; then the outside will be clean also.

Alas for you, lawyers and Pharisees, hypocrites! You are like tombs covered with whitewash; they look well from the outside, but inside they are full of dead men's bones and all kinds of filth. So it is with you: outside you look like honest men, but inside you are brim-full with hypocrisy and crime. (Matthew 23:23–28)

As he passed from there, Jesus saw a man named Matthew at his seat in the customhouse, and said to him, "Follow me"; and Matthew rose and followed him. When Jesus was at table in the house, many bad characters, tax gatherers and others, were seated with him and his disciples. The Pharisees noticed this, and said to his disciples, "Why is it that your master eats with tax gatherers and sinners?" Jesus heard it and said, "It is not the healthy that need a doctor, but the sick. Go and learn what the text means, 'I require mercy not sacrifice.' I did not come to invite virtuous people but sinners." (Matthew 9:9–13)

The Pharisees had their own views on tax collectors, those unjust dealers with the Gentiles.

At first they [the Pharisees] used to say: if an associate [or member] becomes a tax collector, he is deprived of his status as an associate. Later they altered this and said: As long as he is a tax collector, he is not considered reliable; once he has withdrawn from being a tax collector, he is reliable. (Tosefta Demai 3:4)

The tax collector was in effect banned from Pharisaic society.

9. Bans and Excommunication

The Torah recognized that there were certain transgressions for which one might atone. Indeed, the whole principle of sin offerings in Israel is based on such a premise. Other acts, however, are of such gravity that, if they were performed knowingly and deliberately, had irremediable and permanent effects, ranging from the death penalty to the separation of the offender from the community. We can observe the distinction at work in this text from Numbers.

In the case of an individual who has sinned unwittingly, he shall offer a she-goat in its first year as a sin offering. The priest shall make expiation before the Lord on behalf of the person who has erred, for he sinned unwittingly, making such expiation for him that he may be forgiven. For the citizen among the Israelites and for the stranger who resides among them—you shall have one ritual for anyone who acts in error.

But the person, be he citizen or stranger, who acts defiantly reviles the Lord; that person shall be cut off from among the people. Because he has spurned the word of the Lord and violated His commandment, that person shall be cut off—he bears his guilt. (Numbers 15:27–31)

In the post-Exilic period, the following action is ascribed to Ezra in the early days of the restoration of the community in Judea.

. . . Then a proclamation was issued in Judah and Jerusalem that all who had returned from the exile should assemble in Jerusalem, and that anyone who did not come in three days would, by a decision of the officers and elders, have his property confiscated and himself excluded from the congregation of the returning exiles. (Ezra 10:7–8)

Ezra and his fellow leaders of the time, whoever exactly is meant by the latter, must have enjoyed the kind of authority that made such an exclusion both plausible and enforceable. That those conditions lasted very long may be doubted, since we hear little more of such acts of excommunication until the rise of fairly well-defined and voluntary sectarian groups like the Pharisees and the community of Qumran, who could use the weapon of exclusion to preserve their own integrity and discipline. The following bans, for example, like the ban on the tax collector cited in the Tosefta, appear to be from the pre-70 C.E. Pharisaic community.

Akabya ben Mahalaleel testified to four opinions. They answered: Akabya, retract these four opinions you have given and we will make you Ab Beth Din [that is, second officer of the Great Sanhedrin]. He said to them: Better that I be called a fool all my days than that I be made a godless man before God even for an hour; for they shall say of me, he retracted for the sake of (gaining) the office. He declared unclean the residuary hair [in a leprosy symptom], and also the yellow blood, while the Sages declare them clean. If the hair of a blemished firstling fell out and one put it in a wall niche and afterwards slaughtered the animal, he used to permit the hair to be used, while the Sages forbade it. . . . Whereupon they laid him under a ban; and he died while he was still under the ban and they stoned his coffin. (M.Eduyoth 5:6)

The same text continues:

Rabbi Judah said: God forbid that it was Akabya who was under the ban! For the gate of the Temple Court was never shut against the face of any man in Israel so wise and God-fearing as Akabya ben Mahalaleel. But whom did they put under a ban? Eleazer ben Enoch, because he cast doubt on (the teaching of the Sages concerning) the cleaning of hands. And when he died the Court sent and laid a stone on his coffin; whence we learn that if any man is put under a ban and dies while yet under the ban, his coffin must be stoned.

If the grounds in the cases of the tax collector, Akabya, and Eleazer ben Enoch all seem appropriately Pharisaic—all variations on the theme of ritual purity (though the first case has to do with contracting it and the latter two with teaching on the subject)—we do not know what form the ban had or whether it had any set term. It did not, certainly, disqualify one from being thought of as a Jew, and in the case of Akabya there is even some doubt whether he ceased being a respected teacher. After 70 C.E., however, two things occurred to alter the situation. First, the ideals of Pharisaism prevailed as the normative standard of Jewish observance. Second, with the disappearance of all other parties and sects, power was concentrated in Pharisaic hands and wielded through a rabbinic-dominated Sanhedrin, which the Romans themselves acknowledged as the chief judicial body of the Jewish nation.

After 70, then, there were juridical standards—the Pharisees'—for using the ban penalty throughout the community, and there was an authority competent and willing to use it: the Nasi, or head of the Sanhedrin. We are told of two major types of ban: the nidduy of thirty days and the herem of indefinite extension. The person banned was treated juridically like the leper: everyone had to keep a distance of six feet from him. That, at any rate, was the theory. As a matter of fact, the only cases we know of such excommunication have to do with rabbis, and the grounds were incorrect teaching on the matter of ritual purity, insulting another rabbi, or casting ridicule on the Law. Excommunication, as far as we can tell, seems to have remained primarily a weapon in an academic debate.

10. Grave Sins and Light Offenses

The text in Numbers cited above on the subject of inadvertent and presumptuous sin looked primarily at intention. Some later rabbis attempted to be more specific about the deeds themselves, though the penalty of outlawry was now notably postponed to the world to come, as in M.Sanhedrin 10:1. This may indeed have been the venue where excommunication functioned most effectively.

Basing himself on the severe verse, Numbers 15:31, Rabbi Elazar of Modin said: If a man says, "I accept all the Torah with one exception," or if he says, "All the Torah was spoken by God with the exception of one passage, which was spoken by Moses," he has despised the word of God, and is worthy to be thrust out of the world (to come). (Sifre on Numbers, Shelah 112)

Rabbi Elazar of Modin said: He who profanes the Holy Things (of the Temple), and despises the holy days, and breaks the Covenant of Abraham our father, even if he has in his hand many (fulfilled) commandments, he is worthy to be thrust out of the world (to come). (Ibid.)

What is apparently happening in these instances, though still in a somewhat haphazard and unsystematic fashion, is an attempt to define, or at least isolate, what might be considered the fundamentals of a Jewish life, not now in any sectarian fashion, like the threats against the Sadducees already cited above, or in the manner of a homily, like the search for the "great commandment." Implicit in this search is a distinction among moral acts, and we have already seen how instructions regarding proselytes recommended their being introduced to both the "weighty" and the "light" commandments. Whatever those terms might have meant in that particular context—more or less important, more difficult or easier to observe—this distinction of commandments carried an implication that bothered some of the Sages, and they reacted against it. Our first passage is in the form of a reflection on the fact that in Deuteronomy "length of days" is promised to both the one who honors his parents—where disobedience is punishable by stoning—and the one who releases a mother bird found brooding on her nest (Deut. 22:6–7).

Rabbi Abba ben Kahana said: the Scripture has made the lightest command in the Torah equal to the heaviest command; for the reward of length of days is attached to both cases (cited). Rabbi Abun said: If in a commandment (like this), which is, as it were, the payment of a debt, the reward of length of days is added, how much more should it be appended to commandments which involve loss of money or danger to one's life. (JT.Kiddushin 61b)

Rabbi Judah the Prince said: Be as heedful of a light precept as of a grave one, for you know not the reward for each. Reckon the loss incurred by fulfilling a precept against the reward secured by its observance, and the gain gotten by its transgression against the loss that such involves. Reflect upon three things and you will not come within the power of sin: Know what is above you—a seeing eye, and a hearing ear, and all your deeds written in a book. (M.Pirke Aboth 2:1)

Maimonides, in his commentary on this passage, provides some examples of the two types of precept, though with Rabbi Judah's same caveat regarding observation.

This means that one should be just as mindful of a commandment which he considers a minor one, for example the command to rejoice during the festivals, to learn the Holy Tongue [that is, Hebrew], as he is to a commandment of whose major importance we have been informed, the law of circumcision, for example, or that of "fringes" [Num. 15:37–41], or the Passover offering. . . . For as regards the positive commandments, we have never been told what reward the Lord, blessed be He, has set aside for each of them . . . and that is why we must be attentive to all of them. (Maimonides, *Commentary on Mishna Aboth* 2.11)

Not unnaturally, the early Christians were drawn into making the same distinctions in offenses against God's commandments. Here the author is the Alexandrian Origen, struggling ca. 230 C.E. with the Christian's dilemma between faith in Jesus and the deeds that in fact belie that faith.

Whoever dies in his sins, even if he says he believes in Christ, in truth he does not believe in him. Even if it is called faith, it exists without good works and such faith is dead, as we read in the letter that circulates in the name of James. Who is then the believer if not he who comes to such a state . . . without falling into those sins which are called "mortal." (Origen, *Commentary on John* 19, 23)

Those sins were called "deadly" or "mortal" by John in one of his letters included in the New Testament.

If a man sees his brother committing a sin which is not a mortal sin, he should pray to God for him, and He will grant him life, that is, when men are not guilty of mortal sin. There is such a thing as deadly sin, and I do not suggest that he should pray about that; but although all wrongdoing is sin, not all sin is deadly sin. (John, *Letter* 1.2:16–17)

Quite naturally, the rabbis issued the same kind of warning about relying too much on the distinction between "great" and "small" sins. In this instance the caution comes from the Christian Basil of Caesarea (ca. 370–379 C.E.).

How are we to deal with those who avoid the graver sins but commit the smaller ones indiscriminately? First, we should know that this distinction is not found in the New Testament. We have but one statement about all sins, when the Lord said, "Who commits a sin is the slave of sin" (John 8:34). . . . And if we are permitted to speak of a small and a great sin, it must be said that the great sin is the one which exercises dominion over us and the small one is that over which we conquer. As in an athletic contest, the stronger is the one who triumphs and the defeated is weaker than the victor, whoever he happens to be. (Basil, *Shorter Rule* 293)

The classification of sins fell into two different sets of hands in Christianity. First, since the forgiveness of sins was a formal judicial procedure, namely the sacrament of penance, as it came to be called (see below), the specific gravity of sins had to be weighed by those of the clergy delegated to sit in judgment over the sinner and assess the penalties for sin. But it was likewise a matter of concern for the moral theologian—that characteristically Christian figure born of the union of Gospel morality and Greek philosophical ethics. "Mortal sin" is still the subject, but the terms of the discussion are now derived directly from Aristotle's Ethics.

The difference between venial and mortal sin is consequent upon the difference in that lack of order which constitutes the nature of sin. For lack of order is twofold, one that destroys the principle of order and another which, though it does not destroy the principle of order, does bring about a lack of order in the things that follow that principle. Thus, in an animal's body, the frame may be so out of order that the vital principle is destroyed: this is death; while, on the other hand, there is the instance where the vital principle remains but there might be, for example, a disorder of the vital humors: and then there is sickness. Now the principle of entire moral order is the last end, which stands in the same relation to matters of action as an indemonstrable principle does to matters of speculation. Therefore, when the soul is so disordered by sin as to turn away from its last end, to wit, God, to Whom it is united by charity, there is mortal sin; but when it is disordered without turning away from God, then there is venial sin. For even as in the body, the disorder of death which results from the separation of the principle of life is irreparable according to nature, while the disorder of sickness can be repaired because the vital principle itself remains, so it is in matters of the soul. . . . Likewise, in practical matters, he who by sinning turns away from his last end, if we consider the nature of his sin, falls irreparably and is therefore said to sin mortally and to deserve eternal punishment. But when a man sins without turning away from God, by the very nature of his sin his disorder can be repaired because the principle of the order is not destroyed; and therefore he is said to sin venially because he does not sin so as to deserve to be punished eternally. (Thomas Aquinas, *Summa Theologica* I/2, ques. 72, art. 5) [AQUINAS 1945: 2:576–577]

The characterization of certain sins as grave or serious and, by implication, of others as less serious appears in the Quran in the context of forgiveness.

If you keep away from the deadly sins that have been forbidden, We will efface your faults and lead you to a place of honor. (Quran 4:31)

It is narrated on the authority of Abd al-Rahman ibn Abi Bakr that his father said: We were in the company of the Messenger of God, may peace be upon him, when he said: "Should I not inform you about the most grievous of the grave sins?" He repeated it three times, and then he said: "They are: associating anyone with God, disobedience to one's parents, false testimony or false utterance." The holy Prophet was reclining as he spoke, then he sat up, and he repeated it so many times that we wished that he should become silent. (Muslim, *Sahih* 39.158)

Ubaydallah ibn Abi Bakr said: I heard Malik ibn Anas saying that the Messenger of God, may peace be upon him, talked about the great sins, and he observed that they were associating anyone with God, killing a person, disobedience to parents. (Ibid. 39.160)

It is reported on the authority of Abu Hurayra that the Messenger of God, may peace be upon him, observed: "Avoid the seven harmful things." It was said by his hearers, "And what are they, Messenger of God?" He replied, "Associating anything with God, magic, killing someone whom God has declared inviolate without a just cause, consuming the property of an orphan, the consumption of (the fruits of) usury, turning back when the army advances, and slandering chaste women who are believers but unwary." (Ibid. 39.161)

God is indeed a stern judge, but He is also willing to requite charity with mercy and to grant forgiveness in exchange for sincere repentance.

From Abu Tha'laba ... with whom may God be pleased, (quoting) from the Apostle of God, upon whom be God's blessing and peace, that he said: "Truly God, may He be exalted, has laid down ordinances, so neglect them not; he has set limits, so do not exceed them; He has marked certain things as forbidden, so do not commit violations with regard to them; and He has said nothing about certain things, as an act of mercy toward you, not out of forgetfulness, so do not go inquiring into these." An excellent tradition which al-Daraqutni and others have related. (Nawawi, *The Forty Traditions*, no. 29) [JEFFERY 1962: 155]

From Abu Hurayra, with whom God be pleased, from the Prophet, upon whom be God's blessing and peace, who said: "Whoever dispels from a true believer some grief pertaining to this world, God will dispel from him some grief pertaining to the Day of Resurrection. Whoever makes things easy for someone who is in difficulties, God will make things easy both in this life and the next. Whoever shields a Muslim, God will shield him in this world and the next. God is ready to aid any servant so

long as the servant is ready to aid his brother. Whosoever walks a path to seek knowledge therein, God will make easy for him a path to Paradise. No community ever assembles in one of God's houses to recite God's Book and carefully study it among themselves but that tranquillity descends to them and mercy covers them, and the angels surround them, and God makes mention of them among those who are with Him. He whose work detains him will not be hastened by his noble ancestry." Muslim relates this tradition in these words. (Ibid., no. 36)
[JEFFERY 1962: 157–158]

From Anas, with whom may God be pleased, who said: I heard the Apostle of God, upon whom be God's blessing and peace, say: "God, may He be exalted, has said: 'O son of Adam, so long as you call upon Me and hope in Me, I will forgive you for all that comes from you, caring not, O son of Adam, should your sins reach the horizon of the sky. Even then, O son of Adam, if you asked My forgiveness, I should forgive you. O son of Adam, were you to come to Me with enough sins to well nigh fill the earth, and then meet Me without associating anything with Me, I should come to you with a like size of forgiveness.'" Al-Tirmidhi relates it, saying: "It is an excellent, sound tradition." (Ibid., no. 42) [JEFFERY 1962: 160]

Finally, there is an attempt by Baydawi (d. 1286 C.E.), in his commentary on the Quran, to systematize the various Prophetic traditions on the subject.

There is disagreement about the grave sins. The most natural (interpretation) is that a grave sin is one for which the Lawgiver prescribed a specific punishment or pronounced a threat of punishment. Others hold that what is meant is those (commandments) whose inviolability is clearly acknowledged. . . . Some say (further): the lack of gravity (of certain sins) is relative to the sins that are above them and the sins that are below them. The gravest sin is associating (other gods with God), and the lightest is that the soul harbors sinful thoughts. Between these two extremes lie the middle ones that are of the two kinds [that is, the graver and the lighter]. If two (such kinds) present themselves to someone and his soul is drawn toward them because he lacks self-control, and if he restrains his soul from the graver of the two, then what he does commit will be blotted out as a reward for his avoiding the graver sin. This is one of those matters which vary according to the people and situations involved; God, for example, reproved His Prophet for many thoughts which would not be reckoned a sin in another man and certainly would not lead to his punishment. (Baydawi, *Commentary*, on 4:31)

11. The Fundamental Principles of
Jewish Belief

All the rabbinic rulings and advisories on sin shared a conviction that the bond of Jewish cohesiveness was the Law and its observance. That was how the Covenant was understood at the beginning, and the understanding of the Law and its observance continued to be the chief preoccupations of those who were given or assumed responsibility for the community. Some, however, were concerned with belief or, to put it somewhat differently, with what constituted heresy. The earliest statement of a concern expressed in those terms appears to be a text of the Mishna that is addressed quite specifically to the Sadducees, since it is precisely their opinions that here exclude one from a share in the afterlife.

The following are those who do not have a portion in the world to come: the one who says there is no resurrection of the dead, the one who says that the Torah is not from heaven, and the Apiqoros [that is, the "Epicurean," someone who denies divine providence]. (M.Sanhedrin 10:1)

This statement, which responds to a specific and immediate need, does not, obviously, constitute a comprehensive statement of Jewish beliefs, no more than did the attempts at isolating the "weighty" commandments. There were such creed-like statements early in Christianity, as we shall see, prompted by profound differences within the community. But when Judaism too eventually began to produce such statements, the point of departure was not so much a need to define the community and so preserve its integrity as it was an attempt to understand the reality that lay behind what continued to be the pre-eminent good of Judaism, namely, the Law.

For some, that reality was the truths of philosophy—which were of course, the philosophers would quickly add, the truths of God Himself. Those truths could be pursued for their own sake, a course taken by very few of the Children of Abraham; or they could be converted to or reconciled with the Law, a more properly Jewish undertaking. This is what Philo attempted, and Saadya, and Maimonides. In the case of the latter thinker the effort produced not merely reflections or commentary but something that might be regarded as a Jewish creed, a systematic statement of the propositions whose acceptance is fundamental to Jewish belief. Unlike the Christian creeds, however, which, as we shall see, were formally promulgated and at times were administered by the authority of the bishop or of the Great Church as tests for orthodoxy at baptism or elsewhere, Maimonides' list of Thirteen Principles was personal and doctrinal. Despite his conviction that they might serve as such, his principles were never used as either a yardstick or a test for membership in the Jewish community.

The First Fundamental Principle is to believe in the existence of the Creator; that there is an Existent perfect in all the senses of the term "existence." He is the cause of all existence; in Him all else subsists and from Him all else derives. It cannot be that He does not exist. . . .

The Second Fundamental Principle is to believe that God is one, and the cause of all oneness. He is not like a member of a pair, nor a species with respect to a genus, nor a person divided into many discrete elements. Nor is He one in the sense that a simple body is. . . . Rather, God is one in that He is unique. . . .

The Third Fundamental Principle is to believe that He is incorporeal, that His unity is neither potentially nor actually physical; none of the attributes of matter can be predicated of Him, neither motion, nor rest, for example. . . . And whenever Scripture describes Him in corporeal terms, like walking, standing, sitting or speaking, and the like, it is speaking metaphorically. . . .

The Fourth Fundamental Principle is to believe that the One is absolutely eternal. . . .

The Fifth Fundamental Principle is that He alone is rightfully worshiped, exalted and obeyed. One must not pray to anything beneath Him in existence, neither to angels, stars, planets nor the elements, nor to anything composed of these. . . .

The Sixth Fundamental Principle is (the affirmation of) the principle of prophecy, that certain men are so favored and so perfected that they are capable of acquiring pure intellectual form. Their human intellect adheres to the Active Intellect, whither it is gloriously raised. These men are prophets; this is in what prophecy consists. . . .

The Seventh Fundamental Principle is the (fact of) prophecy of Moses our teacher. We must believe that he is the chief of all other prophets before and after him, all of whom were his inferiors. He was the chosen one of all men, superior to all, past and future, in gaining knowledge of God. . . . Moses' prophecy must be distinguished from that of all other prophets in four respects: (1) All other prophets were spoken to by God through intermediaries, only Moses immediately. (2) Prophecy came to all others in their sleep or in daytime when a trance fell on them. . . . This state is called "vision" or "insight," as in the expression "visions of God." But the Word came to Moses in broad daylight, when he stood by the two cherubs, as God had promised. . . . (3) Even if another prophet were to receive a vision of God through the mediation of an angel, his powers would fail; he would be overcome with dread and almost lose his mind, which never happened to Moses. (4) None of the other prophets could attain a vision (of God) whenever they pleased. All depended on God's will. . . . Moses our teacher, on the other hand, could say, whenever he wished, "Wait and I shall hear what the Lord commands you" (Num. 9:8). . . .

The Eighth Fundamental Principal is that the Torah came from God. We must believe that the whole Torah was given us, in its entirety, by God through Moses our teacher. When we call the Torah "God's word" we are speaking metaphorically, since we do not know exactly how it reached us, but only that it came to us through Moses, who acted like a secretary taking dictation. . . . All (its verses) came from God, and all are the Torah of God, perfect, pure, holy and true. . . . The authoritative commentary on the Torah is also the Word of God. The *sukkah* we build today, or the *lulab*, shofar, fringes, phylacteries, etc. we use, all are exact replicas of those which God showed to Moses and which Moses faithfully described for us. . . .

The Ninth Fundamental Principle is the authenticity of the Torah. that is, that this Torah was precisely transcribed from God and no one else. To the Torah, Oral and Written, nothing must be added, nor anything subtracted from it. . . .

The Tenth Fundamental Principle is that God knows all that men do and never removes His eyes from them. . . .

The Eleventh Fundamental Principle is that God rewards those who perform the Torah commandments and punishes those who transgress its admonitions. The greatest reward is the world to come; the worst punishment is extinction. . . .

The Twelfth Fundamental Principle has to do with the the age of the Messiah. We must believe that the Messiah will in fact come and not think of him as delayed. If he does delay, then wait for him without setting a time limit for his coming. One must not make scripturally based conjectures as to when he will come. . . . We must believe that the Messiah will have a higher position and greater honor than all the kings who ever lived, as all the prophets from Moses to Malachi have prophesied. . . . A corollary of this principle is the assertion that the (Messianic) king of Israel must come from the house of David and the seed of Solomon. Anyone who rejects this family contradicts God and the words of His prophets.

The Thirteenth Fundamental Principle is a belief in the resurrection of the dead. The resurrection of the dead is one of the cardinal principles established by Moses our teacher. A person who does not believe in this principle has no real religion, certainly not Judaism. Resurrection is, however, reserved for the righteous. . . . All men must die and their bodies decompose.

Maimonides concludes:

When a man believes in all these fundamental principles, and his faith is thus made clear, he is then one of that "Israel" whom we are to love, pity and treat, as God commanded, with love and fellowship. Even though a Jew might commit every possible sin, whether from lust or because he has been overcome by his lower nature, he will surely be punished for his sins but he will still possess a share in the world to come. He is one of the "sinners of Israel." If, on the other hand, a man surrenders any one of these fundamental principles, he has removed himself from the Jewish community. He is an atheist, a heretic, an unbeliever who "cuts among the plantings." We are commanded to hate him and destroy him. Of him it is said: "Shall I not hate those who hate You, O Lord?" (Ps. 139:21). (Maimonides, *Helek*: Sanhedrin 10)

In the end Maimonides' Thirteen Principles had as little effect on Judaism as the distinction between weighty and light commandments: there is no sign that any Jew was rooted out of the Jewish community or regarded as a non-Jew on the basis of a violation of what surely must be considered as fundamental beliefs, whether thirteen or more or less. On one level, the reverence for the Torah, every word and syllable of it, carried all before it; on another, a tribal community where birth and blood were the essential characteristics of membership found no commodious or convincing way of dissolving the bond of blood on the basis of either belief or behavior, no matter how unlikely or outlandish.

12. The Muslim Articles of Faith

It might be useful here to compare Maimonides' Thirteen Principles with the meditation of another, somewhat later Spanish thinker on the same subject. This one is a Muslim, however. In his Prolegomenon to History, *Ibn Khaldun (d. 1406) offers his list of the articles of the Muslim faith as an illustration for the science of dialectical theology, whose primary purpose was to expand and defend such Scripture-derived articles through rational arguments. He begins, however, with Muhammad's own, far more modest list of the fundamentals of Muslim belief.*

It should be known that the Lawgiver [that is, Muhammad] . . . specified particular matters he charged us to affirm with our hearts and believe in our souls, while at the same time acknowledging them with our tongues. They are the established articles of the Muslim faith. When

Muhammad was asked about his faith, he said, "(Faith is) the belief in God, His angels, His Scriptures, His Messengers, the Last Day, and the belief in predestination, whether it be good or bad" (Muslim, *Sahih* 1.29).

These (following) are articles of faith as established in the science of speculative theology. Let us describe them in summary fashion, so that the real character of speculative theology and the way it originated may become clear. We say:

It should be known that the Lawgiver (Muhammad) commanded us to believe in the Creator whom he considered the sole source of all actions. . . . He informed us that this belief means our salvation, if we have it when we die. However, he did not tell us about the real being of this worshiped Creator, because it is something too difficult for our perception and above our level. He made it our first obligation to believe that He in His essence cannot be compared with created beings. Otherwise, it would not be correct that He was their Creator since in this way there would be no distinction (between Him and them).

Then (He obliged us to believe that) He cannot be described in any way as deficient. Otherwise, he would be similar to created beings. Then, he (obliged us to believe in) His Oneness as divine being. Otherwise, the creation could not have taken place on account of mutual antagonism (between two principles). Then there are the following articles of faith:

God is knowing and powerful. In this way, all actions materialize as witnesses . . . to the perfection of the act of creation.

He has volition. Otherwise, no created thing would be differentiated from the other.

He determines the fate of each created thing. Otherwise volition would be something that comes into being.

He causes our resurrection after death. This constitutes the final touch to His concern with the first creation. If created things were destined to disappear completely, their creation would have been frivolous. They are destined for eternal existence after death.

Further articles of faith are: God sent His Messengers in order to save us from trouble on the Day of Resurrection, because that Day may mean either trouble or happiness, and we would not know that. He wanted to complete His kindness toward us by informing us about this situation and explaining to us the two possibilities and that Paradise means bliss and Hell means punishment. (Ibn Khaldun, *Muqaddima* 6.14) [IBN KHALDUN 1967: 3, 43–45]

Muslim children were taught the elements of Islam by theologians and learned them in the same catechetical fashion that was popular in Christianity. The following excerpt is from a modern example of the genre, though of a highly traditional type going back to the Middle Ages.

Q.: What is the number of the Messengers (of God)?

A.: They are many. No one knows their number save God, may He be exalted. Nevertheless it is incumbent to recognize twenty-five of them by name.

Q.: Who are these twenty-five?

A.: They are Adam, Idris, Noah, Hud, Salih, Lot, Abraham, Ishmael, Isaac, Jacob, Joseph, Shucayb, Aaron, Moses, David, Solomon, Job, Dhu al-Kifl, Jonah, Elijah, Elisha, Zachariah, John, Jesus and Muhammad. May God's blessing and peace be upon them all.

Q.: What is the Last Day, and what is meant by faith in it?

A.: The Last Day is the Day of Resurrection, and the meaning of faith in it is confident assertion of its reality as a coming event, and of all that it will comprise, such as the resurrection of created things, their giving an account (of their deeds), the weighing of their deeds, their passing over the Bridge, and the entering of some of them justly into the Fire [that is, Hell] and some of them by grace into the Garden [that is, Paradise].

Q.: What is the meaning of faith in predestination?

A.: It is that you should firmly believe and confidently affirm that God, may He be exalted, decreed both good and evil before the Creation, that all that has been and all that will be is by the predetermination of God, may He be exalted, by His decree and will. Among the Prophetic traditions (there is one) that faith in this drives away both anxiety and grief.

Q.: What is Islam?

A.: It is that you should bear witness that there is no god but the God and that you should bear witness that Muhammad is the Messenger of God; that you should perform the prayers, pay the alms tax, fast during Ramadan, and go on Pilgrimage to the House, if you are able to make the journey there.

Q.: What is the meaning of the two acts of bearing witness?

A.: The meaning of the first is that you should know, confidently affirm and acknowledge that there is no true object of worship in existence save God, may He be praised and exalted. The meaning of the second is that you should know, confidently affirm and acknowledge that

Muhammad is the Messenger of God, whom He sent to all mankind. His age at that time was forty years. He is the most excellent of created beings, be they in heaven or on earth. He, may God bless him and grant him peace, was born in Mecca, the ennobled city, which he did not leave till he had reached the age of fifty-three years, when God, may He be exalted, bade him emigrate from it to Medina, the illuminated. So he emigrated from it to Medina, where he died at the age of sixty-three.

Q.: What was his genealogy on his father's side?

A.: He was the son of Abdullah, son of Abd al-Muttalib, son of Hashim, son of Abd Manaf, son of Qusayy, son of Hakim, son of Murra, son of Kaʿb, son of Luʾay, son of Ghalib, son of Fihr, son of Malik, son of al-Nadr, son of Kinana, son of Khuzayma, son of Mudrika, son of Ilyas, son of Mudar, son of Nizar, son of Maʿadd, son of Adnan.

Q.: What was his genealogy on his mother's side?

A.: He was the son of Amina, daughter of Wahb, son of Abd al-Manaf, son of Zuhra, son of Hakim, the one mentioned above in the genealogy of his father.

Q.: How many children did he have?

A.: Seven, three males and four females. In order of their birth they were al-Qasim, then Zaynab, then Ruqayya, then Fatima, then Umm Kulthum, then Abdullah, then Ibrahim. All of them were by his wife Khadija, save Ibrahim, who was by his concubine, Mary the Copt.

Q.: How many wives did he have?

A.: They were twelve: Khadija, daughter of Khuwaylid; Sawda, daughter of Zamʿa; Aisha, daughter of Abu Bakr; Hafsa, daughter of Umar; Zaynab, daughter of Khuzayma; Hind, daughter of Abu Umayya; Zaynab, daughter of Jahsh; Juwayriya, daughter of al-Harith, Rayhana, daughter of Zayd; Ramla, daughter of Abu Sufyan; Safiya, daughter of Huyayy; and Maimuna, daughter of al-Harith. Some hold that Rayhana belongs to the concubines and not the wives.

Q.: How many concubines did he have?

A.: They are three: Mary the Copt, who was presented to him by the Muqawqas, ruler of Egypt; Nafisa, whom Zaynab daughter of Jahsh gave him; Zulaykha of the Qurayza. According to those who hold that Rayhana was a concubine, there would have been four. (Jurjani, *The Clear Answers*) [JEFFERY 1962: 460–462]

13. Jews and Gentiles in One Community

The Christian mission to the Gentiles violated in some profound way the Jewish sense of peoplehood. Over the centuries since Abraham, priests, prophets, and doctors of the Law had made every effort to keep the Jewish community separate from those heathen peoples about them, whether that separation was understood as not sharing in their cults, as in the earliest biblical narratives, or not marrying their women, as in Ezra and Nehemiah, or, now under the Pharisees, not failing to observe a degree of ritual purity that extended through all forms of social intercourse and ended at the table. The Christians, perhaps only some Christians at the outset, said that another consideration was more important than the Law and circumcision, namely belief in the Messiahship of Jesus, and that sharing in that belief constituted a new fellowship, a new community of Jew and Gentile, a new people.

Remember your former condition: you, Gentiles, as you were outwardly, you, the "uncircumcised" so called by those who are called "the circumcised"—but only with reference to an outward rite—you were at that time separate from Christ, strangers to the community of Israel, outside God's covenants and the promise that goes with them. Your world was a world without hope and without God. But now in union with Christ Jesus you who were once far off have been brought near through the shedding of Christ's blood. For he is himself our peace. Gentiles and Jews, he has made the two one, and in his own body of flesh and blood has broken down the enmity which stood like a dividing wall between them. For he annulled the Law with its rules and regulations, so as to create out of the two a single new humanity in himself, thereby making peace. This was his purpose, to reconcile the two in a single body to God through the cross, on which he killed the enmity.

So he came and proclaimed the good news: peace to you who were far off, and peace to those who were nearby; for through him we both have access to the Father in the one Spirit. Thus you are no longer aliens in a foreign land, but fellow citizens with God's people, members of God's household. You are built upon the foundation laid by the Apostles and the prophets, and Christ Jesus himself is the foundation stone. In him the whole building is bonded together and grows into a holy temple in the Lord. In him you too are being built with all the rest into a spiritual dwelling for God. (Paul, *To the Ephesians* 2:12–22)

Paul uses another figure.

Christ is like a single body with its many limbs and organs, which, as many as they are, make up one body. For indeed we are all brought into one body by baptism, in the one Spirit, whether we are Jews or Greeks, whether slaves or free men, and that one Spirit has poured out all of us to drink.

A body is not a single organ but many. Suppose the foot should say, "Because I am not a hand, I do not belong to the body," it does belong to the body nonetheless. Suppose the ear should say, "Because I am not an eye, I do not belong to the body," it still belongs to the body. If the body were all eye, how could it hear? If the body were all ear, how could it smell? But in fact God appointed each limb and organ to its own place in the body, as He chose. If the whole were one single organ, there would not be a body at all; in fact, however, there are many different organs and one body. . . . If one organ suffers, they all suffer together. If one organ flourishes, they all rejoice together. (Paul, *To the Corinthians* 1:12–26)

14. Citizens of Heaven in the World of Men

Sometime about 124 C.E. a pagan named Diognetus asked a Christian for some information on his sect. The anonymous author replied with this characterization, a description filled with implicit contrasts with the Jewish communities of that day.

The difference between Christians and the rest of mankind is not a matter of nationality or language or customs. Christians do not live apart in separate cities of their own, speak any special dialect or practice any eccentric way of life. The doctrine they profess is not the invention of busy human minds and brains, nor are they, like some, adherents of this or that school of human thought. They pass their lives in whatever township, Greek or foreign, each man's lot has determined; and conform to ordinary legal usage in their clothing, diet and other habits. Nevertheless the organization of their community does exhibit some features that are remarkable, and even surprising. For instance, though they are residents at home in their own country, their behavior there is more like transients; they take their full part as citizens, but they also submit to everything and anything as if they were aliens. For them, any foreign country is a motherland, and any motherland is a foreign country.

Like other men, they marry and beget children, though they do not expose their infants. Any Christian is free to share his neighbor's table, but never his marriage bed. Though destiny has placed them here in the flesh, they do not live after the flesh; their days are passed on the earth, but their citizenship is above in the heavens. They obey the prescribed laws, but in their own private lives they transcend the laws. They show love to all men, and all men persecute them. They are misunderstood and condemned, and yet by suffering death they are quickened to life. They are poor, yet making many rich; lacking all things, yet having all things in abundance. . . .

To put it briefly, the relations of Christians to the world is that of a soul to the body. As the soul is diffused through every part of the body, so are Christians through all the cities of the world. The soul too inhabits the body, while at the same time forming no part of it; and Christians inhabit the world, but they are not part of the world. . . . The flesh hates the soul and wars against her without any provocation because she is an obstacle to its own self-indulgence; and the world similarly hates the Christians without provocation because they are opposed to its pleasures. . . . The soul, shut up inside the body, nevertheless holds the body together; and though they are confined within the world as in a dungeon, it is the Christians who hold the world together. The soul, which is immortal, must dwell in a mortal tabernacle; and the Christians, as they sojourn for a while in the midst of corruptibility here, look for incorruptibility in the heavens. Finally, just as to be stinted of food and drink makes for the soul's improvement, so when Christians are every day subjected to ill treatment, they increase the more in numbers. Such is the high post of duty in which God has placed them, and it is their moral duty not to shrink from it. (*Letter to Diognetus* 5–6) [STANIFORTH 1968: 176–178]

15. Paul Reflects on the Role of the Jews in History

The overwhelming number of Christians in Paul's day would still have identified themselves in some manner as Jews. Dissociation from their heavily-laden Jewish past, which for some must have seemed like a repudiation, could not have been easy. Was the past worth nothing then? It is possible to discern the question behind Paul's answer.

I am speaking the truth as a Christian, and my own conscience, enlightened by the Holy Spirit, assures me it is no lie. In my heart there is great grief and unceasing sorrow. For I could even pray to be an outcast from Christ myself for the sake of my brothers, my natural kinfolk. They are Israelites; they were made God's sons; theirs is the splendor of the divine presence, theirs the covenants, the Law, the Temple worship, and the promises. Theirs are the patriarchs, and from them, in natural descent, sprang the Messiah. May God, supreme over all, be blessed forever! Amen.

It is impossible that the word of God should have proved false. For not all descendants of Israel are truly Israel, nor, because they are Abraham's sons, are they all his true children, but in the words of Scripture, "Through the line of Isaac your descendants shall be traced." That is to say, it is not those born in the course of nature who are children of God; it is the children born through Abraham's promise who are reckoned as Abraham's descendants. For the promise runs: "At the time fixed I will come, and Sarah shall have a son. . . ."

Brothers, my deepest desire and my prayer to God is for their [that is, the Jews'] salvation. To their zeal for God I can testify; but it is an uninformed zeal. For they ignore God's ways of righteousness, and try to set up their own, and therefore they have not submitted themselves to God's righteousness. For Christ ends the Law and brings righteousness for everyone who has faith. . . .

Scripture says, "Everyone who has faith in him will be saved from shame" (Isa. 52:7)—everyone: there is no distinction between Jew and Greek, because the same Lord is the Lord of all, and is rich enough for the need of all who invoke him. For as it says again, "everyone who invokes the name of the Lord will be saved" (Joel 2:23). How could they invoke one in whom they had no faith? And how could they have faith in one they had never heard of? . . .

What follows? What Israel sought, Israel has not achieved, but the selected few have achieved it. The rest were made blind to the truth, exactly as it stands written: "God brought upon them a numbness of spirit; he gave them blind eyes and deaf ears, and so it is still" (Isa. 29:10). . . .

I now ask, did their failure mean complete downfall? Far from it! Because they offended, salvation has come to the Gentiles, to stir Israel to emulation. But if their offense means the enrichment of the world, and if their falling-off means the enrichment of the Gentiles, how much more their coming to full strength! (Paul, *To the Romans* 10:1–12)

16. The Olive Tree That Is Israel

If this is Paul's consolation to Israel, it is not a source of boasting for the Gentiles who in increasing numbers constituted the new Israel.

But I have something to say to you Gentiles. I am a missionary to you Gentiles, and as such as I give all honor to that ministry when I try to stir emulation in the men of my own race, and to save some of them. For if their rejection has meant the reconciliation of the world, what will their acceptance mean? Nothing less than life from the dead! If the first portion of the dough is consecrated, so is the whole lump. If the root is consecrated, so are the branches. But if some of the branches are lopped off, and you, a wild olive, have been grafted in among them, and have come to share the same root and sap as the olive, do not make yourselves superior to the branches. If you do, remember that it is not you who sustain the root; the root sustains you.

You will say, "Branches were lopped off so that I might be grafted in." Very well: they were lopped off for lack of faith, and by faith you hold their place. Put away your pride and be on your guard; for if God did not spare the native branches, no more will he spare you. Observe the kindness and severity of God—severity to those who fall away, divine goodness to you, if only you remain within its scope. Otherwise you too will be cut off, whereas they, if they do not continue faithless, will be grafted in; for it is in God's power to graft them in again. For if you were cut off from your wild olive and against all nature grafted into the cultivated olive, how much more readily will they, the natural olive branches, be grafted into their native stock! (Paul, *To the Romans* 11:13–24)

17. The Old Priesthood and the New

But you are a chosen race, a royal priesthood, a dedicated nation and a people claimed by God for his own, to proclaim the triumph of him who called you out of the darkness into his own marvelous light. You are now the people of God, who were once not His people; outside His mercy once, you have now received His mercy. (Peter, *Letter* 1.2:9–10)

So Peter, Jesus' chosen Apostle, addressed the newborn community of Christians, on whom he easily bestows the proudest titles of what was already being thought of as "the old Israel." Those same Christians searched the Jewish Bible and found there ample evidence to demonstrate not merely that Jesus was the Messiah but also that his Messianic kingdom was the new Israel, wherein he served as both king and priest. And nowhere perhaps is that stated more clearly than in the passage in 2 Samuel where a "man of God" comes to the priest Eli and speaks as follows.

This is the word of the Lord: You know that I revealed Myself to your forefather (Aaron) when he and his family were in Egypt in slavery in the house of the Pharaoh. You know that I chose him from all the tribes of Israel to be My priest, to mount the steps of My altar, to burn sacrifices and to carry the ephod before Me; and that I assigned all the food offerings of the Israelites to your family. Why then do you show disrespect for My sacrifices and the offerings which I have ordained? What makes you resent them? Why do you honor your sons more than Me by letting them batten on the choicest offerings of My people Israel?

The Lord's word was: "I promise that your house and your father's house shall serve me for all time"; but now His word is: "I will have no such thing; I will honor those who honor Me, and those who despise Me shall suffer contempt. The time is coming when I shall lop off every limb of your own and of your father's family, so that no man in your house shall come to old age. If I allow any to survive to serve my altar, his eyes will grow dim and his appetite fail, his issue will be weaklings and die off. The fate of your two sons shall be a sign to you: Hophni and Phineas shall both die on the same day. I will appoint for Myself a priest who will be faithful and who will do what I have in My mind and My heart. I will establish his house to serve in perpetual succession before my anointed one. Any of your family that still live will come and bow down before him to beg a fee, a piece of silver or a loaf, and will ask for a turn of priestly duty to earn a morsel of bread." (2 Samuel 2:27–35)

Augustine dwells at length on this passage in his City of God.

We cannot say that this prophecy, in which the change of the ancient priesthood is foretold with so great plainness, was fulfilled in Samuel [as the sequel in the biblical account would seem to suggest]; for although Samuel was not of another tribe than that which had been appointed by God to serve at the altar, yet he was not of the sons of Aaron, whose offspring were set apart that the priests might be taken out of it. And thus by that transaction also the same change which should come to pass through Christ Jesus is shadowed forth, and the prophecy itself in deed, not in word, properly belonged to the Old Testament, but figuratively to the New, signifying by the fact exactly what was said by the word to Eli the priest through the prophet. For there were afterwards priests of Aaron's race, such as Zadok and Abiathar during David's reign, and others in succession, before the time came when those things which were predicted so long before about the changing of the priesthood behoved to be fulfilled by Christ. But who that now views these things with a believing eye does not see that they are fulfilled? Since indeed no Tabernacle, no Temple, no altar, no sacrifice, and therefore no priest either, has remained to the Jews, to whom it was commanded in the Law of God that he should be ordained of the seed of Aaron. This too is mentioned by the prophet (in the same text), when he says: "The Lord's word was: 'I promise that your house and your father's house shall serve me for all time'; but now His word is: 'I will have no such thing; I will honor those who honor Me, and those who despise Me shall suffer contempt.'" ... It was of his [that is, Aaron's] lineage, therefore, he has said in this passage that it should come to pass that they would no longer be priests; which already we see fulfilled. If faith is watchful, the things are before us; they are discerned, they are grasped, and forced on the eyes of the unwilling, so that they are seen: "The time is coming," he says, "when I shall lop off every limb of your own and of your father's family, so that no man in your house shall come to old age. If I allow any to survive to serve my altar, his eyes will grow dim and his appetite fail, his issue will be weaklings and die off." Behold, the days which were foretold have already come. There is no priest in the succession of Aaron; and whoever is a man of his lineage, when he sees the sacrifices of the Christians prevailing over the whole world, but that great honor taken away from himself, his eyes and his soul melt away consumed with grief.

... The things which follow are said of Christ Jesus, the True Priest of the New Testament: "I will appoint for Myself a priest who will be faithful and who will do what I have in My mind and My heart. I will establish his house...." The same is the eternal Jerusalem above. "To serve in perpetual succession before my anointed one" [Augustine reads "My Christ"]. (Augustine, *City of God* 17.5) [AUGUSTINE 1948: 2:377]

18. "The Remnant Shall Be Saved"

The final verse of the passage in Samuel turns Augustine to a reflection on the fate of the Jews in the new dispensation.

But what is added, "Any of your family that still live will come and bow down before him," is not said properly of the house of this Eli, but of that of Aaron, the men of which remained even to the coming of Jesus Christ, of which race there are not wanting men even to this present. ... Therefore if it is of these, the predestined remnant, about whom another prophet has said, "The remnant shall be saved" (Isa. 10:21), wherefore the Apostle (Paul) also says, "Even so then at this time also the remnant according to the election of grace is saved"; since, then, it is easily to be understood to be of such a remnant that the present verse speaks, "any of your family that still live," assuredly he believes in Christ. Just as in the time of the Apostle (Paul) very many of that nation (that is, the Jews) believed; nor are there now wanting those (Jews), although very few, who yet believe, and in them is fulfilled what this man of God has here immediately added, "will come and bow down before him to beg a fee," to bow down before whom, if not that High Priest who is also God? For in that priesthood in the succession of Aaron men did not come to the Temple or the altar of God for the purpose of worshiping the priest. (Augustine, *City of God* 17.5) [AUGUSTINE 1948: 2:378–379]

19. The Separation of the Christians from the Jews

As appears from both the Acts of the Apostles and the letters of Paul, Christianity spread through the eastern Mediterranean chiefly through the network of synagogues where Jewish preachers of the Jewish Messiah Jesus had easy access at first. Converts were quickly made among the Gentile populations of those same centers, however, and tension grew between the communities of new Gentile converts and those of the Jewish followers of Jesus. A deeper, though less visible, conflict spread between the Christians and the unconvinced Jews.

One leader who had to deal with the problem in Anatolia, where there were large communities of both Jews and Jewish Christians, was Ignatius, the bishop of Antioch. In his letters he discouraged Jewish practices among Christians who were, or recently had been, themselves Jewish. He died a martyr for his belief in Jesus sometime about 107 C.E.

Never permit yourselves to be misled by the teachings and the worn-out tales of another people [that is, the Jews]. There is nothing useful that can be gotten from them. If we are still following Jewish practices, it is an admission on our part that we have failed to receive the gift of grace. Even the lives of the divinely inspired (biblical) prophets were redolent of Jesus Christ, and the reason they suffered persecution was because they were inspired by his grace so that they might convince future believers that the one sole God has revealed Himself in His Son Jesus Christ, His own Word which came forth from silence, and who in all he was and and all he did gladdened the heart of the One who sent him.

We have seen how those who once followed the ancient customs have attained new hope. They have given up keeping the Sabbath and in its place they now order their lives on the Lord's Day, the day when life first dawned on us, thanks to him and his death. That death, though some deny it, is the very mystery which made believers and enabled us to endure tribulation and so prove ourselves pupils of Jesus Christ, our teacher. How, then, is it possible that we grant him no place in our lives, when even the ancient prophets were themselves his disciples in spirit and looked forward to him as their teacher? That was indeed the very reason why he, whom they were rightly awaiting, came to visit them and raised them from the dead. (Ignatius, *To the Magnesians* 8–9)

The already cited Letter to Diognetus, *written about 124 C.E., shows no inclination to move naturally and persuasively, as Augustine did, from the biblical prophets to a belief in Christ. The author here was almost certainly a Gentile Christian. He was writing to a pagan, perhaps in reply to a request that he explain how Christians differed from Jews.*

Next I expect what you most want to hear about is our Christian unwillingness to accept the faith of the Jews. Admittedly, since they are unwilling to have any truck with the sort of (pagan) religion I have been describing, the Jews may fairly claim to be devotees of the one true God and to acknowledge Him as their sovereign. Nevertheless, insofar as they do him service with rites similar to those of the heathen, they are in error. For if the Greeks must stand convinced of absurdity by the offerings they make to senseless and dumb idols, the Jews ought to realize that it shows equal absurdity, and no true piety, to conceive of God Himself as in want of such things. The maker of heaven and earth and all therein, the supplier of our every need, could never Himself be in any need of the very things which are actually His own gifts to the self-styled givers. Indeed, so long as they believe themselves to be fulfilling their sacrificial duty to Him by means of blood and fat and burnt offerings, and fancy that they are doing Him honor by such rites, I cannot see that there is anything to choose between them and the men who lavish similar attentions on deaf and dumb idols. One party, it seems, makes its offerings to creatures who cannot partake of the gifts, and the other to One who needs none of them.

As for their scrupulousness about meats, and their superstitions about the Sabbath, and their much vaunted circumcision, and their pretentious festivals and new moon observances, all of them too nonsensical to be worth discussing, I hardly think you need instruction from me. For how can it be anything but impious to accept some of the things which God has created for our use and assert their creation to have been commendable, but to reject others as being needless and good-for-nothing? And what can there be but profanity in the slanderous charge that God objects to a good deed being done on a sabbath day? And surely, when they boast that a body mutilation is evidence of their inclusion among the elect, as though it gave them some special claim to God's love, what does this deserve but to be laughed out of court. As for the minute way in which they scrutinize the moon and stars for the purpose of ritually commemorating months and days, and chop up the divinely appointed cycle of the seasons to suit their own fancies, pronouncing some to be times for feasting and others for mourning, could anyone pretend that this indicates true reverence and not simply a deranged intellect?

I imagine that you have heard enough now to see how right the Christians are in repudiating the folly and delusion common to these two cults, as well as the fussy practices of which the Jews are so proud. At the same time, however, you must never expect to learn the inward mystery of their own religion from merely human lips. (*Letter to Diognetus* 3–4) [STANIFORTH 1968: 175–176]

The argument of the Letter to Diognetus *is not a little disingenuous, concealing as it does the affiliation of the Christians to the Jews and the fact that the Jews' "fussy practices" derived from books that the Christians too regarded as divinely inspired Scripture. The problem of affiliation could, however, be dealt with in other, more complex ways than those that suited the innocent Diognetus. Some Christians of his day, for example, were ready to adopt a far more radical procedure for the separation of Christianity from Judaism, to reject not merely the Jewish Scriptures but the very God who had revealed them and had created this world of ours. Though there were others who took the same position, it is most closely associated with Marcion, a native of Pontus in Anatolia who was a member of the Christian community in Rome sometime about 160 C.E.*

Marcion of Pontus succeeded him [Cerdon] and developed his school, advancing the most daring blasphemy against Him who is proclaimed as God by the Law and the Prophets, declaring him to be the author of evils, a lover of war, inconstant in judgment and contrary to Himself. But Jesus being derived from that Father who is above the God who made the world, and coming into Judea in the times of Pontius Pilate the governor, who was procurator of Tiberius Caesar, was manifested in the form of a man to those who were in Judea, abolishing the Prophets and the Law and all the works of the God who made the world, whom he also calls "Ruler of the World."

Besides this, he mutilates the Gospel which is according to Luke, removes all that is written respecting the generation of the Lord and sets aside a great deal of the teaching of the Lord's discourses in which the

Lord is recorded as most clearly confessing that the Maker of this universe is his Father. . . . In like manner too he dismembered the letters of Paul, removing all that is said by the Apostle respecting that God who made the world, to the effect that He is the Father of our Lord Jesus Christ, and also those passages from the prophetic writings which the Apostle quotes in order to teach us that they announced beforehand the coming of the Lord. (Ireneus, *Against the Heresies* 1.27.1–2)

Marcion's special and principal work is the separation of the Law and the Gospel, and his disciples will not be able to deny that their supreme authority has its basis in this (separation), an authority by which they initiate and confirm themselves in this heresy. This is Marcion's "Antitheses" or contradictory propositions, which aim at committing the Gospel to be at variance with the Law in order that from the diversity of the two documents which contain them, they may argue for a diversity of gods as well. (Tertullian, *Against Marcion* 1.19)

20. The Jewish Christians

That there were Jewish believers in the Messiahship of Jesus who nonetheless wished, despite Paul, to continue their observance of the Mosaic laws and commandments is already obvious from the Acts of the Apostles. The leadership of the original community in Jerusalem continued for a while to be closely associated with the family of Jesus (see Chapter 6 below), and the bishops there, as Eusebius calculated them, were all "Hebrews," that is, practicing Jews, down to the second destruction of the city in 135 C.E., "for at that time their whole church consisted of Hebrew believers who had continued from Apostolic times down to the later siege in which the Jews, after revolting a second time from the Romans, were overwhelmed in a full-scale war." Thereafter the history of the Jewish Christians was not a happy one, as the Gentile Christians sought to separate themselves to an ever greater degree from their Jewish origins. In 150 the converted philosopher Justin was still willing to maintain communion with them; by the time in the fourth century that Eusebius wrote his Church History, *those Jewish Christians found, or had placed, themselves in a position that the rest of the Great Church regarded as purely and simply heretical.*

Trypho [a Jewish rabbi] inquired again: If a man, aware that this is so, after he has also plainly known that this (Jesus) is the Christ, and believed and obeyed him, wishes to keep these precepts (of the Mosaic Law) as well, shall he be saved?

In my opinion, Trypho, I answered, such a man will be saved, unless he strenuously does his utmost to persuade others—I mean those Gentiles who have been circumcised by Christ from their error—to keep the same Mosaic commandments that he does, saying that they will not be saved unless they keep them. For this is what you yourself did at the beginning of our discussion, when you declared that I will not be saved unless I keep them.

He answered: Why then do you say: "It is my opinion that such a man will be saved?" Are there any who maintain that such a one will not be saved?

There are, Trypho, I replied, and there are even some who are bold enough not even to join such in social converse and meals, though I do not agree with them. But if they [the Jewish Christians], out of the weakness of their mind, wish to observe such of the sayings of Moses as are now possible—which in our view were ordained because of the hardness of people's hearts—while they still place their hopes in this Christ of ours, and also keep those commandments commending the practice of righteousness and of piety—which are everlasting and in accordance with nature—and who choose to live with Christians and believers without, as I said before, persuading them either to undergo circumcision like themselves, or to keep the Sabbath, or to observe other things of the same kind—I declare that we must fully receive such and have communion with them in all respects, as being of one family and as brothers. But if, Trypho, I said, they who are of your race say they believe in this Christ of ours, and in every way compel those who are of Gentile birth and believe in this Christ to live in accordance with the Law appointed by Moses, or choose not to have communion with them that have such a life in common—these also in like manner I do not accept.

Now they that follow their advice [that is, the advice of the Jewish Christians] and live under the Law, as well as keep their profession in the Christ of God, will, I suppose, be saved. But they that once professed and recognized that this is the Christ, and then for some reason or other passed over into the life under the Law, denying that this is the Christ, and do not repent before death, cannot, I declare, in any wise be saved. (Justin, *Dialogue with Trypho* 47.1–4)

What happened to these Jewish followers of Jesus appears obscurely, and not entirely sympathetically, through the lines of Eusebius' Church History.

There were others whom the evil demon, unable to shake their devotion to the Christ of God, caught in a different trap and made their own. Ebionites they were appropriately named by the first Christians, in view of the poor and mean opinion they held about Christ. They regarded him as plain and ordinary, a man esteemed as righteous through growth of character and nothing more, the child of a normal union between a man and Mary; and they hold they must observe every detail of the (Mosaic) Law—by faith in Christ alone, and a life built upon that faith, (they maintain) they would never win salvation.

A second group went by the same name, but escaped the outrageous absurdity of the first. They did not deny that the Lord was born of a virgin and the Holy Spirit, but nevertheless shared their refusal to acknowledge his pre-existence as God the Word and Wisdom. Thus the impious doctrine of the others was their undoing as well, especially as they placed equal emphasis on the outward observance of the (Mosaic) Law. They held that the letters of the Apostle (Paul) ought to be rejected altogether, calling him a renegade from the Law; and using only the "Gospel of the Hebrews," they treated the rest with scant respect. Like the others they observed the Sabbath and the whole Jewish system; yet on the Lord's day they celebrated rites similar to our own in memory of the Savior's resurrection. (Eusebius, *Church History* 3.27)

21. The Banishment of the Christians from the Synagogue

If the presence of Jewish Christians became increasingly less comfortable within the Church, it was a source of even less comfort in the synagogues, which had been the original locus for the spread of the Christian faith. Sometime during the presidency of Gamaliel II (80–110 C.E.) a remedy of sorts was contrived in the form of a new "benediction," the twelfth, added to those that constituted the normal synagogue prayer of the Tefilla. This was the euphemistically named "blessing of the Minim," the latter some type of apostate group and possibly the Jewish Christians themselves, though these are mentioned separately by name.

For apostates let there be no hope, and the dominion of arrogance do Thou speedily root out in our days; and let the Nazarenes and the Minim perish as in a moment, let them be blotted out of the book of the living and let them not be written with the righteous. Blessed art Thou, O Lord, who humbles the arrogant.

This new "prayer," like the parallel rejection of the Christians' Scriptures, effectively prevented the Jewish followers of Jesus from participating in a central Jewish liturgy in which they were constrained to curse themselves, a fact well known to Jerome in the fourth century. He remarks that "the Jews day and night blaspheme the Savior, and, as I have often remarked, three times daily heap curses on the

Christians under the name of 'Nazarenes.' " The Christian could, of course, decline to repeat it, but his silence would equally surely betray him, as appears in the Talmud's account of the original framing of this formula.

Our Rabbis taught: Simeon the cotton merchant arranged the eighteen benedictions in order before Rabban Gamaliel [II] in Jabneh. Said Rabban Gamaliel to the Sages: Can any among you frame a benediction relating to the Minim? Samuel the Lesser arose and composed it. The following year he forgot it and he tried for two or three hours to recall it, and they did not remove him [from his post as a reader]. Why did they not remove him seeing that Rab Judah had said in the name of Rab: If a reader made a mistake in any of the other benedictions, they did not remove him, but if in the benediction of the Minim, he is removed, because we suspect him of being a Min. (BT.Berakoth 28b–29a)

22. Baptism in the Early Church

Read out of the Jewish congregations, the Christians began to constitute their own. Unlike the Jews, for whom someone born of a Jewish mother was under the Law necessarily Jewish, no one was born a Christian. Every member of the Christian community was in effect a convert, and from the beginning each was treated as the Jews treated their proselytes: they were baptized, just as Jesus had been baptized by John (Matt. 3:13–17) and just as he had commanded his disciples after his resurrection, apparently with a direct reference to the mission to the Gentiles.

The eleven disciples made their way to Galilee, to the mountain where Jesus had told them to meet him. When they saw him, they fell prostrate before him, though some were doubtful. Jesus then came up and spoke to them. He said: "Full authority in heaven and on earth has been committed to me. Go forth therefore and make all nations my disciples: baptize men everywhere in the name of the Father and the Son and the Holy Spirit, and teach them to observe all that I have commanded. And be assured that I am with you always, to the end of time." (Matthew 28:16–20)

From the Acts of the Apostles onward, the practice is attested to as a necessary preliminary to membership in the Church. Here is how the ritual is described in summary in the anonymous Teaching of the Apostles *from early in the second century.*

The way of baptizing is as follows. After completing all the preliminaries, immerse (the candidate) in running water (saying), "In the Name of the Father and of the Son and of the Holy Spirit." If no running water is available, immerse in ordinary water. This should be cold if possible, but otherwise warm water (will do). If neither is practical, then sprinkle water three times on his head (saying), "In the Name of the Father and of the Son and of the Holy Spirit." Both the baptizer and baptized should fast before the baptism, as well as any others who can do so; but the candidate himself should be instructed to observe a fast for a day or two beforehand. (*Teaching of the Apostles 7*)

By the beginning of the third century, as the numbers of would-be Christians increased, more attention was paid to those preliminaries. The following is from the Apostolic Tradition *attributed to Hippolytus (ca. 220 C.E.).*

Those who present themselves for the first time to hear the word should first be brought to the teachers at the house (of prayer) before all the people (of the congregation) arrive. They should be questioned as to why they have come forward to the faith. And their sponsors should witness for them, whether they are able to hear (the word of God). Their life and manner of living should be investigated, and whether they are slave or free.

There follow the rules for different types of candidates for baptism.

If a man is a pimp who supports whores, he should either cease or be rejected (as a candidate for baptism). If a man is a sculptor or a painter, he should be cautioned not to make idols; if he will not leave off this practice, he should be rejected. If a man teaches children worldly [that is, pagan] knowledge, it would be well if he stopped, but if he has no other livelihood, he may be forgiven. If a man is an actor or someone who produces shows in the theater . . . a charioteer likewise, or one who takes part in the games or who attends the games . . . a gladiator or a trainer of gladiators, an animal hunter or someone involved with wild animal shows . . . a priest of idols or a keeper of idols, either he must cease or else be rejected. . . . If a man has a concubine who is a slave, let her too attend the instruction, but only on condition that she has already raised her children, and if she is living with him alone. If not, she should be turned away. If a man has a (free woman) concubine, he should end (the relationship) and contract a legal marriage; if he refuses, he should be rejected.

The catechumen should be instructed for three years; but if a man is earnest and perseveres well in the matter, he may be received (earlier), because it is not the time that is being weighed but his conduct. . . . And when they are chosen who are set apart to receive baptism, then their lives should be examined, whether they are living piously as catechumens, whether they have "honored the widows," visited the sick, fulfilled every good work. If those who sponsored them can bear witness that they have done thus, then let them hear the Gospel. . . .

Those who are to be baptized should be instructed to wash and cleanse themselves on the fifth day of the week; and if any woman is menstruating, her baptism should be postponed till another day. Those who are to receive baptism should fast on Friday and Saturday. And on the Saturday the bishop should assemble all those who are to be baptized in one place, and bid them all to bow and genuflect. And laying his hand on them he shall exorcize every evil spirit to flee from them and never to return to them henceforward. And when he has finished exorcizing, let him breathe on their faces and seal their foreheads and ears and noses and then raise them up.

At the hour when the cock crows they shall first pray over the water. When they come to the water, let the water be pure and flowing. And they shall put off their clothes. And they shall baptize the little children first. And if they can answer for themselves, let them answer; but if they cannot, let their parents answer or someone else from their family. And next they shall baptize the grown men; and last the women, who shall have loosed their hair and laid aside their gold ornaments. Let no one go down to the water having any alien object with them. (Hippolytus, *The Apostolic Tradition*)

At almost the same time, Tertullian (ca. 160–222 C.E.) took up the question of who may perform this ritual of baptism.

It remains also to remind you of the correct observance of the giving and the receiving of baptism. The chief priest, who is the bishop, has the right of giving it; in the second place, the presbyters and deacons, yet not without the bishop's authority, on account of the honor of the Church, for when this has been preserved, peace is preserved. Besides these, even laymen have the right; for what is equally received can be equally given. If there are no bishops, priests, or deacons, other disciples are called. The word of the Lord ought not to be hidden away by anyone. In like manner also, baptism, which is equally God's property, can be administered by all; but how much more is the rule of reverence and modesty incumbent on laymen, since these things belong to their superiors, lest they assume to themselves the specific functions of the episcopate. Emulation of the episcopal office is the mother of schism. (Tertullian, *On Baptism* 17)

23. Faith, Sin, and Repentance

Unlike the Jews, who never lost their strong tribal affiliation and whom both their neighbors and Roman law regarded as a "nation," the Christians constituted nothing else but a community of believers. If a hasty reading of Paul suggested that only faith or disbelief in Christ qualified or disqualified one for continued membership in that society, a more Jewish emphasis on observance appears precisely where we might expect it: in the New Testament Letter of James, that Torah–observant "brother of the Lord" in Jerusalem, who in the course of his advice casts a sidelong and not entirely disinterested glance at Paul's favorite example of justification through faith, Abraham.

My brothers, what use is it for a man to say he has faith when he has nothing to show for it? Can that faith save him? Suppose a brother or a sister is in rags with not enough food for a day and one of you says, "Good luck to you, keep yourselves warm, and have plenty to eat," but does nothing to supply their bodily needs, what is the good of that? So with faith; if it does not lead to action, it is a lifeless thing.

But someone may object: "Here is one who claims to have faith and another who points to his deeds." To which I reply: Prove to me that this faith you speak of is real though not accompanied by deeds, and by my deeds I will prove to you my faith. . . . Can you not see, you quibbler, that faith divorced from deeds is barren? Was it not by his action, in offering his son Isaac upon the altar, that our father Abraham was justified? Surely you can see that faith was at work in his actions, and that by these actions the integrity of his faith was fully proved. Here was the fulfillment of the words of Scripture: "Abraham put his faith in God and it was counted to him as righteousness"; and elsewhere he is called "God's friend." You see then that a man is justified by deeds and not by faith alone. (James, *Letter* 2:14–24)

If good works save, then assuredly sin kills, and for eternity. Such at least is the opinion of the author of the "Letter to the Hebrews."

When men have once been enlightened, when they have had a taste of the heavenly gift and a share in the Holy Spirit, when they have experienced the goodness of God's word and the spiritual energies of the age to come, and after all this have fallen away, it is impossible to bring them once again to repentance; for with their own hands they are crucifying the Son of God and making mock of his death. (Hebrews 6:4–6)

And if one looks at the severity of the penalties in the Mosaic Law, the same conclusion imposes itself.

If we wilfully persist in sin after receiving the knowledge of the truth, no sacrifice for sins remains: only a terrifying expectation of judgment and fierce fire which will consume God's enemies. If a man disregards the Law of Moses, he is put to death without pity on the testimony of two or three witnesses. Think how much more severe a penalty that man will deserve who has trampled under foot the Son of God, profaned the blood of the Covenant by which he was consecrated and affronted God's gracious spirit! For we know who it is who has said "Justice is mine: I will repay"; and again, "The Lord will judge His people." It is a terrible thing to fall into the hands of the Living God. (Hebrews 10: 26–31)

This severe view did not long survive. The Gospels, after all, were filled with encouragement to repentence and forgiveness, and not merely by Jesus. Forgiveness was also available to his followers, as when he said:

I tell you this: no sin, no slander is beyond forgiveness for men; but whoever slanders the Holy Spirit can never be forgiven; he is guilty of eternal sin. (Mark 3:29)

Or here, addressing Peter, or perhaps all the Apostles:

I will give you the keys of the kingdom of Heaven; what you forbid on earth shall be forbidden in heaven, and what you allow on earth will be allowed in heaven. (Matthew 16:19)

Both these passages are difficult, but the Church recognized that sins committed after Christian baptism could be forgiven. Sin was a fact of life, as Tertullion concedes:

We ourselves do not forget the distinction between sins, which was the starting point of our discussion. John has sanctioned it [in the letter cited earlier] and there are in fact some sins of daily committal to which we are all liable; for who is free from the accident of being angry unjustly and after sunset; or even of using bodily violence; or easily speaking evil; or rashly swearing; or forfeiting his promised word; or lying from bashfulness or necessity? In business, in official duties, in trade, in food, in sight, in hearing, by how great temptations are we assailed. But if there were no pardon for such simple sins as these, salvation would be unattainable by any. Of these then there will be pardon through the successful intercessor with the Father, Christ. (Tertullian, *On Shame* 19)

These are the Torah's "inadvertent sins," for which "the priest shall make expiation before the Lord for the said individual, and he shall be forgiven" (Num. 15:27–28). But like the Torah, Tertullian recognizes that there are other, graver sins, perhaps beyond the possibility of forgiveness or atonement.

. . . Wholly different from these, graver and more destructive, such as are incapable of pardon—murder, idolatry, fraud, apostasy, blasphemy, and, of course, adultery and fornication, and whatever other violation of the temple there may be. For these Christ will no more be the successful intercessor; these will not at all be committed by anyone who has been born of God, for he will cease to be the son of God if he commits them. (Tertullian, *On Shame* 19)

Tertullian did not always feel that even those grave sins were unforgiveable. In an earlier essay, "On Penance," he wrestled with the question more hopefully. Conversion and baptism, he knew, wiped the slate clean for the new Christian. But what of the possibility of a second "conversion"—the Greek word for conversion is the same as that used by the Christians for repentance—after baptism? He is not entirely easy with the possibility.

I shrink from mentioning a second, or rather a final, hope, for to treat of any further opportunity of repentance seems almost to suggest another chance to sin. Still . . . though the great gate of forgiveness has been barred and bolted at baptism, second repentance waits in the vestibule to open a postern door once more to those who knock. But once more only, for it is the second time; never again if this once fails. Surely this once is enough; it is a mercy wholly undeserved. . . . The postern is narrow and hard to pass . . . but the alternative is hell.

24. Confession and the Punishment of Sin

By Tertullian's day, then, the Church recognized, if somewhat reluctantly at times, that as far as concerned the "grave sins"—the lesser infractions seem to have required little formality for forgiveness—there existed the possibility of earning a second, postbaptismal forgiveness. This was accomplished through "penance," a word that did service for the confession of one's sins, penalties the Church attached to their forgiveness, and that forgiveness itself, the sinner's reconciliation with the Church. Tertullian continues on the subject of this second chance offered to the sinner.

The second and only remaining penitence is so critical a matter that the testing of it is correspondingly laborious; it is not enough for it to be witnessed by mere admission of guilt; it has also to be carried out in action. This action is more commonly expressed and spoken of under its Greek name, *exomologesis*, by which we confess our sin to the Lord; not indeed as if He were ignorant, but inasmuch as the process of satisfaction is set in motion by confession, and by confession penitence is produced, and by penitence God is appeased.

Thus *exomologesis* is a discipline consisting in prostration and humiliation, imposing on the offender such a demeanor as to attract mercy. With regard also to the very dress and food of the penitent, this discipline enjoins him to go about in sackcloth and ashes, to cover his body in the squalor of mourning, to cast down his spirit with grief, to exchange his self-indulgence for harsh treatment of himself; to have no acquaintance with any food or drink but the plainest, and this not for his stomach's sake but his soul's; in general, to nourish prayers with fasting, to groan, to weep and moan day and night to the Lord his God, to prostrate himself before the presbyter, and to kneel before God's dear ones; to invoke all the brethren as sponsor of his prayers for mercy. The purpose of *exomologesis* is to enhance penitence, to honor God by showing dread of the peril of His anger; by itself pronouncing judgment on the sinner to act as a surrogate for God's indignation; and by temporal affliction, I would not say to frustrate, but to cancel eternal punishment. (Tertullian, *On Penance* 9)

As Tertullian's text reveals, this ecclesiastical punishment was both severe and public. Jerome has left us a rhetorically enhanced picture of just such a case in Rome. Letter 77 was written in 399 C.E. on the occasion of the death of Fabiola, a rich Roman woman under his spiritual care. She had divorced her first husband, "a man of such unspeakable vices that even a whore or a common slave would not have put up with him," Jerome says. Her remarriage was a sin for a Christian woman or man, since, as Jerome points out with pride, "for us what is unlawful for women is equally unlawful for men, and as both sexes serve God they are bound by the same conditions." Fabiola, it appears, was not aware of the prohibtion against remarriage in such cases.

At the death of her second husband she came to herself, and at a time when widows have shaken off the yoke of slavery, live more carelessly and recklessly, frequent the baths, flit here and there across the public places and show off their harlot faces, she put on sackcloth and made a public confession of her mistake. On the eve of Easter, as all of Rome looked on, she took her place with the other penitents in the basilica where once Lateranus perished by Caesar's sword. There in the presence of the bishop and priests and a weeping populace, she exposed her disheveled hair, her wan face, her soiled hands, her dust-stained neck. . . .

This I will say: . . . Fabiola was not ashamed of the Lord on earth and He will not be ashamed of her in heaven. She exposed her wound to all, and Rome tearfully beheld the scar upon her livid body. She uncovered her limbs, bared her head and closed her mouth. Like Moses' sister Mary, she sat alone outside the camp until the priest who cast her out should call her back. She came down from her couch of luxury, she took up the millstone and ground meal, with unshod feet she passed through rivers of tears. She sat upon coals of fire and these were her helpers. She struck the face by which she had won her second husband's love, she abhorred all jewelry, she could not so much as look upon linen, she shrank from all adornment. She grieved as if she had been guilty of adultery, and she expended money on many medicines to cure one wound. (Jerome, *Letter* 77:4–5)

The rite of public penance normally began on Ash Wednesday, when the penitents presented themselves to the bishop at the cathedral door. After the penitents had been led into the church and after the bishop and the clergy had prostrated themselves and tearfully chanted the seven penitential psalms, the bishop sprinkled them with holy water, cast ashes over them, covered their heads with sackcloth, and made formal announcement of their excommunication and the penance required for their readmission to the Church. After the prescribed time, many years in some cases, reconciliation with the Church and readmission to the sacraments took place on Holy Thursday. There were in addition continuing disabilities. Readmission could occur only once in a lifetime, and those who submitted to it could not afterwards marry or, if they already were married, they could not henceforward engage in sexual relations with their spouses. Nor could they enter the army or take up the clerical life. The infamy of the condition and the severity of the penalties made confession and penance a heroic act indeed for most Christians, and there appear to have been few willing to submit to the ordeal. Many preferred to postpone the act of reconciliation to their deathbed. Others, we must think, preferred to throw themselves on the mercy of God.

The reasons are complex, but attitudes and practices began to change in the Western churches in the sixth century. It was no longer thought that repentance and reconciliation were a once-in-a-liftetime possibility, and the bishop was no longer regarded as the Church's sole instrument in effecting that reconciliation. Christians began confessing to their ordinary parish priests; these latter in turn increasingly imposed penances that were, like the confessions that preceded them and the reconciliation or absolution that followed, a private matter. By the beginning of the thirteenth century, frequent private confession was not merely possible, it was required of European Christians, as prescribed by the twenty-first canon of the Fourth Lateran Council.

Every Christian of either sex, after attaining years of discretion, shall faithfully confess all his sins to his own priest at least once a year, and shall endeavor according to his ability to fulfill the penance enjoined him, reverently receive the sacrament of the Eucharist at least at Easter, unless perchance, on the advice of his own priest, for some reasonable cause, he determines to abstain for a time from receiving it. Otherwise he shall both be withheld from entrance into the church while he lives and be deprived of Christian burial when he dies. Wherefore this salutary enactment shall be frequently published in the churches lest anyone assume a veil of excuse in the blindness of ignorance.

The entire proceeding is to be conducted with the most rigorously maintained confidentiality.

Further, he [that is, the confessor] is to give earnest heed that he does not in any way betray the sinner by word or sign or in any other way; but if he needs more prudent advice he shall seek this cautiously, without any divulging of the person, since we decree that whoever shall presume to reveal a sin made known to him in the adjudication of penance is not only to be deposed from the priestly office but also to be thrust into a strict monastery to do perpetual penance. (Acts of the Fourth Lateran Council [1215]) [MCNEILL & GAMER 1938: 413–414]

The desired spiritual, psychological, and even physical circumstances of private confession are succinctly set out in the statutes of a Paris synod of sometime about 1197 C.E.

Priests shall apply the greatest care and caution with regard to confession, namely, that they diligently search out sins, the habitual ones severally, the occasional ones only indirectly or circumstantially, still in such a way that the matter of the confession is supplied from the sins.

Priests shall select for themselves a place easy of access in the church so that they can be seen by all generally; and no one shall hear confessions in a secret place or outside the church, except in great need or sickness.

The priest shall have a humble countenance in confession, and he shall not look at the face of the confessant, especially of a woman, on account of the obligation of honor; and he shall patiently hear what she says in a spirit of mildness and to the best of his ability persuade her by various methods to make an integral confession, for otherwise he shall say it is of no value to her.

Having heard the confession, the confessor shall always ask the confessant if he is willing to refrain from every mortal sin; otherwise he shall not absolve him nor impose a penance upon him. . . .

In imposing slight penances priests shall take heed to themselves, for the nature of the penance ought to be according to the nature of the guilt and the capacity of the confessant.

In confession confessors shall take heed to themselves not to inquire the names of persons with whom the confessants have sinned, but only the circumstances and nature (of the sins), and if the confessant tells the names, the confessor shall rebuke him and shall hold this as secret as the sin of the confessant.

He shall not dare to reveal anybody's confession to any person, from anger or hatred or even from fear of death, by sign or word, generally or specifically. . . . And if he reveals it he ought to be degraded without mercy. (Synodical Constitutions of Odo of Paris [ca. 1197])

[McNEILL & GAMER 1938: 412]

6. Priests, Princes, and Overseers

1. The Governance of Israel

The Hebrews were governed as we should expect them to be, by a tribal shaykh, *and from Abraham onward that elder received directions and occasional visitations from the God who had Himself announced that He was their Lord. But after the sojourn in Egypt, their Lord intervened more frequently in the affairs of His people and often, as in the wilderness of Sinai, in a quite direct fashion. In Sinai, Moses was both a spokesman for the deity and a charismatic tribal leader, but even under those quite extraordinary conditions there are traces of other, more obscure organs of government, many of them doubtless cast back upon that generation of pioneers by later Israelite society. In Numbers, for example, Moses speaks to the Lord:*

"I cannot carry all this people by myself, for it is too much for me. If You would deal thus with me, kill me rather, I beg you, and let me see no more of my wretchedness." Then the Lord said to Moses, "Gather Me seventy of Israel's elders of whom you have experience as elders and officers of the people, and bring them to the Tent of Meeting and let them take their place with you. I will come down and speak with you there, and I will draw upon the spirit that is on you and put it upon them; they shall share the burden of the people with you, and you shall not bear it alone. . . ."

Moses went out and reported the words of the Lord to the people. He gathered seventy of the people's elders and stationed them around the Tent. Then the Lord came down in a cloud and spoke to him; He drew upon the spirit that was on him and put it upon the seventy elders. And when the spirit rested upon them, they spoke in ecstasy, but did not continue. (Numbers 11:14–25)

2. The Establishment of the Priesthood

Whether or not Moses had a prototype Sanhedrin at his side, the early Israelites almost certainly had another institution, again on the direct authority and command of the Lord. This was the body of priests, a group of men—a caste in effect—whose function, mode of life, and even dress set apart them apart from the other Israelites. The first of them was Moses' own brother Aaron. The Lord is once again speaking to Moses.

You shall bring forward your brother Aaron, with his sons, from among the Israelites, to serve me as priests: Aaron, Nadab and Abihu, Eleazar and Ithamar, the sons of Aaron. Make sacral vestments for your brother Aaron, for dignity and adornment. Next you shall instruct all who are skillful, whom I have endowed with the gift of skill, to make Aaron's vestments, for consecrating him to serve Me as priest. These are the vestments they are to make: a breastplate, an ephod, a robe, a fringed tunic, a headdress and a sash. They shall make these sacral vestments for your brother Aaron and his sons, for priestly service to Me; they, therefore, shall receive the gold, the blue, purple, and crimson yarns, and the fine linen. (Exodus 28:1–5)

You shall make the fringed tunic of fine linen. You shall make the headdress of fine linen. You shall make the sash of embroidered work. And for Aaron's sons also you shall make tunics, and make sashes for them, and make turbans for them, for dignity and adornment. Put these on your brother Aaron and on his sons as well; anoint them, and ordain them and consecrate them to serve me as priests.

You shall also make for them linen breeches to cover their nakedness; they shall extend from the hips to the thighs. They shall be worn by Aaron and his sons when they enter the Tent of Meeting or when they approach the altar to officiate in the sanctuary, so that they do not incur punishment and die. It shall be a law for all time for him and for his offspring to come. (Exodus 28:39–43)

If Aaron and his descendants were thus set apart from the other Israelites, it was for a purpose: they were to be, in effect, living paradigms of holiness.

The Lord spoke to Aaron saying: Drink no wine or other intoxicant, you or your sons with you, when you enter the Tent of Meeting, that you may not die—it is a law for all time throughout the ages. For you must distinguish between the sacred and the profane, and between the unclean and the clean; and you must teach the Israelites all the laws which the Lord has imparted to them through Moses.

The priests should perform none of the ordinary tribal functions; rather, they would be supported out of the sacrificial offerings of the people.

Moses said to Aaron and to his remaining sons Eleazar and Ithamar, "Take the meal offering from what is left over from the Lord's offerings by fire and eat it unleavened beside the altar because it is most holy. You shall eat it in the sacred precinct, inasmuch as it is your due, and that of your children, from the Lord's offerings by fire; for so I have been commanded. But the breast of the wave offering and the thigh of the heave offering you, and your sons and daughters with you, may eat in any clean place, for they have been assigned as a due to you and your children from the Israelites' sacrifices of well-being." (Leviticus 10:8–14)

Though there is clear evidence that the entire tribe of Levi was once designated as priests (see, for example, Deut. 18:1ff.), the finished version of the Israelite tradition reproduced in Exodus made a sharp and important distinction. Moses and Aaron were both of that tribe, but other members of Levi under a certain Korath rose up against the two leaders and attempted to seize control of the priestly functions (Num. 16–17). God intervened to punish the rebels, and the sequel defined a new role for the rest of the tribe of Levi.

The Lord said to Aaron: You with your sons and the ancestral house under your charge shall bear any guilt connected with the sanctuary; you and your sons alone shall bear any guilt connected with your priesthood. You shall associate with yourself your kinsmen of the tribe of Levi, your ancestral tribe, to be attached to you and to minister to you and to your sons under your charge before the Tent of the Pact. They shall discharge their duties to you and to the Tent as a whole, but they must not have any contact with the furnishings of the Shrine or with the altar, lest both they and you die. They shall be attached to you and discharge the duties of the Tent of Meeting, all the services of the Tent; but no outsider shall intrude upon you as you discharge the duties connected with the Shrine and the altar, that wrath may not again strike the Israelites.

I hereby take your fellow Levites from among the Israelites; they are assigned to you in dedication to the Lord, to do the work of the Tent of Meeting, while you and your sons are careful to perform your priestly duties in everything pertaining to the altar and to what is behind the curtain. I make your priesthood a service of dedication; any outsider who encroaches shall be put to death. (Numbers 18:1–7)

3. The Support of the Priestly Class

*On this occasion, too, the support of the priestly class out of the offerings for sacrifice
is further defined.*

The Lord spoke further to Aaron: I hereby give you charge of My
gifts, all the sacred donations of the Israelites; I grant them to you and
your sons as a perquisite, a due for all time. This shall be yours from the
most holy sacrifices, the offerings by fire: every such offering that they
render to Me as most holy sacrifices, namely, every meal offering, every
sin offering, and penalty offering of theirs, shall belong to you and your
sons. You shall partake of them as most sacred donations: only males may
eat them; you shall treat them as consecrated.

This too shall be yours: the heave offerings of their gifts, all the wave
offerings of the Israelites, I give to you, to your sons, and to the daughters
that are with you, as a due for all time; everyone of your household who
is clean may eat it.

All the best of the new oil, wine and grain—the choice parts that
they present to the Lord, I give to you. The first fruits of everything in
their land, that they bring to the Lord, shall be yours; everyone of your
household who is clean may eat them. Everything in Israel that has been
proscribed in Israel shall be yours. . . .

And the Lord said to Aaron: You shall, however, have no territorial
share among them or own any portion in their midst; I am your portion
and your share among the Israelites.

And to the Levites I hereby give all the tithes in Israel as their share
in return for the services that they perform, the services of the Tent of
Meeting. Henceforth, Israelites shall not trespass on the Tent of Meeting,
and thus incur guilt and die: only Levites shall perform the services of the
Tent of Meeting; others would incur guilt. It is a law for all time throughout the ages. But they shall have no territorial share among the Israelites;
for it is the tithes set aside by the Israelites as a gift to the Lord that I give
to the Levites as their share. (Numbers 18:8–24)

4. The Purity of the Priesthood

*Since the Jewish priesthood was in effect a tribal caste whose membership was
determined by descent alone, special attention was given to maintaining its ethical
and ethnic purity, particularly with regard to marriage.*

The Lord said to Moses: Speak to the priests, the sons of Aaron, and say to them: None shall defile himself for any (dead) person among his kin, except for the relatives that are closest to him. . . . They shall not shave smooth any part of their heads, or cut the side growth of their beards, or make gashes in their flesh. They shall be holy to their God and not profane the name of their God; for they offer the Lord's offerings by fire, the food of their God, and so must be holy.

A priest shall not marry a woman degraded by harlotry, nor shall they marry one divorced from her husband. For they are holy to their God and you must treat them as holy, since they offer the food of your God. They shall be holy to you, for I the Lord who sanctify you am holy. When the daughter of a priest degrades herself through harlotry, it is her father whom she degrades; she shall be put to the fire.

The priest who is exalted among this fellows [that is, the High Priest], on whose head the anointing oil has been poured and who has been ordained to wear the vestments, shall not bare his head nor rend his vestments. He shall not go where there is any dead body; he shall not defile himself even for his father or mother. He shall not go outside the sanctuary and profane the sanctuary of his God, for upon him is the distinction of the anointing oil of his God, Mine, the Lord's. He may marry only a woman who is a virgin. A widow or a divorced woman or one who is degraded by harlotry—such he may not marry. Only a virgin of his own kin may he take to wife—that he may not profane his offspring among his kin, for I the Lord have sanctified him.

Speak to Aaron in these words: No man among your offspring throughout the ages who has a defect shall be qualified to offer the food of his God: no man who is blind, or lame, or has a limb too short or too long; no man who has a broken leg or a broken arm; or who is a hunchback, or a dwarf, or who has a growth in his eye, or has a boil scar or scurvy, or crushed testes. . . . He may eat the food of his God, of both the most holy as well as of the holy; but he may not enter behind the curtains or come near the altar, for he has a defect. He shall not profane those places sacred to me, for I the Lord have sanctified them. . . .

No man of Aaron's offspring who has an eruption or a discharge shall eat of the sacred donations until he is clean. If one touches anything made unclean by a corpse, or if a man has an emission of semen, or if a man touches any swarming thing by which he is made unclean or any human being by which he is made unclean—whatever his uncleanness— the person who touches such shall be unclean until evening and shall not eat of the sacred donations unless he has washed his body in water. (Leviticus 21:1–22:7)

How seriously the question of priestly descent was taken, to the point even of keeping careful genealogical records, is manifest in what occurred upon the return to Judea after the Exile.

The following were those who returned from Tel-melah, Tel-harsha, Kerub, Addan, and Immer, but could not establish their father's family nor whether by descent they belonged to Israel: the family of Delaiah, the family of Tobiah, and the family of Nekoda, six hundred and fifty-two. Also of the priests: the family of Hobaiah, the family of Hakkoz, and the family of Barzillai who had married a daughter of Barzillai of Gilead and went by his name. These searched for their names among those enrolled in the genealogies, but they could not be found: they were disqualified for the priesthood as unclean, and the governor forbade them to partake of the most sacred food until there should be a priest able to consult the Urim and the Thummim.

The prospects for those thus barred were not good: the practice of consulting the sacred lots called Urim and Thummim (see 1 Sam. 14:38–42) had long since been discontinued, with little expectation that it would soon be restored. At a later stage, and perhaps earlier as well, a claimant to the priesthood, given the proper genealogical certification, had to present himself to the High Council (Sanhedrin) to be certified on physical grounds.

The Chamber of Hewn Stone—there used the Great Sanhedrin of Israel to sit and judge the priesthood; and if in any priest a blemish was found, he clothed himself in black and veiled himself in black and deported and went his way; and he in whom no blemish was found clothed himself in white and veiled himself in white and went in and ministered with his brethren the priests. And they kept it as a festival day that no blemish had been found in the seed of Aaron the priest. And thus they used to say: "Blessed be God, blessed be He, in that no blemish has been found in the seed of Aaron! And blessed be He that chose Aaron and his sons to stand and serve before the Lord in the Holy of Holies!" (M.Middoth 5:4)

5. The Priestly Courses

There were more priests in Israel than were needed for the service at any one time, so the whole number of families who constituted the offspring of Aaron were divided into "courses" (mishmarot), twenty-four of them in all. Their members served in turn, probably from one Sabbath to the next, in the Temple. This is how the first Book of Chronicles explains the arrangement at the time of King David.

The divisions of the Aaronites were: the sons of Aaron: Nadab and Abihu, Eleazar and Ithamar. Nadab and Abihu died in the lifetime of their father, and they had no children, so Eleazar and Ithamar served as priests. David: Zadok of the sons of Eleazar and Ahimelech of the sons of Ithamar divided them into offices by their tasks. The sons of Eleazar turned out to be more numerous by male heads than the sons of Ithamar, so that they divided the sons of Eleazar into sixteen chiefs of clans, and the sons of Ithamar into eight clans. They divided them by lot, both on an equal footing, since they were all Sanctuary officers and officers of God—the sons of Eleazar and the sons of Ithamar. Shemaiah the son of Nathanel, the scribe, who was of the Levites, registered them under the eye of the king, the officers, and Zadok the priest, and Ahimelech son of Abiathar, and the chiefs of clans of the priests and Levites—one clan more taken for Eleazar for each taken of Ithamar.

The list of the heads of the twenty-four courses then follows in order. The text concludes:

According to this allocation of offices by tasks, they were to enter the House of the Lord as was laid down for them by Aaron their father, as the Lord God of Israel had commanded him. (1 Chronicles 24:1–19)

Whatever its beginnings, this arrangement continued until the destruction of the Temple. We catch a glimpse of its operation in the opening chapter of the Gospel of Luke.

In the days of Herod king of Judea, there was a priest named Zechariah, *of the division of the priesthood called after Abiah* [that is, the eighth of the twenty-four courses listed in 1 Chron. 24:7–18]. His wife was also of priestly descent; her name was Elizabeth. Both of them were upright and devout, blamelessly observing all the commandments and ordinances of the Lord. But they had no children, for Elizabeth was barren, and both were well on in years.

Once, *when it was the turn of his division and he was there to take part in the divine service, it fell to his lot, by priestly custom, to enter the sanctuary of the Lord and offer the incense*; and the whole congregation was at prayer outside. It was the hour of the incense offering.

An angel appears to Zechariah and announces to him the future birth of his son, John, the later Baptist.

Meanwhile the people were waiting for Zechariah, surprised that he was waiting so long inside. When he did come he could not speak to them, and they realized that he had a vision in the sanctuary. He stood there making signs to them, and remained dumb.

When his period of duty was completed, Zechariah returned home. After this his wife Elizabeth conceived. (Luke 1:5–24)

6. A King in Israel

We have already seen in Chapter 1 above the Israelite monarchy in its glory under David and Solomon and in less honorable circumstances under some of their successors. But the people had been warned of this institution, which the Lord had granted only reluctantly. We return to the days of Samuel, before there was a king in Israel.

When Samuel grew old, he appointed his sons judges over Israel. The name of the firstborn was Joel, and his second son's name was Abijah; they sat as judges in Beer-sheba. But his sons did not follow in his ways; they were bent on gain, they accepted bribes, and they subverted justice. All the elders of Israel assembled and came to Samuel at Ramah and they said to him, "You have grown old, and your sons do not follow in your ways. Therefore appoint a king for us, to govern us like all other nations." Samuel was displeased that they said "Give us a king to govern us." Samuel prayed to the Lord, and the Lord replied to Samuel, "Heed the demand of the people in everything they say to you. For it is not you they have rejected; it is Me they have rejected as their king. Like everything else they have done since I brought them out of Egypt to this day— forsaking Me and worshiping other gods—so they are doing to you. Heed their demand, but warn them solemnly, and tell them about the practices of any king who will rule over them."

Samuel reported all the words of the Lord to the people who were asking for a king. He said, "This will be the practice of the king who will rule you. He will take your sons and appoint them his charioteers and horsemen, and they will serve as outrunners for his chariots. He will appoint them as his chiefs of thousands and fifties; or they will have to plow his fields, reap his harvest, and make his weapons and the equipment for his chariots. He will take your daughters as perfumers, cooks and bakers. He will seize your choice fields, vineyards and olive groves, and give them to his courtiers. He will take your male and female slaves, your choice young men and your asses, and put them to work for him He will take a tenth part of your flocks and you shall become his slaves. The day will come when you will cry out because of the king whom you yourselves have chosen; and the Lord will not answer you on that day."

But the people would not listen to Samuel's warning. "No," they said. "We must have a king over us, that we may be like all the other nations. Let our king rule over us and go out at our head and fight our battles." When Samuel heard all that the people said, he reported it to the Lord. And the Lord said to Samuel, "Heed their demands and appoint a king for them." (1 Samuel 8:1–22)

7. The Courts and the Judiciary

The king was not the only ruler of Israel. There were the priests, the wardens of God's worship, and other less well-defined groups like "the Elders of Israel, all the heads of tribes who were chiefs of families in Israel" (1 Kings 8:1), who appear from time to time in the royal chronicles, though they do not seem to have had any real power. There was also a judicial machinery, as appears to lie behind these enactments in Deuteronomy.

If a case is too baffling for you to decide, be it a controversy over homicide, civil law or assault—matters of dispute in your courts—you shall promptly repair to the place which the Lord your God will have chosen, and appear before the levitical priests, or the magistrate in charge at the time, and present your problem. When they have announced to you the verdict in the case, you shall carry out the verdict which is announced to you from that place which the Lord chose, observing scrupulously all their instructions to you. You shall act in accordance to the instructions given you and the ruling handed down to you; you must not deviate from the verdict they announce to you either to the right or to the left. Should a man act presumptuously and disregard the priest charged with serving the Lord your God or the magistrate, that man shall die. Thus you will sweep out evil from Israel: all the people will hear and be afraid and not act presumptuously again. (Deuteronomy 17:8–13)

8. The Role of the Priests

The passage in Deuteronomy is strong on exhortation but less generous in explaining means and procedures, perhaps deliberately so. Solomon had put down the foundations of empire, but many years were to pass before the machinery of organization and rule grew to maturity in Jerusalem and the rest of the kingdom. Most of the process is lost to our sight, since it was not of great concern to the anonymous transmitters who stand behind the books called Kings and Chronicles. There are only glimpses. For example, King Jehoshaphat (871–849 B.C.E.) set up a judicial machinery with a competence in matters of both religious and royal statute law, as well as with what appears to be a police function on the part of the Levites.

He appointed judges in the land, in all the fortified towns of Judah, in each and every town. He charged the judges: "Consider what you are doing, for you judge not on behalf of man, but on behalf of the Lord, and He is with you when you pass judgment. Now let the dread of the Lord be upon you; act with care, for there is no injustice or favoritism or bribe-taking with the Lord our God." In Jerusalem Jehoshaphat also appointed some Levites and priests and some heads of the clans of Israelites for rendering judgments in matters of the Lord, and for disputes. Then they returned to Jerusalem. He charged them, "This is how you shall act, in fear of the Lord with fidelity, and with whole heart. When a dispute comes before you from your brothers living in their towns, whether about homicide or about ritual, you must instruct them so that they do not incur guilt before the Lord. . . . See, Amariah the chief priest is over you in all cases concerning the Lord, and Zebadiah son of Ishmael is the commander of the house of Judah in all cases concerning the king; the levitical officers are at your disposal; act with resolve and the Lord be with the good." (2 Chronicles 19:5–11)

9. Judea after the Exile

With exile came the end of the monarchy; but once restored to Judea by Cyrus, the Jews were confronted again with some degree of self-rule, now no longer under the politically unacceptable institution of kingship but in some other form that would serve the community's own needs and represent them vis-à-vis their new sovereigns, Persian, Greek, and Roman. That form was likely an aristocratic council—what the Greeks later called a boule *and the Romans a* senate. *There is no direct evidence from the Persian period (ca. 538–332 B.C.E.). Writing at the very beginning of the Greeks' settlement into the land, Hecateus describes the Jewish form of self-government, an arrangement that he casts back, perhaps with the assistance of a helpful priestly informant, into an idealized Mosaic past.*

Moses chose the men of the greatest refinement and the greatest ability to lead the entire nation, and he appointed them priests; and he ordered that they should have to do with the Temple and the honors and sacrifices offered to their God. These same men he appointed to be judges in all major disputes, and he entrusted to them the guardianship of the laws and customs. For this reason the Jews never have a king, and authority over the people is regularly vested in whichever priest is regarded as superior to his colleagues in wisdom and virtue. This man is called the High Priest, and it is believed that he acts as a messenger to them of God's commandments. It is he, we are told, who in their assemblies and other gatherings announces what has been decreed, and the Jews are so docile in such matters that they straightway fall to the ground and do reverence to the High Priest when he declares the commandments to them. (Hecateus, *Aegyptiaca*)

That is not the picture we are given about a century later, when the Jews' new Greek sovereign, Antiochus III, enters Jerusalem.

King Antiochus to Ptolemy, greetings. Since the Jews, beginning from the time that we entered their territory, have testified to their zeal in our regard, and since, from our arrival in their city they have received us in a magnificent manner and came out to meet us with their senate [*gerousia*, literally "Council of Elders"], have contributed generously to the upkeep of our soldiers and our elephants, and have assisted us in capturing the Egyptian garrison in the citadel, we have judged it proper that we too should respond to those good offices by restoring their city destroyed by the misfortunes of war and repopulating it by bringing back all those people dispersed from it. (Josephus, *Antiquities* 12.3.3)

10. A Hero High Priest of the Second Temple

We are given a vivid, if somewhat idealized, portrait of a High Priest presiding over the Temple ritual in Ecclesiasticus, or the Wisdom of Jesus ben Sira. Simon son of Onias, after whom the portrait was drawn, was High Priest in Jerusalem ca. 225– 200 B.C.E. and was probably personally known to Ben Sira.

It was the High Priest Simon son of Onias in whose lifetime the House [that is, the Second Temple, built by Zerubbabel after the return from the Babylonian exile] was repaired, in whose days the Temple was fortified. How glorious he was, surrounded by the people, when he came from behind the Temple curtain! He was like the morning star appearing through the clouds or the moon at the full; like the sun shining on the Temple of the Most High or the light of the rainbow on the gleaming clouds. . . . When he put on his gorgeous vestments, robed himself in perfect splendor, and went up to the holy altar, he added luster to the court of the sanctuary. When the priests were handing him the portions of the sacrifice, as he stood by the altar hearth with his brothers round him like a garland, he was like a young cedar of Lebanon in the midst of a circle of palms.

All the sons of Aaron in their magnificence stood with the Lord's offering in their hands before the whole congregation of Israel. To complete the ceremonies at the altar and adorn the offering of the Most High, the Almighty, he held out his hand for the libation cup and poured out the blood of the grape, poured its fragrance at the foot of the altar to the Most High, the King of all. Then the sons of Aaron shouted and blew their trumpets of beaten silver; they sounded a mighty fanfare as a reminder before the Lord. Instantly the people as one man fell on their faces to worship the Lord their God, the Almighty, the Most High. Then the choir broke into praise, in the full sweet strains of resounding song, while the people of the Most High were making their petitions to the merciful Lord, until the liturgy of the Lord was finished and the ritual complete. Then Simon came down and raised his hands over the whole congregation of Israel, to pronounce the Lord's blessing, proud to take His name on his lips: and a second time they bowed in worship to receive the blessing from the Most High. (Ecclesiasticus 50:1–21)

11. Hasmonean Sovereignty

In 200 B.C.E., then, there was both a High Priest and a Council of Elders ruling over the Jews, though under the sovereignty of a Greek king in Antioch and whatever delegates and lieutenants he chose to send out to his province of Judea. That arrangement was not a happy one, as we have seen in Chapter 2 above, and Jewish discontent with the Seleucid lords and their policy of Hellenization led first to insurrection and then to a kind of autonomy.

The Maccabees won the effective independence of a Jewish state in Judea through the force of arms; what remained was to negotiate that effective control into recognized and juridical sovereignty, something that could be bestowed only by the Seleucid sovereigns with whom they had been at war. But in the mid-second century B.C.E. the Seleucids were even more deeply engaged in a war among themselves, and in the context of this rivalry the new Judean state appeared not so much as a rebellious vassal but as an ally to be wooed and won—first by the pretender Alexander Balas and then by his rival Demetrius—on terms acceptable to the new Maccabean leader, Jonathan.

King Alexander (Balas) to his brother Jonathan, greeting:

We have heard about you, what a valiant man you are and how fit to be our friend. Now therefore we do appoint you this day to be High Priest of your nation with the title of "King's Friend," to support our cause and to keep friendship with us.

Thus, with the blessings of Alexander Balas, Jonathan assumed the vestments of the High Priest and ruler of the Jewish state on the Feast of Tabernacles in 152 B.C.E.

When this news reached Demetrius, he was mortified. "How did we come to let Alexander forestall us," he asked, "in gaining the friendship and support of the Jews? I too will send them cordial messages and offer honors and gifts to keep them on my side." So he sent a message to the Jews to this effect:

"King Demetrius to the Jewish nation, greeting. . . . Jerusalem and all its environs, with its tithes and tolls, shall be sacred and tax-free. I also surrender authority over the citadel in Jerusalem and grant the High Priest the right to garrison it with men of his own choice. . . .

"Ptolemais and the lands belonging to it I make over to the Temple in Jerusalem, to meet the expenses proper to it. I give 15,000 silver shekels annually, charged on my own royal accounts, to be drawn from such places as may prove convenient. And the arrears of the subsidy, insofar as it has not been paid by the revenue officials, as it formerly was, shall henceforward be paid in for the needs of the Temple. In addition, the 5,000 silver shekels that used to be taken from the annual income of the Temple are also released, because they belong to the ministering priests. . . . The cost of rebuilding and repair of the Temple shall be borne by the royal revenue; also the repair of the walls of Jerusalem and its surrounding fortifications, as well as of the fortresses of Judea, shall be at the expense of the royal revenue." (1 Maccabees 10:18–45)

There was, however, even greater power within the grasp of the house of Hasmon, and it was bestowed on one of them, Simon, not by a foreign sovereign in Antioch but by the Jewish people themselves.

On the eighteenth day of the month Elul, in the year 172 [140 B.C.E.], the third year of Simon's High Priesthood, at Asaramel, in a large assembly of priests, people, rulers of the nation and elders of the land, the following facts were placed on record. . . .

The Jews and their priests confirmed Simon as their leader and High Priest in perpetuity until a true prophet should appear. He was to be their general, and to have full charge of the Temple; and in addition to this the supervision of their labor, of the country, and of the arms and fortifications was to be entrusted to him. He was to be obeyed by all; all contracts in the country were to be drawn up in his name. He was to wear the purple robe and the golden clasp.

None of the people or the priests shall have authority to abrogate any of these decrees, to oppose commands issued by Simon or to convoke any assembly in the land without his assent, to be robed in purple or to wear the gold clasp. Whosoever shall contravene these provisions or neglect any of them shall be liable to punishment. It is the unanimous decision of the people that Simon shall officiate in the ways here laid down. Simon has agreed and consented to be High Priest, General and Ethnarch of the Jews and the priests, and to be the protector of them all. (1 Maccabees 14:25–47)

This was power indeed, more than had been possessed by any previous Jewish leader, whether Moses, David, or Solomon in all his glory. From Simon down to Alexander Janneus, the Hasmonean rulers of Israel were both kings and High Priests.

12. The Pharisees

The surrender to the house of Hasmon of such enormous power, civil and religious, did not obliterate the other sources of authority and autonomy in the Jewish polity: the Gerousia and "the people" still fitfully appear throughout the Hasmonean period, though the former began to show some remarkable changes. Beginning with the reign of John Hyrcanus (134–104 B.C.E.), the Pharisees seem to have enjoyed a more important position in the affairs of state, either as opponents of the crown or, with Alexandra Salome, as its most trusted advisers. Witness Alexander Janneus' (103–76 B.C.E.) deathbed advice to his queen, Alexandra.

She should yield a certain amount of power to the Pharisees, (he said), for if they praised her in return for this sign of regard, they would dispose the nation favorably toward her. These men, he assured her, had so much influence over their fellow Jews that they could injure those whom they hated and help those with whom they were friendly; for they had the complete confidence of the masses when they spoke harshly of any person, even when they did so out of envy; and he himself, he added, had come into conflict with the (Jewish) nation because these men had been badly treated by him. . . .

(After the death of Janneus) Alexandra appointed (her son) Hyrcanus as High Priest because of his greater age but more especially because of his lack of energy; and she permitted the Pharisees to do as they liked in all matters, and also commanded the people to obey them; and whatever regulations, introduced by the Pharisees in accordance with the traditions of their fathers, had been abolished by her father-in-law (John) Hyrcanus, these she again restored. And so, while she had the title of sovereign, the Pharisees had the power. For example, they recalled exiles and freed prisoners, and in a word, in no way differed from absolute rulers. (Josephus, *Antiquities* 13.15.5–16.2)

13. Herod and the Sanhedrin

The pre-eminence of the Pharisees was no match for the ambitions or nakedly wielded power of Herod (37–4 B.C.E.). Although they continue to appear in the narrative of Josephus, it is often in the role of the ill-treated conscience of the king. The tone was set, perhaps, early in Herod's career, when he was still only the teen-aged governor of Galilee on behalf of his father, Antipater. In the course of his stormy stewardship he caught and executed an insurrectionist named Ezekias.

The chief Jews were in great fear when they saw how powerful and reckless Herod was and how much he desired to be dictator. And so they came to Hyrcanus [High Priest and, at the death of Salome, king of Judea], and now openly accused Antipater, saying, "How long will you keep quiet in the face of what is happening? Do you not see that Antipater and his sons have girded themselves with royal power, while you have only the name of king given you? . . . They are openly acknowledged to be masters. Thus Herod, his son, has killed Ezekias and many of his men in violation of our Law, which forbids us to slay a man, even an evildoer, unless he has been first condemned by the Synhedrion [that is, the Sanhedrin] to suffer this fate. He, however, has dared to do this without authority from you."

Having heard these arguments, Hyrcanus was persuaded. . . . Hyrcanus summoned Herod to stand trial for the crimes of which he was accused. Accordingly, after he had settled affairs in Galilee . . . he came with a troop sufficient for the purposes of the journey, and that he might not appear too formidable to Hyrcanus by arriving with a large body of men and yet not be entirely unarmed and unprotected; and so he went to his trial. However, Sextus, the (Roman) governor of Syria, wrote to urge Hyrcanus to acquit Herod of the charge and added threats as to what would happen if he disobeyed. The letter from Sextus gave Hyrcanus a pretext for letting Herod go without suffering any harm from the Synhedrion, for he loved him as a son. But when Herod stood in the Synhedrion with his troops, he overawed them all, and no one of those who had denounced him before his arrival dared to accuse him thereafter; instead there was silence and doubt as to what was to be done. (Josephus, *Antiquities* 14.9.2–4)

Herod later murdered most, if not all, of the Sanhedrin if we are to trust Josephus. The objects of his anger appear not to have been the Pharisees but the priests and aristocracy who shared membership in that council with the Pharisees. The Sanhedrin continued to function during Herod's reign, no longer as a powerful or important political body but simply as a religious court, where the Pharisees' views continued to prevail, which had been one of its functions from the beginning. But then, with the end of the Herodians and the Romans' assumption of direct rule in Judea, the makeup of the Sanhedrin reverted to what it had been before Herod's purge: an aristocratic body dominated by the High Priests, just as it appears on the occasion of the trial of Jesus (see Chapter 3 above).

14. The Great Sanhedrin

Our problems with understanding the Sanhedrin—how many there were (one or two or more), who they were, and what was their competence—are compounded by the fact that there are two bodies of sources that speak of it: the Greek-language testimonies, notably Philo, Josephus, and the New Testament, which often make it sound like a governing as well as a judicial body; and the rabbinic sources, which most often speak of it as a religious court, a Bet Din. In reality, it was probably both. A single body of seventy-one principals, with a mixed priestly and scholarly membership—the "chief priests, scribes, and elders" of the Gospel accounts— undoubtedly held jurisdiction over cases arising from the Mosaic Law, which was in effect the constitution of the Jewish commonwealth, and exercised as much or as little power to govern as the actual ruler—the Hasmoneans, Herodians, or Romans— chose to grant it. The third-, fourth-, and fifth-century rabbis, whose own interests were overwhelmingly legal, saw the Sanhedrin as essentially a judicial and religious body run by people like themselves, and they projected their view of the institution back into a period when its powers were wider and often considerably more secular. The Mishnaic tractate "Sanhedrin," for example, dwells chiefly on cases before the court, but it does occasionally comment more generally.

The greater Sanhedrin was made up of one and seventy (judges) and the lesser by three and twenty. Whence do we learn that the greater Sanhedrin was made up of one and seventy? It is written, "Gather to Me seventy men from the elders of Israel" (Num. 11:16, cited above), and Moses added to them makes one and seventy. (M.Sanhedrin 1:6)

The Sanhedrin was arranged like the half of a round threshing floor so that all might see one another. Before them stood the two scribes of the judges, one to the right and one to the left, and they wrote down the words of them that favored acquittal and the words of them that favored conviction. . . . Before them sat three rows of disciples of the Sages, and each knew his proper place. (Ibid. 4:3–4)

Again, the two sets of sources differ on the presidency of the Great Sanhedrin. The Greek-language testimonies, which speak of the situation before the destruction of the Temple, put the High Priest in charge; the Mishna and Talmud name the "pairs" of scholars who are the heads of the Pharisaic schools (see M.Pirke Aboth 1, cited in Chapter 5 above). The "former (or the senior of the pairs) were Presidents (Nasi), and the others were Fathers of the Court (Ab Bet Din)" (M.Hagigah 2:2).

15. Jesus Commissions the Twelve

Jesus made his public appearance in Israel when the Jewish and Roman organs of government were operating in the land side by side. He was constrained on occasion to advert to the Romans' institutions of sovereignty—their tax collectors, garrisons, and courts—but when his own community began to develop modest institutional organs, it is far more likely that they had Jewish rather than Roman prototypes.

Jesus went round all the towns and villages teaching in their synagogues, announcing the good news of the Kingdom and curing every kind of ailment and disease. The sight of the people moved him to pity; they were like sheep without a shepherd, harassed and helpless; and he said to his disciples, "The crop is heavy, but laborers are scarce; you must therefore beg the owner to send laborers to harvest his crop."

Then he called his twelve disciples to him and gave them authority to cast out unclean spirits and to cure every kind of ailment and disease. These are the names of the twelve apostles: first Simon, also called Peter, and his brother Andrew; James son of Zebedee, and his brother John; Philip and Bartholomew, Thomas and Matthew the tax gatherer; James son of Alpheus, Lebbeus [or Thaddeus]; Simon, a member of the Zealot party; and Judas Iscariot, the man who betrayed him.

These twelve Jesus sent out with the following instructions: "Do not take the road to Gentile lands, and do not enter any Samaritan town; but go rather to the lost sheep of the house of Israel. And as you go, proclaim the message: 'The Kingdom of heaven is upon you.' Heal the sick, raise the dead, cleanse lepers, cast out devils. You received without cost; give without charge." (Matthew 9:35–10:8)

And finally, in an eschatological context:

Peter said, "We have left everything to become your followers. What will there be for us?" Jesus replied, "I tell you this: in the world that is to be, when the Son of Man is seated on his throne in heavenly splendor, you my followers will have thrones of your own, where you will sit as judges over the twelve tribes of Israel." (Matthew 19:27–28)

In at least one celebrated passage (cited in Chapter 3 above) Peter is singled out in a special fashion among the followers of Jesus. The passage describes a conversation at Caesarea Philippi in which Peter, when asked by Jesus, "And you, who do you say I am?" responds, "You are the Messiah, the Son of the Living God."

Then Jesus said, "Simon, son of Jonah, you are favored indeed! You did not learn that from mortal man; it was revealed to you by my heavenly Father. And I say this to you: You are Peter, the Rock; and on this rock I will build my church (*ekklesia*), and the powers of death shall never conquer it. I will give you the keys of the Kingdom of Heaven." He then gave his disciples strict orders not to tell anyone that he was the Messiah. (Matthew 16:17–20)

16. The Bishops of Jerusalem

Whatever else Matthew's Gospel may have meant, or have been intended to mean, it was not understood by Jesus' immediate followers in Jerusalem as anointing Peter as the single head of the new Christian community. Peter is prominent in the events recorded in the Acts of the Apostles, but if there was any implied head of the church there, one is far more likely to think that it was James, "the brother of the Lord."

Then there was James, who was known as the brother of the Lord; for he too was called Joseph's son, and Joseph Christ's father, though in fact the Virgin was his betrothed, and before they came together she was found to be with child by the Holy Spirit, as the inspired Gospel narrative tells us. This James, whom the early Christians surnamed "the Righteous" because of his outstanding virtue, was the first, as the records tell us, to be elected to the episcopal throne of the Jerusalem church. Clement, in his *Outlines* Book VI puts it thus: "Peter, James and John, after the Ascension of the Savior, did not claim pre-eminence because the Savior had specially honored them, but chose James the Righteous as Bishop of Jerusalem." (Eusebius, *Church History* 2.1)

Eusebius kept close track of such matters as the episcopal succession in the various churches of the empire. This is what he has to say of the "Mother Church of all Christians," as it was called.

After the martyrdom of James [ca. 62 C.E.] and the capture of Jerusalem which instantly followed [this actually occurred in 70 C.E.], there is a firm tradition that those of the Apostles and disciples of the Lord who were still alive assembled from all parts of the empire, together with those who, humanly speaking, were kinsmen of the Lord—for most of them were still alive. Then they all discussed together whom they should choose as a fit person to succeed James, and they voted unanimously that

Symeon, son of the Clopas mentioned in the Gospel narrative (John 19:25), was a fit person to occupy the throne of the Jerusalem see. He was, so it was said, a cousin of the Lord. (Eusebius, *Church History* 3.11)

Of the dates of the bishops of Jerusalem I have failed to find any written evidence—it is known that they were very short-lived—but I have received documentary proof of this, that up to Hadrian's siege of the Jews [in 135 C.E.] there had been a series of bishops there. All are said to have been Hebrews in origin [that is, Jewish Christians], who had received the knowledge of Christ with all sincerity, with the result that those in a position to decide such matters judged them worthy of the episcopal office. For at that time their whole church consisted of Hebrew believers who had continued from Apostolic times down to the later siege in which the Jews, after revolting a second time from the Romans, were overwhelmed in a full-scale war. (Ibid. 4.5)

17. Early Christian Elders

James is never actually called "bishop" in the Acts of the Apostles. Eusebius was doubtlessly assimilating James' position to the state of affairs in his own day in the early fourth century. By then the powers and functions of a Christian "overseer" were already well defined. But that organization took some time to develop; early on, both the language and the understanding of who governed the communities of Christians were considerably looser. Indeed, "elder" (presbyteros) and "overseer" (episkopos) sometimes appear to be used interchangeably.

My intention in leaving you behind in Crete was that you should set in order what was left over, and in particular should institute elders [or presbyters] in each town. In doing so, observe the tests I prescribed: is he a man of unimpeachable character, faithful to one wife, the father of children who are believers, who are under no imputation of loose living, who are not out of control? For as God's steward the overseer (*episkopos*) must be a man of unimpeachable character. He must not be overbearing or short-tempered; he must be no drinker, no brawler, no money-grubber, but hospitable, right-minded, temperate, just, devout and self-controlled. He must adhere to the true doctrine, so that he may be well able both to move his hearers with wholesome teaching and to confuse objectors. (Paul, *To Titus* 1:5–9)

There is a popular saying, "To aspire to leadership is an honorable ambition." Our leader, therefore, or overseer, must be above reproach, faithful to one wife, sober, temperate, courteous, hospitable, and a good teacher. . . . He must be one who manages his own household well and wins obedience from his children, and a man of the highest principles. If a man does not know how to control his own family, how can he look after a congregation of God's people? He must not be a convert newly baptized, for fear the sin of conceit should bring upon him a judgment contrived by the devil. He must moreover have a good reputation with the non-Christian public, so that he may not be exposed to scandal and get caught in the devil's snare. (Paul, *To Timothy* 1.3:1–7)

18. A Distinction of Functions and Gifts

If there was some kind of formal authority even in the earliest Christian congregations, there was also both a functional and a charismatic variety.

During this period, when disciples [that is, Christians] were growing in number, there was disagreement between those who spoke Greek and those who spoke the language of the Jews. The former party complained that their widows were being overlooked in the daily distribution. So the Twelve called the whole body of disciples together and said, "It would be a grave mistake for us to neglect the word of God in order to wait at table. Therefore, friends, look out seven men of good reputation from your number, and we will appoint them to deal with these matters, while we devote ourselves to prayer and to the ministry of the Word." This proposal proved acceptable to the whole body. They elected Stephen, a man full of faith and of the Holy Spirit, Philip, Prochorus, Nicanor, Timon, Parmenas and Nicolaus of Antioch, a former convert to Judaism. These they presented to the Apostles, who prayed and laid their hands on them. (Acts of the Apostles 6:1–6)

There are varieties of gifts, but the same Spirit. There are varieties of service, but the same Lord. There are many forms of work, but all of them, in all men, are the work of the same God. In each of us the Spirit is manifested in one particular way, for some useful purpose. One man, through the Spirit, has the gift of wise speech, while another, by the power of the same Spirit, can put the deepest knowledge into words. Another, by the same Spirit, is granted faith; another, by the same Spirit, the gift of healing, and another miraculous powers; another has the gift of prophecy, and another ability to distinguish true spirit from false; yet another has the gift of ecstatic utterance of different kinds, and another the ability to interpret it. But all the gifts are the work of one and the same Spirit, distributing them separately to each individual at will.

For Christ is like a single body with its many limbs and organs, which many as they are, together make up one body. . . . Now you are Christ's body and each of you a limb or organ of it. Within our community God has appointed, in the first place apostles, in the second place prophets, thirdly teachers; then miracle workers, then those who have the gift of healing, or the ability to help others or power to guide them, or the gift of ecstatic utterance of various kinds. Are all apostles? All prophets? All teachers? Do all work miracles? Have all gifts of healing? Do all speak in tongues of ecstasy? Can all interpret them? The higher gifts are those you should aim at. (Paul, *To the Corinthians* 1.12:4–31)

19. The Christian Hierarchy

These charismatic offices eventually disappeared from the Christian community, or perhaps were simply abandoned in the wake of the growing realization that the Second Coming was not as imminent as once had been thought. In any event, the more formal authority prevailed. This is how it appeared to Clement at Rome in the last years of the first Christian century.

The Apostles have preached the Gospel to us from the Lord Jesus Christ; Jesus Christ was sent from God. Christ then is from God, and the Apostles from Christ. Both therefore came in due order from the will of God. Having therefore received his instructions and being fully assured through the Resurrection of our Lord Jesus Christ, they went forth in confidence in the word of God and with the full assurance of the Holy Spirit, preaching the Gospel that the Kingdom of God was about to come. And so, as they preached in the country and in the towns, they appointed their firstfruits, having proved them by the spirit, to be bishops [*episkopoi*: "overseers"] and deacons [*diakonoi*: "ministers"] of them that should believe. And this was no novelty, for of old it had been written concerning bishops and deacons, for the Scripture says in one place, "I will set up their bishops in righteousness and their deacons in faith" [Isa. 60:17, which says in the Greek version "princes" and "overseers" and in the Hebrew "officers" and "taskmasters"]. (Clement of Rome, *To the Corinthians* 42)

And again, from Ignatius, leader of the church at Antioch about 112 C.E.:

Since you are subject to the bishop as to Jesus Christ, you appear to me to live not in the manner of men, but according to Jesus Christ, who died for us in order that by believing in his death you yourselves may escape death. It is necessary then that you do as you do, that without the bishop you should do nothing and that you should also be subject to the presbyters, as to the Apostles of Jesus Christ, our Hope. . . . It is right too that the deacons, being ministers of the mysteries of Jesus Christ, should in every respect be well pleasing to all. For they are not the ministers of meat and drink but servants of the Church of God. It is necessary, then, that they guard themselves from all grounds of accusation as they would from fire.

In like manner, let all reverence the deacons as Jesus Christ, as also the bishop, who is a type of the Father, and the presbyters, who are the Sanhedrin of God and the assembly of the Apostles. Apart from these there is no Church. (Ignatius, *To the Trallians* 2–3)

Avoid divisions as the beginning of evils. All of you follow the bishop as Jesus Christ followed the Father, and follow the presbyters as the Apostles, and respect the deacons as you do the commandment of God. And let no man do anything concerning the church without the bishop. Let that be considered a valid Eucharist over which the bishop presides, or one to whom he commits it. Wherever the bishop appears, there let the people be, just as, wherever Christ Jesus is, there the Catholic Church is. It is not permitted either to baptize or hold a love feast apart from the bishop. But whatever he may approve, that is well pleasing to God, that everything you do may be sound and valid. (Ignatius, *To the Smyrneans* 8)

20. The Apostolic Succession of the Episcopate

By the fourth century, the Christian Church could boast that it was One, Holy, Catholic, and Apostolic. Among those claims, it was probably that of being Apostolic that constituted its own strongest sense of authenticity and validity. It was a trait remarked upon and cherished very early in the history of the community. Here it appears about 175 C.E. in the work of Hegesippus, as cited by Eusebius.

The Church of Corinth remained in the right doctrine down to the episcopate of Primus at Corinth. I spoke with him on my journey to Rome, and we took comfort together in the right doctrine. After arriving in Rome, I made a succession down to Anicetus, whose deacon was Eleutherus. To Anicetus succeeded Soter, who was followed by Eleutherus. In every succession and in every city things are ordered according to the preaching of the Law, the Prophets and the Lord. (Hegesippus, cited by Eusebius, *Church History* 4.22)

Come now, you who wish to indulge a better curiosity, if you would apply it to the business of your salvation, run over the Apostolic churches, in which the very thrones of the Apostles are still pre-eminent in their places, in which their own authentic writings are still read, uttering the voice and representing the law of each of them severally. Achaea is very near you, in which you find Corinth. Since you are not far from Macedonia, you have Philippi and the Thessalonians. Since you are able to cross to Asia, you get Ephesus. Since, moreover, you are close upon Italy, you have Rome, from which there comes even into our own hands the very authority of the Apostles themselves. How happy is that church, on which the Apostles poured forth all their teaching along with their blood! Where Peter endured a suffering like his Lord's; where Paul wins a crown in a death like John's; where the Apostle John was first plunged unhurt into boiling oil, and thence was sent to his island exile [that is, to Patmos]. See what she learned, what taught; what fellowship she had even with our churches in Africa. (Tertullian, *A Ruling against Heretics* 36)

The tracing of this same succession is the very first objective in Eusebius' writing of his monumental Church History *sometime about 312 C.E., as the author explains in its opening lines.*

Since it is my purpose to hand down a written account of the successions of the holy Apostles as well as of the times extending from our Savior to ourselves; the number and the nature of the events which are said to have been treated in church history; the number of those who were her illustrious guides and leaders in especially prominent dioceses; the number of those who in each generation by word of mouth or by writings served as ambassadors of the word of God; the names, the number and the times of those who out of a desire for innovation launched into an extremity of error and proclaimed themselves the introducers of knowledge falsely so called. (Eusebius, *Church History* 1.1)

That the point of the inquiry is not simply a historian's antiquarian curiosity but something essential to the Church's claim to authenticity is clear at almost every point that the "Apostolic Succession" is cited, as here by Ireneus.

Those who wish to discern the truth may observe the apostolic tradition made manifest in every church throughout the world. We can enumerate those who were appointed bishops in the churches by the Apostles, and their successors down to our own day, who never taught, and never knew such absurdities as these (heretical) men produce. For if the Apostles had known hidden mysteries which they taught the perfect in private and in secret, they would surely have committed them to those to whom they entrusted the churches. For they wished these men to be perfect and unblamable whom they left as their successors and to whom they handed over their own office and authority. . . . We point to the apostolic tradition and the faith that is preached to men, which has come down to us through the succession of bishops; the tradition and creed of the greatest, the most ancient church, which was founded and set up at Rome by the two most glorious apostles, Peter and Paul. For with this church, because of its position of leadership and authority, must needs agree every church, that is, the faithful everywhere, since in her the apostolic tradition has always been preserved by the faithful from all parts. (Ireneus, *Against the Heresies* 3.3:1)

Therefore we ought to obey only those presbyters who are in the Church, who trace their succession from the Apostles, as we have shown; who with their succession to the episcopate have received the sure gift of the truth according to the pleasure of the Father. The rest, who stand aloof from the primitive succession, and assemble in any place whatever, we must regard with suspicion, either as heretics and evil-minded; or as schismatics, puffed-up and complacent; or again as hypocrites, acting thus for the sake of gain and vainglory. All these have fallen from the truth. (Ibid. 4.26:2)

21. The Consecration of Bishops, Priests, and Deacons

We have two very early testimonies on the choice and consecration of the bishops who were becoming the paramount rulers of the Church and the true source of all authoritative teaching.

Chose for yourselves bishops and deacons worthy of the Lord, men who are gentle and not covetous, true men and approved; for they also serve you in the service of the prophets and teachers. Therefore do not despise them, for these are they that are honored of you with the prophets and teachers. (*Teaching of the Apostles*)

We turn to the subject of the tradition which is proper for the churches, in order that those who have been rightly instructed may hold fast to that tradition, which has continued until now; and, once they fully understand it from our exposition, they may stand the more firmly in it. . . .

Let the bishop be ordained who is in all respects without fault and who has been chosen by all the people. And when he has been proposed and found acceptable to all, the people should assemble on the Lord's day together with the presbyters and such bishops as may attend, and the choice should be generally approved. Let the bishops lay hands on him (who has been chosen) while the presbyters stand by in silence. And all shall keep silence, praying in their hearts for the descent of the Spirit.

After this, one of the bishops present, at the request of all, should lay his hand on him who is ordained bishop and pray as follows: ". . . Father, who knows the hearts of all, grant to this Your servant whom You have chosen for the episcopate to feed Your holy flock and serve as Your High Priest, that he may minister blamelessly by night and day, that he may unceasingly behold and propitiate Your countenance and offer to You the gifts of Your holy Church. And that by the high priestly Spirit he may have the authority to forgive sins according to Your command, to assign lots according to Your bidding, to loose every bond according to the authority You gave to the Apostles, and that he may praise You in meekness and purity of heart, offering to You a sweet-smelling savor through Your Child Jesus Christ our Lord, through whom to You be glory, might and praise, to the Father and to the Son with the Holy Spirit now and ever and world without end. Amen." . . .

And when a presbyter is ordained the bishop shall lay his hand upon his head, and the presbyters shall also touch him. And he shall pray over him according to the aforementioned form which we gave previously in the case of the bishop, praying and saying, ". . . Look upon this Your servant and impart to him the spirit of grace and counsel, that he may share in the presbyterate and govern Your people with a pure heart. As You looked upon the people of Your choice and commanded Moses to choose presbyters whom You filled with the spirit which You had granted to Your minister, so now, O Lord, grant that there may be preserved among us unceasingly the Spirit of Your grace, and make us worthy that in faith we may minister to You, praising you in singleness of heart through Your Child Jesus Christ our Lord, through whom to You be glory, might and praise, to the Father and to the Son with the Holy Spirit now and ever and world without end. Amen."

And when a deacon is to be appointed, he should be chosen according to what has been said before, the bishop alone laying hands upon him in the same manner. Nevertheless, we order that the bishop alone shall lay on hands at the ordination of a deacon for this reason: that he is not ordained for a priesthood, but for the service of a bishop, that he may do only the things commanded by him. For he is not appointed to be the fellow counselor of the whole clergy but to take charge of property and to report to the bishop whenever necessary. He does not receive the Spirit which is common to all the presbyterate, in which the presbyters share, but rather that which is entrusted to him under the bishop's authority. Nor is he appointed to receive the Spirit of greatness which the presbyters share, but to give attention and to be worthy of the bishop's trust and to be diligent about what is fitting. . . .

But in the appointment of a presbyter, the other presbyters also lay their hands upon him because of the similar Spirit which is common to all the clergy. For the presbyter has authority only to receive, but not to grant, holy orders. Wherefore he does not ordain a man to orders, but by laying on hands at the ordination of (another) presbyter he only blesses while the bishop ordains. (Hippolytus of Rome, *The Apostolic Tradition* 1–9)

22. The Regulation of Church Orders

In addition to publishing a statement of faith to serve as a yardstick for orthodox belief, the first ecumenical council of the Great Church, held at Nicea in Anatolia in 325 C.E., issued various disciplinary decrees or canons regulating the Church orders. Its example was followed by most subsequent synods, that at Antioch in 341, for example.

Nicea, Canon 4: It is most proper that a bishop should be constituted by all the bishops of the province; but if this is difficult on account of some urgent necessity or by the length of the journey, that at all events three (bishops) should meet together at the same place, the absentees giving their suffrages and consent in writing, and then the ordination be performed. The confirming, however, of what is done in each province belongs to its Metropolitan [that is, the presiding bishop of its metropolis].

Antioch, Canon 4: If any bishop is deposed by a synod, or any presbyter or deacon who has been deposed by his bishop, shall presume to perform any function of the ministry, whether it is a bishop acting as a bishop, and the same holds true of a presbyter or a deacon, he shall no longer have any prospect of restoration by another synod nor any opportunity of stating his case; but whoever communicates with him shall be cast out of the Church, and particularly if they have presumed to communicate with any of the persons aforementioned with full knowledge of the sentence that had been pronounced against them.

Another recurrent problem was the movement of the clergy from one jurisdiction to another:

Nicea, Canon 15: On account of the great disturbance and discords that occur, it is decreed that the custom prevailing in certain places contrary to the canon must wholly be done away with; so that neither bishop, presbyter nor deacon shall pass from city to city. But if anyone, after this decree of the holy and great synod, shall attempt any such thing or continue in such a course, his proceedings shall be utterly void, and he shall be restored to the church for which he was ordained bishop or presbyter.

Nicea, Canon 16: Neither presbyters, deacons, nor any others enrolled among the clergy, who, not having the fear of God before their eyes, nor regarding the ecclesiastical canon, shall recklessly remove from their own church, ought by any means to be received by another church; but every constraint should be applied to restore them to their own dioceses; and if they will not go, they must be excommunicated. And if one shall dare to carry off someone in secret and ordain him on his own, though he belongs to another, and this without the consent of the bishop on whose clergy list he was enrolled and then seceded, let the ordination be void.

23. The Episcopal Hierarchy

The same councils, as well as those held at Constantinople in 381 and Chalcedon in 451 C.E., likewise touched upon another delicate question, that of an episcopal hierarchy. It might be argued, as it was, that all bishops were equal; but as Cyprian had already suggested and Nicea acknowledged, some bishoprics were more equal than others.

Nicea (325 C.E.), Canon 6: Let the ancient customs hold good which are in Egypt and Libya and the Pentapolis, according to which the Bishop of Alexandria has authority over all these places. For this is also customary to the Bishop of Rome. In like manner in Antioch and in the other provinces, the privileges are to be preserved to the churches. But this is clearly to be understood, that if any one be made a bishop without the consent of the Metropolitan, the Great Synod declares that he shall not be a bishop. If, however, two or three bishops (of a province) shall from private contention oppose the common choice of all the others, it being a reasonable one and made according to the ecclesiastical canons, let the choice of the majority prevail.

What custom and the ancient tradition could grant, political reality could take away, often in the space of the same sentence.

Nicea (325 C.E.), Canon 7: Since custom and ancient tradition have prevailed that the bishop of Aelia [that is, Jerusalem] should be honored, let him, saving the dignity appropriate to the (provincial) metropolis [that is, Caesarea], have the next place of honor.

Caesarea Maritima was the metropolis or provincial capital of Palestina Prima, where Jerusalem was located as well. Neither custom nor ancient tradition could at this point override that political fact. It took a powerful and aggressive bishop of Jerusalem, Juvenal, to move his see past Caesarea and onto equal footing with the patriarchal sees of Alexandria and Antioch.

The ecclesiastical province would conform, as the next canon makes clear, with the territorial and jurisdictional lines of Roman imperial organization.

Antioch (341 C.E.), Canon 9: It behooves the bishops in each province to acknowledge the bishop who presides in the metropolis and who has to take thought of the entire province, because all men of business come together from every quarter to the metropolis. Wherefore it is decreed that he have precedence in rank (over the other bishops of the province) and that the other bishops do nothing extraordinary without him, according to the ancient canon which prevailed from the time of our fathers, or such things only as pertain to their own particular dioceses and the districts subject to them. For each bishop has jurisdiction over his own diocese, both to manage it with piety, which is incumbent on everyone, and to make provision for the whole district which is dependent upon his city; to ordain presbyters and deacons; and to settle everything with judgment. But let him not undertake anything further without the bishop of the metropolis; neither the latter without the consent of the others.

Constantinople (381 C.E.), Canon 2: The bishops are not to go beyond their dioceses to churches lying outside their bounds, nor bring confusion on churches; but let the bishop of Alexandria, according to the canons, alone administer the affairs of Egypt; and let the bishops of the East administer the East alone, the privileges of the church in Antioch, which are mentioned in the canons of Nicea, being preserved; and let the bishops of the Asian diocese administer the Asian affairs only; and the Pontic bishops only Pontic matters; and the Thracian bishops only Thracian matters. And let the bishops not go beyond their dioceses for ordination or any other ecclesiastical ministrations, unless they are invited. And the aforesaid canon concerning dioceses being observed, it is evident that the synod of each province will administer the affairs of that particular province, as decreed at Nicea. But the churches of God in pagan nations must be governed according to the custom which has prevailed from the time of the Fathers.

What was true on the provincial level proved equally true on the imperial level. Under Constantine the capital of the Roman Empire had been moved from Rome to his new city of Constantinople, the former Byzantium, on the Bosphorus. This political move soon had its effect on the hierarchical organization of the Christian Church.

Constantinople, Canon 3: The bishop of Constantinople, however, shall have the prerogative of honor after the bishop of Rome, because Constantinople is New Rome.

Canon 28 of Chalcedon goes much further in an administrative sense. The bishops of Asia, Pontus, and Thrace, who were being restrained from tampering at Constantinople in 381, now found themselves under the jurisdiction of the imperial Patriarch of the New Rome.

Chalcedon, Canon 28: Following in all things the decisions of the holy Fathers, and acknowledging the canon, which has just been read, of the one hundred and fifty bishops [assembled in Constantinople in 381], beloved by God, we also do enact and decree the same thing concerning the privileges of the most holy Church of Constantinople or New Rome. For the Fathers rightly granted privileges to the throne of the Old Rome, because it was the royal city, and the one hundred and fifty most religious bishops, moved by the same considerations, gave equal privileges to the most holy throne of the New Rome, judging with good reason that the city which is honored with the sovereignty and the Senate, and always enjoys equal privileges with old imperial Rome, should in ecclesiastical matters also be magnified as she [Rome] is, and rank next after her; so that in the dioceses of Pontus, Asia and Thrace the metropolitans and such bishops also of the dioceses aforesaid as are among the barbarians, should be ordained only by the aforesaid most holy throne of the most holy Church of Constantinople; every metropolitan of the aforesaid dioceses, together with the bishops of his province, may ordain bishops of the province, as has been declared by the divine canons, but the metropolitans of the dioceses, as has been said above, shall be ordained by the archbishop of Constantinople, after the proper elections have been held according to custom and have been reported to him.

CHAPTER 6

24. "The Greatest Church": The Issue
of Roman Primacy

The decrees of the Council of Chalcedon in 451 brought the churches of Rome and Constantinople into direct conflict on the issue of the principal and primary bishopric of the Church. The New Rome was manifestly growing at the expense of the Old. Rome protested the expansionist claims of Canon 28 of Chalcedon, but to no great avail. The realities of shifting political power and of deepening cultural differences were drawing East and West into separate spheres and, in the end, separate ecclesiastical jurisdictions.

But there was a matter of principle involved as well: that between an episcopal oligarchical Church and a papal monarchical one. A quasi-monarchical papacy had solid historical claims for many of the early Fathers, whether that pre-eminence was understood as one of honor, as the councils seemed to define it, or whether it rested on Rome as the final court of appeal in ecclesiastical disputes. Sometime about 175 C.E. Ireneus, bishop of Lyons, wrote his Against the Heresies *and invoked the principle of the teaching of the Apostles as the main criterion of truth in the Church. That teaching was transmitted by the Apostles to their successors, the bishops of the various Christian congregations. The authority of these men rested, then, on the validity of their succession from the Apostles. Ireneus assures his readers that Christians can trace that uninterrupted succession in any or all of the churches. But this would be an impractical notion, and so he takes another course.*

But since it would be very long in a book like this to count up the successions in all the churches, we confound all those who, whether through self-pleasing or vainglory, or through blindness and evil opinion, gather together otherwise than they ought by pointing out the traditions derived from the Apostles of the greatest, most ancient and universally known church, one founded and established by the two most glorious Apostles Peter and Paul, and also the faith declared to men which through the succession of bishops comes down to our times. For with this church, on account of its more powerful leadership, every church, that is, the faithful, who are from everywhere, must needs agree, since in it that tradition which is from the Apostles has always been preserved by those who are from everywhere.

The blessed Apostles having founded and established the Church (at Rome), entrusted the office of the episcopate to Linus. Paul speaks of this Linus in his Letters to Timothy. Anacletus succeeded him, and after Anacletus in the third place from the Apostles, Clement received the episcopate. He had seen and conversed with the blessed Apostles, and their

335

teaching was still sounding in his ears and their tradition was still before his eyes. Nor was he alone in this, for many who had been taught by the Apostles still survived. In the times of Clement a serious dissension having arisen among the brethren in Corinth, the Church of Rome sent a suitable letter to the Corinthians, reconciling them in peace, renewing their faith and proclaiming the teaching lately received from the Apostles. . . .

Evaristus succeeded Clement, and Alexander Evaristus. Then Sixtus, the sixth from the Apostles, was appointed. After him Telesphorus, who suffered martyrdom gloriously, and then Hyginus; after him Pius, and after Pius Anicetus, and now, in the twelfth place from the Apostles, Eleutherus [174–189 C.E.] holds the office of bishop. In the same order and succession the tradition and the preaching of the truth which is from the Apostles have continued down to us. (Ireneus, *Against the Heresies* 3.3.2–3)

This same Ireneus, however, admonished the bishop of Rome not to disrupt the unity of the Church by excommunicating the churches of Asia on the matter of the observance of Easter.

25. Tradition and Authority

The practices and beliefs of any given Christian congregation could be validated by showing that they were in conformity with the teaching of the Apostles, a case that was rendered infinitely simpler if it could be demonstrated that the church in question was an Apostolic foundation and that its succession of bishops went back in an unbroken line to one of the Apostles. By the second century the Apostolic tradition was confronted not so much by a challenge in principle as by the presence of other manifestations of authority—a number of bishops acting collegially, for example, or the fact that some churches, and so their bishops, enjoyed a somewhat more intimate connection with the Apostolic tradition than did others.

The conflict implicit in this unfolding of ecclesiastical authority found its sharpest manifestation in a question that had puzzled Christians from the beginning: their relationship with Judaism. The Jews, on their side, dissolved that affiliation rather abruptly by effectively excluding Christians from the synagogue (see Chapter 5 above); for the Christians, however, the separation could never be quite complete—the proofs of the Messiahship of Jesus had no other ground than the Bible. But there remained to be settled other matters of connection with Judaism: their relationship to the Law, for example; certain questions of cult, such as the observance of the Sabbath; and, in the last decade of the second century, the divisive question of the date of Easter. Jesus had died on the eve of Passover and had risen on the day after that feast. The Resurrection, then, would seem to be tied directly to the fourteenth of Nisan in the Jewish calendar.

At this time a question of no small importance arose. For the parishes of all Asia, being from an older tradition, held that the fourteenth day of the moon [that is, of the lunar month], since this was the day on which the Jews were commanded to sacrifice the (Passover) lamb, should be observed as the feast of the Savior's Passover, and that it was necessary, therefore, to end their fast on that day, whatever the day of the week on which it should happen to fall. It was not, however, the custom of the churches elsewhere to end it at this time, but they observed the practice, which from Apostolic tradition had prevailed to the present time, of ending the fast on no other day than that of the Resurrection of the Savior. Synods and assemblies of bishops were held on this account, and all with one consent, by means of letters addressed to all, drew up an ecclesiastical decree that the mystery of the Resurrection of the Lord from the dead should be celebrated on no other day than on the Lord's Day [that is, Sunday], and that we should observe the close of the Paschal fast on that day only. There is still extant a writing of those who were then assembled in Palestine, over whom Theophilus, bishop of the parish [that is, the diocese] of Caesarea, and Narcissus, bishop of Jerusalem, presided; also another of those who were assembled in Rome, on account of the same question, which bears the name of Victor. (Eusebius, *Church History* 5.23)

The bishops of Asia, the chief proponents of the fourteenth of Nisan as the day ending the Passover fast, were not convinced by this assertion of collegial episcopal authority. They were not likely to raise the Jewish precedent, however; rather, they referred to what they regarded as the true Apostolic tradition. Whatever others might do, they had venerable Christian examples on their side.

But the bishops of Asia, led by Polycrates, decided to hold fast to the customs handed down to them. He himself, in a letter addressed to Victor and the church of Rome, set forth the tradition which had come down to him as follows: "We observe the exact day, neither adding nor taking anything away. For in Asia great lights have fallen asleep, which shall rise again on the day of the Lord's coming, when he shall come with glory from heaven and shall seek out all the saints. Of these were Philip, one of the twelve Apostles, who fell asleep at Hierapolis . . . and, moreover, John, who reclined on the Lord's bosom, and being a priest wore the sacerdotal miter, who was both a witness and a teacher; he fell asleep at Ephesus; and further, Polycarp in Smyrna, both a bishop and a martyr. . . . All these observed the fourteenth day of the Passover, according to the Gospel, deviating in no respect, but following the rule of faith. And

I, Polycrates, do the same, the least of you all, according to the tradition of my relatives, some of whom I have closely followed. For seven of my relatives were bishops, and I am the eighth. And my relatives always observed the day when the people put away the leaven. I, therefore, am not affrighted by terrifying words. For those greater than I have said, 'We ought to obey God rather than men.' "

Polycrates, it will be noted, ignored the church in Jerusalem and others that had ruled against him. He seemed to appeal the ruling, or at least chose to present his case, to the bishop of Rome, the presiding bishop at one of the adjudicating synods. And it was from the bishop of Rome that he received his reply.

Thereupon Victor, who was over the church of Rome, immediately attempted to cut off from the common unity the parishes of Asia, with the churches that agreed with them, as being heterodox. And he published letters declaring that all the brethren there were wholly excommunicated. But this did not please all the bishops, and they besought him to consider the things of peace, of neighborly unity and love. Words of theirs are still extant, rather sharply rebuking Victor. (Eusebius, *Church History* 5.24)

One such letter came from Ireneus, bishop of Lyons in the last quarter of the second century, whose views on the validity of Apostolic tradition have already been quoted. Here he underlines some of the dangers of understanding it too monolithically.

The controversy is not merely concerning the day [Ireneus wrote] but also concerning the very manner of the fast. For some think they should fast one day, and others two, yet others more. . . . And this variety of observance has not originated in our times but long before, in the days of our ancestors. It is likely that they did not hold to strict accuracy, and thus was formed a custom for their posterity, according to their own simplicity and their peculiar method. Yet all of these lived more or less in peace, and we also live in peace with one another, and the disagreement in regard to the fast confirms the agreement in faith. . . . Among those were elders before Soter, who presided over the church (of Rome) which you (Victor) now rule. We mean Anicetus, and Pius, and Hyginus, and Telesphorus, and Sixtus. They neither observed it [that is, the fast of the fourteenth of Nisan], nor did they permit others after them to do so. And yet, though they did not observe it themselves, they were nonetheless at peace with those who came to them from the parishes in which it was observed. . . . But none was ever cast out on account of this practice, but the elders before you, who did not observe it, nevertheless sent the eucharist to those parishes who did observe it. (Cited by Eusebius, *Church History* 5.24)

Ireneus' conciliatory view prevailed on this occasion, but the sense of hierarchy was as deeply felt in some churches as the need of unity. Such was the view of Cyprian, the bishop of Carthage in 251 C.E. For him, "the episcopal power was one and undivided"; but the source and type of that unity of both Church and episcopate rested in Peter and the See of Rome, as the sixteenth chapter of Matthew bears unmistakable witness.

The Lord says to Peter, "I say to you, you are Peter and upon this rock I will build my Church, and the gates of hell shall not overcome it. I will give to you the keys of the kingdom of heaven. And what you shall bind upon earth shall be bound also in heaven, and what you shall loose upon earth shall be loosed also in heaven" (Matt. 16:18–19). It is on one man that he builds the Church, and though he assigns a like power to all the Apostles, after his resurrection, saying, "As the Father sent me, I am also sending you. . . . Receive you the Holy Spirit. If you forgive any man his sins, they will be forgiven him; if you retain any man's, they shall be retained" (John 20:21–23). Yet, in order that that unity might be unmistakable, he established by his own authority a source for that oneness having its origin in one man alone. No doubt the other Apostles were all that Peter was, endowed with equal dignity and power. But the beginning comes from him alone, to show that the Church of Christ is unique. (Cyprian, *On the Unity of the Church* 4)

26. Leo, Bishop of Rome

The strongest case for Roman primacy was of course made by the bishops of Rome themselves, and by none more strongly than by Leo, called the Great, who held that see from 440 to 461 C.E. and was one of the moving forces behind the Council of Chalcedon. Early in his tenure, in 444 C.E., Leo put forth the jurisdictional claims of the See of Rome in a letter written to the bishop of Thessalonica.

Those of the brethren who have been summoned to a synod should attend and not deny themselves to the holy congregation. . . . If, however, any more important questions should arise, of a type that cannot be settled there under your presidency, my brother, then send your report and consult us, so that we may respond under the revelation of the Lord, by whose mercy alone we can accomplish anything, because he has breathed favorably upon us. And this so that we might by our decision vindicate our right of recognition in accordance with long-standing tradition and the respect that is due to the Apostolic See. Just as we wish you to exercise your authority in our place, so also we reserve to ourselves issues which cannot be decided on the spot and persons who have appealed to us. (Leo, *Letter* 6 to Anastasius)

Somewhat later, to the same Anastasius of Thessalonica on the principle of hierarchy in the Church:

And from this model [of the differences in rank and order of the Apostles] has arisen a similar distinction among bishops, and by an important ordinance it has been provided that everyone should not claim everything for himself, but that there should be in each province one whose opinion should have priority among the brethren; and again, that those whose appointments are in the greater cities should undertake fuller responsibility, and that through them the care of the universal Church should converge toward Peter's one seat, and nothing anywhere should be separated from its head. (Leo, *Letter* 14 to Anastasius)

The following is from one of Leo's sermons.

From Christ's overruling and eternal providence we have received also the support of the Apostle's aid, which assuredly still operates; and the strength of the foundation, on which the whole lofty building of the Church is reared, is not weakened by the temple that rests upon it. For the solidity of that faith which was praised in the chief of the Apostles is perpetual; and as there survives what Peter believed in Christ, so there also survives what Christ instituted in Peter. For when, as has been read in the Gospel lesson (of the day), the Lord had asked the disciples whom they believed him to be, amid the various opinions that were held, the blessed Peter replied, saying, "You are the Christ. . . ."

The dispensation of the truth therefore abides, and the blessed Peter, persevering in the strength of the rock which he has received, has not abandoned the helm of the Church which he undertook. For he was ordained before the rest in such a way that since he was called the rock, since he is pronounced the foundation, since he is constituted the door-keeper of the kingdom of heaven, since he is set up as the judge to bind and to loose, whose judgments shall retain their validity in heaven, from all these mystical titles we might know the nature of his association with Christ. And even today he more fully and effectually performs what is entrusted to him, and carries out every part of his duty and charge in Christ and with Christ, through whom he has been glorified.

And so if anything is rightly done or rightly decreed by us [that is, Peter's successor], if anything is obtained from the mercy of God by daily supplications, it is his work and merits whose power lives on in his See and whose authority excels. For this, dearly beloved, that confession (of Peter) gained, that confession which, inspired in the Apostle's heart by God the Father, transcends all the uncertainties of human opinions, and was endowed with the firmness of rock, which no assaults could shake. For throughout the Church Peter daily says, "You are the Christ, the Son of the Living God," and every tongue that confesses the Lord is inspired by the teaching authority [*magisterium*] of that voice. (Leo, *Sermon* 3)

Leo's words are homiletic and inspirational, as befits a sermon. The hard edge of polemic emerges more clearly on the issue of the claims of Constantinople and the purport of Canon 28 of Chalcedon. The first text is a letter written by Leo to Emperor Marcian in 452, immediately after the council.

Let the city of Constantinople have, as we desire, its glory, and may it, under the protection of God's right hand, long enjoy the rule of your Clemency. Yet the basis of things secular is one thing and the basis of things divine is another; and there can be no sure building except on the rock that the Lord laid as a foundation. He that covets what is not his due, loses what is his own. Let it be enough for the aforesaid Anatolius [bishop of Constantinople, 449–458 C.E.] that by the aid of your Piety and that with my favorable assent he has obtained the bishopric of so great a city. Let him not disdain a royal city, which he cannot, however, make into an Apostolic See; and let him on no account hope to be able to rise by injury to others. For the privileges of the churches, as determined by the canons of the holy Fathers and fixed by the decrees of the Synod of Nicea, cannot be overthrown by an unscrupulous act, nor disturbed by an innovation. And in the faithful execution of this task by the aid of Christ, it is necessary that I show an unflinching devotion; for it is a charge entrusted to me, and more, it tends to condemnation if the rules sanctioned by the Fathers and laid down under the guidance of God's Spirit at the Synod of Nicea for the government of the whole Church are violated with my connivance—which God forbid—and if the wishes of a single man have more weight with me than the common word of the Lord's entire house. (Leo, *To Marcian* 3)

27. Bishop of Rome, Absolute Primate or First among Equals?

In a letter to Anatolius written in the same year of 452, Leo undertakes to defend the rights of other primatial bishoprics.

Your purpose is in no way whatever supported by the written assent of certain bishops, given, as you allege, sixty years ago [that is, at the Council of Constantinople in 381], and never brought to the knowledge of the Apostolic See (of Rome) by your predecessors; under this present scheme, which from its outset was tottering and has already collapsed, you now wish to place too late and useless props. . . . Metropolitan bishops ought not be defrauded of privileges based on antiquity. The See of Alexandria may not lose any of that dignity which it merited through St. Mark, the evangelist and disciple of the blessed Peter. . . . The Church of Antioch too, in which, at the preaching of the blessed Apostle Peter, the Christian name first was used, must continue in the position assigned to it by the Fathers, and being set in the third place [by Canon 6 of Nicea], must never be lowered therefrom. For the see is one thing and those who preside in it are something different; and an individual's great honor is his own integrity. (Leo, *Letter* 106 to Anatolius)

Leo's vindication of the rights of the other great sees of Constantinople, Alexandria, and Antioch corresponds to the Eastern view of how the highest ecclesiastical authority was distributed in the Church. It is restated here, though with a slightly different nuance, by the monk Theodore of Studium (d. 826), one of the most prominent churchmen of his generation in Constantinople.

It is not the affairs of the world of which we speak: the right to judge them belongs to the emperor and the civil tribunal. Here it is rather a question of divine and heavenly judgments, and these are reserved alone to whom the word of God was addressed: "Whatsoever you shall bind upon earth, will be bound in Heaven, and whatsoever you loose upon earth shall be loosed in Heaven" (Matt. 16:19).

We are at the heart of the matter. This celebrated saying remained the primary proof-text of the Christian Church's spiritual powers and, indeed, of their consequences in the affairs of the secular realm. Theodore continues:

And who are the men to whom this command was given? The Apostles and their successors. And who are their successors? In the first place, whoever occupies the throne of Rome; second, the one who sits on the throne of Constantinople; and after them are those of Alexandria, Antioch and Jerusalem. That is the fivefold authority in the Church. It is to them that all decisions belong in matters of divine dogma. The Emperor and the secular authority have the duty to assist them and to confirm what they have decided. (Theodore of Studium, *Letters*)

It should be recalled, however, that between the time of Leo's letters and that of Theodore, three of those five great patriarchal sees—those of Alexandria, Antioch, and Jerusalem—had fallen under the political sovereignty of Islam, a fact that gave a decidedly theoretical air to the notion of "fivefold authority." There were, in fact, but two effective claimants to primacy: the bishop of Rome and the bishop of Constantinople.

28. Roman Primacy

The occasion for the Pope to assert a far broader claim to absolute primacy in the Great Church arose in a critical form with the appointment of a certain Photius, an immensely learned man but a layman, to the Patriarchate of Constantinople, the highest ecclesiastical post of Eastern Christendom He replaced the monk Ignatius, who had been pressured to resign. The party of Ignatius then appealed to the bishop of Rome. The case grew more complex, but at its heart was the issue of the primacy of the Roman see. Pope and emperor exchanged letters. In his response to Emperor Michael III in 865 C.E., Pope Nicholas I states the Roman case.

. . . The privileges of the Roman church of Christ, confirmed from the mouth of the Blessed Peter, laid down in the church itself, acknowledged even from the earliest days, celebrated by the holy ecumenical councils, and consistently reverenced by all churches, may be diminished in no manner whatsoever, nor altered, since no mortal should dare to move the foundation which God has laid down, and what He has established remains strong and unshaken. . . .

These privileges of this holy church, which were given by Christ and not granted by councils, privileges which are both widely known and highly regarded, which are to us so much an honor as a burden, even though we have come to this honor not through any merits of our own but by command of the grace of God mediated through and in the Blessed Peter, it is these privileges, we say, which oblige us to be solicitous of all the churches of God. For the company of the Blessed Apostle Paul was added to that of the Blessed Peter . . . and these two, like two great heavenly luminaries, placed by the divine ordination in the Roman church, have marvelously lit up the the whole world by the splendor of their brightness. . . .

These things, then, constrain me to come to the assistance of the Patriarch Ignatius as a brother who has been deposed by no rule or ecclesiastical order. . . . These divinely inspired privileges have thus ordained that, since Photius, while Ignatius was still alive, improperly came to the Lord's sheepfold, overthrew the shepherd and dispersed our sheep, he must vacate the position he has usurped and leave the communion of the Christian community. And since we think that nothing would be more discreet, mild or useful to either Ignatius or Photius than that each should come to an investigation to be renewed in Rome, we desire this greatly and we admonish for your own good that you assent. (Nicholas I, *Letter to the Emperor Michael III*)

There was a considerable range of Eastern reactions to this and other Papal asser-tions on the subject of the Roman primacy. Many were willing to concede some form of primacy—of protocol or honor, for example. It was the monarchical principle that was unacceptable. This is one Eastern bishop's careful reading of the problem, expressed during a Greco-Latin debate on the subject in Constantinople in 1136 C.E.

I neither deny nor reject the primacy of the Roman Church. . . . We read in the ancient accounts that there were in fact three Patriarchal Sees closely linked in brotherhood, those of Rome, Alexandria and Antioch, and among them it was Rome, the highest see in the empire, which was granted the primacy. For this reason Rome has been called the first see: it is to her that appeal must be made in doubtful ecclesiastical cases, and it is to her judgment that all matters that cannot be settled according to the normal rules must be submitted. . . .

That is what we discover, my dear brothers, written in the ancient historical documents. But the Roman Church to which we do not deny the primacy among her sisters, and whom we recognize as holding the highest place in any general council, the first place of honor, that Church has separated herself from the rest by her pretensions. She has appropri-ated to herself the monarchy which is not contained in her office and which has split the eastern and western bishops and the churches since the partition of the empire. (Nicetas of Nicomedia, *Discourse*)

One result of this schism over the Roman "monarchy," Nicetas claimed, was that what were once regarded as ecumenical councils were no longer universal in either their representation or their binding power.

When, as a result of these circumstances, she [that is, the Roman Church] assembles a council of the Western bishops without allowing us (in the East) to participate in it, it is perfectly appropriate that her own (Western) bishops should accept the council's decrees and observe them with the veneration that is due to them . . . but as for us (in the East), though we do not disagree with the Roman Church in the matter of the Catholic faith, how can we be expected to accept those decisions which were taken without our advice and of which we know nothing, since we were not present at the council at the time? If the Roman Pontiff, seated upon his lofty throne of glory, wishes to fulminate against us and fire off his orders from the height of his sublime dignity, if he wishes to sit in judgment on our churches with a total disregard of our advice but only in accordance with his own will, as he does seem to wish, what brotherhood and what fatherhood can we discern in such a manner of acting? Who could ever accept such a situation? In such circumstances we could not be called, nor would we really any longer be, sons of the Church but slaves. (Ibid.)

What neither reason nor discussion could accomplish, the political fears of the Eastern Empire did: on two occasions Eastern and Western Christendom came together as one Church, at Lyons in 1274 and at Florence in 1439. The terms were Western, and one of them was the question of Roman primacy. This is the Eastern emperor Michael VIII saying what was required of him in 1274.

The Holy Roman Church likewise possesses the highest and most complete primacy and authority over the universal catholic church, it sincerely and with all humility acknowledges that it has received that primacy, together with the fullness of its power, from the Lord himself in the person of the Blessed Peter, chief or head of the Apostles, whose successor the Roman Pontiff is. And since his chief responsibility is the defense of the truth of the Faith, so it is his judgment that shall prevail in matters of defining that Faith. Anyone who is accused can appeal to his authority in matters pertaining to the tribunals of the Church, and in all that concerns ecclesiastical jurisdiction, there is to be recourse to his judgment. All the churches are subject to his jurisdiction, and the prelates owe obedience and reverence to him. The fullness of his power is such that it invites all the other churches to partake of his solicitude. This same Roman Church has honored many of the churches by bestowing various privileges, and especially the Patriarchal churches. But its prerogative power is always reserved to itself except in general councils or on various other occasions. (Acts of the Council of Lyons [1274])

29. Moscow, the Third Rome

The issue of Roman primacy had been moved forward on the agenda by the transfer of the capital of the Roman Empire from Rome to Constantinople. If Rome's argument was based on the primacy of Peter among the Apostles, Constantinople's rested to some extent on the fact that after 330 C.E. it was the seat of the empire, the New Rome. Whatever the force or validity of that latter argument, it had an unforeseen sequel. When in 1453 Constantinople fell to the Muslim Turks, there was no formal transfer of power to a new Christian capital. But there were those who had no doubts where the mantle descended.

The Church of old Rome fell because of its heresy; the gates of the second Rome, Constantinople, were hewn down by the axes of the infidel Turks; but the Church of Moscow, the Church of the new Rome, shines brighter than the sun in the whole universe. You are the one universal sovereign of all the Christian people, you should hold the reins in awe of God; fear Him who has committed them to you. Two Romes are fallen, but the third stands fast; a fourth there cannot be. The Christian kingdom shall not be given to another. (Philotheus of Pskov) [Cited by ZERNOV 1945: 51]

7. The Church and the State/ The Church as the State

1. God and Caesar

The growth of the institutional Church from assemblies with presiding presbyters to more formal communities governed by episcopal "overseers" with ever-increasing administrative and doctrinal authority took place beyond the care or even the notice of the secular powers of the Roman Empire. Roman administrators were chiefly concerned with good order and took little note of the internal disputes of their sometimes notorious and sometimes obscure sectarians, except when they offended against that order.

The Jews were both notorious and, as we have seen, at times offensive to Roman order. The Christians, once distinguished from the Jews, began to enjoy a notoriety of their own. In the second and third centuries the Church and its leaders had to face an increasingly hostile secular authority; then, in the fourth century, somewhat to its own surprise, the Church found within its communion the emperor himself, first as an ally and then as a competitor.

The Christians, even the first generation of them, were not entirely oblivious of the various magistrates—municipal, provincial, and imperial—who ruled them. Jesus himself had been posed the question of political authority. In the highly charged political atmosphere of first-century Palestine the wonder is not that he should have been confronted with the issue of Roman-Jewish relations that exercised so many of his contemporaries but rather how infrequently it arises in the Gospels. The Synoptics record one such confrontation and Jesus' reply.

Then the Pharisees went away and agreed on a plan to trap him in his own words. Some of their followers were sent to him in company with men of Herod's party. They said, "Master, you are an honest man, we know; you teach in all honesty the way of life that God requires, truckling to no man, whoever he may be. Give us your ruling on this: are we or are we not permitted to pay taxes to the Roman Emperor?" Jesus was aware of their malicious intention and said to them, "Why are you trying to catch me out? Show me the money in which the tax is paid." They handed him a silver piece. Jesus asked, "Whose head is this and whose inscription?" "Caesar's," they replied. He said to them, "Then pay Caesar what is due to Caesar, and pay God what is due to God." This answer took them by surprise and they went away and left him alone. (Matthew 22:15–22)

Outside of Palestine the distinction drawn by Jesus was not so urgent perhaps. Paul, at any rate, saw no snare when in his letter to the Romans he addressed the issue of secular authority in more general terms.

Every person must submit to the supreme authorities. There is no authority but by act of God, and the existing authorities are instituted by Him; consequently anyone who rebels against authority is resisting a divine institution, and those who so resist have themselves to thank for the punishment they will receive. For government, a terror to crime, has no terrors for good behavior. You wish to have no fear of the authorities? Then continue to do right and you will have their approval, for they are God's agents working for your good. But if you are doing wrong, then you will have cause to fear them; it is not for nothing that they hold the power of the sword, for they are God's agents of punishment, for retribution on the offender. That is why you are obliged to submit. It is an obligation imposed not merely by fear of retribution but by conscience. That is also why you pay taxes. The authorities are in God's service, and to these duties they devote their energies. (Paul, *To the Romans* 13:1–6)

Much the same sentiment is echoed by Peter in one of his letters.

Submit yourselves to every human institution for the sake of the Lord, whether to the sovereign as supreme, or to the governor as his deputy for the punishment of criminals and the commendation of those who do right. For it is the will of God that by your good conduct you should put ignorance and stupidity to silence. Live as free men; not however, as though your freedom were there to provide a screen from wrong-doing, but as slaves in God's service. Give due honor to everyone: love to the brotherhood, reverence to God, honor to the sovereign. (Peter, *First Letter* 2:13–17)

2. The Last Great Persecution

The power of the sovereign may not have appeared quite so innocuous to either Peter or Paul, both of whom perished, the tradition relates, in a recklessly offhanded persecution instigated by Nero against the Christians in Rome. Toward the end of the first century such episodic persecutions became better focused, and by the second they were systematic. Churches and property were confiscated, the clergy arrested, and ordinary Christians put to death for public refusal to sacrifice to the emperor. The last great outburst occurred in 303 C.E. under Emperor Diocletian and is graphically described by Eusebius in his Church History.

It was in the nineteenth year of the reign of Diocletian, in the month of Dystus, called March by the Romans, when the feast of the Savior's passion was near at hand, the imperial edicts were published everywhere commanding that the churches be leveled to the ground, the Scriptures be destroyed by fire, and that all holding places of honor be branded with infamy; and that household servants, if they persisted in their profession of Christianity, be deprived of their freedom.

Such was the original edict against us. But not long after other decrees were issued, commanding that all the leaders of the churches everywhere should be thrown into prison and afterward compelled by any means to offer sacrifice. (Eusebius, *Church History* 8.2)

That is what happened at Nicomedia at the beginning of the persecution. But not long after, as persons in the region called Melitene and others throughout Syria attempted to usurp the government, an imperial edict commanded that leaders of the churches everywhere be thrown into prison and chains. What was seen after this defies description. Large numbers were imprisoned everywhere, and all the prisons, which had been set up for murderers and grave robbers, were filled instead with bishops, presbyters and deacons, readers and exorcists, so that there was no longer any room in them for condemned criminals. And as other decrees followed the first, directing that those in prison, if they offered sacrifice, should be set free from prison, but that those who refused should be harassed and tortured, how could any one again number the great host of martyrs in every province (of the Empire), and especially those in Africa and Mauritania and Thebais and Egypt? (Ibid. 8.6)

3. An Edict of Toleration,
311 C.E.

The Emperor Caesar Galerius Valerius, Maximianus, Invictus Augustus, Pontifex Maximus, Germanicus Maximus, Egyptiacus Maximus . . . ; (and) the Emperor Caesar Flavius Valerius, Constantinus Pius Felix Invictus Augustus, Pontifex Maximus . . . ; and the Emperor Caesar Val-

erius Licinianus Licinius Pius Felix Invictus Augustus Pontifex Maximus
. . . to the people of their several provinces, greeting.

Among the other steps that we are taking for the advantage and
benefit of the nation, we have desired hitherto that every deficiency
should be made good, in accordance with the established law and public
order of Rome; and we made provision for this—that the Christians who
had abandoned the convictions of their forefathers should return to
sound ideas. For through some perverse reasoning such arrogance and
folly had seized and possessed them that they refused to follow the path
trodden by earlier generations (and perhaps blazed long ago by their
own ancestors), and made their own laws to suit their own ideas and
individual tastes and observed these, and held various meetings at various
places.

Consequently, when we issued an order to the effect that they were
to go back to the practices established by the ancients, many of them
found themselves in great danger, and many were proceeded against and
punished with death in many forms. Many of them indeed persisted in the
same folly, and we saw that they were neither paying to the gods in
heaven the worship that is their due nor giving any honor to the god of
the Christians. So in view of our benevolence and the established custom
by which we invariably grant pardon to all men, we have thought proper
in this matter also to extend our clemency most gladly, so that the Christians may again exist and rebuild the houses in which they used to meet,
on condition that they do nothing contrary to public order. (Eusebius,
Church History 8.17)

*Two years later the co-emperors Constantine and Licinius—Galerius had died
shortly after the original edict—issued this instruction from Milan.*

When I, Constantine Augustus, and I, Licinius Augustus, had happily met together at Milan, and considered everything that concerns the
welfare and security of the state, we thought that, among other things
which seemed likely to be of general profit to men, we ought first to order
the conditions of the reverence paid to the Deity by granting to the
Christians and to all others full permission to follow whatever form of
worship each of them chooses. In that way whatever Deity there is in
heaven may be benevolent and propitious to us and to all subject to our
authority. Therefore we deemed it right, with the benefit of sound counsel and right reason, to lay down this law, that we in no way deny the legal
right to any man devoted either to the observance or to that worship
which he personally feels best suited to himself, to the end that the

Supreme Deity, whose worship we freely follow, may continue to grant us His accustomed favor and goodwill. . . .

Further, as regards the Christians, we have thought fit to ordain this as well, that if anyone has bought, either from our exchequer or from others, the places in which they were formerly accustomed to congregate . . . that the same be restored to the Christians, without delay or dispute, and without payment or the demand for such. Those who have obtained such places as gifts should likewise restore them to the said Christians without delay. (Lactantius, *On the Death of the Persecutors* 48)

The Christian Church was at last free to pursue its own course—and to discover that it had a new and highly complex relationship with that "Caesar" so effortlessly separated by Jesus three centuries before.

4. The Conversion of Constantine,

312 C.E.

Whether those decrees of toleration were motivated by liberal piety, by simple pragmatism, or by an uncanny reading of the future, and however welcome they were to the Christians, they could scarcely have foretold the course taken by one of those emperors who issued the instruction at Milan only the year before.

The anniversary of Maxentius' accession, the twenty-seventh of October, was near, and his (own first) five years of rule were drawing to a close. Constantine [who was camped opposite Maxentius' forces at the Milvian Bridge near Rome] was directed in a dream to mark the heavenly sign of God on the shields of his soldiers and then to begin the battle. He did as he was ordered, and with the cross-shaped letter X, with its top bent over, he marked Christ on the shields. (Lactantius, *On the Deaths of the Persecutors* 44.3–6)

Accordingly, he [Constantine] prayed to his father's god in heaven, beseeching him and imploring him to tell him who he was and to stretch out his right hand to help him in his present difficulties (with Maxentius). And while he was praying thus fervently, a truly incredible sign appeared to him from heaven, the account of which might have been difficult to believe had it been related by any other person. But since the victorious emperor himself long afterwards described it to the writer of this account, when he was honored with his acquaintance and company, and confirmed his statement with an oath, who could hesitate in accepting the story as true, especially since the testimony that followed has established its truth?

He [Constantine] said that about noon, when the day was already beginning to wane, he saw with his own eyes the victory signal of a cross of light in the heavens, above the sun, and the legend, "Conquer by this," attached to it. At this sight he himself was struck with amazement, and his whole army as well, which was accompanying him on expedition and witnessed the miracle.

He said, further, that he had his own doubts about the meaning of this portent. And while he was pondering and thinking about its meaning, night overtook him; then the Christ of God appeared to him in his sleep and commanded him to make a likeness of the sign which he had seen in the heavens, and to use it as a protection in all engagements with his enemies. (Eusebius, *Life of Constantine* 1.28–29)

5. Christianity as the State Church of the Roman Empire

The results of Constantine's conversion to the Christian faith were quick in coming: benefits and exemptions for the clergy began to be written into Roman law (see below), new churches were endowed out of state funds, and in Palestine in particular Constantine interested himself in the monumental enshrinement of the places associated with the life and death of Jesus. It was Constantine who convened the first ecumenical council of the bishops of the Great Church at Nicea in 325 C.E., and he also presided over its deliberations.

These were only beginnings. Later in that same century other emperors intervened even more directly in the affairs of the Church. The following is an imperial edict, dated 27 February 380 and issued in the names of the co-emperors Gratian and Valentinian II in the West and Theodosius in the East. It undertakes to define, in the formal context of Roman law, the official teaching of the Catholic Church and, in effect, to constitute it the imperial church of the Roman Empire.

It is our will that all the peoples whom the government of our Clemency rules shall follow the religion which a pious belief from Peter to the present declares that the holy Peter delivered to the Romans, and which it is evident that the pontiff Damasus (bishop of Rome) and Peter, bishop of Alexandria, a man of Apostolic sanctity, follow; that is, according to the Apostolic discipline and evangelical teaching we believe in the deity of the Father and the Son and the Holy Spirit of equal majesty, in a Holy Trinity. *Those who follow this law we command shall be comprised under the name of Catholic Christians*; but others, indeed, we require, since they are insane and raving, to bear the infamy of heretical teaching; their gatherings shall not receive the name of churches; they are to be smitten first

with the divine punishment, and after with the vengeance of our indignation, which has the divine approval. (Theodosian Code 16.1.2)

*On the occasion of another ecumenical council, held in the imperial capital of
Constantinople in 381 C.E., the assembled bishops made a final report to Emperor
Theodosius that reveals in its unstated but obvious premises the importance and
prestige of the Roman emperor in the affairs of what had become the state church.*

We begin our letter to your Piety with thanks to God, who has
established the empire of your Piety for the common peace of the
churches and for the support of the True Faith. And after rendering due
thanks to God, as is our duty, we lay before your Piety the things which
have been done in the Holy Synod.

When, then, we had assembled in Constantinople, in accordance
with the letter from your Piety, we first of all renewed our unity of heart
with each other, and then we pronounced some concise definitions, rati-
fying the faith of the Fathers at Nicea and anathematizing the heresies
which have sprung up contrary to that faith. Besides this we also framed
certain canons for the better ordering of the churches, all of which we
have appended to this letter. We therefore beseech your Piety that the
decree of the synod may be ratified, to the end that, as you have honored
the Church by your letter of convocation, so you should set your seal to
the conclusion of what has been decreed. (Council of Constantinople,
Address to Theodosius)

6. The Roman State and the Catholic Church in the Fourth Century

*The course of imperial favor, and of a hardening of attitudes toward other forms of
religion, can be clearly charted in the series of enactments dealing with the Christian
Church that began to appear in Roman law in the fourth century. These start with
a modest decree concerning what was still in 321 C.E. called the "Day of the Sun."*

3 July 321 C.E.: Just as it appears to Us most unseemly that the Day
of the Sun which is celebrated on account of its own veneration should
be occupied with legal altercations and with noxious controversies of the
litigation of contending parties, so it is pleasant and fitting that those acts
which are especially desired shall be accomplished on that day. Therefore
all men have the right to emancipate and to manumit on this festive day,
and the legal formalities thereof are not forbidden. Given on 3 July at
Cagliari in the second consulate of Crispus and Constantine Caesars.
(Theodosian Code 16.2.8)

The Church was also given corporate status, with the obviously beneficial effect that it could thereafter inherit.

3 July 321 C.E.: Every person shall have the liberty to leave at his death any property that he wishes to the most holy and venerable council of the Catholic Church. Wills (to that effect) shall not become void. There is nothing which is more due to men than that the expression of their last will, after which they can no longer will anything, shall be free, and the power of choice, which does not return again, shall be unhampered. (Ibid. 16.2.4)

Paganism was repressed in a number of imperial decrees.

341 C.E.: Superstition shall cease; the madness of sacrifices shall be abolished. For if any man in violation of the law of the sainted Emperor, Our father, and in violation of the command of our clemency, should dare to perform sacrifices, he shall suffer the infliction of a suitable punishment and the effect of an immediate sentence. (Ibid. 16.10.2)

8 November 392 C.E.: Hereafter no one of whatever race or dignity, whether placed in office or discharged therefrom with honor, powerful by birth or humble in condition or fortune, shall in any place or in any city sacrifice an innocent victim to a senseless image, venerate with fire the household deity by a more private offering, and burn lights, place incense or hang up garlands.

If anyone undertakes by way of sacrifice to slay a victim, or to consult the smoking entrails, let him be guilty of lese majesty, receive the appropriate sentence, having been accused by a lawful indictment. . . . If anyone, by placing incense, venerates either images made by mortal labor, or those which are enduring, or if anyone in ridiculous fashion forthwith venerates what he has represented, either by a tree encircled by garlands, or an altar of cut turfs . . . let him be guilty of sacrilege and punished by loss of house or property in which he worshiped according to the heathen superstition. For all places which shall smoke of incense, if they shall be proved to belong to those who burn incense, shall be confiscated. (Ibid. 16.10.12)

399 C.E.: Whatever privileges were conceded by the ancient laws to the priests, ministers, prefects, hierophants of sacred things, or by whatever name they may be designated, are abolished henceforth, and let them not think that they are protected by a granted privilege when their religious confession is known to have been condemned by the law. (Ibid. 16.10.14)

399 C.E.: If there are temples in the fields [that is, outside the cities], let them be destroyed without crowd and tumult. For when these have been thrown down and carried away, the support of superstition will be consumed. (Ibid. 16.10.16)

There was some concern, however, for the magnificent urban temples that by then constituted monuments to local pride or the historical landmarks of an already vanished antiquity.

399 C.E.: We prohibit (pagan) sacrifices, and yet we wish that the ornaments of public works be preserved. And to prevent those who over-throw them from flattering themselves that they do it with some author-ity, if they allege that they possess some rescript or cite some law, let these documents be taken from their hands and referred to Our knowl-edge. (Ibid. 16.10.15)

As for the pagans themselves:

416 C.E.: Those who are polluted by the error or crime of pagan rites are not to be admitted to the army or to receive the distinction and honor of administrator or judge. (Ibid. 16.10.21)

And finally:

423 C.E.: Although the pagans that remain ought to be subjected to capital punishment if at any time they are detected in the abominable sacrifices to demons, let exile and confiscation of goods be their punish-ment. (Ibid. 16.10.23)

Christian clerics, on the other hand, were granted generous privileges and ex-emptions.

319 C.E.: Those who in divine worship perform the services or reli-gion, that is, those who are called clergy, are altogether exempt from public obligations, so that they may not be called away from their sacred duty by the sacrilegious malice of certain persons. (Ibid. 16.2.2)

Such exemptions did not apply to the heretics and schismatics who might lay claim to being Christians.

326 C.E.: Privileges which have been bestowed in consideration of religion ought to be of advantage only to those who observe the Catholic law. It is our will that the heathen and schismatics be not only without privileges but bound by, and subject to, various political burdens. (Ibid. 16.5.1)

26 May 353 C.E.: In order that organizations in the service of the churches may be filled with a great multitude of people, tax exemption

shall be granted to clerics and their acolytes, and they shall be protected from the exaction of compulsory public services of a menial nature. They shall by no means be subject to the tax payments of tradesmen, since it is manifest that the profits which they collect from stalls and workshops will benefit the poor. We decree also that their men who engage in trade shall be exempt from all tax payments. Likewise, the exaction of services for the maintenance of the supplementary post wagons shall cease. This indulgence We grant to their wives, children and servants, to males and females equally, for We command that they also shall continue exempt from tax assessments. (Ibid. 16.2.10)

They were likewise removed in many instances from the jurisdiction of Roman law.

7 October 355 C.E.: By a law of Our Clemency We prohibit bishops from being accused in the courts, lest there should be an unrestrained opportunity for fanatical spirits to accuse them, while the accusers assume they will obtain impunity by the kindness of the bishops. Therefore, if any person should lodge any complaint, such complaint must unquestionably be examined before other bishops, in order that an opportune and suitable hearing may be arranged for the investigation of all pertinent matters. (Ibid. 16.2.12)

Finally, the Roman state began to surrender some of its own authority to the chief executives of the Christian Church. The empire's effective control of its own provincial cities was in notable decline by the sixth century, and the once prosperous urban aristocracies appeared near collapse. The only real government left in those cities was the Church's, and this law of 530 C.E. officially confirms that the Christian bishop was in effect the chief magistrate in many cities.

With respect to the yearly affairs of cities, whether they concern the ordinary revenues of the city, either from funds derived from the property of the city, or from legacies and private gifts, or given or received from other sources, whether for public works, or for provisions, or for aqueducts, or the maintenance of baths or ports, or the construction of walls or towers, or the repairing of bridges and roads, or for trials in which the city may be engaged in reference to public or private interests, we decree as follows: The very pious bishop and three men of good reputation, in every respect the first men of the city, shall meet and each year not only examine the work done, but take care that those who conduct them or have been conducting them, shall manage them with exactness, shall render their accounts, and show by the production of public records that they have duly performed their engagements in the administration of the sums appropriated for provisions, or baths, or for the expenses involved in the maintenance of roads, aqueducts, or any other work. (Code of Justinian 1.4.26)

The "overseer" had become in fact an overseer!

7. The Roman State and the Jews

The newly Christianized empire also paid new attention to Jews.

18 October 315 C.E.: It is our will that the Jews and their elders and patriarchs shall be informed that if, after the issuance of this law, any of them should dare to attempt to assail with stones or with any other kind of madness—a thing which We have learned is now being done—any person who has fled their wild animal sect and has resorted to the worship of God, such assailant shall be immediately delivered to the flames and burned, with all his accomplices. Moreover, if any person from the people should betake himself to their nefarious sect and should join their assemblies, he shall sustain with them deserved punishments. (Theodosian Code 16.8.1)

If the Jews were compelled to show restraint in what were for them dangerously changing circumstances, the new order of things did not mean an end to the longstanding privileges and exemptions accorded them by Roman law. Those now stood as a shield between the Jews and some of the more fanatic Christians.

November 330 C.E.: If any person with complete devotion should dedicate themselves to the synagogues of the Jews as patriarchs and priests and should live in the aforementioned sect and preside over the administration of their law, they shall continue to be exempt from all compulsory public services that are incumbent on persons, as well as those due to the municipalities. Likewise, such persons who are now perchance decurions [that is, members of municipal councils] shall not be assigned to any duties as official escorts, since such men shall not be compelled for any reason to depart from those places in which they are. Moreover, such persons who are not decurions shall enjoy perpetual exemption from the decurionate. (Ibid. 16.8.2)

29 September 393 C.E.: It is sufficiently established that the sect of the Jews is forbidden by no law. Hence We are gravely disturbed that their assemblies have been forbidden in certain places. Your Sublime Magnitude will, therefore, after receiving this order, restrain with proper severity the excesses of those people who, in the name of the Christian religion, presume to commit certain unlawful acts and attempt to destroy and despoil the synagogues. (Ibid. 16.8.9)

398 C.E.: Jews living in Rome, according to the common right, in those cases which do not pertain to their superstition, their court, laws and rights, must attend the (ordinary) courts of justice, and are to bring and defend legal actions according to the Roman laws; hereafter let them be under our laws. If, however, any, by an agreement similar to that for the appointment of arbitrators, decide that the litigation is to be before the Jews or their patriarchs by the consent of both parties and in business of a purely civil character, they are not forbidden by public law to choose their own courts of justice; and let the provincial judges execute their decisions as if the arbitrators had been assigned to them [that is, the Jews] by the decree of a judge. (Ibid. 2.1.10)

6 July 412 C.E.: If it should appear that any places are frequented by conventicles of Jews and are called by the name of synagogue, no one shall dare to violate or to occupy or to retain such places, since all persons must retain their own property in undisturbed right, without any claim of religion or worship.

Moreover, since indeed ancient custom and practice have preserved for the aforesaid Jewish people the consecrated day of the Sabbath, We also decree that it shall be forbidden that any man of the aforesaid faith be constrained by any summons on that day, under the pretext of public or private business, since all the remaining time appears sufficient to satisfy the public laws, and since it is most worthy of the moderation of Our time that the privileges granted should not be violated, although sufficient provision appears to have been made with reference to the aforesaid matter by general constitutions of earlier Emperors. (Ibid. 16.8.20)

8. The City of God and the City of Man

This comfortable political relationship between the Roman state and the Christian Church, though occasionally embarrassing to one side or the other, continued to flourish in the eastern provinces of the Roman Empire. But in the European and African provinces, the Latin-speaking part of the empire, the connection was an increasingly troubling one by the fifth century. The Roman state had come to its term, it was clear, under the attacks of barbarians, and the Church's close association with this other, perishing institution raised questions in the minds of some. Would the collapse of one signal the collapse of the other?

In 426 C.E. Augustine, the learned bishop of Hippo in what is today Algeria, took up the task of distinguishing, and so separating, the two—the dying earthly "City of Man" that was Rome and the celestial "City of God" where all Christians held their true citizenship, as the Letter to Diognetus *had already suggested.*

Augustine accomplished this through a dense meditation on the twin threads of Roman and biblical history. Though in one sense the true heavenly city is the afterlife, the community of saints in the bosom of God, at least one strand of human society, the Israelites, had joined and pursued together the twin aims of justice on earth and beatitude hereafter through the giving of God's Law. But at some point the two became dissociated, and the earthly city of the Israelite kingdom—and its successor states of the Greeks and then the Romans—were no more than worldly kingdoms, subject to the usual laws of sin and corruption, of prosperity followed by collapse and destruction. The heavenly city, still in its earthly passage toward eternity, is thus constrained to find its latter-day abode in human societies that do not share its goal and purposes.

The earthly city, which does not live by faith, seeks an earthly peace, and the end it proposes, in the well-ordered concord of civic obedience and rule, is the combination of men's wills to attain the things that are helpful to this life. The heavenly city, or rather that part of it that sojourns on earth and lives by faith, makes use of this peace only because it must, until the mortal condition which necessitates it shall pass away. Consequently, so long as it lives like a captive and a stranger in the earthly city, though it has already received the promise of redemption and the gift of the spirit as the earnest of it, it makes no scruple to obey the laws of the earthly city, whereby the things necessary for the maintenance of this mortal life are administered: and thus, as this life is common to both cities, so there is harmony between them in regard to what belongs to it. But as the earthly city has had some philosophers whose doctrine is condemned by the divine teaching, and who, being deceived either by their own conjectures or by demons, supposed that many gods must be invited to take an interest in human affairs and assigned to each a separate function and a separate department . . . and as the celestial city on the other hand, knew that one god only was to be worshiped, and to Him alone was due that service which the Greeks call *latreia* and which can be given only to a god, it has come to pass that the two cities could not have common laws of religion, and the heavenly city has been compelled in this manner to dissent, and to become obnoxious to those who think differently, and to stand the brunt of their anger and hatred and persecutions, except insofar as the minds of their enemies have been alarmed by the multitude of Christians and quelled by the manifest protection of God accorded to them.

This heavenly city, then, while it sojourns on earth, calls its citizens out of all nations and gathers together a society of pilgrims of all languages, not scrupling about diversities in the manners, laws and institutions whereby earthly peace is secured and maintained, so long only as no hindrance to the worship of the one supreme and true God is thus introduced. Even the heavenly city, therefore, while in its state of pilgrimage, avails itself of peace on earth, and so far as it can without injuring faith and godliness, desires and maintains a common agreement among men regarding the acquisition of the necessaries of life, and makes this earthly peace bear upon the peace of heaven; for this alone can be truly called and esteemed the peace of reasonable creatures, consisting as it does in the perfectly ordered and harmonious enjoyment of God and of one another in God. (Augustine, *City of God* 19.17) [AUGUSTINE 1948: 2:493–494]

9. "There Are Two Powers"

Augustine's philosophical approach to the dissociation of the Roman City of Man from the Christians' City of God looked to history. The bishop of Rome, who claimed a primacy of ecclesiastical jurisdiction, had to deal with a closer political reality: his relationship with another primate, the emperor in Constantinople. In 494 C.E. the imperial incumbent was Anastasius, and in that year Pope Gelasius wrote to him in an effort to set the emperor straight on the matter of authority.

I implore your Piety not to judge a sense of duty to the divine truth as a form of arrogance. I trust that it will not have to be said of a Roman Emperor that he resented the truth being told him. There are indeed, most august Emperor, two powers by which this world is chiefly ruled: the sacred authority of the Popes and the royal power. Of the two the priestly power is much the more important because it must give an account of the kings of men themselves before the divine tribunal. For you know, our most clement son, that though you have the first place in dignity over the human race, yet you must submit yourself faithfully to those who have the charge of divine things and look to them for the means of your salvation. You know that you should, when it concerns the reception and reverent administration of the sacraments, be obedient to the Church's authority rather than seek to control it. So too in such matters you ought to depend on the Church's judgment instead of seeking to bend it to your own will.

For if, in matters that deal with the administration of public discipline, the bishops of the Church, since they are well aware that the Empire has been conferred on you, are themselves obedient to your laws, so that in purely material matters they ought not to voice contrary opinions, with what willingness, I ask you, should you obey those to whom is assigned the administration of the divine mysteries? So just as there is great danger for the Popes in not saying what is necessary in matters of the divine honor, so there is great danger for those who are obstinate in resistance—which God forbid should happen—at the very time they should be obedient. And if the hearts of the faithful ought to be submitted to all priests in general, who rightly administer holy things, how much more ought assent be given to him who presides over the See which the Supreme Godhead Himself desired to be pre-eminent over all priests, and which the pious judgment of the whole Church has honored ever since? (Gelasius, *Letter to Anastasius*)

10. The Imperial View

The issue of the two spheres of authority, the spiritual and the temporal, argued with such economic finesse by Gelasius, could hardly be gainsaid by any Christian. But even granting the argument, with or without the corollary of Papal primacy, there were other considerations and other equally persuasive responsibilities. These are set forth by Emperor Justinian, who was not unsympathetic to Papal claims, in a letter not just to the bishop of Rome but to all his Roman subjects. The imperial decree, which had the force of law, was dated 17 April 535 C.E.. It begins with a respectful echo of Gelasius' own argument.

The greatest of the gifts which God in His heavenly mercy has given to men are the priesthood and the imperial authority. The former ministers to divine matters and the latter presides and watches over human affairs; both proceed from one and the same source, and together they are adornments of human life. And so nothing is so close to the hearts of emperors as the moral well-being of the priesthood, since it is the priests who have the task of perpetual prayer to God on behalf of the emperors themselves. For if the priesthood is entirely free from vice and filled with faith in God, and if the imperial authority sets in order the commonwealth committed to its charge in justice and efficiency, there will come about an ideal harmony providing whatever is useful for the human race. We therefore have the greatest anxiety for the true doctrines of God and for the moral well-being of the priesthood by which, if it is preserved, we believe that the greatest gifts will be given to us by God and we shall preserve undisturbed those things which we have and moreover gain the benefits which we presently do not possess. But all things are done rightly and efficiently if a beginning is made which is fitting and agreeable to God. We believe that this will come about if there is due care for the observance of the holy canons, which the justly praised Apostles and venerated eyewitnesses and servants of the word of God handed down and which the Fathers preserved and interpreted. (Justinian, *Novella* 6)

11. The Keys of the Kingdom

On 15 March 1081 Pope Gregory VII sent a latter to Hermann, bishop of Metz, on the subject of the Pope's power over the secular authority, in this instance Emperor Henry. The letter's title in the papal archives is "Against those who stupidly maintain that the Emperor cannot be excommunicated by the Roman Pontiff," and that appears to be an adequate summary of both its tone and its contents. None of the themes are new, perhaps, but they are marshaled with marvelous force, ease, and confidence.

It seems hardly necessary for us to comply with your request, namely, that we lend some assistance with a letter of ours and fortify you against the madness of those who keep repeating with perverse mouth that the Holy and Apostolic See has no authority to excommunicate Henry—a man who despises Christian law, destroys the churches and the Empire, sponsors and sustains heretics—and to absolve any from the oaths of fealty sworn to him. Indeed this enterprise seems to us hardly necessary because of the many and perfectly clear proofs that are available in Holy Scripture. . . . To say only a few words out of many, who does not know the words of our Lord and Savior Jesus Christ, who says in the Gospel, "You are Peter and upon this rock I will build my Church, and the gates of hell shall not prevail against it; and I will give you the keys of the kingdom of heaven; and whatsoever you shall bind upon earth will be bound also in heaven; and whatsoever you shall loose upon earth shall be loosed also in heaven"? Are kings excepted here? Are they not among the sheep that the Son of God committed to St. Peter? Who, I ask, can consider himself as exempted from this universal power of binding and loosing conferred on St. Peter, except perhaps some unfortunate who, because he is unwilling to bear the yoke of the Lord, subjects himself to the burden of the devil and refuses to be among Christ's sheep? For such a one it will be a small addition indeed to his wretched freedom if he shakes off from his proud neck the power divinely granted to St. Peter; the more anyone, out of pride, refuses to bear it, the more heavily it shall press upon him and he shall carry it to his damnation at the Judgment.

The Holy Fathers, supporting and serving the Holy Roman Church with great veneration, called her the Universal Mother in the Councils and by other such titles in their writings and acts. In doing this they supported and served this institution of the divine will, this pledge of a dispensation to the Church, this privilege handed on from the beginning to St. Peter, chief of the Apostles, and confirmed to him by a heavenly decree. And in assenting to the proofs of all this and by including them in the confirmation of the faith and in the doctrine of the holy religion, they also accepted her judgments; by their assent in this regard, they also agreed, with one spirit and one voice as it were, that all major affairs and important matters, as well as jurisdiction over all the churches, ought to be referred to her as mother and head; that from her there is no appeal; and that no one should or could retract or repudiate her judgments. . . .

But to return to the point, ought not an authority which has been established by laymen, perhaps even by those who had no knowledge of God, be subjected to an authority which the Providence of Almighty God established for His own honor and which He gave, in His mercy, to the world? For His Son, just as he is believed to be God and man, is also held to be the High Priest, the head of all priests, who sits at the right hand of the Father and is always interceding for us; and he despised a secular kingship, with which the children of this world are so puffed up, and entered freely into the priesthood of the Cross. Who is not aware that kings and princes are sprung from those who, unmindful of God, urged on in fact by the devil, the prince of the world, and by pride, plunder, treachery, murders and by almost every crime, have striven with blind greed, cupidity and intolerable presumption to hold dominion over their equals, that is to say, over men? . . . Who can doubt that the priests of Christ are to be accounted fathers and judges of kings and princes and of all the faithful? Is it not recognized as a form of wretched madness if a son tries to gain ascendancy over his father, or a pupil over his teacher; or to subdue to his own domination, by unlawful pressure, someone to whom, it is believed, has been entrusted not only the earthly but the heavenly power of binding and loosing?

The Emperor Constantine the Great, lord of all the kings and princes throughout almost the entire world, clearly knew this fact . . . when, sitting in the Council of Nicea as the inferior of all the bishops, he did not presume to pass any verdict or judgment upon them; but going so far as to call them gods, he decreed that they were not to be subject to his judgment, but rather that he himself would depend on their opinion.

And finally, on the intrinsic grace of the office:

Therefore all Christians who wish to reign with Christ should be warned not to try to rule with ambition for temporal power. . . . If those who fear God are forced with great misgivings to ascend the Apostolic throne, in which those properly ordained are made better by the merits of blessed Peter the Apostle, with how much more misgiving and appre-hension should the throne of the kingdom be approached, in which even the good and the humble—as is made plain in the cases of Saul and David—are made worse! For what we have said previously about the Apostolic See is contained in the following words found in the decrees of Symmachus the Pope—and we know it well enough from our own expe-rience—"He [that is, the blessed Peter] transmitted to his successors an everlasting gift of merits together with an inheritance of innocence"; and shortly after that he states, "Who may doubt that he is holy whom the loftiness of so great a dignity [as the bishopric of Rome] elevates? In this dignity, if virtues won by his own merits are not present, those suffice which are supplied by his predecessor. For he (St. Peter) either raises eminent men to his exalted office or else enlightens those who are so exalted." (Gregory VII, *To Hermann of Metz*)

12. The Two Swords

The debate went on between the bishop of Rome and the waxing and waning monarchs of Europe, its terms dictated by the personalities on each side and by the extent of the political power each wielded. One of its most explosive fusillades was heard in 1302, when Pope Boniface VIII promulgated his bull called, from its opening words in Latin, Unam sanctam. *It was provoked by his struggle with Philip the Fair of France, but its claims and its echoes far transcended that contest.*

The image of the two swords, which derives from a brief and enigmatic incident just before the arrest of Jesus in Gethsemane, had been invoked in an earlier debate between Church and State to distinguish and above all to separate into two distinct and autonomous spheres the temporal and spiritual powers contested between king and Pope. In Unam sanctam, *however, Pope Boniface VIII firmly grasps both swords in his own pontifical hands.*

We are taught by the words of the Gospel that in this Church and in its power there are two swords, a spiritual, to wit, and a temporal. For when the Apostles said, "Behold, here are two swords" (Luke 22:38)—that refers to the Church since it is the Apostles who are speaking—the Lord does not reply that it was too many, but enough. And he who denies that the temporal sword is in the power of Peter has wrongly understood the word of the Lord when he says (to Peter), "Put up again your sword in its place" (John 18:10–11). It follows then that both (swords) are in the power of the Church, namely, the spiritual and the material swords; the one indeed to be wielded for the Church, the other by the Church; the former by the priest, the latter by the hand of kings and knights, but at the will and sufferance of the priest. For it is necessary that one sword should be under another and that the temporal authority should be subjected to the spiritual. . . . But it is necessary that we affirm all the more clearly that the spiritual power exceeds any earthly power in dignity and nobility, just as spiritual things excel temporal ones. This we can clearly see with our own eyes from the giving of tithes, from the acts of benediction and sanctification, from the recognition of this power and from the exercise of government over these same things. For with the truth as witness, the spiritual power has also to establish the earthly power and judge it, if it is not good. So is verified the prophecy of the prophet Jeremiah concerning the Church and the power of the Church, "Behold, I have set you this day over the nations and over the kingdoms. . . ."

If, then, the earthly power errs, it should be judged by the spiritual power; if the lesser spiritual power errs, it should be judged by the higher competent spiritual power; but if the supreme spiritual power errs, it can be judged only by God, not by man; to which the Apostle (Paul) bears witness: "The spiritual man judges all things; and he himself is judged by no man" (1 Cor. 2:15). It is for this reason that this authority, although given to man and exercised by man, is not human, but rather divine, being given to Peter from God's mouth and founded for him and his successors on the rock by him whom he confessed, when the Lord said to the same Peter, "Whatsoever you shall bind. . . ." Whoever therefore resists this power thus ordained by God, resists the ordination of God. . . . *Consequently we declare, state, define and pronounce that it is altogether necessary to salvation for every human creature to be subject to the Roman Pontiff.* (Boniface VIII, *Unam sanctam*)

13. The Great Schism

Rome's claims to primacy early prevailed over all the other bishoprics in the Latin-speaking European and African provinces of Church and empire. Its Petrine claim, its prestige as an imperial seat, and its lack of serious competition for authority in what were once prosperous Roman provinces but were rapidly becoming Gothic, German and Frankish principalities—all these advantages gave a powerful pre-eminence to the bishop who held the See of Rome and was called "the Pope." But the eastern provinces of that same empire suffered no similar decline. They had, moreover, episcopal sees of great antiquity and prestige. Alexandria and Antioch had long been great cities in their own right, and after Constantine their company was joined by Constantinople, whose rise through the episcopal hierarchy we have already seen. From the beginning, Rome had taken ill to what it saw as episcopal presumption and had protested it, though to no great avail.

The papally inspired formulas of the ecumenical council of Chalcedon in 451 drove a fatal doctrinal wedge between Constantinople, which accepted the formulas, and its eastern sister sees, which did not. The case was rendered moot, perhaps, when in the 630s Muslim armies swept over the provinces of Syria and Egypt and detached them from at least the immediate jurisdiction of Constantinople. Rome and Constantinople were left to pursue their rivalry alone, and they soon found a new venue: the recently converted barbarian tribes in the Balkans, particularly the Bulgarians, whom both great sees struggled to wrestle into their fold.

As time passed, the theological issues between the Greek East and the Latin West multiplied. But in fact, only two mattered, one theoretical and one practical: whether the Roman see had a de jure absolute primacy within the Church; and where, de facto, the jurisdictional line between them was to be drawn. They broke and restored relations a number of times. The first great rupture took place in 866, when Patriarch Photius of Constantinople wrote an encyclical letter to his fellow prelates of the East.

. . . Now the barbarian tribe of the Bulgarians, who were hostile and inimical to Christ, has been converted to a surprising degree of meekness and knowledge of God. Beyond all expectation they have in a body embraced the faith of Christ, departing from the worship of devils and of their ancestral gods, and rejecting the error of pagan superstition.

But what a wicked and malignant design, what an ungodly state of affairs! The previous report of good news has been turned into dejection, delight and joy have been changed into sadness and tears. That people had not embraced the true religion of Christians for even two years, when certain impious and ominous men, or whatever name a Christian might call them, emerged from the darkness, darkness I say because they came from the West. . . . They have villainously devised to lead them away from the true and pure doctrine and from an unblemished Christian faith and in this way destroy them.

The first unlawful practice they have set up is fasting on Saturday. Such slight regard for the traditional teaching usually leads to the complete abandonment of the entire doctrine. They separated the first week of Lent from the rest and allowed them [that is, the Bulgarians] milk, cheese and other gluttonous practices during this time. From here they made the road of transgressions wider and wider and removed the people more and more from the straight and royal road. They taught them to despise the priest living in lawful matrimony, and by rejecting matrimony spread the seed of Manicheism, while they themselves practiced adultery. They did not shrink from reconfirming those who had been anointed by priests with the chrism, and presenting themselves as bishops, they declared the confirmation administered by priests as useless and invalid. . . .

They have not only introduced the committing of such outrages, but now the crown of all evils is sprung up. Besides these offenses that have already been mentioned, they have attempted to adulterate the sacred and holy creed, which had been approved by all the ecumenical synods and has invincible strength, with spurious arguments, interpolated words, and rash exaggerations. They are preaching a novel doctrine: that the Holy Spirit proceeds not from the Father alone, but from the Son as well. . . .

These new forerunners of apostasy, these servants of the anti-Christ, who have deserved death a thousand times, . . . these deceivers and enemies of God, we have by the resolution of the Holy Synod sentenced, or rather declared, that by previous resolutions of synods and by Apostolic laws, they are already condemned, and are made manifest to all. People are so constituted by nature that they are more restrained by present and visible punishments than by previously afflicted ones. Thus because these men persist in their manifold errors, we consider them banished by public proclamation from the company of Christians. (Photius, *Encyclical Letter*)

The response was quick. In the following year Pope Nicholas I wrote a letter to the bishops of the Western empire in which he cast the dispute into a far broader context.

Assuredly among the difficulties which cause us great concern are those, especially disturbing to us, which the Greek emperors Michael and Basil and their subjects inflict on us, and truly on the whole West. Inflamed with hate and envy against us, as we will specify later, they attempt to accuse us of heresy. With hatred indeed, for we not only disapproved but even condemned by deposition and anathematization the advancement attained by Photius, a neophyte, usurper and adulterer of the Church of Constantinople. The ejection from this church of Ignatius [the deposed patriarch of Constantinople], our brother and co-minister, perpetrated by his own subjects and the imperial power, did not receive our approval. And with envy because they learned that Michael, king of the Bulgarians, and his people received the faith of Christ and now desired St. Peter's See to provide teachers and instructors for them.

Instead they wish eagerly to lead the Bulgarians from obedience to the blessed Peter and to subject them shrewdly to their own authority under the pretext of the Christian religion. They preach such things about the Roman Church, which is without spot or wrinkle or anything of the kind, that those ignorant of the faith who hear these things avoid us, shy away, and almost desert us as criminals spotted with the filth of various heresies. . . .

They strive particularly to find fault with our church and generally with every church that speaks Latin, because we fast on Saturdays and profess that the Holy Spirit proceeds from the Father and the Son, whereas they confess that He proceeds merely from the Father. Besides this, they claim that we detest marriage, since we do not allow priests to marry. They blame us because we prohibit priests from anointing the foreheads of the baptized with chrism, which chrism they falsely accuse us of making from fresh water.

They try to blame us because we do not fast, according to our custom, from meat during the eight weeks before Easter, and from cheese and eggs during the seven weeks before the Pasch. They also lie, as their other writings show, when they say that we bless and offer a lamb on the altar, after the Jewish custom, together with the Lord's Body on the feast of Passover. They are certainly pleased with fault-finding! They complain that our priests do not refuse to shave their beards and that we ordain a deacon not yet raised to the priesthood to the episcopacy. They complain even though they appointed as their patriarch a layman, hastily become a monk and tonsured, and then, as they realized, advance him at a leap, without any fear and through the imperial power and favor, directly to the episcopacy. Yet what is more insulting is that they tried to demand a testimony of faith from our messengers, if they wished to be received by them, something which is against every rule and custom. In it [that is, in the required profession of faith] these doctrines of ours and those holding them are anathematized. They even impudently demanded a canonical letter from them, to give to the one they call their "Ecumenical Patriarch." . . .

With what great malice and foolishness those aforementioned Greek leaders and their henchmen are armed against us, because we did not consent to their evil ravings, is clearly revealed. The charges with which they try to stain us are either false or against what has been guarded in the Roman Church, indeed in the whole West, from the earliest times without any contradiction. When great doctors of the Church began to emerge among them, none of them was critical of those practices. Only those among them [that is, the Greeks] who burned not with a just zeal but driven by an evil zeal seek to tear to pieces the traditions of the Church. (Nicholas, *Encyclical Letter*)

A far more grievous schism—one that has never been truly healed—occurred between the Eastern and Western Churches in 1054, when Michael Cerularius was Patriarch and Leo IX Pope. The latter sent a Papal envoy to Constantinople to effect a political alliance between himself and the then emperor, Constantine IX. The envoy, Cardinal Humbert of Silvia Candia, immediately ran afoul of the Patriarch, who opposed the alliance. Humbert himself describes the sequel.

While Michael Cerularius avoided meeting and holding discussions with the (Papal) envoys, and persevered in his folly, those same envoys, defeated by his obstinacy, entered the Church of Hagia Sophia on the Sabbath, July 16, and at about the third hour [that is, about 9 A.M.], when the clergy is customarily preparing for the liturgy, placed the text of an excommunication upon the High Altar under the eyes of the attendant clergy and people. Quickly departing from that place, they also shook the dust from their feet to witness to them, crying out the phrase of the Gospel: May God see and judge.

So the deed was done. This is in part the bill of particulars on the excommunication.

The Holy Roman, First and Apostolic See, to which as the head belongs the special care of all the churches, for the sake of peace and profit of the Church has deigned to make us its messengers to this city (of Constantinople), so that, as our written instructions direct, we might come over and see whether in fact the outcry continues which continuously rises from that city to the Roman See's ears. . . . In what pertains to the pillars of empire and its honored wise citizens, the city is most Christian and orthodox. As to Michael, however, miscalled the Patriarch, and the supporters of his folly, they daily sow abundant tares of heresy in its midst. Whereas like Simoniacs they sell God's gifts and like Valesians they castrate their serfs and not only promote them into the clergy and even to the episcopate; like Arians they rebaptize those baptized, and especially Latins, in the name of the Holy Trinity; like Donatists they declare that, except for the Greek Church, the Church of Christ and true communion and baptism have vanished from the whole world; like the Nicolaites they allow and maintain carnal marriage for ministers of the sacred altar [that is, priests]; like the Severians they call the law of Moses accursed; like the enemies of the Holy Spirit or enemies of God they remove from the Creed the procession of the Holy Spirit from the Son; like the Manicheans, among other things they declare anything fermented alive; like the Nazarenes they hold to Jewish norms of ritual purity to such an extent that they forbid infants who die before the eighth day from their birth [when a Jewish infant would normally be circumcised] to be baptized and forbid women in menstruation or endangered in childbirth to take communion, or, if they are pagans, to be baptized; and being people who cultivate the hair of the head and beard, they do not receive in communion those who cut their hair and shave their beards in accordance with the teachings of the Roman Church.

This Michael, though he had been admonished by the letter of our lord Pope Leo for these errors and many other acts, has contemptuously refused to come to his senses. . . . We thus subscribe to the anathema which our most reverend Pope pronounced alike on Michael Cerularius and his followers, unless they regained their senses, as follows:

"Let Michael the neophyte, miscalled Patriarch, who put on the garb of the monk out of fear alone, and who is now also defamed for most wicked crimes, and with him Leo the archdeacon, called bishop of Ochrida . . . and all their followers in the aforementioned errors and audacities, be *Anathema Maranatha* (1 Cor. 16:22) . . . with all heretics, indeed, with the devil and his angels, unless perchance they recover their sense. Amen. Amen. Amen." (Humbert of Silvia Candia, *Memorandum*)

14. The Caliphate

Islam had no caesar, no ruler inherited from an earlier and different political tradition, as Christianity had. It had no law but its own and no ruler but a Muslim one, called in the years following the death of Muhammad in 632 C.E., the Caliph. The word first appears in the Quran, in a passage already cited in Chapter 1 in connection with the fall of the angels.

Remember, when the Lord said to the angels: "I have to place a deputy on the earth." They said: "Will you place one there who would create disorder and shed blood, while we intone Your litanies and sanctify Your name?" And God said: "I know what you do not know." (Quran 2:30)

This dialogue between God and the angels refers to God's creation of Adam. But the Arabic word used in 2:30 and here translated as "deputy" or "viceroy" is khalifa—*in English, "Caliph"—the same word employed by the early Muslims to designate Muhammad's successor as the head of the Islamic community. The same word appears again in the Quran, in connection with the king and prophet David, and there presents an even more apposite context for the later Islamic office.*

And We said to him: O David, We have made you a trustee (*khalifa*) on the earth, so judge between men equitably and do not follow your lust lest it should lead you astray from the way of God. (Quran 38:26)

There was no question of another prophet after Muhammad. Neither in his Life *nor in the other traditions attributed to him is there anything to suggest that Muhammad appointed a member of the community as his political "viceroy." But a "successor" or Caliph there was, and not without controversy—not about the office but about who should hold it. The historian Tabari (d. 923 C.E.) gives an account of events in Medina immediately after the death of the Prophet.*

Hisham ibn Muhammad told me on the authority of Abu Mikhnaf, who said: Abdullah ibn Abd al-Rahman ibn Abi Umra, the Helper [that is, a Medinese convert], told me:

"When the Prophet of God, may God bless him and save him, died, the (Medinese) Helpers assembled on the porch of the Banu Saʿida and said, 'Let us confer this authority, after Muhammad, upon him be peace, on Saʿd ibn Ubayda.' Saʿd , who was ill, was brought to them, and when they assembled Saʿd said to his son or one of his nephews, 'I cannot, because of my sickness, speak so that all the people can hear my words. Therefore, hear what I say and then repeat it to them so that they may hear it.' Then he spoke and the man memorized his words and raised his voice so that the others could hear.

"He said, after praising God and lauding Him, 'O company of Helpers! You have precedence in religion and merit in Islam which no other Arab tribe has. Muhammad, upon him be peace, stayed for more than ten years (in Medina) amid his people, summoning them to worship the Merciful One and to abandon false gods and idols. But among his own people (in Mecca) only a few men believed in him, and they were not able to protect the Prophet of God or glorify his religion nor to defend themselves against the injustice which beset them. God therefore conferred merit on you and brought honor to you and singled you out for grace. . . . And when God caused him to die, he was content with you and delighted with you. Therefore keep this authority for yourselves alone, for it is yours against all others.'

"They all replied to him, 'Your judgment is sound and your words are true. We shall not depart from what you say and we shall confer this authority on you. You satisfy us and you will satisfy the right believer.' Then they discussed it among themselves and some of them said: 'What if the (Meccan) Emigrants of the Quraysh refuse and say, "We are the Emigrants and the first Companions of the Prophet of God, we are his clan and his friends. Why therefore do you dispute the succession of his authority with us?" ' Some of them said, 'If so, we should reply to them, "A commander from us and a commander from you (then). And we shall never be content with less than that." ' Sa'd ibn Ubayda, when he heard this, said, 'This is the beginning of weakness.'

"News of this reached Umar, and he went to the house of the Prophet, may God bless and save him. He sent to Abu Bakr, who was in the Prophet's house with Ali ibn Abi Talib, upon him be peace, preparing the body of the Prophet, may God bless and save him, for burial. He sent asking Abu Bakr to come to him, and Abu Bakr sent a message in reply saying that he was busy. Then Umar sent saying that something had happened which made his presence necessary, and he went to him and said, 'Have you not heard that the Helpers have gathered in the porch of the Banu Sa'ida? They wish to confer this authority on Sa'd ibn Ubayda, and the best they say is "a commander from among us and a commander from among the Quraysh." ' They made haste toward them, and they met Abu Ubayda ibn Jarrah. The three of them went on together and they met Asim ibn Adi and Uwaym ibn Sa'ida, who both said to them: 'Go back, for what you want will not happen.' They said, 'We will not go back,' and they came to the meeting.

"Umar ibn al-Khattab said: We came to the meeting, and I had prepared a speech which I wished to make to them. We reached them, and I was about to begin my speech when Abu Bakr said to me, 'Gently! Let me speak first and then afterwards say whatever you wish.' He spoke. Umar said, 'He said all I wanted to say and more.'

"Abdullah ibn Abd al-Rahman said: Abu Bakr began. He praised and lauded God and then he said, 'God sent Muhammad as a Prophet to His creatures and as a witness to His community that they might worship God and God alone. . . . It was a tremendous thing for the Arabs to abandon the religion of their fathers. God distinguished the first Emigrants of his people by allowing them to recognize the truth and believe in him and console him and suffer with him from the harsh persecution of his people when they gave them the lie and all were against them and reviled them. . . . They were the first in the land who worshiped God and who believed in God and the Prophet. They were his friends and his clan and the best entitled of all men to this authority after him. Only a wrongdoer would dispute this with them. And as for you, O company of Helpers, no one can deny your merit in the faith or your great precedence in Islam. . . . (But) we are the commanders and you the viziers. We shall not act contrary to your advice and we shall not decide things without you.' . . .

"Abu Bakr said, 'Here is Umar and here is Abu Ubayda. Swear allegiance to whichever of them you choose.' The two of them said, 'No, by God, we shall not accept this authority above you, for you are the worthiest of the Emigrants and the second of the two who were in the cave (Quran 19:40) and the deputy (*khalifa*) of the Prophet of God in prayer, and prayer is the noblest part of the religion of the Muslims. Who would then be fit to take precedence of you or to accept this authority above you? Stretch out your hand so that we may swear allegiance to you.'

"And when they went forward to swear allegiance to him [Abu Bakr], Bashir ibn Saʿd went ahead of them and swore allegiance to him . . . and when the (Medinese) tribe of Aws saw what Bashir ibn Saʿd had done . . . they came to him and swore allegiance to him. . . .''

Hisham said on the authority of Abu Mikhnaf: Abdullah ibn Abd al-Rahman said: People came from every side to swear allegiance to Abu Bakr. (Tabari, *Annals* 1.1837–1844) [LEWIS 1974: 1:3–5]

15. After Abu Bakr

Abu Bakr served as Caliph for two scant years (632–634 C.E.). Although his successor, Umar ibn al-Khattab, held the Caliphate longer (634–644 C.E.), the process of succession still remained uncertain, as illustrated by this tradition attributed to Umar himself.

It has been narrated on the authority of Abdullah ibn Umar who said: I was present when my father was (fatally) wounded (by an assassin). People praised him and said: May God give you a noble recompense! He said: I am hopeful as well as fearful. People said: Appoint someone as your successor. He said: Should I carry the burden of conducting your affairs in my death as well as my life? I wish I could acquit myself (before God) in a way that there is neither anything to my credit nor anything to my discredit. If I should appoint my successor, I would because someone better than I did [that is, Abu Bakr, who appointed Umar]. If I would leave you alone (without a successor), I would do so because one better than I, the Messenger of God, may peace be upon him, did so. Abdullah says: When he mentioned the Messenger of God, may peace be upon him, I realized that he would not appoint anyone as Caliph. (Muslim, *Sahih* 18.755)

But one small problem at least was solved.

I heard from Ahmad ibn Abd al-Samad al-Ansari, who heard from Umm Amr bint Husayn, the Kufan woman, on the authority of her father, who said: When Umar was appointed Caliph [in 634 C.E.], they said to him, "O Deputy of the Deputy of the Prophet of God!" And Umar, may God be pleased with him, said, "This is a thing that will grow longer. When another Caliph comes, they will say 'O Deputy of the Deputy of the Deputy of the Prophet of God.' You are the Faithful and I am your Commander." So he was called Commander of the Faithful. . . .

I heard from Ibn Humayd, who heard from Yahya ibn Wadih, who heard from Abu Hamza, on the authority of Jabir, who said: A man said to Umar ibn al-Khattab, "O Deputy of God!" Umar said, "May God turn you from such a thing!" (Tabari, *Annals* 1.2748) [LEWIS 1974: 1:17]

16. Caliph and Imam

Thus the Muslim community seemed to have taken its first successful steps toward establishing a non-Prophetic ruler, the "Caliph" or "Successor of the Prophet." If the Quran itself gave little or no guidance on this new office in Islam, there were soon circulating Prophetic traditions on the nature and qualifications for the office of Caliph, or the Imam, "he who stands before," as he is more frequently called in theoretical discussions. Ibn Khaldun explains the difference between the two terms.

The Caliphate substitutes for the Lawgiver [that is Muhammad] in as much as it serves, like him, to preserve the religion and to exercise political leadership of the world. The institution is called "the Caliphate" or "the Imamate." The person in charge is called "Caliph" or "Imam." . . .

The name "Imam" is derived from the comparison with the leader of prayer [also called an imam] since he is followed and taken as a model like the prayer-leader. Therefore the institution is called "the Great Imamate." The name "Caliph" is given to the leader because he "represents" the Prophet in Islam. One uses "Caliph" alone or "Caliph of the Messenger of God." There is some difference of opinion on the use of "Caliph of God." Some consider the expression permissible as derived from the general "caliphate" of all the descendants of Adam . . . [based on the Quranic verses cited above]. But in general it is not considered permissible to use the expression since the Quranic verses quoted has no (specific) reference to it.

Ibn Khaldun then reflects briefly on the circumstances under which the office arose.

The position of Imam is a necessary one. The consensus of the men around Muhammad and the men of the second generation shows that the Imamate is necessary according to the religious law. At the death of the Prophet the men around him proceeded to render the oath of allegiance to Abu Bakr and to entrust him with the supervision of their affairs. And so it was with all subsequent periods. In no period were the people left in a state of anarchy. This was so by general consensus, which proves that the position of Imam is a necessary one. (Ibn Khaldun, *Muqaddima* 3.24) [IBN KHALDUN 1967: 1:388–389]

17. Prophetic Traditions on the Caliphate

Consensus on the Caliphate was transmitted, among other ways, through traditions from the Prophet and his Companions. Many of them are frankly redolent of a day when there already was a Caliph—one, it appears, whose authority was being challenged.

Bukhari and Muslim, from Abu Hurayra: The Messenger of God, may God's blessings and peace be upon him, said: "Whoever obeys me obeys God, and whoever disobeys me disobeys God. Whoever obeys the Commander (of the Faithful) obeys me, and who disobeys him disobeys me. The Imam is simply a shield behind whom the fighting takes place, from which one seeks protection. So when he orders fear of God and is just, he shall receive his reward, but if he holds otherwise, it will bring guilt upon him."

Muslim, from Umm al-Husayn: The Messenger, may God bless him and peace be upon him, said: "Even if a mutilated slave is made your Commander, and he leads you in accord with the Book of God, hear him and obey." (Baghawi, *Mishkat al-Masabih*, 17.1.1)

In other traditions, however, the emphasis and the implications for political obedience are quite different.

Bukhari and Muslim from Ibn Abbas: The Messenger of God, may God's blessing and peace be upon him, said: "If anyone sees something hateful in his Commander, let him be patient, for no one separates from the collectivity by so much as a handspan without dying the death of paganism."

Muslim from Awf ibn Malik al-Ashjaʿi, from the Messenger of God, on whom be the blessing of God and peace: "Your best Imams are those you love, who love you, whom you bless and who bless you. The worst are those you hate, who hate you, whom you curse and who curse you."

We said: "Messenger of God, should we not depose them when that happens?" but he said, "No, not so long as they keep the ritual prayers with you; not so long as they keep the prayers. When anyone has a ruler placed over him who is seen doing something which is rebellion against God, he must disapprove of that rebellion, but never withdraw his hand from obedience." (Ibid.)

We cannot be certain exactly when those traditions were put into circulation, but we do know there were serious challenges to both the current Caliph and the office of the Caliphate itself in the wake of the conspiratorial murder of Uthman in 656 C.E. and the accession of the fourth Caliph, Ali ibn Abi Talib. Ali was an early convert to Islam. He was, moreover, a cousin of the Prophet, the husband of his daughter Fatima, and the father of two of the Prophet's favorite grandchildren, Hasan and Husayn. Whatever his advantages, Ali appeared to many to be ambivalent about punishing the assassins of Uthman, the scion of one of the great pre-Islamic houses of Mecca. His hesitation gave his enemies in various camps— Muhammad's wife Aisha and Uthman's relative Mu'awiya prominent among them—an opportunity to drive Ali first out of Medina and then into a kind of Caliphate-in-exile in Iraq, where he had to fight to hold his office. Ali was himself assassinated in 661 C.E. by a schismatic. Over the succeeding years there grew up a body of the "partisans of Ali" (shi'at Ali) who attempted to vindicate not only his claims to the office of Imam but also those of his descendants.

18. The Ruler, Chosen by the People or Designated by God?

With the rise of the Shi'ite movement—never quite politically powerful enough to seize the rulership in Islam but potent enough in its propaganda and ideology to threaten it—the rest of the "Sunni" community, so called because they supported "tradition [sunna] and the commonality," were forced to re-examine and defend their own positions on the nature of sovereignty in Islam. Here one of them, the essayist al-Jahiz (d. 886 C.E.), easily converts necessity into a virtue.

. . . If we were to be asked, which is better for the community, to choose its own leader or guide, or for the Prophet to have chosen him for us? Had the Prophet chosen him, that would of course have been preferable to the community's own choice, but since he did not, it is well for it that he left the choice in its own hands. . . . Had God laid down the procedure for the nomination of the Imam in a detailed formula with its own precise directions and clear signs, that would indeed have been a blessing, for we know that everything done by God is better. But since He did not make specific provision (for the office), it is preferable for us to

have been left in our present situation. How can anyone oblige or constrain God to establish an Imam according to a formula simply because
in your view such a solution would be more advantageous and less troublesome, and better calculated to avoid error and problems? (Jahiz, *The
Uthmanis* 278–279)

*This was the view of most historians, the Shi'ites of course excepted. At least one
Prophetic tradition took no chances and put the choice of a successor directly in the
Prophet's mouth.*

Aisha told that during his illness God's Messenger said to her: "Call
me Abu Bakr your father, and your brother, so that I may write a document, for I fear that someone may desire to succeed me and that one may
say 'It is I,' whereas God and the believers will have no one but Abu
Bakr." Muslim transmitted this tradition. (Baghawi, *Mishkat al-Masabih*
26.30.1)

And again, with even more extended foresight:

Jabir reported God's Messenger as saying, "Last night a good man
had a vision in which Abu Bakr seemed to be joined to God's Messenger,
Umar to Abu Bakr, and Uthman to Umar." Jabir said: When we got up
and left God's Messenger we said that the good man was God's Messenger
and that their being joined together meant that they were the rulers over
the matter with which God had sent His Prophet. (Ibid. 26.34.3)

We return to Jahiz.

There are three different ways of establishing an Imam. The first way
is as I have described [that is, following the overthrow of a usurper],
or, second, under the kind of circumstances in which the Muslims put
into power Uthman ibn Affan [Caliph, 644–656 C.E.], after Umar [Caliph,
634–644 C.E.] had designated (a council of) six person of comparable
worth and they in turn had elected one of their number. . . . A third
possibility is the situation that prevailed when the community made Abu
Bakr Caliph [632–634 C.E.]; the circumstances were different from those
of Uthman's election, since the Prophet had not appointed a council as
Umar did. . . . In Abu Bakr's case the community did not compare the
respective merits of the Emigrants or announce the reasons for the superiority of the person elected; they were, after all, Muslims who had
known each other intimately for twenty-three years . . . and so Abu
Bakr's merits were immediately obvious to them; on the Prophet's death
they had no need to form an opinion, since they already knew. (Jahiz, *The
Uthmanis* 270)

The developed Shi°ite view on this obviously crucial matter of the selection of the Imam or Caliph of the Muslim community is presented in the theological handbook called The Eleventh Chapter, *written by the Shi°ite scholar al-Hilli (d. 1326 C.E.), with a commentary by another later author of the same name. The thesis is set out in the section devoted generally to the Imamate. In the passage immediately preceding our selection, Hilli had demonstrated that the Imam had of necessity to be immune to sin.*

The Third Proposition: It is necessary that the Imam should be designated for the Imamate since immunity to sin is a matter of the heart which is discerned by no one save God Most High. Thus the designation must be made by one who knows that the Imam has the immunity to sin necessary for the office, or else some miracle must be worked through him to prove his truthfulness.

[Commentary:] This refers to the method of appointing the Imam. Agreement had been reached that in appointing the Imam the designation can be made by God and His Prophet, or by a previous Imam in an independent way [that is, without the consent of the people]. The disagreement concerns only whether or not the Imam's appointment can be effected in any way other than by designation. Our fellow Imamites (Shi°ites) deny that absolutely, and hold that there is no way except by designation. For, as we have explained, immunity to sin is a necessary condition of the Imamate, and immunity to sin is a hidden matter, and no one is informed of it except God. In such circumstances, then, no one knows in whom it might be found unless He who knows the unseen makes it known. And that occurs in two ways: first, by making it known to someone else immune to sin, such as the Prophet, and then this latter tells us of the Imam's immunity to sin, and of his appointment; and second, by the appearance of miracles worked through his [the Imam presumptive's] power to prove his truthfulness in claiming the Imamate.

The Sunnis, on the other hand, say that whenever the community acknowledges anyone as its chief, and is convinced of his ability for the Imamate, and his power increases in the regions of Islam, he becomes the Imam. . . . But the truth is contrary to this for two reasons: first, the Imamate is a "Caliphate" [or "succession"] from God and His Messenger and so it cannot be acquired except by the word of them both; and second, the establishment of the Imamate by acknowledging someone as chief and by the latter's claim to the office would result in conflict because of the probability that each faction would acknowledge a different Imam. (Hilli, *The Eleventh Chapter* 186–188)

CHAPTER 7

19. Ali, the First Imam

If, on the Shi͑ite view, the Imam must be "designated" rather than simply "acknowledged," that condition must have occurred in the case of the very first of them, Ali ibn Abi Talib. The Fifth Proposition of Hilli's work takes up that much-disputed question.

The Fifth Proposition: The Imam after the Messenger of God is Ali ibn Abi Talib: First, because of his designation, which has been handed down in a number of distinct lines of Prophetic traditions; and second, because he is the best of his generation, by the word of the Most High . . . ; and third, because it is necessary for the Imam to be immune from sin, and there is no one among those who claim the office who is so immune except Ali, as all agree; and fourth, because he was the most knowledgeable (about Islam), since the Companions consulted him about their problems . . . ; and fifth, because he is more ascetic than any one else, so that he divorced the world three times.

The first point is critical here, since the Shi͑ite proposition of the Prophet's designation of Ali was confronted with the undeniable historical reality that the Muslim community was in fact ruled by three other men—Abu Bakr, Umar, and Uthman—before its choice fell upon Ali. This is how Hilli's commentator deals with that difficulty.

[Commentary:] . . . There are differing opinions regarding the appointment of the Imam. Some claim that after the Messenger of God the Imam was Abbas ibn Abd al-Muttalib because he was his heir. And most Muslims affirm that he was Abu Bakr because the people chose him. And the Shi͑ites maintain that he was Ali ibn Abi Talib because of the designation which came down directly from God and His Messenger to him, and that is the truth. And the author [that is, Hilli] has proved Ali's right in several ways: first, that unbroken tradition of the very words of the Prophet which the Shi͑ites quote regarding the right of Ali, and from which certitude can be elicited, namely, "Greet him as the chief of the believers" and "You are the successor after me," and other words which prove what we intended, to wit, that he is the Imam. (Hilli, *The Eleventh Chapter* 191–192)

To view the Shi͑ite claims from the Sunni side of the Islamic community, we can turn to the popular theological manual by the Sunni scholar al-Nasafi (d. 1114 C.E.).

The objection may be raised that it is related of the Prophet, upon whom be God's blessing and peace, that he once said to Ali, with whom

may God be pleased: "You are to me the same as Aaron was to Moses—
on both of whom be blessings and peace—save that there will be no
prophet after me." Now as the deputyship of Aaron admitted no possibility of substitution, so (the Shiʿites claim) is the case here (between
Muhammad and Ali).

*The Sunni response is not to deny that the Prophet made the statement but to invoke
the circumstances under which it was pronounced.*

The reply is that the Prophet's honoring him was not in the way you
[that is, the Shiʿites] take it, for (it is common knowledge that) the
Prophet, upon whom be God's blessing and peace, appointed Ali as his
deputy over Medina while he went out on one of his raids, and as a result
the evilly-disposed said: "Look, the Prophet has turned his back upon
him and confined him to the house." This grieved Ali, so the Prophet said
to him: "You are to me the same as Aaron was to Moses." Another
indication (that their interpretation is false) is the fact that Aaron died
before Moses, so it would only be sound if he had said: "You are to me
the same as Joshua son of Nun," for he was the real successor to Moses.

*This was one of the contentions of the moderate Shiʿa who looked upon Ali as the
designated, and so the only legitimate successor to Muhammad. Others, however,
would have put Ali above or beside Muhammad in the ranks of the Messengers.*

One group of the Rafidites [that is, one of the radical Shiʿite sects]
teaches that the revelations (brought by Gabriel) were meant for Ali, with
whom may God be pleased, but that Gabriel, on whom be peace, made
a mistake. Another group of them teaches that Ali was associated with
Muhammad in the prophetic office. All these are disbelievers for they
disavow both the text of the Quran and the consensus of the community,
for God has said: "Muhammad is God's Messenger" (Quran 48:29). Some
of them teach that Ali was more learned than the Apostle of God and is
in the position (with regard to him) that al-Khidr held to Moses [that is,
the mysterious figure who serves Moses as mentor in Quran 18:66–83].
The answer to this is that saying of the Prophet which shows such knowledge as Ali had was from the teaching of the Prophet (who said): "I am
the city of learning and Ali is its gate."

Another indication (of the unsoundness of their teaching) is the fact
that Ali was a Saint but the Apostle of God was a Prophet, and a Prophet
ranks higher than a Saint. As for al-Khidr, on whom be peace, he had
direct knowledge (of things divine) for God said: ". . . whom We taught
knowledge such as We have" (Quran 18:66). He means there inspired

knowledge, but even so Moses was superior to him since he had a body of religious Law and a Book, and he who has a religious Law and a Book is superior. A case in point is that of David and Solomon, where David is superior.

Another group of them teaches that there never is a time when there is no Prophet on earth, and that this prophetic office came by inheritance to Ali, with whom may God be pleased, and his progeny, so that anyone who does not regard obedience to him (and his progeny) as an incumbent duty is in unbelief. The truly orthodox people [that is, the Sunnis] teach that there is no Prophet after our Prophet, for this is proved by God's words "and seal of the Prophets" (Quran 33:40). It is related on the authority of Abu Yusuf that the Prophet said: "If a pretender to prophecy comes forward laying claim to the prophetic office, should anyone demand from him proof (of his mission), he [the one who requested proof] would thereby show himself to be in unbelief, for he would have disavowed the text of Scripture." The same is true of anyone who has doubts about him, for one demands a proof in order to make clear what is true from what is false, but if anyone lays claim to the prophetic office after Muhammad, upon whom be blessing and peace, his claim cannot be other than false. (Nasafi, *The Sea of Discourse on Theology*)

[JEFFERY 1962: 445–446]

20. The Pool of Khum

A more detailed version of how the Shi'ites explained the events surrounding the designation of Ali as Imam is provided by al-Majlisi (d. 1700 C.E.). Although he comes late in the tradition, he reproduces a standard Shi'ite contextual exegesis of the Quranic passage in question.

When the ceremonies of the (farewell) pilgrimage were completed, the Prophet, attended by Ali and the Muslims, left Mecca for Medina. On reaching the Pool of Khum he halted, although that place had never before been a stopping place for caravans, because it had neither water nor pasturage. The reason for encampment in such a place (on this occasion) was that illustrious verses of the Quran came powerfully upon him, enjoining him to establish Ali as his successor. He had previously received communications to the same effect, but not expressly appointing the time for Ali's inauguration, which, therefore, he had deferred lest opposition be excited and some forsake the faith. This was the message from the Most High in Sura 5:67:

"O Messenger, publish what has been sent down to you from your Lord, for if you do not, then you have not delivered His message. God will protect you from men; surely God guides not unbelieving people."

Being thus peremptorily commanded to appoint Ali his successor, and threatened with penalty if he delayed when God had become his surety, the Prophet therefore halted in this unusual place, and the Muslims dismounted around him. As the day was very hot, he ordered them to take shelter under some thorn trees. Having ordered all the camel saddles to be piled up for a pulpit or rostrum, he commanded his herald to summon the people around him. When all the people were assembled he mounted the pulpit of saddles, and calling to him the Commander of the Believers [that is, Ali], he placed him on his right side. Muhammad now rendered thanksgiving to God, and then made an eloquent address to the people, in which he foretold his own death, and said: "I have been called to the gate of God, and the time is near when I shall depart to God, be concealed from you, and bid farewell to this vain world. I leave among you the Book of God, to which if you adhere, you will never go astray. And I leave with you the members of my family, who cannot be separated from the Book of God until both join me at the fountain of al-Kawthar."

He then demanded, "Am I not dearer to you than your own lives?" and was answered by the people in the affirmative. He then took the hands of Ali and raised them so high that the white (of his shirt) appeared and said, "Whoever receives me as his master (or ally), then to him Ali is the same. O Lord, befriend every friend of Ali, and be the enemy of all his enemies; help those who aid him and abandon all who desert him."

It was now nearly noon, and the hottest part of the day. The Prophet and the Muslims made the noon prayer, after which he went to his tent, beside which he ordered a tent pitched for the Commander of the Believers. When Ali was rested Muhammad commanded the Muslims to wait upon Ali, congratulate him on his accession to the Imamate, and salute him as the Commander. All this was done by both men and women, none appearing more joyful at the inauguration of Ali than did Umar. (Majlisi, *The Life of Hearts* 334)

21. "Catholic" and "Partisan" in the Muslim Community

The first part of the "creed" of Ibn Hanbal (d. 855 C.E.) concerns matters of doctrine and ritual; then the author turns his attention to a question reflected in the traditions and arguments just cited. By Ibn Hanbal's day, these had already rent the Muslim community with a schism more divisive than any doctrinal heresy: Who was the legitimate head of that community, the actual Caliph or an ideal Imam? The issue began, as we have noted, with a view of history: Who constituted the true leadership of the body of Muslims after the death of the Prophet? Ibn Hanbal undertakes to give the "catholic" (sunni), as opposed to the "partisan" (shi'i), view of that history.

The best of this community (of Muslims), after its Prophet, is Abu Bakr the Just, then Umar ibn al-Khattab, then Uthman ibn Affan [that is, the first three Caliphs]. We give the preference of these three (over Ali) just as the Companions of the Prophet gave preference; they did not differ about it. Then after these three come the five Electors chosen by Umar as he lay dying: Ali ibn abi Talib, Zubayr, Talha, Abd al-Rahman ibn Awf, and Sa'd ibn abi Waqqas. All of them were suited for the Caliphate, and each of them was an Imam [that is, a prayer-leader of the community]. On this we go according to the Prophetic tradition (transmitted) from Umar's son: "When the Messenger of God was living—God bless him and give him peace—and his Companions were still spared, we used to number first Abu Bakr, then Umar, then Uthman and then keep silent." (Ahmad ibn Hanbal, *Creed*) [WILLIAMS 1971: 30]

When it comes to an actual ruler, Ibn Hanbal strongly prefers the acceptance of validly constituted authority in the name of the unity of the community, no matter how personally unacceptable that ruler might be. To set at ease the conscience of the scrupulous believer, Ibn Hanbal assures him that religious obligations performed in the company or under the leadership of such rulers are valid and complete.

And hearing and obeying the Imams and the Commanders of the Faithful (is necessary)—that is, whoever receives the Caliphate, whether he is pious or profligate, whether the people agreed on him or were pleased with him, or whether he attacked them with the sword until he became Caliph and was called "Commander of the Faithful." Going on a holy war is equally efficacious with a pious or a dissolute commander down to the Day of Resurrection; one does not abandon him. Division of the spoils of war and applying the punishments prescribed by the Law belongs to the Imams: it is not for anyone to criticize them or contend with them. Handing over the alms money to them for distribution (is permissible) and efficacious: whoever pays them has fulfilled his obligation (to almsgiving) whether the Imam was pious or dissolute. The collective prayer led by the Imam and those he delegates is valid and complete, both prostrations, and whoever repeats them later is an innovator, abandoning "the tradition" and opposed to it. There is no virtue in his Friday prayer at all, if he does not believe in praying with the Imams, whoever they are, good or bad; the "tradition" is to pray two prostrations with them and consider the matter finished. On that let there be no doubts in your bosom.

Thus, in the eyes of Ibn Hanbal, who prized above all the unity of the Muslim community, secession from that community by rejecting its duly constituted leader is the most grievous sin of all.

Whoever secedes from the Imam of the Muslims—when the people have agreed on him and acknowledged his Caliphate for any reason, either satisfaction with him or conquest, for example, that rebel has broken the unity of the Muslims and opposed the tradition coming from God's Messenger, God's blessing and peace be upon him. If the seceder dies, he dies as ignorant carrion. It is not lawful for anyone to fight against the authority or secede from it, and whoever does so is an innovator, outside "the tradition" and "the way. (Ahmad ibn Hanbal, *Creed*)

[WILLIAMS 1971: 31–32]

22. A Juridical Portrait of the Sunni Caliph

Two centuries after Ibn Hanbal, the Sunnis' understanding of the Caliphate was essentially complete, and the lawyer Mawardi (d. 1058 C.E.) was able to lay out the duties of the office and the qualifications of its tenants with all the clarity typical of a closed issue. It was closed in another sense as well: Mawardi was writing at almost precisely the point when the office of Caliph had lost most of its real powers.

God, whose power be glorified, has instituted a chief of the community as a successor to Prophethood and to protect the community and assume the guidance of its affairs. Thus the Imamate is a principle on which stand the bases of the religious community and by which the general welfare is regulated, so that the common good is assured by it. Hence rules pertaining to the Imamate take precedence over any other rules of government. . . . The Imamate is placed on earth to succeed the Prophet in the duties of defending Religion and governing the World, and it is a religious obligation to give allegiance to that person who performs those duties. . . .

Thus the obligatory nature of the Imamate is established, and it is an obligation performed for all by a few, like fighting in a Holy War, or the study of the religious sciences, and if no one is exercising it, then there emerge two groups from the people: the first being those who should choose an Imam from the community, and the second those who are fitted to be the Imam, of whom one will be invested with the Imamate. As for those of the community who do not belong to either of those two categories, there is no crime or sin if they do not choose an Imam. As to those two categories of people, each of them must possess the necessary qualifications. Those relating to the electors are three:

1. Justice in all its characteristics.

2. Knowledge sufficient to recognize who is worthy to be Imam by virtue of the necessary qualifications.

3. Judgment and wisdom to conclude by choosing the best person, who will best and most knowledgeably direct the general welfare.

As for those persons fitted for the Imamate, the conditions related to them are seven:

1. Justice in all its characteristics.

2. Knowledge requisite for independent judgment about revealed and legal matters.

3. Soundness of the senses in hearing, sight and speech, in a degree to accord with their normal functioning.

4. Soundness of the members from any defect that would prevent freedom of movement and agility.

5. Judgment conducive to the governing of subjects and administering matters of general welfare.

6. Courage and bravery to protect Muslim territory and wage the Holy War against the enemy.

7. Pedigree: he must be of the tribe of the Quraysh, since there has come down an explicit statement on this, and the consensus has agreed. There is no need of taking account of Dirar ibn Amr, who stood alone when he declared that anyone could be eligible. The Prophet said: "The Quraysh have precedence, so do not go before them," and there is no pretext for any disagreement, when we have this clear statement delivered to us, and no word that one can raise against it.

There is some further discussion of the manner of electing an Imam/Caliph, but as a matter of fact the Caliphate had been an inherited office within two families, the Umayyads and the Abbasids, uninterruptedly from 661 C.E. to the time of Mawardi's writing. He briefly averts to this situation and approves.

If the Imamate has been conferred through the designation by the previous Imam of his successor, the consensus is that this is lawful because Abu Bakr designated Umar and Umar designated the electors of his successors. (Mawardi, *The Ordinances of Government*) [WILLIAMS 1971: 84–86].

23. The Shiʿite Succession

For the Sunni, community the partisans par excellence were the Shiʿites, those "followers of Ali." It was not their partisanship for Ali, a revered figure for all Muslims, that made them suspect in Sunni eyes; rather, they rejected the consensus, as the Sunni philosopher and historian Ibn Khaldun (d. 1406 C.E.) explains in his Prolegomenon to History.

Ali is the one whom Muhammad appointed (as head of the community). The Shiʿites transmit texts (of Prophetic traditions) in support of this belief, which they interpret so as to suit their tenets. The authorities on the Prophetic tradition and the transmitters of the religious law do not know these texts. Most of them are supposititious, or some of their transmitters are suspect, or their true interpretation is very different from the wicked interpretation that the Shiʿa give them. (Ibn Khaldun, *Muqaddima* 3.25) [IBN KHALDUN 1967: 1:403]

Although the Shiʿites agreed on the general principle of the Imamate—that it was, for example, a spiritual office that passed by designation from Ali through the line of his descendants—they eventually fell into schismatic disputes on who precisely was the designated heir. By the fourteenth century, Ibn Khaldun could look back and trace an elaborately sectarian Shiʿite heresiography. The first issue to divide them was the matter of the Caliphs who preceded Ali. Were they usurpers or simply inferior?

Some Shiʿa hold the opinion that those texts [that is, the texts supporting Ali's claim to the Imamate] prove both the personal appointment of Ali and the fact that the Imamate is transmitted from him to his successors. They [that is, this group of Shiʿites] are the Imamites. They renounce the two shaykhs (Abu Bakr and Umar) because they did not give precedence to Ali and did not render an oath of allegiance to him, as required by the texts quoted. The Imamites do not take the Imamates of Abu Bakr and Umar seriously. But we do not want to bother with transmitting the slanderous things said about Abu Bakr and Umar by Imamite extremists. They are objectionable in our opinion and (should be) in theirs.

Other Shiʿites say that these proofs require the appointment of Ali not in person but insofar as his qualities are concerned. They say that people commit an error when they do not give the qualities their proper place. They are the Zaydi (Shiʿa). They do not renounce the two shaykhs Abu Bakr and Umar. They do take their Imamates seriously, but they say that Ali was superior to them. They permit an inferior person to be the Imam, even though a superior person may be alive at the same time.

Then there is the far more divisive question of the legitimate succession among Ali's descendants. Here too the Imamite and the Zaydi Shiʿa differ.

The Shiʿa differ in opinion concerning the succession to the Caliphate after Ali. Some have it passed on through the descendants of Fatima [one of Ali's wives and the daughter of Muhammad] in succession, through testamentary designation. . . . They are called Imamites, with reference to their statement that knowledge of the Imam and the fact of his being appointed are an article of faith. That is their fundamental tenet.

Others consider the descendants of Fatima the (proper) successors to the Imamate, but through the selection of an Imam from among the Shiʿa. The conditions governing the selection of that Imam are that he have knowledge, be ascetic, generous and brave, and that he go out to make propaganda for his Imamate. They who believe this are Zaydis, so named after the founder of the sect, Zayd son of Ali son of Husayn, the grandson of Muhammad. He [Zayd; d. 740 C.E.] had a dispute with his brother Muhammad al-Baqir [d. 731 C.E.] concerning the condition that the Imam had to come out openly. Al-Baqir charged him with implying that, in the way Zayd looked at it, their father Ali Zayn al-Abidin [d. ca. 712 C.E.] would not be an Imam because he had not come out openly and had made no preparation to do so. . . . When the Imamites discussed the question of Imamates of the two shaykhs Abu Bakr and Umar with Zayd, and noticed that he admitted their Imamates, they disavowed him and did not make him one of the Imams. On account of this they are called "Rafidites" or "Disavowers." . . .

There are also Shiʿa sects that are called "Extremists." They transgress the bounds of reason and the faith of Islam when they speak of the divinity of the Imams. They either assume that the Imam is a human being with divine qualities, or they assume that he is God in human incarnation. This is a dogma of incarnation that agrees with the Christian tenets regarding Jesus. . . . Some Shiʿa extremists say that the perfection of the Imam is possessed by nobody else. When he dies his spirit passes over to another Imam, so that this perfection may be in him. This is the doctrine of metempsychosis. (Ibn Khaldun, *Muqaddima* 3.26)

[IBN KHALDUN 1967: 1:404–405]

24. Awaiting the Hidden Imam

Ibn Khaldun continues with his exposition of Shiʿism.

Some Shiʿa extremists stop (*waqafa*) with one of the Imams and do not continue (the succession). They stop with the Imam whom they consider to have been appointed last. They who believe this are the Waqifites. Some of them say that the Imam is alive and did not die.

This general typology of "Waqifite" Shiʿites brings Ibn Khaldun to an important feature of developed Shiʿism, the doctrine of the "Hidden Imam."

The extremist Imamites, in particular the Twelvers, hold a similar opinion. They think that the twelfth of their Imams, Muhammad ibn al-Hasan al-Askari, to whom they give the epithet of "The Mahdi," entered the cellar of their house in al-Hilla and was "removed" [or "concealed"] when he was imprisoned there with his mother. He has remained there "removed" [since sometime after 874 C.E.]. He will come forth at the end of time and will fill the world with justice. The Twelver Shiʿa refer in this connection to the Prophetic tradition found in the collection of al-Tirmidhi regarding the Mahdi.

That tradition reads:

The world will not be destroyed until the Arabs are ruled by a man from my family, whose name shall tally with my name.

The text of Ibn Khaldun continues.

The Twelver Shiʿites are still expecting him to this day. Therefore they call him "the Expected One." Each night after the evening prayer they bring a mount and stand at the entrance to the cellar [where the Mahdi was "removed"]. They call his name and ask him to come forth openly. They do so until the stars are out. Then they disperse and postpone the matter to the following night. They have continued the custom to this time. (Ibn Khaldun, *Muqaddima* 3.26) [IBN KHALDUN 1967: 1:406–408]

If we return to the beginning of the process, we can understand somewhat better what gave rise to belief in the hidden Imam, which became normative among the great majority of Shiʿites.

The Shiʿites were the party of both hope and despair in the Islamic community: a hope that the Prophet's message would establish God's justice on earth, and despair that the community as presently constituted could achieve that goal. "As presently constituted" meant governance by the illegitimate Caliphs rather than the Imams, the divinely designated, divinely inspired, and divinely guided descendants of Ali. Those Imams had little ground for hope in the ninth century. As we shall soon *see, there had been a major schism in the Shi*ᶜ*a over the succession to the Imamate among the sons of Ja*ᶜ*far al-Sadiq (d. 765 C.E.), and even the main body of the movement, those moderates called "Imamites" who supported the line from Ja*ᶜ*far's son Musa al-Kazim (d. 800 C.E.), must have grown despondent when the eleventh in that succession, Hasan al-Askari, died in 874 C.E. apparently without issue. A number of views were put forward as a result, among them that there was indeed an infant son but that he had been kept in concealment because of the danger and difficulty of the times. The Shi*ᶜ*ite authority al-Nawbakhti, writing at the beginning of the tenth century, describes what came to be the majority opinion among Shi*ᶜ*ites.*

We have conformed to the past tradition and have affirmed the Imamate of al-Askari and accept that he is dead. We concede that he had a successor, who is his own son and the Imam after him until he appears and proclaims his authority, as his ancestors had done before him. God allowed this to happen because the authority belongs to Him and He can do all that He wills and He can command as He wishes concerning his [that is, the Imam's] appearance and his concealment. It is just as the Commander of the Faithful (Ali) said: "O God, you will not leave the earth devoid of a Proof of Your own for mankind, be they manifest and well known, or hidden and protected, lest Your Proof and Your signs are annulled."

This then is what we have been commanded to do and we have received reliable reports on this subject from the past Imams. It is improper for the slaves of God to discuss divine affairs and pass judgment without having knowledge and to seek out what has been concealed from them. It is also unlawful to mention his [that is, the concealed Imam's] name or ask his whereabouts until such times as God decides. This is so because if he, peace be upon him, is protected, fearful and in concealment, it is by God's protection. It is not up to us to seek for reasons for what God does. . . . The reason is that if what is concealed were revealed and made known to us, then his and our blood would be shed. Therefore, on this concealment, and the silence about it, depends the safety and preservation of our lives. (Nawbakhti, *The Sects of the Shi*ᶜ*a* 92)

[SACHEDINA 1981: 50]

*Nawbakhti wrote when there was some expectation that the Imam might indeed emerge from concealment in some ordinary political sense and assert his claim. But as time passed without an appearance, and at the end of a normal life span, when the hidden Imam could no longer be thought to be alive in any purely human sense, some adjustment in thinking had to be made. What it was is apparent in al-Mufid (d. 1022 C.E.), another Shi*ᶜ*ite authority, writing a century after Nawbakhti.*

When al-Askari died, his adherents were divided into fourteen factions, as reported by al-Nawbakhti, may God be pleased with him. The majority among them affirm the Imamate of his son, al-Qa'im al-Muntazar [The Awaited Redresser of Wrongs, a Messianic title]. They assert his birth and attest his (formal) designation by his father. They believe that he was someone named after the Prophet and that he is the Mahdi of the People. They believe that he will have two forms of concealment, one longer than the other. The first concealment will be the shorter, and during it the Imam will have deputies and mediators. They relate on the authority of some of their leaders that al-Askari had made him [that is, his son and successor] known to them and shown them his person. . . . They believe that the Master of the Command is living and has not died, nor will he die, even if he remains for a thousand years, until he fills the world with equity and justice, as it is now filled with tyranny and injustice; and that at the time of his reappearance he will be young and strong in (the frame of) a man of some thirty years. They proof this with reference to his miracles and take these as some proofs and signs (of his existence). (al-Mufid, *Ten Chapters on the Concealment*) [SACHEDINA 1981: 58]

In the developed form of this tradition, the young son of al-Askari went into concealment, perhaps at his father's death in 874 C.E., perhaps even earlier. During that interval the community—that is, the faithful Shi'ite remnant—was under the charge of four agents, as the theologian Nu'mani (d. 970 C.E.) explains.

As to the first concealment, it is that occultation in which there were the mediators between the Imam and the people, carrying out (the orders of the Imam), having been designated by him, and living among the people. These are eminent persons and leaders from whose hands have emanated cures derived from the knowledge and recondite wisdom which they possessed, and the answers to all the questions which were put to them about the problems and difficulties (of religion). This is the Short Concealment, the days of which have come to an end and whose time has gone by. (Nu'mani, *The Book of the Concealment* 91)
[SACHEDINA 1981: 85–86]

The last of the four of these agents died in 941 C.E. Then there began the Complete Concealment, which will end only with the eschatological appearance, or better, the reappearance of the Mahdi Imam. Until that occurs, the direction of the community rests, as it came to be understood, in the hands of the Shi'ite jurists.

The return of the Mahdi Imam must once have been a vivid expectation among the Shi'ites. But as occurred among the Jews regarding the Messiah and among the Christians on the Second Coming of Christ, so too the Shi'ites relaxed the immedi-

acy of the event into the indefinite future, as is summed up in the tradition attrib-
uted to the fifth Imam, Muhammad al-Baqir (d. 732 C.E.). He was asked about a
saying of Ali that the Shiʿites' time of trial would last seventy years. His response
both explains the delay and counsels, as so many had before and after, that "no man
can know the day or the hour."

God Most High had set a time to seventy years. But when (Ali's son) Husayn was killed [at Karbala in 680 C.E.], God's wrath on the inhabitants of the earth became more severe and that period was postponed up to a hundred and forty years. We had informed you about this, but you re-vealed the secret. Now God has delayed (the appearance of the Mahdi) for a further period for which He has neither fixed a time nor has He in-formed us about it, since "God blots and establishes whatsoever He will; and with Him is the essence of the Book." (Tusi, *The Book of the Conceal-ment* 263) [SACHEDINA 1981: 152–153]

Despite the advice not to be concerned with such matters, the unanimous Shiʿite
tradition knows at least the day and the month of the return of the Hidden Imam:
the Mahdi will return on the anniversary of Husayn's martyrdom on the tenth day
of the month of Muharram.

Ibn Khaldun ended his account with a passing reference to the ritual of
awaiting, at al-Hilla in Iraq, the return of the Hidden Imam to the very house from
which he had originally gone into "occultation." We have an eyewitness report of
the same ceremony from the traveler Ibn Battuta, written ca. 1355 C.E.

Near the principal bazaar of [al-Hilla] there is a mosque, over the door of which a silk curtain is suspended. They call this "the Sanctuary of the Master of the Age." It is one of their customs that every evening a hundred of the townsmen come out, carrying arms and with drawn swords in their hands, and go to the governor of the city after the after-noon prayer; they receive from him a horse or mule, saddled and bridled, and [with this they go in procession] beating drums and playing fifes and trumpets in front of this animal . . . and so they come to the Sanctuary of the Master of the Age. Then they stand at the door and say, "In the name of God, O Master of the Age, in the name of God come forth! Corruption is abroad and tyranny is rife! This is the hour for thy advent, that by thee God may divide the True from the False." They continue to call in this way, sounding the trumpets and drums and fifes, until the hour of the sunset prayer. For they assert that Muhammad ibn al-Hasan al-Askari entered this mosque and disappeared from sight in it, and that he will emerge from it since he is, in their view, the "Expected Imam." (Ibn Battuta, *Travels*) [IBN BATTUTA 1959–1962: 2:325]

25. "Twelvers" and "Seveners" among the Shiʿites

There were many branches of Shiʿites, as Ibn Khaldun describes in detail, but the two most important of them, in terms of the numbers of adherents they could command and the political power they could from time to time wield, were the Imamites called "Twelvers"—the term came to be almost synonymous with "Imamite"—and a group called either Ismaʿilis or "Seveners." Ibn Khaldun explains.

The Imamites consider the following as successors to the Imamate after Ali [d. 661 C.E.] . . . by designation as heirs: Ali's son Hasan [d. 669 C.E.], that latter's brother Husayn [d. 680 C.E.], Husayn's son Ali Zayn al-Abidin [d. 712 C.E.], the latter's son Muhammad al-Baqir [d. 731 C.E.], and his son Jaʿfar al-Sadiq [d. 765 C.E.]. From there on they split into two sects. One of them considers Jaʿfar's son Ismaʿil [d. 760 C.E.] as Jaʿfar's successor to the Imamate. They recognize Ismaʿil as their Imam and they are called Ismaʿilis. The other group considers Jaʿfar's other son, Musa al-Kazim [d. 799 C.E.], as Jaʿfar's successor in the Imamate. They are the Twelvers because they stop the succession with the twelfth Imam [that is, Muhammad al-Mahdi, mentioned above]. They saw that he remains "removed" until the end of time.

That the Shiʿite "designation" was an indelible one and signaled, like the Christians' laying on of episcopal hands, the transmission of an irrevocable spiritual gift is clear from what follows.

The Ismaʿilis say that the Imam Ismaʿil became Imam because his father Jaʿfar designated him to be his successor. Ismaʿil died before his father, but according to the Ismaʿilis the fact that he was designated by his father as his successor means that the Imamate should continue among *his* successors. . . . As they say, Ismaʿil's successor as Imam was his son Muhammad the Concealed One. He is the first of the Hidden Imams. According to the Ismaʿilis, an Imam who has no power goes into hiding. His missionaries remain in the open, however, in order to establish proof (of the Hidden Imam's existence) among mankind.

The Ismaʿili Imam did not recede into some remote metaphysical outback. Sometime about 900 C.E. a certain Ubaydallah appeared in North Africa and convinced enough people that he was the great-grandson of Muhammad "the Concealed One" to carry him to power and his successors to rule over Muslim North Africa and Egypt under the dynastic name of Fatimid. Ibn Khaldun wryly concludes:

The Ismaʿilis are called such with reference to their recognition of the Imamate of Ismaʿil. They are also called "Esotericists" (*batiniyya*) with reference to their speaking about the *batin*, that is, the hidden, Imam. They are also called "heretics" because of the heretical character of their beliefs. (Ibn Khaldun, *Muqaddima* 3.25) [IBN KHALDUN 1967: 1:412–413]

26. The Powers of the Caliph-Imam

As the guardian and transmitter of the Apostolic tradition, the Christian bishop had enormous spiritual powers over his community, and the bishops of Rome claimed that in their case those same powers extended over the entire flock of Christ. But no Christian "overseer" ever possessed the plenitude of what Ibn Khaldun called "the royal power" and "the religious power," which he attributed to the office of the Caliph. Indeed, one has to return to Hasmonean monarchs like Jonathan or Simon to find a parallel authority. And it is in fact no parallel at all, since the Hasmoneans possessed their powers by reason of their simultaneous tenure of two offices, that of king and High Priest, while the Muslim Caliph's flowed from a single investiture. As Ibn Khaldun explains, the Caliph held both of the "two swords" in his single hand.

It has become clear that to be Caliph in reality means acting as a substitute for the Lawgiver [Muhammad] with regard to the preservation of the religion and the political leadership of the world. The Lawgiver was concerned with both things, with religion in his capacity as the person commanded to transmit the duties imposed by the religious laws to the people and to cause them to act in accordance with them, and with worldly political leadership in his capacity as the person in charge of the (public) interests of human civilization. (Ibn Khaldun, *Muqaddima* 3.29) [IBN KHALDUN 1967: 1:448]

We can observe the early Caliphs acting in exactly this fashion. In his brief tenure (632–634 C.E.), Abu Bakr bade his fellow Muslims take up arms against those who sought to withdraw from the community at the death of the Prophet. Immediately after him, Umar (634–644 C.E.) began to set in place many of the long-term institutions of the young Islamic state.

Abu Ja'far said: Umar was the first to fix and write the date (according to the Muslim era), according to what al-Harith told me, having heard it from Ibn Sa'd, on the authority of Muhammad ibn Umar in the year 16 (A.H.) in the month of First Rabi' (March 637 C.E.). And I have already mentioned the reason for writing this and how the affair was. Umar, may God be pleased with him, was the first to date letters and seal them with clay. And he was the first to gather people before a prayer-leader to pray special prayers with them at night in the month of Ramadan, and he wrote concerning this to the provinces and commanded them to do likewise.

The most far-reaching of Umar's measures was his exercise of the "royal power" and his establishment of the first instruments of state to regulate the affairs of a rapidly expanding Islamic empire. Tabari, who is our source here, continues.

I heard from al-Harith, who heard from Ibn Sa'd, who heard from Muhammad ibn Umar, who heard from A'idh ibn Yahya, on the authority of Abu'l-Huwayrith, on the authority of Jubayr ibn al-Huwayrith ibn Nuqayd, that Umar ibn al-Khattab, may God be pleased with him, consulted the Muslims concerning the drawing up of registers, and Ali ibn Abi Talib said to him, "Share out every year whatever property has accumulated to you and do not retail anything." Uthman ibn Affan said, "I see much property, which suffices for all the people and which cannot be counted until you distinguish between those who have taken (from it) and those who have not. I do not like things to be in disorder." Al-Walid ibn Hisham ibn al-Mughira said to him, "O Commander of the Faithful, I have been to Syria and have seen their kings, and they drew up a register and formed a legion. You should draw up a register and form a legion."

In question here was a list of pensioners, a register or divan *of those to whom the spoils of the new Islamic conquests would be distributed in order. Those spoils were now considerable, which explains the controversy about precedence that followed.*

Umar adopted his advice and called Aqil ibn Abi Talib and Makhrama ibn Nawfal and Jubayr ibn Mut'im, who were genealogists of the tribe of Quraysh, and he said to them, "Write (a list) of people according to their ranks!" And they wrote, beginning with the Banu Hashim [that is, Muhammad's family], then following them with Abu Bakr and his kind and then Umar and his kind, that is, following the order of the Caliphate. When Umar looked at it he said, "I wish to God it were as you have written, but begin with the kin of the Prophet of God, may God bless and save him, then continue in order of nearness until you put Umar where God has put him."

I heard from al-Harith, who heard from Ibn Sa'd, who heard from Muhammad ibn Umar, who heard from Usama ibn Zayd ibn Aslam, on the authority of his father, on the authority of his grandfather, who said: I saw Umar ibn al-Khattab, may God be pleased with him, when the writing was shown to him, with the Banu Taym after the Banu Hashim and the Banu Adi after the Banu Taym. And I heard him say, put Umar in his proper place. . . . And the Banu Adi [that is, Umar's kin] came to Umar and said, "You are the deputy of the Prophet of God!" And he answered, "Surely (I am) the deputy of Abu Bakr and Abu Bakr was the deputy of the Prophet of God." And they said, "Why do you not put yourself where these people [that is, the genealogists] have put you?" And Umar said, "Well done, O Banu Adi! Do you want to eat off my back? Do you want me to sacrifice my honor to you? No, by God, not until your turn comes, even though the register close with you and you be written last among the people. I have two masters [Muhammad and Abu Bakr] who followed a certain path, and if I forsake them I shall be forsaken. Whatever of plenty we have attained in this world, whatever reward for our deeds we hope from God in the next world, is from Muhammad alone. He is our nobility, and his kin are the noblest of the Arabs, and then the rest, in order of their nearness to him. Indeed, the Arabs are ennobled with the Prophet of God, and perhaps some of them have many ancestors in common with him. As for us, it is clear that our stems coincide, and right back to Adam there are few ancestors that we do not have in common. But despite that, by God, if the non-Arabs come with deeds, and we come without them, they shall be nearer to Muhammad than we on the Day of Judgment. Let no man look to his ancestry but let him do God's work, and if any man's deeds fall short, his pedigree will not help him." (Tabari, *Annals* 1.2750–2752) [LEWIS 1974: 1:18–20]

27. The Delegation of the Royal Power: The Sultanate

The "royal" or secular powers of the Caliph do not directly concern us here, and they were in any event "delegated" to other, more powerful figures in Islamic history—ministers who rose to dominate a Caliph or generals who simply cowed him. These de facto rulers of the Islamic commonwealth were generally known as "Sultans" and were even more generally former Turkish generals to whom the Caliphs owed the safety of their own houses and the protection of the "Abode of Islam." The Caliph could only hope that the Sultans who lorded it over his narrow base of operations around Baghdad might be Sunni and sympathetic and capable of controlling their troops, as they often in fact were. It fell then to the Islamic lawyers to convert this rather naked usurpation of power into a form of "delegation" and make theory of a necessity, as did Ibn Jama'a (d. 1335 C.E.).

The Imam of the Muslims has the right to delegate authority over any region, country, area or province to whoever is able to hold general authority there, because necessity demands it—not least in a far coun-try. . . . If it is to be a general delegation of power, such as is customary for sultans and kings in our own time, it is lawful for the delegate then to appoint judges and governors and rule the armies, with full disposition of the wealth from all quarters, but not to have anything to do with a region over which he is not delegated, because his is a particular government. The same qualifications apply to the delegate ruler when the Imam selects him that would apply to his own office, except that of Qurayshi descent, because he is standing in the Imam's place.

If a king attains power by usurpation and force in a (Muslim) country, then the Caliph should delegate the affairs of that place to him, in order to call him to obedience and avoid a split with him, lest there be disunity and the staff of the community be broken. In this way usurpation becomes legitimate government, issuing effective orders. (Ibn Jamaʿa, *Statutes*) [WILLIAMS 1971: 91–92].

Ibn Khaldun, who knew well enough how to speak like a lawyer, here chooses to write like a historian.

When royal authority is firmly established in one particular family and tribe supporting the dynasty, and when that family claims all royal authority for itself and keeps the rest of the family away from it, and when the children of that family succeed to the royal authority in turn, by appointment, then it often happens that their wazirs [that is, their ministers] and entourage gain power over the throne. This occurs most often when a little child or a weak member of the family is appointed successor by his father and made ruler by his creatures and servants. It becomes clear that he is unable to fulfill the functions of ruler. Therefore they are fulfilled by his guardian, one of his father's wazirs, someone from his entourage, one of his clients, or a member of his tribe. That person gives the impression that he is guarding the power of the (child ruler) for him. Eventually it becomes clear that he exercises the control, and he uses the fact as a tool to achieve royal authority. He keeps the child away from his people. He accustoms him to the pleasures of his life of luxury and gives him every opportunity to indulge in them. He causes him to forget to look at government affairs. Eventually he gains full control over him. He accustoms the child ruler to believe that the ruler's share in royal authority consists merely in sitting on the throne, shaking hands, being addressed as "Sire" and sitting with the women in the seclusion of the harem. All exercise of actual executive power, and the personal handling and supervision of matters that concern the ruler, such as inspection of the army, finances, and defense of the border regions, are believed to belong to the wazir. He defers to him in all these things. Eventually, the wazir definitely adopts the coloring of the leader, of the man in control.

The royal authority comes to be his. He reserves it for his family and his children after him. (Ibn Khaldun, *Muqaddima* 3.19)

[IBN KHALDUN 1967: 1:377–378]

28. The Religious Powers of the Caliph

To return to the religious powers of this primary political authority in Islam, they are described in brief by Ibn Khaldun.

It should be known that all the religious functions of the religious law, such as (leadership of) prayer, the office of judge, the office of mufti, the Holy War, and market supervision fall under the "Great Imamate," which is the Caliphate. The Caliphate is a kind of great mainspring and comprehensive basis, and all these functions are branches of it and fall under it because of the wide scope of the Caliphate, its active interest in all conditions of the Muslim community, both religious and worldly, and its general power to execute the religious laws relative to both (religious and worldly affairs). (Ibn Khaldun, *Muqaddima* 3.29) [IBN KHALDUN 1967: 1:449]

What Ibn Khaldun saw as powers, the lawyer Ibn Jama'a (d. 1335 C.E.) saw as the Caliph's duties, though both men were writing in an age when the holders of that office had little capacity for either exercising their powers or effectively fulfilling their duties.

As for the ten duties of the ruler to the subjects, the first is to protect the Muslim heritage and defend it, whether in every region, if he is Caliph, or in his own country if he is delegated over it, and to struggle against idolators and put down rebels.

The second is to guard the religion in its principles and beliefs, and put down innovation and heretics and encourage the religious sciences and the study of the Law, venerate learning and religious scholars and raise places from which the light of Islam may shine. . . .

The third is to uphold the rites of Islam, such as the obligation of prayer and the congregational prayers and the call to prayer and performance of it, and the sermons and leadership of the prayers, and the matter of the fast and the feasts, and keeping the calendar, and the pilgrimage; and part of the last is facilitating the pilgrimage from all the districts, and keeping the roads clear and giving people security on the way and appointing people to look after them.

The fourth is to make the final decisions on court cases and sentences, by appointing governors and judges, so as to reduce contentiousness. . . .

The fifth is to wage the Holy War himself and with his armies at least once a year. . . .

The sixth is to apply the punishments imposed by the Law, and make no distinction when doing so between the powerful and the weak. . . .

The seventh is to collect the alms tax and the tribute from those who are to pay it [that is, the People of the Book] and the booty and the land tax, and to use it as the Law stipulates. . . .

The eighth is to supervise pious and family foundations, keep bridges and roads in good repair and make smooth the ways of welfare.

The ninth is to supervise the division and distribution of booty. . . .

The tenth is justice in the ruler in all his affairs. (Ibn Jama'a, *Statutes*) [WILLIAMS 1971: 93–94]

The Caliph, it is clear, was the executor of the religious law and, unlike Muhammad, whose "successor" he was, neither the maker of new laws nor the interpreter of the old. The earliest Caliphs may have exercised some of those religious functions in fact. They certainly led prayers when their personal security permitted it, conducted military campaigns, and acted as judges for the community. But others in that rapidly expanding empire quickly took over in the Caliph's stead: ministers, bureaucrats, and specialists, like the "mufti" on Ibn Khaldun's list—literally "one capable of pronouncing a fatwa," that is, a legal opinion, which, if it was not binding, certainly constituted a legal precedent.

29. The Islamic Judge

The mufti was a legal scholar, someone trained in the increasingly complex legal system of Islamic society. That training took place in one of the numerous colleges of law that arose in Islam from the eleventh and twelfth centuries onward, and most Muslim intellectuals passed through them over the following centuries. These Islamic lawyers constituted an important class in Muslim society, and at least part of their influence derived from the fact that by and large they kept themselves at a distance from the government. They were supported by their own endowments and so could defend or oppose the ruler as circumstances and issues dictated. But a few of them at least were co-opted into government service as judges to administer the Law of Islam as duly constituted delegates of the Caliph.

Nobody may be appointed to the office of judge who does not comply fully with the conditions required to make his appointment valid and his decisions effective.

This is once again al-Mawardi, the constitutional lawyer who died in 1058 C.E.

The first condition is that he must be a man. This condition consists of two qualities, puberty and masculinity. As for the child below puberty, he cannot be held accountable, nor can his utterances have any effect against himself; how much less so against others. As for women, they are unsuited to positions of authority, although judicial verdicts may be based upon what they say. Abu Hanifa said that a woman can act as a judge on matters on which it would be lawful for her to testify, but she may not act as a judge on which it would not be lawful for her to testify. Ibn Jarir al-Tabari, giving a divergent view, allows a woman to act as a judge in all cases, but no account should be taken of an opinion which is refuted by both the consensus of the community and the word of God. "Men have authority over women because of what God has conferred on one in preference to the other" (Quran 4:38), meaning by this, intelligence and discernment. He does not, therefore, permit women to hold authority over men. (Mawardi, *Statutes of Governance* 61–63) [LEWIS 1974: 2:41–42]

Mawardi goes on to rehearse the other qualifications for an Islamic justice: intelligence, freedom, membership in the Islamic faith, rectitude, soundness of sight and hearing, and finally, command of the Islamic Law in both its general principles and its specific applications.

30. The Market Inspector

In any community under Islam the presence of the state was signaled by the judge, the delegate of the religious power, and by the gendarmerie, the delegate of the "royal" power of the distant ruler. But there was a third official as well: the market inspector. The somewhat unexpected presence of this public prosecutor, guardian of public morality, and consumer advocate armed with a religious mandate sounds like a faint echo of Islam's all-inclusive command to its authorities to "summon to good and reject what is disapproved" (Quran 32:17). How the office worked is explained by the Spaniard Ibn Abdun (d. 1100 C.E.).

The judge must not appoint a market inspector without informing the prince of it, so that the judge will have a proof if he later wishes to remove him or keep him. . . . The office of the market inspector is closely akin to that of the judge and thus the occupant should only be a model person. He is the spokesman of the judge, his chamberlain, assistant and successor, and if the judge is prevented, the market inspector may give judgment in his place in what pertains to him and is within his competence. He receives a salary from the public treasury, for he takes care of many matters for the judge which in principle belong to the judge's office, thus sparing the latter fatigue and tiring scenes, and being tried by vulgar and low people, and insolent and ignorant persons from among the artisans and laborers.

The Islamic judge tried cases; the market inspector enforced the law, and his jurisdiction was wide indeed. Inspectors regulated the market, of course, both in regard to fair prices and even in the arrangement of shops and produce. But they could act elsewhere as well, in mosques, for example.

One [that is, the market inspector] must not allow any beggar to beg inside the mosque on Friday; whoever does shall be given corporal chastisement. The mosque servants and muezzins shall be told to prevent it. Also no beggar is allowed to beg at the entrance of the mosque in a loud voice once the prayer-leader of the Friday prayers has gone to the pulpit to preach. The market inspector must not allow any beast of burden to stand near the entrance, for it may make droppings or urine which destroy the ritual purity of the people coming in.

The mosques are the houses of God, places of recollection and worship, and known for purity. They are not for payments of debts, or arguments, or any of the acts of this world, for they are for the acts of the next world. Thus boys should not be taught in them, because they are careless about impurities on their feet and clothing. If it is absolutely necessary, they can be taught in the galleries (of the courtyard). Boys should not be disciplined with more than five blows with the cane for the big ones and three blows for the small ones, with severity proportionate to their ability to bear it.

The inspectors could also intervene in various professions. A number of Ibn Abdun's personal asides are drawn from his own somewhat severe morality.

Schoolmasters must be prevented from attending dinners and funerals and acting as witnesses (for a fee), except on days when they are free, for they are salaried people. They should not increase the numbers of their students: they are forbidden to do it, yet I may say that they will never observe it, for one does not voluntarily rise to serve the community, especially in the matter of teaching school. Also they never teach anything as they should. Most schoolteachers are ignorant of the art of teaching: to know the Quran is one thing and to teach it another.

Moneychangers must be prevented from usury. No currency shall be circulated except that of the land, for differing currencies lead to inflation, higher prices and unstable conditions.

Barbers must not be alone in their shops with a woman, but only in the marketplace, where they may be observed.

Prostitutes shall be forbidden to uncover their faces outside the public houses, to confuse honest women with their adornments, and shall be forbidden to reveal their secrets to married women or come to wedding parties, even if their husbands permit it. Dancing girls shall also be ordered not to uncover their heads (in public).

Pleasure-boys should be expelled from the city and chastised whenever one of them is found (in it). They should not be allowed to circulate among Muslims or participate in festivities, for they are fornicators cursed by God and all men.

And finally, in the matter of the People of the Book living inside the Abode of Islam:

A Muslim may not massage a Jew or a Christian or empty their garbage or clean their latrines, for Jews or Christians are fitter for such work. Also a Muslim may not look after the riding animal of a Jew or a Christian.

Muslim women must be forbidden to enter the infamous churches, for the priests are profligates, adulterers and sodomites. The Frankish [that is, Christian] women too should be forbidden to go in the church except on days of offices or feasts, because they go to eat and drink and fornicate with the priests, and there is not one of the priests who does not have two of them or more to sleep with him. . . . The priests should be ordered to marry, as is done in the eastern lands; if they wanted to, they could do it. . . .

Jews must not butcher an animal for Muslims, and the Jews should be ordered to set aside butcher shops for themselves.

No tax farmer or police agent or Jew or Christian should be allowed to dress like an important person, or as a jurist, or a virtuous person; rather they should be known and avoided. . . . A distinctive badge should be given them by which they may be known, to disgrace them.

No books of learning should be sold to a Jew or a Christian, unless it treats of their own law, for they translate the books and then attribute them to their own people and their bishops, although they are of Muslim authorship. It would be best to allow no Jewish or Christian doctor to treat any Muslim, for they do not have true friendships with Muslims and should treat people of their own community. Since they do not have sincere friendship for Muslims, how shall one trust them with his life? (Ibn Abdun, *On the Implementation of the Law* 59–61) [WILLIAMS 1971: 156–161]

PART II

The Word and the Law and the People of God

Introduction

Judaism, Christianity, and Islam—the three religious communities sprung from the promise to Abraham, or rather, from competition for it—all rest their claims where that promise is recorded, in the Scripture, the Word of God. And yet all three have a complex interscriptural relationship. The Jews have what seems to be the simplest position: the Bible—"our Bible," the Jew would claim, with all the evidence unmistakably on his side—is the sum and substance of God's written revelation. Early on there may have been some question of what precisely that Bible comprised and in what precisely consisted the role of the human "author" in the process. Those issues settled, however, the question, though assuredly not the Book itself, could be closed.

The Christians at first could have no other view but that. They too were Jews, and so the Bible—and that alone—was their Scripture. It was certainly treated as such in the texts that later came to form the New Testament. But Jesus was also the Christ, the Anointed One, and the Son of God, and both he and his redemptive work constituted the fulfillment of the promised New Covenant. That is a theological judgment, but there is a literary consequence not far behind it: the works that "revealed" him, the "Good News of Jesus Christ" and its connected literature, were likewise revelation, and so, it was concluded, Scripture in their own, Christian right.

The nonconverted Jews, the vast majority, would have none of that, of course. If the Christians wandered into their thoughts about Scripture, it was in the context of what these new sectarians had done and were doing with the authentic Scripture, the Bible, and what the Jewish community should do about it. They could retranslate that Scripture, and they could revise some of their interpretations of Messianic passages; but by and large both the Christian double-Scripture theory and their claims more generally could be ignored. The Christians for their part obviously could not afford to ignore the Bible, not because of its clear denomination of the Jews as the Chosen People—that consideration might indeed have counseled them to do precisely that—but because the original body of the followers of Jesus were exclusively Jews. Christians' sense of their own identity—and their legitimacy, when that identity came to be questioned—rested on their conviction that they were the "true Israel," the remnant promised by Scripture that would inherit the Promise. Furthermore, that fulfillment had been accomplished through the coming of the long-awaited Messiah in the person of Jesus of Nazareth. So the Christians had perforce to extend their embrace—half-hearted on the part of some—to what they began to call the "Old Testament."

At first glance the Muslim position on Scripture would seem to be as simple as the Jewish one: the Quran is the sum of the Divine Revelation. Indeed, theirs is perhaps a simpler position than the Jewish one, since there is no real problem of a Quranic canon in Islam and no question at all of authorship: God through His angel Gabriel dictated the Quran—every single word of it—to Muhammad. When we look more closely, however, we discover that the Quran itself acknowledges other and earlier revelations: the "Tawrah" to the Jews through Moses and the "Injil" to the Christians through Jesus. These are undoubtedly authentic revelations, as authentic as the Quran in their way, and the faults that produced the need for the third and final revelation called the Quran lay not in those other books or in their revealer-messengers but in the communities that used them, the "Peoples of the Book," as the Muslims called them.

That interpretation does not, however, constitute the Quran a "New-New Testament" vis-à-vis the other two. On the Muslim view, the Quran resumes and repeats the earlier revelations; the Muslim is thus freed, as the Christian is not, of the obligation of making his case out of the other books, or even of consulting them. Some Muslims did indeed consult them, as our texts will show, but chiefly for polemical purposes: to convict the Jews and Christians of falsifying their own Scriptures, or, chiefly in response to the Christian approach to the Messiah, to find foreshadowings of the Prophet of Islam in those earlier books.

That Scripture was a kind of battleground both within and among the three religious communities should occasion no surprise. The words of God are by their very nature not only the source of every prayer and a guide for all worship and conduct; they provide as well the matter of every brief and the court of last and authoritative appeal. And they are expressed not as we might imagine that God would pronounce, with unmistakable and irrefutable clarity, but in the manner of human discourse—here seemingly clearly, here allusively or ambiguously, or even with apparent self-contradiction. These judgments, shared by Jewish,

Christian, and Muslim interpreters alike, are all tentative. These are, after all, the words of God; one must proceed slowly to judgment.

But judgment there was in all those houses, and a great flood of interpretation: pious and polemical exegesis; exegesis by the number, by color, by letter of the alphabet; exegesis philosophical and philological, pedestrian and poetical, imaginative and impenetrable; exegesis to find the Messiah and not to find him; exegesis to uncover the name of God and to conceal it; and, of course, acres of exegesis to demonstrate that *we*, and we alone, are in fact the true Children of Abraham.

The limits of exegesis are no less than the limits of human ingenuity. But for all its impressive variety and virtuosity, human intelligence is not always convincing as to the truth of Scripture. Far more persuasive was another ally brought into the lists: tradition, or rather, *the* Tradition, since we are not speaking here simply of longstanding or customary ways of thinking or behaving. In the three communities *tradition* has a precise technical meaning: it is the "unwritten Scripture," the body of teaching issued from the same divine source as the Scripture and passed down orally through known channels from generation to generation for the instruction or edification of the believers and, of course, as an authoritative guide for understanding the Scripture, whose companion piece it is.

Scripture and tradition are thus the joint parents not only of exegesis but also of doctrine. Out of them—Scripture as matrix, tradition as the eliciting and shaping agent—comes a great deal of the complex religious culture that we call simply Judaism or Christianity or Islam. In Christianity, where it claimed the authority of the Apostles, tradition underwrote the growth of Christian dogma, which was considered as nothing more than rendering explicit—"defining," as it was said—understandings that went back to Jesus himself and had been passed on through an unbroken Apostolic succession. In Judaism and Islam, however, tradition—the "tradition of the Fathers" in the first, the "custom of the Prophet" in the second—had as its primary task the support of the structure of religious law, from its most general principles to its most detailed prescriptions and prohibitions. Tradition could be, and was, used to modify and even abrogate scriptural precepts, to shrink or extend the legal purview of the Book itself.

Though Christianity appears far more concerned with orthodoxy than orthopraxy, the Christian community as a whole faced a difficult legal problem: What was its position as heir to a Covenant whose warp and woof was a legal system of great detail and complexity, the Torah given to Moses on Sinai? Was there a Covenant without the Law? The beginning of an answer to that troublesome question appears in the Gospels themselves, in a nuanced response of Paul, but the issue was by no means closed—not so long, at least, as there was a highly prescriptive "Old Testament" to confront the now waxing and now waning legal interests of the "New Testament." The Christians eventually disengaged themselves, Covenant still intact, from Torah law. Paul's insight on the spiritual obsolescence of the Jewish Law was maintained, but the connection was not entirely repudiated: from circumcision to the dietary laws, the Christians could have their Pentateuch and allegorize it too.

The question of who or what was a Jew received particular attention after the disruption of the Exile and the wholesale scattering of the Jewish community into colonies all across the Mediterranean and West Asian world. There were, as it turned out, many ways to be Jewish, even the Jesus way, and many ways of looking upon the community. The Jesus way was not long in being rejected, however. The reciprocal rejection of Jew and Christian may have closed the matter for the Jew, but it opened the question in a new and uncharted form for the Christian. Who was a Christian and what was the Christian community were troubling issues from the late first century onward. Tests and definitions of faith were devised and applied, most of them strikingly different from what a contemporary Jew might have judged an appropriate measure. Orthodoxy and orthopraxy are both solutions to a search for normative doctrine. What the Jews had once debated among themselves and then, fleetingly, with the new Christians became in the end a trialog, one held, wondrously, under the auspices of the newest claimants to the heritage of Abraham.

Judaism, and later Islam, had to settle for doctrine; Christianity had within its power the creation of dogma—authoritative teaching *defined* as such by a competent body. Judaism and Christianity were both sacerdotal societies; their chief form of worship was sacrifice, and that primary act was performed by a professional subcommunity of priests: a hereditary caste in Judaism, a designated class in Christianity. But whatever it was in the beginning, the teaching function in Judaism developed laterally into another professional class, the post-Exilic scribes, later the rabbis. Among the Christians it developed upward to a higher level of the priesthood, the episcopate. Whereas the later Muslims savants known as the *ulama* were almost identical functional copies of the rabbis, the Christian bishop owed nothing to either of those types. He taught not from expertise but from authority; and when in synod, he could define—raise teaching from doctrine to dogma.

The new Muslim claimants to "the religion of Abraham," and so the heirs to his Covenant, had no need to interpret either Torah or Gospel, to exorcize or allegorize the Old Law; Islam proceeded directly to an enunciation of the Law of God out of the manifest and exclusive evidence of the Quran and the custom of the Prophet. Nor did it have to engage in that legal enterprise, as the later Jews and earlier Christians did, under the sovereignty and the laws of others. The Muslims' political independence was a right won together with their religious autonomy. For Islam the Law of God was also the law of the state: community and polity were identical from the outset, and so the work of studying, understanding, and refining God's will could proceed under the calm and protective shelter of Islamic sovereignty.

1. The Words of God:
Revelation and Scripture

At diverse times and places and through different agents, as the Scripture itself puts it, God manifested Himself to men. There were epiphanies among those manifestations, startling visions of the Godhead, encounters direct, like that between Moses and Yahweh on Sinai or the three disciples shown Jesus radiantly transfigured on Mount Tabor. But what set off the prophet from the visionary was that those few trusted prophets were given a message for His community, His chosen people. These verbal communications, often of great length, were eventually committed to writing and so constituted a book, or better, the Book, since none could rival God's own words. In this sense all of Scripture has God as its author. The recipients of these revelations nevertheless attempted to puzzle out the relationship of the human prophetic agent to the Book of the Word of God that bore his name on its leaves.

1. Who Wrote the Bible?

We begin apodictically with the rabbis' assured review of the authors of the various books that constituted the Jewish Bible.

Moses wrote his own book [the Torah], the section on Balaam and the Book of Job. Joshua wrote his own book and the last eight verses of the Torah [on the death of Moses]. Samuel wrote his own book and the books of Judges and Ruth. David wrote the Psalms, using compositions of ten sages: Adam, Melchizedek, Abraham, Moses, Heman, Idithun, Asaph, and the three sons of Core. Jeremiah wrote his own book and the book of Kings and Lamentations. Ezekiel and his group wrote Isaiah, Proverbs and the Song of Songs. The men of the Great Synagogue wrote Ezekiel, the Twelve (Minor Prophets), Daniel and Esther; and Ezra wrote his book and the Chronicles up to his own time. (BT.Baba Batra 14b–15a)

2. The Divine Voice on Sinai

The Talmud's account is terse and academic, as befits the academics who composed it. But the Bible itself suggests in this scene between Moses and the Israelites that the problem of authorship was not quite so simple.

The day you stood before the Lord your God at Horeb, when the Lord said to me, "Gather the people to Me that I may let them hear My words, in order that they may learn to revere Me as long as they live on earth, and may so teach their children." You came forward and stood at the foot of the mountain. The mountain was ablaze with flames to the very skies, dark with densest clouds. The Lord spoke to you out of the fire; you heard the sound of words but perceived no shape—nothing but a voice. He declared to you the Covenant which He commanded you to observe, the Ten Commandments; and He inscribed them on two tablets of stone. At the same time the Lord commanded me to impart to you laws and rules for you to observe in the land which you are about to cross into and occupy. (Deuteronomy 4:10–14)

Moses was the Jewish prophet par excellence, and however later generations chose to explain the mode of communication between God and His prophets, Moses or any other, the passage of Deuteronomy represents something else: the direct speech of God to all the people, a public not a prophetic revelation of the divine will. Did God then actually speak? "Perish the thought," Philo says. "God is not a man."

The ten words or oracles [that is, the Ten Commandments], in reality laws or ordinances, were revealed by the Father of All when the nation, men and women alike, were assembled together. Did He utter them Himself in the guise of a voice? Perish the thought: may it never enter our mind, for God is not a man in need of mouth, tongue and windpipe. It seems to me rather that God on that occasion performed a truly holy miracle, by commanding an invisible sound to be created in the air more marvelous than all the instruments and fitted with perfect harmonies, not inanimate, nor yet composed of body and soul like a living creature, but a rational soul full of lucidity and clarity, which, shaping the air and heightening its tension and transforming it into a flaming fire, sounded forth, like breath through a trumpet, an articulate voice so great that those farthest away seemed to hear it with the same distinctness as those nearby. . . . The power of God, breathing on the newly made voice, stirred it up and caused it to blaze forth, and spreading it on every side, rendered its end more luminous than its beginning by inspiring in the soul of each another kind of hearing far superior to that through the ears. For that sense, being in a way sluggish, remains inert until struck by air and put into motion, but the hearing of the mind inspired by God reaches out to make the first advance to meet the spoken words with the swiftest speed. (Philo, *The Ten Commandments* 32–35) [PHILO 1981: 156]

A somewhat less philosophical explanation, indeed no explanation at all, is offered by the rabbi who is made the spokesman for traditional Judaism in Judah Halevi's The Khazar King, *an imaginary dialogue written ca. 1130–1140 C.E. The charge has just been made that the account in Deuteronomy, with its talk of tablets and a voice, smacks of the "personification" that Philo so laboriously attempted to avoid. Halevi's rabbi responds.*

Heaven forbid that I should assume what is against sense and reason. The first of the Ten Commandments enjoins the belief in divine providence. The second command contains the prohibition of the worship of other gods, or the association of any being with Him, the prohibition to represent Him in statues, forms or images, or any personification of Him. How should we not deem Him above personification, since we do so with many of His creations, e.g., the human soul, which represents man's true essence. . . . We must not, however, endeavor to reject the conclusions to be drawn from revelation. We say, then, that we do not know how the intention became corporealized and the speech evolved which struck our ear (on Sinai), nor what new thing God created from nothing, nor what existing thing He employed. He does not lack the power. We say that He created the two tablets and engraved a text on them, in the same way that He created the heavens and the stars by His will alone. God desired it and they became concrete as He wished it, engraved with the text of the Ten Words. We also say that He divided the Red Sea and formed it into two walls, which He caused to stand to the right and the left of the people (on their way out of Egypt), for whom He made easy wide roads and smooth ground for them to walk on without fear and trouble. This rendering, constructing and arranging are attributed to God, who required no tool or intermediary, as would be necessary for human toil. As the water stood at His command, shaped itself at His will, so the air which touched the prophet's ear assumed the form of sounds, which conveyed the matters to be communicated by God to the prophet and the people. . . .

I do not maintain that this is exactly how things occurred; the problem is no doubt too deep for me to fathom. But the result was that everyone who was present at the time became convinced that the matter proceeded from God direct. It is to be compared to the first act of creation. The belief in the Law connected with those scenes (on Sinai) is as firmly established in the mind as the belief in the creation of the world, and that He created it in the same manner in which He—as is known—created the two tablets, the manna, other things. Thus disappear from the soul of the believer the doubts of the philosophers and the materialists. (Judah Halevi, *The Khazar King*) [HALEVI 1905: 62–63]

3. Prophetic Inspiration

At many points in his works Philo attempts to explain how the inspiration of the prophets, of whom Moses is the archetype, operates. Here he uses, as is frequent in ancient philosophy, the method of analogy. The sun as the analog of human reason was already a commonplace in the Platonic tradition from which Philo was drawing, but it was well suited to the particular text under discussion.

Admirably does Moses describe (in the Torah) the inspired Abraham, when he says "about sunset there fell on him an ecstasy" (Gen. 15:12; the Hebrew has: "a deep sleep"). "Sun" is his figurative name for our mind. For what the reasoning faculty is in us, the sun is in the world, since both of them are light-bringers, one sending forth to the whole world that which our senses perceive, the other shedding mental rays upon ourselves through the medium of apprehension. So while the radiance of the mind is still all around us, when it pours as it were a noonday beam into the whole soul, we are self-contained, not possessed. But when it comes to its setting, naturally ecstasy and divine possession and madness fall upon us. For when the light of God shines, the human light sets; when the divine light sets, the human dawns and rises. This is what regularly befalls the fellowship of prophets. The mind is evicted at the arrival of the divine Spirit, but when that departs the mind returns to its tenancy. Mortal and immortal may not share the same home. And therefore the setting of reason and the darkness which surround it produce ecstasy and inspired frenzy. To connect what is coming with what is here written Moses says, "it was said to Abraham" (Gen. 15:13). For indeed the prophet, even when he seems to be speaking, really holds his peace, and his organs of speech, mouth and tongue, as wholly in the employ of Another, to show forth what He wills. Unseen by us, that Other beats on the chords with the skill of a master-hand and makes them instruments of sweet music, laden with every harmony. (Philo, *Who Is the Heir?* 263–266) [PHILO 1945: 74–75]

Philo returns to this notion that the prophet is simply the instrument of God and invokes the same image.

No pronouncement of a prophet is ever his own; he is an interpreter prompted by Another in all his utterances, when, knowing not what he does, he is filled with inspiration, as the (human) reason withdraws and surrenders the citadel of the soul to a new visitor and tenant, the Divine Spirit, which plays upon the vocal organism and raises sounds from it, which clearly express its prophetic message. (Philo, *On the Special Laws* 4.49) [PHILO 1945: 75]

As we shall see, later generation of philosophers, Jewish and Muslim, will prefer other explanations of the phenomenon of prophecy, based on a different, more Aristotelian understanding of how the mind works. We turn now to the result of that prophetic inspiration, the Torah.

4. Moses Writes the Torah

Moses our teacher wrote the book of Genesis together with the whole Torah from the mouth of the Holy One, blessed be He. It is likely that he wrote it on Mount Sinai for there it was said to him, "Come up to Me unto the mount, and be there; and I will give you the tablets of stone and the Torah and the commandments which I have written, to teach them" (Exod. 24:12). The "tablets of stone" include the tablets and the writing that are the Ten Commandments. The "commandment" includes the number of all the commandments, positive and negative. If so, the expression "and the Torah" includes the stories from the beginning of Genesis (and is called Torah-teaching) because it teaches people the ways of faith. Upon descending from the mount, he [Moses] wrote the Torah from the beginning of Genesis to the end of the account of the Tabernacle. He wrote the conclusion of the Torah at the end of the fortieth year of wandering in the desert when he said, "Take this book of the Law and put it in the side of the Ark of the Covenant of the Eternal your Lord" (Deut. 31:26).

This view accords with the opinion of the Talmudic sage who says that the Torah was written in sections (BT.Gittin 60a). However, according to the sage who says that the Torah was given in its entirety, everything was written in the fortieth year when he [Moses] was commanded, "Now write this song for you and teach it to the Children of Israel; put it in their mouths" (Deut. 31:19), and, as he was further instructed,

"Take this book of the Law and put it in the side of the Ark of the Covenant of the Eternal your Lord."

In either case it would have been proper for him to write at the beginning of the book of Genesis: "And God spoke to Moses all these words, saying . . ." The reason it was written anonymously [that is, without that phrase] is that Moses our teacher did not write the Torah in the first person like the prophets who did mention themselves. For example, it is often said of Ezekiel, "And the word of the Eternal came to me saying, 'Son of man . . .' " (Ezek. 3:16–17), and it is said of Jeremiah, "And the word of the Eternal came to me" (Jer. 1:4). Moses our teacher, however, wrote this history of all former generations and his own genealogy, history and experiences in the third person. Therefore he says, "And the Lord spoke to Moses, saying to him" (Exod. 6:2), as if he were speaking about another person. And because this is so, Moses is not mentioned in the Torah until his birth, and even at that time he is mentioned as if someone else was speaking about him. . . .

The reason for the Torah being written in this form [that is, in the third person] is that it preceded the creation of the world, and, needless to say, it preceded the birth of Moses our teacher. It has been transmitted to us by tradition that it [the Torah] was written with letters of black fire upon a background of white fire (JT.Shekalim 13b). Thus Moses was like a scribe who copies from an ancient book, and therefore he wrote anonymously.

However, it is true and clear that the entire Torah—from the beginning of Genesis to "in the sight of all Israel" [that is, the last words in Deut. 34:12]—reached the ear of Moses from the mouth of the Holy One, blessed be He, just as it is said elsewhere, "He pronounced all these words to me with His mouth, and I wrote them down in ink in the book" (Jer. 36:16). The Lord informed Moses first of the manner of creation of heaven and earth and all their hosts, that is, the creation of all things, high and low. Likewise of everything that had been said by prophecy concerning the esoterics of the Divine Chariot (in the vision of Ezekiel) and the process of creation and what has been transmitted about them to the Sages. And also with the account of the four forces of the lower world: the force of minerals, vegetation in the earth, living motion and the rational soul. With regard to all these matters—their creation, their essence, their powers and functions, and the disintegration of those of them that are destroyed—Moses our teacher was apprised, and all of it was written in the Torah, explicitly or by implication. (Nachmanides, *Commentary on Genesis*) [NACHMANIDES 1971: 7–9]

5. Are the Prophets Torah?

The Law was revealed to Moses and to the people by God at Sinai and written down by Moses at the divine command. Thus Moses' five books enjoy a guaranteed authenticity and authority. What then of the second great division of the Bible, the "Prophets"? Are they too "Torah"?

Rabbi Isaac said: The Prophets drew from Sinai the inspiration for all their future utterances, for God spoke "with him who stands here with us this day" (Deut. 29:15), that is, with those who were already created, "and also with those who are not here with us this day"; these latter are the souls which are destined to be created (in the future). So too it does not say "the burden of the Lord to Malachi" (Mal. 1:1), but "by the hand of Malachi," to show that the prophecy was already in his hand at Mount Sinai. So too in Isaiah 48:16 it says, "From the hour when the Torah was given, there am I," that is, "From the hour when the Torah was given, I received this prophecy." This applies not to the Prophets alone, but to all the sages who are destined to arise in after days, for the Decalog is described in Deuteronomy 5:22 as "One great voice," and this was divided first into seven, and then into seventy tongues for all mankind. (*Tanhuma* 11:124a–124b)

Asaph said: "Give ear, O my people, to my Law" (Ps. 78:1), and Solomon said, "Forsake not my Law" (Prov. 4:2). Israel said to Asaph, "Is there another law, that you speak of *my* Law? We have already received the Law on Sinai." He said to them: "There are sinners in Israel who say that the Prophets and the Holy Writings are not Torah and so we will not obey them" (Dan. 9:10). But the Prophets and the Holy Writings are indeed Torah. Hence it says, "Give ear, O my people, to my Law." (*Tanhuma* 10a)

6. The Pre-Mosaic Prophets and Their Works

By the second and third Christian century there were circulating in both Christian and Jewish circles a great many pseudepigraphs—or, somewhat less politely, forgeries—some of them attributed to latter-day scribes like Baruch or Ezra and others purporting to be the works of patriarchal figures like Enoch or a cooperative composition like the "Testament of the Twelve Patriarchs." The Christian bishop Augustine (d. 430 C.E.) takes up the question of their antiquity and their inclusion in the canon. In the course of the discussion he is led to reflect on more general questions of history and revelation, of the canon and the apocrypha.

If I may recall far more ancient times, our patriarch Noah was certainly living even before the great deluge, and I might unreservedly call him a prophet inasmuch as the ark he made, in which he escaped with his family, was itself a prophecy of our times. What of Enoch, the seventh from Adam? Does not the canonical letter of the Apostle Jude declare (Jude 14) that he prophesied? But the writings of these men could not be held to be authoritative either among the Jews or us on account of their too great antiquity, which made it seem needful to regard them with suspicion, lest false things should be set forth instead of true. For some writings which are said to be theirs are quoted by those who, according to their own humor, loosely believe what they please. But the purity of the canon has not admitted these writings, not because the authority of these men who pleased God is rejected, but because the writings are not believed to be theirs.

Nor ought it to appear strange if writings for which so great antiquity is claimed are held in suspicion, seeing that in the very history of the kings of Judah and Israel containing their deeds, which we believe to belong to the canonical Scripture, very many things are mentioned which are not explained there, but are said to be found in other books which the prophets wrote, the very names of these prophets being sometimes given, and yet they are not received in the canon which the people of God received. Now I confess that the reason for this is hidden from me; only I think that even those men, to whom certainly the Holy Spirit revealed those things which ought to be held as of religious authority, might write some things as men of historical diligence and other things as prophets by divine inspiration; and these things were so distinct that it was judged that the former should be ascribed to themselves and the latter to God speaking through them; and so the one pertained to the abundance of knowledge, the other to the authority of religion.

In that authority the canon is guarded. So that, if any writings outside of it are now brought forward under the name of the ancient prophets, they cannot serve as even an aid to knowledge because it is uncertain whether they are genuine; and on this account they are not trusted, especially those of them in which some things are found that are even contrary to the truth of the canonical books, so that it is quite apparent that they do not belong to them. (Augustine, *City of God* 18.38)

[AUGUSTINE 1948: 2:445]

7. David and the Psalms

The Christians, like the Jews before them and the Muslims after, generally attributed the Psalms to David. But that there was discussion on the issue of their authorship and what form it took is revealed by these remarks of Augustine.

In the progress of the city of God through the ages, David first reigned in the earthly Jerusalem as a shadow of that which was to come. Now David was a man skilled in songs, who dearly loved musical harmony, not as a vulgar delight but with a believing disposition, and by it served his God, who is the true God, by the mystical representation of a great thing. For the rational and well-ordered concord of diverse sounds in harmonious variety suggests the compact unity of the well-ordered city. Thus all his prophecy is in psalms, of which one hundred and fifty are contained in what we call the *Book of Psalms*, of which some will have it that those only were composed by David which are inscribed with his name. But there are also some who think none of them was composed by him except those which are marked "Of David," while those which have in the title "For David" have been composed by others who assumed his person. Which opinion is refuted by the voice of the Savior himself in the Gospel, when he says (Matt. 22:44) that David himself by the Spirit said Christ was his Lord; for the 110th Psalm begins thus, "The Lord said to my Lord, you shall sit at My right hand when I make your enemies the footstool under your feet." And truly that very psalm, like many more, has in the title not "Of David" but "For David."

Those seem to me to hold the more credible opinion who ascribe to David the authorship of all these hundred and fifty psalms, and think that he prefixed to some of them the names even of other men who prefigured something pertinent to the matter, but chose to have no man's name in the titles of the rest, just as God inspired him in the management of this variety, which, although dark, is not meaningless. Neither ought it move one not to believe this that the names of some prophets who lived long after the times of King David are read in the inscriptions of certain psalms in that book, and that the things said there seem to be spoken of as it were by them. Nor was the prophetic Spirit unable to reveal to King David, when he prophesied, even these names of future prophets, so that he might prophetically sing something which should suit their persons; just as it was revealed more than three hundred years before the event to a certain prophet, who predicted his future deeds along with his name, that

King Josiah should arise and reign (1 Kings. 13:2; cf. 2 Kings. 23:15–17). (Augustine, *City of God* 17.14) [AUGUSTINE 1948: 2:392]

8. Writing Down the Prophecies of Jeremiah

The Scriptures themselves give an occasional hint about the writing down of revelations, at least as far as the prophets are concerned, as in this text from Jeremiah.

In the fourth year of Jehoiakim son of Josiah of Judah [that is, 605 B.C.E.], this word came to Jeremiah from the Lord: Get a scroll and write upon it all the words that I have spoken to you—concerning Israel and Judah and all the nations—from the time I first spoke to you in the days of Josiah to this day. Perhaps when the house of Judah hear all the disasters I intend to bring upon them, they will turn back from their wicked ways, and I will pardon their iniquity and their sin. So Jeremiah called Baruch, son of Neriah, and Baruch wrote down in the scroll at Jeremiah's dictation all the words which the Lord had spoken to him. Jeremiah instructed Baruch, "I am in hiding; I cannot go to the House of the Lord. You go and read aloud the words of the Lord from the scroll which you wrote at my dictation, to the people in the House of the Lord on a fast day; thus you will be reading them to all the Judeans who come in from the towns. . . ." Baruch son of Neriah did just as the prophet Jeremiah had instructed him—to read the words of the Lord from the scroll in the House of the Lord. (Jeremiah 36:1–8)

As the message of the scroll circulates, Jeremiah and Baruch are warned to go into hiding. The scroll, meanwhile, is locked in one of the rooms of the palace, and its presence is reported to the king.

The king sent Jehudi to get the scroll, and he fetched it from the chamber of the scribe Elishama. Jehudi read it to the king and to all the officials who were in attendance on the king. Since it was the ninth month, the king was sitting in the winter house with a fire burning in the brazier before him. And every time Jehudi read three or four columns, [the king] would cut it up with a scribe's knife and throw it into the fire in the brazier, until the entire scroll was consumed by the fire in the brazier. (Jeremiah 36:21–23)

9. The Cessation of Prophecy in Israel after the Exile

By the second century B.C.E. the Jews had come to realize that the voice of prophecy, at least as that was understood in the days before the Exile, had ceased in Israel. For the philosopher Maimonides (d. 1204), who regarded prophecy as a natural, albeit rare, human function, the cause of the silence was not so much the stilling of God's voice as the troubled times, the "sadness and langor" that affected the entire society.

You know that every bodily faculty sometimes grows tired, is weakened, and is troubled, and at other times is in a healthy state. Accordingly, you will find that the prophecy of the prophets ceases when they are sad or angry, or in a mood similar to one of those two. You know their saying that "prophecy does not descend (during a mood of) sadness or languor" (BT.Shabbath 30b), that prophetic revelation did not come to Jacob our father during the time of his mourning because of the fact that his imaginative faculty was preoccupied with the loss of Joseph; and that the prophetic revelation did not come to Moses, peace be upon him, after the disastrous incident of the spies and until the whole generation of the desert perished, in the way that revelation used to come before, because—seeing the enormity of their crime—he suffered greatly from this matter. . . . Similarly you will find that several prophets prophesied during a certain time and that afterwards prophecy was taken away from them and could not be permanent because of an accident that had supervened. This is indubitably the essential and proximate cause of the fact that prophesy was taken away during the time of the Exile. For what languor or sadness can befall a man in any state that would be stronger than that due to his being a thrall slave in bondage to the ignorant who commit great sins and in whom the privation of true reason is united to the perfection of the lusts of beasts? "And there shall be no might in your hand" (Deut. 28:32). This was with what they had been threatened. And this is what is meant by the saying: "They shall run to and fro to seek the word of the Lord and shall not find it" (Amos 8:12). And it also says: "Her kings and princes are among the nations, the Law is no more; yes, her prophets find no visions from the Lord" (Lam. 2:9). This is true and the cause thereof is clear. For the instrument has ceased to function. This also will be the cause of prophecy being restored to us in its habitual form, as has been promised in the days of the Messiah, may he be revealed soon. (Maimonides, *Guide of the Perplexed* 2.37) [MAIMONIDES 1963: 372–373]

10. The Septuagint

The Hebrew Bible, which was already being interpreted in Aramaic in Palestine at the time of Ezra and Nehemiah, received a full and formal translation into Greek, almost certainly in Egypt and under the impulse of the large colony of Greek-speaking Jews there. Just when this took place is uncertain, though our chief source on the event, the Letter of Aristeas, *claims that it occurred at the time of the king Ptolemy Philadelphus (283–245 B.C.E.). The manner in which it was done was of some importance, particularly to the Christians, who adopted it as their official transcript of the Bible.*

He [Ptolemy Philadelphus] gave orders to (his minister) Demetrius to draw up a memorandum on the writing down of all the books of the Jews. For all the business of state was carried out by decrees and with the utmost accuracy by those Egyptian kings; nothing was done in a careless or haphazard manner. I have inserted here copies of the memorandum and the letters. . . . The following is a copy of the memorandum. The Memorandum of Demetrius to the Great King: "Since you have ordered me, my Lord, O King, to collect the the books required to complete your library (at Alexandria) and to repair those which are defective, I have accordingly taken great pains to fulfill your wishes, and I now have the following proposal to lay before you. The books of the law of the Jews, together with some few others, are missing from the library. They are written in Hebrew characters and language and have been carelessly interpreted [or translated], and I am informed by their experts that they do not represent the original text, since they have never been protected by royal care. What is now required is that they be corrected for your library since the law which they contain, being of divine origin, is full of wisdom and free of all blemish. As a consequence (of this faulty text) literary men and poets and the mass of historical writers have refrained from referring to these books, even those who have lived and are living in accordance with them, because their conception of life is so sacred and religious, as Hecateus of Abdera says. By your leave, my Lord, a letter shall be written to the High Priest in Jerusalem requesting that he send six elders from each of the tribes—men who have lived the noblest life and are most expert in their law—that we may discover the points on which the majority of them are in agreement, and thus, after we have an accurate translation, we can install it in a conspicuous place in a manner that befits both the work and your purpose. May continual prosperity be yours!" (*Letter of Aristeas* 28–32)

It did so please the king. A request and gifts were sent to the High Priest in Jerusalem, Eliezer, who responded by dispatching seventy-two elders, "good men and true," together with a copy of Scripture. They arrive safely, are feted, and the work begins.

Demetrius took the men, and going along the sea wall, which is seven stadia in length, to the island (off the coast at Alexandria), he crossed the bridge and went to the northern districts of Pharos Island. There he assembled them in a beautiful and secluded house which had been built on the shore. He then invited them to carry out the work of translation, and everything they needed for the work was placed at their disposal. So they set to work, comparing their several versions and bringing them into agreement, and whatever they agreed upon was suitably copied out under the direction of Demetrius. . . . Every day they met and worked in a delightfully quiet and sunny place. And so it happened that the work of translation was finished in seventy-two days, just as if it had been planned that way.

When the work was finished, Demetrius assembled all the Jews in the place where the translation had been made and had it read through to all in the presence of the translators, who met with great enthusiasm from the people because of the great benefits which they had conferred upon them. They also warmly praised Demetrius and urged him to have the entire Law transcribed, copied and presented to their leaders. After the books had been read through, the priests and the elders among the translators and the Jewish community and the leaders of the people announced that since the translation was so outstanding and accurate it should properly remain as it was and no alteration be made in it. And when the whole company expressed their agreement, they bade them pronounce, in accordance with their custom, a curse upon anyone who should make any alteration either by adding anything or changing in any way whatever any of the words that had been written or by making any excisions. This was a very wise precaution to ensure that the Book [literally, the Bible, *he Biblos*, the earliest recorded example of this usage] might be preserved unchanged for all future time. (Ibid. 301–311)

Although the Letter of Aristeas *explicitly states that the translation was done at the initiative of the Egyptian king, the same text insists that the version was the product of a consensual effort on the part of the translators and received the cooperation of the High Priest and the enthusiastic and unanimous approval of the Jewish people of Alexandria. Philo, an Alexandrian Jew living at least a century after the* Letter, *tells much the same story about the Greek translation, with even greater emphasis on the miraculous and doubtless divinely inspired unanimity that prevailed among the translators.*

Facing Alexandria lies the island of Pharos (and) . . . because they considered this to be the most suitable place in the district where they might find peace and tranquillity and where the soul could commune with the Laws with none to disturb its privacy, they [that is, the translators] took up their residence there. They took the Sacred Books, lifted them up toward heaven in their hands, and asked God that they might not fail in their purpose. And He heard their prayers, with the result that the greater part, or even the whole, of the human race might be profited and led to a better life by continuing to observe such wise and truly admirable ordinances.

Sitting here in seclusion, with none present save the elements of nature, earth, water, air, heaven—the creation of which was to be the first theme of the sacred revelation, for the Laws begin with the story of the world's creation—they became as it were possessed, and under inspiration, wrote, not each scribe something different, but the word for word identical thing, as though it had been dictated to each by an invisible prompter. Yet who is not aware that every language, and Greek especially, is rich in terms, and that the same thought can be expressed in many ways by changing single words or whole phrases and cutting the expression to the occasion? This was not the case, we are told, with this Law of ours, but the Greek words used corresponded literally with the Chaldean [that is, the Hebrew], and were exactly appropriate to the things they signified. (Philo, *The Life of Moses* 2.45–65)

11. The Septuagint as a Supplementary Revelation

By the fifth century C.E. this Greek version, called the Septuagint, the one used by both Philo and Paul, had won undisputed pride of place in the Christian Church. As Philo had already noted and as Augustine here reaffirms even more strongly, it shared something of the quality of a revelation in its own right.

While there were other interpreters who translated these sacred oracles out of the Hebrew tongue into Greek, as Aquila, Symmachus and Theodotion, and also that translation which, as its author is unknown, is quoted as the fifth edition, yet the Church has received this Septuagint translation just as if it were the only one; and it has been used by the Greek Christian people, most of whom are not aware that there is any other. From this translation there has also been made one in the Latin tongue, which the Latin churches use. Our times, however, have enjoyed the advantage of the presbyter Jerome (d. 419 C.E.), a man most learned and skilled in all three languages, who translated these same Scriptures into the Latin speech, not from the Greek but from the Hebrew.

Augustine was aware that by this time the Jews had long since disavowed the Septuagint; but he also knew the stories we have just reviewed concerning the translation of the latter. For him those stories—and the fact that by then the Christian tradition was irrevocably committed to the Septuagint—were sufficient guarantee of its authenticity and accuracy.

But although the Jews acknowledge this very learned labor of his to be faithful, while they contend that the Septuagint translators have erred in many places, still the churches of Christ judge that no one should be preferred to the authority of so many men, chosen for this very great work by Eleazer, who was then High Priest. For even if there had not appeared in them one spirit, without doubt divine, and the seventy learned men had, after the manner of men, compared together the words of their translation, that what pleased them all might stand, no single translator ought to be preferred to them; but since so great a sign of divinity has appeared in them, certainly, if any other translator of their Scriptures from the Hebrew into any other tongue is faithful, in that case he agrees with those seventy translators, and if he is found not to agree with them, then we ought to believe that it is they who possess the prophetic gift. For the same spirit who was in the prophets when they spoke these things was in the seventy men when they translated them, so assuredly they could also say something else, just as if the prophet himself had said both, because it would be the same spirit who said both; and could say the same thing differently, so that, although the words were not the same, yet the same meaning should shine forth to those of good understanding; and could omit or add something, so that even by this it might be shown that there was in that work not human bondage, which the translator owed to the words, but rather divine power, which filled and ruled the mind of the translator.

Some, however, have thought that the Greek copies of the Septuagint version ought to be emended from the Hebrew copies; yet they did not dare to take away what the Hebrew lacked and the Septuagint had, but only added what was found in the Hebrew copies and was lacking in the Septuagint, and noted them by placing at the beginning of the verses certain stars which they call asterisks. And those things which the Hebrew copies have not and the Septuagint has, they have in like manner marked at the beginning of the verses with horizontal spit-shaped marks like those by which we denote ounces. . . .

If, then, as it behooves us, we behold nothing else in these Scriptures than what the spirit of God has spoken through men, if anything is in the Hebrew copies and not in the version of the Seventy, the spirit of God did not choose to say it through them, but only through the prophets. But whatever is in the Septuagint and not in the Hebrew copies, the same spirit chose to say through the latter, thus showing that both were prophets. (Augustine, *City of God* 18.43) [AUGUSTINE 1948: 2:450–451]

12. The Scriptures and Piety
(ca. 132 B.C.E.)

Among the many books of Jewish piety in general circulation in the two centuries before the Christian era was one titled "The Wisdom of Jesus ben Sira," in Latin called "Ecclesiasticus." It was written in Hebrew sometime about 180 B.C.E. and then translated into Greek by the author's grandson for the benefit of the Egyptian community of Jews, many of whom no longer understood Hebrew. The work begins with the translator's own remarks, in which occurs the earliest reference to all three of the classical divisions of the Bible: the Law, the Prophets, and the Writings.

A legacy of great value has come to us through the Law, the Prophets and the writers who followed in their steps, and for this Israel's traditions of discipline and wisdom deserve recognition. It is the duty of those who study Scripture not only to become expert themselves, but also to use their scholarship for the benefit of the outside world through both the spoken and the written word. So my grandfather Jesus (ben Sira), who had industriously applied himself to the study of the Law, the Prophets and the other writings of our ancestors, and had gained a considerable proficiency in them, was moved to compile a book of his own of themes of discipline and wisdom, so that, with futher help, scholars might make greater progress in their studies by living as the Law directs.

You are asked then to read with sympathetic attention and make allowances if, in spite of all the devoted work I have put into the translation, some of the expressions appear inadequate. For it is impossible for a translator to find precise equivalents for the original Hebrew in another language. Not only with this book, but with the Law, the Prophets and the rest of the writings, it makes no small difference to read them in the original.

When I came to Egypt and settled there in the thirty-eighth year of the reign of King Euergetes [that is, 132 B.C.E.,] I found great scope for education; and I thought it very necessary to spend some energy and labor on the translation of this book. Ever since then I have been applying my skill night and day to complete it and to publish it for the use of those who have made their home in a foreign land, and wish to become scholars by training themselves to live according to the Law. (Wisdom of Jesus ben Sira, Preface)

13. Josephus on the Biblical Canon
(ca. 85 C.E.)

The tract called Against Apion *was written by Josephus, the Pharisee who deserted the cause of the Zealot nationalists in their war against Rome in 66–70 C.E. It is an apologia intended, like most of his other works, not merely to redress certain grievances but to explain Judaism to a Gentile world. Thus it includes a description of the sacred books of the Jews.*

Since among us (Jews) it is not permitted to everyone to write the records, and there is no discrepancy in what is written; and since, on the contrary, the prophets alone had this privilege, obtaining their knowledge of the most remote and ancient history through the inspiration which they owed to God, and committing to writing a clear account of the events of their own time just as they occurred, it naturally and even necessarily follows that we do not possess myriads of inconsistent books in conflict with each other. Our books, those that are justly accredited, are but twenty-two and contain the record of all time.

Of these, five are the Books of Moses [that is, the Torah], comprising the laws and the traditional history from the birth of man down to the death of the lawgiver. This period falls only a little short of three thousand years. From the death of Moses until Artaxerxes who succeeded Xerxes as king of Persia, the prophets subsequent to Moses wrote the history of the events of their own times in thirteen books [that is, the Prophets]. The remaining books [that is, the Writings] contain hymns to God and precepts for the conduct of human life.

From Artaxerxes to our own time the complete history has (also) been written, but it has not been deemed worthy of equal credit with the earlier books because of the failure of the exact succession of the prophets. (Josephus, *Against Apion* 1.7–8)

427

14. Canon and Sanctity

The men who made the actual decisions regarding what was Scripture and what was not were not generous in explaining the grounds for their choices. We must be content with passing remarks, like this one in the Talmud.

That man must be remembered for a blessing, namely Hananiah ben Hezekiah; but for him, the Book of Ezekiel would have been withdrawn (from the canon), for its words contradict the words of the Torah. What did he do? Three hundred measures of oil were brought up to him and he sat in an upper room and expounded it. (BT.Hagigah 13a)

The effect of Hananiah's laborious exegesis presumably reconciled the discrepancies between Ezekiel, Exodus, and Leviticus and permitted it to be included in the scriptural canon.

The rise of the Pharisees, with their emphasis on the extension of ritual purity, placed the question of the sanctity of Scripture in a new context. As a sacred, and hence a taboo object, "all scrolls (of Scripture) render the hands unclean, except the scroll that is used in the Temple court" (M.Kelim 15:6). There were objections to this proscription (see Chapter 3 below), but the Mishna passes directly to the determination of what precisely constituted Scripture—and so could "render the hands unclean"—and what was not. First, there was the physical question.

The blank spaces in a scroll (of the Scriptures) that are above and below (the text), and that are at the beginning and the end, render the hands unclean. Rabbi Judah says: The blank space at the end does not render the hands unclean until the roller is attached to it.

If the writing in a scroll was erased yet there still remained eighty-five letters, as many as there are in the paragraph (beginning) "And it came to pass when the Ark set forward . . . " (Num. 10:35ff.), it still renders the hands unclean. A (single) written sheet (in a Scripture scroll) in which are written eighty-five letters . . . renders the hands unclean. (M.Yadaim 3:4–5)

The same Mishnaic tractate Yadaim then passes directly to the larger question of which books constitute Scripture and which do not, still from the point of view of the transmission of ritual impurity. The controversy has to do with two works in the third division of the Bible, after Torah and the Prophets, called "the Writings."

All the Holy Scriptures render the hands unclean. The Song of Songs and Ecclesiastes render the hands unclean. Rabbi Judah says: The Song of Songs renders the hands unclean, but there is disagreement about Ecclesiastes. Rabbi Yosi says: Ecclesiastes does not render the hands unclean, and there is disagreement about the Song of Songs. Rabbi Simeon says: Ecclesiastes is one of the things about which the School of Shammai adopted the more lenient and the School of Hillel the more stringent ruling. Rabbi Simeon ben Azzai said: I have heard a tradition from the seventy-two elders [that is, of the Great Sanhedrin] on the day when they made Rabbi Eliezer head of the assembly that the Song of Songs and Ecclesiastes both render the hands unclean. Rabbi Akiba said: God forbid! No man in Israel ever disputed about the Song of Songs, that it does not render the hands unclean, for all the ages are not worth the day on which the Song of Songs was given to Israel. For all the Writings are holy, but the Song of Songs is the Holy of Holies. And if there was anything in dispute, the dispute was about Ecclesiastes alone. (M.Yadaim 3:5)

The discussion in Yadaim later returns to the question of translation, whether the few Aramaic passages in Scripture, like Ezra 4:8–7:18 and Daniel 2:4–6:28, enjoy the same sanctity as those in Hebrew. They do, as it turns out, but subsequent translations of the Bible do not share that same holiness.

The (Aramaic) version that is in Ezra and Daniel renders the hands unclean. If this (Aramaic) version is written [that is, translated] into Hebrew, or the Hebrew (passages in Scripture) done in an (Aramaic) version, or in Hebrew script, it does not render the hands unclean. (M.Yadaim 4:5)

15. On the Status of the Christians' So-called Scriptures

Further on in the tractate Yadaim, the later rabbinic tradition reflects upon the earlier Pharisaic one. The point of departure is, as we have just seen, a discussion of the degree of sanctity inherent in the portions of the books of Ezra and Daniel originally written in Aramaic and then translated into Hebrew. The Pharisees maintained that these books were in fact canonical and so shared in the same holiness and the same characteristic of "rendering the hands unclean" as the original Hebrew parts of Scripture. There were those who objected—not, however, on the question of the Aramaic sections of Scripture but on the very idea of Scripture rendering the hands unclean.

The Sadducees say, We cry out against you, O you Pharisees, for you say, "The Holy Scriptures render the hands unclean," but the writings of Hamiram do not render the hands unclean.

"Hamiram" is textually uncertain. It might refer to the "Minim" or heretics; on one view, such references are to the Jewish-Christians. The same text continues:

Rabban Yohanan ben Zakkai said, Have we nothing against the Pharisees save this, for behold, they say, "The bones of an ass are clean and the bones of Yohanan the High Priest are unclean." . . . They [that is, the Pharisees] answered him, "Our love for them is the measure of their uncleanness—that no man should make spoons of the bones of his father or his mother. So it is with the Holy Scripture: our love of them is the measure of their uncleanness; thus since the writings of Hamiram are held in no account, they do not render the hands unclean." (M. Yadaim 4:5–6)

If "Hamiram" is here only an uncertain reference to the Christians, the issue of whether Christian writings in any sense constituted Scripture is more fully and explicitly discussed in the Tosefta. The case in point is a fire that occurs on the Sabbath, and the question is what books may be rescued from the blaze under such circumstances.

All sacred books may be saved from burning (on the Sabbath) whether they are read on the Sabbath or not. Regardless of the language in which they are written, if they become unfit for use they must be hidden away. Why are certain of the biblical books [like the "Writings"] not read? So that they may not nullify the House of Study. The case of a scroll may be saved with the scroll, and the container of the phylacteries together with them, even though there is money in them. Where should they be taken for safety? To an alley which is not a thoroughfare. Ben Bathyra says: even to an alley which is a thoroughfare. (M. Shabbat 16:1)

Thus authentic Scripture may be saved. What else?

We do not save from a fire (on the Sabbath) the Gospels and the books of the Minim. Rather, they are burned in their place, they and their Tetragrammata [that is, occurrences of the sacred name of God that might appear in them]. Rabbi Yosi the Galilean says: During the week one should cut out their Tetragrammata and hide them away and burn the remainder. Rabbi Tarfon said: May I bury my sons! If (these books) should come into my hand, I would burn them along with their Tetragrammata. For even if a pursuer were running after me, I would sooner enter a house [or temple] of idolatry than enter their [that is, the Minim's] houses. For the idolaters do not know Him and deny Him, but these know Him and deny Him. . . . Said Rabbi Ishmael: If for the sake of peace between husband and wife the Ever-Present One has commanded that a book written in holiness be erased by means of water, how much more so should the books of the Minim which bring enmity between Israel and their Father Who is in heaven be erased, they and their Tetragrammata. . . . Just as we do not save them from a fire, so we do not save them from a cave-in, or from water or from anything which would destroy them. (Tosefta Shabbat 13:5)

16. Ezra Rewrites the Scriptures

Among the noncanonical Jewish books circulating under the name of Ezra in the first centuries of the Christian Era is that known as "The Second Book of Esdras"— Esdras is the Greek form of the name Ezra. The book was written in the main by a Palestinian Jew sometime about 100 C.E., and it contains an account of Ezra's work on the Holy Scriptures after the return from the Babylonian Exile. It is Ezra who speaks here.

"May I speak in your presence, Lord? I am about to depart, by your command, after giving warning to those of my people who are now alive. But who will give warning to those born hereafter? The world is shrouded in darkness, and its inhabitants are without light. For your Law was destroyed in the fire [that is, the Babylonian destruction of Jerusalem], and so no one can know about the deeds you have done or intend to do. If I have won your favor, fill me with your holy spirit, so that I may write down the whole story of the world from the very beginning, everything that is contained in your Law; then men will have the chance to find the right path and, if they choose, gain life in the last days."

"Go," He replied, "call the people together, and tell them not to look for you for forty days. Have a large number of writing tablets ready, and take with you Seraiah and Dibri, Shelemiah, Ethan and Asiel, five men all trained to write quickly. Then return here and I will light a lamp of understanding in your mind, which will not go out until you have finished all you are to write. When your work is complete, some of it you must make public; the rest you must give to wise men to keep secret. Tomorrow at this time you shall begin to write."

I went as I was ordered and summoned all the people and said, "Israel, listen to what I say. . . . From this moment no one must talk to me or look for me for the next forty days." I took with me the five men I had been told, and we went away to the field, and there we stayed. On the next day I heard a voice calling me, which said: "Ezra, open your mouth and drink what I give you." So I opened my mouth, and was handed a cup of what seemed like water, except that its color was the color of fire. I took it and drank, and as soon as I had done so my mind began to pour forth a flood of understanding, and wisdom grew greater and greater within me, for I retained my memory unimpaired. I opened my mouth to speak, and I continued to speak unceasingly. The Most High gave understanding to the five men, who took turns in writing down what was said, using characters which they had not known before. They remained at work through the forty days, writing all day, and taking food only at night. But as for me, I spoke all through the day; even at night I was not silent. In the forty days ninety-four books were written. At the end of the forty days the Most High spoke to me. "Make public the (twenty-four) books you wrote first [that is, the twenty-four books of the canonical Hebrew Bible]," He said, "to be read by good and bad alike. But the last seventy books [that is, the apocrypha and pseudepigrapha] are to be kept back and given to none but the wise among your people. They contain a stream of understanding, a fountain of wisdom, a flood of knowledge." And I did so. (2 Esdras 14:19–48)

17. A Christian Insertion in a Jewish Work

Not long after the composition of that Jewish work called 2 Esdras—that is, sometime in the second century C.E.—a prologue (Chapters 1–2) of unmistakable and not very subtly disguised Christian sentiments was added to it by another anonymous hand. Once again it is Ezra who purportedly speaks.

I, Ezra, received on Mount Horeb a commission from the Lord to go to Israel; but when I came they scorned me and rejected God's commandment. Therefore I say to you Gentiles, you who hear and understand: "Look forward to the coming of your shepherd, and he will give you everlasting rest; for he who is to come at the end of the world is close at hand. Be ready to receive the rewards of the kingdom; for light perpetual will shine upon you for ever and ever. Flee from the shadow of the world and receive the joy and splendor that await you. I bear witness openly to my Savior. It is he whom the Lord has appointed; receive him and be joyful, giving thanks to the One who has summoned you to the heavenly realms. Rise, stand up, and see the whole company of those who bear the Lord's mark and sit at His table. They have moved out of the shadow of this world and have received shining robes from the Lord. Receive, O Sion, your full number, and close the roll of those arrayed in white who have faithfully kept the Law of the Lord. The number of Your sons whom You so long desired is now complete. Pray that the Lord's kingdom may come, so that your people, whom He summoned when the world began, may be set apart as His own.

I, Ezra, saw on Mount Sion a crowd too large to count, all singing hymns in praise of the Lord. In the middle stood a very tall young man, taller than all the rest, who was setting a crown on the head of each one of them; he stood out above them all. I was enthralled at the sight and asked the angel, "Sir, who are these?" He replied, "These are those who have laid aside their mortal dress and put on the immortal, those who acknowledged the name of God. Now they are being given crowns and palms." And I asked again, "Who is the young man setting crowns on their heads and giving them palms?" and the angel replied, "He is the Son of God, whom they acknowledged in this mortal life." I began to praise those who had stood so valiantly for the Lord's name. Then the angel said to me, "Go and tell my people all the great and wonderful acts of the Lord God that you have seen." (2 Esdras 2:33–48)

18. Early Testimony on the Gospels

The author to Theophilus: many authors have undertaken to draw up an account of the events that have happened among us, following the traditions handed down to us by the original eyewitnesses and servants of the Gospel. And so I in my turn, your Excellency, as one who has gone over the whole course of these events in detail, have decided to write a connected narrative for you, so as to give you authentic knowledge about the matters of which you have been informed. (Luke 1:1–4)

So begins the Gospel according to Luke. The style is formal, even learned, but the author had no sense that he was writing "Scripture"—as indeed he was not. When an early Christian said "Scripture," he was invariably referring to the Bible. But the Gospels, as the testimony to Jesus' Messianic claims and as an authentic account of his redemptive work, also had a substantial claim on the Christians' attention. Part of that attention was devoted to the question of who wrote those four books.

Five books of Papias [ca. 130 C.E.] are extant, bearing the title *Expositions of the Oracles of the Lord*. Ireneus relates that this is his only work, and adds, "Papias, the hearer of John and the companion of Polycarp, a man of an earlier generation testifies to these things in his fourth book. His work is in five volumes." Now Papias himself in the introduction to his writings makes no claim to be a hearer and eyewitness of the holy Apostles, but to have received the contents of the faith from those who were known to them. He tells us of this in his own words: "I shall not hesitate to set down for you, along with my interpretations, all things which I learned from the elders with care and recorded with care, being well assured of their truth. . . ."

"Now [John] the Elder used to say this also (Papias continues): Mark became the interpreter of Peter and wrote down accurately, but not in order, as much as he remembered of the sayings and doings of Christ. For he was not a hearer or a follower of the Lord, but afterwards, as I said, of Peter, who adapted his teachings to the needs of the moment and did not make an ordered exposition of the sayings of the Lord. And so Mark made no mistake when he thus wrote down some things as he remembered them; for he made it his special care to omit nothing of what he heard and to make no false statements therein." This is what Papias relates concerning Mark.

Now concerning Matthew, it is stated; "So Matthew recorded the oracles in the Hebrew tongue, and each interpreted them to the best of his ability." Papias also makes use of the testimonies of the first letter of John and of the letter of Peter. (Eusebius, *Church History* 3.39)

[According to Ireneus, bishop of Lyons at the end of the second century] Matthew published his Gospel among the Hebrews in their own tongue, when Peter and Paul were preaching the Gospel in Rome and founding the church there. After their departure, Mark, the disciple and interpreter of Peter, himself handed down to us in writing the substance of Peter's preaching. Luke, the follower of Paul, set down in a book the Gospel preached by his teacher. Then John, the disciple of the Lord, who also leaned on his breast, himself produced his Gospel, while he was living in Ephesus in Asia. (Ibid. 5.8)

19. The New Testament Canon

As the Christians came to understand that these writings too constituted a Scripture for the New Covenant, they were faced with the same questions of authenticity and canon that confronted the Jews. A consensus on four Gospels was probably reached early on, but some questions remained, as emerges from the text called the "Muratorian Canon." It was written down in Latin in the eighth century but probably goes back to a Greek original from the end of the second century, that is, to the time of Ireneus.

. . . The third book of the Gospel is the one according to Luke. Luke, the physician, when, after the Ascension of Christ, Paul had taken him to himself as a companion on his travels, wrote in his own name what he had been told, although he had not himself seen the Lord in the flesh. He put down the events as far as he could learn them, and he began his account with the birth of John (the Baptist).

The fourth Gospel is the one by John, one of the disciples. . . . When his fellow disciples and bishops urged him (to write such a work), he said, "Fast with me for three days beginning today, and then let us tell the others whatever may be revealed to each of us." On the same night it was revealed to Andrew, one of the Apostles, that it was John who should narrate all things in his own name as they (all) recalled them. . . .

The Acts of all the Apostles are included in one book. Luke addressed them to the most excellent Theophilus, because some of them occurred when he was present; and he makes this clear by leaving out the sufferings of Peter and the journey of Paul after the latter left Rome for Spain.

As for the Letters of Paul . . . he wrote to no more than seven churches, in this order: the first to the Corinthians, the second to the Ephesians, the third to the Philippians, the fourth to the Colossians, the fifth to the Galatians, the sixth to the Thessalonians, the seventh to the Romans. . . . In addition to these he wrote one (letter) to Philemon, one to Titus, and two to Timothy. They were written in personal affection, but they have been sanctified by being held in regard by the Catholic Church for the regulation of Church discipline. There is extant also a letter to the Laodiceans, and another to the Alexandrians, forged under Paul's name to further the heresy of Marcion. And there are many others which cannot be received into the Catholic Church since it is not fitting for vinegar to be mixed with honey.

The Letter of Jude and the two bearing the name of John are accepted in the Catholic Church; also (the book called) "Wisdom" and written by the friends of Solomon in his honor. We also receive the Apocalypse of John and (one letter) of Peter; [there is a second] which some of us refuse to have read in church. The "Shepherd" is a work written very recently in our own day by Hermas, in the city of Rome, when his brother, Bishop Pius, held the Chair of the Church of Rome. For this reason it too should be read, but not publicly in church to the people, either among the Prophetic books, since their number is complete, or among the Apostles. (Muratorian Canon)

20. There Can Be Only Four Gospels

A good deal of the early discussion on the Christian canon of Scripture was historical in its orientation and method, as we shall see. But the Christian fathers were no less fond of a priori reasoning than contemporary rabbis, and so they were more than willing to demonstrate that there could be no more than four Gospels.

But it is not possible that the Gospels can be either more or fewer in number than they are. For since there are four zones of the world in which we live, and four principal winds, while the Church has been scattered throughout the world, and the pillar and ground of the Church is the Gospel and the spirit of life; it is fitting that she should have four pillars, breathing incorruption on every side, and vivifying men afresh. From this fact it is evident that the Word, the Artificer of all, He that sitteth upon the Cherubim and holds together all things, when he was manifested to men, gave us the Gospel under four forms but bound together by one Spirit.... For the Cherubim too were four-faced, and their faces were images of the dispensation of the Son of God. For it [the Scripture: Rev. 4:7] says, "the first living creature was like a lion," symbolizing His effectual working, His supremacy and royal power [Mark]; "the second was like a calf," signifying His sacrificial and sacerdotal order [Luke]; but "the third had the face of a man," an evident description of His advent as a human being [Matthew]; "the fourth was like a flying eagle," pointing out the gift of the Spirit hovering with His wings over the Church [John]. (Ireneus, *Against the Heresies* 3.11:11)

21. The Historicity of the Gospels

Ireneus' arguments are obviously allegorical; but early in the tradition the Christians also developed arguments that spoke to the Gospels in more historical terms, perhaps, as the following selection suggests, because they were constrained to. Here Origen takes on a pagan polemicist named Celsus.

Unless the Evangelists were devoted to the truth, but were, as Celsus maintains, writing fictions, they would never have made mention of the denial of Peter or the scandal of Jesus' disciples. For even if these things had happened, who could have proved that they happened thus? On the contrary, it was appropriate to pass over such events in silence if the authors had as their intention to teach the readers of the Gospels to despise death, since it was a question of the profession of Christianity that was at stake. (Origen, *Against Celsus* 2.15)

Other arguments for the authenticity of the Gospels were adduced, like these from the Western Christian Arnobius (d. 337 C.E.), and likely too against a pagan polemicist.

You do not believe in these deeds [that is, the miracles of Jesus]? But those who saw them and witnessed them with their own eyes believed them and passed them on as credible to us of a later generation. And who were those men you ask? People of all sorts, incredulous humankind, who, if they had not seen the events out in the open and brighter than the light itself, would never have given their assent to such incredible events. We are not to say, are we, that the men of that time were so vain, lying, stupid and bestial that they imagined they had seen what they had not and which had never occurred, supported it with false testimonies and child-like assertions; and when it was possible to live in peace and harmony, they assumed these gratuitous grounds for hostility and preferred a mal-odorous reputation?

But, you say, the Gospels were written by unlettered and crude men and so it is no easy matter to credit them. But is this not all the more reason to think that they are not cooked up with lies, since they were the products of simple minds incapable of subtle embellishments? (Arnobius, *Against the Heathen* 1.58; 2.5)

And once again in the East:

And if these miracles of Christ were lies which his disciples had conspired to invent, it would indeed be an admirable piece of work, how so many people could have preserved their unanimity on these fictions until they died, and that no one of them was ever moved by the fear of what happened to those who died before him to quit the company and contradict the others by betraying what they had agreed upon among themselves. (Eusebius, *Evangelical Preparation* 3.5)

Often the Evangelists are detected in disagreements. But certainly that is a powerful argument for their veracity. If they had agreed among themselves on every detail, on times and places and words, no one of them would have been believed by their enemies but it would have been thought that these writings had been composed by a human consensus, and that this kind of consensus does not arise from the simple truth. Indeed, that very discrepancy in small details dispels suspicion from them and clearly vindicates the trustworthiness of the writers. (John Chrysos-tom, *Homilies on Matthew* 1.2)

22. Did Paul Write the "Letter to the Hebrews"?

How sophisticated some of the critical reasoning could become is evident in Origen's reflections on the stylistic criterium for authenticity as applied to the New Testament Letter to the Hebrews. *The reporter is Eusebius.*

Furthermore he [Origen; d. ca. 255 C.E.] discusses the *Letter to the Hebrews* in the homily he wrote on it. "That the character of the diction of the letter entitled 'To the Hebrews' has not the Apostle (Paul's) rude-ness in speech, who confessed himself 'rude in speech' (1 Cor. 11:6), that is, in style, but that the letter is better Greek in the framing of its diction, will be admitted by everyone who is able to discern differences of style. But again, on the other hand, that the thoughts of the letter are admira-ble, and not inferior to the acknowledged writings of the Apostle, to this also everyone will consent as true who has given attention to reading the Apostle."

Further on he [Origen] adds the following remarks: "But as for myself, if I were to state my own opinion, I should say that the thoughts are the Apostle's, but that the style and composition belong to one who called to mind the Apostle's teachings and, as it were, made short notes on what his master said. If any church, therefore, holds this letter as Paul's, let it be commended for this also. For not without reason have men of old time handed it down as Paul's. But who wrote the letter, in truth God knows. Yet the account which has reached us [is twofold], some saying that Clement, who was bishop of the Romans, wrote the letter; others that it was Luke, who also wrote the Gospel and the Acts." (Eusebius, *Church History* 6.25)

23. The New Testament Canon in the Fourth Century

Eusebius continues, now speaking in his own voice of his own times.

Now that we have reached this point, it is reasonable to sum up the writings of the New Testament already mentioned. Well, then, we must set in the first place the quartet of the Gospels, which are followed by the book of the Acts of the Apostles. After this we must reckon the letters of Paul; following this we must pronounce genuine the extant first letter of John, and likewise the letter of Peter. After this we must place, if it really seems right, the Apocalypse of John. . . . These then belong to the ac-knowledged writings.

But of those which are disputed, but are nevertheless familiar to most people, there is extant the letter of James, as it is called, and that of Jude; and the second letter of Peter; and the second and third of John, so named, whether they belong to the evangelist or perhaps to some other of the same name as he.

Among the spurious writings there are to be placed also the book of the Acts of Paul, and the Shepherd, as it is called, and the Apocalypse of

Peter; and in addition to these, the extant letter of Barnabas, and the Teachings of the Apostles, as it is called; and moreover, as I said, the Apocalypse of John, if it seems right. This last, as I said, is rejected by some, but others give it a place among the acknowledged writings. And among those some have reckoned also the Gospel of the Hebrews, a work which is especially acceptable to such Hebrews as have received the Christ. (Eusebius, *Church History* 3.25)

24. Orthodox and Heretical Apocrypha

Eusebius continues on the subject of writings rejected from the canon, the so-called apocrypha and pseudepigrapha.

Now all of these (spurious and questionable works) would be among the disputed writings; but nevertheless we have been compelled to make a catalogue of these also, distinguishing those writings which the tradition of the Church has deemed true and genuine and acknowledged from the others outside their number, which, though they are not canonical but even disputed, yet are recognized by most churchmen. [And this we have done] in order that we might be able to know both these same writings and also those which the heretics put forward in the name of the Apostles, whether as containing Gospels of Peter and Thomas and Matthias, or even of some others besides these, or as containing the Acts of Andrew and John and other Apostles. None of these has been deemed worthy of any kind of mention in a treatise by a single member of successive generations of churchmen; and the character and style also is far removed from the apostolic manner, and the thought and intent of their contents is so absolutely out of harmony with true orthodoxy as to establish the fact that they are certainly the forgeries of heretics. For this reason they ought not to be placed among the spurious writings, but refused as altogether monstrous and impious. (Eusebius, *Church History* 3.25)

25. Editing the Christian Scriptures

Though the practice was condemned by the Great Church, some Christians felt free to make their own choice of what was or was not Scripture, while others edited the canonical texts themselves.

Those who are called Ebionites . . . use only the Gospel according to Matthew; they reject the Apostle Paul, calling him an apostate from the Law. The prophetic writings (of the Bible) they strive to expound with special exactness, and persevere in customs according to the Law, and in the Jewish mode of life, even to the extent of worshiping Jerusalem, as if it were the abode of God. (Ireneus, *Against the Heresies* 1.26:2)

If the Ebionites, who were likely the spiritual descendants of the original Jewish Christians, were chiefly concerned with establishing Jesus' claim to be the Jewish Messiah while they continued to observe, in despite of Paul's teaching, the full body of the Jewish law, another group wished to remove all ties with the Jewish past and with the so-called "Old Testament," which enshrined and glorified the malevolent Jewish deity called Yahweh.

Marcion [ca. 160 C.E.] . . . mutilated the Gospel according to Luke, removing all narratives of the Lord's birth, and also removing much of the teaching of the discourses of the Lord where he is most manifestly described as acknowledging the maker of the universe as his Father. Thus he persuaded his disciples that he himself was more trustworthy than the Apostles, who handed down the Gospel; though he gave them not a Gospel but a fragment of a Gospel. He mutilated the Letters of the Apostle Paul in the same manner, removing whatever is manifestly spoken by the Apostle concerning the God who made the world, where he says that He is the Father of our Lord Jesus Christ, and setting aside all the Apostle's teachings drawn from the prophetic writings (of the Bible) which predict the coming of the Lord. (Ireneus, *Against the Heresies* 1.27:2–3)

26. The Latin "Vulgate" Translation of Scripture

Early in the career of Christianity there had been Latin versions of the New Testament for the use of the Christians of Europe and North Africa. But the translation that eventually became "official" was that called the "Vulgate," done by the scholar and monk Jerome (d. 420 C.E.), who spent much of his life in Palestine. Jerome finished translating the New Testament about 386 and then turned to the Old Testament, for which he used the Hebrew text, and finished that in 404. The following passage is from the preface to his translation of the Gospels, addressed to Pope Damasus in Rome.

You urge me to revise the old Latin version and, as it were, to sit in judgment on the copies of Scripture that are now scattered throughout the whole world; and, since they differ one from the other, you ask me to make a judgment about their agreement with the Greek original. The labor is one of love, but at the same time both dangerous and presumptuous; for, in judging others, I must be content to be judged by all; and how dare I to change the language of the world in its hoary old age, and carry it back to the early days of its infancy? When a man, whether he be learned or unlearned, takes this book in his hands and sees that the text differs from the one familiar to him, will he not break out immediately into violent language, and call me a forger and a profane person for having the audacity to add anything to the ancient books, or to make any changes or corrections in them?

There are, however, two consoling reflections which enable me to bear the odium—in the first place the command comes from you, who are the supreme bishop; and, secondly, even on the testimony of those who revile us, readings at variance with the early copies cannot be right. For if we are to put our faith in the (earlier) Latin texts, it is for our opponents to tell us which; for there are almost as many versions of texts as there are copies. If, on the other hand, we are to gather the truth from a comparison of many, why not go back to the original Greek and correct the mistakes introduced by inaccurate translators and the blundering emendations made by confident but ignorant critics, and, further, all the things that have been inserted or changed by copyists more asleep than awake?

This brief preface deals only with the four Gospels—which are to be accepted in the following order, Matthew, Mark, Luke, John—as they have been revised through a comparison of the Greek manuscripts, and only the early ones. But to avoid any great divergences from the Latin (version) which we are accustomed to read, I have used my pen with some restraint; and while I have corrected only such passages as have seemed to convey a different meaning, I have allowed the rest to remain as they are. (Jerome, *Preface to the Gospels*)

27. Jewish and Christian Tampering with Scripture: A Muslim Critique

The Quran insists (3:81; 7:157; 61:6) that both the Jewish and the Christian Scriptures refer to the Prophet of Islam, much in the way, perhaps, that the coming of Jesus had been announced in the Old Testament. A search of those Scriptures failed to reveal any clear reference to Muhammad, however, which left to Muslim apologetes the task of vindicating the Quran and demonstrating that the Jews and Christians had tampered with the texts of the Books of God. One of the first to attempt such a demonstration in a systematic fashion was the Muslim theologian Juwayni (d. 1085 C.E.) in his work entitled The Noble Healing.

Certain clear passages in the Quran, whose information cannot be doubted, show that the texts of the Torah and the Gospel make mention of the Prince of Apostles, that the prayers of God were upon him. It is this motive that has induced Muslim scholars to declare that the texts were altered. The Jews and Christians in fact deny this announcement of the Prophet, and summon to their aid arguments which are like "a mirage in the desert. The thirsty man supposes it is water, but when he comes up to it, he finds that it is nothing" (Quran 24:39). . . .

What astonishes me is that the Jews and the Christians have conceded the fact of the alteration and at the same time regard as senseless someone who speaks of it as a possibility. They defend the impossibility of such a thing after agreeing that it did in fact take place. Listen to this ignorance. According to them, the affirmation of the fact of alteration is conditional to its possibility; but the conditions of such a possibility involve editing copies of the Torah and the Gospel dispersed all over the face of the earth, and of being assured of the willingness of each individual of the two religions, scholars, ascetics, the devout and the pious as well as the sinner, and of their agreement on one single opinion and one common expression, despite the wide differences of opinion. . . .

My position, then, with the aid of God, is that most of the errors that occur in the sciences arise from the fact that arguments are accepted without examination and without reason's making a careful examination of their premises. We shall mention the defects in this argument (of the Jews and Christians) and show wherein the carelessness of their authors lies.

Juwayni first takes the circumstances that show the possibility of altering the Torah.

The Torah which is presently in the hands of the Jews is that which was written by Ezra the scribe after the troubles that Nabuchadnezzar imposed upon them. This latter wrought carnage among the groups of religious Jews, sparing only isolated groups, whose small number allows us to disregard them. He gave over their wealth as booty to his troopers and soldiers and he destroyed their books. Ignorant of the norms of their religious law, he [here, it seems, Antiochus IV] had decided in favor of the corrupt state of the practices of this law: he put up an idol in their place of worship and made public announcement by a herald warning against even a mention of the law. Things remained in this state until an entire generation had passed away. Then those who were in exile found some leaves of the Torah; they took refuge in caves and made pretenses in order to be able to read them in secret.

This (present Torah copy) Ezra wrote 545 years before the mission of the Messiah, upon whom be peace, and when there was not a single Christian upon the earth. It was at this moment that the alteration of the text was possible since it was not a question of re-editing copies of the Torah scattered all over the world, as has been said, nor of counting on the willingness of individuals from different factions, nor were copies of the Torah in the hands of both Jews and Christians. In fact, they only came into Christian hands after they had been altered.

So there was only one doer of this deed, either Ezra himself or, if one puts it after Ezra, whoever it was who recopied Ezra's copy. More, an alteration on his part was possible from the fact that he was eager to see his power extended and by the fact that he was not credited with that kind of impeccability which would have prevented his commission of either light or serious faults. . . . It has been said that the love of power is the last thing to be made to leave the heads of the righteous, and power had considerable importance for the Israelites. And anyone who knows well the chronicles of world history and has followed their extraordinary developments finds there that men greater than Ezra have been moved by the love of power to act senselessly, rejecting the bonds of reason and of religion.

The Jews and the Christians can be convicted each out of the other's mouth on the fact of alteration.

The reason why the Jews and Christians unanimously agree that the text was in fact altered is that the copies that each group has are clearly contradictory. . . . The motive for the difference is, according to the Christians, that the Torah testifies that the Messiah, on whom be peace, would be sent at the time he was, and the copies of the Torah in their hands support the truth of what they say. They maintain, then, that the Jews have changed their copies of the Torah to prevent the recognition of the mission of the Messiah, on whom be peace. The Jews for their part say that the Christians have changed their copies and that the Messiah, on whom be peace, will not come until the end of the seventh period, and their copies support the truth of what they say. Thus both parties agree that the text has been in fact changed, and each group puts a rope around the neck of the other.

For our part, we shall now mention the contradictions between the two versions: In the Jews' Torah, Adam, when he was 130 years old, begot Seth, and in the Christians', he was 230 years old when he begot Seth.

443

Juwayni then goes step by step through the age of the Patriarchs and shows the differences in the chronology of the Jewish and Christian versions of the Torah. He concludes:

These are the very expressions of the Torah, and you see how extraordinary and hateful is this divergence between the two religious groups. And they differ not on the kind of point where opinions vary according to the different points of views of scholars and there arise variations according to how much is assumed. Rather, each group maintains that its text came down to Moses, peace be upon him, and that is the very essence of the tampering.

Finally, there is the matter of the Samaritans' Torah. Its text differs from that in the hands of the two other religious groups, and on the basis of that fact alone one could make a very convincing argument for the fact that the texts were altered.

Juwayni next takes up the Gospels.

There is first of all the enormous error the Christians made in not carefully preserving what they had to transmit, and no reasonable man can hope to correct that. The reason why they fell into this error is that they were careless in a matter that required urgent attention, in times propitious to the alteration and loss of texts, and in the matter of an oral transmission.

Matthew says clearly in his Gospel that he composed it nine years after the Ascension of the Messiah, on whom be peace; as for John, he says explicitly that he assembled his text thirty or more years after the Ascension; likewise Mark, twelve years after the Ascension; and Luke, twenty-two, or according to others twenty years after the Ascension. That is the point made manifestly in the Gospels, and thence arises the error against which there is no defense; more, even if someone attempts to dissemble through the imagination, he cannot achieve what he sets out to do.

Juwayni's first point of attack on the Gospels is the contradictions between and the errors in Matthew and Luke's versions of the genealogy of Jesus. Then he takes up the varying versions of Peter's denial of Jesus, the prediction and the fact after the latter's arrest. He concludes on the matter of this second case:

But the event that took place was unique, as were the moment, the place and the circumstances of the act. But generally when the circumstances in two accounts are identical and yet the accounts differ, one is forced to conclude that one of the two is false. You see then the integrity in the transmission of these Gospels; and how ironic that they pretend that the Evangelists were immune to error and that they transmitted their Gospels from the time of the Messiah, on whom be peace, as one would who personally heard these narratives, preserving what he heard, and carefully keeping the order of the narrative and the very words. According to my opinion, they allowed a great deal of time to pass before composing the Gospels, and both forgetfulness and carelessness got the better of them.

There are other examples of differences among the Gospels. Juwayni concludes with this one.

It is likewise extraordinary that Matthew had mentioned in his Gospel that when the Messiah was crucified and had rendered up his spirit, "the Temple was riven from top to bottom in two pieces, the earth quaked, the stones were shattered, tombs opened, and the bodies of the saints were resuscitated and left their tombs" (Matt. 27:51–53). Those are his own words in his Gospel, and yet no other Evangelist mentions it. But if the facts which he narrated, and which are of such an extraordinary strangeness, took place as he described them, they would be great miracles which one would have great reason to report and which everyone near and far would have recognized. Even people who were incapable of carefully preserving the events of the life of the Messiah, upon whom be peace, or of retaining the accounts, would have loved to have told of such facts and to have immersed themselves in stories on this theme. . . .

All of which shows that Matthew lied or that the three other Evangelists have shown their carelessness by forgetting to mention these extraordinary facts. And they are well charged with negligence since they did not habitually forget. But it would be even stranger that they pretended not to have knowledge of the facts; in effect if such extraordinary miracles actually took place, everybody in the province, near or far, would have known, yes, and in other provinces as well. (Juwayni, *The Noble Healing*) [JUWAYNI 1968: 40–83]

28. A Muslim History of Prophecy

Juwayni can move easily and knowingly across the text and matter of the Bible and the Gospels. It is, in fact, a familiar terrain to the Muslim since it was described in the Quran itself.

We sent down the Torah which contains guidance and light, in accordance with which the prophets who were obedient to God gave instruction to the Jews, as did the rabbis and the priests, for they were the custodians and witnesses of God's writ. . . . Later in the train (of prophets), We sent Jesus son of Mary, confirming the Torah which had been sent down before him, and gave him the Gospel containing guidance and light for those who preserve themselves from evil and follow the straight path. . . . And to you We have revealed the Book containing the truth, confirming the earlier revelations, and preserving them. (Quran 5:44–48)

The Quran, then, is a Book like those other books, and its bearer, Muhammad, a messenger in the tradition of Moses and Jesus—but, for all that, merely a messenger. God's word rests far above his merely mortal powers.

When Our clear messages are recited to them, those who do not hope to meet Us say: "Bring a different Quran, or make amendments in this one." Say: "It is not for me to change it of my will. I follow only what was revealed to me. If I disobey my Lord, I fear the punishment of an awful Day." (Quran 10:15)

Muhammad is only a messenger, and many a messenger has gone before him. So what if he dies or is killed! Will you turn back and go away in haste? He who turns back and goes away in haste will do no harm to God. (Quran 5:144)

These notions became commonplaces in the Islamic tradition, as is evident in this version of sacred history, the details supplied and the lacunae filled in, by the literary virtuoso Jahiz (d. 886 C.E.).

When the situation becomes dangerous because the ancient traditions no longer inspire men's complete confidence, God sets a term at the end of each period of time, a sign to renew the strength of the traditions and renew the teaching of the Messengers when it grows faint. In this manner Noah renewed the traditions dating from the period between Adam and himself by giving true testimony and producing effective signs, so as to safeguard the traditions from corruption and protect them from damage. The (Prophetic) traditions and proofs of earlier generations had not been entirely obliterated or destroyed, but when they were about to be, God sent His signs so that His proofs might not disappear from the earth. That is why the end-time of a period is called "the enfeeblement." There is, however, an unmistakable difference between bending and breaking. Then God sent Abraham at the end of the second period, namely that between the time of Noah and himself; this was the longest "enfeeblement" the world had yet experienced, for Noah remained among his people, expounding and reasoning and explaining, for 950 years, and the first of His signs was also the greatest, namely the Flood, in which God drowned all the people of the earth except Noah and his followers. . . .

Then the Prophets followed one after the other in the period between Abraham and Jesus. Because their proofs followed one upon the other, their signs clear, their acts numerous, and their deeds well known, because all of that took deep root in people's hearts and souls and the whole world spoke of it, their teachings were neither overturned nor diminished nor corrupted during the entire period from Jesus to the Prophet (Muhammad). But when they were on the point of becoming weakened, enfeebled and spent, God sent Muhammad, who renewed the teachings of Adam, Noah, Moses, Aaron, Jesus and John (the Baptist), and gave further detail to them; for Muhammad is righteous, and his witness is true, declaring that the Hour was at hand and that he was the seal of the Prophets. We knew then that his proofs would endure until the term set for it by God. (Jahiz, *The Proofs of Prophecy* 133–134)

Almost any educated Muslim could write such a summary. Witness this example from the Muslim theologian al-Nasafi (d. 1114 C.E.), who is careful to draw the distinction between private or personal written revelations—what he calls the "Scrolls"— from the "Books"—the four revealed codes of Law.

It must be recognized that all the books (of Scripture) which God has sent down (by revelation) to the Prophets and Apostles are the uncreated word of God. Of these there were one hundred Scrolls and four Books. (Of the Scrolls) God sent fifty to Seth the son of Adam, on whom be peace. Thirty were sent to Idris [that is, Enoch], on whom be peace; ten to Abraham, on whom be peace; and ten to Moses, on whom be peace, before the Torah was sent down to him. It was called "The Book of Naming" and was revealed before the drowning of the Pharaoh; then God sent down the Torah after the drowning of the Pharaoh. Later God sent down the Psalter to David, upon whom be peace, and then He sent down the Gospel to Jesus, on whom be peace, who was the last of the Prophets among the Children of Israel. Then God, may He be praised and exalted, sent down the Quran to Muhammad, upon whom be God's blessing and peace, who is the last of the Messengers. Anyone who disavows a (single) verse in any of these Scriptures is in unbelief.

Should anyone say, "I believe in all the Messengers," and then disavow one of the Messengers about whom there is no (scriptural) text, saying, "this one does not belong among them," he would not be in a state of unbelief, but he would be in heresy. This holds so long as he does not enter another religion, but if he enters another religion he is an apostate and may be killed. . . . Be it known, moreover, that the Prophets, upon whom be peace, are 124,000, and the Apostles among them are 313, according to the tradition transmitted from Abu Dharr, with whom may God be pleased, going back to a statement of the Apostle of God, upon whom be God's blessing and peace. In some of the Prophetic traditions the (number of the) Prophets is given as a thousand thousand, or two hundred thousand and more, but the correct thing in this matter is for you to say, "I believe in God and in all the Prophets and Apostles, and in all that has come from God by way of revelation according as God willed." By thus doing you will not affirm someone to be a Prophet who was not, nor will you affirm someone not to be a Prophet who was. (Nasafi, *Sea of Discourse on Theology*) [JEFFERY 1962: 447–448]

29. The Divine Origin of the Quran

The messenger of the Quran may have been a mere mortal, but there was no doubt about the origin of the message he carried to men.

And this (Quran) is a revelation from the Lord of all the worlds,
Which the trusted spirit descended with
To your heart that you may be a warner
In clear Arabic.
(Quran 26:192–195)

As the Quran instructs us, this quality of "trustworthiness" is shared by the heavenly Spirit—identified by the Islamic tradition as Gabriel—with God's chosen Apostle.

This is indeed the word of an honored Messenger,
Full of power, well-established with the Lord and Master of the Throne,
Obeyed and worthy of trust.
Your companion is not mad.
He had surely seen Him on the clear horizon.
And he is chary of making public what is unknown.
(Quran 81:19–24)

It is He who sent His Messenger with guidance and the true faith in order to make it superior to all other religions, though the idolaters may not like it. (Quran 9:33)

The message, the Quran also announces to the world, is not intended only for pagans.

O People of the Book, Our Apostle has come to you announcing many things of the Scripture that you have suppressed, passing over some others. To you has come light and a clear Book from God, through which God will lead those who follow His pleasure to the path of peace, and guide them out of the darkness into light by His will, and to the path that is straight. (Quran 5:15–16)

O you People of the Book, Our Apostle has come to you when Apostles had ceased to come long ago, lest you said: "There did not come to us any messenger of good news or warnings." So now there has reached you a bearer of good tidings and of warnings; for God has the power over all things. (Quran 5:19)

This is the Book free of doubt and involution,
a guidance for those who preserve themselves from evil
and follow the straight path,
who believe in the Unknown, and fulfill their devotional obligations,
and spend in charity of what We have given them;
who believe in what has been revealed to you
and what was revealed to those before you,
and are certain of the Hereafter.
They have found the guidance of their Lord and will be successful.
(Quran 2:1–5)

Thus does God Himself characterize the Book He has sent down to Muhammad, His servant, this very Book in which He is Himself speaking. How and under what circumstances that sending down took place are less easily accessible, though there are clues in that same Book.

It is not given to man that God should speak to Him, except by suggestion or indirectly, or send a messenger to convey by His command whatsoever He please. He is all-high and all-wise.

And so We have revealed to you (Muhammad) the Spirit of Our command. You did not know what the Scripture was before, or faith, and We made it a light by which We show the way to those of Our creatures as We please. (Quran 42:51–52)

And this Quran is not such as could be composed by anyone but God. It confirms what has been revealed before, and is an exposition of what has been decreed for mankind, without any doubt, by the Lord of the worlds.

Do they say (of the Prophet): "He has composed it?" Say to them: "Bring a sura like this, and call anyone apart from God you can to help you, if what you say is true." (Quran 10:37–38)

449

Do they say (of the Prophet): "He has forged (the Quran)?" Say: "Then bring ten suras like it, and call upon anyone except God to help you, if what you say is true."

If they do not answer you, then know it has been revealed with the knowledge of God, and that there is no god but He. (Quran 11:13–14)

These were not the only objections raised by Muhammad's contemporaries. They demanded signs.

We have given examples of every kind of men in this Quran in various ways, and even then most men disdain every thing but disbelief. They say: "We will not believe you until you make a spring of water gush forth from the earth for us; or until you acquire an orchard of date palm trees and grapes, and produce rivers flowing through it, or let chunks of sky fall over us, as you assert." (Quran 17:89–92)

Behind such a request seems to be a more profound doubt: that Muhammad is but a man and thus ill qualified to be a heavenly messenger.

Nothing prevented men from believing when guidance came to them, but they said: "Has God sent (only) a man as a messenger?" Say: "If angels had peopled the earth and walked about in peace and quiet, We would surely have sent to them an angel as a messenger." (Quran 17: 94–95)

To which compare:

And they say: What sort of prophet is this who eats food and walks in the marketplaces? Why was no angel sent to him to act as an admonisher with him? (Quran 25:7)

Those who do not hope to meet Us say: "Why are no angels sent down to us, or why do we not see our Lord?" (Quran 25:21)

30. Muhammad's Ascension into Heaven

There was a way, Muhammad was told by the Quraysh—whether in mockery or sincerity we cannot tell—by which their fellow Meccan could demonstrate his supernatural vocation.

And they say: "We will certainly not believe you until you . . . ascend to the skies, though we shall not believe in your having ascended till you bring down a Book for us which we can read." Say to them: "Glory be to my Lord! I am only a man and a messenger." (Quran 17:95)

Thus Muhammad's opponents at Mecca, the doubting and not entirely unsophisticated Quraysh, demanded two signs validating his claim to prophecy: that he should ascend into heaven and that he should return to them with a book that was intelligible to them. The response lay in the Quran itself. Sura 17:1 contains an enigmatic reference to a miraculous journey whereby Muhammad was carried by God at night from Mecca to another place, eventually identified as Jerusalem. But according to tradition, the voyage did not end there. The source is Ibn Ishaq's Life of the Prophet.

One whom I have no reason to doubt told me on the authority of Abu Saʿid al-Khudri: I heard the Messenger say, "After the completion of my business in Jerusalem (on the occasion of the Night Journey) a ladder was brought to me finer than any I have ever seen. It was that to which the dying man looks when death approaches. My companion mounted it with me until we came to one of the gates of heaven called the Gate of the Watchers. An angel called Ismail was in charge of it, and under his command were twelve thousand angels, each of them having (another) twelve thousand angels under his command." As he told the story the Messenger used to say, "and none knows the armies of God but He" (Quran 74:31). "When Gabriel brought me in, Ismail asked who I was, and when he was told that I was Muhammad, he asked if I had been given a mission, and on being assured I had, he wished me well."

"Then I was taken up to the second heaven and there were the two maternal cousins, Jesus son of Mary and John son of Zakariah. Then to the third heaven and there was a man whose face was as the moon at full. This was my brother Joseph son of Jacob. Then to the fourth heaven and there was a man called Idris, 'and We have exalted him to a lofty place' (Quran 19:56–57). Then to the fifth heaven and there was a man with white hair and a long beard; never before have I seen a more handsome man than he. This was the beloved among his people, Aaron son of Imran. Then to the sixth heaven and there was a dark man with a hooked nose like the Shanuʾa. This was Moses son of Imran. Then to the seventh heaven and there was a man sitting on a throne at the gate of the immortal mansion. Every day seventy thousand angels went in, not to come back until the Resurrection Day. Never have I seen a man more like myself. This was my father Abraham." (*Life* 268–270) [IBN ISHAQ 1955: 184–186]

31. The Night of Destiny

Was this heavenly ascension the occasion when Muhammad received the Book? The text just cited does not seem to suggest it. But on the evidence of the Quran—and of the Bible and the Jewish tradition—Moses certainly received his Book on one single occasion. The Quranic evidence is not so certain for Jesus, but in his case too the Book appears to have been delivered once and for all. Muhammad's circumstances were patently different: both the Quran and the biographical traditions about the Prophet show the Quran being delivered chapter by chapter, and even occasionally verse by verse. That must have prompted remarks, since the Quran averts to this quality that sets Muhammad apart from the other bearers of revelation.

We have divided the Quran into parts that you might recite it to men slowly, with deliberation. That is why We sent it down by degrees. (Quran 17:106)

The Muslim tradition certainly discussed the problem, chiefly in the context of the month of Ramadan, a holy month the Quran itself closely associates with the act of revelation.

Ramadan is the month in which the Quran was revealed as guidance to man and clear proof of the guidance, and a criterion (of falsehood and truth). (Quran 2:185)

The Muslim commentator Zamakhshari (d. 1134 C.E.) supplies additional details on this epochal event.

"In which the Quran was revealed": . . . The meaning of these words is: in which it *began* to be revealed. This occurred during the Night of Destiny. Some say that the Quran may have been sent down as a whole to the lowest heaven (on this night), and then later section by section to the earth. Others say that the meaning is "(the month of Ramadan) on account of which the Quran was revealed." . . . The following is transmitted from the Prophet: the sheets (of writing) of Abraham come down on the first night of Ramadan; the Torah was sent down on the sixth night into the month; the Gospel, the thirteenth; and the Quran, after a lapse of twenty-four (nights into Ramadan). (Zamakhshari, *The Unveiler of the Realities, ad loc.*)

The Quran returns to the same event in another verse, and once again the commentator fills out the narrative.

The perspicuous Book is a witness that We sent it down on a night of blessing—so that We could warn—on which all affairs are sorted out and divided as commands from Us. (Quran 44:2–5)

Most traditions say that the "night of blessing" is the same as the Night of Destiny [that is, the twenty-fourth of Ramadan], for God's word says: "Behold, We sent it [that is, the Quran] on the Night of Destiny" (Quran 97:1). Moreover, His words "on this night every wise bidding is determined" correspond with His words "In it the angels and the spirit descend, by the leave of their Lord, upon every command" (Quran 97:4). Finally, this also corresponds with his words "The month of Ramadan wherein the Quran was sent down" (Quran 2:185). According to most of the Prophetic traditions, the Night of Destiny falls during the month of Ramadan.

If one were to ask what is the significance of the sending down of the Quran on this night, I would respond: It is said that God first sent it down in its entirety from the seventh heaven to the lowest heaven. Then He commanded excellent writers to transcribe it on the Night of Destiny. Gabriel subsequently revealed it piece by piece to the Messenger of God. (Zamakhshari, *The Unveiler, ad loc.*)

32. The Heavenly Book

Islam shares with Judaism belief in a heavenly prototype of Scripture, here called in the Quran's own words "the Mother of the Book," or so the lines were understood by the Muslim commentators.

I call to witness the clear Book, that we made it an Arabic Quran that you may perhaps understand. It is inscribed in the Mother of the Book with Us, sublime, dispenser of (all) laws. (Quran 43:2–4)

Zamakhshari explains:

"Perhaps": This word expresses a wish, because there is a connection between this term and expressions of hoping. So we can say it means: We have created the Book in Arabic and not in any other language because We intended that the Arabs should understand it and not be able to say: "If only the verses of the Book had been sent forth clearly!"

The original text (of the Book) is the tablet corresponding to the words of God: ". . . it is a glorious Quran, in a well-preserved tablet" (Quran 85:21ff.). This writing is designated the "Mother of the Book" because it represents the original in which the individual books are preserved. They are derived from it by copying. (Zamakhshari, *The Unveiler of the Realities, ad loc.*)

Zamakhshari was here simply summarizing what the Quran itself asserts: that the Book of revelation is one and is preserved in Heaven. It contains all God's decrees and sums up all wisdom.

He has the keys of the Unknown. No one but He has knowledge; He knows what is on the land and in the sea. Not a leaf falls without His knowledge, nor a grain in the darkest recesses of the earth, nor any thing green or seared that is not noted in the clear Book. (Quran 6:59)

... There is not the weight of an atom on the earth and in the heavens that is hidden from your Lord, nor is there anything smaller or greater than this but is recorded in the clear Book. (Quran 10:61)

Do you not know that God knows whatever is in the heavens and the earth? This surely is in the Book; this is how God works inevitably. (Quran 22:70)

There is no calamity that befalls the earth or yourselves but that it was in the Book before We created them. This is how God works inevitably. (Quran 57:22)

It is this same Book whose exemplars were given to the earlier peoples of God's choice—to Moses for the Jews (Quran 28:43, 32:23, etc.) and to Jesus for the Christians (Quran 3:43, 19:31)—and whose validity the Quran now validates and confirms.

And this is a revelation from the Lord of all the worlds,
With which the trusted Spirit descended
Upon your heart, that you may be a warner
In clear Arabic.
This was indicated in Books of earlier people.
Was it not a proof for them that the learned men of Israel knew it?
(Quran 26:191–197)

What We have revealed to you in the Book is the truth, and proves what was sent before it to be true. (Quran 35:31)

All the more reason why those "People of the Book" should accept this new exemplar being revealed through the Apostle Muhammad.

Say to them: "O People of the Book, what reason have you for disliking us other than that we believe in God and what was sent down before us?" (Quran 5:59)

33. The Quran: Created or Uncreated?

It was the view that the Quran was in its primal form a book in heaven and thence was sent down to Muhammad, first whole and then in discrete revelations, that embroiled the Muslims' Scripture in an internal theological controversy that has little direct echo in either Judaism or Christianity. If the Quran is the "speech" of God, His Word, then it is necessarily one of His attributes, a subject that provoked lively interest among early Muslim theologians, who were just beginning to explore the connection between essence and accidents as those Greek-defined notions were applied to God. Whether that interest antedated the debate or the debate provoked the interest in a conceptual system that helped the parties to argue or defend their positions is difficult to say. But by the middle of the eighth century the issue had been broached. Indeed, it had gained such notoriety that in the 830s it became the benchmark of one of the few officially promulgated definitions of orthodoxy—and so of heresy—in Islam: the Caliph al-Ma'mun (813–833 C.E.) required Muslims to swear that the Quran was the created speech of God and threatened the recusants with imprisonment.

One who chose not to swear on that occasion was the jurist Ahmad ibn Hanbal (d. 855 C.E.), whose "profession of faith" includes the following article on the Quran.

The Quran is the Word of God and it is not created. It is not wrong to say, "It is not created," for God's Word is not separate from Him, and there is nothing of Him that is created. Beware of discussing this with those who speak about this subject and talk of the "creation of sounds" and such matters, and those who go midway and say "I don't know whether the Quran is created or uncreated, but it is God's Word." Such a one is guilty of a religious innovation, as is the one who says "It is created," for it is God's Word and that is not created. (Ahmad ibn Hanbal, *Creed*) [WILLIAMS 1971: 29]

In despite of Ma'mun and the theologians who may have had the Caliphal ear at the time, it was the position of Ibn Hanbal—that the Quran is uncreated and eternal—that became the normative one in Islam. But whereas Ibn Hanbal simply asserts it in the document just cited, later theologians were willing to argue the case at length and in detail. This, for example, is how the theological argument is integrated into the received accounts of the revelation of the Quran by al-Nasafi (d. 1114 C.E.) in his Sea of Discourse on Theology.

The Quran is God's speaking, which is one of His attributes. Now God in all of His attributes is One, and with all His attributes is eternal and not contingent, (so His speaking is) without letters and without sounds, not broken up into syllables or paragraphs. It is not He nor is it other than He. He caused Gabriel to hear it as sound and letters, for He created sound and letters and caused him to hear it by that sound and those letters. Gabriel, upon whom be peace, memorized it, stored it (in his mind) and then transmitted it to the Prophet, upon whom be God's blessing and peace, by bringing down a revelation and a message, which is not the same as bringing down a corporeal object and a form. He recited it to the Prophet, upon whom be God's blessing and peace, the Prophet memorized it, storing it up (in his mind), and then recited it to his Companions, who memorized it and recited it to the Followers, the

Followers handed it on to the upright, and so on until it reached us. It is (now) recited by tongues, memorized by hearts and written in codices, though it is not contained by the codices. It may be neither added to nor taken from; just as God is mentioned by tongues, recognized by hearts, worshiped in places, yet He is not confined to existence in those places nor in those hearts. It is as He said, "Those who follow the Messenger, the unlettered Messenger, whom they find mentioned in the Torah and the Gospel which they have" (Quran 7:157), for they found (in those Books) only his picture, his description, not his person. Similarly, Paradise and Hell are mentioned, but they are not actually present among us. All this is according to the school of the truly orthodox. (Nasafi, *Sea of Discourse*) [JEFFERY 1962: 398]

34. "Bring a Sura Like It"

We have already seen the Quran's own response to accusations that it represents nothing more than the invention of Muhammad. Go, God challenges the doubters, and produce another Book like it.

This Quran is not such as could be composed by anyone but God. It confirms what has been revealed before, and is an exposition of what has been decreed for mankind, without any doubt, by the Lord of the worlds.

Do they say (of the Prophet): "He has composed it?" Say to them: "Bring a sura like it, and call anyone apart from God you can to help you, if what you say is true." (Quran 10:37–38)

The Quran, then, was not only of heavenly origin; it was, as a direct consequence of that origin, inimitable by mere man, Muhammad or any other, and so the challenge issued in this sura went unanswered. That fact remained the chief probative miracle of Islam, the "sign" that Muhammad resolutely refused to produce but that God produced for him and so verified His religion and His Prophet. The essayist al-Jahiz (d. 868 C.E.) reflects on this.

Muhammad had one unique sign, which affects the mind much in the same manner that (Moses') parting of the seas affected the eyes, namely, when he said to the Quraysh in particular and the Arabs in general—and they included many poets and orators, and eloquent, shrewd, wise, tolerant, sagacious, experienced and farsighted men—"If you can equal me with but a single sura, my claims will be false and you will be entitled to call me a liar." Now it is impossible that among people like the Arabs, with their great numbers, the variety of their tastes, their language, their overflowing eloquence, and their remarkable capacity for elegant language, which has enabled them to describe . . . everything that crawls or runs, and in short everything that the eye can see and the mind picture, who possess every kind of poetic form . . . the same people who were the first to show hatred toward him and make war, suffering losses themselves and killing some of his supporters, that among these people, I say, who were the fiercest in hatred, the most vengeful, the most sensitive to favor and slight, the most hostile to the Prophet, the quickest to condemn weakness and extol strength, no orator or poet should have dared take up the challenge.

Knowing everything we do, it is inconceivable that words should not have been their weapon of choice . . . and yet that the Prophet's opponents should have unanimously refrained from using them, at a time when they were sacrificing their possessions and their lives, and that they should not all have said, or that at least one of them should have said: Why do you kill yourselves, sacrifice your possessions and forsake your homes, when the steps to be taken against him are simple and the way of dealing with him easy: let one of your poets or orators compose a speech similar to his, equal in length to the shortest sura he has challenged you to imitate, or the meanest verse he has invited you to copy? (Jahiz, *Proofs of Prophecy* 143–144)

35. The Earliest Sura

Medieval Muslim and modern Western scholars have long attempted to arrange the suras or chapters of the Quran in some kind of chronological order, chiefly in an effort to integrate them into the biographical data on the life of the Prophet. As this quest proceeded, there were various candidates for the earliest of the revelations, among them Sura 74.

> O you, enfolded in your mantle,
> Arise and warn!
> Glorify your Lord,
> Purify your inner self,
> And banish all trepidation.
> (Quran 74:1–5)

When we turn to the medieval Muslim commentators, we find a variety of opinions on which might have been the earliest sura.

Some say that this [that is, 74:1–5] was the first sura to be sent down. Jabir ibn Abdullah related (the following) from the Messenger of

God: "I was on Mount Hira (near Mecca) when someone called out to me, 'Muhammad, you are the Messenger of God.' I looked to the right and to the left but saw nothing. Then I looked up above me and there I saw something." —In the report according to (his wife) Aisha he says, "I glanced up above me and there I saw someone sitting on a throne between heaven and earth," meaning it was the Angel Gabriel who had called out to him— "I was frightened," the tradition continues, "and returned to Khadija (Muhammad's first wife) and called out: 'Dress me in a mantle, dress me in a mantle!' Then Gabriel came and said 'O you, enfolded in your mantle. . . .' "

From al-Zuhri it is related, on the other hand, that the first sura to come down was "Recite in the name of the Lord" down to the words of God "what he has not known" (Sura 96:1–5). (After the revelation of this sura) the Messenger of God became sad (because the revelations had ceased) and he began to climb to the tops of the mountains. Then Gabriel came to him and said, "You are the Prophet of God." And then Muhammad returned to Khadija and called out: "Dress me in a mantle and pour cold water over me!" Thereupon there came down the sura (which begins) "O you, enfolded in your mantle. . . ."

Still others say that the Prophet heard certain things from the (members of the tribe of) the Quraysh which displeased him, and that this caused him to grieve. Afterwards he was wrapped in his robe reflecting on what grieved him, as is customy with grieving people. Then he was commanded (through the present sura) to warn his countrymen continuously (of the punishment of God), even when they insulted him and caused him injury. (Zamakhshari, *The Unveiler of the Realities, ad loc.*)

36. The Heart of the Quran: The "Throne Verse"

God's throne in heaven plays an important role in both Jewish and Muslim piety, as we shall see in Chapter 2 below. In Islam the explicit mention of God's heavenly seat in the Quran set in train a series of speculations on both the throne and the verses in which it appeared.

God! There is no god but He, the living, the eternal, self-subsisting, ever sustaining. Neither does somnolence affect Him nor sleep. To Him belongs all that is in the heavens and the earth, and who can intercede with Him except by His leave? Known to Him is all that is present before men and what is hidden and that which is to come upon them, and not even a little of His knowledge can they grasp except what He wills. His Throne extends over the heavens and the earth, and He tires not protecting them: He alone is high and supreme. (Quran 2:255)

Qurtubi (d. 1273) relates . . . on the authority of Muhammad ibn al-Hanifiyya: "When the Throne Verse was revealed, every idol and king in the world fell prostrate and the crowns of kings fell off their heads. Satans fled, colliding with one another in confusion until they came to Iblis [their chief]. . . . He sent them to find out what had happened, and when they came to Medina they were told that the Throne Verse had been sent down. . . ."

Tabarsi (d. 1153) relates on the authority of Abdullah ibn Umar that the Prophet said: "Whoever recites the Throne Verse after a prescribed prayer, the Lord of Majesty Himself shall receive his soul at death. He would be as if he had fought with the Prophet of God until he was martyred." . . . Ali also said: "I heard the Messenger of God say, 'O Ali, the chief of humankind is Adam, the chief of the Arabs is Muhammad, nor is there pride in this. The chief of the Persians is Salman [an early Persian convert to Islam], the chief of the Byzantines is Suhayb [Christian convert among the Companions of the Prophet] and the chief of Abyssinia is Bilal [another convert and Islam's first muezzin]. The chief of the mountains is Mount Sinai, and the chief of the trees is the lote tree. The chief months are the sacred months and the chief day is Friday. The chief of all speech is the Quran, the chief of the Quran is the (second) sura, "The Cow," and the chief of "The Cow" is the Throne Verse. O Ali, it consists of fifty words and every word contains fifty blessings.' "

[AYOUB 1984: 247–248]

37. The "Satanic Verses"

If speculation on the Quran's mention of the throne of God is essentially the work of piety, other verses in the Book raised enormously complex exegetical and legal questions. The verses in question, the so-called "Satanic verses," occur in Sura 22 and are addressed to Muhammad.

We have sent no messenger or apostle before you with whose recitations Satan did not tamper. Yet God abrogates what Satan interpolates; then He confirms His revelations, for God is all-knowing, all-wise. This is in order to make the interpolations of Satan a test for those whose hearts are diseased and hardened. (Quran 22:52–53)

In connection with this itself quite extraordinary verse, the Muslim exegetical tradition has preserved a rather startling piece of information, namely, that some of the verses of the Quran originally read quite differently.

The occasion of the revelation of the present verse (22:52) is the following: As the members of the tribe of the Messenger of God turned away from him and took their stand in opposition to him, and as his relatives also opposed him and refused to be guided by what he brought to them, then, as a result of extreme exasperation over their estrangement, and of the eager desire and longing that they be converted to Islam, the Messenger of God hoped that nothing would be revealed to him that would make them shy away. . . . Now this wish persisted until the sura called "The Star" (Sura 53) came down. At that time he (still) found himself with that hope in his heart regarding the members of his tribe. Then he began to recite (53: 19–23):

> "Have you considered al-Lat and al-Uzza
> And Manat, the third, the other?
> Are there sons for you and daughters for Him?
> This is certainly an unjust apportioning.

"These are only names which you and your fathers have invented. No authority was sent down by God for them. They only follow conjecture and will-fulfillment, even though guidance had come already from their Lord."

When, however, he came to God's words "And Manat, the third, the other," Satan substituted something else conformable to the wish that the Messenger of God had been harboring, that is, he whispered something to him which would enable the Messenger to fulfill his wish. In an inadvertent and misleading manner his tongue hurried on ahead of him, so that he said: "These (goddesses) are the exalted cranes. Their intercession (with God) is to be hoped for. . . ." Yet the Messenger of God was not clear at this point until the protection (of God) reached him and he became attentive again.

Some say that Gabriel drew his attention to what had happened, or that Satan himself spoke these words and brought them to the people's hearing. As soon as the Messenger of God prostrated himself in prayer at the end of the sura, all who were present did it with him and felt pleased (that they had had their way). That the opportunity for doing this would be given to Satan constituted a temptation and it was God's test through which the hypocrites should increase in grievance and injury, but the believers should increase in enlightenment and assurance. (Zamakhshari, *The Unveiler of the Realities, ad loc.*)

38. The Revelation and Its Copy

The intrusion of these spurious verses into the Quran, followed by their removal, is mirrored in reverse by the question whether our copies of the Quran—its written exemplars—contain all the material revealed by God to His Prophet. The text itself gives us no reason to think that such is not the case, but the Muslim tradition preserves another recollection. As we shall see shortly, the Shi'ite Muslims have charged that the received text was indeed tampered with for sectarian reasons; but there are other, more fundamental cases of omissions that are more anomalous. The best-known example is that of a verse that prescribed stoning as a penalty for adultery and that was, on unimpeachable testimony, "memorized and recited" as part of the Quran in Muhammad's own lifetime. Yet it occurs nowhere in the text of the Book (see Chapter 5 below). If the "stoning verse" is the most celebrated example of genuine revelation not incorporated into the "copy" of the Quran, it is not the only one, as these canonically accepted traditions suggest.

Ubayy reports: "The Messenger of God said to me, 'God has commanded me to instruct you in the reciting of the Quran.' He then recited 'Did not those who rejected the Prophet among the People of the Book and the associators. . . .' The verse continued, 'Did the offspring of Adam possess a wadi of property,' or 'Were the offspring of Adam to ask for a wadi of property and he received it, he would ask for a second, and if he received that, he would demand a third wadi. Only dust will fill the maw of the offspring of Adam, but God relents to him who repents. The very faith in God's eyes is the original belief, not Judaism or Christianity. Who does good, it will never be denied him.' " (Suyuti, *Perfection in the Quranic Sciences*) [Cited by BURTON 1977: 82–83]

Ibn Abbas said, "Did the offspring of Adam possess two wadis of wealth, he would desire a third. Only dust will fill the maw of the offspring of Adam, but God relents to him who repents." Umar asked, "What is this?" Ibn Abbas replied that Ubayy had instructed him to recite this (as part of the Quran). Umar took Ibn Abbas to confront Ubayy. Umar said, "We don't say that." Ubayy insisted that the Prophet had so instructed him. Umar then asked him, "Shall I write it into the copy in that case?" Ubayy said, "Yes." This was before the copying of the Uthman codices (without the verses in question) and on which the practice now rests. (Burhan al-Din al-Baji, *Responsa*) [Cited by BURTON 1977: 83]

39. Uthman's Recension of the Quran

The assembled and ordered text of the Quran as we now possess it was the result of a cooperative work begun soon after the death of the Prophet. It was brought to completion by Uthman, an early companion of the Prophet and the third Caliph of the Muslim community (644–656 C.E.).

Zayd ibn Thabit said: Abu Bakr (Caliph, 632–634 C.E.) sent for me at the time of the battle of al-Yamama, and Umar ibn al-Khattab (Caliph, 634–644 C.E.) was with him. Abu Bakr said: Umar has come to me and said:

"Death raged at the battle of al-Yamama and took many of the reciters of the Quran. I fear lest death in battle overtake the reciters of the Quran in the provinces and a large part of the Quran be lost. I think you should give orders to collect the Quran."

"What," I asked Umar, "will you do something which the Prophet of God himself did not do?"

"By God," replied Umar, "it would be a good deed."

Umar did not cease to urge me until God opened my heart to this and I thought as Umar did.

Zayd continued: Abu Bakr said to me: "You are a young man, intelligent, and we see no fault in you, and you have already written down the revelation for the Prophet of God, may God bless and save him. Therefore go and seek the Quran and assemble it."

By God, if he had ordered me to move a mountain it would not have been harder for me than his order to collect the Quran. "What," I asked, "will you do something which the Prophet of God himself, may God bless and save him, did not do?"

"By God," replied Abu Bakr, "it would be a good deed."

And he did not cease to urge me until God opened my heart to this as He had opened the hearts of Abu Bakr and Umar.

Then I sought out and collected the parts of the Quran, whether written on palm leaves or flat stones or in the hearts of men. Thus I found the end of the "Sura of Repentance" (Quran 9:129–130), which I had been unable to find anywhere else, with Abu'l-Khuzayma al-Ansari. These were the verses "There came to you a Prophet from amongst yourselves. It grieves me that you sin . . ." to the end.

The leaves were with Abu Bakr until his death, then with Umar for as long as he lived, and then with Hafsa, the daughter of Umar.

Anas ibn Malik said: Hudhayfa ibn al-Yaman went with Uthman

when he was preparing the army of Syria to conquer Armenian and Azerbayjan, together with the army of Iraq. Hudhayfa was shocked by the differences in their reading of the Quran, and said to Uthman, "O Commander of the Faithful, catch this community before they differ about their book as do the Jews and the Christians."

Uthman sent to Hafsa to say, "Send us the leaves. We shall copy them in codices and return them to you."

Hafsa sent them to Uthman, who ordered Zayd ibn Thabit, Abdullah ibn al-Zubayr, Sa'id ibn al-As and Abd al-Rahman ibn al-Harith ibn Hisham to copy them into codices. Uthman said to the three of them who were of the tribe of the Quraysh, "If you differ from Zayd ibn Thabit on anything in the Quran, write it according to the language of the Quraysh, for it is in their language that the Quran was revealed."

They did this, and when they had copied the leaves into codices, Uthman returned the leaves to Hafsa. He sent copies of the codex which they made in all directions and gave orders to burn every leaf and codex which differed from it. (Bukhari, *Sahih* 3.392–394) [LEWIS 1974: 2:1–2]

40. Who Put Together the Suras?

One striking feature of the Quran as we possess it is the fact that only one sura, Sura 9, also called "Repentance" or "Immunity," does not open with the formula "In the Name of God, the Compassionate, the Merciful." The following Prophetic tradition explains the anomaly and sheds some light as well on how the suras might have been put together.

Ibn Abbas said he asked Uthman what had induced him to deal with (Sura 8 called) "The Spoils," which is one of the medium-sized suras, and with (Sura 9 called) "Immunity," which is one with a hundred verses, joining them without writing the line containing "In the Name of God, the Compassionate, the Merciful," and putting it among the seven long suras (at the beginning of the Quran). When he asked again what had induced him to do that, Uthman replied: "Over a period suras with numerous verses would come down to the Messenger of God, and when something came down to him he would call one of those who wrote and tell him to put those verses in the sura in which such-and-such was mentioned, and when a (single) verse came down he would tell them to put it in the sura in which such-and-such is mentioned. Now 'The Spoils' was one of the first to come down in Medina, and 'Immunity' was among the last of the Quran to come down, and the subject matter of one resembled that of the other, so because the Messenger of God was taken (by death) without having explained to us whether it ('Immunity') belonged to it ('The Spoils'), I joined them without writing the line containing 'In the Name of God, the Compassionate, the Merciful," and put it among the long suras." Ahmad ibn Hanbal, Tirmidhi and Abu Dawud transmitted this tradition. (Baghawi, *Mishkat al-Masabih* 8.3)

41. The Seven "Readings" of the Quran

The Quran, with its vowels unmarked in the manner of Semitic writing and transcribed in a still somewhat defective script—the Quran is the earliest Arabic literary text committed to writing—was open to different manners of reading and pronunciation. The Hebrew Bible had gone through similar uncertainties until its own textual standardization. Here we stand at the beginning of the same process as it affected the Quran.

Umar ibn al-Khattab said: I heard Hisham ibn Hakim ibn Hizam reciting the sura (called) "The Criterion" [that is, Sura 25] in a manner different from my way of reciting it, and it was the Messenger of God who taught me how to recite it. I nearly spoke sharply to him, but I delayed until he had finished, and then catching his cloak by the neck, I brought him to God's Messenger and said: "Messenger of God, I heard this man reciting 'The Criterion' in a manner different from that in which you taught me to recite it." He told me to let the man go and bade him to recite. When he recited it in the manner in which I had (earlier) heard him recite it, God's Messenger said, "Thus it was sent down." He then told me to recite it, and when I had done so he said, "Thus it was sent down. The Quran was sent down in seven modes of reading, so recite according to what comes most easily."

Ibn Abbas reported God's Messenger as saying, "Gabriel taught me to recite in one mode, and when I replied to him and kept asking him to give me more, he did so till he reached seven modes." Ibn Shihab said he had heard that these seven modes were essentially one, not differing about what is permitted and what is prohibited. (Baghawi, *Mishkat al-Masabih* 8.3.1)

These Prophetic traditions represent the beginning of one aspect of the textual study of the Quran in Islam, that devoted to a proper "reading." Ibn Khaldun (d. 1406 C.E.), who stands at the end of the process, describes how it evolved.

The Quran is the word of God that was revealed to His Prophet and that is written down between the two covers of copies of the Quran. Its transmission has been continuous in Islam. However, the men around Muhammad transmitted it on the authority of the Messenger of God in different ways. These differences affect certain of the words in it and the manner in which the letters were pronounced. They were handed down and became famous. Eventually, seven specific ways of reading the Quran became established. Transmission of these Quranic readings with their particular pronunciation was also continuous. They came to be ascribed to certain men from among a large number of persons who had become famous as their transmitters. The Seven Quran Readings became the basis for reading the Quran. Later on other readings were occasionally added to the seven. However, they are not considered by the authorities on Quran reading to be as reliably transmitted (as the Seven).

The (Seven) Quran Readings are well known from books which deal with them. Certain people have contested the continuity of their transmission. In their opinion they are ways of indicating the pronunciation, and pronunciation is something which cannot definitely be fixed. This, however, they thought not to reflect upon the continuity of the transmission of the Quran (itself). The majority do not admit their view. The majority asserts the continuity of the transmission of the Seven Readings. Others asserted the continuity of all Seven, save for certain fine points of pronunciation. . . . Quran readers continued to circulate and transmit these readings, until the knowledge of them was fixed in writing and treated systematically. (Ibn Khaldun, *Muqaddima* 6.10)
[IBN KHALDUN 1967: 2:439–440]

The discipline of Quran readings is often extended to include also the discipline of Quran orthography, which deals with usage of the letters in copies of the Quran and with the orthography of the Quran. The Quran uses many letters that are used differently than is usual in writing. . . . When the divergences in the usage and norm of writing made their appearance, it became necessary to deal with them comprehensively. Therefore, they too were written down when scholars fixed the sciences in writing. (Ibid. 6.10) [IBN KHALDUN 1967: 2:442]

42. Textual Corruptions?
The Shi͑ite View

God had helped you during the Battle of Badr at a time when you were helpless. So act in compliance with the laws of God; you may well be grateful. (Quran 3:123)

Some Muslim scholars had difficulty with this particular verse in the transmitted Quran.

"When you were helpless . . . ": al-Qummi and al-Ayyashi say according to (the Imam) Ja'far al-Sadiq: They were not helpless, for the Messenger of God was among them. (Actually the following) came down: "when you were weak. . . ." Al-Ayyashi reports according to Ja'far al-Sadiq that Abu Basir recited the verse in this manner in al-Sadiq's presence. Ja'far said that God had not revealed the verse in that form, but what had come down was "when you were few. . . ." In a Prophetic tradition it is said that God never cast down His Messenger and so what had been revealed was "when you were few. . . ." In several reliable reports it is said that they numbered three hundred and thirteen. (Kashi, *The Pure in the Interpretation of the Quran, ad loc.*)

This kind of textual criticism may have had no other object than to express a reservation on what was considered an unlikely thing for God to have said of His own Prophet. But in other instances the criticism is more direct and more pointed, namely that the text of God's Book had been tampered with in order to advance one sectarian view at the expense of another. The latter was most often the Shi'ites or "Party of Ali," who thought that spiritual leadership in the community had been reserved for Muhammad's cousin Ali ibn Abi Talib and his descendants. The silence of the Quran on this claim inevitably brought forth Shi'ite charges of tampering.

. . . And the oppressors will now come to know through what reversals they will be overthrown! (Quran 26:227)

Al-Qummi says: God mentioned their enemies and those who did wrong against them. He has said (in 26:227), "Those who have done wrong against the law of the family of Muhammad will (one day) know what kind of turning upside down they will experience." This is the way the verse was actually revealed. (Kashi, *The Pure, ad loc.*)

And this is the way the same Muhammad Murtada al-Kashi, a Shi'ite commentator (d. ca. 1505 C.E.), interpreted another critical Quranic passage.

O Messenger, announce what has reached you from your Lord, for if you do not, you will not have delivered His message. God will preserve you from men; for God does not guide those who do not believe. (Quran 5:67)

"Announce what has reached you": that is, concerning Ali. According to the tradition of the authorities on doctrine, this verse was actually revealed in this (extended) form [that is, including "concerning Ali"].

"For if you do not . . . ": If you discontinue the delivery of what has been sent down to you concerning Ali's guardianship (over the believers), and you keep this secret, then it is as if you delivered none of the message of the Lord concerning that which requires reconciliation. Some also read: "His message concerning the confession of the unity of God. . . ."

"God does not guide those who do not believe": In the *Collection* (of al-Tabarsi) it is said on the authority of Ibn Abbas and Jabir ibn Abdullah that God commanded His Prophet to place Ali before men and to (publicly) inform them of his guardianship (over them). The Prophet, however, was afraid that they would say, "He is protecting his cousin," and that a group of his companions might find this distressing. The present verse came down regarding this. On the following day, the Prophet took Ali gently by the hand and said: "Whose protector I am, their protector (also) is Ali." Then he recited the verse in question. (Kashi, *The Pure, ad loc.*)

43. The Proofs of Prophecy

Among the voluminous works of the essayist al-Jahiz (d. 886 C.E.) is one entitled The Proofs of Prophecy. *In it he took up the question of why the earliest generations of Muslims did not, like the Christians, make a systematic collection of the various and many proofs of Muhammad's prophetic calling.*

Let us return to the question of the signs and tokens of the Prophet, and the arguments in favor of his proofs and testimonies. I say this: If our ancestors, who compiled written editions of the Quran, which up to that point had been scattered in men's memories, and united the people behind the reading of Zayd ibn Thabit, while formerly other readings were in free circulation, and established a text free from all additions and omissions, if those early Muslims had likewise collected the signs of the Prophet, his arguments, proofs, and miracles, the various manifestations of his wondrous life, both at home and abroad, and even on the occasion when he preached to a great multitude, to a crowd so large that its testimony cannot be questioned except by ignorant fools or the bigoted opponents (of Islam), if they had done so, today no one could challenge the truth of these things, neither the godless dualist, nor the stubborn materialist, not even the licentious fop, the naive moron, or callow stripling. This tradition of the Prophet would then have been as well known among the common people as among the elite, and all our notables would see the truth (of their religion) as clearly as they see the falsity (of the beliefs) of Christians and Zoroastrians. . . .

The first Muslims were led (to commit this omission) by their confidence in the manifest nature (of the acts of the Prophet); but we ourselves have come to this state because dunces, youths, madmen and libertines lack the proper care and show themselves totally unconcerned, callow and neglectful; also because, before acquiring even the elements of dialectical theology, they filled their heads with more subtleties than their strength can manage or their minds contain. (Jahiz, *The Proofs of Prophecy* 119)

44. Muhammad, the Seal of the Prophets

Christianity rested its claim upon a Messiah who was sent not so much to teach the Kingdom of God as to proclaim it in his own person. For the Christian, Jesus did not belong in the company of the prophets but represented a unique figure in God's plan, the Son of God promised from the beginning and whose redemptive death required no sequel. With Islam we are back on biblical ground, however. Muhammad is one of a line of prophets stretching back to Adam and reaching forward through Abraham and Moses, David and Solomon, until it reached Jesus. And, according to the Quran, although Muhammad had predecessors, he would have no successor.

Muhammad is not the father of any man among you, but a messenger of God and the seal of the Prophets. God has knowledge of every thing. (Quran 33:40)

The commentators took the verse as self-evident.

"But (he is) a messenger of God": Every messenger is the father of his religious community insofar as they are obliged to respect and honor him, and he is obliged to care for them and give them advice. . . .

"And the seal of the Prophets": . . . If one asks how Muhammad (as the seal of the Prophets) can be the last Prophet when Jesus will come down at the end of time [that is, to announce the Day of Judgment and suffer death], then I reply that Muhammad's being the last of the prophets means that no one else will (afterwards) be active as a prophet; Jesus was active as a prophet before Muhammad. And when Jesus comes down he will do this because he devotes himself to the law of Muhammad and performs his prayer according to Muhammad's direction of prayer [that is, facing Mecca], as if he were a member of this community. (Zamakhshari, *The Unveiler of the Realities, ad loc.*)

Another already cited verse opens the perspective somewhat.

We have sent no messenger or apostle before you with whose recitations Satan did not tamper. (Quran 22:52)

The second half of the verse requires its own exegesis, as we have already seen in connection with the "Satanic verses." Our concern here is with the opening phrase, which speaks to an important distinction.

"We have sent no messenger or prophet . . . ": This is a clear proof that there is a difference between a "Messenger" (*rasul*) and a "Prophet" (*nabi*). It is related from the Prophet that once when he was asked about the Prophets, he replied: "There are one hundred and twenty-four thousand." And when he was then asked how many Messengers there were among those, he answered, "The great host of three hundred and thirteen." The distinction between the two is that a Messenger is one of the Prophets to whom the Book is sent down, together with a miracle confirming it. A Prophet, on the other hand, who is not an Apostle, is one to whom no book has been sent down, but who was commanded only to restrain people on the basis of the earlier revealed Law. (Zamakhshari, *The Unveiler, ad loc.*)

45. Muhammad among the Prophets

The question mooted by Zamakhshari is in part exegetical—the occurrence in the Quran of two distinct terms, "Messenger" and "Prophet"—but arises as well from the need to separate and distinguish Muhammad from the other prophets, biblical and nonbiblical, mentioned in the Quran. Zamakhshari's criterion, that the Messenger is the recipient of a public revelation, which separates Muhammad from Jeremiah or Isaiah, for example, and brackets him with Moses and Jesus, was not the only distinction possible. In the passage of Suyuti (d. 1505 C.E.) that follows, the comparison is straightforward, detailed, and obviously popular. The context is said to be a meeting between Muhammad, accompanied by Umar, and the Jews of Medina. When Umar praises Muhammad, the Jews retort that he must be talking about Moses. Umar turns to Muhammad and asks, "Alas for my soul, was Moses better than you?"

Then the Messenger of God, may God bless him and grant him peace, said: "Moses is my brother, but I am better than he, and I was given something more excellent than he was." The Jews said: "This is what we wanted!" "What is that?" he asked. They said: "Adam was better than you; Noah was better than you; Moses was better than you; Jesus was better than you; Solomon was better than you." He said: "That is false. I am better than all these and superior to them." "You are?" they asked. "I am," he said. They said, "Then bring a proof of that from the Torah."

Muhammad agrees but must invoke the assistance of one of his Jewish converts, Abdullah ibn Salam, to check the Torah, presumably because he could read Hebrew, while Muhammad was, as the Muslim tradition maintained, "unlettered." The discussion reported by Suyuti continues.

"Now why," Muhammad asked, "is Adam better than I?" "Because," they answered, "God created him with His own hand and breathed into him of His spirit." "Adam," he then replied, "is my father, but I have been given something better than anything he has, namely, that every day a herald calls five times from the East to the West: 'I bear witness that there is no god but the God and I bear witness that Muhammad is the Messenger of God.' No one has ever said that Adam was the Messenger of God. Moreover, on the Day of Resurrection the Banner of Praise will be in my hand and not in that of Adam." "You speak but the truth," they replied, "that is so written in the Torah." "That," he said, "is one."

Said the Jews: "Moses is better than you." "And why?" he inquired. "Because," they said, "God spoke to him four thousand four hundred and forty words, but never did He speak a thing to you." "But I," he responded, "was given something superior to that." "And what was that?" they asked. Said he: "Glory be to Him who took His servant by night (Quran 17:1), for He bore me up on Gabriel's wing until He brought me to the seventh heaven, and I passed beyond the Sidra tree of the Boundary at the Garden of Resort (Quran 53:14–15) till I caught hold of a leg of the Throne, and from above the Throne came a voice: 'O Muhammad, I am God. Beside me there is no other god.' Then with all my heart I saw my Lord. This is more excellent than that (given to Moses)." "You speak but the truth," they replied, "that is so written in the Torah." "That," he said, "makes two."

Noah is then similarly disposed of. "Well," said Muhammad, "that is three."

They said: "Abraham is better than you . . . God Most High took him as a friend." He answered, "Abraham was indeed the friend of God, but I am His beloved. Do you know why my name is Muhammad? It is because He derived it from His name. He is Al-Hamid, the Praiseworthy, and my name is Muhammad, the Praised, while my community are the Hamidun, those who give praise." "You speak but truly," they replied, "this is greater than that." "That is four."

"But Jesus," they said, "is better than you . . . because he mounted up to the pinnacle of the Temple in Jerusalem, where the satans came to bear him away, but God gave command to Gabriel who with his right wing smote them in their faces and cast them into the fire." "Nevertheless," he said, "I was given something better than that. I returned from fighting with the polytheists on the day of Badr exceedingly hungry, when there met me a Jewish woman with a basket on her head. In the basket there was a roasted kid, and in her sleeve some sugar. She said: 'Praise be to God who has kept you safe. I made a vow to God that if you returned safely from this warlike expedition I would not fail to sacrifice this kid for you to eat.' Then she set it down and I put my hand to it, which caused the kid to speak, standing upright on its four feet, and saying, 'Eat not of me, for I am poisoned.' " "You speak but true," they said. "That is five, but there remains one more, for we claim that Solomon was better than you."

"Why?" he asked. "Because," they said, "God subjected to him satans, jinn, men and winds, and taught him the language of the birds and insects." "Yet," he replied, "I have been given something superior to that. God subjected to me Buraq (the miraculous beast that bore Muhammad on the Night Journey), who is more precious than all the world. He is one of the riding-beasts of Paradise. . . . Between his eyes is written 'There is no god but the God. Muhammad is the Messenger of God.' " "You speak truly," they said, "we bear witness that there is no god but the God and that you are His servant and Messenger." (Suyuti, *Glittering Things*)

[JEFFERY 1962: 334–336]

Finally, in the course of his Night Journey and Ascension to Heaven, Muhammad was given sight of his fellow prophets, whose physical appearance is relayed, on his authority, in his standard biography.

Al-Zuhri alleged as from Sa'id al-Musayyab that the Messenger described to his companions Abraham, Moses and Jesus as he saw them that night, saying: "I have never seen a man more like myself than Abraham. Moses was a ruddy-faced man, tall, thinly fleshed, curly haired with a hooked nose as if he were of the Shanu'a. Jesus son of Mary was a reddish man of medium height with lank hair and with many freckles on his face as though he had just come from a bath. One would suppose that his head was dripping with water, though there was no water on it. The man most like him among you is Urwa ibn Mas'ud al-Thaqafi." (*Life* 266)

[IBN ISHAQ 1955: 183–184]

46. The Prophet-King of the Virtuous City

Muslim contact with Greek philosophical thought introduced other, more rigorous ways of thinking about the question of prophecy, whether of the modalities of the transmission or of the characteristics of the prophet. The first of the Muslim thinkers to integrate Greek political and cognitive theories into a religious system like Islam's, which hinged upon a prophetic revelation, was al-Farabi (d. ca. 950 C.E.). Philo of Alexandria had already done some of the work in the first century by putting Moses and the philosophers side by side as parallel phenomena. Farabi was perhaps the first to resume the discussion in Islam, but now within the framework of Plato's political theories and with considerable help from Hellenic theories of cognition. These enabled Farabi to explain how the process of prophetic revelation occurred.

Since what is intended by man's existence is that he attain supreme happiness, he—in order to achieve it—needs to know what happiness is, make it his end, and hold it before his eyes. Then, after that, he needs to know the things he ought to do in order to attain happiness, and then do the actions. In view of what has been said about the differences of natural dispositions of individual men, not everyone is disposed to know happiness on his own, or the things he ought to do, but needs a teacher and a guide for this purpose.

That teacher and guide is the prophet or, to put it within Farabi's own Plato-derived categories, the ideal ruler of the equally idealized polity called by Farabi "the virtuous city." How that prophet-king receives his own illumination is the next subject taken up by the Muslim philosopher.

The supreme ruler without qualification is he who does not need anyone to rule him in anything whatever, but has actually acquired the sciences and every kind of knowledge, and has no need of a man to guide him in anything. He is able to comprehend well each one of the particular things he ought to do. He is able to guide well all others to everything in which he instructs them, to employ all those who do any of the acts for which they are equipped, and to determine, define and direct these acts toward happiness. This is found only in the one who possesses great and superior natural dispositions, when his soul is in union with the (separate and higher) Active Intellect. He can only attain this (union with the Active Intellect) by first acquiring the passive intellect and the intellect called the acquired; for, as was stated in *On the Soul*, union with the Active Intellect results from possessing the acquired intellect. This man is the true prince according to the ancients; he is the one of whom it ought to be said that he receives revelation. For man receives revelation only when he attains this rank, that is, when there is no longer an intermediary between him and the Active Intellect; for the passive intellect is like matter and substratum to the acquired intellect, and the latter is like matter and substratum to the Active Intellect. It is then that the power that enables man to understand how to define things and actions and how to direct them toward happiness, emanates from the (separate and higher) Active Intellect to the (human) passive intellect. This emanation that proceeds from the Active Intellect to the passive through the mediation of the acquired intellect is revelation. Now because the Active Intellect emanates from the being of the First Cause [that is, God], it can for this reason be said that it is the First Cause that brings about revelation to this man through the mediation of the Active Intellect. The rule of this man is the supreme rule; all other human rulerships are inferior to it and derived from it. Such is his rank. (Farabi, *The Political Regime* 47–50)

[LERNER & MAHDI 1972: 35–37]

47. The Prophet as Lawgiver

This emanation of the intelligible truths from the higher, angelic Active Intellect into the highly developed intellect of an individual man becomes the accepted mode of prophecy among the philosophers. The prophet is, then, a philosopher in his understanding of those truths and becomes a prophet only by turning toward society and converting those truths, or at least some of them, into an idiom comprehensible to the masses who cannot philosophize and so need guidance on their path to happiness and salvation. So it is set forth by one of Farabi's successors in the Islamic philosophical tradition, the physician, statesman, and polymath Ibn Sina (d. 1038 C.E.), or Avicenna as he came to be called in the West. In this passage from his Book of Deliverance it is first established that man is a social animal and will of necessity associate with other men and transact business. These transactions require a code of law, which in turn calls for a lawgiver, someone "in the position to speak to men and constrain them to accept the code; he must therefore be a man." Avicenna continues.

Now it is not feasible that men should be left to their own opinions in this matter so that they will differ each from the other, every man considering as justice that which favors him, and as injustice that which works against his advantage. The survival and complete self-realization of the human race requires the existence of such a lawgiver. . . .

It follows therefore that there should exist a prophet, and that he should be a man; it also follows that he should have some distinguishing feature which does not belong to other men, so that his fellows may recognize him as possessing something which is not theirs, and so that he may stand out apart from them. This distinguishing feature is the power to work miracles.

Such a man, if and when he exists, must prescribe laws for mankind governing all their affairs, in accordance with God's ordinance and authority, God inspiring him and sending down the Holy Spirit upon him. The fundamental principle upon which his [that is, the prophet's] code rests will be to teach them that they have One Creator, Almighty and Omniscient, whose commandments must of right be obeyed; that the Command must belong to Him who possesses the power to create and that He has prepared for those who obey Him a future life of bliss but wretchedness for such as disobey Him. So the masses will receive the prescriptions, sent down upon his tongue from God and the Angels, with heedful obedience. (Avicenna, *Book of Deliverance*) [AVICENNA 1951: 42–44]

48. Avicenna on the Prophethood of Muhammad

There is little in Avicenna's description of the lawgiver to suggest that Muhammad had either a unique role among the prophets or that the possibility of prophetic revelation ended with him. But in one of his works, On the Proof of the Prophecies, *Avicenna appears to take up the case of the prophethood of Muhammad, for reasons he explains as the outset.*

You have asked—may God set you aright—that I sum up for you in a treatise the substance of what I said to you with a view to eliminate your misgivings about accepting prophecy. You are confirmed in these misgivings because the claims of the advocates of prophecy are either logically possible assertions that are treated as necessary without the benefit of (rigorous) demonstrative argument or even of (secondary) dialectical proof, or else impossible assertions on the order of fairy tales, such that the very attempt on the part of their advocate to expound them deserves derision.

Avicenna then gives his own succinct explanation of what prophetic revelation is and how it occurs.

Revelation is the emanation and the angel is the received emanating power that descends on the prophets as if it were an emanation continuous with the Universal Intellect. It is rendered particular, not essentially, but accidentally, because of the particularity of the recipient. Thus the angels have been given different names because (they are associated with) different notions; nevertheless, they form a single totality, which is particularized, not essentially, but accidentally, by the particularity of the recipient. The message, therefore, is that part of the emanation termed "revelation" which has been received and couched in whatever mode of expression is deemed best for furthering man's good in both the eternal and the corruptible worlds as regards knowledge and political govern-ance, respectively. The messenger is the one who conveys what he ac-quires of the emanation termed "revelation," again in whatever mode of expression is deemed best for achieving through his opinions the good of the sensory world by political governance and of the intellectual world by knowledge.

There immediately follows this curiously reticent conclusion.

This, then, is the summary of the discourse concerning the affirma-tion of prophecy, the showing of its essence, and the statements made about revelation, the angel and the thing revealed. As for the validity of the prophethood of our prophet, of Muhammad, may God's prayers and peace be upon him, it becomes evident to the reasonable man once he compares him with the other prophets, peace be on them. We shall refrain from elaboration here. (Avicenna, *On the Proof of Prophecies* 120–124) [LERNER & MAHDI 1972: 113–115]

49. Maimonides on Prophecy

Farabi's thinking on prophecy and prophethood is particularly evident in the phi-losophical works of Maimonides (d. 1204 C.E.). As has been remarked, Islam, like Judaism, mediated its revelation through prophets, and so the Jewish thinker found as much to meditate upon in Hellenic thought on the subject of inspiration as the Muslims had before him.

The opinions of people concerning prophecy are like their opinions concerning the eternity of the world or its creation in time. I mean by this that just as the people to whose mind the existence of the deity is firmly established, have, as we have set forth, three opinions concerning the eternity of the world or its creation in time, so there are three opinions concerning prophecy. . . .

The first opinion—that of the multitude of those among the pagans who considered prophecy as true and also believed by some of the com-mon people professing our Law—is that God, may He be exalted, chooses whom He wishes among men, turns him into a prophet, and sends him with a mission. According to them it makes no difference whether this individual is a man of knowledge or ignorant, aged or young.

However, they also posit as a condition his having a certain goodness and sound morality. For up to now people have not gone so far as to say that God sometimes turns a wicked man into a prophet unless He has first, according to this opinion, turned him into a good man.

The second opinion is that of the philosophers. It affirms that prophecy is a certain perfection in the nature of man. This perfection is not achieved in any individual from among men except after a training that makes that which exists in the potentiality of the species pass into actuality. . . . According to this opinion, it is not possible that an ignoramus should turn into a prophet; nor can a man not be a prophet on a certain evening and be a prophet on the following morning, as though he had made some discovery. Things are rather as follows: When, in the case of a superior individual who is perfect with respect to his rational and moral qualities, his imaginative faculty is in its most perfect state and when he has been prepared in the way that you will hear, he will necessarily become a prophet, inasmuch as this is a perfection that belongs to us by nature. According to this opinion, it is not possible that an individual should be fit for prophecy and prepared for it and not become a prophet, no more than it is possible that an individual having a healthy temperament should be nourished with excellent food without sound blood and similar things being generated from that food.

The third opinion is the opinion of our Law and the foundation of our doctrine. It is identical with the philosophic opinion except for one thing. For we believe that it may happen that one who is fit for prophecy and prepared for it should not become a prophet, namely on account of the divine will. To my mind this is like all the miracles and takes the same course as they. For it is a natural thing that everyone who according to his natural disposition is fit for prophecy and who has been trained in his education and study should become a prophet. But he who is prevented from it is like him who has been prevented, like Jereboam (1 Kings 13:4), from moving his hand or, like the King of Aram's army going out to seek Elisha (2 Kings 6:18), from seeing. As for its being fundamental with us that the prophet must possess preparation and perfection in the moral and rational qualities, it is indubitably the opinion expressed in their dictum: "Prophecy only rests upon a wise, strong, and rich man" (BT. Shabbath 92a). . . . As for the fact that someone who prepares is sometimes prevented from becoming a prophet, you may know from the history of Baruch, son of Neriah. For he followed Jeremiah, who taught, trained and prepared him. And he set himself the goal of becoming a prophet, but was prevented, as he says: "I am weary with my groaning and find no rest" (Jer. 45:3). Thereupon he was told through Jeremiah: "Thus shall you say to him: Thus says the Lord etc. . . . And do you seek great things for yourself? Seek them not" (Jer. 45:2, 5). It is possible to say that this is a clear statement that prophecy was too great a thing for Baruch. Similarly, it may be said, as we shall explain, that in the passage, "Yes, her prophets find no vision from the Lord" (Lam. 2:9), this was the case because they were in exile.

We shall find many texts, some of them scriptural and some of them dicta of the Sages, all of which maintain this fundamental principle that God turns whomever He wills, whenever He wills it, into a prophet, but only someone perfect and superior to the utmost degree. But with regard to one of the ignorant among the common people, this—I mean, that he should turn into a prophet—is not possible according to us except as it is possible that He should turn an ass or a frog into a prophet. It is our fundamental principle that there must be training and perfection, where-upon the possibility arises to which the power of the deity becomes attached. (Maimonides, *Guide of the Perplexed* 2.32) [MAIMONIDES 1963: 360–362]

50. Moses Unique among the Prophets

If what Maimonides says is true of all prophets, he is willing to make the case—the same that Avicenna was apparently reluctant to make regarding Muhammad—that Moses stands apart from all those who went before him or came after him. And the first argument for this, Maimonides insists with a sidelong glance at Islam, is that "to every prophet except Moses our Master prophetic revelation comes through an angel." Then there is Scripture itself.

To my mind the term "prophet" used with reference to Moses and to the others is amphibolous. The same applies, in my opinion, to his miracles and to the miracles of others, for his miracles do not belong to the class of the miracles of other prophets. The proof taken from the Law as to his prophecy being different from that of all who came before him is constituted by His saying: "And I appeared to Abraham, etc., but by My name, the Lord, I made not known to them" (Exod. 6:3). Thus it informs us that his (Moses') apprehension was not like the Patriarchs', but greater—nor, all the more, like that of others who came before. As for the difference between his prophecy and that of all those who came after, it is stated by way of communicating information in the dictum: "And there has not arisen a prophet since in Israel like Moses, whom the Lord knew face to face" (Deut. 34:10). Thus it has been made clear that his apprehension is different from that of all men who came after him in

Israel, which is "a kingdom of priests and a holy nation" (Exod. 19:6) and "in whose midst is the Lord" (Num. 16:3), and, all the more, from the apprehension of those who came in other religious communities.

It is not merely the quality of Moses' apprehension of the divine presence that sets him apart; there is also the evidence of the signs and miracles worked through him.

As for the difference between his miracles in general and those of every prophet in general, it should be said that all the miracles worked by the prophets or for them were made known to very few people only. Thus, for example, the signs of Elijah and Elisha. . . . The same holds good for the signs of all the prophets except Moses our Master. For this reason Scripture makes it clear, likewise by way of information with reference to him, that no prophet will ever arise who will work signs both before those who are favorably and those who are unfavorably disposed toward him, as was done by Moses. (Maimonides, *Guide of the Perplexed* 2.35)
[MAIMONIDES 1963: 367–368]

51. Muhammad on Moses and the Torah

Muhammad, as might be expected, had a quite different view of the matter, as appears in this report attributed to him in the Muslim tradition.

Jabir told how Umar ibn al-Khattab brought God's Messenger a copy of the Torah saying, "Messenger of God, this is a copy of the Torah." When he received no reply he began to read from it to the obvious displeasure of the Messenger of God, so Abu Bakr said, "Confound you, do you not see how the Messenger of God is looking?" So Umar looked at the face of God's Messenger and said, "I seek refuge in God from the anger of God and His Messenger. We are satisfied with God as Lord, with Islam as religion and with Muhammad as Prophet." Then God's Messenger said, "By Him in whose hand my soul rests, were Moses to appear to you and you were to follow him and abandon me, you would err from the right path. Were Moses alive and and came in touch with my Prophetic mission, he would follow me." (Baghawi, *Mishkat al-Masabih* 1.6.3)

52. On the Inspiration of the Quran

European Christian opinion on Islam, its Prophet, and its Sacred Book was generally brutal and ignorant. In some cases there was little excuse for the ignorance since there were not a few Christians who had been and would continue to go to the

Middle East on pilgrimage, and so had been exposed to Islam at first hand. And of those there were even some few who learned Arabic and had studied both Islam and its Scripture. One of those latter was Ricoldo di Monte Croce, a Dominican monk who lived for an extended period in the East from 1288 onwards and who had not only visited Jerusalem but had studied in Baghdad. He had some appreciation of his subject, surely, but he was also an heir to the experience of the Crusades, whose atrocities had coarsened perceptions on both sides. More, Ricoldo was unabashedly a missionary, striving for the conversion of the infidel and awaiting, if need be, his own martyrdom at their hands. His Itinerary *was written in 1294* C.E.

The Saracens can be easily convicted of error and refuted by the Holy Books and the authority of Sacred Scripture, by the books of the philosophers and the way of reason, and even more easily by the Alcoran itself which manifests its own abominable falsity to anyone who reads it. They can also be easily confounded by the scandalous life of their own prophet Muhammad, who led a life consumed by indulgence, adultery and rapine down to his last breath. . . . The Saracens themselves say that Muhammad, a single man, could not produce the Alcoran without God's help, with its many references to the Old and New Testaments. In fact, there are many more things there *against* the Old and New Testaments. And finally, it is known as an absolute certainty in many parts of the East that Muhammad had three teachers, namely two Jews, one of them Salon [Salman] the Persian and the name of the other Abdullah, which means "servant of God," son of Sela. These two became Saracens and taught him a great deal about the Old Testament and the Talmud. The third was a monk and his name was Bahheyin [Bahira], a Jacobite, who narrated to him much from the New Testament and certain information from a book about the infancy of the Savior and about the Seven Sleepers, and Muhammad wrote down those things in the Alcoran. But his chief teacher was, I think, the devil. (Ricoldo di Monte Croce, *Itinerarium*)

[LAURENT 1873: 137–141]

2. On Understanding Scripture

1. "In the Beginning": The Great Exegesis

We have already seen some of the approaches taken toward understanding the Bible. A great deal of attention was given to the cultic and legal matters that loom so large in both the Torah and the Jewish life that flowed from it. But the Book begins with neither cult nor law but with what first the Jews and later the Christians and Muslims recognized as the beginning of God's discourse on His own creation. With the opening verse of Genesis we are standing, quite literally, at the beginning of the universe.

We do not know how these words were understood by the first generation of believers to have heard them, though surely even they struggled for some understanding. For examples of preserved interpretations we must move far later into the tradition, in this instance to a work called the "Book of Jubilees," the work of an anonymous Jewish author of the second century B.C.E. The approach is straightforward, in many instances a summary retelling of Genesis, though with some interesting additions—the angels, for example.

On the first day He created the tall heavens and the earth and the waters and all the spirits who served Him: the angels of the presence, the angels of sanctification, the angels of the spirit of fire, the angels of the spirits of the winds, of the clouds, of darkness, of snow, hail and hoarfrost, the angels of the voices of thunder and lightning, the angels of the spirits of cold and heat, of winter, spring, autumn and summer, and of all the spirits of His creatures in Heaven and on the earth. He created the abysses and darkness, twilight and night, and light, dawn, and day, and He prepared them in the knowledge of His heart. Thereupon we saw His works and praised them.

When the account reaches the fourth day of creation, some of the author's cultic interests appear.

And on the fourth day He created the sun and the moon and the stars, and placed them in the firmament of heaven to give light on earth, to rule over day and night, to separate light from darkness. And God appointed the sun to be a great sign on the earth for days and for sabbaths and for months, for feasts, years, sabbaths of years, for jubilees, and every season of the year. (Jubilees 2:1, 8)

The Law was first given to Moses on Sinai many centuries after the events described in the opening of Genesis. That, however, was the "given" version of the Law; there was another, heavenly Torah that long antedated the Sinai revelation, as Jubilees reveals in speaking of Adam.

After Adam had completed forty days in the land where he was created, he was brought into the Garden of Eden to till and keep it. His wife was brought in on the eightieth day.

Genesis 2:15–25 makes no mention of those intervals, but there is a point to mentioning them here. The author, it appears, has his eyes fixed more closely on Leviticus 12:1–4 than on the text of the second chapter of Genesis.

For that reason the commandment is written on the heavenly tablets in regard to the mother: "She who bears a male shall remain in her uncleanness seven days and thirty-three days in the blood of purification. She shall not touch any hallowed things, nor enter into the sanctuary until the days for the male or female child are accomplished." This is law and testimony written down for Israel. (Jubilees 3:10)

The task of explicating Genesis began before Jubilees and continues to the present day through many different channels and from a great many different perspectives. Typical of what might fairly be called a "consensual" approach is the work called Midrash Rabbah, or the "Great Exegesis." Although that part of it which deals with Genesis—the Midrash Genesis Rabbah—is dated as it stands to the fifth Christian century, it is likely a composite of various opinions of Palestinian rabbis of the two or three preceding centuries. The texture is obviously much richer and more anecdotal, but it does not differ greatly from what one reads in Jubilees: it is a "legalizing," nonsectarian approach to the opening of the Bible.

"In the beginning God created": Six things preceded the creation of the world; some of them were actually created, while the creation of others was already contemplated. The Torah and the Throne of God were created (before the creation of the world). The Torah, for it is written, "The Lord made me as the beginning of His way, prior to His works of old" (Prov. 8:22). The Throne of God, as it is written, "Your throne is established of old . . ." (Ps. 93:2). The creation of the Patriarchs was contemplated, for it is written, "I saw your fathers as the first-ripe in the fig tree at her first season" (Hos. 9:10). (The creation of) Israel was contemplated, as it is written, "Remember Your congregation, which You have gotten aforetime" (Ps. 74:2). (The creation of) the Temple was contemplated, for it is written, "Your throne of glory, on high from the beginning, the place of our sanctuary" (Jer. 17:12). The name of the Messiah was contemplated, for it is written, "His name exists before the sun" (Ps. 72:17). Rabbi Ahabah ben Ze'ira said: Repentance too, as it is written, "Before the mountains were brought forth, etc." (Ps. 90:2), and from that very moment, "You turn man to contrition, and say: Repent, you children of men" (ibid. 90:3). I still do not know which was first, whether the Torah preceded the Throne of Glory or the Throne of Glory preceded the Torah. Rabbi Abba ben Kahana said: The Torah preceded the Throne of Glory, for it says, "The Lord made me as the beginning of His way, before His works of old," that is, before that of which it is written, "Your throne is established of old."

Rabbi Huna, reporting Rabbi Jeremiah in the name of Rabbi Samuel ben Rabbi Isaac, said: The intention to create Israel preceded everything else. This may be illustrated thus: A king was married to a certain lady, and had no son of her. On one occasion the king was found going through the marketplace and giving orders: "Take this ink, inkwell and pen for my son," at which people remarked: "He has no son; what does he want with ink and pen? Strange indeed!" Subsequently they concluded: "The king is an astrologer and has actually foreseen that he is destined to beget a son!" Thus, had not the Holy One, blessed be He, foreseen that after twenty-six generations [that is, from Adam to Moses] Israel would receive the Torah, He would not have written therein, "Command the Children of Israel."

Rabbi Banayah said: The world and the fullness thereof was created only for the sake of the Torah: "The Lord for the sake of wisdom founded the earth" (Prov. 3:19). Rabbi Berekiah said: For the sake of Moses: "And he chose The Beginning [that is, creation] for himself, for there a portion of a ruler was reserved" (Deut. 33:21).

Rabbi Huna said in Rabbi Mattenah's name: The world was created for the sake of three things: the dough offering, tithes and firstfruits, as it is said, "In the beginning God created." Now "beginning" refers to the dough offering, for it is written, "Of the beginning of your dough" (Num. 15:20); again "beginning" refers to tithes, for it is written, "The beginnings of your grain" (Deut. 18:4); and finally, "beginning alludes to firstfruits, for it is written, "The beginning (or firstfruits) of your land, etc." (Exod. 23:19). (*Genesis Rabbah* 1.4–7) [MIDRASH RABBAH 1977: 1:6–7]

2. The Kabbala on Torah, Body and Soul

There is more to explaining the Torah than taking it phrase by phrase and extracting moral or legal lessons from them. Some Greeks believed their myths had an "undersense." In certain Jewish circles it was not so much a question of an "undersense" as an entire "under Torah." So, at any rate, it is expressed in one of the primary documents of what the Jews came to call the "Kabbala." Kabbala—variously Qabbalah and Cabala in the vagaries of English transcription—is quite simply "the tradition," something handed down. What was handed down was somewhat less simple, however: it is a large body of esoteric learning, theosophy of both the alphabetic and the numerical variety—in short, the mysteries of God and His creation.

"Kabbala" is a generic term, but one of the primary works of which it is constituted is the Zohar, or "Book of Splendor," a tract purporting to be the esoteric reflections on the Torah of the second-century C.E. rabbi Simeon ben Yohai, but more likely the editorial work of the Spanish scholar Moses of Leon (d. 1305) operating on older and very heterogeneous material. And it is here that we learn of the body and soul of the Torah.

Rabbi Simeon said: Woe to the man who says that Torah intends to set forth mere stories and common tales. If that were so, then we would ourselves be able at once to put together a torah out of such common tales, and indeed a far more worthy one. And if it is the intention of the Torah to disclose everyday matters, then the rulers of this world have far better books; let us find them and make a torah of them.

We suddenly find ourselves back in the world of Jubilees, with its heavenly tablets of the Law.

All the words of Torah are sublime and lofty mysteries. See how the upper world and the lower world are in perfect balance—Israel below corresponds to the angels above. . . . When the angels descend into the world below they clothe themselves in a manner appropriate to this world, for if they did not do so, they would not be able to remain in this world, nor could the world endure them. And if it is so with the angels, how much more so must it be with the Torah, which created the angels and all the worlds, and through which all the worlds are maintained. When the Torah came down into this world, it clothed itself with the garments of this world, otherwise the world could not have endured it.

So the stories of the Torah are only the Torah's outer clothing. That man is lost who mistakenly thinks that that clothing is the Torah itself, and that there is nothing more to it. He shall have no portion in the world to come. That is why David said: "Open my eyes so that I may see wondrous things of Your Torah" (Ps. 119:18), that is to say, that I may see what is underneath the Torah's outer garment.

You see how a man's clothing is visible to all, and only the fool, when he sees someone clothed in fine raiment, looks no further: he considers the clothing as if it were the body, and then the body as if it were the soul. In like manner the Torah has a body, namely, the commandments of the Torah which are called "the bodies of the Torah." This body is clothed in garments composed of earthly tales. Foolish people look only at those garments, these tales of the Torah. They go no further, nor do they look at what is beneath the outer clothing. But those who are wiser look not at the clothes but at the body beneath them. And the genuine Sages, the servants of the Most High King, those who stood at Mount Sinai, look only at the soul of the Torah, which is the most elemental principle of all, the True Torah, and in the world to come they are destined to look at the soul of the soul of the Torah. (*Book of Splendor* 3.152a)

3. The "Work of Creation"

We have an opportunity to "look at the soul of the soul of the Torah" through the lens of the Zohar itself.

Before the Holy One, blessed be He, had created any image, or fashioned any form, He was alone without any likeness or form. Whoever seeks to apprehend Him as He was, prior to creation, when He existed without image, is forbidden to represent Him with any kind of form or image, whether it be with the letter H or Y, or even with the Holy Name, or with a single letter or sign of any kind. Thus, "You saw no kind of image" (Deut. 4:15) means: you did not see anything which possesses image or form.

But after He had fashioned the image of the Chariot of Supernal Man, He descended into it and was known through the image of YHWH [that is, Yahweh], so that men might apprehend him through His attributes, through each of them severally, and He was called El, Elohim, Shaddai, Zeva'ot, and YHWH, so that men might apprehend Him through His attributes. . . . For if His radiance had not been shed over all creation, how could men have apprehended Him, or how could the verse be true, "The whole earth is full of His glory" (Isa. 6:3)?

Woe to the man who would equate God with any single attribute, even with one that is truly His own. . . . It is like the sea. The waters of the sea in themselves cannot be grasped and give no form, but when they are poured into a vessel—the earth—they receive form. . . . In like manner the Cause of causes formed ten Primordial Numbers. He called Crown the source. In it there is no end of the flow of His radiance, and on this account He called Himself The Infinite. He possesses neither shape nor form, nor does any vessel exist there to contain Him or any means of knowing Him. It is to this that the saying refers, "Do not investigate things too hard for you, or inquire into what is hidden from you" (BT.Hagigah 13a).

The cautionary note cited from the Talmud was neither the beginning nor the end of the matter. The earlier Mishna is somewhat more specific.

The Work of Creation should not be expounded in the presence of two (persons), nor [the Work of] the Chariot in the presence of one, unless he is a sage and already has an independent understanding of the matter. (M.Hagiga 2:1)

The Mishna is obviously not concerned with the unexceptional exposition of Genesis of the type we have already seen from the "Great Exegesis." What is at stake here is what is being called the "Work of Creation," that is, the type of esoteric reading of Genesis already cited from the Book of Splendor. *This kind of theosophic cosmogony must have had a long history, but its classic Jewish formulation is to be found in the* Book of Creation, *composed in Palestine sometime between the third and sixth century* C.E. *God created the world, the brief tract explains, by three principles: by limit, by letter, and by number.*

There are ten Primordial Numbers and twenty-two Basic Letters. . . .

The ten Primordial Numbers are:

One: the Spirit of the Living God.

Two: Air from the Spirit [the same word in Hebrew]. He engraved and carved out of the Air the twenty-two basic letters: three mother letters, seven double and twelve simple letters; and each of them has the same Spirit.

Three: Water from the Air. He engraved and carved out of the Water chaos and disorder, mud and mire. He made them into a kind of seedbed; He raised them as a kind of wall; He wove them into a kind of roof. He poured snow of them and they became earth. . . .

Four: Fire from Water. He engraved and carved out of the Fire the Throne of Glory, the Offanim, the Seraphim, the Holy Creatures and the angels who minister. . . . He chose three of the simple letters, Y, H and W, and made them into His great name [that is, Yahweh]. With them He sealed six extremities. . . . (*Book of Creation* 1–15)

The six extremities are height, depth, east, west, south, and north, and they are the remaining six Primordial Numbers. Thus, in this system the Primordial Numbers 1–10 appear to be the primary emanations of God, with the Spirit of God emerging from 1, then the basic elements Air, Water, and Fire from 2–4. Out of the Air God then "engraves" the twenty-two letters of the Hebrew alphabet, from which come in turn everything from the constellations of the Zodiac to the organs of the human body. Out of Water come the primordial chaos and the physical universe. Finally, out of Fire arrives the spiritual universe, including that Throne-Chariot which became the point of departure for so much of Jewish mysticism. And what is the origin of all this esoteric learning apparently unknown to the Bible? The Book of Creation *concludes:*

When our father Abraham had come, inspected, investigated and understood, and had successfully engraved, combined, carved and computed, then the Lord of all was revealed to him. He set Abraham in His bosom, kissed him on the head, called him His own beloved, and He designated him His son. He made a covenant with him and with his descendants forever, "And Abraham believed in the Lord and He accounted it to him as righteousness" (Gen. 15:6).

This is the Book of the Letters of Abraham our father which is known as "The Laws of Creation." Whoever looks into it, there is no limit to his wisdom. (*Book of Creation* 61, 64)

4. Ramban on Genesis

The thoughts of the rabbis represented in the "Great Exegesis" and of those anonymous sages who stand behind the Kabbala appear to be irreconcilable worlds apart. That they were not—that both the esoteric and the legal-homiletic understanding of Scripture dwelled together at the heart of the Jewish tradition—can be seen in this selection from the great Provençal scholar Nachmanides (d. ca. 1270 C.E.), the universally revered and undoubtedly orthodox "Ramban."

"In the beginning God created": Rashi wrote: "This verse cries aloud for elucidation, as our Rabbis have explained it: 'For the sake of

Torah, which is called "The Beginning," as when it is said, "The Eternal One made me as the beginning of His way"; and for sake of Israel, who is also called "The Beginning," as when it is said, "Israel is the Eternal's hallowed portion, the beginning of His increase." ' "

This exegesis of our Rabbis is very hidden and secret for there are many things the rabbis found that are called "beginnings" and concerning which they give homiletic explanations, and those wanting in faith total up the number (of such things). For example, they [that is, the Rabbis] have said: "For the merit acquired by (fulfilling the commandments associated with) three things has the world been created: for the merit of the dough offering, for the merit of the tithes and for the merit of the first-fruits." "Beginning" surely signifies the dough offering, as it is said, "The beginning of your dough." "Beginning" certainly signifies the tithes, as it is said, "the beginning of your grain." "Beginning" surely signifies the firstfruits, as it is said, "the beginning (or firstfruits) of your land...."

Their intent in the above texts is as follows: the word "beginning" alludes to the creation of the world by Ten Primordial Numbers, and hints in particular to the Primordial Number called Wisdom, in which is the foundation of everything, even as it says "the Eternal has founded the earth by wisdom" (Prov. 3:19). This is the dough offering, and it is holy; it has no precise measure [that is, no fixed amount is prescribed by the Law], thus indicating the little understanding created beings have of it. Now just as a man counts ten measures—this alludes to the Ten Primordial Numbers—and sets aside one measure of the ten as a tithe, so do the wise men contemplate the tenth Primordial and speak about it. The dough offering, which is the single commandment pertaining to the dough, alludes to this. Now Israel, which is called "The Beginning" as mentioned above, is "the congregation of Israel," which is compared in the Song of Songs to a bride and whom Scripture in turn calls "daughter," "sister," and "mother." The Rabbis have already expressed this in a homiletic interpretation of the verse, "Upon the crown wherewith his mother has crowned him" (Song of Sol. 3:11), and in other places. Similarly, the verse concerning Moses, "and He chose The Beginning for himself," which they [that is, the Rabbis] interpret to mean that Moses our teacher contemplated the Deity through a lucid mirror, and he saw that which is called "The Beginning" for himself, and therefore he merited the Torah. Thus all the above interpretations have one meaning. Now it is impossible to discuss this explanation at length in writing, and even an allusion is dangerous since people might have thoughts concerning it which are

untrue. But I have mentioned this (brief explanation cited above) in order to close the mouths of those wanting in faith and of little wisdom, who scoff at the Rabbis. (Nachmanides, *Commentary on Genesis*)
[NACHMANIDES 1971: 20–22]

What Nachmanides intends here is obviously more than simply elucidating the text. He has, of course, to take account of the man who was by then already the major interpreter of the Bible, the French scholar Rashi (d. 1105 C.E.) cited in the text. More will be heard of Rashi throughout Nachmanides' commentary, but in this passage the attempt is to reconcile, and defend, his more homiletically minded predecessors with what he obviously considers the more fundamental esoteric reading of Genesis.

5. A Muslim Creation Story

Just as in Jewish homiletic exegesis God created certain idealized forms of being before turning to the making of material things, so too in Islam certain events preceded the creation of the world. The following account is drawn from a genre that was a rich source of such haggadic narratives in Islam, the "Stories of the Prophets." This one is by the eleventh-century author al-Kisa'i. Unlike either Midrash Rabbah or Nachmanides, the narrative makes no pretense of being a commentary upon the Bible but simply an explanation of an event. One of its intentions is obviously to harmonize the Quranic remarks about creation with the general tenor of the Genesis account, though the actual text of this latter has faded almost invisibly into the background of the Muslim narrative.

Sa'id ibn Abbas, with whom may God be pleased: The first thing that God created was the Preserved Tablet on which is preserved (a record) of all that has been and all that will be till the Day of Resurrection (cf. Quran 85:22). No one knows what is on it save God Most High. It is of white pearl, and God created for it from another jewel a Pen whose length is a five hundred year's journey, whose point is split, and from which light flows as ink flows from the pens of this world. Then a call came to the Pen, "Write," whereat the Pen from the terror of the summoning trembled and shook so that there was a quavering in its "Glory be to God" like the rumbling of thunder, then it entered on the Tablet all that God bade it enter of all that is to be till the Day of Resurrection. So the Tablet was filled up and the Pen ran dry, and he who is to be fortunate was made fortunate, and he who is to be unfortunate was made unfortunate.

Next is created a white pearl "the size of the heavens and the earth," which is transformed into water, reflecting Quran 21:30: "And from water We have produced every living thing." The account then continues, with echoes of Ezekiel 1 and 10 and Isaiah 61:1 (= Matt. 5:34–35).

Then God created the Throne out of a green jewel whose size and whose light no one can describe, and it was put on the billowing waves of the water. Wahb ibn Munabbih [another early Muslim authority] said that none of the former Scriptures failed to mention the Throne and the footstool, for God created them from two mighty jewels. Ka'b al-Ahbar said that the Throne has seventy thousand tongues with which it glorifies God in a variety of languages. It was upon the water, as He says: "Now His throne was upon the water" (Quran 11:7). Ibn Abbas said that every architect builds the foundation first and later sees to the roof, but God created the roof first since He created the Throne (atop the seven heavens) before He created the heavens and the earth. He said that then God created the wind, giving it wings the size and number of which no one save God knows, and He commanded it to bear up the water on which the Throne was, and it did so. So the Throne was upon the water and the water was upon the wind.

The narrative turns to the Throne, with obvious echoes of Ezekiel 1:8–11 and Revelation 4:4, though of which precisely it is impossible to say.

Then, said he [that is, Ibn Abbas], God created the Throne-bearers who at present are four, but when the Day of Resurrection comes God will aid them with four others, as the Most High has said: "And above them eight on that day will bear the Throne of your Lord" (Quran 69:17). They are of such a size as to be beyond description, and each of them has four forms, one in the form of a human, which makes intercession for the sustenance of men, another in the form of a bull, which makes intercession for the sustenance of domestic animals, another in the form of a lion, which makes intercession for the sustenance of wild beasts, and one in the form of an eagle, which makes intercession for the sustenance of the winged creatures.

Ibn Abbas, with whom may God be pleased, said that the footstool is of a jewel other than the jewel from which God created the Throne. Wahb said that there are angels associated with the Throne, some kneeling on their knees, some standing on their feet, bearing the Throne on their necks, but sometimes they get weary and then the Throne is borne up solely by the might of God. (He taught that) the footstool is from the light of the Throne, but others say that the footstool is God's knowledge and that the Throne is God's knowledge with regard to His creation, but this is false in the light of what Abu Dharr al-Ghifari has related of how he asked the Messenger of God, upon whom be God's blessing and peace, which was the most excellent verse in the Quran, and he answered, "the Throne Verse" [2:255; see Chapter 1 above]. Then he said, "The seven heavens would be in the footstool like a bracelet in the desert wastes, and the Throne is as much superior to the footstool as the footstool to a bracelet." (Kisaʾi, *Stories of the Prophets*) [JEFFREY 1962: 161–163]

6. The Divine Purpose in Creation

All these explanations of Creation, Jewish and Muslim alike, have as their objective the integration of other, nonscriptural but authoritative traditions into the account in Genesis. There was, however, another way to proceed, by attempting to rationalize the essentially mythic story in Genesis, to give it cause and purpose and rational shape. Among the first of the "People of the Book" to attempt this was a Hellenized Jew of Alexandria, Philo (ca. 25 C.E.), who had gone to school not only in the Law and Scripture but at the feet of Greek and Roman philosophers.

On the fourth day (of Creation), the earth being now finished, God ordered the heaven in varied beauty. Not that he put the heaven in a lower rank than the earth, giving precedence to the inferior creation [that is, the earth] and accounting the higher and the more divine [that is, the heaven] worthy only of the second place; but to make clear beyond all doubt the mighty sway of His sovereign power. For being aware beforehand of the ways of thinking that would mark the men of future ages, how they would be intent on what looked probable and plausible, with much in it that could be supported by argument, but would not aim at the sheer truth; and how they would trust phenomena rather than God, admiring sophistry rather than wisdom; and how they would observe in time to come the circuits of sun and moon, on which depend summer and winter and the changes of spring and autumn, and would suppose that the regular movements of the heavenly bodies are the causes of all things that year by year come forth and are produced out of the earth; so that there might be none who owing either to shameless audacity or to overwhelming ignorance should venture to ascribe the first place to any created thing, "let them," He said, "go back in thought to the original creation of the universe, when, before the sun or the moon existed, the earth bore plants of all sorts and fruits of all sorts; and having contemplated this, let them form in their minds the expectation that hereafter too shall it bear these at the Father's bidding, whensoever it may please Him." For he has no need of His heavenly offspring [that is, the heavenly bodies] on which he bestowed powers but not independence. . . . This is the reason why the earth put forth plants and bore herbs before the heaven was finished. (Philo, *The Creation of the World* 45–46) [PHILO 1945: 52–53]

7. Jacob's Pillow and Jacob's Ladder and Jacob's Thigh

Philo reasons about Scripture in a straightforward and even dogmatic fashion, with all the ease and elegance of someone well schooled in a self-assured tradition. The rabbinic method is quite different, as we may easily note, though no less assured. We have already seen something of the range of their Scriptural interpretation on Creation in the collective work known as the "Great Exegesis." Here are the same authorities on three objects associated with the story of Jacob in Genesis 28 and 33. The first has to do with the pillow of stones he placed under his head (Gen. 28:11), and is complicated by the textual question of whether there was one or more than one stone, a crux the following explanations indirectly attempt to solve.

Rabbi Judah said: He [Jacob] took twelve stones, saying: "The Holy One, blessed be he, has decreed that twelve tribes should spring forth. Now neither Abraham nor Isaac has produced them. If these cleave to one another, then I know that I will produce the twelve tribes." When therefore the twelve stones united, he knew that he was to produce the twelve tribes. Rabbi Nehemiah said: He took three stones, saying: "The Holy One, blessed be He, united His name with Abraham; with Isaac too He united His name. If these three stones become joined, then I am assured that God's name will be united with me too." And when they did so join, he knew that God would unite His name with him. The Rabbis say: (He took) the least number that (the plural) "stones" can connote, to wit, two, saying, "From Abraham there came forth Ishmael and the children of Keturah; from Isaac there came forth Esau. As for me, if these two stones join, I will be reassured that nothing worthless will come forth from me." (*Genesis Rabbah* 68:11) [MIDRASH RABBAH 1977: 1:623]

In the next passage, having to do with Jacob's dream of a ladder with angels ascending and descending (Gen. 28:12), the manner is allegorical, of the foreshadowing type later much favored by the Christians, and based on a correspondence of details.

Ben Kappara said: No dream is without its interpretation. "And behold a ladder" symbolizes the stairway (leading to the top of the altar in the Temple); "set up on the earth" is the altar, as it says, "An altar of earth you shall make for Me" (Exod. 20:21); "and the top of it reached to heaven" (refers to) the sacrifices, the odor of which reached to heaven; "and behold the angels of God" (refers to) the High Priests; "ascending and descending on it" (refers to) ascending and descending the stairway; "and behold, the Lord stood beside him" (reflects) "I saw the Lord standing beside the altar" (Amos 9:1).

The Rabbis connected it to Sinai. "And he dreamt" and "behold a ladder" symbolizes Sinai; "set up on the earth," as it says "And they stood on the lower part of the mount" (Exod. 19:17); "and the top of it reached to heaven" (compare) "And the mountain burned with fire to the heart of heaven" (Deut. 4:11). "And behold the angels of God" alludes to Moses and Aaron. "Ascending": "And Moses went up to God" (Exod. 19:3); "and descending": "And Moses went down from the mount" (Exod. 19:14). "And behold the Lord stood beside him": "And the Lord came down upon Mount Sinai" (Exod. 19:20). (*Genesis Rabbah* 68:12)
[MIDRASH RABBAH 1977: 1:625]

The last example arises from what must have appeared to the rabbis like an open invitation to commentary, the legal aside that concludes the narrative passage in Genesis 32:22–32: "This is why the Israelites to this day do not eat the sinew of the nerve that runs in the hollow of the thigh; for the man had struck Jacob on that nerve in the hollow of his thigh." The later lawyers were not, in any event, discouraged from believing that the last word had not been said on the matter. The earlier cited passage from the "Great Exegesis" was searching for symbolism in Jacob's ladder; here the quest is legal.

Rabbi Hanina said: Why is it called "the sinew of the nerve" (*gid ha-nashed*)? Because it slipped (*nashah*) from its place. Rabbi Huna said: The branches of the nerve sinew are permitted (to be eaten), but Israel are holy and (so) treat it as forbidden (as well). Rabbi Judah said: He [the angel] touched only one of them and (so) only one of them was forbidden. Rabbi Yosi said: He touched only one of them, but both of them became forbidden. One Mishnaic authority teaches: It is reasonable to suppose that it was the right one, which is Rabbi Judah's view; while another authority teaches: It is reasonable to suppose that it was the left one, which is Rabbi Yosi's view. The opinion that it was the right one (is based on the verse): "And he touched the hollow of his thigh" (ibid. 26), while the opinion that it was the left one is based on the verse "because he

touched the hollow of Jacob's thigh." (*Genesis Rabbah* 78:6)
[MIDRASH RABBAH 1977: 1:719]

8. The Method of the Midrashim

The Midrash Rabbah is but one example of Jewish homiletic commentary, with its edifying motives and occasional flights of interpretation as imaginative as those cited from the Muslim al-Kisaʾi. The genre was long a scriptural commonplace by Nachmanides' day. But it was obviously not to everyone's taste. A fastidiously described critique of the Midrashim and their spirited defense by one of Judaism's principal intellectuals—one whose own interests were as little congruent with these of the Rabbis as were those of Nachmanides—may be observed in the writing of the Spanish philosopher and legal scholar Moses Maimonides (d. 1204 C.E.). The biblical text in question is from Leviticus.

Mark, on the fifteenth day of the seventh month, when you have gathered in the yield of your land, you shall observe the festival of the Lord [that is, of Tabernacles or Sukkoth] (to last) seven days: a complete rest on the first day and a complete rest on the eighth day. On the first day you shall take the product of *hadar* trees [traditionally understood as the citron], branches of palm trees, boughs of leafy trees and willows of the brook, and you shall rejoice before the Lord your God seven days. (Leviticus 23:39–40)

The branches bound together constituted what was called in Hebrew a lulab. *In the Mishna treatise called Sukkah the Rabbis of the first and second century C.E. had explored the legal questions that might arise in connection with it.*

Earlier the *lulab* was carried seven days in the Temple, but in the provinces one day only. After the Temple was destroyed, Rabbi Yohanan ben Zakkai ordained that in the provinces it should be carried seven days in memory of the Temple. . . .

If the first festival day of the feast (of Sukkoth) falls on a Sabbath, all the people bring their *lulabs* to the synagogue (on the day before). The next day they come early and each man identifies his own *lulab* and carries it; for the Sages have said: None can fulfill his obligations on the first festival day of the feast with someone else's *lulab*. But on the other days of the feast a man may fulfill his obligation with someone else's *lulab*. (M.Sukkah 3:12–13)

The homiletic commentaries on Scripture used the same starting point of the verses in Leviticus on the fronds bound into the lulab, *but they proceeded in a very different direction.*

493

". . . The fruit of citrus trees, palm fronds and leafy branches and willows from the riverside. . . ." "The fruit of the citrus tree": these are the Israelites. As the citron has taste and smell, some among the Israelites have both Torah and good works. "Palm fronds": these are the Israelites. As the date has taste but not smell, so are there Israelites who have Torah but not good works. "Leafy branches": these are Israelites. As the myrtle has smell but no taste, so there are Israelites who have good works but no Torah. "Willows from the riverside": these are Israelites. As the willow has neither taste nor smell, so there are Israelites who have neither Torah nor good works. What is God to do with them? God says, "Bind all together in one bundle, and one will atone for the other." (*Leviticus Rabbah* 30:12)

It is apropos of this same passage in the "Great Exegesis" on Leviticus that Moses Maimonides, the Spanish philosopher and scholar of the Law, gives us his reflections on the homiletic approach to Scripture.

As for the four species (of fronds) that constitute a *lulab*, the Sages, may their memory be blessed, have set forth some reason for this in the manner of the Midrashim whose manner is well known to all those who understand their discourses. For these Midrashim have, in their opinion, the status of poetical conceits; they are not meant to bring out the meaning of the text in question. Accordingly, with regard to the Midrashim, people are divided into two classes: A class that imagines that the Sages have said these things in order to explain the meaning of the text in question, and a class that holds the Midrashim in slight esteem and holds them up to ridicule, since it is clear and manifest that this is not the meaning of the (biblical) text in question.

The first class strives and fights with a view to proving, as they deem, the correctness of the Midrashim and to defending them, and they think that this is the true meaning of the biblical text and that the Midrashim have the same status as the traditional legal decisions. But neither of the two groups understands that the Midrashim have the character of poetical conceits whose meaning is not obscure for someone endowed with understanding. At that time this method was generally known and used by everybody, just as the poets used poetical expressions. Thus the Sages, may their memory be blessed, say: "Bar Kappara teaches (concerning the verse) 'With your equipment (*azenekha*) you will have a spike . . .' (Deut. 23:13) [the verse continues: "and when you squat outside (the camp), you shall scrape a hole with it and then turn and cover your excrement"]: do not read *azenekha*, 'your equipment' but *aznekha*, 'your ear.' This teaches us that whenever a man hears a reprehensible thing, he should put a finger into his ear." Would that I knew whether, in the opinion of these ignoramuses, this Tannaite [that is, Bar Kappara] really believed this to be the interpretation of this text, that such was the purpose of this commandment that *yathed*, "spike," means a finger, and that *azenekha*, "your equipment," refers to the two ears. I do not think that anyone of sound intellect will be of this opinion.

This is (actually) a most witty poetical conceit by which Bar Kappara instills a noble moral quality, which is in accordance with the fact that just as it is forbidden to tell them, so it is forbidden to listen to obscene things; and he props it up through a reference to a (biblical) text, as is done in poetical compositions. Similarly, all the passages in the Midrashim enjoining "Do not read thus," but thus, have this (same) meaning. (Maimonides, *Guide of the Perplexed* 3.45) [MAIMONIDES 1963: 572–573]

9. Legal Exegesis

The "Great Exegesis," or Midrash Rabbah, *is an example of the homiletic or "edifying" interpretation of Scripture. Another equally common approach, indeed a necessary one since so much of the Torah is given over to legal matters, is to extract the full legal content and meaning from those prescriptions. In some cases the approach is quite straightforward, as here in Philo's meditation on the allegorical content of the fifth commandment of the Decalog.*

The fifth commandment, which has to do with honoring parents, contains in an allegory many necessary precepts, for old and young, for rulers and ruled, for benefactors and beneficiaries, for slaves and masters. "Parents" here stands for all those in a position of authority: elders, rulers, benefactors and masters, while "children" stands for all those in an inferior station: the young, subject, beneficiaries, slaves. Hence the commandment implies many other injunctions: the young should reverence the old, the old supervise the young; subjects should obey their rulers and rulers consider their subjects' interests; beneficiaries should aim at repaying favor for favor, benefactors not look for a return as if they were moneylenders; servants should exhibit an obedience which expresses love toward the master, masters show themselves gentle and meek and so redress the inequality of status between themselves and their slaves. (Philo, *On the Decalog* 165–166)

Philo is a well-defined and well-known figure from Alexandria at the beginning of the Christian era. But, as was the case with the homiletic exegesis, here too we often have to deal with collective works, where the legal aphorisms of various rabbis, sometimes credited and sometimes not, are arranged, more often by association than by logic, verse by verse through the books of the Torah. The following is an extract from just such a compilation made on Exodus and called Mekilta. *The verse commented upon is Exodus 20:2: "I am the Lord thy God."*

And it was for the following reason that the nations of the world were asked to accept the Torah, in order that they should have no excuse for saying: "Had we been asked, we would have accepted it." For behold, some of them were asked and they refused to accept it, for it is said: "And he said 'The Lord came from Sinai etc.' " (Deut. 33:2). He appeared to the children of Esau, the wicked, and said to them, "Will you accept the Torah?" They said to him, "What is written in it?" He said to them, "You shall not murder." They then said to him, "The very heritage that our father (Esau) left to us was: 'And by the sword you shall live' " (Gen. 27:40). He then appeared to the children of Amon and Moab. He said to them, "Will you accept the Torah?" They said to him, "What is written in it?" He said to them, "You shall not commit adultery." They, however, said to him they were all of them children of adulterers, as it is said, "Thus were both the daughters of Lot with child by their father" (Gen. 19:36). Then he appeared to the children of Ishmael. He said to them, "Will you accept the Torah?" They said to him, "What is written in it?" He said to them, "You shall not steal." They then said to him, "The very blessing that was pronounced upon our father (Ishmael) was: 'And he shall be as a wild ass of a man; his hand shall be upon everything' " (Gen. 40:15). . . . And when He came to the Israelites and "at His right hand was a fiery law for them" (Deut. 33:2), they all opened their mouths and said, "All that the Lord has spoken will we do and obey" (Exod. 24:7). And thus it says, "He stood and measured the earth; He beheld and drove asunder the nations" (Hab. 3:6).

This story of the "offering of the Torah," drawn anonymously from some nonscriptural source and presented without any further justification than that it had happened, is followed by a more formal, attributed argument, which is in turn reinforced by a parable.

Rabbi Simeon ben Eleazer says, "If the sons of Noah could not endure the seven commandments enjoined upon them, how much less could they have endured all the commandments of the Torah! To give a parable. A king had appointed two administrators. One was appointed over the supply of straw and the other over the treasure of silver and gold. The one appointed over the straw supply was held in suspicion. But he used to complain about the fact that they had not appointed him over the treasure of silver and gold. The people then said to him, "Scoundrel! If you were under suspicion in connection with the straw supply, how could they trust you with the treasure of silver and gold?" Behold, it is a matter of reasoning by the method of inference from minor to major. If the sons of Noah could not endure the seven commandments enjoined on them, how much less could they have endured all the commandments of the Torah?

Why was the Torah (given on Mount Sinai and) not given in the Land of Israel? In order that the nations of the world should not have the excuse for saying, "Because it was given in Israel's land, therefore we have not accepted it." Another reason: To avoid causing dissension among the tribes. Else one (tribe) might have said, "In my territory the Torah was given." And another might have said, "In my territory the Torah was given." Therefore the Torah was given in the desert, publicly and openly, in a place belonging to no one. To three things the Torah is likened: to the desert, to fire and to water. This is to tell you that, just as these three things are free to all who come into the world, so also are the words of the Torah free to all who come into the world. (*Mekilta* Bahodesh 5)

10. The Seven Rules of Interpretation

At the end of the parable adduced by Simeon ben Eliezer and cited above, there occurs the brief editorial comment: "it is a matter of reasoning by the method of inference from minor to major." The reference is somewhat offhand, as to something already well known, as indeed it was. Sometime early in the Christian era an attempt had been made to conceptualize what had doubtless long been going on among the rabbis in expounding the legal texts of Scripture. The result was the "Seven Rules of Hillel," a summary of the chief ways of either deriving or harmonizing legal prescriptions from Scripture. It is attributed to Rabbi Hillel the Elder, a somewhat older contemporary of Jesus. The following is how the rules stand in their technically shortened expression in the treatise called The Fathers According to Rabbi Nathan.

Seven rules of interpretation Hillel the Elder expounded before the Bene Bathyra, to wit: (1) a fortiori; (2) analogy; (3) deduction from one verse; (4) deduction from two verses; (5) (inference) from the general and the particular and from the particular and the general; (6) similarity elsewhere; (7) deduction from context. These are the seven rules which Hillel expounded (in his dispute) before the Bene Bathyra. (*The Fathers According to Rabbi Nathan* 37) [ABOTH RABBI NATHAN 1955: 154]

Which means to say: (1) What applies in the lesser case will certainly apply in the greater case; (2) where the same expression is used in two different verses, the same legal considerations will apply; (3) where the same expression is found in a number of verses, legal considerations applicable in one will be applicable in all; (4) a general principle can be deduced from a "family" of at least two texts and be applied more generally; (5) a general principal is limited by a particular instance or a particular instance is raised to the level of a general principle; (6) a problem in one text may be resolved by reference to another, even without the verbal similarities of (2) and (3) above; and (7) a meaning is established by its context.

11. The Conflict of Legal and Homiletic Exegesis

It is readily apparent from the remarks of Maimonides cited above that at least some Jews had problems with the traditional ways of understanding Scripture, particularly with the method known as "haggadic" or "homiletic" exegesis. Although the rationalizing Maimonides was willing to make a defense of sorts of this latter reading of Scripture, it was surely not with a great deal of enthusiasm. The case is only somewhat better made by someone who was far more traditional, the "Rabbi" who is the chief speaker in The King of the Khazars *and the mouthpiece for its author, Judah Halevi. The passage begins with the Rabbi offering an extremely flattering characterization of the Mishna, the written edition of comment upon the Jewish oral law prepared by Rabbi Judah the Prince ca.* 200 C.E.

They [its redactors] treated the Mishna with the same care as the Torah, arranging it in sections, chapters and paragraphs. Its traditions are so reliable that no suspicion of invention could be upheld. Besides this the Mishna contains a large amount of pure Hebrew which is not borrowed from the Bible. It is greatly distinguished by terseness of language, beauty of style, excellence of composition, and the comprehensive employment of homonyms, applied in a lucid way and leaving neither doubt nor obscurity. This is so striking that everyone who looks at it with genuine scrutiny must be aware that mortal man is incapable of composing such a work without divine assistance. Only he who is hostile to it, who does not know it, and never endeavored to read and study it, hearing some general and allegorical utterances of the Sages, deems them senseless and defective.

But the well-informed king of the Khazars, who gives his name to this dialogue of Halevi, raises certain criticisms with his interlocutor.

The Khazar King: Indeed, several details of their sayings [that is, of the Mishna authorities] appear to me inferior to their general principles. They employ verses of the Torah, for example, in a manner without regard to common sense. And one can only say that the application of such verses, now for legal deductions and another time for homiletic purposes, does not tally with their real meaning. Their homiletic stories and tales are often contrary to reason.

The Rabbi: Did you notice how strictly and minutely comments on the Mishna and the Baraitha are given (in the Talmud)? They [that is, the Rabbis represented there] speak with a thoroughness and a lucidity which do equal justice to both the words and the meaning of them.

The Khazar King: I am well aware of the perfection they brought to the art of dialectics, but the argument still stands.

The Rabbi: May we assume that he who proceeds with so much thoroughness should not know as much of the content of a verse as we do?

The Khazar King: This is most unlikely. Two things are possible. Either we are ignorant of their method of interpreting the Torah, or the interpreters of the Rabbinic law are not identical with the exegetes of the Holy Scripture. The latter point of view is absurd. But it is seldom that we see them [that is, the Rabbis] give a verse a rational and literal interpretation (in their exegetical works), but on the other hand, (in the Mishna and Talmud) we never find them interpreting a legal ruling except on the lines of strict logic.

The Rabbi: Let us rather assume two other possibilities. Either they employ secret methods of interpretation which we are unable to discern but which were handed down to them together with the (known) method of the "Thirteen Rules of Interpretation," or else they use biblical verses as a kind of fulcrum of interpretation in a method called "Asmakhta" and make them a sort of hallmark of tradition. An instance is provided by the following verse: "And the Lord God commanded man, saying, Of every tree of the garden you may freely eat" (Gen. 2:16). It forms the basis of the "seven Noachide laws" in the following manner:

"Commanded . . ." refers to jurisdiction.

"The Lord . . ." refers to the prohibition of blasphemy.

"God . . ." refers to the prohibition of idolatry.

"Man . . ." refers to the prohibition of murder.

"Saying . . ." refers to the prohibition of incest.

"Of every tree of the garden . . . ," the prohibition of rape.

"You may freely eat . . . ," a prohibition of flesh from a living animal."

There is a wide difference between these injunctions and the verse (with which they are associated). The people, however, accepted these seven laws as a tradition, connecting them with the verse as an aid to memory.

It is also possible that they applied both methods of interpreting verses, or others which are now lost to us, and considering the well-known wisdom, zeal, and number of the Sages which excludes a common plan, it is our duty to follow them. If we feel any doubt, it is not due to their words, but to our own intelligence. This also applies to Torah and its contents: we must ascribe the defective understanding of it to ourselves. As for the homiletic interpretations, many serve as a basis and introduction for explanations and legal injunctions. . . . Verses of this kind serve as a fulcrum and introduction, rendering a subject eloquent, apposite and showing that it is based on truth. To the same category belong (rabbis') tales of visions of spirits, a matter which is not strange in such pious men. Some of the visions they saw were the consequences of their lofty thoughts and pure minds, others were real apparitions, as was the case with those seen by the prophets. . . .

Other rabbinic sayings are parables employed to express mysterious teachings which are not to be made public. For they are of no use to the masses, and were only handed over to a few select persons for research and investigation, if a proper person—one in an era, or in several—could be found. Other sayings appear senseless on the face of them, but that they have their meaning becomes apparent after but a little reflection. (Judah Halevi, *The Khazar King* 3.67–72) [HALEVI 1905: 191–196]

12. The Scripture Interprets Itself

The description of the construction of the Temple in the Book of Kings (1 Kings 6–7) passes directly from the account of the building to another passage quite different in tone and tenor from the preceding narrative. It is a meditation of Solomon himself and is presented in the form of an interior dialogue on the propriety of God's possessing a house. Almost certainly this text reflects the sensibility of a later, post-Exilic age that had lost the Temple and for whom the transcendent God of Israel dwelled nowhere if not in the universal heaven. It is, in effect, Scripture reflecting upon itself.

(And Solomon continued:) "But will God really dwell on earth? Even the heavens to their uttermost reaches cannot contain You, how much less this House that I have built! Yet turn, O Lord my God, to the prayer and supplication of Your servant, and hear the cry of prayer which Your servant offers before You on this day. May Your eyes be open day and night toward this House, toward the place of which You have said 'My name shall abide there'; may You hear the prayers which Your servant will offer toward this place. And when you hear the supplications which Your servant and Your people Israel offer toward this place, give heed in Your heavenly abode—give heed and pardon."

. . . (Solomon continues:) "When they sin against You—for there is no man who does not sin—and You are angry with them and deliver them to the enemy, and their captors carry them off to an enemy land, near or far; and then they take it to heart in the land to which they have been carried off, and they repent and make supplication to You in the land of their captors, saying, 'We have sinned, we have acted perversely, we have acted wickedly,' and they turn back to You with all their heart and soul, in the land of the enemies who have carried them off, and pray to You in the direction of their land which You gave to their fathers, of the city which You have chosen, and of the House which I have built in Your name—oh, give heed in Your heavenly abode to their prayer and supplication and uphold their cause." (1 Kings 8:27–49)

That Temple destroyed by the Babylonians in 587 B.C.E. was once again rebuilt in the same century, but the notion that God could not be confined to one place persisted. It was encouraged by the prophets; but the transcendence of God, His remoteness in time and place and being from the world of men, received its strongest encouragement from Jewish contact with post-Alexander Hellenism, with its own strongly increasing sense of a spiritual God. That contact is most strongly reflected, as we have already seen, in the works of Philo, a practicing Jew from the deeply Hellenized milieu of Alexandria. This is Philo on the true Temple of God.

The highest and true Temple of God is, we must believe, the whole universe, having for its sanctuary the holiest part of all existence, namely heaven, for its votive offerings the stars, for its priests the angels, who are the servitors of His powers, unbodied souls, not mixtures of rational and irrational natures as ours are, but with the irrational eliminated, completely mind, pure intelligences, in the likeness of the Monad. The other Temple is made by hand; for it was fitting not to inhibit the impulses of men who pay their tribute to piety and wish by means of sacrifices to express their thanks for the good things that befell them or to ask for pardon and forgiveness for errors committed. But he (Moses) provided that there should not be temples built either in many places or many in the same place, judging that since God is one, there should also be only one Temple. (Philo, *The Special Laws* 1.66–67) [PHILO 1981: 279]

This technique of Scripture interpreting itself is a commonplace one. Deuteronomy is in a sense an interpretation of Exodus and Leviticus; Chronicles, of Kings; and the

Exilic prophets, of the whole biblical past. Jewish religious sensibilities changed during and after the Exile, as we have seen, and with them the understanding of the Bible. Here, for example, is how the noncanonical "Wisdom of Solomon" understood the biblical histories of Adam, Cain, Noah, and Abraham.

Wisdom it was who kept guard over the first father of the human race, when he alone had not yet been made; she saved him after his fall, and gave him the strength to master all things. It was because a wicked man forsook her in his anger that he murdered his brother in a fit of rage and so destroyed himself. Through his fault the earth was covered with a deluge, and again wisdom came to the rescue, and taught the one good man how to pilot his plain wooden hulk. It was she, who when heathen nations leagued in wickedness were thrown into confusion, picked out one good man and kept him blameless in the sight of God, giving him strength to resist his pity for his child. (Wisdom 10:1–5)

And of the Exodus from Egypt:

It was she [Divine Wisdom] who rescued a god-fearing people, a blameless race, from a nation of oppressors; she inspired a servant of the Lord, and with his signs and wonders he defied formidable kings. She rewarded the labors of god-fearing men, she guided them on a marvelous journey and became a covering for them by day and a blaze of stars by night. She brought them over the Red Sea and guided them through its deep waters; but their enemies she engulfed, and cast them up again out of the fathomless deep. . . . Wisdom, working through a holy prophet, brought them success in all they did. They made their way across an unpeopled desert and pitched camp in untrodden wastes; they resisted every enemy, and beat off hostile assaults. When they were thirsty they called upon you, and water to slake their thirst was given them out of the hard stone of a rocky cliff. (Wisdom 10:15–11:4)

Or the famous passage in Ecclesiasticus (The Wisdom of Jesus ben Sira) that begins:

Let us now sing the praises of famous men,
the heroes of our nation's history,
through whom the Lord established His renown,
and revealed His glory in each succeeding age.
Some held sway over kingdoms
and made themselves a name by their exploits.
Others were sage counselors,
who spoke out with prophetic power.
Some led the people by their counsels

or by their knowledge of the nation's law;
out of the fund of their wisdom they gave instruction.
Some were composers of music or writers of poetry.
Others were endowed with wealth and strength,
living peacefully in their homes.
All these won fame in their own generation
and were the pride of their times.
Some there were who have left a name behind them
to be commemorated in story.
There are others who are unremembered;
they are dead, and it is as though they never existed,
as though they had never been born
or left children to succeed them.
Not so our forefathers; they were men of loyalty,
whose good deeds have never been forgotten.
Their prosperity is handed on to their descendants,
and their inheritance to future generations.
Thanks to them their children are within the covenants,
the whole race of their descendants.
Their line will endure for all time,
and their fame will never be blotted out.
Nations will recount their wisdom,
and God's people will sing their praises.
(Ecclesiasticus 44:1–15)

There follows (44:16–50:24) a rapid survey of the heroes of Israel from Enoch to the contemporary High Priest, Simon son of Onias. Their chief deeds are mentioned in summary and their praises sung, all for the benefit of a reader who already knows their stories.

The Quran gives a similar review in Sura 21, appropriately called "The Prophets," and here too the listener must be presumed to have heard the stories before.

We gave Moses and Aaron the Criterion (of right and wrong), and a light and a reminder for those who take heed for themselves, who are fearful of their Lord inwardly and dread the Hour. And this is a blessed reminder that We have sent down. Will you deny it?

We had earlier given Abraham true direction, for We knew him well. When he said to his father and his people, "What are these idols to which you cling so passionately?" they replied: "We found our fathers worshiping them." He said: "You and your fathers are in clear error."

They said: "Are you speaking in earnest or only jesting?" He said: "In fact it was your Lord, the Lord of the heavens and the earth, who created them; and I bear witness to this. I swear by God I will do something to your idols when you have turned your back and gone." So he smashed them to pieces. . . .

They wished to entrap him, but We made them greater losers. So We delivered him and Lot, and brought them to the land We had blessed for all the people. And We bestowed on him Isaac, and Jacob as an additional gift, and made them righteous. And We made them leaders to guide the people by Our command; and We inspired them to perform good deeds and perform worship and pay the alms tithe; and they obeyed Us.

To Lot We gave wisdom and knowledge, and saved him from a people who acted villainously and were certainly wicked and disobedient. Thus We admitted him to Our grace. He is surely one of the righteous.

And Noah, when he called to Us before this. We heard him and saved him and those with him from great distress; and We helped him against the people who rejected Our signs as lies. They were a wicked people indeed, so We drowned them one and all.

And David and Solomon, when they pronounced judgment about the field which was eaten up at night by sheep belonging to certain people. We were witnesses to their judgment. We made Solomon understand the case, and bestowed on each wisdom and knowledge. We subdued the hills and the birds to sing his praise along with David. We taught him the art of making coats of mail to shield you from each other's violence. We made tempestuous winds obedient to protect Solomon which blew swiftly to sail at his bidding to the land We had blessed. We are cognizant of every thing. And many of the devils, some dived (for pearls) for him and did other work, and We kept watch over them.

And Job, when he called to his Lord: "I am afflicted with distress, and You are the most compassionate of all." So We heard his cry and relieved him of the misery he was in. We restored his family to him, and along with them gave him others similar to them as a grace from Us and a reminder for those who are obedient.

And mention Ishmael and Idris and Dhu al-Kifl. They were men of fortitude, and they were admitted to Our grace. Verily they were among the doers of good.

And mention the Man of the Fish [that is, Jonah], when he went away in anger and imagined We will not test him. Then he called out in the darkness: "There is no God but You. All glory to You! Surely I was a sinner." We heard his cry and saved him from anguish. That is how We deliver those who believe.

And Zachariah, when he called to his Lord: "Do not leave me alone and childless, for You are the best of givers." So We heard him and gave him John, and cured his wife (of barrenness). These were men who vied in good deeds with one another, and prayed to Us with love and awe, and were meek before Us.

And she who preserved her chastity [that is, Mary, the mother of Jesus], into whom We breathed a life from Us, and made her and her son a token for mankind.

Behold, this, your community is one community and I am your Lord, so worship Me. (Quran 21:48–92)

Finally, there is this instruction from Nehemiah, glossed by the Babylonian Talmud.

They read in the scroll of the Teaching [that is, Torah] of the Lord, translating [or, distinctly] it, giving the sense; so they understood the reading. (Nehemiah 8:8)

"They read in the scroll of the Teaching": this means the written text; "distinctly": this is the Targum; "giving the sense": this has reference to the division into verses; "so they understood the reading": this means the diacritical signs, and some rabbis say that this is the Masora. (BT.Nedarim 37b)

13. "There Are Seven Paths in the Knowledge of the Torah"

The entire range of Scriptural interpretation, from the literal to the most mystical, is laid out by Abraham Abulafia (d. 1292 C.E.), an intellectual follower of Maimonides but a convinced esotericist and student of Kabbala.

There are seven paths in the knowledge of the Torah.

The first path consists in understanding the simple meaning of the Torah text, for a biblical text may not be detached from its simple meaning. This is the way best suited for the multitude of people, men, women and children. Since some people are learned and some altogether unfamiliar with anything except the letters . . . it is appropriate that the uneducated except for the knowledge of the letters be taught some traditions so that they may possess religion in its conventional form. . . .

The second path includes those who study various commentaries, but what they have in common is that they revolve around the simple meaning and pursue it from all angles as in the expositions of the Mishna and the Talmud which expound the surface meaning of the Torah. This is illustrated by the interpretation of the phrase "circumcision of the heart." The Torah ordains that it be circumcised, as it is written (Deut. 10:16), "And you shall circumcise the foreskin of your heart." This commandment cannot be observed literally. It must, therefore, have an explanation. This is to be understood in the light of the verse (Deut. 30:6), "And the Lord your God will circumcise your heart," with the accompanying verse (30:2), "And you shall return to the Lord your God." The term "heart" must, therefore, be taken here as alluding to a return to God.

But this allegorical reading of the text, Abulafia carefully explains, should not replace the literal meaning, as the Christians did with precisely this set of texts.

But the circumcision of the child on the eighth day cannot be understood in the same way, for it cannot be applied to penitence. . . .

The third path embraces the study of the biblical text from the perspective of *midrash* and homiletic exegesis, and the derivatives from these types of study. This is illustrated by the inquiry as to why there is no mention that "God saw that it was good" (only) after the second day of creation, and the answer that it was because the organization of the waters was not completed on the second day. There are other such expositions. This path is called "searching/expounding" (*derash*) to indicate that here there is room to search and probe and also that this subject may be expounded in public. . . .

For Abulafia, as for most students of Scripture, whether Jews, Christians, or Muslims, not all types of explanations are suitable for all believers—"the multitude," as Abulafia calls them. Certain approaches to God's word should be reserved for "the select few."

The fourth path embraces parables and riddles. In this path begins the divergence between the select few and the multitude. The multitude will understand things according to the three paths mentioned earlier. Some will follow the simple text and some will seek explanations for them and some will understand them according to the "searching/expounding" method. But the select few will realize that these are parables and they will search after their meaning, and here they will encounter double-meaning terms, as that subject has been explained in (Maimonides') *Guide of the Perplexed.*

Abulafia lived in an age when the connection of both Christianity and Islam to Judaism was patent to most sophisticated Jews, particularly to those living in Spain. The connection does not, however, diminish Israel's claim to uniqueness, which

*Abulafia locates in its possession of the esoteric teaching known generally as Kab-
bala, or "the Tradition." It was not a notion shared by many of "the multitude,"
who would more likely subscribe to the view that it was the Unwritten Law that was
the characteristic mark of Israel, as will be explained in Chapter 3 below. Abulafia
continues.*

The fifth path includes only the secrets of the Torah. The four paths
mentioned earlier are shared by people of all nations, their masses in the
first three and their wise men in the fourth. The fifth path begins the
levels of secrets possessed by the Jews alone. In this we are differentiated
from the world's general populace as well as its wise men, but also from
the Jewish sages, the rabbis, whose views revolve around the circle of the
latter three of the paths mentioned above.

I cite as an illustration of this (fifth) path the secret meanings disclosed to us by the fact that the (Hebrew) letter "B" with which the
Torah begins is large, and the large letters of the alphabet appear in all
twenty-four books of the Bible . . . or by the inverted form of the base in
the two (forms of) the (Hebrew) letter "N" enclosing the chapter describing the movement of the Holy Ark (Num. 10:35). . . . There are
many similar mysteries handed down by tradition . . . and nothing of the
truths of those mysteries has been disclosed to any people except ours.

*Abulafia shows himself well aware that he is expressing an attitude with which some
Jews, "those who follow the way of the nations"—the Gentile-minded, as he calls
them—would take exception.*

One who follows the way of the nations may mock, thinking that
these letters were written that way without any reason and thus they
misrepresent the tradition, and they are guilty of grave error. But those
who have mastered the truths of these paths recognized their distinction
and these mysteries have been made clear to them, for they are holy. This
path is the beginning of the general wisdom of combining letters. This
path is appropriate only for those who fear God and meditate His name.

*On the sixth path Abulafia passes from simple esotericism to mysticism, or better, an
esotericism directed not toward understanding alone but toward a direct apprehension of God.*

The sixth path is very deep and who can attain it? . . . It is fitting for
those who withdraw from the world in their desire to draw close to God
to the point that they themselves shall experience His active presence in
themselves. These are the people who seek to resemble in their activity
the actions of the Active Intellect [that is, a higher intelligence, of an
angel, the Holy Spirit or of God Himself]. This path embraces the secret

of the "seventy languages" which, by the rules of *gematria* [that is, the system of substituting their numerical equivalents for the letters of a word], is equivalent to the "combination of letters" [that is, they both have a numerical equivalent of 1214]. This involves the return of the letters to their original essence in memory and in thought, analogous to the ten noncorporeal primordial numbers which involve a holy mystery, and all things holy have at least ten constituents.

These are, of course, the same ten primordials already seen in the esoterical account of Genesis called "The Book of Creation," a staple of all Kabbalistic cosmogonies. Abulafia proceeds to illustrate the holiness of ten.

Thus Moses ascended no higher than the ten heavenly realms, and the *Shekina*, the divine presence, descended no more than the ten heavens, and the world was created by ten divine commands, and the Torah was given by Ten Commandments, and there are many cases involving ten which illustrate this. Under the rubric of this path is also involved (the exegetical methods of) *gematria*, *notarikon* [that is, the reading of letters in a word as abbreviations of other words], and the interchange of letters, and then new interchanges to be repeated up to ten times. This halts only because of the weakness of human intelligence, for there is no limit to this process of permutation.

The seventh path is a special path and it includes all the others and it is the Holy of Holies and it is fitting for prophets only. This is the circle that revolves around all things. In attaining it one comprehends the message that descends from the Active Intellect to the power of speech.

Abulafia then gives a brief résumé of the theory of prophecy, which derives, as he says, from Maimonides and which, we may add, Maimonides took up from his Muslim predecessors, themselves the heirs to the theory of Aristotle and his Greek commentators on the existence of a higher and separated intellect. Once united, however temporarily, with this so-called Active Intellect, the human faculty is capable of higher planes of activity, among them prophecy. Abulafia concludes on a cautionary note.

It is improper to describe the manner by which this path, the Holy of Holies, proceeds, by writing about it in a book. It is impossible to disclose this to anyone, not even the main points, unless in his yearning he has learnt as a preliminary, in a direct communication from a teacher, the forty-two and the seventy-two names of God. I have therefore included here in my description, which is the essence of brevity, all that is needed to be said on the subject. (Abulafia, *The Seven Paths of the Torah*)
[BOKSER 1981: 102–104]

14. The Anthropomorphisms in Scripture

What may have first turned believers away from the literal to an "other" under-standing of Scripture was the fact that the plain sense made no sense, or that the plain sense was simply unacceptable. One large category of such "unacceptable" meanings of Scripture, if not for the original recipients of the revelation then assuredly for a later generation of believers with a more spiritually refined view of God, was anthropomorphism, the portrayal of God in grossly material or corporeal or even human terms. The Greeks had early on questioned themselves about their own poets' presentation of the gods in that manner, and they were uneasy with the answers well before the Jews discovered the problem in their own Scripture. The Bible is filled with such anthropomorphisms; and although the Septuagint translators had already softened a number of expressions referring to God's members and very humanlike actions and reactions in their Greek version of the Hebrew, the earliest systematic treatment of the problem is found in Philo.

After all the rest, as has been said, Moses tells us that man was created after the image of God and after His likeness (Gen. 1:26). This is quite well put, for nothing earthborn resembles God more than man. Let no one, however, represent that likeness through the characteristics of the body; for neither is God in human form, nor is the human body Godlike. The word "image" is here used with regard to the mind, the sovereign of the soul; for it is after the pattern of that unique and univer-sal Mind as an archetype that the mind in each individual was formed. It is in a way a god to him who carried it impressed in his mind; for the relationship the great Ruler bears to the world as a whole is precisely that which the human mind holds within man. It is invisible, while itself seeing all things, and though it apprehends the substances of others, its own substance is unknown. (Philo, *The Creation of the World* 69)
[PHILO 1981: 137]

"I will blot out from the face of the earth man whom I made, from man to beast, from reptiles to the winged fowl of heaven, because I was angered that I made him" (Gen. 6:7). Again, some on hearing these words assume that the Existent feels wrath and anger, whereas He is not suscep-tible to any emotion at all. For anxiety is peculiar to human weakness, but neither the irrational emotions nor the parts and limbs of the body are at all appropriate to God.

Nonetheless, such expressions are used by the Lawgiver (Moses) just so far as they furnish an elementary lesson, for the admonition of those who could not otherwise be brought to their senses. For among the laws that consist of commands and prohibitions, laws, that is, in the strict sense of the word, two ultimate summary statements are set forth concerning the First Cause, one that "God is not like a man" (Num. 23:19); the other that He is as a man. But though the former is guaranteed by absolutely secure criteria of truth, the latter is introduced for the instruction of the many. Wherefore it is also said of Him, "like a man He shall discipline His son" (Deut. 8:5). Thus it is for discipline and admonition, not because God's nature is such, that this is said of Him. Among men some are lovers of the soul, some of the body. The companions of the soul, who are able to associate with intelligible and incorporeal natures, do not compare the Existent to any form of created thing. They have excluded Him from every quality, for one of the things that pertains to His blessedness and supreme felicity is that His existence is apprehended as simple, without any distinguishing characteristic; and thus they have allowed a representation of Him only in respect of existence, not endowing Him with any form. But those who have concluded a treaty and a truce with the body are unable to doff the garment of flesh and see a nature uniquely simple and self-sufficient in itself, without admixture or composition. They therefore conceive of the Universal Cause precisely as they do of themselves, not taking into account that while a being that comes into existence through the union of several faculties needs several parts to serve the needs of each, God being uncreated and bringing all the others into being had no need of anything belonging to things generated.

For what are we to think? If He makes use of bodily organs, He has feet to to go forward. But wither will He go, since He fills everything? To whom will He go, when none is His equal. And to what purpose? For it cannot be out of concern for His health, as it is with us. Hands too He must have, both to receive and to give, yet He receives nothing from anyone, for aside from His lack of need, all possessions are His, and He gives by employing as His minister of His gifts the Logos [or Word] through whom He created the world. Nor does He have any needs of eyes. . . . What need is there to speak of the the organs of nourishment? If He has them, He takes nourishment, and after filling up, He rests; and after resting He has another need, and what follows on this I will not even discuss. These are the mythical inventions of the impious who theoretically represent the deity as of human form and as effectively having human emotions.

Why then does Moses speak of feet and hands, of entrances and exits, with regard to the Uncreated, or of His arming to ward off His enemies? For he represents Him as bearing a sword and using shafts and winds and devastating fire—roaring hurricane and thunderbolt the Prophets call them, using different expressions, and say they are the weapons of the Primal Cause. Why again does He speak of His jealousy, His wrath, His transports of anger and similar emotions, which he details and describes in human terms?

To those who make such inquiries he answers thus: "Sirs, who seeks to frame the best laws must have one goal, to profit all those who come in contact with them. Those who have been favored with good natural endowments and a training irreproachable in every respect, and thus find their later course through a highway broad and straight, have truth as their traveling companion; and being initiated by her into the authentic mysteries of the Existent, they do not assign to Him any of the traits of created being. . . . But those who are of a dull and obtuse nature, who have been ill served in their early training, incapable as they are of sharp vision, are in need of monitoring physicians who will devise the proper treatment of their present condition. . . . Let all such learn the lies that will benefit them, if they are incapable of becoming wise through truth. Thus the most esteemed physicians do not dare tell the truth to those dangerously ill in body, since they know that they will thereby become more disheartened and their sickness will not be cured, whereas through the consolation of the opposite approach they will bear their present condition more lightly and the illness will abate. . . .

Now since the lawgiver has become a supreme physician for the morbid states and maladies of the soul, he set himself one task and goal, to excise the diseases of the mind, roots and all, so that nothing remains to bear the germ of incurable disease. In this way he hoped to be able to extirpate them by representing the Primal Cause as employing threats, showing displeasure and implacable anger, and also using weaponry for his assaults on the unrighteous. For only thus can the fool be chided. Accordingly, it seems to me that with the two aforementioned principles, "God is as a man," and "God is not as a man," he has woven together two others closely akin and consistent with them, fear and love. For I know that all the exhortations to piety in the Law refer either to love or fear of the Existent. To those, then, who acknowledge no human part or emotion concerning the Existent, and honor Him for His own sake alone, love is the most appropriate, but fear is most suitable to the others. (Philo, *That God Is Immutable* 51–69)

[PHILO 1981: 139–141]

15. An Allegorical Interpretation of the Promised Land

Philo's exegesis of Scripture, an enterprise that constitutes the bulk of his published work, is profoundly allegorical, seeking out the "deeper" or "spiritual" meaning that lay beneath the literal understanding of the words. Here, for example is his interpretation of the text in Genesis that reads, "On that day He made a covenant with Abraham, saying, To your seed I will give this land from the river of Egypt to the great river Euphrates" (Gen. 15:18).

The literal meaning is that it describes the boundaries of the region between the two rivers, that of Egypt and the Euphrates, for anciently the land and the river were homonymously called "Egypt." . . . But as for the deeper meaning, it indicates felicity, which is the culmination of three goods: the spiritual, the bodily, and those which are external. This (teaching) was praised by some of the philosophers who came afterward, such as Aristotle and the Peripatetics, Moreover, this is said to have (also) been the legislation of Pythagoras. For Egypt is the symbol of the bodily and external goods, while the Euphrates is the symbol of the spiritual, for through them veritable and true joy comes into being, having as its source wisdom and every virtue. And the boundaries rightly take their beginning from Egypt and they end at the Euphrates. For in the end it is difficult to attain those things that pertain to the soul; but first one must proceed through the bodily and external goods, health and keenness of sense and beauty and strength, which are wont to flourish and grow and be attained in youth. And similarly those things that pertain to profitable business and piloting and agriculture and trade. All such things are proper to youth, especially those things that have been rightly mentioned. (Philo, *Questions and Their Solutions on Genesis* 3.16) [PHILO 1981: 228–229]

16. The Pleasures of Paradise

Jews and Christians after Philo struggled with this question of anthropomorphism in Scripture, but none quite so long or so hard as the Muslims. It is not that the Quran is more anthropomorphic than those other revelations; rather, the Muslim was, from his view of the origin and nature of the Book, somewhat less easy with allegorizing God's words for whatever reason. And yet it was done. The Quran, for example, has a great deal to say about the afterlife, and assurances to the pagans of Mecca of the physical reality of both Paradise and Gehenna are part of the earliest revelations in the Quran. Here we may note the words of Sura 76, which dates from the early Meccan period of Muhammad's career.

Was there not a time in the life of man when he was not even a thing? Verily We created man from a sperm yoked (to the ovum) to bring out his real substance, then gave him hearing and sight. We surely showed him the way that he may be either grateful or deny. We have prepared for unbelievers chains and collars and a blazing fire.

Surely the devotees will drink cups flavored with palm blossoms from a spring of which the votaries of God will drink and make it flow in abundance. Those who fulfill their vows and fear the Day whose evil shall be diffused far and wide, and feed the needy for the love of Him, and the orphans and the captives, saying: "We feed you for the sake of God, desiring neither recompense nor thanks. We fear the the dismal day calamitous from our Lord."

So God will protect them from the evil of that day, and grant them happiness and joy, and reward them for their perseverance with Paradise and silken robes where they will recline on couches feeling neither heat of the sun nor intense cold. The shade will bend over them, and low will hang clusters of grapes. Passed round will be silver flagons and goblets made of glass, and crystal clear bottles of silver, of which they will determine the measure themselves. There they will drink a cup flavored with ginger from a spring by the name of Salsabil. And boys of everlasting youth will go about attending them. Looking at them you would think they were pearls dispersed.

When you look around you will see delights and a great dominion. On their bodies will be garments of the finest silk and brocade, and they will be adorned with bracelets of silver; and their Lord will give them the purest draught to drink. (Quran 76:1–21)

The Muslim commentators approach these and other Quranic descriptions of Paradise in a number of different ways. Here, for example, is a cosmology, a laying out of the celestial geography of Paradise in the context of its creation; into its fabulous details have been integrated some of the themes of Islamic theodicy. Often in the three religions this cosmology comes in the form of a vision, but here the details have been supplied in a rather straightforward manner, presumably on the authority of the Prophet, and relayed through his contemporary Ibn Abbas.

Ibn Abbas, may God be pleased with him, said that then [that is, after the creation of the heavens] God created Paradise, which consists of eight gardens. . . . The eight gardens have gates of gold, jewel-encrusted and inscribed. On the first gate is written: "There is no god but the God and Muhammad is the Messenger of God." On the second is written: "The Gate of those who pray the five (liturgical daily) prayers, observing perfectly the ablutions and the prostrations." On the third is written: "The Gate of those who justify themselves by the purity of their souls." On the fourth gate is written: "The Gate of those who encourage the doing of what is approved and discourage the doing of what is disapproved." On the fifth gate is written: "The Gate of him who holds himself back from lusts." On the sixth gate is written: "The Gate of those who perform the Greater and Lesser Pilgrimage." On the seventh gate is written: "The Gate of those who go out on Holy War." On the eighth gate is written: "The Gate of those who desire," that is, those who avert their eyes (from unseemly things) and perform good works such as showing due affection to parents and being mindful of one's kin. By these gates will enter those whose works have been of the kind written on them. (Kisaʾi, *Stories of the Prophets*) [JEFFERY 1962: 172–173]

It is not always easy, or perhaps even useful, to connect a certain exegetical approach with a specific literary genre. The last passage cited above, which has a distinct homiletic flavor, occurs in a collection of narratives, the Stories of the Prophets. *The following sections of the homiletic* Arousing the Heedless *by Abuʾl-Layth al-Samarqandi (d. 983 C.E.) easily combine a Quranically based moral exhortation—the individual Prophetic tradition has already glossed the Quran, and Samarqandi braids a catena of these texts to make his own point—with an undisguised interest in the fabulous elements of Paradise.*

It is related of Ibn Abbas, may God be pleased with him, that he used to say: In Paradise are dark-eyed maidens of the type called "toys," who have been created out of four things, from musk, ambergris, camphor and saffron, stirred into a dough with water of life. All the celestial maidens love them dearly. Were one of them to spit into the ocean its waters would become sweet. On the throat of each of them is written: "He who would desire to have the like of me, let him do the works of obedience to my Lord." Mujahid said that the ground of Paradise is of silver, its dusk of musk, the trunks of its trees are of silver, their branches of pearl and emerald, their leaves and fruits hang low so that he who would eat standing can reach them, and likewise he who would eat sitting or even lying can reach them. Then he recited: "Its fruit clusters hang low" (Quran 86:14), that is, its fruits are near so that both he who is standing and he who is sitting can reach them. Abu Hurayra, may God be pleased with him, said: By Him who sent down the Book to Muhammad, upon whom be God's blessing and peace, the dwellers in Paradise increase in beauty and handsomeness as in this world the inhabitants increase in decrepitude. (Samarqandi, *Arousing the Heedless*) [JEFFERY 1962: 240–241]

There are problems with such anthropomorphisms. They are raised, not unnaturally, by a Christian polemicist.

The sage Abu'l-Fadl al-Haddadi has related to us . . . from Zayd ibn Arqam, who said: There came a man of the People of the Book to the Prophet, upon whom be God's blessing and peace, and said: "O Abu'l-Qasim [that is, Muhammad], do you pretend that the inhabitants of the Garden (really) eat and drink?" "Surely," he replied, "by Him in whose hand is my soul, every one of them will be given the capacity of a hundred men in eating and drinking and having intercourse." The man said: "But someone who eats or drinks has a need of relieving himself, whereas Paradise is too fine a place for there to be in it anything so malodorous." Muhammad replied: "A man's need to relieve himself will be satisfied by perspiring, which will be as sweet-smelling as musk." (Samarqandi, *Arousing the Heedless*) [JEFFERY 1962: 243]

In the following passage the physical delights of Paradise begin to recede into the background, and the exegetical focus turns to the vision of God in the afterlife.

In another tradition it is related that God, may He be exalted, will say to His angels, "Feed my saints," whereupon various kinds of food will be brought, in every bite of which they will find pleasure different from that they found in any other. When they have had their fill of eating, God, may He be exalted, will say, "Give My servants drink," whereupon drinks will be brought, in which they will find a pleasure different from that which they found in any other. When they have finished, God, may He be exalted, will say to them: "I am your Lord. I have made My promise to you come true. Now ask of Me and I will give it to you." They will reply: "O our Lord, we ask that You should be well pleased with us." This they will say two or three times, whereupon He will say: "I am well pleased with you, but today I have an increase (for you). I shall favor you with a token of regard greater than all that." Then the Veil will be removed and they will look upon Him for such a period as God wills. Then they will fall on their faces in a prostration, remaining prostrated for such a time as God pleases, whereat He will say to them: "Raise your heads. This is no place for worshiping." At that they will quite forget all the other enjoyment they have been having, for to see their Lord is the most precious of all their joys. (Samarqandi, *Arousing the Heedless*) [JEFFERY 1962: 242–243]

Samarqandi knows very well that this vision presents a problem, and so he intervenes to offer a correction and his own interpretation.

The lawyer [that is, the author, Abu'l-Layth al-Samarqandi], may God have mercy on him, says: When he [presumably Muhammad, the source of the anonymously transmitted tradition] speaks about the Veil being lifted, he means the veil which is over them [that is, over the glorified souls] which prevents them from seeing Him. As for his statement that they will look upon Him, some say (it means) that they will look on a token such as they had not previously seen. Most of the learned, however, say that it is to be taken according to its literal meaning, and that they will actually see Him, though we know not how, save that it will not be in an anthropomorphic manner, just as here on earth they knew Him, but not in an anthropomorphic manner. (Samarqandi, *Arousing the Heedless*) [JEFFERY 1962: 242–243]

17. Exegesis by the Number

We have already seen that the sixth of Abulafia's "seven paths of knowledge of the Torah" included a technique known as gematria. *The ancients gave each letter of the alphabet a numerical value, and these numerical equivalents of letters provided, of course, an attractive and universally accepted way of penetrating into a sacred text, as both Philo and the Christian Fathers understood and practiced long before the medieval Jewish Kabbalists. The first example is from a Christian author probably but recently converted from Judaism.*

You will say, "But surely this people [the Jews] received circumcision as the seal of their Covenant?" Why, every Syrian and every Arab is physically circumcised, and so are the idol priesthoods; but does that make them members of the Jews' covenant? Even the very Egyptians practice circumcision.

Dear children of love, here is a full explanation of it all. Circumcision was given to us in the first place by Abraham; but he, when he circumcised himself, did so in spiritual prevision of Jesus. He got his instruction from three letters of the alphabet, for the Scripture tells us that "out of his own household Abraham circumcised eighteen and three hundred" (Gen. 14:14, 17:23). How does his spiritual intuition come into this? Well, notice how it specifies the eighteen first, and then, separated from this, the three hundred. Now in writing eighteen, the ten is expressed by the letter "I" and the eight by "E"; and there, you see, you have IE(sus). And then, since grace was to come by a Cross, of which "T" is the shape, it adds "and three hundred." Thus it indicates "Jesus" with two of the letters and "the Cross" with the third. All this is perfectly well known to

Him who has graciously planted the seeds of His teaching in our hearts; and a better interpretation than this I have never given to anybody. I am persuaded, though, that you have every right to know it. (*Letter of Barnabas* [ca. 130 C.E.] 9) [STANIFORTH 1968: 205–206]

Other, better educated Christians and Jews could do much better than this. Augustine, for example, explicates the number six.

The ratio of the single to the double arises, no doubt, from the ternary number, since one added to two makes three. But the whole which these make reaches to the senary number, for one and two and three make six. And this number on that account is called perfect because it is completed in its own parts, for it has these three: one-sixth, one-third and one-half; nor is there any other part found in it. . . . The sixth part of it, then, is one; the third part, two, and the half, three. But one and two and three complete the same six.

Holy Scripture commends to us the perfection of this number, especially in this, that God finished His works in six days, and on the sixth day man was made in the image of God. And the Son of God came and was made the Son of man, that he might re-create us after the image of God, in the sixth age of the human race. For that is now the present age, whether a thousand years apiece was assigned to each age, or whether we trace our memorable and remarkable epochs or turning points of time in the divine Scriptures, so that the first age is to be found from Adam until Noah, and the second thence onwards to Abraham, and then next, according to the division of Matthew the Evangelist, from Abraham to David, from David to the carrying away to Babylon, and from then to the labor of the Virgin, which three ages joined to those other two make five. Accordingly, the birth of the Lord began the sixth, which is now going onwards until the hidden end of time.

We recognize also in this senary number a kind of figure of time, in that threefold mode of division by which we compute one portion before the Law, another under the Law, and a third under grace. In which last time we have received the sacrament of renewal, that we may be renewed also in the end of time, in every part, by the resurrection of the flesh, and so may be made whole of our entire infirmity, not only of soul but also of body. And thence that woman who was made whole and upright by the Lord after she had been bowed by infirmity through the binding of Satan (Luke 13:10–17) is understood to be a type of the Church. . . . And this woman had her infirmity for eighteen years, which is thrice six. . . . Nearly too in the same place in the Gospel (Luke 13:6–9) is that fig tree which was convicted also by the third year of its miserable barrenness. But intercession was made for it, that it might be left alone for that year, that if it bore fruit, well; if otherwise, it should be cut down. For both three years belong to the same threefold division, and the months of three years make a square of six, which is six times six. . . .

And not without reason is the number six understood to be put for a year in the building up of the body of the Lord, as a figure of which he said he would raise up in three days the Temple destroyed by the Jews. For they said, "Forty and six years was this Temple in building" (John 2:20). And six times forty-six makes two hundred and seventy-six. And this number of days completes nine months and six days, which are reckoned, as it were, ten months for the pregnancy of women; not because all come to term on the sixth day after the ninth month, but because the perfection itself of the body of the Lord is found to have been brought in so many days to the birth, as the authority of the Church maintains upon the tradition of the elders. For he is believed to have been conceived on the twenty-fifth of March, upon which day he also suffered; so the womb of the Virgin, in which he was conceived, where no one of mortals was begotten, corresponds to the new grave in which he was buried, "wherein was never man laid" (John 19:41–42), neither before nor since. But he was born, according to tradition, on December twenty-fifth. If, then, you reckon from that day to this you find two hundred and seventy-six days, which is forty-six times six. (Augustine, *City of God* 4.4–5) [AUGUSTINE 1948: 2:735–736]

Or Philo himself on seven:

So august is the dignity inherent by nature in the number seven that it has a unique relation distinguishing it from all other numbers with the first ten: for of these some beget without being begotten; some are begotten but do not beget; some do both of these, both beget and are begotten: seven alone is not found in any of those categories. We must establish this assertion by giving proof of it. Well then, one begets all the subsequent numbers, while it is begotten by none whatever; eight is begotten twice four, but begets no number within the decade; four again holds the place of both, of parent and offspring, for it begets eight by being doubled and is begotten by twice two.

It is the nature of seven alone, as I have said, neither to beget nor to be begotten. For this reason other philosophers liken this number to the motherless virgin Nike, who is said to have appeared out of the head of Zeus, while the Pythagoreans liken it to the principle of all things, for that which neither begets nor is begotten remains changeless; for creation takes place in change, since there is change both in that which begets and in that which is begotten, in the one that it may beget and in the other that it may be begotten. There is only one thing that neither causes change nor experiences it, the original Ruler and Sovereign. Of Him seven may be fitly said to be the symbol. Evidence of what I say is supplied by (the Pythagorean philosopher) Philolaus in these words: "There is," he says, "a supreme Ruler of all things, God, ever One, abiding, without change, Himself (alone) like to Himself, different from all others." (Philo, *On the Creation of the World* 99)

18. The Literal and the Allegorical in the Bible

There were, for all the willingness to indulge in allegorical exegesis in order to avoid the pitfalls of anthropomorphism, grave dangers in pushing that type of interpretation too far, particularly as regards the external observance of the Law, as Philo himself is quick to insist.

There are some who, taking the laws in their literal sense as symbols of intelligible realities, are overprecise in their investigation of the symbol, while frivolously neglecting the letter. Such people, I, for my part, should blame for their cool indifference, for they ought to have cultivated both a more precise investigation of things invisible and an unexceptional stewardship of things visible. As it is, as if living alone by themselves in a wilderness, or as if they had become disembodied souls, knowing neither city nor village nor household nor any company of humans at all, transcending what is approved by the many, they track the absolute truth in its naked self. And yet these men are taught by Sacred Scripture to be concerned with public opinion, and to abolish no part of the customs ordained by inspired men, greater than those of our own day.

For all that the Seventh Day teaches us the power of the Unoriginate and the non-action of created beings, let us by no means annul the laws laid down for its observance, kindling the fire, tilling the earth, carrying burdens, instituting indictments, sitting in judgment, demanding the return of deposits, recovering loans, or doing all else that is permitted on days which are not holy. And though it is true that the holy day is a symbol of spiritual joy and thankfulness to God, let us not bid adieu to the annual seasonal assemblies. And though it is true that circumcision indicates the cutting out of pleasure and all passions and the removal of godless conceit under which the mind supposed itself capable of engendering through its own powers, let us not abrogate the law laid down for circumcising. For we shall be neglecting the Temple service and a thousand other things if we are to pay regard only to that which is revealed by the inner meaning. We ought rather to look on the external observance as resembling the body and the inner meaning as resembling the soul. Just as we then provide for the body, inasmuch as it is the abode of the soul, so we must attend to the letter of the laws. For if we keep these, we shall obtain an understanding of those things of which they are symbols, and in addition we shall escape the censure and the accusations of the multitude. (Philo, *The Migration of Abraham* 89–93) [PHILO 1981: 81–82]

19. Giving a Little Grace to the Scholars

Almost all Jews would assent to the sentiments just cited from Philo, but the majority would likewise agree that, no matter how great the danger, it was impossible or inadvisable to adhere to a literal interpretation in all instances. One who warned of the dangers and at the same time permitted himself and others considerable allegorical space in the body of Scripture was Nachmanides (d. ca. 1270 C.E.). He was by no means a literalist; indeed, he was the first major Jewish commentator on the Torah to regard Genesis through the prism of the Kabbala, that storehouse of Jewish, Hellenic, and Islamic esotericism that was gaining increased attention in Jewish circles. The reader of Nachmanides' commentary could not say, however, that he had not been warned.

Now our Sages have already said (B.Rosh Hashanah 21b): "Fifty gates of understanding were created in the world and all were transmitted to Moses with one exception, as it was said, 'You have made him a little lower than the angels' (Ps. 8:6)." . . . Everything that was transmitted to Moses our teacher through the forty-nine gates of understanding was written in the Torah explicitly or by implication in words, in the numerical value of the letters or in the form of the letters, that is, whether written normally or with some change of form such as bent or crooked letters and other deviations, or in the tips of the letters and their crownlets, as the Sages have said (B.Menachoth 29b): "When Moses ascended to heaven he found the Holy One, blessed be He, attaching crownlets to certain letters of the Torah. He [Moses] said to Him: 'What are these for?' The Lord said to him: 'One man is destined to interpret mountains of Law on their basis.' 'Whence do you know this?' He answered him: 'This is a law given to Moses on Mount Sinai.' " For these hints cannot be understood except from mouth to mouth from Moses, who received it on Sinai.

Based on this tradition, the Sages have said in the Great Commentary on the Song of Songs concerning King Hezekiah (when he was visited by a delegation from the king of Babylon): "He showed them the Book of Crownlets." This book is known and is available to everyone. In it is explained how many crowned *alephs* there are in the Torah, how many *beths*, and the frequency of the rest of the letters and the number of crownlets on each one. The praise which the Sages bestowed on this book and the disclosure of Heze-kiah's secret to the delegation were not for the crownlets themselves but rather for a knowledge of their essence and their meanings, which consist of many exceedingly profound secrets.

There in the Great Commentary on the Song of Songs (1:28), the Sages have also said: "It is written: 'And He declared to you His covenant,' which means, He declared to you the Book of Genesis, which relates the beginning of His creation, 'which He commanded you to perform, even the ten words' (Deut. 4:13), meaning the ten commandments, ten for Scripture and ten for Talmud. For from what source did Elihu the son of Barachel the Buzite come and reveal to Israel the secrets of the behemoth (Job 40:15) and the leviathan (Job 40:25)? And from what source did Ezekiel come and reveal to them the mysteries of the Divine Chariot (Ezek. 1)? It is this which Scripture says, 'The king has brought me into his chambers,' " meaning that everything can be learned from the Torah.

Solomon is, of course, the prime example of the human who drank deeply of secret knowledge and lore. After quoting a number of examples of Solomon's Torah-derived but somewhat more than human wisdom, Nachmanides returns to the main question of his commentary.

And now know and see what I shall answer to those who question me concerning my writing a commentary on the Torah. I shall conduct myself in accordance with the custom of the early scholars to bring peace to the mind of the students, tired of the exile and afflictions, who read in the Seder [that is, Torah selections assigned for reading on Sabbaths and festivals] on the Sabbaths and the festivals, and attract them with the plain meanings of Scripture, and with some things that are pleasant to the listeners and give "grace."

The Hebrew word for "grace" is actually an abbreviation for "hidden wisdom," that is, of the Kabbala.

. . . [T]o the scholars . . .

Now behold I bring into a faithful covenant and give proper counsel to all who look into this book not to reason or to entertain any thought concerning any of the mystic hints which I write regarding the hidden matters of the Torah, for I do hereby firmly make known to him that my words will not be comprehended or known at all by any reasoning or contemplation, except from the mouth of a wise Kabbalist speaking into the ear of an understanding recipient. Reasoning about them is foolish; any unrelated thought brings much damage and withholds the benefit. "Let him not trust in vanity, deceiving himself" (Job 15:31), for these reasonings will bring him nothing but evil, as if they spoke falsely against the Lord, which cannot be forgotten. . . . Rather let such see in our commentaries novel interpretations of the plain meanings of Scripture and Midrashim, and let them take moral instruction from the mouths of our holy Rabbis: "Into that which is beyond you, do not seek; into that which is more powerful than you, do not inquire; about that which is concealed from you, do not desire to know; about that which is hidden from you, do not ask. Contemplate that which is permitted to you, and engage not yourself in hidden things." (Nachmanides, *Commentary on Genesis*)

[NACHMANIDES 1971: 10–16]

20. Dull Masses and Minds Tied Down to Sensibles

Almost from its appearance in the Jewish tradition, the practice of allegorical exegesis was accompanied by warnings that it was not appropriate for every believer, that it should be reserved for the mature and the learned. This advice appears sagacious enough, but it led, not too far down the path, to a profound distinction between "pure truth"—the domain of the philosopher, on the one hand—and the crude and materialistic expressions by which the prophet, who certainly knew far better, was constrained to address the masses in Scripture. What follows is one expression of such a view, in this case from the Muslim philosopher Ibn Sina, or, as the West called him, Avicenna (d. 1038 C.E.).

As for religious law, one general principle is to be admitted, to wit, that religions and religious laws promulgated through a prophet aim at addressing the masses as a whole. Now it is obvious that the deeper truths concerning the real Unity (of God), to wit, that there is one Creator, who is exalted above quantity, quality, place, time, position and change, which lead to the belief that God is one without anyone to share His species, nor is He made of parts, quantitative or conceptual, that neither is He transcendent nor immanent, nor can He be pointed to as being anywhere—it is obvious that these deeper truths cannot be communicated to the multitude. For if this had been communicated in its true form to the bedouin Arabs or the crude Hebrews, they would have refused straightway to believe and would have unanimously proclaimed that the belief to which they had been invited was a belief in an absolute nonentity.

This is why the whole account of the Unity (of God) in religion is (expressed) in anthropomorphisms. The Quran does not contain even a hint to (the deeper truth about) this important problem, nor a detailed account concerning even the obvious matters needed about the doctrine of Unity, for a part of the account is apparently anthropomorphic, while the other part contains absolute transcendence [that is, the total unlikeness of God to His creation], but in general terms, without specification or detail. The anthropomorphic phrases are innumerable, but they [that is, the orthodox interpreters of the Quran] do not accept them as such. If this is the position concerning the Unity (of God), what of the less important matters of belief?

Some people may say: "The Arabic language allows wide use and metaphor; anthropomorphisms like the hand and the face (of God), His coming down in the canopies of clouds, His coming, going, laughter, shame, anger are all correct (linguistically); only the way of their use and their context show whether they have been employed metaphysically or literally." . . . Let us grant that all these (expressions) are metaphors. Where, then, we ask, are the texts which give a clear indication of pure Unity to which doubtlessly the essence of this righteous faith—whose greatness is acclaimed by the wise men of the entire world—invites? . . .

Upon my life, if God the Exalted did charge a prophet that he should communicate the reality about these (theological) matters to the masses with dull natures and with minds tied down to pure sensibles, and then constrained him to pursue relentlessly and successfully the task of bringing faith and salvation to those same masses, and then, to crown all, He charged him to undertake the purifying training of all the souls so they may be able to understand these truths, then He has certainly laid upon him a duty incapable of fulfillment by any man—unless the ordinary man receives a special gift from God, a supernal power or a divine inspiration, in which case the instrumentality of the prophet will be superfluous.

But let us even grant that the Arabian revelation is metaphor and allegory according to the usage of the Arabic language. What will they say about the Hebrew revelation—a monument of utter anthropomorphism from beginning to end? One cannot say that that book is tampered with through and through, for how can this be with a book disseminated through innumerable people living in distant lands, with so different ambitions—like Jews and Christians with all their mutual antagonisms?

All this shows that religions are intended to address the masses in terms intelligible to them, seeking to bring home to them what transcends their intelligence by means of metaphor and symbol. Otherwise, religions would be of no use whatever. (Ibn Sina, *Treatise on Sacrifice*) [RAHMAN 1958: 42–44]

21. Abraham and Sarah as Matter and Form

Philo may have understood how to separate, and at the same time to reverence, both the literal and the allegorical sense of Scripture. But the attractions of the latter at the expense of the plain meaning of God's word continued to be felt in the Jewish community, and an increased familiarity with secular learning, most of it Greek in origin and much of it transmitted to the Jews through Muslim scholars like Ibn Sina, did nothing to lessen the danger. In 1305 C.E. Solomon ben Adret, a leading figure in the struggle between philosophy and the traditional learning, issued the following warning from Barcelona to his fellow Jews in Provence.

It is now some time since our attention was drawn by people from the land of Provence, the chosen remnant, who were jealous for the faith of Moses and the Jews, to the fact that there are men who falsify the Law, and that he is regarded as wise who sits down to demolish the walls and who destroys the words of the Law. They hew out for themselves cisterns, broken cisterns, and they impute to the words of the Law and the words of the sages meanings which are not right. Concerning the two Laws [that is, the written and the oral Torah] they utter in the synagogues and the houses of study words by which none can live. Regardless of the glory of all Israel, they break down all the fences of the Law, and against our holy fathers they put forth their tongue, a thing which even the worshipers of idols have not done. For they say that Abraham and Sarah represent matter and form, and that the twelve tribes of Israel are the twelve constellations. . . . The blasphemers of God further say that the holy vessels which were sanctified, the Urim and the Thummim [cf. Exod. 28:15–21], are the instrument known as the astrolabe, which men make for themselves. . . .

A man who does such things reduces the entire Bible to useless allegories; indeed they trifle with and pervert all the commandments in order to make the yoke of their burden lighter to themselves. Their reports terrify us, and all who arrive here tell us new things. "Truth has stumbled in the street" (Isa. 59:14), for some of them say that all that was written from the section of Genesis as far as the giving of the Law is nothing more than allegory. . . . They show that they have no faith in the plain meaning of the commandments.

The chief reason for all this is that they are infatuated with alien sciences, "of Sidon and Moab" (Judg. 10:9), and pay homage to the Greek books. . . . The children that are consecrated to heaven from their mothers' womb are drawn away from the breasts and are taught the books and the language of the Chaldeans, instead of rising early to study the Jewish faith in the houses of their teachers. Now a boy born upon the knees of natural science, who sees Aristotle's sevenfold proofs concerning it, really believes in it, and denies the Chief Cause. If we refute him, he becomes all the more impious. They read the Law with their lips, but their heart is not sound inwardly, and they pervert it in seven ways. . . . They are ashamed when they speak and they lecture; they speak with their mouths but make hints with the finger that it is impossible to change nature, and they thereby declare to all that they do not believe in the creation of the universe, or in any of the miracles recorded in the Torah. (Solomon ben Adret, *Letter to Provence*)

22. The Past Foreshadows the Future

Tell me now, you who are so anxious to be under law, will you not listen to what the Law says? It is written there that Abraham had two sons, one by his slave and the other by his free-born wife. The slave woman's son was born in the course of nature, the free woman's through God's promise. This is an allegory. The two women stand for two covenants. The one bearing children into slavery is the covenant that comes from Mount Sinai: that is Hagar. Sinai is a mountain in Arabia and it represents the Jerusalem of today, for she and her children are in slavery. But the heavenly Jerusalem is the free woman; she is our mother. For Scripture says: "Rejoice, O barren woman who never bore child; break into a shout of joy, you who never knew a mother's pangs; for the deserted wife shall have more children than she who lives with the husband." (Paul, *To the Galatians* 4:21–27)

This is a capital text for the entire Christian understanding of Scripture, that is, the Jewish Bible, which in the earliest Christian times constituted the only Holy Book. With great ease and confidence Paul asserts, "The two women stand for two covenants" and so teaches all succeeding generations of Christians how they are to read and understand their Jewish past—not simply as a repository of prophecy concerning the Messiah, which Jesus fulfilled in his own life, as the Gospels themselves, and

in particular Matthew, already insisted, but as a testimony to a deeper reality. The
prophecies of the Bible not only predict the New Dispensation of Jesus, but the very
events of biblical history reflect those that are to come: they foreshadow them. A
classic statement of the theory can be found in Augustine (d. 430 C.E.), cast in the
same categories of an earthly and a heavenly Jerusalem invoked by Paul.

Wherefore just as that divine oracle to Abraham, Isaac and Jacob, and all the other prophetic signs and sayings which are given in the earlier sacred writings, so also prophecies from this time of the kings pertain partly to the nation of Abraham's flesh, and partly to that seed of his in which all nations are blessed as fellow heirs of Christ by the New Testament, to the possessing of eternal life and the kingdom of the heavens. Therefore they pertain partly to the bond maid who births to bondage, that is, the earthly Jerusalem, which is in bondage with her children; but partly to the free city of God, that is, the true Jerusalem eternal in the heavens, whose children are all those who live according to God in the earth. But there are (also) some things among them which are understood to pertain to both, to the bond maid properly and to the free woman figuratively. . . .

And this kind of prophecy, as it were compacted and commingled of both the others in the ancient canonical books, containing historical narratives, is of very great significance and greatly exercises the wits of those who search Holy Scripture. For example, what we read of historically as predicted and fulfilled in the seed of Abraham according to the flesh [that is, the Jews], we must also inquire the allegorical meaning of, as it is to be fulfilled in the seed of Abraham according to faith [that is, in the Church]. And so much is this the case that some have thought that there is nothing in these books either foretold and effected, or effected though not foretold, that does not insinuate something else which is to be referred by figurative signification to the city of God on high, and to her children who are pilgrims in this life.

But if this be so, then the utterances of the prophets, or rather the whole of those Scriptures that are reckoned under the title of the Old Testament, will be not of three but of two different kinds. For there will be nothing there which pertains to the terrestrial Jerusalem only, if whatever is there said and fulfilled, or concerns her, signifies something which also refers by allegorical prefiguration to the celestial Jerusalem. . . .

But just as I think that they err greatly who are of the opinion that none of the records of affairs in that kind of writing means anything more than that they happened, so I think those very daring who contend that

526

the whole gist of their contents lies in their allegorical significations. Therefore I have maintained that they are threefold, not twofold. Yet, in holding this opinion, I do not blame those who may be able to draw out of everything there a spiritual meaning, only saving, first of all, the historical truth. (Augustine, *City of God* 12.3) [AUGUSTINE 1948: 2:368–369]

We can observe Augustine the exegete at work and the various types of exegesis in the following passage on the description of Paradise in chapters 2 and 3 of the Book of Genesis. His first concern, though not his chief one, is to save the historical truth.

Some allegorize all that concerns Paradise itself, where the first men, the parents of the human race are, according to the truth of Holy Scripture, recorded to have been. And they understand all its trees and fruit-bearing plants as virtues and habits of life, as if they had no existence in the external world but were only spoken of or related for the sake of spiritual meaning. As if there were no terrestrial Paradise! As if there never existed those two women, Sarah and Hagar, nor the two sons who were born to Abraham, the one of the bond woman, the other of the free, because the Apostle (Paul) says that in them the two covenants were prefigured. . . . No one, then, denies that Paradise may signify the life of the blessed; its four rivers, the four virtues; its trees, all useful knowledge; its fruits, the customs of the godly; its tree of life, wisdom itself, the mother of all good; and the tree of the knowledge of good and evil, the experience of a broken commandment. (Augustine, *City of God* 13.21) [AUGUSTINE 1948: 2:229]

23. Moralizing Exegesis

Augustine's examples of a moralizing exegesis of this passage of Genesis are neither randomly chosen nor invented by him. They come from Philo, the Hellenized Jew who lived and wrote in Alexandria in the first years of the Christian era. Almost all of his works are in the form of an extended philosophical commentary on the Torah, and the one called On the Allegory of the Laws *deals with the same second and third chapters of Genesis.*

And God caused to come forth from the earth every tree, providing delight to the sight and food for nourishment, and in the middle of the garden the tree of life and the tree of the knowledge of good and evil (Gen. 2:9).

Moses then points out what trees of virtue God plants in the soul. These are the various individual virtues, and the acts that correspond to them, total moral victory, and what philosophers call the common duties. These are the plants of the garden. He characterizes these plants to show that what is good is also most delightful amd pleasurable. While some of the arts and sciences are theoretical but not practical, such as geometry and astronomy, and others are practical but not theoretical, like the arts of the carpenter and the coppersmith and all the arts that are called mechanical, virtue is both theoretical and practical; for it obviously involves theory, since philosophy, the road that leads to it, includes theory through its three parts of logic, ethics and physics; but it also involves conduct, for virtue is the art of the whole of life, and life includes all kinds of conduct.

And while virtue embraces both theory and practice, it is also of surpassing excellence in other respects; for indeed the theory of virtue is perfect in beauty, and the practice and exercise of it is a prize to be striven after. Thus Moses says that it is both "beautiful to look upon"—an expression indicating its theoretical side—and "good to eat," words which point to its excellence in use and practice.

Now the tree of life is virtue in the broadest sense, which some call simply "goodness." From it the particular virtues derive their existence. This is also why it is located in the middle of the garden, where it occupies the central, all-encompassing position, so that it might be attended in royal fashion by bodyguards on either side. But some say that it is the heart that is called the tree of life, since it is both the cause of life and it has been given the central place in the body, as it naturally would, being, in their view, the ruling principle. But these people should remember that they are holding an opinion more appropriate to the physician than to the philosopher, while we, as we have said, maintain that virtue in its most generic aspect is called the tree of life. . . .

A river goes forth from Eden to water the garden, thence it is separated into four sources: the name of the first is Pheison; this is what encircles all the land of Havila, where the gold is, and the gold of that land is good; and where there is the ruby and the emerald. And the name of the second is Geon; this encompasses all the land of Ethiopia. And the third river is Tigris; this is the one that runs in front of Assyria. And the fourth river is Euphrates (Gen. 2:10–14).

By these rivers Moses intends to indicate the particular virtues. These are four in number: prudence, self-mastery, courage and justice. The large source, of which the other four are derivatives, is virtue in its general sense, which we have already called goodness. The four derivative rivers are the same number of virtues. The genus virtue first arises from

Eden, that is, the wisdom of God, which is full of joy and brightness and exultation, glorying and priding itself only in God its Father; but the specific virtues, which are four in number, are derived from the generic virtue, which like a river waters the perfect achievements of each of them with an abundant flow of noble actions. (Philo, *On the Allegory of the Laws* 1.56–64)

24. Augustine on the Christian Interpretation of Scripture

Augustine, then, is aware of this rather straightforward Jewish reproduction of Stoic ethical theory. Although he accepts its validity, he has his own, more specifically Christian, and so "more profitable" way of reading the same passage in Genesis.

These things can also and more profitably be understood of the Church, so that they become prophetic foreshadowings of things to come. Thus Paradise is the Church, as it is called in the Song of Songs (Song of Sol. 4:13); the four rivers of Paradise are the four Gospels; the fruit trees, the saints and the fruit of their works; the tree of life is the Holy of Holies, Christ; the tree of the knowledge of good and evil, the will's free choice. For if man despises the will of God, he can only destroy himself; and so he learns the difference between consecrating himself to the common good and reveling in his own. . . . These and other similar allegorical interpretations may be suitably put upon Paradise without giving offense to anyone, while yet we believe the strict truths of history, confirmed by its circumstantial narrative of facts. (Augustine, *City of God* 13.21) [AUGUSTINE 1948: 2:229–230]

25. Origen on the Triple Sense of Scripture

Newly converted Gentile Christians schooled in the methods of Greek literary exegesis became increasingly adept at extracting a variety of understandings from Scripture. One of the first to do so was Origen (d. ca. 254 C.E.), a graduate of the university of Alexandria, who was a pioneer Christian theologian and the foremost Christian biblical scholar of his time.

The cause of false opinions and of impious or ignorant assertions about God appears to be nothing else than that the Scriptures are not understood according to their spiritual meaning but are interpreted according to the mere letter. And therefore to those who believe that the Sacred Books are not the composition of men, but were composed by the inspiration of the Holy Spirit, according to the will of the Father of all things through Jesus Christ, and that they have come down to us, we must point out the modes of interpretation which appear correct to us, who cling to the standard of the heavenly Church according to the succession of the Apostles of Jesus Christ.

Now that there are certain mystical economies made known in the Holy Scriptures, all, even the most simple of those who adhere to the word, have believed; but what these are, the candid and modest confess they do not know. If, then, one were to be perplexed by the incest of Lot with his daughters, and about the two wives of Abraham, and the two sisters married to Jacob, they can return no answer but this, that they are mysteries not understood by us. . . .

The way, then, as it seems to me, in which we ought to deal with the Scriptures and extract from them their meaning is the following, which has been ascertained from the sayings (of the Scriptures) themselves. By Solomon in the Proverbs we find some rule as this enjoined respecting the the teaching of the divine Writings, "and portray them in a threefold manner, in counsel and knowledge, to answer words of truth to those who propose them to you" (Prov. 22:20). One ought, then, to portray the ideas of Holy Scripture in a threefold manner upon his soul in order that the simple man may be edified by the "flesh," as it were, of Scripture, for so we name the obvious sense; while he who has ascended a certain way may be edified by the "soul," as it were. The perfect man, and he who resembles those spoken of by the Apostle (Paul) when he says, "We speak wisdom to those who are perfect, but not the wisdom of the world . . ." (1 Cor. 2:6–7), may receive edification from the spiritual law which is the shadow of things to come. *For as a man consists of body and soul and spirit, so in the same way does the Scripture consist, which has been arranged by God for the salvation of men.* (Origen, *On First Principles* 4.9–11)

Granted that there are three senses of Scripture that correspond to the division of the human person into body, soul, and spirit, how does one know when to depart from the literal or "corporeal" sense of Scripture and interpret it in a spiritual fashion? God himself, Origen responds, has provided the signals.

Since, if the usefulness of the legislation and the sequence and beauty of the history (found in Scripture) were universally evident, we should not believe that anything else could be understood in the Scriptures save what was obvious, the Word of God has arranged that certain stumbling blocks, and offenses and impossibilities should be introduced into the midst of the law and the history, so that we may not, though being drawn away in all directions by the merely attractive nature of the language, either fall away from the true doctrines, as learning nothing worthy of God, or, by not departing from the letter, come to the knowledge of nothing more divine. And this too we must know: that since the principal aim is to announce the "spiritual" connection in these things that are done and that ought to be done, where the Word found that things done according to the history could be adapted to these mystic senses, He made use of them, concealing from the multitude the deeper meaning. . . . And at other times impossibilities are recorded for the sake of the more skillful and inquisitive, in order that they may give themselves over to the task of investigating what is written and so attain a becoming conviction of the manner in which a meaning worthy of God must be sought out in such subjects. (Ibid. 4.15)

26. "Giving a Greek Twist to Foreign Tales"

The effect of Origen on his Christian contemporaries may be gauged by this homage by Gregory, called "the Wonderworker," to the man who converted and instructed him.

He [Origen] himself interpreted and clarified whatever was obscure and enigmatic (in Scripture), as in fact are many utterances of the sacred voices, whether because God is accustomed to speak in that fashion to men so that the divine word may not enter bare and unveiled into some unworthy soul, as most are; or perhaps because time and antiquity have caused the oracles of God, which are by nature most clear and simple, to appear indistinct and dark to us. . . . But Origen made them clear and brought them into the light. This gift was his alone of all men whom I have known personally. (Gregory Thaumaturgus, *To Origen*)

Origen was as well known in pagan intellectual circles as he was in the newly emerging Christian ones. But his methods of Scriptural exegesis did not receive such high marks among the Hellenists, who in the third century were beginning to understand something of the appeal, and the threat, of Christianity. Origen may have attended classes at Alexandria with Plotinus, the chief Platonist of late antiquity, and this is the reaction of one of Plotinus' students, Porphyry (ca. 275 C.E.), to the Christian intellectual and what he represented.

"Enigmas" is the pretentious name given by the Christians to the perfectly plain statements of Moses, thus glorifying them as oracles filled with hidden mysteries and beguiling the critical faculty by their extravagant nonsense. . . . This absurd nonsense should be put to the account of a man I met when I was still quite young, who enjoyed a great reputation and, thanks to the works he left behind him, still enjoys it. I mean Origen, whose fame among teachers of these theories is widespread. He was a pupil of Ammonius (in Alexandria), the most distinguished philosopher of our time. He acquired a great deal of theoretical knowledge with the help of his master, but when it came to choosing the right way of life, he went in the opposite direction. For Ammonius was (born) a Christian and was raised as a Christian by his parents, but when he began to think philosophically he promptly changed to a law-abiding way of life; Origen, on the other hand, a Greek schooled in Greek thought, plunged headlong into un-Greek recklessness. When he was filled with that, he sold himself and his dialectical skills. He lived like a Christian in his defiance of the law, but in his metaphysical and theological ideas he played the Greek, giving a Greek twist to foreign tales. He constantly connected himelf with Plato, and was at home among the writings of Numenius and Cronius, Apollophanes, Longinus, and Moderatus, Nicomachus, and the more eminent disciples of Pythagoras. He also used the books of Chaeremon the Stoic and Cornutus, which taught him the allegorical method of interpreting the Greek mysteries, a method he applied to the Jewish Scriptures. (Porphyry, *Against the Christians*)

27. A Christian Meditation on the Psalms

The Christians elicited those "prophetic foreshadowing of things to come" from all the books of the Bible, but some of the chief and most popular texts were to be found in the Psalms. One of the most commonly cited and commented upon of David's "prophecies" concerning the Messiah who was to issue from his line was Psalm 110.

> The Lord said to my lord,
> "Sit at My right hand
> while I make your enemies your footstool."
> The Lord will stretch forth from Sion your mighty scepter;
>   hold sway over your enemies!
> Your people come forward willingly on your day of battle.
> In majestic holiness, from the womb,
>   from the dawn, yours was the dew of youth.
> The Lord has sworn and will not relent.
>   "You are a priest forever,
>   after the manner of Melchizedek."
> The Lord is at your right hand.

He crushes kings in the day of His anger.
He works judgment upon the nations,
    heaping up bodies,
      crushing heads far and wide.
He drinks from the stream on his way;
    therefore he holds his head high.

For the Jews of the era of its composition this poem or hymn likely had a liturgical function connected with the coronation of an Israelite king. For Augustine, as for most Christians since the days of the Apostles—and for Jesus himself, as the Gospel (Matt. 22:44) would have it—Psalm 110 was a prophecy pure and simple, and as such could be referred immediately to Christ the Messianic priest-king, as it was by Peter in a sermon reported in the Acts of the Apostles.

Men of Israel, listen to me. I speak of Jesus of Nazareth, a man singled out by God and made known to you through miracles, portents and signs, which God worked among you through him, as you well know. When he had been given up to you, by the deliberate plan and choice of God, you used heathen men to crucify and kill him. But God raised him up to life again, setting him free from the pangs of death, because it could not be that death should keep him in its grip. For David says of him:

"I foresaw that the presence of the Lord would be with me always,
For He is my right hand so that I may not be shaken;
Therefore my heart was glad and my tongue spoke my joy;
Moreover my flesh shall dwell in hope,
For You will not abandon my soul to death,
Nor let Your loyal servant suffer corruption.
You have shown me the ways of life,
You will fill me with gladness by Your presence."
(Ps. 16:8–11)

Let me tell you plainly, my friends [Peter continues], that the Patriarch David died and was buried and his tomb is here [that is, in Jerusalem] to this very day. It is clear therefore that he spoke (in those lines) as a prophet, who knew that God had sworn to him that one of his own direct descendants would sit on his throne; and when he said that he was not abandoned to death and his flesh never suffered corruption, he spoke with foreknowledge of the Resurrection of the Messiah.

The Jesus we speak of has been raised by God, as we can all bear witness. Exalted thus with God's right hand, he received the Holy Spirit from the Father, as was promised, and all that we now see and hear flows from him. For it was not David who went up to heaven: his own words

533

are "The Lord said to my Lord, 'Sit at my right hand while I make your enemies your footstool.' " Let all Israel then accept as certain that God has made this Jesus, whom you crucified, both Lord and Messiah. (Acts of the Apostles 2:22–36)

By the time of Augustine the emphasis had shifted from this psalm's prediction of the Messiahship of Jesus to a foreshadowing of his priesthood and the invocation of Melchizedek.

Just as that psalm (Ps. 45) also where Christ is most openly proclaimed as Priest, so even here (in Psalm 110) as King. "The Lord said to my Lord, you shall sit at My right hand when I make your enemies your footstool under your feet." That Christ sits at the right hand of the Father is believed, not seen; that his enemies also are put under his feet does not yet appear; it is being done, it will appear at last; yes, this is now believed; afterward it shall be seen. But what follows, "When the Lord from Sion hands you your scepter, march forth through the ranks of your enemies," is so clear that to deny it would imply not merely unbelief and mistake, but downright impudence. And even the enemies must certainly confess that from Sion has been sent the law of Christ which we call the Gospel, and acknowledge it as the symbol of his power. But that he rules in the midst of his enemies, these same enemies among whom he rules bear witness, gnashing their teeth and being consumed, and having power to do nothing against him.

Then what he says a little later, "The Lord has sworn and will not change His purpose," by which words He intimates that what He adds is immutable, "You are a priest forever in the succession of Melchizedek," who is permitted to doubt of whom these things are said, seeing that now there is nowhere a priesthood and sacrifice after the succession of Aaron, and everywhere men offer under Christ as the Priest, which Melchizedek showed when he blessed Abraham?

Therefore to these manifest things are to be referred, when rightly understood, those things in the same psalm that are set down a little more obscurely, and we have already made known in our popular sermons how these things are to be rightly understood. So also in that where Christ utters through prophecy the humiliation of his Passion, saying, "They have pierced my hands and my feet; they have numbered all my bones; yes, they looked and stared at me" (Ps. 22:16–17). By which words he certainly meant his body stretched out on the Cross, with the hands and feet pierced and perforated by the striking through of the nails, and that he had in that way made himself a spectacle to those who looked and stared. And he [David] adds, "They parted my garments among them, and over my clothing they cast lots" (Ps. 22:8–9). How this prophecy has been fulfilled the Gospel history narrates.

Then, indeed, the other things also which are said there less openly are rightly understood when they agree with those which shine forth with so great clarity, especially because those things also which we do not believe as past but survey as present, are beheld by the whole world, being now exhibited just as they were read of in this very psalm predicted so long before. (Augustine, *City of God* 17.17) [AUGUSTINE 1948: 2:395–396]

28. Explaining Away the Torah

The early Christian was faced with the problem of what to do with that other, sometimes embarrassing Word of God that had been given to the Jews. In many instances the Bible could be read typologically, as we have just seen the Psalms were, but the detailed and concrete provisions of the Law required a more varied treatment. The Letter of Barnabas, *possibly written by an Alexandrian Jewish convert to Christianity sometime about 130 C.E., represents one very early Christian attempt to come to terms with the Torah. The first passage shows how the verses on the scapegoat in Leviticus 16:5ff., quoted in the author's usual freewheeling style, are to be read as a foreshadowing of Christ.*

Notice the directions: "Take a couple of goats, unblemished and well matched; bring them for an offering, and let the priest take one of them for a burnt offering." And what are they to do with the other? "The other," He declares, "is accursed." —Now see how plainly the type of Jesus appears— "Spit on it, all of you; thrust your goads into it, wreathe its head with scarlet wool, and so let it be driven into the desert." This is done and the goat keeper leads the animal into the desert, where he takes the wool off and leaves it there, on a bush we call a bramble, the same plant whose berries we usually eat when we come across it in the countryside; nothing has such tasty fruit as a bramble. Now what does that signify? Notice that the first goat is for the altar and the other is accursed, and that it is the accursed one that wears the wreath. That is because they shall see him on That Day clad to the ankles in his red woolen robe and will say, "Is this not he whom we once crucified, and mocked, and pierced and spat upon? Yes, this is the man who told us that he was the Son of God." But how will he resemble the goat? The point of there being two similar goats, both of them fair and alike, is that when they see him coming on the Day, they are going to be struck with terror

at the manifest parallel between him and the goat. In this ordinance, then, you see typified the future sufferings of Jesus. (*Letter of Barnabas* 7)
[STANIFORTH 1968: 203]

The same author's treatment of the dietary laws is not typological but allegorical.

And now for that saying of Moses, "You are not to eat of swine; nor yet of eagle, hawk or crow; nor of any fish that has not got scales." In this there are three distinct moral precepts which he had received and understood. For God says in Deuteronomy, "I will make a covenant with this people that will embody my rules for holiness" (Deut. 4:1); so, you see, the divine command is in no sense a literal ban on eating, and Moses was speaking spiritually. The meaning of his allusion to swine is this: what he is really saying is "you are not to consort with the class of people who are like swine, inasmuch as they forget all about the Lord while they are living in affluence, but remember him when they are in want, just as a swine, so long as it is eating, ignores its master, but starts to squeal the moment it feels hungry, and then falls silent again when it is given food."

If the method is to work, the author must possess in this instance—the list of prohibited foods in Leviticus is a long one—a considerable knowledge of animal physiology and behavior.

Among other things, He [Moses] also says, "You are not to eat of the hare" (Lev. 11:6), by which he means that you are not to debauch young boys, or become like those who do; because the hare grows a fresh orifice in its backside every year and has as many of these holes as the years of its life. And "you are not to eat the hyena" [this prohibition does not occur in the Bible] signifies that you are to be no lecher or libertine, or copy their ways, since that creature changes its sex annually and is a male at one time and a female at another. The weasel too he speaks of with abhorrence, and not without good reason; his implication being that you are not to imitate those who, we are told, are filthy enough to use their mouths for the practice of vice, nor to frequent the abandoned women who do the same, since it is through its mouth that this animal is impregnated. (*Letter of Barnabas* 10) [STANIFORTH 1968: 206–207]

By his allegorical method the author of the Letter of Barnabas *has freed the Christian from the literal observance of the Law while maintaining the validity of the Mosaic revelation. His moralizing treatment here of Leviticus 11 had a long history in the Christian tradition.*

29. The Fleshly and the Spiritual Understanding
of the Mosaic Law

Augustine, following Paul's lead, had little difficulty in reading the New Testament out of the Old. But as we have already seen in the case of the Letter of Barnabas, *the Jewish Bible posed more particular exegetical problems for the Christian. The Christians early on confronted the possibilities of either rejecting the Bible outright, as Marcion and others suggested, and so completely dissociating themselves from the Jews, or else of accepting the Torah as authoritative and thus binding upon themselves. The first choice was rendered unlikely by the Gospels' own method of arguing the case for the Messiahship of Jesus out of the fulfillment of biblical prophecies, a practice continued by Paul and most of the Christian tradition. The second choice, to remain Torah-observant Jews while accepting the Messiahship of Jesus, recommended itself to many of the early Christians, who were themselves born Jews. It was aborted first by the decision to admit Gentiles into the Christian community and then by Paul's theological accommodation to that fact. Thus the Bible, the Christians' "Old Testament," had to remain authoritative as God's revelation, as could be demonstrated in its typological sense, but it was no longer binding in at least some of its prescriptions.*

Augustine touched upon the problem in more than one of his writings. In the City of God, *he takes it up in theological rather than legal terms.*

In the words "Remember the Law of Moses my servant, which I commanded to him in Horeb for all Israel" (Mal. 4:4), the prophet (Malachi) opportunely mentions precepts and statutes, after declaring the important distinction hereafter to be made between those who observe and those who despise the Law. He intends also that they learn to interpret the Law spiritually, and find Christ in it, by whose judgment that separation between good and bad is to be made. For it is not without reason that the Lord himself said to the Jews, "Had you believed Moses, you would have believed, for he wrote of me" (John 4:46). For by receiving the Law carnally without perceiving that its earthly promises were figures of things spiritual, they fell into such murmurings as audaciously to say (to Malachi), "It is in vain to serve God; and what profit is it that we have kept His ordinance, and that we have walked suppliantly before the face of the Lord Almighty? And now we call aliens happy . . . " (Mal. 3:14). (Augustine, *City of God* 20.27) [AUGUSTINE 1948: 2:556]

Many other Christian exegetes—Jerome for one—wrestled with the legal aspects of the problem of the Christian and the Mosaic Law both before and after Augustine. By the time Thomas Aquinas came to write his Summa Theologica *(1265–1272*

C.E.) the main outlines of a solution were firmly in place. The method of proceeding is the scholastic one developed in the medieval universities.

Question 102, article 2: Whether the Ceremonial Precepts (of the Old Law) Have a Literal Cause or Merely a Figurative Cause?

First Objection: It would seem that the ceremonial precepts have not a literal but merely a figurative cause. For among the ceremonial precepts, the chief were circumcision and the sacrifice of the Passover lamb. But neither of these had any but a figurative cause because each was given as a sign. For it is written: "You shall circumcise the skin of your foreskin, that it may be for a sign of the covenant between Me and you" (Gen. 17:11); and of the celebration of Passover it is written: "It shall be a sign in your hand and as a memorial before your eyes" (Exod. 13:9). Therefore much more did the other ceremonial precepts have none but a figurative reason.

Second Objection: Further, an effect is proportioned to its cause. But all the ceremonial precepts are figurative, as stated above. Therefore they have only a figurative cause.

Third Objection: Further, if it is a matter of indifference whether a certain thing, considered in itself, be done in a particular way or not, it seems that it has not a literal cause. Now there are certain points in the ceremonial precepts which appear to be a matter of indifference, as to whether they are done in one way or in another: for instance, the number of animals to be offered, and other such particular circumstances. Therefore there is no literal cause for the precepts of the Old Law.

On the contrary: Just as the ceremonial precepts foreshadowed Christ, so did the stories of the Old Testament; for it is written that "all (these things) happened to them in figure" (1 Cor. 10:11). Now in the stories of the Old Testament, besides the mystical or the figurative, there is the literal sense. Therefore the ceremonial precepts had also literal, besides their figurative causes.

I answer: As was stated above, the reason for whatever conduces to an end must be taken from that end. Now the end of the ceremonial precepts (of the Mosaic Law) was twofold, for they were ordained to the divine worship for that particular time as well as to the foreshadowing of Christ. . . . Accordingly, the reasons for the ceremonial precepts of the Old Law can be taken in two ways. First, in respect of the worship of God that was to be observed for that particular time; and these reasons are literal, whether they refer to the shunning of idolatry, or recall certain divine benefits, or remind men of the divine excellence, or point out the disposition of mind which was then required in those who worshiped God. Secondly, their reasons can be gathered from the point of view of their being ordained to foreshadow Christ; and thus their reasons are figurative and mystical, whether they refer to Christ himself and the Church, which pertains to the allegorical sense, or to the morals of the Christian people, which pertains to the moral sense, or to the state of future glory, inasmuch as we are brought thereto by Christ, which pertains to the anagogical sense.

Reply to First Objection: Just as the use of metaphorical expressions in Scripture belongs to the literal sense, because the words are employed in order to convey that particular meaning, so also the meaning of these legal ceremonies (like circumcision and Passover) which commemorated certain divine benefits because of which they were instituted, and of other similar ones which belonged to that time, does not go beyond the order or literal causes. Consequently, when we assert that the cause of the celebration of Passover was its signification of the delivery from Egypt or that circumcision was a sign of God's covenant with Abraham, we assign them a literal cause.

Reply to Second Objection: This argument would avail if the ceremonial precepts had been given merely as figures of things to come and not for the purpose of worshiping God then and there.

Reply to Third Objection: As we stated when speaking of human laws, there is a reason for them in the universal, but not in regard to the particular conditions, which depend on the judgment of those who frame them. So too many particular determinations in the ceremonies of the Old Law have no literal cause but only a figurative one; whereas, considered universally, they have a literal cause. (Aquinas, *Summa Theologica* I/2, ques. 102, art. 2) [AQUINAS 1945: 2:862–864]

30. Jesus on Parables and Their Meaning

In common with the rabbis of his own and later times, Jesus often taught in parables. On more than one occasion he also provided a private exegesis of their meaning for the benefit of his disciples.

The same day Jesus went out and sat by the lakeside, where so many people gathered around him that he had to get into a boat. He sat there and all the people stood on the shore. He spoke to them in parables, at some length.

He said: "A sower went out to sow. And as he sowed, some seed fell along the footpath, and the birds came and ate it up. Some seed fell on rocky ground, where it had little soil, and it sprouted quickly because it had no depth of earth; but when the sun rose the young grain was scorched, and as it had no root it withered away. Some seed fell among thistles; and the thistles shot up and choked the wheat. And some of the seed fell into good soil, where it bore fruit, yielding a hundredfold or, it might be, sixtyfold or thirtyfold. If you have ears, then hear."

The disciples went up to him and asked, "Why do you speak to them in parables?" He replied, "It has been granted to you to know the secrets of the kingdom of Heaven, but to those others it has not been granted. For the man who has will be given more, till he has enough and to spare; and the man who has not will forfeit even what he has. That is why I speak to them in parables; for they look without seeing and listen without hearing or understanding. There is a prophecy of Isaiah that is being fulfilled for them: 'You may hear and hear, but you will never understand; you may look and look, but you will never see. For this people's mind has become gross; their ears are dulled, and their eyes are closed. Otherwise their eyes might see, their ears hear and their mind understand, and then they might turn again and I would heal them.' But happy are your eyes because they see, and your ears because they hear! Many prophets and saints, I tell you, desired to see what you now see; to hear what you now hear, but never heard it."

These are strong words and appear to echo Philo's almost contemporary sentiments on the problem of popular misconceptions about Scripture. Then Jesus gives his rather straightforward moral exegesis of the parable to his disciples, and it becomes clear that he was referring to spiritual, not intellectual, ignorance.

You, then, may hear the parable of the sower. When a man hears the word that tells of the Kingdom but fails to understand it, the evil one comes and carries off what has been sown in his heart. There you have the seed sown along the footpath. The seed sown on rocky ground stands for the man who, on hearing the word, accepts it at once with joy; but as it strikes no root in him he has no staying power, and when there is trouble or persecution on account of the word he falls away at once. The seed thrown among thistles represents the man who hears the word, but worldly cares and the false glamour of wealth choke it, and it proves barren. But the seed that fell into good soil is the man who hears the word and understands it, who accordingly bears fruit, and yields a hundredfold or, it may be, sixtyfold or thirtyfold. (Matthew 13:1–23)

31. A Parable of Muhammad

Interestingly, a similar parable, with attached exegesis, is attributed to Muhammad in one of the traditions circulating under his name.

Abu Musa reported that the Messenger of God said: "The guidance and knowledge with which God has commissioned me is like abundant rain which fell on some ground. Part of it was good, and absorbing the water, it brought forth abundant herbage and pasture; and there were some hollows in it which retained the water by which God gave benefit to men, who drank, gave drink and sowed seed. But some of it fell on another portion which consisted only of bare patches which could not retain the water or produce herbage. That [that is, the hollows] is like the one who becomes versed in religion and receives benefit from the message entrusted to me by God, so he knows for himself and teaches others; and (the bare patches) are like the one who who does not show regard for that and does not accept God's guidance with which I have been commissioned. (Baghawi, *Mishkat al-Masabih* 1.6.1)

32. How the Apostles Taught

To return to the Christian tradition, by the time we arrive at the opening decades of the second century, when Origen was writing his summa of Christian teaching called On First Principles, *the question of understanding Christian teachings had been broadened to include the question of intellectual ignorance, or rather its converse, intellectual training. Origen had received just such a training at Alexandria, and it is here factored into the Apostolic tradition.*

Just as there are many among the Greeks and barbarians alike who promise us the truth, and yet we gave up seeking for it from all who claimed it for false opinions after we had come to believe that Christ was the son of God and had become convinced that we must learn the truth from him; in the same way, when we find many who think they hold the doctrine of Christ, some of them differing in their beliefs from the Christians of earlier times, and yet the teaching of the Church, handed down in unbroken succession from the Apostles, is still preserved and continues to exist in the churches up to the present day, we maintain that that only is to be believed as the truth which in no way conflicts with the tradition of the Church and the Apostles.

But the following facts should be understood. The holy Apostles, when preaching the faith of Christ, took certain doctrines, those namely which they believed to be the necessary ones, and delivered them in the plainest terms to all believers, even to such as appeared to be somewhat dull in the investigation of divine knowledge. The grounds of their statements they left to be investigated by such as should merit the higher gifts of the Spirit, and in particular by such as should afterwards receive through the Holy Spirit Himself the graces of language, wisdom and knowledge. There were other doctrines, however, about which the Apostles simply said that things were so, keeping silence as to how or why; their intention undoubtedly being to supply the more diligent of those who came after them, such as should prove to be lovers of wisdom [that is, "philosophers" in the most literal sense], with an exercise on which to display the fruit of their ability. The men I refer to are those who train themselves to become worthy and capable of receiving wisdom. (Origen, *On First Principles* 2–3)

Origen then proceeds to give a summary of basic Christian beliefs, including the divine inspiration of Scriptures, both Old and New Testament. As he puts it, "there was not one Spirit in the men of old and another in those who were inspired at the coming of Christ." That consideration leads in turn to another.

Then there is the doctrine that the Scriptures were composed through the Spirit of God and that they have not only the meaning that is obvious but also another which is hidden from the majority of readers. For the contents of Scripture are the outward forms of certain mysteries and the images of divine things. On this point the entire Church is unanimous, that while the whole Law is spiritual, the inspired meaning is not recognized by all, but only by those who are gifted with the grace of the Holy Spirit in the word of wisdom and knowledge. (Ibid. 8)

33. The Christian Is Instructed on How To Read Scripture

The entire rich body of Scripture contained far more complex matter than rabbinic parables, however. As we have already seen, the Church's new intellectuals, with their professional training in rhetoric, hastened to assist the Christian to a better understanding of the word of God. Augustine devoted an entire treatise to Christian instruction, an instruction that inevitably included guidance on the reading and comprehension of Scripture.

The entire treatment of the Scriptures is based upon two factors: the method of discovering what we are to understand and the method of teaching what has been understood. . . . All teaching is concerned with either things or signs, but things are learned by means of signs. I have defined a thing in the accurate sense of the word as that which is not used to signify anything, for example, wood, stone, animal or others of this kind. But I do not include the tree which we read Moses cast into bitter waters to take away their bitterness (Exod. 15:25), nor the stone which Jacob placed under his head (Gen. 28:11), nor that ram which Abraham sacrificed in place of his son (Gen. 22:13). These are indeed things, but they are also symbols of other things. There are other signs whose whole usefulness consists in signifying. Words belong to this class, for no one uses words except to signify something. From this is understood what I designate as signs, namely those things which are employed to signify something. Therefore, every sign is also a thing—for whatever is not a thing is absolutely nothing—but not every thing is also a sign. So in this division of things and signs, when I speak of things, I shall do so in such a way that, although some of them can be used to signify, they will not disturb the division according to which I am treating first of things and then of signs. (Augustine, *On Christian Instruction* 1.1–2) [AUGUSTINE 1947: 27–29]

The instruction on things and their use in accordance with Scripture constitutes Augustine's teaching of Christian morality. Then, as promised, he takes up the question of signs.

Things which have been written fail to be understood for two reasons; they are hidden by either unknown or ambiguous signs. These signs are either literal or figurative. They are literal when they are employed to signify those things for which they were instituted. When we say *bos* we mean ox, because all men call it by this name in the Latin language, just as we do. Signs are figurative when the very things which we signify by the literal term are applied to some other meaning; for example, we say *bos* and recognize by that word an ox to which we usually give that name; but again, under the figure of the ox, we recognize a teacher of the Gospel. This is intimated by Holy Scripture, according to the interpretation of the Apostle Paul, in the text: "You shall not muzzle the ox that treads out the grain" (Deut. 25:4; cf. 1 Cor. 9:9). (Augustine, *On Christian Instruction* 2.10) [AUGUSTINE 1947: 72]

Jews and Muslims devoted a great deal of attention to establishing a correct text of Scripture. The Christian had an additional problem in that he was coming to God's word via translation—in the case of the Old Testament, through a Greek translation, which was in turn translated into Latin. Even in the case of the New Testa-

ment, most of Augustine's flock would be reading it not in the Greek in which it was written but in a Latin translation.

Obviously, an unknown word or an unknown expression causes the reader to be perplexed. If these come from foreign languages, we must ask about them from men who use those languages, or learn the languages, if we have the time and the ability, or study a comparison of the various translators. . . . The multitude of translators is a very important aid, when they have been considered and debated upon by a comparison of texts. However, avoid all that is positively false. For in correcting texts, the ingenuity of those who desire to know the Sacred Scriptures should be exercised principally in such a way that uncorrected passages, at least those coming from a single source of translation, yield to those that have been rectified.

In emending any Latin translations, we must consult the Greek texts; of these the reputation of the seventy translators [that is, the Septuagint] is most distinguished with regard to the Old Testament. These translators are now considered by the more learned churches to have translated under such sublime inspiration of the Holy Spirit that from so many men there was only one version. . . . Therefore, even if we should discover something in the Hebrew original other than they have interpreted it, it is my opinion that we should yield to the divine direction. This guidance was accomplished through them so that the books which the Jewish nation refused to transmit to other nations, either because of reverence or jealousy, were revealed so far ahead of time, with the aid of the authority of King Ptolemy, to those nations who would believe through our Lord. . . .

However, in reference to figurative expressions, if by chance the reader is caused perplexity by any unknown signs, he must decipher them partly through a knowledge of language, partly through a knowledge of things. The pool of Siloam, where the Lord ordered the man whose eyes he had smeared with clay made of spittle to wash his face (John 9:7), is applicable in some degree as an analogy and unquestionably alludes to some mystery. Nevertheless if the Evangelist had not explained that name from an unknown language, such an essential implication would be hidden from us. So also, many Hebrew names which have not been interpreted by the authors of those books unquestionably have no small power to help toward explaining the obscurities of Scriptures, if someone is able to translate them. Some men, expert in that language, have rendered a truly valuable service to succeeding ages by having interpreted all these words apart from Scripture. . . . Because these have been revealed and translated, many figurative passages in the Scriptures are interpreted. (Ibid. 2.14–16) [AUGUSTINE 1947: 79–82]

For a proper understanding of Scripture, Augustine continues, one must possess a knowledge of many things, including the properties of animals, vegetables, and minerals, of numbers, music, and history, of men, their arts, sciences, and institutions. Thus armed, and forearmed as well against the errors of the pagans who perfected these sciences, the student may then approach what is the main task of the exegete: to understand the ambiguities of Scripture.

When literal words cause Scripture to be ambiguous, our first concern must be to see that we have not punctuated them incorrectly or mispronounced them. Then, when a careful scrutiny reveals that it is doubtful how it should be punctuated or pronounced, we must consult the rule of faith which we have learned from the clearer passages of Scriptures and from the authority of the Church. . . . If both meanings, or even all of them, if there should be several, sound obscure after recourse has been had to faith, we must consult the context of both the preceding and the following passage to ascertain which of several meanings indicated it would consent to and permit to be incorporated in itself.

But when the ambiguity can be explained neither through a principle of faith nor through the context itself, there is nothing to prevent our punctuating the sentence according to any interpretation that is made known to us. . . . The same principles which I proposed for uncertain punctuations must also be followed for undetermined pronunciations. For these also, unless the excess negligence of the reader prevents it, are corrected either by the rules of faith or by the preceding or the succeeding context. (Ibid. 3.1–3) [AUGUSTINE 1947: 117–120]

The obscurities of figurative words, which I must discuss next, require extraordinary attention and persistence. First of all, we must be careful not to take a figurative expression literally. What the Apostle (Paul) said has reference to this: "The letter kills but the spirit gives life" (2 Cor. 3:6). When a figurative expression is understood as if it were literal, it is understood carnally. And nothing is more appropriately named the death of the soul than that which causes the quality of the soul which makes it superior to the beasts—that is, intelligence—to be subjected to the flesh by a close conformity to the literal sense. A man who conforms to the literal meaning considers figurative words as if they were literal and does not transfer what is signified by a literal word to its other sense. If he hears about the Sabbath for example, he thinks only of one day of the seven which are repeated in continuous sequence. When he hears of sacrifice, his thoughts do not rise above the usual sacrifices of the victims of flocks and the fruits of the earth. It is a wretched slavery of soul, indeed, to be satisfied with signs instead of realities, and not to be able to elevate the eye of the mind above the sensible realities to drink in eternal light.

Nevertheless, this slavery of the Jewish people was far different from the usual one of other nations, since the Jews were subjected to temporal things, but in such a way that the One God was honored in all these things. And although they observed the symbols of spiritual things instead of the things themselves, unaware of what they represented, they yet considered it a settled fact that by such servitude they were pleasing the One God of all, whom they did not see. The Apostle (Paul) wrote that this subjection was like that of little children under a tutor (Gal. 3:24ff.). And so those who adhered stubbornly to such symbols could not tolerate the Lord's disdain for those things when the time of their revelation had come. For that reason their leaders stirred up malicious accusations that he healed on the Sabbath, and the people, bound to those signs as if to realities, did not believe that he, who was unwilling to give heed to the signs as they were observed by the Jews, either was God or had come from God. (Ibid. 3.5–6) [AUGUSTINE 1947: 124–125]

To this precept, in accord with which we are careful not to consider a figurative or transferred form of speech as if it was literal, we must add another: That we are not to attempt to interpret a literal expression as if it were figurative. Therefore I must first point out the method of making sure whether a passage is literal or figurative. *In general that method is to understand as figurative anything in Scripture which cannot in a literal sense be attributed either to an upright character or to a pure faith.* Uprightness of character pertains to the love of God and our neighbor; purity of faith, to the knowledge of God and our neighbor. Further, everyone's hope is in his own conscience, so far as he knows that he is advancing in the love and knowledge of God and his neighbor. (Ibid. 3.10) [AUGUSTINE 1947: 129]

Whatever harshness and apparent cruelty in deed and word we read of in Holy Scripture as used by God on His saints is efficacious in destroying the power of lust. If it speaks plainly we must not refer it to another significance as if it were a figurative expression. . . . The things which seem almost wicked to the unenlightened, whether they are only words or whether they are even deeds, either of God or of men whose sanctity is commended to us, these are entirely figurative. . . . (However) what is frequently sinful in other persons is a symbol of some sublime truth in the person of God or a prophet. Certainly union with an adulteress is one thing in the case of corrupt morals, but it is another in the case of the prophesying of the prophet Hosea (Hos. 1:2). It is shameful to strip the body at banquets of the drunken and the lascivious, but it is not for that reason to be naked in the baths. Consequently, we must prudently take into account what is proper for places, circumstances and persons, so that we may not indiscreetly convict them of sin. (Ibid. 3.12) [AUGUSTINE 1947: 132–133]

If a passage is didactic, either condemning vice, or crime, or pre-scribing utility or kindness, it is not figurative. But if it appears to pre-scribe vice or crime, or to condemn utility or kindness, it is figurative. The Lord said, "Unless you eat the flesh of the Son of Man and drink his blood, you shall not have life in you" (John 6:54). This seems to prescribe a crime or vice; therefore it is a figure of speech directing that we are to participate in the Lord's passion and treasure up in grateful and salutory remembrance the fact that his flesh was crucified and wounded for us. Scripture says, "If your enemy is hungry, give him food; if he is thirsty, give him drink" (Prov. 25:21–22). This undoubtedly prescribes a kind-ness, but the part that follows, "for in doing so you will heap coals of fire upon his head," you might suppose was commanding a crime of malevo-lence. So do not doubt that it is a figurative expression. Although it can have a twofold interpretation, by the one intending harm and by the other good, charity should call you away from the former to kindness, so that you may understand that the coals of fire are the burning lamenta-tions of repentance by which that man's pride is healed and he grieves that he has been the enemy of the man who relieves his misery. (Ibid. 3.16) [AUGUSTINE 1947: 136]

Augustine returns to the question of distinguishing where the literal and where the figurative reading is to be applied to Scriptural texts.

We must discover first of all whether the expression we are trying to understand is literal or figurative. When we have made certain that it is figurative, it is easy, by employing the rules concerning (such) things . . . to reflect upon it in all its aspects until we reach the idea of truth, particularly when practice, invigorated by the observance of piety is added to it. . . .

When the expression is seen to be figurative, the words of which it is composed will be discovered to be derived either from similar things or from those related by some affinity. But since things appear similar to each other in many ways, we should not imagine that there is any precept that we must believe that because a thing has a certain analogical meaning in one place, it always has this meaning. For example, the Lord represented leaven in a comdemnatory fashion when he said, "Beware the leaven of the Pharisees" (Matt. 16:10), and as an object of praise when he said, "The kingdom of heaven is like a woman who hid leaven in three measures of flour, until all of it was leavened" (Matt. 13:33).

The rule of this diversity, therefore, has two forms. Anything that is a sign of one thing and then another is such that it signifies either things that are contrary or else things that are only different. They indicate contraries, for instance, when the same thing is expressed by way of analogy at one time in a good sense and at another in a bad sense, like the leaven mentioned above. . . . Yet there are some passages where there is uncertainty with respect to the meaning in which they ought to be understood; for example, "In the hand of the Lord there is a cup of strong wine full of mixture" (Ps. 75:8). It is doubtful whether this signifies the wrath of God, but not to the extreme penalty, that is, to "the dregs"; or whether it signifies the grace of the Scriptures passing from the Jews to the Gentiles, because (it continues) "he has poured out from this to that," although certain practices continue among the Jews which they understand carnally, because "the dregs thereof are not emptied." (Ibid. 3.24–25) [AUGUSTINE 1947: 143–145]

A man who thoroughly examines the Holy Scriptures in an endeavor to find the purpose of the author, through whom the Holy Spirit brought the Scriptures into being, whether he attains his goal or whether he elicits from the words another meaning which is not opposed to the true faith, he is free from blame if he has proof from some other passage of the Holy Scriptures. In fact, the author perhaps saw that very meaning too in the same words which we are anxious to interpret. And certainly, the Spirit of God who produced these words through him also foresaw that this very meaning would occur to the reader or the listener; further, he took care that it should occur to him because it is also based on truth. For what could God have provided more generously and more abundantly in the Holy Scriptures than that the same words might be understood in several ways, which other supporting testimonies no less divine endorse?

When, however, a meaning is elicited that is such that its uncertainty cannot be explained by the unerring testimonies of the Holy Scriptures (themselves), it remains for us to explain it by the proof of reason, even if the man whose words we are seeking to understand was perhaps unaware of that meaning. This is a dangerous practice, however. It is much safer to walk by means of the Holy Scripture. When we are trying to search out those passages that are obscured by figurative words, we may either start out from a passage which is not subject to dispute, or, if it is disputed, we may settle the question by employing the testimonies that have been discovered elsewhere in the same Scripture. (Ibid. 3.27–28) [AUGUSTINE 1947: 147–148]

34. The Catholic Interpretation of Scripture

Augustine was attempting to give practical instruction. Vincent of Lerins, in his Commonitorium *(434 C.E.) had another concern: that Scripture be read and understood according to the mind of the Church Catholic.*

It always was, and it is today, the usual practice of Catholics to test the true faith by two methods: first, by the authority of the divine Canon (of Scripture), and then by the tradition of the Catholic Church. Not that the Canon is insufficient in itself in each case. But because most false interpreters of the Divine Word make use of their own arbitrary judgment and thus fall into various opinions and errors, the understanding of Holy Scripture must conform to the single rule of Catholic teaching, and this especially in regard to those questions upon which the foundations of all Catholic dogma are laid. (Vincent of Lerins, *Commonitorium* 29)

35. How the Muslim Reads the Quran

Instruction on how to read the Quran began with the Prophet himself, or so this tradition circulated under his name would have it.

Abu Hurayra reported God's messenger as saying: "The Quran came down showing five aspects: what is permissible, what is prohibited, what is firmly fixed, what is obscure, and parables. So treat what is permissible as permissible and what is prohibited as prohibited, act upon what is firmly fixed, believe in what is obscure, and take a lesson from the parables." (Baghawi, *Mishkat al-Masabih* 1.6.2)

If that advice seems somewhat schematic for a genuine Prophetic utterance, the highly systematic and scholastic view of the sciences connected with reading and understanding the Quran that the Spanish social philosopher and historian Ibn Khaldun inserted in his Prolegomenon to History *in 1377 C.E. is less cause for surprise.*

It should be known that the Quran was revealed in the language of the Arabs and according to their rhetorical methods. All the Arabs understood it and knew the meaning of the individual words and composite statements. It was revealed in chapters [that is, suras] and verses in order to explain the Oneness of God and the religious duties appropriate to the various occasions.

Some passages . . . are early and are followed by other, later passages that abrogate the earlier ones. The Prophet used to explain these things, as it is said, "So that you may explain to the people what was revealed to them" (Quran 14:46). He used to explain the unclear statements (in the Quran) and to distinguish the abrogating statements from those abrogated by them, and to inform the men around him of this sense. Thus the men around him became acquainted with the subject. They knew why individual verses were revealed and the situation that had required them, and this directly on Muhammad's authority. Thus the verse of the Quran "When God's help comes and the victory" (110:1) refers to the announcement of the Prophet's death, and similar things.

These explanations were transmitted on the authority of the men around Muhammad [that is, the "Companions of the Prophet"; see Chapter 3 below] and were circulated by the men of the second generation (after him). They continued to be transmitted among the early Muslims, until knowledge became organized in scholarly disciplines and systematic scholarly works began to be written. At that time most of these explanations were committed to writing. The traditional information concerning them, which had come down from the men around Muhammad and the men of the second generation, was transmitted farther. That material reached al-Tabari [d. 923], al-Waqidi [d. 823] and al-Tha'alibi [d. 1035] and other Quran interpreters. They committed to writing as much of the traditional information as God wanted them to do.

The linguistic sciences then became technical discussions of the lexicographical meaning of words, the rules governing vowel endings, and style in the use of word combinations. Systematic works were written on these subjects. Formerly these subjects had been habitual with the Arabs, and so no recourse to oral and written transmission had been necessary with respect to them. Now, that was forgotten, and these subjects were learned from books by philologists. They were needed for the interpretation of the Quran, because the Quran is in Arabic and follows the stylistic technique of the Arabs. Quran interpretation thus came to be handled in two ways.

One kind of Quran interpretation is traditional. It is based on information received from the early Muslims. It consists of knowledge of the
abrogating verses and of the verses that are abrogated by them, of the
reasons why a verse was revealed, and the purposes of individual verses.
All this can be known only through the traditions based on the authority
of the men around Muhammad and the men of the second generation.
The early scholars had already made complete compilations on the subject. . . .

The other kind of Quran interpretation has recourse to linguistic
knowledge, such as lexicography and the stylistic form used for conveying
meaning through the appropriate means and methods. This kind of
Quran interpretation rarely appears separately from the first kind. The
first kind is the one that is wanted essentially. The second made its appearance only after language and the philological sciences had become
crafts. However, it has become preponderant, as far as certain Quran
commentaries are concerned. (Ibn Khaldun, *Muqaddima* 6.10)

[IBN KHALDUN 1967: 2:443–446]

36. Where Did the Muslim Commentators
Get Their Information?

Abdullah ibn Amr reported that God's Messenger said: "Pass on
information from me, even if it is only a verse of the Quran; and relate
traditions from the Banu Isra'il, for there is no restriction." . . . Bukhari
transmitted this tradition. (Baghawi, *Mishkat al-Masabih* 2.1.1)

*Ibn Khaldun concurred that such a transmission from Jewish sources had occurred,
particularly when it came to fleshing out some of the narrative material in the
Quran, and he had the social theory to enable him to explain it.*

The early scholars' works (on the Quran) and the information they
transmit contain side by side important and unimportant matters, accepted and rejected statements. The reason is the Arabs had no books or
scholarship. The desert attitude and illiteracy prevailed among them.
When they wanted to know certain things that human beings are usually
curious to know, such as the reasons for existing things, the beginning of
creation, and the secrets of existence, they consulted the earlier People
of the Book and got their information from them. The People of the Book
were the Jews who had the Torah and the Christians who followed the
religion (of the Jews). Now the People of the Torah who lived among the

Arabs at that time were themselves Bedouins. They knew only as much about these matters as is known to ordinary People of the Book. The majority of those Jews were Himyarites [that is, South Arabians] who had adopted Judaism. When they became Muslims, they retained the information they possessed, such as information about the beginning of creation and information of the type of forecasts and predictions. That information had no connection with the (Jewish or Christian) religious laws they were preserving as theirs. Such men were Ka'b al-Ahbar, Wahb ibn Munabbih, Abdullah ibn Salam, and similar people.

The Quran commentaries were filled with material of such tendencies transmitted on their authority; it is information that entirely depends on them. It has no relation to (religious) laws, such that one might claim for it the soundness that would make it necessary to act (in accordance with it). The Quran interpreters were not very rigorous in this respect. They filled the Quran commentaries with such material, which originated, as we have stated, with the People of the Torah who lived in the desert and were not capable of verifying the information they transmitted. However, they were famous and highly esteemed because they were people of rank in their religion and religious group. Therefore, their interpretation has been accepted from that time onward. (Ibn Khaldun, *Muqaddima* 6.10) [IBN KHALDUN 1967: 2:445–446]

37. The Clear and the Ambiguous in the Quran

We have already seen the Bible commenting upon itself and Jesus giving instruction to his disciples on how they were to understand his teaching. The Quran too issued a warning about the problems and dangers in understanding the words of God, and so provided as well an inviting peg upon which later commentators might hang their own theories concerning exegesis.

He has sent down this Book which contains some clear verses that are categorical [or "are from the Mother of the Book"] and others allegorical [or "ambiguous"]. But those who are twisted in mind look for verses allegorical [or "ambiguous"], seeking deviation and giving them interpretations of their own; but none knows their meaning except God; and those who are steeped in knowledge affirm: "We believe in them as all of them are from the Lord"; but only those who have wisdom understand. (Quran 3:7)

The following comments on these verses were written by Zamakhshari in 1134 C.E.

"Categorical verses," namely those whose diction and meaning are sufficiently clear that they are preserved from the possibility of differing interpretations and ambiguity. "And others that are ambiguous," namely those verses that are ambiguous in that they allow differing interpretations.

"The Mother of the Book": that is, the origin of the Book, since the ambiguous verses must be traced back to it and harmonized with it. Examples of such ambiguity include the following: "The vision reaches Him not, but He reaches the vision; He is All-subtle, All-aware" (6:103); or "Upon that day their faces shall be radiant, gazing upon their Lord" (75:22); or "God does not command indecency!" (7:28) compared with "And when We desire to destroy a city, We command its men who live at ease, and they commit ungodliness therein. Then the command is realized against it, and We destroy it utterly" (17:16).

If one then asks whether the (meaning of the) entire Quran might not be (clearly) determined, I answer that men would (then) depend on it since it would be so easily accessible, and thus they would neglect what they lack, namely, research and meditation through reflection and inference. If they did that, then they would be neglecting the only way by which we can attain to a knowledge of God and His unity. Again, the ambiguous verses present a test and a means of distinguishing between those who stand firm in the truth and those who are uncertain regarding it. And great advantages, including the noble sciences and the profit of higher orders of being, are granted by God when scholars stimulate each other and so develop their natural skills, discovering the meanings of the ambiguous verses and harmonizing these with the (clearly) determined verses. Further, if the believer is firmly convinced that no disagreement or self-contradiction can exist in God's words, and then he notices something that appears at least to be a contradiction, and he then diligently searches out some way of harmonizing it (with the clear verses), treating it according to a uniform principle, and by reflecting on it comes to an insight about himself and other things, and with God's inspiration he comes to an understanding of the harmony that exists between the ambiguous verses and the (clearly) determined verses, then his certainty grows and the intensity of his conviction increases.

"As for those whose heart is swerving": These are the people who introduce innovations.

"They follow the ambiguous part," that is, they confine their attention to the ambiguous verses, which give free rein to innovations without harmonizing them with the (clearly) determined verses. But these (same verses) likewise permit an interpretation which agrees with the views of the people of truth.

The following interpretation depends on how one divides—in our parlance, punctu-ates—the text: to wit, whether or not there should be a pause or semicolon after "except God." In Zamakhshari's first interpretation it is not in fact so punctuated, though he concedes the possibility.

"And none knows its interpretation except God and those firmly rooted in knowledge," namely, only God and His servants who have firmly rooted knowledge, that is to say, those who are firm in knowledge and so "bite with a sharp tooth," come to the correct interpretation, according to which one must necessarily explain it. Some, however, place a pause after "except God" and begin a new sentence with "And those firmly rooted in knowledge . . . say." Thus they interpret the ambiguous verses as those whose understanding God reserves to Himself alone as well as the recognition of whatever wisdom is contained in them, as, for example, the exact number of the executioners in hell and similar questions. The first reading is the correct one, and the next sentence begins with "they say," setting forth the situation of those who have a firmly rooted knowledge, namely, in the following sense: Those who know the meaning say "we believe in it," that is, in the ambiguous verses.

"All of them are from our Lord": that is, all the ambiguous verse as well as all the (clearly) determined verse (in the Quran) is from Him. Or (to put it another way), not only the ambiguous verses in the Book but also the (clearly) determined verses are from God, the Wise One, in whose words there is no contradiction and in whose Book there is no discrepancy. (Zamakhshari, *The Unveiler of the Realities, ad loc.*)

One who preferred to read and punctuate this text as Zamakhshari had was the most straightforward Aristotelian produced in Islam, the Spanish philosopher Ibn Rushd, or Averroes (d. 1198 C.E.). In his Decisive Treatise *he develops the argument that, since there is no absolute Muslim consensus on which scriptural verses should be read literally and which allegorically, a certain latitude should be permitted in exegesis (see below). He then turns to this same verse, Sura 3:7.*

It is evident from what we have said (to this point) that a unanimous agreement cannot be established in (theoretical) questions of this kind, because of the reports that many of the believers of the first generation (of Muslims), as well as others, have said that there are allegorical interpretations which ought not to be expressed except to those who are qualified to receive allegories. These are those who "are firmly rooted in knowledge." For we prefer to place a stop after God's words "and those who are firmly rooted and knowledge" (and not before it), because if the scholars did not understand allegorical interpretation (but only God), there would be no superiority in their assent which would oblige them to a belief in Him not found among the unlearned. God has described them as those who believe in Him, and this can only refer to a belief which is based on (scientific or philosophical) demonstration; and this belief only occurs together with the science of allegorical interpretation. For the unlearned believers are those whose belief in Him is not based on demonstration; and if this belief which God has attributed to the scholars (in Quran 3:7) is peculiar to them, it must come through demonstration, and if it comes through demonstration, it only occurs together with the science of allegorical interpretation. For God the Exalted has informed us that those (verses) have an allegorical interpretation which is the truth, and demonstration can only be of the truth. That being the case, it is not possible for general unanimity to be established about allegorical interpretations, which God has made peculiar to scholars. This is self-evident to any fair-minded person. (Averroes, *The Decisive Treatise* 10)

[AVERROES 1961: 53–54]

38. The Outer and Inner Meanings of the Quran

A thinker whose opinions recur throughout the work of Averroes is Ghazali (d. 1111 C.E.), the earlier Baghdad theologian and lawyer whose scathing attack on the rationalist philosophy that was attracting some Muslim thinkers in the tenth and eleventh centuries was, despite its spirited defense by Averroes, the likely cause of its eventual repudiation in Islam. Ghazali too is willing to admit the allegorical interpretation of Scripture, though with considerably more caution than Averroes.

. . . The Prophet said: "Whoever interprets the Quran according to his own opinion will have his place in Gehenna." The people who are acquainted with only the outer sense of exegesis have for this reason discredited the mystics to the extent that these latter practice exegesis, because they explain the wording of the Quran in a manner other than according to the tradition of Ibn Abbas and the (traditional) commentators; and they further maintain that what is involved (in such interpretation) is a matter of unbelief. If the advocates of traditional exegesis are correct, then the understanding of the Quran consists in nothing else than knowing its external meaning. But if they are not right, then what is the

meaning of the Prophet's words: "Whoever interprets the Quran according to his own opinion will have his place in Gehenna"?

It should be noted that whenever someone maintains that the Quran
has no meaning other than that expressed by the external method of
exegesis, then in so doing he is expressing his own limitations. With this
avowal about himself he expresses something which is doubtless correct
(for his own situation), but he is mistaken in thinking that the entire
creation is to be regarded on his level, that is, restricted by his limitations
and situation. The commentaries and traditions show that the meanings
contained in the Quran exhibit a wide scope for experts in the field. Thus,
Ali [the cousin and son-in-law of the Prophet and the fourth Caliph of
Islam] said (that a specific meaning can be grasped) only when God grants
to someone an understanding of the Quran. But if nothing else is involved
except the traditional interpretation, this is not "understanding." Further, the Prophet said that the Quran had a literal meaning, an inner
meaning, an end point and a starting point of understanding. . . . According to the opinion of some scholars, every verse can be understood in
sixty thousand ways, and that what still remains unexhausted (of its
meaning) is still more numerous. Others have maintained that the Quran
contains seventy-seven thousand and two hundred (kinds of) knowledge. . . .

Ibn Mas'ud said: Whoever wishes to obtain knowledge of his ancestors and descendants should meditate upon the Quran. This knowledge does not appear, however, if one restricts the interpretation of the
Quran to its outer meaning. Generally speaking, every kind of knowledge
is included in the categories of actions and attributes, and the description
of the nature of the actions and attributes of God is contained in the
Quran. These kinds of knowledge have no end; yet, in the Quran is found
(only) an indication of their general aspects. Thereby the degrees of the
deeper penetration into the particulars of knowledge are traced back to
the (actual) understanding of the Quran. The mere outer aspect of interpretation gives no hint of this knowledge. Rather, the fact is that the
Quran contains indications and hints, which certain select people with
(correct) understanding can grasp, concerning all that remains obscure in
the more abstract way of thinking and about which men disagree regarding the theoretical sciences and rational ideas. How can the interpretation
and explanation of the outer meaning of the Quran be adequate for this?

*There are, according to Ghazali, additional reasons why one should not be limited
to the mere literal meaning of God's word.*

The Companions of the Prophet and the commentaors disagree on the interpretation of certain verses and put forth differing statements about them which cannot be brought into harmony with one another. That all these statement were heard issuing from the mouth of the Messenger of God is patently absurd. One was obliged to understand one of these statements of the Messenger of God in order to refute the rest, and then it becomes clear that, as concerns the meaning (of the passage of the Quran in question), every exegete has expressed what appeared to him to be evident through his inferential reasoning. This went so far that seven different kinds of interpretations, which cannot be brought into harmony with one another, have been advanced concerning the letters at the beginning of (some of) the suras.

There arises, however, the danger of personal bias.

The prohibition (against interpretation according to personal opinion cited at the outset) involves the following two reasons for its having been sent down: The first is that someone may have a (personal) opinion about something, and through his nature as well as his inclination he may harbor a bias toward it and then interpret the Quran accordingly in order thereby to find arguments to prove that his view is the correct one. Moreover, the meaning (which he links to his view) would not at all have appeared to him from the Quran if he did not have some preconceived opinion and bias. Sometimes this happens consciously, as perhaps in the case of those who use individual verses of the Quran as arguments in support of a heretical innovation and thus know that this is not in accordance with what is meant by the verse. They want rather to deceive their opponents. Sometimes, however, it (also) happens unconsciously. For instance, when a verse admits various meanings, a man inclines in his understanding to what best accords with his own opinion and inclination and thus interprets according to his "individual opinion." That is, it is a person's "individual opinion" which drives one to such an interpretation.

Finally, there is the question of the notorious ambiguity of the Arabic language.

The second reason is that someone may come to an interpretation of the Quran prematurely on the basis of the literal meaning of the Arabic, without the assistance of "hearing" (from earlier sources) and the Prophetic tradition on what is involved in the passages of the Quran which are difficult to understand, on the obscure and ambiguous expressions which are found in the Quran, and on the abbreviations, omissions, implications, anticipations and allusions which are contained in it. Whoever has not mastered the outer aspect of exegesis, but proceeds hastily to conclusions on the meaning (of the Quran) solely on the basis of his understanding of the Arabic language, he commits many errors and aligns himself thereby to the group of those who interpret the Quran according to individual opinion. Prophetic tradition and the "hearing" are indispensable for the outer aspects of exegesis, first of all in order to make one secure thereby against the opportunities for error, and also in order to extend the endeavor to understand and to reach conclusions. (Ghazali, *Revivification of the Sciences of Religion* 1.268)

39. Ghazali on the Sciences of Revelation

It is evident, then, from the differing opinions in the commentaries written on the subject—to say nothing of the received opinion that each verse of the Book "can be understood in sixty thousand ways"—that Muslims found a somewhat greater number of ambiguities in the Quran than the few classical instances cited by the exegetes. The whole range of learning that would eventually be brought to bear on elucidating them is illustrated in textbook fashion by Ghazali.

The praiseworthy sciences have roots, branches, preliminaries and completions. They [that is, the sciences of revelation] comprise, therefore, four kinds.

The "roots," of which there are (in this instance) four, constitute the first kind: (They are) the Book of God, the custom of the Prophet, the consensus of the (Muslim) community and the traditions concerning the Companions of the Prophet [that is, his contemporaries]. The consensus of the community is a "root" because it furnishes indications of the custom of the Prophet; as a "root" it is ranked third. The same is true of the traditions (of the Companions), which likewise provide indications of the custom of the Prophet. The Companions witnessed the inspiration and the sending down (of the Quran) and were able to comprehend much, through a combination of circumstances, which others were not able to observe. Sometimes the explicit statements (of revelation) do not contain something which can be observed through a combination of circumstances. For this reason the men of learning found it beneficial to follow the example of the Companions of the Prophet and to be guided by the traditions regarding them.

The "branches" constitute the second kind. This group deals with that which one comprehends on the basis of the "roots" mentioned above—and indeed cannot be gleaned from the external wording alone—through which the mind is awakened and understanding is thus expanded, so that one comprehends other meanings that are beyond the external wording. Thus one comprehends from the words of the Prophet, "the judge may not judge in anger," that he also would not judge when hungry, needing to urinate, or in the pains of sickness. The "branches" comprise two subtypes, the first of which deals with the requisites of the present world. This subtype is contained in the books of jurisprudence and is entrusted to the lawyers, who are thus the men of learning responsible for the present world. The second subtype deals with the requisites of the hereafter, thus the knowledge of the circumstances of the heart, its praiseworthy and blameworthy characteristics, that which is pleasing to God and that which is abhorrent to Him. . . .

The "preliminaries" constitute the third kind. They are the tools (of scriptural exegesis) such as lexicography and grammar, which are naturally one tool for gaining knowledge of the Book of God and the custom of His Prophet. In themselves lexicography and grammar do not belong to the sciences of revelation; however, one must become engrossed in them for the sake of revelation because the latter appears in the Arabic language. Since no revelation comes forth without language, the mastery of the language concerned becomes necessary as a tool. Among the tools of this kind belong also the skill of writing; however this is not unconditionally required since the Messenger of God was unlettered. If a man were able to retain in his memory everything he hears, then the skill of writing would become unnecessary. Yet, since people are not able to do this, in most cases the skill of writing is essential.

The "completions," that is, in relation to the study of the Quran, constitute the fourth kind. This groups contains the following divisions: (1) that which is connected with the external wording, such as the study of the (various) readings and of the phonetics; (2) that which is connected with the meaning of the contents, such as traditional exegesis, where one must also rely on tradition since the language alone does not yield the meaning; and (3), that which is connected with the "decisions" of the Quran, such as a knowledge of the abrogating and abrogated (verses), the general and the particular, the definite and the probable, as well as the kind and manner, in the same way that one makes one decision in relation to others.

It is already apparent from the listing of the "roots" above that the extra-Quranic traditions attributed to the Prophet rank directly after the Quran itself as part of

God's revelation. They too have their own proper sciences, as Ghazali now explains, and as we shall see in more detail in Chapter 3 below.

The "completions" relating to the traditions of the Prophet and the historical narratives consist of: (1) the study of the authorities, including their names and relationships, as well as the names and characteristics of the Companions of the Prophet; (2) the study of the reliability of the transmitters (of those traditions); (3) the study of the circumstances under which the transmitters lived, in order to be able to distinguish between those who are unreliable and those who are reliable; and (4) the study of the life spans of the transmitters, through which that which is transmitted with defective chains of authorities can be distinguished from that which exhibits unbroken chains. (Ghazali, *Revivification of the Sciences of Religion* 1.254)

40. Truth and Symbol

Thus far the diverse levels of meaning in Scripture flow from the inexhaustibility of God's wisdom. For some, however, there existed the possibility of deliberate conceal-ment on the part of the prophet, chiefly by reason of the inability of the masses for whom Scripture is intended to comprehend any more than mere symbols of the truths that lie beyond.

It is not necessary for the prophet to trouble their minds with any part of the knowledge of God, save that He is One, True and has no like; as for going beyond this doctrine, so as to charge them to believe in God's existence as not to be defined spatially or verbally divisible, as being neither outside the world nor within it, or anything of that sort—to do this would impose a great strain upon them and would confuse the reli-gious system which they already follow. . . . Not every man is ready to understand metaphysics [or theology], and in any case it would not be proper for any man to disclose that he is in possession of a truth which he conceals from the masses; indeed, he must not allow himself to hint at any such thing.

The prophet's duty is to teach men to know the majesty and might of God by means of symbols and parables drawn from things which they regard as mighty and majestic, imparting to them simply this much, that God has no equal, no like and no partner. Similarly he must establish in them a belief in an afterlife in a manner that comes within the range of their imagination and will be satisfying to their souls; he will liken the happiness and misery to be experienced there in terms which they can understand and conceive. As for the truth of these matters, he will only adumbrate it to them very briefly, saying that it is something which "eye has not seen nor ear heard." . . . God certainly knows the beneficent aspect of all this, and it is always right to take what God knows exactly for what it implies. There is therefore no harm in his discourse being interspersed with sundry hints and allusions, to attract those naturally qualified for speculation to undertake philosophical research into the nature of religious observances and their utility in terms of this world and the next. (Avicenna, *Book of Deliverance*) [AVICENNA 1951: 44–45]

This is not a program for exegesis, however. Unlike the masses, the philosopher has little need for the material figures of Scripture; indeed, he would be ill advised to elicit those naked truths so carefully and consciously hidden away from the simple believers.

It has been said that a condition the prophet must adhere to is that his words should be symbols and his expressions hints. Or as Plato states in the *Laws*: Whoever does not understand the apostle's symbols will not attain the Divine Kingdom. [No such sentiments are found in our versions of Plato's *Laws*.] Moreover, the foremost Greek philosophers and prophets made use in their books of symbols and signs in which they hid their secret doctrine, men like Pythagoras, Plato and Socrates. As for Plato, he blamed Aristotle for divulging wisdom and making knowledge manifest, so that Aristotle had to reply: "Even though I had done this, I have still left in my books many a pitfall which only the initiated among the wise and learned can understand." Moreover, how could the prophet Muhammad, may God's prayers and peace be upon him, bring knowledge to the uncouth nomad, not to say to the whole human race, considering that he was sent as a Messenger to all? Political guidance, on the other hand, comes easily to prophets; also the imposition of obligations on people. (Avicenna, *On the Proof of Prophecies* 124) [LERNER & MAHDI 1972: 116]

According to both Farabi and Avicenna, as we have seen in Chapter 1 above, the philosopher and the prophet are both privy to the same God-given truths, but the latter receives the additional responsibility of transmitting them in appropriate forms to the masses. These forms are the material figures and symbols that shadow the higher reality of Truth, as Farabi explains.

The principles of the beings, their ranks of order, happiness and the rulership of virtuous cities are either cognized and intellected by man or he imagines them. To cognize them is to have their essences, as they really are, imprinted on man's soul. To imagine them is to have imprinted on man's soul their images, representations of them, or matters that are imitations of them. . . . Most men, either by nature or by habit, are unable to comprehend and cognize these things; these are the men for whom one ought to represent the manner in which the principles of the beings, their ranks of order, the Active Intellect and the Supreme Rulership [that is, prophecy] exist through things which are imitations of them. Now while the meanings and essences of these things are one (among all nations) and immutable, the matters by which they are imitated are many and varied. Some imitate them more closely, while others do so only remotely.

There is an unmistakable conclusion that follows from this line of reasoning, and Farabi does not hesitate to draw it: the truths of philosophy are universal and unequivocal; those of religion are relative, culturally determined, and limited by the understanding of the recipients.

Therefore it is possible to imitate these things for each group and each nation using matters that are different in each case. Consequently, there may be a number of virtuous nations and virtuous cities whose religions are different, even though they all pursue the very same kind of happiness. For religion is but the impressions of these things, or the impressions of their images, imprinted on the soul. Because it is difficult for the multitude to comprehend these things themselves as they are, the attempt was made to teach them these things in other ways, which are the ways of imitation. Hence these things are imitated [or symbolized by the prophets] for each group or nation through the matters that are best known to them; and it may very well be that the best known to the one may not be the best known to the other.

Most men who strive for happiness follow after an imagined not a cognized form of happiness. Similarly, most men accept such principles as are accepted and followed, and are magnified and considered majestic, in the form of (material) images, not of cognitions. Now the ones who follow after happiness and they cognize it and accept the principles as they cognize them, these are the wise men [that is, the philosophers]. And the ones in whose souls such things are found in the form of (material) images, and who accept them and follow after them as such, these are the believers. (al-Farabi, *The Political Regime* 55–56) [LERNER & MAHDI 1972: 40–41]

41. Allegorical Interpretation as a Resolution of Apparent Contradictions

The Spanish philosopher Ibn Rushd, or Averroes (d. 1198 C.E.), begins his tract entitled The Decisive Treatise Determining the Nature of the Connection be-

tween Religion and Philosophy by demonstrating that the Quran not only permits but even commands the study of philosophy. Whatever the virtues of this exercise, the fact remained that for most Muslims there was a conflict between what they were told in the Book of God and what they read in the Greek and Muslim philosophers. It is to that point that Averroes then turns.

Now since this religion is true and summons to the study which leads to the knowledge of the Truth, we the Muslim community know definitively that demonstrative study [that is, philosophy] does not lead to (conclusions) conflicting with what Scripture has given us; for truth does not oppose truth but accords with it and bears witness to it.

This being so, whenever demonstrative study leads to any manner of knowledge about any being, that being is inevitably either unmentioned or mentioned in Scripture. If it is unmentioned, there is no contradiction, and it is the same case as an act whose category is unmentioned so that the (Muslim) lawyer has to infer it by reasoning from Scripture. If Scripture does speak about it, the apparent meaning of the words inevitably either accords or conflicts with the conclusions of (philosophical) demonstration about it. If this apparent meaning accords, there is no conflict. If it conflicts, there is a call for allegorical interpretation. The meaning of "allegorical interpretation" is: the extension of the significance of an expression from real to metaphorical significance, without forsaking therein the standard metaphorical practices of Arabic, such as calling a thing by the name of something resembling it or a cause or a consequence or accompaniment of it, or other such things as are enumerated in accounts of the kinds of metaphorical speech.

. . . Muslims are unanimous in holding that it is not obligatory either to take all the expressions of Scripture in their apparent [or external] meaning or to extend them all from the apparent meaning by means of allegorical interpretation. They disagree (only) over which of them should and which should not be so interpreted: the Ashʿarites [that is, certain dialectical theologians] for instance give an allegorical interpretation to the verse about God's directing Himself (Quran 2:29) and the Prophetic tradition about His descent (into this world), while the Hanbalites [that is, fundamentalist lawyers and traditionists] take them in their apparent meaning. . . .

It may be objected: There are some things in Scripture which the Muslims have unanimously agreed to take in their apparent meaning, others (which they have agreed) to interpret allegorically, and others about which they have disagreed; is it permissible, then, that demonstration should lead to interpreting allegorically what they [that is, the Muslims] have agreed to take in its apparent meaning, or to taking in its apparent meaning what they have agreed to interpret allegorically? We reply: If unanimous agreement is established by a method which is certain, such (a result) is not sound; but if (the existence of) agreement on those things is a matter of opinion, then it may be sound. This is why Abu Hamid (al-Ghazali) and Abu'l-Ma'ali (al-Juwayni) and other leaders of thought said that no one should be definitely called an unbeliever for violating unanimity on a point of interpretation in matters like these.

For Averroes, that unanimity which absolutely confines one to either a literal or an allegorical interpretation of a verse of Scripture is only rarely achieved, particularly under the stringent conditions he posits. The absence of consensus of course gives considerable latitude to the exegete.

That unanimity on theoretical matters is never determined with certainty, as it can be on practical [or behavioral] matters, may be shown to you by the fact that it is not possible for unanimity to be determined on any question at any period unless that period is strictly limited by us, and all the scholars existing in that period are known to us, that is, known as individuals and in their total number, and the doctrine of each one of them on the question has been handed down to us on unassailable authority. And in addition to all this, unless we are sure that the scholars existing at the time were in agreement that there is not both an apparent and an inner meaning in Scripture, that knowledge of any question ought not to be kept secret from anyone, and that there is only one way for people to understand Scripture. But it is recorded in tradition that many of the first believers used to hold that Scripture had both an apparent and an inner meaning, and that the inner meaning ought not to be learned by anyone who is not a man of learning in this field and who is incapable of understanding it. . . . So how can it possibly be conceived that a unanimous agreement can be handed down to us about a single theoretical question, when we know definitely that not a single period has been without scholars who held that there are things in Scripture whose true meaning should not be learned by all people? (Averroes, *The Decisive Treatise* 7–9)
[AVERROES 1961: 50–53]

3. Scripture and Tradition

Their possession of the Word of God in a written form—that is, a scriptural one—was but one of the shared traits of the "People of the Book." Side by side with those written texts there was another source of revelation, equally ancient, equally authentic, and equally authoritative in the lives of the believers—so authoritative, in fact, that a Jew would readily confirm that there existed not one but two Torahs.

1. "How Many Torahs Do You Have?"

Our Rabbis taught: It happened once that a certain non-Jew came to Shammai and said: "How many Torahs do you have?" He said, "Two: the written Torah and the Torah transmitted by mouth." "I believe you with respect to the Written, but not with respect to the Oral Torah; make me a proselyte on condition that you instruct me on the Written Torah (only)." But Shammai scolded him and repulsed him in anger. When the same man went to Hillel, the latter accepted him as a proselyte. On the first day he taught him his Alef, beth, gimmel, daleths; the following day he reversed their order. "But yesterday you didn't teach me thus," the man protested. "Must you then not trust me? Then trust me with respect to the Oral Torah too." (BT.Shabbat 31a)

2. What Moses Received on Sinai

God said to Moses: "Write these things, for it is by means of these things that I have made a covenant with Israel" (Exod. 34:27). When God was about to give the Torah, He recited it to Moses in proper order, namely, the Scriptures, Mishna, Haggada and Talmud, for God pronounced all these words: God revealed to Moses even the answers to questions which distinguished scholars are destined to ask their teachers in the future, for He said all these things. Then, when God had finished,

He said to Moses, "Go and teach it to My sons." ... Moses said, "Lord, You write it for them." God said, "I did indeed wish to give it all to them in writing, but it was revealed that the Gentiles would in the future have dominion over them, and will claim the Torah as theirs; then would my children be like the Gentiles. Therefore, give them the Scriptures in writing, and the Mishna, Haggada and Talmud orally, for it is they which separate Israel and the Gentiles." (*Tanhuma* 58b)

3. The Unwritten Law as the Distinctive Mark of Israel

In this passage from Tanhuma, *the Gentiles who "in the future will have dominion over them," that is, over the Children of Israel, and "will claim the Torah as theirs" are manifestly the Christians. As the Lord foretold, the same Christians who had expropriated the "Old Testament" for their own purposes refused to accept the oral law of the Mishna, Haggada, and Talmud, which thus became the distinctive marks of the true Israel.*

God gave the Israelites two Laws, the Written Law and the Oral Law. He gave them the Written Law with its 613 ordinances to fill them with commandments and to cause them to become virtuous, as it is said, "the Lord was pleased for His righteousness' sake to increase the Law and make it glorious." And He gave them the Oral Law to distinguish them from other nations. It was not given in writing so that the Gentiles might not falsify it, as they had with the Written Law, and say that they are the true Israel. Therefore it says, "If I were to write for him the many things of My Law, they would be counted as strange" (Hos. 8:12). The "many things" are the Mishna, which is larger than the Law. (*Numbers Rabbah* 14:10)

Rabbi Judah, son of Rabbi Shalom, remarked: Moses wanted the Oral Law to be written as well (as the Torah). But God foresaw that the Gentiles would one day translate the Torah and read it in Greek and say, "They [the Jews] are not (the true) Israel." So God said to Moses, "The Gentiles will say, 'We are (the true) Israel, we are the sons of God,' and Israel will say, 'We are the sons of God. And now the scales are evenly balanced.'" So God said to the Gentiles, "Why do you claim to be My sons? I know only him who has My mystery in his possession; he is My son." Then the Gentiles ask, "What is Your mystery?" God replied, "It is the Mishna." (*Pesikta Rabbati* 14b)

From his perspective long after both these passages had been composed, and long after most of the Jewish tradition had been committed to writing, Maimonides (d.

1204 C.E.) had very mixed reflections on this matter of writing or not writing things down.

Know that many sciences devoted to establishing the truth . . . that have existed in our religious community have perished because the length of time that has passed, because of our being dominated by the pagan nations, and because, as we have made clear, it is not permitted to divulge these matters to all people. For the only thing it is permitted to divulge to all people are the texts of the (scriptural) books. You already know that even jurisprudence was not put down in writing in olden times because of the precept, which is widely known to the nation: "Words that I have communicated to you orally you are not allowed to put down in writing" (BT.Gittin 60b). This precept shows extreme wisdom with regard to the Law, for it was meant to prevent what ultimately came about in this respect: I mean the multiplicity of opinions, the variety of schools, the confusions occurring in the expression of what is put down in writing, the negligence that accompanies what is written down, the divisions of the people, who are separated into sects, and the introduction of confusion with regard to actions. All these matters should be within the authority of the Great Court of Law, as we have explained in our juridical compilations [that is, the *Mishneh Torah*], and as the text of the Torah shows (Deut. 17:8–12).

Maimonides passes from legal matters to the question of esoteric learning, like the "Work of Creation" (see Chapter 2 above) and the "Work of the Chariot."

Now if there was insistence that jurisprudence should not, in view of the harm that would be caused by such a procedure, be perpetuated in a written compilation accessible to all people, all the more could none of the mysteries of the Torah be set down in writing and be made accessible to the people. On the contrary, they were transmitted by a few men belonging to the elite to a few of the same kind, as I explained to you from their saying: "The mysteries of the Torah may only be transmitted to a counselor, wise in crafts . . . " (BT.Hagigah 14a). This was the cause that necessitated the disappearance of those great roots (of knowledge) from the (Jewish) nation. You will not find anything of them except slight indications and pointers occurring in the Talmud and the commentaries on Scripture. These are a few kernels of grain, which are overlaid by many layers of husks, so that people were occupied with these layers of husks and thought that beneath them there was no kernel at all. (Maimonides, *Guide of the Perplexed* 1:71)

4. The Transmission of the Oral Law

If Moses received the entirety of the Law on Sinai, part in writing and part orally, how did the latter descend through many generations of Jews until it finally found written form in the Mishna of Rabbi Judah the Prince about 200 C.E.? Modern scholars offer different answers to that question, but the tradition itself supplies its own answer. Most of the Mishna is relentlessly legal in content, but one of its tractates, the Pirke Aboth, or "Sayings of the Fathers," is a collection of aphorisms. At its very beginning it presents the "chain" by which the Oral Law, here called simply "the Torah," passed from Moses to Rabbi Judah.

Moses received the Torah from Sinai and committed it to Joshua, and Joshua to the Elders, and the Elders to the Prophets, and the Prophets committed it to the men of the Great Assembly. They said three things: Be deliberate in judgment, raise many disciples and make a fence about the Law.

Simon the Just was of the remnants of the Great Assembly. He used to say: By three things is the world sustained: by the Torah, by the (Temple) service and by deeds of loving kindness.

Antigonos of Sokho received (the Torah) from Simon the Just. He used to say: Be not slaves that minister to the master for the sake of receiving a bounty, but be like slaves who minister to a master not for the sake of receiving a bounty; and let the fear of heaven be upon you.

Yosi ben Yoezer of Zeredah and Yosi ben Yohanan of Jerusalem received (the Torah) from them. Yosi ben Yoezer of Zeredah said: Let your house be a meeting place for the Sages and sit amidst the dust of their feet and drink in their words thirstily.

Yosi ben Yohanan of Jerusalem said: Let your house be opened wide and let the needy be members of your household; and talk not much with womankind. They said this of a man's own wife: how much more of his fellow's wife! Hence the Sages have said: He that talks much with womankind brings evil upon himself and neglects the study of the Law and at the last will inherit Gehenna. (M.Pirke Aboth 1:1–5)

The text continues through its list of rabbis, now given in "pairs," who received and transmitted "the Torah" from their predecessors: Joshua ben Perahiah and Nittai the Arbelite; Judah ben Tabbai and Simeon ben Shetah; Shemiah and Abtalion; Hillel and Shammai; Gamaliel and his son Simeon. Some of these scholars of the Law are known. The first of them, Simon the Just, lived about 200 B.C.E.; Simeon ben Shetah appears at the end of the Maccabean period, about 80 B.C.E.; and Hillel and Shammai were slightly older contemporaries of Jesus. This was merely the starting point of a great deal of discussion and speculation, but the tradition was maintained much as it had been enunciated in the Pirke Aboth. It is still present, though much filled out, in this classic presentation of the history of the Oral Law that stands at the beginning of Maimonides' Mishneh Torah.

All the precepts which Moses received on Sinai were given together with their interpretation, as it is said, "And I will give you the tablets of stone, and the law, and the commandment" (Exod. 24:12). The "law" here refers to the Written Law, while the "commandment," refers to its interpretation. God bade us to fulfill the Law in accordance with "the commandment." This commandment alludes to what is called the Oral Law. The whole of the Law was written by Moses our teacher before his death, in his own hand. He gave (a copy of) the scroll to each tribe and deposited one in the Ark for a testimony, as it is said, "Take this book of the law and put it by the side of the Ark of the Covenant of the Lord your God, that it may be there for a witness against you" (Deut. 31:26). "The commandment," which is the interpretation of the Law, he did not write down but gave orders concerning it to the Elders, to Joshua, and to the rest of Israel, as it is said, "All this which I command to you, that you shall do; you shall not add to nor diminish from it" (Deut. 4:2). For this reason it is called the Oral Law.

Though the Oral Law was not committed to writing, Moses taught it in its entirety in his court, to the seventy elders as well as to Eleazer, Phineas, and Joshua—all three of whom received it from Moses. To Joshua, his disciple, Moses delivered the Oral Law and charged him concerning it. So too Joshua, throughout his life, taught orally. Many elders received the Oral Law from Joshua. Eli received it from the elders and from Phineas. Samuel from Eli and his court. David from Samuel and his court. (Maimonides, *Mishneh Torah*, Introduction)

5. The Pharisees and the Oral Tradition

We have few means of verifying the earliest stages of either the Pirke Aboth's version of events or Maimonides' more extended narrative. Where the existence of an oral law, the "traditions of the fathers" as it is also called, comes into firmer focus is with the appearance on the scene of the Jewish party known as the Pharisees, present in Palestinian Judaism at least from the reign of the Hasmonean John Hyrcanus (134–104 B.C.E.). Josephus, who is our chief source for the events of the century immediately preceding and following the life of Jesus, pauses occasionally in his narrative to characterize the Pharisees, among whom he counted himself: "In my nineteenth year I began to govern my life by the rule of the Pharisees, a sect

having points of resemblance to that which the Greeks call the Stoic school"
(Life *12).*

The Pharisees had passed on to the people certain regulations handed down by former generations and not recorded in the Laws of Moses, for which reason they are rejected by the Sadducees, who hold that only those regulations should be considered valid which were written down (in Scripture), and those which were handed down by former generations need not be observed. . . . The Sadducees have the confidence of the wealthy alone but no following among the populace, while the Pharisees have the support of the masses. (Josephus, *Antiquities* 13.10.5–7)

In the course of both the Antiquities *and the* Jewish War, *Josephus cites examples of the Pharisees' piety and their determined dedication to the Law, written and oral, even in the face of grave consequences. This one occurs near the end of the lifetime of Herod, Israel's ruler from 37 to 4 B.C.E. The "unrivaled interpreters of the ancestral laws" may well be the Pharisees, though Josephus himself does not call them such in the text.*

Certain popular figures rose up against him [that is, Herod] for the following reason. Judas, the son of Saripheus, and Matthias, the son of Margalothus, were the most learned of the Jews and unrivaled interpreters of the ancestral laws, and men especially dear to the people because they educated the youth, for all those who made an effort to acquire virtue used to spend time with them day after day.

When these scholars learned that the king's illness could not be cured, they aroused the youth by telling them they should pull down all the works built by the king in violation of the Laws of their Fathers and so obtain from the Law the reward of their pious efforts. It was indeed because of his audacity in making these things in disregard of the Law's provisions, they said, that all those misfortunes, with which he had become familiar to a degree uncommon among mankind, had happened to him, in particular his illness.

Now Herod had set about doing certain things that were contrary to the Law, and for these he had been reproached by Judas and Matthias and their followers. For the king had erected over the great gate of the Temple, as a votive offering and at great cost, a great golden eagle, although the Law forbids those who propose to live in accordance with it to think of setting up images or to make dedications of (the likenesses of) any living things. So these scholars ordered their disciples to pull the eagle down, saying that even if there should be some danger of their being doomed to death, still to those about to die for the preservation and safeguarding of their fathers' way of life, the virtue acquired by them in death would be far more advantageous than the pleasure of living. (Josephus, *Antiquities* 17.6.2)

According to Josephus, the Pharisees were closely allied to the throne during the Hasmonean period until a falling-out with John Hyrcanus on the question of his legitimacy as High Priest (Antiquities 13.10.5–7). The Talmud tells of just such a falling-out over priestly legitimacy. Although the not very historically minded rabbis set it in the reign of Hyrcanus' successor, Alexander Janneus, the account is revealing of the later rabbinic attitude toward those frequently mentioned Perushim, or "Separatists," who are ostensibly and nominally the Pharisees. Clearly here, at least, they are the same "Sages" whom the rabbis identified as their spiritual predecessors. The point of departure for the incident that follows was a rumor that Janneus' mother had been an alien captive, a fact that would have rendered him disqualified for the High Priesthood:

Subsequently the charge (of illegitimacy) was investigated, but not sustained, and the Sages of Israel departed in anger. Then said Eleazer ben Po'irah to King Yannai: "O King Yannai, that is the law for even the humblest man in Israel, and you, a King and a High Priest, shall that be your law too?" "Then what shall I do?" (asked the king). "If you will take my advice, trample them down." "But (if I do,) what shall happen with the Torah?" "Behold it is rolled up and lying in the corner; whoever wishes to study it, let him go and study it." Said Rabbi Nahman ben Isaac: "Immediately a spirit of heresy was instilled in him, for he should have replied, 'That is well for the Written Torah, but what of the Oral Law?' "

Straightway the evil burst forth through Eleazer son of Po'irah, all the Sages of Israel were massacred, and the world was desolate until Simon ben Shetah came and restored the Torah to its pristine glory. (BT.Kiddushin 66a)

6. Jesus and the Pharisees on the Oral Law

Josephus, in addition to writing for a Gentile audience, was also generalizing on the subject of the Pharisaic party. The Gospels too may have been intended in part for Gentiles, but the discussions between Jesus and the Pharisees recorded in them are often quite specific and concrete about points of Jewish observance as embodied in the "ancient tradition" of the Oral Law.

Jesus was approached by a group of Pharisees and lawyers from Jerusalem with the question: "Why do your disciples break the ancient tradition? They do not wash their hands before meals." [Mark 7:3–4 adds by way of explanation: "For the Pharisees and the Jews in general never eat without washing their hands in obedience to an old established tradition; and on coming from the marketplace they never eat without first washing. And there are many other points on which they have a traditional rule to maintain, for example, washing of cups and jugs and copper bowls."] He answered them. "Why do you break God's commandment in the interest of your tradition? For God said, 'Honor your father and your mother,' and 'The man who curses his father and his mother must suffer death.' But you say, 'If a man says to his father or his mother, "Anything of mine which might have been used for your benefit is set apart for God," then he must not honor his father and his mother.' You have made God's law null and void out of respect for your tradition. What hypocrisy! Isaiah was right when he prophesied about you: 'This people pays me lip service but their heart is far from me; their worship of me is in vain, for they teach as doctrines the commandments of men.' "

He called the crowd and said to them, "Listen to me and understand this: a man is defiled not by what goes into his mouth, but by what comes out of it."

Then the disciples came to him and said, "Do you know that the Pharisees have taken great offense at what you have been saying?" His answer was: "Any plant that is not of my heavenly Father's planting will be rooted up. Leave them alone; they are blind guides, and if one blind man guides another, both will fall into a ditch." (Matthew 15:1–14)

On the issue of washing the hands, a number of the Pharisees' enactments are embodied in both the Mishna and the Talmud. Indeed, an entire tract of the Mishna, "Hands" (Yadaim), is given over to the subject, a section of which we have seen in Chapter 1 above in connection with the sanctity of canonical Scripture.

The hands are susceptible to uncleanness, and they are rendered clean (by pouring water over them) up to the wrist. Thus, if a man poured the first water up to the wrist, and the second water above the wrist, and the water flowed back to the hand, the hand becomes clean; but if he poured both the first water and the second water above the wrist, and the water flowed back on the hand, the hand remains unclean. . . .

If there is a doubt whether an act of work was done with the water or not, or whether it was with the prescribed quantity or not, or whether it was unclean or clean, its condition of doubt is deemed clean, for they have said: If there is doubt about the hands, whether they have contracted uncleanness or have conveyed uncleanness or have become clean, they are deemed clean. . . . (M. Yadaim 2:3–4)

7. A History of the Tradition

We are given another extended version of the transmission of the Oral Law in The Khazar King, *written by Judah Halevi ca. 1130–1140 C.E.*

Prophecy lasted about forty years during the Second Temple among those elders who had the assistance of the Shekina [that is, the spirit of God] from the First Temple. Individually acquired prophecy had ceased with the removal of the Shekina (at the destruction of the First Temple) and appeared only in extraordinary times or on account of great force, as that of Abraham, Moses, the expected Messiah, Elijah and their equals. In them the Shekina found a worthy abode, and their very existence helped their contemporaries to gain the degree of prophecy. The people, after their return (from exile), still had Haggai, Zechariah, Ezra and others.

Forty years later these prophets were succeeded by an assembly of Sages, called men of the Great Assembly. They were too numerous to be counted. They had returned with Zerubbabel and inherited their tradition from the prophets, as it is said: "The prophets handed down the Law to the Men of the Great Assembly" (M.Pirke Aboth 1:1).

The next generation was that of the High Priest Simon the Just and his disciples and friends. He was followed by Antigonos of Sokho of great fame. His disciples were Zadok and Boethus, who were the originators of the sects called after them Sadduceans and Boethusans. The next was Yosi ben Yoezer, "the most pious among priests," and Joseph ben Yohanan and their friends. . . . Rabbi Yosi was followed by Joshua ben Porahyah, whose history is known. *Among his disciples was Jesus the Nazarene*, and Nittai of Arbela was his contemporary. After him came Judah ben Tabbai and Simon ben Shetah, with the friends of both. At this period arose the doctrine of the Karaites [see below] in consequence of an incident between the Sages and King (Alexander) Janneus, who was a priest. . . .

The next generation was that of Shemayah and Abtalion, whose disciples were Hillel and Shammai. Hillel was famous for his learning and his gentleness. He was a descendant of David and lived one hundred and twenty years. He had thousands of disciples. . . . The greatest of them was Jonathan ben Uzziel and the least of them was Yohanan ben Zakkai, who left unstudied no verse in the Bible, nor Mishna, Talmud, Haggada, explanatory rules of the Sages and Scribes, nor any word of the law code. Rabbi Yohanan lived a hundred and twenty years like his master and saw the Second Temple.

We have now reached the generation of rabbis in the era of the Temple destruction in 70 C.E. With them begin the attributions, all of them spurious, of written treatises and, notably, the earliest mystical works.

Among his [that is, Yohanan ben Zakkai] disciples was Rabbi Eliezer ben Hyrcanus, the author of the "Chapters of Rabbi Eliezer," a famous work on astronomy, calculation of the spheres and earth and other profound astronomical subjects. His pupil was Rabbi Ishmael ben Elisha, the High Priest. He is the author of works entitled "Hekhaloth," "Hakharath Panim" and the "Science of the Chariot" because he was initiated in the secrets of this science (of mysticism), being worthy of a degree near prophecy.... Another pupil of his was the famous Rabbi Joshua, the same embroiled in the famous affair with Rabbi Gamaliel; further Rabbi Yosi and Rabbi Eleazer ban Arakh.

Besides these famous men and many Sages, priests and Levites whose calling was the study of the Law, there flourished undisturbed in the same period the seventy learned members of the Sanhedrin on whose authority officials were appointed or deposed.... In the next generation after the destruction of the Temple, there lived Rabbi Akiba and Rabbi Tarfon and Rabbi Yosi of Galilee with their friends.... In the next generation lived Rabbi Meir, Rabbi Judah, Rabbi Simon ben Azzai and Rabbi Hananiah ben Teradion and their friends. They were followed by "Rabbi," that is, Rabbi Judah the Prince, our teacher. His contemporaries were Rabbi Nathan, Rabbi Joshua ben Korah, and many others who were the last teachers of the Mishna, also called *Tannaim*. They were followed by the *Amoraim*, who are the authorities of the Talmud.

The Mishna was compiled in the year 530 of the era of the Documents [that is, of the Seleucid era, which began in 312 B.C.E.], which corresponds to the 120th year after the destruction of the (Second) Temple (in 70 C.E.), and 530 years after the termination of prophecy. (Judah Halevi, *The Khazar King* 3.65–67) [HALEVI 1905: 186–191]

8. The Mishna

Thus the Oral Law passed in an unbroken chain from Moses down to the generation of Rabbi Judah, "the Prince," who about 200 C.E. collected and arranged it, and for the first time committed it to writing as the Mishna. Maimonides describes the process of its composition.

Rabbi Judah, our sainted teacher, compiled the Mishna. From the time of Moses to that of our sainted teacher, there had been composed no work from which the Oral Law was publicly taught. Rather, in each generation, the head of the then existing court or the prophet of that era wrote down for his private use an aide-mémoire of the traditions he had heard from his teachers, and which he taught orally in public. In like manner students too transcribed, each according to his ability, the exposition of the Torah and its laws as he heard them, as well as whatever new matter evolved in each generation, material which had not been handed down by tradition but had been deduced by application of the thirteen hermeneutical rules and had been adopted by the Supreme Court. This was the usage current until the time of (Rabbi Judah) our teacher, the saint.

Rabbi Judah gathered together all the traditions, enactments, interpretations, and expositions for every portion of the Torah, material that had either come down from Moses our teacher or had been deduced by the courts in successive generations. All this material was redacted in the Mishna, which was diligently taught in public, and so became generally known among the Jewish people. Copies of it were made and widely disseminated, so that the Oral Law might not be forgotten in Israel.

Why did our saintly teacher behave so rather than leaving matters as they were before? Because he noticed that the number of students was diminishing, fresh disasters were continually occurring, the wicked government was constantly extending its domain and increasing its power, and Israelites were wandering and emigrating to distant countries. So he composed a work to serve as a handbook for all, the contents of which could be studied quickly and not forgotten. Throughout his life, Rabbi Judah and his colleagues busied themselves in giving public instruction in the Mishna. (Maimonides, *Mishneh Torah*, introduction)

How little a "handbook" the Mishna of Rabbi Judah actually is may be seen from its opening. The first division is called "Seeds," and the first tractate, Berakoth or "Blessings," begins thus.

From what time in the evening may the (prayer called) "O hear" be recited? From the time when the priests enter (the Temple) to eat their grain offerings until the end of the first watch. So Rabbi Eliezer. But the Sages say: Until midnight. Rabban Gamaliel says: Until the rise of dawn. His sons once returned after (after midnight) from a wedding feast. They said to him: "We have not recited the 'O hear.'" He said to them: "If the dawn has not risen, you are still bound to recite it. Moreover, wherever the Sages prescribe 'Until midnight' the duty of fulfillment lasts until the rise of dawn." The duty of burning the fat pieces and members (of the animal offerings) lasts until the rise of dawn; and for all that must be consumed "the same day," the duty lasts till the rise of dawn. Why then have the Sages said "Until midnight"? To keep a man far from transgression. (M.Berakoth 1:1)

9. The Talmud

We resume the thread of Maimonides' historical narrative in the introduction of his Mishneh Torah.

All the Sages . . . were the great men of each successive generation, some of them were heads of schools, some Exilarchs, and some were members of the Great Sanhedrin; besides them are thousands and tens of thousands of disciples and fellow students. Ravina and Rav Ashi closed the list of the Sages of the Talmud. It was Rav Ashi who compiled the Babylonian Talmud in the land of Shinar [Babylon, that is, modern Iraq] about a century after Rabbi Yohanan had compiled the Palestinian Talmud. These two Talmuds contain an exposition of the text of the Mishna and an explanation of its obscurities and whatever new subject matter had been added by the various courts from the day of (Rabbi Judah) our saintly teacher, the saint, until the compilation of the Talmud. (Maimonides, *Mishneh Torah*, introduction)

The Talmuds, then, are expositions and a "completion" (gemara) of the Mishna, one done by the rabbis in "Babylonia," that is, Iraq, and the other by their counterparts in Galilee, and finished between 500 and 600 C.E. To illustrate, there follows the text of the Babylonian Talmud elucidating the subject matter of the Mishnaic passage (M.Berakoth 1:1) cited above.

On what does the Mishna authority base himself that he begins: "From what time?" Furthermore, why does he deal with the evening "O hear"? Let him begin with the morning one. The Mishna authority bases himself on the Scripture, where it is written, "(And you shall recite them) . . . when you lie down and when you rise up" (Deut. 6:7), and he states thus: When does the time of the recital of the "O hear" of lying down begin? When the priests enter to eat their grain offerings. And if you like, I can answer: He learns (the priority of evening) from the account of the creation of the world, where it is written, "And there was evening and there was morning, one day" (Gen 1:5). . . .

The Master said: "From the time that the priests enter to eat their grain offerings." When do the priests eat grain offerings? From the time of the appearance of the stars. Let him then say: "From the time of the appearance of the stars." This very thing he wants to teach us, in passing, that the priest may eat the grain offerings from the time of the appearance of the stars. And he also wants to teach us that the expiatory offering is not indispensable, as has been taught: "And when the sun sets, we are clean," the setting of the sun is indispensable (as a condition of purification) to eat the grain offering, but the expiatory offering is not indispensable to enable him to eat the grain offerings. But how do we know that these words "and the sun sets" mean the setting of the sun, and this "we are clean" means that the day clears away? It means perhaps: And when the sun (of the next morning) appears, and "we are clean" means that the man becomes clean. Rabbah, the son of Rabbi Shilah explains: In that case the text would have to read "he becomes clean." What is the meaning of "we are clean"? The day clears away, conformably to the common expression. The sun has set and the day has cleared away. This explanation of Rabbah son of Rabbi Shilah is unknown in the West [that is, in the Palestinian schools], and they raised the question. . . .

The Master said: "From the time that the priests enter to eat the grain offerings." They pointed to a contradiction. From what time may one recite the "O hear" in the evening? From the time the poor man comes home to eat his bread with salt till he rises from his meal. The last clause certainly contradicts the Mishna. Does the first clause also contradict the Mishna? No, the poor man and the priest have the same time.

They pointed to (another) contradiction: From what time may one begin to recite the "O hear" in the evening? From the time the people come home to eat their meal on a Sabbath eve. These are the words of Rabbi Meir. But the Sages say: From the time that the priests are entitled to eat their grain offering. A sign for the matter is the appearance of the stars. And though there is no real proof of it [that is, that the day ends with the appearance of the stars], there is a hint for it. For it is written: "So we continued in the work, half the men holding the spears, from daybreak until the stars came out" (Neh. 4:21). And it says further, "to act as a guard for us at night and as a working party by day" (Neh. 4:22). Why this second citation? If you object and say that the night really begins with the setting of the sun, but that they (the guards) stayed late and came early, (I shall reply): Come and hear the other verse: "To act as a guard for us at night and a working party by day."

Now it is assumed that the "poor man" and "the people" (of these citations) have the same time for their evening meal. And if say that the poor man and the priest also have the same time, then the Sages would be saying the same thing as Rabbi Meir? Hence you must conclude that the "poor man" and the priest have the same time, but the "poor man" and "the people" do not have the same for their evening meal.

But do the priest and the "poor man" really have the same time for supper? They pointed to a contradiction: From what time may one begin to recite the "O hear"? From the time that the Sabbath day becomes hallowed on the Sabbath eve. These are the words of Rabbi Eliezer. Rabbi Joshua says: From the time the priests are ritually clean to eat their grain offering. Rabbi Meir says: From the time the priests take their ritual bath in order to eat their grain offerings. Said Rabbi Judah to him: When the priests take their ritual bath it is still daytime! . . . The objection of Rabbi Judah to Rabbi Meir, was it well founded? Rabbi Meir may reply as follows: Do you think I am referring to the twilight as defined by you? I am referring to the twilight as defined by Rabbi Yosi. For Rabbi Yosi says: The twilight is the twinkling of an eye. The one enters and the other departs and one cannot exactly fix it (that is, the precise point between day and night). . . .

"Until the end of the first watch": . . . Rabbi Isaac ben Samuel says in the name of Rab: The night has three watches, and at each watch the Holy One, blessed be He, sits and roars like a lion and says: Woe to the children, on account of whose sins I destroyed My House and burnt My Temple and exiled them among the nations of the world.

It is worth recalling that when these discussions were recorded it had been many years since there had been a Temple, a functioning priesthood, or sacrifice in ruined Jerusalem, as we are now suddenly and innocently reminded.

It has been taught: Rabbi Yosi says, I was once traveling on the road, and I entered into one of the ruins of Jerusalem to pray. Elijah of blessed memory appeared and waited for me at the door until I finished my prayer. After I finished my prayer, he said to me: Peace be upon you, my master! And I replied, Peace be with you, my master and teacher! And he said to me, My son, why did you go into this ruin? I replied, To pray. He said to me, You ought to have prayed on the road. I said, I feared lest passersby might interrupt me. He said to me, (In that case) you should have said an abbreviated prayer. Thus I learned from him three things: One must not go into a ruin; one may say a prayer on the road; and if one does say his prayer on the road, he recites an abbreviated prayer.

He [Elijah] further said to me: My son, what sound did you hear in this ruin? I replied, I heard a divine voice, cooing like a dove and saying: Woe to the children on account of whose sins I destroyed My House and burnt My Temple and exiled them among the nations of the world! And he said to me: By your life and by your head! Not in this moment alone does this voice so exclaim, but thrice each day does it exclaim thus! And more than that, whenever the Israelites go into synagogues and school-houses and respond, "May His great name be blessed," the Holy One, blessed be He, shakes His head and says: Happy is the king who is thus praised in his house! Woe to the father who had to banish his children, and woe to the children who had to be banished from the table of their father!

Our Rabbis taught: There are three reasons why one must not go into a ruin. (BT.Berakoth 2a–3a)

And more, much more.

10. Safeguarding the Torah

Among those whom the Mishna (M.Sanhedrin 10:1) says will have no share in the afterlife is "he who maintains that the Torah is not divinely revealed." But there is more in the imprecation than what appears at first glance, as the rabbinical discussion of the passage in the Babylonian Talmud reveals. Once the operative scriptural verse has been identified, in this case Numbers 15:31, we can see its application extended beyond the question of revelation to the integrity of the text of the Torah, and finally to the Oral Law and its interpretation.

Our Rabbis taught (regarding the verse) "Because he has despised the word of the Lord, and has broken His commandments, that soul is and will be cut off" (Num. 15:31) that the phrase "despised the word of the Lord" refers to he who maintains that Torah is not from heaven. Another interpretation refers it to an Epikoros; another to one who gives an interpretation of the Torah (not in accordance with the legal prescriptions). "And has broken His commandments": this means one who abolishes the covenant of the flesh [that is, circumcision]. "That soul is and will be cut off": the first "is cut off" implies in this world; the second, "will be cut off," in the next. Hence Rabbi Eliezer of Modin taught: He who defiles the sacred food, despises the festivals, abolishes the covenant of our father Abraham, gives an interpretation of the Torah not in accordance with the legal prescriptions and publicly shames his neighbor, even if he has learning and good deeds to his credit, has no share in the future world.

Another earlier opinion taught: "Because he has despised the word of the Lord," this refers to him who maintains that the Torah is not from heaven. And even if he asserts that the whole Torah is from heaven, excepting a particular verse, which he maintains was not uttered by God but by Moses himself, he too is included in the reference. And even if he admits that the whole Torah is from heaven, excepting a single point, deduction a minori ad majus or inference by analogy [that is, two of the rules of rabbinic exegesis], he is still included in "because he has despised the word of the Lord."

It has been taught: Rabbi Meir used to say: He who studies the Torah but does not teach it is alluded to in "he has despised the word of the Lord." Rabbi Nathan said: It refers to whoever pays no heed to the Mishna. Rabbi Nehorai said: Whoever can engage in the study of the Torah and fails to do so. (BT.Sanhedrin 99a–b)

11. God Is Overruled by a Majority of the Rabbis

The following is only an anecdote, albeit a celebrated one, from the Babylonian Talmud. It reveals something of the complex relationship between the Torah and the Oral Law, God's own words and the rabbis' interpretation of them. The context is a debate concerning whether a certain kind of oven was subject to ritual impurity. A majority of the scholars said it was; Rabbi Eliezer ben Hyrkanos insisted it was not.

On that day Rabbi Eliezer brought forward all the arguments in the world, but they were not accepted. He said to them, "If my ruling is correct, let this carob tree prove it." Thereupon the carob tree was up-rooted (and moved) a hundred cubits from its place, some even say four hundred cubits. The other Sages replied, "No proof may be adduced from a carob tree." Then he said, "If my ruling is correct, let this stream of water prove it." Whereupon the stream of water flowed backward. They replied, "No proof may be adduced from a stream of water." Then he said, "If my ruling is correct, let the walls of the yeshiva prove it." Whereupon the walls of the yeshiva began to totter. But Rabbi Joshua rebuked the walls and said, "When scholars are engaged in legal dispute, what concern is it of yours?" Thus the walls did not topple, in honor of Rabbi Joshua, but neither did they return to their upright position, in honor of Rabbi Eliezer, and to this day they stand inclined. Then he said, "If my ruling is correct, let it be proved from heaven." Whereupon a heavenly voice was heard saying, "Why do you dispute with Rabbi Elie-zer? His rulings are always correct." But Rabbi Joshua said, "It is not in heaven" (Deut. 30:12). What did he mean by that? Rabbi Jeremiah re-plied, "The Torah has already been given at Mount Sinai [and thus is no longer in heaven]. We pay no heed to any heavenly voice, because already on Mount Sinai You wrote in the Torah 'One must incline after the majority' (Exod. 23:2)."

Rabbi Nathan (later) met the prophet Elijah and asked him: "What did the Holy One, blessed be He, do at that moment?" He replied, "God smiled and said, 'My children have defeated Me, My children have defeated Me.' " (BT.Baba Metzia 59b)

12. Codifying the Oral Law

By the beginning of the Middle Ages there was a daunting body of comment and homily on the Oral Torah, much of it legal in nature. Since this was, in the eyes of observant Jews, as binding as the Torah prescriptions themselves, some order had to be put into it, a task that Maimonides proposed to himself sometime about 1177.

I, Moses, son of Maimon the Sefardi, relying on the help of God, blessed be He, resolved myself intently to study all these works, with a view toward assembling the results obtained from them on the question of what is forbidden or permitted, clean or unclean, and the other rules of the Torah—all in plain language and terse style, so that thus the entire Oral Law might become systematically known to all. I would not cite difficulties and solutions or different points of view, one person saying so and another something else, but restrict myself to clear and reasonable statements in accordance with the conclusions drawn from all these compilations and commentaries that have appeared from the time of our Holy Master [that is, Rabbi Judah the Prince] down to the present time, so that all the rules shall be accessible to young and old, whether these pertain to the (scriptural) laws or to the ordinances established by the Sages and prophets, so that there would be no need for any other work to ascertain any of the laws of Israel, but that this work might serve as a compendium of the entire Oral Law, including the ordinances, customs and decrees instituted from the days of our teacher Moses till the compilation of the Talmud, as expounded for us by the Geonim in all the works composed by them since the completion of the Talmud. Hence I have called my work *Mishneh Torah* [that is, "Repetition of the Law"], for the reason that a person who first reads the Written Law and then this compilation will know from it the whole of the Oral Law, without having to consult in the meantime any other book.

I have decided to arrange this compendium in large divisions of the laws according to their various topics. These divisions are distributed in chapters according to subject matter. Each chapter is then subdivided into smaller sections so that they may be systematically memorized. Among the laws on the various topics, some consist of rules in connection with a single biblical precept. This would be the case when such a precept is rich in traditional matter and forms a single topic. Other sections include rules referring to several precepts when these all belong to one topic. For the work follows the order of topics and is not planned according to the number of precepts, as will be explained to the reader.

The total number of precepts that are obligatory for all generations is 613. Of these, 248 are positive, their mnemonic is the number of bones in the body; 365 are negative, and their mnemonic is the number of days in the solar year. (Maimonides, *Mishneh Torah*, introduction)

The result was the Mishneh Torah. *Although most later Jews found it impressive indeed, not all of Maimonides' contemporaries were equally moved. Maimonides was constrained to write to one critic, a judge in Alexandria, and explain his work.*

You should know that every author of a book—whether it deals with the laws of the Torah or with other kinds of wisdom, whether it was composed by one of the ancient wise men among the nations of the world or by physicians—always adopts one of two ways [that is, structures or styles]: either that of the monolithic code or that of the discursive commentary. In a monolithic code, only the correct subject matter is recorded, without any questions, without any answers and without any proofs, in the way which Rabbi Judah adopted when he composed the Mishna. The discursive commentary, in contrast, records both the correct subject matter and other opinions which contradict it, as well as questions on it in all its aspects, answers and proofs as to why one opinion is true and another false, or why one opinion is proper and another improper; this method, in turn, is that of the Talmud, which is a discursive commentary upon the Mishna. Moreover, if someone should object to my distinction between the code and the commentary, and claim that because the names of the Rabbis are cited in the Mishna—as when one Rabbi holds one opinion about a law and another Rabbi holds a contradictory one—this kind of citation of names constitutes proof, it is necessary for me to point out that this is not a proof; a proof explains why one Rabbi holds a certain opinion, while another Rabbi might hold a contradictory one.

You should also understand that if I have caused the names of any Tannaim to be forgotten by recording the correct legal prescription without qualification and anonymously, I have only followed the style of Rabbi

Judah here. He too did this before me, for every legal prescription which he recorded without qualification and anonymously was originated by other scholars, yet even those other Rabbis had not originated the legal prescriptions themselves but had received them from still others, and these others from still others, all the way back to Moses our teacher. And just as the Tannaim and Amoraim did not bother to record the names of all sages from the time of Moses to their own day, because then there would be no end to the citations of names, so I also have not bothered to cite their names. . . .

. . . For this reason I also described in my introduction [to the *Mishneh Torah*] the transmission of the law from one High Court and its chief judge to the succeeding High Court and its chief judge, in order to prove that the tradition of the law did not consist in the traditions of individuals but of the traditions of multitudes. And for this same reason my endeavor and purpose in composing my work was that every ruling (*halakha*) should be cited unqualifiedly [or anonymously], even if in fact it is the opinion of an individual, but it should not be reported in the name of So-and-So. This would destroy the position of the heretics (*minim*) who rejected the entire Oral Law because they saw it transmitted in the name of So-and-So and imagined that this law had never been formulated before, so that the individual had originated it on his own. (Maimonides, *Letter to R. Phineas ben Meshullam*) [TWERSKY 1980: 33–35]

13. The Debate on the Oral Law

Neither before nor after the redaction of the Mishna did all Jews accept the principle of a divinely revealed, continuously transmitted, and authoritative Oral Law. The debate appears to have begun in Maccabean times, possibly when the thesis of the Oral Law began to be advanced in its most rigorous form. For that reason, perhaps, the Mishna had to insist so strongly not merely on the authority but even on the priority of the Oral Law.

Greater stringency applies to the observance of the words of the Scribes than to (the observance of) the words of the (written) Law. If a man said, "There is no obligation to wear phylacteries," so that he transgresses the words of the Law, he is not culpable; (but if he said), "There should be in them [that is, the phylacteries] five partitions," so that he adds to the words of the Scribes, he is culpable. (M.Sanhedrin 11:3)

The dispute is also recorded, now more openly, by Maimonides, though without much sympathy for the opponents or their motives. He is commenting on Mishna

Pirke Aboth 1:3, already quoted above, where the name Antigonos of Sokho occurs.

This sage [Antigonos] has two disciples, one named Zadok and the other Boethus. When they heard him deliver this statement, "Be not like servants etc.," they departed from him. The one said to his colleague, "Behold, the master expressly stated that man has neither reward nor punishment nor is there any expectation at all." (They said this) because they did not understand his intention. The one lent support to his colleague and they departed from the community and forsook the Torah.

A sect banded around one, and another sect around his colleague. The sages termed them "Sadducees and Boethusans." Since they were unable to consolidate the masses according to what they perceived on the faith—for this evil belief divided the consolidated; it certainly did not consolidate the divided—they feigned belief in the matter of the Written Torah because they could not falsify it before the multitude. For had they brought forth their disbelief in the words of the Torah from their own mouths, they [that is, the people] would have killed them. Therefore each said to his party that he believes in the (written) Torah but disputes the (oral) tradition since it is not authentic. They said this in order to exempt themselves from the precepts of the tradition and the decrees and ordinances inasmuch as they could not thrust everything aside, both the written (Torah) and the tradition. Moreover, the path of interpretation was thus broadened for them. Since the interpretation became a matter of their choice, each, according to his intention, could be lenient in what he might wish and stringent in what he might wish. This was possible because he did not believe at all in the fundamental principle. They, however, sought to deceive in matters which were accepted only by some people.

From the time that these evil sects went forth, they have been termed "Karaites" in these lands, meaning to say, Egypt. However, their appellation according to the sages is "Sadducees and Boethusans." They are the ones who began to contest and to interpret all the passages (of the Torah) according to what appeared to them, without at all hearkening to a sage; the reverse of what the One to be blessed stated, ". . . according to the Torah which they shall instruct you and according to the judgment which they shall tell you, you shall do; you shall not turn aside either to the right or to the left from the sentence which they shall declare to you" (Deut. 17:11). (Maimonides, *Commentary on the Mishna*, Aboth 1:3)
[MAIMONIDES 1968]

14. A Jewish Schism over the Oral Tradition

The dispute between the Sadducees and Boethusans on the one side and the Pharisees on the other had long been settled by the time Maimonides was writing at the end of the twelfth century. The history of the controversy was still of interest in Jewish circles, however, because the two points of view in support of and in opposition to the Oral Law were still being sustained. The rabbinic successors to the Pharisees remained faithful to that Law, as their writings from Mishna to Midrash all testify, while the attack upon the oral tradition was mounted from the eighth century onward by a group that called themselves Karaites or "Partisans of Scripture." This is how one Karaite of the early tenth century, Jacob al-Qirqisani, covered the same historical ground as Mishna Pirke Aboth had in the third century and Maimonides would in the late twelfth. Qirqisani takes as given the identification of the Pharisees with the rabbis of his own and an earlier time—the latter, like the former, here qualified as "Rabbanites."

After the Samaritans there appeared the Chiefs of the Community [that is, the men of the Great Assembly], who are the original Rabbanites; this was in the days of the Second Temple. The first of them to be recorded was Simeon, whom they call Simeon the Righteous; they say that he was one of the remaining members of the Great Synagogue. These latter, they say, lived in the days of Ezra and Nehemiah. The Rabbanites [that is, the Pharisees] acknowledged the authority of the Chiefs of the Community solely because they followed the practices and indulgences inherited from Jereboam. In particular they [the Rabbanites] sustained and confirmed these practices, supplied them with argumentative proofs, and wrote down the interpretation of them in the Mishna and in other works. At times one or another of them did set forth the true meaning of a biblical ordinance, but they [the Rabbanites] invariably banished him and sought to do him injury, as was, for example, the case of Gamaliel, who fixed the date of holy days on the basis of the appearance of the new moon, or of Eliezer the son of Hyrkanos, who disagreed with them on the matter of uncleanness of vessels, the construction of which had not been completed; they excommunicated him and kept away from him, despite miraculous proofs of the truth of his opinion. . . .

After the Rabbanites there appeared the Sadducees founded by Zadok and Boethus, who were, according to the Rabbanites, disciples of Antigonos (of Sokho), a successor of Simeon the Righteous and had thus received their learning from the latter. Zadok was the first to expose the errors of the Rabbanites. He openly disagreed with them and he discovered part of the truth; he also composed a book in which he reproved and attacked them. However, he produced no proof of anything that he claimed but merely set it forth in the manner of an assertion.

Jesus too is brought into the lists against the Rabbanites.

Next there appeared Yeshuʿa [that is, Jesus], who the Rabbanites say was the son of Pandera; he is known as Jesus the son of Mary. He lived in the days of Joshua, the son of Perahiah, who is said to have been the maternal uncle of Jesus. This took place in the reign of Augustus Caesar, the emperor of Rome, that is, in the time of the Second Temple. The Rabbanites plotted against Jesus until they put him to death by crucifixion.

Later Qirqisani reaches Islamic times and the beginning of the Karaite movement under Anan ben David.

There appeared Anan (ben David), who is styled the Chief of the Dispersion; this occurred in the days of the Caliph Abu Jaʿfar al-Mansur [754–775 C.E.]. He [Anan] was the first to make clear a great deal of the truth about the divine ordinances. He was learned in the lore of the Rabbanites, and not one of them could gainsay his erudition. It is reported that Hay, the president of the Rabbanite assembly, together with his father, translated the book of Anan from the Aramaic into Hebrew and found nothing in it for which they could not discover the source in Rabbanite lore, excepting his view concerning the firstborn and the difference between a firstling conceived while its mother was owned by a Gentile. . . . The Rabbanites tried their utmost to assassinate Anan, but God prevented them from doing so. (Qirqisani, *Book of Lights*)

[NEMOY 1952: 49–52]

15. Saadya on Scripture and Tradition

The Karaite center was in Iraq, where they took up the weapons of learning and polemic against the "Rabbanites" across a broad front. The principal champion of these latter was Saadya (d. 942 C.E.), the learned Egyptian scholar of Scripture and philosophy who had become Gaon, or head, of the chief rabbinic academy in Iraq. Saadya wrote a number of tracts against the Karaites, who returned the compliment for centuries afterward. Here, in his summa in Arabic entitled The Book of Doctrines and Beliefs, *he outlines his position on the two traditions of the Written and the Oral Law and offers his own utilitarian defense of the latter.*

I will now explain the character of the Holy Scriptures. I declare that God included in His Book a brief record of all that happened in past times in the form of narratives intended to instruct us in the right way of obedience toward him. He further included His laws, and added promises of reward for their obedience. Thus Scripture became a source of everlasting benefit. For all the books of the prophets and the learned books of all nations, numerous though they are, comprise only three principal elements: (1) a list of commandments and prohibitions, which forms one point; (2) the reward and punishment which are the fruits of the former; and (3) an account of those who rendered good service to their country and prospered, as well as those who dealt corruptly and perished. For the instruction necessary for a good life is complete only if these three elements are combined. . . .

I say further that the Wise, may He be exalted and glorified, knew that His laws and the stories of His wondrous signs would, through the passage of time, require people to hand them down to posterity, so that they might become as evident to later generations as they were to the earlier ones. Therefore, He prepared in our minds a place for the acceptance of reliable tradition, and in our souls a quiet corner for trusting it so that His Scriptures and stories should remain safely with us.

I deem it proper to mention a few points in regard to the truth of tradition. Unless men had the confidence that there exists in the world such a thing as a true report, no man would build any expectation on any report he might be told about success in any branch of commerce, or of progress in any art [which we naturally believe], since it is gain which man requires and for which he exerts his strength. Nor would he fear what he should guard against, be it the dangerous state of a road, or a proclamation prohibiting a certain action. But if a man has neither hopes nor fears, all his affairs will come to grief. Unless it is established that there is such a thing as true reports in this world, people will not pay heed to the command of their ruler or his prohibition, except at such time as they see him with their own eyes and hear his words with their own ears; and when no longer in his presence, they will cease to accept his commands and prohibitions.

If things were like this, all management of affairs would be rendered impossible and many people would perish. And unless there is a true tradition in this world, a man would not be able to know if a certain property was owned by his father . . . nor would a man know that he is the son of his mother, let alone that he is the son of his father. . . .

Scripture already declares that reliable tradition is as true as the things perceived by sight. Thus it says, "For pass over to the isles of the Kittites, and see, and send to Kedar, and consider diligently" (Jer. 2:10).

Why does it add the words "and consider diligently" in connection with the matter of report? The answer is because a report [or tradition] is, unlike sense perception, liable to be falsified in two ways, either through a wrong idea or through willful distortion. For this reason Scripture warns, "and consider diligently." Having considered deeply how we can have faith in tradition seeing that there are these two ways (of possible falsification), I found, by way of reason, that wrong ideas and willful distortions can occur and remain unnoticed only if they emanate from individuals, whereas, in a large collective group, the underlying ideas of the individuals who compose it will never be in agreement with one another, and if they willfully decide and agree on inventing a story, this will not remain unnoticed among their people; and whenever their story is put out, there will be related, at the same time, the story of how they came to agree upon it. And when a tradition is safe against these two possibilities (of falsification), there is no third way in which it could possibly be falsified. And if the Tradition of our Fathers is viewed from the aspect of these principles, it will appear sound and safe against any attack, and true, and firmly established. (Saadya, *Book of Doctrines and Beliefs* 3.5) [SAADYA 1945: 109–111]

16. A Karaite Rejoinder to Saadya on the Oral Law

Only one of the many Karaite replies to Saadya will be cited here, that by Salmon ben Jeroham, a somewhat older contemporary of the Egyptian scholar. It is called The Book of the Wars of the Lord *and is written in rhymed quatrains.*

He stated in his misleading discourse,
And he did utter the assertion,
That the Almighty chose to reveal himself to Moses
At Mount Sinai, to give him two Laws for His chosen people
The commandments of the one Law were set down in writing,
While the commandments of the other were kept upon the tongue.
Moreover, they were both to be, into everlasting eternity,
An heirloom for the congregation of the seed of the perfect ones.
My spirit advised me to reply to him in this matter,
And to place my answer among my congregation in a written epistle,
    In order to remove the stumbling block, and to clear the path of stones,

So that the flock of Israel would not go astray into the waterless
desert of heresy.
(Salmon ben Jeroham, *Wars of the Lord*, canto 1, 8–10) [NEMOY 1952: 72–73]

You say that the Rock has given Israel two Laws,
One which is written, and one which was preserved in your mouths.
If this is as you say,
Then indeed your deeds are but falsehood and rebellion against God.
The Holy One has given you an Oral Law
So you can recite it orally,
For, say you, He had deemed it, in His wisdom, a laudable command.
Why, then, did you write it down in ornate script?
Had the Merciful One wished to write it down,
He would have had it written down by Moses.
Now did He not give it to you to be studied orally,
And had He not ordained it not to be inscribed in a book?
Yet they altered God's alleged words and wrote it down,
And instead of studying it orally they transferred it into writing.
How, then, can their words be believed, seeing that they have
                    offended grievously?
They cannot withdraw from this contradictory path.
They wrote down both Laws, thus contemning the commandment of
                    the Almighty.
Where, then, is the Oral Law in which they place their trust?
        Their words have become void and meaningless,
            And out of their own mouths have they testified that they have
drawn God's wrath upon themselves.
(Ibid., canto 1, 18–22) [NEMOY 1952: 74–75]

I have also seen in the Talmud—
Which you Rabbanites regard as if it were your main supporting column,
And which is made by you a partner of the Law of Moses,
And is held beloved and desirable in your hearts—
The bellowing of the School of Shammai against the School of Hillel,
                    to controvert their words,
As well as that of the School of Hillel against the School of Shammai,
                    to refute their interpretations of law.
This one invokes blessings, and that one heaps curses upon their heads,
Yet both are an abomination in the sight of the Lord.
The words of which one of the two shall we accept,

And the views of which one of the two shall we condemn,
Seeing that each of them has attracted a great congregation of adherents,
    And each one of them turns to say, "I am the captain of the ship"?
(Ibid., canto 3, 2) [NEMOY 1952: 79]

17. The Written and the Oral Tradition in the Church

The authentic writings of the Apostles and others of that first generation of Christians constitute one form of the Christian tradition—its Torah, so to speak. But there is more: the unwritten traditions that have no less authority in the life of the Church. Ignatius, for example, the early bishop of Antioch (d. 107 C.E.), grew impatient with those who had to be shown everything in writing "in the archives," here probably the Bible.

I have heard some saying, "Unless I find it in the archives, I will not believe it in the Gospel." And when I say, "It is in Scripture," they reply, "That is precisely the question." As far as I am concerned, Jesus Christ is my "archive" and the inviolable documents are his cross and his death and his resurrection. (Ignatius, *Letter to the Philadelphians* 8.2)

One extended treatment of the theme of the unwritten tradition is found in the tract On the Holy Spirit *written by the Cappadocian bishop Basil (d. 379 C.E.). It should be noted that all of his examples are drawn from the liturgical practices of the Church, and the language suggests a comparison with the pagan "mystery religions" and their secret rites.*

Of the beliefs and public teachings preserved in the Church, some we have from written tradition and others we have received as delivered to us "in a mystery" by the tradition of the Apostles; and both of these have in relation to true piety the same binding force. And these no one will deny, at least no one who is versed even moderately in the institutions of the Church. For were we to reject such unwritten customs as having no great force, we should unintentionally injure the Gospels in their very vitals; or rather, reduce our public definition to a mere name and nothing more. For example, to take the first and most general instance, who is there who has taught us in writing to sign with the cross those who have trusted in the name of our Lord Jesus Christ? What writing has taught us to turn to the East in our prayers? Which of the saints has left us in writing the words at the invocation and at the displaying of the bread in the Eucharist and the cup of the blessing? For we are not, as is well known, content with what the Apostle or the Gospel has recorded; but both before and after, we say other words because of their importance for the (Eucharistic) Mystery, and these we derive from unwritten teaching. Moreover, we bless the water of baptism and the oil of the chrism, and, besides these, the one who is baptized. On the basis of what writings? Is it not from the silent and mystical tradition? What written word teaches the anointing with oil itself? And how is it that a man is baptized three times? And as to other baptismal customs, from what scriptural authority comes the renunciation of Satan and his angels? Does not this come from the unpublished and secret teaching which our fathers guarded in silence, shielded from curious meddling and inquisitive investigation, since they had learned the lesson that the reverence of the mysteries is best preserved in silence? How was it proper to parade in public the teaching of those things which it was not permitted the uninitiated to look at? (Basil, *On the Holy Spirit* 27)

18. The Apostolic Tradition as the Criterion of Truth

The tradition, therefore, of the Apostles, which is apparent throughout the world, is something which all who wish to see the facts can clearly perceive in every church; and we are able to count up those who were appointed bishops by the Apostles and to show their successors to our own time, who neither taught nor knew anything resembling these men's (heretical) ravings. For if the Apostles had known hidden mysteries which they used to teach the perfect, apart from and without the knowledge of the rest, they would have delivered them especially to those to whom they were committing the churches themselves. For they desired them to be very perfect and blameless in all things, and were also leaving them as their own successors, delivering over to them their own proper place of teaching; for if these latter should act rightly, great advantage would result, but if they fell away, the most disastrous calamity would occur. (Ireneus, *Against the Heresies* 3.3.1)

The Apostles first bore witness to the faith of Christ Jesus throughout Judea; they founded churches there, and then went out into the world and preached to the Gentiles the same doctrine of the same faith. They likewise founded churches in every city, from which the other churches derived the shoot of faith and the seeds of doctrine, yes, and are still deriving them, in order to become churches. It is through them that these churches are themselves apostolic, in that they are the offspring of apostolic churches. Every kind of thing must be judged by reference to its origin. Therefore so many and so great churches are all one, being from the first Church which is from the Apostles. . . .

It is therefore on this ground that we put forward our ruling, namely that if Jesus Christ sent out the Apostles to preach, no others are to be accepted as preachers save those whom Christ appointed, since "No one knows the Father except the Son and he to whom the Son has revealed Him" (Luke 10:22). And the Son seems not to have revealed him to any but the Apostles whom he sent out to preach, assuredly to preach what he had revealed to them. But what they preached, namely what Christ revealed to them, this, on my ruling, ought to be established solely through those same churches which the Apostles themselves founded by preaching to them as well by the living voice, as the phrase goes, as by their letters (to them) afterwards. If this is so, it follows immediately that all teaching which agrees with those apostolic churches, the sources and the origins of the Faith, must be judged the truth, since it preserves without doubt what the churches received from the Apostles, the Apostles from Christ, and Christ from God. (Tertullian, *A Ruling on Heretics* 20–21)

If there are any heresies who presume to place themselves in the Apostolic age, that they may thereby seem to have been handed down by the Apostles because they existed at the time of the Apostles, we can say: Let them produce the originals of their churches; let them unfold the roll of their bishops running down in due succession from the beginning in such manner that that first bishop of theirs shall be able to show for his ordainer or predecessor some one of the Apostles or of Apostolic men, a man, moreover, who remained steadfast with the Apostles. For in this manner the Apostolic churches transmit their registers; as the church of Smyrna which records that Polycarp was placed therein by John; as also the church of Rome which makes Clement to have been ordained in like manner by Peter. In exactly the same way the other churches likewise exhibit their several notables, whom, since they were appointed to their episcopal places by the Apostles, they regard as transmitters of the Apostolic seed. (Ibid. 32)

The fully developed position on the role of tradition, the written and the oral, as a criterion of Christian truth is found in the Commonitorium *written by Vincent of Lerins in Gaul in 434 C.E.*

I have often inquired earnestly and attentively of many men eminent for their sanctity and learning, how and by what sure and, so to speak, universal rule I might be able to distinguish the truth of the Catholic faith from the falsehood of heretical depravity, and I have always, and from almost all received an answer to this effect: That whether I or anyone else should wish to detect the frauds of heretics as they arise, or to avoid their snares, and to continue sound and complete in the faith, we must with the help of the Lord fortify our faith in two ways: first, by the authority of the divine Law, and then, by the tradition of the Catholic Church.

But at this point some will perhaps ask, since the canon of Scripture is complete and sufficient for everything, indeed, more than sufficient, what need is there to add to it the authority of the Church's interpretation? For this reason, because, owing to the depth of Holy Scripture, all do not accept it in one and the same sense, but one understands its words in one way, another in another way, so that there are almost as many opinions as there are men. . . . Therefore it is most necessary, on account of so much intricacy and such various errors, that the rule of right understanding of the prophets and Apostles should be framed in accordance with the standard of ecclesiastical and Catholic interpretation. (Vincent of Lerins, *Commonitorium* 2)

Vincent then explains how the tradition is expressed.

With regard to the tradition of the Church, two precautions have to be rigorously and thoroughly observed, adhered to by everyone who does not wish to become a heretic: first, it must be ascertained whether there exists from ancient times a decree established by all the bishops of the Catholic Church with the authority of a universal council; and second, should a new question arise for which no decree can be found, one must return to those Fathers who remained in their own times and places in the unity of communion and faith and were therefore regarded as teaching "probable" doctrine. If we can discover what they held in full agreement and consent, then we can conclude without hesitation that this is the true and Catholic doctrine of the Church.

That tradition, though it had through the watchful care of the Church remained unaltered down to the present time, has nonetheless undergone "development."

The Church of Christ, the careful and watchful guardian of the teachings deposited in her charge, never changes anything in them, never diminishes, never adds; does not cut off what is necessary, does not add what is superfluous, does not lose her own and does not appropriate another's, but while dealing faithfully and judiciously with ancient teaching, keeps this one objective carefully in view: if there is anything which the past has left shapeless and rudimentary, to shape and polish it; if anything is already reduced to shape and polished, to consolidate and strengthen it; if anything is already ratified and defined, to keep and guard it. Finally, what other objectives have councils (of the Church) ever aimed at in their decrees than to provide that what was before believed in simplicity should in the future be believed intelligently; that what was before preached coldly, should in the future be preached earnestly; that what was before practiced negligently, should henceforth be practiced with doubled solicitude? (Ibid. 25)

19. Jahiz on the Usefulness of Tradition

Al-Jahiz (d. 886 C.E.) offered his Muslim readers of the ninth century this explanation of the presence of a large body of traditions from the Prophet that were circulating in Islam.

God knows that man cannot of himself provide for his own needs, and does not intuitively understand the consequences of things without the benefit of the example of messengers, the books of his ancestors, and information about past ages and rulers. And so God has assigned to each generation the natural duty of instructing the next, and has made each succeeding generation the criterion of the truth of the information handed down to it. For hearing many unusual traditions and strange ideas makes the mind more acute, enriches the soul, and gives food for thought and incentive to look further ahead. More knowledge received orally means more ideas, more ideas mean more thought, more thought means more wisdom, and more wisdom means more sensible actions. . . .

Since God did not create men in the image of Jesus, son of Mary, John, son of Zachariah, and Adam, father of humankind, but rather He created them imperfect and unfit to provide for their own needs . . . He sent His Messengers to them and set up His Prophets among them, saying, "Man should have no argument against God after the Messengers" (Quran 4:163). But most men were not eyewitnesses to the proofs of His Messengers, nor did God allow them to be present at the miracles of His Prophets, to hear their arguments or to see their manner of working. And so it was needful that those who were present tell those who were absent, and that they attend to the teaching of the former; and He needed to vary the characters and the motives of those who were doing the transmitting, to show to their hearers and the faithful generally that a large number of people with differing motives and contrasting claims could not all have

invented a false tradition on the same subject without collusion and con-
spiring on the subject. . . . For if they had, it would be known and spoken
of abroad . . . and men would have the greatest of proofs against God, as
He said, "That man should have no argument against God after the Messengers"; for He would be enjoining on them obedience to His Messengers, faith in His Prophets and His Books, and belief in His heaven and
His hell, without giving them proof of tradition or the possibility of
avoiding error. But God is far above such. (Jahiz, *The Proofs of Prophecy*
125–126)

20. Scripture, Tradition, and the Law in Islam

*This mildly rationalizing and utilitarian view of tradition in general and Islamic
tradition in particular may have interested the more sophisticated readers of the
cultured and clever Jahiz. For most Muslims, however, "the tradition" or "the
traditions" had quite another import: by Jahiz' day they already provided the basis
of a great deal of Muslim belief and practice. In Arabic "a tradition" (*hadith*) and
"the tradition" (*sunna*) mean two different things, neither entirely synonymous
with what is understood by the English term "tradition." "A tradition," when it is
used in its technical sense, means a report of some saying or deed of the Prophet that
is transmitted on the witness and authority of one of the men or women around him,
the "Companions of the Prophet," as they came to be called. It will generally be
called here "a Prophetic tradition." "The tradition" is actually "the tradition of the
Prophet," that is, his customary behavior, his teaching, or his example, as it is
reflected in those just mentioned reports. "The tradition of the Prophet" was as
authoritative as the Quran for Muslims, from both a legal and a doctrinal point of
view, as indeed some Prophetic traditions themselves assert.*

Al-Irbad al-Sariya declared that God's Messenger got up and said:
"Does any of you, while reclining on his couch, imagine that God has
prohibited only what is to be found in the Quran? By God, I have commanded, exhorted and prohibited various matters as numerous as what
is found in the Quran, or more numerous." (Baghawi, *Mishkat al-Masabih*
6.1.2)

Aisha said: God's Messenger did a certain thing and gave permission
for it to be done, but some people abstained from it. When God's Messenger heard of it, he delivered a sermon, and after extolling God he said:
"What is the matter with people who abstain from a thing which I do?
By God, I am the one of them who knows most about God and fears Him
most." Bukhari and Muslim transmit this tradition. (Ibid. 6.1.1)

That the earliest Muslims followed the example of their Prophet, "who knows most about God," would seem to need little argument or demonstration. But there were other means of defining moral and legal action for a Muslim: adherence to local custom, for example, or even resort to some kind of analogical reasoning to elicit expanded or additional legal prescriptions from the Quran's "clear declarations." It was in this more polemical context that the role of "the Prophetic tradition" began to be argued in Islam. The earliest and most powerful case for the role of the Prophet's own authentic words and deeds, his "tradition," as the primary instrument for understanding the legal material in the Quran was made by the pioneer Egyptian Muslim jurist al-Shafiʿi (d. 820 C.E.) in his Treatise on the Roots of Jurisprudence. *The argument begins, as always, with the Book itself.*

Shafiʿi said: God has placed His Apostle—(in relation) to His religion, His commands and His Book—in the position made clear by Him as a distinguishing standard of His religion by imposing the duty of obedience to him as well as prohibiting disobedience to him. He has made his merits evident by associating belief in His Apostle with belief in Him. . . . He said:

"They alone are true believers who believe in God and His Apostle, and when they are with him on a matter of common concern, do not depart without obtaining his leave" (Quran 24:62).

Thus God prescribed that the perfect beginning of the faith to which all things are subordinate shall be belief in Him and then in His Apostle. For if a person believes only in Him and not in His Apostle, the name of the perfect faith will never apply to him until he believes in His Apostle together with Him. (Shafiʿi, *Treatise*) [SHAFIʿI 1961: 109–110]

From this principle that belief in God is necessarily accompanied by belief in the Apostle of God, Shafiʿi proceeds to bind the notion of the Prophet's custom into the scriptural proof. This he does by understanding the concept of "wisdom," where it occurs in the phrase "the Book and the Wisdom," as a reference to the words and deeds of the Prophet himself.

Shafiʿi said: God has imposed the duty on men to obey His divine commands as well as the tradition of His Apostle. For He said in His Book:

"Send to them, O Lord, an Apostle from among them to impart Your messages to them, and teach them the Book and the Wisdom, and correct them in every way; and indeed, You are mighty and wise" (Quran 2:129).

After citing a number of almost identical passages, Shafiʿi continues.

So God mentioned His Book, which is the Quran, and Wisdom, and I have heard that those who are learned in the Quran, whom I approve, hold that Wisdom is the tradition of the Prophet of God, which is like what God Himself said; but God knows best! For the Quran is mentioned first, followed by Wisdom; then God mentioned His favor to mankind by teaching them the Quran and Wisdom. So it is not permissible for Wisdom to be called here anything save the tradition of the Apostle of God. For Wisdom is closely linked with the Book of God, and God has imposed the duty of obedience to His Apostle, and imposed on men the obligation to obey his orders. So it is not permissible to regard anything as a duty save that set forth in the Quran and the tradition of the Prophet. (Shafiʿi, *Treatise*) [SHAFIʿI 1961: 110–122]

That what Muhammad said and did reflected nothing but the will of God, Shafiʿi easily demonstrates by reference to passages like the following.

O Prophet, fear God and do not follow the unbelievers and the hypocrites. But follow what is revealed to you from your Lord. Verily, God is All-knowing, All-wise. Truly, God is aware of the things you do. (Quran 33:1–2)

O Apostle, announce what has reached you from your Lord, for if you do not, you will not have delivered His message. God will preserve you from the mischief of men; for God does not guide those who do not believe. (Quran 5:67)

In certifying that the Prophet guides mankind along a straightforward path—the path of God—and that he delivers His message and obeys His commands, as we have stated before, and in ordering obedience to him and in emphasizing all this in the (divine) communications just cited, God has given evidence to mankind that they should accept the judgment of the Apostle and obey his orders. (Shafiʿi, *Treatise*) [SHAFIʿI 1961: 118]

Shafiʿi's argument has now reached a crucial juncture.

Shafiʿi said: Whatever the Apostle has decreed that is not based on any (textual) command from God, he has done so by God's command. . . . For the Apostle had laid down a tradition (on matters) for which there is a text in the Book of God as well as for others concerning which there is no specific text. But what he has laid down in the Prophetic tradition God has ordered us to obey, and He regards our obedience to him [Muhammad] as obedience to Himself, and refusal to obey him as disobedience to Him for which no man will be forgiven; nor is an excuse for failure to obey the Prophet's tradition possible owing to what I have already stated and what the Prophet himself has said:

"Sufyan told us from Salim Abu al-Nadr, a freed slave of Umar ibn Ubaydallah, who heard Ubaydallah ibn Abi Rafiʿ related from his father that the Apostle had said: 'Let me find no one of you reclining on his couch, and when confronted with an order of permission or prohibition from me, say: I do not know (if this is permitted or prohibited); we will follow only what we find in the Book of God.' " (Shafiʿi, *Treatise*)

[SHAFIʿI 1961: 118–119]

So both the Prophetic tradition and the discrete reports that constituted it were carefully studied by Muslim scholars, as Ibn Khaldun explains in his Prolegomenon to History, *written in 1377* C.E.

It should be known that the sciences with which people concern themselves in cities and which they acquire and pass on through instruction are of two kinds: one that is natural to man and to which he is guided by his own ability to think, and a traditional kind that he learns from those who invented it.

The first kind comprises the philosophical sciences. They are the ones with which man can become acquainted through the very nature of his ability to think and in whose objects, problems, arguments and methods of instruction he is guided by his human perceptions, so that he is made aware of the distinction between what is correct and what is wrong in them by his own speculation and research, inasmuch as he is a thinking human being.

The second kind comprises the traditional, conventional sciences. All of them depend upon information based on the authority of the given religious law. There is no place in the intellect for them, save that the intellect may be used in connection with them to relate problems of detail with basic principles. Particulars that constantly come into being are not included in the general tradition by the mere fact of its existence. Therefore, such particulars need to be related (to the general principles) by some kind of analogical reasoning. However, such analogical reasoning is derived from the (traditional) information, while the character of the basic principle, which is traditional, remains valid [that is, unchanged]. Thus analogical reasoning of this type reverts to being tradition itself, because it is derived from it.

It is clear from Ibn Khaldun's remarks that he is not using "traditional" in the sense of "ordinary," "usual," or "the way things have always been done," but rather in the original sense of "handed down" and so, somewhat more awkwardly in English, of the "traditioned" sciences, where it is not so much a question of a science that had been handed down as of a science using "traditioned" data. All those data derive, as he next indicates, from the twin source of the Quran and the reported, or "traditioned," behavior of the Prophet.

The basis of all the traditional [that is, "traditioned"] sciences is the legal material of the Quran and the customary behavior of the Prophet, which is the law given us by God and His Messenger, as well as the sciences connected with that material, by means of which we are enabled to use it. This, further, requires as auxiliary sciences the sciences of the Arabic language [that is, grammar, rhetoric, lexicography, etc.]. Arabic is the language of Islam and the Quran was revealed in it.

The different kinds of traditional sciences are numerous, because it is the duty of the responsible Muslim to know the legal obligations God placed upon him and upon his fellow men. They are derived from the Quran and the reported behavior of the Prophet, either from the text itself or through general consensus, or a combination of the two. Thus he must first study the explicit wording of the Quran. This is the science of Quran interpretation [see Chapter 2 above]. Then he must study the Quran, both with reference to the manner in which it has been transmitted and related on the authority of the Prophet who brought it from God, and with reference to the differences in the readings of the Quran readers. This is the science of Quran reading [see Chapter 1 above].

Then he must study the manner in which the "tradition of the Prophet" is connected with its originator [that is, Muhammad], and he must discuss the transmitters who have handed it down. He must know their circumstances and their probity, so that the information he receives from them may be trusted and so that one may be able to know the part of it in accordance with whose implications one must act. These are the sciences of Prophetic tradition.

Then the process of evolving the laws from their basic principles requires some normative guidance to provide us with the knowledge of how that process takes place. This is the science of the principles of jurisprudence. After one knows the principles of jurisprudence, one can enjoy, as its result, the knowledge of the divine laws that govern the actions of all Muslims. This is jurisprudence proper [see Chapter 5 below].

Furthermore, the duties of the Muslim may concern either the body or the heart. The duties of the heart are concerned with faith and the distinction between what is to be believed and what is not to be believed. This concerns the articles of faith which deal with the essence and the attributes of God, the events of the Resurrection, Paradise, punishment and predestination, and entails discussion and defense of these subjects with the help of intellectual arguments. This is speculative theology. (Ibn Khaldun, *Muqaddima* 6.9) [IBN KHALDUN 1967: 2:436–438]

21. The Inspiration of the Prophetic Traditions

As we have already seen in Chapter 1 above, there was no doubt that the Quran was the inspired word of God. Likewise, for the Prophetic traditions, there is some internal testimony in a few reports that at least some of the words of Muhammad were the result, and enjoyed the authority of, a divine inspiration. The following is reported on the authority of the Prophet's companion Ubayda.

The descent of inspiration was troublesome to the Prophet. His face would go ashen in color. One day inspiration came down on him [possibly just after the revelation of Sura 4:15] and he showed the usual signs of distress. When he recovered, he said: "Take it from me! God has appointed a way for the women: the non-virgin with the non-virgin and the virgin with the virgin. The non-virgin, one hundred strokes and death by stoning; the virgin, one hundred strokes and banishment for a year. (Bayhaqi, *The Great Tradition*) [Cited by BURTON 1977: 74]

The theologian al-Ghazali puts the Muslim position on the Prophetic traditions succinctly.

God does not have two words, one in the Quranic style which we are bidden to recite publicly, and called the Quran, while the other word is not Quran. God has but one word which differs only in the mode of its expression. On occasions God indicates His word by the Quran; on others, by words in another style, not publicly recited, and called the Prophetic tradition. Both are mediated by the Prophet. (Ghazali, *Mustasfa* 1.125) [Cited by BURTON 1977: 57]

22. Transmission of the Prophetic Traditions

Muslim tradition is unanimously agreed that parts at least of the Quran were written down, whether "on palm leaves or flat stones or in the hearts of men," during the Prophet's own lifetime. There is no such unanimity concerning the Prophetic traditions, as these two widely circulated reports testify.

Abdullah ibn Umar reported: "We said, 'O Prophet of God, we hear from you traditions which we cannot remember. May we not write them down?' 'By all means write them down,' he said."

Abu Hurayra reported: "The Prophet of God came to us while we were writing down traditions and said, 'What is this you are writing down?' We said, 'Traditions which we hear from you.' Said he, 'A book other than the Book of God! Do you not know that it was nothing but the writing of books other than the Book of God that led astray the peoples who were before you?' We said, 'Are we to relate traditions from you, O Prophet of God?' He replied, 'Relate traditions from me; there is no objection to that. But he who intentionally speaks falsely on my authority will find a place in hell.' " [Cited by GUILLAUME 1924: 15–16]

23. Tendentious and Sectarian Traditions

That some people were in fact speaking falsely on the authority of the Prophet must have been apparent to everyone who looked into the matter of the Prophetic traditions. The reported words of the Prophet were important not merely for understanding the legal material in the Quran but also for settling various historical claims. The Shi'ites, for example, those partisans of the Imamate of Ali, bolstered their claims to rulership in Islam not merely by charging that the text of the Quran had been deliberately tampered with (see Chapter 1 above); they also interpreted the extant text in a different fashion. How can one determine the truth or falsity of such a claim is the question posed by the essayist al-Jahiz (d. 886 C.E.) in his tract called The Uthmanis.

The radical Shi'ites claim that God revealed several verses regarding Ali, notably the following: "Obey God, obey God's Messenger and those in authority among you" (Quran 4:62), in which "those in authority" refers to Ali and his descendants. In truth, if traditionists were agreed that this verse refers to Ali and his descendants, then we must accept it; but if it [that is, this reported interpretation] is spurious, transmitted on weak authority, it is not only weak but exceptional, and you cannot account it part of your evidence. A Prophetic tradition can derive from a single reliable source and be transmitted on equally sound authority, but it is still reckoned "exceptional" unless it is widely known and a matter of common knowledge. On the other hand, a tradition can be transmitted by two or three persons regarded by traditionists as weak authorities, and in that case it is weak by reason of the weakness of its transmitters; but it still cannot be described as "exceptional" as long as it is transmitted by three authorities. The only sure proof lies in traditions that are transmitted in such a fashion that deliberate forgery or conspiracy to forge can be ruled out. These are the accepted Prophetic traditions.

601

A tradition is accepted not merely because of the number and reliability of its transmitters, but because it has been transmitted by a number of authorities whose motives and inclinations are so different that they could not have possibly conspired together to utter a forged Prophetic tradition. Then the compiler must satisfy himself that these different authorities transmitted the tradition through an equal number of transmitters of equally different motives and tendencies. If the final version then corresponds with the original, conviction is inescapable and doubt and suspicion are excluded.

Turning to the claim that in the verse "Obey . . . " God was referring to Ali to the exclusion of all the (other) Emigrants, the report on which this interpretation rests does not fulfill these conditions or fit this description. Indeed, the commentators suggest that it refers rather to the Prophet's officers and governors, to Muslims in general or to the leaders of expeditions . . . and that it is an injunction to the people to obey the commanders of the army and submit to the civil administration (of the community). (Jahiz, *The Uthmanis* 115)

24. The Criticism of Traditions

Nor was sectarianism the only cause for the multiplication of Prophetic traditions, some of them of very doubtful authenticity. Within less than a hundred years after the death of Muhammad the "traditions of the Prophet" were being invoked ever more frequently and systematically in the elaboration of Islamic law. This new approach to Islamic law, which is typified in the Muslim jurisprudent al-Shafi'i (d. 820 C.E.), created a new demand for traditions, and the supply soon began to rise to meet it.

Some idea of the enormous number of traditions that were eventually credited to the Prophet may be gotten from the fact that when Muslim scholars sat down to collect these reports, one of them, al-Bukhari (d. 870 C.E.), had reputedly accumulated 600,000 such, of which only 7,275 were included in his anthology, a number that may perhaps be reduced to 4,000 or even 2,762 when repetitions are eliminated. Another scholar, Abu Dawud, used only 4,800 out of his collection of some 500,000 Prophetic traditions in his anthology.

One Muslim response to this unchecked growth in the number of Prophetic traditions was, as Jahiz had done, to develop a more critical attitude toward these reports and to attempt to separate, if not the authentic from the spurious, then the "sound" from the "weak." The chief method of proceeding was to scrutinize the chain of transmitters that each tradition now self-consciously bore as a sign of its authenticity. Ibn Khaldun (d. 1406 C.E.) describes the fully developed science of tradition criticism in the survey of Islamic sciences that he incorporated into his Prolegomenon to History.

The purpose of the discipline is a noble one. It is concerned with the knowledge of how to preserve the traditions transmitted on the authority of the Master of the religious law [that is, Muhammad], until it is definite which are to be accepted and which are to be rejected.

It should be known that the men around Muhammad and the men of the second generation who transmitted the traditions were well known in the cities of Islam. There were transmitters in the Hijaz, in Basra and Kufa [the early Muslim garrison towns in Iraq], and then in Egypt and Syria. They were famous in their time. The transmitters in the Hijaz had fewer links in their chains of transmitters and they were sounder, because they were reluctant to accept (as reliable transmitters) those who were obscure and whose conditions were not known. . . .

At the beginning, knowledge of the religious law was entirely based on (oral) tradition. It involved no speculation, no use of opinion, and no intricate reasoning. The early Muslims occupied themselves with it, selecting the sound material, and thus eventually perfected it. Malik wrote the *Kitab al-Muwatta* according to the Hijazi tradition, in which he laid down the principal laws on the basis of sound, generally agreed-upon (material). He arranged the work according to juridical categories. (Ibn Khaldun, *Muqaddima* 6.11) [IBN KHALDUN 1967: 2:452–453]

Another of the sciences of tradition is the knowledge of the norms that leading tradition scholars have invented in order to know the chains of transmitters, the (individual) transmitters, their names, how the transmission took place, their conditions, their classes, and their different technical terminologies. This is because general consensus makes it obligatory to act in accordance with information established on the authority of the Messenger of God. This requires probability for the assumption that the information is true. Thus the independent student must verify all the means by which it is possible to make such an assumption.

He may do this by scrutinizing the chains of transmitters of traditions. For that purpose one may use such knowledge of the probity, accuracy, thoroughness and lack of carelessness or negligence as the most reliable Muslims describe a transmitter as possessing. Then, there are the differences in rank that exist among the transmitters. Further, there is the way the transmission took place. The transmitter may have heard the *shaykh* (dictate the tradition), or he may have read it (from a book) in his presence, or he may have heard it read (by another) in the presence of the *shaykh*, or the *shaykh* may have written it down for him, or he may have obtained the approval of the *shaykh* for written material, or he may have obtained his permission to teach certain materials. (Ibid.)

[IBN KHALDUN 1967: 2:448–449]

25. The Categories of Traditions

This careful scrutiny of the transmitters of any given tradition allowed the scholar to categorize the tradition in question and to rate it according to the criteria he had set up.

There are differences with regard to the soundness or acceptability of the transmitted material. The highest grade of transmitted material is called "sound" (by the tradition scholars). Next comes "good." The lowest grade is "weak." The classification of traditions also includes "missing the original transmitter on Muhammad's authority," "missing one link," "missing two links," "affected with some infirmity," "unique," "unusual" and "unique and suspect." In some cases there is a difference of opinion as to whether such traditions should be rejected. In other cases, there is general agreement that they should be rejected. The same is the case with traditions with sound chains. In some instances there is general agreement as to their acceptability and soundness, whereas, in other instances, there are differences of opinion. Tradition scholars differ greatly in their explanation of these terms. (Ibn Khaldun, *Muqaddima* 6.11)

[IBN KHALDUN 1967: 2:449–450]

26. The Companions of the Prophet

The traditions on the excellence of the generation of Muhammad's contemporaries was not simply an exercise in piety. It was these worthies who were the eyewitness generation and so stood behind every tradition attributed to the Prophet. And it was their character rather than the acuity of their sight or hearing that guaranteed what they transmitted.

The best of mankind after these [that is, after the early Caliphs and the veterans of the Battle of Badr] are the Companions of God's Messenger from the period during which he was among them. Anyone who knew him for a year or a month or a day or an hour, or even saw him, is of the Companions, to the extent that he was with him, took precedence with him, heeded his words and regarded him. The least of these in companionhood is better than the generation which did not see him. If they should come before God with all their works like those who were the associates of the Prophet—God bless him and give him peace—and beheld him and listened to him, the one who saw him with his own eye and believed in him even for a single hour is better for his association than all who followed after, even if they should have performed all the (requisite) good works. (Ahmad ibn Hanbal, *Creed*) [WILLIAMS 1971: 31]

27. Contradictory Traditions

Careful scrutiny of the external transmission mechanisms of a Prophetic tradition was not the only way of investigating Prophetic traditions in Islam. Some attention was also given to the matter of the tradition itself, particularly to the question of contradictory traditions. Al-Shafi'i himself addressed the problem.

As to contradictory Prophetic traditions where no indications exist to specify which is the abrogating and which is the abrogated tradition, they are all in accord with one another and contradiction does not really exist among them. For the Apostle of God, being an Arab by tongue and by country, may have laid down a general rule intended to be general and another general rule intended to be particular. . . . Or a certain question may have been asked to which he gave a concise answer, leading some of the transmitters to relate the tradition in detail and others in brief, rendering the meaning of the tradition partly clear and partly vague. Or (it may happen) that the transmitter of a certain tradition related the answer he heard from the Prophet without knowing what the question had been, for had he known the question he would have understood the answer clearly from the reasoning on which the answer was based.

The Prophet may have likewise laid down a tradition covering a particular situation and another covering a different one, but some of those who related what they had heard failed to distinguish between the two differing situations for which he had laid down the traditions. . . . He may have also provided a tradition consisting of an order or permission or prohibition, the wording of which was general, and he may have provided a second specifying tradition which made it evident that his order of prohibition was not intended to prohibit what he made lawful, nor that his order of permission made lawful what he prohibited. For all possibilities of this kind parallel examples exist in the Book of God. (Shafi'i, *Treatise*) [SHAFI'I 1961: 180–181]

28. The Canonical Collections

We return to Ibn Khaldun's survey of the science of tradition. He now describes the five collections of traditions that had gained the cachet of authority in Islam.

There was Muhammad ibn Isma'il al-Bukhari [d. 870 C.E.], the leading tradition scholar of his time. In his *Musnad al-Sahih* he widened the area of tradition and published the orthodox traditions according to subject. He combined all the different ways of the Hijazis, Iraqis and Syrians, accepting the material upon which they all agreed, but excluding the material concerning which there were differences of opinion. He repeated a given tradition in every chapter upon which the contents of that particular tradition had some bearing. Therefore his traditions were repeated in several chapters, because a single tradition may deal with several subjects, as we have indicated. His work thus comprised 7,200 traditions, of which 3,000 are repeated. In each chapter he kept separate the (different) recensions (of the same tradition), with the different chains of transmitters belonging to each.

Then came the imam Muslim [d. 875 C.E.]. . . . He composed his *Musnad al-Sahih*, in which he followed Bukhari, in that he transmitted the material that was generally agreed upon, but he omitted the repetitions and he did not keep the (different) recensions and chains of transmitters separate. He arranged his work according to juridical categories and the chapter headings of jurisprudence.

How elaborate these judicial categories were may be seen from a glance at Bukhari's Sahih. The whole work is divided into ninety-seven "books." The first contain traditions on the beginning of revelation, on faith and knowledge. The next thirty books are given over to traditions connected with ablution, prayer, alms, pilgrimage, and fasting. These are followed by twenty-two books on matters of business, trusteeship, and in general with conditions of employment and various legal matters. There are three books of traditions on fighting for the faith and dealing with subject peoples, followed by one on the beginning of creation. The next four collect traditions on the Prophets and the admirable traits of various contemporaries of Muhammad, including some account of the Prophet's life up to the Hijra. The next book follows his career at Medina. There are two books with exegetical traditions on the Quran. The three following deal with marriage, divorce, and the maintenance due to one's family. From here to book ninety-five various subjects are treated, among them food, drink, clothing, seemly behavior, medicine, invitations, vows, the expiation of broken vows, blood revenge, persecution, the interpretation of visions, civil strife, and the trials before the end of the world. Book 96 stresses the importance adhering to the Quran and the Sunna, and the last book, which is fairly lengthy, addresses itself chiefly to theological questions on the subject of the Unity of God. We return once more to the text of Ibn Khaldun.

Scholars have corrected the two authors [that is, Bukhari and Muslim], noting the cases of sound traditions not (included in their works). They have mentioned cases where they have neglected (to include traditions which, according to) the conditions governing the inclusion of traditions in their works (should have been included).

Abu Dawud [d. 888 C.E.] . . . al-Tirmidhi [d. 892 C.E.] . . . and al-Nasa'i [d. 915 C.E.] wrote tradition works which included more than merely "sound" traditions. Their intention was to include all traditions that amply fulfilled the conditions making them actionable traditions. They were either traditions with few links in the chain of transmitters, which makes them sound, as is generally acknowledged, or they were lesser traditions, such as (the category of) "good" traditions and others. It was to serve as a guide to orthodox practice. (Ibn Khaldun, *Muqaddima* 6.11) [IBN KHALDUN 1967: 2:454–455]

29. A Tradition Summa: The "Forty" of al-Nawawi

These four great collections of Prophetic traditions, each of which included thousands of separate reports, were made and arranged primarily for the benefit of lawyers, who required a convenient way of finding Prophetic precedents. Their size and complexity made them hardly useful for most Muslims. The needs of piety were met by subsequent smaller collections called "The Forty," since, as one Prophetic tradition reported, there would be a special blessing on whoever assembled that number of reports from the Prophet. One of the best known was the "Forty Sound Prophetic Traditions" of al-Nawawi (d. 1278 C.E.), which served as a kind of catechism in many parts of the Islamic world.

It has come to us on the authority of Ali ibn Abi Talib . . . Ibn Umar and Ibn Abbas and Anas ibn Malik and Abu Hurayra and Abu Saʿid al-Khudri, with whom may God be pleased, through many channels and varied lines of transmission, that the Apostle of God, upon whom may be God's blessing and peace, said: "Whoever preserves for my community forty traditions concerning matters of this religion, God will raise him up on the Last Day in the company of the jurists and the theologians." . . .

The theologians, with whom may God be pleased, have composed innumerable works on this matter (of the Forty Traditions). . . . And now

I have sought God's help in assembling forty Prophetic traditions in imitation of those predecessors, the outstanding traditionists and scholars of Islam. The theologians have agreed that it is permissible to use a weak tradition when it concerns a matter of a meritorious work, yet in spite of this I have not relied on that but rather on the saying of him [that is, Muhammad], upon whom be God's blessing and peace, in the genuine Prophetic traditions: "Let him among us who (was present and) saw, inform him who was absent," and on his saying: "May God brighten life for any man who hears what I say, pays heed to it, and passes it on just as he has heard it."

Among the theologians are some who have assembled forty Prophetic traditions concerning the principles of religion, while others (have made their collections) with reference to the derivative matters of religion. Some about the Holy War, some about ascetic practices, some about rules of conduct, some about practical sermonizing. All these are pious purposes, so may God be pleased with such as have purposed them. My thought, however, was to assemble forty more important than any of these, to wit, the forty traditions which would include all the above mentioned (subjects), and each tradition of which would set forth one of the great points of religious belief, those which the theologians have referred to as "the pivot of Islam" or "the half of Islam" or "the third thereof," or some such title. Then I shall insist that each of the forty be a "sound" Prophetic tradition, for the most part such as will be found in the books called *The Sound* by al-Bukhari and Muslim. I shall record them without their chains of transmitters in order to make it easier to memorize them and make them more generally profitable, if God so wills, and after them I shall add explanations of any obscure expression in them. (Nawawi, *The Forty Traditions*) [JEFFERY 1962: 142–144]

4. The Law of God

1. Moses Receives the Torah

The Covenant had been concluded with Abraham, as the Book of Genesis explains, but it was not until the days of Moses, when the Israelites had been led out of Egypt into the wilderness, that the Law was given to Israel.

On the third new moon after the Israelites had gone forth from the land of Egypt, on that very day, they entered the wilderness of Sinai. Having journeyed from Rephidim, they entered the wilderness of Sinai and encamped in the wilderness. Israel encamped there in front of the mountain, and Moses went up to God. The Lord called to him from the mountain, saying: "Thus shall you say to the house of Jacob and declare to the children of Israel: 'You have seen what I did to the Egyptians, how I bore you on eagles' wings and brought you to Me. Now, then, if you will obey Me faithfully and keep My Covenant, you shall be My treasured possession among all the peoples. Indeed, all the earth is Mine, but you shall be to Me a kingdom of priests and a holy nation.' These are the words that you shall speak to the children of Israel."

Moses came and summoned the elders of the people and put before them all the words that the Lord had commanded him. All the people answered as one, saying, "All that the Lord has spoken we will do." And Moses brought back the people's words to the Lord. And the Lord said to Moses, "I will come to you in a thick cloud, in order that the people may hear when I speak with you and so trust you ever after." Then Moses reported the people's words to the Lord, and the Lord said to Moses, "Go to the people and warn them to stay pure today and tomorrow. Let them wash their clothes. Let them be ready for the third day; for on the third day the Lord will come down, in the sight of all the people, on Mount Sinai. You shall set up bounds for the people round about, saying, 'Beware of going up on the mountain or touching the borders of it. Whoever

609

touches the mountain shall be put to death; no hand shall touch him, but he shall be either stoned or shot; beast or man, he shall not live.' When the ram's horn sounds a long blast, they may go up on the mountain. . . ."

On the third day, as morning dawned, there was thunder and lightning and a dense cloud upon the mountain, and a very loud blast of the horn; and all the people who were in the camp trembled. Moses led the people out of the camp toward God, and they took their places at the foot of the mountain.

Now Mount Sinai was all in smoke, and the Lord had come down upon it in fire; the smoke rose like the smoke of a kiln, and the whole mountain trembled violently. The blare of the horn grew louder and louder. As Moses spoke, God answered him in thunder. The Lord came down upon Mount Sinai, on the top of the mountain, and the Lord called Moses to the top of the mountain and Moses went up. The Lord said to Moses, "Go down, warn the people not to break through to the Lord to gaze, lest many of them perish. The priests also who come near the Lord must purify themselves, lest the Lord break out against them." But Moses said to the Lord, "The people cannot come up to Mount Sinai, for You warned us, saying, 'Set bounds about the mountain and sanctify it.' " So the Lord said to him, "Go down and come back together with Aaron; but let not the priests or the people break through to come up to the Lord, lest He break out against them." And Moses went down to the people and spoke to them.

God spoke all these words, saying:

"I am the Lord your God who brought you out of the land of Egypt, the house of bondage. You shall have no other gods beside Me.

"You shall not make for yourself a sculpted image, or any likeness of what is in the heavens above, or on the earth below, or in the waters under the earth. You shall not bow down to them or worship them. For I, the Lord your God, am an impassioned God, visiting the guilt of the fathers upon the children, upon the third and upon the fourth generations of those who reject Me, but showing kindness to the thousandth generation of those who love Me and keep My commandments.

"You shall not swear falsely by the name of the Lord your God; for the Lord will not clear one who swears falsely by His name.

"Remember the sabbath day and keep it holy. Six days you shall labor and do all your work, but the seventh day is a sabbath of the Lord your God; you shall not do any work—you, your son or daughter, your male or female slave, or your cattle, or the stranger who is within your settlements. For in six days the Lord made heaven and earth and sea, and all that is in them, and He rested on the seventh day; therefore the Lord blessed the sabbath and hallowed it.

"Honor your father and your mother, that you may long endure on the land which the Lord your God is giving you.

"You shall not murder.

"You shall not commit adultery.

"You shall not steal.

"You shall not bear false evidence against your neighbor.

"You shall not covet your neighbor's house; you shall not covet your neighbor's wife, his male or female slave, or his ox or his ass, or anything that is your neighbor's."

All the people witnessed the thunder and the lightning, the blare of the horn and the mountain smoking; and when the people saw it they fell back, and stood at a distance. "You speak to us," they said to Moses, "and we shall obey; but let not God speak to us lest we die." Moses answered the people, "Do not be afraid; for God has come only in order to test you, and that the fear of Him may be ever with you, so that you do not go astray." So the people remained at a distance, while Moses approached the thick cloud where God was. (Exodus 19:1–20:18)

2. "The Covenant Is in These Words"

As the Exodus narrative proceeds, an increased emphasis is placed on the written quality of the Covenant and, apparently in passing, on a distinction that many later interpreters found useful between God's "commands" and His "rules."

Moses went and repeated to the people all the commands of the Lord and all the rules; and all the people answered with one voice and said, "All the things the Lord has commanded we will do!" Moses then wrote down the commands of the Lord.

Early in the morning, he set up an altar at the foot of the mountain, with twelve pillars for the twelve tribes of Israel. He designated some young men from among the Israelites, and they offered burnt offerings and sacrificed bulls as offerings of well-being to the Lord. Moses took one part of the blood and put it in basins, and the other part of the blood he dashed against the altar. Then he took the record of the Covenant and read it aloud to the people. And they said, "All the Lord has spoken, we will do." Moses took the blood and dashed it on the people and said, "This is the blood of the Covenant which the Lord now makes with you concerning all these commands." (Exodus 24:3–8)

The Lord said to Moses, "Come up to me on the mountain, wait there and I will give you the stone tablets with the teachings and commandments which I have inscribed to instruct them." So Moses and his attendant Joshua arose, and Moses ascended the mountain of God. To the elders he had said, "Wait here for us until we return to you. You have Aaron and Hur with you; let anyone who has a legal matter approach them."

When Moses had ascended the mountain, the cloud covered the mountain. The Presence of the Lord abode on Mount Sinai, and the cloud hid it for six days. On the seventh day He called to Moses from the midst of the cloud. Now the Presence of the Lord appeared in the sight of the Israelites as a consuming fire on the top of the mountain. Moses went inside the cloud and ascended the mountain; and Moses remained on the mountain forty days and forty nights. (Exodus 24:12–18)

The Lord gives the tablets to Moses.

Moses turned and went down from the mountain bearing the two tablets of the Pact, tablets inscribed on both their surfaces; they were inscribed on the one side and the other. The tablets were God's work, and the writing was God's writing, incised upon the tablets. (Exodus 32:15–16)

Even before he reaches the camp of the Israelites, Moses hears the sounds of the orgiastic worship of a golden calf the Israelites had made Aaron set up in his absence. In a fit of anger he smashes the tablets of the Law. After the people have been punished and the worship of the True God restored—and Moses makes the extraordinary request of being allowed to gaze on the very Presence of God—the leader of the Israelites once again prepares to ascend the mountain.

The Lord said to Moses, "Carve two tablets of stone like the first, and I will inscribe upon the tablets the words that were on the first tablets, which you shattered. Be ready by morning, and in the morning come up to Mount Sinai and present yourself there to Me, on the top of the mountain; neither shall the flocks and the herds graze at the foot of the mountain."

So Moses carved two stone tablets like the first, and early in the morning he went up on Mount Sinai, as the Lord had commanded him, taking the two stone tablets with him. The Lord came down in the cloud; He stood with him there, and proclaimed the name Lord [that is, YHWH]. The Lord passed before him and proclaimed "The Lord! the Lord! a God compassionate and gracious, slow to anger, abounding in kindness and faithfulness, extending kindness to the thousandth generation, forgiving iniquity, transgression and sin; yet He does not remit all punishment, but visits the iniquity of fathers upon children and children's children, upon the third and fourth generations."

Moses hastened to bow low to the ground in homage, and said, "If I have gained Your favor, O Lord, let the Lord go in our midst, even though this is a stiff-necked people. Pardon our iniquity and our sin, and take us for Your own."

The Lord said: "Hereby I make a Covenant. Before all your people I shall work such wonders as have not been wrought in all the world or in any nation; and all the people who are with you will see how awesome are the Lord's deeds." (Exodus 34:1–10)

The Lord then gives a series of admonitions and advisements (Exod. 34:10–26), and the narrative concludes.

The Lord said to Moses, "Write down these commandments, for in accordance with these commandments I make a Covenant with you and Israel." And Moses was there with the Lord forty days and forty nights; he ate no bread and he drank no water; and he wrote down on the tablets the terms of the Covenant, the Ten Commandments. (Exodus 34:27–28)

3. Moses on Sinai: The Quranic Version

As we have already seen, the Quran pays particular attention to the sojourn of the Israelites in Egypt. One of the longer versions of those events occurs in Sura 7, which resumes its narrative after the escape of Moses and his people across the Red Sea.

When We brought the children of Israel across the sea, and they came to a people who were devoted to their idols, they [that is, the Israelites] said, "Moses, make us a god like theirs." "You are ignorant," he replied. "These people and their ways will surely be destroyed, for false is what they practice. Do you want me to seek for you," he said, "a god other than the God, when He has exalted you over all the nations of the world? Remember the day when he saved you from the people of the Pharaoh who oppressed and afflicted you, and slew your sons and spared your women. In this was a great trial from your Lord."

We made an appointment of thirty nights with Moses (on Mount Sinai), to which we added ten more; so the term set by the Lord was completed in forty nights. Moses said to Aaron, his brother, "Deputize for me among my people. Dispose rightly, and do not follow the way of the authors of evil."

When Moses arrived at the appointed time and his Lord spoke to him, he said, "My Lord, reveal Yourself to me, that I may behold You." "You cannot behold me," he said, "but look at the mountain. If it remains firm in its place, you may then behold Me." But when the Lord appeared on the mountain in His effulgence, it crumbled to a heap of dust, and Moses fell unconscious. When he came to, he said, "All glory be to You! I turn to You in repentance, and I am the first to believe." He said, "O Moses, I raised you above all men by sending my messages and speaking to you."

And We wrote down on tablets admonitions and clear explanations of all things for Moses, and ordered him, "Hold fast to them and command the people to observe the best in them." (Quran 7:138–145)

4. That Moses Was the Best of Lawgivers and His the Best Constitution

Thus Moses received God's Law for His people on Sinai, not merely the written Torah but, as later generations of Jews understood it, the oral Law as well. No one had any doubts that it was the voice of God that had spoken. Where there was some hesitation perhaps was in the role of Moses in the process. Generally speaking, the Jewish tradition gave to Moses a larger share in this deposit of law and precept than Christianity was willing to concede to the Evangelists who wrote down the Gospels or the Muslims to Muhammad. Philo, for example, who had, or chose, in the first century to compete with the sophisticated legal and philosophical theories of the Greeks and the Romans, saw Moses as the ideal legislator, the peer, indeed the superior, of Lycurgus and Pythagoras.

That Moses himself was the best of all lawgivers everywhere, either among the Greeks or the barbarians, and that his laws are the most excellent and truly come from God, since they neglect nothing that is necessary, the following is the clearest proof. If anyone examines the legal usages of other peoples he will find that they have been shaken by innumerable causes—wars, tyrannies or other undesirable events that befall them by the stroke of fortune's turnings. Frequently it is luxury, flowing to excess through unstinting supplies and superfluities, that has destroyed the laws, since the multitudes are unable to bear "an excess of good things" and grow insolent through satiety, and insolence is the antagonist of law. But Moses' laws alone, firm, unshaken, unswerving, stamped as it were by the seals of nature itself, remain solid from the day that they were first enacted to now, and there is hope that they will remain for all future ages as though immortal, so long as the sun and the moon and the entire heaven and universe exist. In any case, though the (Jewish) nation has experienced so many changes both by way of success and the reverse, nothing, not even the smallest part of his ordinances, has been disturbed; since all have clearly accorded high honor to their venerable and godlike character. . . .

But this is not yet the marvel of it, though it may rightly be thought a great matter in itself, that the (Mosaic) laws should have been observed through all time. More wonderful, I believe, is the fact that not only Jews but all other peoples, and particularly those that have taken greater stock of virtue, have grown devout to the point of approving and honoring our laws. In this they have obtained a singular honor, which belongs to no other code. The following is the proof. Among the Greek and barbarian states, there is virtually none that honors the institutions of any other. Indeed, scarcely does any state hold fast lastingly to its own, as it adapts them to meet the vicissitudes of times and circumstances. . . . Virtually all people from the rising of the sun to its setting, every country, nation and state, are hostile to foreign institutions and believe that they increase the approbation of their own by showing disdain for those of others. This is not the case with ours. They draw the attention and win over all barbarians, Greeks, mainlanders and islanders, nations east and west, Europe, Asia, the entire inhabited world from end to end. (Philo, *Life of Moses* 2.12–20) [PHILO 1981: 270–271]

Much the same point regarding Moses and his "constitution" is made, albeit in a more legally nuanced and in perhaps a more Roman than Greek fashion, by the historian Josephus. It occurs in his rejoinder, written in the last years of the first Christian century, to Philo's old Egyptian antagonist Apion and so was directed to a Gentile audience for whom the notion that the law came directly from God would not have been very persuasive.

There is endless variety in the details of the customs and laws which prevail in the world at large. To give but a summary enumeration: some people have entrusted the supreme political power to monarchies, others to oligarchies, yet others to the masses. Our lawgiver [that is, Moses], however, was attracted by none of these forms of polities, but he gave to his constitution the form of what, if a somewhat forced expression be permitted, may be called a "theocracy," placing all sovereignty and authority in the hands of God. To Him he persuaded all to look, as the author of all blessings, both those which are common to all mankind and those which they had won for themselves by prayer in the crises of history. He convinced them that no single action, no secret thought, could be hid from Him. He represented Him as One, uncreated and immutable to all eternity, in beauty surpassing all mortal thought, made known to us by His power, although the nature of His real being passes knowledge.

That the wisest of the Greeks learned to adopt these conceptions of God from principles with which Moses supplied them, I am not now concerned to urge; but they have borne abundant testimony to the excellence of these doctrines, and to their consonance with the nature and majesty of God. In fact, Pythagoras, Anaxagoras, Plato, the Stoics who succeeded him, and indeed nearly all the philosophers appear to have held similar views concerning the nature of God. These, however, addressed their philosophy to the few, and did not venture to divulge their true beliefs to the masses, who had their own preconceived opinions; whereas our lawgiver, by making practice square with precept, not only convinced his own contemporaries but so firmly planted this belief concerning God in their descendants to all future generations that it cannot be moved. The cause of his success was that the very nature of his legislation made it far more useful than any other; for he did not make religion a department of virtue, but the various virtues—I mean justice, temperance, fortitude and mutual harmony in all things between the members of the community—departments of religion. Religion governs all our actions and occupations and speech; none of these things did our lawgiver leave unexamined or indeterminate.

Josephus then turns to more general considerations and to this remarkable appreciation of the Mosaic polity, or rather, its Pharisaic understanding.

All schemes of education and moral training fall into two categories: instruction is imparted in one case by precept, in the other by the practical exercise of the character. All other legislators, differing in their opinions, selected the particular method which each preferred and neglected the other. . . . Our legislator, on the other hand, took great care to combine both systems. He did not leave training in morals inarticulate; nor did he permit the letter of the law to remain inoperative. Starting from the very beginning with the food which we partake from infancy and the private life of the home, he left nothing, however insignificant, to the discretion and caprice of the individual. What meats a man should abstain from and what he may enjoy, with what persons he should associate, what period should be devoted respectively to strenuous labor and to rest—for all this our leader made the Law the standard and the rule, that

CHAPTER 4

we might live under it as a father and a master, and be guilty of no sin through willfulness or ignorance.

For ignorance he left no pretext. He appointed the Law to be the most excellent and necessary form of instruction, ordaining not that it should be heard once for all, or twice, or on several occasions, but that every week men should desert their other occupations and listen to the Law, and obtain a thorough and accurate knowledge of it, a practice which all other legislators seem to have neglected. Indeed, most men, so far from living in accordance with their own laws, hardly know what they are. Only when they have done wrong do they learn from others that they have transgressed the law. Even those of them who hold the highest and most important offices admit their ignorance, for they employ professional legal experts as assessors and leave them in charge of the administration of affairs. But should anyone of our nation be questioned about the laws, he would repeat them all more readily than his own name. The result, then, of our thorough grounding in the laws from the first dawn of intelligence is that we have them, as it were, engraved on our souls. A transgressor is a rarity, evasion of punishment by excuses an impossibility.

To this cause above all do we owe our admirable harmony. Unity and identity of religious belief, perfect uniformity in habits and customs, produce a very beautiful concord in human character. Among us alone will be heard no contradictory statements about God, such as are common among other nations, not only on the lips of ordinary individuals under the impulse of some passing mood, but even boldly propounded by philosophers, some putting forward crushing arguments against the very existence of God, others depriving Him of His providential care for mankind. Among us alone will be seen no difference in the conduct of our lives. With us, all act alike, all profess the same doctrine about God, one which is in harmony with the Law and affirms that all things are under His eye. Even our womenfolk and dependents would tell you that piety must be the motive of all our occupations in life. (Josephus, *Against Apion* 2.16–19)

Our earliest imitators were the Greek philosophers, who, though ostensibly observing the laws of their own countries, yet in their conduct and philosophy were Moses' disciples, holding similar views about God and advocating the simple life and friendly communion between man and man. But that is not all. The masses have long since shown a keen desire to adopt our religious observances; and there is not one city, Greek or barbarian, to which our custom of abstaining from work on the seventh day has not spread, and where the fasts and the lighting of lamps and many of our prohibitions in the matter of food are not observed. Moreover, they attempt to imitate our unanimity, our liberal charities, our devoted labor in the crafts, our endurance under persecution on behalf of our laws. The greatest miracle of all is that our Law holds out no seductive bait of sensual pleasure, but has exercised this influence through its own inherent merits; and as God permeates the universe, so the Law has found its way among all mankind. (Ibid. 2.38)

5. The Precepts of the Law and the Great Commandment

The rabbis had little need and even less desire to construct the kinds of arguments we have just seen Philo and Josephus making for their Gentile readers. The rabbis' concerns were quite different.

Rabbi Hananiah ben Akashya says: The Holy One, blessed be He, was minded to grant merit to Israel. Therefore He multiplied for them the Law and the commandments, as it is written, "It pleased the Lord, for the furtherance of His justice, to make His Law a law of surpassing majesty" (Isa. 42:21). (M.Makkoth 3:16)

Rabbi Simlai said: 613 commandments were given to Moses, 365 negative commandments, answering to the number of the days of the year, and 248 positive commandments, answering to the number of man's members. Then David came and reduced them to 11 [cf. Ps. 15]. Then came Isaiah and reduced them to six [cf. Isa. 33:15]. Then came Micah and reduced them to three [cf. Mic. 6:8]. Then Isaiah came again and reduced the three to two, as it is said, "Keep judgment and do righteousness." Then came Amos and reduced them to one, as it is said, "Seek Me and live." Or, one may say, then came Habakkuk and reduced them to one, as it is said, "The righteous shall live by his faith." (BT.Makkoth 23b–24a)

It happened that a certain non-Jew came before Shammai and said to him, "I wish you to make me a proselyte, but on condition that you teach me the whole Torah while I stand on one foot." Thereupon Shammai drove him off with the builder's cubit measure that he held in his hand. When the same man approached Hillel, the latter said to him, "What is hateful to you, do not do to your neighbor: that is the whole Torah, while all the rest is commentary on it; go and learn it." (BT.Shabbat 31a)

At about the same time, a similar question was posed to another rabbi in the Gospels, perhaps by one of Hillel's own students.

Then one of the lawyers, who had been listening to the discussion and had noted how well he [that is, Jesus] answered, came forward and asked him: "Which commandment is first of all?" Jesus answered, "Hear, O Israel, the Lord our God is the only Lord; love the Lord your God with all your heart, with all your soul, with all your mind and with all your strength (Deut. 6:5). The second is this: Love your neighbor as yourself (Lev. 19:18). There is no other commandment greater than these." The lawyer said to him, "Well said, Master. You are right in saying that God is one and beside Him there is no other. And to love Him with all your heart, all your understanding and all your strength, and to love your neighbor as yourself—that is far more than any burnt offerings or sacrifices." When Jesus saw how sensibly he answered, he said to him, "You are not far from the kingdom of God." (Mark 12:28–34)

Paul, another lawyer, had studied with Hillel's successor, Gamaliel. He is even more terse in his résumé of the Law.

He who loves his neighbor has satisfied every claim of the Law. For the commandments, "Thou shall not commit adultery, thou shall not kill, thou shall not steal, thou shall not covet," and any other commandments there may be, are all summed up in one rule, "Love your neighbor as yourself." Love cannot wrong a neighbor; therefore the whole Law is summed up in love. (Paul, *To the Romans* 13:9–10)

6. There Was, There Will Be, Only One Law

Both the Christians and the Muslims eventually claimed to possess a new and more perfect version of God's Law. Maimonides (1135–1204 C.E.), who had experienced both claims, saw it as part of his task to demonstrate that there was not, nor could there be, any such thing as a new Torah.

Nothing similar to the call addressed to us by Moses our Master has been made before him by any one of those we know who lived in the time between Adam and him; nor was a call similar to that one made by one of our prophets after him. Correspondingly it is a fundamental principle of our Law that there will never be another Law. Hence, according to our opinion, there never has been a Law and there never will be a Law except the one that is the Law of Moses our Master.

The explanation of this, according to what is literally stated in the prophetic books and is found in the tradition, is as follows. Not one of the prophets—such as the Patriarchs, Shem, Eber, Noah, Methuselah and Enoch—who came before Moses our Master has ever said to a class of people: God has sent me to you and has commanded me to say to you such and such things; He has forbidden you to do such and such things and has commanded you to do such and such things. This is a thing that is not attested to by any text in the Torah and that does not figure in any true tradition. These men received only prophetic revelation from God. . . . He who received a great overflow, as for instance Abraham, assembled the people and called them by the way of teaching and instruction to adhere to the truths that he had grasped. Thus Abraham taught the people and explained to them by means of speculative proofs that the world had but one deity, that He had created all the things that are other than Himself, and that none of the forms and no created thing in general ought to be worshiped. This is what he instructed the people in, attracting them by means of eloquent speeches and by means of the benefits conferred upon them. But he never said: God has sent me to you and has given me commandments and prohibitions. Even when the commandment of circumcision was laid upon him, his sons, and those who belonged to him, he circumcised them alone and did not use the form of the prophetic call to exhort the people to do this. . . .

As for the prophets from among us who came after Moses our Master, you know the text of all their stories and the fact that their function was that of preachers who called upon the people to obey the Law of Moses, threatened those who rejected it, and held out promises to those who were firm in observing it.

That there never was such a Law, or such a prophet, either before or after Moses is argued in this passage from an analysis of the texts of Scripture itself. That there never will be is handled differently. Here the argument is based on an analogy with contemporary theories about the physical constitution of living things: that health, for example, is the result of the equilibrium of the humors within the body. Such an argument came easily to the mind of Maimonides, a Spanish biblical and Talmudic scholar who passed much of his later career as court physician to the Muslim rulers of Egypt. Maimonides continues the argument.

We likewise believe that things will always be this way. As it says: "It is not in heaven etc." (Deut. 30:12) . . . "for us and our children forever" (Deut. 29:28). And that is as it ought to be. For when a thing is as perfect as it is possible to be within its species, it is impossible that within that species there should be found another thing that does not fall short of that perfection either because of excess or deficiency. Thus in comparison with a temperament whose composition is of the greatest equibalance possible in the species in question, all other temperaments are not composed in accordance with this equibalance because of either deficiency or excess. Things are similar with regard to this Law, as is clear from its equibalance. For it says: "Just statutes and judgments" (Deut. 4:8). Now you know that the meaning of "just" is equibalanced. For these are manners of worship in which there is no burden and excess, such as monastic life and pilgrimage and similar things, nor any deficiency necessarily leading to greed and being engrossed in the indulgence of appetites, so that in consequence the perfection of man is diminished with respect to his moral habits and to his speculation, which is the case with regard to all the other laws of the religious communities of the past. (Maimonides, *Guide of the Perplexed* 2.39) [MAIMONIDES 1963: 379–380]

The Jewish position was of course well known to the Christians. Here is one Muslim response, by the theologian al-Nasafi (d. 1114 C.E.). If the conclusions would not have been at all acceptable, the terms of Nasafi's argument might have appealed to the physician Maimonides.

The Jews—may God curse them—teach that abrogation of religious Law is not possible, but according to truly orthodox people (in the Muslim community) it is possible. The Jews offer proof and say that the fact that something is commanded (by God) necessarily means that it is helpful, and the fact that something is forbidden (by God) necessarily means that it is harmful. If that is so, then the fact that God has given commands and prohibitions in the Torah indicates that it is concerned with something helpful (to humanity). If then it is possible for Him (later) to forbid something He had commanded in the Torah, that would mean that in the Torah He had commanded something harmful. But that cannot be, for God is wise, He knows the final outcome of affairs, and it is not possible that His action should be described as foolish.

In reply to this we teach that if God gives commands about some matter, that necessarily means it would be helpful at that time, but it does not mean that it would necessarily be helpful at all times. An example is that of food and drink, which are assuredly helpful in a state of hunger but are not necessarily helpful in a state of satiety. Another example is that of the physician who orders for the sick person different medicines at different times, yet that involves no introduction of a new opinion, but is to ensure real helpfulness at that particular time.

By way of confirmation Nasafi concludes with the traditional Muslim view of the revelation of Law (see Chapter 1 above), namely, that between Moses and Muham-

mad revealed Books of Law had been given to David, that is, the Book of Psalms, and to Jesus, that is, the Gospel. Nasafi continues.

So it is here. God is more compassionate to His servants than is a tender physician, and when He appointed the Torah as a religious Law in the time of Moses—on whom be peace—that was something helpful, and (continued to be) until the completion of the Mosaic dispensation. Then (after the completion of the Mosaic dispensation) the helpfulness was in the Psalter until the completion of the Davidic dispensation. Then (after that) the helpfulness was in the Gospel until the completion of the Christian dispensation. Finally, the helpfulness was in the Quran in this age of our Prophet Muhammad—upon whom be God's blessing and peace. (Nasafi, *Sea of Discourse on Theology*)

[JEFFERY 1962: 450–451]

7. The Laws after Moses

If there was no Law after Moses, there was nonetheless a great deal of legal material that evolved, in one fashion or another, out of that original deposit.

The two Talmuds, the Tosefta, the Sifra and the Sifre, and the Toseftot are the sources from all of which it is elucidated what is forbidden and what is permitted, what is unclean and what is clean, what is a penal violation and what involves no penalty, what is fit to be used and what is unfit for use, all in accordance with the traditions received by the sages from their predecessors in an unbroken succession up to the teachings of Moses as he received them on Sinai. From these sources too are ascertained the decrees, instituted by the sages and the prophets, in each generation, to serve as a protective fence about the Law, in accordance with Moses' express injunction, "You shall keep My charge" (Lev. 18:30), that is, "Ordain a charge to preserve My charge." From these sources a clear conception is also obtained of the customs and ordinances, either formally introduced in various generations by their respective authorities or that come into use with their sanction; from these it is forbidden to depart, as it is said, "You shall not turn aside from the sentence which they shall declare to you, to the right hand nor to the left" (Deut. 17:11). So too these works contain the clearly established judgments and rules not received by Moses, but which the Supreme Court of each generation deduced by applying the hermeneutical principles for the interpretation of the Law, and which were decided by those venerable authorities to be the law, all of which, accumulated from the days of Moses to his own time, Rav Ashi put together in the Gemara [that is, the Talmud]. (Maimonides, *Mishneh Torah*, introduction)

Precisely the same point had been made earlier by Judah Halevi in his dialogue entitled The Khazar King, *written ca. 1130–1140 C.E.*

Some of our laws originate, in certain circumstances, "from the place which the Lord shall choose." Prophecy lasted about forty years of the Second Temple. Jeremiah in his prophetic speeches commended the people of the Second Temple for their piety, learning and fear of God. If we did not rely on men like these, on whom should we rely? We see that prescriptions given after Moses' death became law. Thus Solomon hallowed "the middle of the court" (1 Kings 8:64ff.), slaughtered sacrifices on a place other than the altar, and celebrated "the feast seven days and seven nights." David and Samuel appointed the order of the Temple choir, which became a fixed law. Solomon both added to the sanctuary built in the desert and omitted things from it. Ezra imposed the tax of one-third of a shekel on the community of the Second Temple (Neh. 10:33). A stone paving was put in the place of the Ark, hiding it behind a curtain, because they knew that the Ark had been buried in that place.

The objection is then raised that there is a biblical injunction concerning the Law, that "You shall not add thereto nor diminish from it" (Deut. 13:1). How is that to be answered?

This was said only to the masses, that they should not conjecture and theorize and contrive laws according to their own conception. . . . They were recommended to the post-Mosaic prophets, the priests and the judges, as it is written: "I will raise them up a prophet . . . and he will speak to them all that I shall command them" (Deut. 18:18). With regard to the priests and the judges, it is said that their decisions are binding. The words, "You shall not add etc." refer to "that which I commanded you through Moses" as well as any "prophet from among the brethren" who fulfills the conditions of a prophet. They further refer to regulations laid down in common by priests and judges "from the place which the Lord shall choose." For they (too) have divine assistance and would never, on account of their large number, concur in anything which contradicts the Law. Much less likelihood was there of erroneous views because they had inherited vast learning, for the reception of which they were naturally endowed. (Judah Halevi, *The Khazar King* 3.40–41)

[HALEVI 1905: 172–173]

8. How the Law Worked

For most of their history, whether they were under foreign domination or native rulers, the Jews lived under what might be called the Mosaic constitution, the Torah viewed as a body of operational law administered by a court. That court was called the Great Sanhedrin and sat in Jerusalem under the presidency of the High Priest until 70 C.E. But it was not the only religious court in Palestine; there were lesser Sanhedrins, which may have been local bodies or those with limited competence. That there was, in any event, a judicial system with the right of appeal rather than a single court of Jewish law in Greco-Roman times in Palestine is attested to by the Mishna tractate Sanhedrin.

There were three courts (in Jerusalem): one used to sit at the (eastern?) gate of the Temple mount, one used to sit at the gate of the Temple Court (of the Israelites), and one used to sit in the Chamber of Hewn Stone (M.Middoth 5:4). They [that is, local judges from the provinces] used to come first to the court that was at the gate of the Temple Mount, and one would say, "This was the way I interpreted (the Law) and that the way my colleagues interpreted; and in this way I taught and in that my colleagues." If the members of that court had heard of a (precedential) tradition, they told it to them, otherwise they [that is, the appellants] took themselves to the court that was at the gate of the Temple Court. [Here the process is repeated. If no precedent is found in tradition, they proceed upwards.] . . . They come to the Great Court that was in the Chamber of Hewn Stone, whence the Law goes forth to all Israel, as it is written, "From that place which the Lord shall choose" (Deut. 17:10).

When that passage was written, much of the earlier legal system had been swept away in the debacle that overwhelmed Jerusalem. But the work of legal discussion and enlargement went on, chiefly in Galilee, and found its expression in the Mishna. Rabbi Judah's redaction of the Mishna was completed sometime about 200 C.E., and for the next three centuries scholars in the schools of Palestine, notably at Tiberias, and in those of Iraq worked at elucidating and refining it. The work of each group was eventually collected in a gemara or "completion." The gemara of the "Babylonians" of Iraq was connected with the name of Rav Ashi (d. 427 C.E.), and it was, according to Maimonides, a fortuitous event, since the fortunes of the Jewish community were rapidly changing in those days.

After the Court of Rav Ashi, who compiled the ["Babylonian"] Gemara which was finally completed in the days of his son, an extraordinarily great dispersion of Israel throughout the world took place. The people emigrated to remote parts and distant isles. The prevalence of

wars and the march of armies made travel insecure. The study of the
Torah declined. The Jewish people did not flock to the schools in their
thousands and tens of thousands as heretofore; but in each city and country individuals who felt the divine call gathered together and occupied
themselves with the Torah, studied all the works of the sages, and from
these learned the method of legal interpretation.

The extraordinary flexibility of the system is now emphasized.

If a court established in any country after the time of the Talmud
made decrees or ordinances or introduced customs for those residing in
its particular country or for residents of other countries, its enactments
did not obtain the acceptance of all Israel because of the remoteness of
Jewish settlements and the difficulties of travel. And as the court of any
particular country consisted of individuals (whose authority was not universally recognized), while the Supreme Court of seventy-one members
had, several years before the compilation of the Talmud, ceased to exist,
no compulsion is exercised on those living in one country to observe the
customs of another country; nor is any court directed to issue a decree
that had been issued by another court in the same country. So too, if one
of the Gaons [described below] taught that a certain judgment was correct, and it became clear at a later date that this was not in accordance
with the views of the Gemara, the earlier authority is not necessarily
followed but the view is adopted which seems more reasonable, whether
it be that of an earlier or later authority.

But there is, for all that, a cohesive center.

The foregoing observations refer to rules, decrees, ordinances and
customs that originated after the Talmud had been compiled. But whatever is already mentioned in the Babylonian Talmud is binding on all
Israel. And every city and country is bound to observe all the customs
observed by the sages of the Gemara, promulgate their decrees and uphold their institutions, on the ground that all the customs, decrees and
institutions mentioned in the Talmud received the assent of all Israel, and
those sages who instituted the ordinances, issued the decrees, introduced
the customs, gave the decisions and taught that a certain ruling was
correct, constituted the total body or the majority of Israel's wise men.
They were the leaders who received from each other traditions concerning the fundamentals of Judaism in an unbroken succession back to Moses
our teacher, upon whom be peace. (Maimonides, *Mishneh Torah*, Introduction)

The closure of the Talmud did not end the work of either the jurisprudents or the judges. The former continued to study the materials from the oral tradition that Maimonides was to excerpt and arrange in his Mishneh Torah, *while the latter, pressed by requests for judgment on the basis of the laws, were in effect creating new ones. Maimonides explains.*

The sages who arose after the completion of the Talmud, studied it deeply and became famous for their wisdom, are called Gaons. All these Gaons who flourished in the land of Israel, Babylon, Spain and France taught the method of the Talmud, elucidated its obscurities and expounded the various topics with which it deals. For its method is exceedingly profound. . . . Many requests were made to the Gaons of the day by residents of different cities, asking for explanations of difficulties in the Talmud. These the Gaons answered, according to their ability. Those who had put the questions collected the responses which they made into books for study. The Gaons also, at different periods, composed commentaries on the Talmud. . . . They also made compilations of settled rules as to things permitted or forbidden, as to infractions which were penal or were not liable to a penalty. All these dealt with matters in regard to which compendia were needed, that could be studied by one not capable of penetrating to the depths of the Talmud. This is the godly work in which all the Gaons of Israel engaged, from the completion of the Talmud to the present date which is the eighth year of the eleventh century after the destruction of the Second Temple [that is, 1177 C.E.]. (Maimonides, *Mishneh Torah*, Introduction)

9. The Codification of Torah Law

As we have already seen in Chapter 3 above, Maimonides' major legal undertaking was the Mishneh Torah, *his codification of "Jewish Law," where that term is understood as embracing all the prescriptions from Moses to the completion of the Talmud. To Torah in the narrower sense—the written Law given to Moses on Mount Sinai—he devoted far less attention. He did codify it after a fashion, but almost as an afterthought in the wake of the* Mishneh Torah *and chiefly because he disagreed with certain of his predecessors on which commandments belonged to that number of 613. He describes this later project.*

At the completion of our earlier well-known work, which included a commentary on the whole of the Mishna [that is, the *Mishneh Torah*], our objective in writing it was achieved with an explanation of the substance of each and every legal prescription in the Mishna, since our intention there was not to include for every commandment an exhaustive discussion of the law embracing everything that is necessary (to know) of the prohibited and the permissible, liable and free; that much is clear to whoever studies the work. I then decided that it would be advisable to compile a compendium which would include all the laws in the Torah and its regulations, with nothing omitted. In this compendium I would try, as is my custom, to avoid mentioning differences of opinion and rejected teachings, and include there only the established law, so that this compendium would embrace all the laws of the Torah of Moses our teacher, whether they have a bearing in the time of exile or not. . . .

When I first had the idea for this work (of the *Mishneh Torah*), and set to writing it by giving an initial brief list of all the commandments by running through them in the Introduction, I was overcome with a feeling of distress, which in fact I have experienced for a number of years, and which was as follows. Scholars who are engaged in enumerating the commandments, or in writing anything whatsoever on the subject, have all come forward with such strange theories that I could hardly describe their magnitude. . . . Therefore I thought it advisable to precede what I mentioned with a treatise in which I would explain the enumeration of the commandments (of the Torah) and how they are to be counted. To that end I would bring proofs from the verses of the Torah and from the words of the sages, of blessed memory, concerning their interpretation, and I would also precede it with a discussion of the principles that are to guide us in enumerating the commandments. . . . Thus I will explain all the commandments, listing them one after the other, bringing proof wherever there is a doubt, or where one not skilled in the Laws of the Torah might possibly have some unfounded opinion; these I will remove and further explain everything about which there is some doubt. (Maimonides, *Book of the Commandments*, Introduction)

10. Two Classes of Laws:
The Rational and the Revelational

Philo was among the first Jews to explore the path that led through the Greek and Roman theories of law and of cognition, both of which had contributed, as we have seen, to his own understanding of Torah and of the role of Moses in the revelation and the promulgation of the Law. History was not kind to Philo. The Christians expropriated a good deal of his thinking to their own ends, to which it was most congenial. Perhaps more important, the political disasters that descended upon the Jews under Roman sovereignty made the project of recasting Judaism in the then current Hellenic mode an extremely unappetizing one to many religious Jews. The revival of that enterprise had to wait nine centuries, for the passage of the Jews from Roman to Christian to Muslim sovereignty in the Near East and the extraordinary revival of Greek learning in tenth-century Baghdad. That time and that milieu prompted one Jewish scholar, the Gaon Saadya, to cast another look at the legacy of Hellenism. In his Book of Doctrines and Beliefs *(933 C.E.) Saadya attempts to put speculative reason in the service of the Law.*

After these introductory remarks, I now come to the subject proper. I declare that our Lord, may He be exalted and glorified, has informed us through the words of His prophets that He wishes us to lead a religious life by following the religion which He instituted for us. This religion contains laws which He has prescribed for us and which it is our duty to keep and fulfill in sincerity, as it is said, "This day the Lord your God commanded you to do these statutes and ordinances; you shall, therefore, observe and do them with all your heart and all your soul" (Deut. 26:16). His messengers established these laws for us by wondrous signs and miracles, and we commenced to keep and fulfill them forthwith. Later we found that speculation confirms the necessity of the Law for us. It would, however, not have been appropriate to leave us to our own devices.

It is desirable that I should explain which matters and aspects (of the Law) speculation confirms as necessary. I maintain that reason bids us respond to every benefactor either by returning his kindness, if he is in need of it, or by offering our thanks, if he is not in need of recompense. Now since this is a dictate of reason itself, it would not have been fitting for the Creator, be He exalted and glorified, to waive this right in respect of Himself, but it was necessary that He should command His creatures to worship Him and to render thanks to Him for having created them. Reason further lays down that the wise man should not permit himself to be vilified and treated with contempt. It is similarly necessary that the Creator should forbid His servants to treat Him in this way. Reason further prescribes that human beings should be forbidden to trespass upon one another's rights by any sort of aggression. It is likewise necessary that the Wise One should not permit them to act in such a way. Reason, furthermore, permits a wise man to employ a workman for any kind of work and pay him his wages for the sole purpose of allowing him to earn something, since this is a matter which results in benefit to the workman and causes no harm to the employer.

Saadya then shows that these four objectives that reason dictates are in fact the substance of the Law laid down by God in the Torah. They constitute what he later

*calls the class of "Rational Laws," those both revealed and confirmed by reason. He
then turns to a second category, the "Revelational Laws."*

The Second Class of Law consists of matters regarding which reason
passes no judgment in the way of either approval or disapproval so far as
their essence is concerned. But our Lord has given us an abundance of
such commandments and prohibitions in order to increase our reward
and happiness through them, as is said: "The Lord was pleased, for His
righteousness' sake, to make the Law great and glorious" (Isa. 42:21). . . .

The Second Class of Law [that is, "Revelational Laws"] concerns
such matters as are of a neutral character from the point of view of
reason, but which the Law has made the objects of commandment in
some cases and prohibitions in others, leaving the rest in their neutral
state. Instances are the distinguishing of Sabbath and Festivals from ordinary days; the selection of certain individuals to be prophets and leaders;
the prohibition to eat certain foodstuffs; the avoidance of sexual intercourse with certain people; the abstention enforced during periods of
impurity. The great motive for the observance of these principles and the
laws derived and branching out from them is, of course, the command
of our Lord and the promotion of our happiness resulting from it, but I
find for most of them also some minor and partial motives of a useful
character.

*Saadya, then, is not quite willing to surrender this class of Laws to a purely arbitrary
choice on God's part; they too have some practical—and so reasonable—end. He
takes up the question of the Torah's dietary laws. Although they cannot be demonstrated as necessary by human reason alone, they do serve some sensible utilitarian
purpose.*

The prohibition not to eat certain animals has this advantage (for
example): It makes it impossible to liken any of the animals to the Creator, since it is unthinkable that one should permit oneself either to eat or
to declare as impure what one likens to God. Also it prevents people from
worshiping any of the animals, since it is unthinkable that one should
worship either what serves as food or what one declares as impure. . . .

If one examines most of the "Revelational Laws" in the above fashion, one will find in them a great number of partial motives and reasons
of usefulness. But the wisdom of the Creator and His knowledge is above
everything human beings can attain, as is said, "For the heavens are
higher than the earth, as are My ways higher than your ways" (Isa. 55:9).
(Saadya, *Book of Doctrines and Beliefs* 3.2)

[SAADYA 1945: 94–105]

11. Maimonides and Aquinas on the Purposes of the Law

Why was the Law given? The question was not often raised among the rabbis, except perhaps when some of its provisions were attacked by non-Jews, as we shall see. But once the Jews, like the Christians and Muslims, were exposed to philosophy and its claims to be a source of truth and certitude, the issue of the intent and purpose of the Law had to be addressed by anyone who took that claim seriously. One who did address it was Maimonides, who in addition to his training in Torah and Mishna was a profound student of Hellenic philosophy, whether in its Greek or its Islamic versions. He resumes the same theme taken up in his Letter to the Yemen.

The Law as a whole aims at two things: the welfare of the soul and the welfare of the body. As for the welfare of the soul, it consists in the multitude's acquiring correct opinions corresponding to their respective capacity. Therefore some of those opinions are set forth explicitly and some are set forth in parables. For it is not within the nature of the common multitude that its capacity should suffice for apprehending that subject matter as it is. As for the welfare of the body, it comes about by the improvement of their ways of living with one another. This is achieved through two things. One of them is the abolition of their wronging each other. This is tantamount to every individual among the people not being permitted to act according to his will and up to the limits of his power, but being forced to do what is useful to the whole. The second thing consists in the acquisition by every human individual of moral qualities that are useful for life in society so that the affairs of the city may be ordered. (Maimonides, *Guide of the Perplexed* 3.27) [MAIMONIDES 1963: 510]

The Law, then, in Maimonides' view, as in Plato's before him, provides truth for the "multitude" and inculcates the virtues of temperance and justice. Clearly, Maimonides viewed human perfection as essentially political; that is, it was to be achieved by a life in society. Regarding the first objective, the correct opinions that the Law seeks to inculcate, Maimonedes notes:

. . .You should know that in regard to correct opinions through which the ultimate perfection may be achieved, the Law has communicated only their end and issued a call to believe in them in a summary way, that is, to believe in the existence of the deity, may He be exalted, His unity, His knowledge, His power, His will, His eternity. All these points are ultimate ends, which can be made clear in detail and through definitions only after one knows many opinions. In the same way the Law also issues a call to adopt certain beliefs, belief in which is necessary for the sake of political welfare. . . .

What results from what we have now stated as a premise regarding this subject is that whenever a commandment, be it a prescription or a prohibition, requires abolishing reciprocal wrongdoing, or urging to a noble moral quality leading to a good social relationship, or communicating a correct opinion that ought to be believed either on account of itself or because it is necessary for the abolition of reciprocal wrongdoing or for the acquisition of a noble moral quality, such a commandment has a clear cause and is of manifest utility. No question concerning the end need be posed with regard to such commandments. For no one was ever so perplexed for a day as to ask why we were commanded by the Law that God is one, or why we were forbidden to kill and to steal, or why we were forbidden to exercise vengeance and retaliation, or why we were ordered to love each other.

Thus there is no discussion of laws that seem to conform to the dictates of right reason, what another tradition called the "natural law." Where the problem arose was in that category Saadya had called "Revelational Law."

The matter about which people are perplexed and opinions disagree—that some say there is no utility in them except the fact of the mere command, whereas others saw there is a utility in such commandments that is hidden from us—are the commandments from whose external meaning it does not appear that they are useful according to one of the three notions we have mentioned: I mean to say that they neither communicate an opinion nor inculcate a moral quality nor abolish reciprocal wrongdoing. Apparently these commandments are not related to the welfare of the soul, as they do not communicate a belief, or to the welfare of the body, as they do not communicate rules useful for the governance of the household. Such, for example, are the prohibitions of mingled stuff, of the mingling of diverse species, and of meat (boiled) in milk and the commandment concerning the covering of blood, the heifer whose neck was broken, and the firstling of an ass and others of the same kind. However, you will hear my explanation for all of them and my exposition of the correct and demonstrated causes for all of them. (Maimonides, *Guide* 3.28) [MAIMONIDES 1963: 512–513]

Thomas Aquinas (d. 1274 C.E.), a Christian theologian at the University of Paris, was the inheritor and student of a natural law tradition, which reached him by way of the Stoics, Cicero, and Augustine. In that context, he places his discussion of the Torah—the Christians' "Old Law"—in his Summa Theologica.

It belongs to the divine law to direct men to one another and to God. Now each of these belongs, from a universal point of view, to the dictates of the natural law, to which dictates the moral precepts are to be referred; yet each of them has to be determined by divine or human law because naturally known principles are common, both in speculative and practical matters. Accordingly, just as the determination of the common principle about divine worship is effected by ceremonial precepts, so the determination of the common principle of that justice which is to be observed among men is effected by the judicial precepts.

We must therefore distinguish three kinds of precepts in the Old Law, to wit, the moral precepts, which are dictated by the natural law; ceremonial precepts, which are determinations of the divine worship; and judicial precepts, which are determinations of the justice to be maintained among men. Therefore the Apostle (Paul), after saying that "the Law is holy," adds that "the commandment is just, and holy, and good" (Rom. 7:12): "just" in respect to the judicial precepts; "holy" with regard to the ceremonial precepts, since that is holy which is consecrated to God; and "good," that is, conducive to virtue, as to the moral precepts. (Aquinas, *Summa Theologica* I/2, ques. 99, art. 4) [AQUINAS 1945: 822]

But if the moral precepts of the Torah are "dictated by natural law" and so in accordance with reason, what need was there for the revelation of such precepts and their incorporation into the Mosaic Law?

It was fitting that the divine law should come to man's assistance not only in those things for which reason is insufficient, but also in those things in which human reason may happen to be impeded. Now as to the most common principles of the natural law, the human reason could not err universally in moral matters; but through being habituated to sin, it became darkened as to what ought to be done in the particular. But with regard to the other moral precepts, which are conclusions drawn from the common principles of the moral law, the reason of man went astray, to the extent of judging to be lawful things which are evils in themselves. Hence there was need for the authority of the divine law to rescue men from both these defects. Thus among the articles of faith not only are those things set forth to which reason cannot reach, such as the Trinity of the Godhead, but also those things to which right reason can attain, such as that God is one; and this in order to remove the manifold errors in which reason is liable to err. (Ibid., ques. 99, art. 2, ad 2) [AQUINAS 1945: 2:819]

The Old Law showed forth the precepts of the natural law, and added certain precepts of its own. Accordingly, as to those precepts of the natural law contained in the Old Law, all were bound to observe them, not because they belong to the Old Law but because they belong to the natural law. But as to those precepts that were added to the Old Law, they were not binding on any save the Jewish people alone.

The reason for this is because the Old Law was given to the Jewish people that they might receive a prerogative of holiness, in reverence for Christ who was to be born of that people. Now when any laws are enacted for the special sanctification of certain ones, these are binding on them alone. Thus clerics who are set aside for the service of God are bound to certain obligations to which the laity are not bound, and religious are likewise bound by their profession to certain works of perfection to which the secular clergy are not bound. In like manner, this people were bound to certain special observances to which other peoples were not bound. (Ibid., ques. 98, art. 5) [AQUINAS 1945: 2:814]

12. The Example of Circumcision

From an early period it was the practice of circumcision, that seal of the Covenant, that most exercised those Jews who attempted to rationalize the Law, not least because it was used to precisely the opposite end by polemicists among the Gentiles. Both the charge and the retort are already present in Philo in the first century C.E.

The general categories of the special laws, the so-called Ten Commandments, have been carefully investigated in the preceding treatise. Following the sequence of our work, we must now examine the particular ordinances. I shall begin with that which is an object of derision among many people. The circumcision of the genital organs is held in ridicule, though it is most zealously practiced by many other nations, especially by the Egyptians, a people that appears to be populous, ancient and philosophical in the highest degree. It would therefore be proper to let go of the childish banter and investigate more wisely and seriously the causes thanks to which this custom has prevailed, and not hastily pass judgment on the recklessness of great nations. They should reflect that it is unnatural that so many thousands in every generation undergo cutting and mutilate their own bodies and those of their nearest kin while suffering severe pains (without reason), and that there are many conditions that impel them to maintain and discharge a practice introduced by the ancients. The principal reasons are four in number.

The first is that it secures release from the severe and virtually incurable malady of the foreskin called carbuncle, which, I believe, gets its name from the fact that it involves a chronic inflammation and which is more prone to befall those who retain the foreskin. Second, it furthers the cleanliness of the whole body as befits a consecrated order, wherefore the Egyptian priests go even further and have their bodies shaved. For some impurities that ought to be purged collect gradually and retract in the hair and the foreskin. Third, it assures the resemblance of the circumcised member to the heart. For as both are prepared for generation, the cardial pneuma for the generation of thought, the reproductive organ for living creatures, the earliest men deemed it right to assimilate the manifest and visible organ through which sensible things are naturally engendered to the unseen and superior organ by which intelligible things are produced. The fourth and most essential reason is its predisposition to increase fecundity, for it is said that the sperm has free passage without being scattered or flowing into the folds of the foreskin, and consequently the circumcised nations appear to be the most prolific and populous.

Philo is willing to accept these medical and sociological reasons for circumcision on the authority of others more knowledgeable than himself. But he is a philosopher and so has his own reasons that persuade to the purposefulness of circumcision.

These are the explanations that have reached us from the antiquarian studies of inspired men who researched the Mosaic writings with the utmost care. As for myself, in addition to what has been said, I believe that circumcision is a symbol of two things that are particularly essential. One is the excision of pleasures that bewitch the mind. For since among the love-lures of pleasure the prize is carried off by the union of man and woman, the legislators thought it right to dock the organ that serves such intercourse, thus intimating that circumcision signifies the excision of excessive and superfluous pleasure, not of one pleasure alone, but through the one that is most violent also of all the others.

The other reason is that a man should know himself and expel from his soul the grievous malady of conceit. For there are some who boast of their ability to fashion, like good sculptors, the fairest of creatures, man, and puffed up with pride, have deified themselves, ignoring the true Cause of all created things, though they could find a corrective for their delusions in their own acquaintances. For many man among them are sterile and many women barren, whose relations are without issue and who grow old childless. This evil opinion must therefore be excised from the mind together with all others that are not God-loving. (Philo, *The Special Laws* 1.1–11) [PHILO 1981: 277–278]

The moral purpose of the Law, the acquisition of moral qualities, is likewise illustrated by Maimonides' remarks on circumcision.

Similarly, with regard to circumcision, one of the reasons for it is, in my opinion, the wish to bring about a decrease in sexual intercourse and a weakening of the organ in question, so that this activity might be diminished and the organ be in as quiet a state as possible. It has been thought that circumcision perfects what is a congenital defect. This gave the possibility to everyone to raise an objection and say: How can natural things be defective so that they need to be perfected from the outside, all the more because we know how useful the foreskin is for that member? In fact this commandment has not been prescribed with a view to perfecting a congenital defect but to perfecting a moral defect. The bodily pain caused to that member is the real purpose of circumcision. None of the activities necessary for the preservation of the individual is harmed thereby, nor is procreation rendered impossible, but violent concupiscence and lust that goes beyond what is needed are diminished. The fact that circumcision weakens the faculty of sexual excitement and sometimes perhaps diminishes the pleasure is indubitable. For if at birth this member has been made to bleed and has had its covering taken away from it, it must indubitably be weakened.

The Sages, may their memory be blessed, have explicitly stated: "It is hard for a woman with whom an uncircumcised man has had sexual intercourse to separate from him" (Genesis Rabbah 80). In my opinion this is the strongest of the reasons for circumcision. Who first began to perform this act if not Abraham, who was celebrated for his chastity, as has been mentioned by the Sages, may their memory be blessed, with reference to his dictum: "Behold, now I know that you are a fair woman to look upon" (Gen. 12:11).

Maimonides then passes to the social benefits of circumcision.

According to me circumcision has another very important meaning, namely, that all people professing, that is, those who believe in the unity of God, should have a bodily sign uniting them so that one who does not belong to them should not be able to claim that he is one of them, while being a stranger. For he would do this in order to profit by them and to deceive the people who profess this religion. Now a man does not perform this act (of circumcision) upon himself or upon a son unless it be in consequence of a genuine belief. For it is not like an incision in the leg or a burn in the arm, but is a very, very hard thing.

It is also well known what degree of mutual love and mutual help exists between people who all bear the same sign, which forms for them a sort of covenant or alliance. Circumcision is a covenant made by Abraham our father with a view to the belief in the unity of God. This covenant imposes the obligation to believe in the unity of God: "To be a God to you and to your seed after you" (Gen. 17:7). This is also a strong reason, as strong as the first, which may be adduced to account for circumcision; perhaps it is even stronger than the first.

Finally, it is the voice of the physician and the student of human psychology that we hear.

The perfection and perpetuation of this Law can be achieved only if circumcision is performed in childhood. For this there are three wise reasons. The first is that if the child were let alone until he grew up, he would sometimes not perform it. The second is that a child does not suffer as much pain as a grown-up man because his membrane is still soft and his imagination weak; for a grown-up man would regard the thing, which he would imagine before it occurred, as terrible and hard. The third is that the parents of the child that is just born take lightly matters concerning it, for up to that time the imaginative form that compels the parents to love it is not yet consolidated. For this imaginative form increases through habitual contact and grows with the growth of the child, then it begins to decrease and disappear. For the love of the father and the mother for the child when it has just been born is not like their love for it when it is one year old, and their love for it when it is one year old is not like their love when it is six years old. Consequently, if the child were left uncircumcised for two or three years, this would necessitate the abandonment of circumcision because of the father's love and affection for his child. At the time of its birth, on the other hand, this imaginative form is very weak, especially as far as concerns the father, upon whom (the fulfillment of) this commandment is imposed. (Maimonides, *Guide of the Perplexed* 3.49) [MAIMONIDES 1963: 609–610]

When we turn to Aquinas on the same subject, we find that he has built his explanation around Paul's letter to the Romans. He displays borrowings from Maimonides, though with some very different emphases and typical Christian additions.

The chief literal reason for circumcision was in order that man might profess his belief in one God. And because Abraham was the first to sever himself from the infidels by going out from his house and his kindred, for this reason he was the first to receive circumcision. This reason is set forth by the Apostle (Paul) thus: "He received a sign of circumcision, a seal of the justice of the faith which he had, being uncircumcised," because, namely, we are told that "to Abraham faith was reputed unto righteousness," for the reason that "against hope he believed in hope," that is, against the hope that is of nature he believed in the hope that is of grace, "that he might be the father of many nations," when he was an old man, and his wife an old and barren woman (Rom. 4:9ff.). And in order that this declaration and imitation of Abraham's faith might be fixed firmly in the heart of the Jews, they received in their flesh such a sign as they could not forget; and so it is written: "My covenant shall be in your flesh for a perpetual Covenant" (Gen. 16:13). This was done on the eighth day, because until then a child is very tender, and so might be seriously injured. . . . And it was not delayed after that time, lest some might refuse the sign of circumcision because of the pain; and also lest the parents, whose love for their children increases as they become used to their presence and as they grow older, might withdraw their children from circumcision.

A second reason may have been the weakening of concupiscence in that member. A third motive may have been to revile the worship of Venus and Priapus, which gave honor to that part of the body. . . . The Lord's prohibition (against self-mutilation) extended only to cutting oneself in honor of idols, and such was not the circumcision of which we have been speaking.

The figurative reason for circumcision was that it foreshadowed the removal of corruption, which was to be brought about by Christ, and will be perfectly fulfilled in the eighth age, which is the age of those who rise from the dead. And since all corruption of guilt and punishment comes to us, by reason of our carnal origin, from the sin of our first parent, therefore circumcision was applied to the generative member. (Aquinas, *Summa Theologica* I/2, ques. 102, art. 5, ad 1) [AQUINAS 1945: 2:885–886]

13. Rules without Reason

The case of circumcision was by no means the first occasion that questions had arisen about certain prescriptions of the Law. We shall return to Maimonides, and particularly to his suggestions on the origins of the prohibition of mixing meat and milk. In the fourth and fifth Christian centuries, perhaps under the stimulus of Greek and Christian polemic, the rabbis had begun to make a distinction between God's com-

mandments or judgments on the one hand and his "statutes" on the other. Each had the binding force of law, but for different reasons.

It says in Leviticus 18:4, "You shall observe My judgments and execute my statutes." The Rabbis teach: "My judgments" are those things which, if they had not been written, would have had to be written, such as (commandments against) idolatry, unchastity, bloodshed, robbery, blasphemy. "My statutes": these are the things to which Satan and the Gentiles raise objections, such as not eating pig, not wearing linen and woolen together, the law of levirate marriage, the scapegoat. Should you say, "These are empty things," the Scripture adds, "I am the Lord, I have made decrees; you are not at liberty to criticize them." (BT.Yoma 67b)

The point is made even more directly in the conclusion of the following anecdote, which has to do with the ritual of the red heifer described in Numbers 19:1–10.

A heathen said to Yohanan ben Zakkai, "What you do (in the matter of the red heifer) seems like sorcery. You take a red cow and kill it, and burn the corpse and crush its ashes, and then preserve them. Then if one of you becomes unclean by touching a dead body, you sprinkle on the man two or three drops of the water into which the ashes have been cast, and you say to him, 'You are clean.' " Rabbi Yohanan said to him, "Has the demon of madness ever entered into you?" He said, "No." "Have you ever seen a man into whom that demon had entered?" "Yes," he replied. "And what do they do to him?" The man answered, "They take roots and make a smoke underneath the man, then they sprinkle water on him and the demon flies away from him." Rabbi Yohanan said to him, "Let your ears hear what your mouth has just said" [that is, you are refuted out of your own mouth]. . . . When the heathen had gone, his disciples said to Rabbi Yohanan, "You beat him with a feeble reed, but what is your answer to us?" Rabbi Yohanan said, "The dead body does not really defile; the water does not really purify; but God has said, 'I have ordained an ordinance, I have decreed a decree; it is not permitted for you to transgress it.' " (*Numbers Rabbah* 19:8)

Rabbi Yohanan's conclusion could not, surely, have much pleased Maimonides.

There is a group of human beings who consider it a grievous thing that causes should be given for any law; what would please them most is that the intellect would not find a meaning for the commandments and prohibitions. What compels them to feel thus is a sickness that they find in their souls, a sickness to which they are unable to give utterance and of which they cannot furnish a satisfactory account. For they think that if those laws were useful in this existence and had been given to us for that reason, it would be as if they derived from the reflection and the understanding of some intelligent being. If, however, there is a thing for which the intellect could not find any meaning at all and that does not lead to something useful, it indubitably derives from God; for the reflection of man would not lead to such a thing. It is as if, according to these people of weak intellects, man were more perfect than his Maker; for man speaks and acts in a manner that leads to some intended end, whereas the deity does not act thus but commands us to do things that are not useful to us and forbids us to do things that are not harmful to us. But He is far exalted above this; the contrary is the case, the whole purpose consisting in what is useful to us, as we have explained on the basis of the dictum: "For our good always, that He might preserve us alive, as it is at this day" (Deut. 6:24). (Maimonides, *Guide of the Perplexed* 3.31) [MAIMONIDES 1963: 524]

As we have already seen, Maimonides had an attentive reader in the Christian theologian Thomas Aquinas. For Aquinas too, the prescriptions of the Mosaic Law had their reasons. One of them was characteristically Christian: the prefiguring of the New Law in the Old. Thus for him there was not only a literal cause for the sacrifice of the red cow but an elaborate figurative one as well.

The figurative reason for this sacrifice was that the red cow signified Christ in respect of his assumed weakness, denoted by the female sex, while the color of the cow designated the blood of his passion. And the "red cow was of full age" because all Christ's works were perfect; "in which there was no blemish; and which had not carried the yoke" because Christ was innocent and he did not carry the yoke of sin. It was commanded to be taken to Moses because they blamed Christ for transgressing the Law of Moses by violating the Sabbath. And the cow was commanded to be brought to Eleazer the priest because Christ was delivered into the hands of the priests to be slain. It was immolated "outside the camp" because Christ suffered outside the (city) gate. And the priest dipped "his finger in her blood" because in this separation (of the blood from the red cow), symbolized by the finger, the mystery of Christ's passion should be considered and imitated.

The blood was sprinkled "over against . . . the tabernacle," which denotes the synagogue, to signify either the condemnation of the unbelieving Jews or the purification of the believers; and this "seven times" in token either of the seven gifts of the Holy Spirit or of the seven days wherein all time is comprised. . . . The ashes of the burning were gathered by "a man that is clean" because the relics of the Passion came into the possession of the Gentiles, who were not guilty of Christ's death. The ashes were put into water for the purpose of expiation because baptism receives from Christ's Passion the power of washing away sins. The priest who immolated and burned the cow, and he who burned, and he who gathered together the ashes were all unclean, as also he that sprinkled the water. This was the case either because the Jews became unclean through putting Christ to death, whereby our sins are expiated, and this "until evening," that is, until the end of the world when the remnants of Israel will be converted; or else because they who handle sacred things with a view to the cleansing of others contract certain uncleannesses, as Gregory says, and this "until evening," that is, until the end of his life. (Aquinas, *Summa Theologica* I/2, ques. 102, art. 5, ad 5) [AQUINAS 1945: 2:891–892]

14. The Divine Ruse of the Law

In his search for the causes behind apparently arbitrary commandments in the Torah, Maimonides frequently had resort to the explanation that they were promulgated to discourage idolatry. But the "wily graciousness" of God had another intent in mind.

The deity made a wily and gracious arrangement with regard to all the individuals of the living beings that suck. For when born, such individuals are extremely soft and cannot feed on dry food. Accordingly breasts were prepared for them so that they should produce milk with a view to their receiving humid food, which is similar to the composition of their bodies, until their limbs gradually and little by little became dry and solid. Many things in our Law are similar to this very governance on the part of Him who governs, may He be glorified and exalted. For a sudden transition from one opposite to another is impossible. Therefore man, according to his nature, is not capable of abandoning suddenly all to which he was accustomed. And therefore God sent Moses our Master to make of us "a kingdom of priests and a holy nation" (Exod. 19:6). . . . And at that time the way of life generally accepted and customary in the whole world and the universal service on which we were brought up consisted in offering various species of living beings in the temples in which images were set up, in worshiping the latter, and in burning incense before them. . . .

His wisdom, May He be exalted, and his gracious ruse, which is manifest in regard to all His creatures, did not require that He give us a Law prescribing the rejection, abandonment and abolition of all these kinds of worship. For one could not then conceive the acceptance of (such a Law), considering the nature of man, which always likes that to which it is accustomed. . . . Therefore He, may He be exalted, suffered the above-mentioned kinds of worship to remain, but transferred them from created or imaginary and unreal beings to His own name, may He be exalted, commanding us to practice them with regard to Him, may He be exalted. Thus He commanded us to build a Temple for Him . . . to have an altar for His name . . . to have sacrifice offered up to Him . . . to bow down in worship before Him and to burn incense before Him. And He forbade the performance of any of these actions with a view to some-one else. . . . And He singled out priests for the service of His sanctuary. . . . And because of their employment in the Temple and the sacrifices in it, it was necessary to fix for them dues that would be sufficient for them, namely, the dues of the Levites and the priests. Through this divine ruse it came about that the memory of idolatry was effaced and the grandest and true foundation of our belief, namely the existence and the oneness of the deity, was firmly established, while at the same time the souls had no feeling of repugnance and were not repelled because of the abolition of the modes of worship to which they were accustomed and than which no other mode of worship was known at that time.

I know that on thinking about this at first your soul will necessarily have a feeling of repugnance toward this notion and will feel aggrieved because of it, and you will ask me in your heart and say to me: How is it possible that none of the commandments, prohibitions, and great actions—which are very precisely set forth and prescribed for fixed sea-sons—should be intended for its own sake but for the sake of something else, as if this was a ruse invented for our benefit by God in order to achieve His first intention? What was there to prevent Him, may He be exalted, from giving us a Law in accordance with His first intention and from procuring us the capacity to accept this? Hear then the reply to your question that will put an end to this sickness in your heart and reveal to you the true reality of that to which I have drawn your attention. It is to the effect that the text of the Torah tells a quite similar story, namely, in its dictum: "God led them not by the way of the land of the Philistines, although it was near . . . " and so on. "But God led the people about, by way of the wilderness of the Red Sea" (Exod. 13:17–18). Just as God perplexed them in anticipation of what their bodies were naturally inca-pable of bearing—turning them away from the high road toward which they had been going, toward another road so that the first intention should be achieved—so did He in anticipation of what the soul is naturally incapable of receiving prescribe the laws that we have mentioned so that the first intention should be achieved, namely, the apprehension of Him, may He be exalted, and the rejection of idolatry. . . .

As for your question: What was there to prevent God from giving us a Law in accordance with His first intention and from procuring us the capacity to accept this? . . . One may say to you: Inasmuch as God's first intention and His will are that we should believe in this Law and that we should perform the actions prescribed by it, why did He not procure us the capacity always to accept this intention and to act in accordance with it, instead of using a ruse with regard to us, declaring that He will procure us benefits if we obey Him and will take vengeance on us if we disobey Him and performing in deed all those acts of benefiting and all those acts of vengeance? For this too is a ruse used by Him with regard to us in order to achieve His first intention with respect to us. What was there to prevent Him from causing the inclination to accomplish the acts of obedience willed by Him and to avoid the acts of disobedience abhorred by Him, to be a natural disposition fixed in us?

There is one and the same general answer to (these) questions and to all others that belong to the same class: Though all miracles change the nature of some individual being, God does not change at all the nature of human individuals by means of miracles. . . . It is because of this that there are commandments and prohibitions, rewards and punishments. . . . We do not say this because we believe that the changing of the nature of any human individual is difficult for Him, may He be exalted; rather it is possible and fully within His capacity. But according to the foundations of the Law, of the Torah, He has never willed to do it, nor shall He ever will it. For were it His will that the nature of any human individual should be changed because of what He, may He be exalted, wills from that individual, sending of prophets and all giving of a Law would have been useless.

In the end, however, Maimonides is forced to concede that there are some commandments whose precise cause is concealed from us by reason of our ignorance of the historical circumstances or the form of the idolatry they were intended to cure or ameliorate.

In the case of most of the statutes whose reason is hidden from us, everything serves to keep people away from idolatry. The fact that there are particulars the reason for which is hidden from me and the utility for which I do not understand, is due to the circumstance that things known by hearsay are not like things that one has seen. . . . If we knew the particulars of those (idolatrous) practices and heard details concerning those (pagan) opinions, we would become clear concerning the wisdom manifested in the details of the practices prescribed in the commandments concerning the sacrifices and the forms of uncleanness and other matters whose reason cannot, to my mind, be easily grasped. . . .

Consider how great was the extent of this corruption and whether or not it was fitting to spend one's efforts in putting an end to it. Most of the commandments serve, therefore, as we have made clear, to put an end to those opinions and to lighten the grave and oppressive burdens, the toil and the fatigue, that those people imposed upon themselves in their cult. Accordingly, every commandment or prohibition of the Law whose reason is hidden from you constitutes a cure for one of those diseases, which today—thank God—we do not know any more. (Maimonides, *Guide of the Perplexed* 3.49) [MAIMONIDES 1963: 612]

15. Crimes and Their Penalties in the Torah

Inserted in the middle of the account of the giving of the Law in Exodus 20:22–23:33 is a series of regulations, many of which appear to bear upon the life of a settled agricultural community. That would date them after the Israelite entry into Canaan, but they are attached here to the Sinai covenant. Some have to do with criminal acts and carry the death penalty.

21:15–17: He who strikes his mother or father shall be put to death. He who kidnaps a man, whether he has sold him or is still holding him, shall be put to death. He who insults his father or mother shall be put to death.

22:17–20: You shall not let live a sorceress. Whoever lies with a beast shall be put to death. Whoever sacrifices to any god other than the Lord alone shall be proscribed.

"Proscription," according to Leviticus 27:29, is death. Note too the general principle enunciated in Exodus 21:23–25.

If . . . damage ensues (from an act), the penalty shall be life for life, eye for eye, tooth for tooth, hand for hand, foot for foot, burn for burn, wound for wound, bruise for bruise.

Some of the regulations pertain to cult, including this obligation to pilgrimage.

23:14–17: Three times a year you shall hold a (pilgrimage) festival for Me. You shall celebrate the (pilgrimage) feast of Unleavened Bread [Passover]—eating unleavened bread for seven days as I have commanded you—at the set time in the month of Abib, for in it you went forth from Egypt; and none shall come before Me empty-handed. You shall celebrate the (pilgrimage) feast of Harvest [Shabuoth or "Weeks," celebrated fifty days after Passover and so called in Greek "Pentecost"] of the firstfruits of your work, of what you sow in the field, and the (pilgrimage) feast of Ingathering [Sukkoth or "Booths"] at the end of the year, when you gather in the results of your work on the land. These three times a year all your males shall appear before the Sovereign, the Lord.

16. Crimes and Their Penalties in the Quran

As for the thief, whether man or woman, cut off his hand as a punishment from God for what he has done. (Quran 5:38)

Thus the Quran too has its list of crimes and the punishments specified for each. In such cases of Quranically prescribed penalties there was, of course, no room for a judge's discretion, no matter how harsh the punishment might seem. The following legal definitions of certain crimes—the Quran does not so much define the crimes as name them—and their prescribed penalties is from a manual written by the jurisprudent al-Nawawi (d. 1277 C.E.).

Crimes punishable by amputation: For theft the amount necessitating punishment by amputation is (at least) of equal value to a quarter of a (gold) dinar. Two persons stealing together must have stolen twice the minimum amount. There is no amputation if what was stolen was impurity [which cannot constitute property], such as wine, or a pig or dog, or the skin of an animal not ritually slaughtered. But if the container of the wine was worth the minimum amount, amputation follows.

Theft by a minor, an insane person, or one forced against his will is not punished by cutting off the hand, but cutting may be performed on members of a "protected community" [e.g., a Jew or a Christian] subject to our laws. The right hand is cut off for the first offense, even if more than one theft was involved, the left foot for the second, the left hand for the third, and the right foot for the fourth. . . .

Sins not punishable by a prescribed penalty or expiation may be punished by imprisonment, beating, slapping, or threatening. The nature of this is at the discretion of the ruler or his deputy. (Nawawi, *The Goal of Seekers*) [WILLIAMS 1971: 151]

17. The Quran on Jewish Infidelity to the Law

In many instances, then, the Quran simply legislated without a glance backward at those other revealed Books. In at least one case, however, that regarding adultery, Muhammad appears simply to have affirmed the Torah. Moreover, the general theme of Jewish infidelity to the Law given them by God as part of the Covenant is often reflected upon in the Quran.

Remember when We made a Covenant with the people of Israel and said, "Worship no one but God and be good to parents and your kin and to orphans and the needy, and speak of goodness to men, and observe your devotional obligations and pay the alms tithe," you went back on your word, except only a few, and paid no heed.

And remember when We made a Covenant with you whereby you agreed you will neither shed blood among you nor turn your people out of their homes, you promised and are a witness to it too.

But you still kill one another and you turn a party of your people from their homes, assisting one another against them with guilt and oppression. Yet, when they are brought to you as captives, you ransom them, though forbidden it was to drive them away. Do you, then, believe a part of the Book and reject a part? There is no other award for them who so act but disgrace in the world, and on the Day of Judgment, the severest of punishment; for God is not heedless of all you do. (Quran 2:83–85)

18. Muslim and Christian Infidelity to the Torah

The Jews living under Islam were certainly aware of the Muslims' claim to be the inheritors of the true Torah tradition. One reaction to that claim occurs in the dialogue called The Khazar King, *written by Judah Halevi, a Jew from Muslim Spain, sometime about 1130–1140 C.E. Although he recognizes that Islam bears a closer affinity to Judaism than does Christianity, Halevi is not about to surrender the heritage of the Law to Muslims. The point of departure is a remark by the "Rabbi" of the dialogue that Jerusalem is "a divine place, and the law coming forth from it is the true religion." The king of the Khazars, who is making inquiry into the religious claims of Judaism, Christianity, and Islam, then turns to those latter groups.*

The Khazar King: Certainly if later religions admit the truth and do not dispute it, then they all respect the place [that is Jerusalem], and call it the stepping-stone of the prophets, the gate of heaven, the place of the gathering of the souls (on the Day of Judgment). They further admit the existence of prophecy in Israel, whose forefathers were distinguished in a like manner. Finally they believe in the work of creation, the flood, and nearly all that is contained in the Torah. They also perform pilgrimages to this hallowed place.

The Rabbi: I would compare them to proselytes who did not accept the whole Law in all its branches, but only the fundamental principles, if their actions did not belie their words. Their veneration of the land of prophecy consists chiefly in words, and at the same time they also revere places sacred to idols. Such is the case in places in which an assembly happened to meet, but in which no sign of God became visible. Retaining the relics of ancient idolatry and feast days, they changed nothing but the forms. These were indeed demolished (by Muhammad), but the relics were not removed. I might almost say that the verse in the Bible, occurring repeatedly: "You shall not serve strange gods, wood and stone" (Deut. 28:36, 64), contains an allusion to those who worship the wood (of the Cross) and those who worship the stone (of the Kaʿba at Mecca). We, through our sins, incline daily more toward them.

It is true that they, like the people of Abimelech and Nineveh, believe in God, but they philosophize concerning God's ways. The leader of each of these parties [that is, the Muslims and the Christians] maintained that he had found the divine light at its source, to wit, in the Holy Land, and that there he ascended to heaven, and commanded that all the inhabitants of the globe should be guided in the right path. They turned their faces toward that land in prayer, but before long they [that is, the Muslims] changed and turned toward (Mecca) the place where the greatest number of their people lived. . . .

The Khazar King: But the followers of other religions approach you more nearly than the philosophers?

The Rabbi: They are as far removed from us as the followers of a religion from a philosopher. The former seek God not only for the sake of knowing him but also for other benefits which they derive therefrom. The philosopher, however, only seeks Him that he may be able to describe Him accurately in detail, as he would describe the earth. . . . Ignorance of God would be no more injurious than would ignorance concerning the earth be injurious to those who consider it flat. . . . We cannot blame philosophers for missing the mark, since they only arrived at this knowledge by way of speculation, and the result could not have been different. The most sincere among them speak to the followers of a revealed religion in the words of Socrates: "My friends, I will not contest your theology. I say, however, that I cannot grasp it; I only understand human wisdom."

The speculative religions [that is, Christianity and Islam], on the other hand, are now as far removed from us as they were formerly near. If this were not so, Jeroboam and his party would be nearer to us, even though they worshiped idols, since they were Israelites inasmuch as they practiced circumcision, observed the Sabbath and other regulations, with few exceptions which administrative emergencies forced them to neglect. They [that is, the Muslims] acknowledged the God of Israel who delivered them from Egypt, in the same way as did the worshipers of the golden calf in the desert [that is, the Christians]. The former class is at best superior to the latter inasmuch as they [the Muslims] prohibited images. Since, however, they altered the direction of prayer and sought the Divine Influence where it is not to be found [that is, in Mecca], altering at the same time the majority of ceremonial laws, they wandered far from the straight path. (Judah Halevi, *The Khazar King* 4.10–13)

[HALEVI 1905: 215–219]

19. Maimonides on the Counterfeit Children of Abraham

The rather careful argument of The Khazar King *yields to more direct polemic in a letter written by Maimonides to the Jews of the Yemen. In the latter half of the twelfth century this community was not so much perplexed as persecuted and had in its midst both apostates and messianic claimants. The times called not for demonstration but encouragement and support, which Maimonides attempted to provide. He touched, among other things, upon the alleged resemblance of Christianity and Islam to the religion of the Jews.*

Our religion differs as much from other religions for which there are alleged resemblances as a living man endowed with the faculty of reason is unlike a statue which is ever so well carved out of marble, wood, bronze or silver. When a person ignorant of divine wisdom or of God's works sees the statue that superficially resembles a man in its contours, form, features, and color, he believes that the structure of the parts of a statue is like the constitution of a man, because he is deficient in understanding concerning the inner organization of both. But the informed person who knows the interior of both is cognizant of the fact that the internal structure of the statue betrays no skillful workmanship at all, whereas the inward parts of man are truly marvelously made, a testimony to the wisdom of the Creator, such as the prolongation of the nerves in the muscles and their ramifications, the branching out of the sinews and their intersections. . . .

Likewise a person ignorant of the secret meaning of Scripture and the deeper significance of the Law would be led to believe that our religion has something in common with another if he makes a comparison between the two. For he will note that in the Torah there are prohibitions and commandments, just as in other religions there are permitted and interdicted acts, both contain a system of religious observances, positive and negative precepts, sanctioned by reward and punishment.

If he could only fathom the inner intent of the Law, then he would realize that the essence of the true religion lies in the deeper meaning of its positive and negative precepts, every one of which will aid man in his striving after perfection, and remove every impediment to the attainment of excellence. These commands will enable the masses and the elite to acquire moral and intellectual qualities, each according to his ability. Thus the godly community becomes pre-eminent, reaching a twofold perfection. By the first perfection I mean man's spending his life in this world under the most agreeable and congenial conditions. The second perfection would constitute the achievement of intellectual objectives, each in accordance with his native powers.

The tenets of other religions which resemble those of Scripture have no deeper meaning, but are superficial imitations, copied from and patterned after it. They modeled their religions upon ours in order to glorify themselves and indulge their fancy that they are similar to so-and-so. However, their counterfeiting is an open secret to the learned. Consequently they become objects of derision and ridicule, just as one smiles at an ape when it imitates the actions of men. (Maimonides, *Letter to the Yemen*)

20. The Observance of the Sabbath

The Israelites have been led from Egypt by Moses. To sustain them in the desert, God sends down like a miraculous dew in the night a food called manna, which the Israelites collect. The events that follow take place before Sinai.

So they gathered it [that is, the manna] every morning, each as much as he needed to eat; for when the sun grew hot, it would melt. On the sixth day they gathered double the amount of food, two omers for each; and when all the chieftains came and told Moses, he said to them, "This is what the Lord meant: Tomorrow is a day of rest, a holy sabbath to the Lord. Bake what you would bake and boil what you would boil; and all that is left put aside to be kept until the morning." So they put it aside until morning, as Moses had ordered; and it did not turn foul, and there were no maggots in it. Then Moses said, "Eat it today, for today is a sabbath of the Lord; you will not find it today on the plain. Six days you shall gather it; on the seventh day, the sabbath, there will be none."

Yet some of the people went out on the seventh day to gather it [that is, the manna] but they found nothing. And the Lord said to Moses, "How long will you men refuse to obey My commandment and My instructions? Mark that the Lord has given you the sabbath; therefore He gives you two days' food on the sixth day. Let everyone remain where he is: let no man leave his place on the seventh day." And the people remained inactive on the seventh day. (Exodus 16:21–30)

Thus the Sabbath became one of the Israelites' holy days (Lev. 23:2–3), and its observance was incorporated into the Torah legislation given to Moses on Sinai as part of the Ten Commandments. The Exodus version (Exod. 20:8:1–17) of the commandment and the form it assumes in Deuteronomy (Deut. 5:6–21) offer interesting variations on both its origins and its intent.

Remember the sabbath day and keep it holy. Six days you shall labor and do all your work. But the seventh day is a sabbath of the Lord your God: you shall not do any work—you, your son or your daughter, your male or female slave, or your cattle, or the stranger who is within your settlements. For in six days the Lord made heaven and earth and sea, and all that is in them, and He rested on the seventh day; therefore the Lord blessed the sabbath day and hallowed it. (Exodus 20:8–11)

Observe the sabbath day and keep it holy, as the Lord your God has commanded you. Six days you shall labor and do all your work, but the seventh day is a sabbath of the Lord your God: you shall not do any work—you, your son or your daughter, your male or female slave, your ox or your ass, or any of your cattle, or the stranger in your settlements, so that your male and female slaves may rest as you do. Remember that you were a slave in the land of Egypt and the Lord your God freed you from there with a mighty hand and an outstretched arm, therefore the Lord your God commanded you to keep holy the sabbath day. (Deuteronomy 5:12–15)

21. The Sabbath and the
Humanitarian Intent of the Mosaic Law

If we follow the account in Deuteronomy literally, the reason for the injunction to observe the Sabbath was to serve as a remembrance of the Israelites' bondage in Egypt and God's gracious release of them from their ignoble condition of slavery. Such a literal reading did not satisfy all students of Scripture, however. For Philo, among others, God and His lawgiver Moses had other and somewhat more profound lessons in mind.

But it seems that Moses added the other injunctions because of the less obedient who pay little attention to his commandments, and required not only free men to cease from work on the Sabbath, but allowed the same to menservants and handmaids, proclaiming to them security and virtual freedom after every six days, in order to teach both master and servant an admirable lesson. The masters must become accustomed to working with their own hands, not waiting for the services and ministrations of their household slaves, so that if any adverse circumstances should prevail in the course of the vicissitudes of human affairs, they may not through inexperience of personal labor be distressed from the start and renounce the tasks enjoined on them, but use the different parts of their body with greater agility and act with vigor and ease. The servants, on the other hand, should not despair of higher hopes, but possessing in the relaxation that comes after every six days an ember or spark of freedom, look for their complete release if they remain true and loyal to their masters. From the occasional submission of free men to perform the services of slaves and the possibility for the slaves to share in a sense of security, the result will be that human life will advance toward the higher perfection of virtue, when both the seemingly illustrious and the obscurer sort remember equality and owe each other a necessary debt.

But it is not to the servants alone that the Law has granted the Sabbath rest, but also to the cattle. The servants are indeed free by nature, for no man is naturally a slave, but the irrational animals have been made ready for the need and service of men and rank as slaves. (Philo, *The Special Laws* 2.66–69) [PHILO 1981: 238–239]

Nor is this humanitarian purpose limited to the Sabbath regulation.

With these considerations in view, the expounder of the laws proclaimed a day of rest for the land (through the sabbath-year commandment) and restrained the husbandman from his work after every six-year period. But he introduced this regulation not only for the reason just mentioned but also because of his customary humanity, which he thinks fit to interweave into every part of his legislation, thereby impressing on the readers of Sacred Scripture sociable and kindly character traits. For he commands them not to shut off any field during the sabbath-year. All vineyards and olive groves are to be left open, and similarly other properties, whether of sown crops or trees, so that the poor may freely use the wild-growing fruits as much, if not more so, than the proprietors. Thus, on the one hand, he did not allow the masters to till their fields with the aim of sparing them the distress of providing the expenditure (for cultivation) and receiving no profits in return, and, on the other hand, he thought it fit that the needy for that period of time at any rate should enjoy as their own what seemed to belong to others, thus delivering them from any beggarly mien and the reproaches attached to mendicants. Is it not proper that we cherish laws filled with such gentleness, by which the rich are instructed to distribute and share what they have and the poor are exhorted not to be haunting the homes of the affluent on every occasion under the necessity of remedying their indigence, but at times also to derive profit from fruits that, as I said, grow wild and which they can regard as their own? (Ibid. 2.104–107) [PHILO 1981: 239]

22. Maimonides on the Sabbath

The association of the Sabbath now with the work of creation and now with the exodus from Egypt did not escape the commentators on the Law. Maimonides reflects on the reasons in his Guide of the Perplexed *and finds that they verify his own views on the purposes of the Law.*

Perhaps it has already become clear to you what is the cause of the Lord's establishing the Sabbath so firmly and ordaining death by stoning for breaking it. The Master of the Prophets [Moses] has put people to death because of it. It comes third after the existence of the deity and the denial of dualism. For the prohibition of the worship of anything except Him only aims at the belief in His unity. You know from what I have said that opinions do not last unless they are accompanied by actions that strengthen them, make them generally known, and perpetuate them among the multitude. For this reason we are ordered by the Law to exalt this day, in order that the principle of the creation of the world in time be established and universally known in the world, through the fact that all people refrain from working on one and the same day. If it is asked,

What is the cause of this? the answer is: "For in six days the Lord made" (Exod. 20:1).

For this commandment two different causes are given, corresponding to two different effects. In the first Decalog, the cause for exalting the Sabbath is stated as follows: "For in six days the Lord etc." In Deuteronomy, on the other hand, it is said: "Remember that you were slaves in Egypt. . . . For that reason the Lord your God commanded you to keep holy the sabbath day" (Deut. 5:15). This is correct. For the effect, according to the first statement is to regard that day as noble and exalted. . . . This is the effect consequent upon the cause stated in the words: "For in six days etc." However, the order given us by the Law with regard to it and the commandment ordaining us in particular to keep it are an effect consequent upon the cause that we had been slaves in Egypt where we did not work according to our free choice and when we wished and where we had not the power to refrain from working. Therefore we have been commanded inactivity and rest so that we should conjoin two things: the belief in a true opinion—namely the creation of the world in time, which, at the first go and with the slightest of speculations, shows that the deity exists—and the memory of the benefit God bestowed upon us by giving us rest from the burdens of the Egyptians. Accordingly the Sabbath is, as it were, of universal benefit, both with reference to a true speculative opinion and to the well-being of the state of the body. (Maimonides, *Guide* 2.31) [MAIMONIDES 1963: 359–360]

23. Mountains Hanging by a Hair: The Sabbath Prescriptions

(The rules about) release from vows float in the air and have nothing to support them. The rules about the Sabbath, festival offerings and sacrilege are as mountains hanging by a hair, for Scripture is slight but the rules many. (M.Hagigah 1:8)

In the light of the prescriptions as they are set down in Exodus and Deuteronomy, the activities specifically prohibited on the Sabbath appear to be limited to laboring, going abroad, and cooking. But questions must have arisen. In the following case we can note the extension of the commandment, though once again on the basis of a divine decree, to an activity that had been either licit or of indifferent notice up to that point.

During the time that the Israelites were in the wilderness a man was found gathering sticks on the sabbath day. Those who had caught him in the act brought him to Moses and Aaron and all the community, and they kept him in custody, because it was not clearly known what was to be done with him. The Lord said to Moses, "The man must be put to death; he must be stoned by all the community outside the camp." So they took him outside the camp and all stoned him to death, as the Lord had commanded Moses. (Numbers 15:32–36)

There must have been continuous legal discussion of the Sabbath prescriptions over the following centuries. Although most of the debates are invisible to us, some of the development is apparent in the Book of Jubilees, a retelling of the early books of the Bible with a marked emphasis on and extension of the legal material there. It was written in Hebrew, probably by a Pharisee, sometime between 135 and 105 B.C.E. It ends with a redefinition—in the text it is Moses speaking to the people—of the Sabbath regulations.

And behold the commandments about the sabbaths, and all the rules and regulations I have written down for you. Six days you shall work, but on the seventh day is the sabbath of the Lord your God: on it you shall do no work, neither you nor your sons, nor your slave boys nor your slave girls, nor any of your cattle, nor the alien who is among you. And the man who does any work on it shall die: whoever desecrates that day, whoever lies with a woman, or whoever talks on it about anything he intends to do (what, for example, he will buy or sell the next day), and whoever draws water on it because he did not remember to draw it on the sixth day, and whoever lifts any load to carry it out of his tent or out of his house, shall die. You shall do no work whatever on the sabbath: only what you have prepared for yourself on the sixth day shall you eat and drink, so that you may eat and drink and rest and keep sabbath from all work on that day, and bless the Lord your God who has given you a festal day and a holy day. . . . And any man who does any work on the sabbath days, or goes on a journey, or tills a field (whether at home or elsewhere), and whoever lights a fire, or loads any beast, or travels by ship on the sea, and whoever shoots or kills anything or slaughters a beast or a bird, or whoever catches an animal or a bird or a fish, or whoever fasts or makes war on the sabbath—the man who does any of these things on the sabbath shall die, so that the sons of Israel may observe the sabbaths in accordance with the commandments concerning the sabbaths of the land, as it is written on the tablets which He gave into my hands to write out for you the laws of the seasons, and the seasons according to the division of their days. (Jubilees 50:6–13)

By about 200 C.E., the time of the writing down of the Mishna, which devotes an entire tractate to the observance of the Sabbath, the list of prohibited Sabbath activities had been spelled out by the rabbis in enormous detail.

There are thirty-nine main categories of work (outlawed by the Sabbath prohibition against "daily work"): planting, plowing, reaping, binding sheaves, threshing, winnowing, cleaning crops, grinding, sifting, kneading, baking, shearing wool, washing, beating or dyeing it, spinning, weaving, making two loops, plaiting or braiding, separating two threads, tying (a knot), loosening (a knot), sewing two stitches, tearing in order to sew two stitches, hunting a deer or any other animal, slaughtering or flaying or salting the deer, curing its skin, scraping or cutting it up, writing two letters, erasing in order to write two letters, building, pulling down, putting out a fire, lighting a fire, striking with a hammer, and taking anything from one domain to another. These are the main categories of work, thirty-nine in all. (M.Shabbat 7:2)

If a non-Jew lights a lamp on the Sabbath, a Jew may make use of the light. But if he lights it for the sake of the Jew, it is forbidden. If a non-Jew fills a trough with water for his cattle, a Jew may water his own cattle afterwards. But if the non-Jew does it for the Jew, it is forbidden. If a non-Jew sets up a gangplank to go down from a ship, a Jew may go down after him. But if he does it for a Jew, it is forbidden. Rabban Gamaliel and some elders were once traveling on a ship, and a non-Jew set up a gangplank to go down from it. Rabban Gamaliel and the elders did go down by it. (M.Shabbat 16:8)

24. Jesus on the Sabbath

According to the Mishna, reaping, winnowing, and grinding are among the many activities forbidden on the Sabbath. The Talmud discusses another case that had arisen: was it permitted for an individual to pluck grain, rub it in his own hand and eat it?

One may pluck (grain) with the hand and eat (on the Sabbath), but one may not pluck with an implement; and one may rub and eat (grain on the Sabbath), but one may not rub with an implement. These are the words of Rabbi Akiba, but other Sages say that one may rub with one's finger tips and eat, but one may not run a quantity with the hand and eat. (BT.Shabbat 128a–b)

Rabbi Akiba lived in the early second century C.E., but that the rabbinic controversy on this point was at least a century older and that Jesus was embroiled in it, we can read in the Gospel.

One Sabbath he (Jesus) and his disciples were going through the grain fields, and his disciples were plucking the ears of grain, rubbing them in their hands and eating them. Some of the Pharisees said, "Why are you doing what is forbidden on the Sabbath?" Jesus answered, "So you have not read [1 Sam. 21:1–7] what David did when he and his men were hungry? He went into the House of God and took the sacred bread to eat and gave it to his men, though priests alone are allowed to eat it, and no one else." He also said, "The Son of Man is sovereign even over the Sabbath." (Luke 6:1–5)

The two other Synoptics end the same story somewhat differently.

(Jesus continued) have you not read in the Law that the priests in the Temple break the Sabbath and it is not held against them? I tell you, there is something greater than the Temple here. If you had known what that text means, "I require mercy, not sacrifice" (Hos. 6:6), you would not have condemned the innocent. For the Son of Man is sovereign over the Sabbath. (Matthew 12:3–8)

He also said to them [the Pharisees], "the Sabbath was made for the sake of man and not man for the Sabbath: therefore the Son of Man is sovereign even over the Sabbath." (Mark 2:27–28)

In all three of the Synoptics the incident of plucking the kernels of grain on the Sabbath is followed by another instance that brought Jesus into conflict with the Pharisees. The possibility that the prohibitions against certain activities on the Sabbath could be overridden by other, higher considerations already emerges from the first case, and the Mishna makes it explicit.

Rabbi Mattathiah ben Heresh said: If a man has a pain in his throat, they may drop medicine in his mouth on the Sabbath, since there is doubt whether his life is in danger, and whenever there is doubt that life is in danger this overrides the Sabbath. If a building falls down on a man (on the Sabbath) and there is doubt whether he is there or not, or whether he is alive or dead, or whether he is a Gentile or an Israelite, they may clear away the ruin from above him. If they find him alive, they may clear it away (still more) from above him; but if dead, they leave him. (M. Yoma 8:6–7)

Thus the principle was established, but the conditions and circumstances of Sabbath assistance were by no means fixed. According to Mishna Shabbat 22:6 it was not permitted to set a broken limb on the Sabbath or to attend to a sprain, presumably because these were not life-threatening ills. The same general rule probably held with regard to domestic animals: if an animal fell into a pit, it might be made comfortable but not removed, except if its life were threatened—if the pit were filled with water, for example. It must have been that type of debate, then, that lay behind the only cure that Jesus performed on the Sabbath, one that, since it was effected simply by a word, involved no "work" in any defined sense of that term.

He [Jesus] went to another place and entered their synagogue. A man was there with a withered arm, and they asked Jesus, "Is it permitted to heal on the Sabbath?" They wanted to frame a charge against him. But he said to them, "Suppose you had one sheep, which fell into a ditch [or well] on the Sabbath; is there not one of you who would catch hold of it and lift it out? And surely a man is worth more than a sheep! It is therefore permitted to do good on the Sabbath." Turning to the man, he said, "Stretch out your arm." He stretched it out, and it was made sound again like the other. But the Pharisees on leaving the synagogue laid a plot to do away with him. (Matthew 12:9–14)

25. A Gate in the Fence around the Law: The Erub

One of the more widely discussed Sabbath prohibitions was the limitation on travel. "Let each man stay where he is; no one may stir from his home on the seventh day," Exodus 16:29 commands. Using Numbers 35:1–5 as their guide, the rabbis defined a "Sabbath's journey"—the distance comprised by one's domicile or "domain" and so a legitimate area of movement—as 2,000 cubits. There was, however, one alleviation granted by the rabbis to the Mosaic Law by redefining "domain" through the introduction of the notion of an erub, a "mixture" or "fusion" of the boundaries of one's domain or even of an entire town to permit freer movement within it on the Sabbath. This extension was accomplished in one of two ways: by preparing food beforehand and depositing it in the newly "acquired" locality; or by joining the places together with a continuous link, a rope, for example. An entire treatise of the Mishna was devoted to this transparent legal contrivance, and the question was put to the rabbi who spoke for Judah Halevi in The Khazar King: *"How can we make lawful a thing which God has forbidden by means so paltry and artificial?"*

Heaven forbid that all these pious men and Sages should concur in untying one of the knots of the Divine Law. Their intention was to make it tighter and therefore they said: Build a fence around the Law. Part of this (fence building) is the rabbinic prohibition of carrying things out of private to public ground and vice versa, a prohibition not of Mosaic origin. In constructing this fence they introduced this license to prevent their religious zeal from ranking with the Torah and at the same time to give people some liberty in moving about. This liberty was gained in a perfectly lawful way and takes the form of the *Erub*, and marks a line between what is entirely legal, the fence itself, and the secluded part inside the latter. (Judah Halevi, *The Khazar King* 3.51) [HALEVI 1905: 180]

26. The Dietary Laws

You shall not eat anything abhorrent. These are the animals that you may eat: the ox, the sheep, the goat, the deer, the gazelle, the roe buck, the wild goat, the ibex, the antelope, the mountain sheep, and any other animal that has true hoofs which are cleft in two and brings up the cud—such you may eat. But the following, which do not bring up the cud or have true hoofs which are cleft through, you may not eat: the camel, the hare, and the daman—for though they bring up the cud, they have no true hoofs—they are unclean for you; also the swine—for although it has true hoofs, it does not bring up the cud—is unclean for you. You shall not eat of their flesh or touch their carcasses.

These you may eat of, all that live in the water: you may eat anything that has fins and scales. But you may not eat anything that has no fins and scales: it is unclean for you.

You may eat any clean bird. The following you may not eat: the eagle, the vulture and the black vulture; the kite, the falcon, and the buzzard of any variety; every variety of raven; the ostrich, the nighthawk, the sea gull, the hawk of any variety, the little owl, the great owl, and the white owl; the pelican, the bustard, and the cormorant; the stork, any variety of heron, the hoopoe, the bat.

All winged swarming creatures are unclean for you; they may not be eaten. You may eat only clean winged creatures.

You shall not eat anything that has died a natural death. You shall give it to the stranger in your community to eat, or you may sell it to a foreigner. For you are a people consecrated to the Lord your God. (Deuteronomy 14:3–21)

And the Lord spoke to Moses, saying: "Speak to the Israelite people thus: 'You shall eat no fat of ox or sheep or goat. Fat from animals that died (a natural death) or were torn by beasts may be put to any use, but you must not eat it. If anyone eats the fat of animals from which offerings by fire may be made to the Lord, the person who eats it shall be cut off from his kin. And you must not consume any blood, either of bird or of animal, in any of your settlements. Anyone who eats blood shall be cut off from his kin.' " (Leviticus 7:22–27)

The reasons for these prohibitions—and the more specific list in Leviticus 11—have been often discussed in ancient as well as modern times. Here will be cited only two of the many opinions on the subject: one from the beginning of the Christian era, that of the Alexandrian philosopher Philo, who offers a symbolic interpretation; and the other a medieval viewpoint, that of the physician and lawyer Moses Maimonides.

It might perhaps be assumed to be just that all wild beasts that feed on human flesh should suffer from men the same treatment that the beasts inflict on them. But Moses is of the opinion that we should abstain from the enjoyment of these, even though they provide a most pleasant and delectable feast, since he is considering what is appropriate for a civilized soul. For though it is fitting for the perpetrators of such acts to suffer the like, it is not proper for the sufferers to retaliate, lest they become unconsciously brutalized by the savage passion of anger. So cautious is he in this regard that, wishing to have full scope to restrain the impulse for the food just mentioned, he also forbade the use of other carnivores, distinguishing the herbivores as constituting gentle herds, since they are naturally tame and live on the gentle fruits the earth produces and do not engage in scheming against others. They are ten in number . . . for since Moses always held fast to the science of arithmology, which he acutely perceived to be of the greatest import in all that exists, he never legislated any law, great or small, without including and as it were adjusting to his enactments the appropriate number. But of all the numbers from the monad on up, ten is the most perfect, and, as Moses says, most holy and sacred, and with it he marks the kinds of clean animals whose use he wished to assign to the members of his commonwealth.

He subjoins a general test and a verification of the ten species of animals, employing two signs, the parted hoof and chewing the cud. Animals lacking both or one of these are unclean. Now both these signs are symbols of the methods of teaching and learning most conducive to knowledge, by which the better is distinguished from the worse with a view to avoiding confusion. For just as the ruminant animal after chewing up the food fixes it in the gullet, again after a while draws it up and masticates it and then transfers it to the belly, in like manner the student, after receiving from the teacher through his ears the principles and intuitions of wisdom, prolongs the learning process since he cannot straightway apprehend and grasp them with acumen, till by repeating in his memory, through constant exercises which function like the glue of conceptions, he firmly stamps their impression in his soul.

But there appears to be no advantage in having a firm apprehension of ideas unless there is in addition a discrimination and a distinction between them with a view to our choosing what we ought and avoiding their opposites, of which the parted hoof is the symbol. For the path of life is twofold, one branch leading to vice, the other to virtue, and we must learn to turn away from one and never abandon the other. For this reason all animals that are either solid-hoofed or many-hoofed are unclean, the former because they hint at the notion that the good and the bad have one and the same nature, like concave and convex and an uphill and downhill road; the latter because they display before our lives many roads, or rather dead ends, to deceive us, for with a multitude of roads it is no easy matter to perceive the best and most efficient path. (Philo, *The Special Laws* 4.103–110) [PHILO 1981: 282–283]

For the physician Maimonides the reasons for the prohibition are what we might call nutritional or hygienic.

Among all those (foods) forbidden us, only pork and fat may be imagined not to be harmful. But this is not so, for pork is more humid than is proper and contains more superfluous matter. The major reason why the Law abhors it [the pig] is its being very dirty and feeding on dirty things. You know to what extent the Law insists upon the need to remove filth out of sight, even in the field and in a military camp, and all the more within cities. Now if swine were used as food, marketplaces and even houses would have been dirtier than latrines, as may be seen at present in the country of the Franks [that is, the European Christians]. You know the dictum of the Sages, may their memory be blessed: "The mouth of a swine is like walking excrement."

The fat of the intestines also makes us full, spoils the digestion, and produces cold and thick blood. It is more suitable to burn it. Blood, on the one hand, and carcasses of beasts that have died, on the other, are also difficult to digest and constitute a harmful nourishment. It is well known that a beast that has been wounded is close to being a carcass. (Maimonides, *Guide of the Perplexed* 3.48) [MAIMONIDES 1963: 598]

27. From Torah to Code on a Point of Law

You shall not boil a kid in its mother's milk. (Exodus 23:19)

This single dietary injunction, repeated at Exodus 34:26 and Deuteronomy 14:21, provides us with an opportunity to follow the progressive elaboration and interpreta-

tion of a Torah prescription. We begin with the Mishna, where the discussion is already well under way.

No flesh may be cooked in milk excepting the flesh of fish and locusts; and no flesh may be served up on the table together with cheese excepting the flesh of fish and locusts. If a man vowed to abstain from flesh, he is permitted the flesh of fish and locusts. A fowl may be served up on the table together with cheese, but it may not be eaten with it. So the School of Shammai. And the School of Hillel say: It may neither be served nor eaten with it. Rabbi Yosi said: This is one of the cases where the School of Shammai followed the more lenient and the School of Hillel the more stringent ruling. Of what manner of table did they speak? Of a table whereat men eat; but on a table whereon food is (merely) set out, a man may put the one beside the other without scruple. (M.Hullin 8:1)

In its comments on this Mishnaic text the gemara *of the Babylonian Talmud reviews the debate on the subject.*

. . . Agra, the father-in-law of Rabbi Abba, recited: a fowl and cheese may be eaten without restriction. He recited it and he himself explained it thus: it means without washing the hands or cleansing the mouth (between the eating of one and the other).

Rabbi Isaac the son of Rabbi Mesharsheya once visited the house of Rabbi Ashi. He was served with cheese which he ate and then was served with meat which he also ate without washing his hands (between the courses). They said to him: Has not Agra the father-in-law of Rabbi Abba recited that fowl and cheese may be eaten without restriction? A fowl and cheese, yes; but meat and cheese, no! He replied: That is the rule only at night, but by day I can see (that my hands are clean).

It was taught: the School of Shammai say: One must clean (the mouth between meat and cheese courses); the School of Hillel say: One must rinse it. Now what is meant by "one must clean" and "one must rinse"? If one says that it means this, that the School of Shammai say that one must clean the mouth but not rinse it and the School of Hillel say one must rinse the mouth but not clean it, then the statement of Rabbi Zera, to wit, "cleaning the mouth must be done with bread only," would agree with the view of the School of Shammai, would it not? But if you say that it means this, that the School of Shammai say that one must clean the mouth and not rinse it and the School of Hillel say that one must *also* rinse it, then it is a case where the School of Shammai adopt the lenient ruling and the School of Hillel the strict ruling. Why then is this not taught among the cases in which the School of Shammai adopt the lenient ruling

and the School of Hillel the strict ruling? Rather this must be the interpretation: the School of Shammai say that one *must* clean, and this is also
the law with regard to rinsing. And the School of Hillel say that one *must*
rinse, and this is also the law with regard to cleaning. One (school) mentions one requirement, the other (school) another, but they do not really
differ.

The above-cited text stated: Rabbi Zera said: "cleaning the mouth
must be done with bread only." This means only with wheaten bread but
not with barley bread. And even with wheaten bread it is allowed only if
it is cold and not if it is still warm, because of smearing. And it must be
soft and not hard. The law is, cleaning the mouth may be done with
everything except flour, dates, and vegetables.

Rabbi Assi inquired of Rabbi Yohanan: "How long must one wait
between flesh and cheese courses?" He replied: "Nothing at all." But this
cannot be, for Rabbi Hisda said: "If a person ate flesh, he is forbidden to
eat (after it) cheese. If he ate cheese, he is permitted to eat after it flesh."
This indeed was the question: how long must one wait between cheese
and flesh? And he replied: "Nothing at all."

The (above-cited) text (stated): Rabbi Hisda said: "If a person ate
flesh, he is forbidden to eat (after it) cheese; if he ate cheese, he is permitted to eat (after it) flesh." Rabbi Aha b. Joseph asked Rabbi Hisda:
"What about the flesh that is (caught) between the teeth?" He quoted (in
reply) the verse, "While the flesh was yet between their teeth" (Num.
11:33).

Mar Ukba said: "In this matter I am what vinegar is to wine compared to my father. For if my father were to eat flesh now, he would not
eat cheese until this very hour tomorrow, whereas I do not eat cheese
(after flesh) in the same meal, but I do eat it at my next meal." (BT.Hullin
104b–105a)

*Maimonides summed up the state of the question as it was understood in the twelfth
century.*

One who has eaten cheese or milk first is permitted to eat meat immediately afterwards, but he must rinse his hands and cleanse his mouth
between the cheese and the meat. With what shall he cleanse his mouth?
With bread or fruit which he chews and swallows or spits out. And the
mouth may be cleaned with all things except dates, flour or vegetables,
for these do not clean well.

With regard to what (sort of) meat are these rules stated? With
regard to the meat of domesticated or wild animals. But if one ate the

meat of fowl after eating cheese or milk, he is not obligated to either cleanse his mouth or wash his hands.

One who had eaten meat first, whether of animals or of fowl, is forbidden to take milk until he has waited (a period) corresponding to the interval of another meal, which is something like six hours, because of the meat between the teeth which was not dislodged in cleaning. (Maimonides, *Mishneh Torah*: "Laws of Prohibited Foods" 9, 26–28)

One of the earliest attempts to order and codify the rabbinic discussions, the Shulhan Aruch *of Joseph Karo (1488–1575 C.E.), sets forth the law this way.*

If one has eaten meat, even of a wild animal or fowl, he may not eat cheese afterwards until he has waited for six hours. And even if he has waited the required period, if there is meat between his teeth, he must dislodge it. One who chews for an infant must also wait.

If one has eaten cheese, he is permitted to eat meat immediately afterwards, so long as he inspects his hands to see that nothing of the cheese has stuck to them. And if it is night, and he cannot inspect them well, he must wash them, and cleanse his mouth and rinse it. The cleaning consists in chewing bread and cleansing his mouth well with it; he may do the same with anything he wishes, except flour, dates or vegetables, since they adhere to the back of the mouth and do not clean well. Afterwards he should wash his mouth with water or wine. What meat is being referred to here? The flesh of domesticated or wild animals. But if one chooses to eat fowl after cheese, in that case he need not clean (the mouth) or wash (the hands).

If one has eaten a meat-cooked dish, he is permitted to eat a dairy-cooked dish afterwards, and hand washing between them is optional. But if one decides to eat cheese itself after a meat-cooked dish or meat itself after a dairy-cooked dish, the hands must be washed. (*Shulhan Aruch* Yorei De'ah 89)

Finally, in his Guide of the Perplexed *Maimonides returns to the question of meat cooked in milk and offers an opinion of why it was legislated in the first place.*

As for the prohibition against eating meat (boiled) in milk, it is in my opinion not improbable that—in addition to this being undoubtedly very gross food and very filling—idolatry had something to do with it. Perhaps such food was eaten at one of the ceremonies of their cult or at one of their festivals. A confirmation of this may, in my opinion, be found in the fact that the prohibition against eating meat (boiled) in milk, when it is mentioned for the first two times (in the Bible), occurs near the commandment concerning pilgrimage: "Three times a year. . . ." It is as if it is said, When you go on pilgrimage and enter the House of the Lord your God, do not cook there in the way they used to. According to me this is the most probable view regarding the reason for this prohibition. (Maimonides, *Guide* 3.48) [MAIMONIDES 1963: 599]

28. Jesus and the Dietary Laws

The dietary laws were a lively subject of debate in Jesus' day and milieu, or so it would appear from the frequency with which the Pharisees tested him on various aspects of the question. In at least one place Jesus appears to give the answer direct.

Then Peter said, "Tell us what the parable means?" Jesus answered, "Are you still as dull as the rest? Do you not see that whatever goes in by the mouth passes into the stomach and is discharged into the drain? But what comes out of the mouth has its origins in the heart, and that is what defiles a man. Wicked thoughts, murder, adultery, fornication, theft, perjury, slander—these all proceed from the heart; and these are the things that defile a man; but to eat without first washing his hands, that cannot defile him." (Matthew 15:15–20)

Mark, when he tells the same story, adds by way of editorial comment (7:19): "Thus he [that is, Jesus] declared all foods clean." If Mark did indeed receive his Gospel tradition from Peter (see Chapter 1 above), he may have had a privileged understanding of this text from his source, but only well after the event. Peter, it is clear, did not know that Jesus had declared all foods clean by these words, not at any rate until after Jesus' Ascension, when he had a private vision on the matter.

At Caesarea there was a man named Cornelius, a centurion of the Italian Cohort, as it was called. He was a religious man, and he and his whole family joined in the worship of God. He gave generously to help the Jewish people, and was regular in his prayers to God. One day about three in the afternoon he had a vision in which he clearly saw an angel of God, who came into his room and said, "Cornelius!" He stared at him in terror. "What is it, my lord?" he asked. The angel said, "Your prayers and acts of charity have gone up to heaven to speak for you before God. And now send you to Joppa for a man named Simon, also called Peter; he is lodging with another Simon, a tanner whose house is by the sea." So when the angel who was speaking with him had gone, he summoned two of his servants and a military orderly who was a religious man, told them the whole story and sent them to Joppa.

Next day, while they were still on their way and approaching the city, about noon Peter went up on the roof to pray. He grew hungry and wanted something to eat. While they were getting it ready, he fell into a trance. He saw a rift in the sky and a thing coming down that looked like a great sheet of sail cloth. It was slung by the four corners and was being lowered to the ground. In it he saw creatures of every kind, whatever walks or crawls or flies. Then there was a voice which said to him, "Up, Peter, kill and eat." But Peter said, "No, Lord, no: I have never eaten anything profane or unclean." The voice came again a second time: "It is not for you to call profane what God counts clean." This happened three times; and then the thing was taken up again into the sky. (Acts 10:1–16)

The climax, and perhaps the point of this story, occurs somewhat later in Acts, when the authorities of the nascent Church in Jerusalem are asked to rule on the matter of Gentile membership in their fellowship. Should such new believers in the Messiahship of Jesus—men and women who neither knew nor observed Jewish circumcision or Jewish dietary restrictions—be admitted to baptism and community membership? Peter cited his experience, and then James, "the brother of the Lord," spoke for all.

It is the decision of the Holy Spirit, and our decision, to lay no further burden on you beyond these essentials: you are to abstain from meat that has been offered to idols, from blood, from anything that has been strangled, and from fornication. If you keep yourselves free from these things, you will be doing right. (Acts 15:28–29)

29. Clean and Unclean in the Christian Conscience

James' ruling was apparently a decision without a sequel. Paul never refers to it in his letters, and the Gentile Christians seem not to have concerned themselves with the issue of Jewish dietary restrictions thereafter. But they were of concern to some, the Jewish Christians, for example, who still had to resolve for themselves the dietary issue and the larger question of the prescriptions of the Mosaic Law. We have already seen one method of dealing with the Law in Christian circles, through an allegorizing exegesis, in the so-called Letter of Barnabas, *which presents a remarkable specimen of the technique precisely as applied to the dietary code in Leviticus. Then the appropriate conclusion is drawn.*

In these dietary laws, then, Moses was taking three moral maxims and expounding them spiritually; though the Jews, with their carnal instincts, took him to be referring literally to foodstuffs. . . . Moses did say, however, that "you may eat anything that has cloven hoofs and chews the cud" (Lev. 11:3). Why does he say this? Because when a creature of that kind is given provender, it shows its recognition of the giver and takes evident pleasure in him while refreshing itself. So Moses, contemplating what the Lord required, gave it this apt turn of expression. For what these words of his mean is "seek the company of men who fear the Lord; who muse in their hearts on the purport of every word they have received; who receive the statutes of the Lord on their lips and observe them; who know that meditation is a delight; who do in fact 'chew the cud' of the Lord's word." And the "cloven hoof"? That means that a good man is at one and the same time walking in this present world and also anticipating the holiness of eternity. So you see what a master of lawgiving Moses was. His own people did not see or understand these things—how could they?—but we understand his directions rightly, and interpret them as the Lord intended. Indeed, it was to aid our comprehension of them that He "circumcised" our ears and hearts. (*Letter of Barnabas* 10)

[STANIFORTH 1968: 208]

By his allegorical method the author of the Letter of Barnabas *has helped free the Christian from the literal observance of the Law while maintaining the validity of the Mosaic revelation. His moralizing treatment of Leviticus 11 had a long afterlife in the Christian tradition. What is odder to note, however, is the persistence of the older Mosaic tradition of clean and unclean foods.*

Adamnan (ca. 621–704 C.E.) was a potent figure in the establishment of Christianity in Scotland and Ireland in the seventh century. The following canons or disciplinary statutes were passed by one of the Irish church councils of that era and then circulated under his name. Their concern with purity and contamination is little different from that of the Jews.

1. Marine animals cast upon shores, the nature of whose death we do not know, are to be taken for food in good faith, unless they are decomposed.

2. Cattle that fall from a rock, if their blood has been shed, are to be taken; if not, but if their bones and their blood has not come out, they are to be rejected as if they were carrion.

3. Animals that have died in the water are carrion since their blood remains within them. . . .

14. Things that are drowned in water are not to be eaten, since the Lord has prohibited the eating of flesh that contains blood (Lev. 17:10–14; Deut. 12:16, 12:23) for in the flesh of an animal drowned in water the blood remains coagulated. This the Lord prohibits, not because in those days men ate raw flesh, since it would be none too sweet, but because they had been eating drowned and carrion flesh. And the Law written in

metrical fashion says, "Thou shalt not eat carrion flesh" (cf. Lev. 5:2, 17:15).

30. The Quran and the Prophet on Dietary Laws

The matter of clean and unclean foods that was being discussed in Ireland in the seventh century was also the subject of pronouncements, much to the same end, in Arabia of the same era.

Forbidden to you (for food) is carrion and blood and the flesh of the swine, and whatsoever has been killed in the name of some other God, and whatever has been strangled, or killed by a blow or a fall, or a goring, or that which has been mauled by wild beasts, unless slaughtered while still alive; and that which has been slaughtered at altars is forbidden. . . . If one of you is driven by hunger (to eat the forbidden), without the evil intent of sinning, then God is forgiving and kind.

They ask you (Muhammad), what is lawful for them. Say: "All things are lawful for you that are clean, and what the trained hunting animals take for you, as you have trained them in the light of God's teachings, but read over them the name of God, and fear God, for God is swift in the reckoning." (Quran 5:3–4)

There are as well a great many Prophetic traditions on the subject.

Abu Thaʿalaba al-Kushani reported that he said: "Prophet of God, we are in a land belonging to folk who are People of the Book, so may we eat out of their vessels? In a hunting region I hunt with my bow, my dog which is trained and my dog which is not trained, so what is right for me?" Muhammad replied: "Regarding what you have mentioned about the vessels of the People of the Book, if you can get anything else, do not eat out of them; but if you cannot, wash them and eat out of them. Eat what you have hunted with your bow when you have mentioned God's name; eat what you have caught with your trained dog when you have mentioned God's name; eat what you have caught by your untrained dog (only) when you are present at the kill." This tradition was transmitted by Bukhari and Muslim. (Baghawi, *Mishkat al-Masabih* 19.1.1)

Abu Hurayra reported God's Messenger as saying: "Eating any fanged beast of prey is prohibited." Muslim transmitted this tradition.

Ibn Abbas said God's Messenger prohibited every beast of prey with a fang and every bird with a talon. Bukhari and Muslim have transmitted this tradition.

Jabir said that on the day of Khaybar God's Messenger forbade the flesh of domestic asses but permitted horseflesh. Bukhari and Muslim have transmitted this tradition. (Ibid. 19.3.1)

There are also, typically, traditions on the etiquette of eating.

Ibn Umar reported God's Messenger as saying: "When any of you eats, he should eat with his right hand, and when he drinks, he should drink with his right hand." Muslim transmitted this tradition.

He (also) reported God's Messenger as saying: "None of you must ever eat or drink with his left hand, for the devil eats and drinks with his left hand." Muslim transmitted this tradition. (Ibid. 20.1.1)

There was little debate on the general thrust of these Quranic verses and Prophetic traditions. One had to descend to a much lower level of specificity to encounter the "controversial questions." The Quran, for example, includes these verses.

O believers, eat what is good of the food We have given you, and be grateful to God, if indeed you are obedient to Him. Forbidden to you are carrion and blood, and the flesh of swine, and that which has been consecrated [or killed] in the name of any other god. If one is obliged by necessity to eat it without intending to transgress, or reverting to it, he is not guilty of sin; for God is forgiving and kind. (Quran 2:172–173)

No one was likely to commend the eating of swine in the light of such scriptural testimony, but there did arise certain secondary issues, which appear in Razi's Quran commentary.

As to swine, there are certain complex questions. The community is in agreement that all parts of the swine are forbidden. God here refers to the flesh (and not the other parts) of the swine since the chief use (of the swine) has to do with its flesh. This manner of speaking is similar to the words of God: "O believers, when proclamation is made for prayer on the day of assembly [that is, Friday], hasten to the recollection of God and leave off your bargaining" (Sura 62:9), where God specifically forbade bargaining because it represented the main occupation of the people. Thus, though the bristles of the swine are not included in the precise wording (in this verse), they (too) are unanimously regarded as forbidden and impure. There is, however, a difference of opinion concerning whether one may use them in sewing. Abu Hanifa and Muhammad al-Shaybani consider it permissible, while al-Shafi'i does not. Abu Yusuf said, "I regard sewing with swine bristles as objectionable"; but it is also related (elsewhere) that he regarded it as permissible. The arguments of Abu Hanifa and Muhammad al-Shaybani are as follows. We note that the use of swine bristles is conceded to the shoemakers among the Muslims and is not explicitly condemned. There (even) exists an urgent necessity for it. When al-Shafiʿi says that the blood of fleas does not contaminate the clothing because it is difficult to protect oneself from it, why then, by the same reasoning, are not swine bristles permissible since one sews with them? (Razi, *Great Commentary*, *ad loc.*)

31. "What I Tell You Is This"

Whether or not Peter had simply failed to understand his master's teachings on the matter of the dietary laws, Jesus certainly had no hesitation about revising, expanding, or, in the case of divorce, abrogating Torah prescriptions, and in his own name.

You have learned that they were told, "Do not commit adultery." But what I tell you is this: If a man looks upon a woman with a lustful eye, he has already committed adultery in his heart. (Matthew 5:27–28)

Again, you have learned that our forefathers were told, "Do not break your oath," and, "Oaths sworn to the Lord must be kept." But what I tell you is this: You are not to swear at all—not by heaven, for it is God's throne, nor by earth, for it is His footstool, nor by Jerusalem, for it is the city of the great King, nor by your own head, because you cannot turn one hair on it white or black. Plain "Yes" or "No" is all you need to say; anything beyond that comes from the devil. (Matthew 5:33–37)

You have learned that they were told, "Eye for eye, tooth for tooth." But what I tell you is this: Do not set yourself against the man who wrongs you. If someone slaps you on the right cheek, turn and offer him your left. If a man wants to sue you for your shirt, let him have your coat as well. If a man in authority makes you go one mile, go with him two. Give when you are asked to give; and do not turn your back on a man who wants to borrow. (Matthew 5:38–42)

You have learned that they were told, "Love your neighbor, hate your enemy." But what I tell you is this: Love your enemies and pray for your prosecutors, only so can you be children of your heavenly Father, who makes His sun rise on good and bad alike and sends the rain on the honest and the dishonest. If you love only those who love you, what reward can you expect? Surely the tax gatherers do as much as that. And if you greet only your brothers, what is there extraordinary in that? Even the heathen do as much. There must be no limit to your goodness, as your heavenly Father's goodness knows no bounds. (Matthew 5:43–48)

32. Contract or Sacrament: The Case of Divorce

One instance where Jesus clearly separated himself from the Torah tradition was in the matter of divorce, and that issue provides an opportunity for comparing the three religious traditions on a single point of religious law. The classical biblical text on the subject occurs in Deuteronomy, where the law is not stated as a general prescription on the grounds or manner of divorce but rather as the solution of a rather involved case of divorce and remarriage and a contemplated third marriage to the original spouse.

A man takes a wife and possesses her. She fails to please him because he finds something obnoxious [or "indecent"] about her, and he writes her a bill of divorcement, hands it to her, and sends her away from his house; (let us suppose) she leaves his household and becomes the wife of another man; then this latter man (also) rejects her, writes her a bill of divorcement, hands it to her and sends her away from his house; or it may be the man who married her last dies. (Whatever the case) the first husband who divorced her shall not take her to wife again, since she has been defiled (for him)—for that would be abhorrent to the Lord. You must not bring sin upon the land which the Lord your God has given you as a heritage. (Deuteronomy 24:1–4)

The issue of divorce arises in Matthew's Gospel—again not so much as a matter of principle as a detached correction of Torah law amidst a number of "but what I tell you . . ." instructions.

They [that is, the Israelites] were told, "A man who divorces his wife must give her a note of dismissal." But what I tell you is this: If a man divorces his wife for any cause other than unchastity, he involves her in adultery; and anyone who marries a divorced woman commits adultery. (Matthew 5:31–32)

Later, however, the more general question of the grounds for divorce is put to Jesus, why or under what circumstances we do not know, except that it was to test him.

Some Pharisees came and tested him [that is, Jesus] by asking, "Is it lawful for a man to divorce his wife on any and every ground?" He asked in return, "Have you never read that the Creator made them from the beginning male and female?" And he added, "For this reason a man shall leave his father and mother, and the two shall become one flesh. It follows that they are no longer two individuals: they are one flesh. What God has joined together, man must not separate." "Why then," they objected, "did Moses lay it down that a man might divorce his wife by note of

669

dismissal?" He answered, "It was because your minds were closed that Moses gave you permission to divorce your wives; but it was not like that when all began. I tell you, if a man divorces his wife for any cause other than unchastity, and marries another, he commits adultery." (Matthew 19:3–9)

The "note of dismissal" (in Hebrew get; pl. gittin) is the subject of an entire tractate in the Mishna, most of which is devoted to the circumstances governing the validity of such a document.

The essential formula in the bill of divorce is, "Behold, you are free to marry any man." Rabbi Judah says (that it is): "Let this be from me your writ of divorce and letter of dismissal and deed of liberation, that you may be free to marry whomsoever you will." (M.Gittin 9:3)

If a man throws a bill of divorce to his wife while she is within her house or her courtyard, she is divorced. But if he throws it to her while she is in his house or his courtyard, even though he is with her in bed, she is not divorced; but if he throws it into her bosom or her basket, she is divorced. (Ibid. 8:1)

A few passages range a little more widely and touch briefly upon some of the grounds for the action.

If a man put away his wife because of her evil reputation, he may not take her back; and if because of a vow [see M.Ketuboth 7:1ff.], he may not take her back. . . . If a man put away his wife because she was barren, Rabbi Judah says: He may not take her back. But the Sages say: He may take her back. (Ibid. 4:7–8)

In this passage all the differing interpretations of the grounds for divorce rely on exactly the same verse, Deuteronomy 24:1.

The School of Shammai say: A man may not divorce his wife unless he found unchastity in her, for it is written [in Deut. 24:1], "because he has found in her indecency in anything." And the School of Hillel say: He may divorce her even if she spoiled a dish for him, for it is written, "because he has found in her indecency in anything." Rabbi Akiba says: He may divorce her even if he found another fairer than she, for it is written [in the same passage], "she does not win his favor." (Ibid. 9:10)

Some grounds for divorce are so grave that they preclude the return of the property given in the woman's dowry:

These are they who are put away without their marriage settlement: a wife that transgresses the Law of Moses and Jewish custom. What constitutes a transgression of the Law of Moses? If a wife gives her husband untithed food [Num. 18:21ff.], or has intercourse with him while she is unclean [Lev. 18:19], or does not set apart dough offering [Num. 15:18], or utters a vow and does not fulfill it [Deut. 23:21]. And what constitutes a transgression of Jewish custom? If she goes out with her hair unbound, or spins in the street, or speaks with any man. Abba Saul says: Also if she is a scold. And who is deemed a scold? Whoever speaks inside her house and can be heard by her neighbors. (M.Ketuboth 7:6)

Although this text appears to recognize the distinction between religious grounds for divorce ("transgression of the Law of Moses") and more personal and secular reasons (incompatibility, "transgression of Jewish custom"), Jewish thinking about marriage and its dissolution remained contractual and its primary concerns were with validity and equity. Jesus moved it onto other ground by referring its institution in effect to God Himself, but it was Paul above all who shaped Christian thinking about marriage and provided the theological ground that made divorce unthinkable. For the Christian, marriage was eventually formalized as a sacrament, an outward sign that brought divine grace (see Chapter 5 below). This passage in Paul's letter to the Ephesians is crucial in that evolution.

Husbands, love your wives as Christ also loved the Church and gave himself up for it, to consecrate it, cleansing it by water and word, so that he might present the Church to himself all glorious, with no stain or wrinkle or anything of the sort, but holy and without blemish. In the same way men also are bound to love their wives, as they love their own bodies. In loving his wife, a man loves himself. For no one ever hated his own body: on the contrary, he provides and cares for it; and that is how Christ treats the Church, because it is his body, of which we are living parts. Thus it is that, in the words of Scripture, "a man shall leave his father and mother and shall be joined to his wife, and the two shall become one flesh." It is a great truth that is hidden here. I for my part refer it to Christ and to the Church, but it applies also individually; each of you must love his wife as his very self; and the wife must see to it that she pays her husband all respect. (Paul, *To the Ephesians* 5:25–33)

The Pauline view must soon have become standard. Ignatius of Antioch (d. 107 C.E.) counseled that "bridegrooms and brides ought to be married with the recognition of the bishop so that the marriage takes place according to the Lord and not according to lust" (To Polycarp 5:1). By the time Augustine came to write On Marriage and Concupiscence *in 419 C.E., Jesus' remarks on marriage had been joined to his presence at the marriage feast at Cana (John 2:1–11), and both connected with Paul's reflections in his letter to the Ephesians.*

Since it is not only fecundity, whose fruit is in offspring, nor only modesty, whose restraint is faith, but also a kind of sacrament of matrimony is commended to the married faithful, so that the Apostle says, "Husbands, love your wives, just as Christ loved the Church." There is no doubt that this is indeed a sacrament, that a man and woman united in marriage remain together inseparably for as long as they live, nor can one spouse rid himself of the other, except in cases of fornication. . . . If someone should do this [that is, get a divorce], he is not breaking the laws of this age, where divorce and remarriage are permitted, which the Lord testified that holy Moses granted to the Israelites because of the hardness of their hearts, but rather he is guilty, according to the law of the Gospel, of adultery, just as is his wife, if she marries another. . . . There remains something conjugal between those partners as long as they live, which neither separation nor intercourse with others can delete.

In marriages the nuptial goods are cherished: offspring, faith, the sacrament. But not merely that a child should be born, but that he should be reborn, for he is born simply for punishment if he is not reborn to life. And faith, not of the type that the unbelievers possess in their appetite for the flesh. . . . And the sacrament, which they do not lose by separation and adultery but preserve as spouses in concord and chastity. (Augustine, *On Marriage and Concupiscence* 1.10.17)

Augustine's remark on "the laws of this age" acknowledge the presence of another legal system with which the Christians of the Gentile world had to cope: the Roman divorce laws. According to Jewish law, only the man could initiate divorce. Jesus too had spoken of a man's being prohibited from divorcing his wife and so presumably, as Mark 10:12 seems to add, of a wife's being prohibited from divorcing her husband. Roman law, on the other hand, permitted either spouse to divorce the other. Jerome (d. 419 C.E.) took up the Roman notion of the equality of the sexes before the civil law and extended it more broadly into the moral law.

The Lord has commanded that a wife should not be put away except for fornication; and that when she has been put away [that is, divorced], she ought to remain unmarried. Whatever is given as a commandment to men logically applies to women also. For it cannot be that while an adulterous wife is divorced, an incontinent husband must be kept. . . . The laws of Caesar are different, it is true, from the laws of Christ; Papinian [the Roman jurist] commands one thing, our Paul another. Among the Romans the (marriage) bonds are loosed in the case of immodesty on the part of men. But with us, what is unlawful for women is also unlawful for men, and both are bound by the same conditions of service. (Jerome, *Letter 78*)

33. Divorce in Islamic Law

Like the Jewish tradition, Muslim law recognized without debate the possibility of dissolving a marriage contract and devoted most of its attention to regulating and defining the grounds for such action—how it was to be performed in a valid fashion, and what were its legal consequences. Of these latter, it was the establishment of paternity after the divorce and the conditions of the marriage settlement that attracted the most concern. The Quran is already quite detailed on the matter.

Those who swear to keep away from their wives (with intent to divorce) have four months of grace; then if they reconcile (during this period), surely God is forgiving and kind. And if they are bent on divorce, God hears all and knows everything. (Quran 2:226–227)

If the husband's waiting period is intended to prevent rash or hasty action, that prescribed for the wife is to ensure that, if she is pregnant, the father will be established.

Women who are divorced have to wait for three monthly periods, and if they believe in God and the Last Day, they must not hide unlawfully what God has formed within their wombs. Their husbands would do well to take them back in that period, if they wish to be reconciled. Women also have recognized rights as men have, though men are over them in rank. But God is all-mighty and all-wise.

Divorce must be pronounced twice, and then a woman must either be retained in honor or released in kindness. And it is not lawful for you [that is, the husbands] to take anything of what you have given them. . . .

Divorce is (still revokable) after two pronouncements, after which they must either keep them [that is, the men's wives] honorably or part with them in a decent way. You are not allowed to take away the least (part) of what you have given your wives, unless both of you fear that you would not be able to keep within the limits set by God. . . .

If a man pronounces divorce again [that is, for the third time], she becomes unlawful for him (for remarriage) until she has married another man. Then if this latter divorces her, there is no harm if the (original) pair unite again if they think they will keep within the bounds set by God and made clear for those who understand.

When you have divorced your wives, and they have reached the end of the period of waiting, then either keep them honorably or let them go with honor, and do not detain them with the intent of harassing lest you should transgress. (Quran 2:228–231)

What seems to be chiefly envisioned here is the restraint of the financial manipulation of women, perhaps through prolonging the procedure of pronouncing the triple formula of divorce, since only the husband could initiate the divorce, or even of coercing the women to buy themselves out of the contract. A number of Prophetic traditions show other sides of the intent and process of divorce in Islam.

Thawban reported God's Messenger as saying, "If any woman asks her husband to divorce her without some very good reason, the odor of Paradise will be forbidden her."

Ibn Umar reported the Prophet as saying, "The lawful thing which God hates most is divorce."

Abu Hurayra reported God's Messenger as saying, "There are three things which, whether undertaken seriously or lightly, are treated seriously: marriage, divorce, and taking back a wife before a divorce is final."

On the triple repetition of the divorce formula, which was obviously not intended to be done on a single occasion, Prophetic tradition relates the following.

Mahmud ibn Labib told that when God's Messenger was informed about a man who divorced his wife by declaring it three times without any interval between them, he arose in anger and said, "Is sport being made of the Book of God Who is great and glorious even while I am among you?" At that a man got up and said, "Messenger of God, shall I kill him?" (Baghawi, *Mishkat al-Masabih* 12.12.3)

5. The New Covenants

1. Jesus as the Fulfillment of the Law

As we have seen in the previous chapter, Matthew's Gospel presents a number of dicta whereby Jesus appears to be modifying or even abrogating the Mosaic Law. They are preceded, moreover, by Jesus' own most sweeping statement of the connection between his Messianic mission and the Mosaic Law.

Do not suppose that I have come to abolish the Law and the prophets. I did not come to abolish but to complete. I tell you this: so long as heaven and earth endure, not a letter, not a stroke will disappear from the Law until all that must happen has happened. If any man therefore sets aside the least of God's commandments and teaches others to do the same, he will have the lowest place in the kingdom of heaven, whereas anyone who keeps the Law and teaches others so, will stand high in the kingdom of Heaven. I tell you, unless you show yourselves far better men than the Pharisees and the doctors of the Law, you cannot enter the kingdom of heaven. (Matthew 5:17–20)

The fully developed Christian tradition, if it struggled to understand other implications of this passage, had no difficulty with the notion that Jesus was himself the fulfillment and perfection of the Mosaic Law.

Now Christ fulfilled the precepts of the Old Law both in his works and in his teaching. In his works, because he was willing to be circumcised and to fulfill the other legal observances which were binding for the time being. . . . In his teaching he fulfilled the precepts of the Law in three ways. First, by explaining the true sense of the Law. This is clear in the case of murder and adultery, the prohibition of which the Scribes and Pharisees thought to refer only to the exterior act; and so our Lord fulfilled the Law by showing that the prohibition extended also to the interior acts of sin. Secondly, our Lord fulfilled the precepts of the Law by prescribing the safest way to comply with the statutes of the Old Law.

Thus the Old Law forbade perjury, and this is more safely avoided by abstaining altogether from swearing, save in cases of urgency. Thirdly, our Lord fulfilled the precepts of the Law by adding some counsels of perfection, and this is clearly seen in Matthew 19:21, where our Lord said to the man who affirmed that he had kept all the precepts of the Old Law: "One thing is lacking to you: if you will be perfect, go, sell whatever you have and give to the poor, and then you will have riches in heaven; and come, follow me." (Aquinas, *Summa Theologica* I/2, ques. 107, art. 2) [AQUINAS 1945: 2:961]

2. Paul on Torah, Sin, and Redemption

Aquinas in the thirteenth Christian century is at ease with this critical Gospel text on the connection of Jesus and the Law. By then, the separation between Jews and Christians had long since been absolute. But in the days immediately following the death of Jesus, when the community of his followers was made up entirely of Jews, the issue was quite different. It was Paul, in the forefront of the mission to the Gentiles, who attempted to work out the theology of the new relationship between belief in Jesus and the Law of Moses.

It was through one man that sin entered the world, and through sin, death; and thus death pervaded the whole human race, inasmuch as all men have sinned. For sin was already in the world before there was Law, though in the absence of Law no reckoning is kept of sin. But death held sway from Adam to Moses, even over those who had not sinned as Adam did, by disobeying a direct command—and Adam foreshadows the Man who was to come.

But God's act of grace is out of all proportion to Adam's wrongdoing. For if the wrongdoing of that one man brought death upon so many, its effect is vastly exceeded by the grace of God and the gift that came to so many by the grace of one man, Jesus Christ. . . .

It follows, then, that as the issue of one misdeed was condemnation for all men, so the issue of one just act is acquittal and life for all men. For as through the disobedience of one man the many were made sinners, so through the obedience of one man the many will be made righteous.

Law intruded into this process to multiply lawbreaking. But where sin was thus multiplied, grace immeasurably exceeded, in order that, as sin established its reign by way of death, so God's grace might establish its reign in righteousness and issue in eternal life through Jesus Christ our Lord. . . .

For if we have become incorporate with him in a death like his, we shall also be one with him in a resurrection like his. We know that the man we once were was crucified with Christ for the destruction of the sinful self, so that we may no longer be the slaves of sin, since a dead man is no longer answerable for his sin. But if we thus died with Christ, we also believe that we shall come to life with him. We know that Christ, once raised from the dead, is never to die again; he is no longer under the dominion of death. For in dying as he died, he died to sin, once for all, and in living as he lives, he lives in God. In the same way you must regard yourselves as dead to sin and alive to God, in union with Christ Jesus. . . .

You cannot be unaware, my friends—I am speaking to those who have some knowledge of law—that a person is subject to the law so long as he is alive and no longer. For example, a married woman is by law bound to her husband while he lives; but if he dies, she is discharged from the obligations of the marriage law. . . . So you, my friends, have died to the Law by becoming identified with the body of Christ and accordingly you have found another husband in him who rose from the dead, so that we may bear fruit for God. While we lived on the level of our lower nature, the sinful passions evoked by the Law worked in our bodies, to bear fruit for death. But now, having died to that which held us bound, we are discharged from the Law, to serve God in a new way, the way of the spirit, in contrast to the old way, the way of a written code.

What follows? Is the Law identical with sin? Of course not. But except through Law I would never have become acquainted with sin. For example, I should never have known what it was to covet, if the Law had not said, "Thou shall not covet." Through that commandment sin found its opportunity, and produced in me all kinds of wrong desires. In the absence of Law, sin is dead thing. There was a time when, in the absence of Law, I was fully alive; but when the commandment came, sin sprang to life and I died. The commandment which should have lead to life proved in my experience to lead to death, because sin found its opportunity in the commandment, seduced me, and through the commandment killed me.

Therefore the Law is in itself holy, and the commandment is holy and just and good. Are we to say then that this good thing was death to me? By no means. It was sin that killed me, and thereby sin exposed its true character: it used a good thing to bring about my death, and so, through the commandment, sin became more sinful than ever.

We know that the Law is spiritual; but I am not: I am unspiritual, the purchased slave of sin. I do not ever acknowledge my own actions as mine, for what I do is not what I want to do, but what I detest. But if what I do is against my will, it means that I agree with the Law and hold it admirable. But as things are, it is no longer I who perform the action, but the sin that lodges in me. For I know that nothing good lodges in me—in my unspiritual nature, I mean—for the will to do good is there, the deed is not. The good which I want to do, I fail to do; but what I do is the evil which is against my will; and if what I do is against my will, clearly it is no longer I who am the agent, but sin has made its lodging in me.

I discover this principle, then: that when I want to do the right, only the wrong is within my reach. In my inmost self I delight in the Law of God, but I perceive that there is in my bodily members a different law, fighting against the Law that my reason approves and making me a prisoner under the law that is in my members, the law of sin. Miserable creature that I am, who is there to rescue me out of this body doomed to death? God alone, through Jesus Christ our Lord! Thanks be to God! In a word, then, I myself, subject to God's Law as a rational being, am yet, in my unspiritual nature, a slave to the law of sin.

The conclusion of the matter is this: there is no condemnation for those who are united with Christ Jesus, because in Christ Jesus the life-giving law of the spirit has set you free from the law of sin and death. What the Law could never do, because our lower nature had robbed it of its potency, God has done: by sending his own Son in a form like that of our own sinful nature, and as a sacrifice for sin, He has passed judgment against sin within that very nature, so that the commandment of the Law might find fulfillment in us, whose conduct, no longer under the control of our lower nature, is directed by the Spirit. (Paul, *To the Romans* 5:12–8:4)

The same issue is addressed more succinctly in Paul's letter to the Galatians.

You may take it, then, that it is the men of faith who are Abraham's sons. And Scripture, foreseeing that God would justify the Gentiles through faith, declared the Gospel to Abraham beforehand: "In you all nations shall find blessing." Thus it is the men of faith who share the blessing with faithful Abraham.

On the other hand, those who rely on obedience to the Law are under a curse, for Scripture says: "A curse is on all who do not persevere in doing everything that is written in the Book of the Law" (Deut. 27:26).

It is evident that no one is ever justified before God in terms of the Law; because we read "he shall gain life who is justifid through faith" (Hab. 2:4). Now Law is not at all a matter of having faith: we read, "he who does this shall gain life by what he does" (Lev. 18:5).

Christ brought us freedom from the curse of the Law by becoming for our sake an accursed thing; for Scripture says, "A curse is on everyone who is hanged on a gibbet" (Deut. 21:23). And the purpose of it all was that the blessing of Abraham should in Jesus Christ be extended to the Gentiles, so that we might receive the promised Spirit through faith. . . .

Does the Law then contradict the promises? No, never! If a law had been given which had power to bestow life, then indeed righteousness would have come from keeping the Law. But Scripture has declared the whole world to be prisoners in subjection to sin, so that faith in Jesus Christ may be the ground in which the promised blessing is given, and given to those who have such faith.

Before this faith came, we were close prisoners in the custody of the Law, pending the revelation of faith. Thus the Law was a kind of tutor in charge of us until Christ should come when we should be justified through faith; and now that faith has come, the tutor's charge is at an end. (Paul, *To the Galatians* 3:7–25)

We return, finally, to Aquinas.

The end of every law is to make men just and virtuous. Consequently, the end of the Old Law was the justification of men. The Law, however, could not accomplish this, but foreshadowed it by certain ceremonial actions and promised it in words. And in this respect the New Law fulfills the Old by justifying men through the power of Christ's Passion. This is what the Apostle (Paul) says: "What the Law could not do . . . God sending His own Son in the likeness of the sinful flesh . . . has condemned sin in the flesh, that the justification of the Law might be fulfilled in us" (Rom. 8:3–4). And in this respect the New Law gives what the Old Law promised, according to 2 Cor. 1:20: "He," that is, Christ, "is the Yes pronounced upon God's promises, every one of them." Again, in this respect is also fulfilled what the Old Law foreshadowed. Hence it is written concerning the ceremonial precepts that they were "a shadow of things to come, but the body is of Christ" (Col. 2:17); in other words, the reality is found in Christ. Therefore the New Law is called the law of reality, whereas the Old Law is called the law of shadow or of figure. (Aquinas, *Summa Theologica* I/2, ques. 107, art. 2) [AQUINAS 1945: 2:961]

3. The Rabbis on Justification through the Law

If Paul had serious doubts whether anyone could be justified by Torah Law, no matter how carefully observed, the rabbis had no hesitation on the subject. Their chain of reflections takes its starting point from this text in the Mishna.

Anyone who fills one *mitzvah* [that is, a commandment of the Law], God benefits him and lengthens his days and he inherits the land. And everyone who does not fulfill one *mitzvah*, it shall be ill with him and he shall not have length of days and he shall not inherit the land. (M.Kiddushin 1:10)

This is a minimum-maximum case; but in their commentaries on the passage, the Sages broadened the discussion.

About this it is written, "One sinner destroys much good" (Eccles. 9:18). A man should always regard himself as half innocent and half guilty: if he performs one *mitzvah*, happy is he for weighing himself down in the scale of innocence; if he commits one transgression, woe to him for weighing himself down in the scale of guilt. About this one it was written, "One sinner destroys much good." Because of a single sin which he committed, much good is lost to him. Rabbi Simeon ben Eleazer said: Since the individual is judged according to the majority (of his deeds, good and bad), and the world is judged according to its majority, a man should always regard himself as half innocent and half guilty. (Tosefta Kiddushin 1:10)

And in the Jerusalem Talmud:

Ben Azzai gave an interpretation of this verse: "Dead flies makes the perfumer's ointment give off an evil odor" (Eccles. 10:1). One deduces from the use of the singular verb [though the subject is plural] that just as a single fly may infect the perfumer's ointment, so the man who commits only one sin loses thus the merit of his good works. Rabbi Akiba gave an interpretation of this verse: "Therefore Sheol has enlarged its appetite and opened its mouth beyond measure" (Isa. 5:14). It is not written here "beyond measures" but "beyond measure." (It refers to) whoever does not have one *mitzvah* which can prove in his favor (and so make the scales incline) to the side of innocence. This he said with regard to the world to come. But in this world, if even 999 angels declare him guilty and one angel declares him innocent, the Holy One, blessed be He, inclines (the scale) to the side of innocence. (JT.Kiddushin 61d)

4. "The Laws of the Torah Shall Never Be Abrogated"

There is no sign in the passage just cited that the rabbis were arguing, however indirectly, against some Pauline theory of redemption. But when the Jewish theologian Saadya wrote, in Arabic, his Book of Doctrines and Beliefs *in 933 C.E., he was confronted with two distinct and prevalent claims that the Torah had been abrogated—one by the Christians, as we have seen, and another advanced by Islam, in whose very bosom Saadya lived and worked. The issue must have been very much on his mind in the mixed and catholic society of tenth-century Baghdad.*

Having dealt with these matters (of Scripture and tradition), I deem it right to add to my remarks a word on the abrogation of the Law, since this seems to be the place for it. I declare that the Children of Israel, according to an accepted tradition, were told by the Prophets that the laws of the Torah shall never be abrogated. They assert that they heard this in clear terms which allowed no room for misunderstanding or allegorical interpretation. I therefore searched in the Scriptures and found support for this tradition. First, in regard to most of the laws it is written that they are "a covenant forever" and "for your generation." There is, furthermore, a phrase which occurs in the Torah, "Moses commanded us a law, an inheritance of the congregation of Jacob" (Deut. 33:4). Moreover, our people, the Children of Israel, are a people only by virtue of our laws, and since the Creator has declared that our people should exist as long as heaven and earth exist, it necessarily follows that our Law should continue to exist as long as heaven and earth are in being, and this is what He says: "Thus says the Lord . . . if these ordinances depart from before Me, then the seed of Israel also shall cease from being a nation before me forever" (Jer. 31:36).

I found that in the last period of prophecy God exhorted His people that they should keep the Law of Moses until the Day of Judgment, which will be preceded by the advent of Elijah. He says, "Remember the Law of Moses, My servant, which I commanded to him in Horeb for all of Israel, even statutes and ordinances. Behold, I will send you Elijah the prophet before the coming of the great and terrible Day of the Lord" (Mal. 3:22–23).

Then, perhaps with an eye toward the Christians and Muslims, Saadya continues.

Some people say that in the same way as the reason for believing in Moses was his performance of wonders and miracles, so it follows that the reason for believing in some other prophet would be the performance of wonders and miracles by the latter. I was greatly astonished when I heard this remark. For the reason for our belief in Moses lies not in the wonders and miracles only, but the reason for our belief in him and all other prophets lies in the fact that they admonished us in the first place to do what was right, and only after we had heard the prophet's message and found it was right did we ask him to produce miracles in support of it. If he performed them, we believed in him. But if we hear his call and find it, at the outset, wrong, we do not ask him for miracles, for no miracle can demonstrate the impossible. . . .

So it is with anyone who claims to be a prophet. If he tells us, "My Lord commands you to fast today," we ask him for a sign of his prophecy, and if we see it, we believe it and shall fast. But if he says, "My Lord commands you to commit adultery and steal," or, "He announces to you that He will flood the world again," or, "He informs you that He created heaven and earth (literally) in one year," we shall not ask him for a sign because he brings us a message which neither reason nor tradition can sanction. (Saadya, *Book of Doctrines and Beliefs* 3.6) [SAADYA 1945: 111–114]

5. Augustine on Symbol and Reality in the Law

Augustine too wrote on the question of reality and the Law, though in a different context than Aquinas. In On Christian Instruction, *Augustine's remarks flow from his general linguistic, or better rhetorical, theory of sign and thing, of symbol and reality, which he was in the course of applying to the interpretation of Scripture (see Chapter 2 above). For him the Old Testament was symbol, a visible or "carnal" sign of the spiritual reality of the New. To mistake one for the other was to suffer bondage to a sign, a condition shared by both the Jews and the pagans. But the "slavery" of the Old Testament permitted certain nuances.*

He who produces or worships any symbol, unaware of what it means, is enslaved to a sign. On the other hand, he who either uses or esteems a beneficial sign, divinely established, whose efficacy and meaning he knows, does not worship this visible and transitory sign; he worships rather that reality to which all such symbols must be ascribed. Besides, such a man is spiritual and free even during the period of his slavery, when it is not yet advisable to unveil to his mind, carnal as it is, those signs by whose yoke it is to be completely subdued. Such spiritual men are those who were the patriarchs, prophets and all those among the people of Israel, through whom the Holy Spirit gave us the remedies and comforts of the Scriptures. At present, since the evidence of our freedom has been made so clearly apparent in the Resurrection of the Lord, we are not burdened by the heavy labor of even those signs which we understand now. The Lord himself and the Apostolic tradition have transmitted a few observances instead of many, and these are very easy to fulfill, very venerable in their meaning, and most sublime in practice. Examples of these are Baptism and the celebration of the Body and Blood of the Lord. When anyone who has been instructed observes these practices, he understands to what they refer, so that he does not venerate them in a carnal slavery, but rather in a spiritual liberty. (Augustine, *On Christian Instruction* 3.9) [AUGUSTINE 1947: 128]

6. The Law of Fear and the Law of Love

Aquinas approaches the distinction between the Israelites' "Old Law" and the Christians' "New" from another perspective.

(In one respect) the New Law is not distinct from the Old Law because they both have the same end, namely man's subjection to God; and there is but one God of the New and of the Old Testament, according to Romans 3:30: "It is one God that justifies circumcision by faith and uncircumcision through faith." But from another point of view, the New Law is distinct from the Old Law because the Old Law is like a pedagogue of children, as the Apostle (Paul) says (Gal. 3:24), whereas the New Law is the law of perfection, since it is the law of charity, of which the Apostle says that it is "the bond of perfection" (Col. 3:14). . . .

All the differences assigned between the Old and New Laws are gathered from their relative perfection and imperfection. For the precepts of every law prescribe acts of virtue. Now the imperfect, who as yet are not possessed of the habit of virtue, are directed in one way to perform virtuous acts, while those who are perfected by the possession of virtuous habits are directed in another way. For those who as yet are not endowed with virtuous habits are directed in the performance of virtuous acts by reason of some outward cause, for instance by the threat of punishment or the promise of some extrinsic rewards, such as honor, riches or the like. Hence the Old Law, which was given to men who were imperfect, that is, who had not as yet received spiritual grace, was called the Law of Fear, inasmuch as it induced men to observe its commandments by threatening them with penalties; and it is likewise spoken of as containing temporal promises. On the other hand, those who are possessed of (the habit of) virtue are inclined to do virtuous deeds through love of virtue and not because of some extrinsic punishment or reward. Hence the New Law, which derives its pre-eminence from the spiritual grace instilled into our hearts, is called the Law of Love; and it is described as containing spiritual and eternal promises, which are objects of the virtues, chiefly of charity. Accordingly, such persons are inclined of themselves to these objects, not as to something foreign, but as to something of their own. For this reason, too, the Old Law has been described as restraining the hand, not the will, since when a man refrains from some sins through fear of being punished, his will does not shrink absolutely from sin, as does the will of a man who refrains from sin through love of righteousness. Hence the New Law, which is the Law of Love, is said to restrain the will. (Aquinas, *Summa Theologica* I/2, ques. 107)

[AQUINAS 1945: 2:958–960]

7. When Did the Ceremonial Precepts of the Torah Cease To Be Binding on Christians?

These are general distinctions between the Old Law and the New. Aquinas also takes up here and elsewhere the question of the ceremonial and liturgical prescriptions laid out in such detail in the Torah.

All ceremonies are professions of faith, in which the interior worship of God consists. Now man can make profession of his inward faith by deeds as well as by words; and in either profession [that is, by deeds or words], if he make a false declaration he sins mortally. Now, though our faith in Christ is the same as that of the (biblical) fathers of old, yet, since they came before Christ, whereas we came after him, the same faith is expressed in different words by us and by them. . . . Consequently, just as it would be a mortal sin now for anyone, in making a profession of faith, to say that Christ is yet to be born, which the fathers of old said devoutly and truthfully, so too it would be a mortal sin now to observe those ceremonies which the fathers of old fulfilled with devotion and sincerity. (Aquinas, *Summa Theologica* I/2, ques. 103, art. 4)

[AQUINAS 1945: 2:915]

The argument is apparently simple. But Aquinas had also to address the glaringly obvious example of the first generation of Christians, indeed, of the Apostles themselves, who continued to observe the Mosaic Law. Here the going is more complex.

On this point there seems to have been a difference of opinion between Jerome and Augustine. For Jerome distinguished two periods of time (*Against Faustus* 19.16). One was the time previous to Christ's Passion, during which the legal ceremonies (of the Mosaic Law) were neither dead, since they were obligatory and did expiate in their own fashion; nor deadly, since it was not sinful to observe them. But immediately after Christ's Passion they began to be not only dead, so as no longer to be either effectual or binding, but also deadly, so that whoever observed them was guilty of mortal sin. Hence he maintained that after the Passion the Apostles never observed the legal ceremonies in real earnest but only by a kind of pious pretense, lest, namely, they should scandalize the Jews and hinder their conversion. This pretense, however, is to be understood not as if they did not in reality perform those actions but in the sense that they performed them without the intention of observing the ceremonies of the Law, just as a man might cut away his foreskin for health's sake and not with the intention of observing legal circumcision.

But since it seems unbecoming that the Apostles, in order to avoid scandal, should have hidden things pertaining to the truth of life and doctrine, and that they should have made use of pretense in things pertaining to the salvation of the faithful, therefore Augustine more fittingly distinguished three periods of time (*Letter* 82.2). One was the time that preceded the Passion of Christ, during which the legal ceremonies (of the Mosaic Law) were neither dead nor deadly; another period was after the publication of the Gospel, during which the legal ceremonies are both dead and deadly. The third is a middle period, to wit, from the Passion of Christ to the publication of the Gospel, during which the legal ceremonies were indeed dead because they had neither effect nor binding force; but they were not deadly because it was lawful for Jewish converts to Christianity to observe them, provided they did not put their trust in them so as to hold them to be necessary for salvation, as though faith in Christ could not justify without the legal observances. On the other hand, there was no reason why those who were converted from paganism to Christianity should observe them. Hence Paul circumcised Timothy, who was born of a Jewish mother; but he was unwilling to circumcise Titus, who had been born a Gentile.

The reason why the Holy Spirit did not wish the converted Jews to be debarred at once from observing the legal ceremonies, while converted pagans were forbidden to observe the rites of paganism, was in order to show that there was a difference between those rites. For pagan ceremonial was rejected as absolutely unlawful and as prohibited by God for all time, whereas the legal ceremonial (of the Mosaic Law) ceased as being fulfilled through Christ's Passion, being (originally) instituted by God as a prefiguring of Christ.

According to Jerome, Peter withdrew himself from the (company of the) Gentiles (in Antioch) (Gal. 2:12) in order to avoid giving scandal to the Jews, of whom he was the Apostle. Hence he did not sin at all in acting thus. On the other hand, Paul in like manner made a pretense of blaming him (for acting thus) in order to avoid scandalizing the Gentiles, whose Apostle he was. But Augustine disapproves of this solution. For in canonical Scripture [to wit, Gal. 2:12], wherein we must not hold anything to be false, Paul says that Peter was to be blamed. Consequently it is true that Peter was at fault and Paul blamed him in very truth and not with pretense. Peter, however, did not sin by observing the legal ceremonial for the time being, since this was lawful for him who was a converted Jew. But he did sin by excessive minuteness in the observance of the legal rites lest he should scandalize the Jews, with the result that he gave scandal to the Gentiles.

Finally, Aquinas turns to the ruling of the Apostles in Jerusalem whereby Gentile converts are to "abstain from things polluted by contact with idols, from fornication, from anything that has been strangled and from blood" (Acts 15:28–29).

Some have held that this prohibition of the Apostles is not to be taken literally but spiritually. . . . Others maintain that these foods were forbidden literally, not to prevent the observance of legal ceremonies (of the Mosaic Law) but in order to prevent gluttony. . . . We must follow a third opinion and hold that these foods were forbidden literally, not with the purpose of forcing compliance with the legal ceremonies but in order to further the union of Gentiles and Jews living side by side. For blood and things strangled were loathsome to the Jews by ancient custom, and the Jews might have suspected the Gentiles of relapse into idolatry if the latter had partaken of things offered to idols. Hence the things were prohibited for the time being, during which the Gentiles and the Jews were to become united together. But as time went on, with the lapse of the cause, the effect lapsed also, when the truth of the Gospel teaching was divulged, wherein our Lord taught that "not that which enters the mouth defiles a man" (Matt. 15:11), and that "nothing is to be rejected that is received with thanksgiving" (1 Tim. 4:4). (Aquinas, *Summa Theologica* I/2, ques. 103, art. 4, ad 1–3) [AQUINAS 1945: 2:916–918]

8. Old Testament Morality in New Testament Times

For the Christians the difference between the Old and the New Dispensation was not merely that of the abrogation of the precepts of the Old Law. The Christian had to face, as did the Jew, the issue of practices apparently condoned, or at least permitted, in the Bible narrative that were no longer regarded as moral. Augustine advises the Christian reader of the Old Testament on how these are to be understood.

We must also be careful not to think that what is understood in the Old Testament, because of the circumstances of those times, as neither a vice nor a crime, even though it is interpreted not figuratively but literally, can be applied to these times as a mode of life. No one will do this unless he is dominated by a lust which seeks protection even in the very Scriptures by which it should be destroyed. The unhappy man does not realize that those things have been set before his mind for this useful purpose, namely, that men of good hope may understand with profit that a practice which they scorn can have a good use, and one which they adopt can lead to damnation, if charity motivates the use of the first practice, and lust the use of the second.

What lies behind the discussion, as it often does in these circumstances, is the polygamy of the biblical patriarchs.

Thus, even if it were then possible, because of the circumstances, for anyone to possess many wives chastely, it is now possible for another man to be lustful with only one. I have more regard for a man who makes use of the fruitfulness of many wives for the sake of another purpose than for the man who indulges in carnal pleasures with only one wife for the sake of that pleasure. In the first case, a benefit in harmony with the circumstances of the time is sought; in the second instance, lust concerned with temporary sensual pleasure is gratified. Those to whom the Apostle (Paul) "by way of concession" allowed carnal intercourse with one wife because of their "lack of self-control" (1 Cor. 7:2, 6) are less advanced on the road to God than those who, although they had several wives, looked only toward the begetting of children in this union, just as a wise man looks only to the health of his body in the matter of food and drink. And so, if they [that is, biblical polygamists] had been living at the time of the Lord's coming, when the time had come to gather the stones and not to scatter them, they would at once have made themselves eunuchs "for the kingdom of heaven's sake." For there is no difficulty in denying ourselves something, unless there is lust in enjoying it. (Augustine, *On Christian Instruction* 3.18) [AUGUSTINE 1947: 137–139]

And, more generally on the moral differences between the Old and New Testaments:

Although all or nearly all the deeds which are recorded in the Old Testament must be regarded not only in their literal sense but figuratively as well, the reader should interpret as a symbol even those acts which he has taken literally if those who have done them are praised (in the Bible), even though their actions differ from the custom of good men who have kept the divine commands since the coming of the Lord. However, he should not carry that same action over into his own conduct, for there are many deeds which were performed in accordance with duty at that time which can be performed now only through lust.

On the other hand, when he reads of the sins of noble men (in the Bible), even though he can observe and verify in them some figures of future events, he may still apply the proper meaning of the action to this end, namely, that he will by no means venture to boast about his own virtuous deeds nor, because of his own uprightness, look down upon those others as if they were sinners. . . . The sins of those men have been written down for a reason and that is that the following passage of the Apostle (Paul) might be everywhere taken into account: "Therefore let him who thinks he stands take heed lest he fall" (1 Cor. 10:20). There is practically no page of the Holy Books which does not cry out that "God resists the proud but gives grace to the humble" (James 4:6). (Ibid. 3.22–23) [AUGUSTINE 1947: 142–143]

9. Priests and Sin

In both the biblical and the Christian tradition the priesthood serves not merely as the instrument of sacrifice but as the agent of cleansing and reconciliation. "Sins are forgiven," Ambrose said, "through the office of the priest and the sacred ministry" (On Cain and Abel 2.4.15). In the following passage Jerome compares the cleansing powers of the Christian priesthood with its Jewish prototype. His point of departure is the role of the Jewish priest in certifying the disease of leprosy. The text in Leviticus 13:1ff. lists and classifies the symptoms in great detail. If, in the judgment of the priest, the symptoms are those of a malignant condition, he pronounces the afflicted person unclean.

As for the person with a leprous affection, his clothes shall be rent, his head left bare, and he shall cover over his upper lip; and he shall call out "Unclean! Unclean!" He shall be unclean as long as the disease is on him. Being unclean, he shall dwell apart; his dwelling shall be outside the camp. (Leviticus 13:45–46)

Conversely, there might be grounds for thinking that the disease had been healed. Here the procedure for ritual purification is more elaborate.

This shall be the ritual for a leper at the time that he is to be cleansed. When it is reported to the priest, the priest shall go outside the camp. If the priest sees that the leper has been cured of his scaly affection, the priest shall order two live clean birds, cedar wood, crimson stuff, and hyssop to be brought for him who is to be cleansed. The priest shall order one of the birds slaughtered over fresh water in an earthen vessel; and he shall take the live bird, along with the cedar wood, the crimson stuff and the hyssop, and dip them together with the live bird in the blood of the bird that was slaughtered over the fresh water. He shall then sprinkle it seven times on him who is to be cleansed of the eruption and cleanse him; and he shall set the live bird free in the open country.

The one to be cleansed shall wash his clothes, shave off all his hair, and bathe in water; then he shall be clean. After that he may enter the camp but must remain outside his tent for seven days. On the seventh day he shall shave off all the hair of his head, his beard and his eyebrows. When he has shaved off all his hair, he shall wash his clothes and bathe his body in water. On the eighth day he shall take two male lambs without blemish, one ewe lamb in its first year without blemish, three-tenths of a measure of choice flour with oil mixed in for a meal offering, and one measure of oil. These shall be presented before the Lord.

The offering ritual is then described in great detail.

. . . Thus the priest shall make expiation for him before the Lord. The priest shall then offer the sin offering and make expiation for the one being cleansed of his uncleanness. Lastly, the burnt offering shall be slaughtered, and the priest shall offer the burnt offering and the meal offering on the altar, and the priest shall make expiation for him. Then he shall be clean. (Leviticus 14:1–20)

Precisely such an instance is encountered in the Gospels.

After he had come from the hill he [that is, Jesus] was followed by a great crowd. And now a leper approached him, bowed low, and said, "Sir, if only you will, you can cleanse me." Jesus stretched out his hand, touched him and said, "Indeed, I will; be clean again." And his leprosy was cured immediately. Then Jesus said to him, "Be sure to tell nobody; but go and show yourself to the priest, and make the offering laid down by Moses for your cleansing; that will certify the cure." (Matthew 8:1–4)

We turn now to Jerome, commenting on this passage from the Gospel of Matthew.

We read of lepers in Leviticus, where they are ordered to show themselves to the priests; then, if they have leprosy, they are rendered unclean by the priests; not that the priests make them lepers and unclean but because they have some knowledge of the leper and the non-leprous and can distinguish who is clean and who is unclean. Thus just as in that instance the priest renders the leper clean or unclean, so too among us the bishop or the presbyter, not those who are unsound or diseased, but by reason of his office, when he has heard the types of sins committed, knows who is to be bound and who is to be released. (Jerome, *Commentary on Matthew* 16.19)

For the biblical society, leprosy was an actual physical complaint, a disease poised in the shared zone between physical and ritual impurity. For the Christians, however, with their diminished sense of ritual impurity, the connection between sin and disease shaded off into one of their favorite metaphors, the priest as the physician of souls. The same canon of the Fourth Lateran Council of 1215 that prescribed annual confession for all Latin Christians also stipulated the following.

The priest, moreover, shall be discreet and cautious, so that in the manner of a skillful physician he may pour wine and oil upon the wounds of the injured, diligently searching out the circumstances of both the sinner and of the sin, that from these he may prudently understand what manner of advice he ought to offer him and what sort of remedy he ought to apply, employing various measures in order to heal the sick. (Acts of the Fourth Lateran Council) [MCNEILL & GAMER 1938: 414]

By the time of the Fourth Lateran Council the invocation of the priest as physician was, in fact, a metaphor. Both the society at large and the Church had generally separated physical and moral defects, as was obviously not the case with cited instances of leprosy and in this Gospel passage.

As he went on his way Jesus saw a man blind from his birth. His disciples put the question, "Rabbi, who sinned, this man or his parents? Why was he born blind?" "It is not that this man or his parents sinned," Jesus answered; "he was born blind so that God's power might be displayed in curing him." (John 9:1–3)

10. On the Nature of Sin

The anonymous disciples who posed the question to Jesus were making two assumptions: first, that the man's physical defect of blindness was possibly the result of a moral defect, sin; and second, that the effects of sin, in this case blindness, could still be felt in the next generation after its commission, that "the sins of the fathers are visited upon their children, to the third and fourth generation," as a celebrated text of Exodus 20:5 has it. Both assumptions were of capital concern to Christian theologians wrestling with the problem of sin, guilt, and punishment. Thomas Aquinas (d. 1277 C.E.) takes up both. First, on physical defects as a punishment for sin, dealt with under the rubric "Whether death and other bodily defects are the result of sin," Thomas holds that they are the result not of actual sins committed by the person suffering them but of original sin.

The sin of our first parent [that is, Adam] is the cause of death and all such defects in human nature, insofar as by the sin of our first parent the original justice was taken away, by which were not only the lower parts of the soul held together under the control of reason, without any disorder whatever, but also the whole body was held together in subjection to the soul, without any defect. . . . Therefore, when original justice was forfeited through the sin of our first parent, just as human nature was stricken in the soul by the disorder among the powers, so also it became subject to (physical) corruption by reason of disorder in the body.

Now the withdrawal of original justice has the character of punishment, even as the withdrawal of grace has. Consequently, death and all consequent physical defects are punishments of original sin. And although these defects are not intended by the sinner, nevertheless they are ordered according to the justice of God, Who inflicts them as punishments. (Aquinas, *Summa Theologica* I/2, ques. 85, art. 5) [AQUINAS 1945: 2:701]

Are all punishments and defects, birth defects for example, as in the case of the man born blind, the result of sin?

Sometimes a thing seems penal yet has not the nature of punishment absolutely. For punishment is a species of evil . . . and evil is a privation of good. And since man's good is manifold, namely, the good of the soul, the good of the body, and external goods, it happens sometimes that a man suffers the loss of a lesser good that he may profit from a greater; as when he suffers a loss of money for the sake of bodily health, or the loss of both for the sake of spiritual health and the glory of God. In both cases the loss is an evil to a man, not absolutely, but relatively; and hence it does not answer to the name of punishment in the absolute sense, but of medicinal punishment. . . . And since such are not punishments properly speaking, they are not referred to sin as their cause except in a restricted sense; because the very fact that human nature needs treatment with penal medicines is due to the corruption of nature, which is itself the punishment of original sin. . . .

Such defects in those who are born with them, or from which children suffer, are the effects and punishments of original sin, as we have stated above. . . . As for the fact that they are not equally in all, this is due to the diversity of nature which is left to itself, as was stated above. (Aquinas, *Summa Theologica* I/2, ques. 87, art. 7) [AQUINAS 1945: 2:717–718]

And finally, what of the question of inherited guilt, the one raised by the text in Exodus 20:5, to which may be added, as Thomas does, a New Testament parallel. Jesus is reported speaking to the Pharisees.

You snakes, you vipers' brood, how can you escape being condemned to hell? . . . On you will fall all the innocent blood spilt on the ground, from innocent Abel to Zechariah son of Berachiah, whom you murdered between the sanctuary and the altar. Believe me, this generation will bear the guilt of all. (Matthew 23:35–36)

Both passages [Thomas begins] should be referred, apparently, to temporal or bodily punishments, insofar as children are the property of their parents, and descendants of their forefathers. Or, if the reference is to spiritual punishment, they must be understood in reference to the imitation of sin. . . . The sins of the fathers are said to be punished in their children because the latter are more prone to sin through being brought up amid their parents' crimes, both by becoming accustomed to them, and by imitating their parents' example, conforming to their authority, as it were. Moreover, they deserve heavier punishment if, seeing the punishment of their parents, they fail to mend their ways. (Aquinas, *Summa Theologica* I/2, ques. 87, art. 8) [AQUINAS 1945: 2:719–720]

11. Penalties and Penances

Although Paul's new, Christ-centered view of the Law shifted the focus away from the Pharisaic and rabbinic emphasis on observance to the Christian's justification through faith, his letters are likewise filled with admonitions to the new Christians to avoid the practices prevalent in the pagan culture and society that surrounded those early believers. Paul was not legislating; he was simply stating the obvious in condemning murder, fornication, slander, lying, and blasphemy—all crimes overtly and incontestably against the Law of God revealed on Sinai. In the generations immediately after Paul the list of such sins grows into a swelling catalogue of Christian "commandments," like this early example from the anonymous second-century work called the Teaching of the Apostles.

You shall not kill; you shall not commit adultery, sodomy or fornication; you shall not steal; you shall not use magic; you shall not traffic with drugs or procure abortions or kill the newborn child; you shall not covet your neighbor's goods; you shall not forswear yourself; you shall not bear false witness, or slander or bear malice. You shall not be double-minded or doubled-tongued, for a double tongue is a snare of death. Your word shall not be false or empty, but fulfilled in deed. You shall not be coveteous, or extortionate, or hypocritical, or spiteful or arrogant. You shall hate no man; but some you shall rebuke and for some you shall pray and some you shall love more than your own soul.

My child, flee from all evil and from all that resembles it. Be not wrathful, for wrath leads to murder; nor a zealot, nor contentious, nor quick to anger; for from all these things murders are begotten. Be not lustful, for lust leads to fornication; nor a filthy talker nor one of high looks; for from all these things adulteries are begotten. Be not an augur, for it leads to idolatry, nor an enchanter, nor a mathematician [that is, an astrologer], nor one who practices lustrations, nor so much as look upon these things; for from all these things idolatry is begotten. Be not a liar, for the lie leads to theft; nor a lover of money, nor vainglorious; for from all these things thefts are begotten. (*Teaching of the Apostles* 2)

Here too there is little to distinguish a Christian's morality from that of a Torah-observant Jew of the same era, save for the obvious absence of matters of ritual purity. Regarding penalties, the Torah is generally explicit on the subject of crimes against God's Law and their punishment. The punishments, as we have seen, were often severe, but we have little certitude of how often or how rigorously they were carried out to the letter: the same Jews who stoned Stephen to death for blasphemy in 30 C.E. claimed a few weeks before that they had lost the right to capital punishment in the case of Jesus (John 18:28–32).

Temple sacrifice presented the alternative of atoning for sin through sacrifice rather than paying for it with blood or property. But with the final destruction of the Temple in 70 C.E., the possibility of sacrifice, and with it that of sacrificial atonement, becomes moot. There remained, of course, excommunication as a form of retribution for sin, but as we observed, it seems to have been little used in practice. The emphasis in Jewish moral teaching swung markedly and distinctly in the direction of the avoidance of sin.

The Christians of Paul's day were just beginning to experiment with the notion of excommunication, as we shall see in the next chapter, and they certainly had no authority to impose capital punishment. But there was for the Christians a more powerful precedent than the Jewish one. Jesus himself announced his power to forgive sin, and he passed this power "to bind and to loose" to his Apostles after him: "Whatsoever you shall bind on earth shall be bound in heaven, and whatsoever you shall loose on earth shall be loosed in heaven" (Matt. 16:19). That passage was generally understood to mean that the reconciliation of the sinner, and the terms of repentance, rested in the hands of the Church. There remained to be resolved, however, the task of laying out those terms: the definition and distinction of sins and what constituted the penalty or penance for each. The Church's synods and councils eventually took up the first task. The disciplinary canons attached to each council's dogmatic findings constituted a growing body of ecclesiastical statute law, in the first instance regulating the behavior of clerics but gradually extending over the whole body of Christians, as shall be seen below. The matter of penance, however, of prescribing the penalties attached to specific sins, was left in a considerably more unregulated state. Often it was left to individual discretion or local practice to fix such penances. One source of authority on the matter were the bishops, whose guidance was often sought and whose responses to queries, because of the prestige and orthodoxy of the authors, carried weight far beyond their immediate jurisdiction. One such was Basil (ca. 330–379 C.E.), the enormously influential Anatolian bishop whose severe penitential prescriptions often took on the force of law for the Church.

Those who are guilty of sodomy or bestiality, as well as murderers, sorcerers, adulterers and idolaters, all deserve the same penalty. . . . We should receive those who have repented over the course of thirty years. Ignorance, voluntary confession and the long lapse of time provide grounds for forgiveness. (Basil, *Letter* 188)

An intentional homicide, when he repents, should be excommunicated for twenty years. . . . On the completion of this period he will be permitted to share in the sacrament. . . . The unintentional homicide will be excommunicated for ten years. . . . The adulterer for fifteen years; fornicators for seven years. . . . Whoever has denied Christ should weep and remain in penance for his whole life long; he may be given the sacrament only at the moment of death. (Basil, *Letter* 217)

Basil's penances reflect an era when public penance, administered once in a lifetime, was still the norm. But from the sixth century onward, confession, penance, and the reconciliation of the Christian sinner were increasingly a private matter between priest and penitent. It was the parish priest, then, who required guidance on sins, their cures and penalties. This is one early attempt to provide such guidance, from the beginning of the sixth century.

Those who become drunk from ignorance (shall do penance for) fifteen days; from negligence, forty days; from contempt, three forty-day periods. One who constrains another to get drunk for the sake of good fellowship shall do the same penance as the drunken man. One who under the influence of hatred or wantonness constrains others to drunkenness that he may basely put them to confusion or ridicule, if he has not done adequate penance, shall do penance as a slayer of souls. (*Excerpts from the Book of David*) [MCNEILL & GAMER 1938: 172]

The approach taken in the examples just cited look chiefly toward intent in imposing penance for sin. Equally often the quality or condition of the sinner or the victim determined the severity of the penalty, as in the following, a "penitential," or book of penances, compiled for the guidance of confessors sometime about 830 C.E. by one Halitgar of Cambrai. In these handbooks, which become common in Europe from the sixth century onward, the offenses are normally broken down by topic. The following are from the section called "On Fornication."

6. If anyone [that is, a cleric] commits fornication as did the Sodomites, he shall do penance for ten years, three of them on bread and water.

7. If any cleric commits adultery, that is, if he begets a child with the wife or the betrothed of another, he shall do penance for seven years; however, if he does not beget a child and the act does not come to the notice of men, if he is a cleric he shall do penance for three years, one of these on bread and water; if a deacon or a monk, he shall do penance for seven years, three of these on bread and water; a bishop, twelve years, five on bread and water.

9. If anyone commits fornication with a nun or with one who is vowed to God, let him be aware that he has committed adultery; therefore he shall do penance as stated above.

10. If anyone commits fornication by himself or with a beast of burden or with any quadruped, he shall do penance for three years; if he has clerical rank or a monastic vow, he shall do penance for seven years.

These and some following prescriptions in this section have to do with the sexual offenses of clerics. The Penitential *then turns to similar sins committed by laymen.*

13. If any layman commits fornication as the Sodomites did, he shall do penance for seven years.

14. If anyone begets a child of the wife of another, that is, commits adultery and violates his neighbor's bed, he shall do penance for three years and abstain from juicy foods and from his own wife, giving in addition to the husband the price of his wife's violated honor.

15. If anyone wishes to commit adultery and cannot, that is, he is not accepted, he shall do penance for forty days.

16. If anyone commits fornication with a woman, that is, with widows and girls: if with a widow, he shall do penance for a year; if with a girl, he shall do penance for two years.

17. If any unstained youth is joined to a virgin, if the parents are willing, she shall become his wife; nevertheless, they shall do penance for one year and then become man and wife.

18. If anyone commits fornication with a beast, he shall do penance for one year. If he has not a wife, he shall do penance for half a year.

19. If anyone violates a virgin or a widow, he shall do penance for three years. . . .

21. If any one of the women who have committed fornication slays those who are born or attempts to commit abortion, the original regulation forbids communion to the end of her life. What is actually laid down they may mitigate somewhat in practice. We determine they shall do penance for a period of ten years, according to rank, as the regulations state. (Halitgar, *Penitential*) [MCNEILL & GAMER 1938: 302–304]

The "penance" envisioned in these prescriptions is normally some form of fasting or abstinence, typically a diet of bread and water from rising until mid-afternoon. At first it seems probable that the penitent underwent a continuous fast for a prescribed time, with the exception of Sundays and holy days. But from the eighth century onward, the penitential fast was often prescribed for a definite time of the year or of the week, especially the three quadragesimae, or quarantines, and the "required weekdays." The three quarantines corresponded to the three principal festivals of the year, preceding Easter and Christmas (that is, the Advent and Lenten fasts) but following Pentecost. The "required weekdays" were Monday, Wednesday, and Friday. Earlier, all sorts of variations were possible, as in this early sixth-century example.

The penance of a presbyter, a deacon, a subdeacon or a virgin who falls, as well as anyone who puts a man to death, who commits fornication with beasts or with his sister or with another's wife, or who plans to slay a man with poisons, is three years. During the first year he shall lie upon the ground; during the second his head shall be laid upon a stone; during the third, upon a board; and he shall eat only bread and water and salt and some pease porridge. Others prefer thirty periods of three days, or (penances) with special fasts, with food and bed as aforesaid, with food at Nones [that is, about three in the afternoon], until the second year. Another penance is for three years, but with a half-pint of beer or milk with bread and salt every second night with the ration of dinner; and they ought to so supplicate God regularly in the twelve hours of the nights and of the days. (*Excerpts from the Book of David*) [MCNEILL & GAMER 1938: 173–174]

The alternative penances in the text just cited are either early examples of or steps on the way toward a system of "equivalents" that shows up in the penitentials and elsewhere. The commutation of penances may be an attempt at lightening some by intensifying and compressing them. This is a seventh-century example from the disciplinary statutes of the Irish Church and has to do with clerics.

3. The equivalent of a year (of penance): three days with a dead saint in a tomb without food or drink and without sleep, but with a garment about him and with the chanting of psalms and with the prayer of the hours. . . .

4. The equivalent of a year: a three-day period in a church without food, drink, sleep or a garment, and without a seat; and the chanting of psalms with the canticles and the prayer of the hours. . . .

8. The equivalent of a year: forty days on bread and water and a special [that is, an all-day] fast in each week and forty psalms and sixty genuflections and the praying of the hours.

9. The equivalent of a year: fifty days in a long special fast and sixty psalms and genuflections and the praying of the hours.

10. The equivalent of a year: forty days on water and grain and two special fasts each week and forty psalms and genuflections and prayer every hour.

11. The equivalent of a year: a hundred days on bread and water and prayer every hour.

12. All these fasts are without flesh and wine—except a little beer—in another's church during the time. (*The Irish Canons*)

[MCNEILL & GAMER 1938: 123–124]

It was not unknown for penances to be commuted or "redeemed" by monetary payments.

If anyone is not able to fast and has the means to redeem himself, if he is rich, for (every) seven weeks of penance he shall give twenty solidi. But if he has not sufficient means, he shall give ten solidi. But if he is very poor, he shall give three solidi. But let no one be startled because we have commanded to give twenty solidi or a smaller amount, since if he is rich it is easier for him to give twenty solidi than for a poor man to give three solidi. But let everyone give attention to the cause to which he is under obligation, whether it is to be spent on the redemption of captives, or upon the sacred altar, or for poor Christians. And know this, my brethren, that when men or women slaves come to you seeking penance, you are not to be hard on them or compel them to fast as much as the rich, since men and women slaves are not in their own power; therefore lay upon them a moderate penance. (Halitgar, *Penitential*)

[MCNEILL & GAMER 1938: 299]

12. Canons and Canon Law

The first collection and arrangement by topic of the disciplinary canons enacted by the Church councils took place in the sixth century, at the same time as and under the influence of Emperor Justinian's codification of Roman civil law. And just as in the civil process, codification did not end the enactment of new ecclesiastical canons or the making of new collections. Sometime about 1140 C.E. there was a major new addition to the literature, the Decretum, *or more properly* The Concord of Discordant Canons, *by the jurist Gratian. Here for the first time there was an attempt at jurisprudence in addition to mere collection and arrangement. The scholastic and systematic quality of the work is immediately apparent.*

PART I, DISTINCTION III

Part I. All these examples belong to the secular law, but because a civil decree is one thing and an ecclesiastical decree another, and since the civil law is called public or civil, we must inquire by what name an ecclesiastical decree is called. An ecclesiastical decree is denoted by the term "canon." And a canon is defined by Isidore (of Seville) in his *Etymologies*, Book VI, as follows:

Chapter I: What a canon is:
It is called "canon" in Greek, "rule" in Latin
Chapter II: Why is it called a rule?
It is called a rule because it leads correctly and it leads no one astray. Others have said it is a rule either because it governs, or because it provides the norm for right living, or it corrects what is crooked and evil.

Part II. Further, some of the canons are decrees of the pontiffs, others the statutes of councils. Some councils are universal, some are provincial. Some provincial councils are held by the authority of the Roman pontiff, namely, in the presence of a legate of the Holy Roman Church; others in fact by the authority of patriarchs or primates or the metropolitan of the province.

This is what must be understood about the general rules. There are also certain private laws, ecclesiastical as well as secular, which are called privileges. Isidore defines these in Book V (of his work):

Chapter III: What a privilege is:
Privileges are laws for individual persons; they are, in a sense,
private laws. For it is held a privilege because it is held privately.
(Gratian, *Decretum*)

Gratian was a Roman jurist and, of course, a Western Christian writing for the Western Church. He was quite prepared, then, to accept the decretal letters of the

Popes as possessing equal weight with the decrees of the councils in the formulation of the Church's law. Here he draws, in this same connection, an interesting distinction between law and the exegesis of Scripture.

DISTINCTION XX

Part I. It follows that decretal letters must be executed by an authority equal to that of the canons of councils. Now there is a question concerning those who interpret Sacred Scripture. Are they to be followed, or are they subject to these same (decretal letters)? For the more a man depends on reason, the more authority his words would seem to possess. Indeed, many writers of (theological) works, men possessed of a superior knowledge, as if by a more ample grace of the Holy Spirit, are shown to have adhered more to reason. So it would seem that the opinions of Augustine, Jerome and other writers of treatises are to be preferred to the decrees of many of the (Roman) pontiffs.

So it might appear, but such is not necessarily the case, as Gratian argues.

Part II. It is, however, one thing to terminate cases, another to expound Sacred Scripture correctly. In settling litigation not only is wisdom necessary, but also authority. Christ, in order to say to Peter, "Whatever you bind on earth will be bound in heaven, etc.," first gave him the keys of the kingdom of heaven. In one instance he gave him the wisdom to discern between one type of leprosy and another, in the other he gave him the power to cast some out of the Church or to receive others. Since, then, all cases are terminated in either the absolution of the innocent or the condemnation of the guilty, absolution or condemnation require not only wisdom but power on the part of those presiding. It appears that the commentators on Sacred Scripture, even if they excel the (Roman) pontiffs in wisdom and are placed before them in the interpretation of Holy Scripture, nevertheless, because they have not attained to the peak of dignity of the latter, deserve, in defining legal cases, a place after them in rank. (Gratian, *Decretum*)

13. The Derivation of God's Commands: The Muslim View

The Muslim's lot was somewhat simpler than the Christian's. As has been noted, what Jesus or the early Christians understood by "Scripture" was quite simply the Bible. It was only after some time had passed that the body of Christian traditions known collectively as the "New Testament" was regarded as Scripture in its own right and attached, in the manner of a diptych, to the "Old." The Muslim, on the other hand, had neither to explain nor explain away the Torah, since the Quran was quite simply a fresh revelation of those same truths or, from a legal point of view, a restatement of the Law of God that made its earlier expressions not so much abrogated as moot. The Quran, since it is the word of God, and since it obviously includes in its contents a great many prescriptions pertaining to conduct, was also the Law of God. There is no doubt that Muslims thought so from the beginning or that the Prophet's own extra-Quranic teaching and example counted heavily in the early community's efforts at living the life of a believer. That much we can assume; it fell to later Muslims, who lived within a long-established and fully defined version of that life, to explain to themselves just how that had come about. The first example comes from a lawyer, al-Shafiʿi (d. 820 C.E.), who was himself involved in defining the Islamic law.

Shafiʿi said: The sum total of what God declared to His creatures in His Book, by which He invited men to worship Him according to His prior decision, falls in various categories.

One such category is what He declared to His creatures textually (in the Quran), such as the aggregate of duties owed him, namely, that they shall perform the prayer, pay the alms tax, perform the pilgrimage and observe the fast (of Ramadan); and likewise that He has forbidden disgraceful acts, in both public and private, such as the explicit prohibition of adultery, the drinking of wine, eating the flesh of dead things and blood and pork; and finally He has made clear to them how to perform the duty of ablution as well as other matters stated explicitly in the Quran.

A second category consists in those acts the obligation of which He established in His Book but whose manner of performance He made clear by the discourse of His Prophet. The number of prayers (to be said each day), and the (amount) of the alms tax and their time (of fulfillment) are cases in point, but there are similar cases revealed in His Book.

A third category consists of what the Messenger of God established by his own example or exhortation, though there is no explicit rule on them defined by God (in the Quran). For God has laid down in His Book the obligation of obedience to His Prophet and recourse to his decision. So he who accepts a duty on the authority of the Prophet of God accepts it by an obligation imposed by God.

A fourth category consists in what God commanded His creatures to seek through personal initiative (devoted to study of the Quran or the traditions of the Prophet) and by it put their obedience to the test exactly as He tried their obedience by the other duties which He ordered them to fulfill, for the Blessed and Most High said: "And we shall put you on trial in order to know those of you who strive and endure, and We will test your accounts" (Quran 47:33). (Shafiʿi, *Treatise*)

[SHAFIʿI 1961: 67–68]

The same process is described five and a half centuries later by Ibn Khaldun (d. 1406 C.E.), now writing less as a lawyer than as a self-conscious historian.

The basic sources of legal evidence are the Book, that is, the Quran, and then the Prophetic traditions, which clarify the Quran. At the time of the Prophet the laws were received directly from him. He possessed the Quranic revelation, and he explained it directly. No transmission, speculation or analogical reasoning was necessary. After the Prophet's death direct explanation was no longer possible. The Quran was preserved through a general and continuous transmission. As for the Prophetic tradition, the men around Muhammad all agree that it was necessary to act in accordance with whatever of it has reached us, as statement or practice, through a sound report that can be trusted to be truthful. It is in this sense that legal evidence is determined by the Quran and the Prophetic tradition.

Then general consensus took its place next to them. The men around Muhammad agreed to disapprove of those who held opinions different from theirs. They would not have done that without some basis for doing so, because people like the men around Muhammad do not agree upon something without a valid reason. In addition, the evidence attests the infallibility of the whole group. Thus, general consensus became a valid proof in legal matters.

Then we looked into the methods according to which the men around Muhammad and the early generations made their deductions from the Quran and the Prophetic tradition. It was found that they compared similar cases and drew conclusions from the analogy, in that they either all agreed or some of them made concessions in this connection to others. Many of the things that happened after the Prophet are not included [or are not covered] in the established texts. Therefore they compared and combined them with the established indications that are found in the texts, according to certain rules that governed their combinations. This assured the soundness of their comparison of two similar cases, so that it could be assumed that one and the same divine law covered both cases. This became another kind of legal evidence, because the early Muslims all agreed upon it. This is analogy, the fourth kind of evidence. (Ibn Khaldun, *Muqaddima* 6.13) [IBN KHALDUN 1967: 3:23–24]

14. On Consensus

Both Shafiʿi and Ibn Khaldun were discussing what had come to be called the "roots of the law," that is, the sources from which authoritative legal prescriptions may be derived. The Quran is obviously one such source, and in its case the problem was not one of validation but of interpretation (see Chapter 2 above). As for the Prophetic traditions, and indeed for certain practices that find no authority in either the Quran or those same traditions, Ibn Khaldun rests heavily on the principle of consensus, which he pushes back into the "Apostolic age" of Islam, that generation of "men around Muhammad" who "agreed to disapprove of those who held opinions different from theirs." Shafiʿi too had something to say about this principle of consensus, and it is not very different from what Ibn Khaldun said nearly seven centuries after him.

Al-Shafiʿi said, may God have mercy on him: Someone said to me: I have understood your rule concerning the prescriptions of God and the prescriptions of the Prophet, may God bless and save him, and I have understood that whoever follows the Prophet follows God in that God has enjoined obedience to His Prophet. There is also proof of what you say, that no Muslim who knows a Quranic text or a Prophetic tradition may maintain the contrary of either of them, and I have understood that this too is a prescription of God. But what is your proof for following that on which the people are agreed when there is no text to that effect, either as a revelation from God or as a tradition handed down from the Prophet? Do you believe, as some do, that their consensus can rest only on a firm Prophetic tradition, even when that latter has not been handed down?

I answered him: That on which they are in agreement and say that it is a tradition handed down from the Prophet is as they say, if it please God. . . . We maintain what they maintain, following their authority, because we know that even though the tradition of the Prophet may be forgotten by some of them, it cannot be forgotten by all of them, and we know that all of them cannot come to agree on something contrary to the Prophetic tradition, or on any error, please God.

His anonymous questioner requires a proof, and Shafiʿi cites a Prophetic tradition to him.

There are three things which cannot be resented by the heart of a Muslim: sincerity of action for God, good advice to the Muslims, and keeping close to the community of the Muslims. . . .

It was then asked, what is the meaning of the Prophet's command to keep close to the community?

Shafi'i's explanation suggests that the consensus had to do not merely with the first generation of Muslims, those "Companions of the Prophet" on whom so much of the validation of Islamic law rests, but extended into the entire community of believers.

I said [Shafi'i continued] there is but one meaning to it. . . . Since the community of the Muslims is scattered in different countries, one could not keep close to the physical community whose members were scattered, and besides, they were found together with Muslims and unbelievers, with pious men and sinners. Thus it could not mean a physical "closeness" since that was not possible, and because physical nearness would in itself effect nothing, so that there is no meaning in "cleaving to the collectivity" except in agreeing with them in what they make lawful and forbidden, and obedience in both these matters. He who maintains what the community of the Muslims maintains is keeping close to the community, and he who deviates from what the community of the Muslims maintains deviates from that community to which he is commanded to remain close. Error arises in separation. In the community there can be no total error concerning the meaning of the Book, of the Prophetic tradition, or of analogical reasoning, please God. (Shafi'i, *Treatise*)
[SHAFI'I 1961: 285–287]

15. Personal Initiative in the Law

Of all the "roots" on the law, it was the one known as "taking personal initiative" that provoked the most resistance in conservative legal circles. The Quran and the Prophetic tradition both came to be regarded as a form of God's revelation, as we have seen, and the consensus of the community could be seen as the working out of that revelation in social terms: the community could not err on God's and His Prophet's intentions, particularly since there were diffused throughout that community of Muslims so many well-attested and agreed-upon Prophetic traditions that exemplified those intentions. But "personal initiative" was a more nakedly personal judgment on the divine intention, an attempt on the part of a jurist to advance his own reasoned opinion where the Quran provided no text and the tradition and consensus no guidance. Shafi'i accepted it, but under limited circumstances and with a prescribed methodology, namely, analogy, which for him and for most jurists was the only acceptable way of exercising personal initiative in the law.

On all matters touching the Muslim there is either a binding decision (based on the Quran or the tradition) or an indication as to the right answer. If there is a decision, it should be followed; if there is no indication as to the right answer, it should be sought by personal initiative, and that is the same as analogy.

Shafiʿi chose to write his Treatise on the Roots of Jurisprudence *in the form of a dialogue. At this point his imaginary interlocutor has a great many questions and problems about this personal approach to the law.*

He asked: If the scholars apply analogy correctly, will they arrive at the right answer in the eyes of God? And will it be permissible for them to disagree through analogy? Have they been ordered to seek one or different answers for each question? What is the proof for the position that they should apply analogy on the basis of the literal rather than the implicit meaning (of a precedent), and that it is permissible for them to disagree in their answers.

Shafiʿi does not answer directly; he prefers, in his pedagogical fashion, to review the general elements in the law and our knowledge of it.

Legal knowledge is of various kinds. The first consists of the right decisions in both the literal and implied senses; the other, of the right answer in the literal sense only. The right decisions in the first instance are those based either on God's command (in the Quran) or on a tradition from the Apostle related by the public from an earlier public. These two [that is, the Quran and the Prophetic tradition] are the two sources by virtue of which the lawful is to be established as lawful and the unlawful as unlawful. This is the kind of knowledge of which no one is allowed to be either ignorant or doubtful.

Second, the legal knowledge of the specialists consists of Prophetic traditions related by a few and known only to scholars, but others are under no obligation to be familiar with it. Such knowledge may be found among all or a few of the scholars, and it is related by a reliable transmitter from the Prophet. This is the kind of knowledge which is binding on scholars to accept, and it constitutes the right decision in the literal sense insofar as we accept the validity of the testimony of two. This is right only in the literal sense, because it is possible that the evidence of the two witnesses might be false.

Third, there is legal knowledge derived from consensus.

And finally, we come to legal knowledge derived from personal initiative by way of analogy, by virtue of which right decisions are sought. Such decisions are right in the literal sense only to the person who applies the analogy but not to the majority of scholars, since nobody knows what is hidden except God.

The other asked: If legal knowledge is derived through analogy, provided it is rightly applied, should those who apply analogy agree on most of the decisions, although we may find them disagreeing on some?

Shafi'i replied: Analogy is of two kinds: the first, if the case in question is similar in principle to the precedent, no disagreement of this kind is permitted. The second, if the case in question is similar to several precedents, analogy must be applied to the nearest in resemblance and the most appropriate. But in this instance those who apply analogy are likely to disagree (in their answers).

The other asked: Will you give examples? . . . .

Shafi'i replied: If we were in the Sacred Mosque (at Mecca) and the Ka'ba is in sight, do you not say that we should face it in prayer with certainty? . . .

The other replied: That is right.

Shafi'i asked: Are we not under obligation to face the Sacred House in prayer no matter where we happen to be?

That is right.

Do you hold that we could always face the Sacred House correctly?

No, he replied. Not always as correctly as when you were able to see the Sacred House; however, the duty imposed on you was fulfilled [that is, however imperfectly we may have faced the now invisible Ka'ba].

Shafi'i asked: Is, then, our obligation to seek the unknown object different from our obligation to seek the known object?

That is right. . . . On what ground do you hold that the exercise of personal initiative is permitted?

Shafi'i replied: It is on the basis of God's saying:

"From whatever place you come out, turn your face in the direction of the Holy Mosque; and wherever you may be, turn your faces in its direction" (Quran 2:145)

Regarding him who wishes to face the Sacred Mosque in prayer and whose residence is at a distance from it, legal knowledge instructs us that he can seek out the right direction through personal initiative on the basis of certain indications (guiding) toward it. For he who is under obligation to face the Holy House and does not know whether he is facing in the right or wrong direction may be able to face toward the right one through certain indications known to him which help him to face it as accurately as he can, just as another person may know other indications which help to orient him, though the direction found by each person may be differ-ent. . . . Let us assume that you and I know the direction of this road, and that I hold that the prayer-direction is this way and you disagree with me. Who should follow the opinion of the other?

The other replied: Neither is under an obligation to follow the other.

What should each one do then?

The other replied: If I hold that neither should pray until he is certain (of the direction), both might not know it with certainty. Then either the prayer obligation should be abandoned, or the prayer-direction obligation waived so that each can pray in whatever direction he wishes. But I am not in favor of either of those two options. I am rather bound to hold that each one should pray in the direction he believes right and he would be under no obligation to do otherwise. . . .

Shafiʿi replied: You have held that prayer is permissible despite your awareness that one of them is in error; it is even possible that both of them were in error. I have added (the general principle that) such a distinction would be binding on you in the cases of legal witnesses and analogical deduction.

The other replied: I hold that such an error is inevitable but it is not intentional. . . .

Shafiʿi said: It is clear to those of you who are certain of truthful information that personal initiative should never be resorted to except in seeking an unknown object by means of certain indications, although it is permissible for those who exercise such initiative to disagree in their decisions.

The other asked: How is personal initiative to be exercised?

Shafiʿi replied: God, glorified and praised be He, has endowed men with reason by which they can distinguish between differing viewpoints, and He guides them to the truth either by (explicit) texts or by indications (through which they may exercise judgment).

Will you give an example?

God erected the Sacred House and ordered men to face it in prayer when it is in sight, and to seek its direction (by personal initiative) when they are at a distance from it. And He created for them the heaven and the earth and the sun and the moon and the stars and the seas and the mountains and the wind (as guiding indications). For God said:

"It is He who has appointed for you the stars, that by them you might be guided in the darkness of land and sea." (Quran 6:97)

And He said:

"And by landmarks and by the stars they might be guided." (Quran 16:16)

Thus God instructed men to be guided by the stars and other indicators, and by His blessing and help they know the direction of the Sacred House. . . . Thus men should seek, through the reasoning power that God has implanted in them, the direction in which He made it incumbent upon them to face in prayer. If it is thus sought, through their reasoning power and the indications (pointing to it), men can fulfill their duty. (Shafi'i, *Treatise*) [SHAFI'I 1961: 288–303]

If we move forward four centuries, we discover that Shafi'i's carefully wrought argument has come to rest in summary in the legal handbooks, in this instance that written by the Syrian jurist Ibn Qudama (d. 1223 C.E.). It occurs under the heading "The Conditions of Prayer" in the subsection "Facing the Prayer-Direction."

The traveler who is making a supererogatory prayer while mounted may pray in whatever direction he happens to be; likewise, the Muslim who is incapable of turning toward the Ka'ba, by reason of danger or for some other reason, should make his prayer however he is able. But outside these two cases, no prayer is meritorious unless it is made in the direction of the Ka'ba. The Muslim who is in the vicinity should turn toward the Ka'ba itself; if he is at a distance, he should pray in its direction.

The Muslim who is ignorant of the direction of the Ka'ba and is in an inhabited area, should inform himself and base himself on the prayer-niches of the Muslims (there); he is bound, in case of error, to begin the prayer over. When two Muslims must determine the direction on their own personal initiative and they are in disagreement, neither is bound to follow the other. The blind man and uneducated should follow the advice of whoever seems most worthy of confidence. (Ibn Qudama, "The Conditions of Prayer") [IBN QUDAMA 1950: 22–23]

We return to Shafi'i's Treatise, *where he now sets down some summary cautions on the use of personal initiative in the law.*

Nobody should apply analogy unless he is competent to do so through his knowledge of the commands of the Book of God, its prescribed duties and its ethical discipline, its abrogating and abrogated communications, its general and particular rules, and its right guidance. Its ambiguous passages should be interpreted by the tradition of the Prophet; if no tradition is found, then by the consensus of Muslims; if no consensus is possible, then by analogical deduction.

No one is competent to apply analogy unless he is conversant with the established Prophetic tradition, the opinions of his predecessors, the consensus and disagreement of the people, and has adequate knowledge of the Arab tongue. Nor is he regarded as competent in analogical reasoning unless he is sound in mind, able to distinguish between closely parallel precedents, and is not hasty in expressing an opinion unless he is certain of its correctness. Nor shall he refrain from listening to the opinions of those who may disagree with him. (Shafi'i *Treatise*) [SHAFI'I 1961: 306–307]

Shafi'i has enumerated some of the skills required of the the Muslim lawyer if he is to exercise "personal initiative." Ibn Khaldun covers much the same ground.

The transmitted traditions which constitute the "Prophetic tradition" need verification through an investigation of the ways of transmission and the probity of the transmitters [see Chapter 3 above], so that the likelihood of the truthfulness of the transmitted information, which is the basis for the necessity to act in accordance with it, becomes clear. This is also one of the basic subjects of the discipline of jurisprudence. Added to this is the knowledge of abrogating and abrogated traditions, when two traditions are contradictory and the earlier one of the two is taught. This too is another subject of jurisprudence. After that there comes the study of the meaning of words. This is because one depends upon knowledge of the conventional meanings of single or composite utterances, for deriving ideas in general from word combinations in general. The philological norms needed in this connection are found in the sciences of grammar, inflection, syntax and style. . . .

Next, the study of analogy is a very important basis for this discipline. It helps to ascertain the correctness of both principal and special aspects of laws depending on reasoning and analogy; to examine the particular characteristic of a case on which the law is considered probably to depend, as to whether it exists in the principle; and to find out whether that characteristic exists in the special case without anything contradicting it, which would make it impossible to base the law upon it. (Ibn Khaldun, *Muqaddima* 6.13) [IBN KHALDUN 1967: 3:24–27]

16. Legal Knowledge and Legal Obligations

The Islamic law is not simply a body of theory; it is also a code of action defining which among human acts are permissible and which forbidden. In short, it imposes obligations. Shafi'i in his Treatise *undertakes to explain how those obligations differ for various segments of the Muslim community.*

Someone asked me: What is legal knowledge and how much should men know of it?

Shafi'i replied: Legal knowledge is of two kinds: one is for the general public, and no sober and mature person should be ignorant of it. . . . For example, that the daily prayers are five, that men owe to God to fast in the month of Ramadan, to make the pilgrimage to the Holy House whenever they are able, and to pay the legal alms in their estate; that He has prohibited usury, adultery, homicide, theft, wine, and everything of that sort which He has obligated men to comprehend, to perform, to pay in their property, and to abstain from because He has forbidden it to them.

This kind of knowledge may be found textually in the Book of God or may be found generally among the people of Islam. The public relates it from the preceding public and ascribes it to the Apostle of God, no one ever questioning its ascription or its binding force upon them. It is the kind of knowledge that admits of error neither in its narrative nor in its interpretation; it is not permissible to question it.

He asked: What is the second kind?

Shafiʿi replied: It consists of the detailed duties and rules obligatory on men, concerning which there exists neither a text in the Book of God nor, regarding most of them, a Prophetic tradition. Whenever a Prophetic tradition does exist in such a case, it is of the kind that is related by few authorities, not the public, and is subject to different interpretations arrived at by analogy.

17. The Collective Obligation

In addition to the obligation common to every individual and that binding only on specialists, Shafiʿi continues, there is a third type of legal obligation, collective in nature, which rests upon the Muslim community as a whole but not upon every individual within it.

There is a third kind of knowledge. . . . The public is incapable of knowing this kind of knowledge, nor can all specialists obtain it. But those who do obtain it should not neglect it. If some can obtain it, the others are relieved of the obligation of obtaining it, but those who do obtain it (and perform the consequent obligation), they will be rewarded.

The classic example of a "collective obligation" is that of the Holy War (see Chapter 6 below), to which Shafiʿi now turns.

God has imposed the duty of Holy War, as laid down in His Book and uttered by His Prophet's tongue. He stressed the calling to Holy War as follows:

"God has verily bought the souls and possessions of the faithful in exchange for Paradise. They fight in the way of God and kill and are killed. This is a promise incumbent on Him, as in the Torah, so the Gospel and the Quran. And who is more true to his promise than God? So rejoice at the bargain you have made with Him; for this will be triumph supreme." (Quran 9:111)

A number of other Quranic passages on the subject are cited. Then Shafi'i resumes.

These communications mean that the Holy War, and rising up in arms in particular, is obligatory for all able-bodied believers, exempting no one, just as prayer, pilgrimage and alms are performed, and no person is permitted to perform the duty for another, since performance by one will not fulfill the duty for another.

They may also mean that the duty of Holy War is a collective duty different from that of prayer: Those who perform it in a war against the polytheists will fulfill the duty and receive the supererogatory merit, thereby preventing those who remained behind from falling into error.

But God has not put the two categories of men on an equal footing, for He said:

"Such believers who sit at home—unless they have an injury—are not the equals of those who fight in the path of God with their possessions and their selves. . . . God has promised the best of things to both, and He has preferred those who fight to those who sit at home by granting them a mighty reward." (Quran 4:97)

He asked: What is the proof for your opinion that if some people perform the duty, the others would be relieved of the punishment?

It is in the communication I have just cited. . . . God said: "Yet to each God has promised the best of things." Thus God promised "the best of things" for those who stayed behind and could not go to the Holy War, although He clearly specified His preference for those who went to the Holy War over those who stayed at home. If those who stayed at home were in error, while others were fighting, they would be committing a sin, unless God forgives them, rather than receiving "the best of things." (Shafi'i, *Treatise*) [SHAFI'I 1961: 82–86]

18. The Evolution of Islamic Jurisprudence

How had this complex legal system come about? Part of Ibn Khaldun's Prolegomenon to History is given over to a description of the origin and evolution of the various sciences found in Islam. Some of these are what he calls "speculative," that is, they rely on the unaided use of the human intellect for their development and understanding. Others are "traditioned" and are essentially the elaboration of revealed data given in the Quran and the Prophetic traditions (see Chapter 3 above). The former are by and large the legacy of Hellenism in Islam, while the latter are an Arab creation and are indigenous to Islam. Primary among the "traditioned" sciences is the one called jurisprudence.

Jurisprudence is the knowledge of the classification of the laws of God, which concern the actions of all responsible Muslims, as obligatory, forbidden, recommendable, disliked, or permissible. These laws are derived from the Quran and the Prophetic traditions and from the evidence the Lawgiver [that is, Muhammad] has established for a knowledge of the laws. The laws evolved from the whole of this evidence are called jurisprudence.

Then, as he does for all the sciences under discussion, Ibn Khaldun launches into a capsule history of the discipline.

The early Muslims evolved the laws from that evidence, though unavoidably they differed in the interpretation of it. The evidence is mostly derived from texts; the texts are in Arabic. In many instances, and particularly with regard to legal concepts, there are celebrated differences among them as to the meaning implicit in the words. Furthermore, the Prophetic traditions differ widely in respect of the reliability of the recensions; their legal contents, as a rule, are contradictory. Therefore a decision is needed. This makes for differences of opinion. Furthermore, evidence not derived from texts causes still other differences of opinion. Then there are new cases which arise and are not covered by the texts. They are referred by analogy to things that are covered by the texts. All this serves to stir up unavoidable differences of opinion, and this is why differences of opinion occurred among the early Muslims and the religious leaders after them.

Moreover, not all the men around Muhammad were qualified to give legal opinions. Not all of them could serve as sources for religious practice; that was restricted to men who knew the Quran and were acquainted with the abrogating and the abrogated, the ambiguous and the unambiguous verses, and with all the rest of the evidence that can be derived from the Quran, since they have learned these matters from the Prophet directly, or from their higher-ranking colleagues who had learned it from him. These men were called "readers," that is, men who were able to read the Quran. (Ibn Khaldun, *Muqaddima* 6.14)

[IBN KHALDUN 1967: 3:3–4]

19. The Classical Schools

Ibn Khaldun now traces the evolution of the nascent Islamic legal system into distinct "schools," each with its particular point of view. The differences are not

*great, save in the case of Shᶜite jurisprudence, whose principles are, for the Sunni
Ibn Khaldun, "futile."*

It continued to be that way at the beginning of Islam. Then the cities
of Islam grew, and illiteracy disappeared from among the Arabs because
of their constant occupation with the Quran. Now the development of
jurisprudence from its sources took place. Jurisprudence was perfected
and came to be a craft and science. The Quran readers were no longer
called Quran readers but jurists and religious scholars.

The jurists developed two different approaches to jurisprudence.
One was the use of opinion [or reasoning] and analogy; it was represented
by the Iraqis. The other was the use of Prophetic traditions; it was represented by the Hijazis. . . . Few traditions circulated among the Iraqis.
Therefore they made much use of analogy and became skilled in it. That
gave them the name of the "representatives of opinion." Their chief,
around whom and whose followers their school centered, was the Imam
Abu Hanifah [d. 767 C.E.]. The leader of the Hijazis was Malik ibn Anas
[d. ca. 795 C.E.] and, after him, al-Shafiᶜi [d 820 C.E.].

Later on, a group of religious scholars disapproved of analogy and
rejected its use. They were the Zahirites [literally, "partisans of the plain
or 'open' sense"]. They restricted the sources of the law to the texts and
the general consensus. . . . The leader of this school was Dawud ibn Ali
[d. 884 C.E.] and his son and their followers. . . . The Zahirite school has
become extinct today as the result of the extinction of their religious
leaders and the disapproval of their adherents by the great mass of Muslims. . . .

. . . The Alids [that is, the Shiᶜites] invented their own school and
had their own jurisprudence. They based it on their dogma requiring
abuse of some of the men around the Prophet and upon their stated
opinion concerning the infallibility of the Imams and the inadmissibility
of differences in their statements. All these are futile principles. The
Kharijites similarly had their own school. The great mass did not approve
of these schools but greatly disapproved them and abused them. Nothing
is known of the opinions of these schools. Their books have not been
transmitted; no trace of them can be found except in regions inhabited
(by them). The books of the Shiᶜa are thus found in Shiᶜite countries and
wherever Shiᶜite dynasties exist, in the West, the East and in the Yemen.
The same applies to the Kharijites. . . .

Malik ibn Anas was followed by al-Shafiᶜi. He traveled to Iraq after

Malik's time. He met the followers of the Imam Abu Hanifah and learned from them. He combined the approach of the Hijazis with those of the Iraqis. He founded his own school and opposed Malik on many points. Malik and al-Shafi'i were followed by Ahmad ibn Hanbal [d. 855 C.E.]. He was one of the highest-ranking scholars of the Prophetic traditions. His followers studied with those of Abu Hanifah, notwithstanding the abundant knowledge of Prophetic traditions they themselves possessed. They founded another school. (Ibn Khaldun, *Muqaddima* 6.14)

[IBN KHALDUN 1967: 3:4–8]

20. The End of the Age of the Fathers

Just as a consensus developed among medieval Christians that the line of the "Fathers of the Church" had come to an end sometime in the era of John of Damascus (d. ca. 750 C.E.), the Muslims too reflectively closed what was called "the gate of independent judgment" and denied later scholars the same freedom enjoyed by earlier Muslim lawyers to derive fresh legal principles from the data of the Quran and the Prophetic traditions. Ibn Khaldun explains why.

These four authorities [that is, Malik ibn Anas, Abu Hanifah, al-Shafi'i, and Ahmad ibn Hanbal] are the ones recognized by tradition in Muslim cities. Tradition-bound people obliterated all other authorities, and scholars no longer admitted any differences of opinion. The technical terminology became very diversified, and there are obstacles preventing people from attaining the level of independent judgment. It was also feared that the existence of differences of opinion might affect unqualified people whose opinion and religion could not be trusted. Thus, scholars came to profess their inability to apply independent judgment and had the people adopt the tradition of the authorities mentioned and of the respective group of adherents of each. They also forbade one to modify his traditional allegiance (to one of these four schools) because that would imply frivolity. All that remained after basic textbooks had been produced and the continuity of their transmissions had been established was to hand down the respective school traditions and, for each individual adherent, to act in accordance with the traditions of his school. Today jurisprudence means this and nothing else. The person who would claim independent judgment nowadays would be frustrated and have no adherents. (Ibn Khaldun, *Muqaddima* 6.12)

[IBN KHALDUN 1967: 3:8–9]

21. Abrogation in Islamic Law

As both Shafi'i and Ibn Khaldun pointed out more than once, there was no more troublesome issue in Islamic law than that of abrogation, the annulment of one divine ordinance and the substitution of another in its place, "so that what is lawful may become unlawful and what is unlawful may become lawful," as Tabari says. The question is in fact raised by the Quran itself.

When We cancel a message [or "verse"] or throw it into oblivion, We replace it with a better one or one similar. Do you not know that God has power over all things? (Quran 2:106)

When We substitute a revelation for another revelation—God knows best what He reveals—they say, you [Muhammad] have made it up. (Quran 16:101)

This is Shafi'i's view of the passages and the principle behind them.

God indeed created mankind for whatever His established knowledge desired in creating it and for whatever its destiny should be. There is no reversal at all in His judgment, He being swift of reckoning. And He revealed to them the Book that explains everything as a guide and a mercy. In it He laid down some duties which He confirmed and others which He abrogated, as a mercy to His people so as to lighten their burden and to comfort them in addition to the favors which He had begun to bestow upon them. For the fulfillment of the duties which He confirmed, He rewarded them with Paradise and with salvation from His punishment. His mercy has included all of them in what He confirmed and what He abrogated. Praise be to Him for his favors. (Shafi'i, *Treatise*) [SHAFI'I 1961: 123]

The principle of one verse of the Quran abrogating or canceling another, for all its intrinsic interest for the theologian, was not the crucial point with regard to Islamic law, however. For the lawyers the more troublesome question was whether a tradition reported from and attributed to the Prophet could replace a Quranic prescription. At first there was resistance to the notion that one of the Prophet's sayings could invalidate a Quranic prescription, as appears in what Shafi'i says next.

God has declared that He abrogated revelations of the Book only by means of other revelations in it; that the Prophetic tradition cannot abrogate the Book but that it should only follow what is laid down in the Book; and that the Prophetic tradition is intended to explain the meaning of a revelation of a general nature set forth in the Book. For God said:

"When Our clear messages are recited to them, those who do not hope to meet Us say: 'Bring a different Quran, or make amendments in this one.' Say: 'It is not for me to change it of my will. I follow only what was revealed to me. If I disobey my Lord, I fear the punishment of an awful Day.' " (Quran 10:15)

Thus God informed men that He had commanded His Prophet to obey what was revealed to him but that He did not empower him to alter (the Book) of his own accord. (Shafi'i, *Treatise*) [SHAFI'I 1961: 123–124]

And what of the Prophetic tradition itself? May it too be abrogated? Shafi'i replies.

In like manner the tradition of the Prophet states: Nothing can abrogate it except another tradition of the Prophet. If God were to address to His Apostle a revelation on a matter on which Muhammad had provided a tradition different from what God had addressed to him, the Prophet would (then) provide a tradition in conformity with whatever God had revealed to him, and thus he would make clear to men that he was providing a tradition that abrogated one earlier or contrary to it. (Shafi'i, *Treatise*) [SHAFI'I 1961: 125]

But lawyers know that neither life nor law is so simple as that.

Someone may ask: Is it possible to assume that there was a transmitted tradition which was abrogated, while the abrogating tradition was not transmitted?

Shafi'i replied: That is impossible. . . . Were this possible the entire Prophetic tradition might be abandoned by men, for they would then say, "Perhaps it was abrogated." No duty has ever been abrogated unless it was replaced by another. The abrogation of the prayer-direction toward Jerusalem by another in the direction of the Ka'ba is a case in point. (Shafi'i, *Treatise*) [SHAFI'I 1961: 126]

The importance given to those divinely certified traditions by legal scholars— Shafi'i chief among them—eventually prevailed, and what passed into Muslim orthodoxy was the principle that Quran could be abrogated by both the Quran and the tradition of the Prophet. The argument is laid out with great clarity by Ghazali (d. 1111 C.E.).

There is no dispute concerning the view that the Prophet did not abrogate the Quran on his own authority [cf. Quran 10:15]. He did it in response to revelation [cf. Quran 53:3–4: "Nor does he speak of his own desire. It is nothing but an inspiration that is inspired"]. The abrogating text in such cases is not worded in the Quranic style.

715

Even if we consider the Prophet capable of abrogating the Quran on the basis of his own reflection, the authority to exercise his discretion derived from God. Thus God does the actual abrogating, operating through the medium of his Prophet. Consequently one should hold that the rulings of the Quran may (also) be abrogated by the Prophet, rather than solely by (another verse of) the Quran. Although the inspiration in these cases is not Quranic inspiration, the word of God is nonetheless one, and God's word is both the abrogating and the abrogated. God does not have two words, one in the Quranic style which we are bidden to recite publicly, and called the Quran, while the other word is not Quran. God has but one word which differs in the mode of its expression. On occasions God indicates His word by the Quran; on others, by words in another style, not publicly recited, and called the Prophetic tradition.

Both are mediated by the Prophet. In each case the abrogator is God alone who indicates the abrogation by means of His Prophet, who instructs us of the abrogation of His Book. Thus none other but the Prophet is capable of manifesting; none other but God of initiating. Were God in this manner to abrogate a verse by the instrumentality of His Prophet, and subsequently to bring another verse similar to the one that had been abrogated, He would have made good His promise (in Sura 2:106). . . . God did not mean to say that He proposed to bring a verse superior to the first. No part of the Quran is superior to another. He meant to state that He would bring a ruling superior to the first, in the sense of its being easier to perform, or richer in terms of reward. (Ghazali, *Mustasfa* 1.125) [Cited by BURTON 1977: 57]

22. The Case of the Woman Taken in Adultery

This issue of abrogation leads us back to one of the more celebrated incidents recorded in the Gospel of John, that of the woman who was caught in adultery and was then brought to Jesus as a test case.

At daybreak he [that is, Jesus] appeared again in the Temple, and all the people gathered round him. He had taken his seat and was engaged in teaching them when the doctors of the Law and the Pharisees brought in a woman caught committing adultery. Making her stand out in the middle, they said to him: "Master, this woman was caught in the very act of adultery. In the Law of Moses it is laid down [Lev. 20:10; Deut. 22:20–21] that such women are to be stoned. What do you say about it?"

They put the question as a test, hoping to frame a charge against him. Jesus bent down and wrote with his finger on the ground. When they continued to press their question, he sat up straight and said, "That one of you who is faultless shall throw the first stone." Then once again he bent down and wrote on the ground. When they heard what he said, one by one they went away, the eldest first.

And Jesus was left alone with the woman still standing there. Jesus again sat up and said to the woman, "Where are they? Has no one condemned you?" She answered, "No one, sir." Jesus said, "Nor do I condemn you. You may go; do not sin again." (John 8:1–11)

A somewhat similar incident is told of Muhammad, though here a very different point is being made. The story occurs in a tradition going back to Umar and preserved in Bukhari's collection of "sound traditions."

(According to Umar): "They brought to the Prophet, on whom be God's blessing and peace, a Jew and a Jewess who had committed fornication. He said to them, 'What do you find in your Book?' They said, 'Our rabbis blacken the faces of the guilty and expose them to public ridicule.' Abdullah ibn Salam [a Jewish convert] said, 'Messenger of God, tell the Jews to bring the Torah.' They brought it but a Jew put his hand over the verse which prescribes stoning and began to read what came before and after it. Ibn Salam said to him, 'Raise your hand,' and there was the verse about stoning beneath his hand. The Messenger of God gave the order and they were stoned." Ibn Umar added: "They were stoned on the level ground and I saw the man leaning over the woman to shield her from the stones." (Bukhari, *Sahih* 4.300, 309)

23. An Instance of Abrogation: Stoning in Text and Tradition

One of the recurrent charges leveled by Muhammad against the Jews, and echoed in the Quran, was that of the falsification of Scripture. In the example just cited the Prophet shows his fidelity to the Torah-prescribed penalty of stoning, despite the Medinese Jews' attempt to conceal it. The Quran too is explicit on the matter of adultery and fornication, though in a somewhat unexpected way.

The adulterer and the adulteress should be flogged a hundred lashes each, and no pity for them should deter you from the law of God, if you believe in God and the Last Day, and the punishment should be witnessed by a body of believers. (Quran 24:2)

Stoning as a penalty for adultery is nowhere mentioned in the Quran, though the punishment is prescribed by the Torah and apparently practiced by Muhammad. The reconciliation was effected through a Prophetic tradition related on the authority of Ubada. In this case the divine inspiration for Muhammad's utterance is carefully underlined.

The descent of inspiration was troublesome to the Prophet. His face would go ashen in color. One day inspiration came down upon him and he showed the usual signs of distress. When he recovered he said: "Take it from me! God has appointed a way for the women: the non-virgin with the non-virgin and the virgin with the virgin. The non-virgin, one hundred strokes and death by stoning; the virgin, one hundred strokes and banishment for a year." [BURTON 1977: 74]

Put in this fashion, a Prophetic tradition would simply have abrogated the Quran. But some Muslims at least must have had reservations. Another set of traditions, this time reported of Muhammad's companion and the second Caliph of Islam, Umar ibn al-Khattab, intimated that a stoning penalty actually had been revealed as part of the Quran, though it was not in the present copies. According to Umar:

God sent Muhammad with the truth and revealed to him the Book. Part of what God revealed was the stoning verse. We used to recite it and we memorized it. The Prophet stoned and we have stoned after him. I fear that with the passage of time some will say, "we do not find stoning in the Book of God," and will therefore neglect a divine injunction which God revealed. Stoning is a just claim. [BURTON 1977: 77–78]

Why then did not Umar add it to the text of the Quran?

By Him who holds my soul in His hand! Except that men would say, "Umar has added it to the Book of God," I would write it in with my own hand: "The married man and the married woman, when they fornicate, stone them outright." [BURTON 1977: 78]

We are even told where this verse would have occurred.

Ubayy asked Zirr ibn Hubaysh, "How many verses do you recite in the sura (called) 'The Clans' (Sura 33)?" Zirr replied, "Seventy-three verses." Ubayy asked if that was all. "I have seen it," he said, "when it was the same length as (the Sura called) 'The Cow' (Sura 2). It contained the words: 'The married man and the married woman, when they fornicate, stone them outright, as an exemplary punishment from God. God is Mighty, Wise.'" [BURTON 1977: 80]

The question finally comes to rest, all controversy aside, in a jurist's manual of the thirteenth century, in a section on Quranically prescribed penalties. The author is the Syrian al-Nawawi (d. 1277 C.E.).

Fornication: This consists of introducing the male organ into the vagina of a forbidden woman without any ambiguity or doubt, or into the anus of a man or woman as well, according to our (Shafiʿite) school, and it receives a prescribed penalty, regardless of whether it was done for payment or by consent, and is applied as well for (relations with) a woman within the forbidden degrees of kinship or marriage, even if a marriage was performed. The guilty person must be adult, sane, and aware that it was wrong. Drunkenness is no excuse.

1. The prescribed penalty of an adult free Muslim or member of a "protected community" [e.g., a Jew or a Christian], who has consummated a legal marriage previous to the act, is stoning to death. If one of the two partners has not (contracted a marriage), it does not lessen the guilt of the other.

2. The prescribed penalty of a fornicator who is not an adult and free or who has never married is one hundred lashes and banishment for one year, and if the Imam [that is, the ruler] designates a place of banishment, that must be accepted.

3. For a slave the prescribed punishment is fifty lashes and banishment for half a year. (Nawawi, *The Goal of Seekers*) [WILLIAMS 1971: 150–151]

24. Controversial Questions

Although there might be general agreement on the basic principles of the law, there was certainly a great deal of room for debating some of its specifics. Indeed, this area of "controversial questions" debated among the four classical schools of Islamic law constituted an entire subspecies of the discipline of jurisprudence. It is once again Ibn Khaldun who is writing.

It should be known that the jurisprudence just described, which is based upon religious evidence, involves many differences of opinion among scholars of independent judgment. Differences of opinion result from the different sources they use and their different outlooks, and they are unavoidable, as we have stated before.

These differences occupied a very large space in Islam. Originally people could adhere to any juridical authority they wished. Later on the matter was in the hands of the four leading authorities in the Muslim cities. They enjoyed a very high prestige. Adherence was restricted to them, and people were thus prevented from adhering to anyone else. This situation was the result of the disappearance of independent initiative (in the law), because this was too difficult a matter and because, in the course of time, the scholarly disciplines constituting material for independent judgments had multiplied. Also, there existed nobody who might have organized a school in addition to the existing four. Thus, they were set up as the basic schools of Islam.

Differences of opinion among the adherents of these schools and the followers of their laws received equal status with differences of opinion concerning religious texts and legal principles in general. The adherents of the four schools held disputations in order to prove the correctness of their respective founders. These disputations took place according to sound principles and fast rules. Everybody argued in favor of the correctness of the school to which he adhered and which he followed. The disputations concerned all the problems of religious law and every subject of jurisprudence. . . . These disputations clarified the sources of the authorities as well as the motives of their differences and the occasions when they exercised independent judgment. (Ibn Khaldun, *Muqaddima* 6.13) [IBN KHALDUN 1967: 3:30–31]

25. Legal Reasoning on the Prohibition of Wine

Ibn Khaldun's discussion of legal principles is highly abstract and was intended to be so. How the principles he describes were actually applied and controverted may be seen in the instance of the prohibition against wine, recorded in the Quran in the following words.

They question you concerning wine and gambling. Tell them: "There is great sin and (some) profit in them. But the sin in them is greater than the benefit." (Quran 2:219)

The legal commentaries on this brief passage are long and exceedingly complex. This one comes from the Quran commentary of Fakr al-Din al-Razi (d. 1209 C.E.). He begins by attempting to determine the circumstances of this particular revelation.

Some have noted that in God's words "they question you concerning wine and gambling," exactly what the people have asked about is not made clear. It is possible that they inquired about the character and nature of wine. Or they could have asked whether it was permissible to use wine. And finally, they could have asked whether it was permissible or sinful to drink it. But since God answers by indicating the sinfulness of both (wine and gaming), the emphasis in the answer proves that the (original) questions had to do with permission and sinfulness. This verse involves many complex questions.

The first step toward a solution of those questions is to connect this verse with the other Quranic verses that seem to pertain to the same subject, a process that might reveal the evolution of the prohibition.

Four (Quranic) verses have been revealed on the subject of wine. In Mecca the following verse came down: "And (We give you) the fruits of the palms and the vines, from which you obtain an intoxicant as well as wholesome food. Surely this is a sign for people who understand" (Sura 16:67). On the basis of this it would appear that Muslims drank such drinks, since they were (apparently) permitted. Then, however, Umar, Mu'adh and a group of other Companions of the Prophet asked: "Messenger of God, give us an opinion concerning wine, since it seizes a man's mind and steals his wealth!" Then there were revealed the following words of God concerning wine: "In both are great sin and some uses for men." From that point onward some continued to drink wine, while others abstained from it. Then Abd al-Rahman ibn Awf invited some people, and they drank wine together and became drunk. One of them arose in order to perform the prayer and (incorrectly) recited: "Say: O unbelievers, I worship"—the text reads "I do not worship"—"what you worship" (Sura 109:1). At this point the following verse came down: "O believers, do not approach prayer when you are intoxicated until you are aware of what you are saying" (Sura 4:43).

Then some of the Helpers came together, and among them was Sa'd ibn Abi Waqqas. When they became drunk, they began to boast and recite poetry to each other, until finally Sa'd recited a poem that included a slander against the Helpers. Then when one of the Helpers struck Sa'd with the jawbone of a camel and inflicted a deep head wound on him, the latter complained to the Messenger of God, and Umar said: "God, give us a conclusive statement concerning wine!" Then came down the verse: "O believers, wine, games of chance, idols and divining arrows are an abomination and belong to the works of Satan. So avoid it! Perhaps you will (then) prosper. Satan desires only to bring about enmity and hatred among you, with wine and games of chance, and to bar you from the remembrance of God and from prayer. Will you then not desist?" (Sura 5:90–91). Umar added, "Will we desist, Lord?"

Al-Quffal said that the wisdom of issuing the prohibition (against drinking wine) in these stages consists in the fact that God knew that the people had been accustomed to drinking wine and drawing upon its many uses. So He also knew that it would be unbearable for them if He had prohibited wine to them all at once, and thus doubtless He used these stages as a kindness in the prohibition (against drinking wine).

But there are some who hold that God forbids wine and games of chance in the first verse in question (2:219), and that His words "Do not approach prayer when you are intoxicated" came down after it. That is, the request that the drinking of wine be forbidden during the time of prayer is connected with these words, since one who drinks wine would be performing his prayer while intoxicated. If, therefore, intoxication is forbidden, then the prohibition against drinking wine is also included. The verse (regarding the prohibition of wine) in (the sura called) "The Table" [that is, 5:90–91] came down after the verse under discussion and it represents the strongest possible form of the prohibition. According to al-Rabiʿ ibn Anas, however, the present verse (2:219) came down after the prohibition of wine.

My own view is that one should note that the present verse shows the (prior existence of the) prohibition against wine. It lacks, however, a (precise) explanation of what wine is.

What then is the present state of the question among jurists?

. . . al-Shafiʿi said that every intoxicating drink is wine; Abu Hanifah (on the other hand) said that "wine" refers specifically to a strong grape juice that develops foam (as a result of fermentation). The evidence on which Shafiʿa makes his judgment is of several different types.

The first type of evidence that Shafiʿi adduced was that of the Prophetic traditions on the subject.

1. The first (example of the argument from Prophetic tradition) is what is presented on Abu Dawud's testimony in his tradition collection entitled *Sunan*, on the authority of al-Shaʿbi, from Ibn Umar, who was reported to have said: On one particular day the prohibition against wine was revealed, and this was at a time when wine was made of five kinds of things: grapes, dates, wheat, barley and millet. At that time one understood as "wine" a liquid that clouds [the verb here is *khamara*; the noun for wine throughout is *khamr*] the mind.

From this Shafiʿi thought three kinds of conclusions might be drawn: The first is that this shows that all these (substances) were designated as wine; second, the report is the equivalent of an explicit declaration that the prohibition of wine includes the prohibition of these five kinds; third, Umar was speaking of every kind of drink that "clouds" the mind. Umar doubtless knew the correct linguistic usage, and so his tradition indicates that "wine" is a designation for all drinks that "cloud" the mind. And so forth.

2. The second example of Shafiʿi's evidence is this: Abu Dawud relates from al-Nuʿman ibn Bashir the following statement: The Messenger of God said: "Wine is made out of grapes, dates, honey, wheat and barley." From this one can draw two conclusions: first, that this is an explicit explanation that all these things fall in the category of "wine" and thus are also included in the verse that issues the prohibition against wine; and second, that it was not the intention of the lawgiver to give instructions covering all the terms (for wine and similar drinks). Thus, in the present case he had nothing else in mind but to explain that the decision which applies to wine (from grape juice) also applies to these (other types of wine). If the published decision, which refers specifically to wine (made from grape juice), pertains (generally) to the evil of drinking, then it must be applied in like manner to these (other) types of drinks. Al-Khattabi said that the reason the Messenger of God used the word "wine" specifically for these five things was not because wine is produced only from these five, but they are mentioned by name because they were well known at that time. And so the decision concerning these five applies to all that are like them, such as millet, sult and tree sap. . . .

3. Shafiʿi's third example is as follows: Abu Dawud relates also from Nafiʿ who relates from Ibn Umar: The Messenger of God said that every intoxicating drink is wine and that every type of intoxicating drink is forbidden. Al-Khattabi remarked the following: If the Messenger of God states that every type of intoxicating drink is to be considered wine, then this leads to two possible interpretations: first, the word "wine" is being used to designate all drinks that cause intoxication. . . . After the verse had proclaimed the prohibition against "wine," the people did not know the exact meaning which God meant to express by "wine," that is, whether the lawgiver was using the expression according to its usual meaning in Arabic or was producing a legal category by the creation (of a new definition of the word "wine"), as is also the case with the terms "prayer," "fast" and others; and second, the meaning of his statement is that every intoxicating drink is to be treated as sinful as wine. That is, when the Messenger of God says that this intoxicating drink is wine, the literal meaning would be that they are all actually (different kinds of) wine. Now it is clear that this is not what is meant, so one must take it as a figurative expression for whatever is the equivalent (of wine), and this remains as the authoritative decision.

4. The fourth example is this: Abu Dawud relates the following from Aisha: The Messenger of God was asked about a certain concoction and he answered: "Every drink that intoxicates is prohibited." Al-Khattabi remarked: The drink being referred to in the question was one made of honey, and thus this statement of the Messenger of God refutes every interpretation that is put forward by those who declare that such "drinks" are permitted. The statement also refutes the assertion of those who say that a small amount of an intoxicating drink is allowed. The Messenger of God was asked about only a single kind, the honey concoction, but answered with a prohibition against the (entire) class (of intoxicating drinks). This includes not only a large amount of it but a small amount. If separate classifications according to kind and amount were intended here, then the Messenger of God would have mentioned this and not neglected it.

5. The fifth example is this: Abu Dawud related from Jabir ibn Abdullah: The Messenger of God said that whatever intoxicates in large amounts is prohibited in small amounts.

6. The sixth example is this: Abu Dawud related further from al-Qasim, who related from Aisha (who said): I heard how the Messenger of God said: "Every intoxicant is forbidden. Whatever intoxicates in the amount of a bale is also forbidden in a handful." . . . Here then it is most clearly evident that sinfulness extends to all parts of (intoxicating) drinks.

7. The seventh example is this: Abu Dawud also related from Shahr ibn Hawshab who related from Umm Salama that the Messenger of God prohibited every intoxicating and debilitating drink. Al-Khattabi said that by "debilitating" is to be understood every drink that brings about weaknesses and stiffness in the joints. It doubtless includes all kinds of (intoxicating) drinks.

All these Prophetic traditions indicate that every intoxicating drink is wine and is thus prohibited.

Moreover, other types of arguments supported this conclusion, as Razi now explains. The first derives from the etymology of the word "wine" itself.

The second kind of argument which indicates that every intoxicating drink (*muskir*) is wine (*khamr*) is seen when one considers the etymology. The lexicographers mention that the basic meaning of the root *kh-m-r* is "to cover." Thus the head veil is called *khamaar* because it covers the head of a woman, while a *khamar* may be a shrub or a ground depression in a hill, which conceals somebody. . . . The etymology shows that by "wine" we are to understand anything that "veils" [or "clouds"] the mind, just as one designates wine as an intoxicant (*muskir*) because it "closes" (*sakara*) the mind.

The argument from consensus is then put forward.

The third kind of argument which indicates that by "wine" is to be understood whatever intoxicates is based on the fact that the community agrees in the following: There are three (Quranic) verses which refer to wine, in two of which it is explicitly called such (2:219 and 5:90) . . . while the third verse refers to intoxication and contains God's words: "Do not approach prayer when you are intoxicated" (4:43). This shows that by "wine" is meant intoxicants.

And finally, the case can be made from analogical reasoning.

The fourth kind of argument is as follows: The occasion for the prohibition of wine was when Umar and Mu'adh said: "Messenger of God, wine seizes the mind and steals the wealth. Give us an explanation concerning it!" Thus they asked for a judgment from God and His Messenger because wine seizes the mind. Hence it necessarily follows that all that is like wine in this sense is either wine or is equivalent to it in view of the present decision.

The fifth kind of argument is as follows: God has confirmed His prohibition of wine through His words: "Satan desires only to create enmity and hatred among you, with wine and games of chance, and to bar you from a remembrance of God and from prayer" (2:219). Doubtless such kinds of acts are motivated by intoxication. This cause is certain. Accordingly, the present verse (2:219) presents more precise evidence of the fact that the sinfulness of (the use of wine) lies in the fact that it intoxicates. Whether it is now unconditionally necessary that every intoxicating drink is wine or whether this is not so, in all cases the present decision is valid for all intoxicating drinks. Whoever thinks correctly and freely knows that these aspects (of the evidence) are given clearly and distinctly, along with the (clear) statement of the problem. (Razi, *The Great Commentary*, ad loc.)

Once the arguments had all been set forth, the fact remained that the drinking of wine was a Quranically proscribed crime. From this practical perspective the treatment of prosecution and punishment is far more succinct.

Forbidden beverages: Every drink that inebriates in a large quantity is forbidden in a small quantity. The prescribed punishment is not given to a child, an insane person or a non-Muslim subject. One may take wine in case of immediate necessity, according to our (Shafi'ite) school, e.g., to dislodge food in the throat which is choking one, if nothing else is available; one is, however, liable to punishment if he uses wine for medicine or because of thirst.

The prescribed punishment for a free person is forty blows, and that for a slave twenty; by whip, hand, sandal or a rolled-up garment. It is said that it should be with a whip. The Imam [that is, the ruler] may double the punishment if he sees fit. (Nawawi, *Guide for Seekers* 205–244)
[WILLIAMS 1971: 152]

26. The Fast of Ramadan

The fast during the month of Ramadan was one of the precepts laid down in the Quran for all believers. Here we trace the practice from the chief Quranic text, through the prophetic traditions, to the commentators.

O believers, fasting is enjoined on you, even as it was on those before you, so that you might become righteous.

Fast a certain number of days, but if someone is ill or traveling, the same number of other days (he had missed), and those who find it difficult should (as compensation) feed a poor person. For the good they do with a little hardship is better for men. And if you fast, it is good for you, if you knew.

. . . When you see a new moon you should fast for the whole month; but a person who is ill or traveling should fast on other days, as God wishes ease and not hardship for you, so that you complete the (fixed) number and give glory to God for the guidance and be grateful. . . .

You are allowed to sleep with your wives on the nights of the fast: they are your dress as you are theirs. God is aware you were cheating yourselves so He turned to you and pardoned you. So now you may have intercourse with them. Eat and drink until the white thread of dawn appears clear from the dark line, then fast until night falls; and abstain from your wives to stay in the mosques for assiduous devotion. These are the bounds fixed by God, so keep well within them. . . . (Quran 2:183–187)

We begin with some of the Prophetic traditions on the subject of the Ramadan fast.

Ibn Umar, may God be pleased with both of them (both father and son), reported God's Messenger, may peace be upon him, as saying in connection with Ramadan: Do not fast till you see the new moon and do not break fast until you see it; but if the weather is cloudy, calculate it. (Muslim, *Sahih* 6.406.2363)

Sahl ibn Sa'd said that when this verse was revealed, "Eat and drink until the white thread becomes distinct to you from the black thread," a person would take hold of a white thread and a black thread and keep eating until he could find them distinct (in the light of the dawn). It was then that God, the Majestic and Great, revealed (the rest of the phrase) "of the dawn," and then it became clear that "thread" refers to the streak of light in the dawn. (Ibid. 6.412.2397)

Ibn Umar reported that the Messenger of God, may peace be upon him, observed fasts uninterruptedly [that is, night and day] in Ramadan, and the people did this (in imitation of him). But he forbade them to do so. It was said to him: You yourself observe the fasts uninterruptedly (but you forbid us to do so). Upon this he said: I am not like you: I am fed and supplied drink (by God). (Ibid. 6.415.2427)

Abu Hurayra, may God be pleased with him, reported that a person came to the Messenger of God, may peace be upon him, and said: Messenger of God, I am undone. He [Muhammad] said: What brought about your ruin? The man said: I have had intercourse with my wife (during the day) in Ramadan. Upon this Muhammad said: Can you find a slave to set free (by way of atonement)? The man said: No. Muhammad said: Can you fast for two consecutive months? The man said: No. Muhammad said: Can you provide food for sixty poor people? The man said no. The man then sat down and there was brought to the Messenger of God, may peace be upon him, a basket which contained dates. Muhammad said: Give these dates as an alms. The man said: Am I to give to one who is poorer than I. There is no family poorer than mine between the two lava plains of Medina. The Messenger of God laughed so broadly that his back teeth showed and said: Go and give it to your family to eat. (Ibid. 6.418.2457)

Aisha, may God be pleased with her, reported that Hamza ibn Amr al-Aslami thus asked the Messenger of God, may peace be upon him: Messenger of God, I am a person devoted much to fasting. Should I fast during the journey? He said: Fast if you like and break it if you like. (Ibid. 6.421.2488)

Ibn Abbas, may God be pleased with both of them (father and son), reported that when God's Messenger, may peace be upon him, came to Medina, he found the Jews observing the fast on the day of Ashura [that is, the tenth of Muharram]. The Jews were asked about it and they said: It is the day on which God granted victory to Moses and the Banu Isra'il over the Pharaoh and we observe fast out of gratitude to Him. Upon this the Messenger of God, may peace be upon him, said: We have closer connection with Moses than you have, and he commanded (Muslims) to observe fast on this day. (Ibid. 6.423.2518)

Aisha, may God be pleased with her, reported that the Quraysh used to fast on the day of Ashura in the pre-Islamic days and the Messenger of God, may peace be upon him, also observed it. When he migrated to Medina he himself observed the fast and commanded (others) to observe it. But when fasting during the month of Ramadan was made obligatory, he said: He who wishes to observe the fast (of Ashura) may do so and he who wishes to abandon it may do so. (Ibid. 6.423.2499)

The following two traditions, reported from the same authority, show one verse of the Quran abrogating another.

Salama ibn Akwa, may God be pleased with him, reported that when this verse was revealed, "And for those who can afford it there is a ransom, the feeding of a man in need" (2:184), he who liked to fast fasted and he who liked not to observe it ate and expiated till the (following part of the) verse was revealed which abrogated it.

Salama ibn Akwa reported: During the lifetime of the Messenger of God, may peace be upon him, in one month of Ramadan he who wished to fast fasted and he who wished to break it broke it and fed a needy person as an expiation, till this (following) verse was revealed: "But whoever does good of his own accord, it is better for him." (Muslim, *Sahih* 6.428.2547–2548)

The reference to fasting as an obligation imposed upon others before Islam (2:183) elicited these remarks from the exegete Tabari (d. 923 C.E.) on the origins of the Christians' Lenten fast during the fifty days preceding Easter.

As for those who were before us, they were the Christians. The month of Ramadan was prescribed, as it was also prescribed for them neither to eat nor to drink if they wake up after they had gone to sleep. Nor were they allowed to go in to their wives during the entire month of Ramadan. The Christians found the fast of Ramadan hard to endure. Ramadan rotated from winter and summer. As they realized this, they agreed to have the fast between winter and summer. They said: "We shall add twenty days as expiation for what we have done." Thus they made their fast fifty days. Muslims continued to observe the fast in emulation of Christians until the incidents of Abu Qays ibn Sirmah al-Ansari and Umar ibn al-Khattab, when God made lawful for them [that is, the Muslims] eating, drinking and sexual intercourse until the appearance of the dawn. (Tabari, *Commentary* 3.411) [AYOUB 1984: 189]

These "incidents" are described by the commentator al-Wahidi (d. 1076 C.E.).

At first the Muslims used to eat, drink and go in to their wives (after sunset in Ramadan) so long as they had not gone to sleep. Once they slept they did not do any of these things until the following evening. It happened that Qays ibn Sirmah al-Ansari was fasting, so he came to his wife at the time of the breaking of the fast (in the evening), but she had nothing for him to eat. While she went to fetch food for him, he fell asleep. Around noon of the next day he fainted. Likewise, Umar ibn al-Khattab came in to his wife after she had slept. All this was reported to the Prophet. Then this verse (2:187) was sent down and the Muslims were pleased with it. (Wahidi, *The Occasions of Quranic Revelation* 45) [AYOUB 1984: 197]

And on the question of substituting another good work, to wit, feeding a needy person, for the fast during Ramadan:

In sum, abrogation is stipulated only in the case of one in sound health and not on a journey. This is based on God's saying, "Therefore whosoever among you witnesses the moon, let him fast (the month)." The aged one who is near death, however, is allowed not to observe the fast; nor is he obliged to make up fasting by other days. This is because his condition would not change in such a way so as to make up for the days he missed. But if he does break the fast, he should feed a poor man for every day if he has the means to do so. (Ibn Kathir, *Commentary* 1.378–379) [AYOUB 1984: 190–191]

By the time the command to fast had passed into the legal manuals it had been thoroughly discussed by Islamic lawyers, who could then pronounce on almost any conceivable complication. The following commentary from the legal manual of al-Nawawi (d. 1277 C.E.) sets out the conditions of fulfilling the obligation.

To fast one must rigorously avoid intercourse, vomiting . . . or introducing any substance into the "interior of the body." . . . It does not matter if the "interior" is inside the head or the belly or the intestines or the bladder; all can break the fast with the introduction of a substance by snuffing or eating or injection, or through incision in the belly or the head or the like. According to the soundest opinion, putting drops in the nose or the urethra breaks the fast.

It is necessary, however, that the introduction (of a substance) be through an open passage. Thus there is no harm in oil's entering the pores by absorption, or when *kohl* [or eyeliner] is used, and its taste is afterwards perceived in the throat.

Further, the introduction must be intended, so that if a fly or a gnat or dust of the road or flour dust entered (the body) by accident, the fast would not be broken. It also would not be broken if saliva were swallowed carelessly. But the fast is broken if saliva leaves the mouth, and one brings it back into the mouth, or if one moistens a thread in one's mouth and then puts it back in the mouth still moist, or if one swallows saliva in which a foreign substance or something unclean is mixed.

If one swallows saliva in the mouth, then, he does not break the fast, but if he swallows water from the mouth or nose remaining after the ablutions, if it is in any quantity, he does break the fast. If food remaining between the teeth is dislodged by saliva, it does not break the fast. (Nawawi, *Program for Students*) [WILLIAMS 1971: 113–114]

And finally, Ghazali offers a prescription for converting a ritual obligation into a genuinely spiritual act.

When you fast, do not imagine that fasting is merely abstaining from food, drink and marital intercourse. Muhammad, God bless and preserve him, has said: "Many a one who fasts has nothing from his fasting save hunger and thirst." Rather, perfect fasting consists in restraining all the members from what God Most High disapproves. You must keep the eye from looking at things disapproved, the tongue from uttering what does not concern you, and the ear from listening to what God has forbidden—for the hearer shares the guilt of the speaker in cases of backbiting. Exercise the same restraint over all the members as over the stomach and the genitals. A prophetic tradition runs: "Five things make a man break his fast: lying, backbiting, malicious gossip, the lustful glance and the false oath." Muhammad, God bless and preserve him, said: "Fasting is a protection; if one of you is fasting, let him avoid obscene speech, loose living and folly; and if anyone attacks him or insults him, let him say, 'I am fasting.' "

Then endeavor to break your fast with lawful food, and not to take an excessive amount, eating more than you normally eat at night because you are fasting by day; if you take the whole amount you usually take, there is no difference between eating it at one meal at night and eating it at two meals (one by day and one by night, as when one is not fasting). The aim of fasting is to oppose your appetites, and to double your capacity for works of piety. (Ghazali, *The Beginning of Guidance* 27)
[GHAZALI 1953: 129–130]

27. The Menstruant

One Prophetic tradition that invites a direct comparison with Torah law is that on the subject of menstruation.

Anas said that among the Jews, when a woman menstruated, they did not eat with her, and they did not live with such in their houses, so the Prophet's companions questioned him, and God revealed the verse, "They ask you also concerning women during menstruation . . ." (Quran 2:222). The Messenger of God then said, "Do everything except have sexual intercourse." The Jews heard of that and said, "This man does not want to leave anything we do unopposed." Usayd ibn Hudayr and Abbad ibn Bishr came and said, "Messenger of God, the Jews are saying such and such. Shall we not then live with them?" The face of the Messenger of God then underwent such a change that we thought he was angry with the two men. But when they went out they encountered a gift of milk which was being brought for the Prophet; and he sent after them and offered them a drink, whereby they knew he was not angry with them. Muslim transmitted this tradition. (Baghawi, *Mishkat al-Masabih* 3.13)

This tradition suggests that there was no prior Arab custom on the subject of menstruation, or none that was an issue for Muhammad, and that the Quran's remark on it in 2:222 was prompted by someone's awareness of Jewish legislation about menstruation. The Torah indeed speaks of it, and in no uncertain terms, in the midst of a long section of Leviticus on various forms of ritual impurity.

When a woman has a discharge, her discharge being blood from her body, she shall remain in her impurity seven days; whoever touches her shall be unclean until evening. Anything that she lies on during her impurity shall be unclean; and anything she sits on shall be unclean. Anyone who touches her bedding shall wash his clothes, bathe in water and remain unclean until evening; and anyone who touches anything on which she has sat shall wash his clothes, bathe in water and remain unclean till evening. Be it the bedding or be it the object on which she has sat, on touching it he shall be unclean until evening. If a man lies with her, her impurity is communicated to him; he shall be unclean for seven days, and any bedding on which he lies shall become unclean. (Leviticus 15: 19–24)

The laws of ritual purity and impurity were taken seriously indeed by the rabbis of the post-biblical period, and the Mishna has a whole series of tractates, called collectively "Cleannesses," on that subject. One of them, Niddah, or "The Menstru-

ant," is given over to the matter of those few lines in Leviticus. As in most other tracts of the Mishna, when we enter Niddah, we come into a discussion already in progress, and the participants show their usual disinterest in informing us when or under what circumstances it began. The rabbis are discussing when the beginning of the period of impurity is calculated and what tests might be required to determine if a woman is indeed menstruating. They praise women who test themselves often and condemn men who attempt the same thing. The matter of testing is obviously important: it determines, for example, whether a woman may share in consecrated food, which will not be an issue in Islam, and the advisability of having intercourse, which will.

Women may always be assumed clean in readiness for their husbands. When men have come from a journey their wives may be assumed clean in readiness for them. The School of Shammai say: She needs two test cloths for every act (of intercourse), or else on every occasion she should examine it by the light of a lamp. And the School of Hillel say: Two test cloths suffice her throughout the entire night. (M.Niddah 2:4)

The discussion then veers into another related subject. Menstruation and childbirth are both among the causes of a seven-day impurity. Mishna Niddah then attempts to make a determination of when a miscarriage or natural abortion issues in a true childbirth. There is first a general rule.

If a woman suffers a miscarriage and there was blood with it, (it in effect constitutes a childbirth and so) she becomes unclean; but if there was not, (there was no childbirth and so) she remains clean. (Ibid. 3:1)

More elaborate criteria govern this determination, an examination of the aborted fetus, for example.

If the abortion was a fetus filled with water or filled with blood or filled with variegated matter, she need not consider it a human being; but if its (human) parts were formed, she must remain unclean for the number of days prescribed for a male and for a female (birth). (Ibid. 3:3)

Another general rule emerges, this time on the question of when a fetus becomes a human being. The issue is still to determine postpartum ritual purity: a true human birth renders the mother ritually unclean; any other miscarriage leaves her in her original state of ritual purity.

If she suffered a miscarriage on the fortieth day, she need not consider it as a (human) infant; if on the forty-first day, she must continue (unclean for the days prescribed) both for a male and for a female (birth) and also for a menstruant. Rabbi Ishmael says: If (the miscarriage) occurs on the forty-first day, she must continue (unclean for the days prescribed) for a male birth and for a menstruant; but if on the eighty-first day, she must continue (unclean for the days prescribed) for a male and for a female birth and for a menstruant, since a male is fully fashioned after forty-one days but a female only after eighty-one days. But the Sages say: The creation of a male and the creation of a female are alike: each is (fully fashioned) after forty-one days. (Ibid. 3:7)

Finally, menstrual uncleanness is used, by way of analogy, as a type of excommunication from the community of the true Israel, or at least as a disincentive to intermarriage, as here in the case of the Samaritans and the Sadducees.

The daughters of the Samaritans are (considered unclean as) menstruants from their cradle; and thus the Samaritan men convey uncleanness to what lies beneath them in the same degree (as someone who has the flux conveys uncleanness) to what lies above him, since they have connection with menstruants. . . . The daughters of the Sadducees, if they follow in the ways of their fathers, are deemed like the women of the Samaritans; but if they have separated themselves and follow in the ways of the Israelites, they are deemed like the women of the Israelites. (Ibid. 4:1)

Without suggesting that Muhammad or his contemporaries were aware of all of it, this was the background against which Quran 2:222 was revealed.

They ask you about menstruation. Tell them: "This is a pollution. So keep away from women in this state till they are clean of it. When they are free of it, you may go in to them as God has enjoined. For God loves those who seek pardon and those who are clean." (Quran 2:222)

The Quran, then, seems to take the same view as Leviticus: menstruation is a form of ritual impurity, and a man should separate himself from a menstruating woman until the period is over and the woman has purified herself. But that the Muslims understood what has here been translated as "approach" only in sexual terms is made pointedly clear in the traditions handed down from the Prophet on this subject. They occur in the canonical tradition books grouped in a collection called "Menstruation," under the larger juridical category of "Purifications."

Aisha said, "The Prophet and I used to wash from one vessel when we were both ritually unclean from sex. . . . I would drink when I was menstruating, then hand it to the Prophet and he would put his mouth where mine had been and drink; and I would eat flesh from a bone when I was menstruating, then hand it to the Prophet, and he would put his mouth where mine had been. . . ." She also said: "The Prophet would recline in my lap when I was menstruating, then recite the Quran." She also said: "The Prophet said to me, 'Get me the mat from the mosque,' and when I said I was menstruating, he said, 'Your menstruation is not in your hand.' " Maymuna said: "God's Messenger used to pray in a woolen garment which was partly over him and partly over me while I was menstruating." (Baghawi, *Mishkat al-Masabih* 3.13)

There is an entire series of traditions on the theme "Sex above the Waist with a Menstruating Woman."

Aisha reported: "When anyone among us [that is, Muhammad's wives] was menstruating, the Messenger of God, may peace be upon him, asked her to tie a skirt about her and embraced her."

Umm Salama reported: "While I was lying in a bed cover with the Messenger of God, may peace be upon him, I began menstruating, so I slipped away and I picked up my menstrual clothes. Upon this the Messenger of God, may peace be upon him, said: 'Have you begun your period?' I said 'Yes' He called me and I lay down with him on the bed cover." And she further said that she and the Messenger of God used to bathe from the same vessel after sexual intercourse. (Muslim, *Sahih* 119.577, 581)

On the face of it, then, the Prophet appears to have taken menstruation rather lightly. Not so the later Muslim lawyers, who were apparently far closer to Leviticus than to the Prophetic traditions. The jurist Ibn Qudama (d. 1223 C.E.) is one example.

The menstrual periods of women involve ten prohibitions: (1) performance of prayer; (2) obligatory prayer; (3) fasting; (4) circumambulation of the Ka'ba; (5) reading the Quran; (6) touching a copy of the Quran; (7) remaining in a mosque; (8) sexual contacts; (9) formal repudiation of a wife; and (10) being reckoned in a period of voluntary continence. [IBN QUDAMA 1950: 14]

28. A Christian Appraisal of the Islamic Law

Note has already been taken in Chapter 1 above of the judgments rendered on Muhammad and the Quran by the Dominican missionary and veteran Near Eastern traveler Ricoldo di Monte Croce (d. 1320 C.E.). The same scholar and polemicist, who had studied Islam in the schools of Baghdad, offered this summary and appraisal of the Islamic law.

Let us give a brief summary of the Saracens' religious law. Contrary to what is thought, the law of the Saracens is rambling, confused, opaque, lying, irrational and violent. In the first place, it is broad, attacking both the rule of the philosophers of the world who say that it is as difficult to live a virtuous life as it is for an arrow to hit the center of a target as well as the teaching of the Great Philosopher, to wit Christ, who says that narrow is the path that leads to life. For for them the necessity of salvation means nothing except that they say "There is no god but God and Muhammad is the Messenger of God." All the Saracens hold in common that a Saracen has only to say this and he will be saved, even if he should have committed all the sins in the world. Even though they lay down many prohibitions and command many other things in their law, namely in Alcoran, nevertheless the sinner pays no penalty in the next life. It should also be noted that that expression which Muhammad expresses, as it seems to me, in a hundred different ways in the Alcoran, "There is no god but God," is admitted by all religious groups. For that proposition says no more than "There is no dog but dog," or "There is no horse but horse," etc. What the Muslims intend is that the self-evidence of the proposition "there is no god but God" also be extended to "Muhammad is the Messenger of God." But how great an injury they do to philosophical truth by linking the falsest of propositions with the truest of propositions, and how great an injury they do to God by connecting the truth of God with the lie and falsehood of Muhammad, every thoughtful man may judge for himself. And they consider themselves saved if they say that alone. Their law, then, may be called broad. And Satan cunningly foresaw this, so that those people, who are unwilling to ascend by the narrow way to happiness, might take the broad way down to hell.

And how can they observe something which they do not understand? They themselves make their law so confused by their own explanations that their God, who gave the law, almost appears stupid. For it is written there that fornication is prohibited, but every kind of buying and selling is licit and not prohibited and that each may do as he wishes with his own goods. This, then, is what the scrupulous Saracens do. They go to a house of prostitution and say to the whore: "I am filled with desire, but fornication is not permitted. So sell yourself to me." And she sells herself and once the price has been paid, he says to her: "You belong to me." When she agrees that such is indeed the case, he concludes: "According to our law I can do as I wish with my own possessions." Then he can sleep with her with peace of mind. This is indeed what Muhammad himself seems to say in Alcoran, in base and open language: "Wear out the women and it will be no sin as long as you have given the price which you promised." (Ricoldo di Monte Croce, *Itinerary*) [LAURENT 1873: 135–136]

6. One God, One Faith, One Community

1. Unity and Heresy

In the first afterglow of the Ascension and Pentecost, there was only unity and concordance among the followers of the Risen Messiah, as the Acts of the Apostles testifies.

They [the followers of Jesus] met constantly to hear the Apostles teach and to share the common life, to break bread, and to pray. A sense of awe was everywhere, and many marvels and signs were brought about through the Apostles. All whose faith had brought them together held everything in common: they would sell their property and possessions and make a general distribution as the need of each required. With one mind they kept up their daily attendance at the Temple, and, breaking bread in private houses, shared their meals with unaffected joy, as they praised God and enjoyed the favor of the people. (Acts 2:42–47)

The whole body of believers was united in heart and soul. Not a man claimed any of his possession as his own but everything was held in common, while the Apostles bore witness with great power to the resurrection of the Lord Jesus. (Acts 4:32)

That is how the earliest Christian fellowship in Jerusalem appeared to one of its close observers, himself a Christian. But on Luke's own testimony, that pristine unanimity was soon rent, not with sin but with differences of opinion. Sometimes merely administrative matters were in question, as when the "Hebrews" and the "Hellenists" differed over the welfare program in Jerusalem (Acts 6:1–6). More profoundly, Paul and the elders under James did not see eye to eye on the Gentile question. Likewise, a close reading of Paul's letters reveals discord and "divisions," as he calls them, in the communities under his care. Paul was in fact constrained to remonstrate more than once with the brethren at Corinth.

736

I appeal to you, my brothers, in the name of our Lord Jesus Christ: agree among yourselves and avoid divisions; be firmly joined in unity of mind and thought. I have been told, my brothers, by Chloe's people that there are quarrels among you. What I mean is this: each of you is saying, "I am Paul's man" or "I am Apollo's"; "I follow Cephas" or "I am Christ's." Surely Christ has not been divided among you. (Paul, *To the Corinthians* I.1:10–13)

And later in the same letter:

In giving you these injunctions, I must mention a practice which I cannot commend: your meetings do more harm than good. To begin with, I am told that when you meet as a congregation you fall into sharply divided groups; and I believe there is some truth in it, for dissensions are necessary if only to show which of your members are sound. (Ibid. 1.11:17–19)

Indeed, the word "heretic" appears in Paul for the first and only time in the entire New Testament—though assuredly not with the same pointed connotation that it possessed later—when he used it in distinction to a praiseworthy "orthodoxy."

Steer clear of foolish speculations, genealogies, quarrels, and controversies over the Law; they are unprofitable and pointless. A heretic should be warned, once, and once again; after that have done with him, recognizing that a man of that sort has a distorted mind and stands self-condemned in his sin. (Paul, *To Titus* 3:9–10)

Two centuries later, when the life of those same communities was infinitely more complex and the "divisions" ran deeper and more painfully through the body of Christians, Cyprian, the bishop of Carthage, returned to Paul's remarks and enlarged them.

Heresies have often arisen and still arise for this reason, that disgruntled minds will quarrel, or disloyal troublemakers will not maintain the unity. But these things the Lord permits and endures, leaving man's freedom unimpaired, so that when our minds and hearts are tested by the touchstone of truth, the unswerving faith of those who are approved may appear in the clearest possible light. This was foretold by the Holy Spirit through the Apostle, when he says, "Dissensions are necessary if only to show which of your members are sound." Thus are the faithful approved, thus the faithless discovered; thus too, even before the day of judgment, already here below, the souls of the just and the unjust are distinguished, and the wheat is separated from the chaff. This explains why certain people, backed by their hot-headed associates, seize authority for themselves without any divine sanction, making themselves into bishops re-gardless of the rules of appointment, and since there is no one to confer the episcopate on them, they assume the title of bishop on their own authority. (Cyprian, *On the Unity of the Church* 10)

2. The Rule of Faith

How manifestly Jesus intended that there should be one body of believers, and how difficult that intention was to achieve in the face of discordant opinions on the most fundamental questions of faith, is a commonplace theme in early Christian writing. Almost all the early Fathers of the Church touched upon this matter of unity and schism, and by the late second century a number of solutions had been put forward. Both Ireneus (d. ca. 200 C.E.) and Tertullian (d. after 220 C.E.) proposed what they called the "rule of faith," a summary statement of the essential teaching of the Church received from Jesus Christ himself through the Apostles. It alone would suffice for salvation since, as Tertullian put it, "there is no need of curiosity after Christ, nor of inquiry after the Gospels."

The Church, though dispersed throughout the whole world, even to the ends of the earth, has received from the Apostles and their disciples this faith: in one God, the Father Almighty, who made the heaven and the earth and the seas and all the things that are in them; and in one Christ Jesus, the Son of God, who took flesh for our salvation; and in the Holy Spirit, who proclaimed through the prophets the dispensations and the comings, and the birth from a virgin, and the suffering, and the resurrection from the dead, and the fleshly ascension of the beloved Christ Jesus, our Lord, and his future manifestations from heaven in the glory of the Father, "to sum up all things" (Eph. 1:10), and to rise up anew all flesh of the human race, in order that to Christ Jesus, our Lord and God and Savior and King, according to the will of the Invisible Father, "every knee should bend, of things in heaven, and things on earth, and things under the earth, and that every tongue should confess" (Phil. 2:10–11) to him and that he should execute just judgments toward all. . . .

As I have already observed, the Church, having received this preach-ing and this faith, though scattered throughout the whole world, yet as if occupying one house, carefully preserves it. She also believes those points of doctrine as if she had but one soul and one and the same heart, and she proclaims them, and teaches them, and hands them down, all with perfect harmony, as if she possessed a single mouth. For, though the languages of the world are dissimilar, yet the import of the tradition is one and the same. For the churches which have been planted in Germany have not believed or handed down anything different, nor do those in Spain, nor those in Gaul, nor those in the East, nor those in Egypt, nor those in Libya, nor those that have been established in the central regions of the world. . . . Nor will any one of the rulers of the churches, however highly gifted he may be in point of eloquence, teach doctrines different from those, for no one is greater than his Master; nor, on the other hand, will he who is deficient in expression inflict injury on the tradition. For the faith being one and the same, neither does the one who is able to discourse at length upon it make any addition to it, nor does one who can say but little diminish it. (Ireneus, *Against the Heresies* 1.10.1–2)

A half-century later the bishop of Carthage in Africa had a similar vision of the unity of the Church, though now with somewhat more emphasis on the authority of the bishops.

This oneness we must hold to firmly and insist on, particularly those of us who are bishops and exercise authority in the Church, so as to demonstrate that the episcopal power is one and undivided as well. Let none mislead the brethren with a lie, let none corrupt the true content of the faith with a faithless perversion of the truth. The authority of the bishops forms a unity, of which each holds his part in totality; and the Church too forms a unity, however far she spreads and multiplies through the offspring of her fertility, just as the sun's rays are many, yet the strength deriving from its sturdy source is one. So too, though many streams flow from a single spring, and its multiplicity appears to be scattered abroad by the copiousness of its swelling waters, their oneness abides by reason of their point of origin. Try to cut off one of the sun's rays; the unity of that body permits no such division of its light. But if you break a branch from a tree, it can blossom no more, and if you dam up a stream at its source, it dries up in its lower reaches. So too our Lord's Church is radiant with light and pours her rays out over the whole world; but it is one and the same light that is spread everywhere, and the unity of her body suffers no division. She spreads her branches in luxuriant growth all over the earth, she extends her abundant streams still farther; yet one is the headwaters, one the source, one the mother who is prolific in her offspring, generation after generation: of her womb we are born, on her milk are we fed, from her Spirit our souls draw their breath of life. (Cyprian, *On the Unity of the Church* 5)

God is one, and Christ is one, and his Church is one; one is the faith and one the people harmoniously cemented together into the strong unity of a body. This unity cannot be split asunder; that one body cannot be divided by any cleavage of its structure, nor cut up into fragments with its vitals torn apart. Nothing that is separated from the parent stock can ever live or breathe apart; all hope of its salvation is lost. (Ibid. 23)

Cyprian looks back to what already appeared as the golden age of the community.

This common mind once prevailed in the time of the Apostles; this was the spirit in which the new community of the believers obeyed our Lord's commands and maintained charity with one another. The Scriptures are witness to it: "The crowd of those who who had come to believe acted with one mind and soul." . . . But among us that unity of mind has weakened in proportion as the generosity of our charity has crumbled away. In those days they would sell their houses and their estates and lay up for themselves treasures in heaven by giving money to the Apostles for distribution to those in need. But now we do not even give tithes on our patrimony, and whereas our Lord tells us to sell, we buy instead and accumulate. To such an extent have our people lost their steadfastness in belief. That is why our Lord has said in his Gospel, with an eye toward our times, "The Son of Man, when he comes, shall he find, do you think, faith on earth?" We see what he foretold happening before our eyes. As to the fear of God, or a sense of justice, or charity, or good works, faith inspires us to none of them. No one gives thought of the fears that the future holds in store: the Day of the Lord and the wrath of God, the punishments that await unbelievers, the eternal torments appointed for the betrayers of their faith, no one gives them a thought. Whatever a believing conscience should fear, our conscience, because it no longer believes, knows not fear. If only it believed, it would take heed; if it took heed, it would escape. (Ibid. 25)

Cyprian, for one, understood where the cure lay.

Our Lord, whose precepts and admonitions we are bound to observe, ordered the high office of the bishop and the system of his Church when he speaks in the Gospels and says to Peter, "Thou art Peter, and upon this rock I shall build my Church . . ." (Matt. 16:18, 19). Therefore age has followed age and bishop has followed bishop in succession, and the office of the episcopate and the system of the Church has been handed down, so that the Church is founded on the bishops and every act of the Church is directed by these same presiding officers. Since this has been established by divine ordinance, I am astonished that certain persons have been rash and bold enough to choose to write to me in such a manner as to send their letter in the Church's name, when the Church consists of the bishop, the clergy and all the faithful. (Cyprian, *Letter* 33:1)

The unity of the Church would be preserved, then, through the authority of the bishops, those faithful transmitters of Jesus' teaching through their succession back through the Apostles. But such was not the case. In Anatolia charismatics called Montanists asserted the autonomous authority of the Holy Spirit in the face of both bishops and "rules of faith." All around the Mediterranean basin some Christians offered their own, more private and progressive understanding of both Scripture and tradition. And in Cyprian's own Africa a local and indigenous Christian tradition struggled against the very idea of "catholicity" that both Ireneus and Cyprian had been espousing as a cure for divisiveness.

3. Constantine Summons a Council of the Whole Church

The bishops attempted to maintain the unity by acting in concert through the instrument of the synod or council, and they legislated to continue the practice in the first of the great councils of the whole Church, held in 325 C.E..

. . . And in order that this inquiry (into abuses and complaints) may be conveniently made, it is decreed that it is proper that synods should be assembled twice every year in every province, that all the bishops of the province being assembled together, such questions may be looked into, so that those who have confessedly offended against the bishop may appear to be excommunicated with reason by all the bishops, until it shall seem fit to their general assembly to pronounce a more lenient sentence upon them. And let these synods be held, the one before Lent, that the pure gift may be offered to God after all bitterness has been put aside, and let the second be held in the autumn. (Council of Nicea, Canon 5)

These earliest synods of bishops were essentially provincial meetings and so had limited jurisdiction. But the spread of what appeared to be nontraditional teaching, and particularly the opinions of the Alexandrian presbyter Arius, across the eastern Mediterranean far outstripped the reach of either his own bishops or all the bishops of Egypt meeting in synod. The conversion of the Roman emperor to the Christian faith in 312 C.E. seemed to offer a fortuitous solution to this epidemic of heresy. No single bishop had authority over the whole Church, but the ruler of the empire might be thought to have such jurisdiction, or at least the same responsibility of preserving the unity of the Church as he did that of the Roman Empire. Constantine, it appeared, had no hesitation in exercising that responsibility, nor did anyone gainsay it to him. Here it is the emperor who speaks.

It must now be clear to everyone that there is nothing more honorable in my sight than the fear of God. And now because it was earlier

agreed that the Synod of Bishops should meet at Ancyra [Ankara] of
Galatia, it seems good to us for many reasons that another synod assemble
at Nicea [that is, the present Iznik], a city of Bithynia, because the bishops
of Italy and the rest of Europe will be attending, because of the excellent
temperature of the air, and so that I myself might be present as a specta-
tor and participant in those matters that will be treated. And so I give you
public notice, my beloved brethren, that all of you promptly assemble at
that said city, namely Nicea. Let every one of you, therefore, with an eye
to what is best, as I said before, be diligent in attending, promptly and
without delay, that all may be present in person. (Acts of Nicea)

4. A Christian Statement of Belief:
The Creed

*The bishops convened as bidden in the city of Nicea in Anatolia in 325 C.E. What
emerged from their deliberations was a statement of belief that was to provide the
standard of orthodoxy for all Christians. It was not the first such. There was, for
example, the "Apostles' Creed," which, though first cited in this form by Epiphanius
ca. 400 C.E., was nonetheless regarded as the rule of faith composed by the Apostles
themselves in Jerusalem. It, or something quite like it, was certainly in use in various
churches—at Rome, for example—by the fourth century.*

> I believe in the Father Almighty,
> And in Jesus Christ, His only Son, our Lord,
> Who was born of the Holy Spirit and the Virgin Mary,
> Who was crucified under Pontius Pilate and was buried,
> And the third day arose from the dead,
> Who ascended into heaven,
> And sits at the right hand of the Father,
> Whence he comes to judge the living and the dead,
> And in the Holy Spirit,
> The Holy Church,
> The remission of sins,
> The resurrection of the flesh,
> The life everlasting.
> (Epiphanius, *Panarion* 72:3)

*The creed enunciated at Nicea, which we know in the form approved at the Council
of Chalcedon in 451 C.E., seems to have been drawn from the Catechetical Lectures
of Cyril of Jerusalem and to reflect the statement of faith professed early on by the
Jerusalem church.*

742

We believe in one God, the Father All-sovereign, maker of heaven and earth, and all things visible and invisible.

At this point the preoccupations of the Council of Nicea begin to appear in the formulary.

And in one Lord Jesus Christ, the only-begotten Son of God, Begotten of the Father before all ages, Light of Light, True God of True God, begotten not made, of one substance with the Father, through whom all things were made;

Who for us men and for our salvation came down from the heavens, and was made flesh of the Holy Spirit and the Virgin Mary, and became man, and was crucified for us under Pontius Pilate, and suffered and was buried, and rose again on the third day according to the Scriptures, and ascended into heaven, and sits at the right hand of the Father, and comes again with glory to judge the living and the dead, of whose kingdom there will be no end;

And in the Holy Spirit, the Lord and Life-Giver, that proceeds from the Father, who with the Father and the Son is worshiped together and glorified together, who spoke through the prophets;

In one holy, catholic and apostolic church;

We acknowledge one baptism for the remission of sins. We look for a resurrection of the dead, and the life of the age to come. (Acts of Nicea)

5. How the Council Proceeded

The records of the Council of Nicea are not complete, but we can get some idea of how the bishops proceeded from an account by the church historian Eusebius, bishop of Caesarea in Palestine. His formulation, presented to the synod, included the clause: "And (we believe) in One Lord Jesus Christ, the Word of God, God from God, Light of Light, Life from Life, Only-begotten Son, firstborn of all creation, before all ages begotten by the Father, by whom also all things are made." The statement appeared unexceptionable, save that it did not quite address the issue that had brought them all there, that of the essential relationship—the relationship in substance—between Father and Son. Eusebius' account, which is not a little self-serving, proceeds.

On this (statement of) faith being publicly put forth by us, no room for contradiction appeared; for our Most Pious Emperor testified before anyone else that it was most orthodox. He confessed, moreover, that such were his own sentiments, and he advised all present to agree to it and to subscribe to its articles and assent to them, with the insertion of the single word "consubstantial," which, moreover, he interpreted himself, saying that the Son is consubstantial (with the Father) not according to bodily affects, and that the Son subsisted from the Father neither by division nor severance: for the immaterial and intellectual and incorporeal nature (of the Father) could not be the subject of any bodily affect, but that it became us to conceive of such things in a divine and ineffable manner. And our most wise and religious Emperor reasoned but they [that is, the assembled bishops] drew up the following formulary:

"We believe in one God, the Father All-sovereign, maker of heaven and earth, and all things visible and invisible.

"And in one Lord Jesus Christ, the Son of God, Begotten of the Father, the Only-begotten, that is, from the substance of the Father; God from God, Light from Light, True God of True God, begotten not made, consubstantial with the Father, through whom all things were made, those in heaven and those on earth;

"Who for us men and for our salvation came down and was made flesh, suffered and rose again on the third day, ascended into heaven, and is coming to judge the living and the dead.

"And in the Holy Spirit.

"And those who say 'There was time when he was not,' and 'before his generation he was not,' and 'he came to be from nothing' or those who pretend that the Son of God is 'of other hypostasis or substance,' or 'created' or 'alterable,' the Catholic and Apostolic church anathematizes." (Eusebius in Socrates, *Church History* 1.8)

6. Excommunication from the Church Catholic

The Council, then, proposed in almost juridical fashion its own "rule of faith." There remained, however, the question of how to deal with those who did not subscribe to it. This too was taken up, both at Nicea and at subsequent councils.

Concerning those, whether of the clergy or the laity, who have been excommunicated by the bishops in different provinces, let the sentence of the canon prevail, which pronounces that those persons who have been cast out by one bishop are not to be received again into communion by any others. Inquiry should be made, however, whether they have been excommunicated through petty jealousy or contentiousness or other such-like bitterness of the bishop. And in order that this inquiry may be conveniently made, it is decreed that it is proper that synods should be assembled twice every year in every province, that all the bishops of the province being assembled together, such questions may be looked into, so that those who have confessedly offended against the bishop may appear to be excommunicated with reason by all the bishops, until it shall seem fit to their general assembly to pronounce a more lenient sentence upon them. And let these synods be held, the one before Lent, that the pure gift may be offered to God after all bitterness has been put aside, and let the second be held in the autumn. (Council of Nicea [325 C.E.], Canon 5)

All who enter the Church of God and hear the Holy Scriptures, but do not communicate with the people in prayers, or who turn away, by reason of some disorder, from the holy partaking in the Eucharist, are to be cast out of the Church until, after they have made confession, have brought forth fruits of penance, and have made earnest entreaty, they shall have obtained forgiveness; and it is unlawful to communicate with excommunicated persons, or to assemble in private houses and pray with those who do not pray in the church, or to receive in one church those who do not assemble with another church. And if any one of the bishops, presbyters or deacons, or any one in the canon shall be found communicating with excommunicated persons, let him also be excommunicated, as one who brings confusion on the order of the Church. (Council of Antioch [341 C.E.], Canon 2)

If anyone has been excommunicated by his own bishop, let him not be received by others until he has either been restored by his own bishop, or until, when a synod is held, he shall have appeared and made his defense, and, having convinced the synod, shall have received a different sentence. And let this decree apply to the laity, and to the presbyters and deacons, and all those who are enrolled on the clergy list (of a diocese). (Ibid., Canon 6)

Later in the fourth century heresy was made a criminal offense by imperial decree, and thus excommunication from the Church was ratified and reinforced in the law of the state.

20 August 379 C.E.: All heresies are forbidden by both divine and imperial laws and shall forever cease. If any profane man by his punishable teachings should weaken the concept of God, he shall have the right to know such noxious doctrines only for himself but shall not injure others by revealing such doctrines to them. (Theodosian Code 5.5)

25 July 383 C.E.: All persons whatsoever who are tossed about by the false teachings of diverse heresies, namely, the Eunomians, the Arians, the Macedonians, the Pneumatomachi, the Manicheans, the Encratites,

the Apotactites, the Saccophori, and the Hydroparastatae, shall not assemble in any groups, shall not collect any crowds, shall not attract any people to themselves, shall not give the walls of any private houses the appearances of churches, and shall practice nothing publicly or privately which may be detrimental to the Catholic sanctity. Furthermore, if there should exist any person who transgresses what has been so evidently forbidden, he shall be expelled by the common agreement of all good men, and the opportunity to expel him shall be granted to all who delight in the cult and the beauty of the correct observance of religion. (Ibid. 5.11)

11 May 391 C.E.: If any persons should betray the Holy Faith and should profane holy baptism, they shall be segregated from the community of all men, shall be disqualified from giving testimony, and, as We have previously ordained, they shall not have testamentary capacity; they shall inherit from no person, and by no person shall they be designated as heirs. We should also have ordered them to be expelled and removed at a distance if it had not appeared to be greater punishment to dwell among men and to lack the approval of men. (Ibid. 16.7.4)

The crime of heresy is unlike other civil crimes in one important regard: it may be expiated by simple recantation and repentance.

15 November 407 C.E.: Although it is customary for crimes to be expiated by punishment, it is our will, nevertheless, to correct the depraved desires of men by an admonition to repentance. Therefore, if any heretics, whether they are Donatists or Manicheans or of any other depraved belief and sect who have congregated for profane rites, should embrace, by a simple confession, the Catholic faith and its rites, which we wish to be observed by all men, even though such heretics have nourished a deep-rooted evil of long and continued meditation, to such an extent that they seem to be subject to the punishments of the laws formerly issued, nevertheless, as soon as they have confessed God by a simple expression of belief, we decree that they shall be absolved from all guilt. (Theodosian Code 5.41)

7. The Catholic Church

For the first two centuries of Christianity's existence, it was not always a simple matter to distinguish between orthodoxy and heresy in a Church that was still attempting to define itself. But certainly by the time of Constantine there had emerged a kind of Christian consensus that was based on the twin pillars of the Apostolic tradition and the Apostolic succession and that constituted the doctrinal foundation of what was called the Church Catholic. It was a consensus well enough defined and widely enough accepted to constitute an "orthodoxy" against which subsequent opinions, movements, and practices could be measured and judged. This is how it was defined and understood by Vincent of Lerins, writing in 434 C.E.

In the Catholic Church itself, every care should be taken to hold fast to what has been believed everywhere, always, and by all. This is truly and properly "catholic," as indicated by the force and etymology of the name itself, which comprises everything which is truly universal. This general rule will be truly applied if we follow the principles of universality, antiquity and consensus. We do so in regard to universality if we confess that faith alone to be true which the entire Church confesses, all over the world. We do so in regard to antiquity if we in no way deviate from those interpretations which our ancestors and fathers have manifestly proclaimed as inviolable. We do so in regard to consensus if, in this very antiquity, we adopt the definitions and propositions of all, or almost all, the bishops and doctors.

The matter is not so simple, however, as Vincent himself recognizes.

What, therefore, will the catholic Christian do if some members of the Church have broken away from the communion of universal faith? What else but prefer the health of the body universal to the disease of the corrupt member? What if a new contagion strives to infect not only a small part but even the whole Church? Then he will endeavor to adhere to the antiquity which is manifestly beyond the danger of being seduced by the deceit of some novelty. What if in antiquity itself an error is detected, on the part of two or three men, or even on the part of a city or a province? Then he will take care to prefer the decrees of a previous ecumenical council, if there was one, to the temerity and ignorance of a small group. Finally, what if such an error arises and nothing like a council can be found? Then he will take the pains to consult and interrogate the opinions of his predecessors, comparing them with one another only as regards the opinions of those who, though they lived in various periods, and at different periods and different places, nevertheless remained in the communion and faith of the One Catholic Church, and who therefore have become reliable authorities. As he will discover, he must also believe without hesitation whatever not only one or two but all equally and with one consent, openly, frequently, and persistently have held, written and taught. (Vincent of Lerins, *Commonitorium* 2–3)

8. The Holy War against Heresy

The presence of that orthodoxy and of Vincent's pragmatic touchstones of quod ubique, quod semper et quod ab omnibus did not preclude or even much inhibit heresy. The Church authorities continued to argue with, denounce, anathematize, and excommunicate those who were judged deviant from the ever better defined Christian doctrine. Roman law contributed its authority to that same end, as we have seen, but generally the distinction of the two jurisdictions left both the conviction and the punishment of heretics in the hands of the Church. The Fourth Lateran Council convoked by Pope Innocent III in 1215 C.E. marked a radical change in tactics, however. The Albigensians, Cathars, and a number of other dualist and Manichean-inspired churches had entrenched themselves in a broad arc from northern Italy across Languedoc and Provence in southern France and into Spain. Unable to extirpate these beliefs by preaching and teaching, and since excommunication was of little avail where the heretics constituted the community, the third canon of Lateran IV turned to more serious measures, which now involved the secular arm of government.

We excommunicate and anathematize every heresy that raises itself against the holy, orthodox and catholic faith which we have above explained, condemning all heretics under whatever names they may be known, for while they have different faces, they are nevertheless bound to each other by their tails, since in all of them vanity is a common element. Those condemned, being handed over to the secular rulers or their bailiffs, let them be abandoned, to be punished with due justice, clerics being first degraded from their orders. As to the property of the condemned, if they are laymen, let it be confiscated; if clerics, let it be applied to the churches from which they received revenues.

Those who are only suspected (of heresy), due consideration being given to the nature of the suspicion and the character of the person, unless they prove their innocence by a proper defense, let them be anathematized by all until they have made suitable satisfaction; but if they have been under excommunication for one year, let them be condemned as heretics.

Secular rulers who refuse to cooperate may be deposed by papal dissolution of their subjects' oath of allegiance and new rulers invited in.

Secular authorities, whatever offices they may hold, shall be admonished and induced and if necessary compelled by ecclesiastical censure, that if they wish to be esteemed and numbered among the faithful, so for the defense of the faith they ought publicly to take an oath that they will

748

strive in good faith and to the best of their ability to exterminate in the territories subject to their jurisdiction all heretics pointed out by the Church, so that whenever anyone shall have assumed authority, whether spiritual or temporal, let him be bound to confirm this decree by oath. But if a temporal ruler, after having been requested and admonished by the Church, should neglect to cleanse his territory of this heretical foulness, let him be excommunicated by the metropolitan and other bishops of the province. If he refuses to make satisfaction within a year, let the matter be made known to the Supreme Pontiff, that he may declare the ruler's vassals absolved of their allegiance and may offer the territory to be ruled by Catholics.

Finally, an extraordinary privilege is granted: whoever enrolls in this holy war will gain the same spiritual blessings enjoyed by those who take the cross against the Muslims for the liberation of the Holy Land.

Catholics who have girded themselves with the cross for the extermination of heretics will enjoy the indulgences and privileges granted to those who go in defense of the Holy Land. (Fourth Lateran Council, Canon 3)

Nothing was said in that canon of the death penalty, but it is unhesitatingly vindicated by Thomas Aquinas (d. 1274 C.E.), a member of the Dominican order that has been commissioned precisely to do combat with the Albigensians. The question under discussion is: "Whether Heretics Are To Be Tolerated?"

As regards heretics, two points ought to be observed: one from the perspective of the heretics; the other from the point of view of the Church. On the heretics' side there is the sin, whereby they deserve not only to be separated from the Church by excommunication, but also to be severed from the world by death. For it is a much graver matter to corrupt the faith, which quickens the soul, than to forge money, which supports temporal life. Wherefore if counterfeiters and other malefactors are forthwith condemned to death by the secular authority, there is even greater reason for heretics, as soon as they are convicted of heresy, to be not only excommunicated but even put to death.

From the perspective of the Church, however, there is a mercy which looks toward the conversion of those who have strayed, and so she does not condemn immediately, but "after the second and third admonition," as the Apostle directs (Titus 3:10–11). After that, if he is still stubborn, the Church, because she no longer hopes for his conversion, looks rather to the salvation of others, by excommunicating him and separating him from the Church, and furthermore delivers him to the secular tribunal to be exterminated thereby from the world to death. (Aquinas, *Summa Theologica* II/2, ques. 11, art. 3)

9. The Jews and the Church in the Middle Ages

There was very little ambiguity—none in theory and perhaps only a very slight hesitation in practice—in the Church's dealing with heretics. The Jews presented a more complex problem, however. Unlike the heretics, they were overt disbelievers in the basic premise of Christianity, whether that was put forward as a belief in Jesus' divinity or even his Messiahship. Nor were they heathen, since they worshiped the same God the Father and possessed and ratified the very same Scripture out of which the Christians traced their own version of sacred history. The Christians may have claimed those "Hebrews" of the Old Testament for their own progenitors, but they did not, it is clear, venerate contemporary Jews as either spiritual cousins, learned informants, or even cherished fossils of a bygone age. Nor did they attempt to exterminate them or their religious practices. As heirs to a Roman legal tradition whose treatment of the Jews we have already noted, the Christian authorities at-tempted to maintain the status quo, to protect the Jews from generally hostile local populations and at the same time to confine them to their already limited condition, as in this decree issued in slightly differing forms by Popes Alexander III, Innocent III, and here by Gregory X in 1272 C.E.

. . . Even as it is not allowed to the Jews in their assemblies pre-sumptuously to undertake for themselves more than has been permitted to them by law, even so they ought not to suffer any disadvantage in those practices which have been granted to them. Although they prefer to per-sist in their stubbornness rather than to recognize the words of their prophets and the mysteries of Scripture, and thus to arrive at a knowl-edge of the Christian faith and salvation; nevertheless, inasmuch as they have made an appeal for our protection and help, we therefore admit their petition and offer them the shield of our protection through the clemency of Christian piety. In so doing we follow in the footsteps of our predecessors of blessed memory, the Popes of Rome Calixtus, Eugene, Alexander, Clement, Celestine, Innocent and Honorius.

We decree moreover that no Christian shall compel them or any one of their group to baptism unwillingly. . . . For indeed that person who is known to have come to Christian baptism not freely, but unwillingly, is not believed to possess any Christian faith. Moreover, no Christian shall presume to seize, imprison, wound, torment, kill or inflict violence on them; furthermore, no one shall presume, except by judicial action of the authorities of the country, to change the good customs of the land where they live for the purpose of taking their money or their goods from them or from others. In addition, no one shall disturb them in any way during the celebration of their festivals, whether by day or by night, with clubs or stones or anything else. Also no one shall exact compulsory service from them unless it be that they have been accustomed to render it in previous times.

Inasmuch as the Jews are not able to bear witness against the Christians, we decree furthermore that the testimony of Christians against them shall not be valid unless there is among those Christians some Jew who is there for the purpose of offering testimony.

How urgently that protection was needed in some places cries out from what follows in the decree.

Since it sometimes happens that some Christians lose their Christian children, the Jews are accused by their enemies of secretly carrying off and killing these same Christian children and of making sacrifices of the heart and blood of these very children. It also happens that the parents of these children or some other Christian enemies of the Jews secretly hide these same children in order to cause injury to these Jews and to be able to extort from them a certain amount of money by buying themselves out of their difficulties. And most falsely do these Christians claim that the Jews have secretly and furtively carried away these children and killed them, and that the Jews offer sacrifice from the heart and blood of these children, since their law in this matter precisely and expressly forbids Jews to sacrifice, eat or drink the blood, or eat the flesh of animals having claws. This has been demonstrated before our court many times by Jews converted to the Christian faith; but nonetheless a great many Jews are still seized and detained unjustly because of this.

We decree therefore that Christians need not be obeyed against Jews in a case or situation of this type, and we order that Jews seized under such a frivolous pretext be freed from imprisonment, and that they should not be arrested again on such a miserable grounds, unless—which we do not believe—they are caught in the very commission of the crime.

We decree that no Christian should stir up anything new against them, but that they should be maintained in the same status and position which they were in during the time of our predecessors, from antiquity till now. We decree, in order to stop the wickedness and avarice of evil men, that no one shall dare to vandalize or destroy a cemetery of the Jews or dig up human bodies for the sake of getting money.

If anyone, with full knowledge of the contents of this decree, should—which we hope will not happen—be so bold as to act contrary to it, let him suffer punishment in the matter of his rank and position, or let him be punished by the penalty of excommunication, unless he makes amends for his temerity by appropriate compensation. Moreover, we wish that only those Jews who have not attempted to contrive anything toward the destruction of the Christian faith be fortified by the support of such protection. (Gregory X, *Concerning the Jews*)

10. "There Is Only One Holy, Catholic and Apostolic Church"

On 18 November 1302 Pope Boniface VIII issued his bull Unam Sanctam. *Its occasion was another round in the ongoing struggle between the Papacy and the authority of the emperor. But it is also one of the classical medieval statements on the unity and authority of the Church, expressed here from a Western and so Petrine and monarchical point of view. Both the arguments and the scriptural citations, Old Testament and New, are now smooth and supple from long centuries of use.*

We are compelled to believe and to hold that there is only one Holy, Catholic and Apostolic Church. So our faith urges us and so we firmly believe and simply confess; and likewise (we hold) that there is no salvation or remission of sins outside of her—as the bridegroom proclaims in the Song of Songs: "One is my dove, my perfect one is but one; she is the only one of her mother, the chosen of her that bore her" (Song of Songs 6:8), which represents one mystical body whose head is Christ; and of Christ, God is the head. And in it there is "one Lord, one faith, one baptism" (Eph. 4:5). At the time of the Flood there was indeed one ark of Noah, prefiguring one Church; it had been finished in one cubit, had one steersman and commander, namely Noah, and we read that outside it all things existing on earth were destroyed. This Church we venerate, and this alone, as the Lord says through the prophet: "Deliver, O Lord, my soul from the sword, and my only one from the hand of the dog" (Ps. 21:21). He [that is, Jesus] prayed for the soul, that is, for himself—for the head and the body at the same time—which body, namely, he called the one and only Church because of the promised unity of faith, sacraments and charity of the Church. That is the "seamless garment" (John 19:23) of the Lord which was not cut but fell (to one of the soldiers at the crucifixion) by lot. Therefore, in this one and only Church there is one body and one head, not two heads as if it were a monster: namely Christ, and Peter the vicar of Christ, and the successor of Peter; because the Lord said to Peter, "Feed my sheep" (John 21:17). "My sheep," he said, speaking generally and not particularly about these or those sheep; so that it must be understood that he committed to him all his sheep. If therefore the Greeks and others say they were not committed to Peter and his successors, they necessarily confess that they are not the sheep of Christ, for the Lord says in John, "There shall be one flock and one shepherd" (John 10:16).

And, in the concluding sentence in the bull:

Consequently we declare, state, define and pronounce that it is altogether necessary to salvation for every human creature to be subject to the Roman Pontiff. (Boniface VIII, *Unam Sanctam*)

11. The People of the Book

Islam is, on the testimony of the Quran itself, a successor community to those other peoples who had gone before it. They had had their messengers, and they too had been given the benefit of God's Book.

Remember We gave to Moses the Book and sent after him many an apostle; and to Jesus son of Mary We gave clear evidence of the truth, reinforcing him with divine grace. Even so, when a messenger brought to you what did not suit your mood, you turned haughty, and called some impostors and some others you slew.

And they say: "Our hearts are enfolded in covers." In fact, God has cursed them in their unbelief; and only a little do they believe. (Quran 2:87–88)

How many of the followers of the Books having once known the truth desire in their heart to turn you into infidels again, even after the truth has become clear to them! But you forbear and overlook till God fulfills His plan; and God has power over all things.

Fulfill your devotional obligations and pay the alms tithe. And what you send ahead of good you will find with God, for He sees all that you do.

And they say: "None will go to Paradise but the Jews and the Christians," but this is only wishful thinking. Say: "Bring the proof, if you are truthful."

Only he who surrenders to God with all his heart and also does good, will find reward with his Lord and have no regret and fear.

The Jews say, "The Christians are not right," and the Christians say, "The Jews are in the wrong," yet both recite the Scriptures. And this is what the unread had said too. God alone will judge between them in their differences on the Day of Reckoning. (Quran 2:109–113)

12. The Errors of the Jews

The first of those people to have been given Scripture were the Jews.

Men belonged to a single community; and God sent them messengers to give them happy tidings and warnings and sent the Book with them containing the truth to judge between them in matters of dispute; but those who received it disagreed concerning it after receiving clear proofs, on account of waywardness among them. Then God by His dispensation showed those who believed the way to the truth about which they were differing; for God shows whom He pleases the path that is straight. (Quran 2:213)

The Muslim commentators on the Quran were not sure about the duration of the period when "men belonged to a single community." But the Book that was sent down and to whom it was given and why were matters of no dispute.

. . . God means that the Book, that is, the Torah, should decide between the people on matters on which they disagreed. God has assigned the decision to the Book and established it and not the Prophets and the Apostles as the decisive criterion between the people, since whenever one of the Prophets or Apostles had to bring down a judgment, he did it on the basis of the indications which are contained in the Book which is sent down by God. . . .

God's words "disagreed concerning it" mean that they disagreed concerning the Book that God had sent down, that is, the Torah. His words "those who received it" refers to the Jews of the Children of Israel. They are the ones who had been given the Torah and its knowledge. . . . Thus God proclaims that the Jews of the Children of Israel disobeyed the Book, the Torah, and they disagreed concerning it in spite of the knowledge which it contains. In so doing they deliberately disobeyed God since they violated His command and the decision of His Book.

"Then God showed those who believed the way to the truth . . . " means that God granted success to those who are believing, that is, those who support belief in (the one) God and His Apostle, Muhammad, and who put their trust in Him and are convinced that His message, about which the previous recipients of the Book had earlier disagreed, comes from God. The disunity in which God left these people alone, while rightly guiding and helping to the truth those who believe in Muhammad, refers to (Friday as) the "day of gathering" (for worship). Although this day had been enjoined on them [that is, the Jews] as an obligation just as it had been enjoined on us, they deviated from it and changed (their day of worship) to the Sabbath. The Prophet has said: Although we are the last, we surpass (the others in obedience to God's commands), even though the Book was given to them before it was given to us, and so we possessed it after they did. God has rightly guided us even to this day, on matters on which they disagreed. The Jews have taken (as their day of worship) the day following (Friday) and the Christians have taken the day after that.

Concerning the matters about which the people disagreed, Ibn Zayd is reported to have said, according to Yunus ibn Abd A'la, that God's words "then God showed those who believed the way to the truth" mean that He led the believers to Islam. The people disagreed concerning prayer. Some prayed facing toward the East while others faced toward Jerusalem. Then God led us to the right direction of prayer toward Mecca. Also the people disagreed concerning fasting. Some fasted at certain times of the day while others fasted at certain times of the night. Then God led us to the right times for fasting. Also the people disagreed concerning the day of congregational worship. While the Jews chose the Sabbath, the Christians took Sunday; then God led us to the right day [that is, Friday]. Also the people disagreed about Abraham. The Jews considered him a Jew and the Christians considered him a Christian. Then God freed him from such suspicions and demonstrated that he was a *hanif* who was surrendered to God, and that he also was not to be classed among the heathen, as some maintained, who claimed that he had been one of the unbelievers. Finally, the people also disagreed about Jesus. The Jews considered him to be the victim of a lie, while the Christians considered him to be a god. Thereupon God led us to the truth concerning him. (Tabari, *Commentary*, *ad loc.*)

13. The Jews Warned by Their Own Prophets

We sent down the Torah which contains guidance and light; in accordance with which the prophets, who had surrendered themselves [or became *muslims*], gave instructions to [or, judged] the Jews, as well as the masters (of the law) and the rabbis, following the portion of God's Book that had been entrusted to them. (Quran 5:44)

This is one of the central Quranic texts explaining the position of the Jews with respect to God's revelation. As such, it receives full treatment at the hands of the commentators.

". . . [T]he prophets, who had surrendered themselves": Submission [that is, *islam*] is an attribute which is used in praise of the prophets generally and not as a distinguishing characteristic (of the Jewish prophets), just as is the case with attributes one uses in reference to the Eternal One. The use of this attribute (with reference to the biblical prophets) shows that the Jews are far from acknowledging Islam, which is the (true) religion of the prophets in both ancient and modern times, and that Judaism is remote from acknowledging this. God's words, "the prophets, who had surrendered themselves, judged the Jews" emphasizes this in a forceful manner.

"As well as the masters (of the law) and the rabbis": This refers to the ascetics and the learned men among the descendants of Aaron, who remained faithful to the ways of the prophets and have remained aloof from the religion of the Jews.

"Following the portion of God's Book that had been entrusted to them": The portion of God's Book that the prophets had instructed the rabbis and masters (of the Law) to preserve was the Torah. That is, the prophets had ordered them to preserve the Torah from change and distortion. (Zamakhshari, *The Unveiler of the Realities, ad loc.*)

14. The Jewish Falsification of Scripture

Zamakhshari has taken the larger view, but the immediately preceding verses of this same sura were understood by the Islamic tradition to refer to a specific incident with the Jews in the life of the Prophet.

And there are Jews who listen to tell lies, and spy on behalf of others who do not come to you, and who distort the words (of the Torah) out of context, and say: "If you were given (what we say is true), accept it, but if you are not given, beware." . . . Those are the people whose hearts God does not wish to purify. . . . Eavesdropping for the purpose of lying, earning through unlawful means! So if they come to you, judge between them or decline to do so. And if you decline, they can do you no harm; but if you judge, you should do so with justice, for God loves those who are just. But why should they make you a judge when they themselves have the Torah in which is God's Law? Even then they turn away. They are those who will never believe. (Quran 5:41–43)

Ibn Ishaq's Life *sets out the context:*

Ibn Shihab al-Zuhri told me that he heard a learned man of Muzayna telling Saʿid ibn al-Musayyab that Abu Hurayra had told them that Jewish rabbis had gathered in their school when the Messenger (first) came to Medina. A married man had committed adultery with a married woman and they said: "Send them to Muhammad and ask him what the Law about them is and leave the penalty to him. If he prescribes scourging, then follow him, for he is a king and believe in him. If he prescribes stoning, then he is a prophet so beware lest he deprive you of what you hold." . . . The Messenger went out to them and commanded that the two should be stoned and they were stoned at the door of his mosque among the Banu Ghanm ibn Malik ibn al-Najjar. . . .

Salih ibn Kaysan from Nafiʿ, freedman of Abdullah ibn Umar, told me: When the Messenger gave judgment about them he asked for a Torah. A rabbi sat there reading it, having put his hand over the verse of stoning. Abdullah ibn Salam struck the rabbi's hand, saying, "This, O Prophet of God, is the verse of stoning which he refuses to read to you." The Messenger said, "Woe to you Jews! What has induced you to abandon the judgment of God which you hold in your hands?" They answered: "The sentence used to be carried out until a man of royal birth and noble origin committed adultery and the king refused to allow him to be stoned. Later another man committed adultery and the king wanted him to be stoned, but they said, No, not until you stone so-and-so. And then they said that they agreed to arrange the matter by scourging and they did away with all mention of stoning." The Apostle said: "I am the first to revive the order of God and His Book and to practice it." They were duly stoned and Abdullah ibn Umar said, "I was among those that stoned them." (*Life* 393–395) [IBN ISHAQ 1955: 266–267]

Thus the Jews were not merely unfaithful to the Covenant made with God; they had, as this incident testifies, concealed and distorted the revelation that God had given them.

15. The Error of the Christians

The Christians too had been in Muslim eyes unfaithful to God's word.

O People of the Book, do not be fanatical in your faith, and say nothing but the truth about God. The Messiah who is Jesus, son of Mary, was only a Messenger of God, and a word of His which He sent to Mary, as a mercy from Him. So believe in God and His apostles, and do not say "Three." Refrain from this for your own good; for God is only one God, and far from His glory is it to beget a son. (Quran 4:171)

Once again Zamakhshari provides the proper exegetical perspective.

"Do not be fanatical in your faith": The Jews went too far in that they degraded the position of Christ in regarding him as an illegitimate child (of Mary). And the Christians went too far in that they unduly elevated him in considering him a god.

"His word": Jesus is designated as "the word of God" and as "a word of His" (Sura 3:39) because he alone originated through the word and command of God rather than through a father and a sperm. For this reason he is also designated as "the spirit of God" (Sura 66:12) and "a spirit from Him," since Jesus was a spirit-endowed man who originated without any element from a spirit-endowed man, such as the sperm that is discharged from an earthly father. He was created by a new act of creation by God whose power is unlimited.

The word "three" (in this verse) is the predicate of an understood subject. If one accepts the Christian view that God exists in one substance with three divine persons, namely, the Father, the Son and the Holy Spirit, and if one accepts the opinion that the person of the Father represents God's being, the person of the Son represents His knowledge, and the person of the Holy Spirit represents His life, then one must supply the subject (of the clause) as follows: "God is three(fold)." Otherwise, one must supply the subject thus: "The gods are three." According to the evidence of the Quran, the Christians maintain that God, Christ and Mary are three gods, and that Christ is the child of God by Mary, as God says (in the Quran): "O Jesus son of Mary, did you say to men: 'Take me and my mother as gods, apart from God'?" (Sura 5:116) or "The Christians say: 'The Messiah is the Son of God' " (Sura 9:30). Moreover, it is well known that the Christians maintain that in Jesus are (combined) a divine nature derived from his Father and a human nature derived from his mother. God's words (in this verse), "The Messiah who is Jesus, son of Mary, was only a Messenger of God," are also explained on the basis of such an interpretation (of the Christians). These words confirm (the Christian view) that Jesus was a child of Mary, that he had with her the usual relationship between children and their mothers, and that his relationship to God was that he was His Messenger and that he became a living being through God's command and a new act of creation without a father. At the same time these words exclude (the Christian view) that Jesus had with God the usual relationship between sons and their fathers. (Zamakhshari, *The Unveiler of the Realities, ad loc.*)

16. Jews and Christians Compared

In some few instances the Quran weighs Jews and Christians together in the scales of divine justice.

> You will find the Jews and the idolaters most excessive in hatred of those who believe; and the closest in love to the faithful are the people who say "We are followers of Christ," because there are priests and monks among them, and they are not arrogant.
>
> For when they listen to what has been revealed to this Apostle, you can see their eyes brim over with tears at the truth which they recognize, and say: "O Lord, we believe, so put us down among those who bear witness." (Quran 5:82–83)

Zamakhshari spells out the nuances of the sacred text.

Here God is portraying the Jews as unyielding and as acknowledging the truth only grudgingly, while the Christians are of gentle disposition, easily guided and with an inclination toward Islam. Because of their violent animosity toward the believers, God places the Jews together with the idolaters; in fact He goes even further and puts them at the head, since He mentions them before the idolaters. Each of them wishes he could be given a life of a thousand years; but the grant of such life would not save him from chastisement—"for God sees well what they do!" (Sura 2:96). The Jews are surely like this, and even worse! A Prophetic tradition says: "If a Muslim is alone with two Jews, they will try to kill him."

God bases the judgment that the Christians are to be treated kindly and held in high esteem by the Muslims on the fact that there are priests and monks among them, that is, men of learning and servants, and that they are modest and humble people who know no arrogance, while the Jews are just the opposite. Here is a clear example showing the struggle for knowledge is exceedingly useful, leading first to good and then to success, even among the (non-Muslim) priests. The same is likewise true of a concern for the Hereafter and discussions about the End, possibly another characteristic of the monk, just like freedom from arrogance, even though it is a question of a Christian here. (Zamakhshari, *The Unveiler of the Realities, ad loc.*)

17. The Muslim Community

For the Muslims then, on the testimony of the Quran, both the Jews and the Christians constituted defined religious communities, corporate bodies of believers in possession of an authentic revelation. As on most other subjects, the Quran offers no systematic or extended treatment of the subject of the new community of Muslims whose birth it was chartering. But the notion of community occurs often there, sometimes in the context of the Muslims' treatment of each other, sometimes in their distancing themselves from those older communities of "Peoples of the Book."

O believers, if you follow what some of the People of the Book say, it will turn you into unbelievers even after you have come to belief.

And how can you disbelieve? To you are being recited the messages of God, and His Prophet is among you. And whosoever holds fast to God shall verily be guided to the path that is straight.

O believers, fear God as He should be feared, and do not die except as those submitting to him. Hold on firmly together to the rope of God, and be not divided among yourselves, and remember the favors God bestowed on you when you were one another's foe and He reconciled your hearts, and you turned into brethren through His grace. You had stood on the edge of the pit of fire and He saved you from it, thus revealing to you His clear signs, that you might perchance find the right way.

So let there be one community among you who may call to the good, enjoin what is esteemed and forbid what is odious. They are those who will be successful.

So be not like those who became disunited and differed among themselves after clear proofs had come to them. For them is great suffering. . . .

These are the commandments of God We recite to you verily; God does not wish injustice to the creatures of the world. For to God belongs all that is in the heavens and the earth, and to God do all things return. Of all the communities raised among men, you are the best, enjoining the good, forbidding the wrong, and believing in God. If the People of the Book had come to believe, it would have been better for them; but only some believe, and transgressors are many. (Quran 3:100–110)

The foolish will now ask and say: "What has made the faithful turn away from the direction toward which they used to pray?" Say, "To God belongs the East and the West. He guides who so wills to the path that is straight." We have made you a middle community that you act as witness over man, and the Prophet as witness over you. (Quran 2:142–143)

The Quranic notion of Islam as a "central" or "middle" community elicited considerable reflection from the medieval commentators.

I regard the word "middle" in this context as signifying the mean between two extremes. God described the Muslims as a people of the middle path because of their middle position in religion. They are neither people of excess like the Christians, who went to extremes in their monastic practices as well as in what they said concerning Jesus, nor are they people of deficiency like the Jews, who altered the Book of God, killed their prophets, gave the lie to their Lord, and rejected faith in Him. Rather they are people of the middle path and of balance in their religion. God characterized them as people of the middle path because the things which God loves most are those of the middle position. (Tabari, *Commentary, ad loc.*)

And this from the standard authority, Abdullah ibn Umar a-Baydawi, three centuries after Tabari:

The word "middle" or "in the middle" was originally a designation for a position with equal distances on each side. Then it came to refer to certain praiseworthy attributes of character because these lie (in the middle) between extremes of excess and exaggeration on both sides. Thus, generosity lies between wastefulness and stinginess and boldness between foolhardy recklessness and cowardice. The word is now also applied to a person who possesses such characteristics. . . . From the words of God in this verse one can (also) draw the conclusion that consensus is a valid authority (in questions of faith), since if that on which Muslims are agreed were delusion, then a gap would be created in their integrity (and thus they would not stand in the middle). (Baydawi, *The Lights of Revelation, ad loc.*)

18. An Arabic Quran

Islam is a universal community, it is clear from the Quran and Muhammad's own preaching. But it is also true that Muhammad was an Arab sent to preach God's message in the first instance to Arabs. The Arabs were not a "chosen people" the way the Israelites understood themselves to be, but Arabic was in some sense God's "chosen language." A number of verses in the Muslim Scripture lay emphasis on the fact that this is an Arabic Quran. The language is in fact such an important element in interpreting the Book, and particularly in understanding its legal prescriptions, that the jurist al-Shafiʿi (d. 820 C.E.) devoted considerable space to it in his Treatise on the Roots of Jurisprudence. His reflections cast an interesting light on the tension between cultural Arabism and religious Islam.

Someone said: There are in the Quran Arabic and foreign words.

Shafiʿi replied: The Quran indicates that there is no portion of the Book of God that is not in the Arab tongue. He who expressed such an opinion [namely, that there are foreign words in the Quran] . . . perhaps meant that there are certain particular words which are not understood by some Arabs.

Of all tongues that of the Arabs is the richest and most extensive in vocabulary. Do we know any man except a Prophet who apprehended all of it? However, no portion of it escapes everyone, so that there is always someone who knows it. Knowledge of this tongue is to the Arabs what knowledge of the tradition of the Prophet is to the jurists: We know of no one who possesses a knowledge of all the tradition of the Prophet without missing a portion of it. So if the knowledge of all the scholars is gathered together, the entire tradition of the Prophet would be known. However, if the knowledge of each scholar is taken separately, each might be found lacking in some portion of it, yet what each may lack can be found among the others. . . .

In like manner is the (knowledge of the) tongue of the Arabs possessed by the scholars and the public. No part of it will be missed by all of them, nor should it be sought from other people; for no one can learn this tongue save that he has learned it from the Arabs, nor can anyone be as fluent in it as they unless he has followed them in the way they learned it. He who has learned it from them should be regarded as one of the people of that tongue. . . .

Someone may ask: What is the proof that the Book of God was communicated in a pure Arabic tongue, unmixed with others?

Shafiʿi replied: The proof is to be found in the Book of God itself, for God said:

"We never sent a Messenger save in the tongue of his people." (Quran 14:4)

But if someone says: Each of the Messengers before Muhammad was sent to his own people, while Muhammad was sent to all mankind. This may mean either that Muhammad was sent with the tongue of his people and that all others must learn his tongue—or whatever they can learn of it—or that Muhammad was sent with the tongues of all mankind. Is there any evidence that he was sent with the tongue of his own people rather than with foreign tongues?

Shafi'i replied: Since tongues vary so much that different people cannot understand one another, some must adopt the language of others. And preference must be given to the tongues that others adopt. The people who are fit to receive such a preference are those whose tongue is their Prophet's tongue. It is not permissible—but God knows best—for the people of the Prophet's tongue to become the followers of peoples whose tongues are other than that of the Prophet even in a single letter; but rather all other people should follow his tongue, and all people of earlier religions should follow his religion. For God has declared this in more than one communication of His Book:

"Truly, it is the revelation of the Lord of the worlds, brought down by the Faithful Spirit, upon your heart, that you may be one of those who warn, in a clear Arabic tongue." (Quran 26:192–195)

And He also said:

"Thus have We sent it down as an Arabic Law." (Quran 13:37)

And He said:

"And so we have revealed to you an Arabic Quran in order that you may warn the Mother of the Towns and the people of its vicinity." (Quran 42:5)

The "Mother of the Towns" is Mecca, the city of the Prophet and of his people. Thus God mentioned them in His Book as a special people and included them among those who were warned as a whole, and decreed that they were to be warned in their native tongue, the tongue of the Prophet's people in particular.

It is obligatory upon every Muslim to learn the Arab tongue to the utmost of his power in order to be able to profess through it that "there is no god but the God and Muhammad is His servant and Apostle," and to recite in it the Book of God.

Shafi'i finally returns to his lawyer's point.

The reason I began to explain why the Quran was communicated in the Arab tongue rather than in another, is that no one who understands clearly the total meanings of the (legal) knowledge of the Book of God would be ignorant of the extent of that tongue and of the various meanings of its words. . . . Doubts that appear to one who is ignorant (of the Arab tongue) will disappear from him who knows it. . . . Calling the attention of the public to the fact that the Quran was communicated in the Arab tongue in particular is advice to all Muslims. This advice is a duty imposed on them which must not be put aside and is the attainment of a supererogatory act of goodness which no one will neglect. (Shafiʻi, *Treatise*) [SHAFIʻI 1961: 88–94]

19. The Five Pillars of Islam

What then constituted a Muslim? When the Muslim tradition came to define the essentials of Islam, the "pillars of Islam" as they were called, the emphasis clearly lay not upon the modalities of belief—though belief was certainly required—but in the performance of certain ritual and political acts.

It is narrated on the authority of Ibn Abbas that a delegation of (the tribe of) Abd al-Qays come to the Messenger of God, may peace be upon him, and said: Messenger of God, truly ours is a tribe of (the clan) Rabiʻa and there stand between you and us the unbelievers of Mudar and we find no freedom to come to you except in the Sacred Month. Direct us to an act which we should ourselves perform and invite those who live beside us (to perform). Upon this the Prophet remarked: I command you four things and prohibit to you four acts. (The prescribed acts are): Faith in God, and then he explained it for them and said: Testifying the fact that there is no god but the God, that Muhammad is the Messenger of God, establishment of prayer, payment of the alms tax, and that you pay one-fifth of the booty fallen to your lot. And I prohibit you to use the round gourd, wine jars, wooden pots or skins for wine. (Muslim, *Sahih* 1.7.22)

The prohibition against gourds, wine jars, wooden pots, and skins for wine may have been directed against a particular penchant of the Abd al-Qays for drinking. What was far more important, at least as the bedouin tribes outside Mecca were concerned, was the alms tax, as this tradition from the era just following upon the death of the Prophet reveals.

It is narrated on the authority of Abu Hurayra that when the Messenger of God, may peace be upon him, breathed his last and Abu Bakr was appointed as his Caliph after him, those among the Arabs who wanted to become apostates apostatized. Umar ibn al-Khattab said to Abu Bakr: Why would you fight against the people when the Messenger of God declared: "I have been directed to fight against people so long as they do not say: There is no god but the God. . . ." Upon this Abu Bakr said: By God, I would definitely fight against him who separated prayer from the alms tax, for it [that is, the alms tax] is the obligation upon the rich. By God, I would even fight against them to secure the hobbling cord which they used to give to the Messenger of God (as alms tax) but now they have withheld it. Umar ibn al-Khattab remarked: By God, I found nothing but the fact that God opened the heart of Abu Bakr for fighting (against those who refused to pay the alms tax) and I fully recognized that (his stand) was right. (Muslim, *Sahih* 1.9.29)

Adherence to Islam, it is clear, was more than a simple profession of faith in God and His prophet. It also required acts: the ritual acts of prayer, fasting, and pilgrimage, and the social and political act of paying the alms tax. Fasting and the pilgrimage do not occur as part of the obligations mentioned in the traditions cited above, but they are certainly prescribed in the Quran. They are also included in this summary tradition setting out the five pillars of Islam.

It is narrated on the authority of Abdullah ibn Umar that the Messenger of God, peace be upon him said: (The superstructure of) Islam is raised on five (pillars): testifying that there is no god but the God, that Muhammad is His servant and Messenger, and the establishment of prayer, payment of the alms tax, pilgrimage to the House (of God at Mecca) and the fast of (the month of Ramadan). (Ibid. 1.6.20)

20. "Catholic" Islam: Staying Close to the Tradition

In Muhammad's own day membership in the community of Muslims might be understood simply as embracing anyone who acknowledged the unity of God and the Quran as the Word of God and who performed the ritual acts prescribed in the five Pillars. Those grounds had soon to be extended to a detailed affirmation of the teachings of the Quran, as broadened and explained by the various Prophetic traditions attributed to Muhammad himself, as we have already seen in Chapter 3 above. But the process of enlargement did not end there; it soon came to embrace the notion of "consensus," the agreement of Muslims on certain points of belief and practice, even without the authority of a Quranic text or a Prophetic tradition to support them. The validity of "consensus" as an operative element in Islam was argued in what became the classic statement of the position, the Treatise on the Roots of Jurisprudence *of the Egyptian lawyer al-Shafiʿi (see Chapter 5 above). In this passage an anonymous questioner is willing to concede the binding nature of the Quran and the Prophetic traditions, but he requests further proof on the matter of "consensus."*

What is your proof for following what people have agreed upon, where there is no command in a text from God [that is, in the Quran], or related from the Prophet? Would you assert what others have held, that consensus can never occur except on a firm "tradition," even though it may not have been related [that is, even if it has not reached us in the form of a Prophetic tradition]?

I told him [said Shafiʿi]: As to what they agreed upon and say that it has (also) been related from the Prophet, let us hope that it is (accepted) as they say. However, as for what is not related [that is, there is no specific Prophetic tradition on the matter], it may be that it was actually said by the Messenger of God, or it may be otherwise. It is not, however, permissible to attribute sayings to him (without grounds), for one is only permitted to relate what one has heard, and it is not permitted to relate anything one fancies, in which there may be things (the Prophet) did not say.

Therefore we hold to what they held to, following them. We know that if these were practices of the Messenger, they would not be remote to the generality of Muslims, even though they are remote to the few; and we know that the generality of Muslims will not agree on what is contradictory to the customary practice of the Messenger of God, or on an error, please God.

If it is asked, is there anything to indicate or prove that? we reply: Sufyan informs us on the authority of Abd al-Malik ibn Umayr from Abd al-Rahman the son of Abdullah ibn Masʿud, from his father, that the Messenger of God said, "God prospers a servant who listens to what I say, remembers it, pays attention to it, and passes it on. Often one may transmit insight who himself is not perspicacious, and often he transmits it to one with more insight than he. There are three things which cannot be resented by the heart of a Muslim: sincerity of action for God, good advice to the Muslims, and keeping close to the community of the Muslims. . . ."

It was asked, what is the meaning of the Prophet's command to keep close to the community?

I said: There is but one meaning to it. . . . Since the community of the Muslims is scattered in different countries, one could not keep close to the physical community whose members were scattered, and besides, they were found together with Muslims and unbelievers, with pious men and sinners. Thus it could not mean a physical "closeness" since that was not possible, and because physical nearness would in itself effect nothing, so that there is no meaning in "keeping close to the community" except in agreeing with them in what they make lawful and forbidden, and obedience in both these matters. He who maintains what the community of the Muslims maintains is keeping close to the community, and he who deviates from what the community of the Muslims maintains deviates from that community to which he is commanded to remain close. Error arises in separation. In the community there can be no total error concerning the meaning of the Book, of the Prophetic tradition, or of analogical reasoning, please God. (Shafiʿi, *Treatise*) [SHAFIʿI 1961: 285–287].

Much the same point is made in a ninth-century statement of belief from Ahmad ibn Hanbal (d. 855 C.E.). Ibn Hanbal may have differed from the somewhat older Shafiʿi on important points of the law, but he was as convinced as Shafiʿi that the essential truth of the community lay in its adherence to the "tradition." This "creed" begins, then, with what is in effect a conservative's plea for unity, for adherence to "the tradition and the collectivity."

Ahmad ibn Hanbal said: The principles of "the tradition" for us are holding fast to the practice of the Companions of the Messenger of God and seeking guidance from that; and abandoning innovation, for every innovation is an error. Also, abandoning quarrels and not consorting with people who do as they please and leaving off strife and contentiousness in religion. "The tradition" to us means the footsteps of the Messenger of God, may God bless him and give him peace, and "the tradition" explains the meaning of the Quran and is the guide to the Quran. There is no use of logical analogies in "the tradition," nor coining of similitudes nor perception by use of reason or inclination. "Tradition" is nothing more than following, and surrendering up one's own inclinations.

The statement then grows more specific, and we have before us a ninth-century theological agenda: articles of belief that had already been debated to the point of orthodoxy and heresy.

A part of the essential "tradition," such that if one leaves aside any part of it, not accepting and believing it, he cannot be considered as being of the "People of Tradition," is belief in the predestination of good and bad, and the affirmation of the Prophetic traditions about it and belief in them, not saying "Why?" or "How?" but simply affirming them and believing them. If anyone does not know the explanation of these Prophetic traditions or his intelligence does not apprehend them, it is still sufficient, and his sentence is that he shall believe in them and submit to their authority, such as the Prophetic traditions (affirming predestination), and those that the beatific vision is possible, all in their entirety. And even if he turns away from hearing about this, or feels dislike at hearing about it, still he must believe in it, and must not contradict a single letter of it, or any other Prophetic tradition transmitted by dependable narrators. No one should dispute, or speculate about it, or recognize any contention about it, for speaking about predestination and the be-atific vision and the (nature of the) Quran and other matters established by the Prophetic traditions is disapproved of and to be avoided. Whoever speaks of them, if he criticizes "the tradition," is not one of the "People of the Tradition" until he abandons contention and submits and believes in "the tradition."

A number of specifics follow in turn: the Quran as the uncreated Word of God, the vision of God on the Day of Resurrection, the reality of the details of the Final Judgment, the coming of the False Messiah and then the return of Jesus, who will "slay him at the Lydda Gate" of Jerusalem. Finally, there is an article on the nature of faith.

Faith is word and act, and increases and decreases, as is stated in the Prophetic traditions. "The most perfect of believers in faith is the best of them in morality." Also, "He who leaves off the ritual prayers has re-jected God," and there is no act which, when neglected, occasions infide-lity except the ritual prayers. Whoever quits them is an infidel, and God makes killing him lawful. (Ahmad ibn Hanbal, *Creed*)

[WILLIAMS 1971: 28–30]

21. A Shiʿite View of the Community

Shafiʿi's view soon became the orthodox one in Islam, particularly among those Muslims like Ahmad ibn Hanbal who identified themselves as "People of the Tradi-tion [sunna] and the Collectivity" and whom we call "Sunnis." But as Ibn Hanbal stated, "The principles of 'the tradition' [sunna] for us are holding fast to the practice of the Companions of the Messenger of God and seeking guidance from that." There were those among the Muslims, notably the "Partisans [shiʿa] of Ali," generically called "Shiʿites," who preferred not to go the way of the "Companions of the Messenger of God," particularly since these latter had elected first Abu Bakr and then Umar and Uthman to lead the community instead of Ali ibn abi Talib, on whom the divine and Prophetic choice had obviously fallen. This is the way the case is argued by the Shiʿite scholar Ibn Babuya (d. 991 C.E.), beginning with the Quran itself.

Every verse in the Quran which begins with the expression, "O you who believe" refers necessarily to Ali ibn abi Talib as their leader and prince and the most noble among them. And every verse which directs the way to Paradise applies to the Prophet or to the Imams [that is, Ali and his designated successors], the blessings of God be upon them and all their partisans and followers. . . . These (Imams) are immune from sin and error. . . . They may be likened in this community to the Ark of Noah; he who boards it attains salvation or reaches the Gate of Repentance. (Ibn Babuya, *Creed*)

The Shi'ite was not, then, willing to grant infallibility to the "collectivity" in the manner of al-Shafi'i. The community had in fact already erred, or at least part of it allowed itself to be carried into error on the issue of the Imamate. The issue is stated clearly in a Shi'ite creed of the thirteenth century.

The Imam [that is, the head of the community; the officer called "Caliph" by the Sunni Muslims] cannot be elected by the community. He is the absolute ruler, who imposes his final judgment upon his followers. The principle of "consensus" in accepting certain religious laws and practices is completely false. If one were to accept this principle, he should regard Muhammad as not a real Prophet, because all of the people to whom he first addressed himself, or at least the majority of them, did not at first recognize him as such. . . . Only the Imam, appointed by God, is infallible, but the community obviously cannot be considered as infallible. . . .

The community became split and fell into disagreements after the death of the Prophet, thus taking the way of error. This was chiefly due to their reluctance to follow "the Household" [that is, Ali and his descendants]. Only a small group among the Muslims remained faithful to the commandments and the will of the Prophet, suffering for this reason at the hands of different oppressors. . . .

One who follows the religion of his ancestors by "the tradition," without having ascertained for himself whether it is correct or wrong, is not right. He should know and act in accordance with the Quran and "the tradition" as taught by the Imams of the family of the Apostle. . . .

Religion and faith are to be found only in Shi'ism (along with true) following of the tradition of the Prophet. . . . The Prophet predicted the splitting up of the Islamic community into seventy-three sects after his death; and of these only one brings salvation. It is the one which follows the Prophet and his descendants (through the house of Ali), who are the Ark of Noah, giving religious salvation. (*A Shi'ite Creed*)

[WILLIAMS 1971: 40–41]

22. The Prophet Warns against Heresy

The split between Sunni and Shi'ite was only one of a number of fissures that opened within the Muslim community even in the first century of its existence. Some were, like Shi'ism, the result of differing views on such fundamental political questions as "Who is a Muslim?" or "Who shall rule the community?" Others were more theological in their orientation, though not without political implication, like the questions of free will and determination that troubled the early community. Indeed, heresy and schism seemed so unavoidable that there were current a number of traditions from the Prophet himself predicting these torments for his community.

From the Mother of Believers, Umm Abdullah Aisha, with whom may God be pleased, who said: "the Messenger of God, on whom be God's blessing and peace, said: 'Whosoever introduces into this affair of ours [that is, Islam] something that does not belong to it is a reprobate.' " Both Bukhari and Muslim relate it. According to one line of transmission in Muslim (it reads): "Whosoever works a work which has for it no command of ours is a reprobate." (Nawawi, *The Forty Traditions*, no. 5) [JEFFERY 1962: 146]

From Abu Najih al-Irbad ibn Sariya, with whom may God be pleased, who said: The Messenger of God, may God's blessing and peace be upon him, preached a sermon whereby our hearts were made afraid and our eyes dropped tears, so we said: "O Messenger of God, it is as though this were a farewell sermon, so give us a testamentary exhortation." He said: "My testamentary exhortation to you is that you have a pious fear of God, magnified and exalted be He; that you hearken and obey, even though it should be a slave who is appointed over you. He among you who lives long enough will see great disagreement, so take care to observe my custom and the custom of the Rightly Guided Caliphs [that is, the first four: Abu Bakr, Umar, Uthman, and Ali], holding on to them with your molar teeth. Beware of matters newly introduced, for every innovation is an error." So Abu Dawud relates it, as does al-Tirmidhi, who says, "An excellent, sound Prophetic tradition." (Ibid., no. 28) [JEFFERY 1962: 154]

Ibn Mas'ud reported God's Messenger as saying: "There was no Prophet whom God raised up among his people before me who did not have from among his people apostles and companions who held to his Prophetic tradition and followed what he commanded. Then they were succeeded by people who said what they did not practice and did things they were not commanded to do. So he who strives against them with his hand is a believer, he who strives against them with his tongue is a believer, and he who strives against them with his heart is a believer. Beyond that there is not so much faith as a grain of mustard." (Baghawi, *Mishkat al-Masibih* 1.6.1)

Abdullah ibn Amr reported God's Messenger as saying: "My people will experience what the Israelites experienced as closely as one sandal resembles another. . . . The Israelites divided into 72 sects, but my people will divide into 73, all but one of which will go to hell." On being asked which that latter was, he replied, "It is the one to which I and my Companions belong." Tirmidhi transmitted this tradition. A version by Ahmad ibn Hanbal and Abu Dawud from Mu'awiya has: "72 will be in hell and one in Paradise, and that latter is the community." (Ibid. 1.6.2)

23. Wrong Belief and Unbelief

Opinions might differ, but there were differences in substance and importance even among those various opinions. Muslims came to recognize in practice and in theory a juridical distinction between "unbelief," the rejection of one of the basic teachings of Islam and so disqualification as a Muslim, and "heretical innovation," the introduction of some belief or practice unsupported by Islamic teaching or custom and not described in the Prophetic traditions. In matters of doubt an authoritative judicial opinion could be solicited, as Caliph Mustazhir (1094–1118 C.E.) did of the jurist-theologian Ghazali on the subject of certain radical Shi'ite groups. Ghazali carefully builds a legal case for their exclusion from the Muslim community, with all the political consequences of such a judgment.

Their declarations fall into two categories, one of which makes it necessary to declare they are in error, are astray and are guilty of innovation, the other of which makes it necessary to declare that they are unbelievers and (the community) must be cleansed of them.

What constitutes for Ghazali the heretical innovation of the group in question are standard Shi'ite beliefs on the legitimacy and nature of leadership in the Islamic community. Ghazali proceeds with the matter of innovation.

With regard to the first category (of beliefs) which makes it necessary to declare that they are in error, are astray and are guilty of innovation, it is where we encounter those unlearned folk who believe that the leadership (of the community) belongs by right to the immediate family of the Prophet, and that he who should rightly have it in our day is their Pretender [that is, the contemporary descendent of Ali who laid claim to the office]. Their claim is that in the first (Muslim) century the one who should have rightfully had it was Ali [the cousin and son-in-law of Muhammad], may God be pleased with him, but that he was wrongly deprived of it. . . . Nevertheless, they do not believe that it is lawful to shed our blood [that is, the Sunni Muslims who have a different view of the leadership question], nor do they believe that we are in unbelief. What they do believe about us [and, Ghazali might have added, we about them] is that we are iniquitous folk whose minds have erroneously slipped from comprehension of the truth, or that we have turned aside from their leader out of obstinacy and a spirit of contention. It is not permissible to shed the blood of a person in this category or to give judgment that he is in unbelief because he says such things. . . . Judgment should be confined to the declaration that such a one has (merely) gone astray, for he does not express belief in any of the erroneous teachings of their sect . . . concerning certain theological beliefs and matters of resurrection and the Judgment. With regard to all such matters they express no beliefs other than those we express ourselves.

For the Sunnis, the "people of the tradition and the collectivity," the notion of a consensus of the Muslim community was an important one. Does not, then, the Shiʿites' violation of the universal consensus on the question of the early leaders of Islam qualify them as unbelievers?

But someone might ask: But do you not declare them in unbelief because of what they say about the office of community leader in the first years (of Islam), how it belonged by right to Ali and not to Abu Bakr and those who succeeded him, but he was wrongly deprived of it, for in this they go contrary to the consensus of Muslims? Our answer is that we do not deny the dangerous nature of this opposition to the consensus, and for that reason we go beyond charging them with being in undisguised error . . . and charge them with leading others astray, causing heresy and introducing innovation, but we do not go so far as declaring them in unbelief. This is because it is not clear to us that one who goes contrary to the consensus is an unbeliever. Indeed, there is a difference of opinion among Muslims as to whether the proof of a doctrine can rest on consensus alone.

Ghazali pushes the objection a step farther. Some Shiʿites were not content to say merely that Ali had been wrongfully passed over for the leadership on four successive occasions; they went on to denigrate those first four "Successors of the Prophet," men who in the Sunni tradition were called "the Rightly Guided Caliphs."

If someone should ask: Then if someone were to say plainly that Abu Bakr and Umar were in unbelief, ought he to be considered the same as one who calls any other of the Muslim chiefs or judges or leaders who came after them an unbeliever? Yes, we do so teach. To charge Abu Bakr or Umar with unbelief is not different from charging unbelief to any of the leaders or judges of the community, nor, indeed, to any individual who professes Islam, save in two regards. First, it would also be going against and contradicting consensus, though, indeed, one who charges them with unbelief because of some perplexity might not even be contradicting reliable consensus. The second is that there are many traditions from the Prophet passed down concerning the two of them, according to which they were promised Paradise, are eulogized, have judgments expressed as to the soundness of their religion and the steadfastness of their convictions and declaring that they have precedence over the rest of humanity. If these traditions from the Prophet have reached the ears of one who makes the charge (of unbelief against Abu Bakr and Umar), and in spite of it he expresses his belief that they are in unbelief, then he himself is an unbeliever, not because he accused them of unbelief, but because he is giving the lie to the Apostle of God, upon whom be God's blessing and peace, and by general consent anyone who treats any word of his sayings as a lie is an unbeliever.

Ghazali now comes to the rock-bottom issue: Who is a Muslim and who is not? What must one believe to be reckoned a member of the community, secure against all attempts to be read out of the community?

Let us suppose someone asks: What is your teaching with regard to someone who declares a fellow Muslim to be in unbelief, is such a one an unbeliever or not? Our answer is: If such a one is aware that this (fellow Muslim whom he has accused of unbelief) believes in the divine Oneness, had confident trust in the Apostle, upon whom be God's blessing and peace, and held other proper doctrines, then whensoever he declares him an unbeliever with respect to these doctrines, he is himself an unbeliever, since he is expressing an opinion that the true religion is unbelief and is untrue. On the other hand, if he thinks (erroneously) that a fellow Muslim believes that the Apostle was false, or that he denies the Creator, or is a dualist, or some such other that necessarily involves one in unbelief, and so, relying on this opinion, declares him to be in unbelief, then he is in error with respect to his opinion of this person but right in declaring that anyone who so believes is in unbelief.

Ignorance, Ghazali explains, of anything beyond the two propositions in the simple profession of faith does not affect one's position as a Muslim.

It is not a condition of a man's religion that he knows the state of belief of every Muslim or the unbelief of every unbeliever. Indeed, there is no one person who can be imagined who, if we did not know about him, would affect our religious standing. More, if a person believes in God and His Apostle, diligently performs his acts of worship, and yet had not heard of the names of Abu Bakr and Umar, in fact dies before ever hearing of them, he would nevertheless die a Muslim, for belief in what is told about them is not among the pillars of religion, such that any mistake with respect to what must or must not be attributed to them would necessarily strip one of his religion.

What makes this group of Shiʿites infidels, then, is that they have read the Sunni Muslims out of the religion of Islam as unbelievers, despite obvious evidence to the contrary. Ghazali constructs that "obvious evidence" into a small Muslim creed.

They believe that we (Sunnis) are in disbelief, so that it is lawful to plunder our property and shed our blood. This necessarily leads to *their* being declared to be unbelievers. This is unavoidable since they know that we believe that the world has a Maker, Who is One, Powerful, Knowing, Willing, Speaking, Hearing and Seeing; Who has no one like Him; that His Apostle is Muhammad ibn Abdullah, upon whom be God's blessing and peace, who spoke the truth in all that he told about the resurrection and the Judgment, and about Paradise and Hell. These are the doctrines which are pivotal for sound religion. (Ghazali, *On the Disgraceful Doctrines of the Esoteric Sects* 8.1) [JEFFERY 1962: 255–260]

24. The Excommunication and Execution of Unbelievers

Where the Muslims encountered unbelief was not among the "Peoples of the Book," the misguided Jews and Christians who nonetheless possessed the authentic Word of God, but on the part of outright polytheist pagans—the Hindus of India, for example—or among those who had once been, or still claimed to be, Muslims but who nonetheless rejected some basic tenet of Islam—in short, apostates. Apostasy was reckoned a formal crime—the most serious of crimes—and so was subject to the statutory penalties of Islamic law, in this case death, as appears in the law code of Ibn Qudama (d. 1223 C.E.).

Every Muslim, male or female, who apostatizes, should be put to death. The Prophet has said: "When a Muslim denies his religion, kill him."

The apostate should not be executed before he has been three times called upon to make an act of contrition. If he makes an act of contrition, his life should be spared; otherwise he should be decapitated with a sword.

The man who denies the existence of God, or who gives God an associate, a wife, or a son; who calls God a liar or insults Him; who calls a Prophet a liar or insults him; who denies the mission of a Prophet; who denies, in whole or in part, a revealed Book; who rejects one of the Pillars of Islam; or who considers permissible universally recognized prohibitions, such a one is an apostate, or at least does not know the obligations and prohibitions that the law prescribes. In this latter case, he should be instructed; if he refuses to recognize them, he will be considered an apostate. [IBN QUDAMA 1950: 269–270]

We return to Ghazali and the case of the Shiᶜite extremists. He has pronounced them guilty of unbelief; he now proceeds to trace the practical consequences of this judgment.

A concise statement is that they are to be treated in the same manner as apostates [that is, those who were once Muslims but have formally renounced Islam] with regard to blood, property, marriage, slaughtering, execution of judgments and the performing of cult practices. With regard to their spirits, they are not to be treated in the same manner as a born unbeliever, since the Imam (al-Shafiᶜi) gives a choice, when it is the case of a born unbeliever, between four expedients, to wit, (extending him a period of) grace, (allowing him the chance of) ransom, enslaving him, or putting him to death, but he gives no options in the case of an apostate. . . . The only (treatment for such) is that they be put to death and the face of the earth cleansed of them. This is the judgment on those Esotericists who have been adjudged to be in disbelief. Neither the permissibility nor the necessity of putting them to death is limited by being (confined to when we are) in a state of war with them, but we may take them unawares and shed their blood, so that (all the more) when they are involved in fighting is it permissible to kill them.

Should someone ask: "Would you put their women and children to death?" our answer is: As for the children, no, for a child is not to be blamed, and their judgment will come. As for the women, we ourselves would (favor) putting them to death whenever they plainly state beliefs which are (in the category of) unbelief, in accordance with the decision we have already rendered. For the female apostate is, in our opinion, deserving of death in accordance with the all-inclusive statement of him [Muhammad] upon whom be God's blessing and peace: "Whoever changes religion, put that one to death." It is allowable, however, for the leader of the community to follow in this matter the result of his own deliberations, and if he thinks he should follow the way of (the jurist) Abu Hanifa with regard to them and refrain from putting the women to death, the question is one that belongs to the realm of individual deliberation and decision. . . .

As regards the property (of unbelievers), the regulation concerning it is the same as that with regard to the property of apostates. Whatever is taken in conquest, save the corpses of horses and riders, falls wholly under the category of "apostate spoils," which the leader is to distribute rightfully to those to whom such spoils are due, in accordance with the principles of division given in the words of the Most High: "What God has given as spoil to His Messenger from the towns belongs to God and His Messenger etc." (Quran 59:7). . . . When they die their property cannot be inherited, nor can one of them inherit from another. They cannot inherit from a true believer nor can a true believer inherit their property, even though there should have been a kinship between them, for the inheritance relationship between unbelievers and Muslims is severed. Cohabitation with their women is forbidden, just as marriage with a female apostate is illegal. . . .

Closely connected with the unlawfulness of such marriage contracts, is the unlawfulness of (ritual) slaughtering (by an unbeliever). No act of slaughtering by any of them is legally valid any more than a slaughtering by a Magian [that is, a Zoroastrian] or a Manichean. (Ritual) slaughtering and marriage contracts are very similar (in their juristic aspects) and both are unlawful when associated with any group of unbelievers save Jews and Christians, in whose case there is a relaxing of strictness because they are People of the Book which God sent down to a faithful prophet whose trustworthiness is apparent and whose Book is well known.

As for the execution of legal judgments in connection with them, it is invalid and (such judgments) are not to be carried out. Also their testimony is to be refused, for these are all matters whose validity is conditional on the person concerned being a Muslim, for which reason no one among them who has been judged to be in unbelief can properly have a part in such matters. Furthermore, their cult performances are useless. Neither their fastings nor their prayer services have any value, nor do their pilgrimages or almsgivings count for anything, so that whenever one of them repents and cleanses himself of his (erroneous beliefs), and we are satisfied that his repentance is genuine, then he must make up all the cult performances that have slipped by and were performed while he was in a state of unbelief, just as is incumbent in the case of an apostate (who returns to the faith). This is as much as we wished to draw attention to in connection with their legal position. (Ghazali, *On the Disgraceful Doctrines of the Esoteric Sects* 8.2) [JEFFERY 1962: 264–268]

25. "That Was Gabriel.
He Came To Teach You Your Religion"

"Creeds" and statements of belief embodying the essence of Islam become progressively more elaborate even in the Prophetic traditions. This is one reported from Muhammad on the authority of Umar and eventually included among the forty essential traditions of Islam by al-Nawawi (d. 1278 C.E.), which was described in Chapter 3 above.

While we were one day sitting with the Apostle of God, on whom be God's blessing and peace, there appeared before us a man in a very white garment and with very black hair. No traces of journeying were visible on him, and none of us knew him. He sat down close to the Prophet, upon whom be God's blessing and peace, rested his knees against his, put his palms on his thighs, and said: "O Muhammad, inform me about Islam." Said the Apostle of God, upon whom be God's blessing and peace: "Islam is that you should testify that there is no god save the God and that Muhammad is His Apostle, that you should say the prayers, pay the legal alms, fast during Ramadan, and go on pilgrimage to the House [that is, the Ka'ba at Mecca], if you can find a way to do so." Said he: "You have spoken truly." We were astonished at his thus questioning him and telling him he was right, but he went on to say: "Inform me about faith." Muhammad answered: "It is that you should believe in God and His angels and His Books and His Messengers and in the Last Day, and that you should believe in the decreeing of both good and evil." He said: "You have spoken truly." Then he said: "Inform me about the best behavior." Muhammad answered: "It is that you should serve God and as though you could see Him, for though you cannot see Him, He sees you." He said: "Inform me about the Hour." Muhammad said: "About that the one questioned knows no more than the questioner." So he said: "Well, inform me of the signs thereof [that is, of its coming]." Said Muhammad: "They are that the slave girl will give birth to her mistress, that you will see the bare-footed, the naked, the destitute, the herdsmen of the sheep building arrogantly high houses." Thereupon the man went off. I [that is, Umar] waited a while, and then the Prophet said: "O Umar, do you know who that was?" I replied: "God and His Apostle know better." He said: "That was Gabriel. He came to teach you your religion." (Nawawi, *The Forty Traditions*, no. 2) [JEFFERY 1962: 145]

26. Moral Islam

The following Prophetic traditions are from the same collection by al-Nawawi, though here the emphasis is, as it was for most pious Muslims, moral and social rather than dogmatic.

From Abu Hurayra, with whom may God be pleased, who said: Said the Apostle of God, upon whom be God's blessing and peace: "Do not envy one another; do not vie with one another; do not hate one another; do not be at variance with one another; and do not undercut one another in trading, but be servants of God, brothers. A Muslim is a brother to a Muslim. He does not oppress him, nor does he forsake him, nor deceive him nor despise him. God-fearing piety is here," he said pointing to his breast. "It is enough evil for a man that he should despise his brother Muslim. The blood, property and honor of every Muslim is inviolable to a fellow Muslim." Muslim relates this tradition. (Nawawi, *The Forty Traditions*, no. 35) [JEFFERY 1962: 157]

From Abu Hurayra, with whom may God be pleased, who said: Said the Apostle of God, upon whom be God's blessing and peace: "In truth God, may He be exalted, has said: 'Whoever acts with enmity toward a friend of Mine, against him will I declare war. No servant of Mine draws near to Me with anything I like more than that which I have laid upon him as an incumbent duty, and a true servant of Mine will continue drawing near to Me with supererogatory acts of worship so that I may love him. Then when I am living with him, I am his hearing with which he hears, his seeing with which he sees, his hand with which he takes things, his foot with which he walks. If he asks of Me, I will surely give him, and if he takes refuge with Me, I will surely give him refuge.' " (Ibid., no. 38) [JEFFERY 1962: 158–159]

27. Faith and Good Works in Islam

The early problem of unbelief and its political consequences caused Muslims to look closely at the nature of faith and its relationship to good works. The following reflections are from the so-called Testament of Abu Hanifah. *That Muslim jurist died in 767 C.E., but the* Testament *is likely by some later member of his legal school (Chapter 5 above).*

Faith may neither increase nor decrease, for decrease in it could only be conceived of in terms of unbelief, and increase in it in terms of the decrease of unbelief, but how could a single person be at one and the same time both a believer and an unbeliever? The true believer is in truth a true believer and the infidel is in truth an infidel. Faith is not a matter which admits of doubt, nor is unbelief a matter which admits of doubt, for the Most High has said, "These are in truth true believers" (Quran 8:74), and "these are in truth unbelievers" (Quran 4:151). Even the disobedient ones of the community of Muhammad, upon whom be God's blessing and peace, are all of them true believers, and are not to be classified (despite their disobedience) as unbelievers.

Works are something other than faith, and faith is other than works. This is proved by the fact that there are numerous occasions when a true believer is granted exemption from works, whereas it is not permissible to say that he is ever exempted from faith. Thus a women in menstruation or childbirth is granted exemption by God, praised and exalted is He, from prayers, but it is not permissible to say that God has granted her exemption from faith and bidden her abandon her faith. Also to such the Lawgiver says: "Give up fasting but make it up later," but it could not be that one is told to give up faith and make it up later. . . .

We confess that the predetermining of good and evil is from God, exalted be He, for should anyone claim that the predetermining of good and evil is from other than He, he would be one who disbelieves in God and annuls his own confession of the divine unity.

We confess that works are of three kinds, to wit, obligatory, meritorious, and sinful. The obligatory are by God's command and in accordance with His will, His liking, His judgment, His knowledge, His help and His writing on the "Preserved Tablet" (see Quran 85:21). The sinful are not (such) by God's command but in accordance with His will, not in accordance with His liking but by His decreeing and His predetermining, by His creation but not by His help, in accordance with His abandoning and His knowledge, but not with His recognition, and in accordance with His writing on the "Preserved Tablet." (Abu Hanifah, *Testament*)

[JEFFERY 1962: 342–343]

28. Alms and Charity

One of the pillars of Islam, and so an obligation binding upon every Muslim, was the paying of a statutory alms tithe. The complex subject of tithing—how much, to whom, from whom, and for what purpose—is discussed at length in Muslim law books. But there are two Prophetic traditions in al-Nawawi's summary collec-

tion that look at alms not in their legal aspect but as a function of the virtue of charity.

From Abu Dharr, with whom may God be pleased, who said that some from among the Companions of the Apostle of God, upon whom be God's blessing and peace, said to the Prophet, upon whom be God's blessing and peace: "O Apostle of God, the rich take off all the rewards. They say prayers just as we do, they fast just as we do, but they can give in charity out of the superabundance of their wealth (and so surpass us in storing up merit)." He said: "Has not God appointed for you that you should give in charitable alms? Truly, in every ejaculation 'Glory be to God!' there is such an alms, in every 'God is the greatest!' in every 'Praise be to God!' in every 'Hallelujah!' in every bidding what is right and forbidding the doing of what is wrong; even when one of you has sex with his wife, there is an alms in that." They said: "O Apostle of God, (do you mean to say that) when one of us satisfies his desires (with his wife), there will be a reward for that?" He answered: "What do you think? Had He put it among the things forbidden, it would have been sinful for one, so when He put among the allowable things, there was a reward for it also." Muslim relates this tradition. (Nawawi, *The Forty Traditions*, no. 25) [JEFFERY 1962: 153]

From Abu Hurayra, with whom may God be pleased, who said: Said the Apostle of God, upon whom be God's blessing and peace: "An alms is due each day that the sun rises from every finger joint of all the people. If you straighten out some trouble between two individuals, that is an alms. If you help a man with his beast, mounting him thereon or hoisting up onto it his luggage, that is an alms. A good work is an alms. In every step you take in walking to prayer there is an alms. Whenever you remove something harmful from the path, that is an alms." Al-Bukhari and Muslim both relate this tradition. (Ibid., no. 26) [JEFFERY 1962: 153]

29. Militant Islam: War in the Sacred Month

The Messenger sent Abdullah ibn Jahsh off in (the month of) Rajab [624 C.E.] on his return from the (first skirmish) at Badr. He sent with him eight "Emigrants," without any of the "Helpers." He wrote for him a letter, and ordered him not to look at it until he had journeyed for two days and then to do what he ordered him, but not to put pressure on any of his companions (to do likewise). . . . When Abdullah had traveled for two days he read the letter and looked into it and this is what it said:

"When you have read this letter of mine proceed until you reach Nakhla between Mecca and al-Ta'if. Lie in wait there for the Quraysh and find out what they are doing. Having read the letter he said, "To hear is to obey." Then he said to his companions, "The Messenger has commanded me to go to Nakhla to lie in wait there for the Quraysh so as to bring him news of them. He has forbidden me to put any pressure on you, so if anyone wishes martyrdom let him go forward, and he who does not, let him go back; as for me, I am going on as the Prophet has ordered." So he went on, as did all his companions, not one of them falling back. . . .

A caravan of Quraysh passed them carrying dry raisins and leather and other merchandise. . . . When the caravan saw them they were afraid because they had camped near them. But Ukkasha, who had shaved his head, looked down at them, and when they saw him they felt safe and said, "They are only pilgrims, you have nothing to fear from them."

The raiders took council among themselves, for this was the last day of Rajab, and they said, "If we leave them alone tonight they will get into the sacred area and be safe from us; and if we kill them, we will kill them in the sacred month." So they were hesitant and feared to attack the Quraysh. Then they encouraged each other and decided to kill as many as they could and take what they had. . . .

When they returned to the Apostle, he said, "I did not order you to fight in the sacred month," and he held the caravan and the two prisoners in suspense and refused to take anything from them. When the Messenger said that, the men were in despair and thought they were doomed. Their Muslim brethren reproached them for what they had done, and the Quraysh said, "Muhammad and his companions have violated the sacred month, shed blood therein, taken booty and captured men." The Muslims in Mecca who opposed them said it actually occurred in (the month of) Sha'ban and the Jews turned this raid into an omen against the Apostle. . . . When there was much talk about it, God sent down to his Messenger (the verse):

"They will ask you about the sacred month, and war in it. Say, war therein is a heinous thing, but keeping people from the way of God and disbelieving in Him and the sacred shrine and driving out His people therefrom is more heinous with God. And persecution is more heinous than slaying." (Quran 2:217)

That is, if you have killed in the sacred month, they have kept you back from the way of God with their disbelief in Him, and from the sacred shrine, and have driven you from it when you were its people. This is a more serious matter with God than the killing of those whom you have slain. "For persecution is worse than killing," that is, they used to persecute the Muslim in his religion until they made him return to disbelief after believing, and that is worse with God than killing. "And they will not cease to fight you until they turn you back from your religion if they can," that is, they are doing more heinous acts than that and with evil intent.

And when the (verse of the) Quran came down about that and God relieved the Muslims of their anxiety in the matter, the Messenger took possession of the caravan and the prisoners. (Ibn Ishaq, *Life* 423–426)

[IBN ISHAQ 1955: 281–282]

The point is clear: it was permitted to fight for God's cause, even in previously banned time, on the principle of a higher good being served. It was a taking of sides, and the test was a profession of faith in the Lord God of all.

It is reported on the authority of Abu Hurayra that the Messenger of God said: I have been commanded to fight against people so long as they do not declare that there is no god but the God, and he who professed it was guaranteed the protection of his property and life on my behalf, and his affairs rest with God. (Muslim, *Sahih* 1.9.30)

So reads an early tradition reported of Muhammad, justifying the militant quality of his calling—"I have been commanded"—and the test that qualifies one for membership in and protection of the community of Muslims. In this version that test has but a single article, belief in the one true God. Immediately after it, however, another tradition adds a second clause.

It is reported on the authority of Abu Hurayra that he heard the Messenger of God say: I have been commanded to fight against people until they testify the fact that there is no god but the God, and believe (in me) that I am the Messenger (from the Lord), and in all that I have brought. And when they do it, their blood and riches are guaranteed protection on my behalf except where it is justified by law, and their affairs rest with God. (Ibid. 1.9.31)

30. The Sixth Pillar: War in the Path of God

Islam was an activist faith, as the Prophet had demonstrated in both his words and deeds, and the theme of "struggling on the path of God" runs throughout the Quran. In some instances the struggle was a personal one against sin or toward perfection; in others the context was social or communal—in short, as part of a "Holy War" in the quite literal sense of armed combat, what came to be called

Jihad. Thus there came into being another candidate for inclusion among the basic prescriptions of Islam, the "struggle in the path of God" commanded to Muhammad and to all Muslims. The following tradition reported after the death of the Prophet appears to reflect some kind of debate in the community on just how widely that obligation extended. In this tradition at least, war in God's name is quite explicitly denied parity with the other pillars of Islam.

It is reported on the authority of Ta'us that a man said to Abdullah ibn Umar: Why don't you carry out a military expedition? Upon which he replied: I heard the Messenger of God, may peace be upon him, say: In truth Islam is founded on five (pillars): testifying that there is no god but the God, establishment of prayer, payment of the alms tax, the fast of Ramadan and pilgrimage to the House. (Muslim, *Sahih* 1.6.21)

Whether or not Jihad was formally one of the "pillars"—and the lawyers continued to debate the question—militancy on behalf of the cause of Islam, or better of God, was a fundamental duty, as the Quran itself leaves no doubt.

Fight those in the way of God who fight you, but do not be aggressive: God does not like aggressors. And fight those wheresoever you find them, and expel them from the place they had turned you out from. Oppression is worse than killing. Do not fight them by the Holy Mosque unless they fight you there. If they do, then slay them: such is the requital for unbelievers. But if they desist, God is forgiving and kind.

Fight them until sedition comes to an end, and the Law of God (prevails). If they desist, then cease to be hostile, except against those who oppress. (Quran 2:190–193)

Enjoined on you is fighting, and this you abhor. You may dislike a thing, yet it may be good for you; or a thing may haply please you but may be bad for you. Only God has knowledge, and you do not know. (Quran 2:216)

Those who barter the life of this world for the next should fight in the way of God. And We shall bestow on who fights in the way of God, whether he is killed or is victorious, a glorious reward.

What has come upon you that you fight not in the cause of God and for the oppressed, men, women and children, who pray, "Get us out of this city, O Lord, whose people are oppressors; so send us a friend by Your will, and send us a helper."

Those who believe fight in the way of God; and those who do not fight only for the powers of evil; so you should fight the allies of Satan. Surely the stratagem of Satan is ineffective. (Quran 4:74–76)

31. The Prophet's Instructions on the Holy War

Some of the traditions attributed to the Prophet are brief and pointed. Others are schematic, as if they had been pronounced by a lawyer, like this one setting out the terms and conditions governing the conduct of a Holy War.

Sulayman ibn Burayda told on his father's authority that when God's Messenger appointed a commander over an army or a detachment he instructed him to fear God and consider the welfare of the Muslims who were with him. Then he said: "Go forth in God's name in God's path and fight with those who disbelieve in God. Go forth and do not be unfaithful regarding booty, or treacherous, or mutilate anyone, or kill a child. When you meet the polytheists who are your enemy, summon them to three things, and accept whichever of them they are willing to accept and then leave them be. First, summon them to Islam, and if they agree accept it from them and leave them be. Then summon them to leave their abodes and join the ranks of the Emigrants, and tell them that if they do so they will have the same rights and responsibilities as the Emigrants; but if they refuse to join, then tell them they will be like the desert Arabs who are Muslims, subject to God's judgment which applies to believers, but they will have no spoils or booty unless they fight with the Muslims. If they refuse, demand the tribute from them, and if they agree, accept it from them and leave them be; but if they refuse, seek God's help and fight against them.

"When you invest a fortified place and its people wish you to grant them the protection of God and His Prophet, grant them neither but rather grant them your protection and that of your companions, for it is less serious to break your guarantee of protection or that of your companions than to break that of God and His Messenger. If you invest a fortified place and its people offer to capitulate and have the matter referred to God's judgment, do not grant this, but let them capitulate and have the matter referred to your judgment, for you do not know whether or not you will hit God's judgment regarding them."

This tradition was transmitted by Muslim. (Baghawi, *Mishkat al-Masabih* 18.4.1)

And as it did in Christianity, the struggle on behalf of Islam had its rewards in the afterlife. These were considerable, since the duty of the Holy War was a "community obligation," that is to say, it could be fulfilled by a few taking up arms, without the rest of the community being blamed (see Chapter 5 above). Thus it shared the additional merit of being a work of supererogation.

Ibn Abbas reported God's Messenger as saying to his companions: "When your brethren were smitten at the battle of Uhud, God put their spirits in the crops of green birds which go down to the rivers of Paradise, eat its fruits and nestle in lamps of gold in the shadow of the Throne (of God). Then when they had experienced the sweetness of their food, drink and rest, they asked who would tell their brethren about them, that they were alive in Paradise, in order that they (the living believers) might not cease to desire Paradise or recoil in war. God Most High said He would tell them about them so He sent down the verses:

'Never think that those who who are killed in the way of God are dead. They are alive, getting succor from their Lord, rejoicing at what God has given them of His grace, and happy for those who are trying to overtake them and have not joined them yet, and who will have no fear or regret. They rejoice at the kindness and mercy of God; and God does not suffer the wages of the faithful to go to waste' (Quran 3:169–171)."

This tradition has been transmitted by Abu Dawud. (Baghawi, *Mishkat al-Masabih* 3.818)

31. Just War and Homicide

There was, however, a difference between this just war in the cause of religion and the crime of homicide. The distinction is drawn with some care in the Quran.

It is not for a believer to take a believer's life except by mistake; and he who kills a believer by mistake should free a slave who is a believer and pay blood money to the victim's family, unless they waive it as an act of charity. If he belonged to a community that was hostile to you but was himself a believer, then a slave who is a believer should be freed. In case he belonged to a people with whom you have a treaty, then give blood money to his family and free a believing slave. For he who has no means (to do so) should fast for a period of two months continuously to have his sins forgiven by God, and God is all-knowing and all wise.

Anyone who kills a believer intentionally will be cast into Hell to abide there forever, and suffer God's anger and damnation. For him a greater punishment awaits.

O believers, when you go forth (to fight) in the way of God, be discreet and do not say to anyone who greets you in peace: "You are not a believer." You desire the gain of earthly life, but there are prizes in plenty with God. You were also like him (an unbeliever) in the past, but

God has been gracious to you. So be careful and discreet, for God is aware of what you do.

The faithful who sit idle, save those who are disabled, are not equal to those who fight in the way of God with their wealth and lives. God has exalted in rank those who fight for the faith with their wealth and souls over those who sit idle. Though God's promise of good is for all, He has granted His favor of the highest reward to those who struggle in preference to those who sit at home. (Quran 4:92–95)

33. "There Is No Compulsion in Religion"

The Holy War, or Jihad, was fought against unbelievers living in the "Abode of War," that is, the territories outside the political control of the Muslim community. Within the "Abode of Islam" itself lived others who did not accept either the Quran or the Prophet but who were not heathens or polytheists. These were the "Peoples of the Book," the "Scriptuaries" who practiced Judaism, Christianity, and, it will appear, Zoroastrianism. They were not required to embrace Islam; the proof-text is this verse of the Quran.

There is no compulsion in matters of faith. Distinct now is the way of guidance from error. He who turns away from the forces of evil and believes in God, will surely hold fast to a handle that is strong and unbreakable, for God hears all and knows everything. (Quran 2:256)

The interpretation of this famous verse was fairly standard, despite a great deal of uncertainty about the circumstances of its revelation.

Wahidi [d. 1076 C.E.] relates on the authority of Saʿid ibn Jubayr, who related on the authority of Ibn Abbas: "When the children of a woman of the Helpers [that is, early Medinese converts to Islam] all died in infancy, she vowed that if a child were to live, she would bring it up as a Jew. Thus when the Jewish tribe of al-Nadir was evicted from Medina, there were among them sons of the Helpers. The Helpers said, 'O Messenger of God, what will become of our children?' Thus God sent down this (above-cited) verse." Saʿid ibn Jubayr said: "Therefore whoever wished to join them did so and whoever wished not to join them did so likewise." According Mujahid, this (same) verse was sent down concerning a man who had a black male servant called Subayh. The man wished to compel his servant to enter Islam. Al-Suddi said that the verse was sent down concerning a man of the Helpers known as Abu al-Husayn who had two sons. One day merchants from Syria came to Medina to sell oil. The sons of Abu al-Husayn came to the merchants, who converted them to Christianity. They then went to Syria with the merchants. When Abu al-Husayn knew this, he came to the Prophet and asked: "Shall I pursue them?" God then sent down "There is no compulsion in religion." The Messenger of God said: "May God banish them! They are the first two who rejected faith." Mujahid said: "This was before the Messenger of God was commanded to fight against the People of the Book. God's saying 'There is no compulsion in religion' was abrogated and he was commanded to fight against the People of the Book in the Sura 'Repentance' (9:29)." . . .

According to other traditions, the verse was revealed in reference to the People of the Book, who should not be compelled to enter Islam so long as they pay the tribute. The verse is, therefore, not abrogated (by 9:29). Tabari [d. 923 C.E.] relates on the authority of Qatada: "Arab society was compelled to enter Islam because they were an unlettered community, having no book which they knew. Thus nothing other than Islam was accepted from them. The People of the Book are not to be compelled to enter Islam if they submit to paying the (tribute of the) poll tax or the land tax." . . .

Razi [d. 1209 C.E.] . . . comments: "This (verse) means that God did not rest the matter of faith on compulsion or coercion but rather based it on free will and the ability to choose. . . . This is what is intended here when God made clear the proofs of the Divine Unity. He said that there is no longer any excuse for a rejecter of faith to persist in his rejection. That he should be forced to accept faith is not lawful in this world, which is a world of trial. For coercion and compulsion in the matter of faith is the annulment of the meaning of trial and test." [AYOUB 1984: 252–254]

34. The People of the Book: War and Tribute

Whatever recognition was granted to their beliefs and cult, the People of the Book were required to pay tribute in acknowledgment of the Muslims' political sovereignty.

Fight those People of the Book who do not believe in God and the Last Day, who do not prohibit what God and His Apostle have forbidden, or accept divine law, until all of them pay protective tribute in submission. (Quran 9:29)

The standard exegesis explains.

According to this verse, tribute is restricted to the People of the Book. This is confirmed by the fact that Umar [Caliph, 634–644 C.E.]

accepted no tribute from the Zoroastrians until Abd al-Rahman ibn Awf testified that the Prophet had collected tribute from the Zoroastrians of Hajar (in southern Bahrayn) and had said: "Establish for them the same custom as for the People of the Book, for they have a similar Book." Thus they are regarded as possessing the Book. But on our view tribute may not be collected from other unbelievers. According to Abu Hanifa, however, it should be collected from them, from all except the pagan Arabs, for al-Zuhri relates that the Prophet concluded peace treaties with the idolaters who were not Arabs. Finally, according to Malik ibn Anas, tribute should be collected from all unbelievers except apostates.

The minimum tribute is one (gold) dinar per year, with the rich and poor treated equally. Abu Hanifa, however, says that it is forty-eight (silver) dirhams for the rich, half that amount for those who are moderately capable of earning a living, and nothing at all for the poor who are not capable of earning a living. (Baydawi, *The Lights of Revelation, ad loc.*)

35. Guidelines for Christian Behavior under Islam

The following is a very late version of a widely circulated and cited covenant of submission (dhimma) *said to have been originally drawn for the second Caliph, Umar (634–644 C.E.), by the Christians of Syria.*

We heard from Abd al-Rahman ibn Ghanam [d. 697 C.E.] as follows: When Umar ibn al-Khattab, may God be pleased with him, accorded a peace to the Christians of Syria, we wrote to him as follows:

"In the name of God, the Compassionate, the Merciful.

This is a letter to the servant of God Umar (ibn al-Khattab), Commander of the Faithful, from the Christians of such-and-such a city. When you came against us, we asked you for safe conduct for ourselves, our descendants, our property, and the people of our community, and we undertook the following obligations toward you:

We shall not build, in our cities or their neighborhood, new monasteries, churches, convents, or monks' cells, nor shall we repair, by day or by night, such of them as fall in ruins or are situated in the quarters of the Muslims.

We shall keep our gates open for passersby and travelers. We shall give board and lodging to all Muslims who pass our way for three days.

We shall not give shelter in our churches or in our dwellings to any spy, nor hide him from the Muslims.

We shall not teach the Quran to our children.

We shall not manifest our religion publicly or convert anyone to it. We shall not prevent any of our kin from entering Islam if they wish it.

We shall show respect toward the Muslims, and we shall rise from our seats when they wish to sit.

We shall not seek to resemble the Muslims by imitating any of their garments, the *qalansuwa*, the turban, footwear or the parting of hair. We shall not speak as they do, nor shall we adopt their names.

We shall not mount on saddles, nor shall we gird on swords or bear any kind of arms or carry them on our persons.

We shall engrave Arabic inscriptions on our seals.

We shall not sell fermented drinks.

We shall not clip the fronts of our heads.

We shall always dress in the same way wherever we may be, and we shall bind the special cincture about our waists.

We shall not display our crosses or our books on the public ways or the markets of the Muslims. We shall use clappers in our churches only very softly. We shall not raise our voices in our church services or in the presence of Muslims, nor shall we raise our voices when following our dead. We shall not show lights on any of the roads of the Muslims or in their markets. We shall not bury our dead near the Muslims.

We shall not take slaves who have be allotted to the Muslims.

We shall not build houses overtopping the houses of the Mus-lims. . . .

We accept these conditions for ourselves and for the people of our community, and in return we receive a pledge of safe conduct.

If in any way we violate these undertakings, for which we ourselves stand surety, we forfeit our covenant (*dhimma*) and we become liable to the penalties for contumacy and sedition."

Umar ibn al-Khattab replied: Sign what they ask, but add two clauses and impose them in addition to what they have written. They are: "They shall not buy anyone made prisoner by the Muslims," and "Who-ever strikes a Muslim with deliberate intent shall forfeit the protection of this pact." (Tartushi, *Siraj al-Muluk* 229–230) [LEWIS 1974: 2:217–219]

35. A Christian Dress Code for the Other Peoples of the Book

Similar restrictions were in force on the Jews living under Islam, restrictions that were in reality now more severe, now considerably more lenient than they appear on the lawyers' books. Christians too had restrictive codes for the Jews living under their sovereignty, codes that were extended to Muslims as parts of the "Abode of Islam," in Spain for example, began to fall back under Christian control.

In some provinces a difference in dress distinguishes the Jews and Saracens from the Christians, but in others confusion has developed to such a degree that no difference is discernible. Whence it happens sometimes through error that Christians mingle with the women of the Jews and Saracens, and, on the other hand, Jews and Saracens mingle with those of the Christians. Therefore, that such ruinous commingling through error of this kind may not serve as a refuge for further excuse for excesses, we decree that such people of both sexes [that is, Jews and Saracens] in every Christian province and at all times be distinguished in public from other people by a difference of dress, since this was also enjoined on them by Moses. On the days of Lamentations and on Passion Sunday they may not appear in public, because some of them, as we understand, on those days are not ashamed to show themselves more ornately attired and do not fear to amuse themselves at the expense of the Christians, who in memory of the Sacred Passion go about attired in robes of mourning. That we must strictly forbid, lest they should presume in some measure to burst forth suddenly in contempt of the Redeemer. And since we ought not to be ashamed of him who blotted out our offenses, we command that the secular princes restrain presumptuous persons of this kind with condign punishment, lest they presume to blaspheme in some degree the one crucified for us. (Fourth Lateran Council [1215 C.E.], Canon 68)

PART III

The Works of the Spirit

Introduction

Judaism, Christianity, and Islam, in addition to their family affiliation, were also members of the larger community of religions in the Near East. By the time of the advent of Islam, that fellowship had been much diminished, due largely to the spread of Christianity. But at some stages of their history all three were exposed not only to the doubtless powerful attraction of each other—even Judaism, the disinterested progenitor of the other two, had to live for millennia under the political sovereignty of Christianity or Islam—but to the religious beliefs and practices of the pagans, from the theriolatry of Pharaonic Egypt to the Hindu sensibilities of medieval India.

It was not exactly a symmetrical encounter. Most of the pagan cults of the ancient and medieval worlds were officially and actually tolerant of the religious practices of others—there is room for all in a polytheistic world. The Children of Abraham, on the other hand, though grudgingly accepting of each other, were professedly and actually intolerant of all other religious systems. The One True God of Abraham was, on His own witness, a jealous deity who brooked no rivals, and his followers were as fanatic and intolerant as He in their view of the ritual acts and spiritual beliefs of those other "gentiles," "pagans," and "infidels." Conversion or death was a choice that no one of the three hesitated to impose on those unbelievers unhappy enough to be caught under their severe sovereignty.

Yet if acceptance of paganism was out of the question, adaptation was not. Novelty, exoticism, and the political power of unbelievers were all inducements to accepting other modes of worship and other ways of thinking about God. The Israelites did it in a dangerously open fashion on occasion—and paid God's price. More generally, the borrowing was dressed and veiled, not often in a conscious way, in the raiment of tradition.

It is not the purpose here to ferret out these concealed borrowings from the Gentiles. They are assuredly there, even in the oldest parts of the Bible, though in reading the Torah it is difficult to imagine how there could possibly be any room for such, so detailed are God's prescriptions as to how and where and by whom He wished to be worshiped. The rules for priesthood, tabernacle, and sacrifice were all laid out for the Israelites in Sinai, and the books of Kings show how easily and sumptuously those same settings and rituals could be transferred to a new urban setting in Jerusalem.

The Temple and the priesthoods are a source of immense self-congratulation in both the Torah and the later chronicles of Israel, and they are a source of renewed pride when reinstituted after the Exile. But there were anxieties as well, growing uneasiness as to the spiritual validity of animal sacrifice, doubts as to the authenticity of contemporary versions of the priestly line. And there were alternatives, chiefly the synagogue, a place of study and prayer that had developed perhaps during the Exile but stood ready, even if unintended as such, to serve as the center of Jewish community life in all its aspects after the destruction of the Commonwealth and its Temple in 70 C.E.

Study and prayer replaced sacrifice in post-70 Judaism—the ease and rapidity of the changeover appears nothing short of astonishing. And, the survival of the pre-Islamic pilgrimage apart, the same sensibility prevailed in Islam: the mosque is functionally identical to a synagogue as a place of community assembly and prayer. The differences are purely political. Since the Muslim community was a sovereign one, the assembly was overtly political and the prayer publicly and proudly announced by a lofty crier. Christianity, on the other hand, remained faithful to its legacy from Temple Judaism. The Christian Church was not an adaptation of a synagogue but none other than the Temple writ small, and the Christians' primary liturgical act, for all its similarities to a Passover Seder and its eventual borrowing from some synagogue practices, was read by Christians from the beginning as a form of sacrifice, wherein Jesus was both the new victim and the priest of the New Dispensation.

There is borrowing, then, and in plenty, from the cherubim in Exodus to the rites of the Muslim pilgrimage. We have ignored it, since the communities themselves either ignore or deny that any of their cult practices derive from a source other than Scripture and Tradition. But the works of religion extend far beyond ritual. Out in these farther reaches, divine prescription yields to the broader, more elastic, and so, in fact if not in intent, more permissive work of the Holy Spirit, who "listeth where He will." It was there that the Children of Abraham began to move beyond Scripture, and even beyond mere borrowing, onto that terrain which can only be described as the religious heritage of man. The great mass of the faithful, for example, continued to acknowledge God through liturgical, Scripture-sanctioned worship. But there were other paths whereby believers in the three faiths have sought, either individually or in concert, to approach their Creator. Some Jews, Christians, and Muslims chose to withdraw themselves from a society, their own or others', that they judged too devoted to the world or too distanced from God, in order to pursue their own, private visions of perfection. Flight or search, the impulse has carried them into sometimes solitary and sometimes community exercises that range from self-examination and purification to the most extreme forms of ego-abnegation—all with only the most tenuous connection with Scripture.

For many of its practitioners this ascetical regimen has been an end in itself, a form of psychic catharsis or psychic control. For as many others the denial of self is but a preliminary to a higher and more difficult enterprise: the passage of the liberated soul to the very presence of God, "the flight of the alone to the Alone," as the influential pagan Plotinus called it. Mystics too occur in almost all religious communities, though among the Children of Abraham the motifs and texts of meditation are, of course, Scripture-derived: Moses confronting God Himself on Sinai, Ezekiel in trance before his celestial chariot, Jesus transfigured on Tabor, Muhammad borne by night to Jerusalem and thence to the highest heaven. These are the traditional patterns, though the formulas are often startlingly transcended and the mystics' own expressions of what lay in the bosom of God even more startlingly, sometimes shockingly, idiosyncratic.

The legal establishments of Judaism and Islam, the rabbis on both sides of that aisle, were sometimes unhappy with the mystics' often extravagant claims to a higher and more intimate access to God, as were the more highly institutionalized, and so even less flexible, clerics of the Christian Church. For their part, the more prudent among the mystics took refuge in trope and allegory, wrote poetry, or simply put on an antic air. In the end mysticism, like its antecedent asceticism, found some home place in its community. The rabbis discovered to their occasional unease that kabbala and midrash were not antithetical, nor were sufism and hadith. Christianity built cloisters for its ascetics and welcomed into them, and into the control they implied, those who would fly farther and higher still.

To this point we have followed the Children of Abraham in disclaiming all borrowing. Here we shall likewise follow them in acknowledging the adoption, or at very least the close inspection, of the spiritual goods of the pagans—what one Christian sage called, with a nod toward a little biblically sanctioned larceny in the wake of the Exodus, the "spoliation of the Egyptians." The "Egyptians" in question were actually Greeks, the cultural Hellenes who in the wake of Alexander the Great presented to the Jews a different view of the world and its workings. We have already seen something of that encounter of Judaism with Hellenism, how the political version of the latter was repudiated in Palestine by the Maccabees at the same time that many of its intellectual premises were discovered to be both attractive and useful by Jews in Alexandria, for example. Philo found that the rationalized view of the universe that had been carefully crafted by the Greeks and acknowledged as such could be generally reconciled with what his own Scripture had to say on the subject. When Greek philosophy turned to the question of God—to theology, in short—it was found to be useful in defining, explaining, and even, as the Greeks insisted, in proving what God Himself had revealed. The Jewish experiment with Hellenism aborted at that point; political events in Palestine determined the agenda of first- and second-century Judaism. But Christians found it even more congenial; little wonder, since they were increasingly themselves Hellenes born or reared. The Christian Fathers took up with enthusiasm the discarded work of Philo—as the Jews were themselves to do, though not with quite the same enthusiasm or conviction.

Theology was a generally confident and exuberant growth within the bosom of the Christian Church and, from the fourth century onward, the prevailing mode of discourse for orthodox and heretic alike. Its supple dialectic put in the hands of the Christian teacher and the Christian polemicist a powerful instrument indeed. Eventually the polemicist found good use for the weapon against his new Muslim adversary, and the shock of that encounter may have persuaded the Muslim to train himself in the new, for him, intellectual technology. Some did, if only for counterpolemic; some few went even farther down the road where Aristotle beckoned. It was an enterprise not highly thought of in Islam, however, or in traditional Judaism, where a thoroughgoing rationalism, which the Christians thought they had tamed to their own satisfaction, was judged dangerous and, in the end, too inimical to the faith.

Reason and revelation are hoary adversaries among all the Children of Abraham, but not the only ones. Nor are they even likely the most important. Scripture and tradition, orthodoxy and orthopraxy, the rule of the lawyer and the affect of the mystic have likewise struggled for dominance or control in that same arena. But the verities remained: the fact of Creation and of our consequent dependence, and the certitude of the Judgment. The End Time haunts and colors all thought, whether the concern is personal or communal: the sinner quaking before God, the felicitous in Paradise, the apocalyptic Messiah or Mahdi, the Church Triumphant, the sad fate of "those who have no share in the Afterlife." And beyond even That Time is God Himself, the Maker of the Promise and its Fulfillment.

I. The Worship of God: Temple and Synagogue

I. The Cult Prescribed from Sinai

In the book of Exodus the Lord provides Moses with elaborate instructions for the veneration of His presence in the midst of the Israelites.

They shall make an ark of acacia wood, two and a half cubits long, one cubit and a half wide and one cubit and a half high. Overlay it with pure gold—overlay it inside and out—and make upon it a gold molding round about. Cast four gold rings for it, to be attached to its four feet, two rings on one of its side walls and two on the other. Make poles of acacia wood and overlay them with gold, then insert the poles into the rings at the side walls of the ark, for carrying the ark. The poles shall remain in the rings of the ark; they shall not be removed from it. And deposit in the ark the [tablets of] the Pact which I shall give you.

You shall make a cover of pure gold, two and a half cubits long and one cubit and a half wide. Make two cherubim of gold—make them of hammered work—at the two ends of the cover. Make one cherub at one end and the other cherub at the other; of one piece with the cover shall you make the cherubim at its two ends. The cherubim shall have their wings spread out above, shielding the cover with their wings. They shall confront each other, the faces of the cherubim being turned toward the cover. Place the cover on top of the ark, after depositing in the ark the Pact which I will give you. There I will meet with you, and I will impart to you—from above the cover, from between the two cherubim that are on top of the ark of the Pact—all that I will command you concerning the Israelite people. (Exodus 25:10–22)

You shall make a table of acacia wood, two cubits long, one cubit wide, and a cubit and a half high. . . . Make its bowls, ladles, jars and jugs

799

with which to offer libations; make them of pure gold. And on the table you shall set the bread of display, to be before Me always. (Exodus 25: 23–30)

You shall take choice flour and bake it into twelve loaves, two-tenths of a measure for each loaf. Place them on a pure table before the Lord in two rows, six to a row. With each row you shall place pure frankincense, which is to be a token offering for the bread, as an offering by fire to the Lord. He [that is, Aaron] shall arrange them before the Lord regularly every sabbath day—it is a commitment for all time on the part of the Israelites. They shall belong to Aaron and his sons, who shall eat of them in the sacred precinct; for they are his as most holy things from the Lord's offering by fire, a due for all time. (Leviticus 24:5–9)

This sacred bread offered to God in the Temple later provided Jesus with a point of departure for one of his own interpretations of the Law.

Once about that time Jesus went through the wheat fields on the Sabbath; and his disciples, feeling hungry, began to pluck some ears of grain and eat them. The Pharisees noticed this and said to him, "Look, your disciples are doing something which is forbidden on the Sabbath." He answered, "Have you not read (1 Sam. 21:1–7) what David did when he and his men were hungry? He went into the house of God and ate the sacred bread, though neither he nor his men had a right to eat it, but only the priests." (Matthew 12:1–4)

We return to the text in Exodus and its description of how the Menora, or lampstand, should be constructed.

Make a lampstand of pure gold. . . . Six branches shall issue from its sides: three branches from one side of the lampstand and three branches from the other side of the lampstand. . . . Make its seven lamps—its lamps shall be so mounted as to give the light on its front side—and its tongs and fire pans of pure gold. It shall be made, with all these furnishings, out of a talent of pure gold. Note well and follow the patterns for them that are being shown you on the mountain. (Exodus 25:31–40)

2. The Tent of the Presence

As for the tabernacle, make it of ten strips of cloth; make these of fine twisted linen, of blue, purple and crimson yarns, with a design of cherubim worked into them. The length of each shall be twenty-eight cubits, and the width of each cloth shall be four cubits, all the cloths to have the same measurements. . . . You shall make the planks for the tabernacle of acacia wood, upright. The length of each plank shall be ten cubits and the width of each plank a cubit and a half. (Exodus 26:1–16)

It was within this tent that the Ark of the Covenant was to be preserved.

You shall make a curtain of blue, purple and crimson yarns, and fine twisted linen; it shall have a design of cherubim worked into it. Hang it upon four posts of acacia wood overlaid with gold, and having hooks of gold (set) in four silver sockets. Hang the curtain under the clasps and carry the Ark of the Pact there behind the curtain, so that the curtain shall serve you as a partition between the Holy and the Holy of Holies. Place the cover upon the Ark of the Pact in the Holy of Holies. Put the table outside the curtain and the lampstand by the south wall of the Tabernacle, opposite the table, which is placed by the north wall. (Exodus 26:31–35)

3. The Altars

Then the Lord turns to the subject of the liturgy, His ongoing public and community worship. First comes the matter of altars.

You shall make the altar of acacia wood, five cubits long by five cubits wide—the altar is to be square—and three cubits high. Make its horns on the four corners, the horns to be of one piece with it, and overlay it with copper. Make for it pails for removing its ashes, as well as its scrapers, basins, flesh hooks and fire pans—make all its utensils of copper. Make for it a grating of meshwork in copper, and on the mesh make four copper rings at its corners. Set the mesh below, under the ledge of the altar, so that it extends to the middle of the altar. And make poles for the altar, poles of acacia wood, and overlay them with copper. The poles shall be inserted into the rings, so that the poles remain on the two sides of the altar when it is carried. Make it hollow, of boards. As you were shown on the mountain, so shall they be made. (Exodus 27:1–8)

Now this is what you shall offer on the altar: two yearling lambs each day, regularly. You shall offer the one lamb in the morning, you shall offer the other lamb at twilight. There shall be a tenth of a measure of choice flour with a quarter of a *hin* of beaten oil mixed in, and a libation of a quarter *hin* of wine for one lamb; and you shall offer the other lamb at twilight, repeating with it the meal offering of the morning with its libation—an offer by fire for a pleasing odor to the Lord, a regular burnt offering through the generations, at the entrance of the Tent of Meeting before the Lord. For there I will meet with you, and there I will speak with you, and there will I meet with the Israelites, and it shall be sanctified by My Presence.

I will sanctify the Tent of Meeting and the altar, and I will consecrate Aaron and his sons to serve Me as priests. I will abide among the Israelites and I will be their God. And they shall know that I am the Lord their God, who brought them out of the land of Egypt that I might abide among them, I the Lord their God. (Exodus 29:38–46)

There was to be a second altar as well.

And you shall make an altar for burning incense; make it of acacia wood. It shall be a cubit long and a cubit wide—it shall be a square—and two cubits high, its horns of one piece with it. . . . Put it in front of the curtain that is over the Ark of the Pact—where I will meet with you. On it Aaron shall burn aromatic incense; he shall burn it every morning when he tends the lamps, and Aaron shall burn it at twilight when he lights the lamps—a regular incense offering before the Lord throughout the ages. You shall not offer alien incense on it, or a burnt offering or a meal offering; neither shall you pour a libation over it. Once a year Aaron shall perform a purification on its horns with the blood of the sin offering of purification; purification shall be performed on it once a year throughout the ages. It is most holy to the Lord. (Exodus 30:1–10)

4. The Sacrifices

The Lord is to be worshiped by sacrifices, four of which are specified in Leviticus: (1) the whole or burnt offering, (2) the meal or grain offering, (3) the sin offering, and (4) the guilt offering.

The Lord spoke to Moses, saying: Command Aaron and his sons thus:

This is the ritual of the burnt offering. The burnt offering shall remain where it was burned upon the altar all night until morning, while the fire on the altar is kept going on it. The priest shall dress in linen raiment, with linen breeches next to his body; and he shall take up the ashes to which the fire has reduced the burnt offering on the altar and place them beside the altar. He shall then take off his vestments and put on other vestments, and carry the ashes outside the camp to a clean place. The fire on the altar shall be kept burning, not to go out: every morning the priest shall feed wood to it, lay out the burnt offering on it, and turn into smoke the fat parts of the offering of well-being. . . .

This is the ritual of the meal offering. Aaron's sons shall present it before the Lord, in front of the altar. A handful of the choice flour and oil of the meal offering shall be taken from it, with all the frankincense that is on the meal offering, and this token portion shall be turned into smoke on the altar as a pleasing odor to the Lord. What is left of it shall be eaten by Aaron and his sons; it shall be eaten as unleavened cakes, in the sacred precinct; they shall eat it in the enclosure of the Tent of Meeting. It shall not be baked with leaven; I have given it as their portion from My offerings by fire; it is most holy, like the sin offering and the penalty offering. Only the males among Aaron's descendants may eat of it, as their due, for all time throughout the ages from the Lord's offerings by fire. Anything that touches these shall become holy. (Leviticus 6: 7–11)

. . . This is the ritual of the sin offering: the sin offering shall be slaughtered before the Lord, at the spot where the burnt offering is slaughtered: it is most holy. The priest who offers it as a sin offering shall eat of it; it shall be eaten in the sacred precinct, in the enclosure of the Tent of Meeting. Anything that touches its flesh shall become holy; and if any of its blood is spattered on a garment, you shall wash the bespattered garment in the sacred precinct. . . . Only the males in the priestly line may eat of it: it is most holy. But no sin offering may be eaten from which any blood is brought into the Tent of Meeting for expiation in the sanctuary; any such shall be consumed in the fire.

This is the ritual of the guilt offering: it is most holy. The guilt offering shall be slaughtered at the spot where the burnt offering is slaughtered, and its blood shall be dashed on all sides of the altar. All its fat shall be offered: the broad tail; the fat that covers the entrails; the two kidneys and the fat that is on them at the loins; and the protuberance on the liver, which shall be removed with the kidneys. The priest shall burn them into smoke on the alter as an offering by fire to the Lord; it is a guilt offering. Only the males of the priestly line may eat it; it shall be eaten in the sacred precinct: it is most holy.

The guilt offering is like the sin offering. The same rule applies to both: it shall belong to the priest who makes expiation thereby. So, too, the priest who offers a man's burnt offering shall keep the skin of the burnt offering that he offered. Further, any meal offering that is baked in an oven, and any that is prepared in a pan or a griddle, shall belong to the priest who offers it. But every other meal offering, with oil mixed in or dry, shall go to the sons of Aaron all alike. (Leviticus 6:17–7:10)

5. The Temple of Solomon

When David first installed the Ark in his new capital of Jerusalem it was still housed in what must have been a permanent replica of the Tent of the Presence that had been moved from place to place during the long passage from Sinai to the Promised Land. But Solomon had other plans.

Solomon sent this message to King Hiram of Tyre: "In view of what you did for my father David in sending him cedars to build a palace for his residence—see, I intend to build a House for the name of the Lord my God; I will dedicate it to Him for making incense offering of sweet spices in His honor, for the regular rows of bread, and for the morning and evening burnt offerings on sabbaths, new moons, and festivals, as is Israel's eternal duty. The new House I intend to build will be great, inasmuch as our God is greater than all gods." (2 Chronicles 2:2–4)

The building of the House of the Lord began. It was to be, by our best reckoning, 90 × 30 × 45 feet in length, width, and height.

It was in the four hundred and eightieth year after the Israelites left Egypt . . . in the second month, in the fourth year of his reign over Israel [ca. 957 B.C.E.], Solomon began to build the House of the Lord. The house which King Solomon built for the Lord was sixty cubits long, twenty cubits wide and thirty cubits high. The portico in front of the Great Hall of the House was twenty cubits long—along the width of the House— and ten cubits deep to the front of the House. He made windows for the House, recessed and latticed. Against the outside wall of the House—the outside walls of the House enclosing the Great Hall and the Shrine [that is, the Holy of Holies]—he built a storied structure, and he made side chambers all around. . . .

When the House was built, only finished stones cut at the quarry were used, so that no hammer or ax or any iron tool was heard in the House while it was being built. (1 Kings 6:1–7)

At the center of the complex, shielded from the profanity without, was an inner shrine, the "Holy of Holies," which was, like its counterpart in Mecca, a kaʿba or cube. Inside it was placed the sacred Ark of the Covenant.

When Solomon had completed the construction of the House, he paneled the walls of the House on the inside with planks of cedar. . . . Twenty cubits from the rear of the House, he built (a partition) of cedar planks from the floor to the walls [or "the rafters"]; he furnished its interior to serve as a shrine, as Holy of Holies. The front part of the

House, that is, the Great Hall, measured forty cubits. . . . In the innermost part of the House he fixed a shrine in which to place the Ark of the Lord's Covenant. The interior of the shrine was twenty cubits long, twenty cubits wide and twenty cubits high. He overlaid it with solid gold; he similarly overlaid (its) cedar altar. (1 Kings 6:14–21)

Once the building was complete, there followed a ceremony similar to the one that had occurred in David's day to install the Ark of the Covenant in its holy and inviolable housing within Solomon's sanctuary.

Then Solomon convoked the elders of Israel—all the heads of the tribes and the ancestral chieftains of the Israelites—before King Solomon in Jerusalem, to bring up the Ark of the Covenant of the Lord from the City of David, which is called Sion. All the men of Israel gathered before King Solomon at the (pilgrimage) Feast (of Tabernacles) in the month of Ethanim. When all the elders of Israel had come, the priests lifted the Ark and carried up the Ark of the Lord. Then the priests and the Levites brought the Tent of Meeting and all the holy vessels that were in the Tent. Meanwhile King Solomon and the whole community of Israel, who were assembled with him before the Ark, sacrificed sheep and oxen in such abundance that they could not be numbered or counted.

The priests brought in the Ark of the Covenant of the Lord to its place underneath the wings of the cherubim, in the shrine of the House, in the Holy of Holies; for the cherubim had their wings spread over the place of the Ark, so that the cherubim shielded the Ark and its poles from above. The poles projected so that the ends of the poles were visible in the Sanctuary in front of the Shrine, but they could not be seen outside; and there they remain to this day. There was nothing inside the Ark but the two tablets of stone which Moses placed there at Horeb, when the Lord made (a covenant) with the Israelites after their departure from the land of Egypt. (1 Kings 8:1–9)

6. The Temple Liturgy

The full liturgy was then established in the splendid new House of the Lord in Jerusalem.

At that time Solomon offered burnt offerings on the altar which he had built in front of the porch. What was due for each day he sacrificed according to the commandment of Moses for the sabbaths, the new moons and the thrice yearly festivals—the (pilgrimage) Feast of Unleavened Bread [or Passover], of Weeks [or Shabuoth], and of Tabernacles [or

Sukkoth]. Following the prescription of his father David, he set up the divisions of the priests for their duties, and the Levites for their watches, to praise and serve alongside the priests, according to each day's require-ment, and the gatekeepers in their watches, gate by gate, for such was the commandment of David. (2 Chronicles 8:12–14)

The element of praise confided to the Levites in the Temple service had been initiated by David himself even before the Temple was built on Mount Moriah. It included from the beginning the singing of psalms, to the accompaniment of instrumental music and dancing.

David ordered the officers of the Levites to install their kinsmen, the singers, with musical instruments, harps, lyres and cymbals, joyfully mak-ing their voices heard. (1 Chronicles 15:16)

They brought in the Ark of God and set it up inside the tent which David had pitched for it. . . . He [that is, David] appointed Levites to minister before the Ark of the Lord, to repeat the name, to invoke, to praise, and to extol the Lord God of Israel. Their leader was Asaph. . . . It was then on that day that David first commissioned Asaph and his kinsmen to give praise to the Lord:

> "Praise the Lord; call on His name;
> proclaim His deeds among the peoples.
> Sing praises to Him;
> speak of all His wondrous acts."

(1 Chronicles 16:1–9)

7. Liturgical Psalms

A number of the poems collected in the Bible's Book of Psalms were used for liturgical purposes, chiefly, it is supposed, in the Jerusalem Temple rebuilt after the return from the Babylonian Exile. Indeed, the liturgy itself is described in this passage from Psalm 68.

> Men see Your procession, O God,
> the procession of my God, my king, into the sanctuary.
> First come singers, then musicians,
> amidst maidens playing timbrels.
> In assemblies bless God,
> all Israel assembled bless God,
> the Lord, O you who are from the fountain of Israel.
> There is little Benjamin who rules them,

the princes of Judah who command them,
the princes of Zebulon and Naphtali.
(Psalm 68:24–28)

Psalm 47 is described as an "Enthronement Hymn," one of the type sung at Temple festivals like Sukkoth.

All you peoples, clap your hands,
raise a joyous shout to God.
For the Lord Most high is awesome,
great king over all the earth!
He subjects peoples to us,
sets nations at our feet.
He chose our heritage for us,
the pride of Jacob whom He loved.

God ascends amidst acclamation;
the Lord, to the blasts of the horn.
Sing, O sing to our king;
for God is king over all the earth; sing a hymn.
God reigns over the nations,
God is seated on His holy throne.
The great of the peoples are gathered together,
the retinue of Abraham's God;
for the guardians of the earth belong to God;
He is greatly exalted.
(Psalm 47)

Finally, this "Royal Psalm" is one of the songs used liturgically at the coronation ceremony of an Israelite king. Such songs later found particular favor among the Christians, who read them in a Messianic context.

Why do the nations assemble,
and peoples plot vain things;
kings of the earth take their stand,
and regents intrigue together
against the Lord and against His anointed?
"Let us break the cords of their yoke,
shake off their ropes from us!"
He who is enthroned in heaven laughs;
the Lord mocks at them.
Then He speaks to them in anger,
terrifying them in His rage,

"But I have installed My king
　　on Sion, My holy mountain."
Let me tell of the decree:
　　the Lord said to me,
　　"You are My son,
　　I have fathered you this day.
Ask it of Me,
　　and I will make the nations your domain;
　　your estate, the limits of the earth.
You can smash them with an iron mace,
　　shatter them like potter's ware."

So now, O kings, be prudent;
　　accept discipline, you rulers of the earth!
Serve the Lord in awe;
　　tremble with fright,
　　pay homage in good faith,
　　lest He be angered and your way be doomed
　　in the mere flash of His anger.
Happy are those who take refuge in Him.
(Psalm 2)

8. The Daily Whole Offering

The central act of the Temple liturgy was the tamid, *or whole offering, daily slaughtered on the high altar. The details of the ritual were preserved intact in the Mishna tractate called Tamid, written down more than a century after such sacrifices had ceased being offered by Jewish priests in Jerusalem.*

The officer said to them [that is, the assembled priests], "Come and cast lots," (to decide) which of you should slaughter, which should sprinkle the blood, which should clear the inner altar of ashes, which should trim the candlestick, and which should take up the ramp the members (of the daily whole offering, namely) the head and the (right) hind leg, and the two fore legs, the rump and the (left) hind leg, the breast and the neck, and the two flanks, the innards and the fine flour, the baked cakes and the wine. They cast lots, and the lot fell upon whom it fell. . . . He said to them, "Go and bring a lamb from the Chamber of Lambs." Now the Chamber of Lambs was in the northwestern corner. Four chambers were there, one was the Chamber of the Lambs, one was the Chamber

of the Seals, one the Chamber of the Hearth and one the chamber
wherein they made the Bread of the Presence. . . .

He to whom it fell to slaughter the daily whole offering dragged it
along to the slaughterhouse, and they to whom it fell to carry the members followed after. The slaughterhouse lay north of the Altar and there
stood there eight short pillars; upon these were four-sided blocks of cedar
wood into which were fixed iron hooks, three rows to each, whereon
they used to hang (the slaughtered beasts). They used to flay them on
marble tables between the pillars. . . .

The lamb was not (wholly) bound but only tied, and they to whom
it fell to take the members laid hold on it. . . . He whose lot it was to
slaughter slaughtered it; and whose lot it was to receive the blood, received the blood and came to the northeastern corner of the Altar and
sprinkled it to the east and the north; and then he came to the southeast-
ern corner and sprinkled it to the east and the south. The residue of the
blood he poured out at the base (of the Altar) on the south side.

He (that slaughtered it) did not break its hind leg but pierced the
knee joint and so hung it up; he flayed it downwards as far as the breast;
when he reached the breast he cut off the head and gave to him whose
lot it was to take it.

*The slaughtering continues in a highly prescribed fashion, the limbs and liturgical
paraphernalia are distributed to the priests, who take them and place them on the
ramp leading up to the Altar.*

And then they came down and betook themselves to the Chamber
of Hewn Stone to recite the "Hear, O Lord" [that is, the *Shema*; see
below]. The officer said to them, "Recite a benediction!" They recited a
benediction, and recited the Ten Commandments, the *Shema* and the
"And it shall come to pass if you pay heed . . . " (Deut. 11:13–21) and the
"And the Lord spoke to Moses . . . " (Num. 15:37–41). They pronounced
three benedictions with the people: "True and firm" and the Abodah and
the Priestly Blessing (Num. 6:24–26), and on the Sabbath they pronounced a further benediction for the outgoing course of priests.

He said to them. "You that have never drawn the lot to make the
incense preparations, come and cast lots," and the lot fell upon whom it
fell. "Both you who have done it before and you who have not, come and
cast lots, which of you shall take up the members (of the lamb) from the
ramp of the Altar." . . . The other priests they delivered to the servants
of the officer of the Temple. These stripped them of their raiment and left

them with their drawers only. There were wall niches there whereon were written (the names of) the several articles of clothing. . . .

When the High Priest came in (to the Sanctuary) to prostrate himself, three priests held him, one by his right hand and one by his left hand and one by the precious stones; and when the officer heard the sound of the High Priest's feet as he came out (of his own chamber), he raised the curtain (of the Sanctuary) for him, and he went in and prostrated himself and came out. Then his brethren the priests went in and prostrated themselves and came out.

They came and stood on the steps of the Porch. . . . They then pronounced the Blessing (of the Priests) over the people as a single blessing; in the provinces it was pronounced as three blessings, but in the Temple as a single blessing. In the Temple they pronounced the (divine) Name as it was written, but in the provinces by a substituted word. . . . When the High Priest was minded to burn the offering, he used to ascend the ramp having the Prefect (of the priests) at his right hand. When he had reached the half way, the Prefect took him by the right hand and led him up. The first priest stretched out to him the head and the hind leg (of the lamb), and he laid his hands on them and threw them (into the Alter fire). . . . In like manner they held out to him the rest of the members (of the offering) and he laid his hands on them and threw them into the fire. When he was so minded, he only laid his hands on them and others threw them into the fire. Then he walked around the Altar. Where did he begin? From the corner on the southeast, and so to the northeast and to the northwest and to the southwest.

They (then) gave him the wine for the drink offering, and the Prefect stood by each horn of the Altar with a towel in his hands, and two priests stood at the table of the fat pieces (from the lamb) with two silver trumpets in their hands. They blew a prolonged, a quavering, and prolonged blast. Then they came and stood by Ben Arza [that is, the master of the cymbals], the one on his right and the other on his left. When he [that is, the High Priest] stooped to pour out the drink offering the Prefect waved the towel and Ben Arza clashed the cymbal and the Levites broke forth into singing. When they reached a break in the singing they blew upon the trumpets and the people prostrated themselves; at every break there was a blowing of the trumpet and at every blowing of the trumpet a prostration.

This was the rite of the daily whole offering in the service of the House of our God. May it be His will that it shall be built up again speedily, in our days. Amen. (M.Tamid 3:1–7:3)

9. The Pilgrimage Feasts

Three times a year you shall hold a festival for me. You shall observe the Feast of Unleavened Bread [Passover]—eating unleavened bread for seven days as I have commanded you—at the set time in the month of Abib, for in it you went out of the land of Egypt. . . . You shall celebrate the Feast of Harvest [Shabuoth or "Weeks"], of the firstfruits of your work, of what you sow in the field; and the Feast on the Ingathering [Sukkoth or "Tabernacles"] at the end of the year, when you gather in the results of your work from the field. These three times a year shall all your males appear before the Sovereign, the Lord. (Exodus 23:14–17)

There is another, more complete account of the holy days in Leviticus 23, again as part of the instructions imparted to Moses on Sinai.

The Lord spoke to Moses, saying: Speak to the Israelite people and say to them:

These are My fixed times, the fixed times of the Lord, which you shall proclaim as sacred occasions. [SABBATH] On six days work may be done, but on the seventh day there shall be a sabbath of complete rest, a sacred occasion. You shall do no work; it shall be a sabbath of the Lord throughout your settlements. (Leviticus 23:1–3)

. . . [PASSOVER] In the first month on the fourteenth day of the month, at twilight, there shall be a passover offering to the Lord, and on the fifteenth day of the month, the Lord's Feast of Unleavened Bread. You shall eat unleavened bread for seven days. The first day shall be for you a sacred occasion; you shall not work at your occupations. Seven days you shall make offerings by fire to the Lord. The seventh day shall be a sacred occasion: you shall not work at your occupations. (Leviticus 23: 4–8)

. . . [SHABUOTH] When you enter the land which I am giving you and you reap its harvest, you shall bring the first sheaf of your harvest to the priest. He shall wave the sheaf before the Lord for acceptance on your behalf. On the day you wave the sheaf, you shall offer as a burnt offering to the Lord a yearling lamb without blemish. The meal offering with it shall be two-tenths of a measure of choice flour with oil mixed in, an offering by fire of pleasing odor to the Lord; and the libation with it shall be of wine, a quarter of a *hin*. Until that very day, until you have brought the offering of your God, you shall eat no bread or parched grain or fresh ears; it is a law for all throughout the ages in your settlements.

From the day on which you bring the sheaf or wave offering—the day after the sabbath—you shall count off seven weeks. They must be complete: you must count until the day after the seventh week—fifty days [hence, in Greek, Pentecost or "Fifty"]; then you shall bring from your settlements two loaves of bread as a wave offering. . . . They are the Lord's firstfruits. With the bread you shall present, as burnt offerings to the Lord, seven yearling lambs without blemish, one bull of the herd, and two rams, with their meal offerings, and libations, an offering by fire of pleasing odor to the Lord. You shall also sacrifice one he-goat for a sin offering and two yearling lambs as a sacrifice of well-being. . . . On that same day you shall hold a celebration; it shall be a sacred occasion for you; you shall not work at your occupations. This is a law for all time in all your settlements, throughout the ages. (Leviticus 23:10–21)

[SUKKOTH] On the fifteenth day of the seventh month, when you have gathered the yield of your land, you shall observe the Lord's festival [of Tabernacles], for seven days: a complete rest on the first day, and a complete rest on the eighth day. . . . On the first day you shall take the product of *hadar* [traditionally, citrons], branches of palm trees, boughs of leafy trees, and willows of the brook, and you shall rejoice before the Lord your God for seven days. . . . You shall live in booths for seven days, all citizens in Israel shall live in booths, in order that future generations might know that I made the Israelite people live in booths when I brought them out of the land of Egypt, I, the Lord your God. (Leviticus 23:39–43)

The Mishna tractate Sukkah elaborates.

An arbor which is more than twenty ammot in height is not valid, and one which is less than ten handbreadths in height is not valid, or which does not have three walls, or which has a larger area shaded than unshaded, is not valid. If an arbor is old, the School of Shammai consider it invalid, and the School of Hillel says it is valid. What is an old arbor? One constructed thirty days before the festival. But if it was built specifically for the festival, it is valid even if made at the beginning of the year. (M.Sukkah 1:1)

Rabbi Eleazar said: A man is required to eat fourteen meals in the arbor, one during the day and one each evening. The Sages said: there is no prescribed number, but he must eat in the arbor on the first evening of the festival. Rabbi Eleazar also said: If a man has not eaten in the arbor on the first evening of the festival, he must fulfill the obligation on the last evening of the festival. The Sages said: You cannot speak of compensating for a missed obligation, for it is written, "That which is crooked cannot be made straight and that which is lacking cannot be counted" (Ecclesiastes 1:15). (Ibid. 2:6)

"And thus," Leviticus 23 concludes, "Moses announced to the Israelites the appointed seasons of the Lord."

10. Rosh Hashanah

In the seventh month, on the first day of the month, you shall observe a complete rest, a sacred occasion commemorated with loud blasts. You shall not work at your occupations; and you shall bring an offering by fire to the Lord. (Leviticus 23:23–25)

The Mishna notes this same sacred day that marked the beginning of a new year.

If Rosh Hashanah fell on the Sabbath, they blew the Shofar in the Temple, but not elsewhere. After the Temple was destroyed, Rabbi Yohanan ben Zakkai ruled that the Shofar might be blown wherever there was a court. Rabbi Eleazar said: Rabbi Yohanan ben Zakkai made this ruling only for Yabneh [where the Sanhedrin sat after 70 C.E.]. They answered him: It makes no difference whether it was Yabneh or any other place which has a court. (M.Rosh Hashanah 4:1)

11. Yom Kippur

Mark the tenth day of the seventh month as the Day of Atonement. It shall be a sacred occasion for you: you shall practice self-denial, and you shall bring an offering by fire to the Lord; you shall do no work throughout that day. For it is a Day of Atonement, on which expiation is made on your behalf before the Lord your God. Indeed, any person who does not practice self-denial throughout that day shall be cut off from his kin, and whoever does any work throughout that day, I will cause that person to perish from among his people. Do no work whatever; it is a law for all time, throughout the ages in all your settlements. It shall be a sabbath of complete rest for you, and you shall practice self-denial; on the ninth day of the month at evening, from evening to evening, you shall observe this your sabbath. (Leviticus 23:27–32)

Once again the Mishna spells out the legal details of observance.

On Yom Kippur eating, drinking, washing, anointing, putting on sandals, and sexual intercourse are forbidden. A king and a bride may wash their faces, and a woman who has just delivered a child may put on sandals. This was the opinion of Rabbi Eleazar. But the Sages forbade it. (M.Yoma 8:1)

Young children are not required to fast on Yom Kippur. But they should be trained a year or two in advance so that they may become accustomed to the obligation. (Ibid. 8:4)

If ravenous hunger seizes a man (who is fasting), he may be given even non-kosher things to eat until his eyes brighten. If a mad dog bites him, he may not be given a lobe of its liver to eat, but Rabbi Mattathiah ben Heresh permits it. Rabbi Mattathiah also said: If a man has a pain in his throat, they may drop medicine into his mouth (despite the fast) on the Sabbath, since it is possible his life is in danger. Whenever there is a possibility that life is in danger, this overrides the Sabbath. (Ibid. 8:6)

And Jesus on the same point:

On another occasion when he [that is, Jesus] went to synagogue, there was a a man in the congregation with a withered arm, and they were watching to see whether he would cure him on the Sabbath, so they could bring a charge against him. He said to the man with the withered arm, "Come and stand out here." Then he turned to them. "Is it permitted to do good or to do evil on the Sabbath, to save life or to kill?" They had nothing to say; and looking round at them with anger and sorrow at their obstinate stupidity, he said to the man, "Stretch out your arm." He stretched it out and his arm was restored. (Mark 3:1–5)

12. The Scapegoat

The Lord said to Moses: Tell your brother Aaron that he is not to come at will into the Shrine behind the curtain, in front of the cover that is upon the Ark, lest he die; for I appear in the cloud over the cover. Thus only shall Aaron enter the Shrine: with a bull of the herd for a sin offering and a ram for a burnt offering. . . . And from the Israelite community he shall take two he-goats for a sin offering and a ram for a burnt offering. Aaron is to offer his own bull as a sin offering and make expiation for himself and his household. Aaron shall take the two he-goats and let them stand before the Lord at the entrance of the Tent of Meeting; and he shall place lots upon the two goats, one marked for the Lord and the other marked for Azazel [possibly a demon once exorcised from the community]. Aaron shall bring forward the goat designated by lot for the Lord, which he is to offer as a sin offering, while the goat designated by lot for

Azazel shall be left standing alive before the Lord, to make expiation with it and to send it off to the wilderness for Azazel. . . .

(After sacrificing the bull) he shall take a firepan full of glowing embers scooped from the altar before the Lord, and two handfuls of finely ground aromatic incense, and bring this behind the curtain [that is, within the Holy of Holies]. He shall put the incense on the fire before the Lord, so that the cloud from the incense screens the cover over the [Ark of the] Pact lest he die. He shall take some of the bull's blood and sprinkle it with his finger over the cover on the east side; and in front of the cover he shall sprinkle some of the blood with his finger seven times.

There follows a ritual of purification for both the Tent of the Meeting and of the inner shrine, which was the prototype of the later Holy of Holies in Solomon's Temple.

When Aaron has finished purging the Shrine, the Tent of Meeting, and the altar, the live goat shall be brought forward. Aaron shall lay both his hands on the head of the live goat and confess over it all the iniquities and transgressions of the Israelites, whatever their sins, putting them on the head of the goat; and it shall be sent off into the wilderness through a designated man. Thus the goat shall carry on it all their iniquities to an inaccessible region; and the goat shall be set free in the wilderness. (Leviticus 16:3–22)

In most of the Mishnaic texts cited on Leviticus to this point the elaboration has been legal. Here the recollection—the ceremony had not been performed for over a century when these passages were edited—is liturgical.

He [the High Priest] then went to the scapegoat, placed both his hands on it, and confessed. He said: "O God, Thy people, the House of Israel, have committed iniquities, have transgressed, and have sinned before Thee. O God, forgive, I pray, the iniquities, transgressions and sins which Thy people Israel have committed and transgressed and sinned before Thee, as it is written in the Torah of Thy servant Moses: 'For on this day He shall atone for you to cleanse you; from all your sins you shall be clean before the Lord.' " When the priests and the people standing in the Temple court heard the Ineffable Name out of the mouth of the High Priest, they knelt and bowed down and fell on their faces and said: "Blessed by Thy Name, the glory of whose kingdom is forever and ever." (M.Yoma 6:2)

The High Priest was told: "The he-goat has reached the wilderness." How did they know that the he-goat had reached the wilderness? They set up sentinel posts and from these cloths were waved. Thus they knew that the he-goat had reached the wilderness. Rabbi Judah said: Did they not have a better sign? It was three miles from Jerusalem to Beth Haroro. Someone could walk a mile, return a mile, wait enough time to go another mile, and then they would know that the he-goat had reached the wilderness. Rabbi Ishmael said: Did they have another sign? A crimson thread was tied to the door of the Sanctuary. When the he-goat reached the wilderness, the thread turned white, as it is written: "Though your sins be as scarlet, they shall be as white as snow" (Isa. 1:18). (M.Yoma 6:8)

13. The Passover Commandment

Inserted in the description of the historical events surrounding the Israelites' departure from Egypt (Exodus 23ff.), the following instructions are found.

This day shall be to you one of remembrance: you shall celebrate it as a festival of the Lord throughout the ages; you shall celebrate it as an institution for all time. Seven days you shall eat unleavened bread; on the very first day you shall remove leaven from your houses, for whoever eats leavened bread from the first day to the seventh day, that person shall be cut off from Israel.

On the first day you shall hold a sacred convocation, and on the seventh day there shall be a sacred convocation; no work at all shall be done on them; only what every person is to eat, that alone may be prepared for you. You shall observe the [Feast of] Unleavened Bread because this was the very day on which I brought your ranks out of the land of Egypt; you shall observe this day throughout the ages as an institution for all time.

In the first month from the evening which begins the fourteenth day you shall eat unleavened bread until the evening which begins the twenty-first day of the month. No leaven shall be found in your houses for seven days. For whoever eats what is leavened, that person shall be cut off from the assembly of Israel, whether he is a stranger or a citizen of the country. . . . When you enter the land which the Lord will give you, as He promised, you shall observe this rite. And when your children ask you, "What do you mean by this rite?" you shall say, "It is the passover sacrifice to the Lord, because He passed over the houses of the Israelites in Egypt when He smote the Egyptians but saved our houses." (Exodus 12:14–20, 24–27)

14. The Figurative Interpretation of Passover

In the third book of his Guide of the Perplexed *the Torah scholar and philosopher Maimonides (d. 1204 C.E.) lays out what he regards as the reasons for the ceremonial prescriptions of the Torah—the feast days, the appointments of the sanctuary, the priestly vestments, and so on. The exercise is repeated in Questions 101–102 of the* Summa Theologica *of the Christian theologian Thomas Aquinas (d. 1274). In his literal interpretation of these same ceremonies Aquinas follows closely, and even explicitly, the reasons adduced by Maimonides. But for Aquinas, as for most of the Christian tradition, the liturgical prescriptions of the Mosaic Law had, in addition to their principal literal purpose of the suppression of idolatry, a further intent: to figure or foreshadow the New Covenant signaled by the incarnation of Jesus. Thus Aquinas on the literal and figurative cause of Passover.*

The literal reason for the Passover banquet was to commemorate the blessing of being led by God out of Egypt. Hence, by celebrating this banquet, they declared that they belonged to that people which God Himself had taken out of Egypt. For when they were delivered from Egypt they were commanded to sprinkle the lamb's blood on the lintels of their house doors, as though declaring that they were departing from the rites of the Egyptians who worshiped the ram. Hence, by sprinkling or rubbing the blood of the lamb on the doorposts, they were delivered from the danger of extermination which threatened the Egyptians. . . .

The figurative reason is evident, for the sacrifice of the Passover lamb signified the sacrifice of Christ, according to 1 Cor. 5:7, "Christ our Passover is sacrificed." The blood of the lamb, which ensured deliverance from the destroyer, by being sprinkled on the doorposts, signified faith in Christ's Passion in the hearts and on the lips of the faithful, by which same Passion we are delivered from sin and death, according to 1 Pet. 1:18: "You were . . . redeemed . . . with the precious blood . . . of a lamb unspotted." The partaking of its flesh signified the eating of Christ's body in the Sacrament (of the Eucharist); and the flesh was roasted in the fire to signify Christ's passion or charity. And it was eaten with unleavened bread to signify the blameless life of the faithful who partake of Christ's body, according to 1 Cor. 5:8: "Let us feast . . . with the unleavened bread of sincerity and truth." The wild lettuces were added to denote repentance for sins, which is required of those who receive the body of Christ. Their loins were girt in sign of chastity, and the shoes of their feet are the examples of our dead ancestors. The staves they held in their hands denoted pastoral authority; and it was commanded that the Passover lamb should be eaten in one house, that is, in the Catholic Church, and not in the conventicles of heretics. (Aquinas, *Summa Theologica* I/2, ques. 102, art. 5, ad 2) [AQUINAS 1945: 2:886–887]

15. The Upkeep of the Temple

The legislation on Sinai made elaborate and even generous provision, as we have seen, for the support of the priests and Levites dedicated to the service of the Lord. What changed over the centuries was the architectural institutionalization of that service in the Jerusalem Temple, which, with its altar, courts, and outbuildings, constituted an immense liturgical and commercial "industry." The Mosaic Law never envisioned such a permanent complex and had made no provisions for its upkeep or expenses; thus it fell to a later generation of Israelites to address the problem. Solomon himself may have done so, but our first detailed account comes a century and a half later, from the reign of Joash, king of Judah from 837 to 798 B.C.E.

Joash said to the priests, "All the money, current money, which is brought into the House of the Lord as sacred donations, any money a man may pay as the money equivalent of persons [cf. Leviticus 27:2–7] or any other money a man may be minded to bring to the House of the Lord, let the priests receive it, each from his benefactor; they, in turn, shall make repairs on the House, wherever damage may be found." But in the twenty-third year of the reign of Joash (it was found that) the priests had still not carried out repairs to the House. King Joash summoned the priest Jehoiada and the other priests and said to them, "Why have you not kept the House in repair? Henceforth do not accept money from your benefactors any more, but have it donated (directly) to the repair of the House." The priests agreed that they would neither accept money from the people nor undertake repairs on the House.

And the priest Jehoiada took a chest and bored a hole in its lid. He placed it at the right side of the altar as one entered the House of the Lord, and the priestly guards of the threshold deposited there all the money that was brought into the House of the Lord. Whenever they saw that there was much money in the chest, the royal scribe and the High Priest would come up and put the money accumulated in the House of the Lord into bags, and they would count it. Then they would deliver the money that was weighed out to overseers of the work, who were in charge of the House of the Lord. These in turn used it to pay the carpenters and the laborers who worked in the House of the Lord, and the masons and stonecutters. They also paid for the wood and the quarried stone with which to make repairs on the House of the Lord, and for every other expenditure that had to be made in repairing the house. However, no silver bowls and no snuffers, basins or trumpets—no vessels of gold or silver—were made at the House of the Lord from the money brought into the House of the Lord; this was given only to the overseers of the work for the repair of the House of the Lord. No check was kept on the men to whom the money was delivered to pay the workers; for they dealt honestly. Money brought as a guilt offering or a sin offering was not deposited in the House of the Lord; it went to the priests. (2 Kings 12:4–16)

16. Temple Finances after the Exile

After the Exile, in a now impoverished Judea, the question of Temple finances presented itself in a new and urgent form. One rather visionary solution was proposed by Ezekiel.

The burnt offerings, the meal offerings, and the libations on festivals, new moons, sabbaths—all fixed occasions—of the House of Israel shall be the obligation of the prince; he shall provide the sin offerings, the meal offerings, the burnt offerings and the offerings of well-being, to make expiation for Israel. (Ezekiel 45:17)

No Jewish prince arrived, however, to fulfill Ezekiel's vision, and the Temple, without endowed lands or estates, had to make shift as it could. One resource was a new tax voluntarily undertaken by the people at the time of Nehemiah and specifically earmarked for the Temple sacrifices.

We have laid upon ourselves obligations: To charge ourselves one-third of a shekel yearly for the service of the House of our God—for the rows of bread, for the regular meal offering, for the regular burnt offering, (for those of) the sabbaths, the new moons, festivals, for consecrations, for sin offerings to atone for Israel and for all the work in the House of the Lord.

We have cast lots among the priests, the Levites and the people, to bring the wood offering to the House of our God by clans annually at set times in order to provide fuel for the altar of the Lord our God, as is written in the Teaching [that is, the Torah].

We undertake to bring to the House of the Lord annually the first-fruits of our soil and of every fruit tree, also the firstborn of our sons and our beasts, as is written in the Teaching, and to bring the firstlings of our cattle and flocks to the House of our God for the priests who minister in the House of God.

We will bring to the storerooms in the House of our God the first pat of our dough, and our gifts [of grain] and of the fruit of every tree, wine and oil for the priests, and the tithes of our land for the Levites— the Levites who collect the tithes in all our towns subject to royal service. An Aaronite priest must be with the Levites when they collect the tithe; and the Levites must bring up a tithe of the tithes to the House of our God, to the storerooms of the treasury. For it is to the storerooms that the Israelites and the Levites must bring the gifts of grain, wine and oil. The equipment of the sanctuary and of the ministering priests and gate-keepers and the singers is also there. (Nehemiah 10:32–40)

17. Gentile Sacrifice

Gentiles too could offer certain freewill sacrifices in the Temple (M.Shekalim 1:5), but more consequential to the politics of the Temple was the principle that the ruler, Jew or Gentile, could and should contribute to the support of the Temple liturgy. We have explicit testimony in a decree of Antiochus III from about 200 B.C.E., preserved by Josephus.

First we have decided by reasons of piety to furnish for the sacrifices a contribution of sacrificial offerings and wine and oil and incense to the value of 20,000 (drachmas) of silver, and of flour of grain in sacred artabas according to the measure of the country, 1,460 mediamni of wheat and 375 mediamni of salt. I wish all these contributions be furnished them as I have commanded and that the work on the Temple be achieved, the stoas and whatever else needs be built. Let wood be provided from both Judea itself and from among the other peoples and from the Lebanon, without being taxed. Likewise for the other things required to make the restoration of the Temple outstanding. (Josephus, *Antiquities* 12.3.3)

The same point is made somewhat later in Maccabees, with some illuminating comments on the mischief inherent in the system.

During the rule of the High Priest Onias, the holy city (of Jerusalem) enjoyed complete peace and prosperity, and the laws were still observed most scrupulously, because he was a pious man and hated wickedness. The (Greek) kings themselves held the sanctuary in honor and used to embellish the Temple with the most splendid gifts; even Seleucus, king of Asia [Seleucus IV, 187–175 B.C.E.], bore all the expenses of the sacrificial worship from his own revenues.

But a certain Simon, of the clan of Bilgah, who had been appointed administrator of the Temple, quarreled with the High Priest about the regulations of the city market (of Jerusalem). Unable to get the better of Onias, he went to Apollonius son of Thraseus, then governor of Coele-Syria and Phoenicia, and alleged that the treasury at Jerusalem was full of untold riches, indeed the total of the accumulated balances was incalculable and did not correspond to the account of the sacrifices; he suggested that these balances might be brought under the control of the king. When Apollonius met the king, he reported what he had been told about the riches. The king selected Heliodorus, his chief minister, and sent him (to Jerusalem) with orders to remove those treasures. (2 Maccabees 3:1–7)

When the Romans exercised sovereignty over Palestine, they assumed in turn the responsibility of paying for the Temple sacrifices and the honor of having them offered on their behalf. And in 66 C.E., with rebellion brewing in Palestine, that became precisely the issue and, in the sequel, the casus belli *of one of the greatest debacles in Jewish history.*

Some of those most anxious for war made a concerted assault on a fort called Masada, captured it by stealth and exterminated the Roman garrison, installing a garrison of their own in its place. At that same time in the Temple courts Eleazar, son of Ananias the High Priest and a very confident young man, who was Temple Captain, persuaded the ministers of the Temple to accept no gift or offering from a foreigner. And it was this act that made war with Rome inevitable; for they abolished the sacrifices offered for Rome and Caesar himself, and in spite of the earnest appeals of the chief priests and prominent citizens not to cancel the customary offerings for the government, they would not give in.

Among those prominent citizens were the Pharisees, who, if they were unyielding in their punctiliousness in the case of the Jewish king Herod, showed themselves somewhat more pragmatic and accommodating in the case of the Gentile Romans.

Thereupon the principal citizens assembled with the chief priests and the most notable Pharisees to deliberate on the state of affairs, now that they were faced with what seemed like inevitable disaster. . . . They began by expressing their keenest indignation at the audacity of this revolt and their country being threatened with so serious a war. They then proceeded to expose the absurdity of the alleged pretext. Their forefathers, they said, had adorned the sanctuary mainly at the expense of aliens and had always accepted the gifts of foreign nations; not only had they never taken the sacrilegious course of forbidding anyone to offer sacrifices, but they had set up around the Temple the dedicatory offerings that were still to be seen and had remained there for so long a time. But now here were these men, who were provoking the arms of the Romans and courting a war with them, introducing a strange innovation into their religion, and besides endangering the city, laying it open to the charge of impiety, if henceforth it was the Jews alone who allowed no alien the right to sacrifice or worship.

Should such a law be introduced in the case of any private individual, [they continued,] they would be indignant at so inhuman a decree; yet they made light of putting the Romans and Caesar outside the pale. It was to be feared, moreover, that once they rejected the sacrifices for the Romans, they might not be allowed to offer sacrifices even for themselves, and that their city might be placed outside the pale of the empire, unless, with a quick return to discretion, they restored the sacrifices and made amends for the insult before the report reached the ears of those whom they had insulted.

In the course of these pleas, they produced priestly experts on the traditions, who declared that all their ancestors had accepted the sacrifices of aliens. But not one of the revolutionary party would listen to them; even the Temple ministers failed to come to their support and were thus instrumental in bringing about the war. (Josephus, *War* 2.17.1–4)

18. Changing Attitudes toward Sacrifice

Hear the word of the Lord, you chieftains of Sodom;
Give ear to the Lord's instruction,
    You folk of Gomorrah!
"What need have I of all your sacrifices?"
    says the Lord.
"I am sated with the burnt offerings of rams,
    and the suet of fatlings;
    And blood of bulls;
    I have no delight in lambs and he-goats.
That you come to appear before Me—
Who asked that of you?
Trample my courts no more;
    Bringing oblations is futile.
    Incense is offensive to Me.
New moons and sabbaths, proclaiming of solemnities,
    Assemblies with iniquity,
    I cannot abide.
Your new moons and fixed seasons

Fill Me with loathing;
 they are become a burden to Me,
 I cannot endure them.
And when you lift up your hands,
 I will turn my eyes away from you.
Though you pray at length,
I will not listen.
Your hands are stained with crime—
Wash yourselves clean;
Put your evil doings
 Away from My sight.
Cease to do evil;
 Learn to do good.
Devote yourselves to justice;
 Aid the wronged.
Uphold the rights of the orphan;
Defend the cause of the widow."
(Isaiah 1:10–17)

What can I do for you, Ephraim,
What can I do for you, Judah?
When your goodness is like morning clouds
Like dew so early gone?
That is why I have hewn down the prophets,
Have slain them with the words of My mouth:
And the day that dawned brought on your punishment.
For I desire goodness, not sacrifice,
Obedience to God rather than burnt offerings.
(Hosea 6:4–6)

I loathe, I spurn your festivals;
I am not appeased by your solemn assemblies.
If you offer Me burnt offerings—or your meal offerings,
I will not accept them,
I will pay no heed to your gifts of fatlings.
Spare Me the sound of your songs;
And let Me not hear the music of your lutes.
But let justice well up like a river
And righteousness like an unfailing stream.
Did you offer sacrifices and oblations to Me

Those forty years in the wilderness,
O House of Israel?

And you shall carry off your "king"—
Sikkuth and Kiyyun
The images you have made for yourselves
Of your astral deity—
As I drive you into exile beyond Damascus.
(Amos 5:21–27)

19. The Herodian Temple

These late prophetic sentiments did not signal any diminution of popular or official approval of the Temple cult. Zerubbabel's restored Second Temple may have been a relatively modest affair in the wretched circumstances under which it was constructed; but when the resources were available, as they were under Herod (37–4 B.C.E.), a new and more magnificent structure was built upon Mount Moriah in Jerusalem. Josephus is our guide to the inside of the new Jerusalem Temple, which he himself had seen.

Within it [that is, the unrestricted Court of the Gentiles] and not far distant was a second court, accessible by a few steps and surrounded by a stone balustrade with an inscription prohibiting the entry of a foreigner under threat of penalty of death. On its southern and northern side the inner court had three-chambered gateways, equally distant from one another, and on the side where the sun rises it had one great gateway [that is, Nicanor's Gate], through which those of us who were ritually clean used to pass with our wives. Within this court was the sacred court where women were forbidden to enter, and still further within was a third court into which only priests were permitted to go. In this (priests' court) was the Temple (proper), and before it was an altar on which we used to sacrifice whole burnt offerings to God. Into none of these courts did King Herod enter since he was not a priest and was therefore prevented from so doing. But with the construction of the porticoes and the outer courts he did busy himself, and these he finished building in eight years. The Temple (proper) itself was built by the priests in a year and six months, and all the people were filled with joy and offered thanks to God, first of all for the speed (of the work) and next for the king's zeal, and as they celebrated they acclaimed the restoration. (Josephus, *Antiquities* 15.11.5–7)

The Mishna treatise Middoth, which has an elaborate treatment of the chambers of the Temple, also supplies some additional information on the courts.

The Temple Mount measured five hundred cubits by five hundred cubits. Its largest open space was to the south, the next largest to the east, the third largest to the north, and its smallest (open space) was to the west; the place where its measure was greatest was where its use was greatest.

Inside the Temple Mount was a latticed railing, ten handbreadths high. It had thirteen breaches which the Grecian kings had made; they were fenced up again and over against them thirteen prostrations were decreed. Inside this was the Rampart, ten cubits broad. . . .

All the walls there were high, save only the eastern wall, because the (High) Priest that burns the (Red) Heifer and stands on the top of the Mount of Olives should be able to look directly into the entrance of the Sanctuary when the blood is sprinkled. (M.Middoth 2:1, 3, 4)

The careful distinction of the courts, even to the posting of a public warning in Greek and Latin threatening death to intruders beyond the stone balustrade, is the working out in architectural terms of the degrees of holiness focused in that place. The Mishna treatise Kelim sets them out, beginning with the Land of Israel and ending in the inner courts of the Temple.

The Temple Mount is still more holy (than the city of Jerusalem), for no man or woman that has the flux, no menstruant, and no woman after childbirth may enter therein. The Rampart is still more holy, for no Gentiles and none that have contracted uncleanness from a corpse may enter therein. The Court of the Women is still more holy, for none that has immersed himself the selfsame day (because of uncleanness) may enter therein, yet none would thereby become liable to a sin offering. The Court of the Israelites is still more holy, for none whose atonement is yet incomplete may enter therein, and they would thereby become liable to a sin offering. The Court of the Priests is still more holy, for Israelites may not enter therein, save only when they must perform the laying on of hands, slaughtering and waving.

Between the Porch and the Altar is still more holy, for none that has a blemish or whose hair is unloosed may enter there. The Sanctuary is still more holy, for none may enter therein with hands or feet unwashed. The Holy of Holies is still more holy, for none may enter therein save only the High Priest on the Day of Atonement at the time of the (Temple) service. Rabbi Yosi said: In five things is the space between the Porch and the

Altar equal to the Sanctuary: for they may not enter there that have a blemish, or that have drunk wine, or that have hands or feet unwashed, and men must keep far from between the Porch and the Altar at the time of the burning of incense. (M.Kelim 1:8–9)

20. The Sanctuary

And finally, there was the Temple proper, the sanctuary building that housed the Holy of Holies, where the presence of God still dwelled among His people.

Passing within one found oneself in the ground floor of the Sanctuary. This was sixty cubits in height, the same in length, and twenty cubits in breadth. But the sixty cubits of its length were again divided. The front portion, partitioned off at forty cubits, contained within it three most wonderful works of art, universally renowned: a lampstand, a table and and an altar of incense. The seven lamps (such being the number of the branches of the lampstand) represented the planets; the loaves on the table, twelve in number, the circle of the Zodiac and the year; while the altar of incense, by the thirteen fragrant spices from sea and from land, both desert and inhabited, with which it was replenished, signified that all things are of God and for God.

The innermost recess measured twenty cubits, and was screened in like manner from the outer portion by a veil. In this stood nothing whatever; unapproachable, inviolable, invisible to all, it was called the Holy of Holies.

In front of it (the Sanctuary) stood the altar, fifteen cubits high, and with a breadth and length extending alike to fifty cubits, in shape a square with hornlike projections at the corners, and approached from the south by a gently sloping acclivity. No iron was used in its construction, nor did iron ever touch it. (Josephus, *War* 5.5.5–6)

21. The Qumran Community as the Temple of God

There may have been misgivings about Herod both as as a ruler and as a Jew, but the main body of Jews accepted his Temple as a legitimate successor to the Houses of the Lord built by Solomon and Zerubbabel. But not so the priesthoods that served in it. The problem of the legitimacy of the post-Exilic priesthood has nothing to do with Herod but goes back to an earlier era, the Hasmonean monarchy, when a number of Jews refused to accept the validity of the Temple priesthood in the restored

Jewish state and so the validity of the very sacrifices performed by them in the Jerusalem Temple. That, at any rate, is how we read the somewhat opaque allusions that occur in the writings of a body of Jews who withdrew into a separatist community at Qumran at the northwest corner of the Dead Sea. Both the "Community Rule" that formed part of their library, the famous "Dead Sea Scrolls," and another, related document called the "Damascus Rule" make reference to a profanation of the Temple in their day, that is, sometime in the first or second century B.C.E. The Qumran Community Rule describes the consequences in terms of Temple ritual.

In the Council of the Community there shall be twelve men and three Priests, perfectly versed in all that is revealed of the Law, whose works shall be truth, righteousness, justice, loving kindness and humility. They shall preserve the faith in the Land with steadfastness and meekness, and shall atone for sin by the practice of justice and by suffering the sorrows of affliction. They shall walk with all men according to the standard of truth and the rule of time.

When these are in Israel, the Council of the Community shall be established in truth. It shall be an everlasting plantation, a House of Holiness for Israel, an Assembly of Supreme Holiness for Aaron. They shall be witnesses to the truth at the Judgment, and shall be the Elect of Goodwill who shall atone for the Land and pay to the wicked their reward. It shall be that tried wall, that "precious cornerstone" whose foundations shall neither rock nor sway in their place (Isa. 28:16). It shall be a Most Holy Dwelling for Aaron, with everlasting knowledge of the Covenant of justice, and shall offer up a sweet fragrance. It shall be a House of Perfection and Truth in Israel that they may establish a Covenant according to the everlasting precepts. And they shall be an agreeable offering, atoning for the Land and determining the judgment of wickedness, and there shall be no more iniquity. (*The Community Rule* 8)

[VERMES 1968: 85]

When these (initiates) become members of the Community in Israel according to all these rules, they shall establish the spirit of holiness according to everlasting truth. They shall atone for guilty rebellion and for sins of unfaithfulness that they may obtain loving kindness for the Land without the flesh of holocausts and the fat of sacrifice. And prayer rightly offered shall be as an acceptable fragrance of righteousness, and perfection of way as a delectable freewill offering. At that time the men of the community shall set apart a House of Holiness in order that it may be united to the most holy things and a House of Community for Israel, for those who walk in perfection. The sons of Aaron alone shall command in matters of justice and property, and every rule concerning the men of the Community shall be determined according to their word. (Ibid. 9) [VERMES 1968: 87]

22. "Mercy Not Sacrifice Is My Desire"

The tractate Middoth, from which the following reflections upon the Temple and its sacrifices are drawn, was collected into the Mishna sometime about 200 C.E., or 130 years after the physical building of the Temple was utterly destroyed in 70 C.E., so that the Christians could say of it, as Jesus had predicted, "not a stone stood upon a stone." In some sense, on a spiritual or an ideal plane, the Jerusalem Temple still existed for those rabbis. But the ritual conservatism implicit in those carefully preserved details of Temple and courts and now defunct rituals masks a deeper adjustment to a new reality. Those rabbinic sages had also reflected on the prophetic wisdom of Hosea and Amos and begun the painful revision of their thinking. And according to one account, that process was begun almost immediately after the event by Yohanan ben Zakkai himself, the very sage who escaped the city on the eve of its destruction and who gave shape and form to much of the rabbinic thinking that followed.

Once, as Rabban Yohanan ben Zakkai was coming forth from Jerusalem, Rabbi Joshua followed him and saw the Temple in ruins. "Woe unto us," Rabbi Joshua cried, "that this, the place where the iniquities of Israel were atoned for, is laid waste."

"My son," Rabban Yohanan said to him, "be not grieved. We have another atonement as effective as this." "And what is it?" "It is acts of loving kindness, as it is said, 'For mercy not sacrifice is My desire' (Hos. 6:6)." [ABOTH RABBI NATHAN 1955: 4:3]

"Acts of loving kindness" are not further specified in the text. Perhaps there was no need, since another, more practical and concrete theme was soon woven into the meditation: Torah study.

Simeon the Just [perhaps the same High Priest celebrated by Jesus ben Sira in the passage from Ecclesiasticus 50 already cited] was among the last of the men of the Great Assembly. He used to say: By three things is the world sustained: by the Law, by the Temple service and by deeds of loving kindness. (M.Aboth 1:2)

How so the Torah? Behold, it says, "Mercy is my desire and not sacrifice, not whole offerings but the knowledge of God" (Hos. 6:6). Hence we see that the whole offering is the most beloved of sacrifices, for the whole offering is entirely consumed by the flames. . . . But the study of the Torah is more beloved by God than whole offerings. For if a man studies Torah, he comes to know the will of God, as it is said, "Then shall you understand the fear of the Lord and find the will of God" (Prov. 2:5). Hence, when a sage sits and expounds to his congregation, Scripture accounts it to him as though he had offered up fat and blood on the altar. [ABOTH RABBI NATHAN 1955: 4:1]

23. The Nature of Ritual Acts According to Judah Halevi

Freed of the literal obligation to perform a sacrificial liturgy, an even later genera-tion of Jews was also free to contemplate the deeper significance of those acts, as Judah Halevi does in this passage.

All these ceremonies, the remission of sins on the Day of Atonement, the cleansing of the sanctuary from impurities by means of the he-goat of Azazel, with all the accompanying ceremonies; the blessing of Israel through Aaron's uplifted hands, and the reciting of the verse "The Lord bless you"; upon every one of these ceremonies the Divine Influence rested. Religious ceremonies are, like the works of nature, composed of accurately measured proportions of the four elements. A trifle renders them perfect and gives them their proper animal or plant form. Every mixture receives the shape proper to it but can also lose it through a trifle. . . . Who, then, can calculate actions upon which the Divine Influ-ence rests, save God alone? This is the mistake made by alchemists and necromancers [that is, those who sought to duplicate nature]. The former thought, indeed, that they could weigh the elementary fire on their scales and produce what they wished, and thus alter the nature of materials, as is done in living beings by natural heat which transforms food into blood, flesh, bones and other organs. . . .

When these necromancers heard that the appearance of the Deity from Adam down to the Children of Israel was gained by sacrifices, they thought it was the result of meditation and research; that the prophets were but deeply learned persons who accomplished their wonders by means of calculations. Then they, for their part, were anxious to fix sacrifices to be offered up at certain times and astrological opportunities, accompanied by ceremonies and burning of incense which their calcula-tions prescribed. . . . The artificial is not like the natural, however, and religious acts are like nature. Being ignorant of their designs, one thinks of it as nothing but play until the results become apparent. Then one praises their guide and mover and professes belief in Him.

Suppose you heard nothing about intercourse and its consequences, but you feel yourself attracted by the lowest of female organs. If you thought only about the degradation of woman's surrender to you, or the ignominy of surrendering yourself to a woman, you would say wonderingly, this is as vain as it is absurd! But when you see a being like yourself born of a woman, then you marvel and take note that you are one of the preservers of mankind created by God to inhabit the earth. It is the same with religious actions fixed by God. You slaughter a lamb and smear yourself with its blood in skinning it, cleaning its entrails, washing, dismembering it and sprinkling its blood. Then you arrange the wood, kindle the fire, place the body upon it. If this were not done in consequence of a divine command, you would think little of all these actions and think that they estranged you from God rather than bringing you nearer to Him. But as soon as the whole is properly accomplished, and you see the divine fire, or notice in yourself a new spirit, unknown before, or see true visions and great apparitions, you are aware that this is the fruit of the preceding acts, as well as of the great influence with which you have come in contact. (Judah Halevi, *The Khazar King*) [HALEVI 1905: 181–183]

24. Maimonides and Aquinas on Prayer and Sacrifice

Maimonides distinguished between the primary intention of the Law—the inculcation of true opinions about the existence and nature of God—and a secondary intention: the gradual abolition of idolatry. The same distinction may be observed with regard to the specific prescriptions of the Law, and here he applies it to Torah commands to prayer and sacrifice and supplies as well a gloss on the kinds of prophetic texts already cited.

I return to my subject and I say, as this kind of worship—I mean the sacrifices—pertains to a second intention [that is, the abolition of idolatry], whereas invocation, prayer and similar modes of worship come closer to the first intention and are necessary for its achievement, He [that is, God] made a great difference between the two kinds. For one kind of worship, I mean the offering of sacrifices, even though it was done in His name, may He be exalted, was not prescribed to us in the way it existed at first; I mean to say in such a way that sacrifices could be offered in every place and at every time. Nor could a temple be set up in any fortuitous place nor could any fortuitous man offer the sacrifice: "Whosoever would, he consecrated him" (1 Kgs. 13:33). On the contrary, He forbade all this and established one single house (as the Temple), "Unto the place which the Lord shall chose" (Deut. 12:26), so that the sacrifices should not be offered elsewhere: "That you offer not your burnt offerings in every place you see" (Deut. 12:13). Also only the offspring of one particular family can be priests. All this was intended to restrict this kind of worship, so that only the portion of it should subsist whose abolition is not required by His wisdom. On the other hand, invocations and prayers are made in every place and by anyone whoever he may be. This also applies to the fringes, the (prayers on) doorposts, and the phylacteries and other similar modes of worship.

Because of this notion I have revealed to you, people are frequently blamed in the books of the Prophets because of their zeal for sacrifices, and it is explained to them that they are not the object of a purpose sought for its own sake and that God can dispense with them. Thus Samuel says: "Has the Lord as great delight in burnt offerings and sacrifices as in hearkening to the voice of the Lord . . . " (1 Sam. 15:22). And Isaiah says: " 'To what purpose is your multitude of sacrifices to me?' says the Lord . . . " (Isa. 1:11) And Jeremiah says: "For I spoke not to your fathers, nor commanded them in the day I brought them out of the land of Egypt, concerning burnt offerings or sacrifices; but this thing I commanded them, saying: Hearken to My voice and I will be your God and you will be My people" (Jer. 7:22–23). This dictum has been regarded as difficult by everyone whose words I have seen or heard. They say: How can Jeremiah say of God that He has given us no injunctions concerning burnt offerings and sacrifices, seeing that the great part of the commandments are concerned with these things? However, the purpose of the dictum is as I have explained to you. For He says that the first intention consists only in your apprehending Me and not worshiping someone other than Me: "And I will be your God and you will be My people." These laws concerning sacrifices and going to the Temple were given for the sake of the realizing of this fundamental principle. It is for the sake of that principle that I transferred these modes of worship to My name, so that the trace of idolatry be effaced and the fundamental principle of My unity be established. . . .

I have another way of interpreting this verse; it too leads to the very same purpose that we have mentioned. It has been made clear in both the (scriptural) text and in the tradition that in the first legislation given to us there was nothing at all concerning burnt offerings and sacrifices. You ought not to occupy your mind with the passover of Egypt [that is, the sacrifice of the lamb already prescribed in Egypt] for the reason for this is clear and evident, as we shall set forth. . . . The first command given after the exodus from Egypt was the one given us in Marah, namely His saying to us there: "If you will diligently hearken to the voice of the Lord etc." (Exod. 15:26). "There He made them a statute and a judgment etc." (Exod. 15:25). And the correct tradition says: "The Sabbath and the civil laws were prescribed at Marah" (B.Shabbat 87b; B.Sanhedrin 56b). Accordingly, the statute referred to is the Sabbath and the judgment consists in the civil laws, that is, the abolition of mutual wrongdoing. And this is, as we have explained, the first intention: I mean the belief in correct opinions, namely, in the creation of the world in time. For you already know that the foundation of the law addressed to us concerning the Sabbath is its contribution to fortifying this principle, as we have explained in this treatise. Besides the correctness of the beliefs, the intention also included the abolition of wrongdoing among men. (Maimonides, *Guide* 3.32) [MAIMONIDES 1963: 529–531]

Aquinas (d. 1274 C.E.) took Maimonides' argument to its conclusion, driven not so much by logic as by his own Christian reading of God's sacred purpose.

The New Law does not void the observance of the Old Law except in the matter of the ceremonial precepts. Now the latter were figurative of things to come. Therefore, from the very fact that the ceremonial precepts were fulfilled when those things were accomplished which they foreshadowed, it follows that they were no longer to be observed; for if they were to be observed, this would mean that something was still to be accomplished and is not yet fulfilled. Thus the promise of a future gift holds no longer when it has been fulfilled by the presentation of the gift. In this way the legal ceremonies are abolished by being fulfilled. (Aquinas, *Summa Theologica* I/2, ques. 107, art. 2, ad 1) [AQUINAS 1945: 2:961–962]

25. The Synagogue Liturgy

We cannot trace the exact origins of the synagogue, though the existence of some kind of institution combining prayer and Torah study may well go back to the time of the Exile, when the Jews in Iraq had to make do without a Temple and sacrifice. Whatever the case, there were synagogues in Palestine and the Diaspora by the first century. Philo, an eminent Jewish scholar of that era in Alexandria, appears to refer to a service in one such in the following passages.

CHAPTER 1

Innumerable schools of practical wisdom and self-control are opened every seventh day in all cities. In these schools the people sit decorously, keeping silence and listening with the utmost attention out of a thirst for refreshing discourse, while one of the best qualified stands up and instructs them in what is best and most conducive to well-being, things by which their whole life may be made better. (Philo, *On the Special Laws* 2.15)

He [Moses] required them to assemble at the same place on these seventh days, and sitting together in a respectful and orderly manner, hear the laws read so that none should be ignorant of them. And indeed they always assemble and sit together, most of them in silence except when it is the practice to add something to signify their approval of what is read. But some priest who is present or one of the elders reads the holy laws to them and expounds them point by point until about the late afternoon, when they depart, having gained expert knowledge of the holy laws and considerable advance in piety. (Philo in Eusebius, *Evangelical Preparation* 8.7)

This latter passage appears to refer to the homiletic part of a synagogue service. In our earliest accounts from Palestine, which occur in the Gospels, the emphasis is likewise on the guest preacher's discourse on the Scriptures.

They came to Capernaum, and on the Sabbath he [that is, Jesus] went to synagogue and began to teach. The people were astounded at his teaching, for, unlike the doctors of the Law, he taught with a note of authority. (Mark 1:21–22)

Then Jesus, armed with the power of the Spirit, returned to Galilee; and reports about him spread through the whole countryside. He taught in their synagogues and all men sang his praises.

So he came to Nazareth, where he had been brought up, and went to synagogue on the Sabbath day as he regularly did. He stood up to read the lesson and was handed the scroll of the prophet Isaiah. He opened the scroll and found the passage that says, "The spirit of the Lord is upon me because He has anointed me; He has sent me to announce good news to the poor, to proclaim the release for prisoners and recovery of sight for the blind, to let the broken victims go free, to proclaim the year of the Lord's favor" (Isa. 61:1–2).

He rolled up the scroll, gave it back to the attendant, and sat down. And all eyes in the synagogue were fixed on him. He began to speak. "Today," he said, "in your very hearing this text has come true." There was a general stir of admiration; they were surprised that words of such grace should fall from his lips. "Is not this Joseph's son?" they asked. (Luke 4:14–22)

26. The *Shema* ("Hear!")

From these brief texts we cannot conclude what prayers were said as part of the service or even whether the reading from Isaiah was part of the regular cycle of biblical passages that was later characteristic of the synagogue liturgy. That there were standardized prayers from the beginning and that they derived in the main from Scripture seems almost certain. One prayer taken over intact from the earlier Temple liturgy and whose recitation was obligatory, morning and evening, upon every Jew was the Shema, *"Hear!" so called from its opening phrase. The whole was derived directly from the Torah.*

Hear, O Israel! The Lord is our God, the Lord alone. You shall love the Lord your God with all your heart and with all your soul and with all your might. Take to heart these instructions with which I charge you this day. Impress them upon your children. Recite them when you stay at home and when you are away, when you lie down and when you get up. Bind them as a sign on your hand and let them serve as a symbol [or "frontlet"] between your eyes; inscribe them on the doorposts of your house and your gates. (Deuteronomy 6:4–9)

The Lord spoke to Moses as follows: Speak to the Israelite people and instruct them to make for themselves fringes on the corners of their garments throughout the ages; let them attach a cord of blue to the fringe at each corner. That shall be your fringe; look at it and recall all the commandments of the Lord and observe them, so that you do not follow your heart and eyes in your lustful urge. Thus you will be reminded to observe all My commandments and to be holy to your God. I am the Lord your God who brought you out of the land of Egypt to be your God. I, the Lord your God. (Numbers 15:37–41)

The Mishna provides additional details on the recitation of these scriptural prayers.

If a man recites the "O Hear" so softly that he himself cannot hear, he has nevertheless fulfilled the obligation. Rabbi Yosi says: He has not fulfilled it. If he recites it without pronouncing the words distinctly, Rabbi Yosi says he has fulfilled the obligation; Rabbi Judah says he has not. If a man recites the paragraphs in the wrong order, he has not fulfilled the obligation. If he recites it and makes a mistake, he must go back and recite it again. (M.Berakoth 2:3)

Women, slaves and minors are exempt from reciting the "O Hear" and from putting on phylacteries [that is, the "frontlets" of Deuteronomy 6:8]. But they are obliged to say "the Prayer" [that is, the *tefilla*; see below], to perform the obligation of affixing and kissing a mezuza (next to the doorpost) and to say the blessing after meals. (Ibid. 3:3)

27. "The Prayer" (*Tefilla*)

The liturgical "prayer" (tefilla) par excellence was the Amida, said thrice daily while standing. Attested to from about 100 C.E. onward, it comprised the Shemoneh esreh, the "eighteen" benedictions that lay at the heart of the daily synagogue services, and, in a slightly reduced version, those of the Sabbath and other festivals.

God, open my lips, and my mouth shall pronounce Thy praise.

1. Blessed be You, O God, the God of our fathers, the God of Abraham, Isaac and Jacob, the great God, strong and terrible, most exalted One, Creator of heaven and earth, our shield and the shield of our fathers, our trust in every generation. Blessed be You, O God, the shield of Abraham.

2. You are strong, humiliating those who exalt themselves and pronouncing judgment against the oppressors. You live forever, bringing the dead back to life. You cause the wind to blow and the dew to fall. You support the living and revive the dead, and on a sudden You will bring us salvation. Blessed be You, O God, who brings the dead back to life.

3. You are holy and Your name is awe-inspiring. There is no god besides You. Blessed be You, O God, the Holy God.

4. Favor us with the knowledge which comes from You, and with the intelligence and understanding which comes from Your Torah. Blessed be You, O God, who favors us with knowledge.

5. Cause us to return unto You, O God, and we shall return. Renew our days as before. Blessed be You, O God, who delights in our conversion.

6. Forgive us, O Father, for we have sinned against You; wipe out and remove our iniquities from before Your eyes, for great is Your mercy. Blessed be You, O God, who forgives abundantly.

7 Look upon our distress and fight for us; redeem us because of Your Name. Blessed by You, O God, Redeemer of Israel.

8. Cure us, O God, of the wounds of our hearts, of sorrow and longing. Remove them from us and heal our sickness. Blessed be You, who heals the sicknesses of Your people Israel.

9. Bless this year, O our God, on our behalf, so that it shall be good for all kinds of harvests, and let us see soon the time of our redemption. Send dew and rain to the earth, and feed the earth with the treasures of Your goodness and blessings. Blessed be You, O God, who blesses the years.

10. Sound the great trumpet for our freedom, and raise the standard for the calling together of our exiles. Blessed be You, O God, who gathers the scattered members of Your people Israel.

11. Restore our judges and our counselors as at the beginning. And be You alone ruler over us. Blessed be You, O God, who loves justice.

12. Let there be no hope for renegades, and wipe out the kingdom of pride speedily in our days, and may all Nazarenes and heretics perish instantly, may their names be erased from the Book of Life and not be inscribed with those of the righteous. Blessed be You, O God, who humbles the proud.

13. May You have mercy on those who are converted to justice, and give us ample reward together with those who do Your will. Blessed be You, O God, the trust of the righteous.

14. Have mercy on Your people Israel, on Your city of Jerusalem, on Sion the dwelling place of Your glory, on Your Temple, and on the kingship of the house of David, Your truly anointed one. Blessed be You, O God, the God of David, who builds Jerusalem.

15. Hear, O God, the voice of our prayer and have pity on us, because You are a God full of grace and mercy. Blessed be You, O God, who hears prayer.

16. Be gracious to us and dwell in Sion, and may Your servants serve You in Jerusalem. Blessed be You, O God, whom we serve in reverence.

17. We thank You, our God and the God of our fathers, for all Your kindnesses, for Your love and mercy which You have bestowed on us and upon our fathers. When we stumble, Your love supports us. Blessed be You, O God, who loves to be gracious.

18. Send Your peace to Your people Israel and to Your city and Your portion, and bless us all together. Blessed be You, O God, who makes peace.

Certain rabbis attempted to push the origin of these prayers as far back as patriarchal times, though another tradition connected them directly with the destruction of the Temple in 70 C.E.

It has been stated: Rabbi Yosi son of Rabbi Hanina said: The Tefillas were instituted by the Patriarchs. Rabbi Joshua ben Levi says: The Tefillas were instituted (by the men of the Great Assembly) to replace the daily sacrifices. It has been taught in accordance with Rabbi Yosi ben Hanina and it has (likewise) been taught in accordance with Rabbi Joshua ben Levi. According to Rabbi Yosi ben Hanina Abraham instituted the morning Tefilla, as it says, "And Abraham got up early in the morning to the place where he had stood" (Gen. 19:27), and "standing" means only prayer, as it says, "Then stood up Phineas and prayed" (Ps. 106:30). Isaac instituted the afternoon Tefilla, as it says, "And Isaac went out to meditate in the field at eventide" (Gen. 24:63), and "meditation" means only prayer, as it says, "A prayer of the afflicted when he faints and pours out his meditation before the Lord" (Ps. 102:1). Jacob instituted the evening prayer, as it says, "And he lighted upon the place." (BT.Berakoth 26b)

As the same text in the Babylonian Talmud continues, it becomes unmistakable that the thrice-daily prayer in the synagogue was in fact set down next to, in time if not in place, the prescribed Temple rituals.

Why did they say that the morning "Prayer" could be said until midday? Because the regular morning sacrifice could be brought up to midday. . . . And why did they say that the afternoon "Prayer" can be said up to the evening? Because the regular afternoon offering can be brought up to evening. . . . And why did they say that for the evening "Prayer" there is no limit? Because the members and the fat (of the whole offering) which were not consumed (on the altar) by the evening could be brought for the whole of the night. (Ibid.)

28. The Synagogue Cycle of Scriptural Readings

As we saw in the vignette of Jesus in the synagogue of Nazareth, the service in his day included a reading from Scripture, in his case Isaiah, and perhaps some instruction as well, as appears from this example from a Christian source, in this instance concerning Paul and companions in a Diaspora synagogue at Antioch in Pisidia.

On the Sabbath they went to synagogue and took their seats; and after the reading from the Law and the Prophets, the official of the synagogue sent this message to them: "Friends, if you have anything to say to the people by way of exhortation, let us hear it." Paul rose, made a gesture with his hand, and began. (Acts 13:14–16)

As with the synagogue "prayers," the public and liturgical reading of the Law goes back to Temple times—if not to Moses, as some authors claimed, then at least from the time that Ezra stood in the Temple and supervised the reading of the Torah.

Ezra opened the scroll in the sight of all the people, for he was (standing) above the people; as he opened it, all the people stood up. Ezra blessed the Lord, the great God, and all the people answered, "Amen, Amen," with hands upraised. Then they bowed their heads and prostrated themselves before the Lord with their faces to the ground . . . and the Levites explained the Teaching [that is, the Torah] to the people while the people stood in their places. They read from the scroll of the Law of God, translating it and giving it sense; so they understood the reading. (Nehemiah 8:5–8)

And again, at that very Feast of Tabernacles or Sukkoth:

He read from the scroll of the Torah of God each day, from the first to the last day. They celebrated the festival seven days, and there was a solemn gathering on the eighth, as prescribed. (Nehemiah 8:18)

By the middle of the first Christian century, then, the formal reading of the Law was taking place in synagogues on the Sabbath, and presumably on other festivals as well, now accompanied by selections from the Prophets. How formal or structured this practice was we cannot say, but by the time we reach our next witness, the Mishnaic tractate Megillah, the process is formal indeed.

And in the beginnings of the months and during the mid-festival [that is, in the days intervening before the opening and closing days of Passover and Sukkoth] the Law is read by four (readers); they may not take from them or add to them, and they do close with a reading from the Prophets. He that begins the reading of the Law and he that completes it say a Benediction, the one at the beginning and the other at the end. . . . On a festival day it is read by five, on the Day of Atonement by six and on the Sabbath by seven (readers). They may not take from them but they may add to them and they close with a reading from the Prophets. . . .

He that reads in the Law may not read than less than three verses; he may not read to the interpreter [that is, the translator from Hebrew in to Aramaic] more than one verse (at a time), or in (a reading from the Prophets), three verses, but if these three are three separate paragraphs, he must read them out singly. They may leave out verses in the Prophets, but not in the Law. How much may they leave out? Only so much that he leaves no time for the interpreter to make a pause. (M.Megilla 4:2, 4)

All the essentials of the standard synagogue reading practice are here. The Law was to be read continuously from Sabbath to Sabbath—the starting point was celebrated as the feast of Simhat Torah—with no omissions and with a verse-by-verse translation into Aramaic. The minimum was twenty-one verses each Sabbath (three for each of seven readers), but in fact the average number of verses included in each Sabbath's section (a parashah or seder) was far higher. The entire "Palestinian" cycle, divided into 154 sections, probably took somewhat longer than three and a half years to complete. There later arose in Babylonia a different custom, that of distributing the Torah readings in 53 or 54 parashiyot across the single year, and this annual cycle later became the synagogue norm everywhere in the Jewish world.

Each Torah reading, whether in the Palestinian or the Babylonian division, was accompanied by a haftarah, or reading from the Prophets, done not sequentially but by choice, thus providing a kind of exegesis of each Sabbath's Torah text. What precisely composed the haftarah long remained an open question. Often the connection was manifestly verbal. For example, when Genesis 8:1 on Noah was read, the haftarah was Isaiah 54:9: "For it is like in the days of Noah. . . ." Far more often the connection was eschatological and even messianic, particularly in the original Palestinian cycle. Thus the annual reading of the Torah, which began naturally with Genesis 1:1 ("In the beginning of creation, when God created heaven and earth . . . "), was accompanied in the synagogues by a reading of Isaiah 65:17: "For behold, I create new heavens and a new earth. Former things shall no longer be remembered, nor shall they be called to mind." Indeed, almost half of all the haftaroth selected for public reading in the synagogues on the Sabbath were originally taken from Isaiah, and of these more than two-thirds from the deeply messianic chapters 40–66.

29. Jesus' Passover Seder

According to the Synoptics, on the night before his execution Jesus gathered with his disciples in Jerusalem on the fourteenth of Nisan to celebrate the ritual prescribed in Exodus.

The Lord said to Moses and Aaron in the land of Egypt: This month [that is, Nisan] shall mark for you the beginning of the months; it shall be the first of months of the year for you. Speak to the whole community of Israel and say that on the tenth day of this month each of them shall take a lamb to a family, a lamb to a household. . . . Your lamb shall be without blemish, a yearling male. You may equally take a sheep or a goat. You shall keep watch over it until the fourteenth day of this month; and all the aggregate community of the Israelites shall slaughter it at twilight. They shall take some of the blood and put it on the two doorposts and the lintels of the house in which they are to eat it. They shall eat the flesh that same night; they shall eat it roasted over the fire, with unleavened bread and with bitter herbs. Do not eat any of it raw, or cooked in any way with water, but roasted—head, legs and entrails—over the fire. You shall not leave any of it over until morning; if any of it is left until morning, you shall burn it. This is how you shall eat it: your loins girded, your sandals on your feet, and your staff in your hand and you shall eat it hurriedly; it is a passover offering to the Lord. (Exodus 12:1–11)

Just before the Passover that was to mark his own death, Jesus celebrated some kind of ritual—whether the actual Passover meal or some kind of preparatory repast is not entirely clear—with the inner circle of his disciples.

Now on the first day of Unleavened Bread, when the Passover lambs were being slaughtered, his disciples said to him [that is, Jesus]: "Where would you like us to go and prepare for your Passover supper?" So he sent out two of his disciples with these instructions: "Go into the city, and a man will meet you carrying a jar of water. Follow him, and when he enters a house give this message to the owner: 'The Master says, where is the room reserved for me to eat the Passover with my disciples?' He will show you a large room upstairs, set out in readiness. Make the preparations for us there." Then the disciples went off, and when they came into the city they found everything just as he had told them. So they prepared for Passover.

In the evening he came to the house with the Twelve. As they sat at supper Jesus said, "I tell you this: one of you will betray me—one who is eating with me." At this they were dismayed; and one by one they said to him, "Not I, surely?" "It is one of the Twelve," he said, "who is dipping in the same bowl with me. The Son of Man is going the way appointed for him in Scriptures, but alas for that man by whom the Son of Man is betrayed. It would be better for that man if he had never been born."

During the supper, he took bread and having said the blessing, he broke it and gave it to them, with the words, "Take this; this is my body." Then he took a cup, and having offered thanks to God, he gave it to them; and they all drank from it. And he said, "This is my blood, the blood of the Covenant, shed for many. I tell you this, never again shall I drink from the fruit of the vine until that day when I drink it new in the kingdom of God."

After singing the Passover hymn, they went out to the Mount of Olives. (Mark 14:12–26)

30. Paul on the Eucharistic Meal

The account in Mark is not our earliest information on this event. It was already recorded by Paul, though without the Passover context, since it was the central act of that evening that chiefly concerned him.

For the tradition which I handed on to you came to me from the Lord himself: that the Lord Jesus, on the night of his arrest, took bread and, after having given thanks to God, broke it and said, "This is my body, which is for you; do this as a memorial of me." In the same way, he took the cup after supper, and said, "This is the cup of the New Covenant sealed by my blood. Whenever you drink it, do this as a memorial of me." For every time you eat this bread and drink the cup, you proclaim the death of the Lord, until he comes.

It follows that anyone who eats the bread or drinks the cup of the Lord unworthily will be guilty of desecrating the body and blood of the Lord. A man must test himself before eating his share of the bread and drinking from the cup. For he who eats and drinks eats and drinks judgment on himself if he does not discern the Body. (Paul, *To the Corinthians* 1.11:23–29)

31. Jesus as the New High Priest

The following text appears somewhat abruptly in the account of Abraham in Genesis.

Then Melchizedek, king of Salem, brought food and wine. He was a priest of God Most High and pronounced this blessing on Abram: "Blessed be Abram by God Most High, creator of heaven and earth. And blessed be God Most High, who has delivered your enemies into your power." Abram gave him a tithe of all the booty. (Genesis 14:18–20)

The existence of a High Priest of the One True God in the age before Moses and so outside of the line of Aaron was of course known to the early Jewish Christians, particularly since Melchizedek had already been used in a messianic context in Psalm 110. They were quick to make capital of it, as here in the letter to the Hebrews.

Every High Priest is taken from among men and appointed their representative before God, to offer gifts and sacrifices for sins. He is able to bear patiently with the ignorant and the erring, since he too is beset by weakness; and because of this he is bound to make sin offerings for himself no less than for the people. And nobody arrogates the honor to himself: he is called by God, as indeed Aaron was. So it is with Christ: he did not confer upon himself the glory of becoming High Priest; it was granted by God, who said to him, "Thou art my Son; this day have I begotten thee" (Ps. 2:7); and also in another place he says, "Thou art a priest forever, in the succession of Melchizedek" (Ps. 110:4). In the days of his earthly life he offered up prayers and petitions, with loud cries and tears, to God who was able to deliver him from the grave. Because of this humble submission his prayer was heard: son though he was, he learned obedience in the school of suffering, and, once perfected, became the source of eternal salvation for all who obey him, named by God High Priest in the succession of Melchizedek. (Hebrews 5:1–11)

Now if perfection had been attainable through the Levitical priesthood—for it was on this basis that the people were given the Law—what further need would there have been to speak of another priest arising in the succession of Melchizedek, instead of the succession of Aaron? For a change of priesthood must mean a change of law. And the one spoken of here belongs to a different tribe, no member of which has ever had anything to do with the altar. For it is very evident that our Lord is sprung from the tribe of Judah, a tribe to which Moses made no reference in speaking of priests. The argument becomes still clearer if the new priest who arises is one like Melchizedek, owing his priesthood not to a system of earth-bound rules but to the power of a life that cannot be destroyed. For here is the testimony: "Thou art a priest forever, in the succession of Melchizedek." The earlier rules are canceled as impotent and useless, since the Law brought nothing to perfection; and a better hope is introduced, through which we draw near to God. (Hebrews 7: 11–19)

32. Christian Readings: New Sacrifices, a New Temple

Paul had begun to work out the effects of Jesus' redemptive death on the legal provisions of the Torah, while the author of the Letter to the Hebrews took up the complementary question of biblical ritual and its conversion into the matter of the New Covenant.

The first covenant indeed had its ordinances of divine service and its sanctuary, but a material sanctuary. For a tent was prepared—the first tent—in which was the lampstand and the table with the bread of the Presence; this is called the Holy Place. Beyond the second curtain was the tent called the Most Holy Place. Here was a golden altar of incense and the Ark of the Covenant plated all over with gold, in which were a golden jar containing the manna, and Aaron's staff which once budded, and the Tablets of the Covenant; and above it the cherubim of God's glory, overshadowing the place of expiation. On these we cannot now enlarge.

Under this arrangement, the priests are always entering the first tent in the discharge of their duties; but the second is entered only once a year, and by the High Priest alone, and even then he must take with him the blood which he offers on his own behalf and for the people's sins of ignorance. By this the Holy Spirit signifies that so long as the earlier tent still stands, the way into the sanctuary remains unrevealed. All this is symbolic, pointing to the present time. The offerings and worship there prescribed cannot give the worshiper inward perfection. It is only a matter of food and drink and various rites of cleansing—outward ordinances in force until the time of reformation.

But now Christ has come, High Priest of good things already in being. The tent of his priesthood is a greater and more perfect one, not made by men's hands, that is, not belonging to this created world. The blood of his sacrifice is his own blood, not the blood of goats and calves. And thus he has entered the sanctuary once and for all and secured eternal deliverance. For if the blood of goats and bulls and the sprinkled ashes of a heifer have power to hallow those who have been defiled and restore their external purity, how much greater is the power of the blood of Christ. He offered himself without blemish to God, a spiritual and eternal sacrifice; and his blood will cleanse our conscience from the deadness of our former ways and fit us for the service of the living God. (Hebrews 9:1–14)

33. "A Chosen Race, a Royal Priesthood"

The Letter to the Hebrews chooses to dwell on the Temple of the Old Law as prefiguring that of the New, but there was another set of images surrounding Temple and priesthood, derived in the first instance from a striking messianic figure in Psalm 118:22–23. These images are echoed first by Jesus himself in the Gospels and then enlarged and developed in the first letter of Peter, who may have been thinking of his own Jesus-bestowed name of "stone" or "rock."

> The stone which the builders rejected,
> > has become the chief cornerstone.
> This is the Lord's doing;
> > it is marvelous in our sight.
> (Psalm 118:22–23)

Jesus said to them [that is, the "chief priests and elders of the nation"], "Have you never read in the Scriptures: 'The stone which the builders rejected has become the chief cornerstone. This is the Lord's doing and it is marvelous in our eyes'? Therefore I tell you, the kingdom of God will be taken away from you and given to a nation which yields the proper fruit." (Matthew 21:42–43)

Come to him our living Stone, the stone rejected by men but choice and precious in the sight of God. Come and let yourselves be built, as living stones, into a spiritual temple, become a holy priesthood, to offer spiritual sacrifices acceptable to God through Jesus Christ. For it stands written [Isa. 28:16]:

> "I lay in Sion a choice cornerstone of great worth.
> The man who has faith in it will not be put to shame."

The great worth of which it speaks is for you to have faith. For those who have no faith, the stone which the builders rejected has become not only the cornerstone but a stone to trip over, a rock to stumble against. They fall when they disbelieve the Word. Such was their appointed lot!

But you are a chosen race, a royal priesthood, a dedicated nation and a people claimed by God for His own, to proclaim the triumph of him who called you out of the darkness into his own marvelous light. You are now the people of God, who were once not His people; outside His mercy once, you have now received His mercy. (Peter, *Letter* 1.2:4–10)

34. The New Christian Temple

The same question of a new, spiritual Temple, and a criticism of the old, is taken up less than a century later in the Letter of Barnabas *in still another manner.*

We now come to the matter of the Temple; and I will show you how mistaken those miserable folk were in pinning their hopes to the building itself, as if that were the home of God, instead of to God, their own Creator. Indeed, they were scarcely less misguided than the heathen in the way they ascribed divine holiness to their Temple. For mark how completely the words of the Lord Himself dispense with it: "Who is it who can span the whole heaven with the breadth of one hand, or the earth with the flat of his palm? Is it not I, says the Lord. The heaven is a throne for me, and the earth a stool for my feet. What sort of house then will you build for Me, and where is the spot on earth that can serve Me for a resting place?" (Isa. 66:1). You can see that their hope was the purest folly. Besides, He also says, "Behold, those who pulled the Temple down will not rebuild it" (Isa. 49:17), the very thing which is in process of fulfillment now; for after their armed rebellion it was demolished by their enemies, and now they themselves are about to build it up again, as subjects of their foemen. All the same, it has been revealed that city, Temple and Jewish people are all alike doomed to perish one day; for Scripture says, "it will come to pass in the last days that the Lord will deliver up to destruction the sheep of the pasture, with their sheepfold and their watchtower" (Enoch 89:56). And for the Lord to say such a thing is for that thing to come about.

But what we have to ask next is, Can there be any such thing as a temple to God at all? To be sure there can, but where He Himself tells us that He is building it and perfecting it. For it is written, "when the Week draws near its close, then a temple of God will be built gloriously in the Name of the Lord" [source unknown]. And from this I must infer that there is indeed such a thing as a temple. Only, mark that it is to be "built in the Name of the Lord"; for in the days before we believed in God, our hearts were a rotten, shaky abode, and a temple only too truly built with hands, since by our persistent opposition to God we had made them into a chamber of idolatry and a home for demons. . . . But when we were granted remission for our sins and came to put our hopes in His Name, we were made new men, created all over again from the beginning; and as a consequence of that, God is actually dwelling within us in that poor habitation of ours. . . . It is in these ways that He admits us, the bondsmen of mortality, into the Temple that is immortal. (*Letter of Barnabas*)
[STANIFORTH 1968: 215–216]

Augustine's understanding of the new Temple is likewise based on his reading of Scripture, in this case a passage in Haggai. He analyzes it not in the allegorizing moral sense of the Letter of Barnabas *but according to the typological exegesis that he wielded with such sophistication.*

The prophecy of Haggai, in which he said that the glory of the house of God would be greater than the first had been (Hag. 2:9), was not fulfilled in the rebuilding of that (second Temple). For it can never be shown to have had so much glory after it was rebuilt as it had in the time of Solomon; rather, the glory of that house is shown to have diminished, first by the cessation of prophecy and then by the nation itself suffering so great calamities, even to the final destruction made by the Romans. . . . But this house which pertains to the New Testament is just as much more glorious as the living stones, I mean believing, renewed men, of which it is constructed, are better. But it was typified by the rebuilding of that (second) Temple for this reason, because the very renovation of that edifice typifies in the prophetic oracle another testament which is called new. When, therefore, God said to the prophet just named, "And I will give peace in this place" (Hag. 2:9), he is to be understood who is typified by that place; for by that place is typified the Church which was to be built by Christ, nothing else can be accepted as the meaning of the saying "I will give peace in this place" except I will give peace in the place which that place signifies. For all typical things seem in some way to personate those whom they typify, as is said by the Apostle (Paul), "that Rock was Christ" (1 Cor. 10:4).

Therefore the glory of this New Testament house is greater than the glory of the Old Testament house; and it will show itself as greater when it shall be dedicated. For then "shall come the desired of all nations" (Hag. 2:7), as we read in the Hebrew. For before his coming he had not yet been desired by all nations. For they knew not him whom they ought to desire, in whom they had not believed. Then, also, according to the Septuagint version—for it also is a prophetic meaning—"shall come those who are elected of the Lord out of all nations." For then indeed there shall come only those who are elected, whereof the Apostle says, "According as He has chosen us before the foundations of the world" (Eph. 1:4). For the Master Builder who said, "Many are called but few are chosen" (Matt. 22:11–14), did not say this of those, who, on being called, came in such a way as to be cast out of the feast, but would point out the house built up of the elect, which henceforth shall dread no ruin. (Augustine, *City of God* 18.48) [AUGUSTINE 1948: 2:457–458]

35. Idols and Images

You shall not make for yourself a sculpted image, or any likeness of what is in the heavens above, or on the earth below, or in the waters under the earth. (Exodus 20:4–5)

This charge is given to Moses in Deuteronomy:

These are the laws and the rules which you must carefully observe in the land that the Lord, the God of your fathers, is giving to you to possess, as long as you live on earth. You must destroy all the sites at which the nations you are to dispossess worshiped their gods, whether on lofty mountains and on hills or under any luxuriant tree. Tear down their altars, smash their pillars, put their sacred posts to the fire, and cut down

the images of their gods, obliterating their name from that site. (Deuteronomy 12:1–3)

*Throughout most of their history down to the Exile, the problem of idol worship
plagued the Israelites. The Bible makes no effort to dissemble their attraction, from
the golden calf set up during Moses' absence on Sinai to the official policy of idol
worship established by Jeroboam and his successors as kings of Israel. How seriously
the problem was taken emerges clearly from this witheringly sarcastic attack on idols
that occurs in chapter 44 of Isaiah.*

> The makers of idols all work to no purpose;
> And the things they treasure can do no good,
> As they themselves can testify.
> They neither look nor think,
> And so shall they be shamed.
> Who would fashion a god or cast a statue
> That can do no good?
> Lo, all its adherents shall be shamed;
> They are craftsmen, are merely human.
> Let them assemble and all stand up!
> They shall be cowed and they shall be shamed. . . .
>
> The craftsman in wood measures with a line.
> And marks out a shape with a stylus;
> He forms it with scraping tools,
> Marking it out with a compass.
> He gives it a human form,
> The beauty of a man, to dwell in a shrine.
> For his use he cuts down cedars;
> He chooses plane trees and oaks.
> He sets aside trees of the forest;
> Or plants firs, and the rain makes them grow.
> All this serves man for fuel:
> He takes some to warm himself,
> And he builds a fire and bakes bread.
> He also makes a god of it and worships it,
> Fashions an idol and bows down to it!
> Part of it he burns in a fire:
> On that part he roasts meat.
> He eats the roast and is sated.
> He also warms himself and cries, "Ah,
> I am warm! I can feel the heat!"

Of the rest he makes a god—his own carving!
He bows down to it, worships it;
He prays to it and cries,
"Save me for you are my god!"

They have no wit or judgment:
Their eyes are besmeared, and they see not;
Their minds, and they cannot think.
They do not give thought,
They lack the wit to say:
"Part of it I burned in a fire;
I also baked bread on the coals,
I roasted meat and I ate it—
Should I make the rest an abhorrence?
Should I bow to a block of wood?"
He pursues ashes!
A deluded mind has led him astray,
And he cannot save himself,
"The thing in my hand is a fraud!"
(Isaiah 44:9–20)

After the Exile, and with the Jews' exposure to another, Greek form of paganism, the problem appears to have shifted focus from simply idols to the cult of the ruler, the practice of the Greeks and the Romans of deifying their rulers and encouraging, and occasionally requiring, their veneration as an act of political and cultural solidarity. The Jews understood it as no such thing of course, and the Mishnaic tract devoted to idolatry, Abodah Zarah, or "Alien Cult," is quite specific on the matter of what constituted "idols" in the second century C.E.

All images are forbidden, because they are worshiped once a year. So Rabbi Meir. But the Sages say: Only that is forbidden which bears in its hand a staff or a bird or a sphere. Rabbi Simeon ben Gamaliel says: That which bears anything in its hand.

If a man found fragments of images, these are permitted. If he found (a fragment in) the shape of a hand or the shape of a foot, these are forbidden, since an object the like of these is worshiped.

If a man found objects on which is a figure of the sun, a figure of the moon, or a figure of a serpent, he must throw them into the Dead Sea. Rabbi Simeon ben Gamaliel says: If the figures are found on objects of value, these are forbidden, but if on worthless objects, these are permitted. Rabbi Yosi says: One should break them into pieces and scatter them to the winds or throw them into the sea. They said to him: Even so, (in the first case) they would become manure, and it is written, "Let nothing out of all that had been laid under the ban be found in your possession" (Deut. 13:17). (M.Abodah Zarah 3:1–3)

On the face of it, both the stricter and the broader ruling in the first passage appear to be directed against emperor worship. As the Palestinian Gemara on this passage explains, it is primarily regalia from the imperial iconography that is mentioned in 3:1.

A staff because he ruled the world with it, a bird, as it is written, "My hand has found like a nest the wealth of the peoples," a sphere because the world is made in the shape of a sphere. (JT.Abodah Zarah 3.1)

"It refers," as the Babylonian Gemara flatly states, "to the statues of kings." As a matter of fact, synagogue decoration appears to have gone much further, and floor mosaics from Palestinian synagogues depict not only biblical scenes like the "binding of Isaac" but even the sun god riding in his chariot in the center of a zodiacal circle or standing in majesty with a globe and a whip in his hand. Sentiments obviously changed over the years, and the Palestinian Gemara on this same Mishnaic passage reveals two rabbis who took an obviously more lenient view. The "walls" in question would appear to be those of synagogues.

In the days of Rabbi Yohanan [third century C.E.] they began to paint on walls, and he did not prevent them. . . . In the days of Rabbi Abun [fourth century C.E.] they began to make designs on mosaics, and he did not prevent them. (JT.Abodah Zarah 42b)

And there was, finally, an attempt to distinguish act from intent, idolatry from mere decoration. The point of departure is a text in Leviticus.

You shall not make idols for yourselves, or set up for yourselves carved images or pillars or place figured stones in your land to worship upon, for I am the Lord your God. You shall keep My sabbaths and venerate My sanctuary, Mine, the Lord's. (Leviticus 26:1)

One of the Targums paraphrases this passage.

You shall not set up a figured stone in your land, to bow down to it, but a mosaic pavement of designs and forms you may set in the floor of your places of worship, so long as you do not do obeisance [or "prostrate yourselves"] to it. (Targum Pseudo-Jonathan *ad loc.*)

One of the motives for this relative, and by no means universal, leniency was that the Jews were at ease on the issue of idolatry and that image worship was no longer a major problem or concern. Already in the second century B.C.E. the book called Judith was suggesting that:

There is not one of our tribes or clans, districts or towns, that worships man-made gods today. This did happen in days gone by, and that was why our ancestors were abandoned to their enemies to be slaughtered and pillaged, and great was their downfall. But we acknowledge no God but the Lord. (Judith 8:18–19)

The rabbis remained vigilant, however, and the Talmud found it difficult to resist a good, moralizing story on the subject of idolatry.

Our rabbis taught: Sabta, a townsman of Avlas [in Cilicia] once hired out an ass to a Gentile woman. When she came to Peor, she said to him: "Wait till I enter and come out again." When she came out, he said to her, "Now you wait for me until I go in and come out again." "But," she said, "are you not a Jew?" He replied, "What does that concern you?" He then entered (the shrine), uncovered himself before the idol and then wiped himself on the idol's nose, while the shrine attendants praised him, saying, "No man has ever served this idol this way before."

The pleasantry over, the rabbis register their disapproval, since the ways of the Gentiles are inscrutable in this matter of idols.

He who uncovers himself before Baal Peor thereby serves it, even if his intention was to degrade it.

This story, in the associative manner of the Talmud, recalls a similar point and ruling, this one reminiscent of the pre-Islamic ritual of "stoning of the devils," which was incorporated into the Islamic pilgrimage ceremony.

And he who cast a stone at Merculis thereby serves it, even if his intention was to bruise it. Thus, Rabbi Manasseh was going to Be Toratha [a town in Babylonia]. On his way he was told, "An idol stands in that place." He took up a stone and cast it at the idol's statue. Thereupon they said to him, "It is Merculis." . . . So he went and inquired at the House of Study (whether he had done wrong). They informed him, "We have learned, 'He who casts a stone at Merculis thereby serves it,' that is to say, even if it was merely to bruise it." He said to them, "Then I will go and remove it." But they replied, "Whether one casts a stone or removes it, he incurs guilt, because every stone thus removed leaves room for another." (BT.Sanhedrin 64a)

36. Christian Images

It must have taken the Christians some time to adjust their attitudes toward images that depicted some religious subject matter and so might fairly be thought of as either idolatrous or at the very least unseemly. One such image was an imperial portrait. Christians had once been executed for refusing to worship such, and already the New Testament Apocalypse (Revelation 20:4) refers to the fact. But when it was a Christian emperor who was the subject of the portraiture, there appeared to be few misgivings. Far from being scandalized, the Church historian and Constantine's biographer Eusebius took theological comfort in this particular type of image.

One may ascertain the power of that godly faith which sustained his [that is, Constantine's] soul by this consideration, namely that he had his image portrayed on gold coins in such a manner that he appeared to be gazing upward, as if praying to God. These effigies of his circulated throughout the Roman world. Furthermore, at the palaces the statues placed high over the entrance represented him standing upright, gazing up to heaven, and stretching out his arms in the manner of a man praying. (Eusebius, *Life of Constantine* 4.15) [MANGO 1972: 15]

There were limits, however, as appears in this letter addressed by Eusebius, now speaking as a bishop and not as a historian, to Constantine's sister Constantia. She is immediately plunged into the theological dilemma of the two natures of Jesus Christ, one of which, the divine, could obviously not be portrayed, while the other, the human, seemed almost to invite such portraiture.

You also wrote to me concerning a supposed image of Christ, which image you wished me to send you. Now what kind of thing is this that you call the image of Christ? I do not know what impelled you to request that an image of our Savior be delineated. What sort of image of Christ are you seeking? Is it the true and unalterable one which bears his essential characteristics, or the one which he took up for our sake when he assumed the form of a servant (Phil. 2:7)? . . . Granted, he had two forms, even I do not think that your request has to do with the divine form. . . . Surely, then, you are seeking his image as a servant, that of the flesh which he put on for our sake. But that too, we have been taught, was mingled with the glory of his divinity, so that the mortal part was swallowed up by Life. . . . He showed on the mount (Tabor) that nature which surpasses the human one—when his face shone like the sun and his garments like light. Who, then, would be able to represent by means of dead colors and inanimate delineations the glistening, flashing radiance of such dignity and glory, when even his superhuman disciples could not

bear to behold him in this guise and fell on their faces (Matt. 17:1–8). . . .
How can one paint an image of so wondrous and unattainable a form—if
the term "form" is at all applicable to the divine and spiritual essence—
unless, like the unbelieving pagans, one is to represent things that bear no
possible resemblance to anything? . . . For they too make such idols when
they wish to mold the likeness of what they consider to be a god or, as
they might say, one of the heroes or anything else of the kind, yet are
unable even to approach a resemblance and so delineate and represent
some strange human shapes. Surely, even you will agree that such practices are not lawful for us.

*But Jesus was, after all, a man, and as such subject to portraiture. And he was being
portrayed in Eusebius' day. The bishop is constrained in the end to resort to the
biblical argument.*

But if you mean to ask of me the image not of his form transformed
into that of God but that of the mortal flesh before its transformation, can
it be that you have forgotten that passage in which God lays down the law
that no likeness can be made either of what is in heaven or what is in the
earth beneath? Have you ever heard anything of the kind either yourself
in church or from another person? Are not such things banished and
excluded from churches all over the world, and is it not common knowledge that such practices are not permitted to us alone? (Eusebius, *Letter
to Constantia*) [MANGO 1972: 16–17]

*Eusebius' scruples were overwhelmed by events, chiefly, it would appear, by the
growing popularity of the cult of the saints and martyrs and of their relics. Opposition to the cult did not entirely disappear in the East, however. This is a letter sent
by Epiphanius, bishop of Salamis (d. 403 C.E.), to Emperor Theodosius.*

Which of the ancient Fathers ever painted an image of Christ and
deposited it in a church or a private house? Which ancient bishop ever
dishonored Christ by painting him on door curtains? Which one of them
ever made a spectacle of Abraham, Isaac, Jacob, Moses and the other
prophets and patriarchs, of Peter, Andrew, James, John, Paul and the
other Apostles by painting them on curtains or walls? . . . Furthermore,
they lie by representing the appearance of saints in different forms according to their own whim, sometimes delineating the same persons as
old men, sometimes as youths, and so intruding into things they have not
seen. For they paint the Savior with long hair, and this by conjecture
because he is called a Nazarene, and Nazarenes [that is, a sect of Judeo-
Christians called by that name] wear long hair. They are in error, those

who try to attach stereotypes to him; for the Savior drank wine, whereas the Nazarenes did not. . . .

See you not, O most God-loving emperor, that this state of things is not agreeable to God? Wherefore I entreat you . . . that the curtains which may be found to bear in a spurious manner—and yet they do bear—images of the Apostles or prophets or of the Lord Christ himself should be collected from churches, baptisteries, houses and martyria and that you should give them over for the burial of the poor, and as for the images on the walls, they should be whitewashed. As concerns those that have already been represented in mosaic, seeing that their removal is difficult, you know what to ordain in the wisdom that has been granted you by God: if it is possible to remove them, well and good; but if it proves impossible, let that which has already been done suffice and let no one paint in this manner henceforth. For our fathers delineated nothing except the salutary sign of Christ [that is, the cross] both on their doors and everywhere else. (Epiphanius, *Letter to Theodosius*) [MANGO 1972: 41–42]

Christians had earlier been called upon to defend their veneration of images, against pagans whose own spiritual view of the deity had already made them remote from the idolatry of their ancestors, and particularly against Jews, whose own position, though fluid, could hardly countenance the Christians' practice. Eventually there were no more pagans, but the argument with the Jews went on, here taken up by the Christian theologian Leontius. The time is early in the seventh century, not long before the arrival of the first Muslims. Earlier in his tract Leontius points out that the Bible itself shows that the Jews had little reluctance to surround themselves with images, and in the most sacred of places, in the Tent of the Presence—witness the golden cherubim—and in the Temple in Jerusalem. He then takes another course.

You do obeisance to the book of the Law, but you do not make obeisance to the parchments and ink but to the words contained in them. And it is thus that I do obeisance to the icon of God, for when I hold the lifeless representation of Christ in my hands, through it I seem to hold and do obeisance to the Christ. As Jacob kissed the bloody coat of Joseph and felt that he held him in his arms, so Christians think that in holding the image they hold Christ or his Apostles and martyrs. . . . As I have often said, in every greeting and obeisance it is the purpose of the action which is in question. And if you accuse me of doing obeisance to the wood of the cross as though it were God, why do you not say the same of the staff of Joseph? Abraham did obeisance to infamous men who sold a sepulcher, and went on his knees before them, but not as though they were gods. Jacob blessed the idolater Pharaoh and did obeisance to Esau, but not as though they were gods. Do you not see how many salutations and obeisances I have adduced out of the Scriptures, and all without blame? You call us idolaters when it was Christian saints and martyrs who destroyed the temples of the idolaters. (Leontius, *Against the Jews*) [BAYNES 1955: 233]

37. Christian Iconoclasm

In 787 C.E. an ecumenical council was convened at Nicea, the site of the first general council of the Church, to settle the matter of image worship, which had been troubling the Eastern Church for more than half a century. As part of their deliberations, the bishops sitting there requested a report from a certain John, a Jerusalem presbyter, who described for them the events earlier in that century that had led to an outbreak of image smashing in the Byzantine Empire.

When Umar [Umar II, Caliph 717–720 C.E.] had died, he was succeeded by Yazid [Yazid II, Caliph 720–724 C.E.], a frivolous and fickle man. Now there was in Tiberias a certain leader of the lawless Jews, who was a sorcerer and the instrument of soul-destroying demons, called "Forty Cubits High." . . . Being informed of the frivolity of the ruler Yazid, this wicked Jew went up to him and attempted to make some prophecies. Having in this manner gained the tyrant's favor, he said: "I wish, O Caliph, in the light of the good will which I have toward you, to suggest a certain method, easy to accomplish, by which you will gain an extension of your life and will remain here to rule for thirty years, if you put what I say into effect." Won over by the promise of longevity . . . the senseless tyrant replied: "Anything you suggest to me I shall readily do. . . ." Whereupon the Jewish sorcerer said to him: "Give an order without delay or postponement that an encyclical letter be issued throughout your dominions to the effect that every kind of pictorial representation, be it on boards or on wall mosaics or on holy vessels or altar cloths, or anything else of the sort that is found in Christian churches should be obliterated and utterly destroyed; not only these, but also all the effigies that are set up as decoration in the marketplaces of cities." It was a devilish plot on the part of the false prophet to have added "all effigies" because he tried to avoid the suspicion of being hostile to us (Christians).

The wicked tyrant was easily persuaded by him and sent out emissaries throughout his dominions to pull down the holy icons and other images. And in this fashion he denuded God's churches . . . before this plague had reached our country [that is, the Byzantine Empire]. And since the God-loving Christians took to flight (across the frontier) so as not to destroy the icons with their own hands, the Amirs who had been charged with this task imposed it on accursed Jews and miserable Arabs. And so they burnt the holy icons, and some churches they whitewashed, while others they scraped down.

When the unworthy bishop of Nacolia [a see in Anatolia] and his followers heard of this, they imitated the lawless Jews and infidel Arabs and set about insulting the churches of God. . . . And when after doing this, the Caliph Yazid died, no more than two and a half years later, and went into the eternal fire, the images were restored to their original position and honor. And his son Walid [Walid II, Caliph 743–744 C.E.; Yazid's immediate successor was Hisham, Caliph 724–743] was very angry and ordered the magician to be put to death for his father's murder, as just punishment for his false prophecy. (Acts of II Nicea)

[MANGO 1972: 151]

John's report received an immediate confirmation from an eyewitness who was present at the council and said: "I was a young boy living in Syria when the Caliph of the Saracens destroyed the images." This story appears, in one version or another, in most of the Byzantine accounts of the beginning of a reaction to the veneration of images in the Christian Roman Empire. According to it, Byzantine iconoclasm, "image destruction," was inspired by a Jew living under Islam who convinced the Muslim Caliph Yazid to ban images and image worship in his realms. This probably occurred in 721 C.E. Not long afterward the "infection" spread across the frontier, where a number of bishops succumbed, and they in turn caught the ear of Emperor Leo III (717–741 C.E.), who was himself a native of the Syrian frontier region and, as one Byzantine historian had it, a notorious "Saracen sympathizer." A number of edicts against images were issued beginning in 726 C.E., and the effects are described in the life of a contemporary holy man, Stephen.

In every village and town one could witness the weeping and lamentation of the pious, whereas, on the part of the impious, one saw sacred things trodden upon, (liturgical) vessels turned to other use, churches scraped down and smeared with ashes because they contained holy images. And wherever there were venerable images of Christ or the Mother of God or the saints, these were consigned to the flames or were gouged out or smeared over. If, on the other hand, there were pictures of trees or birds or senseless beasts, and in particular of satanic horse races, hunts, theatrical and hippodrome scenes, these were preserved with honor and given greater lustre.

Somewhat later, under Leo's son and successor, Constantine V (741–775 C.E.):

The tyrant [Constantine V] scraped down the venerable church of the all-pure Mother of God at the Blachernae (in Constantinople), whose walls had previously been decorated with pictures of God's coming down to us, and going on to His various miracles as far as His Ascension and the Descent of the Holy Spirit. Having thus suppressed all Christ's mysteries, he converted the church into a storehouse of fruit and an aviary: for he covered it with mosaics (representing) all kinds of birds and beasts, and certain swirls of ivy leaves (enclosing) cranes, crows and peacocks, thus making the church, if I may say so, altogether unadorned. (*Life of Saint Stephen the Younger*) [MANGO 1972: 152]

It was Constantine V who in 754 convened a council to make the prohibition of images part of the official teaching of the Church. This is part of its Definition of Faith *on that occasion.*

We have considered it proper to demonstrate in detail by the present Definition the error of those who make and reverence images. . . . How senseless is the notion that the painter, who from sordid love of gain pursues the unattainable, namely to fashion with his impure hands things that are believed by the heart and confessed by the mouth. This man makes an image and calls it Christ. Now the name "Christ" means both God and man. Hence he has either included, according to his vain fancy, the uncircumscribable Godhead in the circumscription of created flesh, or he has confused that unconfusable union . . . and in so doing has applied two blasphemies to the Godhead, namely through the circumscription and the confusion. So also, he who reveres images is guilty of the same blasphemies.

The same argument does not pertain to images of the Virgin and the saints, it might be argued. The Council replies:

How indeed do they dare depict through the gross art of the pagans the all-praised Mother of God who was overshadowed by the plenitude of divinity, through whom an unapproachable light did shine for us, who is higher than the heaven and holier than the cherubim? Or the saints who will reign with Christ, and sit beside Him to judge the world, and share in His glory . . . are they not ashamed to depict them through pagan art? For it is not lawful for Christians who believe in the resurrection to adopt the customs of demon-worshiping Gentiles, and to insult by means of inglorious and dead matter the saints who will be adorned with much glory.

The Definition *concludes:*

Let no man dare to pursue henceforth this impious and unholy practice. Anyone who presumes from now on to manufacture an icon, or to
worship it, or to set it up in a church or a private house, or to hide it, if
he is a bishop or a presbyter or deacon, he shall be deposed; if he is a
monk or a layman, he shall be anathematized and deemed guilty under
imperial law as a foe of God's commands and an enemy of the doctrines
of the Fathers. (*Definition of Faith of the Council of 754*) [MANGO 1972: 166–168]

*Among those who rallied to the defense of the veneration of images was John of
Damascus, scion of a Christian family that had long served in the Muslim civil service
in Damascus. John followed another course, however; he retired to a monastery near
Jerusalem, where he wrote tirelessly in defense of Christian orthodoxy. For him that
included the veneration of images of Jesus, his mother, and the saints.*

Since some find fault with us for showing reverence and honoring
the image of our Savior and that of our Lady, and also of the rest of the
saints and servants of Christ, let them hear that from the beginning God
made man after His own image. On what other grounds, then, do we
show reverence to each other than that we are made after God's image?
For as Basil, that most learned expounder of things divine, says, "The
honor given to the image passes over to the prototype." Now a prototype
is that which is imaged, from which the form is derived. Why was it that
Moses' people showed reverence round about the tabernacle which bore
an image and type of heavenly things, or rather the whole of creation?
God indeed said to Moses, "See that you make all things after the pattern
that We showed you on the mountain" (Exod. 33:10). The cherubim also,
which overshadowed the seat of mercy, are they not the work of men's
hands? What is the renowned Temple at Jerusalem? Is it not made by
hands and fashioned by the skill of men?

*The veneration that the Christians pay to their images is different from that given
by the pagans to idols: witness the fact that God permitted the sacrifices of the Jews
but banned those of the Greeks.*

The divine Scriptures, however, blame those who show reverence to
graven images, but also those who sacrifice to demons. The Greeks sacrificed and the Jews also sacrificed; but the Greeks to demons; the Jews,
however, to God. And the sacrifice of the Greeks was rejected and condemned, but the sacrifice of the just was acceptable to God. For Noah
sacrificed, and God smelled a sweet savor of a good purpose, receiving
also the fragrance the right choice and goodwill toward Him. And so the

graven images of the Greeks, since they were the images of demon deities, were rejected and forbidden. But besides this, who can make an imitation of the invisible, incorporeal, uncircumscribed and formless God? Therefore to give form to the Deity is the height of folly and iniquity. And therefore in the Old Testament the use of images was repressed.

What has changed from the biblical circumstances is the enfleshing of God in the person of Jesus Christ.

But after God, in the depths of His mercy, became for our salvation in truth man, not as He was seen by Abraham in the semblance of man, or by the Prophets, but He became in truth man, according to substance, and after He lived upon earth and dwelt among men, worked miracles, suffered and was crucified, He rose again and was received up into heaven; since all these things actually took place and were seen by men, they were written for the remembrance and instruction of us who were not present at that time in order that, though we saw not, we may still, hearing and believing, obtain the blessing of the Lord.

John passes to a new argument, the educational value of images, which serve the same purpose for the illiterate as books do for the educated.

But since all have not a knowledge of letters or time for reading, it appeared good to the Fathers, that these events, as acts of heroism, should be depicted on images to be a brief memorial of them. Often, doubtless, when we have not the Lord's Passion in mind and see the image of Christ's crucifixion, we remember the Passion and fall down and show reverence not to the material but to that which is imaged; just as we do not show reverence for the material of the Gospel, or to the material of the cross, but that which these typify. For wherein does the cross that typifies the Lord differ from a cross that does not do so? It is the same also in the case of the Mother of God. For the honor which is given her is referred to Him who was incarnate of her. And similarly also the brave acts of holy men stir us to bravery and to emulation and imitation of their valor and to the glory of God.

Finally, there is an appeal to the unwritten tradition of the Church, with a considerable debt to Basil's On the Holy Spirit.

The honor rendered the image passes over to the prototype. But this is an unwritten tradition, just as is also the demonstration of reverence toward the East and to the cross and very many similar things. Moreover, that the Apostles handed down much that was unwritten, Paul the Apostle of the Gentiles writes: "Therefore, brethren, stand fast and hold the traditions which you have been taught by us, whether by word or by letters" (2 Thess. 2:14). And to the Corinthians he writes, "Now I praise you, brethren, that you remembered me in all things and keep the traditions as I have delivered them to you" (1 Cor. 2:2). (John of Damascus, *On the Orthodox Faith* 4.16)

The issue of image worship was apparently settled by the seventh ecumenical council, that held in Nicea in 787 C.E. It rejected the policy of Leo III and the theology of Constantine V. This is the pertinent part of its Confession of Faith.

To make our confession short, we keep unchanged all the ecclesiastical traditions handed down to us, written or unwritten, and of these one is the making of pictorial representations, agreeable to the history of the preaching of the Gospel, a tradition useful in many respects, but especially in this, that so the incarnation of the Word is shown forth as real and not merely fantastic, for these have mutual indications, and without doubt also have mutual significations.

We, therefore, following the royal pathway and the divinely inspired authority of our holy Fathers and the traditions of the Catholic Church for, as we all know, the Holy Spirit dwells in her, define with all certitude and accuracy, that just as the figure of the precious and life-giving cross, so also the venerable and holy images, as well in painting and mosaic, as of other fit materials, should be set forth in the holy churches of God, and on the sacred vessels and on the vestments and on hangings and in tablets both in houses and by the wayside, to wit, the figure of our Lord God and Savior Jesus Christ, of our spotless lady, the Mother of God, and of all pious people. For by so much the more frequently as they are seen in artistic representation, by so much the more readily are men lifted up to the memory of their prototypes, and to a longing after them; and to these should be given due salutation and honorable reverence (*proskynesis*), not indeed the true worship (*latreia*) which pertains to the divine nature alone; but to these, as to the figure of the precious and life-giving cross, and to the book of the Gospels and to other holy objects, incense and lights may be offered according to ancient pious custom. For the honor which is paid to the image passes on to that which the image represents, and he who shows reverence to the image shows reverence to the subject represented in it. (Acts of II Nicea, *Confession of Faith*) [MANGO 1972: 166–168]

This was by no means the end of the controversy over images, neither in the Eastern Church, where it first arose and was to arise again shortly after this council, nor in the Western, where the Roman Church's veneration of images became part of the agenda of the reformers.

38. Islam and the Graven Image

Ibn Ishaq's biography of the Prophet provides an account of both the origins and some of the modalities of idol worship among the pagan Arabs of Mecca and its vicinity in the days before Islam.

They say that the beginning of stone worship among the sons of Ishmael was when Mecca became too small for them and they wanted more room in the country. Everyone who left town took with him a stone from the sacred area to do honor to it. Wherever they settled they set it up and walked around it as they had around the Ka'ba. This led them to worship what stones they pleased and those which made an impression on them. Thus as generations passed they forgot their primitive faith and adopted another religion for that of Abraham and Ishmael. They worshiped idols and adopted the same errors as the people before them. Yet they retained and held fast practices going back to the time of Abraham, such as honoring the temple [that is, the Ka'ba] and going round it, the great and the little pilgrimage [that is, the *hajj* and the *umra*], and the standing on Arafat and Muzdalifa, sacrificing the victims, and the pilgrim cry at the great and little pilgrimage, while introducing elements which had no place in the religion of Abraham. . . .

Every household had an idol in their house which they used to worship. When a man was about to set out on a journey he used to rub himself against it as he was about to ride off; indeed, that was the last thing he used to do before his journey; and when he returned from his journey the first thing he did was to rub himself against it before he went to his family. . . .

Now along with the Ka'ba the Arabs had adopted Tawaghit, which were temples which they venerated as they venerated the Ka'ba. They had their guardians and their overseers and they used to make offerings to them as they did to the Ka'ba and to circumambulate them and sacrifice at them. Yet they recognized the superiority of the Ka'ba because it was the temple and mosque of Abraham the friend of God. (Ibn Ishaq, *Life*) [IBN ISHAQ 1955: 35–38]

The Prophet made no secret of his intentions regarding these idols of the Arabs. When he finally entered Mecca after his long emigration to Medina, he put his intentions into action, as described in a passage in Ibn Ishaq's Life.

The Messenger after arriving in Mecca, once the populace had settled down, went to the shrine and went round it seven times on his camel, touching the black stone with a stick which he had in his hand. This done, he summoned Uthman ibn Talha and took the keys of the Ka'ba from him, and when the door was opened for him, he went in. There he found a dove made of wood. He broke it in his hands and threw it away. . . . (According to another account) the Messenger entered Mecca on the day of the conquest and it contained 360 idols which Iblis [or Satan] had strengthened with lead. The Messenger was standing by them with a stick in his hand saying, "The truth has come and falsehood has passed away" (Quran 17:81). Then he pointed at them with his stick and they collapsed on their backs one after another.

When the Messenger had prayed the noon prayer on the day of the conquest (of Mecca) he ordered that all the idols which were around the Ka'ba should be collected and burned with fire and broken up. . . . The Quraysh had put pictures in the Ka'ba including two of Jesus son of Mary and Mary, on both of whom be peace. Ibn Shihab said: Asma the daughter of Shaqr said that a woman of the Banu Ghassan had joined in the pilgrimage of the Arabs and when she saw a picture of Mary in the Ka'ba she said: "My father and my mother be your ransom! (Mary), you are surely an Arab woman!" The Messenger ordered that the pictures be erased, except those of Jesus and Mary. (Ibn Ishaq, *Life*) [IBN ISHAQ 1955: 552]

We know little of what to make of that last curious event. What we can say, on the basis of the Quran, is that, for all Muhammad's opposition to idolatry, there is no sign in that Book of any preoccupation, no open approval or disapproval even, of pictures or images. But conditions must soon have changed. The collections of Prophetic traditions are filled with condemnations of images and image making.

Abu Talha reported the Prophet as saying, "The angels do not enter a house which contains dogs or pictures." Bukhari and Muslim transmit this tradition.

Aisha told that she had screened a storeroom of hers with a curtain on which there were figures and the Prophet tore it down; so she made two cushions out of it and had them in the house for sitting on. Bukhari and Muslim transmit this.

She also reported the Prophet as saying, "Those who will receive the severest punishment on the Day of Resurrection will be those who imitate what God has created."

Sa'id ibn Abi Hasan said: "When I was with Ibn Abbas a man came to him and said, 'Ibn Abbas, I am a man whose livelihood comes only from the work of my hands, and I make these representations of things.' Ibn Abbas replied that he would tell him only what he had heard from

861

God's Messenger. He had heard him say, 'If anyone makes a representation of anything, God will punish him until he blows a spirit into it, and he will never be able to do that.' Then when the man gasped and became pale, he said to him, 'Out upon you! If you must do so, make representations of these trees or of anything which does not possess a soul.' " Bukhari transmitted this tradition.

Ibn Abbas reported God's Messenger as saying, "The one who receives the severest punishment on the Day of Resurrection will be he who kills a prophet, or who is killed by a prophet, or kills one of his parents, or who makes representations of things, and a learned man who derives no benefit from his learning." (Baghawi, *Mishkat al-Masabih* 21.5.1–3)

We do not know when those traditions were put into circulation. If they are authentic, we are faced with the same kind of dilemma that the figuratively decorated synagogues of Palestine posed to a supposedly aniconic Jewish tradition: Muslim coinage bore representations of the Caliph down to the reign of Abd al-Malik (685–705 C.E.), and even after that date Muslim sovereigns continued to build Syrian steppe palaces decorated in a style that was not merely figurative but even aggressively and suggestively secular. It is perhaps safer to conclude that Islam came to its iconophobia gradually and that the Prophetic traditions reflect a later and not a primary stage in that evolution. The later official Islamic sentiment on images is clear enough, however. This is how it is expressed in one of the standard Islamic law books, that written by the Syrian jurist al-Nawawi (d. 1377 C.E.). Now all fear of idolatry is gone, and the reasons for the prohibition are overtly theological.

The learned authorities of our (Shafi'ite) school and others hold that painting a picture of any living thing is strictly forbidden, because it is threatened with grievous punishment as mentioned in the Prophetic traditions, whether it is intended for common domestic use or not. So the making of it is forbidden under every circumstance, because it implies a likeness to the creative activity of God. . . . On the other hand, the painting of a tree or of camel saddles and other things that have no life is not forbidden. Such is the decision on the actual making of a picture.

Similarly, it is forbidden to make use of any object on which a living thing is pictured, whether it is to be hung on a wall or worn as a dress or a turban or on any other object of common domestic use. But if it is on a carpet trampled underfoot, or on a pillow or cushion . . . then it is not forbidden. Whether such an object will prevent the angels of God from entering the house in which it is found is quite another matter.

In all this there is no difference between what casts a shadow and what does not cast a shadow. This is the decision of our school on the question, and the majority of the Companions of the Prophet and their immediate followers and the learned of succeeding generations accepted it. . . . Some later authorities make the prohibition refer only to objects that cast a shadow, and see no harm in objects that have no shadow. But this view is quite wrong, for the curtain to which the Prophet objected was certainly condemned, as everyone admits, yet the picture on it cast no shadow; and the other traditions make no distinction between one picture and another. Al-Zuhri holds that the prohibition refers to pictures in general, and similarly to the use of them and to entrance into a house in which they are found, whether it is a case of design on a dress or any other design, whether the picture hangs on a wall or is on a robe or a carpet, whether in common domestic use or not, as is the clear meaning of the Prophetic traditions. (Nawawi, *Guide to an Understanding of Muslim* 8.398) [Cited by ARNOLD 1928: 9–10]

2. The Worship of God: Church and Mosque

1. Early Christian Worship

For our first glimpse of the Christians at worship we must return to Paul.

To sum up, my friends: when you meet for worship, each of you contributes a hymn, some instruction, a revelation, an ecstatic utterance, or the interpretation of such an utterance. All of these must aim at one thing: to build up the Church. If it is a matter of ecstatic utterance, only two should speak, or at most three, one at a time, and someone must interpret. If there is no interpreter, the speaker had better not address the meeting at all but speak to himself and to God. Of the prophets, two or three may speak, while the rest exercise their judgment upon what is said. If someone else, sitting in his place receives a revelation, let the first speaker stop. You can all prophesy, one at a time, so that the whole congregation may receive instruction and encouragement. It is for prophets to control prophetic inspiration, for the God who inspires them is a God not of disorder but of peace.

As in all congregations of God's people, women should not address the meeting. They have no license to speak, but should keep their place as the law directs. If there is something they want to know, they can ask their husbands at home. It is a shocking thing that a woman should address the congregation. (Paul, *To the Corinthians* 1.14:26–35)

Early community worship is also discussed in the letter Paul sent to Timothy.

First of all, then, I urge that petitions, prayers, intercessions and thanksgivings be offered for all men, for sovereigns and all in high office, that we may lead a tranquil and quiet life in full observance of religion and high standards of morality. Such prayer is right and approved by God our Savior, whose will it is that all men should find salvation and come to know the truth. . . . It is my desire, therefore, that everywhere prayers be said by the men of the congregation, who shall lift up their hands with pure intention, excluding angry and quarrelsome thoughts. . . . A woman must be a learner, listening quietly and with due submission. I do not permit a woman to be a teacher, nor must woman domineer over man; she should be quiet. (Paul, *To Timothy* 1.2:1–12)

Earlier in the same letter to the Corinthians just cited, Paul touched upon one of the problems that had arisen in the still rather spontaneous Christian liturgy: the role of the ecstatic in community worship.

I say, then, that the man who falls into ecstatic utterance should pray for the ability to interpret. If I use such language in my prayer, the Spirit in me prays, but my intellect lies fallow. What then? I will pray as I am inspired to pray, but I will also pray intelligently. I will sing hymns as I am inspired to sing, but I will sing intelligently too. Suppose you are praising God in the language of inspiration; how will the plain man who is present be able to say "Amen" to your thanksgiving when he does not know what you are saying? Your prayer of thanksgiving may be all that could be desired, but it is of no help to the other man. Thank God I am more gifted in ecstatic utterance than any of you, but in the congregation I would rather speak five intelligible words, for the benefit of others as well as myself, than thousands of words in the language of ecstasy. (Paul, *To the Corinthians* 1.14:13–19)

2. How Christians Worship: An Explanation to the Gentiles

Sometime about 150 C.E. the former philosopher Justin, now converted to the Christian faith, wrote an open letter to Emperor Antoninus Pius explaining and defending Christianity and its practices. This is how he set forth the Christians' manner of worship.

After washing [that is, baptizing] him who has been convinced and has given his assent, we bring him to those who are called the brethren, where they are assembled, to offer prayers in common, both for ourselves and for him who has been enlightened as well as for all men everywhere, with all our hearts, that, just as we have learned the truth, so we may be counted worthy to be found good citizens and guardians of the commandments to the end that we find eternal salvation.

When we have finished our prayers we salute one another with a kiss. Then there is brought to the president of the brethren bread and a cup of water and wine. And he takes them and offers up praise and glory to the Father of all things, through the name of the Son and the Holy Spirit, and gives thanks at length that we are deemed worthy of these things at His hand. When we have finished the prayers and thanksgiving, all those present assent by saying *Amen*, which in the Hebrew tongue means "So be it." When the president has given thanks and all the people have assented, those who are called deacons among us give to those present a portion of the Eucharistic bread and wine and water, and carry it away to those who are absent.

This food is called among us the Eucharist, and none is allowed to partake of it except he believe that our teachings are true, and has been washed with the washing for the remission of sins and for regeneration, and who lives as Christ directed. For we do not receive them as ordinary food or ordinary drink, but as the Word of God, Jesus Christ, our Savior; as he took flesh and blood for our salvation, so too, we are taught, the food blessed by the prayer of the word which we received from him, by which, through its transformation, our blood and flesh are nourished, this food is the flesh and blood of Jesus who was made flesh. For the Apostles in the memoirs made by them, which are called Gospels, have thus narrated that the command was given: that Jesus took bread, gave thanks, and said, "Do this in remembrance of me; this is my body." And he took the cup in like manner and said, "This is my blood," and gave it to them alone. This very thing the evil demons imitated in the mysteries of Mithras, and commanded to be done. For, as you know or can discover, bread and a cup of water are set out in the rites of initiation with the repetition of certain words.

And on the matter of the "Lord's Day," formerly the "Sun's Day":

. . . On the day which is called the day of the sun there is an assembly of all those who live in the towns or in the country; and the memoirs of the Apostles or the writings of the prophets are read, as long as time permits. Then the reader ceases and the president speaks, admonishing us and exhorting us to imitate these excellent examples. Then all arise together and offer prayers; and, as we have said before, when we have concluded our prayer, bread is brought and wine and water, and the president in like manner offers up prayers and thanksgivings with all his might; and the people assent with *Amen*. And there is the distribution and partaking by all of the Eucharistic elements; and to them who are not present they are sent by the hand of the deacons. And they that are prosperous and wish to do so give what they will, each as he wishes.

Whatever is collected is deposited with the president, who gives aid to the orphans and widows and such as are in want because of sickness or some other cause; and to those also who are in prison, and to strangers from abroad; he is in fact a protector to all who are in need.

We hold our common assembly on the day of the sun because it is the first day, on which God put to flight darkness and chaos and made the world, and on the same day Jesus Christ our Savior rose from the dead; for on the day before that of Saturn they crucified him; and on the day after Saturn's day, the day of the sun, he appeared to his Apostles and disciples and taught them these things, which we have also handed on to you for your consideration. (Justin, *Apology* 1.65–67)

3. The Christian Celebration of the Sabbath

Although the first day of the week, the "Lord's day," was early marked as a peculiarly Christian holy day, the Sabbath continued to be observed in Christian circles, as this prayer from the Apostolic Constitutions *bears witness.*

O Almighty Lord, who did create the world through Christ, and did ordain the Sabbath as a memorial of creation, because on it You rested from Your work . . . You, O Lord, brought our fathers out of Egypt . . . (and) commanded them to keep the Sabbath, not providing thereby an excuse for idleness but an occasion for godliness. (*Apostolic Constitutions* 7.36)

Or again in Origen's somewhat idealized vision, with its reminiscence of synagogue attendance:

Leaving on one side the Jewish observance of the Sabbath, let us see of what kind the observance of the Sabbath ought to be for the Christian. On the Sabbath no worldly affairs ought to be undertaken. If, then, you abstain from all secular works and do nothing worldly, but employ yourself in spiritual works, and come to church and give ear to the Scripture readings and to sermons, if you think on heavenly things and are concerned with your future hope, if you have before your eyes the coming judgment, and do not look to the present and the visible, but to the invisible and the future, this is the observance of the Sabbath for the Christians. (Origen, *Sermon on Numbers* 23.4)

By the fourth century the Sabbath was everywhere yielding place to Sunday as the Christians' holy day; but its attraction, and the letter of the Law, still operated on Augustine.

"Observe the Sabbath day": This commandment concerns us even more than it concerns them [that is, the Jews]. The Jews observe the Sabbath in a servile fashion, spending it in riotousness and drunkenness. How much better could their women be employed at the spinning wheel than in dancing on that day in the balconies of their houses. Let us not concede for a moment, my brothers, that they observe the Sabbath. The Christian observes the Sabbath spiritually, by abstaining from servile work. For what is "from servile work"? From sin. How do we prove this? Ask the Lord: "Whoever commits sin is the servant of sin" (John 8:34). So that on us likewise is enjoined spiritually the observance of the Sabbath. (Augustine, *On the Gospel of John* 3.19)

The consecration of Sunday as the Christians' holy day was finally sealed by the Roman state's own recognition.

[7 March 321 C.E.]: Constantine to Elpidius. All judges, city people and craftsmen shall rest on the venerable day of the Sun. But countrymen may without hindrance attend to agriculture, since it often happens that this is the most suitable day for sowing grain or planting vines, so that the opportunity offered by divine providence may not be lost, for the right season is of short duration. (Code of Justinian 3.12.3)

[3 July 321 C.E.]: The Emperor Constantine to Elpidius. Just as we thought it most unfitting that the day of the Sun, with its venerable rights, should be given over to swearing and counter-swearing of litigants and their unseemly brawls, so it is a pleasant and a joyful thing to fulfill petitions of special urgency on that day. Therefore on the festal day let all be allowed to perform manumission and emancipation (of slaves); and let nothing that concerns this be forbidden. (Theodosian Code 2.8.1)

4. Two Eucharistic Liturgies

The Teaching of the Apostles *is an anonymous Christian tract, perhaps from the second century, that already has a developed Eucharistic liturgy between its lines.*

Concerning the Eucharist, give thanks in this way. First for the cup: "We give thanks to You, our Father, for the holy vine of David Your servant, which You have made known to us through Your servant Jesus. To You be the glory forever." And for the broken bread: "We give thanks to You, our Father, for the life and knowledge which You have made known to us through Your servant Jesus. To You be the glory forever. As this broken bread was scattered upon the hills, and was gathered together

and made one, so let Your Church be gathered together into Your kingdom from the ends of the earth; for Yours is the glory and the power
through Christ Jesus forever."

Let none eat or drink Your Eucharist, save such as are baptized into
the name of the Lord. For concerning this the Lord has said: "Give not
that which is holy to the dogs."

And after you are filled, give thanks as follows: "We give thanks,
Holy Father, for Your holy name, which You have made a tabernacle in
our hearts, and for the knowledge, faith and immortality which You have
made known to us through Your servant Jesus. To You be the glory
forever. You, Lord Almighty, created all things for Your name's sake and
gave food and drink to men for their enjoyment, that they might give You
thanks; and to us You granted spiritual food and drink and life eternal,
through Your servant. Above all we thank You that You are mighty. To
You be glory forever. Remember, Lord, Your Church, to deliver us from
all evil and to make her perfect in Your love, and to gather from the four
winds her that is sanctified into Your kingdom which You have prepared
for her; for Yours is the power and the glory forever. Let grace come, and
let this world pass away. Hosanna to the God of David. If any is holy, let
him approach; if any be not holy, let him repent. *Maranatha* Amen."
(*Teaching of the Apostles* 9–10)

The following liturgy, drawn from the Apostolic Tradition *of Hippolytus and
dating from about 225 C.E., is more explicit and more formal than that in the*
Teaching.

THE BISHOP: The Lord be with you.
PEOPLE: And with your spirit.
BISHOP: Lift up your hearts.
PEOPLE: We lift them up to the Lord.
BISHOP: Let us give thanks to the Lord.
PEOPLE: It is right and just.
BISHOP: We give You thanks, O God, through Your beloved Son
Jesus Christ, whom You sent to us in the last times to be a savior and a
redeemer and a messenger of Your will; who is Your inseparable Word,
through whom You made all things and in whom You were well pleased.
You did send him from heaven into the Virgin's womb; he was conceived
and became incarnate and was shown to be Your Son, born of the Holy
Spirit and the Virgin; who, fulfilling Your will and preparing for You a
holy people, stretched out his hands in suffering, that he might free from
suffering all who believed in You.

When he was being betrayed to his voluntary suffering, that he might destroy death, break the chains of the devil, tread Hell underfoot, bring forth the righteous from it, and set a boundary to it, and that he might show forth his Resurrection, Our Lord took bread and gave thanks to You and said: "Take, eat: This is my body which is broken for you." So too the cup, saying: "This is my blood which is shed for you. As often as you do this, you shall do it in remembrance of me."

And so we, who are mindful of his death and resurrection, offer You this bread and this cup, giving thanks to You that You considered us worthy to stand before You and minister as Your priest. And we beseech You that You should send Your Holy Spirit upon the offering of the Holy Church; and that You should grant it to all the saints who partake, making them one, for fulfillment of the Holy Spirit and for the confirmation of their faith in truth; that we may praise and glorify You through Your Son Jesus Christ, through whom be honor and glory to You, to the Father and to the Son with the Holy Spirit in Your Holy Church, both now and forever. Amen. (Hippolytus, *The Apostolic Tradition* 8:4)

5. The Service of the Word of God

In its developed form, the Eucharistic liturgy was a composite ceremony, and the Eucharist proper, of the type described in the Teaching of the Twelve Apostles *and the* Apostolic Tradition, *was preceded by a service of prayer and worship and followed by a communion or the distribution of the consecrated bread and wine to the faithful. The opening prayers, sometimes called "the Service of the Word of God" or, in its Western form, "the Mass of the Catechumens," was open to all Christians—those under instruction for baptism (that is, the "catechumens"), as well as the baptized—and it owed much of its form and conduct to the synagogue service from which it doubtless derived. This description of such a service is from a work entitled* The Apostolic Constitutions *and dates from the fourth century* C.E. *It is addressed to the bishop of a community.*

When you call an assembly of the church as one that is the commander of a great ship, appoint the assemblies to be made with all possible skill, charging the deacons as sailors to prepare places for the brethren as passengers, with all due care and decency. First, let the building be long, with its head [that is, the apse] toward the east end, so that it will be like a ship. In the middle let the bishop's throne be placed, and on each side of him let the presbyters sit down; and let the deacons stand near, in close and girt garments, for they are like the sailors and managers of the ship. Let the laity sit on the other side, with all quietness and good order. And let the women sit by themselves, they also keeping silence.

In the middle let the reader stand upon some raised place: let him read the book of Moses, of Joshua son of Nun, of the Judges and of the Kings and Chronicles, and those written after the return from the captivity; and besides these, the books of Job and of Solomon, and of the sixteen prophets. When there have been two lessons severally read, let some other person sing the hymns of David, and let the people join at the conclusion of the verses. Afterwards let our Acts be read, and the Letters of Paul our fellow worker, which he sent to the churches under the conduct of the Holy Spirit; and afterwards let a deacon or presbyter read the Gospel, both those which I [that is, Peter], Matthew and John have directed to you and those which the fellow workers of Paul received and handed on to you, Luke and Mark. And while the Gospel is read, let all the presbyters and deacons and all the people, stand up in great silence; for it is written: "Be silent and hear, O Israel" (Deut. 27:9), and again, "Stand there and hear" (Deut. 5:31).

In the next place, let the presbyters one by one, not all together, exhort the people, and the bishop last of all, since he is the commander. Let the doorkeepers stand at the entries of the men and observe them. Let the deaconesses also stand at those of the women, as sailors. For the same description and pattern was in both the Tent of the Witnessing and in the Temple of God (Deut. 23:1). But if anyone is out of his place, let him be rebuked by the deacon . . . and removed into the place proper for him; for the church is not only like a ship, but also like a sheepfold. For as the shepherds place all the animals distinctly, I mean goats and sheep, according to their age and kind, and still every one runs together, like with like; so it is to be in the church. Let the young persons sit by themselves, if there is a place for them; if not, let them stand up. But let those that are already advanced in years sit in order. . . . Let the younger women also sit by themselves, if there is a place for them; if there is not, let them stand behind the other women. Let those women who are married and have children be placed by themselves, but let the virgins and the widows and the older women stand or sit before all the rest; and let the deacon be the assigner of places, that every one who comes in may go to his proper place and may not sit around the entrance. In like manner, let the deacon oversee the people, that nobody may whisper, or sleep, or laugh, or nod; for all ought to stand wisely and soberly and attentively in church, with all his attention on the word of the Lord.

This marks the end of the Service of the Word of God. Then, after the departure of some lay persons, the offertory ceremony preparatory to the Eucharist begins.

After this let all arise as one, and looking toward the east, after the catechumens and penitents [that is, those under a temporary ban] have left, pray toward the east to God, who ascended up to the heaven of heavens to the east, from the same direction that the first humans, when they had yielded to the persuasion of the serpent and disobeyed the command of God, were expelled. As for the deacons, after the prayer is over, let some of them attend upon the offering of the Eucharist, ministering to the Lord's body with fear. Let others of them watch the multitude and keep them quiet. But let the deacon who is at the High Priest's side say to the people, "Let no one have any quarrel with another; let no one come in hypocrisy." Then let the deacon pray for the whole Church, for the whole world and the several parts of it, and the fruits of it; for the priests and the rulers, for the High Priest and the king, and the peace of the universe. After this, let the High Priest pray for peace upon the people, and bless them, as Moses commanded the priests to bless the people, in these words: "The Lord bless you and keep you; the Lord make His face to shine upon you and give you peace." Let the bishop also pray for the people and say: "Save Your people, O Lord, and bless Your inheritance, which You have obtained with the precious blood of Your Christ, and have called a royal priesthood and a holy people."

After this let the sacrifice [that is, the Eucharist proper] follow; and when the offering has been made, let every rank by itself partake of the Lord's body and precious blood in order, and approach in reverence and holy fear, as toward the body of their king. Let the women approach with their heads covered, as is becoming the order of women; but let the door be watched, lest any unbeliever, or one not initiated, come in. (*Apostolic Constitutions* 57)

6. Pentecost in Jerusalem

The Constitutions' *presentation of the liturgy was intended to be instructional and normative. How the Christians actually conducted their liturgical life is better learned from eyewitnesses. Here the witness is Egeria, a Western visitor to Jerusalem in 380 C.E. The occasion is Pentecost, as Egeria herself explains.*

And finally, Pentecost, fifty days after Easter, the day on which the Holy Spirit descended on Jesus' disciples who were patiently and fearfully collected in an upper room, as it was believed, on Mount Sion.

When it is the morning (of Pentecost Sunday) all the people assemble in their usual way in the Great Church, the Martyrium [that is, what was later called the Church of the Holy Sepulcher], and have sermons from the presbyters and then the bishop, and the offering is duly made in the way that is usual on the Lord's day, except that the dismissal at the Martyrium is hurried, so that it is over before nine o'clock. And soon after the dismissal at the Martyrium all the people escort the bishop with singing to Sion, where they arrive in time for nine o'clock. When they arrive, they have a reading of the passage from the Acts of the Apostles where the Spirit descends so that all nations might understand the things that were spoken, after which the Mass proceeds as usual.

The presbyters read this passage from the Acts of the Apostles because this place on Sion, though it has now been altered into a church, is the very spot where what I have mentioned was done by the multitude who were assembled with the Apostles after the Lord's Passion.

After that the service proceeds as usual, and they make the offering there. Then as the people are dismissed the archdeacon makes this announcement: "Let us all be ready today on the Mount of Eleona at the Imbomon immediately after midday."

So all the people return home for a rest. And as soon as they have had their meal, they go up to Eleona, the Mount of Olives, each at his own pace, till there is not a Christian left in the city. Once they have climbed Eleona, the Mount of Olives, they go to first to the Imbomon, the place from which the Lord ascended into heaven, where the bishop and the presbyters take their seats, and likewise all the people. They have readings, and between them hymns and antiphons suitable to this day and to the place. . . . When this has been done, the catechumens are blessed, and also the faithful.

It is now already three o'clock, and they go down singing hymns from there to another church, also on Olivet, and in it is the cave where the Lord used to sit and teach the Apostles. By the time they get there it is after four, and they have vespers. The prayer is said, the catechumens are blessed, and then the faithful.

From there all the people go down with their bishop, singing hymns and antiphons suitable to the day, and so, very slowly and gently, they make their way to the Martyrium. When they arrive at the city gate it is already night, and the people have brought hundreds of church candles to help them. But since it is quite a way from the gate to the Great Church, the Martyrium, they arrive there at about eight at night, going very slowly all the way so that the walk does not weary the people. The great doors which face the market street are opened, and the bishop and all the people enter the Martyrium with hymns.

Once inside the church they have hymns and a prayer, and the catechumens are blessed, and also the faithful. Then they set off once more with hymns to the Anastasis. Again in the Anastasis [or "Resurrection"] they have more hymns and antiphons and a prayer, and the catechumens are blessed, and also the faithful. Then the same is done again at the Cross. And once more all the Christian community conducts the bishop with hymns to Sion. Once there, they have suitable readings, psalms and antiphons, a prayer, the blessing of the catechumens and the faithful, and so they are dismissed. After the dismissal everyone goes to have the bishop's hand laid on him, and about midnight everybody returns to his home. Thus this is a very tiring day for them, for they have never stopped all day since they kept vigil in the Anastasis at cock-crow, and the services have taken so long that it is midnight by the time they are dismissed at Sion and all return to their homes. (Egeria, *Pilgrimage* 70–71)

7. An Eastern Eucharistic Liturgy

Egeria gives us a glimpse of the liturgical life of the Church while still in its formative period. Although its central element, the re-enactment of Jesus' "Last Supper," did not much vary, there grew up around this act different combinations of readings, prayers, commemorations, and petitions, depending on local tradition and practice. Eucharistic liturgies in Rome or Milan, for example, or Alexandria, Edessa, or Constantinople all displayed an elemental similarity with considerable local variants of language and style.

Eventually the growing power of the great ecclesiastical centers and the concentration of authority and prestige there led to the decline, and in some instances the disappearance, of local liturgical traditions. The "Mass" of the Roman Church replaced many of the Western variants, while the liturgies called after St. Basil and St. John Chrysostom, the preferred forms in Constantinople, had a similar, though perhaps not so thoroughgoing effect in the East.

The "John Chrysostom" is the form celebrated in the daily Eucharistic liturgy of the Eastern Church; the "St. Basil" is used on feast days. The former is divided, like its Western counterparts, into two sections: a "Eucharistic liturgy"—the "canon" of the Western "Mass"—preceded by a "liturgy of the catechumens" open to those undergoing "catechesis," the instruction prior to baptism, and to the excommunicated cut off from full participation in the life of the Church. This "liturgy of the catechumens," composed chiefly of prayers, hymns, and the daily prescribed readings from Scripture, has a distinct Hellenic nuance. The emphasis on knowledge as light and on membership in the Kingdom as citizenship can be heard in this prayer, said between the reading of Paul and the Gospel.

O Merciful Master, cause the pure light of the knowledge of you to shine into our hearts, and open the eyes of our mind to discern your message of Good Tidings; fill us with the fear of your blessed commandments, that in treading under foot our fleshly desires, we may seek a heavenly citizenship, and may do and consider all those things that are pleasing to you. For you, Christ our Lord, are the source of light to our souls and bodies, and to you we ascribe glory, together with your Eternal Father, and your All-Holy, Righteous and Life-Giving Spirit, now and forever, and from all ages to all ages.

There follows, as in the West, a series of prayers for the living—the emperor and the imperial family prominently to the fore—and a commemoration for the dead. Then comes another of the remarkable hymns that typify the Eastern liturgy, in this instance the "Cherubic Hymn," traditionally attributed to the eighth-century theologian John of Damascus.

> Let us, the mystic counterparts of the Cherubim,
> Who sing the thrice-holy hymn to the life-creating Trinity
> Now put aside all earthly cares,
> That we may welcome the King of all,
> Invisibly escorted by the Angelic Hosts.
> Alleluia, Alleluia, Alleluia.

Although the basic structure is one in both East and West—the Creed and the Offertory, for example, which now follow—there are distinguishing emphases. Thus at the Eastern offering of the bread and the wine, they are wafted by a gold or silver fan representing the wings of the Cherubim: the presence of the invisible angelic host is strongly felt and often expressed in word and in symbol in the Eastern liturgies. The liturgy of the catechumens is completed, and the celebrant, priest or bishop, performs the central eucharistic act, first with the bread, then with the wine.

Take, eat: this is my body, which is broken for you, for the remission of sins. . . . Drink you all of this; this is my blood of the New Covenant, which is shed for you and for many for the remission of sins.

There then occurs in the Eastern liturgy a prayer that is undoubtedly the theological crux between East and West, a "summoning" of the Holy Spirit to transform the bread and wine into the body and blood of Christ—the "transubstantiation" of the Western theologians—a miracle that occurs, according to the Latin Church, at the simple pronouncing of the words, "This is my body . . . This is my blood. . . ." The "summoning" is something more as well: a prayer for the communion of all the faithful, the Old Testament knit into the New.

Unite us all [prays the priest], as many as are partakers of the one bread and cup, each with the other, in the participation of the one Holy Spirit; allow no one of us to share in the holy Body and Blood of Your Christ to our judgment or our condemnation, but to the end that we may all find in it mercy and grace, together with all the saints who have been well pleasing to You ever since the world began, our forefathers and fathers, the patriarchs, prophets, apostles, preachers, evangelists, martyrs, confessors, teachers, and with all the spirits of the saints who have been made perfect in faith.

At the completion of this and other prayers, first the priest and then the deacon shares in the Eucharistic bread and wine. Then, before he distributes them likewise to the congregation, the priest prays on the communicants' behalf.

I believe, O Lord, and I confess that you are truly the Christ, the Son of the Living God, who came into the world to save sinners, of whom I am the chief. I also believe that this is indeed your most precious blood. Wherefore, I pray you, have mercy on me, forgive me my offenses, voluntary and involuntary, whether in word or in deed . . . and account me worthy to partake without condemnation in your most pure mysteries, for the remission of my sins and the attainment of everlasting life.

Each member of the congregation approaches the sanctuary of the temple-church of the New Dispensation and receives the bread and wine, now transformed into the Body and Blood of Christ. And although there are additional prayers and hymns, the liturgy, whether Eastern or Western, is in effect completed. "Go," the Latin worshiper is told, "the Mass is over."

8. Worship Compared

According to a story told in the Russian Primary Chronicle, Prince Vladimir of Kiev, who was about to declare an official religion for his princedom, wished to inform himself about the forms of worship in use among his neighbors of different faiths. In 987 C.E. he sent envoys to the Muslim Bulgars, the Western Christian Germans, and the Eastern Christian Greeks at Constantinople to observe and compare. The envoys' reactions, which may have had as much to do with cultural differences and political considerations as with prescribed manners of worship, are reported by the same Chronicle.

Thus they returned to their own country, and the prince [that is, Vladimir] called together his vassals and elders. Vladimir then announced the return of the envoys, and suggested that their report be heard. He thus commanded them to speak out before his vassals. The envoys reported: "When we journeyed among the (Muslim) Bulgarians, we beheld how they worship in their temple, called a mosque, while they stand ungirt. The Bulgarian bows, sits down, looks hither and thither like one possessed, and there is no happiness among them, only sorrow and a dreadful stench. Their religion is not good. Then we went among the (Roman Catholic) Germans, and saw them performing many ceremonies in their temples; but we beheld no glory there. Then we went on to Greece, and the (Byzantine) Greeks led us to the edifices where they worship their God, and we knew not whether we were in heaven or on earth. For on earth there is no such splendor or such beauty, and we are at a loss how to describe it. We know only that God dwells there among men, and their service is fairer than the ceremonies of other nations. For we cannot forget that beauty. . . ."

Then the vassals spoke and said: "If the Greek faith were evil, it would not have been adopted by your grandmother Olga, who was wiser than all other men." Vladimir then inquired whether they should all accept baptism, and they replied that the decision rested with him. (*Russian Primary Chronicle*) [ZENKOVSKY 1963: 68]

9. "When You Pray . . . "

The Eucharist is the chief form of liturgical worship among Christians; but in common with Jews and Muslims, they petition and thank God through a great variety of private prayers. Although there is no liturgical instruction in the Gospels, Jesus not only advised his followers on how they should pray but also gave them the very words they should use.

When you pray, do not be like the hypocrites; they love to say their prayers standing up in the synagogue and at the street corners, for everyone to see them. I tell you this: they have their reward already. But when you pray, go into a room by yourself, shut the door, and pray to your Father who is there in the secret place; and your Father, who sees what is secret, will reward you.

In your prayers do not go babbling on like the heathen, who imagine that the more they say the more likely they are to be heard. Do not imitate them. Your Father knows what your needs are before you ask Him.

This is how you should pray:

877

Our Father in heaven,
thy name be hallowed;
thy kingdom come,
on earth as in heaven.
Give us this day our daily bread.
Forgive us the wrong we have done,
  as we have forgiven those who have wronged us.
And do not bring us to the test,
  but save us from the evil one.
(Matthew 6:5–13)

Those words continued to be used, of course, and others as well—some taken directly from the Gospels or the Greek or Latin version of the Bible, some the products of private piety or individual inspiration, in prose and poetry, in all the languages in use among Christians, now recited, now chanted or sung. Again, some of these prayers were inserted in the Eucharistic and other liturgies and so became "public" or "official" prayers of the Church; others remained the subject of private devotion.

All Christian preaching and instruction urges prayer on the faithful, but only rarely has the exhortation been accompanied by formal instruction. In the sixteenth century the degeneration, and the revival, of private devotion and popular forms of piety was a source of growing concern in Church circles. As a consequence, there arose a concerted effort to revitalize Christian piety and particularly the practice of prayer. Two influential figures in that movement were the Spaniards Ignatius of Loyola (1491–1556 C.E.) and Teresa of Avila (1515–1582). The latter, who spent nearly fifty years of her life in a Carmelite convent, explains in direct and compre-hensible terms the difference between the simple recitation of words and what she calls "mental prayer."

You must understand that the mere opening or closing of the mouth does not determine whether a prayer is vocal or mental. If, while I am praying vocally, I am entirely absorbed in God to whom I am speaking, and if I concentrate my attention more on Him than on the words I am uttering, I am combining therein both vocal and mental prayer. (Teresa of Avila, *The Way of Perfection*)

One of the more popular forms of religious instruction in the sixteenth-century Catholic revival was that found in the Spiritual Exercises written by Ignatius of Loyola, the religious innovator who founded the Society of Jesus, or Jesuits, in 1534. The "spiritual exercises" were precisely that, a set of exercises to be administered by his followers to the Christian faithful to raise their spiritual consciousness and so their devotion to Jesus and their dedication to the Roman Church. The carefully structured and detailed exercises, which are nothing less than a clinical course on prayer carried out under the supervision of a skilled practitioner—the Christian was intended to "make" the exercises, not merely study them—are filled with practical instruction, a great deal of it on prayer, including what Loyola called "Three Methods of Prayer." The first is a kind of examination of conscience with regard to the Ten Commandments and so on; the second is what Teresa of Avila called "mental prayer," a thoughtful reflection, an interior realization of the words of a well-known prayer like the "Our Father."

The second method of prayer is that the person, kneeling or seated, according to the greater disposition in which he finds himself, and as more devotion accompanies him, keeping the eyes closed or fixed on one place, without going wandering with them, says "Father" [that is, the first word of the prayer], and remains on the consideration of this word as long as he finds meanings, comparisons, relish and consolation in considerations pertaining to such a word. At let him do likewise with each word of the "Our Father" or of any other prayer he wishes to say in this way.

First Rule: The first rule is that he will be an hour on the whole "Our Father" in the manner just mentioned. If he finishes, he will say a "Hail Mary," "Creed," "Soul of Christ" and "Hail, Holy Queen," vocally or mentally, according to the usual way.

Second Rule: The second rule is that, should the person who is contemplating the "Our Father" find in one word, or in two, matter so good to think over, and relish and consolation, let him not concern himself to pass on, even though the hour ends on what he finds there. The hour ended, he will say the rest of the "Our Father" in the usual way.

Third Rule: The third is that if one has lingered for a whole hour on one word or two of the "Our Father," when he will want to come back on another day to the prayer, let him say the above-mentioned word or two as he is accustomed, and on the word which immediately follows, let him begin to contemplate according to what was said in the second rule. (Ignatius of Loyola, *Spiritual Exercises*, "The Fourth Week")

10. The Recollection of the Name of God

It is uncertain which Eastern Christian composed the following text, whether Symeon the New Theologian in the eleventh century or somebody else somewhat later. It gives rather explicit directions for the type of rhythmic prayer just described.

One must acquire, above all else, three things: death to everything, a pure conscience which preserves you from every self-accusation, and freedom from every passion that might incline you toward the present age, or even toward your own body. Then, seated in a peaceful cell, apart, in a corner, do as I instruct you: close the door and raise your spirit above every vain and temporal object; then, resting your beard on your breast, and turning your physical eye and your entire spirit toward the middle of your belly, also called the navel, restrain the air that passes through your nose in such a way as to render your breathing difficult, and mentally explore within your entrails to find there the heart where it pleases all the faculties of the soul to abide.

In the beginning you will find darkness and a stubborn dullness, but if you persevere and carry out this exercise day and night, you will discover, O wonder! a happiness without limit. As soon, in fact, as the spirit discovers the place of the heart, it will suddenly perceive what it has never known: it will perceive the air that exists at the center of the heart, and it will perceive itself whole and full of discernment, and henceforward, as soon as a thought issues forth, even before it is completely formed, by the invocation of Jesus Christ the spirit tracks it down and destroys it. . . . The rest you will understand with the help of God by keeping guard over your spirit and holding Jesus in your heart.
[Cited by HAUSHERR 1927: 68–69]

The "invocation of Jesus," here associated with rhythmic breathing techniques, is doubtless the "Jesus prayer," or "single-word prayer," favored by Eastern Christian masters of the spirituality of stillness. John Climacus was already using it familiarly in the seventh century.

Let the remembrance of death and the concise Jesus Prayer go to sleep with you and get up with you, for nothing helps you as these do when you are asleep. (John Climacus, *The Ladder of Divine Ascent*, Step 15)
[JOHN CLIMACUS 1982: 178]

In a definition of stillness (hesychia), the "remembrance of Jesus" is connected with breathing.

Stillness is worshiping God unceasingly and waiting on Him. Let the remembrance of Jesus be present with your every breath. Then indeed you will appreciate the value of stillness. (Ibid., Step 27)
[JOHN CLIMACUS 1982: 269–270]

The "Jesus prayer" is, then, formulaic, repetitive, and rhythmically connected with breathing. It occurs in a number of similar formulas, of which "Lord Jesus Christ, have mercy on me" is one of the more common.

A parallel phenomenon occurs in Islam, and mutual borrowings between Eastern Christians and Muslims are by no means to be ruled out. In Muslim circles this type of prayer is called "remembrance" or "recollection" of the name of God.

"Recollect God often," the Quran commands (Quran 33:40), for "the recollection of God makes the heart calm" (Quran 13:28). The Quran does not say what form that recollection is to take, but it eventually became centered, as it did in Christianity, upon the divine Name; and one or another form of such recollection was built into the liturgy of every Sufi fraternity in Islam. "Recollection" is, quite simply, the most common form of noncanonical Muslim piety and perhaps the best known in non-Muslim circles, since its practice as a communal and public devotion from the twelfth century down to modern times has drawn the attention of Western pilgrims and travelers in the Near East. How closely the Muslim "recollection" resembles its Christian counterpart is clear from this very early testimony to the practice by Sahl al-Tustari (d. 896 C.E.).

Sahl said to one of his disciples: Strive to say continuously for one day "O God! O God! O God!" and do the same the next day and the day after that—until he became habituated to saying those words. Then he bade him repeat them at night also, until they became so familiar that he uttered them even during his sleep. Then he said: Do not repeat them any more but let all your faculties be engrossed in remembering God. The disciple did this, until he became absorbed in the thought of God. One day, when he was in his house, a piece of wood fell on his head and broke it. The drops of blood which trickled to the ground bore the legend "O God!" (Hujwiri, *The Unveiling of the Hidden*) [HUJWIRI 1911: 195]

In this text directions do not go much beyond urging the continuous repetition of the formula, here simply the divine name "Allah, Allah, Allah." But with the passage of time both the physical directions and the formulas become more complex. Thus Ibn Iyad in the mid-thirteenth century provides recitation instructions on the very common prayer formula drawn from the first part of the profession of faith: La illaha ill'Allah, "There is no god but The God."

Its recitation is begun from the left side of the breast, which is like the niche enclosing the lamp of the heart, the center of spiritual brightness. It continues going down and around the base of the breast, up the right side to its top. Continue until you reach the starting position. (Ibn Iyad, *Lofty Deeds*) [Cited by ANAWATI & GARDET 1961: 202]

Ibn Iyad belonged to a Sufi group called the Shadhilis, and he is describing their characteristic method of "recollection." Another account of the same method comes from Muhammad al-Sanusi (d. 1859 C.E.), a collector of Sufi traditions and himself the founder of one the last two great Sufi fraternities, the Sanusis.

The positions to be taken in a Shadhili "recollection" consist in squatting down on the ground, legs crossed, knees raised, arms around the legs, head lowered between the two knees, eyes closed. The head is then raised while reciting *la ilaha* during the interval between the arrival of the head at the height of the heart from its (starting) position on the right shoulder. One should be careful to banish from the soul whatever is alien to God. When the head reaches the level of the heart, the *illa* should be enunciated with vigor so that it makes its impression there and its effect spreads thence to all the members of the body. That is what one calls the prayer of compassion and expulsion. . . . One then says the *Allah* directly into the heart in a manner even more energetic: the formula then has the effect of compressing there the principles of the fear of God and of affirming His Oneness. (Sanusi, *The Gushing Spring*)

[Cited by ANAWATI & GARDET 1961: 202–203]

The Muslim's private "recollection" has, then, its obvious resemblances to the East-ern Christian practice of the single-phrase "Jesus prayer." The Muslim manifesta-tion, however, was often enlarged to embrace a litany of the "Ninety-nine Beautiful Names of God," whose recitation was commonly assisted by a chaplet of thirty-three or ninety-nine beads, an obvious ancestor to the Western Christian's "rosary beads."

11. Spiritual Concerts

Equally characteristic of Islamic piety was the performance of the "recollection" ritual in unison by groups of Sufis, often accompanied by music and even dancing. Such a devotion, called an "audition" and perhaps best understood as a kind of spiritual concert, was widespread—though by no means universally approved of— across the entire Islamic world down to modern times. One of the earliest apprecia-tions we have of the spiritual concert comes from Ahmad Ghazali (d. 1126 C.E.), the brother of the more famous lawyer and theologian. The Sufis gather, and their master gives them a spiritual exegesis of some passage from the Quran. Then a singer begins the chanting of Sufi poetry.

When they [that is, the assembled Sufis] experience within them a stirring which affects them like the commotion of one who is called to the service of a mighty king and to appear before God, he who falls into ecstasy does not rise until he is overpowered, and the rest do as he does. The dance is not to be affected or feigned; no, their movements must be in accordance with the state, like one who is overcome by terror or unavoidable trepidation. Then when their spirits receive a mystical appre-hension of the unseen states, and their hearts are softened by the lights of the Divine Essence and are established in purity and the spiritual lights, they sit down, and the chanter chants a light chant to bring them forth by degrees from the internal to the external. . . . Then they get up from the place of the audition and go to their dwellings and sit watching for the revelation of what appeared to them in the state of their absorption in ecstasy. After the audition some of them dispense with food for days on account of the nourishment of their spirits and hearts with unseen mystical experiences. (Ahmad Ghazali, *On the Audition*) [TRIMINGHAM 1971: 196]

"Things went on that way," Ghazali continues, fully aware that he is describing a devotion undergoing rapid changes, "till the common people imitated them, and the good was mingled with the corrupt and the system was disordered." What may have disordered the system was the transformation of these "spiritual concerts" into celebrations that seemed little different from a party or a carouse. One who was notorious for the lavish entertainments of his "concerts" at Nishapur was Abu Saʿid ibn Abi al-Khayr (d. 1049 C.E.). Once approached by another Sufi who questioned him about this innovation of "permitting the young men to dance and sing," Abu Saʿid responded with this lesson in sublimation.

As for the young men's dancing in the spiritual "audition," the souls of young men are not yet purged of lust—indeed it may be the prevailing element—and lust takes possession of all the limbs. Now if a young dervish claps his hands, the lust of his hands will be dissipated, and if he tosses his feet, the lust of his feet will be lessened. When by this means the lust fails in their limbs, they can preserve themselves from great sins, but when all lusts are united—which my God forfend—they will sin mortally. It is better that the fire of their lust should be dissipated in the "audition" than in something else. (Abu Saʿid, *The Secrets of Holiness* 269) [NICHOLSON 1921: 58]

The answer is undoubtedly orthodox and may have been calculated to appease, unlike another response reported to a similar objection.

There was at Qaʾin a venerable Prayer Leader, whose name was Khwaja Muhammad Qaʾini. When Abu Saʿid arrived at Qaʾin, Khwaja Muhammad spent most of his time in waiting upon him, and he used to attend all the parties to which Abu Saʿid was invited. On one of these occasions, during the "audition" which followed the feast, Abu Saʿid and all the company had fallen into transports of ecstasy. The muezzin gave the call to noonday prayers, but Abu Saʿid remained in the same rapture and the dervishes continued to dance and shout. "Prayers! Prayers!" cried the Prayer Leader Muhammad Qaʾini. "We *are* at prayers," said Abu Saʿid, whereupon the Prayer Leader left them in order to take part in the prayer service. When Abu Saʿid came out of his trance, he said, "Between its rising and its setting the sun does not shine upon a more venerable and learned man than Khwaja Muhammad. But his knowledge of Sufism is less than the tip of a hair." (Abu Saʿid, *The Secrets of Holiness* 293) [NICHOLSON 1921: 60–61]

Ghazali may have had Abu Saʿid's practices in mind when he expressed some reservations about "spiritual concerts." He would certainly not have approved of the late medieval form of the devotion that Edward Lane witnessed in Cairo in 1836. Here the Sufis belonged to the Mawliyya or Mevlana order, the famous "whirling dervishes" founded by Jalal al-Din Rumi (d. 1273 C.E.) at Konya in Turkey.

Most of the dervishes [*darwish* is the Persian word to describe the Arabic *Sufi*, the Muslim ascetic/mystic; see Chapter 3 below] were Egyptians, but there were among them many Turks and Persians. I had not waited many minutes before they began their exercises. . . . The dervishes who formed the large ring (which enclosed four of the marble columns of the portico) now commenced their *zikr* [Arabic *dhikr*: "recollection"], exclaiming over and over again "Allah" and, at each exclamation, bowing the head and the body and taking a step to the right, so that the whole ring moved rapidly round. As soon as they commenced this exercise, another dervish, a Turk of the order of Mowlawees, in the middle of the circle, began to whirl, using both his feet to effect this motion, and extending his arms; the motion increased in velocity until his dress spread out like an umbrella. He continued whirling thus for about ten minutes; after which he bowed to his superior, who stood within the great ring, and then, without showing any signs of fatigue or giddiness, joined the dervishes in the great ring; who had now begun to ejaculate the name of God with great vehemence, and to jump to the right instead of stepping.

After whirling, six other dervishes, within the great ring, formed another ring, but a very small one, each placing his arms on the shoulders of those next to him; and thus disposed they performed a revolution similar to that of the larger ring, except in being more rapid; repeating also the same exclamation of "Allah!" but with a rapidity proportionately greater. This motion they maintained for about the same length of time that the whirling of the single dervish before had occupied; after which the whole party sat down to rest. They rose again after the lapse of about a quarter of an hour and performed the same exercise a second time.
[LANE 1836: 172–174]

12. The Sacraments

To return to Christian worship, the Eucharist and baptism were but two, albeit the most important, of a number of acts and ceremonies that took on a special religious significance for Christians. These were called, from the fourth century onward, mysteria by the Greeks and sacramenta by the Latins. Their distinguishing characteristic was that they were exterior signs of the operation of an invisible, interior grace. Or, as Augustine put it, speaking expressly of the bread and wine of the Eucharist: "They are called sacraments because one thing is seen in them, another understood. What is seen is a bodily appearance, but what is understood has a spiritual fruit."

The definition of a sacrament was sufficiently elastic—"an indication, by means of signs and symbols, of invisible and ineffable realities," according to one— that the number of them seems to have fluctuated in the early Church. Where there was agreement was that Christ was the principal agent in working that invisible grace; the priest was simply an instrument, whence it followed that the virtue or spiritual condition of the officiating cleric had no effect on the operation of that grace. There was dispute, however, over how that connection between the realm of spirit and that of matter was effected. That it came about through the words of the officiating priest serving as Jesus' deputy was the general view in the West; in the Eastern churches the prevailing sentiment was for a more direct divine intervention in the form of a descent of the Holy Spirit. That difference in viewpoints long separated the Eastern and Western churches.

Eventually the number of sacraments became stabilized at seven: Baptism, Confirmation, Unction, Penance, Eucharist, Holy Orders, and Matrimony. Reflection on each of them became more complex, particularly as it became more theological. Here, for example, is the treatment of the sacraments in what became one of the classic textbooks of the Middle Ages, the Four Books of Sentences *of Peter Lombard, written sometime about 1150 C.E. Further, it bears the unmistakable signs of the method characteristic of Hellenically derived theology: a carefully systematic presentation and reliance on what had already become the Church's authorities, the "Fathers."*

ON SACRAMENTS

The Samaritan who tended the wounded man (Luke 10:30–37) applied to his wounds the dressings of the sacraments, just as God instituted the remedies of the sacraments against the wounds of original and actual sin. Concerning the sacraments, four questions first present themselves for consideration: what a sacrament is, why it was instituted, wherein it consists, and how it is performed; and what the difference is between the sacraments of the Old and New Covenant.

WHAT A SACRAMENT IS

"A sacrament is the sign of a sacred thing" (as Augustine says). However, a sacred mystery is also called a sacrament, so that a sacrament may be (both) the sign of something sacred and the sacred thing signified.

So (as Berengar of Tours says) "a sacrament is the visible form of an invisible grace." . . .

HOW A SIGN AND A SACRAMENT DIFFER

Furthermore, "some signs are natural, as smoke which signifies fire; others conventional" (as Augustine says); of those which are conventional, some are sacraments and some are not. For every sacrament is a sign, but the converse is not true. A sacrament bears a resemblance to the thing of which it is the sign. "For if sacraments did not bear a resemblance to things of which they are the sacraments, they could not be properly called sacraments." For a sacrament is properly so called because it is a sign of the grace of God and the expression of invisible grace, so that it bears its image and its cause. Sacraments, therefore, were not instituted merely to signify something, but also as a means of sanctification. For things which were instituted only to signify are signs only, and not sacraments; such were the sacrifices of the flesh and the ceremonial observances of the Old Law, which could never justify those who offered them, because, as the Apostle (Paul) says: "The blood of goats and of oxen and the ashes of a heifer being sprinkled sanctify such as are defiled, to the cleansing of the flesh" (Heb. 9:13), but not of the spirit. Now this uncleanness (referred to in the Old Law) was the touching of a dead body. . . . These legal observances also cleansed sometimes from bodily leprosy; but no one was ever justified by the works of the Law, as the Apostle says (Rom. 3:20; Gal. 2:16), even if he performed them in faith and charity. Why? Because God has ordained them for servitude, not for justification, so that they might be the types of things to come, wishing that these offerings should be made to Him rather than to idols. They therefore were signs, yet also sacraments, although they are often called so incorrectly in the Scriptures, because they were rather signs of a sacred thing than availing anything themselves. These moreover the Apostle calls "works of the Law," which were instituted only to signify something, or as a yoke.

Peter Lombard shortly returns to this question of the "sacraments" of the Old Law, which in turn leads him to those of the New.

OF THE DIFFERENCE BETWEEN
THE OLD AND THE NEW SACRAMENTS

Now it remains to note the difference between the old and the new sacraments, since we call sacraments what anciently they called sacred things, such as sacrifices and oblations and the like. The differences between these Augustine indicated briefly when he said, "because the former only promised and signified salvation, while the latter gave it."

OF THE SACRAMENTS OF THE NEW LAW

Let us now come to the sacraments of the New Covenant, which are baptism, confirmation, the blessing of bread, that is, the eucharist, penance, extreme unction, ordination, marriage. Of these some offer a remedy for sin and confer a helping grace, like baptism; others are merely a remedy, like marriage; others strengthen us with grace and virtue, such as the eucharist and ordination. If indeed we are asked why these sacraments were not instituted immediately after the fall of man (through Adam's sin), since in them are justification and salvation, we say that before the coming of Christ, who brought grace, the sacraments of grace could not be granted, for they have derived their virtue from his death and passion. Now Christ was unwilling to come (into this world) before man was convinced that he could find help in neither natural nor written law. (Peter Lombard, *Sentences* 4.1.1–2)

[PETER LOMBARD 1917: 79–82]

13. A Famous Relic

This Christian sanctification of matter, whose theoretical ground rested in the Incarnation and which is so systematically apparent in the doctrine of the sacraments, was another potent element in kindling Christian piety. The veneration of relics, for example, both in the cult of the martyrs and saints and in the question of images and icons was a popular and widespread form of devotion among Christians, and one that profoundly separated them, in theory if not always in fact, from Jews and Muslims. The matter of relics arose early in the history of the Church, in a quite spectacular fashion.

When the business at Nicea [that is, the ecumenical council there in 325 C.E.] was finished, the priests returned home. The Emperor (Constantine) rejoiced greatly at the restoration of unity of opinion in the Catholic Church, and in his desire to express, on behalf of himself, his children and the empire, the gratitude toward God which the unanimity of the bishops inspired, he directed that a house of prayer should be erected to God at Jerusalem near the place called Calvary. At the same time his mother Helena went to the city for the purpose of offering up prayer and of visiting the sacred places. Her zeal for Christianity made her anxious to find the wood which formed the adorable Cross. But it was no easy matter to discover either this relic or the Lord's sepulcher; for the pagans, who in former times had persecuted the Church and who, at the first promulgation of Christianity, had had recourse to every artifice to exterminate it, had concealed that spot under much heaped-up earth and built up what before had been a depression, the way it appears now, and the more effectively to conceal them had enclosed the entire place of the Resurrection and Mount Calvary within a wall and had moreover ornamented the whole area and paved it with stone. . . .

At length, however, the place was discovered, and the fraud about it that had been so zealously maintained was detected; some say that the facts were first disclosed by a Hebrew who dwelt in the East and who derived his information from some documents which had come to him by paternal inheritance; but it seems more likely to suppose that God revealed the fact by means of signs and dreams. . . . When by command of the emperor the place was excavated deeply, the cave whence our Lord arose from the dead was discovered; and at no great distance three crosses were found and another separate piece of wood on which were inscribed in white letters in Hebrew, Greek and Latin the following words: "Jesus of Nazareth, the king of the Jews." These words, as the sacred book of the Gospels relates, were placed by command of Pilate, governor of Judea, over the head of Christ.

There remained a difficulty, however, in distinguishing the Divine Cross from the others, for the inscription had been wrenched from it and thrown aside and the cross itself had been cast aside with the others, without any distinction, when the bodies of the crucified were taken down. . . . It was no concern of theirs [that is, the Roman executioners] to deposit the crosses in their original order, since it was growing late, and as the men were dead they did not think it worthwhile to remain to attend to the crosses. A more divine indication than could be furnished by man was therefore necessary in order to distinguish the Divine Cross from the others and this revelation was given in the following manner. There was a certain lady of rank in Jerusalem who was afflicted with a most grievous and incurable disease. Macarius, bishop of Jerusalem, accompanied by the mother of the emperor and her attendants, went to her bedside. After engaging in prayer, Macarius signaled the spectators that the Divine Cross would be the one which, on being brought in contact with the invalid, would cure the disease. He approached her with each of the three crosses in turn, but when two of the crosses were laid upon her, it seemed but folly and mockery to her for she was at the gates of death. When, however, the third cross was in like manner brought to her, she suddenly opened her eyes, regained her strength, and immediately sprang from her bed well. It is said that a dead person was, in the same way, restored to life. The venerated wood having thus been identified, the greater portion of it was deposited in a silver case, in which it is still preserved in Jerusalem; but the empress sent part of it to her son Constantine, together with the nails by which the body of Christ had been fastened. (Sozomen, *Church History* 2.1)

Thus were discovered the remains of the "True Cross," the premier relic of Christendom. When Egeria visited Jerusalem about fifty years after Helena, she found the cross already the subject of a considerable cult. The time is Easter week, and the place is Constantine's shrine at Golgotha, the site of Jesus' crucifixion.

The people are dismissed at the Cross (after the dawn service) even before the sun is up, and those who are more ardent go to Mount Sion to pray at the pillar at which the Lord was scourged. They then go home for a short rest, but it is not long before everyone is assembled for the next service. The bishop's chair is placed on Golgotha behind the cross which stands there now. He takes his seat and a table is placed before him with a linen cloth on it. The deacons stand round, and there is brought to him a gold and silver box in which is the Holy Wood of the Cross. It is opened and the Wood of the Cross and the Title are taken out and placed on the table.

As long as the Holy Wood is on the table, the bishop sits with his hands resting on either end of it and holds it down, and the deacons round him keep watch over it. They guard it like this because the custom is that all the people, catechumens as well as the faithful, come up one by one to the table. They lean down over it, kiss the Wood and move on. And it is said that on one occasion one of them bit off a piece of the Holy Wood and stole it away, and for this reason the deacons stand round and keep watch in case anyone dares to do the same again.

Nor are the remains of the cross the only relic displayed and venerated.

Thus all the people go past one by one. They stoop down, touch the Holy Wood and the inscription with their forehead and then their eyes, then kiss it, but no one dares put out his hand to touch it. When they have kissed the Cross they go to a deacon who stands holding the Ring of Solomon, and the Horn with which the kings of Israel were anointed. These they venerate by kissing them, and they start around about eight o'clock, with everyone going by, entering by one door and going out by the other, until midday. (Egeria, *Pilgrimage* 67)

14. The Christian Cult of Martyrs

Jews, Christians, and Muslims all reverenced their holy men, dead as well as alive, but what sets Christianity apart from the other two religions is the development of an approved and official cult of the saints, and particularly the martyrs for the faith. If there were such cults among Jews and Muslims, as there certainly were, they remained on the level of popular practice and were viewed with suspicion and even hostility by the guardians of orthodoxy. The following is Augustine's defense of the Christian practice, not in the face of a Jewish objection but against a pagan one.

We do not build temples and ordain priests, rites and sacrifices to the martyrs; for they are not our gods, but their God is our God. Certainly we honor their reliquaries, as the memorials of holy men of God who strove for the truth even to the death of their bodies, that the true religion might be made known, and false and fictitious religions exposed. For if there were some before them who thought that these religions were really false and fictitious, they were afraid to give expression to their convictions. But who ever heard of a priest of the faithful, standing at an altar built for the honor and worship of God over the body of some holy martyr, say in his prayers, "I offer to you a sacrifice, O Peter, or O Paul, or O Cyprian"? It is to God that sacrifices are offered at their tombs, the God who made them both men and martyrs, and associated them with the angels in celestial honor.

And the reason why we pay such honors to their memory is that by so doing we may both give thanks to the true God for their victories, and by recalling them afresh to remembrance, may stir ourselves to imitate them by seeking to obtain like crowns and palms, calling to our help the same God on whom they called. Therefore, whatever honors the religious may pay in the places of the martyrs, they are but honors rendered to their memory, not sacred rites or sacrifices offered to dead men as to gods. And even such as bring thither food—which indeed is not done by the better Christians, and in most places in the world is not done at all—do so in order that it may be sanctified to them through the merits of the martyrs, in the name of the Lord of the martyrs, first presenting the food and offering prayer, and thereafter taking it away to be eaten, or to be in part bestowed upon the needy. But he who knows the one sacrifice of Christians, which is the sacrifice offered in those places, also knows that these are not sacrifices offered to the martyrs. It is, then, neither with divine honors nor with human crimes, by which they [that is, the pagans] worship their gods, that we honor our martyrs; neither do we offer sacrifices to them or convert the crimes of the gods into their sacred rights. (Augustine, *City of God* 8.27) [AUGUSTINE 1948: 2:134–135]

15. Muslim Canonical Prayer

Another visitor from the Christian West to the Muslim East was Ricoldo di Monte Croce, who was there not simply to make pilgrimage but rather to confute and convert the Muslims. Ricoldo was not, then, a disinterested visitor, but he nonetheless found something in Islamic practice to admire.

What can I say of their prayers? For they have such great care and devotion in their prayers that I was amazed when I saw and experienced it firsthand. For I spent three and a half months with the camel nomads in the deserts of Arabia and Persia and never for any reason did I ever see these camel Arabs neglect to pray at the prescribed hours of the day or night, and particularly in the morning and the evening. They manifest such a devotion in their prayers that they put all other things from them. (Ricoldo, *Itinerarium*) [LAURENT 1873: 131–132]

What Ricoldo found so impressive was the performance of the liturgical prayers obligatory upon all Muslims, male and female, who have attained the use of reason. They had to be performed facing the direction of Mecca five prescribed times daily. According to the classic Letter on the Roots of Jurisprudence *of al-Shafiʿi, the Egyptian legal scholar who died ca. 820 C.E., the obligations imposed by God on men can be derived (1) explicitly from the Quran, though with progressive abrogations; (2) in general terms from the Quran and explicitly regarding its modalities from the Prophet; (3) from the Prophet's teachings alone, which are also binding; and (4) deductively from the Quran or the teachings of the Prophet, the famous "personal initiative" of Islamic jurisprudence. How the first two operated in the question of liturgical prayer is made clear in the following passage from the same* Letter.

Shafiʿi said: I have heard some scholars who related that God had imposed a certain duty for prayer before He laid down that for the five prayers. For He said:

> O you wrapped in your mantle,
> Stay up the night, except a little,
> Half of it, or a little less
> Or a little more,
> And chant the Quran distinctly.
> (Quran 73:1–4)

God abrogated this duty by another, which may be found in the same Sura, and it reads as follows:

891

"The Lord knows that you stay up nearly two-thirds of the night, or half of it, or a third of it, and a party of those with you likewise, and God determines the night and the day. He knows that you will never count it up, so He has turned toward you in mercy. So recite what may be convenient for you of the Quran; He knows that some of you will be sick and others journeying about in the land, seeking the bounty of God, and others fighting in the path of God. So recite what is convenient of it, and observe the prayer and pay the alms." (Quran 73:20)

Even these latter modifications are not entirely clear, Shafiʿi argues, and so it is necessary to turn to the Prophetic tradition for clarification.

Shafiʿi said: In such a case it is obligatory to seek the evidence of the Prophetic tradition for determining which of the meanings is valid. Thus the Prophetic tradition has indicated that no duty other than that of the five prayers is obligatory and that any earlier prayers have been abrogated by that tradition. (Shafiʿi, *Risala*) [SHAFI'I 1961: 128–129]

Shafiʿi resumes the standard teaching.

God, Blessed and Most High, said: "Truly prayer has become for the believers a thing prescribed at stipulated times" (Quran 4:103). And He said, "Observe the prayer and pay the alms tax" (Quran 2:43 etc.). And He said to His Prophet, "Take of their wealth an alms tax to cleanse and purify them thereby and pray for them" (Quran 9:103). And He said: "Pilgrimage to the House [that is, the Kaʿba] is a duty to God from the people, whoever is able to make his way there" (Quran 3:97).

Thus God has laid down in the Quran the duties of prayer, alms tax and pilgrimage and specified the modes of their performance through His Prophet's tongue.

So the Apostle specified that (each day) prayers shall number five, that the number of the cycles in the noon, afternoon and evening prayers shall number four repeated twice in the towns, and the cycles at the sunset prayer shall number three and at the dawn prayer two.

He decreed that in all (the prayers) there should be recitals (from the Quran), audible at the sunset, evening and dawn prayers, and silent recitals at the noon and afternoon prayers.

He specified that at the beginning of each prayer there shall be the declaration "God is great" and at the ending salutations on the Prophet and his house, and that each prayer consists of the "God is great," the recital (from the Quran), the bowing and two prostrations after each inclination, but that beyond these nothing is obligatory.

He decreed that prayer while one is on a journey can be shorter, if the traveler so desires, in the three occasions that have four cycles, but he made no change in the sunset and dawn prayers when those prayers are performed in town. However, all prayers must be (performed) in the direction of Mecca, whether one is in town or on a journey. (Shafiʿi, *Risala*) [SHAFIʿI 1961: 158–159]

The turning toward Mecca in prayer provides Shafiʿi with an illustrative example of the use of "personal initiative" in a matter of law.

Shafiʿi said: (God ordered the performance of prayer) in the direction of the Sacred Mosque [in Mecca; that is, the Kaʿba] and said to His Prophet: "Sometimes We see you turning your face about toward the heaven. So We will turn you in a direction that will satisfy you. Turn your face in the direction of the Sacred Mosque, and wherever you are, turn your faces in that direction" (Quran: 2:144). And He said: "And from whatever place you have gone forth, turn your face in the direction of the Sacred Mosque; and wherever you may be, turn your faces in its direction" (Quran 2:149).

Thus God, glorified be His praise, guided men, should they be at a distance from the Sacred Mosque, by using the reasoning powers which He has implanted in men and which discriminate between things and their opposites and the landmarks which He set up for them when the Sacred Mosque, to which He commanded them to turn their faces, is out of sight. For God said, "For it is He who made for you the stars, that you might be guided by them in the darkness of land and sea" (Quran 6:98). And He said, "And by the landmarks and by the stars they are guided" (Quran 16:16).

Shafiʿi said: Such landmarks may be the mountains, the nights and the days, which have winds of known names though they blow from different directions, and the sun and the moon and the stars whose risings and settings and whose places in the sky are known.

Thus God prescribed to men the use of personal reasoning in turning in the direction of the Sacred Mosque by means of guidance to them, which I have described; so long as men use their personal reasoning they will not deviate from His command, glorious be His praise; but He did not permit them to pray in any direction they wished if the Sacred Mosque were out of sight. And He also instructed them about His will and providence and said, "Does man think that he will be left roaming at will?" (Quran 75:36). "Left roaming at will" means one who is neither commanded nor prohibited. (Shafiʿi, *Risala*) [SHAFIʿI 1961: 69–70]

Shafiʿiʾs is the voice of the lawyer, a powerful one in Islam, but by no means the only accent heard in religious circles. There was also the voice of the mystic, in this case the Spaniard Ibn al-Arabi (1165–1240 C.E.). He read the matter of the direction of prayer in a very different way indeed.

Consider this matter, for as men know God (in this world), so they will see Him on the Day of Resurrection. . . . So beware lest you restrict yourself to a particular tenet (concerning the Reality) and so deny any other tenet (equally reflecting Him), for you would forfeit much good; indeed, you would forfeit the true knowledge of what is. Therefore, be completely and utterly receptive to all doctrinal forms, for God Most High is too All-embracing and Great to be confined within one creed rather than another, for He has said, "Wheresoever you turn, there is the face of God" (Quran 2:115), without mentioning any particular direction. He states that there [that is, "wheresoever you turn"] is the face of God, the face of a thing being its reality.

. . . The perfect servant, despite his knowledge of this [that is, the omnipresence of God], nevertheless maintains himself, in his outer and limited form, in prayer, his face turned toward the Sacred Mosque (in Mecca), believing God to be in that direction when he prays; the Sacred Mosque is in truth representative of a facet of the Reality, as in the verse, "Wheresoever you turn, there is the face of God," and in facing it one is face to face with God in it. However, do not tell yourself that He is in that direction only, but rather maintain both your attitude (of prayer) in facing the Sacred Mosque and your attitude (of understanding) the impossibility of confining His face to that particular direction, it being merely one of the points toward which men turn. (Ibn al-Arabi, *The Bezels of Wisdom*, "Hud") [IBN AL-ARABI 1980: 137–138]

If these sentiments of the mystic seem to undermine the uniqueness and absoluteness not only of Mecca but even of Islam itself, Ibn al-Arabi apparently had little hesitation in making his views on worship even clearer.

> My heart is capable of every form,
> a cloister of the monk, a temple for idols,
> a pasture for gazelles, the votary's Kaʿba,
> the tables of the Torah, the Quran.
> Love is the creed I hold: Wherever turn
> His camels, love is still my creed and faith.
> (Ibn al-Arabi, *Tarjuman* 11.13–15)

16. Prophetic Traditions on Prayer

When Shafi'i speaks of Muhammad "decreeing" the specifics of the obligation to prayer set down in general terms in the Quran, he is referring to the "traditions" or reports originally transmitted by Muhammad's contemporaries and professing to recount the Prophet's teachings or conduct. Even in Shafi'i's own lifetime these were beginning to be collected for legal purposes. In the end they provided, together with the Quran, the chief foundation of Islamic law. The following are some typical and widely circulated Prophetic traditions on the subject of prayer. First, as to its times:

Burayda told of a man asking the Apostle of God about the time of prayer, to which he [Muhammad] replied: "Pray with us these two," meaning two days. When the sun passed the meridian he summoned Bilal, who uttered the call to prayer, then he commanded him and he made the announcement declaring that the time to begin the afternoon prayer had come when the sun was high, white and clear. Then he gave him command and he made the announcement declaring that the time to begin the sunset prayer had come when the sun had set. Then he gave command and he made the announcement declaring that the time to begin the night prayer had come when the twilight had ended. Then he gave command and he made the announcement declaring that the time to begin the dawn prayer had come when the dawn appeared.

The next day he commanded him to delay the (summons to the) noon prayer until the extreme heat had passed and he did so, and he allowed it to be delayed until the extreme heat had passed. He observed the afternoon prayer when the sun was high, delaying it beyond the time when he had previously observed it. He observed the sunset prayer before the twilight had ended; he observed the night prayer when a third of the night had passed; and he observed the dawn prayer when there was clear daylight. Then asking where the man was who had inquired about the time of prayer and receiving from him a reply that he was present, he said, "The time for your prayer is within the limits of what you have seen." Muslim has transmitted this report. (Baghawi, *Mishkat al-Masabih* 4.2.1)

Ibn Mas'ud said that the extent of the shadow when the Apostle of God prayed the noon prayer was three to five feet in summer and five to seven feet in winter. Abu Dawud and Nasa'i have both transmitted this report. (Ibid. 4.2.3)

Abu Hurayra reported the Apostle of God as saying, "No prayer is more burdensome to the hypocrites than the dawn and the evening prayer; but if they knew what blessings lie in them, they would come to them even if they had to crawl to do so." Muslim transmits this report. (Ibid. 4.4.1)

Amr ibn Shuʿayb on his father's authority reported his grandfather as saying that God's Messenger prohibited the recitation of poems in a mosque, buying and selling in it, and sitting in a circle in a mosque on Friday before the prayer. Abu Dawud and Tirmidhi transmitted this report.

Ibn Umar said that there were seven places where the Apostle of God forbade men to pray: a dunghill, a slaughterhouse, a graveyard, the middle of the road, a bath, places where camels kneel to drink, and the roof of God's House. Tirmidhi and al-Maja have transmitted this report. (Ibid. 4.8.2)

Anas ibn Malik reported the Apostle of God as saying, "A man's prayer in his house is equivalent to a single observance of prayer, his prayer in a tribal mosque is worth twenty-five, his prayer in a Friday mosque is equivalent to five hundred, his prayer in the Aqsa mosque (in Jerusalem) is equivalent to fifty thousand, his prayer in my mosque (in Medina) is (also) equivalent to fifty thousand, and his prayer in the Sacred Mosque [that is, the Haram at Mecca] is equivalent to a hundred thousand." Ibn Maja has transmitted this report. (Ibid. 4.8.3)

Ibn Umar reported the Apostle of God as saying, "Do not prevent your women from coming into mosques, but their houses are better for them." Abu Dawud transmitted this report.

Ibn Masʿud reported the Prophet as saying, "It is more excellent for a woman to pray in her house than in her courtyard, and more excellent for her to pray in her own room than (elsewhere) in the house." Abu Dawud transmitted this report. (Ibid. 4.24.2)

Jabir ibn Samura said: The Apostle of God came out to us . . . and said, "Why do you not draw yourselves up in rows (for prayer) as the angels do in the presence of the Lord?" We asked, "Apostle of God, how do the angels draw themselves up in rows in the presence of the Lord?" He replied, "They make the first rows complete and keep close together in the row." Muslim transmitted this report.

Anas reported the Apostle of God as saying, "Complete the front row, then the one that comes next, and if there is any incompleteness, let it be in the last row." Abu Dawud transmitted this report.

Abu Hurayra reported the Apostle of God as saying, "The best of the men's rows (in prayer) is the first and worst is the last, but the best of the women's rows is the last and the worst is the first." Muslim transmitted this report. (Ibid. 4.25.1–2)

Abu Saʿid reported the Apostle of God as saying, "When there are three people (praying together), one of them should lead them. The one among them most worthy to act as prayer leader is the one most versed in the Quran." Muslim transmitted this report. (Ibid. 4.27.1)

Abu Hurayra reported the Apostle of God as saying, "When one of you leads the people in prayer he should be brief, for among them are the sick, the weak and the aged. But when one of you prays by himself, he may be as long as he likes." This report has been transmitted by Bukhari and Muslim. (Ibid. 4.28.1)

Tariq ibn Shihab reported the Apostle of God as saying, "The Friday prayer in congregation is a necessary duty for every Muslim, with four exceptions: a slave, a woman, a boy and an invalid." Abu Dawud transmitted this report. (Ibid. 4.44.2)

Salman reported the Apostle of God as saying, "If any man bathes on Friday, purifies himself as much as he can with ablution, anoints himself with oil or puts on a touch of perfume which he has in his house, then goes out and, without squeezing between two men, prays what is prescribed for him, then remains silent when the prayer leader preaches, his sins between that time and the next Friday will be forgiven him." Bukhari has transmitted this tradition. (Ibid. 4.45.1)

17. The Institution of the Call to Prayer

The standard Life of Muhammad *provides the setting for the institution of many of the practices that became standard in the devotional life of the Muslim community, among them the public call to prayer.*

When the Apostle was firmly settled in Medina and his brethren the "Emigrants" were gathered to him and the affairs of the "Helpers" were arranged, Islam became firmly established. Prayer was instituted, the alms tax and fasting were prescribed, legal punishments fixed, the forbidden and the permitted prescribed, and Islam took up its abode with them. . . . When the Apostle first came (to Medina), the people gathered about him for prayer at the appointed times without being summoned. At first the Apostle thought of using a trumpet like that of the Jews who used it to summon to prayer. Afterwards he disliked the idea and ordered a clapper to be made [like the Christians'], so that it was duly fashioned to be beaten when the Muslims should pray.

Meanwhile Abdullah ibn Zayd ibn Tha'laba . . . heard a voice in a dream and came to the Apostle saying: "A phantom visited me at night. There passed by me a man wearing two green garments carrying a clapper in his hand, and I asked him to sell it to me. When he asked me what I wanted it for I told him that it was to summon people to prayer, where-upon he offered to show me a better way: it was to say thrice: 'God is great. I bear witness that there is no god but the God. I bear witness that Muhammad is the Apostle of God. Come to prayer. Come to prayer. Come to success. Come to success. God is great. God is great. There is no god but the God.' " When the Apostle of God was told of this he said that it was a true vision if God so willed it, and that he should go to Bilal and communicate it to him so that he might call to prayer thus, for he had a more penetrating voice. When Bilal acted as muezzin Umar heard him in his house and came to the Apostle dragging his cloak on the ground and saying he had seen precisely the same vision. The Apostle said, "God be praised for that!" (Ibn Ishaq, *Life* 346–347) [IBN ISHAQ 1955: 235–236]

18. On the Sublimity of Ritual Prayer

One of the great Muslim reformers was the lawyer and theologian Ghazali (d. 1111 C.E.). In many of his works, and most notably in his Revivification of the Sciences of Religion, *Ghazali attempted to breathe a deeper spirituality into the practice of ordinary Muslims by heightening their awareness in the performance of ritually prescribed actions. It was necessary to prepare the soul for ritual acts, Ghazali insisted, and to perform them with proper and explicit intention. Here, for example, is the appropriate way to fulfill the obligation of washing before prayer, with all the lawyer's attention to detail but accompanied by the spiritual awareness of the saint.*

Make the intention of removing filth from the body or of fulfilling the ceremonial preparation for worship. The making of the intention must not be omitted before the washing of the face, for otherwise the ablution is invalid. Then take a handful of water for your mouth and rinse your mouth three times, making sure that the water reaches the back of it—unless you are fasting, in which case, act gently—and say: "O God, I am purposing to read Your Book and to have Your name many times on my lips; through the steadfast word make me steadfast in this life and the world to come." Then take a handful of water for your nose, draw it in three times and blow out the moisture in your nose; while drawing it in say, "O God, make me breathe in the fragrance of Paradise, and may I be pleasing to You," and while blowing it out, "O God, I take refuge with You from the odors of Hell and from the evil abode." Then take a handful for your face, and with it wash from the beginning of the flattening of the forehead to the end of the protuberance of the chin, up and down and from ear to ear across. . . . Make the water reach the four places where hair grows: the eyebrows, the moustache, the eyelashes and the cheeks. . . . As you wash your face say, "O God, make my face white through Your light on the day when You whiten the faces of Your elect, and do not blacken my face with darkness on the day when You blacken the faces of your enemies." Do not omit wetting the thick part of the beard.

Then wash your right hand, and after that the left, together with the elbow and half the upper arm; for the adornment in Paradise reaches to the places touched in ablution. As you wash your right hand say, "O God, give me my book (of accounting) in my right hand and grant me an easy reckoning." As you wash your left say, "O God, I take refuge with You from being given my book in my left hand or behind my back." Then, moistening the fingers, rub all over your head, keeping the fingertips of right and left hands close together, placing them on the fore part of the head and moving them back to the nape of the neck and forward again. Do this three times—and similarly with the other parts of the body— saying, "O God, cover me with Your mercy, send down Your blessing upon me, shelter me beneath the shadow of Your Throne on the day when there is no shadow save Yours; O God, make my hair and my flesh forbidden things to the Fire."

Then run your ears outside and inside with clean water; place your fingers in your earholes and rub the outside of your ears with the ball of your thumbs and say, "O God, make me one of those who hear the word and follow the good in it; O God, make me hear the crier of Paradise along with the righteous in Paradise." Then rub your neck and say, "O God, deliver my neck from the Fire; O God, I take refuge with You from the chains and fetters."

Then wash your right foot and after that the left, together with the ankles. With the little finger of your left hand wash between your toes, beginning with the little toe on the right foot and finishing with the little toe on the left. Approach the toes from below and say, "O God, establish my feet on the straight path along with the feet of Your righteous servants." Similarly, when you wash the left say, "O God, I take refuge with

You that You may not cause my feet to slip from the path into the Fire on the day when You cause the feet of the hypocrites and idolaters to slip."

If a man says all these prayers during his ablution, his sins will have departed from all parts of his body, a seal has been set upon his ablution, it has been raised to beneath the Throne of God and unceasingly praises and hallows God, while the reward of that ablution is recorded for him to the Day of Resurrection. (Ghazali, *The Beginning of Guidance* 8–9)
[GHAZALI 1953: 95–97]

Although Ghazali was a mystic of considerable stature in Islam, he was here writing for the Muslim layman, converting, so to speak, the religious sensibilities of the "spiritual" Muslim into common practice. The mystics' own characteristic view of the deeper significance of ritual practices like daily prayer—and how remote it is from mere compliance—is on more explicit display in this page from a book by the Sufi al-Kharraz (d. 890 C.E.) on the etiquette of prescribed prayer.

When entering on prayer you should come into the Presence of God as you would on the Day of Resurrection, when you will stand before Him with no mediator between, for He welcomes you and you are in confidential talk with Him, and you know in whose presence you are standing, for he is the King of kings. When you have lifted your hands and said "God is most great," then let nothing remain in your heart save glorification and let nothing be in your mind in the time of glorification than the glory of God Most High, so you forget this world and the next when glorifying Him.

When a man bows in prayer, then it is fitting he should afterwards raise himself, then bow again and make intercession, until every joint of his body is directed toward the throne of God Most High, until there is nothing in his heart greater than God Most Glorious and he thinks so little of himself that he feels himself to be less than a mote of dust.
[SMITH 1950: no. 26]

19. A Muslim Philosopher on the "Uses" of Prayer and Ceremonial Observances

Both the theologian and the mystic were well within what the Muslim tradition understood as orthodoxy. Philosophers too prayed in Islam, and perhaps with the same fervor as a Ghazali or a Kharraz. But they had access to another, non-Muslim strain of thought that affected their attitudes even on prayer and ritual observance.

In the course of his account of the role of the prophet, Avicenna offers his coolly detached reflections, somewhat in the manner of Plato, on the "uses" of religion, specifically of prayer and other acts of worship.

Now this person, the prophet, is not of the kind that often comes into this world, or in every age: the gross (human) matter able to receive his sort of perfection occurs in but few temperaments. It follows from this that the prophet must devise means of securing the survival of his code and laws in all the spheres of human welfare. . . . He must therefore prescribe certain acts which men should repeat at close intervals, so that if the time for the performance of one is missed, there may soon be an opportunity for performing the next like act while the memory is still fresh and has not yet been obliterated. These acts must of course be linked up with some means of calling God and the afterlife to mind, else they will be useless: this mnemonic can only consist of set words to be uttered, or set resolves to be intended in the imagination. Men must be told that these acts are means of winning God's favor and of qualifying for great and generous reward. . . . In a word, these acts should be reminders; and these reminders must be either certain motions, or the denial of certain motions resulting in other motions. The former category may be illustrated by the instance of formal prayers, the latter by fasting. . . .

He should also if possible mix in with these observances other interests, in order to strengthen and extend the code, and to make their practice generally advantageous in a material sense also. Examples of this are Holy War and pilgrimage. He should specify certain places in the world as the most suitable for worship, stating that they belong exclusively to God; certain obligatory acts must also be specified as being done for God's sake only—as for instance the offering of sacrifices, which are a great help in this connection. The place which is advantageous in this context, if it be the town where the lawgiver took refuge and dwelt, will also serve the purpose of bringing him to mind, an advantage second only to that of remembering God and the Angels. . . .

The noblest of these observances from a certain point of view is that one in which the performer assumes that he is addressing God in private converse, that he is turning to God and standing before Him. This observance is prayer. Certain steps preparatory to prayer must also be prescribed, similar to those which a man customarily undertakes of his own accord before entering the presence of a human ruler; namely, purification and cleansing. The regulations laid down for these should be effective and impressive. The act of prayer should further be accompanied by those attitudes and rules of conduct usually observed in the presence of kings: humility, quietness, lowering the eyes, keeping the hands and feet withdrawn, not turning about and fidgeting. For every moment of the act of worship appropriate and seemly rules should be prescribed. All these conditions of religious observance serve the useful purpose of keeping the people's thoughts fixed firmly upon the recollection of God, and in this way they will continue in their close attachment to the laws and ordinances of the Faith. (Avicenna, *Book of Deliverance*) [AVICENNA 1951: 45–47]

20. The Friday Service

The noon prayer on Friday, "when the sun passes over the meridian," was the congregational prayer obligatory on all Muslims. As might be expected, a number of Prophetic traditions are reported on the subject.

Abu Hurayra reported the Messenger of God, may peace be upon him, as saying: The best day on which the sun has risen is Friday: on it Adam was created, on it he was made to enter Paradise, on it he was expelled from it. And the Last Hour will take place on no other day but Friday.

Abu Hurayra reported God's Messenger, may peace be upon him, as saying: We are the last (religious community) but we would be the first on the day of Resurrection and we would be the first to enter Paradise except that they [that is, the Jews and Christians] were given the Book before us and we were given it after them. They disagreed regarding the truth. And it was this day of theirs about which they disagreed, but God guided us to it, and that day is Friday for us; the next day is for the Jews and the day following for the Christians. (Muslim, *Sahih* 4.302, 1857, 1860)

Ghazali, as we have just seen, took as his goal the revivification of religious practices in Islam, which he hoped to accomplish by emphasizing both their spiritual content and the intent of the worshiper. This, for example, is his treatment of the Friday prayer.

Friday is the festival of the believers. It is an excellent day, ordained specially for this community by God, may He be magnified and exalted. In the course of it there is a period, the exact time of which is unknown; and if any Muslim, making request to God Most High for what he needs, chances to do so in this period, God grants his request. Prepare then for it [Friday] on Thursday by cleansing of the clothes, by many acts of praise and by asking forgiveness on Thursday evening, for that is an hour equal in merit to the (unknown) hour of the Friday. Make the intention of fasting on Friday, but do so on Saturday or Thursday as well, since there is no prohibition on fasting on Friday alone.

When the morning breaks, wash, since Friday washing is obligatory on every adult, that is, it is "established" and "confirmed." Then array yourself in white clothes, for these are the most pleasing to God. Use the best perfume you have. Cleanse your body thoroughly by shaving, cutting your hair and nails, using the toothpick and practicing other forms of cleanliness, as well as by employing fragrant perfumes. Then go early to the mosque, walking quietly and calmly. . . . It is said that, in respect to nearness to the beholding of the face of God, people come in the order of their early arrival for the Friday observance.

When you have entered the mosque, take your place in the first [that is, the nearest] row. If the congregation has assembled, do not step between their necks and do not pass in front of them while they are praying. Place yourself near a wall or pillar so that the people do not pass in front of you. Before sitting say the prayer of "greeting." Best of all, however, is to perform four prostrations, in each of which you recite the Sura of Purity (Sura 112). There is a tradition to the effect that whoever does that will not die until he has seen, or, in a variant reading, has been shown, his place in Paradise. . . .

When the leader has come out to commence the worship, break off your private worship and conversation and occupy yourself with responding to the muezzin, and then by listening to the sermon and taking it to heart. Do not speak at all during the sermon. It is related in a Prophetic tradition that "whoever says 'Hush!' to his neighbor while the leader is giving the sermon, has spoken idly, and whoever speaks idly has no Friday observance (credited to him)." The point is that in saying "Hush" he was speaking, whereas he ought to have checked the other man by a sign, not by a word. . . .

After the Friday observance perform two prostrations, or else four or six in pairs. All this is traditionally related of the Messenger of God, God bless him and preserve him, in various circumstances. Then remain in the mosque until the sunset worship, or at least until the late afternoon service. Watch carefully for the "excellent hour," for it may occur in any part of the day, and perhaps you will light upon it while making humble supplication to God. In the mosque do not go to the circle of people or the circle of storytellers, but to the circle of profitable knowledge, that is, the knowledge that increases your fear of God Most High and decreases your desire for this world; ignorance is better for you than all the knowledge which does not draw you away from this world toward the next.

Take refuge with God from unprofitable knowledge. Pray much at the rising, declining and setting of the sun (on Fridays), at the formal institution of worship, at the preacher's ascending the pulpit, and at the rising of the congregation for worship; the likelihood is that the "excellent hour" will be at one of those times. Endeavor on this day to give such alms as you can manage, even if it is little. Divide your time between the worship, fasting, almsgiving, reciting the Quran, recollection of God, solitary devotions, and "waiting for prayer." Let this one day of the week be devoted to what pertains to the future life, and perhaps it will be an atonement for the rest of the week. (Ghazali, *The Beginning of Guidance* 26) [GHAZALI 1953: 127–128]

21. The Two Liturgical Festival Days

In addition to Friday, other days liturgically commemorated by Muslims are the Feast of the Immolation, or Great Festival, celebrated during the pilgrimage month in honor of Abraham's sacrifice of Isaac—an event re-enacted on the pilgrimage itself—and the Feast of Breaking the Fast, or Lesser Festival, at the end of Ramadan. Both have their social and popular aspects in Muslim societies, as they do in the following traditions, but liturgically they resemble the Friday service with sermon.

Jabir ibn Abdullah reported: The Messenger of God, may peace be upon him, stood up on the day of the Breaking of the Fast and observed prayer. And he began the prayer before the sermon. He then delivered the sermon. When the Messenger of God, may peace be upon him, had finished the sermon, he came down from the pulpit and made his way to the women and exhorted them (to do good acts), and he was leaning on the arm of (his muezzin) Bilal. Bilal had stretched out his cloth into which women were throwing alms. (Muslim *Sahih*, 4.313, 1925)

Another tradition specifies:

He then walked on till he came to the women (in the mosque) and preached to them and admonished them and asked them to give alms, for most of them are the fuel for Hell. A woman having a dark spot on her cheek stood up and said: Why is it so, O Messenger of God? He said: For you grumble often and show ingratitude to your spouses. And then they began to give alms out of their ornaments such as their earrings and rings which they threw onto the cloth of Bilal. (Ibid. 4.313, 1926)

Umm Atiya reported: We were commanded to bring out on the feast days sequestered women and those unmarried. Menstruating women (also) came out but remained behind people and pronounced the "God is Great!" along with them. (Ibid. 4.314, 1933)

Aisha reported: Abu Bakr came to see me (at the Prophet's house) and I had two girls with me from among the girls of the Helpers; they were singing what the Helpers recited to one another at the Battle of Buʿath. They were not, however, (professional) singing girls. Abu Bakr said: What, the playing of this wind instrument of Satan in the house of the Messenger of God, may peace be upon him, and this too on the Festival Day? Upon this the Messenger of God, may peace be upon him, said: Abu Bakr, every people have a festival and this is ours. (Ibid. 4.317, 1938)

22. A Muslim Holy Day: The Tenth of Muharram

Like the religious calendars of the Jews and the Christians, the Muslims' was filled with days commemorating past events of special significance to the community. One of the most important, on a scale similar to Passover for the Jews or Easter for the Christians, was the tenth day of the lunar month of Muharram. Biruni (d. 1048 C.E.) explains its significance in his Traces of the Past.

The tenth (of Muharram) is called Ashura, a most distinguished day. The Prophet is reported to have said: "O men, hasten to do good works on this day for it is a grand and blessed day, on which God had mercy on Adam."

The day was, and is, of special significance to Shiʿite Muslims, since it marked the martyrdom of Husayn, the son of Ali and the grandson of the Prophet, at Karbala in Iraq in 680 C.E.

People marked this day with celebration until the murder of Husayn ibn Ali ibn Abi Talib occurred on it, when he and his adherents were treated in such a way as never in the whole world the worst criminals have been treated. They were killed by hunger and thirst, through the sword; they were burned and their heads roasted, and horses were made to trample over their bodies. Therefore people came to consider this day as an unlucky one.

On the contrary, the Umayyads [that is, the Muslim dynasty in power that engineered the slaughter] dressed themselves on this day in new garments, with various kinds of ornaments, and painted their eyes with kohl; they celebrated a feast, and gave banquets and parties, eating sweetmeats and pastries. Such was the custom in the nation during the rule of the Umayyads, and so it remained also after the downfall of the dynasty [in 750 C.E.].

The Shiʿite people, however, lament and weep on this day, mourning over the protomartyr Husayn in public, in Baghdad, for example, and in other cities and villages; and they make a pilgrimage to the blessed soil [that is, the burial site of Husayn] in Karbala. As this is a mourning day, their common people have an aversion to renewing the vessels and utensils of the household on this day.

And as with most of the other sacred days in the three religions, there was an attempt to connect Ashura back to biblical prototypes, and here with Gospel ones as well.

People say that on this day (of Ashura) God took compassion on Adam, that the Ark of Noah stood still on the mountain, that Jesus was born, that Moses was saved (from the Pharaoh). . . . Further, on this day Jacob regained his eyesight, Joseph was drawn out of the well, Solomon was invested with the royal power, the punishment was taken away from the people of Jonah, Job was freed from his plague, the prayer of Zachariah was granted and John (the Baptist) was given to him. . . .

Though it is possible that all these events should have occurred on this day, we must state that all this rests on the authority of popular storytellers, who do not draw upon learned sources or upon the consensus among the Peoples of the Book.

Some people say that Ashura is an Arabicized Hebrew word, to wit, Ashur, that is, the tenth of the Jewish month of Tishri, in which falls the fasting of (Yom) Kippur; that the date of this fasting was compared with the months of the Arabs, and that it was fixed on the tenth day of the Arabs' first month, as it falls with the Jews on the tenth day of their first month.

The Prophet gave order to fast on this day in the first year of the Hijra, but afterwards this fast was abrogated by the other law, to fast during the month of Ramadan, which falls later in the year. People relate that the Prophet of God, on arriving in Medina, saw the Jews fasting on Ashura. On inquiring of them, he was told that this was the day on which God had drowned Pharaoh and his people and had saved Moses and the Israelites. Then the Prophet said, "We have a nearer claim on Moses than they." In consequence he fasted on that day and ordered his followers to do the same. But when he afterwards issued the law regarding the fasting of Ramadan, he no longer ordered them to fast on Ashura, but neither did he forbid them.

This tradition is not correct, however, since scientific examination proves against it. . . . You could not maintain that the Prophet fasted on Ashura on account of its coincidence with the tenth of Tishri in this year, unless you transfer it from the first of the Jewish months to the first of the Arab months so as to make them fall together. Also in the second year of the Hijra the Jewish Ashura and the day of Muhammad's arrival cannot have coincided. (Biruni, *Traces of the Past*) [BIRUNI 1879: 326–328]

23. Adam at Mecca

All three religions possess a rich haggadic store of legend concerning the events described, or imagined, in the Book of Genesis, and Adam is not unnaturally the focus of many of those stories. In this one a Promethean Adam is connected with an antediluvian pilgrimage to Mecca.

Hashim ibn Muhammad has informed us, relating from Ubayy, from Abu Salih, from Ibn Abbas, who said: Adam departed from (the heavenly) Paradise between the time of noon prayers and the time of afternoon prayers, and was sent down to the earth. He had been dwelling in Paradise for half a day of the days of the Other World, that is, five hundred years of those days whose measure is twelve hours, for a day there is a thousand years as people count them in this world. Adam was cast down on a mountain in India called Nawdh [traditionally identified on Ceylon], and Eve fell at Jedda [the Red Sea port of Mecca]. Adam brought down with him some of the scented air of Paradise, which clung to the trees and valleys and filled all that place with perfume. It is thus that the perfumes known to us are derived from that scented air of Adam, upon whom be God's blessing and peace.

It is said that there was sent down along with Adam some of the myrtle of Paradise, also the Black Stone, which was then whiter than snow, and Moses' rod, which was of celestial myrtle wood, ten cubits long, that is, the height of Moses, upon whom be God's blessing and peace, as well as some myrrh and frankincense. Afterwards there was sent down to him the anvil, the blacksmith's hammer and pinchers. Then, from where he had fallen on the mountain, Adam looked and saw an iron shoot growing out of the mountainside, and he said: "This [the anvil] is from this [the iron shoot]." So he began to break down with the hammer trees that had grown old and had dried up, and upon them he heated that shoot till it melted. The first thing that he hammered out of it was a long knife with which he might work. Then he fashioned an earthen oven, the same one that Noah later inherited and the one that boiled over in India, bringing the punishment (of the Flood).

When (presently) Adam went on pilgrimage (to Mecca), he placed the Black Stone on (the mountain there called) Abu Qubays, where it gave light to the inhabitants of Mecca on dark nights, just the moon gives light (on clear nights). About four years before Islam the Quraysh brought it down from Abu Qubays, but meanwhile it had become black because of menstruating women and polluted persons mounting up to it and rubbing it with their hands. Adam made the pilgrimage from India to Mecca forty times. (Ibn Sa'd, *The Great Classes* 1.11–12) [JEFFERY 1962: 189–191]

24. Abraham as the Founder of the Cult at Mecca

Stories of Adam's connection with Mecca are pervasive in Muslim religious legend. The Quran, however, knows only Abraham's role there, and it is a major one.

Remember, We made the House (at Mecca) a place of congregation and safe retreat, and said: "Make the spot where Abraham stood a place of worship"; and enjoined upon Abraham and Ishmael to keep Our House immaculate for those who shall walk around it and stay in it for contemplation and prayer, and for bowing in adoration. . . .

And when Abraham was raising the foundations of the house with Ishmael, (he prayed): "Accept this from us, O Lord, for You hear and know every thing." (Quran 2:125, 127)

What then of all the haggadic traditions in Islam that connect the House of God or the Ka'ba at Mecca with Adam, the first prophet? The two strains of tradition are harmonized in the following commentary by Zamakhshari (d. 1144 C.E.) on these verses.

God sent down the House, which was one of the rubies of Paradise, with two emerald doors, one on the eastern and one on the western side. Then God said to Adam: "I have sent down for you that which must be circumambulated just as My Throne is circumambulated." Adam then set out on foot for the House (at Mecca) from the Land of India. Angels met him on the way, saying, "Blessed be your pilgrimage, O Adam; we too have made pilgrimage to the House of God, two thousand years before you." Adam subsequently performed the pilgrimage forty times on foot to the House of God from India. The House remained as it was until God took it up to the fourth heaven during the Flood. This was what was known as the "populous house." God later ordered Abraham to rebuild it, and Gabriel showed him the location. It is said that he built it from materials taken from five mountains: Mount Sinai, Mount Olivet, Mount Lebanon, Mount Ararat and Mount Hira, from which he took its foundation stone. Gabriel brought him the Black Stone from heaven. (Zamakhshari, *The Unveiler of the Realities, ad loc.*)

A more forthrightly "spiritualizing" reading of the Adam-Abraham-Ka'ba stories is given by the Spanish Sufi master Ibn al-Arabi (d. 1240 C.E.), who begins his account with a brief summary of traditions concerning the early history of the Ka'ba.

"And when Abraham was raising the foundations of the House" (Quran 2:127): It is said that the Ka'ba was brought down from Heaven during the time of Adam. It had an eastern and a western door. Adam made the pilgrimage from the land of India. The angels turned toward it (from a distance of) 40 parasangs. He circumambulated the House and entered it. Then, it was raised up (to heaven) during the time of the Flood of Noah. It was brought down a second time during the time of Abraham. He visited it and raised up its foundations. He made its two doors into one. It is said that (Mount) Abu Qubays shook violently, and split off from the Black Stone, which was a white sapphire from the Garden that Gabriel had brought down and had hidden in it [that is, Mount Abu Qubays] at the time of the Flood until the time of Abraham. Abraham put it in its place. Then it turned black from the fingering of menstruating women.

Then Ibn al-Arabi begins to spell out the interpretation, item by item.

Its [that is, the Ka'ba's] descent during the time of Adam signifies the appearance of the heart [that is, the spiritual faculty] during his time and its presence within him. Its having two doors—the east and the west—signifies knowledge of Creation and the Afterlife and the gnosis of the knowledge of light and the knowledge of darkness during his time, though without the knowledge of the Oneness of God. His setting out to visit it from the land of India signifies his turning toward creation and moderation, from knowing the physicality of dark natural things to the place of the heart. The turning of the angels signifies the dependence of the animal and vegetable powers upon the body, and the appearance of their traces upon it before the traces of the heart in the forty that were created in it by intention and its substance became fermented. Or its turning away, through conduct and behavior, from knowing the darkened self toward the place of the heart. . . .

Its being raised up in the time of the Flood to Heaven signifies the concealment of people in the victory of whim and caprice. The Flood is folly and ignorance in the time of Noah rather than the place of the heart.

Its remaining in the Fourth Heaven, is The Inhabited House [that is, the heavenly archetype of the Ka'ba] which is the heart of the world. Its coming down again during the time of Abraham signifies leading the people to the place of the heart during his time through his guidance. Abraham's raising the foundations and his making one door signifies accepting the heart through his conduct from his place to the place of the spirit, which is the secret. (It is also a sign of) the raising up of his high stations and his arrival to the place of proclaiming the unity of God. For he is the first who had the idea of the Oneness of God, as he said: "As for me, I have turned my face as a hanif to Him Who cleaved the heavens and the earth. I am not a polytheist!" (Quran 6:79).

The Black Stone signifies the spirit. The violent shaking of (Mount) Abu Qubays and its splitting off from it signifies its appearance as a spiritual exercise and the setting in motion the instruments of the body for meditation in the search for its appearance. Because of that it is said: it is hidden within it. That means, it has disappeared within the body. Its turning black from the touching of menstruating women signifies its disappearance and its becoming troubled and angry by reason of the idle chatter of the mental faculty in preference to the heart and its becoming the master over it. Its blackening is the spiritually luminous way that the spirit draws near to it. (Ibn al-Arabi, *Commentary*, 86–87 [translated by Reuven Firestone])

25. The Pilgrimage of Islam

This mix of local and biblical traditions surrounding the boxlike building called "the Ka'ba" in Muhammad's Mecca was the result of an attempt to link what was patently a very old, and in Muhammad's day a pagan, religious tradition in Mecca with the past age of the "religion of Abraham." The process begins, as we have just seen, in the Quran, where first Abraham and then, as a post-Quranic reflex, Adam are identified as the builders of the Ka'ba. The linkage goes further, however, and the chief pilgrimage rituals of both Mecca and its immediate environs are confirmed as Muslim rituals.

When We chose the site of the House for Abraham (We said): Associate no one with Me and clean My House for those who will circumambulate it, stand (in reverence), and bow in homage.

Announce the Pilgrimage to the people. They will come to you on foot and riding along distant roads on lean and slender beasts, in order to reach the place of advantage for them, and to pronounce the name of God on appointed days over cattle He has given them as food; then eat the food and feed the needy and the poor.

Let them attend to their persons and complete the rites of pilgrimage, fulfill their vows and circuit around the ancient House. . . .

There are advantages for you in these (animals to be sacrificed) up to a time, then their place is in the ancient House for sacrifice.

For every community We have ordained certain rites that they may commemorate the name of God by reciting it over the cattle We have given them for sacrifice. Your God is One God, so be obedient to Him. (Quran 22:26–34)

Known are the months of pilgrimage. If one resolves to perform the pilgrimage in these months, let him not indulge in concupiscence, sin or quarrel. And the good you do shall be known to God. Provide for the journey, and the best of provisions is piety. O men of understanding, obey Me.

It is no sin to seek the favors of your Lord (by trading). When you start from Arafat in a concourse, remember God at the monument that is sacred, and remember Him as He has shown you the way, for in the olden days you were a people astray. Then move with the crowd impetuously, and pray God to forgive you your sins. God is surely forgiving and kind.

When you have finished the rites and ceremonies, remember God as you do your fathers, in fact with greater devotion. (Quran 2:197–200)

26. Muhammad's Farewell Pilgrimage

Since the pilgrimage was a known and ongoing rite in Muhammad's day, the Quran has no need of prescribing its rituals in inclusive detail: what was done before will continue to be done, though now under Islamic auspices. But when another, later generation of Muslims needed more guidance, they could find it in the circumstantial account of the Prophet's farewell pilgrimage in the year of his death. Not unnaturally it became the model for the performance of this obligation, incumbent on all competent Muslims, to at least once in a lifetime to go to Mecca and perform the ceremonies described here.

Ja'far ibn Muhammad [the sixth Shi'ite Imam, d. 765 C.E.] reported on the authority of his father [Muhammad al-Baqir, the fifth Imam, d. 732 C.E.]: We went to Jabir ibn Abdullah [one of the last surviving Companions of the Prophet, d. 693 C.E., aged ninety-four] and he had begun inquiring about the people till it was my turn. I said: I am Muhammad ibn

Ali ibn Husayn [that is, the grandson of Husayn, Muhammad's own grandson]. Jabir placed his hand upon my head and opened my upper button and then my lower one and then placed his palm on my chest (to bless me), and I was, during those days a young boy, and he said: You are welcome, my nephew. Ask whatever you want to ask. . . .

I said to him: Tell me about the Pilgrimage of God's Messenger, may peace be upon him. He held up nine fingers and then stated: The Messenger of God, may peace be upon him, stayed at Medina for nine years but did not perform the Pilgrimage; then he made public announcement in the tenth year to the effect that God's Messenger, may peace be upon him, was about to perform the Pilgrimage. A large number of persons came to Medina, and all of them were anxious to follow the Messenger of God, may peace be upon him, and do according to his doing. We set out till we reached Dhu al-Hulayfa [in the vicinity of Mecca]. Asma daughter of Umays gave birth (there) to Muhammad ibn Abi Bakr. She sent a message to the Messenger of God, may peace be upon him, asking him: What should I do (in my present state of ritual impurity)? He said: Take a bath, wrap up your private parts and put on the (pilgrim's) garment of purification. The Messenger of God, may peace be upon him, then prayed in the mosque (there) and after that mounted al-Qaswa [his she-camel] and it stood up with him on its back at al-Bayda.

And I saw as far as I could see in front of me nothing but riders and pedestrians, and also on my right and my left and behind me. And the Messenger of God, may peace be upon him, was prominent among us, and the (revelation) of the Quran was descending upon him, and it is he who knows its (true) significance. And whatever he did, we also did that. He pronounced the Oneness of God, saying: "At Your service, O Lord, at Your service, at Your service. You have no partner. Praise and Grace is Yours, and Sovereignty too. You have no partner." And the people also pronounced this invocation, which they (still) pronounce today. . . .

We had no intention but that of making the (formal) Pilgrimage, being unaware of the Lesser Pilgrimage, but when we came with him to the House [that is, the Ka'ba], he touched the pillar [that is, the black stone] and made (seven) circuits, running three of them and walking four. And then going to the Place of Abraham (in the Haram), he recited: "And adopt the Place of Abraham as a place of prayer" (Quran 2:125). And this place was between him and the House. . . . He recited in two prostrations "Say: He is God, One" (Sura 112) and "Say: O unbelievers . . . " (Sura 109). He then returned to the pillar and kissed it. He then went out the gate to al-Safa [a place adjoining the Haram], and as he reached it he said: "Al-Safa and al-Marwa are among the signs appointed by God" (Quran 2:158), (adding) I begin with what God has commanded me to begin. He first mounted al-Safa until he saw the House, and facing in the direction of the Ka'ba, he declared the Oneness of God and glorified Him, and said: "There is no god but the God, One; there is no partner with Him. His is the Sovereignty, to Him praise is due, and He is powerful over everything. There is no god but the God alone, who fulfilled His promise, helped His servant and routed the confederates alone." He then made supplication in the course of that, saying such words three times. He then descended and walked toward al-Marwa, and when his feet came down in the bottom of the valley, he ran, and when he began to ascend he walked until he reached al-Marwa. There he did as he had done at al-Safa.

And when it was his last running at al-Marwa, he said: If I had known beforehand what I have come to know afterwards, I would not have brought sacrificial animals and would have performed a Lesser Pilgrimage. So he who among you has not the sacrificial animals with him should put off the (pilgrim's) garment of purification and treat it as Lesser Pilgrimage. Suraqa ibn Malik ibn Ju'sham got up and said: Messenger of God, does it apply to the present year or does it apply forever? Thereupon the Messenger of God, may peace be upon him, intertwined his fingers and said twice: The Lesser Pilgrimage has become incorporated in the (formal) Pilgrimage, adding: "No, but forever and ever." . . . Then all the people, except the Messenger, may peace be upon him, and those who had with them sacrificial animals, put off the garment of purification and got their hair clipped.

When it was the eighth day of the Pilgrimage Month they went to Mina and put on the garment of purification for the Pilgrimage, and the Messenger of God, may peace be upon him, rode forth and led the noon, afternoon, sunset, evening and dawn prayers. He then waited a little till the sun rose, and commanded that a tent should be pitched at Namira [a place at the limits of the territory of Mecca]. The Messenger of God, may peace be upon him, then set out, and the Quraysh did not doubt that he would halt at the (hillock called) "the sacred site" as they used to do in the pre-Islamic period. The Messenger of God, may peace be upon him, passed on, however, until he reached (the hill of) Arafat and he found that the tent had been pitched for him at Namira. There he halted until the sun had passed the meridian; he commanded that his camel be brought and saddled for him. Then he came to the bottom of the valley (there) and addressed the people.

There follows Muhammad's farewell discourse to the Muslims, after which the narrative continues:

The Messenger of God, may peace be upon him, then mounted his camel and came to the halting place, making his camel turn toward the side where there were rocks, with the path taken by those on foot in front of him, and faced toward the Ka'ba. He kept standing there (from the time of the noonday prayer) till the sun set, and the yellow light had somewhat gone and the disk of the sun had disappeared. He made Usama sit behind him, and he pulled the nosestring of the camel so forcefully that its head touched the saddle, and he pointed out to the people on his right hand to be moderate (in their pace) . . . and this is how he reached al-Muzdalifa.

There he led the evening and sunset prayers. . . . The Messenger of God, may peace be upon him, then lay down till dawn and then offered the dawn prayer . . . when the morning light was clear. He again mounted his camel, and when he came to "the holy site" he faced toward the Ka'ba, supplicated God, glorified Him, and pronounced His Uniqueness and Oneness, and kept standing until the daylight was very clear. He then went quickly before the sun rose . . . till he came to the bottom of Muhassir [between Muzdalifa and Mina]. He urged his camel a little, and following the middle road, which comes out at the greatest pile of stones, he came to the pile near the tree. At this he threw seven small pebbles, saying "God is Great" while throwing each one of them in the manner in which small pebbles are thrown (with the fingers), and this he did at the bottom of the valley.

He then went to the place of sacrifice, and sacrificed sixty-three camels with his own hand. Then he gave the remaining ones to Ali, who sacrificed them, and he made him share in his sacrifice. He then commanded that a piece of flesh from each animal sacrificed should be put in a pot, and when it was cooked, both of them [that is, Muhammad and Ali] took some meat of it and drank its broth. The Messenger of God, may peace be upon him, again rode and came to the House (of God) and offered the sunset prayer at Mecca. He came to the tribe of Abd al-Muttalib, who were supplying (pilgrims) the water of the (sacred spring) Zamzam, and said: Draw water, O tribesmen of Abd al-Muttalib; were it not that people would usurp this right of supplying themselves with water from you (if I did so), I would have drawn it along with you. So they handed him a container and he drank from it. (Muslim, *Sahih* 7.462, 2803)

There were, then, as the text reveals, two distinct rituals: the hajj, or pilgrimage properly so called; and another set of practices called the ʿumra, or so-called lesser pilgrimage, which, as it turns out, was the genuine Meccan pilgrimage. This latter fell during a different sacred month and was celebrated in and around the Meccan Haram and not, as was the case with the hajj, at various sites in the neighborhood of but outside Mecca. But the two were formally combined on the occasion of Muhammad's first and only pilgrimage as a Muslim: "The ʿumra has become incorporated in the hajj," as he reportedly said on that occasion.

27. Pagan Survivals and Muslim Misgivings

Although the Quran was reassuring on the point that the "greater" and the "lesser" pilgrimage were both part of God's original revelation to Abraham, there was a common sense at Mecca that the associated rituals were remnants of a pagan past. We can read the source of the concern between the lines of Quran 2:158 and even more clearly in the anecdotes prompted by clarifications of that verse.

Surely Safa and Marwa are among the signs of God. Whoever goes on Pilgrimage to the House (of God), or performs the Lesser Pilgrimage, is not guilty if he walks around [or "circumambulates"] them; and he who does good of his own accord will find appreciation with God who knows everything. (Quran 2:158)

Thus, as appears from the texts themselves ("is not guilty . . . "), Muhammad's Muslim contemporaries felt some uneasiness about these pilgrimage rituals, and the Quranic commentators scanned the Prophetic traditions for evidence of it.

Wahidi [d. 1076 C.E.] relates that when asked about al-Safa and al-Marwa, Anas ibn Malik said: "We were of the opinion that they belonged to the era of heathenism. Thus when Islam came we ceased running between them. God therefore sent down this verse (2:158)."

Qurtubi the jurist [d. 1273] relates that Urwah ibn al-Zubayr said to (Muhammad's wife) Aisha: "I see nothing against anyone who does not run between al-Safa and al-Marwa, nor would I be concerned if I myself did not run between them." She answered: "Ill is that which you speak, O son of my sister! The Messenger of God ran between them and so did the Muslims. It was rather those who sacrificed to Manat, the idol that was in the Mushlal who did not run between them. Thus God sent down (2:158). Had it been as you say, the verse would have read 'in him there is no blame if he does not run between them.' "

Al-Shaʿbi said: "During the era of heathenism there was an idol on al-Safa called Isaf and another on al-Marwa called Naʾilah. People used to touch them when they ran (between the two hills). The Muslims did not wish to run between them on that account; hence God sent down this verse." [AYOUB 1984: 177]

Somewhat in the same vein is this tradition concerning the kissing of the black stone embedded in the corner of the Ka'ba.

Abdullah ibn Sarjis reported: I saw the bald one, that is, Umar ibn al-Khattab, may God be pleased with him, kissing the stone and saying: By God, I am kissing with the full knowledge that you are a stone and that you can do neither harm nor good; if I had not seen the Messenger of God, upon whom be peace, kissing you, I would not have kissed you. (Muslim, *Sahih* 7.434, 2914)

28. Substitution, Surrogation, and Sublimation

There is a long and well-established tradition in Islam that in those cases where ritual obligations cannot be fulfilled, other pious acts may be substituted for them— feeding a poor person in lieu of fasting during Ramadan, for example. Even in the case of the pilgrimage, which was site-determined rather than merely time-fixed, some degree of substitution was permissible, as the Quran itself explains.

Perform Pilgrimage (*hajj*) and the Lesser Pilgrimage (*'umra*) in the service of God. But if you are prevented, send an offering which you can afford as sacrifice, and do not shave your heads until the offering has reached the place of sacrifice. But if you are sick or have an ailment of the scalp (preventing the shaving of the head), then offer expiation by fasting or else give alms or a sacrificial offering. When you have security, then those of you who wish to perform the Lesser Pilgrimage along with the Hajj, should make a sacrifice according to your means. But he who has nothing should fast for three days during the Pilgrimage and seven on return, completing ten. This applies to him whose family does not live near the Holy Mosque. (Quran 2:196)

The circumstances envisioned for the commutation or substitution of one pious act for another, ritually required one are inevitably those where it is impossible to perform the required prayer, fasting, and so on. Here just such a case is made for pilgrimage commutation by a Sufi master of the early tenth century. The setting, however, is a juridical process presided over by the Caliphal Grand Vizier and reported by the son of one of the clerks at the hearing.

Each day the Vizier Hamid was brought a few of the notebooks found in the homes of Hallaj's disciples; they were put before him, and he handed them to my father to read them to him. Now it so happened that on one of those days my father read to him, in the presence of the justices Abu Umar and Abu Husayn ibn al-Ushnani, from one of Hallaj's writings in which it was reported that "when a man wants to carry out the legally required pilgrimage and has no way of doing it, he must set aside a room in his home that no impurity touches, where no one goes, and which no one may pass through; then, at the time of the pilgrimage, he must walk around in a circle, as one does at the Sacred House; once that is done he must perform the rituals as at Mecca. After that he will gather together thirty orphans, prepare them the best possible meal, invite them into this place and serve them this meal himself. When they have finished their meal and washed their hands, he will dress each one of them in a (new) shirt and give each seven drachmas. . . . And all of that, when it is carried out, will take the place of the hajj for him."

[MASSIGNON 1982: 1:546]

The "Hallaj" of the text is the celebrated mystic and martyr Husayn ibn Mansur al-Hallaj, whose life will be regarded more closely in Chapter 4 below. The doctrinal position cited from his notebooks, which Hallaj claimed had precedent in the writings of the earlier master Hasan al-Basri and which the justice Abu Umar insisted did not (there is in fact none such in any of Hasan's preserved texts), led quickly to Hallaj's death sentence—"it is lawful to shed his blood"—a sentence signed, not without hesitation, by the same Abu Umar and with a great deal of pressure from the Grand Vizier Hamid. After some delays the sentence was confirmed by the Caliph and carried out, with extreme cruelty, on 26 March 922 C.E.

There was obviously more at stake in Baghdad in 922 C.E. than a mere case of substitution of one pious act for another. What Hallaj was suggesting was an alternative setting for the pilgrimage, an approach that struck many of his contemporaries as usurpation rather than substitution. And indeed, such may have been his intent, carried out in the name of that same interior spiritualization already witnessed in Ghazali. For Ghazali, however, the spiritualization of a ritual act did not lead to the latter's destruction, as it inevitably did for Hallaj.

God prescribed two kinds of religious duties: one concerning intermediate things [that is, religious rituals] and the other concerning the Realities [that is, the transcendental truths of God]. Now duties to the Realities involve knowledge that flows from God and returns to Him. Whereas duties respecting intermediate things involve knowledge that, flowing from objects below Him, is able to rejoin Him only by transcending them and destroying them. Now one must include the building of the Haram and of the Ka'ba among duties to "intermediate things," just as it is said: "the first sacred enclosure established for the people was that at Bakka [Mecca], a blessed enclosure . . . " (Quran 3:96). As long as you remain attached to this enclosure, you will remain separated from God. But when you have really detached yourself from it, then you will reach the One who built and established it; then meditating on the temple (destroyed) in yourself, you will possess the real presence of its Founder.

. . . Shaykh Husayn ibn Mansur Hallaj, may God be merciful to him, recited the following to me:

O you who censure me for loving Him, how much you crush me;
If only you could see the One I mean, you would no longer censure me.
People make the pilgrimage; I am going on a (spiritual) pilgrimage to
       my Host;
While they offer animals in sacrifice, I offer my heart and my blood.
Some of them walk in procession around the Temple, without their
       bodies,
For they walk in procession in God, and He has exempted them from
       the Haram.

[MASSIGNON 1982: 1:543]

3. Withdrawal from the World

1. Judah Halevi on Jewish Asceticism

For the benefit of a fictional king who was conducting an inquiry into the claims of different religions, Judah Halevi put in the mouth of his own alter ego, a traditionalist rabbi, some remarks on the subject of Jewish asceticism. Halevi's work, entitled The King of the Khazars, *was composed between 1130 and 1140 C.E.*

The divine law imposes no asceticism on us. It rather desires that we should keep the equilibrium and grant to every mental and physical faculty its due, as much as it can bear, without overburdening one faculty at the expense of another. If a person gives way to licentiousness, he blunts his mental faculty; he who is inclined to violence injures some other faculty. Prolonged fasting is no act of piety for a weak person who, having succeeded in checking his desires, is not greedy. For him feasting is a burden and self-denial. Neither is diminution of wealth an act of piety, if it is gained in a lawful way, and if its acquisition does not interfere with study and good works, especially for him who has a household and children. He may spend part of it in almsgiving, which would not be displeasing to God; but to increase it would be better for himself.

Our Law, as a whole, is divided between fear, love and joy, by each of which one can approach God. Your contribution on a fast day does nothing nearer to God than your joy on the Sabbath and the holy days, if it is the outcome of a devout heart. . . . The observance of the Sabbath is itself an acknowledgment of His omnipotence (in its recollection of the Exodus), and at the same time an acknowledgment of the creation by the divine Word. . . . The observance of the Sabbath is therefore nearer to God than monastic retirement and asceticism. (Judah Halevi, *The King of the Khazars*) [HALEVI 1905: 113–114]

2. Jewish Monasticism

Judah Halevi was reflecting on the Jewish tradition as he knew and understood it from the perspective of the twelfth century. That tradition had already forgotten, or had chosen to ignore, many of the forms of Jewish piety and observance that our sources reveal in the centuries immediately preceding and following the beginning of the Christian era. We do not always know what to make of some of them, whether they are constructs, idealizations, or reality, but they are described in great detail, particularly the two examples of what can only be called "Jewish monasticism" that we find in the pages of Philo and Josephus. The first group, called the Therapeutae, or "Healers," had their "houses" around Lake Mereotis near Alexandria.

The houses of the society are exceedingly simple, providing protection against two of the most pressing dangers of the site, the fiery heat of the sun and the icy cold of the air. They are neither near together, as in towns, since living at close quarters is troublesome and displeasing to people who are seeking to satisfy their desire for solitude, nor yet at a great distance, because of the sense of friendship they cherish and to render help to each other if robbers attack them. . . . Twice each day they pray, at dawn and at eventide: at dawn they pray for a fine bright day in the true sense of heavenly daylight which they pray may fill their minds. At sunset they ask that the soul may be wholly relieved from the burden of the senses and the objects of sense, and sitting in a place where she is both consistory and council chamber to herself, she may pursue the quest of truth. The interval between each morning and evening is spent entirely in spiritual exercises. They read the Holy Scriptures and seek wisdom from their ancestral philosophy by taking it as an allegory, since they think that the words of the literal text are symbols of something whose hidden nature is revealed by studying the underlying meaning. They have also the writings of men of old, the founders of their way of thinking, who left many memorials of the form used in allegorical interpretation, and these they take as a kind of archetype and imitate the method in which this principle is carried out. And so they do not confine themselves to contemplation, but also compose hymns and psalms to God in all sorts of meters and melodies, which they write down with the rhythms made necessarily more solemn. (Philo, *The Contemplative Life* 24–30)

Philo then describes how the Therapeutae meet together each seventh day in assembly, where the senior man among them, "who also has the fullest knowledge of the doctrines which they profess," delivers a discourse. Women too attend the general assembly, though they are separated by a head-high partition.

They lay self-control to be, as it were, the foundation of their soul and on it build the other virtues. None of them would put food or drink to his lips before sunset, since they hold that philosophy finds its right place in the light, the needs of the body in darkness and therefore they assign the day to one and a small part of the night to the other. Some in whom the desire of studying wisdom is even more deeply implanted remember to take food only after three days. . . . But on the seventh day [that is, the Sabbath], as they consider it to be sacred and festal in the highest degree, they have awarded special privileges as its due; and on it, after providing for the soul, refresh the body also, which they do as a matter of course with the cattle too, by releasing them from their continuous labor. (Ibid. 34–36)

On every seventh Sabbath there is a special feast, a banquet, which Philo compares favorably with the licentious symposia of the Greeks and Romans. Here too women are present.

. . . [M]ost of them are aged virgins, who have kept their chastity not under compulsion, like some of the Greek priestesses, but of their own free will in their ardent yearning for wisdom. Eager to have her for their life mate, they have spurned the pleasures of the body; and they desire no mortal offspring but those immortal children which only the soul that is dear to God can bring to birth unaided because the Father has sown in her spiritual rays enabling her to behold the truths of wisdom. (Ibid. 68)

At this banquet—I know some will laugh at this, but only those whose actions call for tears and lamentation—no wine is served . . . but only water of the brightest and clearest, cold for most of the guests but warm for such of the older men as live delicately. The table too is kept pure from flesh of animals; the food that is laid on it is loaves of bread with salt as a seasoning, sometimes also flavored with hyssop as a relish for the daintier appetites. Abstinence from wine is enjoined by right reason, as for the priest when sacrificing, so for these for their lifetime. For wine acts like a drug, producing folly, and costly dishes stir up that most insatiable of animals, desire. (Ibid. 73–74)

After the supper they hold the sacred vigil, which is conducted in the following way. They rise up all together and standing in the middle of the refectory, form themselves first into two choirs, one of men and one of women, the leader and preceptor chosen from each being the most honored among them and also the most musical. Then they sing hymns to God composed of many measures and set to many melodies, sometimes chanting together, sometimes taking up the harmony antiphonally, hands and feet keeping time in accompaniment and, rapt with enthusiasm, reproduce sometimes the lyrics of the procession, sometimes of the halt and of the wheeling and counterwheeling of a choral dance. (Ibid. 83–84)

If there is something utopian in this portrait of Platonic sages interrupting their contemplation of wisdom to celebrate the Sabbath with a spiritual symposium, there is something more authentically Jewish perhaps about the group Josephus calls the Essenes, who were also known to Philo under the same name.

There are three philosophical sects among the Jews. The followers of the first are the Pharisees, of the second the Sadducees, and the third sect, which pretends to a severer discipline, are called Essenes.

These Essenes are Jews by birth and seem to have a greater affection for one another than the other sects have. They reject pleasures as evil, but esteem continence and the conquest over our passions as a virtue. They neglect wedlock, but choose out other persons' children while they are still pliable and docile, and esteem them as their own kindred, and form them according to their own way of life. They do not absolutely deny the the propriety of marriage and the succession of mankind that flows therefrom, but they guard against the lewd behavior of women and are persuaded that none of them preserve their fidelity to one man.

These men are despisers of riches . . . nor is anyone to be found among them who possesses more than any other, since it is a law of theirs that those who come to them must allow whatever they have to become the common property of the entire group, so that among them there is no appearance of poverty or superabundance of riches, but everyone's possessions are mixed in with everyone else's and there is, so to say, one inheritance among all the brothers. . . .

As for their piety toward God, it is very extraordinary. Before sunrise they speak not a word on profane matters but offer up certain prayers, which they have received from their forefathers, as if beseeching the sun to rise. After this each is sent off by their curators to exercise one of the skills they possess. They work hard at this until the fifth hour, when they assemble once again in one place. Then, when they have put on white veils, they bathe in cold water. After this purification, they all meet in a chamber of their own, into which no one of any other sect is admitted. They go thus purified into a refectory, as if entering a temple, and quietly seat themselves. The baker lays out loaves in order and the cook brings a single plate of one kind of food and sets it before each one of them. A priest says a blessing before the meal and it is forbidden for anyone to taste of the food until the blessing has been said. The same priest says a blessing again after the meal. . . . Afterwards they put off their white garments and return to their labors until evening, when they return home to a supper in the same fashion. . . .

In other things, they do only what they are enjoined by their curators, and there are only two things that are done according to each's free will, namely, to assist those in need and to show mercy, since they are permitted of their own accord to give assistance to deserving cases when they need it and to give food to those in want; they cannot, however, give anything to their kin without permission of the curators. . . . They take great pains in studying the writings of the ancients and select from them what is most helpful for their souls and bodies, and they inquire after such roots and stones as may cure their ills. . . .

The Essenes are stricter than any other Jews in resting from their labors on the Sabbath, for they not only get their food ready on the day previous, that they may not have to kindle a fire on the Sabbath itself, nor will they remove any vessel from its place or use it for defecation. Even on days other than the Sabbath they dig a small pit a foot deep with a scoop, a kind of hatchet that is given them when they are first admitted in that company, and covering themselves round about with their garments, that they may not affront the divine rays of light, they defecate in that pit, after which they pile the earth back in again; and even this they do in remote places, which they select for this purpose. And even though emptying the bowels is a natural act, yet it is their rule to wash themselves afterward, as if it defiled them. . . .

There is another community of Essenes who agree with the rest in their manner of life and customs and laws, but who differ from them on the subject of marriage, since they consider that in not marrying they are cutting off the principal part of human life, which is the hope of succession; indeed, they maintain, if all men were of the same mind (as the celibates), the whole human race would fail. They do, however, make trial of their spouses for three years, and if they find that they have their menstrual periods three times, as a test of their likely fertility, then they actually marry them. But they do not cohabit with their wives during pregnancy to demonstrate that they do not marry for pleasure but for the purpose of procreation. (Josephus, *War* 2.8.2–13)

3. The Monks of Qumran

The Essenes of Philo and Josephus long remained purely a literary phenomenon. Then some forty years ago the well-preserved traces of a very similar community were discovered at Qumran, at the northwest corner of the Dead Sea. Those traces included not only a community complex of buildings but also, hidden away in nearby caves, the writings of the sect, including their "Community Rule." It is by no means certain that this Jewish community at Qumran, which was occupied from the second century B.C.E. down to the destruction of the Temple in 70 C.E., is identical with Josephus' Essenes, but the similarities are such to suggest that we are dealing with, if not the same, then a very similar example of believers who had withdrawn from the mainstream of Jewish life in Palestine and had adopted a regimen of purity and of unquestioning obedience in a rigorously hierarchical community.

Every man, born of Israel, who freely pledges himself to join the Council of the Community shall be examined by the Guardian at the head of the Congregation concerning his understanding and his deeds. If he is fitted to the discipline, he shall admit him into the Covenant that he may be converted to the truth and depart from all falsehood; and he shall instruct him in all the rules of the Community. And later, when he comes to stand before the Congregation, they shall all deliberate his case, and according to the decision of the Council of the Congregation, he shall either enter or depart.

After he has entered the Council of the Congregation he shall not touch the pure Meal of the Congregation until one full year is completed, and until he has been examined concerning his spirit and his deeds; nor shall he have any share in the property of the Congregation. Then when he has completed one year within the Community, the Congregation shall deliberate his case with regard to his understanding and his observance of the Law. And if it be his destiny, according to the judgment of the Priests and the multitude of the men of the Covenant, to enter the Community, his property and earnings shall be handed over to the Bursar of the Congregation who shall register it to his account and shall not spend it for the Congregation. He shall not touch the Drink of the Congregation until he has completed a second year among the men of the Community. But when the second year has passed, he shall be examined, and if it is his destiny, according to the judgment of the Congregation, to enter the Community, then he shall be inscribed among his brethren according to his rank for the Law, and for justice, and for the pure Meal; his property shall be merged and he shall offer his counsel and judgment to the Community. (*The Community Rule* 6) [VERMES 1968: 81–82]

And this is the Rule for the men of the Community who have freely pledged themselves to be converted from all evil and to cling to all His commandments according to His will.

They shall separate from the congregation of men of falsehood and shall unite, with respect to the Law and possessions, under the authority of the sons of Zadok [the High Priest of the era of David; cf. 2 Sam. 8:17], the Priests who keep the Covenant, and of the multitude of the men of the Community, who hold fast to the Covenant. Every decision concerning doctrine, property and justice shall be determined by them.

They shall practice truth and humility in common, and justice and uprightness and charity and modesty in all their ways. No man shall walk in the stubbornness of his heart so that he strays after his heart and eyes and evil inclination, but he shall circumcise in the Community the foreskin of his evil inclination and of stiffness of neck that they may lay a foundation of truth for Israel, for the community of the everlasting Covenant. They shall atone for all of those in Aaron who have freely pledged themselves to holiness, and for those in Israel who have freely pledged themselves to the House of Truth, and for those who join them to live in community and to take part in the trial and the judgment and condemnation of all those who transgress the precepts.

On joining the Community, this shall be their code of behavior with respect to all these precepts. Whoever approaches the Council of the Community shall enter the Covenant of God in the presence of all who have pledged themselves. He shall undertake by a binding oath to return with all his heart and soul to every commandment of the Law of Moses in accordance with all that has been revealed to the sons of Zadok, the Keepers of the Covenant and the seekers of His will and to the multitude of the men of their Covenant who together have freely pledged themselves to His truth and to walking in the way of His delight. And he shall undertake by the Covenant to separate from all men of falsehood who walk in the way of wickedness. (*The Community Rule* 5) [VERMES 1968: 78–79]

They shall eat in common and pray in common and deliberate in common.

Whenever there are ten men of the Council of the Community they shall not lack a priest among them. And they shall sit before him according to their rank and shall be asked their counsel in all things in that order. And when the table has been prepared for eating, and the new wine for drinking, the Priest shall be the first to stretch out his hand to bless the firstfruits of the bread and the new wine.

And where the ten are, there shall never lack a man among them who will study the Law continually, day and night, concerning the right conduct of a man with his companion. And the Congregation shall watch in community for a third of every night of the year, to read the Book and study and Law and pray together. (Ibid., no. 6) [VERMES 1968: 80–81]

4. The Following of Christ

At about the same time, we read this in the Gospels, which incidentally make no mention of either the Essenes or Qumran.

Jesus then said to his disciples, "If anyone wishes to be a follower of mine, he must leave self behind; he must take up his cross and come with me. Whoever cares for his own safety is lost; but if a man will let himself be lost for my sake, he will find his own true self. What will a man gain by winning the whole world at the cost of his true self? Or what can he give that will buy that self back?" (Matthew 16:24–26)

And now a man came up and asked him, "Master, what good must I do to gain eternal life?" "Good?" said Jesus, "Why do you ask me that? One alone is good. But if you wish to enter into life, keep the commandments." "Which commandments?" he asked. Jesus answered, "Do not commit murder; do not commit adultery; do not steal; do not give false evidence; honor your father and your mother; and love your neighbor as yourself." The young man answered, "I have kept all these. Where do I still fall short?" Jesus said to him, "If you wish to go the whole way, go, sell all your possessions and give to the poor, and then you will have riches in heaven; and come, follow me." When the young man heard this, he went away with a heavy heart, for he was a man of great wealth. (Matthew 19:16–22)

These two passages from Matthew constitute in an exemplary way the Christians' invitation to a special piety and a special vocation, to "go the whole way": a call, in the first example, to the peculiarly Christian task of "taking up the cross," if not in fact, then, even more terribly, in spirit. The commentator is Thomas à Kempis (d. 1471 C.E.), the author of one of the most influential works of spirituality in the long Christian tradition.

Why are you afraid to take up the Cross, which is the road to the Kingdom? In the Cross is salvation; in the Cross is life; in the Cross is protection against our enemies; in the Cross is the infusion of heavenly sweetness; in the Cross is strength of mind; in the Cross is joy of spirit; in the Cross is the height of virtue; in the Cross is perfection of sanctity.

There is no salvation of soul, no hope of eternal life, but in the Cross. Take up the Cross, therefore, and follow Jesus, and go forward into eternal life. Christ has gone before you bearing His Cross, and He died for you on the Cross, that you also may bear your cross and desire to die on the Cross. Because if you die with Him, you shall also live with Him; And if you share His sufferings, you will also share His glory.

See how in the Cross all things consist, and all things depend on dying on it. There is no other way to life, and to true inner peace, than the way of the Cross, and of daily self-denial. Go wherever you will, seek whatever you will, you will find no higher way above or safer way below than the road of the Holy Cross. Arrange and order things to your own ideas and wishes, yet you will find suffering to endure, whether you will or not; so you will always find the Cross. For you will either endure bodily pain or suffer anguish of mind and spirit.

At times God will withdraw from you; at times you will be troubled by your neighbor, and, what is more, you will often be a burden to yourself. Neither can any comfort or remedy bring you any relief, but you must bear it as long as God wills. For God desires that you learn to bear trials without comfort, that you may yield yourself wholly to Him, and grow more humble through tribulation. No man feels so deeply in his heart the Passion of Christ as he who has to suffer in like manner. The Cross always stands ready, and everywhere awaits you. You cannot escape it, wherever you flee; for wherever you go, you bear yourself, and always find yourself. Look up or down, without you and within, and everywhere you will find the Cross. (Thomas à Kempis, *The Imitation of Christ* 2:12)

Although Thomas à Kempis was himself a monk, his preaching—and the passage just cited is a good illustration—was on behalf of a kind of populist piety, a spirituality for all Christians. But Jesus' remarks just cited from Matthew were generally read not as a populist manifesto but as a distinction drawn by Jesus himself between the Christian in search of "mere" salvation—for him the observance of the Law will bring life—and someone searching for a higher level of perfection. We are at the starting point of Christianity's double life, salvation or perfection, prescriptions or counsels, observance or asceticism, the secular or the religious vocation?

5. Celibacy: The Gospels and Paul

The cited passages in Matthew's Gospel are quite explicit: Jesus makes poverty the barrier that distinguishes the Christian seeker after perfection from the mere observer of what came to be understood as Christian morality. But poverty, not only of the spirit but actual poverty, soon had a companion along this high road to perfection: celibacy. Jesus' remarks on divorce in Mark are followed in the parallel version in Matthew 19 by a more general discussion of marriage.

The disciples said to him [Jesus], "If that is the position with husband and wife, it is better not to marry." To this he replied, "That is something which everyone cannot accept, but only those for whom God has appointed it. For while some are incapable of marriage because they were born so, or were made so by men, there are others who have themselves renounced marriage for the sake of the kingdom of Heaven. Let those accept it who can." (Matthew 19:10–12)

The early Christians of Corinth, the site of a major cult center of Aphrodite, may already have been debating this question. Such at any rate seems to be the implication behind Paul's letter to them.

You say that it is a good thing for a man to have nothing to do with women; but because there is so much immorality, let each man have his own wife and each woman her own husband. . . . Do not deny yourselves to one another, except when you agree upon a temporary abstinence in order to devote yourselves to prayer; afterwards you may come together again; otherwise, for lack of self-control, you may be tempted by Satan.

All this I say by way of concession, not command. I should like you all to be as I am myself; but everyone has the gift God has granted him, one this gift and another that.

To the unmarried and the widows I say this: it is a good thing if they stay as I am myself; but if they cannot control themselves, they should marry. Better be married than burn with vain desire. . . .

On the question of celibacy, I have no instructions from the Lord, but I give my judgment as one who by God's mercy is fit to be trusted. It is my opinion, then, that in a time of stress like the present this is the best way for a man to live—it is best for a man to be as he is. Are you bound to a marriage? Do not seek a dissolution. Has your marriage been dissolved? Do not seek a wife. If, however, you do marry, there is nothing wrong with it. . . .

I want you to be free from anxious care. The unmarried man cares for the Lord's business: his aim is to please the Lord. But the married man cares for worldly things: his aim is to please his wife; and he has a divided mind. The unmarried or celibate woman cares for the Lord's business; her aim is to be dedicated to him in body as in spirit; but the married woman cares for worldly things; her aim is to please her husband.

In saying this I have no wish to keep you on a tight rein. I am thinking simply of your own good, of what is seemly, and of your freedom to wait upon the Lord without distraction. (Paul, *To the Corinthians* 1.7:1–35)

I asked him again, saying, "Sir, since you have been so patient with me, will you explain this also?" "Speak," he said. And I said, "If a wife or husband die, and the widow or widower marry again, does he or she commit sin?" "There is no sin in marrying again," he said, "but if they remain unmarried, they gain greater honor and glory with the Lord; but if they marry, they do not sin. Guard therefore your chastity and purity, and you will live to God." (Hermas, *The Pastor* 4.4)

The ambiguity about celibacy and marriage that runs unresolved through these early texts left a lasting mark on Christian moral teaching. Not merely was the permanently vowed celibate state the Christian ideal; temporary celibacy was advocated within the married state. "Do not deny yourselves to one another, except when you agree upon a temporary abstinence in order to devote yourselves to prayer," Paul had said in the letter cited above. The progress of the idea may be seen in this example from a manual for confessors from about 525–550 C.E.

We advise and exhort that there be continence in marriage, since marriage without continence is not lawful but sin, and [marriage] is permitted by the authority of God not for lust but for the sake of children, as it is written, "And the two shall be in one flesh" [Matt 19: 5], that is, in unity of the flesh for the generation of children, not for the lustful concupiscence of the flesh. Married people, then, must mutually abstain during three forty-day periods in each single year [possibly the three "quarantines," the forty-day fasts before Christmas and Easter and following Pentecost] by consent for a time that they may be able to have time for prayer for the salvation of their souls; and on Sunday night or Saturday night they shall mutually abstain, and after the wife has conceived he shall not have intercourse until she has borne her child, and they shall come together again for this purpose, as the Apostle (Paul) says [1 Cor. 7:5]. (*Penitential of Finnian*) [MCNEILL & GAMER 1938: 96]

6. Clerical Celibacy

In the case of Christian clerics, the connection with celibacy was present from a very early date, though its application varied considerably from one jurisdiction to another.

Those who have been made deacons, declaring when they were ordained that they must marry because they were not able to continue as they were (in the celibate state), and who afterwards did marry, shall continue in the ministry because it was conceded to them by the bishop. But if they were silent on the matter, undertaking at their ordination to abide as they were, and then afterwards proceeded to marry, they shall cease from the diaconate. (Council of Ancyra [314 C.E.], Canon 10)

If any shall maintain concerning a married presbyter [or priest], that it is not lawful to partake of the oblation that he offers, let him be anathema. (Council of Gangra [355–381 C.E.], Canon 4)

Since it is declared in the Apostolic Canons that of those who are advanced to the clergy unmarried, only lectors and cantors are able to marry, we also, maintaining this, determine that henceforth it is nowise lawful for any subdeacon, deacon or presbyter after his ordination to contract matrimony; but if he shall have dared to do so, let him be deposed. And if any of those who enter the clergy wishes to be joined to a wife before he is ordained subdeacon, deacon or presbyter, let it be done.

Moreover it has come to our knowledge that in Africa and Libya and in other places the most God-beloved bishops in those parts do not refuse to live with their wives, even after consecration, thereby giving scandal and offense to the people. Since therefore it is our particular care that all things tend to the good of the flock placed in our hands and committed to us, it has seemed good that no such thing shall in any way occur. . . . But if any shall have been observed to do such a thing, let him be deposed.

Since we know it to be handed down as a rule of the Roman Church that those who are deemed worthy to be advanced to the diaconate and presbyterate should promise no longer to cohabit with their wives, we, preserving the ancient rule and apostolic perfection and order, will that lawful marriage of men who are in holy orders be from this time forward firm, by no means dissolving their union with their wives or depriving them of their mutual intercourse at a convenient season. . . . For it is meet that they who assist at the divine altar should be absolutely continent when they are handling holy things, in order that they may be able to obtain from God what they ask in sincerity. (Quinquisext Council [692 C.E.], Canons 6, 12–13)

If deacons and priests might continue, in despite of Roman practice, in the married state contracted before ordination, the same was not true of bishops.

The wife of him who is advanced to the episcopal dignity shall be separated from her husband by mutual consent, and after his ordination and consecration to the episcopate she shall enter a monastery situated at a distance from the abode of the bishop, and there let her enjoy the bishop's support. And if she is deemed worthy, she may be advanced to the dignity of deaconess. (Ibid., Canon 48)

The first Western legislation prohibiting the cohabitation of the Christian clergy with the wives they took before ordination—and this pertained to all the clergy, from deacon to bishop—appears to have been promulgated by the Council of Elvira in Spain in 306 C.E. An even clearer expression is found in a Papal decretal of 385 C.E. that connects clerical celibacy directly with the Jewish priesthoods. These decretals had the force of law in the Western Church.

Why did He admonish them to whom the Holy of Holies was committed, "Be you holy, because I the Lord your God am holy" (Lev. 20:7)? Why were they commanded to dwell in the Temple during the year of their turn to officiate, far from their own homes? Obviously it was for the reason that they might not be able to continue to have marital relations with their wives, so that, adorned with a pure conscience, they might offer to God an acceptable sacrifice. After the time of their service was completed they were permitted to resume their marital relations for the sake of continuing the (priestly) succession, because only from the tribe of Levi was it ordained that anyone should be admitted to the priesthood. . . . Wherefore also our Lord Jesus, when by his coming he brought us light, solemnly affirmed in the Gospel that he had come not to destroy but to fulfill the Law. And therefore, he who is the bridegroom of the Church wished that its form be resplendent with chastity, so that on the Day of Judgment, when he should come again, he might find it without a spot or blemish, as he taught by his Apostle. And by the rule of its ordinances which may not be denied, we who are priests and Levites are bound from the day of our ordination to keep our bodies in soberness and modesty, so that in those sacrifices which we offer daily to our God we may please Him in all things. (Pope Siricius, *Decretal*, Chapter 7)

The final and abiding position of the Western Church on clerical celibacy, now including its extension to the grade of subdeacon, is set forth in two letters of Pope Leo (440–461 C.E.), called "the Great."

Although they who are not within the ranks of the clergy are free to take pleasure in the companionship of wedlock and the procreation of children, yet, for the sake of exhibiting the purity of complete continence, even subdeacons are not allowed carnal marriage; that "both they that have wives be as though they had none" (1 Cor. 7:29) and they that have not may remain single. But if in this order (of the subdiaconate), which is the fourth from the head, this is worthy to be observed, how much more is it to be kept in the first [the episcopate], the second [the presbyterate or priesthood], and the third [the diaconate], lest anyone be reckoned fit for the deacon's duties, or the presbyter's honorable position, or the bishop's pre-eminence, who is discovered as not yet having bridled his uxorious desires. (Leo, *To Athanasius*, 5)

The same law of continence is for the ministers of the altar as for the bishops and priests, who, when they were laymen, could lawfully marry and procreate children. But when they had attained to the said ranks, what was before lawful became unlawful for them. And thus, in order that their wedlock may become spiritual instead of carnal, it is necessary that they do not put away their wives but have them "as though they had them not," whereby both the affection of their married life may be retained and the marriage function cease. (Leo, *Rusticus* 3)

7. Radical Celibacy in the Early Church

We return to early Christian discussions about celibacy. Some Christians went very far indeed in their interpretation of Jesus and Paul and simply rejected the institution of marriage, a position that found no support in the Church as a whole.

Others who style themselves Encratites [or the "Self-Controlled"] acknowledge some things concerning God and Christ in accordance with the Church, but in respect to their mode of life they pass their time inflated with pride; thinking that by meat they might glorify themselves, they abstain from all animal food, drink water, and, forbidden to marry, they devote the rest of their lives to asceticism. (Hippolytus, *Refutation of All Heresies* 8.13)

There are those who spring from Saturninus and Marcion and who are called Encratites. They preach the unmarried state, thus setting aside the original creation of God, and indirectly condemn Him who made male and female for the propagation of the human race. Some reckoned as among their number have also introduced abstention from animal food, thus showing their ingratitude to God who created all things. (Ireneus, *Against the Heresies* 1.28)

8. A Christian Holy Man

Although the Encratites had their successors and later imitators here or there in the Christian world, these remain for us obscure and marginal movements. Christian self-denial found its champion elsewhere, in the simple Egyptian named Antony who died in 356 C.E., aged 105. His life was written, and widely disseminated, shortly thereafter.

The blessed Antony was a native Egyptian, and he was descended from a noble family, and in fact he owned slaves. His ancestors were (Christian) believers, and from his earliest days he was brought up in the fear of our Lord, and when he was a child and was being reared among his own relatives, he knew nothing of his father or of what went on among his own family: he was so naturally silent and his mind was so humble that he did not even trouble his parents by questioning them. He was exceedingly modest, modest beyond measure. He was unable to read or write because he could not bear the rough behavior of the boys in the school; his whole desire was to be nothing more than what was written of Jacob, "a simple man, a dweller in tents." He clung closely to his parents, and when they came to church he would run before them in the flow of his affection. He was not like an ordinary child, whose usual routine is broken by the childish amusements. He never neglected the observance of any of the seasons of the Church. . . .

After the death of his parents, Antony was left alone with one little sister. He was about eighteen or twenty years old, and on him rested the responsibility of caring for both the household and his sister. Six months after the death of his parents, when he was going, as usual, into the Lord's house, and was reflecting within himself, he thought as he walked how the Apostles had left all and followed the Savior, and how in Acts, men sold their possessions and brought and laid them at the Apostles' feet for distribution to the needy, and what and how great a hope was laid up for them in heaven. While he was thinking of these matters he went into the church just as the Gospel was being read, and he heard the Lord say to the rich man: "If you would be perfect, go and sell what you have and give to the poor; and come and follow me and you shall have treasure in heaven." Antony, as though God had put him in mind of the saints and the passage had been read for his benefit, immediately left the Lord's house and gave the possessions which he had from his ancestors to the villagers—they were three hundred acres, productive and rich—that they should no more be a burden upon himself and his sister. And all the

rest that was unmovable he sold, and the considerable money thus collected he gave to the poor, saving a little, however, for his sister's sake.
He went back to the Lord's house, and hearing the Lord say in the
Gospel, "Be not anxious for the morrow," he could remain no longer, but
went and gave even that to the poor.

Antony committed his sister to known and faithful virgins, installing
her in a maidens' house for upbringing, and henceforth he devoted himself outside his own house to ascetic discipline, paying attention to himself and patiently training himself. For there were not as yet many monasteries in Egypt, and no monk at all had experience of the remote desert;
but every one of those who wished to have a care for himself practiced
the ascetic discipline in solitude near his own village.

There was in the next village to Antony an old man who had lived
from his youth the life of a hermit. Antony, after he had seen this man,
imitated him in piety and at first he began to live in places outside the
village. Then, if he heard of any good man anywhere else, like the prudent
bee he went forth and sought him out and did not return to his own place
until he had seen him; and he returned only after he had gotten from the
good man provisions, as it were, for his journey on the road to virtue. So
at first he lived thus and steadfastly held to his purpose not to return to
the home of his parents or to the remembrance of his family, but to
devote all his desire and energy to the perfection of his discipline. He
worked, however, with his hands, having heard that "he who is idle, let
him not eat," and part (of his wages) he spent on bread and part he gave
to the needy. And he prayed constantly, because he had learned that a
man ought to pray unceasingly in private. For he had given such heed to
what was read that none of those things that were written fell from him
to the ground; he remembered everything, and afterwards his memory
served him as Scripture. . . .

Now Saint Antony was a storehouse of fasting, and of prayer, and of
ascetic labors, and of patient endurance, and of love and of righteousness,
which is the mother of them all, but he did not compete with those others
who were young monks like himself, except in one matter only, that is to
say, he would not suffer himself to be second to any of them in good
works. . . . And when the Enemy, that hater of the virtues and the lover
of evil things, saw all this great perfection in the young man, he could not
endure it, and he surrounded himself with his slaves, as is his custom, and
began to work on Antony. At the beginnings of his tempting of the saint,
he [that is, Satan] approached him with flattery and caused him to feel
anxiety about his possessions, and solicitude and love for his sister, and

for his family, and to experience the love of money and lusts of various kinds, and to think of the rest of the things of the life of this world, and finally of the hard and laborious life that he lived, and the weakness of body which would come upon him in the course of time. . . .

Now when the Enemy saw that his craftiness in this matter was without profit, and that the more he tempted Saint Antony, the more strenuous the saint was in protecting himself with the armor of righteousness, he attacked him by means of the (sexual) vigor of early manhood which is bound up in the nature of our humanity. He used to trouble him at night with the goadings of passion, and in the daytime as well he tried him and pained him with the same desires, and to such an extent that even those who just looked upon him knew from his appearance that he was waging war against the Adversary. But the more the Evil One plagued him with filthy and maddening thoughts, the more Saint Antony took refuge in prayer and in abundant supplication, and amidst them all he remained wholly chaste. And the Evil One was working upon him every shameful deed according to his custom, and at length he even appeared to Saint Antony in the form of a woman—other similar feats he performed with ease, for such things are a subject of boasting for him.

None of these temptations are of any avail, however. Antony perseveres in virtue and soon begins to pay the price of fame.

It happened that in the course of time Antony's fame reached all the monks who were in Egypt and even all the others there who did not live the life of the ascetic and the recluse, and men of distinction and monks in Egypt began to come to him in large numbers. The Egyptian monks came to him that they might copy the manner of his life and deeds, and the laity came that he might pray over them, and might heal certain of them of their illnesses. One day, when a crowd of people had come there in a body to see him and they had besought him repeatedly to speak to them, and he had answered them not a word, they lifted the door out of its socket, and threw themselves down on their faces before him, and implored him, and then each man among them stood up and made known his request to him. And when he had gone out to them, like a man who issues from the bowels of the earth, they saw that his appearance was like that of an angel of light, and they marveled that his body had not been weakened by all his confinement and why it was that his understanding had not become feeble, and rather, on the contrary, in appearance, physique and countenance he was exactly as they had known him in the past. (Athanasius, *Life of Antony*)

9. Antony Goes into the Desert

When Antony saw the great crowds of people who had collected about him and realized that the trouble which those men and women caused him was increasing, he began to fear that he should become unduly puffed up in his mind because of the things that God had accomplished through him, or that others might esteem him beyond proper bounds and more than he deserved. And so he determined to go away from that place and enter the Thebaid [that is, the desert area around Egyptian Thebes]. So he took a little bread and sat down on the river bank and waited for a boat going to the district that was his destination. And as he was reflecting there, he suddenly heard a voice from heaven: "Antony, where are you going? Why are you leaving this place?" Now he was not frightened by this voice but spoke to it like a man doing what was customary. "Because, my Lord," he replied, "the people will not allow me a little silent contemplation here. And so I intend to go to the Thebaid, and I am particularly eager to go because the people here are asking me for things which are totally beyond my powers."

God instead counseled going not to the Thebaid but into the "innermost desert" and showed Antony the way. On his journey he was assisted by the only inhabitants of the place, the local bedouin, who supplied him with bread and water.

Then the Blessed Antony was alone in that wilderness, for the place where he chose to live was desolate in the extreme. But he was thus able to reflect the more on exalted things, and he was content. And the brothers who used to visit him earlier now begged him to allow them to bring to him there every month some garden greens and olives and oil, and though he opposed them, they overcame him with their entreaties and forced him to receive them. Thus they began to pay him visits, one at a time. And the blessed man grew exceedingly elderly and advanced in years. And even there in the desert the blessed man was engaged in struggle, not with flesh and blood, but with the demons and impure spirits, as we have learned from those who visited him. They used to hear there the sounds of cries and tumult, to see flashing spears, and at night the whole mountain was filled with fiery demons and his visitors were filled with fear. . . . But he encouraged the brethren who were with him not to be frightened or tremble at such apparitions. For, he told them, "They are only empty phantoms which at the name of the Cross perish as if they had never existed." (Athanasius, *Life of Antony*)

CHAPTER 3

10. Cells in the Wilderness

There were many who followed where Antony led, and for spiritual motives as varied as those traced by the seventh-century master of Eastern monasticism, John Climacus.

Some enter this harbor, this sea, or indeed the abyss of solitary life because they cannot control their tongues or because of some previous bad habit of the flesh. Others do so because they have a bad temper, which they cannot restrain in company, or because they arrogantly think it better to sail on their own rather than under the guidance of someone else. Others do so because if they live amid material things they cannot do without them. Some think a life of solitude will enhance their zeal, and some wish to punish themselves in secret for their faults. Some think of the glory a solitary life will earn them. And there are some—may the Son of Man find them on earth when He returns—who undertake this holy way of life because of a delight in, a thirst for the love and sweetness of God. (John Climacus, *The Ladder of Divine Ascent*, Step 27)

[JOHN CLIMACUS 1982: 265]

Like Antony, these seekers after solitary perfection took themselves in the first instance to the desert and wildernesses of Egypt.

Beyond Nitria there is another place in the inner desert, about nine miles distant; and this place is called, by reason of the great number of monastic dwellings scattered through the wilderness, "The Cells." To this place those who have already had their first initiation, and who desire to live a more remote life, stripped of all its trappings, withdraw themselves: for the desert is vast, and the cells are separated one from another by so wide a space that no one is in sight of his neighbor, nor can any voice be heard.

The monks abide singly in their cells, and there is a great silence and a great tranquillity among them: they come together at the church only on Saturdays and Sundays, where they see each other face to face like people restored in heaven. If anyone happens to be absent from that gathering, they immediately understand that he has been detained by some bodily ailment, and so they all go to visit him, not indeed all of them together but at different times, and each carries with him whatever he may have with him at his abode that might be appreciated by the ill person. But for no other reason does any dare disturb the silence of his neighbor, unless occasionally to strengthen someone with a good word,

937

or, it might be, to anoint with the comfort of counsel the athletes set for the struggle. Many of them go three and four miles to church, and the distance separating one cell from another is no less great. But so great is the love that is in them . . . that if anyone should wish to dwell with them, as soon as they are aware of it, each man offers his own cell. (Rufinus, *History of the Monks of Egypt*)

Rufinus is writing history, or at least collecting anecdotes, at second hand. One who had the immediate experience and left us his own rather rhetorical account—he was also the translator of the Bible into Latin—was Jerome, who took up the monastic life in Palestine in the fourth century.

I dwelt in the desert, in the vast solitude which gives the hermit his savage home, parched by the burning sun. . . . Sackcloth disfigured my unshapely limbs, and my skin from long neglect became as black as the Ethiopian's. Tears and groans were every day my portion; if drowsiness chanced to overcome my struggle against it, my bare bones, which hardly held together, crashed against the ground. Of my food and drink I say nothing; for even in sickness the solitaries have nothing but cold water, and to eat one's food cooked is looked upon as an indulgence. . . . My face is pale and my frame chilled with fasting. (Jerome, *Letter* 22.7)

11. Pirke Aboth, Christian Style

The growth of Christian monasticism produced a parallel body of literature to instruct and edify monks and laymen alike with accounts of the struggles and the triumphs of these "athletes of God." One popular form of this literature was "the sayings of the Fathers," aphorisms on the life of self-denial by those engaged in trying to lead it.

A certain man asked the abbot Antony, "What shall I observe, that I may please God?" And the old man answered him: "Observe what I tell you. Wherever you go, have God ever before your eyes. Whatever you do, hold by the example of the Holy Scriptures. And wherever you are staying, do not be quick to leave it. These three things observe and you shall be saved."

They said of the abbot Pambo, that in the hour of his departing this life, he said to the holy men who stood about him: "From the time I came into this place of solitude and built my cell and dwelt in it, I do not recall that I have eaten bread save what my hands have toiled for, or repented of any word I have spoken to this hour. And so I go to the Lord as one who has not yet made a beginning of serving God."

The abbot Antony said: "Fish out of water die; even so monks out-side their cells or who stay with men of the world fall away from their vow of quiet. As a fish must return to the sea, so must we to our cells, lest in being out, we forget the watch within."

A certain brother came to the abbot Moses in Scete, seeking a word from him. And the old man said to him: "Go and sit in your cell, and your cell will teach you everything."

An old man saw someone laughing and said to him: "In the presence of heaven and earth we have to give an account of our whole life to God, and you laugh?"

At one time the abbot Achilles came into the cell of the abbot Isaiah in Scete and found him eating. For he had put salt and water in the pot. And seeing that he hid it behind the plaits of palm leaves, Achilles said to him, "Tell me what you were eating?" Isaiah answered, "Forgive me, father, but I was cutting palm leaves and I grew warm. And so I dipped a morsel of bread in salt and put it in my mouth; and my throat was parched and the morsel did not go down, and so I was compelled to pour a little water on the salt so that I could swallow it. But forgive me." And thereafter the abbot Achilles used to say, "Come and see Isaiah supping consommé in Scete! If you really want consommé, go down into Egypt."

A monk met certain handmaidens of God upon the road, and at the sight of them he turned aside. But the abbess said to him, "If you were a perfect monk, you would not have looked so closely as to notice that we were women."

The abbot Cyrus of Alexandria was questioned about lustful fanta-sies. He answered: "If you have not the fantasies, you are without hope, because you have either the fantasies or the deed. . . . He who sins in the flesh has no trouble with sexual fantasies."

The abbot Daniel used to say, "Even as the body flourishes, the soul grows withered; and when the body is withered, then does the soul put forth leaves."

There came to the abbot Lucius in Enna certain monks of the type called "Pray-ers," and the old man asked them: "What kind of handwork do you do?" They said: "We touch no kind of handwork, but as the Apostle says, we pray without ceasing." The old man said to them: "So you do not eat?" They said: "Yes, we eat." And the old man asked: "And while you are eating, who prays for you?" And again he questioned them: "You do not sleep either?" And they said: "We sleep." And the old man said: "And when you sleep, who prays for you?" And he said to them: "Forgive me, my brothers, but you do not do as you said; but I shall now show you how in working with my hands, I pray without ceasing. For I sit, with the help of God, steeping my few palm leaves and from them I weave a mat, and I say all the while, 'Have mercy on me, O God . . . ' Is this not a prayer?" And they said: "Yes." And he said: "And when I stay all day long working and praying with heart and mouth, I make sixteen denarii more or less (from my work), and out of that sum I leave two at the door and spend the rest on food. And whoever finds the two denarii prays for me while I eat and sleep. And thus by God's grace there is fulfilled in me what Scripture says, 'Pray without ceasing.' "

Thieves once came into an old monk's cell and said to him: "We have come to take whatever you have in this cell." And he said: "Take whatever you see, my sons." So they took whatever they could find in the cell and went away. But they overlooked a little bag that was hidden in the cell. So the old man went chasing after them, shouting, "My sons, you have overlooked this. Take it." But they marveled at the patience of the old man and brought everything back, saying to one another, "Truly, this is a man of God." (*The Sayings of the Fathers*)

12. States of the Soul

If the earliest literature produced by the monastic movement appears largely anecdotal, it quickly came of age. A notable effect of the monastic preoccupation with conscience and recollection was a new awareness of the interior states of the soul, of how the affective and volitional life worked. Here the general psychological landscape is laid out by John Climacus in his Ladder of Divine Ascent, *a work written for an early-seventh-century monastic audience in the Near East. In it he gives his own version of the catalogue of the "seven deadly sins" and contrasts them with their virtuous extremes.*

If the height of gluttony is that you force yourself to eat even when you are not hungary, then the height of temperance in a hungry man is that he restrains even the justifiable urges of nature. If the height of lechery is that one raves even over animals and inanimate things, then the height of purity is to look on everyone in the same way that one would regard inanimate objects. If the ultimate stage of cupidity is to gather without ever being satisfied, the ultimate stage of poverty is the willingness to dispense with one's own body. If the final point of despondency is to have no patience even while living in total peace, the final point of patience is to consider oneself to be at rest even in the midst of affliction. If to be furious even in solitude is talked of as a sea of wrath, then calmness, whether your slanderer be present or not, will be a sea of long-suffering. If the high point of vainglory is for a person to put on airs even when no one is present to praise him, the sure proof of its absence is that you keep your thoughts under control when someone is praising you to your face. If it is a sign of perdition, that is, pride, to be arrogant even when poorly dressed, then surely among high doings and great success lowly thoughts betoken saving humility. (John Climacus, *The Ladder of Divine Ascent*, Step 29) [JOHN CLIMACUS 1982: 283–284]

Since they dealt with extreme psychological states, the analyses of the religious writers are often graphic and arresting, as illustrated in this sophisticated fourth-century description of what John called "despondency" and what we might term monastic depression.

Our sixth struggle is with what the Greeks call accidie (*akedia*), and which we may describe as tedium or perturbation of heart. It is akin to dejection and is particularly experienced by wandering monks and solitaries, a persistent and obnoxious enemy to such as dwell in the desert, disturbing the monk especially about midday, like a fever mounting at a regular time, and bringing its highest tide of inflammation at definite accustomed hours to the sick soul. And so some of the Fathers declare it to be the demon of noontide which is spoken of in the 90th Psalm.

When this besieges the unhappy mind, it begets aversion to the place, boredom with one's cell, and scorn and contempt for one's brethren, whether they are dwelling with one or some way off, as careless and unspiritually minded persons. Also, toward any work which must be done within the enclosure of our own place, we become listless and inert. It will not permit us to stay in our cell, or to attend to our reading: we lament that in all this while, living in the same spot, we have made no progress; we sigh and complain that bereft of sympathetic fellowship we have no spiritual fruit; and bewail ourselves as empty of all spiritual profit, abiding vacant and useless in this place.... We praise other and far distant monasteries, describing them as more helpful to one's progress, more congenial to the health of the soul. We paint the fellowship of the brethren there, its suavity, its richness in spiritual conversation, contrasting it with the harshness of all that is at hand, where not only is there no edification to be had from any of the brethren who dwell here, but where one cannot even procure one's victuals without enormous toil. Finally, we conclude that there is no health for us so long as we stay in this place....

Toward eleven o'clock or midday it induces such lassitude of body and craving for food as one might feel after the exhaustion of a long journey and hard toil, or the postponing of a meal throughout a two- or three-day fast. Finally, one gazes anxiously here and there, and sighs that no one brother of any description is seen approaching: one is forever in and out of one's cell, gazing at the sun as though it were tarrying at its setting. One's mind is an irrational confusion, like the earth befogged in a mist, one is slothful and vacant in every spiritual activity, and no remedy, it seems, can be found in this state of siege except a visit from some brother or the solace of sleep. Finally, our malady suggests that in common courtesy one should salute the brethren, and visit the sick, near or far. It dictates such offices of duty and piety as seeking out this relative or that and making haste to visit them; or there is that religious and devout lady, destitute of any support from her family, whom it is pious to visit now and again and supply in holy fashion with the necessary comforts, neglected and despised as she is by her own relations.

The directors of souls could not only diagnose such spiritual ills; they also had at hand the cure.

And so the wise Fathers in Egypt would in no way suffer the monks, especially the younger, to be idle, measuring the state of their heart and their progress in patience and humility by their steadiness at work; and not only might they accept nothing from anyone toward their own support, but out of their own toil they supplied such brethren as came by, or were from foreign parts, and sent huge stores of victuals and provisions throughout Libya, a barren and hungry land, and to those who pined in the squalor of the prisons in the towns.

The preceding is amply confirmed by example.

So the abbot Paul, so revered among the Fathers, was living in the vast desert of Porphyrio secure in his daily sustenance from the date palms there and from his small garden. Though he had no other way of keeping himself—his dwelling in the desert was seven day's journey and more from any town or human habitation, so that the cost of carrying the produce to market would be more than the work he had sweated over would fetch—he nevertheless collected palm leaves (for plaiting into mats) and every day he exacted from himself just such a measure of work that would be required to earn a living (if he sold them). And when his cave was filled with his handiwork of an entire year, he would then set fire to it and burn each year the work he had so carefully done. And thus he proved that a monk cannot endure to remain in his place without doing some manual work, nor can he climb any nearer the summit of holiness. And even though the necessity of earning a living in no way demands it, the work should nonetheless be done for the sole purging of the heart, the steadying of thought, perseverance in the cell, and the conquest and final overthrow of accidie itself. (Cassian, *Collations*)

13. The Cenobites

Antony is the archetype of the hermit monk, the Christian who has withdrawn from the world to pursue perfection in solitude. But as was apparent in his own life, the charismatic power of holy men was such that they were only rarely unaccompanied by others who pursued them even into the "inner deserts" in order to sit at their feet and imitate their ascetical style of life. It was, then, a natural development that individuals who shared this common goal should begin to live not in the scattered cells already described but in genuine communities, koinobia. *In 420 C.E. the monk Palladius wrote his* Paradise of the Holy Fathers, *which includes this version of the beginning of the cenobitic movement among Christian ascetics.*

In the country of (Egyptian) Thebes, and in the district there called Tabenna, there was a certain blessed man whose name was Pachomius [ca. 292–346 C.E.], and this man led a beautiful life of ascetic excellence, and he was crowned with the love of God and of man. Now as this man was sitting in his cell, an angel appeared to him who said: "Since you have completed your apprenticeship it is unnecessary for you to dwell here; go and gather together to you all those who are wandering and make your dwelling with them, and lay down for them such laws as I shall tell you." And the angel gave him a book wherein was written the following.

So came into existence the Rule of Pachomius, the first collection of ordinances regulating the common life of Christian monks and the forerunner of the better-known rules of Basil in the Eastern and Benedict in the Western Church. The rules are not complex, but they are unmistakably regulatory; and they instituted practices that were to last from that day to this. The monks, for example, were instructed to take their meals in common.

And he [that is, the angel] commanded that "a monk who was a stranger and had a different garb from theirs should not enter in with them to the table; the man who sought to be accepted as a monk in that monastery was obliged to labor there for three years, after which he should receive the tonsure [that is, a ritual cutting of the hair]. When the monks were eating together they were to cover up their faces with their cowls so that they might not see each other eating and not hold converse together over the table, and not gaze about from one side to the other." And he further commanded that during the course of each day they should repeat twelve sections of the Book of Psalms, and during each evening twelve additional sections of the Book of Psalms, and that when they came to eat they should repeat the Great Psalm.

And the blessed Pachomius said to the angel: "The sections of the Book of Psalms which you have appointed for us for repetition are far too few." And the angel said to him, "The sections of the Book of Psalms which I have appointed are indeed few, so that even the monks who are weak may be able to fulfill the rules, and may not be distressed thereby. For there is no law laid down for the perfect, because their mind is at all seasons occupied with God, but this law which I have laid down is for those who have not a perfect mind, so that, though they fulfill only such things as are prescribed by the rules, they can thereby acquire openness of face." . . .

And there were living in that mountain [that is, at Tabennesi] about 7,000 brethren, and in the monastery in which the blessed Pachomius himself lived, there were living 1,300 brethren; and besides these there were also other monasteries, each containing about 300 or 200 or 100 monks, who lived in common; and they all worked with their hands and lived by that toil; and their superfluities they gave to the nunneries there. Each day those monks whose week of service it was rose up and attended to their work; others attended to the cooking, and others set out the tables and laid upon them bread and cheese, and vessels of vinegar and water. And there were some monks who went in to partake of food at the third hour of the day, and others at the sixth, and others at the ninth hour, and others in the evening, and others who ate once a day only; and there were some who ate only once a week. . . . Some worked in the orchard, some in the garden, some in the blacksmith's shop, some in the baker's shop, the carpenter's shop or the laundry; some wove baskets and mats of palm leaves, and one was a maker of nets, and one was a maker of sandals, and one was a scribe. Now all these men as they were performing their work were repeating the Psalms and the Scriptures in order.

And there were large numbers of women who were nuns, and who closely followed this same rule of life, and they came from the other side of the river [that is, the Nile] and beyond it, and there were also married women who came from the other side of the river close by. And whenever any one of them died, the other women would bring her and lay her down on the bank of the river and go away. Then certain of the brethren would cross over in a boat and bring her over with the singing of psalms and with lighted candles, and with great ceremony and honor. And when they had brought her over they would bury her in their cemetery. Without priest or deacon no man would go to that nunnery, however, and then only on Sundays. (Palladius, *Paradise of the Holy Fathers*)

14. Basil on the Superiority of Community Life

The standards of Eastern monasticism were set by Basil of Caesarea in Cappadocia (330–379 C.E.). His Rule *discusses, among other topics, whether the ascetic life of the solitary or the cenobite is preferable. For Basil, the second is the better, and he starts with the most pragmatic of all reasons.*

I think that the life of several persons in the same place is preferable (to that of the solitary). First, because for bodily wants no one is sufficient for himself, but we need each other in providing what is necessary. But just as the foot has one ability, but is wanting another, and without the help of the other members it would find its own power neither strong nor sufficient of itself to continue, nor any supply for what it lacks, so too in the solitary life: what is of use to us and what is wanting we cannot provide for ourselves, for God who created the world has so ordered all things that we are dependent upon each other, as it is written that we may join ourselves to one another (Wisdom 13:20).

But in addition to this, reverence for the love of Christ does not permit each one to have regard only for his own affairs, for love, he says, seeks not her own (1 Cor. 13:5). The solitary has only one goal, the service of his own interests. That clearly is opposed to the law of love, which the Apostle (Paul) fulfilled when he did not in his own eyes seek his own advantage but the advantage of many, that they might be saved (1 Cor. 10:33).

Further, no one in solitude recognizes his own defects, since he has no one to correct him and in gentleness and mercy direct him on his way. For even if correction is from an enemy, it may often, in the case of those who are well disposed, rouse the desire for healing. . . . Also the commandments may be better fulfilled by a larger community and not by one alone. For while this thing is being done, another is neglected; for example, by attendance upon the sick the reception of strangers is neglected; and in the bestowal and distribution of the necessities of life, especially when they are time-consuming, the care of the work is neglected. . . .

There are dangers that we say accompany the solitary life, but the first and foremost is that of self-satisfaction. For he who has no one to test his work easily believes that he has completely fulfilled the commandments. . . . For how shall he manifest his humility, when he has no one to whom he can show himself the inferior. (Basil, *Shorter Rule*, ques. 7)

15. The Monks and the Great Church

So long as the monks remained in remote wildernesses it was their reputation rather than their actual presence that impressed itself on Christian consciences. But the monastic life, if inimical to the pagan cities of the third and fourth centuries, found the climate of the fifth-century Christian city and its environs somewhat more agreeable. It was also in the fifth century that the monks, rural or urban, began to intervene more directly in Church affairs. A single charismatic wonder-worker like Simeon Stylites, the famous pillar-saint of northern Syria, or that other Syrian monk Barsauma, the destroyer of synagogues, might influence members of the imperial house; more troublesome in both principle and practice were the hordes of monks who descended, like a fourth estate, upon the deliberations of synods and councils to demonstrate in the council chambers and on the streets outside. The Council of Chalcedon in 451 C.E. addressed this new problem and attempted to bring the monks under the control of the Church by placing them and their monasteries directly under the jurisdiction of the local bishops.

They who lead a true and worthy monastic life shall enjoy the honor that belongs to them. But since there are some who assume the monastic condition only as a pretense, and will upset the ecclesiastical regulations and affairs, and run about without distinction [or identification] in the cities and want to found monasteries for themselves, the synod therefore has decreed that no one shall build a monastery or a house of prayer or erect anything without the consent of the bishop of the city; and further, that also the monks of every district and city shall be subject to the bishop, that they shall love peace and quiet and observe the fasts and prayers in the places where they are assigned continually; that they shall not encumber themselves with ecclesiastical and secular business and shall not take part in such; that they shall not leave their monasteries except when, in cases of necessity, they may be commissioned by the bishop of the city with such; that no slave shall be admitted into the cloister in order to become a monk without the permission of his master. Whoever violates this our order shall be excommunicated, that the name of God be not blasphemed. The bishop of the city must keep a careful oversight of the monasteries. (Acts of the Council of Chalcedon, Canon 4)

16. Monasticism Comes to the West

The Church in the West was kept well informed about the development of Christian asceticism in the Near East through frequent visits of Westerners to Egypt and Palestine and the presence in Rome of the Alexandrian bishop Athanasius, the author of the Life of the Blessed Antony, *as well as by the rapid translation of the classics of the desert into Latin by Jerome and Rufinus among others. Jerome, in particular, was strenuous in encouraging on his Italian correspondents the ascetic life style, the "way of perfection" that he himself had embraced in Palestine. It is not necessary, in fact, to go to the desert; the ascetic's virtues of self-denial, of voluntary celibacy and poverty, are equally at home in the city, even, as he counsels the celibate maiden Eustochium (Letter 27), in one's mother's house: "you avoid wine as you would poison. . . . An empty stomach and fevered lungs are indispensable for the preservation of chastity. . . . Let your companions be women pale and thin from fasting; rarely go out of the house. . . . Give away your property; it is now no longer yours."*

The formal life style of the monk was introduced into the West, where Augustine, not yet a Christian but interested in the new faith, encountered it in Milan, as he describes in a famous and critical passage in his Confessions. *In August 386 C.E. he had a visitor, a certain Ponticianus, an imperial agent and himself a converted Christian, who discovered Augustine reading Paul and was both surprised and delighted. Augustine continues.*

When, then, I told him that I bestowed much pains upon these writings, a conversation ensued on his speaking of Antony, the Egyptian monk, whose name was in high repute among God's servants, though up to that time unfamiliar to us. When he came to know this he lingered on the topic, imparting to us who were ignorant a knowledge of this so eminent man and marveling at our ignorance. But we were amazed, hearing God's wonderful works most fully manifested in such recent times, indeed almost in our own day [Antony had died only about thirty years earlier], wrought in the true faith and the Catholic Church. We all wondered—we that they were so great, and Ponticianus that we had never heard of them.

From this his conversation turned to the companies in the monasteries, and their way of life so fragrant to God, and of the fruitful deserts of the wilderness, of which we knew nothing. And there was a monastery at Milan full of good brethren, outside the walls of the city, under the care of Ambrose [bishop of Milan, 373–397 C.E.], and we were ignorant of it.

Augustine relates a story told by Ponticianus, how one day at the imperial court at Trier, when a number of officials went out for a walk, two of his companions strolled off by themselves.

In their ramblings they came upon a certain cottage where lived some of God's servants [that is, Christians], "poor in spirit" to whom "belongs the Kingdom of Heaven," and they found there a book in which was written the life of Antony. This one of them began to read, then marvel at, and be inflamed by it; and in reading to think about embracing such a life, and giving up his worldly employments to serve God. . . . Then Ponticianus and the other who was walking with him through other parts of the garden, came searching for the two in the same place, and when they found them, they advised them to return as the sun was setting. . . . But the other two, with their thoughts on heavenly things, remained in the cottage. And both of them were affianced to brides who also, when they heard of this, dedicated their virginity to God. (Augustine, *Confessions* 8.6)

17. Benedict on the Monastic Life

The position held by Basil in the annals of Eastern monasticism was occupied in the Latin Church by Benedict of Nursia (ca. 480–544 C.E.), whose Rule became the model for most of the others that followed down to the Counter-Reformation. Benedict's work opens with a review of the various forms of Christian monasticism.

It is manifest that there are four kinds of monks. The first is that of the cenobites, that is the monastic, serving under a rule and an abbot. The second kind is that of the anchorites, that is the hermits, those who have learned to fight against the devil not by the new fervor of a conversion but by a long probation in a monastery, having been taught already by association with many; and having been well prepared in the army of the brethren for the solitary fight of the hermit, and secure now without the encouragement of another, they are able, God helping them, to fight with their own hand or arm against the vices of the flesh or their own thoughts. But a third and very bad kind of monk is that of the sarabites, not tried as gold in a furnace by a rule, experience being their teacher, but softened after the manner of lead; keeping faith with the world by their works, they are known by their tonsure to lie to God. Being shut up by twos and threes alone and without a shepherd, in their own and not in the Lord's sheepfold, they have their own desires for a law. For whatever they think good and choose, that they deem holy; and what they do not wish, that they consider unlawful. But the fourth kind of monk is the kind called the "wanderers around" (*gyrovagi*), who during their whole life are guests for three or four days at a time in the cells of various monasteries throughout the various provinces; they are always wandering and never stationary, serving their own pleasures and the allurements of the palate, and in every way worse than the sarabites. (Benedict, *Rule*, Chapter 1)

According to Benedict, then, the two besetting vices of the ascetical way of life are self-indulgence and that tendency to roam already noted with disapproval in the

Sayings of the Fathers. *The cure for self-indulgence was, as already discussed by Basil, the life in a community under both a rule and a monastic superior. In Benedict the matter is set out with great clarity: the superior, or abbot, is Christ's representative, and the primary monastic virtue is obedience to the rule and to the abbot who is its embodiment.*

The first degree of humility is prompt obedience. This is required of all who, whether by reason of the holy servitude to which they are pledged, or through fear of hell, or to attain to the glory of eternal life, hold nothing more dear than Christ. Such disciples delay not in doing what is ordered by their superior, just as if the command had come from God. Of such our Lord says, "At the hearing of the ear he has obeyed Me" (Ps. 17:45). And to the teachers he likewise says, "He that hears you, hears me" (Luke 10:16).

For this reason such disciples, surrendering forthwith all they possess, and giving up their own will, leave unfinished what they were working at, and with the ready foot of obedience in their acts follow the word of command. Thus, as it were, at the same moment comes the order of the master and the finished work of the disciple: with the speed of the fear of God both go jointly forward and are quickly effected by such as ardently desire to walk in the way of eternal life. These take the narrow way, of which the Lord says, "Narrow is the way which leads to life" (Matt. 7:14). That is, they live not as they themselves will, neither do they obey their own desires and pleasures, but following the command and direction of another, and abiding in their monasteries, their desire is to be ruled by an abbot. (Benedict, *Rule*, Chapter 5)

18. The Ladder of Perfection

The ladder of perfection was the favorite image of Christian writers on progress in the spiritual life. And if John Climacus did not invent the image, as he surely did not, it was widely popularized by his Ladder of Divine Ascent, *a book read aloud and often in Eastern and Western monasteries for the instruction of the brethren.*

I have put together a ladder of ascent, though my meager knowledge makes me something of a second-rate architect. Still, let each one take note of the step on which he is standing. (John Climacus, *The Ladder of Divine Ascent*, Step 27) [JOHN CLIMACUS 1982: 265]

There are perhaps as many ladders as there are writers on the spiritual life, and with almost as many steps. Benedict's rule for his monks arranges the steps in terms of ascending grades of humility.

Brothers, if we would scale the summit of humility and swiftly gain the heavenly height which is reached by our lowliness in this present life, we must set up a ladder of climbing deeds like that which Jacob saw in his dream, whereon angels were descending and ascending. Without doubt that descending and ascending is to be understood by us as signifying that we descend by exalting ourselves and ascend by humbling ourselves. But the ladder itself thus set up is our life in this world, which by humility of heart is lifted by our Lord to heaven. Our body and soul we may indeed call the sides of the ladder in which our divine vocation has set up the divers steps of humility and discipline we have to ascend.

The first step of humility, then, is reached when a man, with the fear of God always before his eyes, does not allow himself to forget but is ever mindful of all of God's commandments. He remembers, moreover, that such as contemn God fall into hell for their sins, and that life eternal awaits such as fear Him. And warding off at each moment all sin and defect in thought and word, of eye, hand and foot, of self-will, let such a one bestir himself to prune away the lusts of the flesh.

If this is the degree of perfection incumbent upon all Christians, the ladder quickly mounts to higher and more difficult levels of self-control.

The second step of humility is reached when any one not loving self-will takes no heed to satisfy his own desires but copies in his life what our Lord said, "I came not to do my own will, but the will of Him who sent me" (John 6:3–8). Scripture likewise proclaims that self-will engenders punishment and necessity purchases a crown.

The third step of humility is reached when a man, for the love of God, submits himself with all obedience to a superior, imitating our Lord, of whom the Apostle (Paul) says, "He was made obedient, even to death" (Phil. 2:8).

The fourth step in humility is reached when any one in the exercise of his obedience patiently and with a quiet mind bears all that is inflicted on him, things contrary to nature, and even at times unjust, and in suffering all these he neither wearies nor gives up the work. . . .

The fifth stage of humility is reached when a monk manifests to his abbot, by humble confession, all the evil thoughts of his heart and his secret faults. . . .

The sixth step of humility is reached when a monk is content with all that is mean and vile, and with regard to everything enjoined him accounts himself a poor and worthless workman. . . .

The seventh step is reached when a man not only confesses with his tongue that he is most lowly and inferior, but in his innermost heart believes so. . . .

The eighth step of humility is reached when a monk does nothing but what is the common rule of the monastery, or what the example of his seniors enforces.

The ninth step in humility is reached when a monk restrains his tongue from talking, and practicing silence, speaks not until a question is asked of him. . . .

The tenth step of humility is attained when one is not easily and quickly moved to laughter. . . .

The eleventh step of humility is reached when a monk, in speaking, does so quietly and without laughter, humbly, gravely, and in a few words and not with a loud voice. . . .

The twelfth step of humility is reached when a monk not only has humility in his heart, but even shows it on his exterior to all who behold him. Thus, whether he be in the oratory at the "Work of God" in the monastery, or in the garden, on a journey, or in the fields, or wheresoever he is, sitting, standing or walking, always let him, with head bent and eyes fixed upon the ground, bethink himself of his sins and imagine that he is arraigned before the dread judgment of God. . . .

When all these steps have been mounted the monk will presently attain to that love of God which is perfect and casts out fear. By means of this love everything which he had observed before not without fear, he shall now begin to do by habit, without any trouble and, as it were, naturally. He acts now not through fear of hell, but for the love of Christ, out of a good habit and a delight in virtue. All this our Lord will vouchsafe to work by the Holy Spirit in his servant, now cleansed from vice and sin. (Benedict, *Rule*, Chapter 7)

19. Monks at Prayer

The prayer life for those Christians who chose to live in monastic communities was different in length and complexity from that of the ordinary Christian. Monks assembled at fixed hours of the day and night to join in reciting and chanting in unison what came to be called the "Divine Office" (what Benedict just referred to as the "Work of God"). Thus life in the Benedictine monastery chiefly comprised manual labor and the monastic liturgy par excellence, the recitation in common of Sacred Scripture, principally the Psalms, in sessions distributed across the day and night hours, so that in the course of a week the entire body of 150 psalms might be completed.

The Prophet says, "Seven times have I sung Your praises" (Ps. 118: 164). This sacred number of seven will be kept by us if we perform the duties of our service in the Hours of Matins [or daybreak], Prime [or full light], Terce [about 9 A.M.], Sext [about noon], None [about 3 P.M.], Vespers or Evensong and Compline. It was of these daytime Hours that the Prophet said, "Seven times a day I have sung Your praises," and of the nighttime vigils [begun about 2 A.M.] the same Prophet says, "At midnight I arose to confess to You" (Ps. 118:62). (Benedict, *Rule*, Chapter 16)

The Divine Office was celebrated in Western and Eastern monasteries with equal fervor. Here Symeon (949–1022 C.E.), surnamed "the New Theologian," a monastic reformer and mystic of the Eastern Church, describes the attitudes toward the Office appropriate to the monk.

Let it be noted that he who has already outwardly laid aside the earthly man with his attitude of mind, and by assuming the monastic habit has clothed himself with the heavenly man (1 Cor. 15:47–49), must rise at midnight before the Night Office and recite the prescribed (individual) prayer. After doing so he must rise with all to go to the service of praise, and with attention and vigilance go through the whole service. He must pay particular attention to the beginning of the hymnody, that is, the six psalms [Psalms 3, 38, and 63, then 88, 103, and 143], the psalm verses (usually chanted at this service) and the lections [that is, readings from the lives of the saints or the writings of the Fathers], with great concentration, without relaxation of body or putting one foot in front of another or leaning on walls or pillars, but holding the hands securely together, the feet equally on the ground, and the head immobile without nodding here and there. The mind must not wander nor the thoughts be occupied with curiosity or interest in the more careless brethren as they talk or whisper to each other. On the contrary the eye and the soul must be kept free from distraction and pay attention to nothing else but to the psalmody and the reading, and, as far as possible, to the meaning of the words of the Divine Scripture that are being sung or read. . . .

Once the morning Office of praise is finished do not, as soon as you have left the (monastery) church, start talking to one man or the other and so be distracted in idle talk. Rather pray in the solitude of your cell, and when you have recited the appointed prayers with tears and great recollection, take on some physical labor and at once go off to perform it. If it is some appointed task, go off to that task; if it is manual labor, go off to it; if it is study, go off to study. Refuse altogether to sit in your cell without some occupation, lest idleness teach you every kind of evil of which one may not even speak. Do not go about the monastery to inspect those who work or perform services, but observe that silence and detachment from all things in which true solitude consists. Take heed of yourself alone and of your manual work, whatever it is. (Symeon, *Discourses* 26: 2–3) [SYMEON NEOTHEOLOGUS 1980: 274–276]

Bonaventure (1221–1271 C.E.), a Franciscan monk, cardinal in the Roman Church and, like Symeon, a considerable mystical theologian, explores in the didactic fashion of the West the motives behind the monastic Divine Office.

The Holy Spirit has commanded the recitation of the Divine Office in the Church for five reasons. The first is to imitate the heavenly choirs. The saints and angels are ceaselessly engaged in singing His praises in the presence of God. "Blessed are they," says the Psalmist, "that dwell in Your house, O Lord; they shall praise You for ever and ever." Christ, according to His promise, "Behold, I am with you all days even to the consummation of the world," deigns to be truly with us here sacramentally as well as spiritually, and so it behooves us to the best of our ability to render Him honor and praise according to the example of the celestial spirits, so that even though we do not praise Him continuously, as those heavenly chanters do, we sing His praises at least from time to time despite our frailty.

The Divine Office has been established in the second place that we might render thanks to God at certain hours, mindful of His blessings and, praying for His grace, from time to time turn to Him, who was born of the Virgin Mary at night, dragged before the Sanhedrin at early morn, arose at daylight, was scourged at the third hour and a little latter (after the third hour) sent the Holy Spirit upon the Apostles, was crucified at the sixth hour, died upon the cross at the ninth, and being at supper in the afternoon gave us the Sacraments and was buried at Compline [that is, in the evening]. . . .

In the third place the Divine Office was established in order that through it we may be continuously incited to devotion and kindled with the love of God, to prevent our indolence and the great number of our occupations make our love grow lukewarm. In the Book of Leviticus the Lord says: "This is the perpetual fire which shall never go out on the altar . . . the priest shall feed it, putting wood on it every day in the morning." This fire is the fervor of devotion, which ought always to burn on the altar of our heart, which the devout priest ought to nourish con-

953

stantly by putting on it the fuel of divine praises, that it may never be extinguished.

The fourth reason for which the Divine Office was instituted is that through it we may draw the faithful, who might thereby know how to set aside certain hours for prayer, to the practice of devotion, so that they may assemble in church at least when the offices of divine praise are being performed inside, and be less easily distracted when they see the clerics celebrating the Divine Office. . . . Most people would scarcely ever devote themselves to prayer if they were not called to church from worldly occupations at stated times to engage in divine service and listen to the word of God.

The fifth purpose of the Divine Office is to exhibit the beauty of the Christian religion. Jews, Gentiles and heretics from time to time assemble in their churches to celebrate their false rites. It is obviously far more proper and fitting for those who have the true and holy mysteries of the Sacraments to assemble often for the purpose of celebrating and venerating them and performing the solemn service of praise due to the Creator. (Bonaventure, *The Virtues of a Religious Superior* 6:5–9)

20. The Franciscan Spirit

In addition to celibacy and obedience, the other great wellspring of Christian ascet-icism flowing forth from the Egyptian deserts was that of poverty. It had its Gospel proof-texts, to be sure, and the Desert Fathers fervently cultivated the casting off of possessions. But theirs was an essentially private world of seclusion. Where the ideal of poverty was broadcast to society as a whole was in the life and work of Francis of Assisi (d. 1226 C.E.). He attempted, as many holy men before and after him, to convert that vision of spiritual perfection into a formal way of life, which in the Christian tradition meant the creation of a monastic order. This is how it was expressed in the version of the Franciscan Rule of the "Minor Brothers" submitted to and approved by Pope Honorius III in 1223 C.E.

In the name of the Lord thus begins the life of the Minor Brothers [or Friars Minor].

The Rule and Life of the Minor Brothers is this, namely to observe the Gospel of our Lord Jesus Christ, by living in obedience, without property and in chastity. Brother Francis promised obedience and reverence to the Lord Pope Honorius and to his canonically elected successors and to the Roman Church. And let the other brothers be bound to obey Brother Francis and his successors.

If any wish to embrace this life and come to our brothers, let them send them to their provincial ministers, to whom alone and not to others is accorded the power of receiving brothers. But let the ministers diligently examine them regarding the Catholic faith and the Sacraments of the Church. And if they believe all these things, and if they will confess them faithfully, and observe them firmly to the end, and if they have no wives, or, if they have and their wives have already entered a monastery, or have, with the authority of the diocesan bishop, given them permission to do so after having made a vow of continence, and if their wives be of a certain age that no suspicion may arise concerning them, let the ministers say to them the words of the Holy Spirit, that they should go and sell all their goods and strive to distribute them to the poor. If they should not be able to do this, their goodwill suffices. . . .

Afterwards let them give them clothes of probation, to wit, two tunics without a hood and a cord and breeches and a chaperon reaching to the cord. . . . The year of probation being finished, they shall be received to obedience, promising always to observe this life and this rule. . . . And let all the brothers be clothed in poor garments and they may patch them with pieces of sackcloth and other things, with the blessing of God. I exhort and admonish them not to despise and judge men whom they see clothed in fine and showy garments, using dainty meats and drink, but rather let each one judge and despise himself. . . .

I strictly enjoin on all the brothers that in no wise they receive coins or money, either themselves or through a third party. Nevertheless, for the necessities of the sick and for clothing the other brothers, let the ministers and guardians alone take watchful care through spiritual friends, according to places and times and cold climates, as they shall see expedient in the necessity, saving that, as I have said, they receive no coins or money. . . .

The brothers shall appropriate nothing to themselves, neither a house nor a place nor anything. And as pilgrims and strangers in this world, serving the Lord in poverty and humility, let them go confidently in quest of alms, nor ought they be ashamed, because the Lord made himself poor for us in this world. This, my dearest brothers, is the height of the most sublime poverty which has made you heirs and kings of the kingdom of heaven; poor in goods but exalted in virtue. Let that be your portion, for it leads to the land of the living; adhere to it without reservation, my best beloved brothers, for in the name of our Lord Jesus Christ, it never desires to possess anything under heaven. (*Franciscan Rule*)

21. This World and the Next: The Islamic Preaching

Much in the manner of developed Christianity, the preaching of Islam drew a sharp distinction between this world and its values and that other world that is both the Hereafter and the abode of God.

Know that the life of this world is only a frolic and a mummery, an ornamentation, boasting and bragging among yourselves, and lust for multiplying wealth and children. It is like rain so pleasing to the cultivator for his vegetation which sprouts and swells, and then begins to wither, and you see it turn to yellow and reduced to chaff. There is severe punishment in the Hereafter, but also forgiveness from God and acceptance. As for the life of this world, it is no more than the merchandise of vanity. (Quran 57:20)

Al-Mustawrid ibn Shaddad told that he heard God's Messenger say, "I swear by God that this world in comparison to the world to come is just like one of you putting your finger in the sea. Let him consider what he brings out on it." (Baghawi, *Mishkat al-Masabih* 25.1.1)

Abu Hurayra reported God's Messenger as saying, "The world is the believer's prison and the infidel's Paradise." (Ibid.)

Abu Hurayra reported God's Messenger as saying, "The world is accursed and what it contains is accursed, except remembrance of God and what He likes, a learned man or a learner." (Ibid.)

Ibn Mas'ud told that God's Messenger slept on a reed mat and got up with the marks of it on his body, so Ibn Mas'ud said, "Messenger of God, I wish you would order us to spread something out for you and make something (on which you might rest)." He replied, "What do I have to do with the world? In relation to the world I am just like a rider who shades himself under a tree, and then goes off and leaves it." (Ibid. 25.1.2)

Ibn Umar told that God's Messenger caught hold of him and said, "Be in the world as though you were a stranger and a wayfarer, and reckon yourself to be among the inhabitants of the grave." (Ibid. 25.2.1)

There are echoes too of "Blessed are the poor . . . "

Usama ibn Zayd reported God's Messenger as saying, "I stood at the gate of Paradise, and the majority of those who entered it were poor, the rich being held back, except that those who were to go to Hell were ordered to be sent there. I stood at the gate of Hell, and the majority of those who entered it were women." This tradition is reported by Bukhari and Muslim. (Baghawi, *Mishkat al-Masabih* 25.2.1)

Anas told that the Prophet said: "O God, grant me life as a poor man, cause me to die as a poor man and resurrect me in the company of the poor." Aisha asked him why he said this, and he replied, "Because they will enter Paradise forty years before the rich. Do not turn away a poor man, Aisha, even if all you can give him is half a date. If you love the poor and bring them near you, Aisha, God will bring you near Him on the day of resurrection." (Ibid. 25.2.2)

Amr ibn al-Awf reported God's Messenger as saying, "I swear by God that it is not poverty I fear for you, but I fear that worldly goods may be given to you as lavishly as they were to your (pagan) ancestors, that you may vie with with one another in desiring them as they did, and that they may destroy you as they destroyed them." (Ibid. 25.1.1)

A belief in this Other World of God meant of course embracing its values. The classical collections of Prophetic traditions are filled with reported sayings of the Prophet on the virtues of prayer and fasting, not merely the canonically prescribed prayers and the equally obligatory fast of Ramadan, but the supererogatory performance of these spiritual exercises, though with cautious awareness that any practice attributed to the Prophet might be construed as a precedent for an additional obligation upon all Muslims.

Abu Hurayra and Abu Sa'id reported God's Messenger as saying, "People will not sit remembering God without angels surrounding them, mercy covering them, peace descending upon them, and God mentioning them among those who are with Him." (Baghawi, *Mishkat al-Masibih* 9.2.1)

Abu al-Darda reported God's Messenger as saying, "Would you like me to tell you the best and purest of your deeds in the estimation of your King, those which raise your degrees highest, those which are better for you than spending gold and silver, and better for you than that you should meet your enemy and cut off one another's head?" On receiving a reply in the affirmative, he said, "It is remembering God." (Ibid. 9.2.2)

Abdullah ibn Busr told of a desert Arab coming to the Prophet and asking who was the best among men, to which he replied, "Happy is he whose life is long and whose deeds are good." He asked God's Messenger what deed was most excellent, and he replied, "That you should leave the world with the mention of God fresh on your tongue." (Ibid.)

Abu Sa'id said God's Messenger was asked who would be the most excellent and most exalted in degree in God's estimation on the day of resurrection, and he replied, "The men and women who make frequent mention of God." He was asked if they would be superior even to the man who had fought in the path of God, and he replied, "Even though he plied his sword among infidels and polytheists till it was broken and smeared with blood, the one who made mention of God would have a more excellent degree than he." (Ibid. 9.2.3)

Abdullah ibn Shaqiq said than when he asked Aisha whether the Prophet used to fast the whole month of Ramadan, she replied, "I never knew him to fast a whole month except Ramadan, or to refrain from fasting some part of every month until he died." (Ibid. 7.7.1)

Aisha said that God's Messenger used to fast on Mondays and Thursdays. Abu Hurayra reported God's Messenger as saying, "Men's deeds are presented to God on Mondays and Thursdays, and I like mine to be presented when I am fasting." (Ibid. 7.7.2)

Abu Hurayra reported God's Messenger as saying, "There is an almsgiving that is applicable to everything, and the almsgiving of the body is fasting." (Ibid. 7.7.3)

22. The Catholic Tradition in Asceticism

True to its heritage as a "successor" religion to Judaism and Christianity, Islam entered early and easily into the "catholic" tradition of asceticism, as that was understood in the eighth century C.E. The authority cited here is Hasan al-Basri (d. 728), of the generation immediately following the Prophet and one of the founding fathers of the movement that was already being called "Sufism" in his day.

This world has neither worth nor weight with God; so slight is it, it weighs not with God so much as a pebble or a clod of earth. As I am told, God has created nothing more hateful to him than this world, and from the day He created it He has not looked upon it, so much He hates it. It was offered to our Prophet with all its keys and treasures . . . but he refused to accept it; and nothing prevented him from accepting it—for there is naught that can lessen him in God's sight—but that he knew God hated a thing and therefore he hated it. . . .

. . . As for Muhammad, he bound a stone upon his belly when he was hungry; and as for Moses, the skin of his belly showed as green as grass because of it all: he asked naught of God, the day he took refuge in the shade, save food to eat when he was hungry, and it is said of him in the stories that God revealed to him, "Moses, when you see poverty approaching you, say, Welcome to the badge of the righteous! And when you see wealth approaching, say, Behold! A sin whose punishment has been put on aforetime."

The next ascetic exemplar adduced by Hasan is Jesus, though there is no other record of the saying attributed to him here.

If you should so wish, you might name as a third the Lord of the Word and the Spirit [that is, Jesus], for in his case there is a marvel. He used to say, "My daily bread is hunger, my badge is fear, my raiment is wool, my mount is my foot, my lantern at night is the moon, my fire by day is the sun, and my fruit and fragrant herbs are such things as the earth brings forth for the wild beast and cattle. All the night I have nothing and yet there is none richer than I!"

And if you should so wish, you might name as a fourth instance David, who was no less wonderful than these others: he ate barley bread in his chamber and fed his family upon bran meal, but his people on fine grain. And when it was night, he clad himself in sackcloth, and chained his hand to his neck, and wept until dawn; eating coarse food and wearing robes of hair.

All these men hated what God hates, and despised what God despises; then the righteous thereafter followed in their path and kept close to their tracks. (Abu Nuʿaym, *The Ornaments of the Saints* 2:134–140)
[Cited by ARBERRY 1950: 34–35]

The same broad Judeo-Christian horizons are apparent in the formation of the Baghdad master Junayd (d. 910 C.E.) when he attempts to explain what Sufism is.

Sufism is founded on eight qualities exemplified in eight apostles: the generosity of Abraham, who sacrificed his son; Ishmael, who submitted to the command of God and gave up his dear life; the patience of Job, who patiently endured the affliction of worms and the jealousy of the Merciful; the symbolism of Zachariah [that is, the father of John the Baptist], to whom God said: "Thou shall not speak to men for three days save by signs" (Quran 3:36); and again to the same effect: "When he called upon his Lord with a secret invocation" (Quran 19:2); the strangerhood of John (the Baptist), who was a stranger in his own country and an alien to his own kind among whom he lived; the pilgrimhood of Jesus, who was so detached from worldly things that he kept only a cup and a comb—the cup he threw away when he saw a man drinking in the palms of his hand, and the comb likewise when he saw another man using his fingers instead of a comb; the wearing of wool by Moses, whose garment was woolen; and the poverty of Muhammad, to whom God Almighty sent the key of all treasures that are upon the face of the earth, saying, "Lay no trouble on yourself, but procure every luxury by means of these treasures," and he answered, "O Lord, I desire them not; keep me one day full fed and one day hungry." (Junayd, *Treatise*)

[Cited in HUJWIRI 1911: 39–40]

23. The Historical Origins of Sufism

Many of the early names to which the title of "Sufi" is attached in Muslim hagiography are little more than that, names alone. Hasan al-Basri is a firmly historical witness, however, and he stands close to the top of the page in every attempt, medieval and modern, to get back to the beginnings of the spiritual discipline that the Muslims call Sufism. And so he appears in the work of the Spanish philosopher-historian Ibn Khaldun (d. 1406 C.E.), who provides in his Prolegomenon to History *a schematic view of the origins of Sufism.*

The Science of Sufism. This science belongs to the sciences of religious law that originated in Islam. Sufism is based on the assumption that the method of those people (who later came to be called Sufis) had always been considered by the important early Muslims, the men around Muhammad and the men of the second generation, as well as those who came after them, as the path of true and right guidance. Their approach is based upon constant application to divine worship, complete devotion to God, aversion to the false splendor of the world, abstinence from pleasure, property and position to which the great mass aspires, and retirement from the world into solitude for divine worship. These things were general among the men around Muhammad and the early Muslims. (Ibn Khaldun, *Muqaddima* 6.10) [IBN KHALDUN 1967: 3:76]

The habit of a simple and unworldly life, if not actually the practice of what a later generation understood as asceticism, was traced back, then, to the earliest generation of Muslims, and even to the most eminent and powerful of them, as this account by the early Sufi author al-Kharraz (d. 890 C.E.) illustrates.

When Abu Bakr [Caliph, 632–634 C.E.] succeeded to the leadership, and the world in its entirety came to him in abasement, he did not lift up his head on that account, or make any pretensions; he wore a single garment, which he used to pin together, so that he was known as "the man of the two pins." Umar ibn al-Khattab [Caliph, 634–644 C.E.], who also ruled the world in its entirety, lived on bread and olive oil; his clothes were patched in a dozen places, some of the patches being of leather; yet there were opened to him the treasures of Khusraw and Caesar. As for Uthman [Caliph, 644–656 C.E.], he was like one of his slaves in appearance; of him it is related that he was seen coming out of one of the gardens with a faggot of firewood on his shoulders, and when questioned on the matter, he said, "I wanted to see whether my soul would refuse." Ali [Caliph, 656–661 C.E.] bought a waistband for four dirhams and a shirt for five dirhams; finding the sleeve of his garment too long, he went to a cobbler and taking his knife, he cut off the sleeve level with the tips of his fingers; yet this same man divided the world right and left. (Kharraz, *The Book of Truthfulness*) [Cited by ARBERRY 1950: 32]

It was at that point, at the death of Ali and the accession of the dynasty called the Umayyads, that there occurred a turning in the spiritual direction of Islam, according to what later became a commonly held view of the history of the community. Ibn Khaldun resumes.

Then worldly aspirations increased in the second century [that is, the eighth century C.E.] and after. People now inclined toward worldly affairs. At that time, the special name of "Sufis" was given to those who aspired to divine worship. . . . The most obvious etymology (of the term *Sufi*), if one uses one, is that which connects the word with *al-suf*, because Sufis as a rule were characterized by the fact that they wore woolen garments. They were opposed to people wearing gorgeous garments, and, therefore, they chose to wear wool.

Ibn Khaldun then passes to the transition within the still young Sufi movement from asceticism to mysticism, the latter here characterized by its possession of a "particular kind of perception."

The Sufis came to represent asceticism, retirement from the world and devotion to divine worship. Then, they developed a particular kind of perception which comes about through ecstatic experience. This comes about as follows. Man, as man, is distinguished from all the other animals by his ability to perceive. His perception is of two kinds. He can perceive sciences and matters of knowledge, and these may be certain, hypothetical, doubtful or imaginary. Also, he can perceive "states" persisting in himself, such as joy and grief, anxiety and relaxation, satisfaction, anger, patience, gratefulness and similar things. (Ibn Khaldun, *Muqaddima* 6.16) [IBN KHALDUN 1967: 3:76–78]

These "states" of self-awareness represent stages in the Sufi's training, as we shall see, and lead eventually to the mystical experience. All of this had been worked out in great detail by Ibn Khaldun's day. But the road to that point was a long one;

the Sufi had to make a place for himself in the Islamic experience, a process that was accompanied by opposition, rejection, suffering, and even on occasion death.

24. Conversions and Affirmations

By all accounts the earliest Muslims to bear the name "Sufi" were ascetics: Muslims whose rejection of "this world" bore all the signs of a religious conversion. Such was certainly the case for the early and much celebrated holy man Ibrahim ibn Adham, a prince of Balkh in eastern Iran who died sometime about 777 C.E.

My father was of Balkh, Ibrahim ibn Adham is reported to have said, and he was one of the kings of Khurasan. He was a man of wealth and taught me to love hunting. One day I was out riding with my dog, when a hare or a fox started. I spurred on my horse; then I heard a voice behind me saying, "It was not for this that you were created. It was not this you were charged to do." I stopped and looked right and left, but I saw no one; and I said, "God curse the devil!" Then I spurred on my horse again; and I heard a voice clearer than before, "O Ibrahim! It was not for this that you were created; it was not this you were charged to do." I stopped once more and looked right and left, but still I saw no one. And I re-peated, "God curse the devil!" Then I spurred on my horse once again; and I heard a voice from the bow of my saddle, "O Ibrahim, it was not for this that you were created. It was not this that you were charged to do." I stopped and said, "I have been roused! I have been roused! A warning has come to me from the Lord of the Worlds. Truly, I will not disobey God from this day on, so long as the Lord shall preserve me." Then I returned to my people, and abandoned my horse. I came to one of my father's shepherds, and took his robe and cloak, and put my rai-ment upon him. Then I went toward Iraq, wandering from land to land. (Abu Nuᶜaym, *The Ornaments of the Saints* 7:368) [Cited by ARBERRY 1950: 36]

Or, in the manner of the holy in every religion, the saint is marked as such from birth. The following is told, with an interesting prologue, of Rabiᶜa, a famous holy woman of Basra in Iraq who died in 752 or 801 C.E.

If anyone asks, "Why have you included Rabiᶜa in the rank of men?" my answer is that the Prophet himself said, "God does not regard your outward forms." The root of the matter is not form, but intention, as the Prophet said, "Mankind will be raised up according to their intentions." Moreover, if it is proper to derive two-thirds of our religion from Aisha [referring to the great bulk of Prophetic traditions reported on the au-thority of the Prophet's wife Aisha], surely it is permissible to take religious instruction from a handmaiden of Aisha. When a woman becomes a "man" in the path of God, she is a man and one cannot any more call her a woman.

The night when Rabiʿa came to earth, there was nothing whatsoever in her father's house; for her father lived in very poor circumstances. He did not possess even one drop of oil to anoint her navel; there was no lamp, and not a rag to swaddle her in. He already had three daughters, and Rabiʿa was his fourth, which is why she was called Rabiʿa, "the fourth."

"Go to our neighbor So and So and beg him for a drop of oil so I can light the lamp," his wife said to him. Now the man had entered into a covenant that he would never ask any mortal for anything. . . . The poor woman wept bitterly. In that anxious state the man placed his head on his knees and went to sleep. He dreamed that he saw the Prophet.

"Be not sorrowful," the Prophet bade him. "The girl child who has just come to earth is a queen among women, who shall be the intercessor for seventy thousand of my community." . . .

When Rabiʿa had become a little older, and her mother and father were dead, a famine came upon Basra, and her sisters were scattered. Rabiʿa ventured out and was seen by a wicked man who seized her and sold her for six dirhams. Her purchaser put her to hard labor.

One day as she was passing along the road a stranger approached her. She fled and, as she ran, she fell headlong and her hand was dislocated. "Lord God," she cried, bowing her face to the ground, "I am a stranger, orphaned of mother and father, a helpless prisoner fallen into captivity, my hand broken. Yet for all this I do not grieve; all I need is Your good pleasure, to know whether You are well pleased or not." "Do not grieve," she heard a voice say. "Tomorrow a station will be yours such that the cherubim in heaven will envy you."

So Rabiʿa returned to her master's house. By day she continually fasted and by night she worshiped standing until day.

Her owner one night sees Rabiʿa at her prayers, a lantern suspended without chain above her head, and whose light fills the house. He is moved and chastened and gives her her freedom.

She left the house and went into the desert. From the desert she proceeded to a hermitage where she served God for a while. Then she determined to perform the pilgrimage and set her face toward the desert (road from Basra to Mecca). She bound her bundle of possessions on a donkey. In the middle of the desert her donkey died. . . . "O God," she cried, lifting her head, "do kings so treat the powerless? You have invited

me to Your House, then in the midst of the way, You have suffered my
donkey to die, leaving me alone in the desert."

Hardly had she completed her prayer when her donkey stirred and
rose up. Rabi'a placed her load on its back and continued on her way. . . .
She traveled on through the desert for some days, then she halted. "O
God," she cried, "my heart is weary. Where am I going? I am a lump of
clay and Your house is a stone! I need You here."

God spoke unmediated in her heart. "Rabi'a, you are traveling in
the lifeblood of eighteen thousand worlds. Have you not seen how Moses
prayed for the vision of Me? And I cast a few motes of revelation upon
the mountain, and the mountain shivered into forty pieces. Be content
here in My name!" (Attar, *Recollections of the Saints* 1:73)

[ATTAR 1966: 40–43]

25. Ibn Khaldun Analyzes the Sufi Experience

*The long process of experience and meditation upon that experience that constituted
the beginnings of the Sufi path in Islam is largely concealed from our eyes. But, as
occurred in Christianity, the "path" eventually became a broad and well-posted
highway whose every turning had been charted by those who had gone before. That
much is readily apparent in Ibn Khaldun's systematic and highly rationalized
treatment.*

Knowledge originates from evidence, grief and joy from the perception of what is painful or pleasurable, energy from rest, inertia from being
tired. In the same way, the exertion and worship of the Sufi novice must
lead to a "state" which is the result of his exertion. That "state" may be
a kind of divine worship. Then it will be firmly rooted in the Sufi novice
and become a "station" for him. Or, it may not be divine worship, but
merely an attribute affecting the soul, such as joy or gladness, energy or
inertia, or something else.

The "stations" form an ascending order. The Sufi novice continues
to progress from station to station, until he reaches the (recognition of
the) Oneness of God and the gnosis which is the desired goal of happiness. Muhammad says: "Whoever dies confessing that there is no god but
the God, enters Paradise."

*"Gnosis," a special intuitive understanding that differs radically from ordinary
reflective knowledge, is the heart of the mystic's experience, as we shall observe in
Chapter 4 below. It is the end of the quest. Ibn Khaldun returns to the novice
standing at the very beginning.*

964

Thus the novice must progress by such stages. The basis of them all is obedience and sincerity. Faith precedes and accompanies them all. Their result and fruit are states and attributes. They lead to others, and again to others, up to the station of the (recognition of the) Oneness of God and of gnosis. If the result [that is, the "state"] shows some shortcoming or defect, one can be sure that it came from some shortcoming that existed in the previous stage. The same applies to the ideas of the soul and inspirations of the heart.

The hallmark of Sufism is, according to Ibn Khaldun, the practice of self-scrutiny.

The novice therefore must scrutinize himself in all his actions and study their concealed import, because the results of necessity originate from actions, and shortcomings in the results thus originate from defects in the actions. The Sufi novice finds out about that through his mystical experience, and he scrutinizes himself as to its reasons. Very few people share the self-scrutiny of the Sufis, for negligence in this respect is almost universal. Pious people who do not get that far perform, at best, acts of obedience freed from the juridical study of how to be satisfactory and conforming. The Sufis, however, investigate the results of the acts of obedience with the help of mystical and ecstatic experience in order to learn whether they are free from deficiency or not. Thus it is evident that the Sufis' path in its entirety depends upon self-scrutiny with regard to what they do or do not do, and upon discussion of the various kinds of mystical and ecstatic experience that result from their exertions. This, then, crystallizes for the Sufi novice in a "station." From that station he can proceed to another, higher one. (Ibn Khaldun, *Muqaddima* 6.16)

[IBN KHALDUN 1967: 3:78–79]

26. A Quick Sketch of the Sufi Tradition

None of this analysis is original to Ibn Khaldun. By the time he was writing his Prolegomenon in 1377 there was already an extensive body of Sufi literature, much of it highly theoretical in nature. Indeed, Sufism constituted a well-defined discipline with its own somewhat ambivalent place in the hierarchy of Muslim religious disciplines, as Ibn Khaldun explains.

Thus the Sufis had their special discipline, which is not discussed by other representatives of the religious law. As a consequence, the science of the religious law came to consist of two kinds. One is the special field of jurists and muftis. It is concerned with the general laws governing the acts of divine worship, customary action and mutual dealings. The other is the special field of the "people" [that is, the Sufis]. It is concerned with pious exertion, self-scrutiny with regard to it, discussion of the different kinds of mystical and ecstatic experience occurring in the course of it, the mode of ascent from one mystical experience to another, and the interpretation of the technical terminology of mysticism in use among them.

When the sciences were written down systematically, and when the jurisprudents wrote works on jurisprudence and the principles of jurisprudence, on speculative theology, Quran interpretation and other subjects, the Sufis too wrote on their subject. Some Sufis wrote on the laws governing asceticism and self-scrutiny, how to act and not act in imitation of model (saints). That was done by Muhasibi [ca. 781–825 C.E.] in his *Consideration of the Truths of God*. Other Sufi authors wrote on the behavior of Sufis and their different kinds of mystical and ecstatic experiences in the "states." Al-Qushayri [986–1072 C.E.] in his *Letter* and Suhrawardi [1145–1234 C.E.] in his *Connoisseurs of Wisdom*, as well as others, did this. Al-Ghazali combined the two matters in his book called *The Revivification*. In it he dealt systematically with the laws governing asceticism and the imitation of models. Then he explained the behavior and customs of the Sufis and commented on their technical vocabulary. (Ibn Khaldun, *Muqaddima* 6.16) [IBN KHALDUN 1967: 3:79–80]

27. Two Sufi Autobiographies

All these authors regarded by Ibn Khaldun as critical in the formulation of the canons of Sufism are known to us, and one could easily compose a history of Sufism, particularly of its more moderate type, from their theoretical writings on the subject. Let us turn instead to personal statements by two very different men who experienced the Sufi life and left us their recollections: Abu Sa'id ibn Abi al-Khayr (967–1049 C.E.) and al-Ghazali (d. 1111 C.E.).

Whatever else it might eventually become, Sufism began, and to some extent always remained, an exercise in the same kind of self-restraint and even self-chastisement that was present in the early Christian tradition. The annals of Christianity, particularly as that faith was understood and practiced in Syria, are filled with tales of the most extraordinarily severe asceticism. Although Islamic piety rarely indulged in such extremes of self-abasement, physical and psychological severity were not entirely alien to it, as witnessed by this account of the early days of Abu Sa'id ibn Abi al-Khayr. The narrator at the outset is his father, who was curious about the doings of his son and one night followed him.

My son walked on till he reached the Old Cloister. He entered it and shut the gate behind him, while I went up on the roof. I saw him go into a chapel which was in the convent and close the door. Looking through the chapel window, I waited to see what would happen. There was a stick lying on the floor, and it had a rope fastened to it. He took up the stick and tied the end of the rope to his foot. Then, laying the stick across the top of a pit that was in a corner of the chapel, he slung himself head downwards, and began to recite the Quran. He remained in that posture until daybreak, when, having recited the whole Quran, he raised himself from the pit, replaced the stick where he found it, opened the door, came out from the chapel, and commenced to perform his ablution in the middle of the convent. I descended from the roof, hastened home and slept till he came in. (Abu Sa'id, *The Secrets of Oneness* 32:4)

[Cited by NICHOLSON 1921: 13–14]

Here Abu Sa'id himself explains his manner of life in those earliest days of his career as a Sufi, and incidentally provides an explanation of why he recited the Quran hanging upside down.

When I was a novice, I bound myself to do eighteen things: I fasted continually; I abstained from unlawful food; I practiced recollection of the name of God uninterruptedly; I kept awake at night; I never reclined on the ground; I never slept but in a sitting posture; I always sat facing the Ka'ba; I never leaned against anything; I never looked at a handsome youth or a woman whom it would have been unlawful for me to see unveiled; I did not beg; I was content and resigned to God's will; I always sat in the mosque and did not go into the market because the Prophet said that the market is the filthiest of places and the mosque the cleanest. In all my acts I was a follower of the Prophet. Every twenty-four hours I completed a recitation of the Quran.

In my seeing I was blind, in my hearing deaf, in my speaking dumb. For a whole year I conversed with no one. People called me a lunatic, and I allowed them to give me that name, relying on the Tradition that a man's faith is not made perfect until he is supposed to be mad. I performed everything I had read or heard of as having been done or commended by the Prophet. Having read that when he was wounded in the foot at the battle of Uhud, he stood on his toes in order to perform his devotions—for he could not set the sole of his foot on the ground—I resolved to imitate him, and standing on tiptoe I performed a prayer of forty genuflections. I modeled my actions, outward and inward, upon the Custom of the Prophet, so that habit at last became nature.

Whatever I heard or found in books concerning the acts of worship performed by the angels, I performed the same. I had heard and seen in writing that some angels worship God on their heads. Therefore I placed my head on the ground and bade the blessed mother of Abu Tahir tie my toe with a cord and fasten the cord to a peg and then shut the door behind her. Being left alone, I said "O Lord! I do not want myself; let me escape from myself!" and I began a recitation of the entire Quran. When I came to the verse, "God shall suffice you against them, for He hears and knows all" (Quran 2:131), blood poured from my eyes and I was no longer conscious of myself.

At that point began Abu Sa'id's conversion from mere asceticism to the life of a mystic saint. As he himself tells us, what had previously been simply his efforts were now transformed into God's spiritual gifts, the "graces" and "blessings" with which Sufi literature is filled.

Then things changed. Ascetic experiences passed over me of a kind that cannot be described in words, and God strengthened and aided me therein, but I had fancied that all these acts were done by me. The grace of God became manifest and showed me this was not so, and that these acts were acts of divine favor and grace. I repented of my belief and realized that it was mere self-conceit. Now if you say that you will not tread this path because it is self-conceit, I reply that your refusal to tread it is likewise self-conceit, and until you undergo all this, its self-conceit will not be revealed to you. Self-conceit appears only when you fulfill the Law, for self-conceit lies in religion and religion is of the Law. To refrain from religious acts is unbelief, but to perform such acts self consciously is dualism, because if "you" exists and "He" exists, then two exist, and that is dualism. You must put your self away altogether.

I had a cell in which I sat, and sitting there I was enamored of passing away from myself. A light flashed upon me, which utterly destroyed the darkness of my being. God Almighty revealed to me that I was neither that nor this: that this was His grace even as that was His gift.

Abu Sa'id was well aware of the sudden adulation that accompanied Sufi "celebrity" in medieval Islam, and the equally swift reversal to which all such celebrity is subject.

Then the people began to regard me with great approval. Disciples gathered round me and converted to Sufism. My neighbors too showed their respect for me by ceasing to drink wine. This proceeded so far that a melon skin I had thrown away was bought for twenty pieces of gold. One day when I was riding on horseback, my horse dropped dung. Eager to gain a blessing, the people came and picked up the dung and smeared their head and faces with it.

After a time it was revealed to me that I was not the real object of their veneration. A voice cried from the corner of the mosque, "Is not your Lord enough for you?" (Quran 41:53). A light gleamed in my breast and most veils were removed. The people who had honored me now rejected me, and even went before the judge to bear witness that I was an infidel. The inhabitants of every place that I entered declared that their crops would not grow on account of my wickedness. Once, while I was seated in a mosque, a woman went up on to the roof and bespattered me with filth; and still I heard a voice saying, "Is not your Lord enough for you?" The congregation desisted from their prayers, saying, "We will not pray together so long as this madman is in the mosque." . . .

This joyous transport was followed by a painful contraction of spirit. I opened the Quran and my eye fell on the verse, "We will prove you with evil and with good, to try you; and to Us shall you return" (Quran 21:36), as though God said to me, "All this which I put in your way is a trial. If it is good, it is a trial, and if it is evil, it is a trial. Do not stoop to good or to evil but swell in Me!" Once more my self vanished and His grace was all in all. (Abu Saʿid, *The Secrets of Oneness* 37:8)

[Cited by NICHOLSON 1921: 15–17]

What affected people's attitude toward Ibn Abi al-Khayr were changes in his external behavior. From a severe asceticism, he turned to what appeared to be a profligate life style, complete with luxurious feasts and splendid entertainments filled with song and dance (see Chapter 4 below). The turnabout caused another ambitious but somewhat naive Sufi to think that perhaps the famous Abu Saʿid had been overrated, a serious miscalculation. He approached the Master.

O Shaykh, (he said) I have come in order to challenge you to a forty days' fast. The poor man was ignorant of the Shaykh's novitiate and of his forty years of austerities: he fancied that the Shaykh had always lived in this same manner. He thought to himself, "I will chasten him with hunger and put him to shame in the eyes of the people, and I shall be the object of their regard." On hearing this challenge, the Shaykh said, "May it be blessed!" and spread his prayer rug. His adversary did the like, and they both sat down side by side.

While the ascetic, in accordance with the practice of those who keep a fast of forty days, was eating a certain amount of food, the Shaykh Abu Saʿid ate nothing; and though he never once broke his fast, every morning he was stronger and fatter and his complexion grew more and more ruddy. All the time, by his orders and under his eyes, his dervishes feasted luxuriously and indulged in spiritual concerts, and he himself danced with them. His state was not changed for the worse in any respect. The ascetic, on the other hand, was daily becoming feebler and thinner and paler, and the sight of the delicious viands which were served to the Sufis in his presence worked more and more upon him. At length he grew so weak that he could scarcely rise to perform the obligatory prayers. He repented of his presumption and confessed his ignorance.

When the forty days were finished the Shaykh Abu Saʿid said, "I have complied with your request: now you must do as I say." The ascetic acknowledged this and said, "It is for the Shaykh to command." Abu Saʿid said, "We have sat for forty days and eaten nothing and gone to the privy; now let us sit another forty and eat nothing but never go to the privy." His adversary had no choice but to accept the challenge, though he thought to himself that it was impossible for any human to do such a thing. (Abu Saʿid, *The Secrets of Oneness* 160:18) [Cited by NICHOLSON 1921: 71–72]

The man ended, of course, by becoming the disciple of Abu Saʿid ibn Abi al-Khayr.

Ghazali, whose distinguished intellectual career spanned philosophy, theology, and law, was a Sufi as well, and it was chiefly his moderate and sympathetic writing on the subject of Sufism that made the Islamic world a safer place for the sometimes extravagant likes of Ibn Abi al-Khayr. In addition to the extended treatment of Sufism in his Revivification of the Sciences of Religion, *Ghazali gives a personal but still highly schematic and intellectualized sketch of his own search for certitude in the autobiographical* Deliverer from Error. *After experimenting with the other disciplines, Ghazali tells us, he came at length to Sufism.*

When I had finished with those sciences, I next turned with set purpose to the method of Sufism. I knew the complete mystic "way" includes both intellectual belief and practical activity; the latter consists of getting rid of obstacles in the self and stripping off its base characteristics and vicious morals, so that the heart may attain to freedom from what is not God and to constant recollection of Him.

Ghazali, ever the intellectual, begins by reading the Sufi classics.

. . . I thus comprehended their fundamental teachings on the intellectual side, and progressed, as far as is possible by study and oral instruction, in the knowledge of Sufism. It became clear to me, however, that what is most distinctive of Sufism is something which cannot be apprehended by study, but only by tasting, by ecstasy and by moral change. . . . From the sciences I had labored at and the paths I had traversed in my investigation of the revelational and revealed sciences, there had come to me a sure faith in God Most High, in prophethood and the Last Day. These three credal principles were firmly rooted in my being, not through any carefully argued proofs, but by reason of various causes, coincidences and experiences which are not capable of being stated in detail.

It has already become clear to me that I had no hope of the bliss of the world to come save through a God-fearing life and the withdrawal of myself from vain desire. It was clear to me too that the key to all this was to sever the attachment of the heart to worldly things by leaving the mansion of deception and returning to that of eternity.

Next Ghazali, the distinguished professor on the faculty of Islamic law at the university of Baghdad, takes stock of his life.

I considered the circumstances of my life, and realized that I was caught in a veritable thicket of attachments. I also considered my activities, of which the best was my teaching and lecturing, and realized that in them I was dealing with sciences that were unimportant and contributed nothing to the attainment of eternal life. After that I examined my motive in my work of teaching, and realized that it was not a pure desire for the things of God, but that the impulse moving me was the desire for an influential position and public recognition. I saw for certain that I was on the brink of a crumbling bank of sand and in imminent danger of hell fire unless I set about to mend my ways. . . .

For nearly six months beginning in July 1095 I was continuously tossed about between the attractions of worldly desires and the impulses toward eternal life. In that month the matter ceased to be one of choice and became one of compulsion. God caused my tongue to dry up so that I was prevented from lecturing. One particular day I would make an effort to lecture to gratify the hearts of my following, but my tongue would not utter a single word nor could I accomplish anything at all.

Now in the full grip of spiritual impotence, Ghazali quits Baghdad, his family, and his post there and disappears into a ten-year seclusion, some of it spent in Jerusalem, some on pilgrimage to Mecca, and two years on spiritual retreat in Damascus.

In due course I entered Damascus and there I remained for nearly two years with no other occupation than the cultivation of retirement and solitude, together with religious and ascetic exercises, as I busied myself purifying my soul, improving my character and cleansing my heart for the constant recollection of God Most High, as I had learnt from my study of Sufism. I used to go into retreat for a period in the mosque of Damascus, going up the minaret of the mosque for the whole day and shutting myself in so as to be alone. . . .

I continued at this stage for the space of ten years, and during these periods of solitude there were revealed to me things innumerable and unfathomable. This much I shall say about that in order that others may be helped: I learnt with certainty that it is above all the Sufis who walk on the road of God; their life is the best life, their method the soundest method, their character the purest character; indeed, were the intellect of the intellectuals and the learning of the learned and the scholarship of the scholars, who are versed in the profundity of revealed truth, brought together in the attempt to improve the life and character of the Sufis, they would find no way of doing so; for to the Sufis all movement and all rest, whether external or internal, brings illumination from the lamp of prophetic revelation; and behind the light of prophetic revelation there is no other light on the face of the earth from which illumination may be received. (Ghazali, *Deliverer* 122–132) [GHAZALI 1953: 54–60]

28. "No Monasticism in Islam"

Christian monks in the Near East were to some extent characterized by their association with a woolen cloak—their version of the "religious habit" of Western Christendom—an association that at least suggests that "Sufism" owed more than a passing resemblance to Christian monastic practices on the Syrian steppe. Monks and monasticism are in fact mentioned in the Quran. In two of the citations it is not so much a question of the institution of monasticism as of praise for monks who "are not proud" (5:82) or the condemnation of those Christian monks "who devour the wealth of mankind wantonly" or "hoard up gold and silver and spend it not in the way of God" (9:34). If this were the end of it, one would assume that Muhammad neither admired nor condemned Christian monasticism as such. But there is another, somewhat longer passage on the subject that is far more problematic. It occurs in the midst of the now familiar history of God's revelation.

We sent Noah and Abraham, and We gave prophethood to their progeny and the Book, and some of them were well-directed, but many of them were disobedient. Then in their train We sent Our apostles, and succeeding them Jesus, son of Mary, and gave him the Gospel, and put into the hearts of his followers and caused Our messengers," God declares, "to follow in their [that is, Noah and Abraham and their seed] footsteps; and We caused Jesus, son of Mary, to follow, and gave him the Gospel, and in the hearts of those who followed him We placed compassion and kindness. And monasticism, they created it, which had not been prescribed for them by Us except for seeking the pleasure of God; yet they did not observe it as it should have been rightly observed. (Quran 57:27)

"And monasticism. . . ." The meaning, and so the translation, of this bit of the verse is by no means certain. Is "monasticism" in parallel with "compassion and kindness," a virtuous practice begun by the Christians of their own volition, or is "monasticism" contrasted with what immediately precedes, a blameworthy human innovation? In Arabic the verse yields both meanings, and its inherent ambiguity is reflected in early Muslim comments upon it, as in this example from Muhasibi (d. 837 C.E.).

God blamed those among the Israelites [that is, the Christians] who, having instituted the monastic life to which He had not previously obliged them, did not observe it in an exact fashion. And He said, "this monastic life which they instituted; We ordained it not for them." . . .

There is disagreement on this verse. Mujahid interprets it as "We have not ordained it for them only to make them desire to conform themselves to the divine pleasure," that is to say, "We have prescribed it. . . . God placed in them, for their own good, the seeds of the monastic life, and then reprimanded them for abandoning it." But Abu Imama al-Bahili and others comment upon it as follows: "We have not prescribed, that is to say, it was not We who ordained this. They instituted it only to please God and even so God blamed them for abandoning it." This latter opinion is the more probable and one which embraces most of the scholars of the community. [MASSIGNON 1968: 149]

We cannot say which in fact is the more probable interpretation. Muhasibi is certainly correct in maintaining that the reading of the verse in a pejorative sense, namely that monasticism is a Christian innovation, unrequired, even undesired, by God, became the common interpretation of this verse among Muslims. It is no surprise, then, that there soon began to circulate a tradition on the subject attributed to Muhammad himself. "No monasticism in Islam," the Prophet is reported to have said.

29. Monks and Sufis

There was in fact no monasticism in Islam, not in the Christian sense of individuals or groups removing themselves from the world and society and living under perpetual vows of poverty, chastity, and obedience. But the spirituality of Muslims and Christians often took parallel paths, and both the similarities and differences appear in this advice given to an aspiring Sufi novice by one of the great masters, Ibn al-Arabi (1164–1240 C.E.) of Murcia.

Among the things you must possess, my brother, is (the grace) not to live at the expense of other people, to be a burden to no one, to accept no support from man either for yourself or anyone else, but to practice your own trade and be abstemious in the matter of your living expenses. (Exercise restraint) also in your words and glances on all occasions, whether you are moving about or are stationary. Be not extravagant in matters of housing or dress or food, for what is lawful (therein) is but little and leaves no room for lavishness. . . .

Among the things you must possess, my friend, is (the grace of doing with but) little food, for (abstinence) in this and cheerfulness in obedience drives away laziness. You must be careful to apportion out your time by day and by night. As for the hours when the religious law summons you to stand before God, they are the five prayer periods for the canonical prayers. But beyond them are the other times consecrated by the custom of the Prophet. So if you are a craftsman, labor diligently to make enough in one day to provide your needs for several days. If you are a businessman, do not hasten away from your place of prayer after the dawn prayer until the sun has risen, nor after the afternoon prayer until the sun has set. . . . Do not sleep until you are quite overcome by slumber. Do not eat save what is needful, nor dress save as is necessary to guard against heat and cold, with the intention of covering the genitals and removing a peremptory impediment to the worship of God. . . .

Among the things you must possess is (the grace of) having an accounting with yourself, a seasonable examination of your innermost thoughts, putting a shamefacedness before God as the raiment on your heart, for if you possess a true feeling of shame before God you will prevent your heart from harboring fancies which God would find blameworthy, or from being moved by emotions with which God Most High would not be pleased. We ourselves used formerly to have a master who was accustomed to record his emotional states during the day in a book that he had, and when night came he would set the pages in front of him and have an accounting with himself for what was written therein. . . .

Take care to be continent. That is, avoid everything that would leave an impression on your soul. . . . If you live in that state of continence which is the foundation of religion and the path to God, your works will thrive and your undertakings be successful, your condition in life will prosper, supernatural blessings will hasten toward you, and you will be guided by divine care in all your affairs. We have no doubt about it. But whenever you turn aside from the path of continence and go straying in every valley (of desire), God departs from you and leaves you to yourself, so that Satan gets the mastery of you. (Ibn al-Arabi, *A Treatise on What the Novice Must Possess*) [JEFFERY 1962: 643–645, 653]

At times even the externals of the two types of spiritual endeavor, that of the monk and that of the Sufi, bore remarkable similarities, as one Muslim had occasion to observe. The era is the eleventh century, the Latin Crusader century in Palestine, and it is a community of Christian monks that first attracts the attention of the Muslim Usama.

I visited the tomb of John [the Baptist], the son of Zachariah—God's blessing on both of them—in the village of Sebaste in the province of Nablus [that is, the biblical Samaria]. After I said my prayers, I went into the square that was bounded on one side by the holy precinct (where the tomb was located). I found a half-closed gate, opened it and entered a church. Inside were about ten old men, their bare heads as white as combed cotton. They were facing eastward, and wore [embroidered?] on their breasts staffs ending in crossbars turned up like the rear of a saddle [that is, some form of a cross, as Usama likely knew very well]. They swore their oaths on this sign, and gave hospitality to those who needed it. The sight of their piety touched my heart, but at the same time it displeased and saddened me, for I had never seen such zeal and devotion among the Muslims.

I brooded on this experience for some time, until one day, as Muʿin al-Din and I were passing the Peacock House, he said to me, "I want to dismount here and visit the shaykhs." "Certainly," I said, and so we dismounted and went into a long building set at an angle to the road. At first I thought that there was no one there. Then I saw about a hundred prayer mats and on each one of them a Sufi, his face expressing a peaceful serenity, and his body humble devotion. This was a reassuring sight, and I gave thanks to Almighty God that there were among Muslims men of even more zealous devotion than those Christian priests. Before this I had never seen Sufis in their convent and so was ignorant of the way they lived. (Usama, *Book of the Staff* 528–529)

A century later, in 1183 C.E., the Muslim traveler Ibn Jubayr likewise had occasion to note communities of ascetics, now in Damascus, and he too was impressed and edified.

Ribats for Sufis, which are here called *khanaqas*, are numerous. They are adorned residences; water flows through all of them and they present the most delicious prospect imaginable. The members of this type of Sufi organization live like kings here since God has provided for them even beyond the necessities and so freed their minds from any concern for earning a living, and thus they can devote themselves entirely to His service. He has lodged them in halls which give them a foretaste of those of Paradise. So these fortunate men, the most favored of the Sufis, enjoy by God's favor the blessings of both this world and the next. They follow a praiseworthy vocation and their life in common is conducted in an admirable fashion.

Ibn Jubayr observed, and obviously approved of, something new and unusual about the Sufi life, their manner of prayer.

Their manner of worship is peculiar to them. Their custom of assembling for highly charged musical recitals is most pleasant. Sometimes, so carried away are some of these rapt ascetics when they are under the influence of this condition, that they can scarcely be thought of as belonging to this world at all. (Ibn Jubayr, *Travels* 284)

30. Sufi Communities

Ibn Jubayr had a name for the Sufis' common lodging, a ribat, *a familiar term to him, though in Damascus, he explains, the less familiar* khanaqa *is used. This latter, a Sufi cloister or convent, was the third, and in the end the most common, of a trio of institutions that served the needs and ends of ascetics and mystics in Islam. The oldest of the three was, as Ibn Jubayr intimates, the* ribat. *By tradition this was originally a fortified keep to protect the lands and coasts of Islam. In time, it evolved into a kind of cloistered hospice for Muslims who for reasons of need—widows were often housed in them—or by preference chose to separate themselves from the world. In the end the* ribat *became totally identified with Sufism, though it had neither the personal stamp of the shrine-tomb (zawiya) nor the official character and internal organization of what seems very akin to a Christian monastery—the text of Usama already suggests the comparison—the* khanaqa.

If the Sufi convent had some of the features of the Pachomian monastery, the shrine-tomb corresponded to an earlier development in Christian spirituality. As we have seen in the case of Antony and others, the earliest Christian holy men attracted others to themselves and provided both a model and an ideal for those admirers to follow. The shaykh of the Islamic tradition had much the same effect: his sanctity drew others to himself. At the same time, his quarters, perhaps enlarged to permit others to lodge there, became at once a very loosely organized "school" and shrine of sanctity. At the shaykh's death he was often buried in the same place, and so in the final stage of its evolution the zawiya was both a shrine and a tomb, and not always on a modest scale. Ibn Battuta describes a shrine-tomb he visited near Wasit in Iraq in 1327 C.E.

This gave me the opportunity of visiting the grave of the saint Abu al-Abbas Ahmad al-Rifaʿi [d. 1182 C.E.], which is set at a village called Umm Ubayda, one day's journey from Wasit. . . . It is a vast convent in which there are thousands of poor brethren. . . . When the afternoon prayers have been said, drums and kettle drums were beaten and the poor brethren began to dance. After this they prayed the sunset prayer and brought in the repast, consisting of rice bread, fish, milk and dates.

After the meal there begins the community "recollection," a widespread Sufi devotion already noted by Ibn Jubayr; it is performed in this instance under the direction of the master of the shrine-tomb together with his adepts. Shaykh Ahmad, as is noted, was a linear descendant of the saint buried there. Finally, the "Rifaʿi" version of a "spiritual concert" was considered notorious even in its own day.

When all had eaten and prayed the first night prayer, they began to recite their "recollection," with the shaykh Ahmad sitting on the prayer carpet of his ancestor above mentioned, when they began the musical recital. They had prepared loads of firewood which they kindled into a flame, and went dancing into the midst of it; some of them rolled in the fire, and others ate it in their mouths, until finally they extinguished it entirely. This is their regular custom, and it is the peculiar characteristic of this corporation of Ahmadi brethren. Some of them will take a large snake and bite its head with their teeth until they bite it clean through. (Ibn Battuta, *Travels*) [IBN BATTUTA 1959–1962: 273–274]

The community resident within one of these convents or shrine-tombs might be formal or informal, loosely or tightly structured, made up of permanent members or with transient "sojourners." Where the life and the community was more formal was where it was associated with a "way," practices and blessings modeled on and derived from a saintly master. These are Islam's "religious orders," similar in some respects to the monastic confraternities of Christianity, though far more charismatic and with a greater orientation toward a master-novice relationship than their Christian, and particularly their Western Christian, counterparts. In the Sufi reception and training of postulants, for example, we can observe both the similarities to and the differences from Christian practice. Ibn Battuta describes the arrival at the gates of a Cairo convent of a postulant who has already had some training.

When a new arrival makes his appearance, he has to take up his stand at the gateway of the convent, girded about the middle, with a prayer rug slung over his back, his staff in his right hand and his ablution jug in his left. The gatekeeper informs the steward, who goes out and ascertains from what country he has come, what convents he has resided in during his journey [or earlier training], and who was his initiator. If he is satisfied with the truth of his replies, he brings him into the convent, arranges a suitable place for him to spread out his prayer mat and shows him the washroom. The postulant then restores himself to a state of ritual cleanliness, goes to his mat, ungirds himself and prays two prostrations. After this he clasps the hands of the shaykh [that is, the spiritual master] and of those who are present and takes his seat among them. (Ibn Battuta, *Travels* 1.20) [Cited by TRIMINGHAM 1971: 171]

The postulant has become a novice and is set upon the course of his spiritual training.

The Sufi masters observe the following rule. When a novice joins them with the purpose of renouncing the world, they subject him to a spiritual training for the space of three years. If he fulfills the requirements of this discipline, well and good; otherwise they declare that he cannot be admitted to the Path. The first year is devoted to the service of the people, the second year to service of God, and the third year to watching over his own heart.

At the end of his three-year training and probation, the novice is ready for investiture with the patched Sufi cloak, the "religious habit" of this way of life.

The adept, then, who has attained the perfection of saintship takes the right course when he invests the novice with the Sufi cloak after a period of three years during which he has educated him in the necessary discipline. In respect of the qualifications which it demands, the Sufi cloak is comparable to a winding sheet: the wearer must resign all his hopes of the pleasures of life, and purge his heart of all sensual delights, and devote his life entirely to the service of God. (Hujwiri, *The Unveiling*)
[HUJWIRI 1911: 54–55]

31. Convent Rules and Charters

Like their Christian counterparts, the earliest rules governing the life of Sufis living under a single convent roof were apparently quite simple. This set is attributed to Abu Saʿid ibn Abi al-Khayr (d. 1047 C.E.), a pioneer of the Sufi life in eastern Iran.

1. Let them keep their garments clean and themselves always pure.
2. Let them not sit in the mosque or in any holy place for the sake of gossiping.
3. In the first instance let them perform their prayers in common.
4. Let them pray much at night.
5. At dawn let them ask forgiveness of God and call upon Him.
6. In the morning let them read as much of the Quran as they can and let them not talk until the sun has risen.

7. Between the evening prayers and the bedtime prayers let them occupy themselves with repeating some litany.

8. Let them welcome the poor and the needy and all who join their company, and let them bear patiently the trouble of waiting upon them.

9. Let them not eat anything except when participating with another.

10. Let them not absent themselves without receiving permission from one another.

Furthermore, let them spend their hours of leisure in one of three things: either in the study of theology or in some devotional exercise or in bringing comfort to someone. Whoever loves his community and helps them as much as he can is a sharer in their merit and future recompense. (Abu Saʿid, *The Secret of Oneness*) [NICHOLSON 1921: 46]

The guidelines just cited are the teachings of an individual on the conduct of the spiritual life. More often in the Islam the monastic "rules" were the result of stipulations built into the founding charter of a convent by the founder-donor. The monasteries and convents of Islam were supported, like most other Muslim religious institutions, out of endowments. Generally, the details of both the finances and the internal organization of the institution were spelled out in the original endowment charter, as in this example preserved in inscriptional form from one of the convents of Jerusalem.

In the name of God, the Merciful, the Compassionate: the devoted servant of Almighty God, Ibn Abd Rabbihi ibn Abd al-Bari Sanjar al-Dawadari al-Salihi ordered the construction of this blessed convent called the House of the Saints. He made it a pious foundation for the sake of Almighty God and for the benefit of thirty members of the Sufi community and their disciples, both Arabs and Persians, of whom twenty are celibate and ten married. They are to live here and not depart, neither in summer nor in winter, neither spring nor fall, except in urgent cases and in order to extend hospitality to those Sufis and disciples who desire it for a period of ten days. He made its endowment (the income of) the village of Bir Nabala (of the territory of) the blessed Jerusalem and of the village of Hajla of (the territory of) Jericho; and also (the income of) a bakery and a mill and what is above these two enterprises in Jerusalem; of a soap factory, six shops and a paper factory in Nablus; of three gardens, three shops and four mills in Baysan. This is all endowment for the benefit of this convent and for instruction in the Shafiʿite rite; for a professor of Prophetic traditions and a reader to recite same; for ten persons who will memorize traditions and ten who will recite the Book of God in its

979

entirety each day; also for a eulogist who will glorify the Prophet. All of this (latter) is to be done in the Aqsa mosque.

This (was done) on the first day of the year 695 [1295 C.E.], in the governorship of the devoted servant of God Sanjar al-Qaymari, may God grant him pardon. [VAN BERCHEM 1922: no. 70]

32. Convent Life in Islam

Sufi convent life evolved over a long period of time, from the most informal, almost anarchical arrangements, to institutions that rivaled Christendom's orderly monasteries. The first example here is from Muqaddasi, a professional traveler roaming the "Abode of Islam" sometime before 980 C.E., when Sufi congregations were still grasping for a sense of themselves.

When I entered Sus [a town in southwestern Iran] I went to the main mosque to seek out a shaykh whom I might question concerning certain points of Prophetic tradition. It happened that I was wearing a cloak of Cypriot wool and a Basran waist wrapper and so I was directed to a congregation of Sufis. As I approached they assumed that I too was a Sufi and welcomed me with open arms. They settled me among them and began questioning me. Then they sent a man with food. I felt uneasy about taking the food since I had had nothing to do with such (Sufi) congregations before this. They expressed surprise at my reluctance and my not joining in their rituals. But I felt drawn to associate myself with this congregation and find out about their method, and learn the true nature of Sufism. I said to myself, "This is your chance, here where nobody knows you."

I cast off all restraint in their regard. . . . At one time I joined in their antiphonal singing, on another occasion I shouted with them, and on another recited poems with them. I went with them to visit hospices and to engage in religious recitals, with the result that I won a remarkably high place in the affections of both the Sufis and the people there. I gained a great reputation; I was visited for my virtue and was sent presents of clothes and money, which I accepted but straightway handed over untouched to the Sufis, since I was well off. I spent every day in my considerable devotions, and they imagined that I did it out of piety. People began touching me and spreading reports of my fame, saying that they had never seen a more excellent ascetic. So it continued until, when the time came that I had penetrated into their secrets and learned all that I wished, I just ran away from them in the middle of the night and by the morning I was well away. (Muqaddasi, *The Best of Climes*, 415)

Three and a half centuries later, when Ibn Battuta describes the convents of Cairo ca. 1355 C.E., the institutional landscape looks very different.

Each convent in Cairo is affected to the use of a separate congregation of ascetics [here in Arabic, a *fakir*; the Persian equivalent is a dervish] most of whom are Persians, men of good education and adepts in the "way" of Sufism. Each has a shaykh and a warden, and the organization of their affairs is admirable. It is one of their customs in the matter of their food that the steward of the house comes in the morning to the dervishes, each of whom then specifies what food he desires. When they assemble for meals, each person is given his bread and soup in a separate dish, none sharing with another. They eat twice a day. They receive winter clothing and summer clothing and a monthly allowance varying from 20 to 30 dirhams each. Every Thursday evening they are given sugar cakes, soap to wash their clothes, the price of admission to the bathhouse and oil to feed their lamps. These men are celibate; the married men have separate convents. Among the stipulations required of them are attendance at the five daily prayers, spending the night in the khanaqa and assembly in mass in a chapel within the convent. (Ibn Battuta, *Travels*) [IBN BATTUTA 1959–1962: 44]

Or here, in even broader strokes, is Damascus of the same era.

The people of Damascus vie with one another in the building and endowment of mosques, religious houses, colleges and shrines. . . . Every man who comes to the end of his resources in any district of Damascus finds without exception some means of livelihood opened to him, either as a prayer leader in a mosque, or as a reciter in a law school or by occupation [of a cell] in a mosque, where his daily requirements are supplied to him, or by recitation of the Quran, or employment as a keeper at one of the blessed sanctuaries, or else he may be included in the company of Sufis who live in the convent, in receipt of a regular allowance for upkeep and clothing. Anyone who is a stranger there living on charity is always protected from [having to earn it at] the expense of his self-respect and dignity. Those who are manual workers or in domestic service find other means of livelihood, for example, as guardian of an orchard or intendant of a mill or in charge of children, going with them in the morning to their lessons and coming back with them in the evening, and anyone who wishes to pursue a course of studies or devote himself to the religious life receives every aid to the execution of his purpose. (Ibid.) [IBN BATTUTA 1959–1962: 149–150]

4. The Mystics' Ascent
to God

Mysticism is sometimes taken as the esoteric understanding of God and His works given to a few chosen souls, or as the immediate apprehension of, and even identity with, God Himself. In either case, mysticism found a profound, if occasionally troubled, place in Judaism, Christianity, and Islam.

The sources of the trouble are not far to seek. For one thing, such a privileged understanding seemed to create "a church within a church," an elite group of believers who, if they did not often trouble those latter members of the flock, certainly troubled their shepherds. And among some of the adepts, their special understanding, their "gnosis," which they at least thought was more profound, and perhaps even more authentic, than that possessed by the ordinary believer, had the effect of reducing what might be called "ordinary revelation" to an inferior status and, as an occasional corollary, of freeing the adept from the "ordinary observance" prescribed by that other, public revelation. And finally, the mystic's intuitive leap into the neighborhood, or even the very bosom, of God seemed to violate one of the most profound and strongly held beliefs of the three monotheistic faiths, that in the utter transcendence, the absolute otherness, of God.

1. "O, Let Me Behold Your Presence"

The biblical worlds of God and man were unalterably separate. "The heavens are the Lord's heavens, but the earth He has given to the sons of man," as Psalm 115:16 put it. What, then, was the origin of this extraordinary idea that men could somehow approach God, could fathom His inscrutable secrets? The notion is not so wondrous, perhaps, as it might first appear. The seeds of it are already present at Sinai. It was during the sojourn of the Israelites in the wilderness of Sinai that the basic document of what later came to be called Judaism was given them. But there also occurs in the Sinai narrative an illuminating passage on the nature of God, His presence among His people, and the desire of at least some of the latter to draw closer to Him.

Now Moses would take the Tent and pitch it outside the camp, at some distance from the camp. It was called the Tent of Meeting, and whoever sought the Lord would go out to the Tent of Meeting that was outside the camp. Whenever Moses went out to the Tent, all the people would rise and stand, each at the entrance of his tent, and gaze after Moses until he had entered the Tent. And when Moses entered the Tent, the pillar of cloud would descend and stand at the entrance of the Tent, while He spoke to Moses. When all the people saw the pillar of cloud poised at the entrance of the Tent, all the people would rise and bow low, each at the entrance of his tent. The Lord would speak to Moses face to face, as one man speaks to another. And he would then return to the camp, but his attendant, Joshua son of Nun, a youth, would not stir out of the Tent.

Moses said to the Lord, "See, You say to me, 'Lead this people forward,' but You have not made known to me whom You will send with me. Further, You have said, 'I have singled you out by name, and you have indeed gained my favor.' Now, if I have truly gained Your favor, pray let me know Your ways, that I may know You and continue in Your favor. Consider, too, that this nation is Your people." And He said, "I will go in the lead and will lighten your burden." And he said to Him, "Unless You go in the lead, do not make us leave this place. For how shall it be known that Your people have gained Your favor unless You go with us, so that we may be distinguished, Your people and I, from every people on the face of the earth?" The Lord said to Moses, "I will also do this thing that you have asked; for you have truly gained My favor and I have singled you out by name."

Moses said, "O, let me behold Your Presence!" And He answered, "I will make all My goodness pass before you and I will proclaim before you the name Lord [that is, YHWH]."

Written, of course, in the Semitic fashion without vowels and generally vocalized as Yahweh. But there was a strict prohibition about pronunciation of the divine name, and one way of avoiding that was to substitute other vowels, thus "Yehoweh" or "Jehoveh." The text continues.

". . . [A]nd the grace that I grant you and the compassion that I show. But," He said, "you cannot see My face, for man may not see Me and live." And the Lord said, "See, there is a place near Me. Station yourself on the rock and, as My Presence passes by, I will put a cleft in the rock and shield you with My hand until I have passed by. Then I will take My hand away and you will see My back; but My face must not be seen." (Exodus 33:7–23)

The Quran likewise recalls this incident.

When Moses arrived at the appointed time and his Lord spoke to him, he said: "O Lord, reveal Yourself to me that I may behold You." "You cannot behold Me," He said, "But look toward the mountain: if it remains firm in its place, then you may behold Me." But when his Lord appeared on the mountain in His effulgence, it crumbled to a heap of dust, and Moses fell unconscious. When he came to, he said: "All glory to You. I turn to You in repentance, and I am the first to believe." (Quran 7:143)

This protracted and intimate exposure to the presence of the Lord had its unmistakable physical effect, however.

Moses came down from Mount Sinai. And as Moses came down from the mountain bearing the two tablets of the Pact, Moses was not aware that the skin of his face was radiant, since he had spoken to Him. Aaron and all the Israelites saw that the skin of Moses' face was radiant; and they shrank from coming near him. But Moses called to them, and Aaron and all the chieftains in the assembly returned to him, and Moses spoke to them. Afterwards all the Israelites came near, and he instructed them concerning all the Lord had imparted to him on Mount Sinai. And when Moses had finished speaking with them, he put a veil over his face. (Exodus 34:29–35)

2. Visions of the Throne

The Israelites' "public" revelation was given not merely to Moses on Sinai but both before and after: from Adam and Enoch, Abraham and Jacob at one end of the biblical record to Daniel at the other, God had appeared or spoken to or otherwise communicated with, in a waking state or in dreams, many in Israel. Direct access to God was not, then, thought extraordinary among the Israelites, though some of its modalities and some of its effects certainly were, as in the case of Isaiah.

In the year King Uzziah died [742 B.C.E.], I beheld my Lord seated on a high and lofty throne, and the skirts of His robe filled the Temple. Seraphs stood in attendance on Him. Each had six wings: with two he covered his face, with two he covered his legs and with two he would fly.

And one would call to the other,
"Holy, holy, holy!
The Lord of Hosts!
His presence fills all the earth!"

The doorposts would shake at the sound of the one who called, and the House kept filling with smoke. I cried,

"Woe to me; I am lost!
For I am a man of unclean lips
And I live among a people
Of unclean lips;
Yet my eyes have beheld
The King Lord of Hosts."

Then one of the seraphs flew over to me with a live coal, which he had taken from the altar with a pair of tongs. He touched it to my lips and declared,

"Now that this has touched your lips,
Your guilt shall depart
And your sin be purged away."

Then I heard the voice of my Lord saying: "Whom shall I send? Who will go for Us?" And I answered: "Here am I; send me." (Isaiah 6:1–8)

The following far more circumstantial, and obscure, account—the vision is highly personalized and idiosyncratic, and it is not always certain what the prophet was seeing or envisioning—is found in the opening chapter of the Book of Ezekiel. The prophet himself is speaking; the time is a few years into the Babylonian Exile.

In the thirtieth year, on the fifth day of the fourth month, when I was in the community of exiles by the Chebar Canal (in Babylonia), the heavens opened and I saw visions of God. On the fifth day of the month—it was the fifth year of the exile of King Jehoiachin [that is, 593 B.C.E.], the word of the Lord came to the priest Ezekiel son of Buzi the priest, by the Chebar Canal in the land of the Chaldeans. And the hand of the Lord came upon him there.

I looked, and lo, a stormy wind came sweeping out of the north—a huge cloud and flashing fire, surrounded by a radiance; and in the center of it, in the center of the fire, a gleam as of amber [or, "electrum"]. In the center of it were also the figures of four creatures. And this was their appearance:

They had the figures of human beings. However, each had four faces, and each of them had four wings. . . . The four of them had their faces and their wings on their four sides. Each one's wings touched those of the other. They did not turn as they moved; each could move in the direction of any of its faces.

Each of them had a human face (at the front); each of the four had the face of a lion on the right; each of the four had the face of an ox on the left; and each of the four had the face of an eagle (at the back). Such were their faces. . . . With them was something that looked like burning coals of fire. This fire, suggestive of torches, kept moving about among the creatures; the fire had a radiance, and lightning issued from the fire. Dashing to and fro (among) the creatures was something that looked like flares.

And here, as often, there is an ambiguity in the Hebrew between "wind" and what is called in English "spirit."

As I gazed on the creatures, I saw one wheel on the ground next to each of the four-faced creatures. As for the appearance and structure of the wheels, they gleamed like beryl. All four had the same form; the appearance and structure of each was as of two wheels cutting through each other. And when they moved, each could move in the direction of any of its four quarters; they did not veer when they moved. Their rims were tall and frightening, for the rims of all four were covered all over with eyes. And when the creatures moved forward, the wheels moved at their sides; and when the creatures were borne above the earth, the wheels were borne too. Wherever the spirit [or "the wind"] impelled them to go, they went—wherever it impelled them—and the wheels were borne alongside them; for the spirit of the creatures was in the wheels. . . .

Above the heads of the creatures was a form: an expanse, with an awe-inspiring gleam as of crystal, was spread out above their heads. . . . When they moved, I could hear the sound of their wings like the sound of mighty waters. . . . When they stood still, they would let their wings droop. From above the expanse over their heads came a sound. . . .

Above the expanse over their heads was the semblance of a throne, in appearance like a sapphire; and on top, upon this semblance of a throne, was the semblance of a human form. From what appeared as his loins up, I saw a gleam as of amber [or "electrum"]—what looked like a fire encased in a frame; and from what appeared as his loins down, I saw what looked like fire. There was a radiance all about him. Like the appearance of which shines in the clouds on a day of rain, such was the appearance of the surrounding radiance. That was the appearance of the semblance of the Presence of the Lord.

When I beheld it, I threw myself down on my face. And I heard the voice of someone speaking. And He said to me: "O mortal man, stand on your feet that I may speak to you." As He spoke, a spirit entered into me and set me on my feet; and I heard what was being spoken to me. (Ezekiel 1:1—2:3)

The Lord delivers to Ezekiel his commission, a warning to a rebellious Israel, and it is only then that Ezekiel begins to be transported. At the phrase "These are the words of the Lord God," the narrative continues.

Then a spirit [or wind] carried me away, and behind me I heard a great roaring sound: "Blessed is the Presence of the Lord, in His place," with the sound of the wings of the creatures beating against one another, and the sound of wheels beside them—a great roaring sound. A spirit seized me and carried me away. I went in bitterness, in the fury of my spirit, while the hand of the Lord was strong upon me. (Ezekiel 3:12—14)

3. Heavenly Journeys

The mere fact of God's revelations to Moses in person on Sinai, to various prophets like Isaiah and Ezekiel and Daniel in dreams or ecstatic states, and to any number of individuals through His angels makes it abundantly clear that God Most High was content to descend on occasion to that "earth He has given to the sons of man." Ezekiel's vision had shown him the highest heavens and the throne and very form of God, but he himself had remained on earth during the experience. More extraordinarily, the Bible records a number of cases where men were physically taken up alive into "the Lord's Heaven." Enoch, it appears from Genesis 5:24, did not die, as was said of all the other patriarchs in the biblical narrative, but was taken up by God.

All the days of Enoch came to 365 years. Enoch walked with God, then he was no more, for God took him. (Genesis 5:24)

Many centuries later, the Christian author of the "Letter to the Hebrews" can cite Enoch along with Abraham as a witness to the power of faith.

And what is faith? Faith gives substance to our hopes, and makes us certain of realities we do not see. It is for their faith that the men of old stand on record. . . . By faith Enoch was carried away to another life without passing through death; he was not to be found because God had taken him. For it is the testimony of the Scripture that before he was taken he had pleased God, and without faith it is impossible to please God. (Hebrews 11:1, 5–6)

The case of Elijah is considerably less mysterious, though no less miraculous. Elijah and his disciple Elisha are in Jericho.

The disciples of the prophets who were at Jericho came over to Elisha and said to him, "Do you know that the Lord will take your master away from you today?" He replied, "I know it too; be silent."

Elijah and Elisha approach the Jordan. Elijah strikes the waters with his cloak and they part so the two men can pass over on dry land.

As they were crossing, Elijah said to Elisha, "Tell me, what I can do for you before I am taken from you?" Elisha answered, "Let a double portion of your spirit pass on to me." "You have asked a difficult thing," he said. "If you see me as I am being taken from you, this will be granted to you; if not, it will not."

They kept on walking and talking; a fiery chariot with fiery horses suddenly appeared and separated one from the other; and Elijah went up to heaven in a whirlwind. Elisha saw it, and he cried out, "Oh, father, father! Israel's chariots and horsemen!" When he could no longer see him, he grasped his garments and rent them in two. (2 Kings 2:5–12)

The biblically certified presence of these two mortals alive in God's abode set in train a number of consequences. Enoch, as we shall see, became the central figure in a great many visionary accounts of the upper world, while the return of Elijah was associated in post-Exilic times with the End of Days. Here the Lord speaks through the mouth of His prophet Malachi.

Lo, I will send the prophet Elijah to you before the coming of that awesome, fearful day of the Lord. He shall reconcile fathers to sons and sons to fathers, so that, when I come, I do not strike the whole land with utter destruction. (Malachi 3:23)

The expectation of Elijah's return was still very much in the front of men's minds in Jesus' day.

When he came to the territory of Caesarea Philippi, Jesus asked his disciples: "Who do men say that the son of man is?" They answered: "Some say John the Baptist, others Elijah, others Jeremiah or one of the prophets." (Matthew 16:13)

Whatever others may have thought, Jesus himself publicly identified John the Baptist, recently imprisoned by Herod Antipas, with the returned Elijah.

I tell you this: never has there appeared on earth a mother's son greater than John the Baptist, and yet the least in the Kingdom of Heaven is greater than he. Ever since the coming of John the Baptist the Kingdom of Heaven has been subjected to violence and violent men are seizing it. For all the prophets and the Law foretold things to come until John appeared, and John is the destined Elijah, if you will but accept it. (Matthew 11:12–14)

And so he revealed to Peter, James, and John, immediately after they had beheld the transfigured Jesus in the company of Moses and Elijah.

On their way down the mountain, Jesus enjoined them not to tell anyone of the vision until the Son of Man had been raised from the dead. The disciples put a question to him: "Why then do our teachers say that Elijah must come first?" He replied, "Yes, Elijah will come and set everything right. But I tell you that Elijah has already come, and they failed to recognize him, and worked their will upon him; and in the same way the Son of Man is to suffer at their hands." Then the disciples understood that he meant John the Baptist. (Matthew 17:9–13)

The presence of Moses in the company of Jesus and Elijah on that hilltop in Galilee indicates that by Jesus' day he too had begun to be reckoned among those who had not suffered death but had been taken directly up into heaven. Moses did ascend Sinai to the presence of God in Exodus 24, but he descended as well, and the last chapter of Deuteronomy leaves no doubt that he later died.

Moses went up from the steppes of Moab to Mount Nebo, to the summit of Pisgah, opposite Jericho, and the Lord showed him the whole land. . . . "This is the land of which I swore to Abraham, Isaac and Jacob I will give to your offspring. I have let you see it with your own eyes, but you shall not cross there."

So Moses the servant of the Lord died there in the land of Moab, at the command of the Lord. He buried him in the valley in the land of Moab, near Beth Peor; and no one knows his burial place to this day. (Deuteronomy 34:1–6)

We cannot know why the final, apparently offhanded remark was added to the account, but it left open considerable space for the growth of a Moses ascension legend, and there certainly was such in full vigor in later times. This, for example, is how Josephus describes the final earthly moments of Moses.

And while he bade farewell to Eleazar and Joshua and was yet speaking with them, a cloud suddenly descended upon him and he disappeared into a ravine. But he has written of himself in the sacred book that he died, for fear that they might say by reason of his surpassing virtue he had gone back to the deity. (Josephus, *Antiquities* 4:48)

In all these cases it is more a matter of an assumption, a being taken up, rather than an ascension, a circumstantial voyage from earth to heaven. The earliest example of the latter occurs beyond the limits of Bible, in a third- or second-century B.C.E. work attributed to Enoch, the patriarch who had escaped death. The fourteenth chapter of the composite work that is now called the "First Book of Enoch" relates a fully articulated journey through the heavens.

Behold, clouds called me in the vision, and mist called me, and the path of the stars and flashes of lightning hastened me and drove me, and in the vision winds caused me to fly and hastened me and lifted me up into heaven. (1 Enoch 14:8)

And this is what he saw when he entered the heavens.

I proceeded until I came near to a wall which was built of hailstones, and a tongue of fire surrounded it, and it began to make me afraid. And I went into the tongue of fire and near to a large house which was built of hailstones, and the wall of that house was like a mosaic made of hailstones, and its floor was snow. Its roof was like the path of the stars and flashes of lightning, and among them fiery cherubim, and their heaven was like water. And there was a fire burning around its wall, and its door was ablaze.

And I went into that house, and it was hot as fire and cold as snow, and there was neither pleasure nor life in it. Fear covered me and a trembling took hold of me. And as I was shaking and trembling, I fell on my face. And I saw in the vision, and behold another house, which was larger than the former, and its doors were open before me, and it was built of a tongue of fire. And in everything it so excelled in glory and splendor and size that I am unable to describe to you its glory and its size.

If the model for this double-chambered house in heaven is likely the earthly Temple in Jerusalem, with its interior Holy of Holies, what follows is unmistakably drawn from Ezekiel's prophetic vision.

And I looked and I saw in it a high throne and its appearance was like ice and its surrounds like the shining sun and the sound of cherubim. And from beneath the high throne there flowed out rivers of burning fire so that it was impossible to look at it. And He who is great in glory sat upon it, and His raiment was brighter than the sun and whiter than any snow. And no angel could enter, and at the appearance of the face of Him who is honored and praised no creature of flesh could look. A sea of fire burnt round Him and a great fire stood before Him, and none of those round Him came near to Him. Ten thousand times ten thousand stood before Him, but He needed no holy counsel. And the Holy Ones who were near Him did not leave by night or day, and did not depart from Him.

And until then I had been prostrated on my face, as I trembled. And the Lord called me with His own mouth and said to me, "Come hither, Enoch, to My holy word." And He lifted me up and brought me near the door. And I looked, with my face down. (1 Enoch 14:9–25)

There are heavenly journeys attributed to others among the biblical patriarchs in the post-Exilic literature called "Pseudepigrapha" and not included in the Bible. One such work with one such journey is the so-called "Testament of Levi." It is later than 1 Enoch and adds another important motif to the genre, the voyage through the various heavens, with a description of the sights seen en route. It contains a some-what confused description of the seven heavens, confused chiefly because the various versions of the "Testament of Levi" stand midway between belief in a three-tiered and a seven-tiered upper world. The doctrine of the seven heavens, founded on the domains of the seven planetary spheres of contemporary astronomy, was common-place in Greco-Roman circles. The Jewish tradition supplied its own version of the function and contents of each, here set forth, not for the first time certainly, in rather crisp summary fashion in the Talmud.

Rabbi Judah said: There are two firmaments, for it is said: "Behold, to the Lord your God belongs heaven and the heaven of heavens" (Deuteronomy 10:14). Resh Lakish said: (There are) seven, namely, the Curtain, the Firmament, the Clouds, the Lofty Abode, the Dwelling, the Fixed Place and the Thick Darkness. (BT.Hagigah 12b)

4. The "Work of the Chariot"

Whatever the inherent interest of the accounts of cosmic and celestial voyages, it was Ezekiel's experience of the heavenly chariot that made the strongest impression on Jewish sensibilities. The Babylonian Talmud tells the following story.

Once Rabbi Yohanan ben Zakkai was riding on an ass when going on a journey, and Rabbi Eleazar ben Arak was driving the ass from behind. Rabbi Eleazar said to him: "Master, teach me a chapter from the 'Work of the Chariot.'" He answered: "Have I not taught you all thus: 'Nor the "Work of the Chariot" in the presence of one, unless he is a sage and understands of his own knowledge'?" (BT.Hagigah 14b)

Yohanan ben Zakkai, the sage who escaped Jerusalem just before its destruction by the Romans in 70 C.E., is here quoting his own words in order to discourage the request for instruction on the "Work of the Chariot." The full text of his ruling occurs in Mishna Hagigah and provides a little more context for the implied reprimand. The Mishna's caution about the "Work of Creation" begins with a warning against public discussion of the forbidden degrees of sexual relations and includes in its strictures the "Work of the Chariot."

The (subject of) forbidden relations may not be expounded in the presence of three persons, nor the Work of Creation in the presence of two, nor the (Work of) the Chariot in the presence of one, unless he is a sage and already has an independent understanding of the matter. (M.Hagigah 2:1)

We return to Yohanan ben Zakkai.

Rabbi Eleazar then said to him: "Master, then permit me to say [or perhaps "repeat"] to you something which you have taught me." He answered: "Say on!" Rabbi Yohanan ben Zakkai immediately dismounted from the ass, wrapped himself up (in his prayer shawl) and sat upon a stone beneath an olive tree. Rabbi Eleazar said to him: "Master, why did you dismount from the ass?" He answered: "Is it proper that while you are expounding the 'Work of the Chariot' and the Divine Presence is with us, and the ministering angels accompany us, I should be riding on the ass?"

Immediately Rabbi Eleazar ben Arak began his exposition of the "Work of the Chariot" and fire came down from heaven and encompassed all the trees in the field, and thereupon they all began to utter song. . . . An angel then said from the fire: "This is the very 'Work of the Chariot,' " whereupon Rabbi Yohanan ben Zakkai rose and kissed him on the head and said: "Blessed be the Lord God of Israel, who has given to Abraham our father a son who knows how to speculate upon, and to investigate, and to expound the 'Work of the Chariot.' " (BT.Hagigah 14b)

What is this "Work of the Chariot" that is subject to so many cautions and yet is so holy that Yohanan puts on his prayer shawl to hear it explained and that it summons down to earth the Shekina, the Divine Presence of God? The "Work of Creation," mentioned in the same cautions, was an esoteric exposition of what is sketched in Genesis, a kind of filling in the blanks of the biblical account out of a mélange of ideas, some of them palpably non-Jewish in origin, in circulation in late antiquity. The "Work of the Chariot" is a similar explanation of the first chapter of Ezekiel. The matter becomes clear as the Talmud begins to gloss Mishna Hagigah 2:1.

"Nor (the Work of) the Chariot in the presence of one": Rabbi Hiyya taught: But the headings of the chapters may be transmitted to that one person. Rabbi Zera said: The headings of chapters may be transmitted only to the Head of the Religious Court and to one whose heart is careful within him. Others say: *Only* if his heart is careful within him. Rabbi Ammi said: The mysteries of the Torah may be transmitted to "captains of companies, men of rank, counselor, magician and cunning enchanter" (Isa. 3:3).

Although there was some debate on how closely the circle was to be drawn, instruction on the "Work of the Chariot" was obviously to be restricted to individuals of maturity and sagacity. Whether the instruction was orally derived is unclear; it is conceivable, as some later commentators thought, that the "Work of the Chariot" was already an assembled and edited collection of teachings. The same Talmud passage continues.

Rabbi Joseph was studying the "Work of the Chariot"; the elders (of the Babylonian academy) of Pumbeditha were studying the "Work of Creation." The latter said to the former: Let the master teach us the "Work of the Chariot." He replied: Teach me the "Work of Creation." After they had taught him, they said to him: Let the master instruct us in the "Work of the Chariot." . . . We have already studied therein as far as "And He said to me: Son of Man . . ." (Ezek. 2:1). He replied: This is the very "Work of the Chariot."

The "Work of the Chariot" was, then, a certain understanding of the first chapter of the Book of Ezekiel.

An objection was raised: How far does the "Work of the Chariot" extend? Rabbi said: As far as the second "I saw" (in 1:27). Rabbi Isaac said: As far as "amber" (in 1:28). As far as "I saw" may be taught (publicly); thenceforward only the heads of the chapters may be transmitted. Some, however, say: As far as "I saw" the heads of chapters may be transmitted; thenceforward, if he is a sage capable of independent speculation, yes; if not, no.

This exchange seems to suggest that the heart of the esoteric understanding of the first chapter of Ezekiel turns on the word "amber" in 1:27 and 28. Two anecdotes are adduced to confirm this.

May one expound the mysteries of "the amber"? For behold, there was once a child who expounded the (mysteries of) "the amber" and a fire went forth and consumed him —The child is different, for he had not reached (the fitting) age. . . . The Rabbis taught: There was once a child who was reading at his teacher's house the Book of Ezekiel, and he apprehended what "the amber" was, whereupon a fire went forth from "the amber" and consumed him. So they sought to suppress the Book of Ezekiel, but Hananiah ben Hezekiah said to them: If he was a sage, all are sages! (BT.Hagigah 13a)

The two children were thus judged exceptional cases, and the Book of Ezekiel was left in the canon, its public reading and glossing permitted—the text of the Talmud proceeds to do exactly that—while the esoteric understanding of it was limited to those to whom it would do no harm.

Finally, there is a Christian testimony from the early third century. The author is Origen, the Alexandrian Christian who was well acquainted with the Hebrew Scriptures. The passage occurs in the prologue to his commentary on the biblical Song of Songs.

It is said that the custom of the Jews is that no one who has not reached full maturity is permitted to hold this book [that is, Song of Songs] in his hands. And not only this, but even though their rabbis and teachers are accustomed to teach all the Scriptures and their oral traditions to young boys, they postpone till last the following four texts: The opening of Genesis, where the creation of the world is described; the beginning of the prophecy of Ezekiel, where the teaching about the angels is expounded; the end (of the same book) which contains the description of the future Temple; and this present book, the Song of Songs. (Origen, *Commentary on the Song of Songs*, Prologue)

5. Jewish Gnosticism: The Temple-Palaces of God

The main line of Jewish mysticism, from late biblical times through the rabbinic and medieval eras, appears to be a type of what has come to be known by the convenient rubric of Gnosticism, that is, a special knowledge (gnosis) or, better, a special or esoteric understanding of exoteric texts, which is reserved for a chosen few and which, in the classical gnostic style, is closely associated with redemption.

The "Work of Creation" is esotericism purely and simply, secret meanings of public texts, in this case of the first chapter of Genesis. But that same kind of understanding of the first chapter of the Book of Ezekiel, the "Work of the Chariot," was linked, via a heavenly, Ezekiel-inspired journey, to the vicinity of the Throne of God. This is how it is described in summary—and how it came to be divulged—in a work known as "The Greater Treatise on the Temple-Palaces." The landscape is that of Ezekiel's vision.

Rabbi Ishmael said: When Rabbi Nehunyah ben ha-Qanah saw that wicked Rome had taken counsel to destroy the great ones of Israel, he at once revealed the secret of the world, the measure that appears to one who is worthy of gazing on the King, on His Throne, on His majesty and His beauty, on the Holy Creatures, on the mighty Cherubim, on the Offanim of the Shekina, on the swift lightning, on the terrible electrum, on Rigyon [that is, the river of fire] which surrounds His Throne, on the bridges, on the fiery flames that blaze up between one bridge and the next, on the dense smoke, on the bright wind that raises from the burning coals the pall of smoke which covers and conceals all the chambers of the Temple-Palace of Arabot, the (seventh) heaven, on the fiery clouds, on Surya, the Prince of the Divine Presence, the servant of TVTRKY'EL YHVH, the Majestic one. (*The Greater Treatise* 15:1) [ALEXANDER 1984: 120]

Although the word "chariot" does not occur in this passage, there are present many of the elements of what the rabbis were talking about when they referred to the "Work of the Chariot." The focus of the journey is manifold. There is the arrival in "Arabot," the seventh heaven and the site of the seven Hekalot, *or "Temple-Palaces," which give their name to the literature. Each palace has its own guardian, and there is a considerable lore of gaining entry, chiefly by knowing the correct name of the guardian or seal. The names, many of them undecipherable or deliberately unintelligible at this remove, clearly owe a great deal to formula magic, as in this example.*

When you come and stand at the gate of the sixth palace, show the three seals of the Gatekeepers of the sixth palace, two of them to Qizpiel the Prince, whose sword is unsheathed in his hand and from it lightning bolts shoot out, and it is drawn against anyone unworthy to gaze upon the King and on the Throne. . . . Show one seal to Dumiel. Is Dumiel really his name? Is not Abirghydrhm [or Abirghhydrpyr] his name? (*The Greater Treatise* 20:5) [ALEXANDER 1984: 123–124]

Here at any rate we understand. Dumiel, which straightforwardly means "the silence of God," is not only the guardian of this palace but also the ruler of the four elements. He has as well a magical title, Abirghhydrpyr, composed of a Hebrew transliteration of the elements' four Greek names: aer (air), ge (earth), hydor (water), and pyr (fire).

The Temple-Palaces writings have been called "a manual for mystics," and they do indeed contain what appear to be practical instructions for achieving the same difficult ascent as that undertaken by the famous four who, as we shall see, were thought to have entered Paradise. In the eleventh century Hai Gaon, the head of the Iraqi yeshiva, was asked to comment on a famous and difficult passage in the

Talmud that, whatever its original sense, was understood in his day to refer to a mystical ascent to Paradise. The Talmud passage begins: "Four men entered the Garden. . . ." Pardes, the Hebrew word borrowed from Persian via Greek and signifying "garden," is also used, as we have seen, in the sense of the same word in English, "Paradise," the abode of the blessed, or even of God. The text continues: "namely, Ben Azzai and Ben Zoma, and Somebody Else and Rabbi Akiba." The "Somebody Else" had a name, and it is used later in the passage: Elisha ben Abuya. He apostatized, however, and so even the mention of his name was avoided. The Talmud continues with Akiba's caution that they not confuse the marble walls of the heavenly palaces with the glitter of water.

Rabbi Akiba said to them: When you arrive at the stones of pure marble, do not say "Water! Water!" . . . Ben Azzai cast a look and died. . . . Ben Zoma looked and became demented. Somebody Else "mutilated the shoots" [that is, apostatized]. Rabbi Akiba departed unhurt. (BT.Hagigah 14b)

The outcome is not entirely clear. The implication is that Ben Azzai and Ben Zoma failed the ordeal and suffered accordingly, while both Rabbi Akiba and Elisha ben Abuya (his apostasy occurred after this incident) were successful and returned safely from the "Paradise." Already in this opaque passage the emphasis is on methodology, and it is precisely that aspect that Hai Gaon reflects upon in his comment on it.

You may be aware that many of the sages were of the opinion that an individual who possesses certain explicitly defined worthy characteristics, and who wants to look at the Chariot and to peer in the palaces of the celestial angels, has ways to achieve this. He must sit fasting for a specified number of days, place his head between his knees, and whisper to the earth many prescribed songs and hymns. He thus peers into the inner rooms and chambers as if he were seeing the seven palaces with his own eyes, and he observes as if he were going from palace to palace and seeing what is in all of them. The rabbis of the Mishna have taught two texts on this subject, called *The Greater Treatise on the Temple-Palaces* and *The Lesser Treatise on the Temple-Palaces*. (Hai Gaon)

[Cited by HALPERIN 1984: 543–544]

There are passages in the Temple-Palace texts that seem to confirm this prescription. In one of the best known a sage named Nehunyah ben ha-Qanah is described as experiencing a kind of mystic trance or transport, in which he witnesses "a marvelous majesty and strange dominion, a majesty of exaltation and a dominion of radiance, which is aroused before the Throne of Glory." He is "brought back" by members of his "brotherhood" to explain why not everyone is successful in what was begin-

ning to be called, somewhat inexplicably, "descent to the Chariot." The answer, as always, depends on showing the right seals to the right gatekeepers. But since these are rabbis, the account concludes on an appropriately legal note.

Dumiel [that is, the keeper of the gate leading out of the sixth of the Temple-Palaces] says to him: I testify and warn you of two things. He who descends does not descend to the Chariot unless he has these two qualities: (either he has read) the Torah, the Prophets and the Writings, and he studies Mishna, the statutes and the homiletic exegeses, and the legal decisions concerning what is forbidden and what is permitted, or else he has fulfilled every negative command that is written in the Torah, and keeps all the prohibitions of the statutes and judgments and teachings which were spoken to Moses on Sinai.

If a man says "I have one of these two qualities," immediately Dumiel summons Gabriel the scribe who writes for the man a document and hangs it on the shaft of the carriage of that man. It says: "Such and such is the learning of this person, and such and such are his deeds. He requests permission to enter before the Throne of Glory."

As soon as the gatekeepers of the seventh Temple-Palace see Dumiel, Gabriel and Qizpiel proceeding in front of the chariot of that man who is worthy to descend to the Chariot, they cover their faces and sit down—for they were standing erect. They loosen their strung bows and return their sharp swords to their sheaths. Nevertheless, it is necessary to show them a great seal and a fearful crown—T'DS VBR MNVGYH VK'SH YHVH the God of Israel. Then they enter before the Throne of Glory and bring out before him [that is, the "descender"] all kinds of melody and song, and, making music, they proceed before him till they lead him in and seat him with the Cherubim, the Offanim and the Holy Creatures and he sees wonders, powers, majesty, greatness, holiness, dread, humility and righteousness in that hour. (*The Greater Tractate* 21:4–22:2) [ALEXANDER 1984: 124–125]

We have no overwhelming conviction that either the authors of these texts or their readers held the achievement of such a heavenly ascent as a practical goal. The objective may well have been some more commonplace earthly good, a blessing perhaps, or even the acquisition of magical powers. So these passages associated with Rabbi Akiba seem to suggest.

Rabbi Akiba said: When I set forth this method of ascending and descending to the Chariot, they fixed for me a daily blessing in the heavenly court and in the earthly court. . . . A heavenly voice announced to me from beneath the Throne of Glory, "For my friend, who endures the

suffering of descending and ascending to the Chariot, I have fixed a blessing [to be recited] three times a day in the heavenly court and in the
earthly court. I will love and I will redeem any household where it is
repeated." (*Lesser Treatise on the Temple-Palaces* [SCHAEFER 1981: nos. 422–423]

*Akiba then describes what is required for this vicarious enjoyment of the fruits of the
heavenly ascent.*

Rabbi Akiba said: Anyone who wants to repeat this tradition and to
utter the name explicitly must sit fasting for forty days. He must put his
head between his knees until the fast gets control of him. He must whisper toward the earth and not toward heaven, so that earth may hear and
not heaven. If he is an adolescent, he may say it as long as he does not
have an emission. If he is married, he must be prepared [that is, conti-
nent] three days in advance, as it is written "Be prepared for the third
day" (Exodus 19:15).

The magical quality of what is being transmitted then becomes evident.

If he tells it to a friend, he must tell him one letter from among the
first ones and one letter from among the last ones. He should not make
the combination for him, lest he make a mistake and destroy's God's
world. If he wants to test him, he may test him once but not twice. He
must supervise him carefully, lest he make a mistake and destroy God's
world. He should make regular use of it month by month and year by
year, thirty days before Rosh Hashanah [to cover the forty-day period?]
from the first of Elul to Yom Kippur, to keep Satan from accusing him
and ruining his entire year. (*Lesser Treatise on the Temple-Palaces*)
[SCHAEFER 1981: no. 424]

6. The Divine Names

We have yet another mystical tradition that the whole Torah is comprised of names of the Holy One, blessed be He, and that the letters of
the words separate themselves into Divine Names when divided in a different manner, as you may imagine by way of example that the verse of
bereshit [that is, the first verse of Genesis] divides itself into these other
words: *berosh/yithbareh/Elohim*. This principle likewise applies to the entire
Torah, aside from the combinations and the numerical value of the Holy
Names. Our Rabbi Shlomo [that is, Rashi; d. 1105 C.E.] has already written in his commentaries on the Talmud concerning the manner in which
the Great Name of seventy-two letters is derived from the three verses

(Exod. 14:19–21): "And He went," "And He came," "And He stretched out." It is for this reason that the scroll of the Torah in which a mistake has been made in one letter being added or subtracted is disqualified, for this principle [namely, that the whole Torah is comprised of the Divine Names] obligates us to disqualify a scroll of the Torah in which one letter *vav* is missing from the word *otham*, or in which there are thirty-nine fully spelled [that is, spelled with *vav*] examples in the Torah, or if someone were to add a *vav* to any of the deficiently spelled ones. So it is in similar cases even though it matters not one way or the other for the sense. It is this principle that has caused scholars to count every fully and defectively spelled word in the Torah and Scripture and to compose books on the fully punctuated text, going back as far as Ezra the scribe and the prophet, so that we should be heedful of this, as the Sages derived it from the verse (Neh. 8:8): "And they read in the book of the Law of the Lord distinctly; and they gave the sense, and caused them to understand the reading."

It would appear that the Torah, "written with letters of black fire upon a background of white fire" (JT.Shekalim 13b) was in the form we have mentioned, namely that the writing was continuous, with break of words, which made it possible for it to be read by way of Divine Names and also by way of our normal reading which makes explicit the Torah and the commandment. It was given to Moses our teacher using the division of words which express the commandment, and orally it was transmitted to him in the rendition which consists of the Divine Names. Thus masters of the Kabbala write the letters of the Great Name I have mentioned all close to each other, and then these are divided into words consisting of three letters and many other divisions, as is the practice among the masters of the Kabbala. (Nachmanides, *Commentary on Genesis*) [NACHMANIDES 1971: 13–15]

7. Ascent by Intuition

The mystic was not the only one possessed of the conviction that it was possible to leap across revelation to an individual understanding of God. As we shall see in Chapter 5 below, the philosophers too shared that view. One such was Philo, who as a Jew as well as a philosopher had before him a double paradigm of an approach to God. Here he reflects upon biblical figures like Abraham, Jacob, and Moses who were particularly close to God.

These no doubt are truly admirable persons and superior to the other classes. They have, as I have said, advanced from down to up by a sort of heavenly ladder and by reason and reflection happily inferred the Creator from His works. But those, if such there be, who have had the power to apprehend Him through Himself without the cooperation of any reasoning process to lead them to the sight, must be recorded as holy and genuine worshipers and friends of God in truth. In their company is he who in the Hebrew is called Israel, but in our tongue the God-seer, who sees not His real nature—for that, as I said is impossible—but that He is. (Philo, *On Rewards and Punishments* 43)

Moses, of course, is the best-known example of someone who approached God and was rewarded with a vision of the deity, an event that Philo can treat in a bold allegorical fashion for the benefit of a wider audience of believers: the ascent of Sinai signifies a scaling of the heights of heaven itself.

Ex. 24 12a: What is the meaning of the words "Come up to Me to the mountain and be there"? This signifies that a holy soul is divinized not by ascending to the air or to the ether or to heaven higher than all but to a region above the heavens. And beyond the world there is no place but God. (Philo, *Questions on Exodus* 40)

In these instances Philo is meditating on Scripture, an unmistakably Jewish Scripture. But he could speak more generally, and more philosophically, as well. Earlier, the Greeks may have thought that it was possible to demonstrate the essence of the ultimate principle with the same ease and assurance as a theorem in geometry, but by the time that philosophical tradition reached Philo, its earlier intellectual optimism had necessarily to be trimmed to permit some place for intuitive knowledge, that sudden unreasoned and unreasoning seizure by understanding. Plato had already cleared a place for an intuitive leap in his own theology, and Philo, who stood in the midst of a still vital Platonic tradition in first-century B.C.E. Alexandria, describes just such an experience in his personal progress as a theologian.

The harvest of spontaneous good things is called "release," inasmuch as the mind is released from working on its own projects and is, we may say, emancipated from self-chosen tasks, by reason of the abundance of the rain and ceaseless shower of blessings. And these are of a most marvelous nature and passing fair. For the offspring of the soul's own travail are for the most part poor abortions, things untimely born; but those which God waters with the snow of heaven come to birth perfect, complete and peerless.

I feel no shame in recording my own experience, a thing I know from its having happened to me a thousand times. On some occasions, after making up my mind to follow the usual course of writing on philosophical doctrines, and knowing definitely the substance of what I was to set down, I have found my understanding incapable of giving birth to a single idea, and have given it up without accomplishing anything, reviling my understanding for its self-conceit and filled with amazement at the might of Him That Is, to Whom is due the opening and closing of soul-wombs. On other occasions, I have approached my work empty and suddenly became full, the ideas falling in a shower from above and being sown invisibly, so that under the influence of divine possession I have been filled with corybantic frenzy and been unconscious of anything, place, persons present, myself, words spoken, lines written. For I obtained language, ideas, an enjoyment of light, keenest vision, pellucid distinctness of objects, such as might be received through the eyes as a result of the clearest showing. (Philo, *The Migration of Abraham* 32–35) [PHILO 1945: 72–73]

And again, less personally, but in an even more deeply Platonic vein, albeit taking his point of departure as usual from a biblical text:

"He who shall come out of you," Scripture says, "shall be your heir" (Gen. 15:4). Therefore, my soul, if you feel any yearning to inherit the good things of God, leave not only your land, that is, the body, your kinsfolk, that is, the senses, your father's house, that is, speech, but be a fugitive from yourself also and issue forth from yourself. Like persons possessed and corybants, be filled with inspired frenzy, even as the prophets are inspired. But it is the mind which is under the divine afflatus, and no longer in its own keeping, but is stirred to its depths and maddened by heavenward yearning, drawn by the Truly Existent and pulled upward thereto, with truth to lead the way and remove all obstacles before its feet, that its path may be smooth to tread, such is the mind which has this inheritance.

To that mind I say, "Fear not to tell us the story of your departure from the first three. For to those who have been taught to give ear to the things of the mind, you ever repeat the tale." "I migrated from the body," she answers, "when I ceased to regard the flesh; from sense, when I came to view all the objects of sense as having no true existence, when I denounced its standards as spurious and corrupt and steeped in false opinion, and its judgments equipped to ensnare and deceive and ravish truth away from its place in the heart of nature; from speech, when I sentenced it to long speechlessness, in spite of all its self-exaltation and self-pride. Great indeed was its audacity, that it should attempt the impossible task to use shadows to point me to substances, words to point me to facts. And, amid all its blunders, it chattered and gushed about, unable to present with clear expression the distinctions in things. (Philo, *Who Is the Heir?* 69–73) [PHILO 1945: 73–74]

8. The Direct Apprehension of God

Thus Philo was schooled in a Greek philosophical tradition that, for all its relentless intellectualism, nonetheless conceded the possibility of a final direct approach to God, not by analogy or as the term of the final syllogism in the long process of discursive reasoning, but by a kind of sudden leap of the mind to God—the "flight of the alone to the Alone," as one of Philo's pagan successors in that same tradition put it. This is the gift enjoyed by the prophets; but according to Philo, it not restricted to them alone.

There is a mind more perfect and more purified, which has been initiated into the great mysteries, a mind that discovers the First Cause not from created things, as one may learn of the abiding object from its shadow, but transcends creation and obtains a clear impression of the Uncreated, so as from Him to apprehend both Himself and his shadow, that is, the Word (of God) and the world. This mind is Moses, who says, "Manifest Yourself to me that I may see You clearly" (Exod. 33:13). (Philo, *The Allegory of the Laws* 3.100–101) [PHILO 1981: 126–127]

This would not have been possible, for Moses or for anyone else, had not God previously "inspired" man in the very act of creation.

"Breathed into" (Gen. 2:7) is equivalent to "inspired" or "ensouled" the soulless; for heaven forbid that we should be infected with such far-out nonsense as to think that God employs for inbreathing organs such as mouth or nostrils; for God is without every quality, not only without human form. . . . And to what purpose, save that we may obtain a conception of Him? For how could the soul have conceived of God had He not infused it and taken hold of it as far as possible? For the human mind would never have made bold to soar so high as to apprehend the nature of God had not God Himself drawn it up to Himself, so far as it was possible for human mind to be drawn up, and imprinted it in accordance with the (divine) powers accessible to its reasoning. (Ibid. 1.36–38) [PHILO 1981: 127]

This "ensoulment" is given to all men. But there is something higher, the joint effect of human striving and God's graciousness. It is expressed by Philo in terms and images drawn directly from Plato.

After the self-taught, who enjoyed rich natural endowments, the third to reach perfection is the Man of Practice, who receives as his special reward the vision of God. For having applied himself to all aspects of human life and dealt with them in no offhand manner, and having evaded no toil or danger on the chance that he might be able to track down the truth, which is well worth pursuing, he found among mortal kind a profound darkness on land, water, air and ether. For the ether [that is, the fifth element and the substance of the heavenly bodies] and the entire heaven presented to him the appearance of night, since the whole sensible realm lacks determination, and the indeterminate is the brother of darkness and its kin. In his earlier period he kept the eye of his soul shut, but through unremitting struggles he laboriously began to open it and to part and throw off the obscuring mist. For an incorporeal beam purer than ether suddenly flashed over him and disclosed the intelligible world led by its charioteer. That charioteer, irradiated by a circle of undiluted light, was difficult to discern or divine, for the eye is enfeebled by the sparkling lights. Yet in spite of the abundant light that flooded it, it held its own in its extraordinary yearning to behold the vision. The Father and Savior, perceiving his genuine longing and desire, felt pity and, lending strength to the penetration of his sight, did not begrudge him a vision of Himself, to the extent that it was possible for created and mortal nature to contain it. Yet it was not a vision showing what He was, but only that He is. For the former, which is better than the good, more venerable than the monad, and purer than the unit, cannot be discerned by anyone else; but for Him alone is it allowed to comprehend Himself. . . .

This knowledge (that God exists) he has gained from no other source, not from things terrestrial or celestial, nor from the elements or compounds, mortal or immortal, but summoned by Him alone who is pleased to reveal His own proper existence to the suppliant. How this means of approach has come about is worth looking at through the use of a similitude. Do we see the sense-perceptible sun by anything other than the (light of the) sun or the stars by anything other than the (light of the) stars, and in general is not light seen by light? Similarly, God too has His own splendor and is discerned through Himself alone, without anything else assisting or being capable of assisting with a view to the perfect apprehension of His existence. They are but makers of inferences who strive to discern the Uncreated and the Creator of all from His creation, acting similarly to those who search out the nature of the One from the Two, whereas observation of the dyad should begin with the monad, which is its source. The pursuers of truth are they who form an image of God through God, light through light. (Philo, *On Rewards and Punishments* 36–46) [PHILO 1981: 127–129]

9. The Kabbalists' Torah and the Rabbis' Torah

In Philo, the mystic mounted up to God through man's purity and God's grace. Later Jewish works on "temple-palaces" show a much greater interest in esoteric techniques for the successful achievement of the journey to the throne of God. Many of those techniques appear magical—incantations, for example—but later Jewish mystics of the type interested in Kabbala, or The Tradition, were likewise concerned with techniques, though not always or necessarily magical ones.

One of the primary centers of Kabbala in the Muslim Near East was at Safed in Galilee, where many of the Jewish scholars exiled from Spain had migrated in the early years of the sixteenth century. One of the most illustrious there and in the entire history of Kabbala was Isaac Luria, dead at the age of thirty-eight in 1572 C.E.. His reflections on the acquisition of mystical knowledge are here passed on by one of his students.

My teacher's [that is, Isaac Luria's] comprehension of this knowledge proceeded along the following course. At first he studied the *Zohar*, and sometimes a whole week went by as he sought to grasp what he had studied. He studied one subject many times in order to understand in depth. He did this on many occasions. At times it was told to him that he still had not grasped that subject in its essence, and he continued to labor on the subject. Sometimes he was told the explanation of the subject according to Rabbi Simeon bar Yohai [that is, the second-century C.E. sage to whom the *Zohar* was attributed]. Sometimes he was told that this is how Rabbi Simeon bar Yohai understood the subject but that he [that is, Isaac Luria] still needed to go more deeply into it. Then did the prophet Elijah reveal himself to him, and then he understood everything, the great and the small, of all kinds of knowledge.

My teacher used to expound matters of the Law, according to their literal meaning, each of the six days of the week. But then he used to expound secret meanings in honor of the Sabbath.

(According to Isaac Luria,) the study of the Torah must have as its primary motive to attach the soul to its source through the Torah, in order to complete the supernal tree (of the Ten Primordial Numbers) and to complete and perfect the supernal man. This is the reason for the creation of man and the goal of his Torah study.

Commenting on Deuteronomy 22:3, "Thus you shall do with every lost object of your brother," Luria reveals another aspect of Kabbalism.

Know that a person may at times be perfected through "conjunction" [that is, a temporary joining to or indwelling in the body of another] or at times he may require reincarnation, which is much more painful. The penalty for anyone who finds a lost object and does not return it is that he cannot find justification through "conjunction" after his death but he must render it in some form of reincarnation. And this is the meaning of the concluding section of the verse cited above: "You may not hide yourself." This refers to "conjunction" alone, which involves being hidden in his neighbor's soul. Rather, he will require reincarnation, which is much more painful than "conjunction."

The eschatological punishment of reincarnation is also applied by Isaac Luria to the subject of mystical study.

If a person has not perfected himself by fulfilling all the 613 commandments in action, speech and thought, he will of necessity be subject to reincarnation (so that he may fulfill them). . . . And whoever has not studied Torah according to the four levels indicated by PRDS [= *pardes* = Paradise], (an acronym) which is a composite of the initial letters from four (Hebrew) words, *peshat* [that is, the literal], *remez* [the allegorical], *derash* [the homiletic], and *sod* [the mystical], will have his soul returned for reincarnation, so that he might fulfill each of them. (Jacob Zemah, *The Shulhan Arukh of the Divine Rabbi Isaac*) [BOKSER 1981: 145–146]

For all this patent esotericism, the rabbis' more intellectualistic tradition continued to run strongly through the writings of Luria and the most convinced Kabbalists. Moses of Cordova (1522–1570 C.E.), for example, was one of Luria's contemporaries and teachers at Safed. He too speaks of the need and the means of mystical study.

Undoubtedly, one of the duties laid down by the Torah is for a person to know God, in accordance with his powers of comprehension. Thus the text states, "I am the Lord your God" (Exod. 20:2), on which Maimonides offers the following comment in the beginning of his work (*Mishneh Torah*): The chief foundation and basis of all wisdom is to know that there is a First Cause, who brought all beings into existence. . . . And there is no doubt that our master intended to convey to us that included in this commandment is the understanding of the process by which existing things derived from Him, to the extent that this is within our human comprehension.

There can be no doubt concerning this, for how could one assume that the call to know as here used means only to believe in God's existence? The text would have stated that we have a positive commandment to *believe* that there is a God. But it is not written thus, it is written to *know*. This means specifically to attain knowledge, a comprehension of God in accordance with human intellectual capacity. And similarly did the Bible specify (Jer. 22:15): "Know the God of your fathers and serve Him." This is intended to teach us that to serve Him properly we must know Him, that is, know His Primordial Numbers and how He directs them and His unity with them. This is proper service, the unification of the Holy One, praised be He, and His Divine Presence. . . .

As to the appropriate time for commencing such study, I saw that the subject lends itself to a threefold division. First, there is the matter of preparing oneself to be fit to enter this holy domain. It is indeed true that it is not seemly that everyone who reaches out to robe himself in the holy garments in order to serve in the holy place shall come and so robe himself. One must first remove from oneself the coverings of crude pride which impede one from grasping the truth, and direct his heart toward heaven so that he shall not stumble. . . .

Second, it is important that a person train himself in the method of profound textual analysis so that he be accustomed and skillful in detaching from a text the illustrative elaborations, and this will enable him to reach the goal in this knowledge.

Thirdly, he shall dedicate himself to full acquisition of the laws of the Gemara [that is, the Talmudic discussions of the Mishna text], and the explanation of the commandments according to their simple meaning, as explained by Maimonides in the *Mishneh Torah*.

Fourth, he should also accustom himself to study Bible, whether much or little, so that he is perfected with sound knowledge, with Bible and Mishna, and he stumble not, and that he be not one of the group lost in error. . . .

After this, a person is to cleanse his mind of the follies and pleasures of the times, to the extent possible nowadays, and then will the gates of wisdom open to him. . . . Second, there is no doubt that a person will be unfit to pursue this knowledge unless, at the proper time, he marries and cleanses his thoughts. . . .

It is also necessary that a person reach at least his twentieth year, which brings him to the minimum of half the time fixed for the age of discernment [that is, forty, in M.Pirqe Aboth 5:24]. It is true that some held off until they reached their fortieth year, but we do not agree with this, for many followed our view and were successful. . . .

Third, as to the right time for engaging in this study, certainly it is easy to study any time in the day, but the time that is most conducive to study matters in depth is during the long nights, after midnight; or on the Sabbath, for the Sabbath itself lends predisposition to it; and on the holy days, especially Weeks [Shabuoth or Pentecost, that is, the holy day commemorating the giving of the Torah; see Chapter 1 above], for I have tried it many times and found this a time of wondrous propitiousness; and on the days of Tabernacles, in the "shelter" (*sukkah*) itself, for there it is most conducive. The times here mentioned were tested by me, and I speak from experience. (Moses of Cordova, *Deborah's Palmtree* 3:1–2) [BOKSER 1981: 139–141]

10. Jesus' Transfiguration

Perhaps even as Philo was pondering the immediate contemplation of God, this event occurred, the Gospels tell us, in another, quite different Jewish milieu in Galilee.

Six days later Jesus took Peter, James and John, the brother of James, and led them up to a high mountain, where they were alone. And in their presence he was transfigured; his face shone like the sun and his clothes became as white as the light. And they saw Moses and Elijah appear, conversing with him. Then Peter spoke: "Lord," he said, "how good it is that we are here! If you wish it, I will make three shelters here, one for you, one for Moses and one for Elijah." While he was still speaking, a bright cloud overshadowed them, and a voice called from the cloud: "This is my Son, my Beloved, on whom my favor rests; listen to him." At the sound of the voice the disciples fell on their faces in terror. Jesus then came up to them, touched them, and said, "Stand up; do not be afraid." And when they raised their eyes they saw no one, but only Jesus. (Matthew 17:1–8)

In Matthew's Gospel this event occurs just after Peter's acknowledgment of Jesus' messiahship. The epiphany may have served to confirm and validate that acknowledgment, with at least the suggestion that Jesus too would be taken up to heaven alive, as those other figures in the scene, Moses and Elijah, were. If that was its original intent, what came to be called the Transfiguration in the Christian tradition eventually served a quite different end: what Peter, James, and John witnessed on Mount Tabor was the paradigm of the Christian mystic's face-to-face experience of God.

11. Prophecy, Ecstasy, and Heresy

But before the Tabor experience could be elevated into a prototype of the mystic experience there were problems to be faced and misunderstandings to be resolved. To begin with, the earliest Christian communities were far more charismatic and ecstatic than those that followed. Paul provides the context.

Put love first; but there are other gifts of the Spirit at which you should aim also, and above all prophecy. When the man is using the language of ecstasy he is talking with God, not with men, for no man understands him; he is no doubt inspired, but he speaks mysteries. On the other hand, when a man prophesies, he is talking to men, and his words have power to build; they stimulate and they encourage. The language of ecstasy is good for the speaker himself, but it is prophecy that builds up a Christian community. I should be pleased for you all to use the tongues of ecstasy, but better pleased for you to prophesy. The prophet is worth more than the man of ecstatic speech—unless indeed he can explain its meaning, and so help to build up the community. Suppose, my friends, that when I come to you I use ecstatic language; what good shall I do you, unless what I say contains something by way of revelation, or enlightenment, or prophecy, or instruction? (Paul, *To the Corinthians* 1.14:1–6)

Prophesy, then, and ecstatic visions and utterances were not uncommon phenomena in the Christian congregations of the first and second centuries. Indeed, they were reckoned a kind of revelation—but cautiously, and with controls, as also appears in that same letter of Paul to the Corinthians.

To sum up, my friends, when you meet for worship, each of you contributes a hymn, some instruction, a revelation, an ecstatic utterance, or the interpretation of such an utterance. All of these must aim at one thing, to build up the church. If it is a matter of ecstatic utterance, only two should speak, or at most three, at one time, and someone must interpret. If there is no interpreter, the speaker had better not address the meeting at all, but speak to himself and to God. Of the prophets, two or three may speak, while the rest exercise their judgment upon what is said. If someone else receives a revelation while still sitting in his place, let the first speaker stop. You can all prophesy, one at a time, so that the whole congregation may receive instruction and encouragement. It is for prophets to control prophetic inspiration, for the God who inspires them is a God not of disorder but of peace. (Paul, *To the Corinthians* 1.14:26–33)

Paul does not say who the interpreter was to be. With the increasing organization and institutionalization of Christian communities under a bishop, there is little doubt that eventually it was he who first controlled, and eventually suppressed, this freewheeling form of individual revelation. But not always and everywhere successfully.

There is said to be a certain village named Ardabau, in Mysia, on the borders of Phrygia. There they say that when Gratus was Proconsul in Asia, a recent convert named Montanus . . . first became inspired; and falling into a sort of frenzy and ecstasy raved and began to babble and utter strange sounds, prophesying in a manner contrary to the traditional and constant custom of the Church from the beginning. . . . And he stirred up in addition two women [Priscilla and Maximilla] and filled them with the false spirit so that they talked frantically, at unseasonable times, and in a strange manner, like the person already mentioned. . . . And the arrogant spirit taught them to revile the universal and catholic church under heaven, because the spirit of false prophecy received from it neither honor nor entrance into it; for the faithful in Asia met often and in many places throughout Asia to consider this matter and to examine the recent utterances, and they pronounced them profane and rejected the heresy, and thus these persons were expelled from the Church and shut out from the communion. (Eusebius, *Church History* 5.16)

These (next) are Phrygians by birth and they have been deceived, having been overcome by certain women called Priscilla and Maximilla, and they regard them as prophetesses, saying that in them the Paraclete Spirit dwelled. And they likewise glorify one Montanus before these women as a prophet. So with their endless books from these people they go astray, and they neither judge their statements by reason nor pay any attention to those who can judge them. But they rather behave without judgment in the faith they place in them, saying they have learned something more through them than through the Law and the Prophets and the Gospels. But they glorify these women above the Apostles and every gift, so that some of them presume to say that there was something more in them than in Christ. These confess God the Father of the universe and the creator of all things, like the Church, and all that the Gospel witnesses concerning Christ. But they invent new fasts and feasts and meals of dry food and meals of radishes, saying that thus they were taught by their women. (Hippolytus, *Refutation of All Heresies* 8.19)

12. From Asceticism to Mysticism

If one, perhaps aborted, source of Christian mysticism was the charismatic tradition present from the beginning in Christian communities, then another, and in the end a far more fruitful one, lay in the bosom of Christian asceticism. As we have already seen in Chapter 3 above, asceticism was for some early Christians an end in itself, a voluntary fulfillment of Jesus' invitation, "If you would be perfect . . ." But very early on it was understood, if not to have another end beyond itself, then to serve another joint purpose. Basil of Caesarea, the pioneer of Christian monasticism, points the direction.

There is only one way out of this, namely, total separation from the world. But withdrawal from the world does not mean physical removal from it. Rather, it is the withdrawal by the soul of any sympathy for the body. One becomes stateless and homeless. One gives up possessions, friends, ownership of property, livelihood, business connections, social life and scholarship. The heart is made ready to receive the imprint of sacred teaching, and this making ready involves the unlearning of knowledge deriving from evil habits. To write on wax, one must first erase the letters previously written there, and to bring sacred teaching to the soul one must begin by wiping out the preoccupations rooted in ordinary habits. (Basil, *Letter* 2)

The expectation that there were rewards beyond the practice of self-denial, rewards in this life and not in the hereafter, is already present in homilies attributed, falsely, to Macarius, one of the principal figures in Egyptian asceticism.

This is something that everyone ought to know, that we have eyes within, more penetrating than these eyes; and a hearing more acute than this hearing. As the eyes of sense behold and recognize the face of a friend or a loved one, so the eyes of the true and faithful soul, spiritually illumined with the light of God, behold and recognize the True Friend. (Macarius, *Homily* 28:5)

Christians behold as in a mirror the good things of eternity. . . . The sight of an earthly king is an object of desire to all men. Everyone in his capital longs to catch even a glimpse of his beauty, the magnificence of his apparel, the glory of his purple. . . . Thus carnal men desire to see the glory of the earthly king. But what of those upon whom has fallen the dew of the Spirit of life in the Godhead, smiting their hearts with a divine passion for Christ, their heavenly king? How much more are they bound fast to that beauty of that ineffable glory . . . of Christ the eternal King . . . and desire to obtain those unspeakable blessings which by the Spirit they see in a mirror? (Ibid. 5:4–5)

This expectation that monastic ritual might lead to visions, spiritual or otherwise, was by no means extraordinary, as witnessed by this encounter between Olympius, a monk of Skete in Egypt, and a pagan priest who paid him a visit. It is Olympius speaking in this anonymously recollected anecdote.

When he [that is, the pagan priest] had observed the life of the monks, he said to me: "With a life of this kind do you receive no visions from God?" "No," I said to him. Then the priest said to me: "As we minister our god conceals nothing from us but rather reveals to us his mysteries. And you, after you have endured so many labors and sleepless nights and days of silence and mortification, do you say 'We see nothing'? Why, then, if you see nothing, the thoughts of your heart must be evil that they separate you from your God." So I went and reported his words to the elders; and they were amazed and said: "So indeed it is. Unclean thoughts do indeed separate God from man." (*The Sayings of the Fathers* 1:583)

At times the experiences undergone by the early monks put us in the presence of genuine mystical transports and an intimate connection with God Himself (see the example of John Cassian below). Others simply received visions, glimpses of the spiritual world beyond this, as here in the deathbed recollections of the monk Anuph.

From the day when I [Anuph] first confessed my Redeemer under persecution, never has an untrue word passed my lips. Never have I allowed earthly desire to dim my spiritual longings. But God's grace has never failed me, and I have needed no earthly thing. Angels have given me all the sustenance I have craved. And God has hidden from me nothing that happens on earth. . . . Often He shows me the hosts of angels that stand before Him: often I behold the glorious company of the righteous, the martyrs and the monks, such as had no purpose but to honor and praise God in singleness of heart. And there too I behold Satan and his angels delivered to eternal torment, while the righteous for their part enjoy eternal bliss. (Rufinus, *Monastic History* 10)

13. Prayer and Contemplation

Spiritual "events" sometimes took the form of visions; more often the experience was associated with prayer. This is Cassian's description of the highest form of prayer, a "prayer without images," a "flame of fire" assisted by an illumination from on high.

It transcends all human thoughts and is distinguished, I will not say by no sound of the voice, but by no movement of the tongue, no utterance of words. It is a prayer which the mind, enlightened by the infusion of heavenly light, does not confine within stilted human speech but pours forth richly in an accumulation of thoughts, as from a plentiful fountain, and ineffably speaks to God, expressing in the shortest possible time such great things as the mind, when it returns to itself, could not easily speak or tell. (Cassian, *Collations* 9:25)

These more personal experiences, are amplified by Cassian sometime about 400 C.E. and echoed in the Homilies *attributed to Macarius and likewise dating from the fourth or fifth century.*

I was often caught up into such an ecstasy as to make me forget that I was clothed with the burden of a weak body. Suddenly my soul forgot all external notions and entirely cut itself off from all material objects so that neither my eyes nor my ears performed their proper functions. And my soul was so filled with devout meditations and spiritual contemplation that often in the evening I did not know whether I had taken any food, and on the next day I was very doubtful whether or not I had broken my fast on the day before. (Cassian, *Collations* 19:4)

(In this prayer) the soul leaves herself, as it were, and is transported into the heavenly regions. All earthly cares are buried in oblivion. The spirit is captivated by things divine, things infinite and incomprehensible, marvels which cannot be expressed in human words. At last it breaks out in longing: "O that my soul might leave the earth and soar away with my prayer!" (Macarius, *Homily* 8:1)

The Macarian Homilies give a graphic description of the act of contemplation. For others, contemplation might have been an intellectual act; here it is quite unmistakably visionary, albeit through the eyes of the soul.

This is something everyone ought to know, that there are eyes that are more inward than these eyes and hearing more inward than this hearing. As the eyes sensibly behold and recognize the face of a friend or loved one, so the eyes of the faithful and worthy soul, once spiritually enlightened by the light of God, behold and recognize the true friend, the sweetest and longed-for bridegroom, the Lord, while the soul is shone upon by the adorable Spirit; and thus beholding with the mind the desirable and only expressible beauty, it is smitten with a passionate love of God, and is directed into all the virtues of the Spirit, and thus possesses an unbounded, unfailing love for the Lord it longs for. (Macarius, *Homily* 28:5)

As time passed and experiences grew more profound, the essential difference between the prayer that is the obligation of every Christian and the mystic's characteristic activity of contemplation could be scored more clearly, as here by one of the Eastern masters of the the spiritual life, Isaac, monk and bishop of Nineveh in newly Muslim-occupied Iraq of the seventh century C.E.

Sometimes from prayer a certain contemplation is born which makes prayer disappear from the lips. And he to whom this contemplation happens becomes a corpse without a soul, in ecstasy. . . . The motions of the tongue and the heart during prayer are keys. What comes after them is the entering into the treasury. Here then all mouths and tongues are silent, and the heart, the treasurer of the thoughts, the mind, the governor of the senses, the daring spirit, that swift bird, and all their means and powers and the beseeching persuasions have to stand still there: for the master of the house has come.

Just as the whole force of the laws and the commandments which God has laid down for mankind have their term in purity of the heart, according to the words of the Fathers, so all kinds and habits of prayer with which mankind prays to God have their term in pure prayer. Lamentations and self-humiliations and beseechings and inner supplications and sweet tears and all other habits which prayer possesses have their boundary, and the domain within which they are set into motion is pure prayer.

As soon as the spirit has crossed the boundary of pure prayer and proceeded onward, there is neither prayer nor emotions nor tears nor authority nor freedom nor beseeching nor desire nor longing after any of those things which are hoped for in this world or in the world to be. Therefore there is no prayer beyond pure prayer . . . but beyond this limit it passes into ecstasy and is no longer prayer. From here onward the spirit desists from prayer; there is sight, but the spirit does not pray. (Isaac of Nineveh, *Mystical Treatises* 112–114)

Much the same type of distinction, though with more emphasis on the affects of contemplation, is drawn by the Spanish Carmelite nun Teresa of Avila (1515–1582 C.E.) in her Way of Perfection.

Do not mistakenly believe that one draws but little profit from vocal prayer when it is well made. I assure you that it is quite possible for our Lord to raise you to perfect contemplation while you are reciting the "Our Father" or some other vocal prayer. And thus His Majesty shows that He hears one who prays in such a manner. This Sovereign Master speaks to the soul in return, suspends its understanding, checks its thoughts and, as it were, forms the very words before they are pronounced. And thus one cannot utter a single word by oneself without the greatest effort. The soul then realizes that the Master teaches it without any sound of words. He suspends the activities of the faculties which, instead of gaining benefits, would only cause harm if they attempted to operate.

In this state the faculties are filled with delight, without knowing why it is they rejoice. The soul is inflamed with an increasing flow of love without perceiving how it loves. It knows that it enjoys the object of its love, but it does not understand the nature of this enjoyment. Nevertheless, it realizes that the understanding could not, of itself, yearn for so ineffable a good. It realizes too that the will embraces the good without the soul's knowing how the will does this. If the soul can understand anything at all, it is the fact that nothing could possibly merit this benefit. It is a gift of the Master of heaven and earth who in the end bestows this boon in a manner worthy of Him. This is contemplation. (Teresa of Avila, *The Way of Perfection*)

14. Origen: The Christian Platonist in Search of God

Early monastic mysticism appears highly personal, remote from any currents save those swirling in the mystic's own soul. But once those impulses moved from desert and wilderness to the wider world inhabited by Christianity in the fourth century, the Christian mystic had a double heritage upon which to draw: the biblical and the philosophical. For the third-century Christian, no less than for the first-century Jew Philo, Moses and Plato were the two principal guides along the mystical path, Moses as a paradigm, Plato as an instructor.

The Platonic tradition held firmly to the immortality of the highest faculty of the soul, that is to say, the human intellect. It also affirmed what has been called "the great chain of being," a linked and graduated unity from the First Cause at the head of creation to the lowest form of being at its base. This chain of being was the royal staircase by which creation proceeded gradually outward and downward from God by way of emanation; it was also the ladder by which men struggled, likewise gradually, back up to God by way of purification, understanding, and contemplation.

These were commonplaces of the tradition when the Philo was active in Alexandria and two centuries later when Origen (185–254 C.E.) was enrolled as the first known Christian in the philosophy faculty there. They provided Origen, as they had Philo, the theoretical bases for an approach to God.

That study is called "moral" which inculcates a seemly manner of life and lays down a foundation for virtuous habits. The study called "natural" is that in which the nature of each single thing is considered to the end that nothing may be done in life contrary to nature but rather that everything be assigned to those uses intended by the Creator in bringing it into being. The study called "inspective" is that by which we go beyond things seen and contemplate something of the heavenly and the divine, looking upon them with the mind alone, for they are beyond the range of bodily sight. (Origen, *Commentary on the Song of Songs*, Prologue)

The nature of these studies becomes clearer when Origen links them with what were to be the texts in a Christian version of an academic curriculum, namely, the three biblical books ascribed to Solomon: Proverbs, Qohelet or Ecclesiastes, and the Song of Songs.

So as to distinguish each of these three branches of learning from the other, that is, the moral, the natural and the inspective, and to differentiate among them, Solomon issued them in three books, arranged in the proper order. First, in Proverbs, he taught the moral science, casting the rules for living into the form of brief and pithy maxims, as was appropriate. Second, he covered the science known as natural in Ecclesiastes. There he discussed at length the things of nature, and by distinguishing the useless and vain from the profitable and the essential, he counsels us to forsake vanity and to cultivate useful and upright things. Similarly, the inspective science he has explained in this little book now before us, that is, the Song of Songs. In it he instills into the soul the love of things divine and heavenly, using to this end the figures of the Bride and the Bridegroom, and he teaches us that communion with God must be attained by the paths of charity and love.

If then a man has completed his course in the first subject, as it is taught in Proverbs, by emending his behavior and keeping the commandments, and then, once he has seen how empty the world is and realized how brittle are transitory things, he renounces the world and all that is in it, he will proceed from that point to contemplate and desire the things that are not seen and are eternal. But to attain these, we need God's mercy, so that, once having beheld the beauty of the Word of God, we may be kindled with a saving love for Him, and He Himself may deign to love the soul whose longings for Himself He has discerned. (Ibid., Prologue)

This state cannot be achieved, of course—and here the voices of the Platonist and the Christian mingle in harmony—until after death, when the intellect is finally freed of the carnal weight of the body and the earthbound soul.

And so the rational being, growing at each successive stage, not indeed as it grew in this life, in the flesh or body and in the soul, but rather increasing in mind and intellect, advances as a mind already perfect to a perfect knowledge, now no longer hindered by its former carnal senses, but developing in intellectual power, ever more closely approaches the pure and it gazes "face to face," so to speak, on the causes of things. (Origen, *On First Principles* 2.11.7)

15. Moses Enters the Darkness

What once seemed fitting and natural to Origen no longer seemed so to Christians a century later. The attraction of the emanationist theory of creation and the figure of the ladder had induced some to follow a certain Arius and place the person of Jesus a step or grade below the Father. The reaction against the Arians—and at the Council of Nicea in 325 C.E. this reaction was constituted Christian orthodoxy—was to insist once again, as Genesis itself seemed to insist, on an absolute creation of the universe from nothing: God—Father, Son, and Holy Spirit—stood on one side of what was now the great divide of being, all of creation on the other.

There would appear to be no hope of approaching God across that great abyss, none save that provided by the example of Moses on Sinai. Here the Christian Gregory of Nyssa (ca. 335–394 C.E.) follows Moses up Sinai. In the first, lighted stages of the ascent he walks step by step with Origen. Although Gregory speaks of Moses and Exodus, he is here commenting on what Origen taught the Christians should be the mystics' biblical vade mecum, the Song of Songs.

Moses' vision of God began with light; afterwards God spoke to him in a cloud. But when Moses rose higher and became more perfect, he saw God in the darkness. Now the doctrine we are taught here is as follows. Our initial withdrawal from wrong and erroneous ideas of God is a transition from darkness to light. Next comes a closer awareness of hidden things, and by this the soul is guided through sense phenomena to the world of the invisible. And this awareness is a kind of cloud, which overshadows all appearances, and slowly guides and accustoms the soul to look toward what is hidden. Next, the soul makes progress through all these stages and goes on higher, and as she leaves below all that human knowledge can attain, she enters within the secret chamber of the divine knowledge, and here she is cut off on all sides by the divine darkness. Now she leaves outside all that can be grasped by sense or by reason, and the only thing left for her contemplation is the invisible and the incomprehensible. And here God is, as the Scriptures tell us in connection with Moses: "But Moses went into the dark cloud wherein God was" (Exod. 20:21). (Gregory of Nyssa, *Commentary on the Song of Songs* 11)

Moses, then, is the type of the believer who crossed the abyss, who penetrated into that profound "otherness" that characterizes the divine and is hereafter represented in the Christian tradition by the figure of impenetrable darkness or a dense cloud. Gregory of Nyssa spoke of that darkness at length, and many of his thoughts on it are found in his Life of Moses. *Here he reflects on Moses' entry into the cloud on the summit of Sinai, as described in Exodus 24.*

What now is the meaning of Moses' entry into the darkness and the vision of God that he enjoyed in it? . . . The sacred text is here teaching us that . . . as the soul makes progress, and by a greater and more perfect concentration comes to appreciate what the knowledge of truth is, the more it approaches this vision, and so much the more does it see that the divine nature is invisible. It thus leaves all surface appearances, not only those that can be grasped by the senses but also those which the mind itself seems to see, and it keeps on going deeper until by the operation of the spirit it penetrates the invisible and the incomprehensible, and it is there that it sees God. The true vision and the true knowledge of what we seek consists precisely in not seeing, in an awareness that our knowledge transcends all knowledge and is everywhere cut off from us by the darkness of incomprehensibility. Thus that profound evangelist, John, who penetrated into this luminous darkness, tell us that "no man has seen God at any time," teaching us by this negation that no man—indeed, no created intellect—can attain a knowledge of God.

We can conceive of no limitation in an infinite nature, and that which is without limit cannot by its nature be understood. And so every desire for the Beautiful which draws us on in this ascent is intensified by the soul's very progress toward it. And this is the real meaning of seeing God: never to have this desire satisfied. By fixing our eyes on those things which help us to see, we must ever keep alive in us the desire to see more and more. And so no limit can be set on our progress toward God: first of all, because no limitation can be put upon the beautiful, and secondly, because the increase of our desire for the beautiful cannot be stopped by any sense of satisfaction. (Gregory of Nyssa, *Life of Moses* 2)

The figure is biblical, of course; and if the ethical and intellectual theory is still Platonic, the easy optimism of Plato, and of Origen, is gone. Aspiration has been converted into a series of paradoxes—the vision that consists in not seeing, a knowledge that transcends knowledge. These sentiments are the product of something new, a later and less confident Platonism perhaps, a Platonism at the same time more esoteric and more religious than that which Philo and even Origen knew, a Platonism tempered in its Christian form by the lessons learned from the Arian heresy condemned at Nicea. And it was profoundly to shape not so much the Christian experience of God as the understanding of the mode and meaning of that experience.

16. The Negative Theology of Dionysius the Areopagite

The classic exposition of later Platonic mysticism in Christian raiment is found in a series of works attributed to a certain Dionysius the Areopagite, one of Paul's converts mentioned in passing in Acts 17:34. In fact, he had nothing to do with the body of works circulating under his name; they were, as far as we can tell, an anonymous product of the early decades of the sixth Christian century. The essential themes of that system appear early in the tract entitled The Mystical Theology.

. . . As you look for a sight of the mysterious things, leave behind you everything perceived and understood, everything perceptible and understandable, all that is not and all that is, and, with your understanding laid aside, strive upward as much as you can toward union with Him who is beyond all being and knowledge. By an undivided and absolute abandonment of yourself and everything, shedding all and freed from all, you will be uplifted to the ray of the divine shadow which is above everything that is.

Equally characteristic is the emphasis on the esoteric nature of the mystic's knowledge. "Dionysius" is no more eager than his rabbinic contemporaries in the Talmud that this kind of speculation fall into the hands of the uninitiated.

See to it that none of this comes to the hearing of the uninformed, that is to say, to those caught up with the things of the world, who imagine that there is nothing beyond instances of individual being and who think by their own intellectual resources they can have a direct knowledge of Him who has made the shadow His hiding place. And if initiation into the divine is beyond such people, what is to be said of those others, still more uninformed, who describe the transcendent cause of all things in terms derived from the lowest order of being. . . . What has actually to be said about the cause of everything is this. We should posit and ascribe to it all the affirmations we make in regard to beings, and, more appropriately, we should negate all those affirmations, since it surpasses all being. Now we should not conclude that the negations are simply the opposites of the affirmations, but rather that the cause of all is considerably prior to this, beyond privations, beyond every denial, beyond every assertion.

This, at least, is what was taught by the Blessed Bartholomew. He says that the Word of God is vast and minuscule, that the Gospel is wide-ranging yet restricted. To me it seems that in this he is extraordinarily shrewd, for he has grasped that the good cause of all is both eloquent and taciturn, indeed wordless. It has neither word nor act of understanding, since it is on a plane above all this, and it is made manifest only to those who travel through foul and fair, who pass beyond the summit of every holy ascent, who leave behind them every divine light, every voice, every word from heaven, and who plunge into the darkness where, as Scripture proclaims, there dwells the One who is beyond all things.

The author now stands at the outer limit of paradox, and he is forced to resort more and more often to new and unusual compounds in hyper- ("super-" or "trans-") to express what he wants to but cannot say about God.

I pray we could come to this darkness so far above the light! If only we lacked sight and knowledge so as to see, so as to know, unseeing and unknowing, that which lies above all vision and knowledge. For this would be really to see and to know: to praise the Transcendent One in a transcending way, namely through the denial of all beings. We would be like sculptors who set out to carve a statue. They remove every obstacle to the pure view of the hidden image, and simply in this act of clearing aside they show up the beauty which is hidden.

Now it seem to me that we should praise the denials (concerning the First Cause) quite differently than we do the assertions. When we made assertions we began with the first things, moved down through the intermediate terms until we reached the last things. But now as we climb from the last things up to the most primary, we deny all things so that we may unhiddenly know that unknowing which is itself hidden from all those possessed of knowing amid all beings, so that we may see above being that darkness concealed from all the light among beings.

The figure of the sculptor abstracting, "clearing aside" to reveal the form inherent in the marble brings the author to a discussion of the "negative theology" that was to prove so useful in so many subsequent Christian explorations of mystical theology.

When we assert what is beyond every assertion, we must then proceed from what is most akin to it. . . . But when we deny that which is beyond every denial, we have to start by denying those qualities which differ most from the goal we hope to attain. . . . So this is what we say. The Cause of all is above all and is not inexistent, lifeless, speechless, mindless. It is not a material body, and hence has neither shape, nor form, quality, quantity, or weight. It is not in any place and can be neither seen nor touched. It is neither perceived, nor is it perceptible. . . . Again, as we climb higher we say this. It is not soul or mind, nor does it possess imagination, conviction, speech or understading. . . . It does not live nor is it life. It is not a substance nor is it eternity or time. . . . It falls within the predicate neither of non-being nor of being. . . . It is beyond assertion and denial. We make assertions and denials of what is next to it, but never of it, for it is both beyond every assertion, being the perfect and unique cause of all things, and, by virtue of its pre-eminently simple and absolute nature, free of every limitation, beyond every limitation; as it is also beyond every denial. (Dionysius the Areopagite, *Mystical Theology* 997b–1048b) [(PSEUDO)-DIONYSIUS 1987: 135–141]

17. God Experienced, East and West

The theology of "Dionysius the Areopagite" is, like most theological analyses, highly abstract, while the mystical experience is by its nature an intensely personal one. Here two Christians, one from Eastern Christendom, the other from the beginning of the European Middle Ages, attempt to describe it. The account of Symeon, the so-called "New Theologian" (949–1022 C.E.) who is closely linked with the Dionysian tradition in the Eastern Church, is here reported through one of his students.

As Symeon was praying one night, and his purified mind was thus united with the First Intelligence, he experienced a brilliant light coming from above, pure and great and casting its radiance over all, as bright indeed as the light of the day itself. He too was illumined by it, and it appeared to him as if the entire building, and his own cell within it, had all been annihilated in the merest instant. He was borne aloft into the air, forgetful of his own body, and in this condition—as he later told and wrote to his close associates, he experienced both happiness and scalding tears. He was lost in wonder at this extraordinary event, since he had never had such an experience before, was both filled with great happiness and overcome with hot tears. Amazed by the strangeness of this marvelous happening—for he had as yet no similar revelations—he cried out repeatedly, "Lord, have mercy on me." He was aware of this only after he returned to his normal state since at the time he was unaware that he was speaking or that his words were audible outside his cell. It was likewise during this state of illumination that the grace of (spiritual) sight was bestowed upon him, and a great a brilliant cloud, without form but suffused with the nameless presence of God, appeared to him. To the right of this cloud there appeared to him his (deceased) spiritual father, Symeon of Studium, standing erect and wearing his customary habit.

Symeon stared fixedly at the divine light and prayed without distraction, but since he had been in this ecstatic state for some time, he was unaware of whether he had left his own body or whether he was still within it, as he later told us. At length the great light began gradually to draw away and Symeon once more found himself conscious of his body and his cell. . . . Such is the effect of purity of heart and so great the operation of divine love in virtuous souls. (Nicetas Stethatus, *Life of Symeon the New Theologian*)

An equally circumstantial description is given to monastic brethren by Bernard of Clairvaux (1090–1153 C.E.), who had begun his career as a Cistercian in 1112 C.E.

Bear awhile with my foolishness. I would tell you, as indeed I promised, how it is with me in these matters. I confess, then, that the Word has come to me—I speak as a fool—and has come many times. Yet though He has often come in unto me, I never perceived the moment of His coming; I have perceived Him present, I remember he has been present; sometimes I have actually been able to have a premonition of His entry, but never to be aware of it when it happens, nor of His going out from me. For whence He came into my soul, and whither He went when He left it again, by what way He came in or went out, even now I confess I do not know. . . .

Certainly it was not by the eyes that He entered, for He has no color; nor by the ears, for He made no sound; nor by the nostrils, for He blends not with the air but with the soul; nor did He make the air fragrant—He *made* it. Nor again did He enter through the mouth, for He is not to be eaten or drunk; nor could He be discerned by touch, for He is impalpable. By what way then did He enter? Can it be that He did not enter at all because He did not come from outside? For He is not one of the things that is without. Yet again, He did not come from within me, for He is good and I know that "no good thing dwells within me."

I have gone up to the highest point in my powers, and behold, the Word was towering yet higher. My curiosity took me to my lowest depth to look for Him, nevertheless He was found still deeper. If I looked outside of me, I found He was beyond my farthest reach; if I looked within, He was more inward still. . . .

You ask, then, since His ways are thus beyond all searching out, how did I know the Word was present? Because He is living, and powerful to act and to do; and as soon as He came within He roused my sleeping soul. He stirred and softened and wounded my heart, for it was dry and stony and poor in health. He began, too, to pluck out and to destroy, to build up and to plant, to water the dry places, to lighten the dark corners, to throw open the closed doors, to enkindle the chilled regions, "to make the crooked straight and the rough places plain," so that "my soul blessed the Lord, and all that was within me praised His holy Name." So then the Word, the Bridegroom, though several times He has come unto me, had never made known His entry by any signs or tokens, either by voice or by sight or by step. In fine, it was by no movements of His that He became known to me, nor could I tell by any senses of mine that He had passed into my inmost parts; only by the movement of my heart, as I said at the outset, did I recognize His presence; and by the flight of all vices from me, and by the suppression of all carnal desires, I was aware of the power of His might; and from the discovery and conviction of my secret faults I came to wonder at the depth of His wisdom; and from the amendment, small though it was, of my life and conversation I learned of His goodwill and loving kindness; and through the renewing and refashioning of the spirit of my mind, that is, my inner man, I perceived in some measure His excellent beauty; and from gazing on all these things together, I was filled with awe at His abundant greatness. (Bernard of Clairvaux, *Sermons on the Song of Songs* 74:5–6)

18. Conjugal and Other Loves

Christian mystics of the Latin West took to heart Origen's advice to make the biblical Song of Songs—a rhapsody of conjugal, indeed of sexual, love—their guide to the spiritual life. Thus the mystics' quest for God is often expressed in terms of love of bridegroom and bride, as in Bernard of Clairvaux's meditation on the Song of Songs.

It is this conformity [that is, of the mystic with Jesus, the Word of God] that brings about the marriage of the soul with the Word, when the soul, which is already like Him in nature, shows itself like Him also in will, loving as itself is loved. Thus, if it loves so perfectly, it is wedded to Him. Is there anything more joyful than this conformity? Is there anything more to be desired than charity, charity which makes you, O soul, no longer content with human instruction, go forward on your own with full confidence to approach the Word, to cleave steadfastly to the Word, to address your questions to Him as a friend, to ask His counsel on every matter, as receptive in your intelligence as you are fearless in your desire? This is the marriage contract of a truly spiritual and holy union. No, contract is too weak a description; it is an embrace. . . .

The Bridegroom is not only loving, He is love. . . . God demands to be feared as Lord; to be honored as Father; as Bridegroom to be loved. Which of these is the highest, which the noblest? Love, we cannot doubt. Without love fear torments and honor has no grace. Fear remains servile because love does not set it free; and honor which does not flow from love is not real honor but mere flattery. Truly, honor and glory are due to God alone; but God will not accept either unless they are sweetened

with the honey of love. Love is sufficient of itself, pleasant of and for itself.
Love is a merit and love is its own reward. Love seeks neither cause nor
outcome outside itself; the outcome is identical with the practice of it. I
love because I love; I love that I may love. . . . Of all the movements of
the soul, of all its feelings and affects, it is by love alone that the creator
responds to its Creator, though in less than equal measure, and pays Him
back something of what it has received. . . .

Love then is the great reality; but there are degrees of love, and
highest of all is the love of the bride. Children love their fathers, but they
are thinking of the inheritance they expect to get. . . . I am suspicious of
that love which I see is animated by the hope of getting something. It is
weak. . . . It is impure. . . . Pure love is not mercenary. Pure love does not
draw its strength from hope, nor is it injured by distrust. This is the love
the bride has; for all and everything she has is this: all her being, all her
hope is love and love alone. The bride overflows with love, and the
Bridegroom is content therein. He seeks nothing else from her; she has
nothing else to give. It is this which makes Him the Bridegroom, her the
bride. This is the love that belongs only to those who are joined in marriage, the love which none other but the bride, not even a son, can attain.

Rightly then does the bride renounce all other affections and give
herself up wholly to love and to love alone, for she is able to make some
return to love by loving him back again. For when she has poured her self
forth in love, how little this is when compared with that fountain which
flows in a never failing stream! Truly, they do not flow in equal volume,
the lover and Love Himself, the soul and the Word, the bride and the
Bridegroom, the Creator and the creature: it is as though we were to
compare a thirsty man with the spring he drinks from. (Bernard, *Homilies
on the Song of Songs* 83:3–6)

*Elsewhere, in Bernard's analysis of the progressive types of love, there can be little
doubt that in the fourth and highest stage he is speaking of the mystic's, and his
own, personal experience.*

Happy is the one who has deserved to gain the fourth stage, where
a man does not love even himself except for the sake of God. Your justice,
O Lord, is like the mountains of God. This love is a mountain, and a high
mountain. . . . Who shall ascend into the mountain of the Lord? . . .
When will the mind experience such an affection as this so that, inebri-
ated with divine love, forgetful of self, and having become in its own eyes
like a shattered vessel, the whole of it may continue on to God and, being
joined to God, become one spirit with Him. . . .

Blessed and holy, I would say, is he to whom it has been granted to experience such a thing in this mortal life at rare intervals, or even once, and this suddenly and scarcely for the space of a single moment. In a certain manner to lose yourself as though you were not, and to be utterly unconscious of yourself and be emptied of yourself, and, as it were, brought to nothing, this, I say, belongs to heavenly intercourse and not human affection. And if indeed, a mortal is suddenly from time to time, as has been said, even for the space of a moment admitted to this, straightway the wicked world grows envious, the evil of the day throws everything into confusion, the body of death becomes a burden, the necessity of the flesh causes unrest, the fainting away of corruption offers no support; and what is more vehement than these, fraternal charity recalls one. Alas, he is forced to return to himself, to fall back upon his own, and in his wretchedness to cry out, "Unhappy man that I am, who shall deliver me from the body of this death?"

. . . O love, holy and chaste! O sweet and pleasing affection! O pure and undefiled intention of the will! The more surely undefiled and purer, as there is now mixed with it nothing of its own; so much the sweeter and more pleasing, as its every feeling is wholly divine. To be thus affected is to become one with God. Just as a little drop of water mixed with a lot of wine seems entirely to lose its own identity, while it takes on the taste and the color of the wine; just as iron, heated and glowing, looks very much like fire, having divested itself of its original and characteristic appearance; and just as air flooded with the light of the sun is transformed into the same splendor of light that it appears not so much lighted as to be light itself; so it will inevitably happen that in saints every human affection will in some ineffable manner melt away from self and will be entirely transfused in the will of God—be all in all, if in man there is left anything at all of man himself. The substance indeed will remain, but in another form, another glory, and another power. (Bernard of Clairvaux, *On the Love of Good* 10)

The love imagery drawn from the Song of Songs and elaborated by Bernard of Clairvaux occurs again and again in the writings of Christian mystics of the West. But occasionally the theme and image of love take other turns, as in this early-fifteenth-century meditation by Dame Julian of Norwich.

Jesus Christ that doeth good against evil is our Very Mother: we have our Being of Him—where the ground of Motherhood beginneth—with all sweet Keeping of Love that endlessly followeth. As verily as God is our Father, so verily God is our Mother; and that shewed He in all, and especially in those sweet words where He saith: I it am. That is to say, I it am, the Might and Goodness of the Fatherhood; I it am, the Wisdom of the Motherhood; I it am, the Light and the Grace that is all blessed Love; I it am, the Trinity. . . .

In these three is all our life: Nature, Mercy, Grace: whereof we have meekness and mildness; patience and pity; and hating of sin and of wickedness. And thus is Jesus our Very Mother in Nature by virtue of our first making. And He is our Very Mother in Grace, by taking on our nature made. All the fair working, and all the sweet natural office of dearworthy Motherhood is impropriated to the Second Person. . . . I understand three manners of beholding Motherhood in God: the first is grounded in our Nature's making; the second is tasking of our nature—and there beginneth the Motherhood of Grace; the third is the Motherhood of working—and therein is a forth-spreading by the same Grace, of length and breadth and height and of deepness without end. And all is one Love. (Julian of Norwich, *Revelations of Divine Love* 59)

The theme of the mystic's love of God appears early and urgently in Islam in the prayers of Rabiʿa (d. 801 C.E.), the Baghdad mystic who replied, when her hand was sought in marriage:

The contract of marriage is for those who lead a phenomenal existence. But in my case, there is no such existence, for I have ceased to exist and have passed out of self. I exist in God and I am altogether His. I live in the shadow of his command. The marriage contract must be asked of Him, not from me. (Attar, *Recollections of the Saints* 1:66)

[Cited by SMITH 1931: 186]

Rabiʿa was also the author of one the most famous poems in all Sufi literature, a brief meditation on the love of God.

I have loved you with two loves, a selfish love and a love that is worthy of You.

As for the love which is selfish, therein I occupy myself with You, to the exclusion of all others.

But in the love which is worthy of You, You raise the veil that I may
see You.

Yet is the praise not mine in this love or that,

But the praise is Yours in both that love and this.

(Rabiʿa)   [Cited by SMITH 1931: 223]

The golden age of Sufism produced, this elegant little parable of mystic love from the pen of the Persian poet Attar, written in 1177 C.E.

A girl fell in a river—in a flash
Her lover dived in with a mighty splash,
And fought the current till he reached her side.
When they were safe again, the poor girl cried:
"By chance I tumbled in, but why should you
Come in after me and hazard your life too?"
He said: "I dived because the difference
of 'I' and 'you' to lovers makes no sense—
A long time passed when we were separate,
And now that we have reached this single state
When you are me and I am wholly you,
What use is it to talk of us as two?"
All talk of two implies plurality—
When two has gone there will be Unity.
(Attar, *The Conference of the Birds*) [ATTAR 1984: 194]

The tone of Attar's poetic parable is romantic but sober, and unmistakably hetero-sexual. It by no means exhausted the Sufis' emotional repertoire on the subject, however. The most famous of the Muslim poets of mystic love wrote much of his best work in the grip of an extraordinary passion for a fellow Sufi. Indeed, the love of Jalal al-Din Rumi (1207–1273 C.E.) for Shams al-Din Tabrizi was so all-consum-ing that in the end Rumi's son and disciples murdered the beloved Shams al-Din and told the master that he had simply disappeared. But not from Rumi's heart: the presence of Shams al-Din haunts the epic of love that is called the Mathnawi. *It opens with these lines.*

Hearken to this reed forlorn,
Breathing, ever since 'twas torn
From its rushy bed, a strain
Of impassioned love and pain.

The secret of my song, though near,
None can see and none can hear.
Oh, for a friend to know the sign
And mingle all his soul with mine!

'Tis the flame of Love that fired me,
'Tis the wine of Love inspired me.
Wouldst thou learn how lovers bleed,
Hearken, hearken to the Reed!
(Rumi, *Mathnawi*, Prologue) [Cited by ARBERRY 1950: 111]

And in these celebrated lines on human and divine love:

A certain man knocked at a friend's door: his friend asked:
> "Who is there?"

He answered: "I." "Begone," said his friend, "tis too soon!
> At my table there is no place for the raw.

How shall the raw be cooked but in the fire of absence? What else
> will deliver him from hypocrisy?"

He turned sadly away, and for a whole year the flames
> of separation consumed him;

Then he came back and again paced to and fro beside the house
> of his friend.

He knocked at the door with a hundred fears and reverence lest any
> disrespectful word might escape from his lips

"Who is there?" cried the friend. He answered: "Thou, O charmer
> of all hearts."

"Now," said the friend, "since thou art I, come in, there is no room
> for two I's in this house."

(Rumi, *Mathnawi*) [RUMI 1925–1940: 1:3056–3064]

19. The Spiritual Light

The path to God's presence traced by Gregory of Nyssa and "Dionysius," namely, the one that led into the realm of ineffable darkness that was the abode of the divine, continued to have its devotees in both the Eastern and the Western branch of Christendom. In the end, however, the Eastern Church came to prefer another way, that of God as Light. It is already clearly expressed in the fourth- or fifth-century Homilies *attributed to the Egyptian desert master Macarius.*

The soul which has been perfectly illuminated by the ineffable beauty of the glory of the light of the face of Christ, has achieved perfect participation in the Holy Spirit and has become worthy to be an abode and throne of God, that soul becomes wholly eye and wholly face and wholly Spirit, being so made by Christ who drives and guides and carries it about, and graces and adorns it with spiritual beauty. (Macarius, *Homilies* 1:2)

And if Moses on Sinai is the type of the mystic entering the cloud of unknowing, Jesus transfigured on that other mountain called Tabor in Galilee provides the most powerful image for the mysticism of light.

As the body of the Lord was glorified when he went up into the mountain, and was transfigured into the divine glory and into the infinite light, so are the bodies of the saints glorified and shine like lightning. The glory that was within Christ was spread out upon his body and shone forth there, and likewise the power of Christ in the saints shall on that day be poured outwardly upon their bodies. (Ibid. 15:38)

"That day" was for the author the day of the Last Judgment, but for later mystics the transfiguration could be achieved in this life in the mystic's transport. So it was in the tenth century for Symeon, the "New Theologian," whose Discourses gave the Byzantine Church a clear and highly personal understanding of what had by then come to be the single most powerful characterization of the mystic's encounter with God: to stand in the presence of God was to be bathed in and suffused with an ineffable immaterial light. Symeon, here referring to himself in the third person, informs the reader that he first had this experience while still living as a layman in Constantinople, though he was already well embarked upon a personal conversion.

During the day he managed a patrician's household and daily went to the palace, engaged in worldly affairs, so that no one was aware of his pursuits. Every evening tears welled from his eyes; more and more frequently he prostrated himself with his face to the ground, with his feet together, without moving from the spot where he stood. With all diligence he recited prayers to the Mother of God accompanied with groans and tears. . . . So as his prayer grew longer every evening he continued until midnight. Not a member of his body moved, his eye did not turn or look up, but he stood motionless as though he were a statue or an incorporeal spirit.

One day, as he stood and recited, "God have mercy upon me, a sinner," uttering it with his mind rather than his mouth, suddenly a flood of divine radiance appeared from above and filled all the room. As this happened he lost all awareness (of his surroundings) and forgot that he was in a house or that he was under a roof. He saw nothing but light all round him and did not know if he was standing on the ground. He was not afraid of falling; he was not concerned with the world, nor did anything pertaining to men and corporeal beings enter into his mind. Instead, he was wholly in the presence of immaterial light and seemed to himself to have turned into light. Oblivious of all the world, he was filled with tears and with ineffable joy and gladness. His mind then ascended to heaven and beheld yet another light, which was clearer than that which was close at hand. (Symeon, *Discourses* 22:3–4)
[SYMEON NEOTHEOLOGUS 1980: 245–246]

He describes, now in the first person, how it happened again not long after he had taken up the life of the monk.

I entered the place where I usually prayed and . . . I began to say "Holy God." At once I was so greatly moved to tears and loving desire of God that I would be unable to describe in words the joy and delight I then felt. I fell prostrate on the ground, and at once I saw, and behold, a great light was immaterially shining on me and seized hold of my mind and soul, so that I was struck with amazement at the unexpected marvel, and I was, as it were, in ecstasy. Moreover, I forgot the place where I stood, who I was, and where, and could only cry out, "Lord, have mercy," so that when I came to myself I discovered I was reciting this. . . . Who it was that was speaking, or who moved my tongue, I do not know—only God knows.

"Whether I was in the body or outside the body" (2 Cor. 12:2–3), I conversed with the light. The Light itself knows it; it scattered whatever mist there was in my soul and cast out every earthly care. It expelled from me all material denseness and bodily heaviness that made my members sluggish and numb. What an awesome marvel! It so invigorated and strengthened my limbs and muscles, which had been faint through great weariness, that it seemed to me as though I was stripping myself of the garment of corruption. Besides, there poured into my soul in unutterable fashion a great spiritual joy and perception and a sweetness surpassing all taste of visible objects, together with a freedom and forgetfulness of all thoughts pertaining to this life. In a marvelous way there was granted to me and revealed to me the manner of the departure from this present life. Thus all the perceptions of my mind and soul were wholly concentrated on the ineffable joy of the Light.

. . . When it [that is, the Light] appears, it fills one with joy, when it vanishes it wounds. It happens close to me and carries me up to heaven. It is a pearl (of great price) (Matt. 13:46). The light envelops me and appears to me like a star, and it is incomprehensible to all. It is radiant like the sun, and I perceive all creation encompassed by it. It shows me all that it contains, and enjoins me to respect my own limits. I am hemmed in by roof and walls, yet it opens the heavens to me. I lift up my eyes sensibly to contemplate the things that are on high, and I see all things as they were before.

The experience is over, but not the instruction.

I marvel at what has happened and I hear a voice speaking to me secretly from on high. "These things are but symbols and preliminaries, for you will not see that which is perfect as long as you are clothed in flesh. But return to yourself and see that you do nothing that deprives you of the things that are above. Should you fall, however, it is to recall you to humility! Do not cease to cultivate penitence, for when it is united with My love for mankind it blots out past and present failures." (Symeon, *Discourses* 16:3–5) [SYMEON NEOTHEOLOGUS 1980: 200–202]

Stepping back a bit from the immediacy of the event, Symeon explains that, for the believer who experiences it, this is nothing less than a kind of deification.

Let no one deceive you. God is light (1 John 1:5), and to those who have entered into union with him He imparts of His own brightness to the extent that they have been purified. When the lamp of the soul, that is, the mind, has been kindled, then it knows that a divine fire has taken hold of it and inflamed it. How great a marvel! Man is united to God spiritually and physically, since the soul is not separated from the mind, neither the body from the soul. By being united in essence man also [that is, like God] has three hypostases. He is a single god by adoption with body and soul and the divine Spirit, of whom he has become a partaker. . . . How He abides in us and how we in turn abide in Him, the Lord Himself taught us when He said, "You, Father, are in Me and I in You" (John 17:21) and "they are in Me and I in them" (John 17:23). (Symeon, *Discourses* 15:3) [SYMEON NEOTHEOLOGUS 1980: 195]

20. Jesus, the Eucharist, and the Transfiguration

Since the Son of God, in His incomparable love for man, not only united His divine hypostasis with our nature, by clothing Himself in a living body and a soul gifted with intelligence, but also united Himself . . . with the human hypostases themselves, in mingling Himself with each of the faithful by communion with His Holy Body, and since He becomes one single body with us (Eph. 3:6), and makes us a temple of the undivided Divinity, for in the very body of Christ dwells the fullness of the Godhead bodily (Col. 2:9), how should He not illuminate those who commune worthily with the divine ray of His Body, which is within us, lighting their souls, as He illumined the bodies of the disciples on Mount Tabor? For on the day of the Transfiguration, that Body, source of the light of grace, was not yet united with our bodies; it illuminated from the outside those who worthily approached it, and sent the illumination into the soul by the intermediary of the physical eyes; but now, since it is mingled with us and exists in us, it illuminates the soul from within. (Gregory Palamas, *The Triads* 1.3.38) [PALAMAS 1983: 19]

Thus, what was called by the Jews the Shekina, the Divine Presence, became for Eastern Christians the Divine Light, which "illuminates the soul from within." It is, as Palamas (1296–1359), the most influential mystical theologian of the Eastern Church, attempts to explain, neither a sensible light nor yet only a symbol.

The monks know that the essence of God transcends the fact of being inaccessible to the senses, since God is not only above all created things but is even beyond the Godhead. The excellence of Him who surpasses all things is not only beyond all affirmation but also beyond all negation, it exceeds all excellence that is attainable by the mind.

It is impossible to carry the Dionysian paradoxes much farther. Is God then totally unknowable? For an answer Palamas turns to the Divine Light, which he verifies from the experience of the saints:

This hypostatic light, seen spiritually by the saints, they know by experience to exist, as they tell us, and to exist not symbolically only, as do manifestations produced by fortuitous events, but it is an illumination immaterial and divine, a grace invisibly seen and ignorantly known. *What it is, they do not pretend to know.*

. . . This light is not the essence of God, for that is inaccessible and incommunicable; it is not an angel, for it bears the marks of the Master. Sometimes it makes a man go out from the body, it elevates him to an ineffable height. At other times it transforms the body, and communicates its own splendor to it when, miraculously, the light which deifies the body becomes accessible to the eyes of the body. Thus indeed did . . . Stephen (appear) when being stoned (Acts 6:15), and Moses, when he descended from the mountain (Exod. 34:29). Sometimes the light "speaks" clearly, as it were with ineffable words, to him who contemplates it. Such was the case with Paul (2 Cor. 12:4). According to Gregory the Theologian, "it descends from the elevated place where it dwells, so that He who in His own nature from eternity is neither visible nor containable by any being may in a certain measure be contained by a created nature. He who has received this light, by concentrating upon himself, constantly perceives in his mind that same reality which the children of the Jews called manna, the bread that came down from on high (Exod. 16:14 ff.)." (Gregory Palamas, *The Triads* 2.3.8–9) [PALAMAS 1983: 57–58]

21. The Lamp in the Niche

The scriptural accounts of Moses on Sinai and Jesus on Tabor served, when and where needed, as Jewish and Christian paradigms of the vision of God. The Muslim had no such straightforward narrative text in the Quran to certify Muhammad for the same purpose. The mystics of Islam turned instead for their inspiration to the famous "Light Verse."

> God is the Light of the heavens and the earth.
> The semblance of His Light is that of a niche
> in which is a lamp, the flame within the glass,
> the glass as it were a glittering star, lit with the oil
> of a blessed tree, the olive, neither of the East
> nor of the West, whose oil appears to light up
> even though fire touches it not—light upon light.
> God guides to His Light whom He will.
> So does God advance precepts [or "allegories"] for men,
> For God has knowledge of everything.
>
> (Quran 24:35)

The last sentence in the verse reads like an open invitation to allegorical exegesis, and so it was generally interpreted. One example is the work entitled The Pure in the Interpretation of the Quran, *by the Shiʿite scholar al-Kashi (d. 1505 C.E.). His interpretation, which is overtly Shiʿite in intent, goes back, as he tells us, to another, much earlier eminence in that tradition, Ibn Babuya al-Qummi (d. 939). Qummi's authorities are no less than the fifth and sixth Shiʿite Imams, Muhammad al-Baqir (d. 731) and Jaʿfar al-Sadiq (d. 756).*

In "The Oneness" (of al-Qummi) it is reported, on the authority of al-Sadiq: What is at question here is a simile that God has fashioned for us.

"God is the Light of the Heavens and the Earth": Just so, said al-Sadiq.

"His Light": al-Sadiq said: This refers to Muhammad.

"That of a niche": al-Sadiq said that what is meant here is Muhammad's breast.

"In which is a lamp": al-Sadiq said: In which is the light of knowledge, that is, of prophecy.

"The flame within the glass": al-Sadiq said: The knowledge of the Messenger of God went forth from the latter into the heart of Ali.

". . . neither of the East nor of the West": According to al-Sadiq these words refer to the Commander of the Believers, Ali ibn Abi Talib, who was neither a Jew nor a Christian.

"Whose oil appears to light up even though fire touches it not": al-Sadiq said: The knowledge would issue forth from the mouth of the knowing one of the family of Muhammad [that is, Ali] even if Muhammad had not spoken it.

"Light upon light": al-Sadiq said that this means from one Imam to the next.

Then Kashi turns to another Shi°ite commentator, al-Tabarsi (d. 1153 C.E.), for a somewhat more general interpretation of the same verse.

It is said . . . (by Tabarsi) from the Imam al-Baqir in a Tradition that the verse "God is the Light of the heavens and the earth" means: "I [that is, God] am the rightly guided director of the heavens and the earth. The knowledge that I have given, namely, My light through which the guidance results, 'is like a niche wherein is a lamp.' The niche is the heart of Muhammad, and the lamp is his light, wherein lies knowledge." Further, God's words "the flame in the glass" mean: "I [that is, God] want to lay hold of you and what is with you so that I might manifest the Executor [a standard Shi°ite designation for Ali] like the flame in the glass, 'as it were a glittering star.' Then will I give men news of the excellence of the Executor."

"Lit with the oil of a blessed tree": The root of that blessed tree is Abraham. This is referred to in God's words: "The mercy of God and His blessings be upon you, O people of the House. Surely he [that is, Abraham] is worthy of praise and glory" (Quran 11:76).

"That is neither of the East nor of the West" means: You are neither Jews, so that you would perform the prayer facing toward the west [that is, Jerusalem] nor Christians, so that you would face toward the east. Rather you follow the creed of Abraham, of whom God has said: "No, in truth Abraham was neither a Jew nor a Christian, but a *hanif* who had submitted to God. Certainly he was never one of the idolaters" (Quran 3:60). (Kashi, *The Pure, ad loc.*)

22. What Is the Mystic Way?

In Chapter 3 above we followed the jurist and theologian Ghazali (d. 1111 C.E.) on his voyage of discovery of Sufism as he described it in his Deliverer from Error. At the end of his quest, in attempting to define what he has found, he begins with a comparison with the ablution that purifies a Muslim for prayer.

In general, then, how is the mystic way described? The purifying which is the first condition of it is the purification of the heart completely from what is other than God Most High; the key to it, which corresponds to the opening act of adoration in prayer, is the sinking of the heart completely in the recollection of God; and the end of it is complete annihilation in God. At least this is its end relative to those first steps which almost come within the sphere of choice and personal responsibility; but in reality in the actual "way" it is the first step, what comes before it being, as it were, the antechamber for those who are journeying toward it.

With this first stage of the "way" there begin the revelations and visions. The mystics in their waking state now behold angels and the spirits of the prophets; they hear these speaking to them and are instructed by them. Later, as a higher stage is reached, instead of beholding forms and figures, they come to stages in the "way" which it is hard to describe in language; if a man attempts to express these, his words inevitably contain what is clearly erroneous.

In general what the mystics manage to attain is nearness to God; some, however, would conceive of this as "infusion," some as "union," and some as "identity" (with God). All that is erroneous. He who has attained the mystic state need do no more than say that "Of the things I do not remember, what was, was; think it good; do not ask an account of it." . . .

In general, the man to whom He has granted no immediate experience at all apprehends no more of what prophetic revelation really is than the name alone. The miraculous graces given to the saints are in truth the beginnings of the prophecy, and that was the first "state" of the Messenger of God, peace be upon him, when he went out to Mount Hira, and was given up entirely to his Lord, and worshiped Him so that the bedouin said, "He loves his Lord passionately."

Now this is a mystical "state" which is realized in immediate experience by those who walk in the way leading to it. Those to whom it is not granted to have the immediate experience can become assured of it by trial [that is, observation of Sufis] and by hearsay, if they have sufficiently numerous opportunities of associating with mystics to understand that [that is, the mystical experience] with certainty by means of what accompanies the states. Whoever sits in their company derives from them this faith; and no one who sits in their company is pained. (Ghazali, *Deliverer* 132–135) [GHAZALI 1953: 60–62]

Ibn Khaldun too attempts to explain the Sufi experience, though now not through the sensibilities of one who had himself traveled the path but from the perspective of the cultural historian.

Mystical exertion, retirement, and the recollection exercise are as a rule followed by the removal of the veil of sensual perception. The Sufi beholds divine worlds which a person subject to the senses cannot. The spirit belongs to those worlds. The reason for the removal of the veil is the following. When the spirit turns from external sense perception to inner perception, the senses weaken and the spirit grows strong. It gains predominance and a new growth. The recollection exercise helps to bring that about. It is like food to make the spirit grow. The spirit continues to grow. It had been knowledge; now it becomes vision. The veil of sensual perception is removed, and the soul realizes its essential existence. This is identical with perception. The spirit now is ready for the holy gifts, for the sciences of divine presence, and for the outpouring of the Deity. Its essence realizes its own true character and draws close to the highest sphere, the sphere of the angels.

The removal of the veil often happens to people who exert themselves in mystical exercise. They perceive the realities of existence as no one else does. They also perceive many future happenings in advance. With the help of their minds and psychic powers they are active among the lower existents, which thus become obedient to their will. The great Sufis do not think much of the removal of the veil and of activity among the lower existents. They give no information about the reality of anything they have not been ordered to discuss. They consider it a tribulation when things of that sort occur to them, and try to escape them whenever they afflict them.

By the "great Sufis" Ibn Khaldun means the earliest generation of Muslims, beginning with the men of Muhammad's own generation. Although they received abundant visitations of the divine grace, they paid little attention to such manifestations. The self-conscious pursuit of such experiences set in only at a later date, among more recent mystics.

Recent mystics have turned their attention to the removal of the veil and the discussion of perceptions beyond sensual perception. Their ways of mystical exercise in this respect differ. They have taught different methods of mortifying the sensual perception and nourishing the reasoning spirit with recollection exercises, so that the soul might fully grow and attain its own essential perception. When this happens they believe that the whole of existence is encompassed by the perceptions of the soul, that the essences of existence are revealed to them, and that they perceive the reality of all the essences from the divine throne to light rain. This was said by al-Ghazali in the Revivification, after he had mentioned the forms of spiritual exercises. . . .

The recent Sufis who have occupied themselves with this kind of removal of the veil talk about the real character of the higher and lower existents and about the real character of the kingdom, the spirit, the throne, the seat, and similar things. Those who did not share their approach were not able to understand their mystical and ecstatic experiences in this respect. The muftis partly approve of these Sufis and partly accept them. Arguments and proofs are of no use in deciding whether the Sufi approach should be rejected or accepted, since it belongs to intuitive experience. (Ibn Khaldun, *Muqaddima* 6.16) [IBN KHALDUN 1967: 3:81–83]

23. Junayd on Oneness of and with God

It is not always easy to understand where Ibn Khaldun is drawing his systematic line between the "earlier" and "later Sufis," but the Baghdad master Junayd (d. 910 C.E.) certainly falls in the very heart of the earlier category. He stands midway between the Sufi pioneer Muhasibi (d. 837) and his erstwhile disciple, the far more extreme Hallaj, executed at Baghdad in 922 C.E. Like Muhasibi and most of the other "sober" Sufis, Junayd was a skilled director of souls, as this brief analysis indicates.

There are three types of people: the man who seeks and searches, the man who reaches the door and stays there, and the man who enters and remains.

As for the man who seeks God, he goes toward Him guided by a knowledge of the religious precepts and duties (of Islam), concentrating on the performance of all external observances toward God. Regarding the man who reaches the doorway and stays there, he finds his way there by means of his internal purity, from which he derives his strength. He acts toward God with internal concentration. Finally, as for the man who enters into God's presence with his whole heart and remains before Him, he excludes the vision of anything other than God, noting God's every sign to him, and is ready for whatever his Lord may command. This readiness is characteristic of the man who recognizes the Oneness of God. (Junayd, *Treatises*) [JUNAYD 1962: 176]

This last perception of the "Oneness of God," an expression that in Arabic also does service as "Oneness with God," was for Junayd and his ninth-century Baghdad contemporaries both the touchstone and the climax of the mystical experience. It was not an easy notion either to grasp or to describe. Although Junayd defined the "Oneness of/with God" in typically aphoristic fashion as "the separation of the Eternal from the contingent"—a phrase not uncommonly offered by his successors as a definition of Sufism, or rather of mysticism purely and simply—he also addressed the central concept of Oneness in a somewhat fuller fashion.

Know that the first condition of the worship of God—may He be exalted and magnified—is the knowledge of God, and the basis of the knowledge of God is the recognition of His being One, and that His Oneness precludes the possibility of describing God in terms of responses to the questions "How?" or "Where?" or "When?" . . .

God's Oneness connotes belief in Him. From belief follows confirmation which in turn leads to knowledge of Him. Knowledge of Him implies obedience to His commands, obedience carries with it the ascent toward Him, which leads ultimately to reaching Him.

This apparent success in the mystical quest leads only to a further paradox, however.

When God is attained His manifestation can be expounded, but from His manifestation there also follows bewilderment which is so overwhelming that it inhibits the possibility of the exposition of God, and as a result of losing this manifestation of God the elected worshiper is unable to describe God. And there, when the worshiper is unable to describe God, he finds the true nature of his existing for God. And from this comes the vision of God, together with the loss of his individuality. And with the loss of his individuality he achieves absolute purity . . . he has lost his personal attributes: . . . he is wholly present in God . . . wholly lost to self.

But then there is an inevitable return to a more normal condition, though not without permanent alterations in spiritual temperament.

He is existent in both himself and in God after having been existent in God and non-existent in himself. This is because he has left the drunkenness of God's overwhelming presence and come to the clarity of sobriety. Contemplation is once again restored to him, so that he can put everything in its right place and assess it correctly. Once more he assumes his individual attributes, after the "obliteration" his personal qualities persist in him and in his actions in this world, when he has reached the height of spiritual perfection granted by God, he becomes a pattern for his fellow men. (Junayd, *Treatises*) [JUNAYD 1962: 171–172]

Know that this sense of the Oneness of God exists in people in four different ways. The first is the sense of Oneness possessed by ordinary people. Then there is the sense shared by those well versed in formal religious knowledge. The other two types are experienced by the elect who have esoteric knowledge. (Ibid.) [JUNAYD 1962: 176]

God's Oneness is in fact the cornerstone of Islam—every Muslim's profession of faith begins with the statement that "There is no god but the God"—and Junayd bases his analysis on its simple assertion.

As for the sense of Oneness possessed by ordinary people, it consists in the assertion of God's Oneness, in the disappearance of any notion of gods, opposites, equals or likenesses to God, but with the persistence of hopes and fears in forces other than God. This level of Oneness has a certain degree of efficacy since the simple assertion of God's Oneness does in fact persist.

As for the conception of Oneness shared by those who are well versed in religious knowledge, it consists not only in the assertion of God's Oneness, in the disappearance of any conception of gods, opposites, equals or likenesses to God, but also in the performance of the positive commands (of religion) and the avoidance of that which is forbidden, so far as external action is concerned, all of this being the result of their hopes, fears and desires. This level of Oneness likewise possesses a degree of efficacy since there is a public demonstration of the Oneness of God.

As for the first type of esoteric Oneness, it consists in the assertion of the Oneness of God, the disappearance of the conception of things referred to, combined with the performance of God's command externally and internally, and the removal of hopes and fears in forces other than God, all of this is the result of ideas that conform with the adept's awareness of God's presence with him, with God's call to him and his answer to God.

A second type of esoteric Oneness consists in existing without individuality before God with no intermediary between, becoming a figure over which His decrees pass in accordance with His omnipotence, a soul sunk in the flooding sea of His Oneness, all sense lost of himself, God's call to him and his response to God. It is a stage wherein the devotee has achieved a true realization of the Oneness of God in true nearness to Him. He is lost to both sense and action because God fulfills in him what He has willed of him. . . . His existence now is like it was before he had existence. This, then, is the highest stage of the true realization of the Oneness of God in which the worshiper who sustains this Oneness loses his own individuality. (Junayd, *Treatises*) [JUNAYD 1962: 176–178]

24. Self-Obliteration

Obliteration, the loss of one's personal or individual characteristics before God, is also the key to attaining that same state: It is both the method and the goal of the mystic's pursuit, as Ghazali explains in his great work of spiritual renewal, The Revivification of the Sciences of Religion.

Whoever looks upon the world only because it is God's work, and knows it because it is God's work, and loves it because it is God's work, does not look except to God and knows nothing except God, and loves naught except God—he is the true One-maker who does not see anything but God, indeed, he does not regard even himself for his own sake but because he is God's servant, and of such a person it is said that he is annihilated in Oneness and he is annihilated from himself. (Ghazali, *Revivification* 4:276)

According to Junayd, the first step on the path to self-annihilation consists in training the will.

The obliteration of attributes, characteristics and natural inclinations in your motives when you carry out your religious duties, making great efforts and doing the opposite of what you may desire, and compelling yourself to do the things which you do not wish to do.

Nor must asceticism be neglected.

The obliteration of your pursuit of pleasure and even the sensation of pleasure in obedience to God's commands; so that you are exclusively His, without intermediary means of contact.

Finally, the mystic achieves true obliteration, a complete loss of self-awareness, and with it, a higher level of existence.

The obliteration of the consciousness of having attained the vision of God at the final stage of ecstasy when God's victory over you is complete. At this stage you are obliterated and have eternal life with God, and you exist only in the existence of God because you have been obliterated. Your physical being continues but your individuality has departed. (Junayd, *Treatises*) [JUNAYD 1962: 81]

25. Oneness with God Is Not Identity with God

Sufi theoreticians on the one hand cut their definitions of annihilation of self and Oneness with God exceedingly fine; ecstatics on the other, the "drunken Sufis" who did not share Junayd's measured sobriety, followed whither their fevered experience and expressions led them. The result was, not unpredictably, a conservative reaction, or at least a degree of caution, and in the first instance on the part of certain Sufi masters themselves. One such was al-Sarraj (d. 988 C.E.), whose great systematic treatise on Sufism ends with a kind of syllabus of errors directed at Sufi theory and practice.

Some mystics of Baghdad have erred in their doctrine that, when they pass away from their qualities, they enter into the qualities of God. This involves "infusion" or leads to the Christian belief concerning Jesus. The doctrine in question has been attributed to some of the earlier (Muslim) mystics, but its true understanding is this: when a man goes forth from his own qualities and enters into the qualities of God, he goes forth from his own will, which is a gift to him from God, and enters into the Will of God, knowing that his will has been given to him by God, and that by virtue of this gift he can stop regarding himself and become entirely devoted to God. This is one of the stages of those who seek after Oneness. Those who have erred in this teaching are the ones who have failed to note that the qualities of God are not the same as God. To make God identical with His qualities is to be guilty of infidelity, because God does not descend into the heart but what does descend into the heart is faith in God and belief in His Oneness and reverence for the thought of him. (Sarraj, *The Splendor of Sufism* 432) [Cited in JUNAYD 1962: 84]

Some have abstained from food and drink because they fancy that, when a man's body is weakened, it is possible that he may lose his humanity and be invested with the attributes of divinity. The ignorant persons who hold this doctrine cannot distinguish between humanity and the innate qualities of humanity. Humanity does not depart from a man any more than blackness departs from that which is black or whiteness from that which is white, but the innate qualities of humanity are changed and transmuted by the all-powerful radiance that is shed upon them from the Divine Realities. The attributes of humanity are not the essence of humanity. Those who speak of the doctrine of obliteration mean the cessation of our regarding our own actions and works of devotion through continuously regarding God as the doer of those acts on behalf of His servants. (Ibid. 426) [Cited in JUNAYD 1962: 84–85]

26. "All That Matters for the Ecstatic Is That His Only One Bring Him to His Oneness"

We have already seen Ghazali's reflections on his spiritual career. But these are thoughts recollected and reshaped in tranquillity. Indeed, some Sufi lives may have been tranquil, but certainly not that of Islam's most notorious seeker after God, the Baghdad saint and mystic, Husayn ibn Mansur, surnamed al-Hallaj, "the carder," who was put to death, a martyr of esoteric Sufism, in 922 C.E. A brief memorial of his father's much troubled, peripatetic life was set down by Hallaj's son Hamd.

CHAPTER 4

My father, Husayn ibn Mansur, was born in Bayda (in Iran), in a place called al-Tur. He was brought up in Tustar, and for a period of two years he became the disciple of Sahl ibn Abdullah Tustari, after which he went to Baghdad. He walked around sometimes dressed in hairshirts, other times in two coats of dyed material, other times in a woolen robe with a turban, or in a greatcoat with sleeves, like a soldier.

He left Tustar first for Basra (in Iraq) and was eighteen years old at the time. Next he left dressed in two coats to see Amr al-Makki and Junayd and he lived near Amr for eighteen months. After that he married (in Basra) my mother Umm al-Husayn, daughter of Abu Ya'qub Aqta; but Amr al-Makki was unhappy about this marriage and a great quarrel flared up between Abu Ya'qub and Amr over this subject. My father went at that time alone to Junayd and told him how unbearable the crisis ... was making the situation in Baghdad. Junayd advised him to keep calm and to show them respect, which he did patiently for some time.

Next he left for Mecca and remained there a year on a pious visit. Afterwards he returned to Baghdad with a group of Sufi ascetics. He went to Junayd to pose a question, which the latter did not, however, answer, judging it to be motivated by the desire for a personal mission.

The break with Junayd, at this point or later, was more substantial, as we shall see. The account of Hallaj's son continues.

My father, hurt by this, returned, together with my mother, to Tustar, where he remained for nearly two years. And there he received such a warm personal welcome that all his (Sufi) contemporaries hated him, particularly Amr ibn Makki, who persisted in sending letters about him to eminent persons in Khuzistan in which he accused him of very grave errors. To such a degree and so effectively that my father put aside the religious garb of the Sufis, rejected it, and put on a sleeved coat, frequenting the company of worldly society.

He left Tustar after that and we saw no more of him for five years. During this time he traveled through Khurasan and Mawaranahr (in eastern Iran); from there he went (southward) into Sijistan and Kirman, and afterwards returned to (his home region of) Fars. He began to speak in public, to hold meetings, to preach God to the people. In Fars people knew him as "the ascetic" and he wrote several works for them. Then he went from Fars back to Ahwaz, and called for her who brought me into the world to come to him. He spoke in public and everyone, great and small, approved of him. He spoke to his listeners of their consciences, of what was in their hearts, which he unveiled for them. They called him "the carder of consciences," and the name "the carder" (*al-hallaj*), for short, stayed with him.

Next he left for Basra; he stayed there only a little while, leaving me in Ahwaz with his disciples. He went a second time to Mecca, dressed this time in a coat of rags and patches and an Indian cloak. Many people accompanied him on this journey, during which Abu Yaʿqub Nahrajuri, out of hatred, spread the charge against him (of being a magician) with which people are familiar.

Hallaj returns to Basra and then installs himself, with his family and a number of disciples, in Baghdad. But he does not rest there for long. He is soon off once again, this time to the "land of idolatry," India and Turkestan. And, his son adds, "the gossip about him increased after this journey."

He departed again after that and made a third pilgrimage, including a two-year spiritual retreat in Mecca. He returned this time very changed from what he had been before. He purchased property in Baghdad and built a house. He began to preach in public a doctrine only half of which which I understood. In the end (the lawyer) Muhammad Dawud rose against him, together with a whole group of *ulama*; and they took their accusations against his views to (the Caliph) al-Muʿtadid. . . . Some people said: he is a sorcerer. Others: he is a madman. Still others: he performs miracles and his prayer is granted (by God). And tongues wrangled over his case up to the moment when the government arrested and imprisoned him.

At that time (the Grand Chamberlain) Nasr Qushuri went to the Caliph, who authorized him to build my father a separate cell in prison. Then a little house was constructed for him adjoining the prison; the outside door to the building was walled up, the building itself was surrounded by a wall, and a door was made opening into the interior of the prison. For about a year he received visits from people there. Then that was forbidden him, and he went for five months without anyone being able to see him. . . . At that time I was spending my night with my maternal family outside, and staying during the day near my father. Then they imprisoned me with him for a period of two months. At that time I was eighteen years old.

And when the night came in which my father was to be taken, at dawn, from his cell (for execution), he stood up for the prayer, of which he performed one of two prostrations. Then, with this prayer completed, he continued repeating over and over again the word "illusion . . . illusion," until the night was almost over. Then for a long time he was silent, when suddenly he cried out "truth . . . truth." He stood up again, put on his head cloak and wrapped himself in his coat, extended his hands, turned toward the prayer-direction and went into ecstatic prayer. . . .

When the morning came, they led him from the prison, and I saw him walking proudly in his chains. . . . They led him then (to the esplanade) where they cut off his hands and feet, after having flogged him with 500 lashes of the whip. Then he was hoisted up onto the cross, and I heard him on the gibbet talking ecstatically with God: "O my God, here I am in the dwelling place of my desires, where I contemplate Your marvels. O my God, since You witness friendship even to whoever does You wrong, how is it You do not witness it to this one to whom wrong is done because of You?" . . .

At the time of the evening prayer, the authorization by the Caliph to decapitate Hallaj came. But it was declared: "It is too late; we shall put it off until tomorrow." When morning came, they took him down from the gibbet and dragged him forth to behead him. I heard him cry out then, saying in a very high voice: "All that matters for the ecstatic is that his Only One bring him to his Oneness." Then he recited this verse: "Those who do not believe in the Final Hour call for its coming; but those who believe in it await it with loving shyness, knowing that this will be (the coming of) God" (Quran 42:17). These were his last words.

His head was cut off, then his trunk was rolled up in a straw mat, doused with fuel and burned. Later his ashes were carried to Lighthouse Point (on the Tigris) to disperse them to the wind. [MASSIGNON 1982: 10–18]

27. "I Am the Truth"

Hallaj's son's account of his father's life and death makes no mention of his trial, which, as we have seen in Chapter 2, had to do with the examination of Hallaj's views on the pilgrimage. This apparent attack on Islamic ritual may indeed have merited Hallaj the death sentence in 922, but it was by no means his only, or perhaps even his most scandalous, view of Islamic religious teaching. What attracted even more attention in later generations was another remark let drop, in what appears to be utter simplicity, to Junayd.

It is related that Hallaj met Junayd one day, and said to him, "I am the Truth." "No," Junayd answered him, "it is by means of the Truth that you are! What gibbet will you stain with your blood!" [MASSIGNON 1982: 127]

That appears to be the full extent of the incident and the exchange. But there is little doubt as to how Hallaj intended Junayd to understand the expression "I am the

Truth"—or, as it has been translated, "My 'I' is God"—or how Junayd understood it. "The Truth" is a title of God, and Hallaj was arrogating it to himself, and not, it is noted, in a state of ecstatic "intoxication" but in its aftermath, the believer's normal state of "sobriety," a distinction that meant little to Hallaj but was of crucial importance to Junayd. Our source is the Persian Sufi Hujwiri (fl. 1057 C.E.).

I have read . . . that when Husayn ibn Mansur, in a sort of trance, broke with Amr al-Makki and came over to Junayd, the latter said: "Why did you come?"

"To live in community with you as a master."

"I do not live in community with madmen; community life requires balance, otherwise what happened to you with Sahl Tustari and Amr occurs."

"O master, sobriety and intoxication are only the two human aspects of the mystic, who remains separated from his Lord as long as these two aspects are not both annihilated."

"O Ibn Mansur, you are wrong in your definition of those states, sobriety and intoxication; the first means the state of normal equilibrium of the faithful before God; it is not a qualification of the faithful that he may get it through his own effort as a creature; likewise the second, which signifies extremes of desire and love. O Ibn Mansur, I see in your language an indiscreet curiosity and some expressions that are useless."
(Hujwiri, *The Unveiling* 235) [Cited by MASSIGNON 1982: 125–126]

28. Ecstatic Utterances

What Junayd tactfully characterized as "some expressions that are useless" many other Muslims called "ecstatic utterances," cries like Hallaj's "I am the Truth" or Bistami's "Glory be to Me," uttered in a moment of mystical transport—valid for the mystic, no doubt, but the cause of some disturbance, and even scandal, to the ordinary Muslim. Both Ghazali and Ibn Khaldun tried to put the best face upon what was admittedly a difficult subject.

Those gnostics, when they return from their ascent into the heaven of Reality, confess with one voice that they saw no existent there save the One Real Being. Some of them arrived at this scientifically, others experimentally and subjectively. For these last the plurality of things entirely fell away; they were drowned in the absolute Oneness, and their intelligences were lost in Its abyss. . . . They became like persons struck dumb, and they had no power within them except to recall God, not even the power to recall themselves. So there remained with them nothing save

God. They became drunk with a drunkenness wherein the sense of their own intelligence disappeared, so that one cried out "I am the Truth," and another "Glory be to Me! How great is My Glory!" and still another "Within this robe is nothing but God!" ... But the words of lovers passionate in their intoxication and ecstasy must be hidden away and not spoken of. (Ghazali, *Niche for Lights*)

There are the suspect expressions which the Sufis call "ecstatic utterances" and which provoke the censure of orthodox Muslims. As to them, it should be known that the attitude that would be fair to the Sufis is that they are people who are removed from sense perception. Inspiration grips them. Eventually, they say things about their inspiration that they do not intend to say. A person who is removed from sense perception cannot be spoken to. More, he who is forced to act is excused. Sufis who are known for their excellence and exemplary character are considered to act in good faith in this and similar respects. It is difficult to express ecstatic experiences, because there are no conventional ways of expressing them. This was the experience of Abu Yazid al-Bistami and others like him. However, Sufis whose excellence is not known and famous deserve censure for utterances of this kind, since the (data) that might cause us to interpret their statements (so as to remove any suspicion attached to them) are not clear to us. Furthermore, any Sufis who are not removed from sense perception and are not in the grip of a (mystical) state when they make such utterances, also deserve censure. Therefore the jurists and the great Sufis decided that al-Hallaj was to be killed, because he spoke (ecstatically) while not removed from sense perception but in control of his state. And God knows better. (Ibn Khaldun, *Muqaddima* 6.16) [IBN KHALDUN 1967: 3:102]

29. The Face in the Mirror

Ghazali's moderating influence won for Sufism a respected, if always somewhat suspect, place in the Sunni household, and Nasafi's libertines were banished to the realm of the heterodox. But as the Sufi movement continued to develop, instances of what Juyawni would doubtless have considered "indiscreet curiosity" and "useless expressions" continued to occur in Sufi circles. Even the fate of Hallaj did nothing to dampen the adventuresome thought of some Sufi masters. His example, however, when accompanied by continuing vigil on the part the Sunni authorities, may have counseled some mystics to resort to the somewhat safer ground of allegory or inference.

One of the more prolonged and celebrated of the Sufi allegories is a long poem in Persian, The Conference of the Birds, *written by Farid al-Din Attar in 1177 C.E. Its premise is that the birds of the world collect to go in search of an ideal king. In the end they discover him, but not before they tell and have told to them a great number of stories illustrative of the Sufi life, whose path they are themselves in fact allegorically tracing. Attar's allegorical birds finally reach their goal, the abode of a mythical king called Simorgh, whose Persian name derives etymologically from si =* "thirty" *and morgh =* "birds."

> A world of birds set out, and there remained
> But thirty when the promised goal was gained,
> Thirty exhausted, wretched, broken things,
> With hopeless hearts and tattered, trailing wings.

The king's herald counsels them to turn back.

> The herald said: "The blaze of Majesty
> Reduces souls to unreality,
> And if your souls are burnt, then all the pain
> That you have suffered will have been in vain."
> They answered: "How can a moth flee fire
> When fire contains its ultimate desire?
> And if we do not join Him, yet we'll burn,
> And it is for this that our spirits yearn—
> It is not union for which we hope;
> We know that goal remains beyond our scope." . . .

> Though grief engulfed the ragged group, love made
> The birds impetuous and unafraid;
> The herald's self-possession was unmoved,
> But their resilience was not reproved—
> Now gently he unlocked the guarded door;
> A hundred doors drew back, and there before
> The birds' incredulous, bewildered sight
> Shone the unveiled, the inmost Light of Light.
> He led them to a noble throne, a place
> Of intimacy, dignity and grace,
> Then gave them all a written page and said
> That when its contents had been duly read
> The meaning that their journey had concealed,
> And of the stage they'd reached, would be revealed. . . .

> The thirty birds read through the fateful page
> And there discovered, stage by detailed stage,

Their lives, their actions, set out one by one—
All their souls had ever been or done. . . .

The chastened spirits of these birds became
Like crumbled powder, and they shrank with shame.
Then, as by shame their spirits were refined
Of all the world's weight, they began to find
A new life flow toward them from that bright
Celestial and ever-living Light—
Their souls rose free of all they'd been before;
The past and all its actions were no more.
Their life came from that close and insistent sun
And in its vivid rays they shone as one.
There in the Simorgh's radiant face they saw
Themselves, the Simorgh of the world—with awe
They gazed, and dared at last to comprehend
They were the Simorgh and the journey's end.
They see the Simorgh—at themselves they stare,
And see a second Simorgh standing there;
They look at both and see the two are one,
That this is that, that this, the goal is won.
They ask (but inwardly; they make no sound)
The meanings of these mysteries that confound
Their puzzled ignorance—how is it true
That "we" are not distinguished here from "You"?
And silently their shining Lord replies:
"I am a mirror set before your eyes,
And all who come before my splendor see
Themselves, their own unique reality."
(Attar, *The Conference of the Birds*) [ATTAR 1984: 214–219]

The image of the face in the mirror was not original with Attar. It had appeared in one of its most striking forms in the work of the dominant figure in all of Islamic mysticism, the Spaniard Muhyi al-Din ibn al-Arabi (1165–1240 C.E.). It is introduced at the very beginning of his Bezels of Wisdom, *in the expression of one of his fundamental themes: the ultimate and primordial unity of Reality or Being, polarized into the God and the Cosmos only after and because of the Reality's desire to experience itself in another.*

The Reality wanted to see the essences of His Most Beautiful Names, or, to put it another way, to see His own Essence in an all-inclusive object encompassing the whole (divine) Command, which, qualified by existence, would reveal to Him His own mystery. For the seeing of a thing, itself by itself, is not the same as its seeing itself in another, as it were in a mirror; for it appears to itself in a form that is invested by the location of the vision by that which would only appear to it given the existence of the location and its [that is, the location's] self-disclosure to it.

The reality gave existence to the whole Cosmos (at first) as an undifferentiated thing without anything of the spirit in it, so that it was like an unpolished mirror. It is in the nature of the divine determination that He does not set out a location except to receive a divine spirit, which is also called "the breathing into him" (Quran 21:91). The latter is nothing other than the coming into operation of the undifferentiated form's (innate) disposition to receive the inexhaustible overflowing of Self-Revelation, which has always been and will ever be. . . .

Thus the (divine) Command required (by its very nature) the reflective characteristic of the mirror of the Cosmos, and Adam was the very principle of reflection for that mirror and the spirit of that form. (Ibn al-Arabi, *Bezels of Wisdom*, "Adam") [IBN AL-ARABI 1980: 50–51]

Here the image is turned around, and it is God who is the mirror.

If you are a believer, you will know that God will manifest Himself on the Day of Resurrection, initially in a recognizable form, then in a form unacceptable (to ordinary belief), He alone being the Self-manifesting One in every form, although it is obvious that one form is not the same as another.

It is as if the single Essence were a mirror, so that when the observer sees in it the form of his belief about God, he recognizes and confirms it, but if he should see it in the doctrinal formulation of someone of another creed, he will reject it, as if he were seeing in the mirror His form and then that of another. The mirror is single, while the forms (it reveals) are various in the eye of the observer.

None of the forms are in the mirror wholly, although a mirror has an effect on the forms in one way and not in another. For instance, it may make the form look smaller, larger, taller or broader. Thus it has an effect on their proportions, which is attributable to it, although such changes occur only due to the different proportions of the mirrors themselves. Look, then, into just one mirror, without considering mirrors in general, for it is the same as your beholding (Him) as being one Essence, albeit that He is beyond all need of the worlds. Insofar as He is Divine Names, on the other hand, He is like (many) mirrors. In which Divine Name have you beheld yourself, or who is the one who beholds? It is only the reality of the Name that is manifest in the beholder. Thus it is, if you will but understand. (Ibn al-Arabi, *The Bezels of Wisdom*, "Elias")

[IBN AL-ARABI 1980: 232–233]

Ibn al-Arabi returns to the relationship of the Reality and the Cosmos, now in terms of light and shadow.

Know that what is "other than the Reality," which is called the Cosmos, is, in relation to the Reality, as a shadow is to what casts the shadow, for it is the shadow of God, this being the same as the relationship between Being and the Cosmos, since the shadow is, without doubt, something sensible. What is provided there is something on which the shadow may appear, since if that whereon it appears should cease to be, the shadow would be an intelligible and not something sensible, and would exist potentially in the very thing that casts the shadow.

The thing on which this divine shadow, called the Cosmos, appears is the (eternally latent) essences of contingent beings. The shadow is spread out over them, and the (identity of the) shadow is known to the extent that the Being of the (original) Essence is extended upon it. It is by His Name, the Light, that it is perceived. This shadow extends over the essences of contingent being in the form of the unknown Unseen. Have you not observed that shadows tend to be black, which indicates their imperceptibility (as regards content) by reason of the remote relationship between them and their origins? If the source of the shadow is white, the shadow itself is still so [that is, black].

This is how the universe exists. Ibn al-Arabi then begins to move from its existence to our way of knowing both this world of ours called the Cosmos and its source.

No more is known of the Cosmos than is known from a shadow, and no more is known of the Reality than one knows of the origin of a shadow. Insofar as He has a shadow, He is known, but insofar as the form of the one casting the shadow is not perceived in the shadow, the Reality is not known. For this reason we say that the Reality is known to us in one sense and unknown in another.

We are, then, seriously misled about the "real existence" of the sensible universe.

If what we say is true, the Cosmos is but a fantasy without any real existence, which is another meaning of the Imagination. That is to say, you imagine that it [that is, the universe] is something separate and self-sufficient, outside the Reality, while the truth is that it is not so. Have you not observed (in the case of the shadow) that it is connected to the one who casts it, and would not its becoming unconnected be absurd, since nothing can be disconnected from itself?

It is, Ibn al-Arabi immediately continues, in the mirror we should look.

Therefore know truly your own self [that is, your own essence], who you are, what is your identity and what your relationship with the Reality. Consider well in what way you are real and in what was (part of) the Cosmos, as being separate, other, and so on.

Thus God is seen in many different modes: in one way—"green"—by the ordinary believer relying on the givens of Scripture, in another—"colorless"—by the theologian with his refined deductive portrait. And they are both correct, and, of course, both wildly wrong.

The Reality is, in relation to a particular shadow, small or large, pure or purer, as light in relationship to the glass that separates it from the beholder to whom the light has the color of the glass, while the light itself has no particular color. This is the relationship between your reality and your Lord; for, if you were to say that the light is green because of the green glass, you would be right as viewing the situation through your senses, and if you were to say it is not green, indeed it is colorless, by deduction, you would also be right as viewing the situation through sound intellectual reasoning. That which is seen may be said to be a light projected from a shadow, which is the glass, or a luminous shadow, according to its purity. Thus, he of us who has realized in himself the Reality manifests the form of the Reality to a greater extent than he who has not. . . .

God created shadows lying prostrate to right and left only as clues for yourself in knowing yourself and Him, that you might know who you are, your relationship with Him, and His with you, and so you might understand how or according to which divine truth all that is other than God is described as being completely dependent on Him, as being (also) mutually independent. Also that you might know how and by what truth God is described as utterly independent of men and all worlds, and how the Cosmos is described as both mutually independent with respect to its parts and mutually dependent. (Ibn al-Arabi, *The Bezels of Wisdom*, "Joseph") [IBN AL-ARABI 1980: 123–126]

30. Al-Jili and the Perfect Man

Sufism from Ibn al-Arabi onward developed a repertory of esoteric learning that was as vast and at times as impenetrable as the Kabbala. This was theosophy pure and simple, an arcane and transcendental way of looking at this world in terms of a higher reality, a blend of knowing and doing, of gnosis and theurgy, with strong derivative roots in the late Platonic tradition of the fifth and sixth century C.E. One of the central themes of this world view was the theory of the "Perfect Man," a figure who simultaneously embraces the Holy Spirit, the Word, Adam, Muhammad, and the fully enlightened mystic himself. Ibn al-Arabi was one of the pioneers in the development of this motif, but it found its classic expression in the treatise called The Perfect Man *by Abd al-Karim al-Jili (d. ca. 1410 C.E.).*

God created the angel called Spirit from His own light, and from him He created the world and made him His organ of vision in the world. One of his names is the Word of God. He is the noblest and most exalted of all existent beings. The Spirit exercises a Divine guardianship, created in him by God, over the whole universe. He manifests himself in his perfection in the Ideal Muhammad: therefore the Prophet is the most excellent of all mankind. While God manifests Himself in His attributes to all other created beings, He manifests Himself in His essence to this angel [that is, the Spirit] alone. Accordingly, the Spirit is the Pole of the present world and the world to come. He does not make himself known to any creature of God but to the Perfect Man. When the saint knows him [that is, the Perfect Man] and truly understands the things which the Spirit teaches him, then he too becomes a pole around which the entire universe revolves. But Poleship belongs fundamentally to the Spirit, and if others hold it, they are only his delegates. (Jili, *The Perfect Man* 2:12)

[Cited by NICHOLSON 1921: 110–111]

The Perfect Man is the Pole on which the spheres of existence revolve from first to last, and since things came into being he is one forever and ever. He has various guises and appears in diverse bodily tabernacles: in respect of some of these his name is given to him, while in respect to others it is not given to him. His original name is Muhammad, his name of honor is Abu al-Qasim [that is, "father of Qasim," the latter the name of Muhammad's first son], his description is Abdullah [that is, "servant of God"], and his title is Shams al-Din [that is, "the sun of religion"]. In every age he bears a name suitable to his guide in that age. I once met him [that is, the Perfect Man, Muhammad] in the form of my Shaykh, Sharaf al-Din Isma'il al-Jabarti, but I did not know that he [that is, the Shaykh] was the Prophet, though I knew the Prophet was the Shaykh. . . . The real meaning of this matter is that the Prophet has the power of assuming every form. When the adept sees him in the form of Muhammad which he wore during his life, he names him by that name, but when he sees him in another form but knows him to be Muhammad, he names him by the name of the form in which he appears. The name Muhammad is not applied except to the Real Muhammad. . . . If you perceive mystically that the Reality of Muhammad is displayed in any human form, you must bestow upon the Reality of Muhammad the name of that form and regard its owner with no less reverence than you would show our Lord Muhammad, and after having seen him therein you may not behave toward it in the same manner as before.

This appearance of the Real Muhammad in the form of another could be miscon-strued as the condemned doctrine of the transmigration of souls, and so al-Jili hastens to dissociate the two.

Do not imagine that my words contain any tincture of the doctrine of metempsychosis. God forbid! I mean that the Prophet is able to assume whatever form he wishes, and the Tradition declares that in every age he assumes the form of the most perfect men (of that age) in order to exalt their dignity and correct their deviation: they are his Caliphs externally and he is their reality inwardly.

In the Perfect Man himself are identified all the individualizations of existence. With his spirituality he stands with the higher individualizations, in his corporeality with the lower. His heart is identified with the Throne of God, his mind with the Pen, his soul with the Well-Guarded Tablet, his nature with the elements, his capability of receiving form with matter. . . . He stands with the angels with his good thoughts, with the demons and the devils with the doubts that best him, with the beasts in his animality. . . .

You must know that the Perfect Man is a copy of God, according to the saying of the Prophet, "God created Adam in the image of the Merciful," and in another Tradition, "God created Adam in His own image." . . . Further, you must know that the Essential names and the Divine attributes belong to the Perfect Man by fundamental and sovereign right in virtue of a necessity inherent in his essence, for it is he whose "reality" is signified by these expressions and whose spirituality is indicated by these symbols: they have no other subject in existence (to which they might be attached) except the Perfect Man.

Once again the figure of the mirror is adduced, and in a manner familiar from Ibn al-Arabi: man, and in particular the Perfect Man, is the mirror in which God sees and recognizes and admires Himself, as does man.

As a mirror in which a person sees the form of himself, and cannot see it without the mirror, such is the relation of God to the Perfect Man, who cannot possibly see his own form but in the mirror of the name "God." And he is also a mirror to God, for God laid upon Himself the necessity that His names and attributes should not be seen save in the Perfect Man. (Jili, *The Perfect Man* 2:58) [Cited by NICHOLSON 1921: 105–107]

31. Ibn Khaldun: An Evaluation of the Sufi Tradition

Ibn Khaldun had all these developments before him, from the earliest Muslim ascetics, through the "ecstatic utterances" of Bistami and Hallaj, to the daring "existential monism" of Ibn al-Arabi and the theosophical speculation of his successors, when he composed his thoughts on Sufism for the Prolegomenon *to History. He was well aware of the strong current of disapproval, or at least of reservation, that many in the Islamic legal establishment had expressed on the subject of Sufis and Sufism. For his part, however, Ibn Khaldun attempts to isolate the dubious areas in Sufi speculation, in the first instance by laying out the topics with which Sufis generally concerned themselves.*

Many jurists and muftis have undertaken to refute these . . . recent Sufis. They summarily disapproved of everything they came across in the Sufi "path." The truth is that discussion with the Sufis requires making a distinction. The Sufis discuss four topics. (1) Firstly, they discuss pious exertions, the resulting mystical and ecstatic experiences, and self-scrutiny concerning one's actions. They discuss these things in order to obtain mystical experience, which then becomes a station from which one progresses to the next higher one. . . . (2) Secondly, they discuss the removal of the veil and the perceivable supernatural realities, such as the divine attributes, the throne, the seat, the angels, revelation, prophecy, the spirit, and the realities of everything in existence, be it supernatural or visible; furthermore, they discuss the order of created things, how they issue from the Creator Who brings them into being. . . . (3) The third topic is concerned with activities in the various worlds and among the various created things connected with the different kinds of divine grace. (4) The fourth topic is concerned with expressions which are suspect if understood in their plain meaning. Such expressions have been uttered by most Sufi leaders. In Sufi technical terminology they are called "ecstatic utterances." Their plain meaning is difficult to understand. They may be something that is disapproved of, or something that can be approved, or something that requires interpretation.

Now that the territory has been charted, Ibn Khaldun can proceed to his critique. First, on the matter that by all accounts constituted the main stream of Sufism and that had won, at least since the time of Ghazali, a recognized place among accept-able Islamic practices and experiences.

As for their discussion of pious exertions and stations, of the mystical and ecstatic experiences that result, and of self-scrutiny with regard to shortcomings in the things that cause these experiences, this is something that nobody ought to reject. These mystical experiences are sound ones. Their realization is the very essence of happiness.

Ibn Khaldun then reverses the second and third points he had established above, treating first the Sufis' perceptions about the operation of divine grace, which he is inclined to accept, and their description, after the "removal of the veil," of that other, higher world where God and His angels and the other higher realities have their being, about which he is much less certain.

As for their discussion of the acts of divine grace experienced by the Sufis, the information they give about supernatural things, and their activity among created things, these are sound and cannot be disapproved of, even though some religious scholars tend to disapprove . . . since they might be confused with prophetic miracles.

There is no problem here. The scholastic apparatus of theology had its distinctions well in order.

Competent orthodox scholars have made a distinction between (miracles and acts of divine grace) by referring to "the challenge (in advance)" that is, the claim made (by the prophet in advance) that the miracle would occur in agreement with the prophetic revelation. It is not possible, they said, that a miracle could happen in agreement with the claim of a liar. Logic requires that a miracle indicate truthfulness. By definition a miracle is something that can be verified. If it were performed by a liar it could not be verified and thus would have changed its character, which is absurd. In addition, the world of existence attests the occurrence of many such acts of divine grace. Disapproval of them would be a kind of negative approach. Many such acts of divine grace were experienced by the men around Muhammad and the great early Muslims. This is a well-known and famous fact.

The Sufis' charting of the higher realities, on the other hand, might appear to constitute a kind of private, intuitive, and so unverifiable revelation. In this case Ibn Khaldun recommends a kind of circumspect neglect.

Most of the Sufi discussion about the removal of the veil of the reception of the realities of the higher things, and of the order in which the created things issue, falls, in a way, under the category of ambiguous statements. It is based upon the intuitive experience of the Sufis, and those who lack such intuitive experience cannot have the mystical experience that the Sufis receive from it. No language can express what the Sufis want to say in this connection, because languages have been invented only for the expression of commonly accepted concepts, most of which apply to sensible reality. Therefore, we must not bother with the Sufi discussion of those matters. We ought merely to leave it alone, just as we leave alone the ambiguous statements in the Quran and the Prophetic custom. Those to whom God grants some understanding of these mystical utterances in a way that agrees with the plain meaning of the religious law do, indeed, enjoy happiness. (Ibn Khaldun, *Muqaddima* 6.16) [IBN KHALDUN 1967: 3:99–101]

32. Sufis and Shiʿites

Ibn Khaldun then turns his attention to trends that began to develop in Sufism after its heroic period. In his reading of Sufi history it was the Shiʿites who led Islamic mysticism astray.

The ancient Sufis did not go into anything concerning the Mahdi [that is, the expected Muslim messiah]. All they discussed was their mystic activity and exertion and the resulting ecstatic experiences and states. It was the Imamite and extremist Shiʿa who discussed the preferred status of Ali, the matter of his Imamate, the claim made on his behalf to have received the Imamate through the last will of the Prophet, and the rejection of the two Shaykhs [that is, Abu Bakr and Umar]. . . . Among the later Sufis, the removal of the veil and matters beyond the veil of sense perception came to be discussed. A great many Sufis came to speak of incarnation and oneness. This gave them something in common with the Imamites and the extremist Shiʿa who believed in the divinity of the Imams and the incarnation of the deity in them. The Sufis also came to believe in the "Pole" and in "saints." This belief looked like an imitation of the opinions of the extremist Shiʿa concerning the Imam and the Alid "chiefs."

Ibn Khaldun will return to the Shiʿa-Sufi theory of "Poles" and "saints." He continues:

The Sufis thus became saturated with Shiʿa theories. Shiʿa theories entered so deeply into their religious ideas that they based their practice of using a cloak on the fact that Ali clothed al-Hasan al-Basri in such a cloak and caused him to agree solemnly that he would adhere to the mystic path. This tradition (begun by Ali) was continued, according to the Sufis, through al-Junayd, one of the Sufi shaykhs.

However, it is not known for a certainty whether Ali did any such thing. The mystic path was not reserved to Ali, but all men around Muhammad were models of the various paths of religion. The fact that the Sufis restrict precedence in mysticism to Ali smells strongly of pro-Shi'a sentiments. This and other aforementioned Sufi ideas show that the Sufis have adopted pro-Shi'a sentiments and have become enmeshed in them. (Ibn Khaldun, *Muqaddima* 3.51) [IBN KHALDUN 1967: 2:186–187]

And so, on Ibn Khaldun's view as a Sunni historian, the chief tenets of the "recent Sufis" that show the influence of Shi'ism are, first, their discussions of the God-head's becoming incarnate in certain chosen souls and, second, their insistence on the Divine Oneness to the extent that it became in effect pantheism.

Tradition scholars and jurists who discuss the articles of faith often mention that God is separate from His creatures. The speculative theologians say that He is neither separate nor connected. The philosophers say that He is neither in the world nor outside it. The recent Sufis say that He is one with the creatures in the sense that He is incarnate in them or in the sense that He is identical with them and there exists nothing but Himself either in the whole or in any part of it. . . .

A number of recent Sufis who consider intuitive perceptions to be scientific and logical hold the opinion that the Creator is one with His creatures in His identity, His existence and His attributes. They often assume that this was the position of philosophers before Aristotle, such as Plato and Socrates. . . . The Oneness assumed by the Sufis is identical with the incarnation the Christians claim for the Messiah. It is even stranger, in that it is the incarnation of something primeval in something created and the Oneness of the former with the latter.

The Oneness assumed by the Sufis is also identical with the stated opinion of the Imamite Shi'a concerning their Imams. In their discussions, the Shi'a consider the ways in which the oneness of the Deity with the Imams is achieved. (1) The essence of the primeval Deity is hidden in all created things, both sensible and intelligible, and is one with them in both kinds of perception. All of them are manifestations of it, and it has control over them—that is, it controls their existence in the sense that, without it, they would not exist. Such is the opinion of the people who believe in incarnation.

(2) There is the approach of those who believe in absolute Oneness. It seems as if in the exposition of those who believe in incarnation, they

have sensed the existence of an (implicit) differentiation contradicting the concept of Oneness. Therefore, they disavowed the (existence of any differentiation) between the primeval Deity and the creatures in essence, existence, and attributes. In order to explain the difference in manifestations perceived by the senses and the intellect, they used the specious argument that those things were human perceptions that are imaginary. By imaginary . . . they mean that all those things do not exist in reality and exist only in human perception. Only the primeval Deity has real existence and nothing else, either inwardly or outwardly. (Ibn Khaldun, *Muqaddima* 6.16) [IBN KHALDUN 1967: 3:83–86]

Ibn Khaldun has no doubts about whence these notions derived, or about their essential falsehood.

The recent Sufis who speak about the removal of the veil and supersensory perception have delved deeply into these subjects. Many of them have turned to the theory of incarnation and oneness, as we have indicated. They have filled many pages with it. That was done, for instance, by al-Harawi [ca. 1010–1089 C.E.] in the *Book of Stations* and by others. They were followed by Ibn al-Arabi [1165–1240 C.E.] and Ibn Sab'in [1226–1271 C.E.] and their pupils, and then by Ibn Afif [ca. 1260–1289 C.E.], Ibn al-Farid [d. 1235 C.E.] and Najm al-Din al-Isra'ili [1206–1278 C.E.] in the poems they composed.

The early Sufis had had contact with the Neo-Isma'ili Shi'ite extremists who also believed in incarnation and in the divinity of the Imams, a theory not known to the early Isma'ilis. Each group came to be imbued with the dogmatics of the other. Their theories and beliefs merged and were assimilated. In Sufi discussion there appeared the theory of the "Pole," meaning the chief gnostic. The Sufis assumed that no one can reach his station in gnosis until God takes him to Himself and gives his station to another gnostic. . . .

The theory of successive "Poles" is not, however, confirmed by logical arguments or evidence from the religious law. It is a sort of rhetorical figure of speech. It is identical with the theory of the extremist Shi'a about the succession of the Imams through inheritance. Clearly, mysticism has plagiarized this idea from the extremist Shi'a and come to believe in it.

The Sufis furthermore speak about the order of existence of the "saints" who come after the "pole," exactly as the Shi'a speak of their "representatives." They go so far (in the identification of their own concepts with those of the Shi'a) that when they construed a chain of transmitters for the wearing of the Sufi cloak as a basic requirement of the mystic way and practice, they made it go back to Ali. This points in the same direction. Among the men around Muhammad, Ali was not distinguished by any particular practice or way of dressing or by any special condition. Abu Bakr and Umar were the most ascetic and pious people after the Messenger of God. Yet, none of these men was distinguished by the possession of any particular religious practice peculiar to him. In fact, all the men around Muhammad were models of religion, austerity, asceticism, and pious exertion. This is attested by their way of life and history. Indeed, with the help of these stories, the Shi'a try to suggest that Ali is distinguished from the other men around Muhammad by being in possession of certain virtues, in conformity with well-known Shi'a beliefs. (Ibn Khaldun, *Muqaddima* 6.16) [IBN KHALDUN 1967: 3:92–93]

5. Thinking about God

1. The Birth of Philosophy

If God's revelation through Scripture was an unveiling of Himself to man, there were other ways of coming to a knowledge of God, ways that had been equally deliberately provided by the Creator, as Philo, the Hellenized Jew of Alexandria, explains in his meditation on the Torah. The theme is not new: Philo's Greek and Roman mentors all had their eyes cast heavenward, seeking traces of God. But for a Jew to attempt to elicit such a rationalized portrait from Scripture was a novel enterprise, one with enormous consequences: Yahweh, who had been for the Jews pre-eminently the purposeful God of history, their history, was about to begin His equally purposeful career as the God of philosophy, and so the common property of all men, with or without the benefit of revelation.

Its Maker arrayed the heaven on the fourth day with a most divine adornment of perfect beauty, namely the light-giving heavenly bodies; and knowing that of all things light is best, He made it the indispensable means of sight, the best of the senses; for what the intellect is in the soul, this the eye is in the body; for each of them sees, the one the things of the mind, the other the things of sense; and they have need, the mind of knowledge, that it may become cognizant of incorporeal objects, the eye of light, for the apprehending of bodily forms. Light has proved itself the source of many other boons to mankind, but pre-eminently of philosophy, the greatest boon of all. For man's faculty of vision, led upward by light, discerned the nature of the heavenly bodies and their harmonious movement. He saw the well-ordered circuits of the fixed stars and planets, how the former moved in unchanging orbit and all alike, while the latter sped round in two revolutions out of harmony with each other. He marked the rhythmic dances of all these, how they were marshaled by the laws of perfect music, and the sight produced in his soul an ineffable delight and pleasure. Banqueting on sights displayed to it one after another, his soul was insatiate in beholding. And then, as usually happens, it went on to busy itself with questioning, asking what is the essence of these visible objects? Are they in nature unoriginated or had they a beginning of existence? What is the method of their movement? And what are the principles by which each is governed? It is out of the investigation of these problems that that philosophy grew, than which no more perfect good has come into the life of mankind. (Philo, *The Creation of the World* 53–54) [PHILO 1945: 53–54]

2. Saadya on Reason and Revelation

Opening the door to philosophy—that is, to all the demonstrative sciences of the Greeks, "than which no more perfect good has come into the life of mankind," as Philo put it in such an apparently unself-conscious manner—seemed upon reflection to close the door to other avenues of truth, or at least to raise questions about their usefulness or necessity, as we shall see shortly. Christianity would have its own debate about this scientific certitude offered by the Greek sciences, but its claims were essentially messianic and not prophetic. And so the burden of the resolution of the conundrum of reason and revelation fell most heavily on the Jews and the Muslims.

The response of both groups begins from a simple proposition: truth is one, whether discovered by philosophy or revealed by a special act of God. In his Book of Doctrines and Beliefs, *Saadya (d. 942 C.E.), the chief luminary of the Jewish community in Muslim Baghdad, begins by describing the "bases of truth and the vouchers of certainty, which are the sources of all knowledge and the mainspring of all cognition." Three of them could have come from any textbook on Greek philosophy: empirical observation, intellectual intuition, and logical demonstration. But there is a fourth, and it is there that the Jew and the scripturalist begins to speak.*

As for ourselves, the community of monotheists, we hold these three sources of knowledge to be genuine. To them, however, we add a fourth source, which we have derived by means of the (other) three, and which has thus become for us a further principle. That is, the validity of authentic tradition, by reason of the fact that it is based upon the knowledge of the senses as well as that of reason. . . . At this point, however, we remark that this type of knowledge, I mean that which is furnished by authentic tradition and the books of prophetic revelation, corroborates for us the validity of the first three sources of knowledge. (Saadya, *Book of Doctrines and Beliefs*, Introduction) [SAADYA 1948: 18]

This is a relatively modest role assigned to revelation, that of confirming the other sources of true and certain knowledge. But Saadya has not finished with the topic. When he returns to it, he deftly moves the cart out before the horse.

Now someone might, of course, ask: "But how can we take it upon ourselves to indulge in speculation about objects of knowledge and their investigation to the point where these would be established as convictions according to the laws of geometry and become firmly fixed in the mind, when there are people who disapprove of such an occupation, being of the opinion that speculation leads to unbelief and is conducive to heresy?" Our reply is that such an opinion is held only by the uneducated among them. Thus you see the masses of this country [that is, Baghdad] labor under the impression that whoever goes to India becomes rich. . . . It is also related that some of the ignorant people in Arabia are under the impression that whoever does not have a she-camel slaughtered on his grave, is brought to the Last Judgment on foot. And many other such ridiculous stories are circulated.

Should one say, however, "But did not the greatest of the sages of Israel forbid this sort of occupation, and especially speculation on the beginning of time and place, saying, 'Whosoever speculates on the following four matters would have been better off had he not been born; namely, "What is below and what is above, what was before and what will be behind" (M.Hagigah 2:1)?'" Our answer is this, and we ask the Merciful One to stand by us, that it is inconceivable that the sages should have prohibited us from (rational inquiry). For did not our Creator Himself command us to do this very thing apropos of authentic tradition, as is evident from the declaration (of the prophet): "Know you not? Hear you not? Has it not been told to you from the beginning? Have you not understood the foundations of the earth?" (Isa. 40:21). . . .

What, however, the sages forbade was only to lay the books of the prophets aside and to accept any private notion that might occur to an individual about the beginning of place and time. For whoever speculates in this wise may either hit the mark or miss it. Until he hits it, however, he would be without religious faith, and even when he has hit upon the teaching of religion and has it firmly in hand, he is not secure against being deprived of it again by some uncertainty that might arise in his mind and corrupt his belief. We are agreed, then, on charging one who behaves in this fashion with sin, even though he be a professional thinker. As for ourselves, the congregation of the Children of Israel, we engage in research and speculation in a way other than this. It is this method of ours which I wish to describe and clarify with the help of the Merciful One.

Know then, and may God direct you aright, you who studies this book, that we inquire into and speculate about the matters of our religion with two objectives in mind: (1) in order to have verified in fact what we have learned from the prophets of God theoretically; and (2) in order to refute him who argues against us in anything pertaining to our religion. For our Lord, may He be blessed and exalted, instructed us in everything which we require by way of religion, through the medium of His prophets, after having established for us the truth of prophecy by signs and miracles. Thus He enjoined us to accept these matters as binding and observe them. He has furthermore informed us, however, that if we would engage in speculation and diligent research, inquiry would produce for us in each instance the complete truth, tallying with His announcements to us by the speech of His prophets. Besides that He has given us the assurance that the godless will never be in a position to offer a proof against our religion, nor the skeptics (to produce) an argument against our creed. (Ibid., Introduction) [SAADYA 1948: 27–28]

3. On the Usefulness of Revelation

If, then, speculative knowledge can produce "the complete truth, tallying with His announcements to us by the speech of His prophets," what need was there of revelation in the first place? This is the classic question for the scripturalist, Jewish, Christian, or Muslim, and Saadya faces it directly and responds.

Inasmuch as all matters of religious belief, as imparted to us by our Lord, can be attained by means of research and correct speculation, what was the reason that prompted (divine) wisdom to to transmit them to us by way of prophecy and support them by means of visible proofs and miracles rather than by intellectual demonstrations? We say: the All-Wise knew that the conclusions reached by means of the art of speculation can be attained only in the course of a certain measure of time. If, therefore, He had referred us for our acquaintance with His religion to that art (of speculative knowledge) alone, we should have remained without religious guidance for some time, until the process of reasoning was completed so that we could make use of its conclusions. But many of us might never complete the process because of some flaw in his reasoning. Again, he might not succeed in making use of its conclusions because he was overcome by worry or overwhelmed by uncertainties that confuse and befuddle him. That is why God, may He be exalted and magnified, afforded us a quick relief from all these burdens by sending us His messengers through whom He transmitted messages to us, and by letting us see with our own eyes the signs and proofs supporting them, about which no doubt could prevail and which we could not possibly reject. . . . Thus it became immediately incumbent upon us to accept the religion, together with all that was embraced in it, because its authenticity has been proven by the testimony of the senses. Its acceptance is also incumbent upon anybody to whom it has been transmitted because of the attestation of authentic tradition. . . . Furthermore women and children and people who have no aptitude for speculation can thus have a perfect and accessible faith, for the knowledge of the senses is common to all human beings. (Saadya *Book of Doctrines and Beliefs*, Introduction) [SAADYA 1948: 31–32]

4. On the Necessity of Revelation

In the tractate on Command and Prohibition, *Saadya divided the Law into "revelational" and "rational" precepts, and it is in connection with these latter that he makes his strongest and most direct case, not merely for the usefulness of revelation but for its necessity.*

. . . I have heard that there are people who say that men have no need for divine messengers and prophets because their reason is enough of a guide for them to distinguish between good and evil. I, therefore, went back to the touchstone of truth and I noted that if the matter were really as they said it was, the Creator would have known it best and He would not have sent any messengers to mankind, since He does nothing that has no purpose. Then I pondered the matter deeply and I found that there was considerable need for the dispatch of messengers to God's creatures, not only that they might be informed by them about revealed laws, but also on account of the rational precepts. For these latter too are carried out practically only when there are messengers to instruct men concerning them.

Thus, for example, reason calls for gratitude toward God for His kindness, but does not define how this gratitude is to be expressed or at what time or in what form it is to be shown. There was, then, need for messengers who defined it and designated it as "prayer" and assigned to it certain set times and gave it a particular formulation and prescribed a specific posture and direction. . . .

Another instance is the measure of punishment for crimes. Reason considers it proper that whoever commits a crime should expiate for it, but it does not define what form this expiation ought to take: whether a reprimand alone is sufficient, or should include the defamation of the evildoer, or include, in addition, flogging. In the event that the punishment take the form of flogging, again, the question is how much, and the same applies to the defamation and the reprimand. Or whether nothing short of the death of the criminal would suffice. And again it might be asked whether the punishment should be the same for whoever commits a certain crime or whether it should vary from person to person. So the prophets came and fixed for each crime its own penalty, and grouped some of them with others under certain conditions, and imposed monetary fines for some. For these considerations, then, that we have enumerated and other such reasons, it is necessary for us to have recourse to the mission of God's messengers. (Saadya, *Book of Doctrines and Beliefs* 3.3)

[SAADYA 1948: 146]

5. Moses the Philosopher

If human reason requires revelation as its necessary complement for the attainment of the end of man, the way of reason and the way of revelation were in some respects parallel paths to that end, the one being traveled by the philosopher, the other by the prophet. Did it follow, then, that the philosopher, the pagan wise man, was the peer of the prophet? Was Plato the equal of Moses? The germ of one response appears in Philo's attempt to make the prophetic experience an ecstatic one. On this view prophecy occurred only when the soul dispossessed its normal intellectual faculty and permitted the divine afflatus to take over and give light and even voice to the prophet. An "unlettered" prophet, a spiritual "natural" uninstructed in worldly wisdom, might serve very well for this purpose, and this was in fact the Muslim point of view with regard to Muhammad. But it was not Philo's with respect to Moses. For the Jewish thinker, prophecy was not another, alternative way to the truth but a phenomenon superadded to the philosopher's apprehension of truth.

I intend to record the life of Moses, whom some consider the law-giver of the Jews, others as the interpreter of the Holy Laws, a man who is in every respect the greatest and most perfect, and whom it is my wish to make known to those who deserve not to be uninformed of him. For while the fame of the laws he left behind has traveled throughout the inhabited world and reached the ends of the earth, the man himself as he was in reality is known to few. This was due to the unwillingness of Greek men of letters to consider him worthy of mention, probably through envy and also the disagreement of his laws in many instances with those ordained by the legislators of many states. (Philo, *Life of Moses* 1.1–2)

[PHILO 1981: 267]

Later in the same treatise, part of an ongoing commentary on the Jewish Scriptures, Philo takes up Moses' education in Egypt. Jesus was God-taught, as his youthful instruction of the rabbis on the Law illustrates (Luke 2:46–47), and so too was the "unlettered" Muhammad. But Moses had other teachers. Even though his education "seemed to be a case of recollection rather than of learning," Philo's description of those teachers and what they taught him effectively integrates Moses into the intellectual tradition of the ancient world, particularly that of Egypt, which in Philo's day was regarded as the birthplace and font of wisdom.

Teachers arrived forthwith from various places, some unbidden from the bordering areas and the Egyptian provinces, others summoned from Greece under promise of great bounty. But he [Moses] soon outstripped their capacities, for his happy natural gifts anticipated their instruction, so that it seemed to be a case of recollection rather than of learning, and he himself even further devised conundrums for them. For great natures open up new spheres of knowledge . . . and the naturally endowed soul goes forward in advance to meet its instruction and derives more profit from itself than from its teachers, and having grasped some first principles of knowledge rushes forward, as the saying goes, like the horse to the pasture. Arithmetic, geometry, the theory of rhythm, harmony, meter, and the entire field of music as exhibited by the use of instruments or in the accounts of more specialized manuals and expositions, were transmitted to him by learned Egyptians. They further instructed him in the philosophy conveyed through symbols, which they display in the so-called "holy characters" [that is, the hieroglyphs] and through the approbation accorded animals, to which they [the Egyptians] even pay divine honors. Greeks taught him the rest of the universal curriculum, and savants from the bordering lands taught him Assyrian letters and the Chaldean science of the heavenly bodies. The latter he also acquired from the Egyptians, who especially pursue astronomy. And when he had learned with precision from either nation both that on which they agree and that on which they disagree, avoiding politics and strife, he sought the truth, since his mind was incapable of accepting anything false, as is the wont of sectarians, who maintain the doctrines proposed, whatever they happen to be, without examining whether they are trustworthy, thus acting exactly like hired lawyers who have no concern for justice. (Ibid. 1.21–24) [PHILO 1981: 267–268]

6. The Prophet Is Also a Philosopher

Moses was, then, the most learned man of his time and, on the chronological evidence, the predecessor of vaunted Greek masters like Plato. It was Plato who was the borrower, as the sequel to the argument shows, and the point was taken up with avidity by the Christian Fathers, Augustine among others.

Certain partakers with us in the grace of Christ wonder when they hear and read that Plato had conceptions concerning God in which they recognize considerable agreement with the truth of our religion. Some have concluded from this that when Plato went to Egypt he had heard the prophet Jeremiah or, while traveling in the same country, had read the prophetic Scriptures, which opinion I myself have expressed in certain of my writings.

Augustine has, however, reinvestigated the chronological question and concluded that Plato was in Egypt too late to have encountered Jeremiah and too early to have been able to read the Septuagint translation of the Scriptures commissioned by King Ptolemy.

. . . [U]nless, indeed, we say that, as Plato was most earnest in the pursuit of knowledge, he also studied those writings [that is, the Bible] through an interpreter, as he did those of the Egyptians . . . or learned as much as he possibly could concerning their contents by means of conversation. What warrants this supposition are the opening verses of Genesis, "In the beginning God made heaven and earth. And the earth was invisible and without order; and darkness was over the abyss: and the Spirit of God moved over the waters." For in the *Timaeus*, when writing on the formation of the world, Plato says that God first united heaven and fire; from which it is evident that he assigns fire a place in heaven. This opinion bears a certain resemblance to the statement, "In the beginning God made heaven and earth." Plato next speaks of those two intermediary elements, water and air, by which the other two extremes, namely, earth and fire, were mutually united; from which circumstances he is thought to have so understood the words, "The Spirit of God moved over the waters." For, not paying sufficient attention to the designations given by those Scriptures to the Spirit of God, he may have thought that the four (physical) elements are spoken of in that place, because the air is also called "spirit."

Then, as for Plato's saying that the philosopher is a lover of God, nothing shines forth more conspicuously in those Sacred Writings. But the most striking thing in this connection, and that which most of all inclines me almost to assent to the proposition that Plato was not ignorant of those Writings, is the answer which was given to the question elicited from the holy Moses when the words of God were conveyed to him by the angel; for, when he asked what was the name of that God who was commanding him to go and deliver the Hebrew people out of Egypt, this answer was given: "I am who am; and you shall say to the Children of Israel, He who is sent me to you" (Exod. 3:14); as though compared with Him who truly is, because He is unchangeable, these things which have been created mutable are not—a truth which Plato zealously held and most diligently commended. And I know not whether this sentiment is anywhere to be found in the books of those who are before Plato, unless in that Book where it is said, "I am who am; you shall say to the Children of Israel, He who is sent me to you." (Augustine, *City of God* 8.11)

[AUGUSTINE 1948: 2:112–113]

Many centuries later Maimonides pursues the argument much in the same vein.

Know that the true prophets indubitably grasp speculative matters, though by means of his speculation alone man is unable to grasp the causes from which what a prophet has come to know necessarily follows. . . . For the very overflow that affects the imaginative faculty, with the result of rendering it perfect so that its activity brings about its giving information about what will happen and its apprehending those future events as if they were things perceived by the senses and had reached the imaginative faculty through the senses, this is the same overflow that renders perfect the activity of the rational faculty so that its activity brings about its knowing things that are real in their existence, and it achieves this apprehension as if it had apprehended it by starting from speculative premises. . . . The overflow of the Active Intellect goes in its true reality only to it [the human rational faculty], causing it to pass from potentiality to actuality. It is from the rational faculty that the overflow comes to the imaginative faculty. How then can the imaginative faculty be perfected in so great a measure as to apprehend what does not come to it from the senses without the rational faculty being affected in a similar way so as to apprehend without having apprehended by way of premises, inference and reflection? (Maimonides, *Guide of the Perplexed* 2.39)

[MAIMONIDES 1963: 377]

7. Philo on the Limits of Speculative Theology

Philo stands at the beginning of a long debate on reason and revelation among the Peoples of the Book, but he too had before him an already long tradition of attempts to reason about God. It had begun among the Greeks with an attempt to arrive at the principle of all things, a quest that pondered various material possibilities. Once the basic distinction between matter and spirit had been established, however, the investigation took a new course. It accepted that its object was God, the same supernatural presence or force or power commemorated under various human guises by the Greeks' own mythology. Thereafter theology, the "science of God," attempted to apply its refined tools of conceptual analysis and demonstrative proof—methods that had been spectacularly vindicated in the science of mathematics—to understanding, in as rigorous a way as possible, the essence, attributes, and operations of God.

As we have already seen in Chapter 4 above, Philo was willing to concede the possibility of an intuitive knowledge of God to the man endowed with both a rigorous training in philosophy and the gift of God's grace. But he was careful to insist that this was a knowledge of God's existence only; knowledge of His essence was restricted to God Himself. For Philo, the substance of God was not only unknown but unknowable, which was likely a new position in the Greek philosophical tradition from which he had come, though after him it became a commonplace in Jewish, Christian, and Muslim theology.

Do not suppose that the Existent, which truly exists, is apprehended by any man; for we have in us no organ by which we may form any image of It, neither sense organ, for it is not sense-perceptible, nor mind. So Moses, the student of invisible nature—for the divine oracles [that is, Scripture] say that he entered the darkness (Exod. 20:21), a figure intimating the invisible and incorporeal existence—searched everywhere and into everything and sought to see with distinct clarity the object of his great yearning and the only good. But finding nothing, not even an idea that resembled what he hoped for, in despair and learning from others, he flies for refuge to the object of his search itself and makes the following supplication: "Reveal Yourself to me that I may see You clearly" (Exod. 33:13). And yet he does not attain his purpose, since the knowledge of things both material and immaterial that come after the Existent is considered a most ample gift for the best race among mortals. For we read: "You will see what is behind Me, but My face will not be seen by you" (Exod. 33:23), meaning that all that comes after the Existent, both material and immaterial, is accessible to apprehension, even if it is not all already apprehended, but He alone by His very nature cannot be seen. And why is it astonishing if the Existent is inapprehensible to men when even the mind in each of us is unknown to us? For who has seen the true nature of the soul, whose obscurity has bred innumerable disputes among the sophists who propose opinions contrary to each other or even completely opposed in kind?

The very name of God is, then, unknown.

It follows that not even a proper name can be given to the Truly Existent. Observe that when the prophet earnestly inquires what he must answer those who ask about His name, He says, "I am He that is" (Exod. 3:14), which is equivalent to "My nature is to be, not to be spoken." But that mankind should not be in complete want of a designation for the Supremely Good, He allows them to use analogically, as though it were His proper name, the title of Lord God of the three natures, teaching, perfection and practice, whose recorded symbols are Abraham, Isaac and Jacob. For this, He continues (Exod. 3:15), is "My name through the ages," inasmuch as it belongs to our time period, not to the precosmic, "and My memorial," not a name set beyond memory and thought, and again, "for generations," not for beings ungenerated. For those who have entered the realm of mortal creation require the analogical use of the divine name, so that they may approach, if not the facticity, then at least the name of the Supremely Good, and be ruled according to it.

This is also shown by an oracle revealed as from the mouth of the Ruler of the universe that no proper name of Him has been disclosed to anyone. "I appeared," He says, "to Abraham, Isaac and Jacob, being their God, and My name of 'Lord' I did not reveal to them" (Exod. 6:3). For if the order of the words is changed back to the normal grammatical sequence, the meaning would be as follows: "My proper name I did not reveal to them," but only the one for analogical use, for the reasons already mentioned. So ineffable indeed is the Existent that not even the ministering powers tell us a proper name. Thus after the wrestling match that (Jacob) the Man of Practice fought in his quest for virtue, he says to the unseen master, "Declare to me your name," and He said, "Why do you ask this My name?" (Gen. 32:29), and He does not disclose His personal and proper name. "Suffice it for you," He says, "to profit from My blessing, but as for names, those symbols of created things, seek them not among imperishable natures." Do not then be thoroughly perplexed if you find the highest of all things to be ineffable, when His Word too, cannot be expressed by us through His own name. And indeed, if He is ineffable, He is also inconceivable and incomprehensible. (Philo, *On the Changing of Names* 7–15) [PHILO 1981: 141–143]

8. Paul on the Wisdom of the World and the Wisdom of God

Paul, like Philo, was a Diaspora Jew living in a world suffused with Greek philosophical ideas and ideals. Both men could use those ideas as seemed appropriate, but Paul had public reason to condemn them to the new Christians.

This doctrine of the cross is sheer folly to those on their way to ruin, but to those of us who are on our way to salvation, it is the power of God. Scripture says, "I will destroy the wisdom of the wise, and bring to nothing the cleverness of the clever." Where is your wise man now, your man of learning, or your subtle debater—limited, all of them, to this passing age? God has made the wisdom of this world look foolish. As God in His wisdom ordained, the world failed to find Him by its wisdom, and He chose to save those who have faith by the folly of the Gospel. Jews call for miracles, Greeks look for wisdom; but we proclaim Christ—yes, Christ nailed to the cross. And though this is a stumbling block for the Jews and folly to the Greeks, yet to those who have heard his call, Jews and Greeks alike, he is the power of God and the wisdom of God. . . .

As for me, brothers, when I came to you, I declared the attested truth of God, without display of fine words or wisdom. I resolved that while I was with you I would think of nothing but Jesus Christ—Christ nailed to the cross. I came before you weak, nervous and shaking with fear. The word I spoke, the Gospel I proclaimed, did not sway you with subtle arguments; it carried conviction by spiritual power, so that your faith might not be built upon human wisdom but upon the power of God. (Paul, *To the Corinthians* 1.1:18–2:5)

9. Christ and Socrates

In the generation after Paul the wisdom of Hellenism did not appear quite so threatening, particularly to intellectuals like Justin who were raised in that tradition. Christ was immeasurably greater than Socrates; but truth is one, and even the pagan Greeks had some share in it.

Our teachings appear to be greater than all human teaching, because Christ, who appeared for our sakes, became the whole rational being, body and reason and soul. For whatever either lawgivers or philosophers uttered well they elaborated by finding and contemplating some part of the Logos. But since they did not know the whole of the Logos, which is Christ, they often contradicted themselves. And those who by human birth were older than Christ, when they attempted to consider and prove things by reason, were brought before the tribunals of the impious and busybodies. And Socrates, who was more zealous in this direction than all of them, was accused of the very same crimes as ourselves. For they said he was introducing new divinities, and did not consider those to be gods whom the state recognized. But Socrates cast out from the state

Homer and the rest of the poets, and taught men to reject the wicked demons and those who did the things which the poets related; and he exhorted them to become acquainted with the God who was unknown to them, by means of the investigation of reason, saying that "it is not easy to find the Father and Maker of all, nor, having found him, to declare Him to all."

But these things our Christ did through his own power. For no one trusted in Socrates to the point of dying for this teaching, but in Christ, who was partially known to Socrates—for he was and is the Logos who is in every man, and who foretold the things that were to come to pass both through the prophets and in his own person when he was made of like passions and taught these things—not only philosophers and scholars believed, but also artisans and people entirely uneducated, despising alike glory and fear and death, since he is the power of the ineffable Father, and not the mere instrument of human reason. . . .

I prayed and strove with all my might to be found a Christian, not because the teachings of Plato are contrary to those of Christ, but because they are not in all respects like them, as is the case with the doctrines of the others, Stoics, poets and prose authors. For each discoursed rightly, seeing that which was kin to Christianity through sharing in the seminal divine reason; but they who have uttered contrary opinions seem not to have had the invisible knowledge and the irrefutable wisdom. Whatever has been uttered aright by any man in any place belongs to us Christians; for next to God we worship and love the Logos which is from the unbe-gotten and ineffable God, since on our account He has been made man so that, being partaker of our sufferings, He may also bring us healing. For all the authors were able to see that truth darkly, through the implanted seed of *logos* dwelling in them. For the seed and imitation of a thing, given according to a man's capacity, is one thing; far different is the thing itself, the sharing of which and its representation is given according to His grace. (Justin, *Apology* 2.10, 13)

10. The Fathers Debate the Role of Greek Philosophy

With a greater familiarity with this "wisdom of the world," as Paul called it, a new generation of Christians pondered somewhat more carefully the attractions and the dangers of the demonstrative, discursive, and at times utterly convincing science of the Greeks. To some it seemed almost like a form of revelation.

Philosophy was necessary for the Greeks for righteousness, until the coming of the Lord. And it now helps toward true religion as a kind of preparatory training for those who come to faith by the way of demonstration. For "your foot shall not stumble" if you assign all good to Providence, whether it belongs to the Greeks or to us. For God is the source of all good things; of some in a primary sense, like the Old and New Testaments; of others by way of consequence, like philosophy. But it may be that philosophy was given to the Greeks immediately and primarily, until the Lord should call the Greeks. For philosophy served as a pedagogue to bring the Greek mind to Christ, as the Law brought the Hebrews. Thus philosophy was a preparation, paving the way toward perfection in Christ. (Clement of Alexandria, *Stromateis* 1:5)

If that was the view from highly Hellenized Alexandria at the beginning of the third century, the matter appeared somewhat differently in the nearly contemporary Latin-speaking Western Church.

These are the teachings of men and of demons born of the spirit of this world's wisdom, for itching ears; and the Lord called this foolishness, choose the foolish things of this world to the confusion of philosophy. It is this philosophy which is the subject matter of this world's wisdom, that rash interpreter of the divine nature and order. In fact, heresies are themselves prompted by philosophy. It is the source of the "Aeons" and I know not what infinite "forms" and the "trinity of man" in the system of Valentinus. He was a Platonist. It is the source of Marcion's "better God," "better" because of his tranquillity. Marcion came from the Stoics. Again, when it is said that the soul perishes, that opinion is taken from the Epicureans. The denial of the restoration of the flesh is taken over from universal teaching of the philosophers; the equation of matter with God from Zeno, and when any assertion is made about a God of fire, then Heraclitus comes in. Heretics and philosophers handle the same subject matter; both treat of the same subjects: Whence came evil? And why? Whence came man? And how? And the question lately posed by Valentinus: Whence came God? His answer: From *enthymesis* and *ektroma*! Wretched Aristotle who taught them dialectic, that art of building up and demolishing, so protean in statement, so far-fetched in conjecture, so unyielding in controversy, so productive of disputes; self-stultifying since it is ever handling questions but never settling anything. . . . What is there in common between Athens and Jerusalem? Between the Academy and the Church? Between heretics and Christians? Away with all projects for a "Stoic" or a "Platonic" or a "dialectical" Christianity! After Christ Jesus we desire no subtle theories, no acute inquiries after the Gospel. (Tertullian, *On the Prescription of Heretics* 7)

By the fifth Christian century, however, an accommodation had been made, even in Latin circles, though with continuing echoes of Paul's warnings.

Although a Christian man instructed in ecclesiastical literature may perhaps be ignorant of the very name of the Platonists, and may not even know that there have existed two schools of philosophers speaking the Greek tongue, to wit, the Ionian and Italic, he is nevertheless not so deaf with respect to human affairs as not to know that philosophers profess the study, and even the possession, of wisdom. He is on his guard, however, with respect to those who philosophize according to the elements of this world and not according to God, by whom the world itself was made; for he is warned by the precept of the Apostle (Paul) and faithfully hears what has been said, "Beware that no one deceive you through philosophy and vain deceit, according to the elements of the world" (Col. 2:8). Then, that he may not suppose that all philosophers are such as do this, he hears the same Apostle say concerning certain of them, "Because that which is known of God is manifest among them, for God has manifested it to them. For His invisible things from the creation of the world are clearly seen, being understood by the things which are made, also by His eternal power and Godhead" (Rom. 1:19–20). And, when speaking of the Athenians, after having spoken a mighty thing concerning God, which few are able to understand, "In Him we live and move and have our being" (Acts 17:28), he goes on to say, "as certain also of your own people have said."

Paul knows well too to be on his guard even against these philosophers (who understand the truth) in their errors. For where it has been said by him that God has manifested to them His invisible things by those things which are made that they might be seen by the understanding, there it has also been said that they did not rightly worship God Himself because they paid divine honors, which are due to Him alone, to other things also to which they ought not to have paid them, "because, knowing God, they glorified Him not as God: neither were they thankful, but became vain in their imaginings and their foolish hearts were darkened. Professing themselves to be wise, they became fools and changed the glory of the incorruptible God into the likeness of the image of corruptible man, and of birds, and of four-footed beasts, and of creeping things" (Rom. 1:21–23), where the Apostle would have us understand him as meaning the Romans, the Greeks and the Egyptians, who gloried in the name of wisdom; but concerning this, we will dispute with them afterwards.

With respect, however, to that wherein the philosophers agree with us, we prefer them to all others, namely, concerning the one God, the author of this universe, who is not only above everybody, being incorporeal, but also above all souls, being incorruptible: our principal, our light, our good. And though the Christian man, being ignorant of their writings, does not use in disputation words which he has not learned—not calling that part of philosophy natural, which is the Latin term, or physical, which is the Greek one, which treats of the investigation of nature; or that part rational or logical which deals with questions of how truth may be discovered; or that part moral or ethical which concerns morals and shows how the good is to be sought and evil to be shunned—he is not for all that ignorant that it is from the one true and supremely good God that we have that nature in which we are made in the image of God, and that doctrine by which we know Him and ourselves, and that grace through which, by cleaving to Him, we are blessed. This, then, is the reason why we prefer these to all others, because while other philosophers have worn out their minds and powers in seeking the causes of things, and endeavoring to discover the right mode of learning and of living, these, by knowing God, have found where resides the cause by which the universe has been constituted, and the light by which truth is to be discovered, and the fountain at which felicity is to be drunk. All philosophers, then, who have had these thoughts concerning God, whether Platonists or not, agree with us. But we have chosen to argue our case with the Platonists, because their writings are better known. For the Greeks, whose tongue holds the highest place among the languages of the Gentiles, are loud in their praise of their writings; and the Latins, likewise taken by their excellence or their renown, have studied them more heartily than other writings, and by translating them into our tongue, have given them greater celebrity and notoriety. (Augustine, *City of God* 8.10) [AUGUSTINE 1948: 2:111–112]

11. Despoiling the Egyptians

As is clear in the case of Clement, and even earlier of Philo, philosophy and science inspired no terror in many of the religious intellectuals of the eastern, Greek-speaking provinces of the Roman Empire. They themselves had been to Greek schools before their conversion, had learned the methods, literary and philosophical, in use there, and had begun to apply them, and teach others to apply them, to their newly found Christian faith. One of them, Origen, a graduate of the philosophy faculty of the university of Alexandria, composed ca. 225 C.E. the first systematic treatment of the principles of the Christian faith. Here we see this pioneer Christian theologian and his work through the eyes of one of his students, Gregory, called "the Wonderworker," whom Origen not only converted to the Christian faith but whose view of the world he had altered forever.

He [Origen] taught us to consider not only the obvious and evident arguments, but sometimes even erroneous and sophistical ones, to probe and sound each to see whether it gave any echo of hollowness. Thus he provided us with a reasonable training for the critical part of our soul. . . . He also raised within us a humility of the soul, as we were amazed by the great and marvelous and manifold and all-wise workmanship of the universe. . . . By physics he established a reasonable, in place of an unreasonable, wonder in our souls. This divine and lofty science is taught by the study of nature, a subject most delectable to all. What need to mention the sacred studies, geometry dear to all and irrefragable, and astronomy, whose path is on high? . . . He made heaven accessible to us by "the ladder reaching up to heaven" of either study.

He was the first and only one to direct me to Greek philosophy, persuading me by his own manner of life to listen and adhere to the study of ethics. He thought it right that we should philosophize, and collate with all our powers every one of the writings of the ancients, whether philosophers or poets, excepting and rejecting nothing, save only those of the atheists. (Gregory Thaumaturgus, *To Origen*)

Origen responded to Gregory's encomium and, in the course of his reply, contrived what was to become Christianity's most familiar scriptural justification for helping itself to the riches of Greek philosophy and science, namely, the example of the Israelites' "despoiling of the Egyptians" described in Exodus 11:2–35.

Greetings in God, sir, my most excellent and revered son Gregory, from Origen: . . . Your abilities are such as to make you an accomplished Roman lawyer, or a Greek philosopher in one of the most prestigious of the schools. But my desire has been for you to focus all the force of your abilities on Christianity as your end, and to this effect I implore you to take from Greek philosophy whatever matters are capable of being generalized into serving as studies preparatory to Christianity, and likewise from geometry and astronomy such things as might be useful for the exposition of Holy Scripture, so that what the sons of the philosophers said about geometry and music and grammar and rhetoric and astronomy, namely, that they are the handmaidens of philosophy, we may also say of philosophy in relation to Christianity.

It is possibly just something of this sort that is hinted at in Exodus, which was written from the mouth of God, where it is said that the Children of Israel were to ask from their neighbors and their fellow residents silver and gold vessels as well as clothes, so that having thus despoiled the Egyptians, they might have material for the construction of the (prescribed) things . . . in the Holy of Holies, the ark with its cover, and the cherubim, and the seat of mercy, and the golden vessel in which was stored the manna, the bread of angels.

But, my son, make your first and foremost concern the reading of the Holy Scriptures. For we need great attention in reading the Scriptures, that we may not speak or think too rashly about them. . . . Do not be satisfied with merely knocking and seeking; what is most important is our prayer to understand divine matters. (Ibid.)

12. Faith and Knowledge

Early in the encounter with the wisdom of the Hellenes, the new breed of Christian theologians had to address the issue of adherence to the truth through faith and its understanding through knowledge. Here one of the first of them, Clement of Alexandria, speaks to the point.

Knowledge [*gnosis*] is, so to speak, the perfecting of man as man, which is accomplished through acquaintance with divine things; in character, life and word it is harmonious and consistent with itself and with faith. For by it faith is made perfect, since it is through it alone that the man of faith becomes perfect. Faith is an internal good, and without searching for God confesses His existence and glorifies Him as existent. Hence, by starting with this faith, and being developed by it through the grace of God, the knowledge of Him is likewise to be acquired to as great an extant as possible. . . .

But it is not doubt about God but rather belief that is the foundation of knowledge. Christ is both the foundation and the superstructure, through whom both the beginning and the end come to be. And the beginning and the end, by which I mean faith and love, are not taught. Knowledge [*gnosis*], which is conveyed as a deposit through communication by the grace of God, is entrusted to those who show themselves worthy of it. . . .

Faith is, then, a kind of compendious knowledge of the essentials, while knowledge is the sure and firm demonstration of what is received by faith, built upon faith by the Lord's teaching and carrying us onward to unshaken conviction and certainty. And, as it seems to me, the first saving change is that from paganism to faith; and the second, that from faith to knowledge. And this latter passing on to love thereafter brings about a mutual friendship between that which knows and that which is known. And he who has arrived at this state has already perhaps attained equality with the angels. He continues to advance, at any rate, after he has reached the final ascent in the flesh, and passes on through the Holy Sevenness into the Father's house, to that which is indeed the Lord's abode. (Clement, *Stromateis* 7.10)

13. "Knowing Not What He Is, But Knowing What He Is Not"

Clement understands the passage from faith to knowledge not as a simple progress to a more profound understanding of what one had previously simply accepted but as a true ascent, out of and beyond the flesh, into the realms of an almost mystical theology.

The sacrifice acceptable to God is unchanging alienation from the body and its passions. This is the really true piety. And is not philosophy, therefore, rightly called by Socrates the meditation on death? For he who neither applies his eyes in the exercise of thought nor draws upon his other senses but rather applies himself to objects purely with mind practices the true philosophy. . . .

. . . In the great mysteries concerning the universe nothing remains to be learned; we have only to contemplate and comprehend with the mind nature and things. We shall understand more about purification by confession and more about contemplation by analysis, advancing through analysis to the first notion, beginning with the properties underlying it; abstracting from the body its physical properties, taking away the dimension of depth, then of breadth, then of length. The point that remains is the unit, possessing only position. If we abstract position, what remains is the conception of unity.

If, then, we abstract all that belongs to bodies and things called incorporeal, we cast ourselves in the greatness of Christ, and thence advancing into immensity by holiness, we may reach somehow to the conception of the Almighty, knowing not what He is, but knowing what He is not. And form and motion, or standing, or a throne or place, or right hand or left, are not at all to be conceived as belonging to the Father of the universe, although it is so written. . . . The First Cause is not in space but above time and space and name and conception. (Clement, *Stromateis* 5.11)

14. The Father and the Son: Some Preliminary Proposals

It was one thing, perhaps, to lay down as Origen did the philosophical bases upon which the Christian faith might rest; it was quite another to take Christian teach-ings themselves, couched, as they inevitably were, in the language of Scripture, and attempt to explain them in philosophical terms. One attractive area of investigation was the nature of the relationship of Jesus to his "Father who is in heaven," or, somewhat more elusively, how Jesus could be eternal and one with the Father and at the same time man. Hippolytus, in his Refutation of All Heresies, *presents two sharply contrasting second-century views of the matter, which bear within them the seeds of a great many later theological postures. In the first, which Hippolytus identifies as coming from heretical Jewish-Christian circles, the Ebionites, the human Jesus is made to appear as a kind of "adopted" son of the Father.*

Jesus [it was alleged] was a man, born of a virgin, according to the counsel of the Father, and after he had lived in a way common to all men and had become pre-eminently religious, he afterwards at his baptism in the Jordan received Christ, who came from above and descended upon him. Therefore miraculous powers did not operate in him prior to the manifestation of that Spirit which descended and proclaimed him as the Christ. But some others (who share this view) are disposed to think that this man never was God, even at the descent of the Spirit, whereas others of them maintain that he was made God after the resurrection from the dead. (Hippolytus, *Refutation of All Heresies* 7.35)

Almost exactly the opposite view of the Father and the Son was proposed by one Noetus of Smyrna, "a reckless babbler and trickster," as Hippolytus calls him.

There is one Father and Son of the universe, and that He who had made all things was, when He wished, invisible to those who existed, and when He wished, He became visible; that He is invisible when He is not seen and visible when He is seen; that the Father is unbegotten when He is not generated but begotten when He was born of a virgin; that He is not subject to suffering and is immortal when He does not suffer and die, but when His passion came upon Him, Noetus admits that the Father suffers and dies. The Noetians think that the Father is called the Son according to events at different times. (Hippolytus, *Refutation of All the Heresies* 10.27)

15. An Early Theological Discussion in Christian Circles

These views of Jesus and the Father are already identified as heretical in the source that transmits them to us. To pass from a condemnation of what is false to a statement of what actually constituted an orthodox view of the matter was a more complex task, however, and one that required considerable discussion. We are given some insight into one such dialectical inquiry that took place at the ecumenical council of Nicea in 325 C.E. As we have already seen, the bishops put forth a draft statement of the Christian faith as follows.

We believe in one God, the Father All-sovereign, maker of heaven and earth, and all things visible and invisible.

And in one Lord Jesus Christ, the Son of God, Begotten of the Father, the Only-begotten, that is, from the substance of the Father; God from God, Light from Light, True God of True God, begotten not made, consubstantial with the Father, through whom all things were made, those in heaven and those on earth;

Who for us men and for our salvation came down and was made flesh, suffered and rose again on the third day, ascended into heaven, and is coming to judge the living and the dead.

And in the Holy Spirit.

And those who say "there was time when he was not," and "before his generation he was not," and "he came to be from nothing," or those who pretend that the Son of God is "of other hypostasis or substance," or "created" or "alterable," the catholic and apostolic church anathematizes.

Eusebius, the Church historian and bishop of Caesarea who was present at the synod, and who had earlier proposed his own formula, reports on what followed.

At their suggesting this formula, we did not let it pass without inquiry in what sense they were using the expressions "of the substance of the Father" and "consubstantial with the Father." Accordingly, questions and explanations took place and the discussion tested the meaning of these phrases. And they professed that the phrase "of the substance" meant the Son's being indeed from the Father, yet without being as it were a part of Him. And with this understanding we thought good to assent to the meaning of the pious teaching suggesting that God was from the Father, though not a part of His substance. On this account we too assented to this meaning, without declining even the term "consubstantial," since peace was the aim we set before us and in fear of deviating from the correct meaning.

In the same way, we also accepted "begotten, not made," since they [the proposers] said that "made" was an appellation to the other creatures which came to be through the Son, to whom the Son bore no likeness. Wherefore the Son was not a work resembling the things which through him came to be, but was an essence too high for any level of work, and which the Divine Oracles [that is, the Scriptures] teach to have been generated from the Father, the mode of generation being ineffable and inexplicable to every originated nature.

And so too on examination there are grounds for saying that the Son is "consubstantial" with the Father; not in the way of bodies, or like mortal beings, for he is not by division of essence or by severance, no, nor by any affect or alteration or changing of the Father's substance and power, since from all such the unoriginate nature of the Father is alien; but because "consubstantial with the Father" suggests that the Son of God bears no resemblance to the originated creatures, but that to his Father alone who begot him is he in every way assimilated, and that he is not of any other hypostasis and substance but from the Father. To this term too, understood in such a way, it appeared well to assent, since we were aware that even among the ancients some learned and illustrious bishops and writers have used the term "consubstantial" in their theological teaching concerning the Father and the Son.

So much then for the (statement of) Faith which was published, to which we all assented, not without inquiry, but according to specified meanings mentioned before the most religious Emperor himself and justified by the aforementioned considerations. And as for the anathemas published by them at the end of the Faith, we thought them without offense because they forbade the use of expressions not found in Scripture, from which almost all the confusion and disorder in the Church have come. Since, then, no divinely inspired Scripture has used the phrase "out of nothing" and "once he was not" and the rest which follow, there appeared no ground for using or teaching them; to which also we assented as a good decision since it had not been our (own) custom hitherto to use these terms.

Moreover, to anathematize "before his generation he was not" did not seem preposterous in that it is confessed by all, that the Son of God existed before the generation according to the flesh. Nay, our most religious Emperor proved in a speech made on that occasion that he [the Son] was in being even according to his divine generation which is before all ages, since even before he was generated in actuality, he was potentially with the Father ingenerately, the Father being always the Father, as King always, as Savior always, being all things potentially, and always being in the same respects and in the same way.

This we have been forced to transmit to you, beloved brethren, to make clear to you the deliberations that surrounded our inquiry and assent, and how reasonably we resisted even to the last minute, so long as we were offended at statements which differed from our own, but received without contention what no longer pained as soon as, on candid examination of the sense of the words, they appeared to us to coincide with what we ourselves have professed in the (statement) of Faith which we previously declared. (Eusebius in Sozomen, *Church History* 1.8)

16. The Divine Trinity

Trinitarian—or better, triadic—thinking about the primary principle or principles of being was not a Christian innovation. Dyads and triads were philosophical commonplaces among the later Platonist philosophers, and Philo's triune, "Lord God of three natures, teaching, perfection and practice, whose recorded symbols are Abraham, Isaac and Jacob," is a notion that can be found, as a whole or in its distinct parts, scattered through many passages in his writings, here, for example, in his work called Abraham.

Spoken words are symbols of that which is apprehended by the intellect alone. When, therefore, at high noon, the soul is fully illuminated and, entirely filled with intelligible light, it is rendered shadowless by the rays of light diffused all around it, it perceives a triple vision of a single object, one representing it as it really is, the other two like shadows reflected from it. This occurs also for those living in the sensible light; whether standing or moving, objects often cast two shadows simultaneously. No one, however, should suppose that the shadow can properly be referred to God. It is only an analogical use of words in order to afford a clearer view of the fact being set forth, for the truth is not so. Rather, as anyone who stands closest to the truth would say, in the central position is the Father of the Universe, who in Holy Scriptures is properly called the Existent One, and on either side are the senior powers that are nearest to Him, the Creative and the Regent. The Creative is designated God, since through it He established and ordered the universe; the Regent is called Lord, for it is right that the Creator should rule and hold sway over what He has brought into being.

The central Being, then, attended by each of His powers, presents to the mind that has vision the appearance, now of one, now of three: of one when perfectly purified and transcending not only the multitude of numbers but even the dyad, neighbor to the unit, it hastens to the form that is unmixed and uncombined, and is in itself in need of nothing whatever; of three, when as yet uninitiated into the greater mysteries, it still celebrates the lesser ones, and is unable to apprehend the Existent by Itself alone and apart from anything else, but only through Its actions, either creative or ruling. This is, as they say, a "second best voyage"; yet it shares in a view that is no less dear to God. But the former mode has not merely a share, it is itself the God-beloved view, or rather it is truth, more venerable than any point of view, more precious than any act of thinking. (Philo, *Abraham* 119–125) [PHILO 1981: 222–223]

Although in other places Philo identifies what is here called "the Creative" with the Word of God, or even His Son, the difference between his notion and the Christian Trinity is readily apparent. For Philo, the "triune God" is a matter of human perception, a useful analogical way of grasping the nature of God through secondary affects of creating and ruling rather than immediately through His essence. For the Christian, the Trinity is a mode of being, and its three constituents of Father, Son, and Holy Spirit are fully articulated existential persons, as Augustine explains.

All those Catholic expounders of the divine Scriptures, both Old and New, whom I have been able to read, who have written before me concerning the Trinity, Who is God, have purposed to teach, according to the Scriptures, this doctrine, that the Father, and the Son, and the Holy Spirit intimate a divine unity of one and the same substance in an indivisible equality; and that therefore they are not three Gods but one God: although the Father has begotten the Son, and so He who is the Father is not the Son; and the Son is begotten by the Father, and so He who is the Son is not the Father; and the Holy Spirit is neither the Father nor the Son, but only the Spirit of the Father and the Son, Himself co-equal with the Father and the Son, and pertaining to the unity of the Trinity; . . . the Father and the Son and the Holy Spirit, as they are indivisible, so work indivisibly. This is also my faith, since it is the Catholic faith.

Some persons, however, find a difficulty in this faith; when they hear that the Father is God and the Son God and the Holy Spirit God, and yet that the Trinity is not three Gods but one God; and they ask how they are to understand this, especially when it is said that the Trinity works indivisibly in everything that God works, and yet that a certain voice of the Father spoke, which is not the voice of the Son; and that none except the Son was born in the flesh, and suffered, and rose again, and ascended into heaven; and that none but the Holy Spirit came (upon Jesus at his baptism) in the form of a dove. (Augustine, *On the Trinity* 1.4–5)

[AUGUSTINE 1948: 2:672–673]

17. A Scriptural Demonstration of the Trinity

Parts of Augustine's proof for a triune God are derived from Scripture, many of them from the New Testament, with its frequent references to "Father" and "Son." But a number too are drawn from the Bible, the Christians' Old Testament, where there appear to be distinct and multiple manifestations of God on occasion.

In that which is written in Genesis, to wit, that God spoke with man whom He had formed out of the dust, if we set apart the figurative meaning and treat it so as to place faith in the letter of the narrative, it should appear that God spoke with man in the appearance of a man. This is not indeed expressly laid down in the Book, but the general tenor of its reading sounds in this sense, especially in that which is written, that Adam heard the voice of the Lord God, walking in the garden in the cool of the evening. . . . Adam too says that he hid himself from the face of God. Who then was He? Whether the Father, or the Son or the Holy Spirit? Whether altogether indiscriminately did God the Trinity speak to man in the form of man? The context itself of Scripture nowhere, it would seem, indicates a change from person to person, but He seems still to speak to the first man who (earlier) said, "Let there be light" and "Let there be firmament," and so on through each of those days, (the One) whom we usually take to be God the Father, making by a word whatever He willed to make. For He made all things by His word, which Word we know, by the right rule of faith, to be His only Son. . . . Why are we not to go on to understand that it was He also [that is, the Father] who appeared to Abraham and to Moses, and to whomever He would, through the changeable and visible creature subjected to himself, while He Himself remains in Himself and in His own substance, in which He is unchangeable and invisible? But possibly it might be that the Scripture passed over in a hidden way from person to person, and while it related that the Father said, "Let there be light," and the rest which it mentioned Him to have done by the Word, went on to indicate the Son as speaking to the first man; not unfolding this openly, but intimating it to be understood by those who could understand it.

Augustine passes to the Christians' most cogent and frequently cited biblical proof-text, Abraham's encounter with the three men in Genesis 18:1ff.

Under the oak at Mamre he [Abraham] saw three men, whom he invited and hospitably received and ministered to them as they feasted. Yet Scripture at the beginning of that narrative does not say that three men appeared to him but "The Lord appeared to him." And then, setting forth in due order after what manner the Lord appeared to him, it has added the account of the three men, whom Abraham invites to his hospitality in the plural number, and afterwards speaks to them in the singular number as one; and as one He promises Abraham a son by Sarah, namely, the one whom the Scripture calls "Lord" in the beginning of the same narrative. "The Lord," it says, "appeared to Abraham." He invites them then, and washes their feet, and leads them forth at their departure, as though they were men; but he speaks as with the Lord God, whether when a son is promised to him or when the destruction is shown to him that was impending over Sodom.

There is a subtext to Augustine's argument throughout this section of On the Trinity: *whether or not Jesus, the pre-existent Son of God in the Christians' Trinity, had appeared in human form before his birth. And that is the first issue addressed in his reflections on the scene of Abraham at Mamre.*

That place in Scripture demands neither a slight nor a passing consideration. For if one man had appeared (to Abraham), what else would those at once cry out, who say that the Son was visible also in His own substance before He was born of the Virgin, but that it was He? . . . And yet I would go on to demand in what manner "He was found in fashion as a man" before He had taken our flesh, seeing that His feet were washed and He fed upon earthly food? How could that be, when He was still "in the form of God and thought it not robbery to be equal to God" (Phil. 2:6–7)? For, tell me, had He already "emptied Himself, taking upon Him the form of a servant, and made in the likeness of man and found in fashion as a man" (ibid.) when we know when it was that He did this through His birth of the Virgin? How, then, before He had done this, did He appear as one man to Abraham? Or was not that form a reality?

I could put these questions if it had been one man that appeared to Abraham, and if that one were believed to be the Son of God. But since three men appeared, and no one of them is said to be greater than the rest either in form or age or power, why should we not here understand, as visibly intimated by the visible creature, the equality of the Trinity and one and the same substance in three persons? For, lest anyone should think that one among the three is in this way intimated to have been the greater, and that this one is understood to have been the Lord, while the other two were His angels, because, whereas three appeared, Abraham there speaks to one as the Lord: Holy Scripture has not forgotten to anticipate, by a contradiction, such future thoughts and opinions, when a little while after it says (Gen. 18:33) that two angels came to Lot, among whom that just man also . . . speaks to one as to the Lord. For so Scripture goes on to say, "And the Lord went His way, as soon as He left communing with Abraham; and Abraham returned to his place." (Augustine, *On the Trinity* 2.10–11) [AUGUSTINE 1948: 2:711–714]

18. A Jewish Rebuttal

The Jews' first polemical concern with the Christians was, of course, with Jesus' messianic claims simply as such and then perhaps, as Christian theology progressively unfolded, with the anomaly represented by the Christians' assertion that Jesus was also the eternal Son of God. There was not much incentive for the Jews to continue the debate in the overwhelmingly Christian Roman Empire after Constantine. But six centuries later Jews and Christians once again stood as political equals, now as protected minorities under Islam, and the dialogue was resumed, particularly when the changed circumstances and the Muslim example brought Jewish thinkers once again to explore the possibilities of a scriptural theology in the manner of Philo. The pioneer in that enterprise was Saadya (d. 942 C.E.), head of the Jewish schools in Iraq, and its chief testament is his Book of Doctrines and Beliefs, *where he confronts the Christians directly on the matter of the Trinity.*

Let me say that in this matter (of God's attributes) the Christians erred when they assumed a distinction in God's personality which led them to make of him a trinity and to deviate from the orthodox belief. I shall, therefore, take occasion here to make note of what refutation of their doctrine is offered by reason, invoking the aid of the truly One and His Uniqueness.

Now I do not have in mind when I present this refutation the uneducated among them who profess only a crass materialistic trinity. For

I would not have my book occupy itself with answering people like that, since what that answer must be is quite clear and the task simple. It is rather my intention to reply to their elite, who maintain that they adopted their belief in the trinity as a result of rational speculation and subtle understanding, and it was thus that they arrived at these three attributes and adhered to them. Declaring that only a thing that is living and omniscient is capable of creating, they recognized God's vitality and omniscience as two things distinct from His essence, with the result that these became for them a trinity. (Saadya, *Doctrines and Beliefs* 2.5)

[SAADYA 1945: 103]

Part of Saadya's rebuttal of the doctrine of the Trinity is dialectical, as were the Christians' own arguments on the matter; but part too is addressed to the Christians' use of Scripture. He was not concerned with what use the Christians made of their own writings; the question of biblical interpretation, on the other hand, is one he must and does contend.

If, again, they derive their proof from Scripture, as for example, some one of them might assert, I see that Scripture says that God is possessed of a spirit and a word, as is borne out by the statement, "The spirit of the Lord spoke to me and His word was upon my tongue" (2 Sam. 23:2), our answer is that this "spirit" and "word" are things specially created by God, constituting the detailed speech revealed by God to His prophet. We know, in fact, that the Scripture calls the name of God "soul," as Scripture says, "Who has not taken My soul in vain" (Ps. 24:4) instead of "My name." Now inasmuch as in the case of creatures "soul" and "spirit" have one connotation, and the Creator also has a "soul" by which is meant His name, the "spirit" which is attributed to Him means "revelation" and "prophecy." This misinterpretation of these terms on the part of these individuals is, then, due to their unfamiliarity with the Hebrew language.

Similarly, I find that some of these (trinitarians) cite as proof (of their doctrine) the fact that the Scriptures declare that the spirit of God engages in Creation. They say (for example): "The spirit of God has made me, and the breath of the Almighty gives me life" (Job 33:4). Also they assert that the word of God engages in Creation. That is the import of their statement, "By the word of the Lord were the heavens made, and by the breath of His mouth" (Ps. 33:6). I note, however, that this too is due to unfamiliarity with the language of Scripture. For the Scriptures mean to say by these assertions only that the Creator created all things by means of His word, His command, His will or His wish, that He created them with intent, not wantonly, unintentionally or from necessity. This is borne out by the scriptural remark: "But He is at one with Himself, and who can turn Him? And what His soul desires, even that He does" (Job 23:13). (Ibid. 2.5) [SAADYA 1948: 105–106]

And on the celebrated incident at Mamre:

Others, conjecturing about the implication of the passage, "And the Lord appeared to him by the terebinths of Mamre," declare that the thing that appeared to Abraham and was designated by this name was a trinity, because Scripture later explicitly states: "And behold, three men stood before him." Let me explain, then, that these are more ignorant than all of those who have been mentioned earlier, because they did not wait until they reached the end of the passage. For had they patience until they heard the verse, "And the men turned from there and went toward Sodom; but Abraham yet stood before the Lord" (Gen. 18:22), they would have realized that the men had departed while the light of God remained stationary with Abraham, who was in its presence. The thought, therefore, that God was identical with these men is completely refuted.

The truth of the matter is that the light of God appeared to Abraham first in order that he might infer therefrom that his visitors were good and saintly men. That is why Abraham said to them: "My Lord, if I have now found favor in your sight" (Gen. 18:3). What was actually meant was angels of the Lord or messengers of the Lord, by way of ellipsis, which is of frequent occurrence in the language of the Children of Israel, as well as in other languages. (Ibid. 2.6) [SAADYA 1948: 107–108]

19. And a Muslim Rebuttal

The theologian Ghazali interpreted the prologue of the Gospel of John in a manner consistent with Muslim beliefs. These opening verses of John were a capital text for the Christians' assertion of the divinity of Jesus; and so after his new exegesis of the text, Ghazali turns to some more general reflections on the Christian view of the Trinity.

In interpreting the doctrine of the hypostases, the Christians have followed a procedure which has obliged them to proclaim the existence, conceptually and objectively, of three Gods, distinct in their essence and natures, or else deny the Essence of God, glorious is His Name. For they use the term "Father" for the Essence as defined by fatherhood, "Son" for the Essence as defined by sonship, and "Holy Spirit" for the Essence as defined by the aspect of "proceeding." And after all that they still speak of One God!

If they are cornered in this matter and realize that the Essence of the Father as particularized by the attribute of fatherhood cannot admit the attribute of sonship—and the same argument applies to the Son and the Holy Spirit—and that it is not one of those relative essences, so as to be considered a father to one person and a son to another, they then state that the Essence is one, but that it is perfectly possible to describe it by all of those attributes; except that when we describe it by one attribute, we apply the negation of whatever is different from it. That is the pitch of their ignorance and stupidity: they proclaim the pre-eternity of these Essences and their attributes. So the Essences are inseparably attached to the attributes and the attributes are inseparably attaching to the Essences: whenever the thing attached exists, the thing attaching to it exists as well; and whenever the thing attaching to it is removed, the thing attached to is removed also. So if we suppose that the attribute attaching to the Essence is negated, we must also suppose the Essence itself is negated. This is the meaning behind that solemn reference in the Holy Book:

> They are unbelievers
> Who say, "God is the Third of Three." (Quran 5:73)

(Ghazali, *The Elegant Refutation*) [ARBERRY 1964: 306–307]

20. The Philosopher and the Rabbi

The premise of Judah Halevi's The Khazar King, *which was written as an apologia for traditional Judaism sometime between 1130 and 1140 C.E., was that the ruler of the Crimean people called the Khazars was visited by God in a dream and told that his actions were not pleasing to God. In an effort to practice the true religion, he summoned to his presence a philosopher, a Muslim and a Christian theologian, and a rabbi to explain their positions to him. The first three make only a token appearance in the work, but at the outset the philosopher sets forth his creed, with particular emphasis on the points that separated him from the adherents of the scriptural religions.*

There is no favor or dislike in the nature of God because He is above desire and intention, since a desire intimates a want in the person who feels it, and not until it is satisfied does he become, so to speak, complete; if it remains unfulfilled, he lacks completion. In the same way God is, in the opinion of the philosophers, above the knowledge of individuals, because the latter change with the times, while there is no change in God's knowledge. He, then, does not know you, much less your thoughts or actions, nor does He listen to your prayers or see your movements. If philosophers say that He created you, they only use a metaphor, because He is the Cause of causes in the creation of all creatures, but not because this (specific act) was His intention from the beginning. He never created man. For the world is without beginning, and there never arose a man except through one who came into existence before him, in whom are united forms, gifts, characteristics inherited from father, mother and other relations, besides the influences of climate, countries, food and water, spheres, stars and constellations. Everything is reduced to a Prime Cause, not to a Will proceeding from this, but an Emanation from which emanated a second, a third, and a fourth cause. (Judah Halevi, *The Khazar King*) [HALEVI 1905: 36]

The rabbi responds:

There is an excuse for the philosophers. Being Greeks, science and religion did not come to them as inheritances. They belong to the descendants of Japheth, who inhabited the north, while that knowledge coming from Adam, and supported by the divine influence, is only to be found among the progeny of Shem, who represented the successors of Noah and constituted, so to speak, his essence. This knowledge has always been connected with this essence, and will always remain so. The Greeks only received it when they became powerful, from Persia. The Persians had it from the Chaldeans [or Babylonians]. It was only then that the famous Greek philosophers arose, but as soon as Rome assumed political leadership, they produced no philosopher worthy of the name.

The Khazar King: Does this mean that Aristotle's philosophy is not deserving of credence?

The Rabbi: Certainly. He exerted his mind, because he had no tradition from any reliable source at his disposal. He meditated on the beginning and end of the world, but found as much difficulty in the theory of a beginning as in that of the eternity of the world. Finally, these abstract speculations which made for the eternity of the world prevailed, and he found no reason to inquire into the chronology or derivation of those who had lived before him. Had he lived among a people with well-authenticated and generally acknowledged traditions, he would have applied his deductions and arguments to establish a theory of creation, however difficult, instead of the eternity of the world, which is even more difficult to accept.

The Khazar King: Is there any decisive proof?

The Rabbi: Where could we find one for such a question? Heaven forbid that there should be anything in the Bible to contradict that which is manifest or proved! On the other hand, it tells of miracles and changes of ordinary things, newly arising, or changing one into the other. This proves that the Creator of the world is able to accomplish what He wills, and whenever He wills. The question of eternity and creation is obscure, while the (rational) arguments on either side are evenly balanced. But the theory of creation derives greater weight from the prophetic tradition of Adam, Noah and Moses, which is more deserving of credence than mere speculation. If, after all, a believer in the Law finds himself compelled to admit an eternal matter and the existence of many worlds prior to this one, this would not impair his belief that this world was created at a certain epoch, and that Adam and Noah were the first human beings. (Judah Halevi, *The Khazar King*) [HALEVI 1905: 53–54]

21. Theology among the Jews, Christians, and Muslims

Halevi attempted to put philosophy and theology into some kind of historical perspective for the Khazar king. The Spaniard Maimonides (d. 1204 C.E.) attempted much the same, though in a far more analytical fashion, for the Jewish readers of his Guide of the Perplexed. *He begins by discussing the condition of theology in Judaism.*

As for that small bit of dialectical theology concerning the question of the Oneness of God and what depends from this notion, which you will discover in the writings of some of the Gaons [that is, the heads of the Jewish academies] and in those of the Karaites, that the subject matter of this argument was taken over by them from the dialectical theologians of Islam, and they are brief indeed when compared to what the Muslims have also had to say on this subject.

Furthermore, it happened that the first Muslims to follow this path belonged to a certain sect, namely the Muʿtazilites, from whom our (Jewish) coreligionists borrowed and whose way they followed. After a time another sect arose in Islam, namely the Ashʿarites, who had other opinions, none of which will be discovered among our coreligionists. The reason is not because they preferred the first opinion to the second, but simply because they happened to have taken over and adopted the first opinion and assumed that it was something that had been proven by demonstration.

Maimonides now moves back to the era before Islam and lays out his understanding of the origins of dialectical theology among the Christians, both the Hellenized Christians and the Syriac-speaking ones of the interior Near East.

You should realize that all the statements that the Muslims—both the Muʿtazilites and the Ashʿarites—have made on these subjects [that is, on the Oneness of God and its consequences] are all of them opinions founded on premises that were derived from the books of the (Christian) Greeks and the Syrians who had wished to disagree with the opinions of the (pagan) philosophers and to disprove their statements. Why this occurred was because when the Christian community came to include those communities (of Greeks and Syrians)—the Christian doctrine being what it is—and since the opinions of the (pagan) philosophers were widespread in those communities—philosophy had first risen there, and there were kings who protected religion—the learned of the time from among the Greeks and the Syrians saw that those (Christian) doctrines were strongly and obviously opposed to philosophical opinion. Thus there arose among them this science of dialectical theology.

They [that is, the early Christian theologians] began to establish premises that would be useful for (establishing) their beliefs and for countering those opinions that might undermine the foundations of their Law. Thus when the community of Islam later arrived on the scene and the books of the (pagan) philosophers were translated for them, those (same Christian) polemics that had been composed against the books of the (Greek) philosophers were likewise translated for the Muslims. Thus the Muslims discovered the dialectical theology of John Philoponus (ca. 525 C.E.) and Yahya ibn Adi (d. 974 C.E.) and others with regard to those notions, made it their own, and thought they had achieved something great. . . .

Afterwards dialectical theology became broader in scope and these people [that is, the Muslim theologians] went down other peculiar roads that had never been taken by the dialectical theologians from among the (Christian) Greeks and others, for these (roads) were near to those of the philosophers. There subsequently appeared among the Muslims statements of the Law that were particular to them and that they necessarily had need to defend. Furthermore, differences occurred among them with regard to these questions, so that every one of their sects attempted to establish premises that would be useful for the defense of its opinion.

There is no doubt that there are things that are shared by all three of us (religious communities), I mean the Jews, the Christians and the

THE WORKS OF THE SPIRIT

Muslims: namely, the assertion of the creation of the world in time, the validity of which entails the validity of miracles, and other things. As for the other matters into which these two latter communities chose to plunge—for instance the notion of the Trinity into which the Christians plunged and the dialectical theology into which certain sects of the Muslims plunged—so that they found it necessary to establish premises and to establish, by means of these premises . . . the notions that are peculiar to each of the two communities, these are things that we (Jews) do not in any way require. (Maimonides, *Guide of the Perplexed* 1:71)

22. Ibn Khaldun on the Origins of Theology in Islam

Somewhat later than Maimonides, Ibn Khaldun gives his own rapid survey of what he calls the "traditioned sciences." In the Prolegomenon to History *he takes up the question of theology, first offering his rather general definition of its nature and function.*

The duties of the Muslim may concern either the body or the heart. The duties of the heart are concerned with faith and the distinction between what is to be believed and what is not to be believed. This concerns the articles of faith which deal with the essence and the attributes of God, the events of the Resurrection, Paradise, punishment and predestination, and entails discussion and defense of these subjects with the help of intellectual arguments. (Ibn Khaldun, *Muqaddima* 6.9)
[IBN KHALDUN 1967: 2:438]

Islam in fact knew two theologies. The first was the Greeks' science about God, often called metaphysics after the Aristotelian work that was the Muslims' chief source of instruction in it. The second was what was called in Arabic by Jews, Muslims, and Christians kalam *and has been translated here throughout as "dialectical theology." Unlike the Greeks' metaphysics, which began with the premises of pure reason, the method of dialectical theology in Islam more closely resembled that of the Christians' "sacred theology," which, as Maimonides pointed out, took the givens of revelation as its starting point and then attempted to demonstrate dialectically the conclusions that flowed from them. These two aspects of Islamic dialectical theology are clearly underlined in Ibn Khaldun's description of it, which includes both the Quranic menu of its subject matter and a generic characterization of its method, to wit, "intellectual arguments."*

Ibn Khaldun returns to the earliest days of Islam and undertakes to provide a sketch of the conditions that brought this discipline into being, though with a notable, and understandable, reluctance to trace it to Christian origins, as Maimo-

nides had. Ibn Khaldun begins by summing up what might be called the "articles of faith," the propositions that every Muslim must believe in order to be saved. He then continues.

These main articles of faith are proven by the logical evidence that exists for them. Evidence for them from the Quran and the Prophetic traditions also is ample. The scholars showed the way to them and the religious leaders verified them. However, later on, there occurred differences of opinion concerning the details of these articles of faith. Most of the difference concerned the "ambiguous verses" of the Quran. This led to hostility and disputation. Logical argumentation was used in addition to the traditional material. In this way, the science of dialectical theology originated.

We shall now explain this summary statement in detail. In many verses of the Quran the worshiped Master is described as being absolutely devoid (of human attributes), and this in absolute terms requiring no interpretation. All these verses are negative (in their statements). They are clear on the subject. It is necessary to believe them, and statements of the Lawgiver (Muhammad) and the men around him and the men of the second generation have explained them in accordance with their plain meaning.

Then there are a few verses in the Quran suggesting anthropomorphism, with reference to either the essence or the attributes of God. The early Muslims gave preference to the evidence for God's freedom from human attributes because it was simple and clear. They knew that anthropomorphism is absurd, but they decided that those (anthropomorphic) verses were the word of God and therefore believed them, without trying to investigate or interpret their meaning. . . . But there were a few innovators in their time who occupied themselves with those "ambiguous verses" and delved into anthropomorphism. One group operated with the plain [that is, literal] meaning of the relevant verses. They assumed anthropomorphism for God's essence, in that they believed that He had hands, feet and a face. Thus they adopted a clear-cut anthropomorphism and were in opposition to the verses stating God is devoid of human attributes. . . . The people who gave consideration to the anthropomorphic verses then tried to escape from the anthropomorphic abomination by stating that God has "a body unlike (ordinary human) bodies." . . . Another group turned to anthropomorphism with regard to the attributes of God. They assumed direction, sitting, descending, voice, letter (sound) and similar things on the part of God. Their stated opinions imply anthropomorphism, and like the former group they took refuge in statements like "a voice unlike voices," "a direction unlike directions," "descending unlike descending." . . .

Later on the sciences and the crafts increased. People were eager to write systematic works and to do research in all fields. The speculative theologians wrote on God's freedom from human attributes. At that juncture the Muʿtazila innovation came into being. The Muʿtazila extended the subject (of God's freedom from human physical attributes) to the negative verses and decided to deny God's possession of the ideational attributes of knowledge, power . . . and life, in addition to denying their consequences. . . . The Muʿtazila further decided to deny God's possession of volition. This forced them to deny predestination, because predestination requires the existence of a volition prior to the created things. They also decided to deny God's hearing and vision, because both hearing and vision are corporeal accidents. . . . They further decided to deny God speech for reasons similar to those they used in connection with hearing and vision. . . . Thus the Muʿtazila decided that the Quran was created. This was an innovation; the early Muslims had clearly expressed the contrary view. The damage done by this innovation was great. Certain leading Muʿtazilites indoctrinated certain Caliphs with it, and the people were forced to adopt it. The Muslim religious leaders opposed them. Because of their opposition, it was permissible to flog and kill many of them. This caused orthodox people to rise in defense of the articles of faith with logical evidence and to push back the innovations.

The leader of the speculative theologians, Abu al-Hasan al-Ashʿari [d. 935 C.E.] took care of that. He mediated between the different approaches. He disavowed anthropomorphism and recognized the (existence of the) ideational attributes. He restricted God's freedom from human attributes to the extent to which it had been recognized by early Muslims, and which had been recognized by the proofs stating the general applicability (of the principle) to special cases. He recognized the four ideational attributes [that is, of knowledge, power, volition, and life], as well as hearing, vision and speech, as an essential function of God, and this with the help of both logical and traditional methods. He refuted the innovators in all these respects. He discussed with them their stated opinions with regard to (God's concern for) human welfare and what is best for man, and their definition of good and evil, which they had invented on the basis of their innovation. He perfected the dogmas concerning the rising of the dead, the circumstances of the Resurrection, Paradise and Hell, and reward and punishment. Ashʿari added a discussion of the Imamate because the Imamite Shi'ites at that time suggested the novel idea that the Imamate was one of the articles of faith and that it was the duty of the Prophet as well as of the Muslim nation to fix (the succession to) the Imamate and to free the person who would become the Imam from any responsibility in this respect. However, the Imamate is at best a matter of public interest and social organization; it is not an article of faith. But it was added to the problems of this discipline. The whole was called "the science of dialectical theology." (Ibn Khaldun, *Muqaddima* 6.14) [IBN KHALDUN 1967: 3:45–50]

23. The Intrusion of Philosophy into Dialectical Theology

Even as this rationalist tradition was developing in Islamic circles, during the century and a half spanning the Mu'tazilite beginnings about 800 C.E. and the death of Ash'ari in 935, a great many Greek philosophical works were translated into Arabic, as Maimonides had pointed out in his summary. This project proceeded under the patronage of the very Caliph Ma'mun (813–833 C.E.) who had given an ear to the Mu'tazilites. The effects were not long in being felt on the nascent discipline of dialectical theology, not directly from the translations but from the adaptation of the analytical method into their own work by certain Muslim thinkers, as Ibn Khaldun continues.

Thus Ash'ari's approach was perfected and became one of the best speculative disciplines and religious sciences. However, the forms of its arguments are, at times, not technical [that is, not scientifically rigorous] because the scholars (of Ash'ari's time) were simple and the science of logic which probes arguments and examines syllogisms had not yet made its appearance in Islam. Even if some of it had existed, the theologians would not have used it because it was so closely related to the philosophical sciences, which are altogether different from the beliefs of the religious law and were, therefore, avoided by them. . . . After that the science of logic spread in Islam; people studied it. And they made a distinction between it and the philosophical sciences in that logic was merely a norm and yardstick for arguments and served to probe the arguments of the philosophical sciences as well as those of other disciplines.

Then, (once they had accepted the legitimacy of logic) scholars studied the premises the earlier theologians had established. They refuted most of them with the help of arguments leading them to a different opinion. Many of these (earlier) arguments were derived from philosophical discussions of physics and metaphysics, and when the scholars now

probed them with the yardstick of logic, it showed that the earlier arguments (like those used by Ashʿari) were applicable only to those other
(philosophical) disciplines and not to dialectical theology. But they did
not believe that if the arguments were wrong, the conclusion was also
wrong. . . . This approach differed in its technical terminology from the
earlier one; it was called "the school of recent scholars" [or, "the modern
school"], and their approach often included a refutation of the philosophers as well, where the opinions of the latter differed from the articles
of faith. They considered the philosophers the enemies of the articles of
faith because in most respects there is a relationship between the opinions
of the innovators and the opinions of the philosophers.

The first scholar to write in accordance with the (new) theological
approach was al-Ghazali [d. 1111 C.E.]. He was followed by the imam Ibn
al-Khatib [Fakhr al-Din al-Razi; d. 1209]. A large number of scholars
followed in their steps and adhered to their tradition. (Ibn Khaldun,
Muqaddima 6.14) [IBN KHALDUN 1967: 3:50–52]

*Ibn Khaldun follows the evolution of dialectical theology down closer to his own
time.*

If one considers how this discipline (of dialectical theology) originated and how scholarly discussion was incorporated in it step by step,
and how, during this process, scholars always assumed the correctness of
the articles of faith and paraded proofs and arguments in their defense,
one will realize that the character of this discipline is as we have established it, and that the discipline cannot go beyond those limits. However,
the two approaches have been mixed up by recent scholars: the problems
of theology have been confused with those of philosophy. This has gone
so far that one discipline is no longer distinguishable from the other. The
student cannot learn theology from the books of the recent scholars, and
the same situation confronts the student of philosophy. Such mixing was
done by Baydawi [d. 1286 C.E.] . . . and by later, non-Arab scholars in all
their works. . . .

The approach of the early Muslims can be reconciled with the beliefs
of the science of dialectical theology only if one follows the old approach
of the theologians (and not the mixed approach of more recent scholars).
The basic work here is the *Right Guidance* of al-Juwayni [d. 1083 C.E.], as
well as works that follow its example. Those who want to inject a refutation of the philosophers into their dogmatic beliefs must use the books of
Ghazali and Fakhr al-Din Razi. These latter do show some divergencies
from the old technique, but do not make such a confusion of problems

and subjects as is found in the approach of the recent scholars who have come after them.

Ibn Khaldun then sums up with his own reflections on speculative or dialectical theology. The year, it will be recalled, is 1377 C.E.

In general, it must be known that this science, the science of dialectical theology, is not something that is necessary to the contemporary student. Heretics and innovators have been destroyed. The orthodox religious leaders have given us protection against heretics and innovators in their systematic works and treatments. Logical arguments were needed only when they defended and supported (their views with them). Now, all that remains of those arguments is a certain amount of discussion, from most of whose ambiguities and inferences the Creator can be considered to be free. (Ibn Khaldun, *Muquaddima* 6.14)

[IBN KHALDUN 1967: 3:53–54]

24. The Limited Role of Dialectical Theology

It was not, then, an entirely successful enterprise in Islam, this dialectical theology. The fundamentalists regarded its use of intellectual arguments as unnecessarily rationalistic, while more philosophically sophisticated Muslims criticized its lack of scientific rigor. Ghazali—for Ibn Khaldun the first of the "modernists" in theology— was a scholar who understood the methods of discursive reasoning used by Greek and Muslim philosophers, and he recognized both the usefulness and the limits of dialectical theology. Like Ibn Khaldun, he emphasized its essentially defensive function.

God sent to His servants by the mouth of His Messenger, in the Quran and the Prophetic traditions, a creed which is the truth and whose contents are the basis of man's welfare in both religious and secular affairs. But Satan too sent, in the suggestions of heretics, things contrary to orthodoxy; men tended to accept his suggestions and almost corrupted the true creed for its adherents. So God brought into being the class of (dialectical) theologians, and moved them to support traditional orthodoxy with the weapon of systematic theology by laying bare the confused doctrines invented by the heretics at variance with traditional orthodoxy. This is the origin of (dialectical) theology and theologians.

In due course a group of theologians performed the task to which God invited them; they successfully preserved orthodoxy, defended the creed received from the prophetic source and rectified heretical innovations. Nevertheless in so doing they they based their arguments on premises which they took from their opponents and which they were compelled to admit by naive belief or the consensus of the community or bare acceptance of the Quran and the Prophetic traditions. For the most part their efforts were devoted to making explicit the contradictions of their opponents and criticizing them in respect of the logical consequences of what they admitted.

This method might serve with Muslims who were willing to start at the same shared premises, but it would hardly do with those other philosophers and theologians trained in the Hellenic mode and committed to beginning with the first principles of reason.

This method was of little use in the case of one who admitted nothing at all save logically necessary truths. . . . It is true that, when theology appeared as a recognized discipline and much effort had been expended on it over a considerable period of time, the theologians, becoming very earnest in their endeavors to defend orthodoxy by the study of what things really are, embarked on the study of substances and accidents with their natures and properties. But since that was not the (principal) aim of their science, they did not deal with the question thoroughly in their thinking and consequently did not arrive at results sufficient to dispel universally the darkness of confusion due to the different views of men. I do not exclude the possibility that for others than myself these results have been sufficient; indeed, I do not doubt that this has been so for quite a number. But these results were mingled with naive beliefs in certain matters which are not included among first principles. (Ghazali, *Deliverer from Error* 81–83) [GHAZALI 1953: 27–29]

25. Theology Is to Piety as Scansion Is to Poetry

As Maimonides pointed out, medieval Jewish theology from Saadya onward went through many of the same stages of excitement and doubt as its Islamic counterpart. There is little surprise in this, since the enterprise was being pursued by Muslims and Jews with a similar, sometimes an identical, culture, often writing in the same language in the very same cities. And, of course, both Muslims and Jews were attempting to protect revelation from a rationalism that at times threatened to overwhelm it. Thus Judah Halevi shared many of his contemporary Ghazali's reservations about dialectical theology and incorporated them in his dialogue with the Khazar king. Tell me, the king asks, about the "masters of dialectical theology." His Jewish interlocutor responds.

This theology has no value, save as an exercise in dialectics. . . . A simple, wise man, such as a prophet, can impart to others little by way of formal instruction, nor can he solve a problem by dialectical methods, while the master of dialectical theology possesses such an aura of learning that those who hear him consider him as superior to the simple pious man whose learning consists of beliefs which no one can induce him to abandon. Yet the supreme achievement of the master of dialectical theology, in all that he learns and teaches, would be that there should come into his own soul and the souls of his students those very same beliefs which are present by nature in the soul of the simple man.

It happens that the science of dialectical theology destroys many true beliefs in a man's heart by leading him into doubts and conflicting opinions. The masters of dialectical theology are like experts on poetic meters who investigate scansion. Such experts make a great fuss and use a lot of formidable terms to describe a skill which comes easily to someone naturally gifted in poetry, who senses the meter and so never breaks in any way the rules of scansion. . . . The same may be said about those who possess a natural aptitude for living according to the divine law and for drawing near to God: through the words of the pious sparks are kindled in their souls, which become rays of illumination in their hearts. A man not endowed with such a natural gift has necessarily to resort to dialectical theology, which may not bring him any benefit, and indeed may conceivably cause him positive harm. (Judah Halevi, *The Khazar King* 5.16) [HALEVI 1905: 56–57]

26. The Fundamentalist Position: "Without Howing" versus Dialectical Theology

One of the areas in which the early Muslim proponents of dialectical theology used their newly discovered skills was in explaining the various attributes attached to God in the Quran: "merciful," "compassionate," "powerful," "seeing," "knowing," "hearing," and so on. Some raise an immediate problem: How indeed can God see without eyes, or shall we credit Him with eyes as well? The problem is anthropomorphism, a problem that, upon closer inspection, all the attributes raise in one form or another. The early dialectical theologians attempted to address the problem in the same time-honored fashion invoked by Jewish and Christian theologians, the prudent use of allegorical exegesis.

The allegorizing of the divine attributes is an issue that never quite disappeared in Islam, and it was one of the grounds of choice for Muslim conservatives— the overwhelming number of them lawyers—to confront the theologians. Among the lawyers, it was the followers of Ahmad Ibn Hanbal (d. 855 C.E.) who took the most conservative positions of all. A Hanbalite spokesman in late-twelfth-century Damas-

cus was Ibn Qudama (d. 1223 C.E.), whose works include one pointedly entitled The Prohibition of the Study of the Works of the Dialectical Theologians. Here he concludes.

We have already pointed out by the preceding, the evil of the science of dialectical theology that originates in its very source, the censure of it by our religious leaders, the unanimous agreement of the learned men that its advocates are partisans of heretical innovations and error, that they are not regarded as belonging to the ranks of learned men, and that whoever occupies himself with it becomes a heretic and will not prosper. (Ibn Qudama, Prohibition 90)

The issue is a familiar one, and it serves to clarify what precisely constitutes heresy in Islam.

Allegorical interpretation is an innovation in religion. Now an innovation is any doctrine in religion which the Companions [that is, the generation of Muhammad's "contemporaries," the latter term construed broadly] had died mentioning. Innovation in religion is the heresy against which our Prophet has cautioned us, and which he informed us was the most evil of things. He has said (in a tradition): "The most evil things are the innovated ones." He has also said (likewise in a tradition): "Keep to my course of conduct and the course of conduct of the (first four) rightly guided Caliphs after me; hold fast to it." "Beware of innovations; for every innovation is a heretical innovation, and every heretical innovation is an error." Now, the allegorical interpreter has deserted the course of conduct of the Apostle of God and that of the rightly guided Caliphs; he is an inventor of heretical innovations, and has gone astray by virtue of the aforementioned tradition. (Ibn Qudama, Prohibition 56)

How, then, is one to deal with all the apparent anthropomorphisms used to characterize God in the Quran and the Prophetic traditions? Simply by accepting them, Ibn Qudama asserts. He offers a clear exposition of the conservative position in theology, the doctrine known in shorthand fashion as "Without Howing." The authority is no less than the eponym of the school himself.

An (earlier) Hanbalite has said: I asked Abu Abdullah Ahmad ibn Muhammad ibn Hanbal about those traditions which say that God will be seen, and that He plants His foot and other statements similar to these. Whereupon Abu Abdullah answered: We believe in them, and accept them as true, without rejecting any part of them, whenever their chains of transmitters are sound; nor do we deny the statements of the Apostle, for we know that what he has brought to us is true.

God should not be described in excess of His own description of Himself, boundless and immeasurable: "There is nothing like Him! He is the Hearing, the Seeing" (Quran 42:11). Therefore we say precisely what He has said, and describe Him as He has described Himself, without going beyond His description, or depriving Him any of His attributes merely for fear of some possible slander which might be leveled against us. We believe in these traditions, we acknowledge them, and we allow them to stand exactly as they have come down to us, without being able to understand the how of them, or fully understand their intended sense, except in accordance with His own description of Himself; and He is, according to His own description, the Hearing, the Seeing, boundless, immeasurable. His attributes proceed from Him and are His own. We do not go beyond the Quran or the traditions of the Prophet and his Companions; nor do we know the how of these, save by the acknowledgment of the Apostle and the confirmation of the Quran. (Ibn Qudama, *Prohibition* 19)

27. Ash'ari on the Charge of Heretical Innovation

Ibn Qudama's view that dialectical theology constituted a reprehensible innovation in Islam was hardly novel. The charge had been leveled against theologians almost from the beginning. Indeed, Ash'ari himself (d. 935 C.E.), one of the fathers of the discipline, had taken up arms against this allegation in a tract called On Thinking Well of Engaging in the Science of Theology. *The Prophet, it was said by the opponents of theology, knew nothing about such new-fangled notions, a "motion and rest, body and accident, accidental modes and states." Wrong, says Ash'ari.*

The Apostle of God did know these questions about which they have asked, and he was not ignorant of any detail involved in them. However, they did not occur in his time in such specific form that he should have, or should not have, discussed them—even though their basic principles were present in the Quran and the tradition of the Prophet. But whenever a question arose which was related to religion from the standpoint of the Law, men discussed it, and inquired into it, and disputed about it, and debated and argued. . . . Such questions, too numerous to mention, arose in their days, and in the case of each one there had come no explicit determination from the Prophet. For if he had given explicit instructions concerning all that, they would not have differed over those questions, and the differences would not have lasted till now.

The mere fact of these differences of opinion shows that men investigated, and will continue to investigate, matters of importance on which neither the Quran nor the tradition gives guidance. Moreover, Ash ͨari continues, the analogical method so typical of theology was the same one used in these investigations.

But even though there was no explicit instruction of the Apostle of God regarding each one of these questions, they referred and likened each to something which had been determined explicitly in the Book of God, and the Tradition, and their own independent judgment. Such questions, then, which involved judgments on unprecedented secondary causes, they referred to those determinations of the Law which are derivative, and which are to be sought only along the line of revelation and the Prophetic tradition. But when new and specific questions pertaining to basic dogmas arise, every intelligent Muslim ought to refer judgment on them to the sum of principles accepted on the grounds of reason, sense experience, intuition, etc. . . .

Judgment on legal questions which belong to the category of what is passed down by tradition is to be based on reference to legal principles which likewise belong to the category of the traditioned, and judgment on questions involving the data of reason and the senses should be a matter of referring every such instance to (something within) its own category, without confounding the rational with the traditioned or the traditioned with the rational. So if dialectical theology on the creation of the Quran and on the atom . . . had originated in those precise terms in the Prophet's time, he would have discussed and explained it, just as he explained and discussed all the specific questions which did originate in his time. (Ash ͨari, *The Science of Dialectical Theology* 21–22)

[ASH ͨARI 1953: 130–131]

28. The Fatal Flaw of Sacred Theology

Judah Halevi thought dialectical theology dangerous; Ibn Qudama regarded it as an unjustified and heretical innovation. But for the philosophically more astute Maimonides, who "knew the difference between demonstration, dialectic, and sophistry," this theology based on revelation had a fatal flaw: in truth it could not demonstrate anything.

All the first dialectical theologians from among the Greeks who had adopted Christianity and from among the Muslims did not conform to the appearance of that which exists, but considered how existence ought to be in order that it should furnish a proof for the correctness of a particular opinion, or at least should not refute it. And when such a fantasy held good, they assumed that what exists corresponds to that form and started to argue in order to establish the truth of the assertions from which are taken the premises that show the correctness of the doctrine, or at least do not refute it.

This was the way of the men of intellect who first used this method, put it down in books, and claimed that speculation alone impelled them to do so, and that they did not seek thereby to protect a doctrine or a preconceived opinion. Men of later periods who study these books know nothing about all this and consequently find in these ancient books a vigorous argument and a powerful endeavor to establish the truth of a certain thing or to refute a certain thing. . . . (They also believe) that their predecessors did what they did only in order to confuse the opinions of the philosophers and to make them doubt that which they regarded as a demonstration. Those who say this are not aware, and do not know, that the matters are not as they thought, but that their predecessors toiled to establish what they desired to establish and to refute what they desired to refute because of the harm that would come if this were not done— even if it were after a hundred propositions—to the opinion whose recognition as correct was desired by them. These ancient dialectical theologians did away with the disease starting with its root. . . .

When I studied the books of these dialectical theologians, as far as I had the opportunity—and I have likewise studied the books of the philosophers, as far as my capacity went—I found that the method of all the dialectical theologians was one and the same in kind, though subdivisions differed from one another. For the foundation of everything is that no consideration is due to how that which exists is, for it is merely a custom [or, the way it happens to be], and from the point of view of the intellect, it could well be different. Furthermore, in many places they follow the imagination [that is, the faculty wherein likely or probable truths reside] and call it intellect [that is, the faculty of necessary truths].

To illustrate his case, Maimonides chooses what was the absolute base issue between the philosophers on the one hand and the dialectical theologians and, indeed, all the partisans of revelation on the other. Genesis said, and the latter maintained, that the universe had been created in time; reason demonstrates, the philosophers had argued from the beginning, that the universe is eternal. Maimonides continues.

Thus when they [that is, the dialectical theologians] propound the premises that we will let you hear, they found by their demonstrations the (affirmative) judgment that the world is created in time. And when it is thus established that the world is created in time, it is likewise undoubtedly established that it has a Maker who has created it in time.

Then they infer that this Maker is One; whereupon, basing themselves on His being One, they affirm that He is not a body. This is the way of every dialectical theologian from among the Muslims in anything concerning this subject. Thus also do those belonging to our community who imitate them and follow their ways. . . .

Now when I considered this method of thought, my soul felt a very strong aversion to it, and had every right to do so. For every argument deemed to be a demonstration of the temporal creation of the world is accompanied by doubts and is not a decisive demonstration except to those who do not know the difference between demonstration, dialectic and sophistry. As for those who know these arts, it is clear and evident to them that there are doubts with regard to all these proofs and that premises that have not been demonstrated have been used in them. . . .

If you are one of those who are persuaded by what the dialectical theologians say, and if you believe that the demonstration with regard to the creation of the world in time is correct, bravo for you. If, however, it is not demonstrated in your opinion, and if you take over from the prophets, through obeying their authority, the doctrine that it was created in time, there is no harm in that. . . .

There may be no harm in allowing oneself to be convinced by the dialectical theologians, or even in simply taking one's beliefs straight out of Genesis, but that is not what Maimonides had in mind. His was a far more adventuresome project, one that Ibn Qudama would surely have objected to and one that many of Maimonides' own Jewish successors did in fact have grave doubts about. Maimonides explains.

The correct way, according to me, which is the method of demonstration about which there can be no doubt, is to establish the existence and the oneness of the deity and the negation of corporeality through the methods of the philosophers, which methods are founded upon the doctrine of the eternity of the world—not because I believe in the eternity of the world or because I concede this point to the philosopher, but because it is through this method that the demonstration becomes valid and perfect certainty is obtained with regard to those three things: I mean the existence of the deity, His oneness and His not being a body; all this without regard to reaching a judgment as to the world's being eternal or created in time. When these three great and sublime problems have been validated for us through a correct demonstration, we shall thereafter return to the question of the creation of the world in time and we shall enounce with regard to it all the argument that is possible. (Maimonides, *Guide of the Perplexed* 1: Chapter 71) [MAIMONIDES 1963: 178–183]

29. Rationalist Theology

Maimonides was assuredly not the only one aware of the dark little secret of the dialectical theology of the medieval Muslims and their Jewish imitators: that it was mostly dialectic, with very little theology. There were also those who, as Ghazali described them, "admitted nothing at all save logically necessary truths," to wit, the partisans of metaphysics or rationalistic theology on the Greek model. In his auto-biographical Deliverer from Error Ghazali offers a capsule history of this kind of theology from its point of origin among the Hellenes.

The study of philosophy began, Ghazali explains, with the "Materialists," who simply denied a Creator and posited an eternal cycle of everlasting generation, "animals from seed and seed from animals." The second group, the "Naturalists," were constrained by the order and excellence of nature to admit the existence of a Creator God, but they denied any spiritual existence and so the immortality of the soul and an afterlife. Finally, there are the "more modern" philosophers, called "Theists," who include Socrates, Plato, and Aristotle, the latter of whom "systematized logic for them and organized the sciences, securing a higher degree of accuracy and bringing them to maturity."

The Theists in general attacked the two previous groups, the Materialists and the Naturalists and exposed their defects so effectively that others were relieved of the task. . . . Aristotle, moreover, attacked his predecessors among the Theistic philosophers, especially Plato and Socrates, and went so far in his criticisms that he separated himself from them. Yet he too retained a residue of their unbelief and heresy from which he did not manage to free himself. We must therefore reckon as unbelievers both those philosophers themselves and their followers among the Islamic philosophers, such as Ibn Sina [or Avicenna], al-Farabi and others; in transmitting the philosophy of Aristotle, however, none of the Islamic philosophers has accomplished anything comparable to the two men named. (Ghazali, *Deliverer from Error* 87–88) [GHAZALI 1953: 31–32]

The principal area of unbelief lay, according to Ghazali, in the science called theology or metaphysics.

Here occur most of the errors of the philosophers. They are unable to satisfy the conditions of proof they lay down in logic and consequently differ much from one another here. The views of Aristotle, as expounded by Farabi and Avicenna, are close to those of the Islamic writers. All their errors are comprised under twenty heads, on three of which they must be reckoned infidels and on seventeen heretical innovators. . . . The three points on which they differ from all Muslims are as follows:

(1) [On the physical reality of Paradise and Hell], they say that for bodies there is no Resurrection: it is bare spirits which are rewarded or punished; and the rewards and punishments are spiritual, not bodily. They certainly speak true in affirming the spiritual ones, since these do exist as well; but they speak falsely in denying the bodily ones and in their pronouncements disbelieve the revelation.

(2) [On divine providence], they say that God knows universals, but not particulars. This too is plain unbelief. The truth is that "there does not escape Him the weight of an atom in the heavens or in the earth" (Quran 34:3).

And what Maimonides too had earmarked has a basic disagreement.

(3) [On the eternity of the world], they say that the world is everlasting, without beginning. But no Muslim has adopted any such view on this question. (Ghazali, *Deliverer from Error* 96–97) [GHAZALI 1953: 35–36]

30. Farabi on God's Providence

We note the issue between theology and Islam on the subject of the afterlife in Chapter 6 below. Here we see one of Islam's premier philosophers, al-Farabi, attempting to pick his careful way through the thorny and dangerous subject of divine providence.

Different beliefs are held by many people about the care of the Lord for His creation. Some maintain that He cares for His creation as a king cares for his subjects and their welfare, without conducting personally the affairs of any of them, and without connection between Him and partner or wife, but by appointing for the task one who will undertake it and discharge it, and do in regard to it what right and justice demand.

Farabi makes no comment on that view, so it may be his own, though we cannot be certain. The second is distinctly not his opinion, however.

Others think that the Creator is not sufficient unless He undertakes the personal management of each one of His creatures in each one of their actions, and directs them aright, and leaves none of his creatures to (the care of) others. It would follow that He is responsible for many actions which are defective, blameworthy, ugly actions, errors and abominable words and deeds, and when any of His creatures aims at attacking one of His clients—a reversal of truth by way of argument—He is his helper and responsible for leading him and guiding him. . . . And if they deny that He directs and helps such for some things, they must deny the whole doctrine. Such principles give rise to wrong ideas and give rise to vicious and abominable ways. (Farabi, *Aphorisms of the Statesman* 82) [FARABI 1961: 69]

31. Ghazali on Theology and Muslim Belief

Ghazali remained unconvinced by explanations such as Farabi's.

Among the most extreme and extravagant of men are a group of scholastic theologians who dismiss the Muslim common people as unbelievers and claim that whoever does not know scholastic theology in the form they recognize and does not know the prescriptions of the Holy Law according to the proofs which they have adduced is an unbeliever.

These people have constricted the vast mercy of God to His servants and made paradise the preserve of a small clique of theologians. They have disregarded what is handed down by the Prophetic traditions, for it is clear that in the time of the Prophet, may God bless and save him, and in the time of the Companions of the Prophet, may God be pleased with them, the Islam of whole groups of rude Arabs was recognized, though they were busy worshiping idols. They did not concern themselves with the science of analogical proof and would have understood nothing of it if they had.

Whoever claims that theology, abstract proofs and systematic classification are the foundations of belief is an innovator. Rather is belief a light which God bestows on the hearts of His creatures as a gift and a bounty from Him, sometimes through an explainable conviction from within, sometimes because of a dream in sleep, sometimes by seeing the state of bliss of a pious man and the transmission of his light through association and conversation with him, sometimes through one's own state of bliss. (Ghazali, *The Decisive Criterion* 202) [LEWIS 1974: 2:20–21]

32. The Truth of Philosophy

And yet Ghazali was by no means a fundamentalist in the mold of Ibn Qudama. He understood both the attractions and the dangers of philosophy and science, but he was unwilling to permit the dangers to be used as a reason for dismissing the truth and the certitude that philosophy brought. Mathematics provides an almost classic instance.

None of its results are connected with religious matters, either to deny or affirm them. They are matters of demonstration which it is impossible to deny once they have been understood and apprehended. Nevertheless there are two drawbacks which arise from mathematics. The first is that every student of mathematics admires its precision and the clarity of its demonstrations. This leads him to believe in the philosophers (and scientists generally) and to think that all their sciences resemble this one in clarity and cogency. Further, he has already heard the accounts on everyone's lips of their unbelief, their denial of God's attributes and their contempt for revealed truth; he becomes an unbeliever merely by accepting them as authorities, and says to himself, "If (revealed) religion were true, it would not have escaped the notice of these men since they are so precise in this science."

That is one extreme: seduction by mathematics. The other is no more attractive.

The second drawback arises from the man who is loyal to Islam but ignorant. He thinks that religion must be defended by rejecting every science connected with the philosophers, and so rejects all their sciences and accuses them of ignorance therein. He even rejects their theory of the eclipse of the sun and the moon, considering that what they say is contrary to religion. . . . A grievous crime indeed against religion has been committed by the man who imagines that Islam is defended by the denial of the mathematical sciences, seeing that there is nothing in revealed truth opposed to these sciences by way of either negation or affirmation, and nothing in these sciences opposed to the truths of revelation. (Ghazali, *Deliverer from Error* 90–91) [GHAZALI 1953: 33–34]

33. Rationalist Ethics and Revealed Morality

Ghazali had no brief for or interest in mathematics; it simply provided him, by the clarity and cogency of its demonstrations, a casebook model for the truth of science, even the foreign and often heretical science of the Greeks and the Muslim followers. Ethics, on the other hand, with its judgments about conduct and morality, is a rival and competitor of revealed religion, and so a more interesting and complicated case. There are, for example, the instances where the teachings of philosophical ethics, a well-defined branch of the Hellenic philosophical tradition, are identical with those of the Muslim moral theologians working with the data of revelation, as Ghazali saw himself doing. Two explanations are possible: that the former borrowed from the latter—an argument already familiar from Philo—or that the truth of God is essentially one and so there should be little wonder that different groups can reach it by different means. "Ethics," Ghazali begins, "consists in defining the characteristics and moral constitution of the soul and enumerating the various types of soul and the method of moderating and controlling them." He continues.

This they [that is, the philosophers] borrow from the teaching of the mystics, those men of piety whose chief occupation is to meditate upon God, to oppose the passions, and to walk in the way leading to God by withdrawing from worldly pleasure. In their spiritual warfare they have learned about the virtues and vices of the soul and the defects in its actions, and what they have learned they have clearly expressed. The philosophers have taken over this teaching and mingled it with their own disquisitions, furtively using this embellishment to sell their rubbishy wares more readily. . . .

From this practice of the philosophers of incorporating in their books conceptions drawn from the prophets and the mystics, there arise two evil tendencies, one in their partisans and one in their opponents.

The evil tendency in the case of the opponent is serious. A crowd of men of slight intellect imagines that, since these ethical conceptions occur in the books of the philosophers mixed with their own rubbish, all reference to them must be avoided, and indeed any person mentioning them must be considered a liar. They imagine this because they heard of the conceptions in the first place only from the philosophers, and their weak intellects have concluded that, since their author is a falsifier, they must be false.

We have heard the argument before from Ghazali, in the case of those who wished to throw out all of mathematics, baby, bathwater, and eclipses of the sun and moon. Here, however, the instance is different.

This is like a man who hears a Christian assert, "There is no god but the God, and Jesus is the Messenger of God." The man rejects this, saying, "This is a Christian conception," and does not pause to ask himself whether the Christian is an infidel only in respect of his denial of the prophethood of Muhammad, peace be upon him. If he is an infidel only in respect of his denial of the prophethood of Muhammad, then he need not be contradicted in other assertions, true in themselves and not connected with his unbelief, even though these are also true in his eyes (like the Christian statement cited above).

Ghazali then passes on to far more personal terrain than a defense of the Christians' right to be correct on certain religious matters.

To some of the statements made in our published works on the principles of the religious sciences an objection has been raised by a group of men whose understanding has not fully grasped the sciences and whose insight has not penetrated to the fundamentals of the systems. They think that these statements are taken from the works of the ancient philosophers, whereas the fact is that some of them are the product of reflections which occurred to me independently—it is not improbable that one foot should fall on another footprint—while others come from the revealed Scriptures, and in the case of the majority the sense, though perhaps not the actual words is found in the works of the mystics.

After this not entirely spirited defense of his own originality, Ghazali comes to the difficult heart of the matter, the spoliatio Aegyptorum, *or, to use Ghazali's own figure, honey in a cupping glass.*

Suppose, however, that the statements [that is, certain moral teachings] are found only in the philosophers' books. If they are reasonable in themselves and supported by proof, and if they do not contradict the Book and the Custom of the Prophet, then it is not necessary to abstain from using them. If we open this door, if we adopt the attitude of abstaining from every truth that the mind of a heretic has apprehended before us, we should be obliged to abstain from much that is true. We should be obliged to leave aside a great number of verses of the Quran and the traditions of the Messenger and the accounts of the early Muslims, and all the sayings of the philosophers and the mystics. . . . The lowest degree of education is to distinguish oneself from the ignorant ordinary man. The educated man does not loathe honey even if he finds it in the surgeon's cupping glass; he realizes that the cupping glass does not essentially alter the honey. The natural aversion from it in such a case rests on popular ignorance, arising from the fact that the cupping glass is made only for impure blood. Men imagine that the blood is impure because it is in the cupping glass, and are not aware that the impurity is due to a property of the blood itself. (Ghazali, *Deliverer from Error* 99–105) [GHAZALI 1953: 38–42]

34. Ibn Rushd: The Law Commands the Study of Philosophy

There were few in Islam who were willing to dispute Ghazali on this point; indeed, as is clear from Ibn Qudama's position, many Muslims found Ghazali's stance far too liberal when it came to the use of reason in thinking about God. The one voice raised against Ghazali in the name of philosophy was that of the Spanish scholar Ibn Rushd (d. 1198 C.E.), demonstrably the greatest student of the Hellenic philosophical tradition ever produced in Islam. Ghazali's Incoherence of the Philosophers *was countered point by point in Ibn Rushd's* Incoherence of the Incoherence. *Here, however, we hear the man the West knew as Averroes speaking to the issue*

*of philosophy in Islam in more general, and very Muslim, terms. We are now at the
opposite pole from Ibn Qudama: not only is intellectual investigation not heresy; it
is commanded by the Islamic law.*

Praise be to God with all due praise, and a prayer for Muhammad,
His chosen servant and Messenger. The purpose of this treatise is to
examine, from the standpoint of the study of the (Islamic) Law, whether
the study of philosophy and logic is allowed by the Law, or prohibited,
or commanded, either by way of recommendation or as obligatory.

We say: If the activity of philosophy is no more than the study of
existing beings and the reflection on them as indications of the Artisan [or
Creator], that is, inasmuch as they are products of art, for beings also
indicate the Artisan through our knowledge of the art in them, and the
more perfect this knowledge is, the more perfect the knowledge of the
Artisan becomes, and if the Law has encouraged and urged reflection on
beings, then it is clear that what this name (of philosophy) signifies is
either obligatory or recommended by the Law.

That the Law summons us to reflection on beings, and the pursuit
of knowledge about them by the intellect is clear from the several verses
of the Book of God, blessed be He and exalted, such as the saying of the
Exalted, "Reflect, you have vision" (Quran 59:2); this is textual authority
for the obligation to use intellectual reasoning, or a combination of intellectual and legal reasoning. Another example is His saying, "Have you not
studied the kingdom of the heavens and the earth, and whatever things
God has created?" (Quran 8:185); this is a text urging the study of the
totality of beings. Again, God the Exalted has taught that one of those
whom He singularly honored by this knowledge was Abraham, peace be
upon him, for the Exalted said, "So we made Abraham see the kingdom
of the heavens and the earth, that he might be . . . " etc. (Quran 2:5–6).
The Exalted also said, "Do they not observe the camels, how they have
been created, and the sky, how it has been raised up?" (Quran 2:6–7); and
He said, "and they gave thought to the creation of the heavens and the
earth" (Quran 2:7), and so in countless other verses.

Since it has now been established that the Law has rendered obligatory the study of beings by the intellect, and reflection on them, and since
reflection is nothing more than inference and drawing out of the unknown from the known, and since this is reasoning or at any rate done
by reasoning, therefore we are under an obligation to carry on our study
of beings by intellectual reasoning. It is further evident that this manner
of study, to which the Law summons and urges, is the most perfect kind

of study using the most perfect kind of reasoning; and this is the kind called "demonstration."

The Law, then, has urged us to have demonstrative knowledge of God the Exalted and all the beings of His creation. But it is preferable and even necessary for anyone who wants to understand God the Exalted and the other beings demonstratively to have first understood the kinds of demonstration and their conditions (of validity), and in what respects demonstrative reasoning differs from dialectical, rhetorical and fallacious reasoning. But this is not possible unless he has previously learned what reasoning as such is, and how many kinds it has, and which of them are valid and which invalid. This in turn is not possible unless he has previously learned the parts of reasoning, of which it is composed, that is, the premises and their kinds. Therefore he who believes in the Law and obeys its commands to study beings, ought prior to his study to gain a knowledge of these things, which have the same place in theoretical studies as instruments have in practical activities. (Ibn Rushd, *The Decisive Treatise* 1–2) [AVERROES 1961: 44–46]

One objection can be easily dispensed with.

It cannot be objected: "This kind of study of intellectual reasoning is a heretical innovation since it did not exist among the first believers." For the study of legal reasoning and its kinds is also something which has been discovered since the (time of) the first believers, yet it is not considered a heretical innovation. So the objector should believe the same about the study of intellectual reasoning. For this there is a reason, which is not the place to answer here. But most (masters) of this religion (that is, Islam) support intellectual reasoning, except a small group of gross literalists, who can be refuted by (sacred) texts. (Ibid. 3) [AVERROES 1961: 46]

Ibn Rushd is not naive; he is well aware of the dangers to the faith, real or alleged, that are associated with the study of Greek philosophy.

From (all) this it is evident that the study of the books of the ancients is obligatory by (Islamic) Law, since their aim and purpose in their books is just the purpose to which the Law has urged us, and that whoever forbids the study of them to anyone who is fit to study them, that is, anyone who unites the two qualities of natural intelligence and religious integrity and moral virtue is blocking people from the door by which the Law summons them to knowledge of God, the door of theoretical study which leads to the truest knowledge of Him; and such an act is the extreme of ignorance and estrangement from God the Exalted.

And if someone errs or stumbles in the study of these books owing to a deficiency in his natural capacity, or bad organization of his study of them, or being dominated by his passions, or not finding a teacher to guide him to an understanding of their contents, or a combination of all or more than one of these causes, it does not follow that one should forbid them to anyone who is qualified to study them. For this manner of harm which arises owing to them is attached to them by accident, not by essence; and when a thing is beneficial by its nature and essence, it ought not to be shunned because of something harmful contained in it by accident. This was the thought of the Prophet, peace be upon him, on the occasion when he ordered a man to give his brother honey to drink for his diarrhea, and the diarrhea increased after he had given him the honey; when the man complained to him about it, he said, "God spoke the truth; it was your brother's stomach that lied." We can even say that a man who prevents a qualified person from studying books of philosophy, because some of the most vicious people may be thought to have gone astray through their study of them, is like a man who prevents a thirsty person from drinking cool, fresh water until he dies from thirst because some people have choked to death on it. For death from water by choking is an accidental matter, but death by thirst is essential and elementary. (Ibid. 5–6) [AVERROES 1961: 48–49]

35. The Ban on the Greeks

As we have already seen, the ninth-century discovery, via translation, of the works of Greek philosophers like Plato and Aristotle encouraged the growth of a rationalist movement in Islam. We have also noted the reaction that soon appeared in traditionalist circles, particularly among the Hanbalites. The balance between faith and reason was indeed a perilous one, and when a thinker like Ibn Sina or Maimonides was seen to have conceded too much to the claims of reason, disclaiming voices were soon raised. Ibn Sina provoked the reaction of Ghazali, and Maimonides too, for his part, provoked a great many protests, especially among Western Jews.

Maimonides was a particularly complicated case, since he stood behind, as Ibn Sina did not, a large body of impeccably orthodox writing on the subject of the Mosaic Law. But the tone and the argument of the Guide of the Perplexed *delivered a quite different message to many. Notable among the defenders of the traditional approach to Judaism was Solomon ben Adret, a prestigious rabbi of Barcelona, here writing in response to a query sometime about a generation after the death of Maimonides in 1204 C.E.*

You have made inquiry about my attitude toward that traditional story according to which the world will come to an end after a certain time; you say that you have discovered statements in the writings of Rabbi Moses Maimonides which contradict this (traditional belief).

You should know that in these and all similar matters, when we attempt to investigate them through pure science, the latter view must inevitably prevail; thus we are indeed forced to conclude that the world will never cease to exist, since science is based upon perceptions and observations of nature, and we can observe that all the planets as well as the earth are in perpetual motion without alteration. But the belief in an end to the world is not founded on any sense perception but on the evidence of the sages, with the result that this belief cannot be undermined.

What has been founded on tradition or prophetic inspiration cannot be undermined by any science in the world, since science ranks (in certitude) far below prophetic inspiration. This is a principle agreed upon by the adherents of all positive religions, and in particular by the adherents of our own true faith. We believe in the entire tradition, as we believe in the supernatural miracles which were done for the patriarchs, for example, as we believe in the passing through the Red Sea and the Jordan, in the sun's standing still, etc. To be sure, all this is denied by the philosophers, and for them neither Moses nor any of the prophets avails anything.

The philosophers pure and simple are one thing, but what of those Jews who were attempting to reconcile tradition and philosophy?

If Jewish scholars were to accept the point of view maintained by science in general, they would be constrained to interpret many passages of Scripture in a forced way in order to bring them into agreement with science, and to explain many things allegorically because philosophy cares not at all for prophets or commandments. If we wish, then, as true Jewish scholars, to remain in agreement with tradition, we must explain the words of the Bible without concern as to whether or not they agree with the conclusions of science. It is possible, for example, to interpret all the passages in the Bible which refer to resurrection allegorically, particularly the narrative of the dry bones (Ezek. 37). But though there is in this way no necessity to apply any particular verse of Scripture to an actual general resurrection, tradition nevertheless obliges us to do so, and this is enough to oblige us to interpret the respective verses in a corresponding way, since divine wisdom is of far greater value to us than human wisdom, and as we must give unconditional preference to a tradition preserved by our forefathers, which is deeply rooted and founded in the prophets, rather than to the results of our limited human knowledge. (Solomon ben Adret, *Letter to an Anonymous Inquirer*)

For some, these public pronouncements of private sentiments were not enough. Ben Adret was urged to act more officially in this situation when "the sanctuary is being consumed by rotten books," as one partisan put it. He did. Solomon wrote to various communities advising them to forbid the study of philosophy to men under thirty. The advice provoked in 1304 C.E. the following retort from Jacob ben Machir, a mathematician of Montpellier.

. . . If such (scientific) studies do damage to faith, why then do you permit them at all and require only that a line should be drawn between youth and maturity? Is a man of advanced years, then, entitled to expose his faith in religious truths which he learned in his youth to the temptations of philosophical scepticism later on? I am perfectly aware that your true but secret intention is to deny the validity of science altogether, because you have often spoken in a derogatory manner about it and its pioneers, and have even declared that Maimonides' positions on cosmology are without foundation. . . .

I concede that there are some unacceptable notions expressed in the writings of the philosophers, but this hardly justifies your refusal to allow us to acquaint ourselves with the good ideas they contain. Our scientific efforts demonstrate to the nations [that is, the Gentiles] that we have an open mind and an appreciation for everything that is beautiful and good. We might even take them as an example in this regard, since they honor the scholars of other denominations who translate their writings into the languages spoken by those denominations even though they may be in profound disagreement with the latter's ideas. The convictions of a people are in no way weakened by such an attitude, and their faith is nowhere and never undermined, and certainly not ours, for the truth of which we possess the best possible proofs. Besides, there is no one among us who wants to dissolve all biblical stories into allegories; I myself know very well the frontier which philosophy must not cross in its criticism of the Bible, and the most ardent fanatic has no grounds for criticizing me for going too far in this respect. I neither overestimate nor underestimate the value of philosophy, and I am thankful to anybody who can give me a satisfactory explanation of one of those wondrous Talmudic legends.

Solomon ben Adret responded almost immediately.

. . . I regret the injury to your dignity, which you yourself endanger by lowering yourself to practices unworthy of the height to which your peers rightly elevated you by reason of your learning, and by joining the children who can scarcely cry "Daddy" or "Mommy" but who nonetheless throw themselves into the arms of secular science and make a hobby of astrological reveries and overhasty syllogisms. It is true that such studies may be of profit to men of experience whose hair has grown gray while they studied Torah, and that they offer to reasonable people a somewhat deeper insight into the essence of religion, than which no better evidence can be found than Maimonides himself. Besides, mathematics and medicine do not at all belong to the sciences interdicted by me. Even so, a complete peace between philosophy and revealed religion is inconceivable. (Solomon ben Adret, *To Jacob ben Machir*)

In Barcelona in July 1305 C.E. Solomon ben Adret published the final version of his interdiction. A formal ban or excommunication was pronounced upon all those Jews under the age of twenty-five who studied the books of the Greeks on natural science—medicine excepted—or the first philosophy or metaphysics, whether in the original or in translation. It is difficult to measure the effects of the ban in either the short or the long term. Ben Adret died in 1310 and his edict does not seem to have long survived him.

36. The Mystic's Gnosis and the Theologian's Science

The philosopher and the theologian both claimed, then, a privileged access to a knowledge of God, claims resting essentially on the primacy and autonomy of reason. But there was another such claim in Islam, as there had been in the two Abrahamic faiths that preceded it: the mystic too claimed the benefit of a privileged knowledge of God, primary, authentic and immediate, visionary, intuitive—a genuine gnosis.

Ghazali, who was in the unique position of being both a theologian and a mystic, has left us a comparative evaluation of the mystic's inspired gnosis and the theologian's discursively developed understanding in his Revivification of the Sciences of Religion. *Both ways of knowing do indeed open a way to God, but there are fundamental and crucial differences between them, as he pedagogically explains in a chapter subtitled: "Wherein there is set forth the difference between inspiration and study, between the way of the Sufis in discovering the truth and the way of those given over to speculative knowledge."*

Be aware that the types of knowledge which are not necessarily possessed by everyone come into the heart in different ways and the mode by which they arrive varies. At times they appear unexpectedly in the heart as if they had been thrown in from the heart knows not what source. At other times they are acquired by the method of intellectual elaboration and study. The knowledge which arises neither by way of acquisition nor by the operation of a deductive chain is called inspiration;

that which comes about from intellectual elaboration is called examination or reflection.

The knowledge which presents itself in the heart of a sudden and without striving, study or work on the part of the subject is of two types: the first is of the kind that a man is unaware how it came to him or whence; the second carries with it an understanding of the means whereby it came, that is, the vision of the angel who cast it into the heart. The first type is called inspiration and breathes in the depths of the heart; the second is called revelation and properly belongs to the prophets. As for the first, it is characteristic of the saints and the pure of heart, while the previously mentioned type of knowledge, the kind acquired by means of intellectual elaboration, that is proper to the learned.

After this somewhat scholastic introduction, Ghazali turns to more Quranic—and more mystic—images and language.

What can be truly said of the subject (of such inspired knowledge) is that his heart is ready to receive the irradiation of the Truth of Truths which is in all things. Nothing in effect can interpose itself between the heart and things . . . a kind of veil which puts itself between the mirror of the heart and the Well-Guarded Tablet upon which is inscribed all that God has decreed until the Day of Resurrection. The truths of knowledge radiate from the mirror of the tablet onto the mirror of the heart, as an image produced on a mirror will imprint itself on another placed in front of it.

The veil which is between the two mirrors is sometimes drawn aside by the hand, sometimes by the breaths of air that move it. Thus there blow at times the breaths of grace; the veils are then lifted from before the eyes of the heart and certain of the things inscribed on the Well-Guarded Tablet are reflected in him. That occurs from time to time in sleep and by this means one knows what will happen in the future. As for the complete removal of the veil, that will occur at the point of death when there will be removed that which conceals. But it also happens that the veil is drawn aside during the waking state to the extent of being lifted by a hidden grace of God Most High, and then something of the marvels of knowledge gleams in hearts from behind the veil of the Mystery. At times it is like a quick lightening flash; at other times a whole series of them, but limited, and it is extremely rare that this condition is much prolonged.

Just as it is only the mode of its acquisition that distinguishes the mystic's grace-inspired knowledge from the scholar's—whether he is one of the philosophers or one of the ulama class—the same distinction prevails between inspiration—God's gift to the saint—and revelation, God's gift to the prophet.

Inspired knowledge differs from acquired knowledge by neither its nature nor its locus nor its cause but only with respect to the removal of the veil: that is not within the power of man. And revelation in turn does not differ from inspiration with respect to any of these but only by the vision of the angel who brings the knowledge, which comes into our hearts only through the agency of angels. God Most High alludes to it in His words, "It is not given to man that God should speak to him, except by a revelation, or from behind a veil, or by sending an apostle in order that this latter, by God's permission, reveals to man what God wishes" (Quran 42:50–51).

With these preliminaries out of the way, the mystics' most influential and respected spokesman in Islam comes to the parting of the paths and follows the one that leads to his real subject, the Sufi way to God.

With this introduction, know that Sufis prefer the knowledge that comes by inspiration, to the exclusion of that acquired by study. Again, they desire neither to study such learning nor to learn anything of what authors have written on the subject: to inspect neither their teachings nor their arguments. They maintain on the contrary that the "way" consists in preferring spiritual combat, in getting rid of one's faults, in breaking one's ties and approaching God Most High through a single-minded spiritual effort. And every time those conditions are fulfilled, God for His part turns toward the heart of His servant and guarantees him an illumination by the lights of understanding.

Since God Most High has reserved to Himself the power of governing the heart, when the Mercy of God is extended upon this latter, light shines there, his breast expands, the secret of the Kingdom is revealed to him, the veil which blinded him disappears from before his face by the grace of the Mercy and the Truths shine out before him. The only thing in the power of the believer is that he prepare by the purification that strips him clean and that he arouse in himself a care for such things, as well as a sincere will, a consuming thirst and an attentive observation in the constant expectation of what God most High will reveal to him of His Mercy.

As for the prophets and the saints, this object was never revealed to them and the light was never expanded in their breasts either by dint of study or intellectual labors or by things written in books, but they arrived at it by renouncing the world to lead an ascetic life, by freeing themselves of their attachments, by emptying their hearts of their earthly occupations and by approaching God Most High by a single-minded spiritual effort. And he who is God's, God is his.

The Sufis say that the way that leads to such an end consists first of all in cutting off all one's attachments to the world, to cease preoccupying oneself with family, wealth, children, one's homeland, as well as with learning, with authority, with honor; and more, to bring the heart to a state where the existence or non-existence of everything is a matter of indifference. Then the Sufi retires into his own company, into a cell, obliging himself to fulfill the obligatory religious precepts and obligations. He remains thus, his heart empty, concentrating on a single objective. He does not dissipate his thoughts either by reading the Quran or meditating on one of its commentaries, or on the books of Prophetic traditions or any other. He attempts to achieve just the opposite, that nothing should enter his spirit save God Most High.

When he is seated in solitude, he does not cease to say "God, God" continuously and with a recollected heart. And he carries on until he comes to a state where he abandons the movement of his tongue and imagines the word [that is, the name of God] rolling off his tongue. Then he arrives at the point of obliterating any trace of the word from his tongue and he finds his heart continuously applied to (the exercise of) recollection. And he perseveres in it with determination until he reaches the point where he effaces the image of this word from his heart, the letters and the form of the word, and only the sense of the word remains in his heart, present within him, as if joined to him and never leaving him.

It is within his power to arrive at this point and to make this stage endure while resisting temptations. He cannot, however, draw upon himself the Mercy of God Most High. Rather, by his efforts he makes himself ready to receive the breaths of the divine Mercy and there remains nothing else for him to do but to await what God will reveal to him of His Mercy, as He revealed it, by this same way, to the prophets and the saints.

Then, if the will (of the Sufi) has been sincere, his spiritual effort a pure one, and his perseverance perfect; if he has not been carried in the opposite direction by his passions or preoccupied by an unrest arising from his attachments to the world, then the rays of the Truth will shine in his heart. At the outset this will be like a sudden lightening that does not last, then returns, but slowly. If it does return, sometimes it remains and sometimes it is only passing. If it remains, sometimes its presence is extended and sometimes not. And at times illuminations like the first appear, one following the other; at other times they are reduced to a single experience. The saints' "resting" in that state are without number, just as their natures and characters are innumerable.

In sum: this way leads solely, insofar as it concerns you, to a complete purity, purification and clarity, and then to being ready, expectant.

Finally, Ghazali returns to the opening theme, the difference between the inspired knowledge of the Sufi and the discursive knowledge of the theologian.

As for those who practice speculation and discursive examination, they do not deny the existence of this way (of the Sufi), or its possibility, or that it can arrive at such an end on rare occasions: it is, after all, the state often achieved by the prophets and the saints. But they have looked upon it as an arduous way, slow to yield its fruits, requiring a complex of conditions rarely achieved. They have maintained that at this point it is almost impossible to break one's attachments to the world and that to arrive at a "state" and remain there is more difficult still. . . . As a consequence of this kind of spiritual struggle (they say), the temperament is spoiled, the reason disordered and the body made ill. If the soul has not been exercised (by the practices of piety) and formed by the realities of the sciences to begin with, the heart is monopolized by corrupt imaginings in which the soul takes its rest over an extended period of time, to the point that one's life is past and over without success having been achieved. How many Sufis who have followed this route have remained for twenty years in the grip of some imaginary fantasy, while someone who had previously been solidly grounded in learning would have immediately recognized the dubious quality of this product of the imagination. To devote oneself to following a course of study is the surest way of proceeding and accomplishing the end.

(The dialectical theologians) say that this attitude of the Sufis is like that of a man who neglects the study of the religious law by maintaining that the Prophet, may the peace and blessing of God be upon him, did not study but became expert in this discipline by revelation and inspiration, without studying texts or writing commentaries on them, and so will I, perhaps, by the practice of asceticism and sheer perseverance. Whoever thinks that way, they maintain, does ill to himself and is squandering his life. Indeed, he is like a man who leaves off trying to earn a living and cultivating the soil in the hope of chancing upon some buried treasure or other, something that is possible but highly improbable. (Ghazali, *Revivification* 3:16–17)

37. Ibn al-Arabi on the Irrelevance of Ibn Rushd

Jewish respect for Maimonides may have prevented a more radical reaction to the rationalist tradition that he so brilliantly and profoundly represented. In Islam, too, the scholastics' reverence for Ghazali and Ghazali's moderating influence may have prevented a full-scale reaction to the rationalist strain. But there are responses other than reaction, and the more radical mystical thinkers in Islam—more radical than al-Ghazali at any rate—illustrate another view of rationalism. For example, Ibn al-Arabi (1165–1240 C.E.), from his own supremely confident position—the text of his book The Bezels of Wisdom, *he informs the reader at the outset, was handed to him by no other than Muhammad himself in Damascus in the month of Muharram, 1230 C.E.—simply dismisses the rationalizing and rationalist ways of trying to understand God as at worst ignorant and at best irrelevant. In his* Meccan Revelations *Ibn al-Arabi tells this highly revealing anecdote about a meeting in Cordova between himself, the still very young patron saint of Islamic theosophy, and Ibn Rushd, the "second Aristotle" of Islam.*

I spent a good day in Cordova at the house of Abu al-Walid ibn Rushd. He had expressed a desire to meet with me in person, since he had heard of certain revelations I had received while in retreat, and had shown considerable astonishment concerning them. In consequence, my father, who was one of his close friends, took me with him on the pretext of business, in order to give Ibn Rushd the opportunity of making my acquaintance. I was at the time a beardless youth.

As I entered the house the philosopher rose to greet me with all the signs of friendliness and affection, and embraced me. Then he said to me, "Yes!" and showed pleasure on seeing that I had understood him. I, on the other hand, when I became aware of the motive of his pleasure, replied, "No!" At this Ibn Rushd drew back from me, his color changed and he seemed to doubt what he had thought of me. He then put to me the following question: "What solution have you found as a result of mystical illumination and divine inspiration?" I replied "Yes and No. Between the Yea and the Nay the spirits take their flight beyond matter, and the necks detach themselves from their bodies." At this Ibn Rushd became pale, and I saw him tremble as he muttered the formula, "There is no power save from God." This was because he had understood my allusion. (Ibn al-Arabi, *Meccan Revelations* 1:153) [IBN AL-ARABI 1980: 2]

We are somewhat less certain than Ibn Rushd about the meaning of the allusion, but there is no mistaking Ibn al-Arabi's views on what and how we know about God—or better, the Reality. He begins with an attack on the very foundation of the rationalist enterprise, the principal of causality.

An indication of the weakness of intellectual speculation is the notion that a cause cannot be (also) the effect of that to which it is a cause. Such is the judgment of the intellect, while in the science of divine Self-revelation it is known that a cause may be the effect of that for which it is a cause. . . . The most that the intellectual will admit to on this matter, when he sees that it contradicts speculative evidence, is that the essence, after it is established that it is one among many causes, in some form or other, of a (given) effect, cannot be an effect to its effect, so that that effect should become its cause, while the first still remains a cause, but that if its determination becomes changed by its transformation in forms, then it may thus become an effect to its own effect, which might then become its cause. This then is as far as he will go, when he perceives that the matter does not agree with his rational speculation.

There have been none more intelligent than the Apostles, God's blessing be on them, and what they brought us derives from the divine Majesty. They indeed confirmed what the intellect confirms, but added more that the intellect is not capable of grasping, things the intellect declares to be absurd, except in the case of one who has had an immediate experience of divine manifestation; afterwards, left to himself, he is confused as to what he has seen. If he is a servant of the Lord, he refers his intelligence to Him (to respond to his perplexities), but if he is a servant of reason, he reduces God to reason's yardstick. This happens only so long as he is in this worldly state, being veiled from his otherworldly state in this world. (Ibn al-Arabi, *The Bezels of Wisdom*, "Elias") [IBN AL-ARABI 1980: 234]

The "servant of the Lord" and the "servant of reason" are thus neatly distinguished. Other similar distinctions, all to the same point, appear often in his work.

For the believers and men of spiritual vision it is the creation that is surmised and the Reality that is seen and perceived, while in the case of those not in these two categories, it is the Reality Who is surmised and the creation that is seen and perceived by the senses. . . .

Men are divided into two groups. The first travel a way they know and whose destination they know, which is their "Straight Path" (of Quran 11:56). The second group travel a way they do not know and of whose destination they are unaware, which is equally the Straight Path. The gnostic calls on God with spiritual perception, while he who is not a gnostic calls on Him in ignorance and bound by a tradition.

Such a knowledge is a special one stemming from "the lowest of the low" (Quran 95:5), since the feet are the lowest part of the person, what is lower than that being the way beneath them. He who knows that the

Reality is the way knows the truth, for it is none other than He that you progress and travel, since there is naught to be known save Him, since He is Being Itself and therefore also the traveler himself. Further, there is no Knower save Him; so who are you? Therefore, know your true reality and your way, for the truth has been made known to you on the tongue of the Interpreter [that is, Muhammad], if you will only understand. He is a true word that none understands, save that his understanding be true; the Reality has many relations and many aspects. . . .

. . . You may say of Being what you will; either that it is the creation or that it is the Reality, or that it is at once both the creation and the Reality. It might also be said that there is neither creation nor the Reality, as one might admit to perplexity in the matter, since by assigning degrees the difficulties appear. But for the limitation (that arises in defining the Reality), the Apostles would not have taught that the Reality transforms Himself in cosmic forms nor would they have described Him (at the same time) as abstracting Himself from all forms. . . .

Because of this (inevitable limitation by definition), He is both denied and known, called incomparable and compared. He who sees the Reality from His standpoint, in Him and by Him, is a gnostic. He who sees the Reality from His standpoint, in Him, but with himself as the seer, is not a gnostic. He who does not see the Reality in this way, but expects to see Him by himself, he is ignorant.

In general most men have perforce an individual concept of their Lord, which they ascribe to Him and in which they seek Him. So long as the Reality is presented to them according to it, they recognize Him and affirm Him, whereas if it is presented in any other form, they deny Him, flee from Him and treat Him improperly, while at the same time imagining that they are acting toward Him fittingly. One who believes (in the ordinary way) believes only in a deity he has created in himself, since a deity in "beliefs" is a (mental) construction. They see (in this deity) only themselves and their own constructions within themselves. (Ibn al-Arabi, *The Bezels of Wisdom*, "Hud") [IBN AL-ARABI 1980: 132–133]

6. The Last Things

All religions agree on the fact that souls experience states of happiness and misery after death, but they disagree in the manner of symbolizing these states and explaining their existence to men. (Ibn Rushd, *Unveiling of the Programs of Proof* 122) [AVERROES 1961: 76]

So Ibn Rushd, a Muslim philosopher of Spain in the waning years of the twelfth century. It is the beginning of a chapter on the "Future Life." His mood in writing it was more defensive, perhaps, than philosophical, as we shall see, but he knew whereof he spoke. Again, referring to the future life, Ibn Rushd remarks:

This is a problem which is not found in the older philosophers, although resurrection has been mentioned in different religions for at least a thousand years, and the philosophers whose theories have come to us are of more recent date. The first to mention bodily resurrection were the prophets of Israel after Moses, as is evident from the Psalms and many books attributed to the Israelites. Bodily resurrection is also affirmed in the New Testament and attributed by tradition to Jesus. (Ibn Rushd, *Incoherence of the Incoherence* 580) [AVERROES 1954: 359]

And, the Muslim Ibn Rushd had no need of adding, resurrection sounds like a trumpet throughout the Quran.

1. The Darkness Below

The Israelites unmistakably had some notions of a type of survival beyond the grave, although, despite Ibn Rushd's flat assertion, the concept does not seem to have been integrated into God's or their own thinking about the Covenant or the Law. Indeed, there is no sure biblical reference to a resurrection or an authentic form of life after death until the Book of Daniel, the last work included in the Bible. Enoch and Elijah were immortal only in the sense that they did not die. The fear of eternal punishment or the promise of an eternal reward are never offered in the Torah as motives for fidelity to the Covenant.

According to the biblical evidence, the dead were thought to survive, after a fashion, and they may have been the subject of some kind of tomb cult in Israel. This passage in Deuteronomy addressed to the Lord seems to imply that untithed food offered to the dead is right and appropriate.

I have neither transgressed nor neglected any of Your commandments. I have not eaten any of the tithe while in mourning; I have not cleared out any of it while I was unclean, and I have not deposited any of it with the dead. (Deuteronomy 26:13–14)

The abode of these not-quite dead—the "strengthless dead," as they are later called—where the Bible does give it a name, is Sheol. Descriptions of it and its location are vague. Sheol is generally a dark, underground place—its other names are "the grave" or "the abyss"—and its principal inhabitants seem to be those who died violently or did not receive appropriate burial, as here in Isaiah and Ezekiel.

> Once you thought in your heart,
> "I will climb to the sky,
> Higher than the stars of God
> I will set my throne.
> I will sit on the mount of assembly,
> On the summit of Zaphon:
> I will mount the back of a cloud—
> I will match the Most High."
> Instead, you are brought down to Sheol,
> To the bottom of the Pit . . .
> All the kings of nations
> Were laid, every one,
> Each in his tomb.
> While you were left unburied,
> Like loathesome carrion,
> Like a trampled corpse
> In the clothing of the slain gashed by the sword
> Who sink to the very stones of the Pit.
> (Isaiah 14:13–19)

Thus said the Lord God: On the day he [that is, the Pharaoh] went down to Sheol, I closed the deep over it and covered it; I held back its streams and great waters were checked. . . . When I cast him down to Sheol with those who descend into the Pit. . . . You too shall be brought down . . . to the lowest parts of the netherworld; you shall lie among the uncircumcised and those slain by the sword. Such shall be the fate of Pharaoh and all his hordes—declares the Lord. (Ezekiel 31:15–18)

O mortal, (the Lord said) wail (the dirge)—along with the women of the mighty nations—over the masses of Egypt, accompanying their descent to the lowest part of the netherworld, among those who have gone down into the Pit. Whom do you surpass in beauty? Down with you, and be laid to rest with the uncircumcised! . . .

From the depths of Sheol the mightiest of warriors speak to him [that is, the Pharaoh] and his allies; the uncircumcised, the slain by the sword, have gone down and lie there. (Ezekiel 32:18–21)

Israelite malefactors too are plunged into Sheol.

Scarcely had Moses finished speaking all these words when the ground under them burst asunder, and the earth opened its mouth and swallowed them up with their households, all Korah's people and all their possessions. They went down alive into Sheol with all that belonged to them; the earth closed over them and they vanished from the midst of the congregation. (Numbers 16:31–33)

But there is another, more neutral view of Sheol as a "quiet grave" shared by high and low alike.

Why did I not die at birth, expire when I came forth from the womb? . . . For now I would be lying in repose, asleep and at rest, with the world's kings and counselors who rebuild ruins for themselves, or with nobles who possess gold and fill their houses with silver. Or why was I not like a buried stillbirth, like babies who never saw the light? There the wicked cease from troubling; there rest those who strength is spent. Prisoners are wholly at ease; they do not hear the taskmaster's voice. Small and great alike are there, and the slave is free of his master. (Job 3:11–19)

2. The Resurrection

Then, in the Book of Daniel, written sometime about 165 B.C.E., when Israel was in the grip of what appeared might be a fatal pogrom at the hands of Antiochus Epiphanes, this apparently new perspective appears in Daniel's vision.

At that time, the great prince, Michael, who stands beside the sons of your people, will appear. It will be a time of trouble, the like of which has never been since the nation came into being. At that time the people will be rescued, all who are found inscribed in the book. Many of those who sleep in the dust of the earth will awake, some to eternal life, others to reproaches, to everlasting abhorrence. And the knowledgeable will be radiant like the bright expanse of sky, and those who lead the many to righteousness will be like the stars forever and ever. (Daniel 12:1–4)

Thus the first unmistakable reference to a future life is connected, as it will often be in subsequent references, with righting life's wrongs—the collective wrongs to Israel, as here, or the injustices suffered by an individual. In the Jewish tradition at least, a belief in immortality was born of a desire for theodicy.

But there is something else in the text as well. Unless the word "like" is here signaling only a metaphor, there is a connection of the just with heaven and the stars. We are perhaps at the Jewish beginning—it was fairly commonplace among the pagans—of the notion that the good "go to heaven."

3. Sadducees, Pharisees, Rabbis, and Others on the Afterlife

The point of view put forward in Daniel 12, though it was taken up and elaborated by many in the period between the two Testaments, did not entirely drive out the old Israelite denial of a life after death, not at least until 70 C.E. and the triumph of the Pharisees. Chief among the Jews who denied an afterlife were the Sadducees, the conservative and aristocratic party who constituted the ruling group in the Sanhedrin for most of the period. Opposing them on the issue of immortality were the Pharisees. Josephus first offers this general characterization of the two parties.

The Pharisees had passed on to the people certain regulations handed down by former generations and not recorded in the Laws of Moses [that is the Torah, the Pentateuch], for which reason they are rejected by the Sadducees, who hold that only those regulations should be considered valid which were written down (in Scripture), and those that were (only) handed down by former generations need not be observed. (Josephus, *Antiquities* 13:297)

As a consequence of that fundamental difference in deriving the Law there followed these opposed views of the afterlife.

The Pharisees . . . believe that souls have the power to survive death and that there are rewards and punishments under the earth for those who have led lives of virtue or vice: eternal imprisonment is the lot of evil souls, while the good souls receive an easy passage to a new life. . . . The Sadducees hold that the soul perishes along with the body. (Josephus, *Antiquities* 18:14–16)

Paul plays upon that same fundamental difference of opinion when he is taken in custody before the council of the Sanhedrin for a hearing.

Paul was well aware that one section of them [that is, of the San-hedrin] were Sadducees and the other Pharisees, so he called out in the Council, "My brothers, I am a Pharisee, a Pharisee born and bred; and the true issue in this trial is our hope of the resurrection of the dead." At these words the Pharisees and the Sadducees fell out among themselves, and the assembly was divided—the Sadducees deny that there is any resurrection, or angel or spirit, but the Pharisees accept them. So a great uproar broke out; and some of the doctors of the Law belonging to the Pharisaic party openly took sides and declared, "We can find no fault with this man; perhaps an angel or spirit has spoken to him." The dissen-sion was mounting, and the (Roman) commandant was afraid that Paul would be torn to pieces, so he ordered the troops to go down and bring him into the barracks. (Acts 23:6–10)

Paul was in fact a Pharisee, or at least educated as one, as he tells us elsewhere, and so it is not remarkable that he should follow the Pharisaic position on the question of life after death. But what of his master, Jesus? In Mark 12 Jesus is approached by some Sadducees, who, as the Gospel remarks, "say that there is no resurrection" (Mark 12:18). They pose him a legal conundrum: a woman has married seven different husbands in series, all of whom predecease her. To which of them will she be married at the resurrection, "when they all come back to life"? The intent was probably to demolish belief in the afterlife by a legal reduction to the absurd, but Jesus takes the question seriously and gives a serious answer.

Jesus said to them, "You are mistaken, and surely this is the reason: you do not know either the Scriptures or the power of God. When they rise from the dead, men and women do not marry; they are like angels in heaven. But about the resurrection of the dead, have you never read in the Book of Moses, in the story of the burning bush, how God spoke to him and said, "I am the God of Abraham, the God of Isaac and the God of Jacob" (Exod. 3:6). God is not the God of the dead but the God of the living.

Thus Jesus' answer too is in perfect agreement with the teaching of the Pharisees, and his attempt to establish it out of the Torah is precisely the polemical tack taken by the later rabbis when they debated the resurrection question in the tractate "Sanhedrin" in the Talmud. "Debate" is not perhaps the word. The Sadducees were no longer a force in Jewish life after 70 C.E., and so the Pharisaic view that there was an afterlife, a place of punishment and reward, had become in fact Jewish "orthodoxy." Witness, for example, the second of the Eighteen Blessings introduced into standard synagogue worship in this era (see Chapter 1 above).

You, O Lord, are mighty forever, You quicken the dead, are mighty to save. You sustain the living with loving kindness, quicken the dead with great mercy, support the falling, heal the sick, loose the captive, and keep Your faith with those who sleep in the dust. Who is like You, Lord of mighty deeds, and who resembles You, O King, who kills and quickens and causes salvation to spring forth.

Yes, faithful You are to quicken the dead. Blessed are You, O Lord, who quickens the dead. (Shemoneh Esreh 2)

The starting point of the Talmudic discussion was, in any event, this Mishnaic text.

All Israel have a portion in the world to come, for it is written, "Your people are all righteous; they shall inherit the land forever, the branch of My planting, the work of My hands, that I may be glorified" (Isa. 60:22). But the following have no portion therein: he who maintains that resurrection is not a biblical doctrine, the Torah was not divinely revealed and an Apiqoros [that is, an "Epicurean"]. (M.Sanhedrin 10:1)

He who holds that "resurrection is not a biblical doctrine" is obviously the Sadducee or a connected group. "Epicurean" here and elsewhere in the Talmud seems to extend farther than the Greek philosophical school of that name, and at times it seems to be used generically as "heretic." But there was a connection between the philosophy and the Talmud's "Apiqoros," and nowhere more clearly than here, since a central tenet of Greco-Roman Epicureanism was its denial of the afterlife.

So the discussion proceeds in BT.Sanhedrin 90b–92b. Texts are brought forth; and although there is no clear-cut statement to that end, there is an attempt to show that the resurrection can at least be deduced from or was intimated in the Bible. Many of the adduced texts depend on allegorical interpretations or the presence in a cited text of an indefinite future tense that is then construed to refer to the afterlife. There is a passing, almost casual reference to Daniel 12 but, interestingly, no use of Exodus 3:6, the text cited by Jesus.

If we cannot hear Jesus' rabbinic voice in BT.Sanhedrin 90b–92b, we can certainly hear Paul's. First, Rabbi Meir (d. ca. 175 C.E.) responds to a query not from the queen of Egypt but from the name that stood in the text at that point before it got garbled, the chief of the Samaritans.

Queen Cleopatra [that is, the Samaritan patriarch] asked Rabbi Meir: "I know that the dead will revive, for it is written, 'And they [that is, the righteous] shall blossom forth out of the city like the grass of the earth' (Ps. 72:16). But when they arise, shall they be nude or in their clothes?" He replied: "You may deduce an answer a fortiori from a grain of wheat: if a grain of wheat, which is buried naked, sprouts in so many robes, how much more so the righteous, who are buried in their raiment?"

And Paul, in response to a very similar question:

You may ask, how are the dead raised? In what kind of a body? How foolish! The seed you sow does not come to life unless it has first died, and what you sow is not the body that shall be, but a naked grain; and God clothes it with the body of His choice, each seed with its own particular body. All flesh is not the same flesh: there is flesh of men, flesh of beasts, of birds, and of fishes—all different. . . . So it is with the resurrection of the dead. What is sown in the earth as a perishable thing is raised imperishable. Sown in humiliation, it is raised in glory; sown in weakness, it is raised in power; sown as an animal body, it is raised as a spiritual body. (Paul, *To the Corinthians* 1.15:35–44)

4. Gehinnom

Together with a growing conviction from the second century B.C.E. onward that there was an afterlife went the elaboration of its function and features, largely through the agency of the "heavenly journey" discussed in Chapter 4 above. There was, to begin with, the older Sheol; but although the Septuagint and the Christian Latin version of the Bible both translate "Sheol" by "Hades" and "Infernus," respectively, it does not appear that Sheol was the Hell of those somewhat later traditions. It was not created for punishment, and if there was torment in Sheol, it was the torment of privation, aloneness, ineffectiveness.

A place of explicit damnation does eventually appear in the Jewish tradition, as a separate phenomenon from Sheol. There was a valley immediately to the south of Jerusalem known as "the valley of the Children of Hinnom," in Hebrew, Ge ben Hinnom or Ge Hinnom. Under the the later monarchy, during the reigns of Ahaz and Menasseh, the place called "the Valley of Hinnom" was used as the site of ritual sacrifice, where Jews offered their children as burnt sacrifice to the god Moloch. Then, with the restoration of the Law under Josiah, official action was taken concerning the shrine called Topheth in the Gehinnom.

He [Josiah] desecrated Topheth in the valley of the Ben Hinnom, so that no one might make his son or daughter pass through the fire in honor of [or: as an offering to] Moloch.

The people of Judah have done what displeases Me—declares the Lord. They have set up their abominations in the House which is called by My name, and they have defiled it. And they have built the shrines of

Topheth in the Valley of Ben Hinnom to burn their sons and daughters in fire—which I never commanded, which never came to My mind.

Assuredly, a time is coming—declares the Lord—when men shall no longer speak of Topheth or the Valley of Ben Hinnom, but of the Valley of Slaughter; and they shall bury in Topheth until no room is left. The carcasses of this people shall be food for the birds of the sky and the beasts of the earth, with none to frighten them off. (Jeremiah 7:30–33)

Possibly Isaiah is thinking of this same place of filth, pollution, and smoldering fires in a passage where the Lord predicts His final victory over His enemies. A later generation of Jews certainly understood it to mean Gehinnom, as we shall see.

All flesh . . . shall go out and gaze on the corpses of the men who rebelled against Me; their worms shall not die, nor their fire be quenched; they shall be a horror to all flesh. (Isaiah 66:23–24)

And this passage too from Zechariah was read by later rabbis as referring to a judgment after death, though there is no sign in the text itself that it refers to such an eschatological event.

Throughout the land—the Lord declares—two-thirds shall perish, shall die, and one-third of it shall survive. That third I will put into the fire, and I will smelt them as one smelts silver and test them as one tests gold. (Zechariah 13:8–9)

5. A Moral Hell

When we turn to "The Wisdom of Solomon," a work composed by an Alexandrian Jew of the first century B.C.E., we can see the new notions at work on the moral plane. The case is put forward by "the wicked" that life is short and there is nothing afterwards, so come, let us enjoy.

A passing shadow, such is our life, and there is no postponement of our end, man's fate is sealed and none returns. Come then and let us enjoy the good things while we can, and make full use of creation, with all the eagerness of youth. Let us have costly wines and perfumes to our heart's content and let no flower of spring escape us. (Wisdom of Solomon 2:5–8)

So they argued, and very wrong they were; blinded by their own malevolence, they did not understand God's hidden plan; they never expected that holiness of life would have its recompense; they thought that innocence had no reward. But God created man for immortality, and made him the image of His own immortal Self; it was the devil's spite that brought death into the world, and the experience of it is reserved for those who take his side.

But the souls of the just are in God's hand, and torment shall not touch them. In the eyes of foolish men they seemed to be dead; their departure was reckoned as defeat, and their going from us disaster. But they are at peace, for though in the sight of men they may be punished, they have a sure hope of immortality; and after a little chastisement they will receive great blessings, because God has tested them and found them worthy to be His. Like gold in a crucible he put them to the proof and found them acceptable like an offering burnt whole upon the altar. (Wisdom of Solomon 2:21–3:6)

The hope of the godless man is like down flying on the wind, like spindrift swept before a storm, and smoke which the wind whirls away, or like the memory of a guest who stayed for one day and passed on. But the just live forever: their reward is in the Lord's keeping and the Most High has them in His care. Therefore royal splendor shall be theirs, and a fair diadem from the Lord Himself. (Wisdom of Solomon 5:14–16)

In 2 Maccabees, likewise written in Egypt ca. 124 B.C.E., King Antiochus is depicted as bent on executing seven brothers for their fidelity to the Law. They respond:

Fiend though you are, you are setting us free from this present life, and since we die for His laws, the King of the universe will raise us up to a life everlastingly made new. (2 Maccabees 7:9)

Or again:

Better to be killed by men and cherish God's promise to raise us again. There will be no resurrection to life for you. (2 Maccabees 7:14)

The passage in 2 Maccabees that most interested later Christians in the Latin West seemed like a scriptural verification—the Books of Maccabees were included in the Christian canon of Scripture—of their belief in Purgatory as a place of temporary punishment where the pains of the dead sinner could be alleviated by the prayers of the living.

Regrouping his forces, he [that is, Judah Maccabeus] led them to the town of Adullam. The seventh day was coming on so they purified themselves, as custom dictated, and kept the Sabbath there. Next day they went, as had now become necessary, to collect the bodies of the fallen (in battle) in order to bury them with their relatives in the ancestral graves. But on every one of the dead, they found, under the tunic, amulets sacred to the idols of Jamnia, objects which the Law forbids to Jews. It was evident to all that here was the reason why these men had fallen. Therefore they praised the work of the Lord, the Just Judge who reveals what is hidden; and turning to prayer, they asked that this sin might be entirely blotted out.

The noble Judah called on the people to keep themselves free from sin, for they had seen with their own eyes what had happened to the fallen because of their sin. He levied a contribution from each man and sent the total of two thousand silver drachmas to Jerusalem for a sin offering. (2 Maccabees 12:38–44)

A sin offering is normal; what is unusual here is that it is for the dead. It is perhaps the novelty of it that elicits the immediately following remark, or defense, from the author of 2 Maccabees.

. . . [A] fit and proper act in which he took due account of the resurrection. For if he had not been expecting the fallen to rise again, it would have been foolish and superfluous to pray for the dead. But since he had in view the wonderful reward reserved for those who die a godly death, his purpose was a holy and pious one. And this is why he offered an atoning sacrifice to free the dead from their sin. (2 Maccabees 12:45)

6. The New Testament Vision of the Beyond

A later generation of Christians combed the Bible as carefully as the rabbis did for texts in support of their vision of the afterlife as a place of punishment and reward. And like the rabbis they found them. But save for the one example of Daniel, the exegesis seems forced in the extreme. Yet if the Israelites had no such view of the afterlife, many post-Exilic Jews certainly did, including Jesus and Paul. The later Christians were correct in supposing that they had inherited their notions of the afterlife from the Jews, but the legacy came from those generations of Jews who composed the Apocrypha, the Mishna, and the Talmud and who believed firmly in an eternal Hell and an eternal Paradise and described them in a series of vivid apocalypses.

The Synoptic Gospels all have their apocalyptic chapters, as we have seen. Taken as a whole, their view of the afterlife was a traditional one, as that word was understood in conservative Jewish circles after the Exile: there was a life after death characterized by God's judgment, His punishments, and His rewards in places set aside for that purpose. This, for example, is Enoch's version of the end from the second century B.C.E.

And in those days the earth will return what has been entrusted to it, and Sheol will return what has been entrusted to it, that which it has received, and destruction will return what it owes. And he [that is, the

Chosen One] will choose the righteous and holy from among them, for the day has come near that they must be saved. And in those days the Chosen One will sit on his [or "My"] throne, and all the secrets of wisdom will flow from the counsel of his mouth, for the Lord of the Spirits has appointed him and glorified him. And in those days the mountains will leap like rams, and the hills will skip like lambs satisfied with milk, and all will become angels in heaven. Their faces will shine with joy, for in those days the Chosen One will have risen; and the earth will rejoice, and the righteous will dwell upon it, and the chosen will go and walk upon it. (1 Enoch 61)

Such visions of future glory doubtless colored the Christians' expectation of the coming Kingdom, but the Gospels show the darker side of the End Time as well. Its themes are already present in the teaching of John the Baptist.

The people were on the tiptoe of expectation, all wondering about John, whether he was perhaps the Messiah, but he spoke out and said to them all: I baptize you with water; but there is one to come who is mightier than I. I am not fit to unfasten his shoes. He will baptize you with the Holy Spirit and with fire. His threshing fork is ready in his hand, to winnow his threshing floor and gather the wheat into his granary; but he will burn the chaff on a fire that will never go out. (Luke 3:15–17)

On Jesus' own teaching there can be no doubt. These remarks are from the Sermon on the Mount. The place of eternal punishment is now firmly "Gehenna," the Bible's Gehinnom.

Anyone who nurses anger against his brother must be brought to judgment. If he abuses his brother he will have to answer for it to the court; if he sneers at him he will have to answer for it in the fires of Gehenna. (Matthew 5:22)

If your right eye is your undoing, tear it out and fling it away; it is better for you to lose one part of your body than for the whole of it to be thrown into Gehenna. (Matthew 5:29)

To which there is added, in Mark's version of the saying, the characterization already cited from Isaiah 66:24.

. . . Gehenna, where the devouring worm never dies and the fire is not quenched. (Mark 9:48)

Not everyone who calls me "Lord, Lord" will enter the kingdom of Heaven but only those who do the will of my heavenly Father. (Mark 7:21)

And on curing the servant of the Gentile centurion:

Many, I tell you, will come from east and west to feast with Abraham, Isaac and Jacob in the kingdom of heaven. But those who were born to the kingdom will be driven out into the dark, the place of wailing and grinding of teeth. (Matthew 8:11–12)

The same theme and images show up in the parables, in the story of a man's enemy sowing weeds among his wheat, for example. Both crops are allowed to grow together until harvest time, when they are harvested separately, first the weeds for burning and then the wheat for storage in barns.

His disciples came to him [that is, Jesus] and said, "Explain to us the parable of the weeds in the field." And this was his answer: "The sower of the good seed is the Son of Man. The field is the world; the good seed stands for the children of the Kingdom, the weeds for the children of the evil one. The enemy who sowed the weeds is the devil. The harvest is the end of time. The reapers are angels. As the weeds, then, are gathered up and burnt, so at the end of time the Son of Man will send out his angels, who will gather out of his kingdom whatever makes men stumble and all whose deeds are evil, and these will be thrown into the blazing furnace, the place of wailing and grinding of teeth. And then the righteous will shine as brightly as the sun in the kingdom of their Father. If you have ears, then hear." (Matthew 13:36–43)

When the Son of Man comes in his glory and all the angels with him, he will sit in state upon his throne, with all the nations gathered before him. He will separate men into two groups, as a shepherd separates the sheep from the goats, and he will place the sheep on his right hand and the goats on his left. Then the king will say to those on his right hand, "You have my Father's blessing; come, enter and possess the kingdom that has been ready for you since the world was made." . . . Then he will say to those on his left hand, "The curse is upon you; go from my sight to the eternal fire that is ready for the devil and his angels." . . . And they will go away to eternal punishment and the righteous will enter eternal life. (Matthew 25:31–46)

Like the place of torment, Gehenna, the place of eternal life has also been localized. Jesus refers to it in his final moments of life. As he hangs on the cross, the criminal crucified next to him turns to Jesus.

And he said, "Jesus, remember me when you come to your throne." He answered, "I tell you this. Today you shall be with me in Paradise." (Luke 23:43)

It was, as we shall see, a promise fulfilled.

7. The Charting of Hades

The Gospels do not offer many details of Paradise and Gehenna, but Jewish apoca-
lypses from 1 Enoch in the second century B.C.E. to 4 Ezra in the late first century
C.E. provide elaborate "eyewitness" reports, particularly of the now elaborate geog-
raphy of the underworld of the damned.

Enoch was the enigmatic biblical presence described simply in Genesis 5:24:
"Having walked with God, Enoch was seen no more, because God took him away."
Where God took him is not explained in the Bible. But in the period after the Exile,
and for long afterwards, Enoch became the subject of an elaborate visionary litera-
ture among the Jews, part of which professed to describe, in his name, the regions
of the afterlife. The shadowy biblical Sheol has now been fleshed out with many of
the features, geographical and cosmological, of the Greek underworld.

And they took me to a place where those who were there were like
burning fire, and when they wished, they made themselves look like men.
And then they led me to a place of storm and a mountain the tip of whose
summit reached to heaven. And I saw lighted places and thunder in the
outermost ends, in its depths a bow of fire and arrows and their quivers,
and a sword of fire, and all the flashes of lightning. And they took me to
the water of life, as it is called, and to the fire of the west which receives
every setting of the sun. And I came to a river of fire whose fire flows like
water and pours into the great sea which is toward the west. And I saw
all the great rivers, and I reached the great darkness and went where all
flesh walks. And I saw the mountains of the darkness of winter and the
place where all the water of the deep pours out. And I saw the mouths
of all the rivers of the earth and the mouth of the deep.

This is, then, the subbasement of the universe. It is also the place of future punish-
ment. In Enoch's account, as in almost all its successors, it will be populated by
exemplary sinners, here the immortal "sons of the gods" who had defiled themselves
by intercourse with the "daughters of men" in Genesis 6:4, as is explained to Enoch
by the archangel Uriel.

And Uriel said to me: "The spirits of the angels who were promis-
cuous with women will stand here; and they, assuming many forms, made
men unclean and will lead men astray so that they sacrifice to demons as
gods—that is, until the great judgment day on which they will be judged
so that an end will be made of them. And their wives, having led astray
the angels of heaven, will become sirens. And I, Enoch, alone saw the
sight, the ends of everything, and no man has seen what I have seen." (1
Enoch 17–19)

As happened later in Christian and Muslim circles, though Gehenna had its un-
doubted interest for visionaries and storytellers, it fell to the rabbinic lawyers to
extract the appropriate judicial conclusions from the mass of scriptural and tradi-
tional material that lay before them. Here the question is twofold: who is in
Gehenna and what is the duration of their punishments?

Rabbi Shammai teaches this: that there will be three groups at the
judgment: one of the truly holy, another of the truly wicked, and a third
in between. It is immediately written and sealed that the truly holy shall
live until the end of time, and it is likewise written that the truly wicked
shall remain in Gehenna, as it is written (Dan. 12:2). As for the third
group, they shall go down to Gehenna for a time and then come up again,
as it is written (Zech. 13:9 and 1 Sam. 2:6). But the Hillelites say: He who
is abundant in mercy inclines toward mercy, and it is of them that David
speaks (Ps. 116:1) to God, who hears him and responds in these terms:
. . . Sinners, Jew and Gentile alike having sinned in their body, shall be
punished in Gehenna for twelve months and then reduced to nothingness.
(BT.Rosh Hashanah 16b–17a)

Or as the Tosefta to Sanhedrin refines it, making it very clear that Gehenna is not
a Purgatory but rather the antechamber to annihilation:

. . . [T]heir souls are reduced to nothing and their bodies burned and
Gehenna vomits them up; they become ash and the wind disperses them
to be trodden underfoot by the holy. (Tosefta Sanhedrin 13:3)

8. A Rabbinic Discussion of Gehenna

By the time the Babylonian Talmud was assembled in the sixth or early seventh
century C.E., the notion of a Hell for grave sinners was a familiar one in Jewish
circles, learned and unlearned. Here in Talmud "Erubin" the subject of Gehenna
comes up, entirely naturally, in the course of a discussion of other matters. The par-
ticipants deal with both the scriptural topoi and the legal issues with practiced ease.

Rabbi Joshua ben Levi has said: What (is the meaning of) what is
written (in Ps. 65:2): "Passing through the valley of Baca they make it a
place of springs; yes, the early rain clothes it with blessings"?

Joshua ben Levi's exegesis, which follows, is not so arbitrary as perhaps it appears
in translation. Each interpretation is based on the root of the Hebrew word under
examination.

"Passing" is an allusion to men who transgress the will of the Holy
One, blessed be He; "valley" (is an allusion to these men) for whom
Gehenna is made deep; "of Baca" (signifies) that they weep and shed

tears; "they make it a place of springs," like the constant flow of the altar drains; "the early rains clothe it with blessings," that is, they acknowledge the justice of their punishment and declare before Him, "Lord of the universe, You have judged well. You have condemned well and provided Gehenna for the wicked and Paradise for the righteous."

It would seem, then, on the basis of Rabbi Joshua ben Levi's exegesis of the verse in Psalms that even the wicked acknowledge the justice of God's judgment. We are not entirely surprised, however, to discover that there is another point of view, here expressed through Simeon ben Lakish, relying on his own understanding of the famous passage in Isaiah 66:24. The apparent conflict of opinions is soon resolved in favor of Joshua ben Levi.

[It might be objected that] this is not (so). For did not Rabbi Simeon ben Lakish state: The wicked do not repent even at the gate of Gehenna, for it is said, "And they shall go forth and look upon the carcasses of men who rebel against me . . . " (Isa. 66:24), where it is not said "who have rebelled" but "who rebel" (implying) that they go on rebelling forever? There is no contradiction since the former [that is, Ben Levi] refers to transgressors in Israel and the latter [Ben Lakish] to transgressors among idol worshipers. Logical argument also leads to this conclusion, since otherwise a contradiction would arise between two statements of Resh Lakish. For Resh Lakish (also) stated: The fire of Gehenna has no power over the transgressors in Israel, as may be inferred *a minori ad majus* from the golden altar: if (the gilt veneer) on the golden altar, which was only the thickness of a dinar, lasted for many years and the fire had no power over it, how much more would that be the case with the transgressors in Israel who are as full of good deeds as a pomegranate (with seed), as is said in Scripture, "Your temples are like a pomegranate" (Song of Songs 6:7), and Rabbi Simeon ben Lakish remarked: Do not read "Your temples" but "Your empty ones" (signifying) that even the worthless among you are as full of good deeds as a pomegranate.

If one is to follow Resh Lakish in this matter and maintain that Israelites do not suffer in Gehenna, are we forced to go back and reinterpret "passing through the valley of Baca"? No, the text continues.

. . . [T]hat (refers to the fact) that they [that is, the wicked Israelites] are at the time under sentence to suffer in Gehenna, but our father Abraham comes, brings them up and receives them, except such an Israelite as had immoral intercourse with the daughter of an idolater, since his foreskin is drawn forward and he cannot be discovered (by Abraham). Rabbi Kahana demurred. Now that you have laid down that "who rebels" implies that they go on rebelling, would you also maintain that where it is written in Scripture "who brings out" or "who brings up," that (the meaning is) "who always brings up" or "who always brings out"? So you must admit that (the meaning is) "who brought up" or "who brought out" and so too here "who rebelled."

The thread of the discussion returns to the authority with whom it began, Rabbi Jeremiah ben Eleazar, but it remains firmly on the last subject, Gehenna.

Rabbi Jeremiah further stated: Gehenna has three gates: one in the wilderness, one in the sea and one in Jerusalem. In the wilderness since it is written in Scripture, "Since they [Korah and his sons], and all that belongs to them, went down alive into the pit" (Num. 16:33). In the sea, since it is written in Scripture, "Out of the belly of the underworld I cried, and You heard my voice" (Jon. 2:3). In Jerusalem, since it is written in Scripture, "Says the Lord, whose fire is in Sion and His furnace in Jerusalem" (Isa. 31:9), and the school of Rabbi Ishmael taught that "whose fire is in Sion" refers to Gehenna and "His furnace in Jerusalem" refers to the gate of Gehenna.

Are there no more (gates) than that? Has not Rabbi Meryon in fact stated in the name of Rabbi Joshua ben Levi . . . : There are two palm trees in the Valley of Ben Hinnom and between them smoke rises, and it is (in connection with) this spot that we have learned "The stone palms of the iron mountain are fit (for the lulab), and this is the gate of Gehenna"? Is it possible that this is the same as "the one in Jerusalem"?

Rabbi Joshua ben Levi stated: Gehenna has seven names, and they are Sheol, Destruction, the Pit, Tumultuous Pit, Miry Clay, Shadow of Death and the Underworld. . . . Are there no more (names) than this? Is there not in fact the name of Gehenna? (This means) a valley that is as deep as the valley of Hinnom and into which all go down for gratuitous acts. . . .

(As for) Paradise, Resh Lakish said: If it is in the Land of Israel, its gate is Beth Shean; if it is in Arabia, its gate is Beth Gerem; and if it is Between the Rivers [that is, Syria-Mesopotamia], its gate is Damascus. (BT.Erubin 19a)

Sheol survives in Jewish thought as a dark and underground place, the world of graves and tombs, the abode of the dead. But it is Gehinnom, or Gehenna as it is called when it appears in the Greek of the Gospels, that is the place of punishment. It is somewhere far below, under the abyss or the ocean, but its original geographical site stays firm: the vent hole of Hell remains in the Ge ben Hinnom south of Jerusalem.

9. The Heavenly Garden

As we have seen, the "good thief" in Luke's Gospel is told that he will be with Jesus in Paradise. "Paradise," the Greek term borrowed from the Persian word for "royal park" or "plantation," was there and thereafter doing service as a translation for the Hebrew "Gan Eden," the Garden of Eden: Jesus' kingdom, and the abode of the blessed in the afterlife, is identical with the biblical Eden.

Throughout the Bible the name Eden is used only of Genesis' terrestrial paradise of Adam. Eventually, however, in post-Exilic times, the Garden of Eden became the name for the abode of the just after death. This was a new development. At first a place had been reserved, almost as a kind of celestial storage, for Enoch and Elijah, the two mortals taken up alive to heaven. By the first century B.C.E., when the later parts of the first Book of Enoch came to be written, there were others as well: "the elect who dwell in the garden of life" (1 Enoch 61:12). It is Enoch who speaks.

And he was lifted on the chariots of the spirit, and his name vanished from among men. And from that day I was not counted among them, and he placed me between two winds, between the north and the west, where the angels took the cords to measure for me the place of the chosen and the righteous. And there I saw the first fathers and the righteous who from the beginning of the world dwelt in that place. (1 Enoch 70: 2–4)

At about the same time, the Garden was being relocated from some not very certain site on earth into the remote heavens. The point was probably to move His saints closer to God after death. Indeed, some refer to Paradise as the abode of both God and the just, while others place the righteous and their Paradise in the third heaven, or even the seventh heaven, the highest of the firmaments and just below the abode of God. The following is Enoch's version of Paradise: it is located in the third heaven, and its physical features are now considerably more detailed than Genesis' rather spare account of the earthly Garden of Eden.

And these men [that is, Enoch's angel guides] led me from there to the third heaven and set me in the midst of Paradise. And that place is more beautiful than anything there is to see—all trees in full bloom, all fruit ripe, every kind of food always in abundance, every breeze fragrant. And there are four rivers flowing by in silent course: the whole garden is good, producing what is good to eat.

And the tree of life is in that place, where the Lord rests, when He goes into Paradise. And that tree is indescribable for the quality of its fragrance. . . . And every tree is laden with good fruit: there is no tree that is without fruit; and the whole place is blessed.

Paradise appears swept and garnished, but as yet uninhabited. Enoch's guides explain.

And I said, how very blessed is this place. The men answered me, This place, Enoch, is prepared for the righteous, who will endure hardships in this life, and mortify themselves, and turn their eyes away from unrighteousness, and execute true justice, to give bread to the hungry, and to cover the naked with a garment, and to lift up anyone who has fallen, and to help those who have been wronged, who live their lives in God's presence and serve Him alone. For them is this place prepared as their eternal inheritance. (2 Enoch 5:1–10)

This vision remained, in its essence, the standard Jewish conception of the positive side of the afterlife throughout the rabbinic period: there was a heavenly garden called Paradise whose still palpably physical pleasures were reserved for the righteous after the Judgment. Although who precisely might be included among its residents was debated, neither the reality nor the location of Paradise was cast into doubt by the masters of the Talmud.

10. Signs of the Times

Far more consequential than changes in Jewish ideas about the habitat of the dead and what befell them there was a radically new view of the destiny of God's creation. In the literature produced after the Exile there appears the entirely novel idea that this world will come to an end; and that end, far from being the outcome of a theorem, was sensed as imminent. It was assuredly a physical event. More important, it was God's providentially ordered moral happening: the End Time, though accompanied by unimaginable hardships and trials, would represent the Lord's vindication of His people. And it would be achieved by an agent from on high: a Messiah.

These themes begin in the prophets, but they find their most urgent and vivid presentations in the anonymous or pseudepigrapical works that were in wide circulation in Jewish circles from the second century B.C.E. onward. Since this End Time was felt, in varying degrees in different circles, to be rapidly approaching, one of the most popular themes in the new literature of eschatological visions and warnings was a description of the signs that would precede the End. There would be, the prophets and others warned, a time of troubles before the resolution. Joel, for example, describes in graphic terms both that "great and terrible day" and the ingathering of "the remnant" that will follow.

> After that,
> I will pour out My Spirit on all flesh;
> Your sons and your daughters shall prophesy,
> Your old men shall dream dreams,
> And your young men shall see visions;

I will even pour out My Spirit
Upon male and female slave in those days.
I will set portents in the sky and on the earth,
Blood and fire and pillars of smoke;
The sun shall be turned to darkness
And the moon into blood.

But everyone who invokes the name of the Lord shall escape, for there shall be a remnant on Mount Sion and in Jerusalem, as the Lord promised. Anyone who invokes the Lord will be among the survivors.

For lo! in those days and in that time,
When I restore the fortunes of Judah and Jerusalem,
I will gather all the nations,
And bring them down to the Valley of Jehoshaphat.
There I will contend with them
Over My very own people, Israel,
Which they scattered among the nations.
For they divided My land among themselves
And cast lots over My people;
And they bartered a boy for a whore,
And sold a girl for wine, which they drank.
(Joel 3:1–4:3)

11. "No Man Knows the Hour": The Second Coming of the Christ

For the Christians, with their ambiguity on whether the Kingdom had come or was still to be expected, the coming of the Messiah had to be converted into a twofold event: the historical incarnation of Jesus and a second, eschatological return to complete the messianic work. Indeed, Jesus himself foretold it: all three Synoptics have versions of Jesus' discourse about the Last Day, when the Son of Man will return for a second time. He will be preceded by the almost unimaginable catastrophes that Joel had already predicted for the "Day of the Lord." There will be impostors and false prophets, but then at last the true Messiah will come to gather his chosen ones to himself. This is Jesus' apocalyptic vision as Mark recounts it in his Gospel.

As he was leaving the Temple, one of his disciples exclaimed, "Look master, what huge stones! What fine buildings!" Jesus said to him, "You see these great buildings? Not one stone will be left upon another. All will be thrown down."

When he was sitting on the Mount of Olives facing the Temple, he was questioned privately by Peter, James, John and Andrew. "Tell us," they said, "when this will happen. What will be the sign when the fulfillment of this is at hand?"

Jesus began: "Take care that no one misleads you. Many will come claiming my name and saying, 'I am he'; and many will be misled by them. When you hear news of battle near at hand and the news of battles far away, do not be alarmed. Such things are bound to happen; but the end is still to come. For nation will make war upon nation, kingdom upon kingdom; there will be earthquakes in many places; there will be famines. With these things the birth pangs of the new age begin. . . . Those days will bring distress such as never has been until now since the beginning of the world which God created—and will never be again. If the Lord had not cut short that time of troubles, no living thing could survive. However, for the sake of his own, whom He has chosen, He has cut short the time.

"Then if anyone says to you, 'Look, here is the Messiah,' or, 'Look, there he is,' do not believe it. Impostors will come claiming to be messiahs, or prophets, and they will produce signs and wonders to mislead God's chosen, if such a thing were possible. But you, be on your guard; I have forewarned you of it all.

"But in those days, after that distress, the sun will be darkened; the moon will not give her light; the stars will come falling from the sky, the celestial powers will be shaken. Then will you see the Son of Man coming in the clouds with great power and glory, and he will send out his angels and gather his chosen from the four winds, from the farthest bounds of earth to the farthest bounds of heaven. . . .

"But about that day or that hour no one knows, not even the angels in heaven, not even the Son; only the Father." (Mark 13:1–32)

The Christian congregation that Paul committed to his care still had a vivid expectation of the "Day of the Lord." Paul's own interest in the Last Things was not particularly strong, as we shall see, but he did his best to reassure his flock at Thessalonica, who seemed particularly preoccupied with the Second Coming. Paul seeks to restrain their anxieties by referring them to Jesus' own pointing to the signs, as we have just seen in Mark.

And now, brothers, about the coming of our Lord Jesus Christ and his gathering us to himself: I beg you, do not suddenly lose your heads or alarm yourselves, whether at some oracular utterance, or pronouncement, or some letter purporting to come from us, alleging that the Day of the Lord is already here. Let no one deceive you in any way whatever. That day cannot come before the final rebellion against God, when wickedness will be revealed in human form, the man doomed to perdition. He is the enemy. . . . You cannot but remember that I told you this when I was still with you; you must now be aware of the restraining hand which ensures he shall be revealed only at the proper time. For already the secret power of wickedness is at work, secret only for the present until the Restrainer disappears from the scene. And then he will be revealed, that wicked man whom the Lord Jesus will destroy with the breath of his mouth and annihilate with the radiance of his coming. But the coming of that wicked man is the work of Satan. It will be attended by all the powerful signs and miracles of the Lie, and all the deception that sinfulness can impose on those doomed to destruction. Destroyed they shall be, because they did not open their minds to love of the truth, so as to find salvation. Therefore God puts them under a delusion, which works upon them to believe the lie, so that they may all be brought to judgment, all who do not believe the truth but make sinfulness their deliberate choice. (Paul, *To the Thessalonians* 2.2:1–12)

There were other questions as well. What of those believers who died before that Final Coming, for example?

This we tell you as the Lord's word: we who are left alive until the Lord comes shall not forestall those who have died; because at the word of God's command, at the sound of the archangel's voice and God's trumpet call, the Lord himself will descend from heaven; first the Christian dead will rise, then we who are left alive shall join them, caught up in clouds to meet the Lord in the air. Thus we shall always be with the Lord. Console one another, then, with these words.

About dates and times, my friends, we need not write to you, for you know perfectly well that the Day of the Lord comes like a thief in the night. . . . Sleepers sleep at night, and drunkards are drunk at night, but we, who belong to the daylight, must keep sober, armed with faith and love for coat of mail, and hope of salvation for helmet. For God has not destined us to the terrors of judgment, but to the full attainment of salvation through our Lord Jesus Christ. He died for us so that we, awake or asleep, might live in company with him. Therefore hearten one another, fortify one another, as indeed you do. (Paul, *To the Thessalonians* 1.4:15–5:13)

12. A Christian Apocalypse

The brief apocalypses in the three Synoptic Gospels were later fleshed out in highly imaginative detail by the final work included in the New Testament canon, the Revelation of John, from the pen of someone generally thought to be identical with the "beloved disciple" of Jesus and the author of the fourth Gospel, though the date of composition of the Revelation was probably close to the end of the first century. Here too the terrors of the Day of the Lord are spelled out, but there is the glory and the resurrection as well. The narrative begins with Jesus' return at the final act of the End Time.

I saw heaven open wide, and there was before me a white horse; and its rider's name was Faithful and True, for he was just in judgment and just in war. His eyes flamed fire and on his head were many diadems. Written upon him was a name known to none but himself, and he was robed in a garment drenched in blood. He was called the Word of God, and the armies of heaven followed him on white horses, clothed in fine linen, clean and shining. . . . And on his robe and on his thigh was written the name "King of Kings and Lord of Lords."

Then I saw an angel standing in the sun, and he cried aloud to all the birds flying in mid-heaven: "Come and gather for God's great supper, to eat the flesh of kings and commanders and fighting men, of horses and their riders, the flesh of all men, slave and free, great and small!" Then I saw the beast [that is, Rome and its divinized emperor] and the kings of the earth and their armies mustered to do battle with the Rider and his army. The beast was taken prisoner, and so was the false prophet who had worked miracles in its presence and deluded those that had received the mark of the beast and worshiped its image. The two of them were thrown alive into the lake of fire with its sulphurous flames. The rest were killed by the sword which went out of the Rider's mouth; and all the birds gorged themselves on their flesh.

Then I saw an angel coming down from heaven with the key of the abyss and a great chain in his hands. He seized the dragon, that serpent of old, the Devil or Satan, and chained him up for a thousand years; he threw him into the abyss, shutting and sealing it over him, so that he might seduce the nations no more until the thousand years were over. After that he must be let loose for a short while.

Then I saw thrones, and upon them sat those to whom judgment was committed. I could see the souls of those who had been beheaded for the sake of Christ's word and their testimony to Jesus, those who had not worshiped the beast and its image or received its mark on their forehead or hand. These came to life again and reigned with Christ for a thousand years, though the rest of the dead did not come to life until the thousand years were over. This is the first resurrection. Happy indeed, and one of God's own people, is the man who shares in this first resurrection! Upon such the second death has no claim; but they shall be priests of God and of Christ, and shall reign with him for the thousand years.

At the end of the thousand years Satan will return, according to this vision, and muster his forces for the final battle. The battle is ended by God himself in a great rain of fire from heaven; Satan is consigned to hell forever together with the Antichrist. It is then that the Final Judgment begins.

Then I saw a great white throne, and the One who sat upon it; from His presence earth and heaven vanished away, and no place was left for them. I could see the dead, great and small, standing before the throne; and the books were opened, the roll of the living. From what was written in these books the dead were judged upon the record of their deeds. . . . Then Death and Hades were flung into the lake of fire. This lake of fire is the second death, and into it were flung any whose names were not to be found in the roll of the living.

Then I saw a new heaven and a new earth, for the first heaven and the first earth had vanished, and there was no longer any sea. I saw the Holy City, the New Jerusalem, coming down out of heaven from God, made ready like a bride adorned for her husband. I heard a loud voice proclaiming from the throne, "Now at last God has His dwelling among men! He will dwell among them and they shall be His people, and God Himself will be with them. He will wipe every tear from their eyes; there shall be an end to death, and to mourning and crying and pain; for the old order has passed away."

Then He who sat on the throne said, "Behold, I am making all things new!" And He said to me, "Write this down for these words are trustworthy and true. Indeed, they are already fulfilled. 'I am Alpha and Omega, the beginning and the end. A draught from the water springs of life will be My free gift to the thirsty. All this is the victor's heritage; and I will be his God and he will be My son. But as for the cowardly, the faithless, and the vile, murderers, fornicators, sorcerers, idolaters and liars of every kind, their lot will be the second death, in the lake that burns with sulphurous flames.' " (Revelation 19:11–21:9)

13. The Second Coming: The Muslim Tradition

Muslims believed that Jesus did not die on the cross, as the Christians alleged, but had been taken up alive by God to heaven. He would, then, have to return to earth and suffer the death that is the common fate of all mankind. But his return had for the Muslims as much eschatological significance as it did for the Christians, and it was closely connected with the events of the End Time, as appears in this summary statement of Muslim messianism by Ibn Khaldun (d. 1406 C.E.).

It has been well known by all Muslims in every epoch, that at the end of time a man from the family of the Prophet will without fail make his appearance, one who will strengthen the religion and make justice triumph. The Muslims will follow him, and he will gain domination over the Muslim realm. He will be called the Mahdi [that is, the "Guided One"]. Following him, the Antichrist will appear, together with all the subsequent signs of the Hour (of the Last Judgment), as established in the sound tradition. After the Mahdi, Jesus will descend and kill the Antichrist. Or, Jesus will descend with the Mahdi, and help him kill the Antichrist, and have him as the leader in his prayers. (Ibn Khaldun, *Muqaddima* 3.51) [IBN KHALDUN 1967: 2:156]

The matter did not rest there, of course. The Muslim tradition had filled in many of the details regarding Jesus' return.

Abu Salih Shuʿayb ibn Muhammad al-Bayhaqi has informed us with a chain of authorities back to Abu Hurayra how this latter related that the Messenger of God, upon whom be God's blessing and peace, said: "The Prophets are brethren, though of different mothers, and their religion is one and the same. I am the nearest of mankind to Jesus son of Mary, on both of whom be peace, because there has been no Prophet between him and me. It will come to pass that the son of Mary will descend among you as a just ruler. He will descend to my community and be my deputy [or Caliph] over them, so when you see him, give him recognition. He will be a man symmetrical in stature, of reddish-white (complexion), lank-haired, as though his hair were dripping perfume though it had not been moistened. He will come down in a greenish-yellow garment, will break crosses and kill swine, will put an end to the poll tax [that is, the tax paid by non-Muslims under Islam], will raise the welcoming cry from al-Rawha when he comes for the Greater and the Lesser Pilgrimage, undertaking them both with zeal. He will make war on behalf of Islam, until in his time he destroys all religions save that of Islam, and there will thenceforward be but one single prostration of obeisance, namely that to God,

Lord of the Worlds. Also in his time God will destroy the Antichrist, the lying al-Dajjal. Then there will be such security on earth that lions will pasture freely with camels, tigers with cattle, wolves with sheep, children will play with serpents and no one will do harm to anyone. Then he will die, and the Muslims will pray over him and bury him at Medina beside the grave of Umar. Read, if you will, the words 'There are none of the People of the Book but will believe in him before his death, and on the Day of Resurrection he will be a witness against them' (Quran 4:159)." (Tha῾alibi, *Stories of the Prophets*) [JEFFERY 1962: 596–597]

Additional specifics are given in a series of traditions cited by Ibn Khaldun.

The final descent of Jesus will be at the time of the afternoon prayer, when three-fourths of the Muslim day has passed. . . . It has been stated in the tradition that Jesus will descend at the white minaret east of Damascus. He will descend between two yellowish-colored ones, that is, two light-saffron-yellow-colored garments. He will place his hands upon the wings of two angels. His hair is as long as though he had just been released from a dungeon. When he lowers his head, it rains, and when he lifts it up, jewels resembling pearls pour down from him. He has many moles on his face. Another tradition has: "Square built and reddish white." Still another has: "He will marry in the *gharb*," *gharb* meaning a bucket as used by the Bedouins. Thus the meaning is that he will take a woman from among the Bedouins as his wife. She will bear his children. The tradition also mentions that Jesus will die after forty years. It is also said that Jesus will die in Medina and be buried at the side of Umar ibn al-Khattab. And it is said that Abu Bakr and Umar [that is, the first two Caliphs of the Muslim community] will rise from the dead between two Prophets (Muhammad and Jesus). (Ibn Khaldun, *Muqaddima* 3.51)

[IBN KHALDUN 1967: 2:193–194]

14. "A Man from My Family"

Thus, the Muslims' expectation of the End Time included the return of Jesus. What is new in the Islamic tradition is that he will come in the company of, or following upon, another messianic figure, the Mahdi, or "Guided One." There were in circulation a great many Prophetic traditions on the subject, the chief of which are reported and analyzed by Ibn Khaldun in his Prolegomenon to History. Typical of the simplest and most direct of them are the two following, which occur in canonical collections of the traditions of the Prophet by al-Tirmidhi and Abu Dawud and are reported here by Ibn Khaldun.

With their chain of transmitters going back to Ibn Mas'ud, al-Tirmidhi and Abu Dawud have published the following tradition . . . on the authority of the Prophet: "If no more than one day remained of the world . . . God would cause the day to last until there be sent a man from me—or: from my family—whose name will tally with my name, and the name of whose father will tally with the name of my father." . . . The version of al-Tirmidhi has: "The world will not be destroyed until the Arabs are ruled by a man from my family, whose name will tally with my name." . . . Al-Tirmidhi states in connection with both versions that it is a good and sound tradition. (Ibn Khaldun, *Muqaddima* 3.51)

[IBN KHALDUN 1967: 2:159–160]

Muhammad could not serve as his own messiah; he was a mortal man and he was dead. The Islamic focus on the messiah as restorer came to rest, then, on one of the Prophet's family. The messiah will be, the traditions begin to insist, a descendant of one of the offspring of Muhammad's daughter Fatima. This was a tribute not so much to Fatima as to her husband Ali, the cousin of the Prophet and the figure about whom the major schism in Islam, that between Sunnis and Shi'ites, had developed.

Abu Dawud published a tradition relating to Ali in his chapter on the Mahdi . . . on the authority of Abu al-Tufayl, on the authority of Ali, on the authority of the Prophet, who said: "If only one day in the whole duration of the world remained, God would send a man of my family who would fill the world with justice, as it has been filled with injustice." With a chain of transmitters going back to Ali, Abu Dawud also published the following tradition . . . on the authority of Abu Ishaq al-Sabi'i, who said that Ali, looking at his son al-Hasan, said, "This son of mine is a lord, as he was called by (his grandfather) the Messenger of God. From his spine there will come forth a man who will be called by the name of your prophet and who will resemble him physically, but will not resemble him in character. . . ."

The following tradition, furthermore, was published by Abu Dawud, as well as by Ibn Maja and al-Hakim through Ali ibn Nufayl . . . on the authority of Umm Salima, who said: I heard the Messenger of God say: "The Mahdi is one of my family, one of the descendants of Fatima." This is Abu Dawud's version. He did not make any critical remarks concerning it. Ibn Maja's version has: "The Mahdi is one of Fatima's descendants." Al-Hakim's version has: "I heard the Messenger of God mention the Mahdi. He said, 'Yes, he is a fact, and he will be one of the children of Fatima.' " (Ibn Khaldun, *Muqaddima* 3.51) [IBN KHALDUN 1967: 2:162–165]

Shi ͨite speculation about the return of the Mahdi centered more and more on the return of their "concealed" Imam, but Sunni and Shi ͨite alike devoted considerable time and energy to what Ibn Khaldun obviously considered a useless pursuit.

There are many similar such statements. The time, the man and the place (of the Mahdi's return) are clearly indicated in them. But the time passes, and there is not the slightest trace (of the prediction coming true). Then some new suggestion is adopted which, as one can see, is based upon linguistic equivocations, imaginary ideas, and astrological judgments. The life of every one of those people is spent on such things. (Ibn Khaldun, *Muqaddima* 3.51) [IBN KHALDUN 1967: 2:195]

15. The Resurrection of the Flesh

As we have read, Paul addressed the question of the Final Judgment in letters to his flock at Thessalonica. There he was chiefly concerned, because the Thessalonians were, with the imminence of the Second Coming of Jesus. But the new Christians elsewhere had different queries, regarding the resurrection of the dead, for example.

You may ask, how are the dead raised? In what kind of body? How foolish! The seed you sow does not come to life unless it has first died; and what you sow is not the body that shall be, but a naked grain, perhaps of wheat, or of some other kind; and God clothes it with the body of His choice, each seed with its own particular body. All flesh is not the same flesh: there is flesh of men, flesh of beasts, of birds and of fishes, all different. There are heavenly bodies and earthly bodies. . . . So it is with the resurrection of the dead. What is sown in the earth as a perishable thing is raised imperishable. Sown in humiliation, it is raised in glory; sown as an animal body, it is raised as a spiritual body. If there is such a thing as an animal body, there is also a spiritual body.

To explain this "spiritual body," Paul invokes one of his more familiar notions, the parallelism between Adam and Jesus.

If there is such a thing as an animal body, there is also a spiritual body. It is in this sense that Scripture says, "The first man, Adam, became an animate being," whereas the last Adam has become a life-giving spirit. Observe, the spiritual does not come first; the animal body comes first, and then the spiritual. The first man was made of the "dust of the earth"; the second man is from heaven. The man made of dust is the pattern of all men of dust, and the heavenly man is the pattern of all heavenly men. As we have all worn the likeness of the man made of dust, so we shall wear the likeness of the heavenly man.

What I mean, my brothers, is this: flesh and blood can never possess the kingdom of God, and the perishable cannot possess immortality. Listen, I will unfold a mystery: we shall not all die (before the return of Christ), but we shall all be changed in a flash, in the twinkling of an eye, at the last trumpet call. For the trumpet will sound, and the dead will rise immortal, and we shall be changed. This perishable being must be clothed with the imperishable, and what is mortal must be clothed with immortality. (Paul, *To the Corinthians* 1.15:35–53)

Paul's metaphor of the seed sown and reborn is taken up and elaborated by Gregory of Nyssa (ca. 335–394 C.E.), brother of Basil of Caesarea and himself a prominent theologian.

It seems to me that the argument of the Apostle (Paul) [that is, in the text just cited] is in perfect accord with our own idea of the resurrection, and manifests much the same notion as our definition, which asserted that the resurrection is nothing other than the reconstitution of our nature to its pristine state. For as we learn from Scripture, in the first cosmogony [that is, in Genesis], the earth first brought forth a green plant, and then a seed was produced from this plant, and this latter seed, once it had fallen to the ground, produced another plant in the same form as the original growth. Now the inspired Apostle says that this is what happens also at the resurrection. Thus we learn from him not only that human nature is changed into a far nobler state, but also what we are to hope for is just this: the return of human nature to its pristine condition. The original process was not that of an ear from the seed, but of the seed from the ear, the ear thereafter growing from the seed.

The order of events in this simile clearly shows that all the happiness which will be ours through the resurrection will be a return to our original state of grace. Originally we too were, in a sense, a full ear, but we were withered by the torrid heat of sin; and then on our dissolution by death the earth received us. But in the spring of the resurrection the earth will again display this naked grain of our body in an ear, tall, luxuriant and upright, reaching up as high as heaven, and, for stalk and beard, decked with incorruption and all the other godlike characteristics. . . . The first ear was the first man, Adam. But with the entrance of evil, human nature was divided into a plurality; and, as happens with ripened grain in the ear, each individual person was stripped of the beauty of the ear and mingled with the earth. But in the resurrection we are reborn in that pristine beauty, becoming the infinite number of harvest fields instead of that single original ear. (Gregory of Nyssa, *On the Soul and the Resurrection*)

Augustine too speaks to Paul's text, not to the seed simile but to the difficult notion of a "spiritual body."

When the spirit is subservient to the flesh it is appropriately called carnal, and when it is subject to the spirit it is rightly called spiritual, not because it has become spirit, as some have inferred from the text of Scripture that says "sown as an animal body, it is raised as a spiritual body," but rather because it will be subject to the spirit, readily offering total and wonderful obedience. And this will lead to the fulfillment of their [that is, the souls of the dead saints] desire, the secure attainment of assured immortality, the removal of all feeling of discomfort, all corruptibility and reluctance. (Augustine, *The City of God* 13.20)

16. Creation Restored

There were Christians whose expectations of a physical renewal in the End Time went beyond the mere resurrection of individuals' bodies. Ireneus (d. ca. 200 C.E.), for example, had this broad vision of "the restored creation of the righteous."

Some men hold beliefs which have been introduced from heretical discourses; they are ignorant of God's ways and of the mystery of the resurrection of the just and of their kingdom, the first of which is the beginning of immortality, while the kingdom is the means by which such as have proved worthy are gradually accustomed to receive God. For this reason we must say something on this subject and explain that in the restored creation the righteous must rise first at the appearance of God to receive the inheritance promised by God to the fathers, and to reign in it; then follows the Judgment. For it is only right that they should receive the reward of their endurance in that (same) created order in which they suffered trouble and pain and were much tested by sufferings. . . . Therefore this created order must be restored to its first condition and be made subject to the righteous without hindrance. (Ireneus, *Against the Heresies* 5.32.1)

This understanding that at the Judgment all of physical creation will be restored to a pristine glorified state casts light for Ireneus on a remark made by Jesus to his disciples at the Last Supper.

I tell you, never again shall I drink from the fruit of the vine until that day when I drink it new with you in the kingdom of my Father. (Matthew 26:29)

Jesus promised [Ireneus resumes] to "drink from the fruit of the vine" with his disciples and in so doing he indicated two things: the inheritance of the earth in which the new fruit of the vine will be drunk, and the physical resurrection of his disciples. For it is the body which arises anew which receives the new wine, and we cannot conceive of him drinking from the fruit of the vine once he has taken his place with his followers in the region above the heavens. And more, those who drink it are not disembodied, since to drink wine belongs to the body rather than to the spirit. (Ireneus, *Against the Heresies* 5.33.1)

17. A Millennial Kingdom

Ireneus' reflections on "the resurrection of the just and their kingdom," while they are presented as a simple, almost matter-of-fact extension of the belief in a return to life of the bodies and souls of the elect, are nourished by another New Testament text that had a profound influence on later Christian thinking and imagining about the Last Things. It comes from the apocalyptic Book of Revelation.

Then I saw an angel coming down from heaven with the key of the abyss and a great chain in his hands. He seized the dragon, that serpent of old, the Devil or Satan, and chained him up for a thousand years; he threw him into the abyss, shutting and sealing it over him, so that he might seduce the nations no more until the thousand years were over. After that he must be let loose for a short while.

Then I saw thrones, and upon them sat those to whom judgment was committed. I could see the souls of those who had been beheaded for the sake of God's word and their testimony to Jesus, those who had not worshiped the beast and its image or received its mark on their forehead or hand. These came to life again and reigned with Christ for a thousand years, though the rest of the dead did not come to life until the thousand years were over. This (raising of the martyrs) is the first resurrection. Happy indeed, and one of God's own people, is the man who shares in this first resurrection! Upon such the second death has no claim; but they shall be priests of God and of Christ, and shall reign with him for the thousand years.

After the millennium Satan is once again released, only to be defeated once again and consumed by fire sent down from heaven. There follows the Final Judgment.

Then I saw a great white throne, and the One who sat upon it; from His presence earth and heaven vanished away, and no place was left for them. I could see the dead, great and small, standing before the throne; and the books were opened. Then another book was opened, the roll of the living. From what was written in these books the dead were judged upon the record of their deeds. . . . Then Death and Hades were flung into the lake of fire. This lake of fire is the second death, and into it were flung any whose names were not to be found in the roll of the living. (Revelation 20:1–15)

The notion of a thousand-year reign of Christ's kingdom before the Final Judgment and the beginning of eternity took strong hold in certain Christian quarters. Here are Tertullian's reflections on the Millennium from about 207 C.E.

It is also our belief that a kingdom has been promised to us on earth, and before we attain heaven; but in a condition other than this, namely, in the (first) resurrection. That resurrection will last for a thousand years, in a city of God's making, a Jerusalem sent down from heaven, which the Apostle (Paul) also describes as "our mother from above" (Gal. 4:26); and when he proclaims that our . . . citizenship "is in heaven" (Phil. 3:20), he is surely ascribing it to a heavenly city. . . . We maintain that this is the city designed by God for the reception of the saints at the (first) resurrection, and for favoring them with abundance of all goods, spiritual goods to be sure, in compensation for the goods we have despised or lost in this present age. For indeed it is right and worthy of God that His servants should also rejoice in the same place where they suffered affliction in His name. This is the purpose of the kingdom; it will last a thousand years, during which the saints will arise sooner or later, according to their degrees of merit, and then, when the resurrection of the saints is completed, the destruction of the world and the just conflagration will be accomplished; we shall be "changed in a moment" into the angelic substance, by the "putting on of incorruption" (1 Cor. 15:52–53), and we shall be transferred to the celestial kingdom. (Tertullian, *Against Marcion* 3:24)

18. Paul in the Third Heaven

For the Christians, as for the Jews, what awaited both saint and sinner in the afterlife was justice, justice that would be meted out not merely in another time but in another place. For Paul, that "other place" was already located in the world above. Here in his letter to the flock at Corinth he speaks of himself, as often, in the third person.

I am obliged to boast. It does no good; but I shall go on to tell of visions and revelations granted by the Lord. I know a Christian man who fourteen years ago (whether in the body or out of it, I do not know—God knows) was caught up as far as the third heaven. And I know that this same man (whether in the body or out of it, I do not know—God knows) was caught up into Paradise and heard words so secret that human lips may not repeat them. (Paul, *To the Corinthians* 2.12:1–4)

This is oblique boasting at best, unmistakable as to the fact but with no revelation of what Paul saw in the third heaven. The early Christian tradition did not scruple to fill in the details. In the so-called Apocalypse of Paul we can see how fourth-century Christians combined Genesis' description of Adam's earthly garden with Greek features and moved the entire landscape to the world above. Paul's alleged account begins exactly where the letter to the Corinthians ends.

I peered up into the height and I saw there other angels whose faces shone like the sun. Their limbs were girt with girdles of gold, and they bore palms in their hands, and the sign of God; they were clothed in garments on which was written the name of the Son of God. (*Apocalypse of Paul* 12)

And he [that is, Paul's angel guide] took me away from where I had seen all these sights, and there before me was a river of white, whiter than the whiteness of milk. I said to the angel, "And what is this?" And he replied: "Before you is Lake Acherusia, where the City of Christ is located. But it is not permitted to every man to go into that city, since this is the way which leads to God. And so if anyone is a fornicator and ungodly but turns and repents and produces the appropriate fruits of repentance, then when first he leaves the body he is brought here and worships God and is then handed over at God's command to the angel Michael, who baptizes him in Lake Acherusia and leads him into the city with those who have not sinned." . . .

Then the angel said to me: "Follow me and I shall lead you into the city of Christ." He took his stand by Lake Acherusia and put me in a golden boat; then about three thousand angels sang hymns in my presence until I reached the city of Christ.

The city of Christ is surrounded by the same four rivers found in Eden (Gen. 2: 10–14), though they now flow, as they did for Enoch, in a more allegorical fashion.

And in the round of the city there were found twelve gates of great beauty, and four rivers which encircled it. . . . And I asked the angel: "What are these rivers which encircle this city?" And he replied: "These are the four rivers whose abundant flow is for those who are in this land of promise; as for their names, the river of honey is called Phison; and the river of milk, Euphrates; and the river of oil, Gihon; and the river of wine, the Tigris. Since the righteous, during their time in the world did not exert the power they had over these things and so went hungry without them and afflicted themselves for the name of the Lord God, so when they enter this city the Lord will bestow these same upon them beyond number or measure." (*Apocalypse of Paul* 22–23)

19. An Angelic Account of the Afterlife

Like Paul before him, and like many others in an even earlier Jewish tradition, Muhammad too was taken on a heavenly journey. The original intent of the account of his ascension, hinted at in Quran 17:1 and fleshed out in some detail in Ibn Ishaq's Life, may have been to validate Muhammad's credentials as a prophet. But when that no longer seemed necessary, the heavenly journey could serve, as it had for any number of figures from Enoch to Paul, as an occasion to lay out both the geography and the demography of the afterlife. In this thirteenth-century example, however, it is not Muhammad who has the vision but his guide upon that journey, the angel Gabriel, a fact that makes it possible to give a view of Gehenna as well as of Heaven.

Yazid al-Raqashi has related from Anas ibn Malik that Gabriel came to the Prophet, may God's blessing and peace be upon him, at an unwonted hour and with a changed countenance. The Prophet, God's blessing and peace be upon him, said: "How is it that I see your countenance changed?" He answered: "O Muhammad, I have come to you in that hour when God has given command that the bellows blow up the Fire. No man who knows that Gehenna is a reality, that the fire therein is a reality, that the torment of the tomb is a real thing, and that God's punishment is even greater (than thought) ought to be in tranquillity till he is secure therefrom." The Prophet, upon whom may God bestow His blessing and peace, said: "O Gabriel, describe Gehenna to me." He replied, "Very well. When God, may He be exalted, created Gehenna He had it stoked for a thousand years till it grew red. Then he had it stoked for another thousand years till it grew white. Then He had it stoked for another thousand years till it went black. So it is black as the darkest night, but its flames and burning coals may never be put out."

The physical description of Gehenna continues until Gabriel reaches the gates of the descending circles of Hell, where he has an opportunity of sorting out the Islamic hierarchy of sinners. "Are they like our gates?" Muhammad asks.

"No!" Gabriel said. "They open one below the other, gate after gate, between a seventy years' journey, and each gate is seventy times hotter than the gate that preceded it. God's enemies are driven to it, and as they reach its gate the Zabaniya [or infernal attendants] meet them with fetters and chains. The chain is inserted in the man's mouth and brought out his rectum. His left hand is fettered to his neck and his right hand is thrust through his heart and pulled out between his shoulders, where it is fastened with chains. Moreover, every human will be chained to a satan." . . .

The Prophet, upon whom be God's blessing and peace, said: "Who are the dwellers in those gates?" Gabriel answered: "The lowest section has in it the Hypocrites [that is, those Medinese who pretended to believe in the Prophet; Quran 4:145], those of the People of the Table who disbelieved [that is, disbelieved in Jesus' miracle; Quran 5:115], and the People of the Pharaoh's household [that is, those who disbelieved in Moses' miracle; Quran 40:46]. Its name is Hawiya (101:9). The second section (upward) has in it the polytheists. Its name is Jahim (69:30). The third in it has the Sabians. Its name is Saqar (74:26ff.). The fourth section has in it Iblis [that is, the Fallen Angel] and his followers, and the Magians [that is, the Zoroastrians]. Its name is Laza (70:15). The fifth section has the Jews in it. It is called Hutama (104:4). The sixth section has the Christians in it. Its name is Saʿir (4:10)."

At this point Gabriel held back out of respect for the Messenger of God, may God's blessing and peace be upon him, but he, may God's blessing and peace be upon him, said: "Are you not going to inform me about the dwellers in the seventh (or uppermost) section?" So he replied: "In it are those of your community who have committed grave sins and have died without having repented." At this the Prophet, may God's blessing and peace be upon him, fell down in a swoon, but Gabriel set his head on his own breast until he recovered. When he recovered he said: "O Gabriel, great is my affliction and violent is my grief. Can it be that any of my community will enter the Fire?" "Yes," he said, "those of your community who are guilty of grave sins." At that the Messenger of God, upon whom be God's blessing and peace, wept, and Gabriel also wept. (Samarqandi, *Arousing the Heedless*) [JEFFERY 1962: 233–235]

20. Hades and Hell

It is clear from the Jewish apocalypses of the second century B.C.E. onward that Jewish ideas of the afterlife, in details if not in substance, were being affected by Greek notions of the underworld. Orpheus in Greek mythology, Odysseus in the Odyssey, and finally Aeneas in Virgil's epic all made circumstantial trips into Hades, journeys that fixed in literary form both popular and learned ideas about the afterlife. Thus

*the biblical Sheol passed into a punitive but still Jewish Gehinnom and then, from
1 Enoch onward, to a composite Gehenna-Hades.*

*The Gospels reflect a view that is still somewhat more Gehenna than Hades;
but once the Christian movement passed out of its native Jewish environment, more
and more elements of Greco-Roman eschatology began to appear in the Christians'
accounts. So close was the resemblance, in fact, that Tertullian had to defend himself
against the charge that the Christians had stolen their ideas of the afterlife from the
pagans.*

We are also derided because we maintain that that God is going to
judge the world, just as the (pagan) poets and philosophers place a judgment seat in the underworld. And if we threaten Gehenna, which is a
store of hidden subterranean fire for purpose of punishment, we are
received with hoots of derision, though they too have a (fiery) river
Pyriphlegethon in the abode of the dead. And if we would mention Paradise, a place of divine delight appointed to receive the spirits of the saints
which is separated from the knowledge of this everyday world by a kind
of fire zone, then the Elysian Fields have anticipated the Faith. Whence,
I ask you, come these similarities to our teachings in the (pagan) philosophers and poets? They are simply taken from our holy teachings, which,
since they are earlier, are the more trustworthy and the more credible.
(Tertullian, *Apology* 47)

*Tertullian is not terribly embarrassed by the resemblance, then; nor apparently were
the many other Christians who continued to elaborate on both the geography and
the theodicy of the underworld. The late-fourth-century* Apocalypse of Paul *has
already been cited on its revelations about the "city of Christ" that awaits the
virtuous in the next world; it is even more explicit on what awaits the damned.
"Come," says Paul's angel guide, "follow me and I shall show you the souls of the
godless and sinners that you may know what the place is like."*

I saw a river boiling with fire, and in it was a great crowd of men and
women immersed up to their knees, while others were immersed up to
their navels, and others up to their lips and hair. I asked the angel: "Sir,
who are these people in the river of fire?" And the angel answered and
said to me: "These are they who are neither hot nor cold because they
were found neither among the number of the righteous nor among the
number of the godless. They spent the period of their sojourn on earth
by passing some days in prayer but other days in sin and fornication right
up to the moment of their deaths." And I asked him: "And who are the
ones who are immersed up to their knees in fire?" "These are those who,
after they have left the church spend their time indulging in strange dis-

courses. Those, however, who are immersed up to the navel are those who, after they have received the body and blood of Christ, go away off and fornicate and do not leave off sinning until they die. And those who are immersed up their lips are the ones who, on meeting in God's church, spend their time slandering one another. Those immersed up to the eyebrows are those who nod signs to each other and so secretly prepare evil against their neighbor." (*Apocalypse of Paul* 31)

These are relatively mild punishments compared to what follows.

. . . I saw girls wearing black clothing and four fearsome angels with blazing chains in their hands. They placed the chains on the girls' necks and led them into the darkness. I tearfully asked the angel: "Who are these, sir?" And he said to me: "They are women who, though they were appointed as virgins, defiled their virginity before being given to their husbands, and that without the knowledge of their parents. And it is for that reason they continuously pay their own particular penalty." . . .

And I saw other men and women suspended by their eyebrows and their hair, and they were dragged along by a river of fire. I asked: "Who are those, sir?" And he said to me: "They are those who did not give themselves to their own husbands and wives but rather to adulterers, and for that reason they continuously pay their own particular penalty."

And I saw other men and women covered with dust, and their faces were like blood, and they were in a pit of tar and brimstone, and they were running along in a fiery river. And I asked: "Who are those, sir?" And he said to me: "These are the ones who have committed the iniquity of Sodom and Gomorrah, men with men, and for that reason they continuously pay the penalty." (*Apocalypse of Paul* 39)

Next Paul sees men and women being strangled in the fire. They are, he is told, those who killed their own children.

But their children appealed to the Lord God and to the angels who oversee the punishments, saying: "Defend us from our parents, for they have defiled what God has fashioned; they bear the name of God but they do not keep His commandments, and they give us as food to dogs and to be trampled by pigs; and they threw others of us into the river." But those children were handed over to the angels of Tartarus who were in charge of the punishments, so that they might lead them to a spacious place of mercy. Their fathers and mothers were, however, strangled in an everlasting punishment.

Paul is aghast and breaks into tears.

The angel said to me. "Why are you weeping? Are you more com-passionate than the Lord God, who is blessed forever, who has assigned judgment, and has allowed every man to choose good or evil and act as he wishes?" Again I wept even more vehemently, and he said to me: "You are weeping and you have not yet seen the greater punishments? Follow me and you will see some that are seven times greater than these."

And he brought me to the north, to the place of all punishments, and he placed me above a well, which I found was sealed with seven seals. . . . And when the well was opened, there instantly arose from it a foul and evil smell which was far worse than all the punishments. And I looked into the well and saw on all sides fiery masses burning. . . . The angel said to me: "If someone is sent down into this well of the abyss, and it is sealed above him, no reference is ever made to him in the presence of the Father and the Son and the Holy Spirit and the holy angels." And I said: "And who is it who is sent into this well?" And he said to me: "Here are all those who have not confessed that Christ entered into the flesh and that the Virgin Mary bore him, and who say that the bread of the Eucharist and the cup of the blessing are not the body and blood of Christ."

And I looked away from the north and toward the west, and there I saw the worm that never rests, and in that place there was gnashing of teeth. The worm was a cubit in length and had two heads. And I saw there men and women amidst the cold and gnashing of teeth. And I asked and said: "Sir, who are these people in this place?" And he said to me: "These are those who say that Christ has not risen from the dead and that this flesh does not rise." (*Apocalypse of Paul* 40–42)

21. The Harrowing of Hell

This graphic approach to the afterlife arises in part from a juridical and pastoral concern to have eschatological punishments seem to fit the offenses to which they are attached, simply as a matter of God's justice. It was this same concern, as we shall see, that caused some to think there was a place between Heaven/Paradise and Gehenna/Hell, which came to be called Purgatory, where God's justice might be ful-filled, or even perhaps tempered, through remedial rather than punitive punish-ments. On the same score, room had to be found for the Limbo of Children, that "spacious place of mercy" hinted at in the Apocalypse of Paul *as the final resting place of minors incapable of sin or virtue and so incapable of either meriting Heaven or deserving Hell. Finally, the Limbo of Patriarchs was reserved as the resting place of the souls of the righteous who died before the coming of Jesus and whose release was the object of Jesus' "harrowing of Hell." There is a prediction in the Gospels that Jesus would descend into the underworld after his death, though with no details as to how or why that might be accomplished.*

"I tell you this: there is not a thoughtless word that comes from men's lips but that they will have to account for it on the day of judgment. For out of your own mouth you will be acquitted and out of your own mouth condemned."

At this some of the doctors of the law and the Pharisees said, "Master, we should like you show us a sign." He answered, "It is a wicked, godless generation that asks for a sign. The only sign that will be given it is the sign of the prophet Jonah. Jonah was in the sea monster's belly for three days and three nights, and in the same way the Son of Man will be three days and three nights in the bowels of the earth." (Matthew 12: 36–40)

By the turn from the second into the third Christian century there was no doubt— indeed, there may have been none from the beginning—as to what this "sign" meant.

Among us the underworld is thought of as a bare cavity or some kind of cesspool of the world open to the sky; rather, it is a vast space in a deep pit beneath the earth, a hidden depth in the very bowels of the earth, since we read that Christ spent three days "in the bowels of the earth" (Matt. 12:40), that is, in the innermost recess which is concealed within the earth itself, and hollowed out within it and lying atop the abysses which stretch away underneath. Now Christ is God, because he both died as man according to the Scriptures and was buried according to those same Scriptures, and here too he fulfilled the law of humanity by complying with the condition of human death in the underworld; nor did he "ascend to the heights" of heaven until he had previously "descended into the depths" (Eph. 4:8–9) of the earth that he might make the prophets and the patriarchs sharers of himself. (Tertullian, *On the Soul* 55)

22. The Bosom of Abraham

Matthew's reference to Jesus' descent into the "bowels of the earth" was connected with the place called the "Bosom of Abraham" in this celebrated parable in Luke.

There was once a rich man who dressed in purple and the finest linen and feasted in great magnificence every day. At his gate, covered with sores, lay a poor man named Lazarus, who would have been glad to satisfy his hunger from the scraps from the rich man's table. Even the dogs used to come and lick his sores.

One day the poor man died and was carried away by the angels to Abraham's bosom. The rich man also died and was buried, and in Hades, where he was in torment, he looked up, and there far away was Abraham and Lazarus at his side. "Abraham, my father," he called out, "take pity on me. Send Lazarus to dip the tip of his finger in water, to cool my tongue, for I am in agony in this fire." But Abraham said, "Remember, my child, that all the good things fell to you while you were alive and all the bad to Lazarus; now he has his consolation here and it is you who is in agony. But that is not all: there is a great chasm between us; no one from our side who wants to reach you can cross it, and none can pass from your side to us." (Luke 16:19–26)

Where Abraham and Lazarus lay, then, was in the Limbo of Patriarchs, patiently awaiting the coming of Christ for their release; the rich man was begging some assistance from another place, the remote ancestor of what would become in Western Christianity Purgatory. How Abraham and others found their release is described in the third- or fourth-century popular account of Jesus' trial and execution called The Gospel of Nicodemus. *In this apocryphal gospel Jesus' descent to Hell and the substance of the Lazarus parable have been brought together into a single dramatic narrative. The source for this account is said to be that Simeon who performed the circumcision rite on Jesus (Luke 2:25–35); he had died and had been in the underworld when Jesus arrived there. The time is midnight on the Friday of Jesus' crucifixion.*

We were then in Hades with all who have died since the beginning of the world. And at the hour of midnight there shone forth in the darkness there a light like the light of the sun, and the light fell upon all of us and now we saw one another. And immediately our father, Abraham, together with the patriarchs and the prophets, was filled with joy, and they said to one another: "This shining comes from a great light." The prophet Isaiah, who was present there, said: "This shining comes from the Father and the Son and the Holy Spirit. I prophesied this when I was still living, when I said 'The land of Zabulon and the land of Nephthalim, the people that sat in darkness saw a great light.' " Then there came into our midst another figure, a hermit from the wilderness. The patriarchs asked him: "Who are you?" He replied: "I am John, the last of the prophets, who made straight the ways of the Son of God . . . the only begotten Son of God comes here so that whoever believes in him should be saved, and whoever does not believe in him should be condemned. Therefore I say to you all: When you see him, do you all worship him. For it is only now that you have an opportunity for repenting the fact that you worshiped idols in the vain world above and sinned. At another time it will be impossible." (*Gospel of Nicodemus* 18–19)

Jesus at length appears at the entrance of Hades.

. . . [T]he gates of brass were shattered, and the gates of iron were crushed, and all the dead who were bound up were loosed from their chains, and we with them. And the King of Glory entered in like a man and all the dark places of Hades were filled with light. . . . The King of Glory stretched forth his right hand and took hold of our forefather Adam and raised him up. Then he turned also to the rest and said: "Come with me, all you who have suffered death through the tree which this man [that is, Adam] touched. For behold, I raise you all up again through the tree of the cross." . . . The Savior blessed Adam with the sign of the cross on his forehead. And he did likewise to the patriarchs and prophets and martyrs and all the forefathers, and he took them and leaped up from out of Hades. And as he went the holy fathers sang his praises, trailing behind him and saying: "Blessed be he who comes in the name of the Lord. Alleluia. To him be the glory of all the saints." (Ibid. 21–24)

They mount up to the heavenly Paradise. In their company is "a humble man carrying a cross on his shoulder."

The holy fathers asked him: "Who are you, you who have the appearance of a thief, and what is the cross you carry on your shoulder?" He answered; "I was, as you say, a robber and thief in the world, and therefore the Jews took me and delivered me to the death of the cross together with our Lord Jesus Christ. . . . And he said to me, 'Truly, I say to you, today you shall be with me in Paradise' (Luke 23:43). So I came to Paradise carrying my cross and found Michael the Archangel. . . . And when the flaming sword saw the sign of the cross, it opened to me and I entered in. Then the archangel said to me: 'Wait a short while. For Adam also, the forefather of the race of men, comes with the rest of the righteous that they also may enter here.' And now that I have seen you, I have come to meet you." When the saints heard this they all cried with a loud voice: "Great is our Lord and great is his power!" (Ibid. 26)

We stand here near the narrative and descriptive beginning of the Christian understanding of the punitive and purgatorial states of the afterlife. How they are shaped at the end of the process of their systematization appears in this theological handbook from 1268 C.E.

In order to know what Hell Christ descended to, we must remember that Hell has two meanings, and refers either to the punishment or the place of punishment. . . . If Hell designates the place of punishment, then a distinction must be drawn among four places. There is the Hell of the damned, in which one endures both the punishments of the senses and punishment of damnation [that is, deprivation of the divine presence] and in which there is both inner and outer darkness, i.e., absence of grace; it is eternal mourning. Above it is the Limbo of the Children, where one endures the punishment of damnation but not the punishment of the senses, and there is both inner and outer darkness.

Above this place is Purgatory, where there is the punishment of the senses and the punishment of damnation (but only) for a certain period, and there is outer darkness, but not inner darkness, for by grace one has inner light there, because one sees that one will be saved. The upper place is the Limbo of the Holy Fathers [that is, the Patriarchs] where there was the punishment of damnation but not of the senses, and there was outer darkness but not the darkness of the deprivation of grace. It is into this place that Christ descended and liberated his own and thus "swallowed up" Hell, for he completely destroyed death. . . . This place is also called the Bosom of Abraham; it is the heaven of the empyrean, for Abraham is there forevermore. Between these places there is no passage, except in the past from the third to the fourth, that is, from Purgatory to the Limbo of the Holy Fathers. (*Compendium of the True Theology* 4:22)

[Cited by LE GOFF 1984: 264–265]

23. Punishment as Purgation

The thirteenth-century Compendium *takes Purgatory as a given, as indeed it was in the Western Church at that point. The origins of the idea are much earlier, of course, and lay perhaps in that interval between the death of the individual Christian and the universal judgment of the Last Day. What occurred then, it seemed to many early Christians, was some purely temporary state of punishment for those who required it, punishment that was purgative rather than punitive. That Tertullian believed in such is certain.*

"Are all souls then," you ask, "in the realm of the underworld?" Yes, whether it pleases you or not. And there are (both) punishments and refreshments there. . . . Why cannot you imagine that the soul experiences either punishment or comfort in the underworld, in the period while it is awaiting the judgment, whether punishment or reward, with a kind of anticipation? . . . Otherwise, what will happen in that interval? Shall we be sleeping? But souls cannot sleep. . . . Or do you think that nothing happens there? . . . Surely it would be the height of injustice if in that place the souls of the wicked continued to prosper and the good were still deprived of happiness. . . . And so, since we understand that "prison" indicated in the Gospel as the underworld and the expression "last penny" (Matt. 5:25) to refer to the fact that every small sin will be expiated there in the interval before the resurrection, no one will doubt that the soul in the underworld pays some price, without prejudice to the fulfillment of the process at the resurrection, which also will be effected through the medium of the flesh. (Tertullian, *On the Soul* 58)

Nor was the Latin Tertullian the only Christian Father who subscribed to the notion of remedial chastisement in the afterlife. The Christian Hellenists of Alexandria also viewed it that way.

All who are virtuous change to better dwellings, the reason for this change being the choice of knowledge. . . . But strict chastisements, through the goodness of the great judge, the overseer, compel (the wicked), through increasing suffering, to repent. The punishments are inflicted through the attending angels, through the various previous (individual) judgments and by the general judgment. (Clement of Alexandria, *Stromateis* 8.2)

If . . . they will not listen to the song . . . let them be disciplined by God's hand, suffering paternal correction before the judgment, until they are ashamed and repent and so do suffer the final condemnation by their stubborn unbelief. For these are only partial disciplinings, called chastisements, which most of us who have lapsed into sin incur, though we belong to the Lord's people. But our chastisement by Providence is like that of children by a teacher or a father. God does not take vengeance, which is the repayment of evil by evil; rather, He chastises for the benefit of the chastised. (Ibid. 7.16)

Clement's fellow Alexandrian, Origen (ca. 185–255 C.E.), likewise believed in the remedial nature of divine punishment.

Just as an excess of food causes fevers (in the body) . . . so the soul accumulates an abundance of sins, and in due time this buildup of evils comes to a boil for the sinner's punishment and catches fire for his retribution. This is when the mind itself, or the conscience, which through divine power keeps a record of all things . . . sees set out before its eyes the story of its misdeeds. . . . God acts in dealing with sinners like a physician . . . and the fury of His anger is useful for the purging of souls. Even that penalty which is said to be imposed by fire is understood as applied to a sinner to assist his health. (Origen, *On First Principles* 2.10.4, 6)

Moreover, Origen was willing to take the next step, though with a great deal of hesitation: if punishment after death is remedial rather than punitive, then one must think it will at some point end, when all the wicked among God's creatures will have been rehabilitated by their chastisements.

We speak very tentatively and uncertainly on this subject, more by way of promoting discussion than of drawing definite conclusions. . . . The end and consummation of the world will occur, and then each being will have to undergo the punishment which his sins have merited. God alone knows that time. . . . We suppose that the goodness of God will restore the unity of the whole creation in the end, through His Christ, when all His enemies have been subdued and overcome. . . . Whether any of those ranks who act under the devil's leadership will be able in some future time to be converted to goodness, inasmuch as they still have the power of free will; or whether a persistent and inveterate evil becomes their very nature from long habit, I leave to the reader's judgment. . . . Meanwhile both in time and in eternity all these matters will be dealt with in due order and proportion according to their deserts; so that some are restored in the first ages, some in later, some even in the last times; restored through greater and graver punishments, and long-term penalties that are endured, it may be, through many ages. (Origen, *On First Principles* 1.6.1–3)

Basil (330–379 C.E.), bishop of Caesarea in Anatolia, regarded such speculations as pernicious: hell is as eternal as heaven will be.

Many men have forgotten such important sayings and pronouncements of the Lord, and on their own initiative set a time limit to punishment, in order that they may sin with greater confidence. This is a result of the devil's trickery. But if there is any time limit for eternal punishment, it follows that there must be a time limit for eternal life itself. And since we cannot imagine this with regard to eternal life, what case can be made for ascribing a limit to eternal punishment? The adjective "eternal" applies equally to both. (Basil, *Shorter Rule* 267)

Augustine is equally opposed to this view. Although he is censuring pagan Platonists, his remarks would pertain with similar point to Origen's position.

Now the Platonists, while refusing to believe than any sins go unpunished, hold that all punishments are directed toward purification, whether they are punishments inflicted by human laws or those imposed by divine decree, and whether the latter are suffered in this life or after death, when someone is spared in this life or when his affliction does not result in his correction. . . . Those who hold this view will have it that the only punishments after death are those intended to purify, so that the soul may be cleansed from any infection contracted by contact with the earth. . . .

For our part, we acknowledge that even in this mortal life there are indeed some purificatory punishments; but penalties inflicted on those whose life is not improved thereby, or is even made worse, are not purificatory. Punishments are a means of purification only to those who are disciplined and corrected by them. All other punishments, whether temporal or eternal, are imposed on every person in accordance with the treatment he is to receive from God's providence; they are imposed either in retribution for sins, whether past sins or sins in which the person so chastised is still living, or else they serve to exercise and to display the virtues of the good; and they are administered through the agency of men or of angels, whether good or evil angels. . . . As for temporal pains, some people suffer them in this life only, others after death, others both in this life and the other; yet all this precedes that last and strictest judgment. However, not all men who endure temporal pains after death come into those eternal punishments which are to come after the judgment. Some in fact will receive forgiveness in the world to come for what is not forgiven in this. (Augustine, *City of God* 21.13)

Finally, Aquinas (d. 1277 C.E.) devotes an article of his Summa Theologica *to the question of the penalties of the afterlife and the possibility that they might be purely remedial, and so finite, in nature. First he responds directly to the issue of the eternity of punishment for sin.*

I answer that: Sin incurs a debt of punishment because it disturbs an order, and the effect remains for as long as the cause remains. Therefore as long as the disturbance of the order continues, so too must the debt of punishment. Now sometimes the disturbance of an order is reparable and sometimes it is irreparable because a defect which destroys the principle is irreparable, while, if the principle is saved, defects can be repaired by virtue of that principle. For instance, if the principle of sight is destroyed, sight cannot be restored except by divine power; whereas, if the principle of sight is preserved, while there might arise certain impediments to seeing, these can be remedied by nature or art.

Now in every order there is a principle by which one becomes a member of that order. Consequently, if a sin destroys the principle of the order by which man's will is subject to God, the disorder will be such as to be considered in itself irreparable, though it is possible to repair it by the power of God. Now the principle of this order is the last end, to which man adheres by charity. Therefore, whenever sin turns man away from God so as to destroy charity, considered in themselves, such sinners incur a debt of eternal punishment.

But in responding to the corollary issue of the possibility of penal rehabilitation in the afterlife, Aquinas prefers to invoke the example of human criminal justice.

Punishment is proportioned to sin in point of severity, both in divine and in human judgments. In no judgment, however, as Augustine says (*City of God* 21.11), is it requisite for the punishment to equal the fault in point of duration. For the fact that adultery or murder is committed in a moment does not call for a momentary punishment; in fact, they are punished sometimes by imprisonment or banishment for life—sometimes even by death. Now this does not take into account the time occupied in the homicide but aims at removing a murderer from the society of the living; so that this (capital) punishment represents, in its own way, the eternity of punishment inflicted by God. Now according to Gregory (*Moralia* 34.19), it is just that he who has sinned against God in his own eternity should be punished in God's eternity. A man is said to have sinned in his own eternity not only because he has sinned throughout his whole life, but also because, from the very fact that he fixes his end in sin, he has the will to sin everlastingly. . . .

Even the punishment that is inflicted according to human laws is not always intended as a remedy for the one who is punished, but sometimes only for others. Thus when a thief is hanged, this is not for his own amendment, but for the sake of others, who at least may be deterred from crime through fear of the punishment, according to Proverbs 19:25: "The wicked man being scourged, the fool shall be wiser." Accordingly, the eternal punishments inflicted by God on the reprobate are remedial punishments for those who refrain from sin through the thoughts of these punishments. (Aquinas, *Summa Theologica* I/2, ques. 87, art. 3)
[AQUINAS 1945: 2: 711–712]

24. Purgatory

The point being argued by both Augustine and Aquinas is that at least some of the punishments of the afterlife are eternal. Neither would deny that other punishments inflicted on men between their death and the Final Judgment are indeed remedial and so will come to an end, at that Judgment or possibly sooner. What had occurred between the writings of the two men was that the remedial punishment of the afterlife had been localized in a fixed place, Purgatory. At the Second Council of Lyons in 1274 C.E., which marked the reunion, however temporary, of the Western and Eastern branches of Christendom, the Western position on Purgatory was defined and explicated for Eastern acceptance.

Because of various errors that have been introduced by the ignorance of some and the malice of others, we state and publicly pronounce that those who lapse into sin after baptism ought not to be rebaptized but that they obtain pardon for theirs sins through a true penitence. That if, truly penitent, they die in charity before having, by worthy fruits of penance, rendered satisfaction for what they have done by commission or omission, their souls . . . are purged after their death, by purgatorial or purificatory penalties, and that, for the alleviation of these penalties they are served by the suffrages of the living faithful, to wit, the sacrifice of the mass, prayers, alms and other works of piety that the faithful customarily offer on behalf of others of the faithful according to the institutions of the Church. The souls of those who, after receiving baptism, have contracted absolutely no taint of sin, as well as those who, after contracting the taint of sin, have been purified either while they remained in their bodies, or after being stripped of their bodies, are, as we stated above, immediately received into heaven. The souls of those who die in mortal sin or only with original sin, soon descend into Hell, to be chastised with differing punishments, however. The same Roman Church nonetheless firmly believes and firmly asserts that on the day of judgment all men will appear in their bodies before the tribunal of Christ to give an account of their own deeds. (Profession of Faith of Michael Palaeologus)

25. The Preaching of God's Final Judgment

The very foundations of Islam are cast on eschatology, and the earliest suras of the Quran ring incessantly with the certainty of the Judgment and threats and promises of the future life.

> Has news of the Overpowering Event reached you?
> Many faces will be contrite on that day,
> Laboring, wearied out,
> Burning in scorching fire,
> Given water from the boiling spring to drink.
> They will have no food except bitter thorn,
> Neither nourishing nor banishing hunger.
> Well-pleased with their endeavor,

In the high empyrean,
Never hearing idle talk.

There is a stream of running water in it;
And within it are couches placed on high,
Goblets set,
Cushions arranged,
And rich carpets spread.
(Quran 88:1–16)

Surely for those who persecute believers, men and women, and do not repent afterwards, there is the punishment of Hell, and the punishment of burning.

Surely for those who believe and do the right there are gardens with rivers running by. That is the greatest success. (Quran 85:10–11)

Ah, the woe that day for those who deny,
Who call the Day of Judgment a lie!
None denies it but the sinful transgressors.
When Our revelations are recited before him,
    he says: "These are fables of long ago."
No. In fact what they have been doing has rusted their hearts.
Therefore they will be screened off from their Lord that day,
Then they will indeed burn in Hell.
They will then be told:
"This is what you had denied." . . .

Verily the pious will be in heaven,
On couches face to face.
On their faces you will see
    the glow of beatitude.
They will be served the choicest wine, sealed
With a sealing of musk.
(Quran 83:10–26)

Surely a time is fixed for the Day of Judgment.
The day the trumpet blast is sounded you will come in hordes;
The heavens will be opened wide and turn into so many doors.
The mountains put into motion turning into mirage.
Certainly Hell lies in wait,
The rebels' abode,
Where they will remain for aeons,
Finding neither sleep nor anything to drink there

Except boiling water and benumbing cold:
A fitting reward.
They were those who did not expect a reckoning,
And rejected our signs as lies.
We have kept an account of everything in a book.
So taste, for We shall add nothing but torment.

As for those who preserve themselves from evil and follow
     the straight path, there is achievement for them:
Orchards and vineyards,
And graceful maidens ever of the same age,
And flasks full and flowing.
They will hear no blasphemies there or disavowals:
A recompense from your Lord, a sufficient gift.
(Quran 78:17–36)

The whole of Sura 82 is in fact an early Muslim résumé of the Last Things.

THE CLEAVING

In the name of God, most benevolent, ever-merciful.

When the sky is split asunder.
When the stars dispersed,
When the oceans begin to flow,
When the graves are overturned,
Each soul will know what it had sent ahead and what it had left behind.
O man, what seduced you from your munificent Lord,
Who created you, then formed your symmetry, then gave you the
               right proportion,
Shaping you into any form He pleased?
Even then you deny the Judgment.
Surely there are guardians over you,
Illustrious scribes
Who know what you do.
The pious will surely be in heaven,
The wicked certainly in Hell:
They will burn in it on the Day of Judgment,
And will not be removed from it.
How then can you comprehend what the Day of Judgment is?
It is the day when no soul will have the power to do the least for a soul,
        and God's will alone will be done.

(Quran 82:1–19)

Yet, as Jesus himself had warned, no man knows the day or the hour.

They ask you about the Hour: When is its predetermined time? Say: "Only my Lord has the knowledge. No one can reveal it except Him. Oppressive for the heavens and the earth will it be. When it comes, it will come unawares." They ask you about it as if you knew. You tell them: "Only God has the knowledge." (Quran 7:187)

But there will be signs of its immediate approach. Those cited in Sura 82 were chiefly cosmological, but elsewhere in the Quran (e.g., 22:2) they are social as well. The graves will be emptied of the dead. There will be a judgment: every man's deeds have been recorded by angels, and each individual will be confronted with his own account. The righteous will henceforth lead a life of pleasure in what is elsewhere called "the Garden" or "the Garden of Eden"; the evildoers are condemned to a fiery Gehenna. God alone will be the judge.

When the single blast is sounded on the trumpet,
And the earth and the mountains heaved and crushed to powder with
               one leveling blow,
On that Day will come what is to come.
The sky will cleave asunder on that day and fall to pieces.
On its fringes will be angels, eight of them, bearing their Lord's
               throne aloft.
You will then be set before Him, and no one of you will remain
               unexposed.
He who is given his ledger in his right hand, will say: "Here, read
               my ledger.
I was certain I will be given my account."
So he shall have an agreeable life
In high empyrean
With fruits hanging low within reach;
"Eat and drink to your fill as a reward for deeds you have done in
               days of yore."
But whoever gets his ledger in his left hand, will say: "Would that I were
               never given my ledger,
And not known my account!
I wish death had put an end to me.
Of no use was even my wealth.
Vanished has my power from me."
"Seize him and manacle him,
Then cast him to be burnt into Hell;
And string him to a chain seventy cubits long.

He did not believe in God the supreme,
Nor urged others to feed the poor.
And that is why he has no friend today,
Nor food other than suppuration
Which none but the hellish eat."
(Quran 69:13–37)

And from the Sura called "The Inevitable":

When what is to happen comes to pass—
Which is bound to happen undoubtedly—
Degrading some and exalting others;
When the earth is shaken up convulsively,
The mountains bruised and crushed,
Turned to dust, floating in the air,
You will become three kinds:
Those of the right hand—how happy those of the right hand!
Then those of the left hand—how unhappy those of the left hand!
Then those who go before, how pre-excellent,
Who will be honored
In gardens of tranquillity;
A number of the earlier peoples,
But a few of later times,
On couches wrought of gold,
Reclining face to face.
Youths of never-ending bloom will pass round to them
Cups and decanters, beakers full of sparkling wine,
Unheady, unebriating;
And such fruits as they fancy
Bird meats that they relish,
And companions with big beautiful eyes
Like pearls within their shells,
As recompense for all they have done.
They will hear no nonsense there or talk of sin,
Other than "peace, peace," the salutation.

As for those on the right hand—how happy those on the right hand—
They will be in the shade of the thornless lote tree
And acacia covered with heaps of bloom,
Lengthened shadows,
Gushing water,
And fruits numberless,

Unending, unforbidden,
And maidens incomparable.
We have formed them in a distinctive fashion,
And made them virginal,
Loving companions matched in age,
For those of the right hand,
A crowd of earlier generations
And a crowd of the later.

But those of the left hand—how unhappy those of the left hand—
Will be in the scorching wind and boiling water,
Under the shadow of thick black smoke
Neither cool nor agreeable.
They were endowed with good things
But persisted in that greater sin,
And said "What! When we are dead and turned to dust and bones,
        shall we be raised again?
And so will our fathers?"
Say: "Indeed, the earlier and the later generations
Will be gathered together on a certain day which is predetermined.
Then you, the erring and the denyers,
Will eat of the tree of Zaqqum,
Fill your bellies with it,
And drink over it scalding water,
Lapping it up like female camels raging of thirst with disease."
Such will be their welcome on the Day of Judgment. . . .

If he is one of the honored,
There will be peace and plenty, and gardens of tranquillity for him.
And if he is one of those of the right hand,
There will be the salutation by those of the right hand: "Peace be
        upon you."
But if he is of the denyers and the errants,
The welcome will be boiling water
And the roasting in Hell.
This is indeed the ultimate truth.
Then praise your Lord, the most supreme.
(Quran 56:1–95)

There is more than one problem of interpretation here. The first has to do with the identity of the "three kinds" of men who will face judgment. They seem to corre-

1174

spond to those who stand on the right and on the left and "those who go before,"
but they do not appear to match three distinct types of punishment or reward.
Zamakhshari (1134 C.E.) attempts to explain.

. . . "Those on the right side . . . left side" . . . : It may be a question
of those of high rank and those of low rank. . . . The right side constitutes
a good sign and the left side constitutes a bad sign. . . . Others say that
those on the right and those on the left are those who experience happiness and unhappiness: the blessed are happy with themselves because of
their obedience, while the damned are unhappy with themselves because
of their disobedience. Still others say that the inhabitants of Paradise
come to stand on the right and those of hell fire on the left.

"Those who go before" (are) those with pious hearts who arrived
there first, for God summoned them and they were not surpassed in
striving as God's pleasure indicated. There are some who say that there
are three classes of men: (1) the one who enters into the good early in his
life and perseveres in it until he leaves this world. This is the one who
"goes before" and stands near God. (2) Then there is the man who enters
into sin early in his life and is remiss for a long time, but then turns in
repentance toward God. This is the one on the right side. (3) Finally,
there is the man who enters into evil early in life and who is thereafter
incapable of refraining from it until his death. This is the one on the left
side. (Zamakhshari, *The Unveiler of the Realities, ad loc.*)

The second problem has to do with the two apparently contradictory verses: "A
number of the earlier peoples / But a few of later times" (13–14) and "A crowd
of earlier generations / And a crowd of the later" (40). Zamakhshari's commentary
on Sura 56 continues.

The word "number" designates a numerous community. . . . What
is meant is: "those who go before" are numerous among the former
generations. These are the communities from Adam's day to Muhammad.
"But a few of later times" refers to the community of Muhammad. Others say that the former and later times refer to the older and younger
members of the (Muslim) community.

This latter interpretation would seem to refer respectively to the Meccan and then
the Medinese converts to Islam. That reading would lead naturally to the interpreta-
tion of verse 40 cited disapprovingly by Zamakhshari.

It is related that the Muslims were severely persecuted when this
verse "But a few of later times" (verse 14) was revealed, and that for this
reason the Messenger of God once again took counsel with his Lord until

there was revealed (the later verse): "And a crowd of the later." To this I answer: This is not likely for two reasons. In the first place, the verse under discussion (verse 14) refers clearly to "those who go before," while the second verse (verse 40) refers to "those on the right side" ... and second, because abrogation (of one verse by another) is possible (in the case of commands), but not in the case of simple information.

The following sura represents a somewhat more schematic, and considerably clearer, view of the afterlife as the place where God's justice will be fulfilled.

For those who fulfill their covenant with God and do not break
                their agreement,
Who keep together what God has ordained held together, and fear their
                Lord and dread the hardship of the Reckoning,
Who persevere in seeking the way of their Lord, who fulfill their
                devotional obligations, and spend of what We have given
                them, secretly and openly, who repel evil with good:
                For them is the recompense of Paradise:
Perpetual gardens which they will enter with those of their fathers, wives
                and children who are virtuous and at peace. . . .
    As for those who break God's covenant after validating it, and sever relations which God enjoined cohered, and spread corruption in the land, there is condemnation for them and an evil abode.
    God increases or decreases the fortunes of whosoever He will, and they rejoice in the life of this world. Yet the life of this world is nothing but a trifle as compared to the life of the next. (Quran 13:20–26)

In the passage just cited, the moral quality of the afterlife is stressed. There is no lack of passages, however, where the emphasis is on the physical details of both the punishments of the sinner and the rewards of the just. In the translation of this next graphic sura the refrain verse, "How many favors of your Lord will you then deny?" which is repeated after every verse, has been omitted after the first occurrence.

O society of demons and men, cross the bounds of heaven and the earth
                if you have the ability, then pass beyond them; but
                you cannot unless you acquire the law.
How many favors of your Lord will you then deny?
Let loose at you will be smokeless flames of fire so that you will not be
                able to defend yourselves.
When the sky will split asunder, and turn rosy like the dregs of
                anointing oil.

Neither men nor demons will be questioned on that day about his sin.
The sinners will be recognized by their marks and seized by the forelock
                    and their feet.
This is Hell the sinners called a lie.
They will go round and round between it and boiling water.
But for him who has lived in awe of the sublimity of his Lord,
                    there will be two gardens,
Full of overhanging branches,
With two springs of water flowing through them both.
In both of them will be every kind of fruit in pairs.
Reclining on carpets lined with brocade, fruits of the garden hanging
                    low within reach.
In them maidens with averted glances, undeflowered by men or demons
                    before them,
As though rubies and pearls.
Should the reward of goodness be anything but goodness?
And beside these are two other gardens,
Of darkest verdant green,
With two fountains gushing constantly,
With fruits in them,
And dates and pomegranates.
In them good and comely maidens,
Houris cloistered in pavilions,
Undeflowered by men or demons before them.
Reclining on green cushions and rich carpets excellent.
Blessed by your Lord, full of majesty and beneficence.
(Quran 55:33–76)

The tree of Zaqqum will indeed be the food of sinners.
It is like pitch. It will fume in the belly
As does boiling water.
"Seize him and drag him into the depths of Hell," (it will be said).
"Then pour over his head the torment of scalding water."
"Taste it, you were indeed the mighty and the noble!
This is certainly what you had denied."
Surely those who fear and follow the straight path will be in a place
                    of peace and security
In the midst of gardens and of springs,
Dressed in brocade and shot silk,
        facing one another.

Just like that. We shall pair them with companions with large black eyes.
They will call for every kind of fruit with satisfaction.
There they will not know any death apart from the first death they
　　　　　　had died.
(Quran 44:43–56)

26. The End Defined

*These extended selections from the Quran reveal at once a highly developed and
central view of the Last Things: the Last Judgment, Heaven, and Hell all have a
vivid, if sometimes highly allusive, reality. The details were filled in, as they were
in Judaism and Christianity, by popular preaching and the collections of Prophetic
traditions, while the dogmatic issues began to emerge from the workshops of the
theologians in the eighth and ninth centuries. We join that latter tradition in the
mid-ninth century in a series of statements of what then passed as Islamic orthodoxy,
collectively called* The Testament of Abu Hanifah. *The eschatological articles,
buttressed with appropriate Quranic support, begin with number 17.*

Article 17: We confess that God ordered the pen to write. Then the
pen said, "What shall I write, my Lord?" God said: "Write what shall
happen every day till the Resurrection," as He says: "Everything that they
do is in the books kept by the guardian angel; every action, whether small
or great, is written down" (Quran 54:52ff.).

Article 18: We confess that the punishment in the tomb shall without fail take place.

Article 19: We confess that, in view of the traditions on the subject,
the interrogation by Munkar and Nakir is a reality.

Article 20: We confess that Paradise and Hell are a reality and that
they are created and existing at present, that neither they nor their inhabitants shall vanish, since the Scripture says regarding the Faithful: "It [that
is, Paradise] is prepared for the God-fearing" (Quran 3:127), and regarding the infidels: "It [that is, Hell] is prepared for the infidels" (Quran 2:22,
3:126). They were created with a view to reward and punishment respectively.

Article 21: We confess that the balance is a reality, since Scripture
says: "And we will appoint balances for the Day of Resurrection" (Quran
21:48).

Article 22: We confess that the reading of the book on the Day of
Resurrection is a reality, since the Scripture says: "Read your book, there
is needed none but yourself to make out an account against you this day"
(Quran 17:15).

Article 23: We confess that God will restore to life those souls after death, and cause them to rise, on a day of which the duration will be fifty thousand years, for retribution and reward and paying of duties, as Scripture says, "In truth God will wake up to life those who are in the tombs" (Quran 22:7).

Article 24: We confess that the meeting of God with the inhabitants of Paradise will be a reality, without description, comparison or modality.

Article 25: The intercession of our Prophet Muhammad, upon whom be God's blessing and peace, is a reality for all those who belong to the inhabitants of Paradise, even though they should be guilty of mortal sins. . . .

Article 27: We confess that the inhabitants of Paradise will dwell there forever, and that the inhabitants of Hell will dwell there forever, as the Scripture says regarding the Faithful: "They are the companions of Paradise, they shall dwell there forever" (Quran 2:76), and regarding the infidels: "They are the companions of the fire, they shall dwell there forever" (Quran 2:75, 214). (*Testament of Abu Hanifah*) [WENSINCK 1932: 129–131]

27. The Torments of the Grave

Each of these articles has its own background and history. Articles 18 and 19, for example, offered without Quranic support but with a generic reference to the Prophetic traditions, look like this in one of the traditions. It is highly wrought into a careful narrative, assembled by Abu'l-Layth al-Samarqandi (d. 983 C.E.) and reported with a full chain of authorities reaching back to al-Bara ibn Azib.

[Muhammad said, on the occasion of the funeral of one of his Medinese followers:] When a man who is a true believer is drawing near to the next world and is about to be cut off from this world, there descend to him angels whose faces are as white as the sun, bringing with them a shroud from Paradise and celestial aromatics, and take their seat just within his vision. Then the Angel of Death arrives, takes a seat at his head and says: "O you tranquil soul, come forth to God's favor and God's forgiveness." Then, said the Prophet, upon whom be God's blessing and peace, it [that is, the soul of the believer] comes forth, flowing as easily as a drop from a waterskin, whereupon those angels take it, not leaving it in his hand more than the twinkling of an eye before they take it, wrap it in the aforementioned shroud and aromatics so that the odor from it is more redolent than the finest musk to be found on the face of the earth, and mount up with it. . . . At last they come to the gate of the lowest heaven and ask that it be opened for it. It is opened to them and the chief personages in each heaven receive it and accompany it to that which lies beyond it, till at last they arrive with it at the seventh heaven. There God, exalted be He, says: "Write its record in Illiyun (Quran 83:18–21) and return it to the earth from which I created men, into which I make them return, and out of which I will bring them a second time" (Quran 20:55). The spirit is then returned to its body, whereupon two angels [that is, Munkar and Nakir, unmentioned in the Quran] come to it and ask: "Who is your Lord?" It replies: "God is my Lord." They ask: "What is your religion?" "Islam is my religion," it replies. Then they say: "And what say you about this man who was sent among you?" and it answers: "He is the Apostle of God, upon whom be God's blessing and peace." They ask: "What works have you?" and it answers: "I have read God's Book, believed it and in it put my trust." Then a herald will call: "He has believed My servant [that is, Muhammad]. Spread for him a bed from the Garden, clothe him in a celestial garment, open for him a door giving onto the Garden through which may come to him its breezes and its aroma and expand his grave for him as far as the eye can reach. . . ."

But when an unbeliever is drawing near to the next world and being cut off from this world, there descend to him from heaven angels whose faces are black, bringing with them haircloth, and take their seats just within his vision. Then the Angel of Death arrives, takes his seat at his head and says: "O you pernicious soul, come forth to God's discontent and wrath." Thereupon his soul is scattered all through his members and the angel drags it forth like the dragging of an iron spit through moist wool, tearing the veins and sinews. Thus he takes it, but it is not in his hand more than the twinkling of an eye before those angels take, put it in the haircloth where the odor from it is like the stench of a decomposing carcass. They mount up with it . . . and at last they come with it to the gate of the lowest heaven, and ask that it be opened for it, but it is not opened for it. . . . Then God will say: "Write his record in Sijjin (Quran 83:7–9), then let his spirit be thrown out." . . . So his spirit is returned to his body, whereupon two angels come and sit by him. They ask him, "Who is your Lord?" and he replies, "Alas, I know not." And they ask him: "What is your religion?" to which he again replies: "Alas, I know not." They ask: "Well, what do you say about this man who was sent among you?" but again he replies: "Alas, I know not." At which a herald cries from heaven: "He has given My servant (Muhammad) the lie. Spread him a bed from the Fire, clothe him in fire, open for him a door giving out on the Fire, through which its heat and smoke may enter to him, and contract his grave so his ribs pile one upon the other." Then there approaches him a man, ugly of countenance, ill-dressed and foul-smelling, who says to him: "Receive tidings of that which will grieve you. This is your day which you were promised." He will ask: "And who are you?" to which the man will reply: "I am your evil deeds," whereat he will say: "O Lord, let not the Hour arrive, let not the Hour arrive." (Samarqandi, *Arousing the Heedless*) [JEFFERY 1962: 208–210]

The narrative is smooth and reassuring, but there were doctrinal problems here, at least early on in Islam. They can still be heard echoing in this theological manual written by al-Nasafi (d. 1114 C.E.).

The Muʿtazilites, the Jahmites and the Najjarites [that is, the ninth-century rationalizing groups of theologians] teach that neither intelligence nor analogy can accept the reality of the torments of the tomb or the questioning of Munkar and Nakir. (Their argument is that) if He punishes man it must be either that He torments the flesh without the spirit or that He causes the spirit to re-enter the body (after death) and then torments it. Now it would be useless to punish the flesh without the spirit for (then) it would not feel the pain, yet it is not possible to think that He causes the spirit to re-enter the flesh and then torments it, for if He caused the spirit to re-enter the flesh, it would make necessary a second dying, which is not possible, for God has said, "Every soul shall taste death" (Quran 3:185), and this verse informs men that they will not taste of death more than once. Since these two possibilities are shown to be hopeless, there remains but the third, namely, that there is no torment in the tomb.

Having stated the objection, Nasafi now supplies the rejoinder.

There is a proof that the torment of the tomb is something which the intelligence can accept. Do you not see that a sleeper's spirit goes out from him (in sleep) and yet remains connected with the body, so that he may suffer pain in a dream, and both the pain and the relief (from it) reach him? Also conversations take place in dreams because the spirit is (still) connected with the body. It is related of the Prophet, upon whom be God's blessing and peace, that he was asked how the flesh suffers pain in the grave when there is no spirit in it, and he answered: "In the same way that your tooth suffers pain though there is no spirit in it." (Thus) the Prophet informed his (questioner) that the tooth may be subject to pain because it is connected with the flesh, even though there is no spirit in it, and so, in like manner after death, because a man's spirit is (still) connected with his body, the body may feel pain. (Nasafi, *The Sea of Discourse on the Science of Theology*) [JEFFERY 1962: 436–438]

28. The Resurrection of the Body Demonstrated

They say: "O Lord, twice You made us die, and twice You made us live. We admit our sins. Is there still a way out for us?" (Quran 40:11)

*The resurrection of the body, to which this Quranic verse was generally thought to refer, was as difficult a conceptual question for the Muslims as it was for the Christians. Al-Ash*ari (d. 935 C.E.), one of the first proponents of theology in Islam, attempted a demonstrative proof of its possibility with the new weapons of rational science. At the same time, to defend the usefulness and validity of that science, he made God the theologian in this instance.*

All dialectical theology which treats in detail of questions deriving from the basic dogmas of God's Oneness and Justice is simply taken from the Quran. Such is also the case with theological discourse on the possibility and impossibility of the resurrection (of the body). This question had been disputed by intelligent Arabs (of Muhammad's day) and by others before them until they were amazed by the possibility of that and said, "What! When we have died and become dust? That is an incredible return!" (Quran 50:3) . . . and "Who will quicken bones when they have decayed?" (Quran 36:78). . . . Apropos of such theological discussion of theirs God put into the Quran arguments designed to confirm, from the viewpoint of reason, the possibility of the resurrection after death. He taught and instructed His Prophet how to argue against their denial in two ways, according to the two groups of adversaries. For one group admitted the first creation but denied the second, while the second group denied both (creations) on the ground that the world is eternal [that is, both *a parte ante* and *a parte post*].

So against him who admitted the first creation, God argued by saying, "Answer: He will quicken them who produced them the first time" (Quran 36:79), and by saying, "It is He who gives life by a first creation and then restores it; and it is very easy for Him" (Quran 30:27), and by His words, "As He first made you, you will return" (Quran 7:29). By these verses He called their attention to the fact that he who was able to effect something [to wit, the original creation] without reference to a pre-existing exemplar is all the more able to effect something which has already been produced. Indeed, the latter is easier for him, as you know from your own experience. But in the case of the Creator, it is not "easier" for Him to create one thing than to create another. . . .

As for the group which denied both the first creation and the second [that is, the "re-creation" of the resurrection] and maintained the eternity of the world, a doubt entered their minds simply because they said: "It is our experience that life is wet and hot and death is cold and dry, akin to the nature of earth. How then can there be any combination of life and earth and decayed bones, resulting in a sound creation, since two contraries do not combine?" For this reason, then, they denied the resurrection.

It is certainly true that two contraries do not combine in one substratum, or in one direction, or in what (already) exists in the substratum. But they can exist in two substratums by way of propinquity. So God argued against them by saying: "He who makes fire for you from a green tree—for behold, you kindle fire from it" (Quran 38:80). In saying that, God was referring to their own knowledge and experience of the emergence of fire from green trees, notwithstanding the heat and dryness of the former and the coldness and wetness of the latter. Again, God made the possibility of the first production a proof of the possibility of the last production, because it is a proof of the possibility of the propinquity of life to earth and decayed bones and of making it a sound creation, for He said, "Just as We created man a first time, so We shall restore him" (Quran 21:104). (Ash'ari, *The Science of Dialectical Theology* 9–12)

[ASH'ARI 1953: 123–125]

29. The Resurrection of the Body Contested

Neither Ash'ari's attempted demonstration nor the later distinction of a spirit that is not in the flesh but somehow remains connected with it to a sufficient extent to allow the body to suffer the physical pains and enjoy the physical pleasures of the afterlife solved the problem. The early rationalizing sectarians may have denied the literal truth of the torment of the tomb, but once the full impact of Greek philosophy began to be felt in Islam, a far greater problem arose: the resurrection of the corruptible body and its reunion with the incorruptible soul. And if this seemed improbable, then equally improbable would be the body's share in either the physical pains of Hell or the physical pleasures of Paradise. Ibn Sina (d. 1038 C.E.), a thinker deeply imbued with Greek philosophy but a Muslim withal, here attempts to solve the problem in terms of Paradise. He is speaking of the fate of the middle range of souls, neither recognized saints nor inveterate sinners.

It may be true, as some theologians state, that when souls, supposing they are pure, leave the body, having firmly fixed within them some such beliefs concerning the future life as are appropriate to them, being the sort of picture that can properly be presented to the ordinary man, when souls such as these leave the body, lacking both the force to draw them upward to complete perfection . . . but all their spiritual dispositions are turned toward the lower world and drawn to the corporeal . . . these souls may well imagine all those afterlife circumstances in which they believed as actually taking place before them, the instrument reinforcing their imagination being some kind of celestial body.

It is then in the deceased soul's imaginative faculty that the physical pleasures of Paradise appear to occur, with an assist from a higher body, one of the immortal heavenly bodies. This is no ersatz pleasure, or ersatz pain, Ibn Sina continues.

In this way the pure souls will really be spectators of the events of the grave and the resurrection about which they were told in this world, and all the good things of the afterlife; while the wicked souls will similarly behold, and suffer, the punishment which was portrayed to them here below. Certainly the imaginative picture is no weaker than the sensual image; rather it is the stronger and clearer of the two. This may be observed in dreams: the vision seen in sleep is often of greater moment in its kind than the impression of the senses. . . . As you know, the image seen in dreams and that sensed in waking are alike simply impressed upon the soul; they differ only in this, that the former kind originates from within and descends into the soul, while the latter sort originates from without and mounts up to the soul. It is when the image has already been impressed that the act of contemplation is consummated. It is this impression, then, that in reality pleases or pains the soul, not any external object. (Ibn Sina, *The Book of Deliverance*) [AVICENNA 1951: 74–75]

30. The Incoherence of the Philosophers

Avicenna's argument was ingenious, but it was not very convincing to Ghazali, who pointed out in his Incoherence of the Philosophers, *as we have already seen in Chapter 5 above, that the issue of the literal resurrection of the body, and the literal truth of the pains of Gehenna and the pleasures of Paradise, was one of the irreconcilable issues that separated the philosophical from the Islamic tradition. And the chief offender in the Muslim camp was no less than Ibn Sina himself, who is here reflecting more generally on the question of the afterlife.*

The afterlife is a notion received from religious teaching; there is no way of establishing its truth save by way of religious dogma and acceptance of the prophets' reports as true; these refer to what will befall the body at the resurrection, and those corporeal delights or torments which are too well known to require restating here. The true religion brought into this world by our Prophet Muhammad has described in detail the state of happiness or misery awaiting us hereafter so far as the body is concerned. Some further support for the idea of the hereafter is attainable through reason and logical demonstration—and this is confirmed by prophetic teaching—namely, that happiness or misery posited by spiritual apprisement, though it is true that our conjecture falls short of realizing a full picture of them now, for reasons which we shall explain. Metaphysicians have a greater desire to achieve this spiritual happiness than the happiness which is purely physical; indeed, they scarcely heed the latter, and were they granted it would not consider it of great moment in comparison to the former kind, which is proximity to the First Truth, in a matter to be described presently. Let us therefore consider this (spiritual) state of happiness, and of contrasting misery; the physical sort is fully dealt with in the teachings of religion. (Ibn Sina, *Book of Deliverance*) [AVICENNA 1951: 64]

If this seems innocuous enough, we should recall a text of the same work, where Avicenna remarks on the methods of the prophet-lawgiver.

The prophet's duty is to teach men to know the majesty and might of God by means of symbols and parables drawn from things which they regard as mighty and majestic, imparting to them simply this much, that God has no equal, no like and no partner. Similarly he must establish in them a belief in an afterlife in a manner that comes within the range of their imagination and will be satisfying to their souls; he will liken the happiness and misery to be experienced there in terms which they can understand and conceive. (Ibid.) [AVICENNA 1951: 44–45]

Ibn Rushd (d. 1198 C.E.), a Spanish philosopher who took his Muslim faith seriously, attempted to answer Ghazali. He too begins where Ibn Sina had, on the very nature of eschatological revelation, in a text cited in part at the very beginning of this chapter.

All religions agree on the fact that souls experience states of happiness or misery after death, but they disagree in the manner of symbolizing these states and explaining their existence to men. And it seems that the kind of symbolization that is found in this religion of ours is the most perfect means of explanation to the majority of men and provides the greatest stimulus to their souls to the life beyond; and the primary concern of religions is with the majority. . . . It seems that corporeal symbolization provides a stronger stimulus to the life beyond than the spiritual kind; the spiritual (kind) is more acceptable to the class of debating theologians, but they are the minority.

For this reason we find the people of Islam divided into three sects with regard to the understanding of the symbolization which is used in (the texts of) our religion referring to the states of the future life. One sect holds that existence is identical with this existence here with respect to bliss and pleasure, i.e., they hold that it is the same sort and that the two existences differ only in respect to permanence and limit of duration, i.e., the former is permanent and the latter is of limited duration. Another group holds that there is a difference in the kind of existence. This group has two subdivisions. One subgroup holds that existence symbolized by these sensible images is spiritual, and it has been symbolized thus [that is, in sensible material images] only for the purpose of exposition; these people are supported by many well-known arguments from Scripture, but there would be no point in enumerating them. Another subgroup thinks that it is corporeal, but think that the corporeality of the life beyond differs from the corporeality of this life in that the latter is perishable while the former is immortal. They too are supported by arguments from Scripture. . . .

It seems that this opinion is more suitable to the elite, for the admissibility of this opinion is founded on facts which are not discussed in front of everyone. One is that the soul is immortal. The other is that the return of the soul (after death) to other bodies does not involve the same absurdity as its return to these same (earthly) bodies. This is because it is apparent that the material of the bodies that exist here is successively transferred from one body to another. . . . Bodies like these cannot possibly all exist actually (at the same time), because their material is one. A man dies, for instance, his body is transformed into dust, that dust is transformed into a plant, another man feeds on that plant; then semen proceeds from him, from which another man is born. But if other bodies are supposed, this state of affairs does not follow as a consequence. (Ibn Rushd, *Unveiling of the Programs of Proof*) [AVERROES 1961: 76–77]

And this is in fact Ibn Rushd's own view, expressed when he takes Ghazali on directly, in his Incoherence of the Incoherence.

What Ghazali says against them [that is, the philosophers] is right, and in refuting them it must be admitted that the soul is immortal, as is proved by rational and religious proofs, and it must be assumed that what arises from the dead are simulacra of these earthly bodies, not these bodies themselves, for that which has perished does not return individually and a thing can only return as an image of that which has perished, not as a being identical with what has perished, as Ghazali declares. (Ibn Rushd, *Incoherence of the Incoherence 586*) [AVERROES 1954: 1:362]

31. An End to Hell?

Another trace of Purgatory in Islam, or at least a discussion of the premises—namely that punishment after death is (1) remedial in its intention, and hence (2) temporary and finite—occurs in Zamakhshari's treatment of Sura 11:103–110.

In this surely is a sign for him who fears the torment of the Hereafter, the day when mankind will be assembled together, which will be a day when all things would become evident. We are deferring it only for a time ordained. The day it comes no soul will dare say a word but by His leave; and some will be wretched and some will be blessed. And those who are doomed will be in Hell; for them there will be sighing and sobbing, where they will dwell so long as heaven and earth endure, unless your Lord wills otherwise. Surely, your Lord does as He wills. Those who are blessed will be in Paradise, where they will dwell so long as heaven and earth endure, unless your Lord wills otherwise: this will be a gift uninterrupted. (Quran 11:103–108)

Is it conceivable, then, as this sura seems to suggest, that Paradise and Gehenna will survive only so long as this finite heaven and earth of ours? Zamakhshari comments.

"So long as heaven and the earth endure": There are two possible meanings here. First, the heaven and the earth of the Hereafter are being referred to, since these endure forever. That the Hereafter does possess heaven and earth is shown by the words of God [14:48 and 39:74]. . . . Since it is essential for the inhabitants of the Hereafter that something exist that will bear and shelter them, then either there must exist a heaven or else the Throne (of God) must shelter them. Anything that shelters someone is, in effect, a kind of heaven. Or second, this ("so long as") is an expression for affirming (perduration) and for denying termination. Thus the Arabs say . . . "so long as a star shines" and other similar formulas affirming (perduration).

Could God end Paradise and Gehenna by His own will then? Zamakhshari continues.

Someone may now ask: What is the meaning of the exception referred to in God's words "unless your Lord wills otherwise"? For it is certain that the inhabitants of Paradise and those of hell fire will remain there forever without exception. My response is that the exception refers to eternal persistence in the punishment by fire and eternal stay in the blessing of the Garden. The inhabitants of the hell fire will not continue to be punished only by fire; rather, they will also be punished through severe frost and in other ways, and especially by a punishment which is stronger than all these kinds, namely, that God will be angry with them, will reject them, will regard them as contemptible. By the same token, the inhabitants of Paradise will enjoy, in addition to the Garden, something more important and more moving than that, namely the complaisance that God will have in them. Thus God says:

"God has promised men and women who believe gardens with streams of running water where they will abide forever, and beautiful mansions in the Garden of Eden, and the blessings of God above all. That will be happiness supreme" (Quran 9:72).

Thus, in addition to the reward of the Garden, they receive yet another gift of God, the nature of which no one knows but Him. This is what is meant by the exception.

But the exegesis of the passage is not yet complete. The phrase "verily, your Lord does as He wills" raises another possibility, the one that makes the Christian position on Purgatory possible. Zamakhshari dismisses it immediately, however.

The meaning of God's words "Surely, your Lord does as He wills" . . . is as follows: He allots whatever he wills as punishment to the inhabitants of hell fire, just as He grants his gifts unceasingly to the inhabitants of Paradise. One should reflect upon this, since one part of the Quran explains another. One should not be deceived here by the assertion of the Mujbira [that is, those who oppose the doctrine of free will], who maintain that the (first) exception means that the people of grave sins will be brought out of hell fire through intercession. For the second exception [that is, "Surely your Lord does as He wills"] clearly accuses them of falsehood and proves they lie.

There is also a Prophetic tradition much to the same point as the contention of the Mujbira—and earlier of Origen. Zamakhshari now turns to it.

But what are we to think of those who repudiate the Book of God on the basis of a Prophetic tradition which has come down to them from a non-expert like Abdullah ibn Amr ibn al-As? According to this tradition, a day will come when the gates of Gehenna will be closed and no longer will anyone be inside. And this is supposed to happen after the inhabitants have been there for a very long time. It has come to my attention that those who let themselves be misled by this tradition and believe that the unbelievers will not remain forever in hell fire have fallen prey to this error. This and similar views are clear deceptions, from which may God preserve us! . . . If this tradition according to Abdullah ibn Amr ibn al-As is sound, then its meaning can only be that the unbelievers will come out of the heat of the fire and into the cold of severe frost. Only in this sense would Gehenna be empty and its gates closed. (Zamakhshari, *The Unveiler of the Realities, ad loc.*)

32. The Vision of God

That the afterlife of the blessed consisted, in some degree and in some manner, of the vision of God does not seem to have been doubted by the first generation of Jesus' followers.

Now we see only puzzling reflections in a mirror, but then we shall see face to face. My knowledge now is partial; then it will be whole, like God's knowledge of me. (Paul, *To the Corinthians* 1.13:12)

How great is the love that the Father has shown us! We were called God's children, and such we are; and the reason why the godless world does not recognize us is that it has not known Him. Here and now, dear friends, we are God's children; what we shall be has not been disclosed, but we know that when it is disclosed, we shall be like Him because we shall see Him as He is. (John, *Letters* 1.3:1–3)

By the time of Ireneus, bishop of Lyons in the late second century c.e., the Mosaic experience on Sinai had to be addressed as part of the scriptural context of what the Christians called "the beatific vision."

Because of His greatness and His wonderful glory, "no mortal man may look upon God and live" (Exod. 33:30); for the Father is beyond comprehension. But because of His love and His compassion, and because all things are possible for Him, this too He granted to those who love themselves, that is, to see God. . . . Man of himself does not see God. It is He who is willingly seen by those whom he wishes, and when He wishes, and how He wishes. For God is powerful in all things: He is seen by the spirit of prophecy; He is seen by the Son by way of adoption; and

He will be seen in the kingdom of heaven paternally, while the Spirit prepares man in the Son of God, the Son brings him to the Father, and the Father gives incorruptible life for all eternity, which occurs to each in that he sees God. (Ireneus, *Against the Heresies* 4.20.5)

Augustine had somewhat greater difficulty with the ocular vision of God in the afterlife, and far less confidence in his ability to explain it. He begins with Paul's "now . . . puzzling reflections in a mirror . . . then face to face."

This [that is, face to face] is the way the holy angels now see, the ones called our angels. . . . The way they now see is the same way we will see; but not yet, so Paul says "now . . . puzzling reflections in a mirror. . . ." That vision is preserved for us as the reward of our faith, and it was of that John was speaking when he said "we shall see Him as He is." The face of God ought to be understood as His manifestation and not as some body part as such, like the one we have and call by that name. So when I am asked what the blessed will do in that spiritual body of theirs, I do not say that I see but rather that I believe. . . . And so I say that they will see God in that body, but whether with it, the way we now through our body see the sun, the moon, the stars and the earth and all the things in it, is no insignificant question. (Augustine, *City of God* 22.29.1)

The incorporeal God who rules all will be seen by us also by our bodies. Whether God will be seen by those eyes by reason of their possessing a degree of excellence like the mind's whereby they too might perceive incorporeal natures is difficult or impossible to show on the basis of examples or texts from the Sacred Scriptures; or, what is easier to understand, God will be known and obvious to us in such a way that He will be seen by the Spirit in and by each of us: He will be seen by one man in another, He will be seen in Himself, and He will be seen in the new heaven and the new earth, and in every creature that will then exist. (Ibid. 22.29.6)

The Quranic proof-text on the vision of God occurs in Sura 75.

> You love this transient life,
> And neglect the Hereafter.
> How many faces will be refulgent on that Day,
> Looking toward their Lord;
> And how many faces on that day will be woe-begone
> Thinking that some great disaster is about to fall upon them.
> (Quran 75:20–25)

The theologian Ash°ari (d. 935 C.E.) offers his direct and succinct exegesis of a text that already in his day had become the subject of controversy. He begins by rejecting the parallel to other Quranic uses of the same verb "looking toward" in contexts where it means "considering as an example" or "feeling sympathy for" or "expecting." "And so," Ash°ari concludes:

. . . [I]t is certain that His words "looking toward their Lord" here mean "seeing" since they cannot refer to any of the other kinds of "looking toward." For if "looking" is limited to four kinds, and three are impossible in the present case, the fourth kind must be certain, namely, the "look" of the seeing of the eye which is in the face.

But there is a possible objection arising from the next phrase. Ash°ari's exegesis now takes the form of a scholastic disputation with an anonymous opponent.

But has not God (also) said, "And on that day other faces will be despondent thinking that 'some great disaster will fall upon them' " (Quran 75:24–25)? But thinking is not done with the face, and so similarly His words ". . . looking toward their Lord" must mean the "look" of the heart.

Your objection has no force [Ash°ari responds] because thinking is not done with the face but only with the heart [that is, with an interior faculty]. Hence, since God coupled thinking with a mention of the face, it must refer to the thinking of the heart because thinking is done only with the heart. And if "looking" were (likewise) restricted to the heart, His mentioning it in connection with the face would have to refer to the heart. But since "looking" may be done with the face and in others ways, in connecting it with a reference to the face, He must mean by it the "looking" of the face.

The anonymous objector brings another text into play.

Question: Then what is the meaning of His words, "Eyes do not attain Him but He attains to eyes" (Quran 6:103)?

Response [by Ash°ari]: They refer to this life and not the next. Hence, when God says in another verse that eyes *will* look at Him, we know that the time of which He says that eyes do not attain Him must be different from the time in which He has revealed that they will be looking at Him. (Ash°ari, *The Science of Dialectical Theology* 75–79)

[ASH°ARI 1953: 48–50]

Few were probably convinced by such highly wrought dialectic. The mystics knew they would see God in the Hereafter because some of their number had in fact seen

Him in this life. The theologians had to be content to struggle with the mere possibility, something that their metaphysical premises suggested was not beyond reach, no matter how little the Quran, the traditionists, and general Muslim sensibilities encouraged them to entertain that thought. For the Christian, the God-man Jesus provided an inviting bridge by which to cross over to the Godhead Itself. Most Muslims, like the great majority of Jews, paused gravely on the hither side, uncertain whether the enormous chasm that separated creature and Creator could ever be transcended, here or even hereafter.

Short Titles

ABOTH RABBI NATHAN 1955. *The Fathers According to Rabbi Nathan.* Translated by Judah Goldin. New Haven: Yale University Press.

ALEXANDER 1984. P. S. Alexander, *Textual Sources for the Study of Judaism.* New York: Barnes and Noble.

ANAWATI & GARDET 1961. G. C. Anawati and Louis Gardet, *Mystique musulmane.* Paris: Librairie philosophique J. Vrin.

AQUINAS 1945. *Basic Writings of Thomas Aquinas.* Edited and annotated by Anton Pegis. 2 vols. New York: Random House.

ARBERRY 1950. A. J. Arberry, *Sufism: An Account of the Mystics of Islam.* London: George Allen & Unwin, Ltd., 1950; rpt. New York: Harper & Row, 1970.

ARBERRY 1964. A. J. Arberry, *Aspects of Islamic Civilization, as Depicted in the Original Texts.* London: George Allen & Unwin, Ltd., 1964; pbk. Ann Arbor: University of Michigan Press, 1976.

ARNOLD 1928. T. Arnold, *Painting in Islam.* Oxford: Oxford University Press, 1928; rpt. New York: Dover Books, 1965.

ASH'ARI 1953. Richard J. McCarthy, S.J., *The Theology of al-Ash'ari.* Beirut: Imprimerie Catholique.

ATTAR 1966. *Muslim Saints and Mystics: Episodes from the Tadhkirat al-Awliya ("Memorials of the Saints") by Farid al-Din Attar.* Translated by A. J. Arberry. Chicago: University of Chicago Press.

ATTAR 1984. Farid ud-Din Attar, *The Conference of the Birds.* Translated by Afkham Darbandi and Dick Davis. Harmondsworth: Penguin.

AUGUSTINE 1947. *Writings of Saint Augustine,* vol. 4: *Christian Instruction.* Translated by J. J. Gavigan. New York: Cima Publishing Company.

AUGUSTINE 1948. *Basic Writings of Saint Augustine.* Edited by Whitney J. Oates. 2 vols. New York: Random House.

AVERROES 1954. *Averroes' Tahafut al-Tahafut (The Incoherence of the Incoherence).* Translated by Simon van den Bergh. 2 vols. London: Luzac & Company.

AVERROES 1961. *Averroes on the Harmony of Religion and Philosophy.* Translated by G. F. Hourani. London: Luzac & Company.

AVICENNA 1951. A. J. Arberry, *Avicenna on Theology.* London: John Murray.

AYOUB 1984. M. Ayoub, *The Qur'an and Its Interpreters.* Vol. 1. Albany: State University of New York Press.

BAYNES 1955. N. H. Baynes, "Idolatry and the Early Church." In N. H. Baynes, *Byzantine Studies and Other Essays,* pp. 116–143. London: Athlone Press.

BIRUNI 1879. Al-Biruni, *The Chronology of Ancient Nations. . . .* Translated and edited by C. E. Sachau. London: 1879; rpt. Frankfurt: Minerva, 1969.

BOKSER 1981. Ben Zion Bokser, *The Jewish Mystical Tradition*. New York: Pilgrim Press.

BURTON 1977. John Burton, *The Collection of the Qur'an*, Cambridge: Cambridge University Press.

(PSEUDO)-DIONYSIUS 1987. *Pseudo-Dionysius: The Complete Works*. Translated by Colm Luibheid with Paul Rorem. New York: Paulist Press.

FARABI 1961. Al-Farabi, *Fusul al-Madani: Aphorisms of the Statesman*. Edited and translated by D. M. Dunlop. Cambridge: Cambridge University Press.

GHAZALI 1953. W. Montgomery Watt, *The Faith and Practice of al-Ghazali*. London: George Allen & Unwin, Ltd.

GUILLAUME 1924. Alfred Guillaume, *The Traditions of Islam: An Introduction to the Study of the Hadith Literature*. Oxford: Clarendon Press, 1924; rpt. Lahore: Universal Books, 1977.

HALEVI 1905. Judah Halevi, *The Kuzari: An Argument for the Faith of Israel*. Translated by H. Hirschfeld. 1905; rpt. New York: Schocken Books, 1964.

HALPERIN 1984. D. J. Halperin, "A New Edition of the Hekhalot Literature." *Journal of the American Oriental Society* 104 (1984), 543–552.

HAUSHERR 1927. I. Hausherr, *Le méthode d'oraison hésychaste*. Rome: Orientalia Christiana.

HUJWIRI 1911. *The "Kashf al-Mahjub," the Oldest Persian Treatise on Sufism by al-Hujwiri*. Translated by Reynold A. Nicholson. London: Luzac & Company, 1911; rpt. London: Luzac, 1959.

IBN AL-ARABI 1980. Ibn al-Arabi, *The Bezels of Wisdom*. Translated and edited by R.W.J. Austin. New York: Paulist Press.

IBN BATTUTA 1959–1962. *The Travels of Ibn Battuta, A.D. 1325–1354*. Translated and edited by H.A.R. Gibb. 2 vols. Cambridge: Cambridge University Press.

IBN ISHAQ 1955. *The Life of Muhammad: A Translation of Ishaq's Sirat Rasul Allah*. Translated and edited by A. Guillaume. London: Oxford University Press.

IBN KHALDUN 1967. Ibn Khaldun, *The Muqaddimah: An Introduction to History*. Translated by Franz Rosenthal. 3 vols. 2nd corrected ed. Princeton: Princeton University Press.

IBN QUDAMA 1950. H. Laoust, *Le Précis de droit d'Ibn Qudama*. Beirut: Institut Français de Damas.

JEFFERY 1962. A. Jeffery, *A Reader on Islam: Passages from Standard Arabic Writings Illustrative of the Beliefs and Practices of Muslims*. 's-Gravenhage: Mouton and Company.

JOHN CLIMACUS 1982. *John Climacus, The Ladder of Divine Ascent*. Translated by Colm Luibheid and Norman Russell. New York: Paulist Press.

JUNAYD 1962. Ali Hassan Abdel-Kader, *The Life, Personality and Writings of al-Junayd*. London: Luzac & Company.

JUWAYNI 1968. M. Allard, *Textes apologétiques de Juwaini*. Beirut: Dar al-Machreq.

LANE 1836. Edward Lane, *Manners and Customs of the Modern Egyptians* (1836). 5th ed. rpt. New York: Dover Publications.

LAURENT 1873. J.C.M. Laurent, *Peregrinatores Medii Aevi Quattuor*. 2nd ed. Leipzig: J. C. Hinrichs.

LE GOFF 1984. Jacques Le Goff, *The Birth of Purgatory*. Chicago: University of Chicago Press.

LERNER & MAHDI 1972. R. Lerner and M. Mahdi (eds.), *Medieval Political Philosophy: A Sourcebook*. Glencoe, Ill.: Free Press, 1963; pbk. Ithaca: Cornell University Press, 1972.

LEWIS 1974. Bernard Lewis, *Islam from the Prophet Muhammad to the Capture of Constantinople*. 2 vols. New York: Harper & Row.

LEWIS 1976. Bernard Lewis, "On That Day: A Jewish Apocalyptic Poem on the Arab Conquests." In *Mélanges d'Islamologie . . . de Armand Abel*, pp. 197–200. Leiden: E. J. Brill, 1974. Reprinted in Bernard Lewis, *Studies in Classical and Ottoman Islam (7th–16th Centuries)*. London: Variorum Reprints, 1976.

MCNEILL & GAMER 1938. J. T. McNeill and H. M. Gamer, *Medieval Handbooks of Penance*. New York: Columbia University Press.

MAIMONIDES 1963. Moses Maimonides, *The Guide of the Perplexed*. Translated and edited by Shlomo Pines. Chicago: University of Chicago Press.

MAIMONIDES 1965. *The Code of Maimonides: Book XIV*. New Haven: Yale University Press.

MAIMONIDES 1968. *The Commentary to Mishneh Aboth*. Translated by Arthur David. New York: Bloch Publishing Company.

MANGO 1972. Cyril Mango, *The Art of the Byzantine Empire, 312–1453: Sources and Documents*. Englewood Cliffs, N.J.: Prentice-Hall.

MASSIGNON 1968. Louis Massignon, *Essai sur les origines du lexique technique de la mystique musulmane*. Paris: J. Vrin.

MASSIGNON 1982. Louis Massignon, *The Passion of al-Hallaj: Mystic and Martyr of Islam*. Translated by Herbert Mason. 4 vols. Princeton: Princeton University Press.

MIDRASH RABBAH 1977. *The Midrash Rabbah*. Translated by H. Freedman et al. 5 vols. London, Jerusalem, New York: Soncino Press.

NACHMANIDES 1971. Ramban (Nachmanides), *Commentary on the Torah: Genesis*. Translated by C. B. Chavel. New York: Shilo Publishing House.

NEMOY 1952. *Karaite Anthology: Excerpts from the Early Literature*. Translated by Leon Nemoy. New Haven: Yale University Press.

NICHOLSON 1921. Reynald A. Nicholson, *Studies in Islamic Mysticism*. Cambridge: Cambridge University Press.

PALAMAS 1983. Gregory Palamas, *The Triads*. Edited by John Meyendorff; translation by Nicholas Gendle. New York: Paulist Press.

PESIKTA RABBATI 1968. *Pesikta Rabbati*. Translated by William G. Braude. 2 vols. New Haven and London: Yale University Press.

PETER LOMBARD 1917. E. F. Rogers, "Peter Lombard and the Sacramental System." Ph.D. diss., Columbia University.

PHILO 1945. Philo, *Selections*. Edited and translated by H. Lewy. In *Three Jewish Philosophers*. Philadelphia: Jewish Publication Society, 1945; rpt. New York: Meridian Books, 1960.

PHILO 1981. Philo of Alexandria, *The Contemplative Life, The Giants, and Selections*. Translated by David Winston. New York: Paulist Press.

PINES 1971. S. Pines, *An Arabic Version of the Testimonium Flavianum and Its Implications*. Jerusalem: Israel Academy of Sciences and Humanities.

RAHMAN 1958. F. Rahman, *Prophecy in Islam: Philosophy and Orthodoxy*. London: George Allen & Unwin, Ltd.

RUMI 1925–1940. Jalal al-Din Rumi, *Mathnawi*. Edited, translated, and annotated by R. A. Nicholson. 8 vols. London: Luzac & Company.

SAADYA 1945. Saadya Gaon, *Book of Doctrines and Beliefs*. Abridged translation by A. Altman. In *Three Jewish Philosophers*. Philadelphia: Jewish Publication Society, 1945; rpt. New York: Meridian Books, 1960.

SAADYA 1948. Saadya Gaon, *The Book of Beliefs and Opinions*. Translated by S. Rosenblatt. New Haven: Yale University Press.

SACHEDINA 1981. A. Sachedina, *Islamic Messianism: The Idea of the Mahdi in Twelver Shiʿism*. Albany: State University of New York Press.

SAHAS 1972. D. J. Sahas, *John of Damascus on Islam: The "Heresy of the Ishmaelites."* Leiden: E. J. Brill.

SCHAEFER 1982. P. Schaefer, *Synopse zur Hekhalot-Literatur*. Tübingen: J.C.B. Mohr.

SHAFIʿI 1961. *Islamic Jurisprudence: Shafiʿi's Risala*. Translated by Majid Khadduri. Baltimore: Johns Hopkins University Press.

SMITH 1931. Margaret Smith, *Studies in Early Mysticism in the Near and Middle East*. London: Sheldon Press, 1931; rpt. Amsterdam: Philo Press, 1973.

SMITH 1950. Margaret Smith, *Readings in the Mystics of Islam*. London: Luzac & Company.

SOKOLOW 1981. M. Sokolow, "The Denial of Muslim Sovereignty over Eretz-Israel in Two 10th Century Karaite Bible Commentaries." In J. Hacker (ed.), *Shalem*, 3: 309–318. Jerusalem: Yad Izhak Ben-Zvi Institute.

STANIFORTH 1968. *Early Christian Writings: The Apostolic Fathers*. Translated by Maxwell Staniforth. Harmondsworth: Penguin.

SYMEON NEOTHEOLOGUS 1980. *Symeon the New Theologian: The Discourses*. Translated by C. J. Catanzaro. New York: Paulist Press.

TRIMINGHAM 1971. J. Spencer Trimingham, *The Sufi Orders in Islam*. London: Oxford University Press.

TWERSKY 1980. I. Twersky, *Introduction to the Code of Maimonides (Mishneh Torah)*. New Haven and London: Yale University Press.

VAN BERCHEM 1922. Max Van Berchem, *Corpus inscriptionum arabicarum. Syrie du Sud*, vol. 2: *Jerusalem, "Ville."* Cairo: Institut français d'archéologie orientale.

VERMES 1968. Geza Vermes, *The Dead Sea Scrolls in English*. Harmondsworth: Penguin

WENSINCK 1932. A. J. Wensinck, *The Muslim Creed: Its Genesis and Historical Development*. Cambridge: Cambridge University Press.

WILLIAMS 1971. J. A. Williams, *Themes of Islamic Civilization*. Berkeley: University of California Press.

WRIGHT 1848. T. Wright, *Early Travels in Palestine*. London: H. G. Bohn.

ZENKOVSKY 1963. Serge A. Zenkovsky, *Mediaeval Russia's Epics, Chronicles and Tales*. New York: E. P. Dutton.

ZERNOV 1945. N. Zernov, *The Russians and Their Church*. London and New York: Macmillan.

Index